The Prophet

The Prophet

THE LIFE OF
LEON TROTSKY

THE ONE-VOLUME EDITION

———————

Isaac Deutscher

VERSO

London • New York

This one-volume edition first published by Verso 2015
The Prophet Armed, The Prophet Unarmed, and *The Prophet Outcast*
first published by Verso 2004

The Prophet Armed first published by Oxford University Press 1954
The Prophet Unarmed first published by Oxford University Press 1959
The Prophet Outcast first published by Oxford University Press 1963

3 5 7 9 10 8 6 4 2

Verso
UK: 6 Meard Street, London W1F 0EG
US: 20 Jay Street, Suite 1010, Brooklyn, NY 11201
www.versobooks.com

Verso is the imprint of New Left Books

ISBN-13: 978-1-78168-560-0
eISBN-13: 978-1-78168-562-4 (US)
eISBN-13: 978-1-78168-721-5 (UK)

British Library Cataloguing in Publication Data
A catalogue record for this book is available from the British Library

Library of Congress Cataloging-in-Publication Data
A catalog record for this book is available from the Library of Congress

Printed in the US by Maple Press

CONTENTS

Volume III: The Prophet Outcast 1929–1940

LIST OF ILLUSTRATIONS

VOLUME I

THE PROPHET ARMED

1879–1921

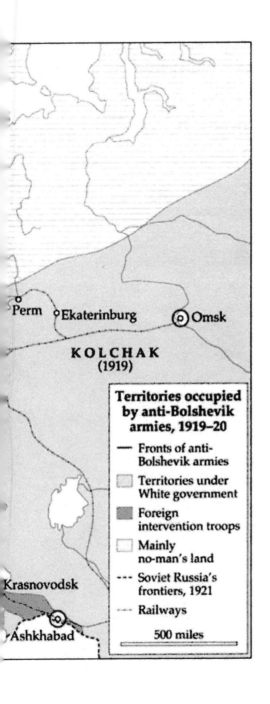

Perm

Ekaterinburg

Omsk

KOLCHAK
(1919)

Territories occupied
by anti-Bolshevik
armies, 1919–20

— Fronts of anti-
Bolshevik armies

☐ Territories under
White government

■ Foreign
intervention troops

☐ Mainly
no-man's land

--- Soviet Russia's
frontiers, 1921

⋯ Railways

500 miles

Krasnovodsk

Ashkhabad

PREFACE

WHEN I first contemplated the writing of a biographical trilogy on the leaders of the Russian revolution I intended to include a study of Trotsky in Exile, not a full-scale biography of Trotsky. Trotsky's later years and the tragic close of his life stirred my imagination more deeply than did the earlier and more worldly part of his story. On second thoughts, however, I began to doubt whether Trotsky in Exile could be made at all comprehensible if the earlier part of the story was not told. Then, pondering historical materials and biographical sources, some of them new to me, I came to realize more clearly than before how deeply the drama of Trotsky's last years was rooted in the earlier and even the earliest stages of his career. I therefore decided to devote to Trotsky two separate yet interconnected volumes: *The Prophet Armed* and *The Prophet Unarmed*, the first giving what might be described as Trotsky's 'rise', the second his 'fall'. I have refrained from using these conventional terms because I do not think that a man's rise to power is necessarily the climax of his life or that his loss of office should be equated with his fall.

The titles to these volumes have been suggested to me by the passage from Machiavelli printed on page xii. The present study illustrates the truth of what is there said; but it also offers a somewhat ironical commentary on it. Machiavelli's observation that 'all armed prophets have conquered and the unarmed ones have been destroyed' is certainly realistic. What may be doubted is whether the distinction between the armed prophet and the unarmed one and the difference between conquest and destruction is always as clear as it seemed to the author of *The Prince*. In the following pages we first watch Trotsky conquering without arms in the greatest revolution of our age. We then see him armed, victorious, and bent under the weight of his armour—the chapter portraying him at the very pinnacle of power bears the title 'Defeat in Victory'. And when next the Prophet Unarmed is contemplated, the question will arise whether a strong element of victory was not concealed in his very defeat.

My account of Trotsky's role in the Russian revolution

will come as a surprise to some. For nearly thirty years the powerful propaganda machines of Stalinism worked furiously to expunge Trotsky's name from the annals of the revolution, or to leave it there only as the synonym for arch-traitor. To the present Soviet generation, and not only to it, Trotsky's life-story is already like an ancient Egyptian sepulchre which is known to have contained the body of a great man and the record, engraved in gold, of his deeds; but tomb-robbers and ghouls have plundered and left it so empty and desolate that no trace is found of the record it once contained. The work of the tomb-robbers has, in this present instance, been so persistent that it has strongly affected the views even of independent Western historians and scholars.

Despite all this, the record of Trotsky's life is still intact, preserved in his own voluminous but now mostly forgotten writings and in his Archives; in numerous memoirs of friendly and of hostile contemporaries; in files of Russian periodicals published before, during, and after the revolution; in minutes of the Central Committee; and in verbatim reports of the Congresses of the party and of the Soviets. Nearly all these documentary sources are available in public libraries in the West, although a few of them can be found only in private libraries. I have drawn on all these sources. Together with my wife, who shared equally with me in research and has in many other respects contributed greatly to this work, I made a special study of the rich collection of Russian pre-revolutionary periodicals in the Hoover Library at Stanford, California, where I found sources scarcely used before by historians of Russian revolutionary movements. Together with my wife I also studied the Trotsky Archives at the Houghton Library, Harvard University, by far the most important collection of original documents on Soviet history existing outside the U.S.S.R. (A brief description of the Archives is given in the bibliography at the end of this volume.)

I have therefore no ground for complaining here, as I complained in the Preface to my *Stalin*, about paucity of biographical material. This is due largely to the contrast between my chief characters. Trotsky was as communicative about his life and activities as Stalin was secretive. He allowed complete strangers to delve freely into almost every aspect of his life; he himself wrote an autobiography; and, what is more important, a strong, unconscious autobiographical streak runs through his scores of published volumes, through his innumerable articles and essays not reprinted in book form, and through some of his unpublished writings. Wherever he went he left footprints so firm that nobody could later efface or blur them, not even he himself, when on rare occasions he was tempted to do so.

A biographer is not usually expected to apologize for narrating the life of a political leader who has himself written an autobiography. I feel that this case may be an exception to the rule, for after a close and critical examination I still find Trotsky's *My Life* as scrupulously truthful as any work of this kind can be. Nevertheless, it remains an apologia produced in the middle of the losing battle its author fought against Stalin. In its pages the living Trotsky wrestled with his tomb-robbers. To wholesale Stalinist denigration he responded with a peculiar act of self-defence which savoured of self-glorification. He did not and could not satisfactorily explain the change in the climate of the revolution which made his defeat both possible and inevitable; and his account of the intrigues by which a narrow-minded, 'usurpatory', and malignant bureaucracy ousted him from power is obviously inadequate. The question which is of absorbing interest to the biographer is: to what extent did Trotsky himself contribute to his own defeat? To what extent was he himself compelled by critical circumstances and by his own character to pave the way for Stalin? The answer to these questions reveals the truly classical tragedy of Trotsky's life, or rather a reproduction of classical tragedy in secular terms of modern politics; and Trotsky would have been more than human if he had been able to reveal it. The biographer, on the other hand, sees Trotsky at the climax of his achievement as being as guilty and as innocent and as ripe for expiation as a protagonist in Greek drama. This approach, presupposing sympathy and understanding, is, I trust, as free from denunciation as from apologetics.

In *My Life* Trotsky sought to vindicate himself in terms imposed upon him by Stalin and by the whole ideological situation of Bolshevism in the 1920s, that is, in terms of the Lenin cult. Stalin had denounced him as Lenin's inveterate enemy, and Trotsky was consequently anxious to prove his complete devotion to, and his agreement with, Lenin. His devotion to

Lenin after 1917 was undoubtedly genuine; and the points of agreement between them were numerous and important. Nevertheless, Trotsky blurred the sharp outlines and the importance of his controversies with Lenin between 1903 and 1917, and also of later differences. But another and much stranger consequence of the fact that Trotsky made his apologia in terms of the Lenin cult was that in some crucial points he belittled his own role in comparison with Lenin's, a feat extremely rare in autobiographical literature. This applies especially to the account of the part he played in the October uprising and in the creation of the Red Army, where he detracted from his own merits in order not to appear as Lenin's detractor. Free from loyalties to any cult, I have attempted to restore the historical balance.

Finally, I have paid special attention to Trotsky the man of letters, the pamphleteer, the military writer, and the journalist. Most of Trotsky's literary work is now wrapt in oblivion and inaccessible to a wider public. Yet this is the writer of whom Bernard Shaw, who could judge Trotsky's literary qualities only from poor translations, said that he 'surpassed Junius and Burke'. 'Like Lessing', Shaw wrote of Trotsky, 'when he cuts off his opponent's head, he holds it up to show that there are no brains in it; but he spares his victim's private character. . . . He leaves [his victim] without a rag of political credit; but he leaves him with his honour intact.'[1] I can only regret that considerations of space and composition have not allowed me to show this side of Trotsky's personality in greater detail; but I hope to return to it in *The Prophet Unarmed*.

I. D.

October 1952

[1] *The Nation*, London, 7 Jan. 1922.

ACKNOWLEDGEMENTS

I AM greatly indebted for criticism and friendly encouragement to Professor E. H. Carr and Mrs. Barbara Ward-Jackson, who read parts of my manuscript; and to Mr. Donald Tyerman, who read the whole. Mr. Bernard Singer helped me with his intimate knowledge of Russian life. To Mr. D. M. Davin and members of the Editorial Staff of the Oxford University Press I am grateful for many suggestions for improvements in style. Mr. Hugo Dewar and Mr. Jon Kimche kindly assisted me with materials and books, some of which are now bibliographical rarities. My thanks are given to Professor Wm. A. Jackson and his assistants at the Houghton Library, Harvard University, who helped my wife and me to find our way through the dossiers of the Trotsky Archives. I am similarly obliged to the Staffs of the Hoover Library, the London Library, the British Museum, and the National Central Library.

The generosity of the Oxford University Press and the Humanities Department of the Rockefeller Foundation enabled my wife and me to spend many months in the United States and to carry out that part of our research programme which depended entirely on our access to the above-mentioned American libraries.

My debt to other authors is acknowledged in footnotes. The quotation from Machiavelli's *The Prince* on page xii is taken by permission of J. M. Dent & Sons Ltd., from the translation by W. K. Marriott in the Everyman's Library.

I. D.

'. . . there is nothing more difficult to take in hand, more perilous to conduct, or more uncertain in its success, than to take the lead in the introduction of a new order of things. Because the innovator has for enemies all those who have done well under the old conditions, and lukewarm defenders in those who may do well under the new. . . .

'It is necessary, therefore, if we desire to discuss this matter thoroughly, to inquire whether these innovators can rely on themselves or have to depend on others: that is to say, whether, to consummate their enterprise, have they to use prayers or can they use force? In the first instance they always succeed badly, and never compass anything; but when they can rely on themselves and use force, then they are rarely endangered. Hence it is that all armed prophets have conquered, and the unarmed ones have been destroyed. Besides the reasons mentioned, the nature of the people is variable, and whilst it is easy to persuade them, it is difficult to fix them in that persuasion. And thus it is necessary to take such measures that, when they believe no longer, it may be possible to make them believe by force.

'If Moses, Cyrus, Theseus, and Romulus had been unarmed they could not have enforced their constitutions for long—as happened in our time to Fra Girolamo Savonarola, who was ruined with his new order of things immediately the multitude believed in him no longer, and he had no means of keeping steadfast those who believed or of making the unbelievers to believe.'

MACHIAVELLI, *The Prince*, CHAPTER VI

CHAPTER I

Home and School

THE reign of Tsar Alexander II (1855–81) was drawing to its gloomy end. The ruler whose accession and early reforms had stirred the most sanguine hopes in Russian society, and even among émigré revolutionaries, the ruler who had, in fact, freed the Russian peasant from serfdom and had earned the title of the Emancipator was spending his last years in a cave of despair—hunted like an animal by the revolutionaries, and hiding in his imperial palaces from their bombs and pistols.

The Tsar was paying the penalty for the frustration of the hopes he had stirred: he had deceived the expectations of almost every class in society. In the eyes of many landlords he was still subversion itself, crowned and dressed in imperial robes. They had never forgiven him the reform of 1861, which had deprived them of their feudal mastery over the peasants. From the peasants he had lifted the burden of serfdom only to let them be crushed by poverty and debts: the ex-serfs had, on their emancipation, to yield to the gentry much of the land they had tilled, and for the land they retained they had over the years to pay a heavy ransom. They still looked up to the Tsar as to their well-wisher and friend and believed that it was against his intentions that the gentry cheated them of the benefits of the emancipation. But already there had been aroused in the peasantry the hunger for land, that great hunger which for more than half a century was to shake Russia and to throw her into a fever, body and mind.

The gentry and the peasantry were still the main classes of Russian society. Only very slowly was the urban middle class growing. Unlike the European bourgeoisie, it had no social ancestry, no tradition, no mind of its own, no self-confidence, and no influence. A tiny portion of the peasantry was detaching itself from the countryside and beginning to form an industrial working class. But, although the last decade in the reign of Alexander brought the first significant industrial strikes, the urban working class was still looked upon as a mere displaced branch of the peasantry.

From none of these classes could there come an immediate threat to the throne. Each class hoped that its claims would be met and its wrongs redressed by the monarch himself. In any case, no class was in a position to air its grievances and make its demands widely known. None could rally its members and muster its strength in any representative institution or political party. These did not exist. State and Church were the only bodies that possessed a national organization; but the function of both, a function which had determined their shape and constitution, had been to suppress not to express social discontent.

Only one group, the intelligentsia, rose to challenge the dynasty. Educated people in all walks of life, especially those who had not been absorbed in officialdom, had no less reason than had the peasantry to be disappointed with the Tsar—the Emancipator. He had first aroused and then frustrated their craving for freedom as he had aroused and deceived the muzhiks' hunger for land. Alexander had not, like his predecessor Nicholas I, chastised the intelligentsia with scorpions; but he was still punishing them with whips. His reforms in education and in the Press had been half-hearted and mean: the spiritual life of the nation remained under the tutelage of the police, the censorship, and the Holy Synod. By offering the educated a semblance of freedom he made the denial of real freedom even more painful and humiliating. The intelligentsia sought to avenge their betrayed hopes; the Tsar strove to tame their restive spirit; and, so, semi-liberal reforms gave way to repression and repression bred rebellion.

Numerically the intelligentsia were very weak. The active revolutionaries among them were a mere handful. If their fight against the ruler of ninety million subjects were to be described as a duel between David and Goliath, that would still exaggerate their strength. Throughout the 1870s, this classical decade of the intelligentsia's rebellion, a few thousand people at the most were involved in the peaceful, 'educational and propagandist' phase of the *Narodnik* (Populist) movement; and in its final, terroristic phase less than two score men and women were directly engaged. These two score made the Tsar a fugitive in his own realm, and kept the whole might of his empire in check. Only against the background of a discontented but mute nation could so tiny a group grow to so gigantic a stature. Unlike the basic classes of society, the intelligentsia were articulate; they had the training indispensable for an analysis of the evils that plagued the nation; and they formulated the programmes that were supposed to remedy those evils. They would hardly have set out to challenge the ruling power if they had thought that they were speaking for themselves alone. They were at first inspired by the great illusion that they were the mouth-piece of the nation, especially of the peasantry. In their thoughts their own craving for freedom merged with the peasants' hunger for land, and they called their revolutionary organization *Zemlya i Volya*—Land and Freedom. They eagerly absorbed the ideas of European socialism and strove to adjust them to the Russian situation. Not the industrial worker but the peasant was to be the pillar of the new society of their dreams. Not the publicly owned industrial factory but the collectively owned rural commune—the age-old *mir* which had survived in Russia—was to be the basic cell of that society.

The 'men of the 1870s' were foredoomed as precursors of a revolution. No social class was in fact prepared to support them. In the course of the decade they gradually discovered their own isolation, shed one set of illusions only to adopt another, and tried to solve dilemmas, some peculiar to their country and generation and some inherent in every revolutionary movement. At first they attempted to move the peasantry to action, either by enlightening the muzhiks about the evils of autocracy, as did the followers of Lavrov, or by inciting them against the Tsar, as Bakunin had urged them to do. Twice in this decade men and women of the intelligentsia abandoned homes and professions and tried to settle as peasants among the peasants in order to gain access to their mind. 'A whole legion of socialists', wrote a general of the gendarmerie, whose job it was to watch this exodus, 'has taken to this with an energy and a spirit of self-sacrifice, the like of which cannot be found in the history of any secret society in Europe.' The self-sacrifice was fruitless, for the peasantry and the intelligentsia were at cross purposes. The muzhik still believed in the Tsar, the Emancipator, and received with suspicious indifference or outright hostility the words of *Narodnik* 'enlightenment' or 'incitement'. Gendarmerie and police rounded up the idealists who had 'gone to the people';

the courts sentenced them to long terms of imprisonment, hard labour, or deportation.

The idea of a revolution through the people was gradually replaced by that of a conspiracy to be planned and carried out by a small and determined minority from the intelligentsia. The forms of the movement changed accordingly. The exodus of the intelligentsia to the countryside had been spontaneous; it had not been guided from any centre. The new conspiracy required a strictly clandestine, closely knit, strongly led, and rigidly disciplined organization. Its leaders—Zhelyabov, Kibalchich, Sofia Perovskaya, Vera Figner, and others—were not at first inclined to terroristic action; but the logic of their position and the events drove them that way. In January 1878 a young woman, Vera Zasulich—one day she was to influence the chief character of this book—shot General Trepov, head of the gendarmerie in Petersburg, in protest against his maltreatment and humiliation of a political prisoner. At her trial horrible abuses of which the police had been guilty were revealed. The jury were so shocked by the revelations and so moved by the sincere idealism of the defendant that they acquitted her. When the police attempted to seize her outside the court, a sympathetic crowd rescued her and enabled her to escape. The Tsar ordered that henceforth military tribunals, not juries, should try political offenders.

Zasulich's unpremeditated deed and the response it evoked pointed the way for the conspirators. In 1879, the year in which this narrative begins, the party of *Land and Freedom* split. One group of members, bent on pursuing terroristic attempts until the overthrow of autocracy, formed themselves into a new body, the *Narodnaya Volya*, the *Freedom of the People*.[1] Their new programme placed far greater emphasis on civil liberties than on land reform. Another and less influential group, setting no store by the terroristic conspiracy, broke away to advocate *Black Partition* (*Chornyi Peredel*)—an egalitarian distribution of the land. (From this group, headed by Plekhanov, who presently emigrated to Switzerland, was to come the first Marxist and Social Democratic message to the revolutionaries in Russia.)

The year 1879 brought a rapid succession of spectacular

---

[1] *Narodnaya Volya* is often translated as the *Will of the People*. *Volya* means in fact both 'will' and 'freedom' and can be translated either way.

terroristic attempts. In February Prince Kropotkin, the Governor of Kharkov, was shot. In March an attempt was made on the life of General Drenteln, head of the political police. In the course of the year the Tsar himself narrowly escaped two attempts: in March a revolutionary fired five shots at him; and in the summer, while the Tsar was returning from his Crimean residence, several mines exploded under his train. Mass arrests, hangings, and deportations followed. But on 1 March 1881 the conspirators succeeded in assassinating the Tsar.

To the world Tsardom presented a glittering façade of grandeur and power. Yet in April 1879 Karl Marx in a letter written from London to a Russian friend pointed to the disintegration of Russian society concealed behind that façade; and he compared the condition of Russia at the close of Alexander's reign with that of France under Louis XV.[1] And, indeed, it was in the last decade of Alexander's reign that most of the men were born who were to lead the Russian revolution.

. . . .

Far away from the scenes of this grim struggle, in the peaceful and sunlit steppe of the southern Ukraine, in the province of Kherson, near the little town of Bobrinetz, David Leontievich Bronstein was—in the year 1879—settling down on a farm which he had just bought from a Colonel Yanovsky, after whom the farm was called Yanovka. The Colonel had received the land, about a thousand acres, from the Tsar as a reward for services. He had not been successful as a farmer and was glad to sell 250 acres and to lease another 400 to Bronstein. The deal was completed early in the year. In the summer the new owner and his family moved from a nearby village to the thatched cottage which they had acquired together with the farm.

The Bronsteins were Jews. It was rare for a Jew to take up farming. Yet about two score of Jewish farming colonies—an overspill from the crowded ghettoes of the 'pale'—were scattered over the Kherson steppe. Jews were not allowed to live in Russia outside the pale, outside, that is, the towns that lay mostly in the western provinces annexed from Poland. But they were allowed to settle freely in the southern steppe near the Black Sea. Russia had come into possession of that sparsely

[1] *Perepiska K. Marxa i F. Engelsa s Russkimi Politicheskimi Deyatelami*, p. 84.

populated but fertile land towards the end of the eighteenth century, and the Tsars were anxious to promote colonization. Here, as so often in the history of colonization, the foreign immigrant and the outcast were the pioneers. Serbs, Bulgarians, Greeks, Jews were encouraged to conquer the wilderness. Up to a point, the Jewish settlers improved their lot. They struck roots in the country; they enjoyed certain privileges; and they were relieved of the menace of expulsion and violence which always hung over the Jewish pale. It had never been quite clear just how far that pale extended. Alexander I had allowed it to spread a little. Nicholas I had no sooner ascended the throne than he ordered the Jews to be driven back. Towards the middle of the century he expelled them again from Nikolayev, Sebastopol, Poltava, and the towns around Kiev. Most of those expelled resettled within the shrunken and congested pale, but a few went out to the steppe.[1]

It was probably during one of these expulsions, in the early 1850s, that Leon Bronstein, the father of the new owner of Yanovka, had left with his family a small Jewish town near Poltava, on the east side of the Dnieper, and settled in the Kherson province. His sons and daughters when they grew up stayed on the land; but only one, David, became prosperous enough to detach himself from the Jewish colony and set up as an independent farmer at Yanovka.

As a rule, the colonists came from the lowest orders of the Jewish population. Jews had been town dwellers for centuries; and farming was so foreign to their way of life that very few of those able to eke out a living in town would take to it. The merchant, the craftsman, the money-lender, the middle-man, the pious student of the Talmud, all preferred living within the pale, in an established if miserable Jewish community. They despised rural life so much that in their idiom *Am Haaretz*, 'the man of the land', also meant the boor and the vulgar who did not even have a smattering of the Scriptures. Those who went out into the steppe had had nothing to lose; they were not afraid of hard and unfamiliar work; and they had few or no ties with the Synagogue.

The new owner of Yanovka would certainly have been described by his co-religionists as an *Am Haaretz*: he was

---

[1] S. M. Dubnov, *History of the Jews in Russia and Poland*, vol. ii, pp. 30–34 and *passim*.

illiterate, indifferent to religion, and even a little contemptuous of the Synagogue. Although a ploughman in the second generation only, he had in himself so much of the peasant and of the child of nature as to appear almost completely un-Jewish. At his home not Yiddish, that amalgam of old German, Hebrew, and Slavonic, was spoken but a mixture of Russian and Ukrainian. Unlike most muzhiks, however, the Bronsteins had no memories of serfdom; here in the open steppe serfdom had never been firmly established. David Bronstein was a free and ambitious, tough, and hard-working farmer, of the frontiersman type. He was determined to develop his farm into a flourishing estate, and he drove himself and his labourers hard. His opportunities still lay ahead: when he moved to Yanovka he was only about thirty.

His wife Anna came from different stock. She had been brought up either in Odessa or in some other southern town, not in the country. She was educated enough to subscribe to a lending library and occasionally to read a Russian novel—few Russian Jewish women of the time could do that. In her parental home she had imbibed something of the orthodox Jewish tradition; she was more careful than her husband to observe the rites, and she would not travel or sew on the Sabbath. Her middle-class origin showed itself in an instinctive conventionality, tinged with a little religious hypocrisy. In case of need, she would sew on the Sabbath, but take good care that no stranger should see her doing so. How she had come to marry the farmer Bronstein is not clear; her son says that she fell in love with him when he was young and handsome. Her family was distressed and looked down upon the bumpkin. This was, nevertheless, not an unhappy marriage. At first the young Mrs. Bronstein fretted at rustic life, but then she did her best to shed her urban habits and to become a peasant woman. Before they came to Yanovka, she had borne four children. A few months after the family had settled at Yanovka, on 26 October 1879, a fifth was born, a boy. The child was named after his grandfather, Lev or Leon, the man who had left the Jewish town near Poltava to settle in the steppe.[1]

By a freak of fate, the day on which the boy was born, 26 October (or 7 November according to the new calendar) was

[1] L. Trotsky, *Moya Zhizn*, vol. i, chapter ii.

the precise date on which thirty-eight years later, as Leon
Trotsky, he was to lead the Bolshevik insurrection in Petrograd.[1]

.   .   .   .

The boy spent his first nine years at Yanovka. His childhood,
as he himself put it, was neither like a 'sunny meadow' nor like
a 'dark pit of hunger, violence, and misery'. The Bronsteins led
the stern life of industrious and thrifty upstarts. 'Every muscle
was strained, every thought set on work and savings.' 'Life at
Yanovka was entirely governed by the rhythm of the toil on the
farm. Nothing else mattered, nothing except the price of grain
in the world market';[2] and this was just then falling rapidly.
However, the Bronsteins's preoccupation with money was no
heavier than that of most farmers; they were not stingy where
their children were concerned, and were doing their best to
give them a good start in life. When Lyova[3] was born, the elder
children were at school in town; the baby had a nursemaid, a
luxury very few peasants could afford. Later there would be a
teacher of music at Yanovka, and the boys would be sent to the
universities. Both the parents were too absorbed in their work
to give their youngest child much tenderness, but for this he
had instead the affectionate care of his two sisters and of his
nanny. Lyova grew into a healthy and lively boy, delighting his
parents and sisters and the servants and labourers on the farm
with his brightness and good temper.

By the standards of his environment, he had a comfortable
childhood. The Bronsteins's cottage was built of clay and had
five rooms; some of these were small and dim, with uncovered
clay floors and ceilings which leaked in heavy rain; but peasant
families usually lived in mud huts and hovels of one or two
rooms. During Lyova's childhood the family grew in wealth and
importance. The crops and the herds of cattle were on the
increase; new farm buildings sprang up around the cottage.
Next to the cottage stood a big shed containing a workshop, the
farm kitchen, and the servants' quarters. Behind it was a cluster
of small and large barns, stables, cowsheds, pigsties, and other
outbuildings. Farther off, on a hill beyond a pond, stood a big
mill, apparently the only one in this part of the steppe. In the

---

[1] In the same year, more than two months later, Joseph Djugashvili Stalin was
born in the little Georgian town of Gori.
[2] Trotsky, op. cit., loc. cit.   [3] Lyova is the diminutive of Lev or Leon.

summer, muzhiks from nearby and remote villages would come to have their corn ground. For weeks they waited in queues, slept in the fields when the weather was dry or in the mill when it rained, and paid the mill owner a tithe in kind for the grinding and threshing. David Bronstein traded with local merchants at first; but later, as his wealth grew, he sold his goods through his own wholesaler at Nikolayev, the grain harbour rapidly developing on the Black Sea. After a few years at Yanovka, he could easily have afforded much more land than he owned, were it not for the new *ukase* of 1881 which forbade Jews to buy land even in the steppe. He could now only rent it from neighbours; and this he did on a large scale. The neighbours belonged to the 'downstart' Polish and Russian gentry, who lightheartedly wasted their fortunes and were deep in debt, even though they still lived in splendid country residences.

Here the boy watched for the first time a social class in decay. 'The quintessence of aristocratic ruin was the Ghertopanov family. A large village and the entire county were once called by their name. The whole district had belonged to them. Now the old Ghertopanov owned only a thousand acres, and these were mortgaged over and over again. My father leased this land, and paid the rents into the bank. Ghertopanov lived by writing petitions, complaints, and letters for the peasants. When he came to see us, he usually hid tobacco and lumps of sugar up his sleeve. His wife did the same. Dribbling, she would tell us stories about her youth, and about the serfs, pianos, silks, and perfumes she had possessed. Their two sons grew up almost illiterate. The younger, Victor, worked as an apprentice in our workshop.'[1] It is easy to imagine the sense of their own competence and dignity that the Bronsteins felt when they compared themselves with such neighbours. Much of their own self-confidence and optimistic industriousness they passed on to their children.

Parents and sisters tried to keep the little Lyova in or near the cottage, but the bustle and commotion on the farm were too much for him, except during the quiet monotonous winter months, when family life centred on the dining-room. The magic of the workshop next door lured the boy: there Ivan Vassilyevich Grebien, the chief mechanic, initiated him into the

[1] L. Trotsky, *Moya Zhizn*, vol. i, pp. 46–47.

uses of tools and materials. Ivan Vassilyevich was also the family's confidant; he lunched and supped at the cottage, at his master's table, a thing almost unimaginable in an ordinary Jewish home. The mechanic's tricks and jokes and his jovial temper captivated Lyova: in *My Life* he recollects the mechanic as the main influence of his early childhood. But at the workshop the boy now and then also came up against an outburst of puzzling ill temper on the part of other labourers. Time and again he would overhear harsh words about his parents, words which shocked him, set him thinking, and sank into his mind.

From the workshop he would wander to the barns and cow-sheds, play and hide in shady lofts, grow familiar with men and animals, and with the wide spaces of the prairie. From his sister he learned the alphabet, and got his first inkling of the importance of figures as he watched the peasants and his father wrangling in the mill over grain and money. He stared at scenes of poverty, cruelty, and helpless rebellion; and he watched the strikes of half-starved labourers in the middle of the harvest. 'The labourers left the fields and gathered in the courtyard. They lay in the shade of the barns with their faces turned downward, brandishing their bare, cracked, straw-pricked feet in the air, and waited to see what would happen. Then my father would give them some whey, or water melons, or half a sack of dried fish, and they would go back to work and even sing.'[1] Another scene he was to remember was that of a group of labourers coming from the fields, in the twilight, with uncertain steps and with their hands stretched out in front of them—they had all been struck by night-blindness from undernourishment. A health inspector came down to Yanovka, but found nothing wrong there: the Bronsteins treated their labourers no worse than did the other employers; the food, soup and *kasha*, was not inferior to that served on any other farm. The impression all this made on the child need not be exaggerated. Many have seen such and worse scenes in their childhood without later becoming revolutionaries. Other and more complex influences were needed to kindle in Lyova indignation against social injustice and to turn his mind against the established order. But when those influences appeared, they recalled vividly the

[1] L. Trotsky, *Moya Zhizn*, vol. i, p. 42.

pictures and scenes stored in his memory, and played all the more strongly on his sensitivity and conscience. The child took his environment for granted. Only when he was disturbed by an extreme instance of his father's harshness would he burst into tears and hide his face in the pillows on the sofa in the dining-room.

He was seven when his parents sent him to school at Grom-okla, a Jewish-German colony only a couple of miles away from Yanovka. There he stayed with relatives. The school he atten-ded may be described as a *kheder*, a Jewish private religious school, with Yiddish as its language. Here the boy was to be taught to read the Bible and to translate it from Hebrew into Yiddish; the curriculum also included, as sidelines, reading in Russian and a little arithmetic. Knowing no Yiddish, he could neither understand his teacher nor get along with his school-mates. The school was almost certainly a dirty and fetid hole, where the boy accustomed to roam the fields must have nearly choked. The ways of the adults also bewildered him. Once he saw the Jews of Gromokla driving a woman of loose morals through the main street of the village, pitilessly humiliating her and shouting vehement abuse. Another time the colonists meted out stern punishment to a horse-thief. He also noticed a strange contrast: on one side of the village stood the wretched hovels of Jewish colonists; on the other shone the neat and tidy cottages of German settlers. He was naturally attracted to the gentile quarters.

His stay at Gromokla was brief, for after a few months the Bronsteins, seeing the boy was unhappy, decided to take him back home. And so he said goodbye to the Scriptures and to the boys who would go on translating, in a strange sing-song, versets from the incomprehensible Hebrew into the incomprehensible Yiddish.[1] But, during his few months at Gromokla, he had learned to read and write Russian; and on his return to Yanovka he indefatigably copied passages from the few books at hand and later wrote compositions, recited verses, and made rhymes of his own. He began to help his father with accounts and book-keeping. Often he would be shown off to visiting neigh-bours and asked to recite his verses and produce his drawings.

[1] Later, during his stay in Odessa, he once again took lessons in Hebrew, but the result was not much better.

At first he ran away in embarrassment, but soon he grew accustomed to receiving admiration and looked for it.

A year or so after he had left the Jewish school there came to Yanovka a visitor who was to have a decisive influence on him as boy and as adolescent. The visitor was Moissei Filipovich Spentzer, Mrs. Bronstein's nephew, one of the remote, town-dwelling, middle-class branch of the family. 'A bit of a journalist and a bit of a statistician', he lived in Odessa, had been touched by the liberal ferment of ideas, and had been debarred from the University for a minor political offence. During his stay at Yanovka, which lasted a whole summer—he had come there for his health—he gave much of his time to the bright but untutored darling of the family. Then he volunteered to take him to Odessa and to look after his education. The Bronsteins agreed; and so, in the autumn of 1888, equipped with a brand new school uniform, loaded with parcels containing all the delicacies that the Yanovka farm-kitchen could produce, and amid tears of sadness and joy, Lyova left.

The Black Sea harbour of Odessa was Russia's Marseilles, only much younger than Marseilles, sunny and gay, multi-national, open to many winds and influences. Southern ebullience, love of the spectacular, and warm emotionalism predominated in the temperament of the people of Odessa. During the seven or so years of his stay there it was not so much the city and its temper, however, as the home of the Spentzers that was to mould Lyova's mind and character. He could hardly have come into a family which contrasted more with his own. At first the Spentzers were not too well off; Spentzer himself was handicapped by his expulsion from the University, and, for the time being, his wife, headmistress of a secular school for Jewish girls, was the family's mainstay. Later Spentzer rose to be an eminent liberal publisher. Max Eastman, the American writer who knew the couple about forty years later, described them as 'kindly, quiet, poised, intelligent'.[1] They began by teaching the boy to speak proper Russian instead of his homely mixture of Ukrainian and Russian; and they polished his manners as well as his accent. He was impressionable and eager to transform himself from a rustic urchin into a presentable pupil. New interests and pleasures were opening before him. In the

[1] Max Eastman, *Leon Trotsky: The Portrait of a Youth*, p. 14.

evenings the Spentzers would read aloud the classical Russian poets—Pushkin and Lermontov and their favourite Nekrasov, the citizen-poet, whose verses were a protest against the miseries of Tsardom. Lyova would listen entranced and would demur at being compelled to descend from the golden clouds of poetry to his bed. From Spentzer he first heard the story of Faust and Gretchen; he was moved to tears by *Oliver Twist*; and stealthily he read Tolstoy's drastic and sombre play, *The Power of Darkness*, which the censorship had just banned and which was the topic of much hushed conversation among the grown-ups.

The Spentzers had chosen a school for him, but he was too young. This difficulty was overcome, however, when the registrar at home made out a birth certificate declaring him to be a year older than he was. A greater obstacle was that the year before, in 1887, the government had issued the ill-famed *ukase* on *numerus clausus*, under which admittance of Jews to secondary schools was so restricted that they might not exceed 10 and in some places 5 or 3 per cent. of all pupils. Jewish entrants had to sit for competitive examinations. At the examination Lyova, who had not attended any primary school, failed. For a year he was sent to the preparatory class at the same school, whence Jewish pupils were admitted to the first form with priority over outside Jewish applicants.

At St. Paul's *Realschule*—this was the name of the school—no Greek or Latin was taught, but pupils got a better grounding than in the ordinary *gymnasium*, in science, mathematics, and modern languages, German and French. To the progressive intelligentsia this curriculum seemed best calculated to give their children a rationalistic and practical education. St. Paul's had been founded by the German Lutheran parish of Odessa, but it had not escaped Russification. When Lyova joined it the teaching was in Russian, but pupils and teachers were of German, Russian, Polish, and Swiss origin—Greek Orthodox, Lutheran, Roman Catholic, and Jewish. This variety of nationalities and denominations resulted in a degree of liberalism uncommon in Russian schools. No single nationality predominated, and no denomination, not even the Greek Orthodox, was favoured. At the worst, a Russian teacher would surreptitiously pester a Polish pupil, or a Roman Catholic priest would annoy with subdued malice a Jewish boy. But there was no open discrimination or persecution to give a sense of inferiority to non-Russian pupils. To be sure, the discrimination was inherent in the fact that Russian had been made the official language; but only German parents and children would have been likely to resent this. And, in spite of the *numerus clausus*, the Jewish pupil, once he had been admitted, was treated with fairness. In a sense, St. Paul's gave Lyova his first taste of cosmopolitanism.

He at once became the top pupil in his class. 'No one had to take charge of his training, no one had to worry about his lessons. He always did more than was expected of him.'[1] His teachers were quick to acknowledge his gifts and diligence, and soon he also became popular with the boys of the higher forms. Yet he shunned sports and physical exercise, and during his seven years on the Black Sea he never went fishing, rowing, or swimming. His aloofness from the school playground was perhaps due to an accident during an early escapade, when he fell from a ladder, hurt himself badly, and 'wriggled on the ground like a worm', and perhaps also to his feeling that the proper place for outdoor exercise was Yanovka: 'the city was for studying and working.' His excellence in the class-room was enough to establish his self-confidence.

In the course of the seven years of the *Realschule* he was involved in a few school rows, none of which ended too badly. Once he produced a school magazine, nearly all written by himself; but, as such magazines had been forbidden by the Ministry of Education, the teacher to whom he presented a copy warned him to desist. Lyova paid heed to the warning. In the second form, a group of boys, including Lyova, booed and hissed a disliked teacher. The headmaster detained some of the offenders, but he let off the first pupil as being quite above suspicion. Some of the detained boys then 'betrayed' Lyova. 'The best pupil is a moral outcast', said the insulted teacher, pointing at the boy of whom he had been proud; and the 'outcast' was expelled. The shock was softened by the understanding and sympathy which the Spentzers showed their ward and by the indulgence of his own father, who was more amused than indignant.

Next year Lyova was readmitted, after examination; he became again the favourite and the pride of the school and took

[1] M. Eastman, *Leon Trotsky: The Portrait of a Youth*, p. 17.

care to avoid further trouble, though in one of the upper forms, together with other pupils, he refused to write compositions for a sluggish teacher who never read or returned the exercise-books; but this time he suffered no punishment. In the auto-biography, he himself describes, in a somewhat self-indulgent tone, the sequel to his expulsion: 'Such was my first political test, as it were. The class was henceforth divided into distinct groups: the talebearers and the envious on one side, the frank and courageous boys on the other, and the neutral and vacillating mass in the middle. These three groups never quite disappeared even in later years. I was to meet them again and again in my life....'[1] In this reminiscence the second form at the Odessa school is indeed made to look like the prototype of the Communist party in the 1920s with its divisions for and against Trotsky.

The boy's appearance and character were now becoming formed. He was handsome, with a swarthy complexion and sharp but well-proportioned features, short-sighted eyes lively behind their spectacles, and an abundant crop of jet black, well-brushed hair. He took unusual care with his appearance: neat and tidy, well and even stylishly dressed, he looked 'highly bourgeois'.[2] He was buoyant, sprightly, but also dutiful and well mannered. Like many a gifted youth, he was also strongly self-centred and eager to excel. To quote his own words, he 'felt that he could achieve more than the others. The boys who became his friends acknowledged his superiority. This could not fail to have some effect on his character.'[3] Max Eastman, his not uncritical admirer, speaks about his strong and early de-veloped instinct of rivalry, and compares it to a well-known instinct in race-horses. 'It makes them, even when they are ambling along at a resting pace, keep at least one white eye backwards along the track to see if there is anything in the field that considers itself an equal. It involves an alert awareness of self, and is upon the whole a very disagreeable trait—especially as it appears to those horses who were not bred for speed.'[4] Although Lyova had many followers among his school mates, none became his intimate friend.

At school he came under no significant influence. His teachers,

[1] L. Trotsky, *Moya Zhizn*, vol. i, p. 94.
[2] M. Eastman, *Leon Trotsky: The Portrait of a Youth*, pp. 15, 31.
[3] L. Trotsky, op. cit., vol. i, p. iii.   [4] M. Eastman, op. cit., p. 19.

whose personalities he sketches so vividly in the autobiography, were a mixed lot: some reasonably good, others cranky, or notorious for taking bribes; even the best were too mediocre to stimulate him. His character and imagination were formed at the Spentzers' home. There he was loved as well as admired, and he responded with warmth and gratitude. From his first weeks there, when he watched rapturously the Spentzers' baby and observed its first smiles, until the last days of his stay nothing clouded the affectionate relationship. The only discordant story his mentors would tell after many years was how once, at the beginning of his stay, Lyova sold a few of their most precious books to buy himself sweets. As he grew, he appreciated more and more his good fortune in having found such excellent guides and he shared increasingly in their intellectual interests. Editors of local liberal newspapers and men of letters were frequent visitors. He was mesmerized by their talk and by their mere presence. To him 'authors, journalists and artists always stood for a world more attractive than any other, open only to the elect';[1] and this world he beheld with a thrill known only to the born man of letters when he first comes into contact with the men and the affairs of his predestined profession.

Odessa was not one of the leading or most lively literary centres; the giants of Russian literature were not among the friends of the Spentzers. All the same, the boy of fifteen or sixteen stood reverently at the threshold of the temple, even if he saw none of the high priests at the altar. The local liberal press, much molested by the censorship, had its courageous and skilful writers such as V. M. Doroshevich, the master of that semi-literary and semi-journalistic essay at which Bronstein himself was one day to excel. Doroshevich's *feuilletons* were Lyova's and his elders' favourite reading. After Spentzer had started his publishing business, the house was always full of books, manuscripts, and printers' proofs which Lyova scrutinized with devouring curiosity. It excited him to see books in the making, and he inhaled with delight the fresh smell of the printed word, for which he was to retain a fond weakness even in the years when he was conducting vast revolutionary and military operations. Here he fell ardently in love with words; and here he first heard an authentic author, a local authority on Shakespeare who had

[1] L. Trotsky, *Moya Zhizn*, vol. i, p. 86.

read one of his compositions, express rapturous admiration for the way the boy handled and marshalled words.

He was spellbound by the theatre as well. '. . . I developed a fondness for Italian opera which was the pride of Odessa. . . . I even did some tutoring to earn money for theatre tickets. For several months I was mutely in love with the coloratura soprano, bearing the mysterious name of Giuseppina Uget, who seemed to me to have descended straight from heaven to the stage boards of Odessa.'[1] The intoxication with the theatre, with its limelight, costumes, and masks, and with its passions and conflicts, accords well with the adolescence of a man who was to act his role with an intense sense of the dramatic, and of whose life it might indeed be said that its very shape had the power and pattern of classical tragedy.

From Odessa, Lyova returned to Yanovka for summer holidays and for Christmas, or sometimes to repair his health. At every return he saw visible signs of growing prosperity. The home he had left was that of an ordinary well-to-do farmer; the one he came back to looked more and more like a landlord's estate. The Bronsteins were building a large country house for themselves and their children; yet they still lived and worked as of old. The father still spent his days bargaining with muzhiks over sacks of flour in the mill, inspecting his cowsheds, watching his labourers at the harvest, and occasionally himself grasping the scythe. The nearest post-office and railway station were still twenty or so miles away. Nobody read a newspaper here—at the most his mother would slowly and laboriously read an old novel, moving her toil-worn finger across the pages.

These homecomings filled Lyova with mixed feelings. He had remained enough of a villager to feel constricted in the city and to enjoy the wide and open steppe. Here he uncoiled himself, played, walked, and rode. But at each return he also felt more and more a stranger at Yanovka. His parents' pursuits seemed unbearably narrow, their manners coarse, and their way of life purposeless. He began to perceive how much ruthlessness towards labourers and muzhiks went into the making of a farmer's prosperity, even if that ruthlessness was, as it seems to have been at Yanovka, softened by patriarchal benevolence. While on holidays, Lyova helped with book-keeping and calculating wages; and some-

[1] L. Trotsky, op. cit., vol. i, p. 85.

times father and son quarrelled, especially when the calculations seemed to the old Bronstein unduly favourable to the
wage-earners. The quarrels did not escape the attention of the
labourers, and this incensed the farmer. The boy was not inclined to behave with discretion, and his spirit of contradiction
was enhanced by a feeling of superiority, not unusual in the
educated son of an illiterate peasant. Rural life in general
struck him now as repulsively brutal. Once he tried, unavail-
ingly, to protest against the rudeness of a policeman who came
to deport two labourers because their passports had not been
quite in order. He had a glimpse of the savage cruelty with
which the poor themselves treated one another. He felt a vague
sympathy for the underdog and an even vaguer remorse for his
own privileged position. Equally strong, or perhaps even more
so, was his offended self-esteem. It hurt him to see himself as the
son of a rustic moneygrubber and illiterate upstart, the son, one
might say now, of a *kulak*.

His stay in Odessa ended in 1896. A *Realschule* normally had
seven forms, but St. Paul's only six, so he had to attend a
similar school at Nikolayev to matriculate. He was now nearly
seventeen, but no political idea had so far appealed to him. The
year before, Friedrich Engels had died; the event did not register in the mind of the future revolutionary—even the name of
Karl Marx had not yet come to his ears. He was, in his own
words, 'poorly equipped politically for a boy of seventeen of that
time'. He was attracted by literature; and he was preparing for
a university course in pure mathematics. These two approaches
to life, the imaginative and the abstract, lured him—later he
would strive to unite them in his writings. But for the time being
politics exercised no pull. He pondered the prospects of an
academic career, to the disappointment of his father, who would
have preferred a more practical occupation for him. Least of
all did he imagine himself as a revolutionary.

In this the spirit of the time undoubtedly showed itself. At
other times young people often plunged into clandestine revolutionary groups straight from school. This happened when such
groups were astir with new ideas, animated by great hopes, and
naturally expansive. During the 1880s and the early 1890s the
revolutionary movement was at its nadir. In assassinating
Alexander II the *Freedom of the People* had itself committed

suicide. Its leaders had expected that their deed would become the signal for a nation-wide upheaval, but they failed to evoke any response and the nation maintained silence. Those directly and indirectly connected with the conspiracy died on the gallows, and no immediate successors came forward to continue it. It was revealed once again that, despite its discontent, the peasantry was in no revolutionary mood: to the peasants the assassination of Alexander II was the gentry's revenge on the peasants' benefactor.

The new Tsar, Alexander III, abolished most of his predecessor's semi-liberal reforms. His chief inspirer was Pobedonostsev, his tutor and the Procurator of the Holy Synod, in whose sombre and shrewd mind were focused all the dread and fear of revolution felt by the ruling class. Pobedonostsev egged on the Tsar to restore the unimpaired 'domination of the father over his family, of the landlord over his countryside and of the monarch over all the Russias'. It became an offence to praise the previous Tsar for the abolition of serfdom. The gentry's jurisdiction over the peasantry was restored. The universities were closed to the children of the lower classes; the radical literary periodicals were banned; the nation, including the intelligentsia, was to be forced back into mute submission.

Revolutionary terrorism proved itself impotent, and thus another *Narodnik* illusion was dispelled. An attempt to assassinate Alexander III—Alexander Ulyanov, Lenin's elder brother participated in it—failed. The survivors of the *Freedom of the People* languished in prisons and in places of exile, cherished their memories and were lost in confusion. Characteristic of the time was the repentance of one of the *Narodnik* leaders, Tikhomirov, who came out, in western Europe, with a confession under the title 'Why have I ceased to be a revolutionary?' Some former rebels found an outlet for their energies and talents in industry and commerce, which were now expanding at a quicker tempo than before. Many found their prophet in Leo Tolstoy, who rejected with disgust the evils of autocracy but preached that they should not be resisted with force. Tolstoy's doctrine seemed to give a moral sanction to the intelligentsia's disillusioned quiescence.

In *My Life* Trotsky ascribes his political indifference to this general mood. The explanation is only in part correct. The truth is that well before 1896, the year in which he left Odessa, a revival had begun in the revolutionary underground. The Marxists expounded a new programme and method of action; and groups of students and workers who considered themselves social democrats were rapidly springing up. From a contemporary Russian report to the Socialist International we know that by the middle of the decade such groups had been active in Odessa.[1] The young Bronstein was not aware of their existence. Evidently no socialist circle existed among the pupils of St. Paul's, otherwise it would have tried to attract the school's most popular and gifted pupil. Nor did the stirrings of the new movement find any echo in the prosperous and well-sheltered home of the Spentzers. The Spentzers belonged to those on whom the *Narodnik* débâcle had left a deep impression. They shunned the really dangerous topics or spoke about them in muffled voices. Their radicalism shaded off into a broad-minded but timid liberalism which was, no doubt, implicitly opposed to Tsardom. This was too little to impress their ward. Only clear-cut, bold, and expressly stated ideas can enthuse young minds and hearts. When in 1895 Nicholas II ascended the throne and bluntly told the very moderate 'liberal' *Zemstvos* to give up 'nonsensical dreams', Lyova's heart was with the 'dreamers'; but, like the Spentzers, he took it for granted that it was quixotic to strive for any change in the established system of government.

In this ill-defined, quiescently liberal mood one sentiment was felt very keenly: a wistful yearning for Europe and its civilization, for the West at large and its freedoms. That 'West' was like a vision of the promised land—it provided compensation and comfort for the sorry and shabby reality of Russia. Especially on the Jewish intelligentsia, that part of the world which knew no pogroms, no pale, and no *numerus clausus*, exercised immense fascination. To a large section of the gentile intelligentsia, also, the West was the antithesis of all they detested at home: the Holy Synod, the censorship, the *knout*, and *katorga*.[2] Many of the educated Russians first approached the West with that exalted reverence with which the young Herzen had

---

[1] *Doklad Russkikh Sots. Demokratov Vtoromu Internatsionalu* (Geneva 1896) states that in Odessa these groups had been more active than elsewhere in the south of Russia. See also P. A. Garvi, *Vospominanya Sotsialdemokrata*, pp. 20–1.

[2] *Katorga*: hard labour, penal servitude.

viewed it before bourgeois liberalism, seen at close quarters, disillusioned him. In later years Lyova, too, would, as a Socialist, grow aware of the limitations of liberal Europe and turn against it: but something of his youthful enthusiasm for the 'West' was to survive and colour his thoughts to the end.

This, then, was the frame of mind in which he left Odessa, 'the most police-ridden city in police-ridden Russia'. His only vivid political memory of the city was that of a street scene dominated by Odessa's Governor, Admiral Zelenoy, a man who exercised 'absolute power with an uncurbed temper'. 'I saw him but once and then only his back. But that was enough for me. The Governor was standing in his carriage, fully erect, and was cursing in his hoarse voice across the street, shaking his fist. Policemen, with their hands at attention, and janitors, caps in hand, marched past him in review, and behind curtained windows frightened faces peeped out. I adjusted my school bag and hurried home.'[1]

The spark of rebellion had not yet been kindled in the young man who watched the satrap—he merely shrank in horror from the ruling power and went his way, as if in a mood of Tolstoyan non-resistance.

[1] L. Trotsky, *Moya Zhizn*, vol. i, p. 79.

CHAPTER II

In Search of an Ideal

IT was a casual influence that first set the young Bronstein on his revolutionary road. In the summer of 1896 he arrived at Nikolayev to complete his secondary education. He was lodging with a family whose sons had already been touched by Socialist ideas. They drew him into argument and tried to impress their views on him. For several months they seemed to make no headway. He superciliously dismissed their 'Socialist Utopia'. Assailed with arguments, he would adopt the posture of a somewhat conservative young man, not devoid of sympathy with the people but distrusting 'mob ideology' and 'mob rule'. His passion was for pure mathematics and he had no time or taste for politics. His hostess, apprehensive because of her sons' dangerous views, was delighted by this good sense and tried to induce them to imitate him. All this did not last long. The talks about prevailing social injustice and about the need to change the country's whole way of life had already started a ferment in his thoughts. The Socialists' arguments brought out and focused the scenes of poverty and exploitation that had since childhood been stored in his mind; they made him feel how stifling was the air he had breathed; and they captivated him by their novelty and bold high-mindedness. Yet he continued to resist. The stronger the pull of the new ideas the more desperately he clung to his assumed conservatism and indifference to politics. His spirit of contradiction and his eagerness to excel in argument did not easily allow him to yield. But his defences and vanity had to give way. In the middle of the school year he suddenly acknowledged his 'defeat', and at once began to argue for socialism with an ardour and acuteness which took aback those who had converted him.[1]

Again and again we shall see this psychological mechanism at work in him: He is confronted with a new idea to which up to a point he is conditioned to respond; yet he resists at first with stubborn haughtiness; his resistance grows with the attraction; and he subdues incipient doubt and hesitation. Then his inner

[1] Trotsky, op. cit., vol. i, p. 120.

defences crumble, his self-confidence begins to vanish; but he is still too proud or not convinced enough to give any sign of yielding. There is no outward indication yet of the struggle that goes on in his mind. Then, suddenly, the new conviction hardens in him, and, as if in a single moment, overcomes his spirit of contradiction and his vanity. He startles his erstwhile opponents not merely by his complete and disinterested surrender, but by the enthusiasm with which he embraces their cause, and sometimes by the unexpected and far-reaching conclusions which he draws from their arguments.

The cause to which he had just adhered was dim in his mind. He had embraced a mood rather than an idea. He would 'side with the underdog'. But who was the underdog? How did he become one? And what was to be done? Nobody could offer him guidance. No significant Socialist group or organization existed in Nikolayev. Immediately, his socialism showed itself in a freshly awakened interest in social and political matters and in a corresponding weakening of his passion for mathematics. He began to seek those with similar views and interests; but in doing so he at once stepped out of the sheltered environment in which he had spent his childhood and adolescence.

Through his co-lodgers he met a certain Franz Shvigovsky, a poor gardener renting an orchard on the outskirts of the town, who, in his hut in the orchard, held a small discussion-club for radically minded students and working men. Shvigovsky, a Czech by origin, was a curious character. He read in many languages, was well versed in the classics of Russian and German literature, subscribed to foreign newspapers and periodicals, and was always ready to oblige his friends with a banned political book or pamphlet. Old *Narodniks*, living in the town under police surveillance, would sometimes join the group at the orchard. There were no prominent men among these *Narodniks*, and they formed no organization; but they imparted something of their own romantic revolutionary outlook to Shvigovsky's circle. Nearly all its members considered themselves to be *Narodniks*. The meetings, as one of the participants says, had a 'harmless character'. People came to the orchard because they felt at ease there and could speak freely. In the town Shvigovsky's garden soon had 'a most odious reputation ... as a centre of all sorts of the most terrible conspiracies'. The police sent in spies, disguised as labourers working in the garden; but these could only report that Shvigovsky kept serving his visitors apples and endless cups of tea and having harmless and cranky discussions with them.[1]

These, we know, were years of revolutionary revival. In March 1895 the Minister of the Interior, Durnovo, wrote to Pobedonostsev that he was alarmed by the new trends, especially among students who had zealously and with no expectation of reward taken to lecturing on all sorts of social themes. In the Minister's eyes this idealistic disinterestedness augured nothing good. All the repressive legislation of previous years had failed to make the schools and universities immune from subversive influences. For years now the ministry had been appointing professors over the heads of the faculties, dismissing suspects, and promoting obedient nonentities. Scholars of world fame such as D. Mendeleyev, the chemist, I. Mechnikov, the biologist, and M. Kovalevsky, the sociologist, had been found disloyal and dismissed or forced to resign their chairs. The eminent historian Klyuchevsky had had to recant his liberal opinions. The works of John Stuart Mill, Herbert Spencer, and Karl Marx had been forbidden. Students' libraries and clubs had been closed; and informers had been planted in the lecture halls. Entry fees had been raised fivefold to bar academic education to children of poor parents. Yet in spite of everything resurgent rebellion stalked the universities. At the end of 1895 and at the beginning of 1896 students were asked to take an oath of loyalty to the new Tsar, Nicholas II. In Petersburg, Moscow, and Kiev most students refused. The Tsar's coronation (during which thousands of onlookers were trampled upon, maimed, and killed in a stampede for which the police were blamed) was followed, in May 1896, by a strike of 30,000 Petersburg workers, the first strike on this scale.[2]

In these events the influence was already felt of the Union of Struggle for the Emancipation of the Working Class recently founded by Lenin, Martov, and Potresov. The revived movement was wholly influenced by the Marxists—the *Narodniks* scarcely took part in it. The new socialism relied primarily on the industrial worker. It repudiated terrorism. It recognized

---

[1] G. A. Ziv, *Trotsky, Kharakteristika po Lichnym Vospominanyam*, p. 8.
[2] Sibiryak, *Studencheskoye Dvizhenie v Rosii*.

the need for further capitalist industrialization in Russia, through which the working class would grow in numbers and strength. Its immediate purpose, however, was to fight for civil liberties and to move the workers to economic and political action and organization.

These developments had so far made only a ripple on the Nikolayev backwater. At the time when Bronstein joined Shvigovsky's circle (in the late autumn or early winter of 1896) its members must still have been agitated by the events that had taken place earlier in the year. They collected information and discussed it. But they did not go beyond that. They were not in a position to gauge the import of the new movement, and they had only a hazy notion of the Marxist critique of the *Narodnik* doctrines. They went on calling themselves *Narodniks*. Only one member of the circle, a young woman, Alexandra Sokolovskaya, herself the daughter of a *Narodnik*, claimed to be a Marxist and tried to persuade the circle that proletarian socialism offered them the real philosophy and science of revolution. She made little impression at first. But soon the hut in the orchard resounded with heated arguments. When Bronstein entered he found himself at once in the middle of a fierce controversy. At once he was pressed to make a choice. At once he labelled himself a *Narodnik*. And almost at once he assailed the solitary Marxist. G. A. Ziv (a friend of his youth and later his enemy, who has written vivid reminiscences of these days) tells us that when he, Ziv, first came to the orchard in the winter of 1896 Bronstein, not yet eighteen, 'was, because of his eminent gifts and talents, already attracting the attention of all Franz's visitors'; he was already the 'most audacious and determined controversialist' of the group and spoke with 'pitiless sarcasm' about the theories of Karl Marx, as expounded by the young woman.

He had only very little knowledge of either of the two contending doctrines. He had just borrowed from Shvigovsky a few outdated clandestine pamphlets, the first he ever read, and some files of radical periodicals; and he had scanned these nervously, impatient to grasp at a glance the substance of the arguments they contained. The authors who excited his enthusiasm were John Stuart Mill, Bentham, and Chernyshevsky, though their books had no direct bearing on the new controversy.

For a time Bronstein proudly described himself as a Benthamist and had no inkling how ill his infatuation fitted any revolutionary, whether *Narodnik* or Marxist. Of Marx himself and of the lesser lights of the Marxist school he had not even a smattering of knowledge. A more cautious or reflective young man would have sat back, listened to the arguments, perhaps gone to the sources and weighed the pros and cons before he committed himself. (It was in this manner that Lenin first approached the teachings of Marx.) But Bronstein was precocious and had a volatile and absorptive mind. He had, 'like richly intellectual people who can think rapidly, a wonderful gift of bluff. He could catch so quickly the drift of an opponent's thought, with all its . . . implications, that it was very difficult to overwhelm him with mere knowledge.'[1] From school he had brought the self-confidence of the brilliant pupil and the habit of outshining his fellows. The last thing he would do when buttonholed by his new associates and urged to take sides was to plead ignorance. He did take sides; and, incapable of lukewarm reserve, he dashed headlong into the fray.

He made his choice instinctively. The *Narodnik* outlook appealed to him precisely through that which distinguished it from the Marxist. The Marxists insisted that all social phenomena are directly or indirectly determined by society's economic condition. The *Narodniks* did not altogether reject this view— they had twenty years earlier been the pioneers of historical materialism in Russia. But they did not dwell on it with the same implacable emphasis; and many of them accepted the so-called subjectivist philosophy, which stressed the supremacy of the 'critical mind' and of the will of the individual. This philosophy accorded well with the traditions and the legends of a party which had refused to defer its assault on Tsardom until the economic conditions had 'ripened' or until the mass of the people had been aroused, and which had sent out its lonely fighters and martyrs, its strong-minded and strong-willed conspirators, to hunt down, bomb in hand, the Tsar, his ministers, and his governors. To the young Bronstein Marxism seemed narrow and dry as dust—an offence to the dignity of man, whom it portrayed as the prisoner of economic and social circumstances,

---

[1] Max Eastman, *Leon Trotsky, The Portrait of a Youth*, p. 68; A. G. Ziv, op. cit., pp. 9–12; L. Trotsky, op. cit., vol. i, chapters vi–vii.

the plaything of anonymous productive forces. This, he himself was to say later, was a simplification and a parody of Marxism; and, at any rate, no other modern political creed was to inspire as many people as Marxism would with the will and determination to fight, to suffer, and to die for their cause.[1] But the parody was not altogether unreal. Many of those who professed Marxism were indeed adopting the dry and quietist parody as their creed. The first version of Marxism which the young Bronstein encountered was probably of that sort. Against this the attraction of the romantic *Narodnik* tradition was overwhelming. It held up inspiring examples to imitate, the memory of heroes and martyrs to cherish, and a plain, unsophisticated promise for the future. It offered glories in the past and it seemed to offer glories in the future. It only seemed so. In its decay, the *Narodnik* movement was incapable of repeating its past exploits, incapable, at any rate, of repeating them with the old, pure, and heroic illusions. But even while the sun of that great romantic movement was setting, it cast a purple afterglow on to the Russian skies. The eyes of the young Bronstein were filled with that glow.

Having thrown himself into the controversy he was Sokolovskaya's most bitter antagonist. Into their relationship there crept an ambivalent emotion almost inevitable between two young and close political opponents of different sex, meeting regularly in a tiny group, attracted and repelled by each other and incapable of escaping from each other. Sokolovskaya, several years older than Bronstein—six according to some, ten according to others—had, of course, a wider and more serious political experience than had the pupil of the top form of the *Realschule*. Modest, firm in her convictions, and altogether free from vanity, she would stubbornly explain her views and keep her temper even when her adolescent opponent was making her the butt of his jibes. The situation took on a farcical twist. Everybody in the orchard was a little infatuated with the girl; and some of the boys wrote love poems. The great 'isms' and problems, the budding love and the rhymes all became mixed up—and the more perverse grew the discussions. 'You still think

[1] In his late years, Trotsky often compared Marxism with Calvinism: the determinism of the one and the doctrine of predestination of the other, far from weakening or 'denying' the human will, strengthened it. The conviction that his action is in harmony with a higher necessity inspires the Marxist as well as the Calvinist to the highest exertion and sacrifice.

you are a Marxist?' Bronstein teased her, 'How on earth can a
young girl so full of life stand that dry, narrow, impractical
stuff!'—'How on earth', Sokolovskaya would answer, 'can a
person who thinks he is logical be contented with a headful of
vague idealistic emotions?' Or Bronstein would mock at her girlish
sentimentality which scarcely harmonized with her adherence to
Marxism, that 'doctrine for shopkeepers and traders'.[1]

Yet her arguments were beginning to find their way to his
mind. His inner confidence was shrinking. All the more 'relentless' was he in debate, and all the more boorish were his
jibes. On the last day of December 1896 the group met for a
discussion and celebration of the New Year. Bronstein came and,
to the surprise of his friends, declared that he had been won over
to Marxism. Sokolovskaya was elated. Toasts were drunk to
the rapid emancipation of the working classes, to the downfall
of Tsarist tyranny, and so on. When Bronstein's turn came, he
stood up, lifted his glass, and turning towards Sokolovskaya,
without apparent reason or provocation, burst out: 'A curse
upon all Marxists, and upon those who want to bring dryness
and hardness into all the relations of life!' The young woman
left the orchard swearing that she would never shake hands
with the brute. Soon afterwards she left the town.[2]

The new year had come, and the group had not yet gone
beyond talk. Bronstein wrote a polemical article against Marxism, 'more epigrams, quotations, and venom than content' and
sent it off to a periodical with *Narodnik* leanings. The article
never appeared. Jointly with Sokolovskaya's brother, he was
writing a drama on the Marxist-*Narodnik* controversy, but got
stuck after the first or second act. The play was intended to show
the *Narodnik* in a favourable light and to contrast him with the
Marxist. As the plot was unfolding the authors noticed with
astonishment that it was the Marxist who was shaping into the
attractive character: he was almost certainly endowed with
some of Sokolovskaya's features. The group also staged a 'revolt' in the local public library, the board of which had intended
to raise readers' fees. The 'orchard' rallied the 'public', brought

---

[1] G. A. Ziv, op. cit., p. 15; M. Eastman, op. cit., p. 46.
[2] These incidents are related by both Eastman and Ziv. In *My Life* Trotsky
omits them; but as in his preface to Eastman's book he confirms its factual accuracy,
he thereby also testifies to the truthfulness of these stories, for which Ziv is the
original source.

in new subscribers and overthrew the board at an annual meeting—no small event in the dormant town.[1]

Bronstein now neglected his school work; but he had learned enough to graduate in the summer of 1897 with first-class honours. However, his father sensed that something had gone wrong. On a vacation at Yanovka Lyova had talked about freedom and the overthrow of the Tsar. 'Listen, boy. That will never happen, not even in 300 years!' the farmer replied, wondering where his son had picked up such ideas. Soon he was on the track of Lyova's new associates and briskly ordered him to keep away from Shvigovsky's orchard. Lyova now asserted his 'critical mind' and 'free will'. He was free, he said, to choose his own friends; but as he would not submit to paternal authority he would not go on living on his father's money. He gave up his allowance, took up private tutoring, and moved from his comfortable lodgings to Shvigovsky's hut, where six students, some tubercular, had already been living. The change was exhilarating; freedom at last! Gone was the neat and dutiful bourgeois son, the object of admiration and envy to other boys' parents. His place was taken by a real *Narodnik*, who, like the pioneers of old, 'went to the people' to become one of them, lived in a little commune where everybody dressed like a farm labourer, put his few *kopeyks* into the pool, drank the same thin soup, and ate the same *kasha* from a common tin bowl.

Old Bronstein sometimes came from Yanovka to see whether Lyova, weary of privation and discomfort, might not mend his ways. There was no sign of this. One of Shvigovsky's lodgers, later a well-known communist editor, was to remember the 'big, whiskered farmer . . . coming into the hut at dawn and standing over him aggressive and implacable. "Hello!" he shouts with a loud voice like a bugle: "You, too, ran away from your father?" '[2] Angry scenes alternated with half-hearted reconciliation. The father, seeing the ruin of his fond hopes for Lyova, was inconsiderate and impatient. The son, humiliated in front of his comrades, among whom he aspired to be the leading light, reacted with vehemence and disrespect. On both sides came into play the same temperaments, the same sense of righteousness, the same stubbornness, the same pride, and the same bugle-like voices. When Lyova entered the University of

[1] L. Trotsky, loc. cit.   [2] M. Eastman, op. cit., p. 55.

Odessa to study mathematics, it seemed that things might yet
be patched up: even pure mathematics was in his father's eyes
preferable to playing in obscure company at the overthrow of the
Tsar. At the university Lyova began to show an exceptional
gift for his subject.[1] But the university could not compete in
attraction with Shvigovsky's orchard; nor could calculus get
the better of revolution. His stay in Odessa was brief, but long
enough for him to make contact with revolutionaries there and
to get from them clandestine papers and pamphlets, with which
he returned in triumph to Nikolayev.

Then came the turbulent spring of 1897. In March a student-
girl imprisoned for her political convictions in the Peter–Paul
fortress in St. Petersburg committed suicide by burning herself in her cell. The event provoked a storm of protests and
demonstrations in the universities. In reprisal the authorities
deported large numbers of undergraduates. New protests and
demonstrations followed. Even 'police-ridden' Odessa was astir.
Students coming from Kiev brought fresh excitement and indignation to Shvigovsky's orchard. This, Bronstein and his
friends felt, was the time to pass from words to deeds.

'Bronstein . . . suddenly called me aside and proposed in
great secrecy that I join a working-men's association, organized by himself', writes Ziv, then a student of medicine just
arrived from Kiev. 'The *Narodnik* idea, Bronstein said, had been
discarded; the organization was planned to be social democratic, although Bronstein avoided using this term . . . and proposed to call it the *Southern Russian Workers' Union.*' 'When I
joined the organization', Ziv goes on, 'everything had already
been arranged. Bronstein had already established his contacts
with the workers and also with revolutionary circles in Odessa,
Ekaterinoslav, and other towns. . . .'[2]

About 10,000 workers were employed in the docks and factories of Nikolayev, mostly skilled and well-paid craftsmen with
enough leisure to read books and newspapers. So far, however,
they had had no organization, not even a trade union. The

---

[1] Eastman quotes a prominent Russian technician, one of Trotsky's university
colleagues, who, even after the revolution, regretted the loss to science of so exceptionally gifted a mathematician. Ibid., p. 59.

[2] A. G. Ziv, op. cit., p. 18. About this time social democratic groups were reviving
or being formed in most towns in the south. See M. N. Lyadov, *Kak Nachynala Skła-
dyvatsia R.K.P. (Istorya Ross. Sots.-Dem. Rab. Partii),* pp. 310 ff.

working-class quarters were teeming with religious sects opposed to the Orthodox Church. These sectarians Bronstein approached. He quickly saw which of them were concerned with religious dogma mainly and which were more preoccupied with the political implications of their opposition to Greek Orthodoxy. Among the latter he recruited the first members of the South Russian Workers' Union. He grouped them in small circles which met regularly to discuss current events and read clandestine papers. Before the year was out the Union counted about 200 members. From a contemporary Russian report, published after their arrest, we have a detailed view of the organization. Its members were locksmiths, joiners, electricians, seamstresses, and students, most of them in their early or middle twenties but some well over forty.[1] Among the founding members was also Sokolovskaya. Unmindful of the New Year's Eve scene, she returned to the orchard as soon as she had learned about the new beginning.

The name of the organization was evidently borrowed from another which had existed a quarter of century before and had had its centre in Odessa. The old South Russian Workers' Union, founded by a student, E. O. Zaslavsky, had been *Narodnik* in character and followed Lavrov's educational-propagandist line. It had been, as far as can be ascertained, roughly of the same size as its successor. In 1875 it was routed out by the police. Its leaders were tried by the Senate and most of them were convicted to forced labour. Zaslavsky and some of his associates died in prison. One of the founders, N. P. Shchedrin, was twice condemned to death and twice had his sentence commuted to life-long forced labour. For many years the prisoner was chained to his wheel-barrow, until his mind became deranged; then he was transferred to the Schlusselburg fortress, where for another fifteen years he was subjected to the sort of torture of which Dostoyevsky's *Notes from the House of the Dead* perhaps gives an idea. The legend of this martyrdom lived on in southern Russia; and it was probably as a tribute to it that Bronstein called his organization the South Russian Workers' Union. He himself assumed his first pseudonym—Lvov.

---

[1] *Rabocheye Delo, Organ Soyuza Russkikh Sotsial-Demokratov*, Geneva, 1 April 1899, pp. 150–2, gave a long and detailed list of the arrested members of the Union, with data about age, occupation, &c.

This transformation of the boy, who only the year before seemed a rich man's worldly son, into the founder of a clandestine organization, volunteering to take the revolutionary's thorny path, was startlingly rapid. He had evidently been overflowing with an inborn exuberant energy and with an ardour and imagination for which conventional pursuits provided little or no outlet. He needed a cause to serve, a cause exacting sacrifice; and when he found it, his youthful and passionate temperament came into the open. Both his friends and his enemies agree that he was the moving spirit, the mouthpiece, the organizer, and also the most energetic and devoted worker of the Union. 'Our group was the first social democratic organization at Nikolayev', says Ziv in reminiscences coloured by retrospective hostility. 'We were so excited by our success that we were in a state . . . of chronic enthusiasm. For the major part of these successes we were undoubtedly indebted to Bronstein, whose energy was inexhaustible and whose many-sided inventiveness and untiring drive knew no bounds.' The organization, Ziv goes on, many years afterwards looked back with pride to its hey-day when it was led by the eighteen-year-old boy, who by his faith, eloquence, and personal example cast a spell upon its members and induced them to forget all their private attachments and preoccupations and wholly devote to the cause themselves, their thoughts, energies, and time. After Bronstein's departure the nerve of the organization snapped. The Union could not recapture the ardour of its beginnings.[1]

The Union was, of course, a tiny group compared with any normal party or organization. In relation to the power against which it set itself it was like a microbe assailing a huge and decaying body; it was in fact one of a score or so of the microbes of revolution that were just going into action.

The groups set up in the docks and factories circulated leaflets and a sheet called *Nashe Delo (Our Cause)*. The leaflets commented on matters of local interest, conditions in factories and shipyards, and abuses by employers and officials. The exposures made an impression; those exposed were compelled to reply; and the Union fought back with new leaflets. 'What satisfaction I had when I received the information from factories and workshops that the workers avidly read the mysterious leaflets

[1] A. G. Ziv., op. cit., p. 21 and *passim*.

printed in purple ink. . . . They imagined the author as a strange
and powerful person who had . . . penetrated into all the
factories, knew what was happening in the workshops, and
within twenty-four hours reacted to events with fresh leaflets.'[1]
Nashe Delo, the 'organ' of the Union, also met with encouraging
response. The group was too poor to print the clandestine sheet.
Bronstein is said to have proposed to produce it secretly in
Spentzer's printing shop in Odessa—in his fervour he was unmindful of the harm he might have done to his relative—but
his own comrades persuaded him not to. Then a somewhat
cranky well-wisher came along with a 'scheme' for revolution:
what was needed to overthrow the Tsar, he said, was 100,000
roubles, for which a thousand little clandestine printing shops
could be set up all over Russia to flood the working-class quarters with anti-Tsarist proclamations. As a beginning the well-
wisher presented the group with a mimeograph; and Bronstein
set to work. He himself wrote the sheet and the leaflets; he himself calligraphed them in purple ink (so that the workers should
not need to strain their eyes); he himself illustrated the text with
cartoons; he himself produced, in the wretched dwelling of a
blind comrade, the stencils and the several hundred copies of
each issue; and he himself looked after the distribution.[2] It
used to take him about two hours to print a page. 'Sometimes
I did not even unbend my back for a week, interrupting my
work only for meetings and group discussions.'

Politically, the Union was a parochial fraternity of rebels,
innocent of any sophistication. Some members still described
themselves as *Narodniks*, others called themselves Marxists; but
this division did not interfere with their work. They could act
together because they acted on a narrow basis. They called the
workers to fight for higher wages and for shorter hours and in
this no difference showed itself between the *Narodnik* and the
Marxist. They avoided addressing the workers on the political
issues over which they were arguing at the orchard. This sort of
activity, at this time characteristic of most of the clandestine
groups, was later labelled 'Economist', because of its one-sided
concentration on matters of 'bread-and-butter'. But it was its

---

[1] L. Trotsky, op. cit., vol. i, pp. 133-4.
[2] 'All the important technical, not to speak of the literary part of the work was
done by Bronstein.' A. G. Ziv, op. cit., p. 21 and *passim*.

one-sidedness that secured its rapid success. If two groups, each advocating another 'ism', had come out and tried in competition with each other to win the workers, the result would have been confusion and failure. Only within a broader and more firmly established movement could the differences be seriously fought out. All the same, the Union of Nikolayev became known to the leaders of more advanced groups in other centres, who were preparing to call a Congress and to found the Social Democratic Workers' Party. They wondered whether to invite the Nikolayev group to send its delegate: would his age not detract from the solemnity of the occasion? Before the doubt was resolved the Nikolayev group was in prison.[1]

The success of this first venture demonstrated to the young revolutionary the 'power of the written word'. The town was astir with rumour; the Union, admired or feared, was a factor to be reckoned with; and friend and foe imagined it to be much stronger than it was. All this was the effect of his, Bronstein's, written word. The belief in the power of the word was to remain with him to the end. In every situation he would turn to it as to his first and his last resort; and throughout his life he would wield that power sometimes with world-shaking effect, and sometimes with lamentable failure. In this small fraternity of rebels he also first tried out his oratory; but the first attempt ended in humiliation and tears. It was one thing to speak sharply and bitingly in argument and quite another to make a set speech. 'He quoted Gumplowitz and . . . John Stuart Mill . . . and he got himself so terribly wound up in a sliding network of unintelligible big words and receding hopes of ideas that his audience sat bathed in sympathetic perspiration, wondering if there was any way under the sun they could help him to stop. When he finally did stop and the subject was opened for general debate, nobody said a word. Nobody knew what the subject was.' The speaker 'walked across the room and threw himself face down in the pillow on the divan. He was soaking with sweat, and his shoulders heaved with shame and everybody loved him.'[2]

In this small group none of Bronstein's qualities, good or bad,

---

[1] L. Trotsky, *Pokolenie Oktyabrya*, p. 20; M. N. Lyadov, *Kak Nachala Skladyvatsia RKP*, p. 324; Akimov, *Materialy dla Kharakteristiki Razvitya RSDRP*, pp. 39, 75.

[2] M. Eastman, op. cit., p. 70; Ziv relates that Bronstein carefully studied the techniques and tricks of polemics in Schopenhauer's *The Art of Debating*.

escaped his comrades. Their recorded observations agree with one another in almost everything except the emphasis. Sokolovskaya, who was to become his wife and whom he was to abandon, recollected after nearly thirty years that he could be very tender and sympathetic but also very assertive and arrogant; in one thing only he never changed, in his devotion to the revolution. 'In all my experience I have never met any person so completely consecrated', she said. His detractor speaks with more emphasis about his self-centredness and domineering temper: 'Bronstein's Ego', writes Ziv, 'dominated his whole behaviour', but, he adds, 'the revolution dominated his Ego.' 'He loved the workers and loved his comrades . . . because in them he loved his own self.' Having cheerfully given up the comforts of a settled life and the prospects of a good career he could not see how others could behave differently. When Ziv, anxious to finish his university course, began to neglect the group, Bronstein gave him a telling though tactful admonition. He presented Ziv with a picture on which he wrote a dedication: 'Faith without deeds is dead.'[1]

The hero who inspired him more than anybody else was Ferdinand Lassalle, the founder of the first mass movement of German socialism. In those days Lassalle's influence on European socialism was very strong—later the disclosure of his ambiguous political dealings with Bismarck dimmed the lustre. That the young Bronstein should have been so strongly impressed by Lassalle was due to an indubitable affinity. Lassalle, too, had been the son of a wealthy Jewish family and had abandoned his class to strive for the emancipation of the workers. He had been one of the greatest orators and one of the most colourful and romantic characters of his age. His meteoric career had come to a tragic end: he found his death in a romantic duel. As the founder of the first modern Labour party—the first not only in Germany—he had made history. The greatness, the brilliance, and the drama of such a life could not but stir the young Bronstein's imagination. He spoke about his hero with rapturous admiration; he swore to follow in his footsteps; and, if we are to believe Ziv, he boasted that he would become the Russian Lassalle. The young man was not addicted to modesty, false or real. He hid neither his faults nor his pretensions.

[1] M. Eastman, op. cit., p. 87; A. G. Ziv, op. cit., pp. 12, 19-21.

He used to think and dream and indulge his ambition—aloud.

. . . .

The first spell of his clandestine activity lasted from the spring of 1897 till the end of the year. The police at first refused to believe that all the agitation in the factories and docks emanated from the few adolescents and cranks in Shvigovsky's garden; and they searched for a more impressive source. This gave the Union time to spread its influence, until the police recovered from incredulity and began to watch the comings and goings of Bronstein and his friends. Towards the end of the year the leaders of the Union, expecting repression, agreed to disperse and to resume work after an interval. They decided, however, to reappear in town if in their absence the police arrested workers belonging to the Union: the police must not be in a position to tell the rank and file that the leaders had deserted them.

In the first weeks of 1898 Bronstein left Nikolayev to seek refuge on an estate in the country, where Shvigovsky had just taken a new job. No sooner had he arrived there than both he and Shvigovsky were seized by the police. Most members of the Union were arrested in Nikolayev and in the neighbourhood. From the country Bronstein was transferred to the prison at Nikolayev and then to a prison at Kherson, where he was kept for several months. The police had no doubt that he was the animator of the group. Through a bitterly cold winter they kept him in strict isolation in a tiny, unheated, unaired, and vermin-ridden cell. A straw mattress was brought for the night and removed at dawn so that in daytime he had neither couch nor seat. He was not allowed to walk and take exercise in the prison yard, nor to receive a newspaper, a book, soap, or a change of linen. Starved, dirty, covered with lice, he paced his cell, knocked at the walls to see whether there was a living soul in the neighbouring cells—there was none; he resumed his walk, counted his steps and tried to shake off the vermin. The monotony of these months was not even interrupted by an official interrogation; the prisoner was not even told what were the charges brought against him. This treatment, intended to break his spirit, was still milder than that meted out to a few other members of the Union, who under torture were committing suicide, becoming insane, or breaking down and agreeing to serve as informers. 'There were times . . . when I was sick with loneliness', he confessed. But he found moral satisfaction in his sacrifice and he composed revolutionary limericks which later were sung as folk-songs. Towards the end of his stay in this prison the police relented, and his mother succeeded in bribing his guards and sending in food parcels and such 'luxuries' as soap, linen, and fruit.

For depositions and examination he was at last transferred to a prison in Odessa, in which he was to remain a year and a half, until the end of 1899. There, too, he was kept in solitary confinement, but he could secretly communicate with his friends.[1] The prison was overcrowded and alive with constant movement, plotting, and practical jokes. He was in high spirits and poked fun at the colonel of the gendarmerie who conducted the investigation. To prepare himself for his interrogator he had to ascertain how much the gendarmes had discovered about the Union and he communicated about this with his associates in other cells. 'His task . . . was not easy . . . he had to tell me the the whole story of his arrest and the circumstances attending it and to summarize his own deposition. . . . All this had to be expressed so that I should get the fullest possible idea of what had happened and so that the communication should contain no clue against himself in case of interception. He performed this in a masterly fashion. He wrote an essay full of scintillating wit and satirical irony, a brilliant pamphlet.'[2] He began to transform his own experience into literature.

The interrogation dragged on without producing incriminating evidence. In the meantime Bronstein avidly read whatever he could lay hands on, at first only books and periodicals available in the prison library but, later, books sent from outside as well. The prison library contained only religious literature and church periodicals. For linguistic exercise he read the Bible simultaneously in German, French, English, and Italian. Then he got hold of files of Greek Orthodox periodicals, which were full of polemics against agnostics, atheists, and especially freemasons. 'The polemics of the learned Orthodox writers', he

---

[1] It was in this prison that the members of the Union learned about the founding 'Congress' of the Social Democratic Party, which had just taken place in Minsk; and in excitement they passed on this news from window to window. L. Trotsky, *Pokolenie Oktyabrya*, p. 20.

[2] A. G. Ziv, op. cit., p. 28.

wrote later, 'against Voltaire, Kant, and Darwin, led me into
a world of theological thoughts which I had never touched before and I had never even distantly imagined in what fantastic,
pedantic, droll forms these thoughts poured out.' 'The research on the devils, daemons, their princes, Satan himself and
the Kingdom of Darkness constantly amazed me. . . . The
copious descriptions . . . of Paradise with details about its . . .
internal lay-out ended on a melancholy note: "Exact directions
about the location of Paradise are not available"; and at dinner
and tea and during my walks I kept repeating this sentence: as
to the geographical location of Paradise precise directions are
lacking.'[1] Theological bickering with a bigoted jailor was his
favourite diversion. Rationalistic rejection of religion was, generally speaking, characteristic of the educated Russian of this time,
whether he was Radical or Socialist or only moderately Liberal,
whether he came from a Greek Orthodox or a Jewish family.
In Bronstein's upbringing the Jewish creed had played no part
at all, and only in the prison did he acquaint himself with Greek
orthodoxy. Both the Jewish and the Greek orthodoxies were so
obscurantist and stubborn in their refusal to take notice of any
new idea—they were in this respect far behind the Protestant
and even the Catholic Churches—that they violently repelled
the educated or even half-educated man. He could not compromise with a religion which itself refused to compromise with
any modern trend in the human mind.

As he delved with amusement into this theological literature
he also tried to extract from its polemical summaries and distortions the main lines of the unfamiliar philosophies and sociological systems which the Church condemned. He searched for
clues which would enable him to reconstruct his own versions
of these evil theories and then to evaluate them, according to
his lights, in a Marxist manner. From outside he received a few
books which helped him more directly. He read Darwin's
works, and these confirmed him in his instinctive atheism.
Twenty-five years later he recalled how Darwin's description
of the way in which the pattern on the peacock's feathers
formed itself naturally, banished for ever the idea of the Supreme Being from his mind; and how shocked he was to learn

---

[1] See Trotsky's letter to Eastman in Eastman, op. cit., p. 113, and L. Trotsky,
Moya Zhizn, vol. i, p. 141.

that Darwin himself had not been an atheist.[1] Then the philosophical essays of Arturo Labriola, the Italian Marxist, brought him a little nearer to his goal: Labriola's thought and style, undogmatic, lucid, and graceful, left a lasting impression. He now only half understood the subject matter of Labriola's book, but he obtained more solid clues to Marxist theory.

From such precarious points of view, and using a loose tissue of fact drawn from Greek Orthodox sources, he then attempted to write a materialist history of freemasonry and in this concrete historical analysis to put to a test his homespun version of Marxism. This was his first copious literary work and one for which he preserved a lifelong attachment: he remained unconsoled after its loss in one of his early wanderings. We need not share the author's tenderness for his first-fruits; but we may assume that in these writings he first tried his hand at Marxist history writing. Among his many essays, which he used to put into a hiding place in the prison latrine for his friends to read, was one on the role of the individual in history, the subject of ever-absorbing debate for the Marxist and the *Narodnik*. 'I made no new discoveries; all the conclusions . . . at which I arrived had been made long ago by others. . . . But I reached them gropingly and, up to a point, independently. This influenced the whole course of my development. In the writings of Marx, Engels, Plekhanov, and Mehring, I later found confirmation for what in prison seemed to me only a guess. . . . I had not at the outset accepted historical materialism in a dogmatic form.'[2]

These efforts occupied his mind and kept his spirit buoyant as his second year in prison was drawing to a close. Mentally, the adolescent was passing into manhood; and the transition was hastened by the fact that nothing was left to the captive in his cell but thought and reflection.

. . . .

[1] In an address to the students of the Sverdlov University in Moscow, in 1923, he said: 'To the end of my life I shall wonder whether Darwin was sincere in this, or whether he merely paid his tribute to conventional beliefs.' *Pokolenie Oktyabrya*, pp. 55–56.

[2] L. Trotsky, *Moya Zhizn*, vol. i, p. 147. Ziv claims that in the Odessa prison Bronstein also wrote a treatise on wages, in which he argued that piece-wages were preferable to time-wages, because they were more conducive to high productivity. It seems almost impossible that he should have dealt with so specific an economic subject at this time. Ziv was again imprisoned with Bronstein in St. Petersburg in 1906–7; and he probably ascribes to his friend in Odessa an essay written several years later.

Towards the end of 1899 the prisoners received their administrative verdict, that is, a verdict without trial. Bronstein and three of his associates were to be deported to Siberia for four years; others were exiled for shorter terms; some were released. Soon the trek of the deportees began. They were first taken to Moscow, and there they waited six months in a 'transfer prison'. Not only had they been given no fair hearing or trial, the two and a half years of their detention were not to be deducted from their terms.

In the prison in Moscow Bronstein met older and more experienced revolutionaries from all parts of Russia who were also awaiting final deportation. New faces, new impulses, new ideas. Here he first heard about Lenin and read his solid book, just published, *The Development of Capitalism in Russia*. Here he first became aware of the more advanced stages the clandestine movement had reached in the north of the country. Even battles of ideas fought in western Europe found an immediate echo within the walls of this prison. Among the many books passed on from cell to cell was Edouard Bernstein's famous work *The Premisses of Socialism*, the first explicit attempt made by an eminent German Social Democrat to dissociate the labour movement from the revolutionary conceptions of Marxism and to impart to it an evolutionary, reformist character. Bernstein's work provoked what seemed at the time a Homeric struggle between two wings in European socialism, the 'orthodox Marxist' and the 'revisionist'. It caused no flurry among the inmates of the transfer prison: not one of them was in a mood to abandon the road of revolution for a peaceful pedestrian march towards socialism.

In these new surroundings Bronstein lost none of his self-confidence. He went on reading and arguing, and produced a continuous stream of essays and pamphlets. He planned to set up a printing shop inside the prison under the very noses of the police. This seemed too risky to his comrades and he had to content himself with circulating his output in manuscript. Already to his fellows his imagination at times seemed too bold and his willingness to challenge authority too rash. At Kherson he had, in the teeth of opposition, persuaded his comrades to start a hunger strike in protest against a proposal from the police that juvenile prisoners be released on condition that their

parents would give them a good thrashing and keep them from
meddling in politics—this was 'an insult to the honour of the
juvenile revolutionary'. Here again, in Moscow, he defended
with *bravura* the prisoner's dignity. A prisoner had failed to take
off his cap to the governor of the prison and had been punished
with solitary confinement. Bronstein at once staged a demonstration of solidarity:

At a brief meeting it was decided that we should all come out
with our hats on and ask the guard to give the alarm signal for the
governor. When the governor comes we shall, of course, not take
off our hats. Circumstances will dictate what to do next. The guard
. . . refused to give the alarm signal. We crowded around him, and
Bronstein, standing in front of us, took out his watch and said with
supreme confidence: 'I give you two minutes to make up your mind.'
. . . Then . . . pushing aside the disconcerted jailor, he pressed the
button with a magnificent flourish. We put on our hats and went out
to the yard. The governor, surrounded by a huge band of armed
guards, came running into the yard. 'Why don't you take your hat
off?', he burst out, jumping at Bronstein, who stood in front of us
with the most defiant mien. 'And you, why don't you take off yours?',
Bronstein replied proudly.[1]

A few giant guards carried away the struggling rebel to solitary
confinement.

Harsh and defiant towards authority, or, as he himself would
have said, towards the class enemy, he was warm-hearted and
even sentimental with his comrades and their relatives. The
convicts were allowed to receive their relatives twice a week.
At these visits Bronstein 'showed a moving tenderness not only
to his own girl and future wife . . . but to all the other women
who came to see their husbands or brothers; he charmed them
all with his chivalry'.[2] The women usually took home the men's
linen; but Bronstein refused to benefit from such comforts,
washed and repaired his own linen, and mocked at revolutionaries so ensnared in bourgeois habits and prejudices as to burden their womenfolk with such work. Returning from the
visitors' room to the cell, he 'used to spend all the excess of his
tenderness on us, caressing and kissing and embracing us'. So
much was he remembered for the warmth of his friendship that
years later his friends, who had in the meantime become his

[1] A. G. Ziv, op. cit., p. 39.　　　　　　　　　[2] Ibid., p. 36.

opponents, were puzzled by his ruthlessness in the revolution and in the civil war.

During this spell in the Moscow prison, in the spring or summer of 1900, he married Alexandra Sokolovskaya. A Jewish chaplain conducted the wedding in the cell; and the bridegroom borrowed a wedding ring from one of his jailors. The story of this marriage is a little obscure. Quite often political deportees arranged fictitious marriages, because a married couple were entitled to be deported to the same place and could thus escape complete isolation. The fictitious connexions often developed into real ones. It is not clear how Bronstein and Sokolovskaya at first viewed their marriage. In *My Life* he devoted to this only one curiously detached and cool phrase, suggesting that it was meant to be a sham. 'Common work', he says, 'had bound us closely together, and so, to avoid separation, we married. . . .'[1] The eye-witness account denies the prosaic character of the connexion. It describes how the ambivalent feeling between the former antagonists had given place to love, how in the prison and *en route* from Moscow to Siberia Bronstein was full of affection, and how, during the journey under military escort which lasted nearly a fortnight, he was so absorbed in that affection that he completely neglected his friends and discussions. This eye-witness account seems, on internal evidence, truthful. The marriage, incidentally, was not easily concluded. Bronstein first thought of it in the Kherson prison, but not having yet come of age he had to get parental permission. His father objected: he would not allow his son to marry a girl so much older, a girl who—the old Bronstein had no doubt about this—had led his son on to the evil path. 'Lyova raged and thundered' writes Ziv, 'and fought with all the energy and stubbornness of which he was capable. But the old man was no less stubborn, and having the advantage of being on the other side of the prison bar, he won.' In Moscow Lyova renewed his efforts and this time he succeeded. He would perhaps not have 'raged and thundered' so much for the sake of a fictitious wedding.

The journey from Moscow to the place of exile, interrupted by short stops in various transfer prisons, lasted from the summer till the late autumn. The whole party of deportees travelled by

[1] Trotsky, op. cit., vol. i, p. 148.

rail to Irkutsk, where they were separated and dispatched in different directions. The Bronsteins were sent down the Lena river on a large barge, which was crowded with Skoptsy,[1] dressed in white clothes, chanting prayers, and dancing wildly. The Bronsteins were ordered to disembark in the village of Ust-Kut, which during the gold rush on the Lena had served as a base for east Siberian settlers. The gold-diggers had by now moved farther east and north, and Ust-Kut was a god-forsaken place with about a hundred peasant huts, dirty and plagued by vermin and mosquitoes. The inhabitants, sick with unfulfilled dreams of wealth, were madly addicted to *vodka*. Here the Bronsteins stayed for a time, during which he studied *Das Kapital*, 'brushing the cockroaches off the pages' of Karl Marx. Later they obtained permission to move to another place, 150 miles farther east, where he worked as book-keeper for an illiterate millionaire peasant–merchant. His employer conducted business over a vast area and was the uncrowned ruler of its Tunguz inhabitants. Bronstein watched this huge capitalist enterprise growing on virgin Siberian soil—he would cite it in the future as an illustration of that combination of backwardness and capitalist development which was characteristic of Russia. Sociological observation and attentive book-keeping did not go well together, and an error in the accounts cost Bronstein his job. In the middle of a severe winter, with temperatures about ninety degrees below freezing-point, the Bronsteins went on sledges back to Ust-Kut. With them was their baby daughter, ten months old, wrapped in thick furs. At the stops the parents had to unwrap the baby to make sure that in protecting her from freezing to death they had not suffocated her.

From Ust-Kut they moved to Verkholensk, half-way on the road to Irkutsk, in the mountains towering over the Baikal Lake. There they occupied a little house and settled down in relative comfort. Verkholensk was one of the oldest eastern Siberian settlements—thirty-five years earlier Polish insurgents had been

[1] The Skoptsy were a persecuted sect of fanatics who castrated themselves to live in saintliness ('Holy eunuchs'). They lived in communes and were mostly gardeners, dressed in white, and spent night hours in prayer. The sect based itself on Isaiah: 'For thus saith the Lord unto the eunuchs that keep my sabbaths, and choose the things that please me, and take hold of my covenant; even unto them will I give in mine house and within my walls a place and a name better than of sons and of daughters.' (lvi. 4, 5.) According to legend, some of the Tsars (e.g. Alexander I) belonged to the sect.

deported there to build roads—and it now had a large colony
of deportees and good postal connexions with Irkutsk, the most
important town in this part of Siberia. Here Bronstein had a
fair opportunity to continue his studies and develop his ideas,
to establish useful contacts and to make himself known in more
ways than one. Soon he was up to his ears in the disputes which
were going on in the exiles' colonies and he wielded a growing
influence. He lectured, argued, and wrote, pleading for socialism against anarchism, for mass struggle against terrorism, and
for Marxism against the subjectivist philosophy. In the preceding years he had accepted the main lines of the Marxist philosophy: now, in Siberia, he finally and firmly identified himself
with the social-democratic trend. A Social Democratic Siberian
Union was just then growing up, recruiting members among
deportees and among workers employed in the building of the
Trans-Siberian Railway. The Union approached Bronstein and
asked him to write leaflets. He readily agreed, and soon the
organization came to regard him as their leader and mouthpiece. Two years later he was to represent this Siberian Union
in Brussels and London at the momentous Congress during
which the party split into Mensheviks and Bolsheviks.

The spring of 1901 brought one of those sudden commotions
which marked the flux and reflux of public opinion in the Tsarist Empire. There were again stormy demonstrations in the
universities and strikes in the factories. Thousands of students
were arrested; many were conscripted into the army—this was
a new punishment decreed in 1899—and many were deported.
The Holy Synod excommunicated Leo Tolstoy. In February
1901 an undergraduate named Karpovich shot the Minister
of Education, Bogolepov. The Writers' Association protested
against brutal police control over academic life. The Socialist
International denounced the Tsar in a solemn manifesto.
The clandestine groups got fresh blood, and new deportees
brought a fresh breeze into the Siberian colonies. From the new-
comers' tales Bronstein tried to gauge the strength of the anti-
Tsarist opposition. He reached the conclusion that the political
ferment, intense though it was, was about to fizzle out largely
because the clandestine groups did not know what use to make
of it or how to direct it against autocracy. The mushrooming
underground organizations led a disjointed existence, each being

engrossed in local affairs and ambitions. National co-ordination and leadership were needed. Bronstein was not the first to advance this idea. Abroad older Marxists, Plekhanov, Lenin, Martov, and others were expounding it in the newly-founded *Iskra* (*The Spark*). But *Iskra*, the first issue of which had appeared in Germany a few months before, had not yet reached the exiles at Verkholensk. Bronstein set down his views in an essay which was widely circulated and hotly debated in the Siberian colonies. The biographical interest of this now little-known essay lies in the fact that in it he expounded broadly a view of the organization and the discipline of the party identical with that which was later to become the hall-mark of Bolshevism, and which he himself then met with acute and venomous criticism.[1]

The revolutionary movement, so he argued in 1901, would be a Frankenstein monster, unless it came under the rule of a strong Central Committee which would have the power to disband and expel any undisciplined organization or individual. 'The Central Committee will cut off its relations with [the undisciplined organization] and it will thereby cut off that organization from the entire world of revolution. The Central Committee will stop the flow of literature and of wherewithal to that organization. It will send into the field . . . its own detachment, and, having endowed it with the necessary resources, the Central Committee will proclaim that this detachment is the local committee.' Here, one might say, was in a nutshell the whole procedure of purge, expulsion and excommunication, by which he himself was eventually to be 'cut off from the entire world of revolution'. Yet, it was true that at this time the revolutionary movement in Russia could not advance a single step without national integration and discipline and that a national leadership was sometimes bound to impose this discipline sternly on reluctant groups.[2] When Bronstein first formulated this view, he brought down upon himself the very charges with which he

[1] See his *Vtoroi Syezd RSDRP* (*Otchet Sibirskoi Delegatsii*), p. 32. He quoted his Siberian essay in 1903 in an appendix to his report to the Siberian Union on the second congress of the party, in which he tried to explain why he sided with the Mensheviks against the Bolsheviks, despite the views he had advocated in Siberia. The Siberian Union at first was, like the South Russian Union, 'economist' in character; and only in 1902 did it recognize the supremacy of revolutionary politics over economics and join, under Bronstein's influence, the *Iskra* organization. Later it was affiliated with the Mensheviks.

[2] L. Martov, *Istorya Ross. Sotsial-Demokratii*, pp. 62–72.

would one day confront Lenin. Some of the deportees argued that
Bronstein's view was a relapse from the Marxist into the *Narodnik* attitude; that Social Democrats set their hopes on the mass
of the workers and not on a handful of leaders; and that they
had, consequently, no need to invest a Central Committee with
those dictatorial powers which had been indispensable in a
narrow conspiracy. We shall not now go farther into the controversy which at its more advanced stage will become one of
the major motifs of this narrative. But it is important to notice
that its first appearance goes back as far as 1901.

These activities are, however, less well known to us than
Bronstein's literary achievements of the Siberian years. Very
soon after his arrival he began to write for the *Eastern Review*
(*Vostochnoye Obozrenie*), a progressive newspaper appearing at
Irkutsk. He signed his contributions Antid Oto. The pen-
name (from the Italian *antidoto*) well suited the spirit of opposition which permeated his writings. As Antid Oto he became
very popular in the Siberian colonies and through exiles returning to Russia his fame presently reached revolutionary
circles in Petersburg, Kiev, and even the émigrés in western
Europe.[1] His contributions, which are reprinted in volumes iv
and xx of his *Works*, were on the borderline of literature and
journalism—by the standards of the short-winded, asthmatic
journalism of the mid-twentieth century they would certainly
be classed as literature. He wrote social reportage and literary
criticism. The former consisted of essays mainly on the life of the
Siberian peasantry, composed in a mixed style at once leisurely
and descriptive and sharply satirical. In these writings he was
strongly influenced by Gleb Uspensky, the talented and tragic
Narodnik whose realistic yet profoundly melancholy descriptions
of the life of peasants, artisans, and petty officials tore open the
wounds and revealed the miseries of the Tsarist empire, and set
a very high standard for the 'literature of exposure'.

'Nearly a quarter of a century has passed since the old writer
surveyed the scene, and it is time to see how much has changed
in the Russian countryside and small town since his days': with
this direct invocation Antid Oto stepped into Uspensky's shoes.

[1] The author knew personally old ex-deportees, who, in the 1920s and 1930s
would in conversation still refer to Trotsky as Antid Oto and ask, for instance, 'What
does Antid Oto say about the situation?'

He dealt with the same characters, the peasants and the petty officials, the injured and the dejected; and he treated them with the same sympathy and pity—only his indignation was sharper and more bitter. As his writings had to be laid before the censor, he did not directly attack the Government. But this restraint made his subdued anger and mockery even more effective. His language was easy and fluent, and despite its mannerisms—it was often verbose, sometimes pompous and over-elaborate—it was colourful and expressive; and full, penetrating observation, vivid portraiture, and unexpected contrasts and images made up for his mannerisms. 'Our village is economically devastated by the *kulaks*, physically by syphilis and all sorts of epidemics, and spiritually it lives in a dense concentrated darkness . . .', he wrote in an essay on the insanitary state of the Siberian countryside and on the lot of the village doctor. 'In thoughtful silence our village is dying from disease.' The mentally ill were kept for observation in the prisons, which, because of the lack of hospitals, formed 'the psychiatric department of the local sanitary authority'. In one case two homeless invalids, an old insurgent and an old gendarme—the same gendarme who had once escorted the insurgent to the place of deportation—lived in the same prison cell, for lack of any other asylum. The doctors were cut off from the world, helpless and dejected. Perhaps regional conferences of the medical personnel would shake them from their apathy.[1] Another time he demanded local government for Siberia. In European Russia, he wrote, the *Zemstvos* (rural assemblies) had at least some say in local matters. But east of the Urals the administration sensed rebellion in every *Zemstvo*, and even if a nucleus of local government existed here and there, the peasants were in it as 'silent symbols' only. The gentry sent one representative for every 3,000 roubles of income, while the peasants sent one for every 43,000.

He illustrated the anachronistic nature of the administration in a character-sketch of a clerk in a Siberian *volost* (an administrative district comprising several villages). The clerk was burdened with an incredible variety of jobs: he acted on the spot for the Ministry of the Interior; he was responsible to the Ministry of War for the call-ups; he collected taxes for the Ministry of Finance; he prepared statistics for the Ministry of

[1] L. Trotsky, *Sochinenya*, vol. iv, pp. 17–42.

Agriculture; he was the local agent for the Department of Justice, and for the Ministry of Education and Religious Denominations. Only the Navy and the Foreign Office left him in peace; but even this was not sure. Financial agent, statistician, agronomer, road engineer, architect, notary, legal officer, all in one person, the clerk did not even receive his salary regularly. The result? 'The half-fictitious statistical figures he supplies to higher authority are processed there, made the basis of many an official . . . survey or investigation, which then becomes the object of passionate polemics for the responsible leaders of opinion.'[1] A series of Bronstein's articles was devoted to the 'martyrdom of the womenfolk': the muzhik beat his wife mercilessly, and so did the wealthy Siberian merchant.

Half a century later these essays still retain their documentary value, and one can imagine the effect they produced at the time. The censor pored over them with increasing suspicion and more and more often cut out paragraphs or entire sections. The writer was constantly compelled to resort to new tricks of evasion and to convey his purpose by hint and allusion. When his 'unprotected fingers' were no longer able to grasp the nettle of fact, he would, with an apology, make his style shade off into semi-fiction.

Opposition writers often found in literary criticism some refuge from the assaults of censorship. This was so with Bronstein, yet to him literary criticism was much more than a convenient pretext for expounding political views. He was a literary critic as by vocation. Even his first attempts to approach literature from the Marxist angle were untainted by that narrow political utilitarianism which so-called Marxist criticism often makes its chief virtue. His approach was analytical rather than didactic, and it was enriched by a vivid appreciation and enjoyment of aesthetic values. He was a voracious reader. In the course of his two years in Siberia he wrote on Nietzsche, Zola, Hauptmann, Ibsen, D'Annunzio, Ruskin, Maupassant, Gogol, Herzen, Belinsky, Dobrolyubov, Uspensky, Gorky and others. The range of his historical and literary reminiscence and allusion was extremely wide, even if some of it must be dismissed as a youthful showing-off of erudition. His prime interest was, as with the Marxist it must be, in the social impulse behind the literary

---

[1] L. Trotsky, *Sochinenya*, vol. iv, pp. 3–7 and *passim*.

work, in the moral and political climate to which the poet or the novelist gives his individual expression, and in the effect which the literary work, in its turn, has on that climate.

But there was nothing in this of the vulgar Marxism which pretends to discover an economic or political class-interest hidden in every poem or play or novel. He was also exceptionally free (quite exceptionally for a man of 20–22 years) from the sectarian attitude which may induce a revolutionary to denounce any spiritual value which he cannot fit to his own conception and for which he has therefore no use. In the young Marxist this attitude is usually a symptom of inner uncertainty: he has not genuinely assimilated his new-found philosophy; the principles he professes are up to a point external to his thinking; and he is an historical materialist from duty rather than from natural conviction. The more fiercely he denounces anything that seems to contradict his ill-digested philosophy, the easier is his conscience, the more gratified is his sense of duty. In the young Bronstein it was therefore a sign of how intimately he had made the Marxist way of thinking his own, and a measure of his confidence in it, that he was singularly free from that dutiful sectarianism. He usually paid generous tribute to the talent or genius of a writer whose ideas were remote from or directly opposed to the doctrines of socialism. He did so not merely from fairness but from the conviction that the 'spiritual estate of man is so enormous and so inexhaustible in its diversity' that only he who 'stands on the shoulders of great predecessors' can utter a truly new and weighty word. The twenty-one-year-old writer insisted that revolutionary socialism was the consummation, not the repudiation, of great cultural traditions—it repudiated merely the conservative and conventional conception of tradition. He was not afraid of finding that Socialist and non-Socialist views might overlap or coincide and of admitting that there was a hard core, or a grain, of truth in any conception which as a whole he rejected.[1]

His first literary essay, a critical obituary on Nietzsche,

---

[1] He concluded an essay on Gogol, 'the founder of the Russian novel' as follows: 'If Gogol tried to weaken the social significance of his own writings . . . let us not hold this against him. If in his publicist writings he tried to appeal to the petty minds—let us forgive him this! And for his great inestimable artistic merits, for the loftily humane influence of his creative work—eternal, inextinguishable glory to him!' *Sochinenya*, vol. xx, p. 20.

appeared in the *Eastern Review,* in several instalments, in December 1900, a month or two after his arrival in Siberia. He could have chosen no subject more embarrassing than the work of Nietzsche whose hatred of socialism was notorious and whose cult of the Superman was repugnant to the Socialist. Bronstein began his obituary with an apology for its critical tenor: 'We ought to behave dispassionately towards the personalities of our . . . adversaries, and we ought to . . . pay due tribute to their sincerity and other individual merits. But an adversary—sincere or not, alive or dead—remains an adversary, especially if he is a writer who survives in his works. . . .' He showed how the idea of the Superman grew out of normal bourgeois morality and in what way it was opposed to that morality. Nietzsche, he held, generalized and drew to its last logical, or rather illogical, conclusion the contempt of the masses which was deeply rooted in normal bourgeois thinking. To prove this point, the critic showed how many of Nietzsche's views were either implied or expressly stated in the writings of Herbert Spencer, that representative philosopher and sociologist of the Victorian middle class. The idea of the Superman was opposed to bourgeois morality only as the excess is opposed to the norm. The immoral Superman stood in the same relation to the virtuous middle class in which the medieval *Raubritter* (with his maxim: Rauben ist keine Schande, das tuhn die Besten im Lande) had stood to the feudal lord. Nietzsche's ideal was the rapacious bourgeois freed from inhibition and stripped of pretences. Despite this, the Socialist could not but admire the brilliant originality with which Nietzsche had shown how brittle were the normal workaday ethics of the middle class.[1]

To this issue Bronstein returned in an essay on Ibsen, in whom he saw the immortal artist at loggerheads with the false moralist.[2] 'The historian of European social thought will never forget the slaps, those truly glorious slaps, which Ibsen has inflicted on the well washed, neatly brushed, and shiningly complacent physiognomy of the bourgeois philistine.' In *An Enemy of the People,* for instance, Ibsen had shown how subtly, without committing a single act of violence, a bourgeois democracy could isolate and destroy a heretic ('as effectively as if they had deported him to Siberia'). But the Socialist cannot approve the

---

[1] L. Trotsky, *Sochinenya,* vol. xx, pp. 147–62.   [2] Ibid., pp. 181–95.

superman-like attitude of Ibsen's hero, his distrust of the people, and his contempt of government by majority. The people, the majority—the Socialist agrees—is not the fount of all-embracing wisdom: 'If the "crowd" were called upon to pronounce on the merits of a scientific theory or of a philosophical system . . . Ibsen would have been a thousand times right. . . . The view of a Darwin on problems of biology is a hundred times more important than the collective opinion expressed at a meeting by a hundred thousand people.' (The author did not imagine that fifty years later it would be customary in his country for mass meetings to denounce 'disloyal' biologists or linguists.) 'But when we go out into the field of practical social policy, where so many deeply antagonistic interests are at play, the problem is quite different. . . . There the subordination of the minority to the majority, if it corresponds to the genuine balance of social forces and is not temporarily brought about by artificial means, is of infinitely superior merit.' Nevertheless, Ibsen's distrust of 'the people' expressed an artistic opposition to bourgeois society, an opposition towards which Marxists ought to behave with understanding and sympathy, although they themselves revolted against that society from different premises and in a different way.

As a Marxist, Bronstein was not impressed by the pretensions of art for art's sake. 'Like a paper kite [that art] can soar to heights from which all earthly matters are drowned in grey indifference. But even after it has reached the clouds, this poor "free" art still remains tied to a strong rope, the earthly end of which is tightly gripped by the philistine.'[1] 'Literature without the power of great synthesis', he wrote on another occasion, 'is the symptom of social weariness and is characteristic of sharply transitional epochs.'[2] He therefore viewed critically the then fashionable symbolist trend; but he did so not because he favoured narrow realism. On the contrary: 'Artistic creation, no matter how realistic, has always been and remains symbolist. . . . The purpose of art . . . is not to copy reality in empirical detail but to throw light on the complex content of life by singling out its general typical features. . . . Every artistic type is broadly a symbol, not to speak of such highly symbolical images as

---

[1] See the essay on Hauptmann, ibid., pp. 170–81.
[2] Essay on Balmont, ibid., pp. 167–70.

Mephisto, Faust, Hamlet, Othello, artistically embodying definite "moments" of the human soul. . . .' The symbolist school,
however, he held, was trying to elevate the means into an end
in itself and, so, was degrading the symbol from an intensified
expression of human experience into a means of escaping from
that experience.

His interest in European letters was as intense as was his
reaction against the national self-centredness of official, and in
part also of *Narodnik*, Russia. He ridiculed the boast of the
Slavophiles that they had no need to learn from the West and
that the Russians themselves made all the great discoveries
and inventions—'the Russian land can rear its own Platos and
quick-witted Newtons'.[1] This 'westernizing', then common to
all Marxists and liberals, did not imply any repudiation of the
Russian spiritual heritage of the nineteenth century—Russia's
great literary tradition did not go back any farther. Most of
Russia's thinkers and writers had been rebels, and the revolutionary intellectual was steeped in their works. It was the influence of the literature of rebellion that helped Bronstein to cut
himself adrift from his own childhood and adolescence in which
there had been so little experience likely to make of him a
revolutionary. He had been, we know, profoundly impressed by
Gleb Uspensky. In 1902, when Uspensky died insane, Bronstein
quoted with self-revealing approval Uspensky's remark that
there had been almost no link between his adult life as a rebel
and his childhood and adolescence, and that he had had 'to forget his own past' before he could form his new identity. This was,
of course, even truer of the writer of the obituary. 'With terrible
suicidal perspicacity', he wrote, 'Uspensky grasped life such as
it was and he burned himself out in the craving for life such as it
should be. He searched for truth and found the lie; he searched
for beauty and found ugliness; he searched for reason and found
unreason.'[2]

In the other leaders of the literary revolt, Belinsky, Dobrolyubov, and to a lesser extent in Herzen, Bronstein admired their
identification with the oppressed, their indifference to worldly

[1] L. Trotsky, *Sochinenya*, vol. xx, pp. 116–18, the satirical article on 'The
Russian Darwin' published in November 1901.
[2] Bronstein wrote two obituary essays on Uspensky, one for the *Eastern Review*
and another for *Nauchnoye Obozrenie* (Scientific Survey), *Sochinenya*, vol. xx, pp. 33–
40 and 41–67.

success, their imperviousness to banality, and the self-immolating integrity with which they searched for truth. Uspensky, the *Narodnik*, had risen above *Narodnik* prejudices and illusions: 'A lonely figure, the martyr of his own fearless thought, he looks with painfully penetrating eyes above the heads of his contemporaries and comrades . . . into the face of the future.' Belinsky, 'the godfather of modern Russian literature' held that 'nothing that appears and succeeds at once and is met with . . . unconditional praise can be important or great—significant and great is only that which divides opinion . . . which matures and grows through genuine struggle, which asserts itself . . . against living resistance'. In Dobrolyubov the critic valued the extreme sensitivity to any false note and the impatience with platitudes, even when they were innocuous. Nothing was more embarrassing to Dobrolyubov than to have to listen to a man who argued heatedly about the inhumanity of cannibalism or the usefulness of education. Dobrolyubov's satire, Bronstein concluded, would remain acutely topical 'as long as the great heroism for petty affairs raised its head so high . . . and as long as it was considered a social merit to preach the rudiments of a cheap liberalism'.[1]

This summary of Bronstein's literary criticism may, through inevitable compression, give a somewhat exaggerated idea of the maturity of his writings. His style, over-elaborate, over-rhetorical, and over-witty, was still adolescent; but his judgement was, on the whole, mature. To the biographer the value of these essays is enhanced by the many flashes of the author's implied self-analysis and self-portrayal. However, the young Bronstein epitomized more directly his own outlook in an invocation to the twentieth century (written early in 1901, under the title 'On Optimism and Pessimism, on the Twentieth Century, and on Many Other Things').[2] There he analysed various types of optimism and pessimism and stated his preference for the view which was pessimistic about the present but optimistic about the future. It is, Bronstein argues, the man who holds this view who opens new vistas to the human mind and makes history. More than once this peculiar optimist has had to brave a Holy Inquisition. 'More than once has the collective Torquemada devoted exclusive attention to him.' Yet he, the optimist, rises

[1] Ibid., pp. 12, 29–31.   [2] Ibid., pp. 74–79.

from the ashes and 'as passionate, as full of faith and as militant as ever, confidently knocks at the gate of history'. On his way he meets the philistine, whose strength lies in numbers and undiluted vulgarity and who is 'armed to the teeth by an experience which does not range beyond the counter, the office desk, and the double bedroom'. To the mockery of the philistine and to his pseudo-realistic conservatism ('There is nothing new under the moon'), the optimist who looks to the future replies:

Dum spiro spero! . . . If I were one of the celestial bodies, I would look with complete detachment upon this miserable ball of dust and dirt. . . . I would shine upon the good and the evil alike. . . . But I am a *man*. 'World history which to you, dispassionate gobbler of science, to you, book-keeper of eternity, seems only a negligible moment in the balance of time, is to me everything! As long as I breathe, I shall fight for the future, that radiant future in which man, strong and beautiful, will become master of the drifting stream of his history and will direct it towards the boundless horizon of beauty, joy and happiness! . . .

The nineteenth century has in many ways satisfied and has in even more ways deceived the hopes of the optimist. . . . It has compelled him to transfer most of his hopes to the twentieth century. Whenever the optimist was confronted by an atrocious fact, he exclaimed: What, and this can happen on the threshold of the twentieth century! When he drew wonderful pictures of the harmonious future, he placed them in the twentieth century.

And now that century has come! What has it brought with it at the outset?

In France—the poisonous foam of racial hatred; in Austria—nationalist strife . . .; in South Africa—the agony of a tiny people, which is being murdered by a colossus; on the 'free' island itself—triumphant hymns to the victorious greed of jingoist jobbers; dramatic 'complications' in the east; rebellions of starving popular masses in Italy, Bulgaria, Rumania. . . . Hatred and murder, famine and blood. . . .

It seems as if the new century, this gigantic newcomer, were bent at the very moment of its appearance to drive the optimist into absolute pessimism and civic nirvana.

—Death to Utopia! Death to faith! Death to love! Death to hope! thunders the twentieth century in salvoes of fire and in the rumbling of guns.

—Surrender, you pathetic dreamer. Here I am, your long awaited twentieth century, your 'future'.

—No, replies the unhumbled optimist: You—you are only the *present*.

. . . .

After four and a half years of prison and exile Bronstein longed for a scene of action broader than the Siberian colonies. In the summer of 1902, the underground mail brought him a copy of Lenin's *What is to be done?* and a file of *Iskra*. He read these with mixed feelings. Here he found ideas on the shape and character of the party, ideas which had been maturing in him, set out with supreme confidence by the brilliant émigré writers. The fact that he had in his backwater reached the same conclusions independently could not but give him a thrill and confirm him in his self-reliance. But he was intensely restless: he could no longer bear the sight of the muddy, cobble-stoned, narrow streets of Verkholensk. Even the arguments within the colonies of deportees and his literary successes with the *Eastern Review* filled him with boredom. If only he could get away to Moscow or Petersburg . . . and then perhaps to Geneva, Munich, or London, the centres where the intellectual weapons of the revolution were being forged. . . .

He shared his impatience and his secret ambition with his wife. Alexandra had no doubt that her husband was destined to greatness, and that at twenty-three it was time for him to do something for immortality. She urged him to try to escape from Siberia and in doing so she shouldered the burden of a heavy sacrifice. She had just given birth to their second daughter and was now undertaking to struggle for her own and her children's lives, unaided, with no certainty of a reunion. In her own conviction she was, as his wife and as a revolutionary, merely doing her duty; and she took her duty for granted without the slightest suggestion of melodrama.[1]

On a summer night in 1902, Bronstein, hidden under loads of hay in a peasant cart rumbling along bumpy Siberian fields, was on his way to Irkutsk. In his bed, in the loft of his house at Verkholensk, there lay the dummy of a man. Next evening the police inspector who came, as usual, to check whether the Bronsteins were in, climbed a ladder to the loft, glanced at the bed and, satisfied that everything was in order, went away. In

[1] L. Trotsky, *Moya Zhizn*, vol. i, p. 157; Ziv, op. cit., p. 42; M. Eastman, op. cit., pp. 142–3.

the meantime the fugitive, supplied by his friends at Irkutsk with new, respectable-looking clothes, boarded the Trans-Siberian railway.

Before he left Irkutsk his comrades provided him with a false passport. He had to inscribe hastily the name he was to assume, and he scribbled that of one of his former jailors in the Odessa prison. In this hazardous escape did the identification with his jailor perhaps gratify in the fugitive a subconscious craving for safety? It may be so. Certainly the name of the obscure jailor was to loom large in the annals of revolution: it was—Trotsky.[1]

The journey west was unexpectedly quiet. The passenger killed time reading Homer's hexameters in a Russian translation. He alighted at Samara on the Volga, where *Iskra's* organization had its Russian headquarters. He was heartily welcomed by Kzhizhanovsky-Clair, the prominent technician, Lenin's friend and future chief of the Soviet *Gosplan* (State Planning Commission). Bronstein's literary reputation had preceded him, and Kzhizhanovsky-Clair nicknamed him *The Pen* (*Piero*) and sent a glowing report on his talents and activities to *Iskra's* headquarters in London. Straightway Bronstein was sent to Kharkov, Poltava, and Kiev to inspect groups of Socialists. He found that most of the groups persisted in their local patriotisms and refused to co-operate with one another or to submit to any central authority. With a report to this effect he returned to Samara. There an urgent message from Lenin was awaiting him: The Pen was to report as soon as possible at *Iskra's* foreign headquarters.

---

[1] Ziv, op. cit., pp. 25–26; M. Eastman, op. cit., p. 143. In his autobiography Trotsky does not mention the bizarre origin of his pseudonym. As if a little ashamed of it, he merely says that he had not imagined that Trotsky would become his name for the rest of his life.

CHAPTER III

At the Door of History

EARLY one morning, almost at dawn, in October 1902, the fugitive from Siberia knocked violently at a door in London, at 10 Holford Square, near King's Cross. There, in one room and a kitchen, lived Vladimir Ilyich Lenin and his wife, Nadezhda Konstantinovna Krupskaya—Mr. and Mrs. Richter to their lower-middle-class neighbours. The early hour was hardly suitable for a visit, but the caller was too full of the importance of his mission and too impatient and self-confident to think of the minor courtesies. He had travelled in feverish excitement from Irkutsk to London, stealing across frontiers and surmounting all obstacles on the way. In Vienna he had roused the famous Victor Adler, the founder of the Austrian Socialist Party, from a Sunday rest and got from him the help and the money he needed for the rest of his journey. In Zurich he had knocked, in the middle of the night, at the door of Paul Axelrod, the veteran of Russian Marxism, in order to introduce himself and make arrangements for the last lap. Now, at his final destination, alone in the grey mist of an early London morning, with only a cabman waiting behind him for the fare— the passenger had no money—he expressed his inner agitation by his loud knocking. He was indeed 'knocking at the door of history'.

Krupskaya, guessing a countryman in the early and noisy visitor, and a little worried lest her English neighbours might be annoyed by this instance—not the only one—of the extravagant behaviour of the foreigners in the house, hurried out to meet the newcomer. From the door she exclaimed: 'The Pen has arrived!' Lenin, she later recollected, 'had only just awakened and was still in bed. Leaving them together I went to see to the cabman and prepare coffee. When I returned I found Vladimir Ilyich still seated on the bed in animated conversation with Trotsky on some rather abstract theme. But the cordial recommendations of the "young eagle" and this first conversation made Vladimir Ilyich pay particular attention to the newcomer.'[1] The visitor was to remember the 'kindly expression on Lenin's face . . . tinged with a justifiable amazement'.

Breathlessly the visitor made his report on the political trends and moods among the Siberian exiles; on the impressions he had formed from his recent trip to Kiev, Kharkov, and Poltava; on the reluctance of local groups there to consider themselves as parts of an integrated national movement; on the work at Samara headquarters; on the degree of reliability of the clandestine channels of communication; on defects in the arrangements for illegal frontier crossings; and on much more. Lenin, who had recently been exasperated by the unbusiness-like and muddled communications that had been reaching him from the underground in Russia, was delighted to obtain from the young man an unusual amount of precise and definite information, to listen to his 'lucid and incisive' remarks and to find in him a convinced adherent of the idea of a centralized party.[2]

Anxious to examine him more closely, Lenin took him for long walks and talks, in the course of which he showed him London's historical and architectural landmarks. But Trotsky—so he began to be called—was so full of the clandestine struggle in Russia that his mind was closed to anything that had no direct bearing on it. He noticed the peculiar mannerism Lenin used in trying to acquaint him with some of the landmarks: 'This is *their* Westminster' or 'This is *their* British Museum', he would say, conveying by the inflection of his voice and by implication both his admiration for the genius embodied in the grand buildings and his antagonism to the ruling classes, to whose spirit and power those buildings were a monument. Trotsky was eager to return from these digressions to topics nearer to his heart: In what way did the *Iskra* men propose to weld the disconnected groups into a centralized party? How were they faring in the campaign against the Economists, who were trying to keep the movement within the bounds of non-political trade unionism? How would they counter the attempts just begun by others to revive a *Narodnik*-like terrorist party? What were they going to do to combat Peter Struve's 'legal

[1] N. K. Krupskaya, *Memories of Lenin*, p. 60.
[2] Lenin, *Sochinenya*, vol. xxxiv, pp. 89–92; Krupskaya, loc. cit.; L. Trotsky, *Moya Zhizn*, vol. i, chapter xi.

Marxists', who were drifting away from revolutionary Marxism? Lenin listened with discreet satisfaction to the story of how in jail Trotsky and others had studied his *Development of Capitalism in Russia*, how impressed they had been by the enormous mass of statistical material he had marshalled to show that capitalist industry had been transforming Russian society so radically that it had killed all hope of agrarian socialism and set the scene for the proletarian movement. And above all there was the question: Why was Trotsky so urgently asked to report to London and what was he to do here?

In truth, no special assignment had been awaiting him. Lenin was usually anxious to meet everyone who had gained distinction in underground work. Only a few weeks before he had written: 'In order that the centre should always be able not only to advise, persuade, and argue . . . but actually to conduct the orchestra, it is necessary that it should be known precisely who is playing which fiddle, and where, and how he does it; where any person has been trained to wield an instrument and which instrument; who strikes a false note, and where and why . . ., who ought to be shifted, and how and whither, in order to eliminate the discordant tone. . . .'[1] His idea of the centralized party included a close interest in the living people who were fighting the party's battles on the spot, an interest characteristic of the true leader of men. Trotsky, he knew, had 'played first fiddle' in Siberia, and so he wished to meet him, to find out 'where and how he had learned to wield his instrument'. At this time Lenin was complaining, in letters to friends, about the inadequacies of *Iskra*'s editorial staff, and he must have pondered whether The Pen would not be best employed on *Iskra*. On the day of Trotsky's arrival Lenin found him accommodation in a neighbouring house, where the other editors of *Iskra*, Martov and Zasulich, were living. No sooner had the newcomer moved in than he wrote his first contribution to the paper—it appeared in the issue published immediately after his arrival and dated 1 November 1902.[2]

The editorial board of *Iskra* consisted of six: Plekhanov, Vera Zasulich, and Axelrod, the three émigré pioneers of social democracy; and the much younger Lenin, Martov, and Potresov,

[1] Lenin, *Sochinenya*, vol. vi, pp. 205-24.   [2] *Iskra*, no. 27.

who had only recently left Russia. Most of the editors were living in London, in the borough of St. Pancras; Plekhanov and Axelrod lived in Switzerland, but Plekhanov made frequent trips to London. From this group, especially from Lenin's home, ran all the threads to the underground movement in Russia, whose agents appeared at Holford Square with messages and went back with instructions. Thus, the young Trotsky found himself transferred from Verkholensk straight into the directing centre of Russian socialism and placed under the constant influence of outstanding and contrasting personalities.

Zasulich and Martov shared with him their home, their meals, and their thoughts. It was Vera Zasulich who had, the year before Trotsky's birth, fired at General Trepov, and had unwittingly inspired the *Freedom of the People* to follow her example. After the jury acquitted her she escaped abroad, kept in touch with Karl Marx, and, although she did not accept his teaching without mental reservations, became one of the founders of the Russian Marxist school. Disregarding Marx's doubts, she was among the first to proclaim that the proletarian socialism he had advocated for western Europe would suit Russia as well.[1] She was not only a heroic character. Well read in history and philosophy, she was essentially a heretic, with a shrewdly feminine mind working by intuitive impulses and flashes rather than by reasoning. In all the portraits of her drawn by contemporaries, we also find the comic touches of the old-style Russian Bohemian. 'She wrote very slowly, suffering truly all the torments of literary creation'; and as she wrote or argued she paced thoughtfully up and down her room, with her slippers flapping, rolling cigarettes, chain-smoking, throwing butts on the window sills and tables, scattering ash over her blouse, arms, and manuscripts or into her cup of tea, and sometimes over her interlocutor. To the young Trotsky she was the heroine of a glorious epic—he had come to stay under one roof with the living legend of revolution.

Martov was only a few years older than Trotsky. He, too, was a Jew. The descendant of an old family of great Hebrew scholars—his real name was Zederbaum—he had been one of the initiators of the Bund, the Jewish Socialist party; but then he abandoned the idea of a separate Jewish Labour party, and,

---

[1] *Perepiska K. Marxa i F. F. Engelsa s Russkimi Politicheskimi Deyatelami*, pp. 240–2.

together with Lenin, founded the *Association for the Struggle for the Emancipation of Workers,* in Petersburg. He followed Lenin into exile, where they joined hands with the veteran émigrés to found *Iskra*. A suble analyst, a writer with a satirical bent, a fluent and prolific commentator on the topics of the day, he was *Iskra's* journalistic mainstay, while Lenin was its political inspirer and organizer. Both Martov and Zasulich belonged to the romantic breed of rebels, guided less by theoretical principle than by moral indignation at social injustice. Full of charm, generosity, and modesty, both were by temperament artists rather than politicians.

Lenin was made of different stuff. Not that he was entirely free from romanticism—no one who was so could be a revolutionary while the revolution was still nothing but idea and dream. But Lenin had suppressed the romantic streak in himself and was contemptuous of the usual unworldliness of the Russian rebel. The brother of the *Narodnik* martyr, he knew the price in blood and frustration which revolutionaries had paid for that unworldliness. His task, as he saw it, was to infuse in them a spirit of realism, to blend their fervour with sobriety, and to train them in precise, efficient methods of work. For this he reserved his own energy and time. Self-disciplined, absorbed in study and work, he was rarely seen at the gatherings of the exiles and rarely took part in their interminable, often fruitless arguments. He appreciated and enjoyed discussion as preparation for action, not for its own sake. In a sense, his mind moved along a single track, but that track was as broad as society itself and it led to the transformation of society.

It was almost inevitable that Trotsky should be drawn closer to Zasulich and Martov, whose roof he shared and who exercized their influence on him constantly, than to Lenin whose influence was intermittent only. Still in his formative years, he needed close social intercourse and argument on which he could whet his mind. This need Zasulich and Martov, but not Lenin, generously satisfied. They also struck a deeper chord in him, the chord which the *Narodniks* had struck when he had first joined Shvigovsky's circle. Lenin's conduct, for all the curiosity and respect it aroused, could not but seem to him dry and prosaic. Years were to pass before he discovered greatness in that prosaic character.

Soon after he had arrived in London, he also met Plekhanov, who, like Zasulich, had been an almost legendary figure to him. Plekhanov, too, had been one of the founding fathers of Russian Marxism and had stood close to Engels. He was the philosopher and ideologue of the new school, its great, erudite stylist and orator, enjoying European fame. But Plekhanov was also full of his own fame and brilliance—remote and haughty. At their first meeting he showed an instinctive dislike of the new contributor to *Iskra*, and the dislike grew into intense antipathy. The too men possessed many similar gifts and characteristics. Both were imaginative writers and sharp-witted controversialists; both had a theatrical manner of speaking and behaving; both were full of themselves, their ideas, and their doings. But while the junior's star was only beginning to rise, the senior's had just begun to decline. Trotsky was overflowing with immature yet captivating enthusiasm; Plekhanov was becoming sceptical and over-ripe. Lunacharsky relates an anecdote, current among the émigrés, which, though obviously untrue, does in part indicate Plekhanov's attitude. When he arrived in London, Zasulich expansively praised in his presence Trotsky's talents. 'The lad', she exclaimed, 'is undoubtedly a genius.' Plekhanov sulked, turned aside and said: 'I shall never forgive him this.'[1]

The *Iskra* team still spoke with one voice. But it had its dissensions, of which Trotsky presently became aware, and in which he was unwittingly becoming involved. The editorial board was equally divided between the three veterans and the three younger editors. Controversial matters were decided by vote and, as each group voted solidly against the other, a deadlock arose. Issues of editorial policy had often to be left in abeyance. Lenin, anxious to break the deadlock, thought of adding a new, a seventh, member to the board. As early as March 1903, four months after Trotsky's arrival, Lenin, in a memorandum sent to all editors, emphatically recommended his appointment. Beforehand he disposed of objections concerning Trotsky's age and qualifications: he underlined Trotsky's 'rare abilities', 'conviction and energy', and added that his

[1] A. Lunacharsky, *Revolutsionnye Siluety*, pp. 19–22. Some memorists (Zelikson-Bobrovskaya) say that when Trotsky's first unsigned articles appeared in *Iskra*, readers attributed them to Plekhanov.

contributions were 'not only very useful but absolutely necessary'.[1] Zasulich and Martov agreed. 'His [Trotsky's] literary works', Martov wrote to Axelrod, 'reveal indubitable talent . . . and already he wields great influence here thanks to his uncommon oratorical gifts. He speaks magnificently. Of this both I and Vladimir Ilyich [Lenin] have had sufficient proof. He possesses knowledge and works hard to increase it. I endorse Lenin's proposal without reservation.'[2] Axelrod, too, accepted the candidature. On this at least there was no division between the veterans and the others. The whole team, with one exception, eagerly welcomed Trotsky. The exception was Plekhanov. He objected vehemently on the ground that Trotsky's contributions, with their florid rhetoric, lowered the standard of the paper. That Trotsky's style was flowery and full of flourishes was true. Lenin had gently tried to prune it; and, in recommending Trotsky's appointment, he wrote that if the latter became a regular member of the editorial team it would be easier to impress on him the need for stylistic simplicity: he would then see that this was the view of the whole team, not merely Lenin's preference for austerity. But, to the indignation of all his colleagues, Plekhanov was unmoved. After much bickering, Zasulich brought the unsuspecting Trotsky to an editorial conference, hoping that Plekhanov would give in. Plekhanov snubbed the 'intruder' and persisted in his veto.

In *My Life* Trotsky says that Plekhanov suspected that he, Trotsky, would join Lenin in his opposition to the veterans. This could hardly have been Plekhanov's main motive. All the other veterans treated Trotsky with almost paternal pride and tenderness; and he in his turn showed them an affectionate reverence, becoming the Benjamin of the group. Such was his attitude not only towards Zasulich but also, and especially, towards Axelrod, whose home in Zurich presently became Trotsky's favourite retreat during his trips to the Continent. It is difficult to imagine characters more contrasting than those of Plekhanov and Axelrod, who had for nearly twenty-five years worked together in close friendship. Axelrod was a south Ukrainian Jew, like Trotsky. He had started as a *Narodnik* in the original South Russian Workers' Union, from which Trotsky had

---

[1] Krupskaya, op. cit., p. 65; Trotsky, *Moya Zhizn*, vol. i, chapter xii.
[2] *Pisma Axelroda i Martova*, pp. 79–80.

borrowed the name of his first organization. Then he had emigrated and pioneered for Marxism. With none of Plekhanov's gifts, poor as a writer and poorer still as a speaker, he was the inarticulate originator of many of the ideas which his friend brilliantly expounded. While Plekhanov's socialism was intellectual, Axelrod's sprang from absolute confidence in the working class. He believed fanatically that the workers would find their way to socialism and emancipation, and he instinctively distrusted the intelligentsia's aspiration to lead them— this was later the main motive of his unflagging opposition to Bolshevism. While Plekhanov, a polished European and an aristocrat in appearance, led a rather bourgeois life, Axelrod earned his living as a worker, producing in his home a special kind of buttermilk and delivering it to his customers. Over his milk-cans he argued with fugitives from Russia to whom his home was a haven of rest, and whom he fed and often clad. With his broad dishevelled beard, he looked more like a saintly Russian rabbi than a revolutionary politician. Yet the revolutionary leaders, including until quite recently Lenin, had all regarded him as their teacher and inspirer. To this man the young Trotsky became strongly attached, and the attachment was to have a bearing on his political fortunes.[1]

Ties of mutual friendship also bound him to another pioneer, Leon Deutsch, once also a southern Russian *Narodnik*, who had recently, after thirteen years of *katorga*, escaped from Siberia and made a journey around the world. Although at the height of his fame—his courageous escape had earned him world-wide admiration—Deutsch was regarding the new time, its problems, and its men, with weary and somewhat uncomprehending eyes. A little uneasy about Trotsky's exuberant radicalism and optimism, he nevertheless attached himself tenderly to the brilliant 'Benjamin', as if to the embodiment of his own youthful hopes, watched his first steps abroad with admiration, and sought to help him and to advance him in every way.

The dissension inside the *Iskra* team had as yet no political significance. Only a short time before, Lenin and Martov,

---

[1] L. Trotsky, loc. cit. and *Lenine*, pp. 9–60; A. Lunacharsky, op. cit., pp. 35–40; F. Dan, *Proiskhozhdenie Bolshevisma*, pp. 191–4, 288–9; N. Alexeyev in *Proletarskaya Revolutsia*, no. 3, 1924; L. N. Meshcheryakov in *Pechati Revolutsia*, vol. ii, 1924; V. Medem, *Von Mein Leben*, vol. ii, chapter i; John Mill, *Pioneers and Builders*, vol. i, pp. 205–7.

as we have seen, had sat at the veterans' feet with the same feelings which animated Trotsky now. But their apprenticeship had come to an end; and, as often happens, the pupils were more acutely aware of this than the masters. The whole work now centred on *Iskra*, and as editors and contributors the veterans, with the exception of Plekhanov, were more or less ineffectual. They wrote rarely and not very well; and they took little or no part in organizing the clandestine movement in Russia. Lenin and Martov shared day-to-day editorial duties; and Lenin, assisted by Krupskaya, bore the brunt of the drudgery that had to be done in order to keep and develop the contacts with Russia.[1] Inevitably, the veterans felt that they were being by-passed.

The jealousies were focused in the antagonism between Plekhanov and Lenin, each of the two being the most assertive man in his group. This antagonism had appeared at the moment of *Iskra*'s foundation, and it had grown since. Lenin was acquiring confidence in his own ideas and methods of work, and he did not conceal it. Plekhanov treated him with patronizing irony or with schoolmasterly offensiveness. Some months before Trotsky's arrival, in May 1902, Lenin had written to Plekhanov: 'You have a fine idea of tact. . . . You do not hesitate to use the most contemptuous expressions. . . . If your purpose is to make mutual work impossible, then the way you have chosen will very rapidly help you to succeed. As for our personal relations . . . you have finally spoilt them, or more exactly, you have achieved their complete cessation.'[2] This rift had since been patched up by Zasulich and Martov. But clashes recurred and the latest was connected with Trotsky's work for *Iskra*. 'Once [Lenin] returned from an editorial meeting', writes Krupskaya, 'in a terrific rage. "A damned fine state of affairs", he said, "nobody has enough courage to reply to Plekhanov. Look at Vera Ivanovna [Zasulich]! Plekhanov trounces Trotsky, and Vera just says 'Just like our George. All he does is to shout.'" "I cannot go on like this", Lenin burst out.'[3]

---

[1] In a hostile memoir, written in 1927, Potresov admitted: 'And yet . . . all of us who were closest to the work . . . valued Lenin not only for his knowledge, brains, and capacity for work but also for his exceptional devotion to the cause, his unceasing readiness to give himself completely, to take upon himself the most unpleasant functions and without fail to discharge them with the utmost conscientiousness.' A. N. Potresov, *Posmertnyi Sbornik Proizvedenii*, p. 299.

[2] *The Letters of Lenin*, pp. 155–6.   [3] Krupskaya, op. cit., p. 65.

Almost imperceptibly this dissension was being superseded by another arising from it. Lenin, Martov, and Potresov (the latter's role, important at first, was now insignificant) still acted and voted together against the veterans. But as the rivalry developed, Lenin began to alienate his contemporaries also, especially Martov. Convinced that he was right, he would not turn back, and went on in total disregard of the veterans' susceptibilities. Martov, less definite in his views and less determined to enforce them, tried to make peace. His ideas were usually the same as Lenin's; but as soon as he tried to put them into effect and met with resistance, he began to vacillate, and, swayed by second thoughts, to retreat. This was so not only in the quarrel with the veterans. In other matters as well, he usually first agreed with Lenin to 'strive uncompromisingly' for a certain objective. Then he would balk at Lenin's uncompromising manner, and would finally abandon the objective. He was by temperament 'soft' and was repelled by Lenin's 'hardness'. At meetings 'Lenin would glance at Martov, for whom he had a high esteem, with a critical and slightly suspicious eye, and Martov, feeling this glance, would look down and his shoulders would twitch nervously. . . . Lenin would look beyond Martov as he talked, while Martov's eyes grew glassy behind his drooping and never quite clean pince-nez.'[1]

These, then, were the influences under which Trotsky came. The fact that Lenin defended him and tried to promote him, against Plekhanov's opposition, might have brought him close to Lenin and turned him against the veterans. But this did not happen. For one thing, the veterans, as we know, did not on this point support Plekhanov—they, too, did their best to sponsor and encourage Trotsky. For another, he was nearly ten years younger than Lenin and ten times as sensitive to the veterans' romantic appeal. So far he had had no time to become disillusioned with them and to notice that, for all their virtues, they were ineffectual in day-to-day work. Lenin's opposition to them seemed to him boorish, and his motives personal and mean.

However, he considered the discord as the trivial side of a glorious and momentous venture. The internal squabbles did not prevent *Iskra* from being the great rallying centre of the nascent party—its name alone was a stirring summons to

[1] Trotsky, *Moya Zhizn*, vol. i, p. 176.

revolutionaries. Nobody believed in *Iskra*'s mission more ardently than Trotsky; and his writings pulsated with this belief. The distinctive mark of his early contributions to *Iskra* lies not so much in originality of ideas as in the force of the emotional current that runs through them, in the passionate character of his revolutionary invocations, and in the almost dramatic vehemence of the invective which he poured out on Russia's rulers and on socialism's enemies. He was now writing without the inhibitions of censorship, and he gave free vent to his temperament, a fact which did not necessarily improve the quality of his writing—his articles for *Iskra* were often inferior to his Siberian essays.

His first contribution to *Iskra* was devoted to the bi-centenary of the ill-famed Schlüsselburg fortress, which Peter the Great had built near his capital—'his window on Europe and his most important prison'. The writer evoked the shades of the martyrs who had been murdered or driven to madness within its walls, among them Alexander Ulyanov, Lenin's brother. And he ended with a ringing apostrophe to the Tsar and his servants: 'You may still indulge in your patriotic bacchanals—to-day you are still the masters of Schlüsselburg.' In the same issue he flayed the quasi-liberal gentry, who in the *Zemstvos* hardly dared to breathe a word against authority: 'What other Egyptian plagues, what other Russian scorpions are needed to straighten the meekly bent backs of the liberal *Zemstvo* men?'[1] In connexion with Slavophile demonstrations against Turkey, sponsored by the Tsar, he wrote about the 'Sharks of Slavophilism': 'Again, O Russian citizen, an attempt is made to open the safety valve of official Slavophilism and to provide an outlet for the excess of your civic emotions. Again, as twenty-five years ago [during the Russo-Turkish war of 1878], the journalistic purveyors of patriotism drag out of their archives . . . ideas of Pan-Slav fraternity and put them into circulation with pomp and chiming of bells.' Yet the Tsarist government treats its own people no better than the Sultan treats his non-Moslem subjects. 'Are our own prisons', the writer asked, 'better than the Turkish . . . have the soldiers of our punitive expeditions not raped the wives and daughters of the Poltava peasants? Have they not looted their property?' Why then were so-called Liberals

[1] *Iskra*, no. 27, 1 November 1902.

lending support to the Tsar's 'civilizing mission' in Turkey, why 'do not they call for a crusade against the barbarians . . . of Tsardom?' The semi-liberal opposition, 'that lawful opposition to a lawless government' was already, and would remain for many years, the favourite butt of his irony.[1] In the *Zemstvos*, whose function it should be to judge the actions of the administration, the 'defendant in fact assumes the role of the presiding judge and arrogates the right to adjourn the court at any moment'. Tsardom was offering the *Zemstvos* 'the *knout* wrapped in the parchment of Magna Charta', and the *Zemstvos* were contented. What do they understand by freedom—'freedom from political freedom?' 'One may confidently say that if Russian freedom were to be born from the *Zemstvos*, it would never come to life. Fortunately Russian freedom has more reliable parents: the revolutionary proletariat and the inner, self-destructive logic of Russian absolutism.' 'Many political trends will succeed one another, many "parties" will emerge and fade, each pretending to improve upon the Social Democratic programme and tactics, but the future historian will say: these trends and these parties were only insignificant, secondary incidents in the great struggle of the awakened working class . . . already advancing with clumsy but faithful steps on the road of political and social emancipation.'[2]

In a similar vein he wrote about the Tsar's attempts to force the Russian language on the Finns and to destroy their autonomy; the expulsion of Maxim Gorky from the Imperial Academy; the futility of the newly formed Social Revolutionary party, reverting to *Narodnik* terrorism; or the attempt by the police to set up puppet clandestine organizations to compete with the real underground. His attacks on the terrorism of the Social Revolutionaries, especially one made after the execution of a young student Balmashev, who had killed Sypiagin, the Minister of the Interior, provoked indignant protests from Liberals and Socialists. The Liberal intelligentsia had much more sympathy with the terrorists than had the Marxists. But

---

[1] *Iskra*, no. 28, 15 November and no. 29, 1 December 1902. It is noteworthy that as early as March 1901 Trotsky wrote in the *Eastern Review*: 'Pure liberalism with all its Manchester symbols of faith has faded in our country before it has blossomed: it did not find any social ground for itself. It was possible to import Manchester ideas . . . but it was impossible to import the social environment which produced those ideas.' *Sochinenya*, vol. xx, pp. 85–86.   [2] *Iskra*, no. 29, 1 December 1902.

even Socialists held that Trotsky's polemics were too vehement and that he ought to have written with more respect or warmth about the executed Social Revolutionary.[1]

Only nine months were to elapse between his arrival in London and the opening of the second congress of the Russian Social Democratic party. In this short time his reputation was established firmly enough to allow him, at the age of twenty-three, to play a leading role at the congress, in the momentous split between Bolsheviks and Mensheviks. This was perhaps due more to his lecturing and speech-making than to his writing. No sooner had he arrived in London than Lenin and Martov pitted him in debate against venerable old *Narodnik* and anarchist émigrés in Whitechapel. The novice was pleasantly surprised at the ease with which he swept the floor with his grey-bearded opponents. After that he toured the Russian colonies in western Europe. Contemporaries have described the first sudden and irresistible impact of his oratory, the élan, the passion, the wit, and the thunderous metallic voice, with which he roused audiences and bore down upon opponents. This appears all the more remarkable as only a few years before he could only stammer in blushing perplexity before a tiny, homely audience and as he had spent most of the time since in the solitude of prison and exile. His oratory was quite untutored: he had hardly yet heard a single speaker worthy of imitation. This is one of those instances of latent unsuspected talent, bursting forth in exuberant vitality to delight and amaze all who witness it. His speech, even more than his writing, was distinguished by a rare intensity of thought, imagination, emotion, and expression. The rhetoric which often spoilt his writing made his speaking all the more dramatic. He appeared, as it were, with the drama in himself, with the sense of entering a conflict in which the forces and actors engaged were more than life-size, the battles Homeric, and the climaxes worthy of demi-gods.[2]

---

[1] In the summer of 1902, Miliukov, the future leader of the Constitutional Democrats, paid a visit to *Iskra*'s editors in London, praised *Iskra* but objected to its campaign against terrorism. 'Why', he said, 'let there be another two or three such attempts on the Tsar's ministers and we are going to get a constitution.' The moderate constitutionalist often regarded the terrorist as a useful agent for exerting pressure on the Tsar. N. Alexeyev in *Proletarskaya Revolutsia*, no. 3, 1924.

[2] In August 1902, just before his flight from Siberia, he had written in the *Eastern Review*: 'The laws of social life and the principles of party . . . are also a force

Elevated above the crowd and feeling a multitude of eyes centred
on him, himself storming a multitude of hearts and minds
below—he was in his element. A contemporary describes the
lean, tallish man, with large fierce eyes and large, sensual,
irregular mouth, perched on the platform like a 'bird of prey'.[1]

. . . .

In the admired speaker and writer there lived on, as he
himself put it, a 'barbarian struggling for self-preservation'.
Having found himself among the élite of the movement, he had
to lift himself intellectually by his bootstraps. He diligently
studied Marxism, which in this its golden age gave the adept a
solid mental equipment. Just before he escaped from Siberia
he had explored the intricacies of 'capitalistic circulation', with
its periodic crises, as they are analysed with seeming dryness and
yet with the utmost dramatic effect in the second volume of
Das Kapital. Abroad he resumed this study. But the fascination
of Marxism kept his mind closed to any extraneous idea or
phenomenon. On his arrival in London it had seemed to him
strange that Lenin should try to interest him in English historical monuments. When he first visited Paris he similarly
defended himself against the assault of novel impressions. He
summed up his first view of Paris grotesquely: 'Very much like
Odessa, but Odessa is better.' The art treasures of the Louvre
bored him. What excited him most in France was the controversy between the orthodox Marxists, led by Jules Guesde, and
the reformists who followed Jaurès. He plunged into a crowd of
Parisian workers demonstrating against Millerand, the first
Socialist to become a minister in a bourgeois government and
then engaged in suppressing strikes. Marching in the crowd he
shouted 'all sorts of unpleasant things against Millerand'.

In Paris he met his second wife. She was Natalya Sedova, a
girl student who had taken him to the Louvre and tried to open
his eyes to paintings and sculpture. A few years younger than his
first wife, she, too, was a revolutionary. She had been expelled
from a boarding school for young ladies of noble birth at
Kharkov, where she had persuaded her classmates not to attend

not second in its grandeur to the antique Fatum. Social principles in their pitiless
compulsion, not less than Aeschylus' Fate, can grind into dust the individual soul
if it enters into a conflict with them.' Sochinenya, vol. xx, p. 241.
   [1] V. Medem, op. cit., vol. ii, pp. 7–9; P. A. Garvi, Vospominanya Sotsialdemokrata, p. 385.

prayers and to read, instead of the Bible, Russian radical literature.[1] She was at this time studying the history of art at the Sorbonne. She was to remain his companion for the rest of his life and to share with him to the full triumph and defeat. Sokolovskaya, however, remained his legal wife and bore his name. To all three the legal niceties of their connexion did not matter at all—like other revolutionaries they disregarded on principle the canons of middle-class respectability. At heart, perhaps, Trotsky never quite freed himself from a qualm over the manner of his separation from Sokolovskaya; and this, more than alleged reluctance to expatiate on his private life, may explain why in his autobiography he devoted no more than a single sentence to the whole affair. As an émigré he himself could not do much for his wife and two children. His parents, who in 1903 went to Paris for a reconciliation, took care of the children, helping to bring them up. As far as we know, the question of a reunion between Trotsky and his first wife never arose. When he and Sedova returned to Russia there was no suggestion of discord. Ties of respect and of a high-minded friendship were to bind the three of them to the end; and eventually his political fortunes affected with equal tragedy both the women and the children of both.

.   .   .   .

While he was working and lecturing in France, Switzerland, and Belgium, there came from clandestine headquarters in Russia insistent demands that he should be sent back. The Russian underground and the émigré centre competed intensely for personnel. Trotsky knew nothing of these demands. When old Leon Deutsch learned about them, he used all his influence to prevent Trotsky's return. With the burden of his own thirteen years of hard labour in Siberia still on his mind, he pleaded with the editors of *Iskra* to leave the 'Benjamin' abroad, so that he might widen his education, see the world, and develop his talents. Deutsch found an ally in Lenin, who was reluctant to lose his contributor. Lenin wrote back to Russia that Trotsky was showing no desire to return. This was a subterfuge by which Lenin hoped to put off Russian headquarters, and Krupskaya leaves no doubt that it was Lenin who decided against sending Trotsky back. Thus, Trotsky's fate was settled for the

[1] Eastman, op. cit., p. 153.

time being: he would stay abroad for the forthcoming congress
of the party.[1]

.   .   .   .

In July 1903 the congress was at last convened in Brussels.
This was actually to be the foundation assembly—the so-called
first congress of 1898 had been a meeting at Minsk of eight
people only, who were soon arrested, and had left nothing
behind except a stirring *Manifesto*, written by Peter Struve.
Only now, in 1903, had the network of clandestine organizations become close enough, and the contacts of *Iskra* with it
solid enough, for everybody to feel that the time had come to
form a regular party with a well-defined constitution and an
elected leadership. It was taken for granted that that leadership
would remain with the *Iskra* team, which alone had supplied
the organizations with a political idea and alone had co-
ordinated their activities. For the whole team the congress was
a solemn occasion. To the veterans it was the materialization of
a dream long cherished in prisons, and in places of deportation
and exile.

It was also taken for granted that the *Iskra* men would appear
at the congress as a single body, bound by solidarity in ideas, in
achievement, and in the aspiration to leadership. Before the
congress there was some discord over the drafting of a programme, but this was easily settled. Opposition was expected
from two groups: from the Economists, who would fight a
rearguard skirmish against the triumphant advance of revolutionary politics; and from the Jewish Bund, claiming for itself
a special status within the party. These two groups were in a
minority, and all *Iskra* men were united against them. Just
before the opening of the congress the editors of *Iskra* began to
wrangle over the manner in which the leading bodies of the
party should be set up; but this seemed a minor detail of
organization.

At the beginning of July forty-four delegates with voting
rights, and fourteen with consultative voice, met at the Socialist
Maison du Peuple in Brussels. Trotsky arrived from Geneva to
represent, together with another delegate, the *Siberian Social
Democratic Workers' Union*.[2] Seated in a drab warehouse in the

---

[1] N. Krupskaya, *Memories of Lenin*, p. 60; Lenin, *Sochinenya*, vol. xxxiv, p. 114.
[2] In *My Life* he describes humorously how he and Dr. Ulyanov, Lenin's younger

back of the *Maison du Peuple*, the delegates listened in exaltation to Plekhanov's opening speech. By their presence, they felt, they were creating a landmark in the history of that submerged Russia which had for more than three-quarters of a century struggled against the Tsars and was now heading for the final battles. Neither the humble setting of the congress, nor its obscurity from the world, could, in the eyes of the participants, deprive the moment of its historic consequence.

The first controversy on the floor concerned the Bund. The Jewish organization demanded autonomy within the party, with the right to elect its own central committee and to frame its own policy in matters affecting the Jewish population. It asked further that the party should recognize the Bund as its sole agency among the Jewish workers. It urged the party that it should advocate not merely equal rights for Jews, as it had done, but that it should acknowledge the right of the Jews to 'cultural autonomy', their right, that is, to manage their own cultural affairs and to maintain their own schools in the Jewish (Yiddish) language. On behalf of the *Iskra* men, Martov, who had been one of the Bund's founders, indignantly repudiated these demands. Trotsky repeated the repudiation even more vehemently. The debate was taking place only a few months after the great pogrom of the Jews at Kishynev. Jewish susceptibilities and suspicions were aroused; and they were indirectly reflected in the Bund's attitude.[1] The non-Jewish spokesmen of *Iskra* kept in the background in order to spare those susceptibilities; and so the rebuff to the Bund came from the Jews. Martov tabled the motion against the Bund; and only Jewish delegates put their signatures to it. Trotsky himself spoke on behalf of the *Iskra*ites of Jewish origin, and, making the most

brother, at a small station near Geneva, hurriedly boarded an express train for Brussels after the train had begun to move, and how the station-master stopped the train to take the strange passengers off the buffers. Trotsky travelled on a false Bulgarian passport as Mr. Samokovlieff. These precautions were intended to keep the Russian secret police in the dark. But the *Okhrana* had its agents among the delegates, and the Belgian police closely watched the congress and its participants. Trotsky describes, in the style of a good film scenario, his race with a police agent through the empty streets of Brussels in the middle of the night. Finally, the congress was transferred to London.

[1] An illuminating account of the mood among Jewish socialists after the pogrom is found in the correspondence of Y. M. Sverdlov, the future Soviet President, in *Pechat i Revolutsia*, vol. ii, 1924. See also Medem, op. cit., vol. ii, pp. 29–32.

of this circumstance, he lashed the delegates of the Bund into a
fury. They protested vehemently against his speech, suggested
that he was out to affront the Jews, and appealed to the chairman to protect them. When the chairman found Trotsky's
remarks unexceptionable, the Bundists tabled a motion censur-
ing the chairman.

This was one of the stormiest scenes at the congress, and one
of the very rare occasions on which Trotsky referred to himself
as a Jew and spoke on a specifically Jewish issue That he was
doing so only to refute Jewish demands must have seemed almost
caddish to the highly-strung delegates of the Bund. He pleaded,
however, that more than a Jewish issue was at stake. Claiming
for itself autonomy within the party, with the right to elect its
own Central Committee, the Bund was, in fact, setting a
precedent for others: if the party had granted such privileges to
the Bund it could not later refuse them to other groups. It would
then have to abandon the idea of an integrated organization
and to transform itself into a loose federation of parties and
groups. In short, the Bund was trying by devious means to
induce the *Iskra* men to abandon their guiding principle and
the practical work they had done to put it into effect. The other
demand that the Bund be recognized as the party's sole agency
among Jewish workers amounted to a claim that only Jews
were entitled to carry the Socialist message to Jewish workers
and to organize them. This, Trotsky pointed out, was an
expression of distrust in the non-Jewish members of the party,
a challenge to their internationalist conviction and sentiment.
'The Bund', Trotsky exclaimed amid a storm of protests, 'is free
not to trust the party, but it cannot expect the party to vote
no confidence in its own self.'[1] The party as a whole could not
renounce its right to address the Jewish toiling masses without
yielding to Jewish separatism. The Bund's demand for 'cultural
autonomy' sprang from the same separatism, confronting with
its claims first the party and then the state and the nation.
Socialism was interested in sweeping away barriers between
races, religions, and nationalities—it could not turn its hand to
putting up such barriers. He granted the Jews the right to have
schools in their own language, if they so desired. But these, he
added, should not be outside the national educational system,

[1] *Vtoroi Syezd RSDRP*, pp. 52–55.

and Jewish cultural life at large should not be centred on and closed in itself. He tabled a motion to this effect, supplementing Martov's general resolution. Both resolutions were carried by an overwhelming majority.[1]

Like Martov, Axelrod, Deutsch, and other Socialists of Jewish origin, Trotsky took the so-called assimilationist view, holding that there was no future for the Jews as a separate community. The ties that had kept the Jews together were either those of religion, which, according to the prevalent Socialist conviction, were bound to dissolve; or those of a semi-fictitious nationalism culminating in Zionism. The Bund was strongly opposed to Zionism, for it conceived the future of the Jews to lie in the countries of the so-called diaspora. But, Trotsky argued, in its opposition to Zionism the Bund absorbed from the latter its nationalist essence.[2] He saw the solution of the Jewish problem not in the formation of a Jewish state, still less in the formation of Jewish states within the non-Jewish ones, but in a consistently internationalist reshaping of society. The premiss for this was mutual unreserved confidence between Jews and non-Jews, whether in the party or in the state. To this attitude he was to adhere till the end of his life—only the impact of Nazism was to induce him to soften a little his hostility towards Zionism.[3] He would not grant the tragic truth contained in the Jews' distrust of their gentile environment. Neither he nor any other Socialist could imagine even in a nightmare that the working classes of Europe, having through generations listened to the preachings of international solidarity, would, forty years later, be unable or unwilling to prevent or stop the murder of six

[1] Ibid., p. 198.
[2] Some time after the congress Trotsky published in *Iskra* a bitter attack on Zionism. The occasion was a conflict between the original Zionists who were led by Theodore Herzl and those Zionists who, led by Max Nordau, were prepared to abandon Palestine for Uganda as a Jewish homeland. Herzl tried to buy the land of Palestine from the Sultan, while Nordau conducted a campaign for the acquisition of Uganda. A fanatical follower of Herzl made an attempt on Nordau's life. Trotsky wrote in this connexion about Herzl as a 'shameless adventurer' and about 'the hysterical sobbings of the romanticists of Zion'; and he saw in the conflict the bankruptcy of Zionism. (*Iskra*, no. 56, 1 January 1904.)
[3] In an interview with the American-Jewish *Forward* (28 January 1937) Trotsky stated that after the experience of Nazism, it was difficult to believe in the 'assimilation' of the Jews, for which he had hoped. Zionism by itself, he went on, would not solve the problem; but even under Socialism, it might be necessary for the Jews to settle on a separate territory.

million Jewish men, women, and children in Hitler's gas chambers. To this problem the formulas of the Bund could, of course, provide no answer. Trotsky came out as a Jew against Jewish separatism, because his vision of the future was as remote from mid-century European 'civilization' as heaven from earth.

The next dispute at the congress was between the *Iskra* men and the Economists. The Economists protested against the supremacy which revolutionary politics had gained in the mind of the party over trade unionism and the struggle for reforms. They also objected to the centralized organization in which they, the Economists, were reduced to impotence. Their spokesmen, Martynov and Akimov, upbraided *Iskra* for its dictatorial, 'Jacobin-like' attitude.[1] It should be noted that this is the first time the charge appears in the records. The *Iskra* men answered the critics in unison. Trotsky spoke against the Economists with an aggressive zeal which earned him the epithet of 'Lenin's cudgel'.[2] The struggle for small economic gains and reforms, he said, made sense only in so far as it helped to muster the forces of the working classes for revolution. 'The Social Democratic Party, as it struggles for reforms, carries out a fundamental reform of itself—a reform in the minds of the proletariat, which is being prepared for a revolutionary dictatorship.' The ruling classes, in any case, agree to reforms only when they are confronted by a threat of revolution, and so the supremacy of revolutionary politics was needed even in the struggle for reforms.[3] He defended the centralistic mode of organization, saying that the party needed strict statutes, enabling the leadership to keep out noncongenial influences. Ridiculing the charges of Jacobinism, he said that the statutes should express '*the leadership's organized distrust*' of the members, a distrust manifesting itself in vigilant control from above over the party.[4]

This idea was soon to become Lenin's exclusive property, the hallmark of Bolshevism. Trotsky, we remember, had advocated it as early as in 1901; and this idea was still *Iskra*'s common property. It summed up, to quote the most authoritative Menshevik historian, the reaction of all forward-looking Socialists against the 'shapelessness and federative looseness' of the move-

[1] *Vtoroi Syezd RSDRP.*, p. 137.   [2] N. K. Krupskaya, op. cit., p. 70.
[3] *Vtoroi Syezd RSDRP.*, pp. 136-7.   [4] Ibid., p. 168.

ment.[1] But this was the last time that all *Iskra* men, including the future Mensheviks, were in complete accord in defending this idea, although perhaps none of them spoke for it as vigorously as Trotsky did. None of them would have been more surprised than he if he had been told that a few sessions later he would angrily renounce his own words. It was, generally speaking, not Lenin but the future leaders of Menshevism, especially Plekhanov, who at this congress, during the debate on the programme, spoke with the greatest determination for proletarian dictatorship. Plekhanov urged the delegates to adopt formulas that left no doubt that in a revolutionary situation they would not shrink from the destruction of parliamentary institutions or from restricting civil liberties. *Salus revolutionis suprema lex esto*—Plekhanov used these words as his text when he argued that if, after the overthrow of Tsardom, a constituent assembly hostile to the revolutionary government were to be elected, that government should, after the manner of Cromwell, disperse the assembly. It was on this principle that Lenin and Trotsky acted in 1918, unmoved by the vituperation of an old and sick Plekhanov. The latter now also pleaded that the revolutionary government should not abolish capital punishment—it might need it in order to destroy the Tsar. These views evoked one single protest from an obscure delegate and gave rise to a feeble doubt in a few others, but they were generally received with acclamation.

Behind the scenes, however, the solidarity of the *Iskra* men was beginning to vanish. The discord did not at first appear over any problem of policy, not even over the famous paragraph 1 of the statutes, on which they were eventually to divide, but over a matter in which no principle of policy or organization was involved. Lenin proposed to reduce the number of *Iskra*'s

---

[1] L. Martov, *Istorya Rossiiskoi Sotsial-Demokratii*, pp. 62–72. Martov describes how much the concept of a centralized organization was then 'in the air'. The idea was first formulated in detail not by Lenin but by an underground worker in Petersburg, who wrote a letter to Lenin about this, and who after the split joined the Mensheviks. In the year before the congress a scheme of organization similar to Lenin's was proposed to *Iskra* by Savinkov, who later left the Social Democrats to form the Social Revolutionary Party. Even after the split Martov wrote: 'In the problem of organization we are first of all adherents of centralism, which as revolutionary social democrats we must be.' Ibid., p. 11. See also Lenin, *Sochinenya*, vol. vi, pp. 205–24, Martov's preface to Cherevanin, *Organizatsionnyi Vopros*, and V. L. Akimov, *Materialy dla Kharakteristiki Razvitya RSDRP*, p. 104.

editors from six to three. The three editors were to be: Plekhanov, Martov, and himself. Axelrod, Zasulich, and Potresov
were to be left out. Historians of the opposed schools are eager
retrospectively to read into this proposal profound, far-reaching
intentions, baleful or benign, according to the viewpoint. In its
actual setting, Lenin's intention was simple. He was seeking to
make the editorial work of *Iskra* more efficient than it had lately
been. As the board of six had tended to divide equally, he had,
in order to break the deadlock, proposed Trotsky's appointment;
but, since Plekhanov's objections had ruled this out, he now
tried to achieve his purpose by reducing, instead of increasing,
the number of editors. The three whom he was proposing had
been *Iskra*'s real pillars. Zasulich, Axelrod, and Potresov had contributed very little—none of them was a fluent writer—and had
done even less in the work of administration and organization.[1]
On grounds of efficiency alone, Lenin's proposal was justified.
But considerations of efficiency clashed, as they often do, with
acquired rights and sentiment. Lenin had his qualms before he
decided on this step; Plekhanov had little or no scruple. To
Trotsky this attempt to eliminate from *Iskra* Axelrod and
Zasulich, two of its founders, seemed 'sacrilegious'; he was
shocked by Lenin's callousness.

This narrow issue at once became entangled with other and
wider questions. *Iskra*'s editorial board was to remain, as it had
been, the party's virtual leadership. A central committee, to be
elected at the congress, was to operate in Russia. But, working
underground and exposed to arrest, it could not secure continuity in leadership—only an émigré centre, such as the
editorial board, could do that. Lenin further proposed the election of a Council which was to act as arbiter between the
central committee and the editorial board. That Council was
to consist of five members: two from *Iskra*, two from the central
committee, and a chairman who was to be elected by congress.
It was a foregone conclusion that Plekhanov would be the
chairman; and so *Iskra*'s editorial board was sure to wield the
decisive influence in the Council. It was because of this scheme

---

[1] Explaining in a letter to his follower his own motives, Lenin stated that to the
45 issues of the 'old' *Iskra* Martov had contributed 39 articles, Lenin 32, Plekhanov
24; Zasulich had written only 6 articles, Axelrod 4, and Potresov 8. Lenin, *Sochinenya*,
vol. xxxiv, p. 164.

that Lenin brought upon himself the charge that he was seeking to dominate the party. Yet, as events showed, the scheme by itself could not give Lenin more influence than he had had under the old dispensation. If it tended to accord a privileged position to any single person then that person was Plekhanov, Lenin's future enemy. All that was to be achieved was the elimination of the least effective members of the old team, in the first instance of Axelrod and Zasulich. Lenin was willing to pay these veterans the homage they had well deserved; but he was not prepared to do so in a manner that would have interfered with the effective conduct of business, the brunt of which he himself had anyhow borne. The two veterans, not unnaturally, were shocked. Martov was anxious to soothe them. Trotsky, not well informed about the inner workings of the team, could not understand Lenin's motives. He sensed a sinister conspiracy.

While behind the scenes the initiated whispered about the 'family scandal', the statutes of the party came up for debate in full session. The *Iskra* team had discussed them before the congress and had noticed a difference between Lenin and Martov. Lenin's draft ran as follows: 'A member of . . . the Party is any person who accepts its programme, supports the Party with material means, and *personally participates* in one of its organizations.' Martov's draft was identical with Lenin's, except that where Lenin demanded that a member should 'personally participate' in one of the party's organizations, Martov required him more vaguely to 'co-operate personally and regularly under the guidance of one of the organizations'. The difference seemed elusively subtle. Lenin's formula pointed towards a closely-knit party, consisting only of the actual participants in the clandestine bodies. Martov's clause envisaged a looser association, including those who merely assisted the underground organization without belonging to it. When the two formulas were first compared, the difference did not seem important; and Martov was prepared to withdraw his draft.[1] There seemed to be no reason why the party should split over two words of a paragraph in its rules and regulations.

In the meantime the personal clashes connected with Lenin's editorial scheme generated behind the scenes ill feeling and

[1] Pavlovich, *Pismo k Tovarishcham o Vtorom Syezde*, p. 5.

bitterness which caused the protagonists to approach one another with petulance and growing suspicion.[1] Martov, Trotsky, and others angrily assailed Lenin for his rudeness and lust for power, while Lenin could not see why this abuse should be heaped on him when all he had done was to suggest a workable and self-explanatory plan for *Iskra*'s overhaul. Each side began to scent intrigue and machination in every move made by the other. Each side was on the look-out for the traps that the other was laying for it. Each began to rehash old and half-forgotten differences; and although these had seemed puny only yesterday, they now appeared meaningful and portentous. In this mood the antagonists faced one another when the congress moved on to examine the statutes. There could be no question now of patching up the different formulas and submitting only one draft. On the contrary, the author of each draft was bent on bringing out the most deeply hidden implications of his clause, on making them as explicit as possible, on impressing the bewildered delegates with the gulf, the unbridgeable gulf, between the alternatives; and on emphasizing and over-emphasizing the practical consequences that the adoption of the one clause or the other would entail. Martov and Lenin, the two friends and comrades, confronted each other as enemies. Each spoke as if in a trance; each wondered at his own strange behaviour; each was surprised and bewildered by it; yet neither was capable of pausing and retracing his steps.[2]

The mood of the chief protagonists communicated itself to the delegates. The congress was split. Instead of founding one party it gave birth to two. At this moment, Plekhanov, the future irreconcilable enemy of the Bolshevik revolution, was Lenin's closest ally; while Trotsky was one of Lenin's most vocal opponents. He charged Lenin with the attempt to build up a closed organization of conspirators, not a party of the working

---

[1] The *Iskra* men held their closed sessions outside the congress. At one of these, when the division first became apparent, Trotsky presided because the opponents could not agree on any other chairman. Trotsky, *Moya Zhizn*, vol. i, chapter xii.

[2] In a letter to Potresov, Lenin wrote shortly after the Congress: 'And now I am asking myself: for what reason should we part to become life-long enemies? I am reviewing all the events and impressions of the congress, I am aware that often I acted and behaved in terrible irritation, 'madly', and I am willing to admit this my guilt to anybody—if one can call guilt something that was naturally caused by the atmosphere, the reactions, the retorts, the struggle, etc.' Lenin, *Sochinenya*, vol. xxxiv, p. 137.

class. Socialism was based on confidence in the workers' class-instinct and in their capacity to understand their historical mission—why then should the party not open its gates wide to them, as Martov advised? Lenin, surprised to see his 'cudgel' turning against him, made repeated attempts to detach Trotsky from Martov. In full session he mildly and persuasively appealed to Trotsky, saying that from lack of experience Trotsky was confusing the issues and misinterpreting the differences. In the working class, too, he went on, there was confusion, wavering, and opportunism; and if the party were to open its gates as widely as Martov urged it to do, then it would absorb into its ranks all those elements of weakness. They should organize only the 'vanguard of the proletariat', its most class-conscious and courageous elements. The party must lead the working class; it could not, therefore, be as broad as the class itself.

This argument failed to persuade Trotsky. Lenin then met him outside the conference hall and for hours tried to answer charges and to explain his behaviour. Later he sent his followers and his own brother to 'bring over Trotsky'.[1] All was in vain. Trotsky was stiffening in hostility.

The congress adopted by a majority Martov's draft of the statutes. But this majority included the delegates of the Bund and the Economists, who, having been defeated by the votes of all *Iskra* men, were about to leave the congress and secede from the party. After their secession Lenin presented his scheme for the overhaul of *Iskra*'s staff. Trotsky countered the scheme with a motion emphatically confirming in office the old editorial board.[2] This time Lenin won with a majority of only two votes. With the same majority the congress elected Lenin's candidates to the Central Committee. The opposition abstained from voting. Thus it came about that Lenin's followers were labelled *Bolsheviki* (the men of the majority), while his opponents were described as *Mensheviki* (the men of the minority). The leaders of the minority, shocked and almost horror-stricken by the audacity with which Lenin had deprived Axelrod and Zasulich of their status in the party, announced that they would boycott the newly elected Central Committee and *Iskra*. Martov at once resigned from the editorial board. Lenin denounced this as intolerably anarchic behaviour. He was determined to enforce

[1] L. Trotsky, loc. cit. [2] *Vtoroi Syezd RSDRP*, p. 364.

the authority of the newly-elected bodies: he insisted that, however narrow the margin by which they had been chosen, they constituted the legitimate leadership: in any democratic body, the majority, be it ever so slight, is the repository of constitutional power. The congress broke up in uproar and chaos.

In spite of its outwardly fortuitous character, this division initiated a long and irreversible process of differentiation, in the course of which the party of the revolution was to become separated from the party of the moderates. In western Europe the most moderate elements in the Labour movements were already frankly describing themselves as reformists, opposed to revolution. It was natural that such a division should appear in Russia as well. But under Tsarist autocracy even the most moderate of Socialists could not openly constitute themselves into a party of reform: the parliamentary democratic setting for this was lacking. They went on to profess, more or less sincerely, revolutionary socialism and Marxist orthodoxy. This, even more than the bewildering circumstances of the split, concealed its true nature. The division assumed an involved, irrational, and befogged aspect. What Trotsky saw in 1903 was two groups professing the same principles of policy and organization. He perceived nothing that would cause them to drift apart, except Lenin's ruthlessness in dealing with comrades, with such exalted comrades as Axelrod and Zasulich. This superfluous split, he reasoned, could not but become a source of weakness to the party and the working class.

On the face of things this was quite true. So far the protagonists were divided only by a difference in temper, although every one of them would soon try to rationalize this difference into a deeper controversy over ideas and conceptions. But the difference in temper was not without significance. In his 'disrespect' for the veterans, Lenin had shown that he would subordinate every sentiment, no matter how praiseworthy, and every other consideration to higher requirements of policy and organization. If the founding fathers of the party had to be sacrificed to efficiency, he would sacrifice them. An underground movement, assailing the ramparts of Tsardom and savagely persecuted, could not afford to give honorary sinecures even to those who had started the movement. This was, of course, a fanatical and in a sense an inhuman attitude. The man who so acted would not hesitate to sacrifice other persons and other considerations to what he regarded as the vital interest of the revolution. But a revolutionary party cannot do without a large dose of fanaticism of this sort. It must take seriously the maxim, proclaimed by Plekhanov, that the preservation of the revolution is its supreme law. Lenin's opponents, on the other hand, gave to their private sentiments the same weight which they had promised to attach to that law alone. They would, in the future, give the same weight to all sorts of other sentiments and considerations, clashing with their avowed revolutionary aspiration. They would prove themselves conciliators, not revolutionaries.

It is no wonder, however, that the symptomatic significance of this difference, so obvious in retrospect, was hidden from many, if not from most, of the actors. Trotsky did not perceive the revolutionary frame of mind behind Lenin's personal ruthlessness. Other motives probably confirmed him in his attitude. By Lenin's side he saw the haughty, aggressive Plekhanov, who had snubbed him on every occasion for no apparent reason. On the other side were all the warm-hearted and unassuming men and women to whom he had owed so much. His choice was clear; it was a choice he would one day grievously regret.

Almost immediately after the congress, 'not yet cooled off from the heat of the clash', he wrote the *Report of the Siberian Delegation*, 'a human document for the future historian', as he described it. In it he expressed with much affectation his disillusionment, his new hostility towards Lenin, and the contradictions in his own attitude.

The congress thought that it was doing constructive work; it was only destructive. . . . Who could suppose that this assembly, convened by *Iskra*, would mercilessly trample over *Iskra*'s editorial board . . .? Which political crystal gazer could forecast that Martov and Lenin would step forth . . . as the hostile leaders of hostile factions? All this has come like thunder from the blue[1] . . . this man [Lenin], with the energy and talent peculiar to him, assumed the role of the party's disorganizer. . . . Behind Lenin . . . stood the new compact majority of the 'hard' *Iskra* men, opposed to the 'soft' *Iskra* men. We, the delegates of the Siberian Union, joined the 'soft' ones, and

[1] N. Trotsky, *Vtoroi Syezd RSDRP* (*Otchet Sibirskoi Delegatsii*), pp. 8–11.

. . . we do not think that we have thereby blotted our revolutionary
record. . . . The confirmation of the old editorial board of *Iskra* had
been taken for granted. . . . The next day, comrades, we were burying
Iskra. . . . *Iskra* is no longer, comrades. About *Iskra* we can speak
only in the past tense, comrades.

Echoing Martov, he wrote that Lenin, impelled by a yearning
for power, was imposing upon the party a 'state of siege' and his
'iron fist'.[1] 'We suffered defeat because fate has decreed victory
not for centralism but for [Lenin's] self-centredness.' Like a new
Robespierre, Lenin was trying to 'transform the modest Council
of the party into an omnipotent Committee of Public Safety';
and, like Robespierre, he was preparing the ground for the
'Thermidorians of socialist opportunism'.[2] For the first time,
Trotsky now made this significant analogy, to which, throughout his life, in different contexts and changed circumstances,
he would come back over and over again. What he now intended to convey was this: Robespierre's terror brought about
the Thermidorian reaction, which was a setback not merely
to the Jacobins but to the French Revolution at large. Similarly,
Lenin was carrying the principle of centralism to excess, and in
doing so he would not only bring discredit upon himself, but
provoke a reaction against the principle of centralism, a reaction
which would favour the opportunists and the federalists in
the movement. In a postscript Trotsky added mockingly that
he had not intended to compare Lenin with Robespierre: the
Bolshevik leader was a mere parody of Robespierre, whom he
resembled as 'a vulgar farce resembles historic tragedy'.[3] Once
he had made up his mind against Lenin he did not mince his
words. He attacked with all his intensity of feeling and with all
the sweep of his invective.

The leaders of the minority, the Mensheviks, carried out their
threat to boycott the Central Committee and *Iskra*. Trotsky,
among others, ceased to contribute. In September 1903 the
Mensheviks assembled in Geneva to decide on the forms of
further action: how far should they carry the boycott? Should
they incur the risk of expulsion, and, if expelled, form a rival
party? Or should they conduct themselves so as to remain
within the party and try to unseat Lenin at the next congress?

---

[1] N. Trotsky, *Vtoroi Syezd RSDRP* (*Otchet Sibirskoi Delegatsii*), pp. 20–21.
[2] Ibid., p. 30.   [3] Ibid., p. 33.

Views were divided. For all the violence of his public attacks on Lenin, Trotsky advocated moderation. The purpose of the boycott, in his view, was to exert pressure on Lenin and Plekhanov, to bring back the veterans to their positions of influence and to re-establish unity. The conference adopted a resolution written jointly by Martov and Trotsky. That part of the declaration of which Trotsky was the author stated: 'We consider it our moral and political duty to conduct . . . the struggle by all means, without placing ourselves outside the party and without bringing discredit upon the party and the idea of its central institutions. . . . [We shall strive] to bring about a change in the composition of the leading bodies, which will secure to the party the possibility of working freely towards its own enlightenment.'[1] But, although the Mensheviks stopped short of final schism, they formed a shadow central committee which was to conduct the campaign against the Leninist committee and against *Iskra*, and which, in case of a final break, would undoubtedly have emerged as the leadership of the new party. That committee, or 'bureau', consisted of Axelrod, Martov, Trotsky, Dan, and Potresov. Except for Trotsky, these men were to lead Menshevism to the end.

The Mensheviks had, in fact, no need to take upon themselves the odium of breaking up the party. The boycott which they waged with a loud hue and cry quickly yielded results. Plekhanov, who had at first so firmly sided with Lenin, became anxious to appease the opposition and to remove its grievance. He tried to persuade Lenin that they should restore the old editorial board. Lenin would not budge: he could not, he said, under the pressure of informal émigré groups, reverse a formal decision taken by a national congress.[2] From the point of view of the procedure by which any party is normally guided, Lenin's argument was irrefutable. But Plekhanov was in a position to disregard it. He was the chairman of the party's Council, and he was still the more authoritative man on *Iskra*'s editorial board, which, after Martov's resignation, consisted of himself and Lenin only. Plekhanov decided to invite Axelrod, Zasulich, Martov, and Potresov to rejoin the editorial staff. Lenin resigned. The Mensheviks thus took over *Iskra*, still in a position of the greatest

---

[1] *Pisma Axelroda i Martova*, p. 94.
[2] Lenin, *Sochinenya*, vol. xxxiv, pp. 162–6.

influence. Soon Lenin's own followers wondered whether Lenin had not gone too far and whether it was not wiser to seek peace with their adversaries. Lenin was defeated and isolated, yet even more than before convinced of the rightness of his attitude and determined to defend it.

With the Mensheviks Trotsky returned to *Iskra*, much to Plekhanov's annoyance. But having made it possible for the veterans to return in triumph, Plekhanov could not straightway slam the door on their most devoted defender and protégé. At first he merely urged Martov, now the actual editor, to keep Trotsky in a more subordinate place than he had held in the old *Iskra* or the one which Martov would have liked to assign to him. Trotsky was apparently confined to commenting on more or less indifferent topics, especially after readers in Russia had objected to the offensive tone of his polemics against Lenin.[1] Plekhanov, although he himself was now severely attacking Lenin, would not countenance this tone in Trotsky. At length, he demanded that *Iskra* should cease to publish Trotsky's contributions; and he threatened to resign from the paper if his demand was rejected. It was 'morally repugnant' to him, he stated, to be editor of a paper for which Trotsky was writing.

The occasion of this 'ultimatum' was an article by Trotsky on the war between Russia and Japan, which had just broken out. The article, published in *Iskra* in the middle of March 1904, was confused in content and style—Plekhanov's objections to it were not quite groundless—but it also contained a few significant ideas. Much of it was devoted to an exposure of Russian liberalism, 'half hearted, vague, lacking in decision and inclined to treachery'. This attitude of the middle classes was bound to harm the cause of democracy, but it would have one redeeming consequence: liberalism would not be able to place itself at the head of the revolution; and it would by its behaviour speed up 'the self-determination of the proletariat'. In the main, however, the argument was a criticism of the party's attitude, a criticism which did not quite tally with Trotsky's anti-liberal invective. He attacked 'the majority of the party committees' for the crudities of their propaganda, which claimed that the war against Japan was being waged in the interest, and with the

[1] See, for instance, the protest from the party committee of Tver, *Iskra*, no. 60.

support, of the Russian bourgeoisie. This, Trotsky argued, was not true; the Tsar conducted the war in the exclusive interest of autocracy—the bourgeois liberals were in 'an anti-patriotic mood'. He protested against the 'pseudo-Marxist cliché' rampant in the party: 'The vital criterion of class interest is being transformed into a dead and deadening cliché . . . into a Procrustean bed for problems which are no longer analysed but chopped around . . . for the proletariat's consumption.' The criticism was directed mainly, though not exclusively, against the Bolsheviks.[1]

Plekhanov's 'ultimatum' placed the Menshevik *Iskra* team in a quandary. They had all approved the incriminated article. They were reluctant to dispense with Trotsky's services: he was one of their chief spokesmen and a member of their shadow central committee. They had, on the other hand, recaptured *Iskra* thanks to Plekanov; and to him, as to the chairman of the Council, they owed their newly-won predominance, as Plekhanov was constantly reminding them. At first they rejected his pretensions and chafed at his 'undignified behaviour', 'blackmail', and 'personal spite'. Trotsky, nevertheless, offered to resign and expressed the desire to return to clandestine work in Russia. Martov and the other Mensheviks prevailed upon him to ignore the insult and to go on working for *Iskra*. But Plekhanov, having staked his prestige in this vendetta, could not put up with this; he carried out his threat of resignation. At length, the Mensheviks, afraid of losing their most important ally, who had just enabled them to defeat and humiliate Lenin, came to terms with Plekhanov: Trotsky's name disappeared from *Iskra*.[2]

Thus began Trotsky's estrangement from the Mensheviks. Although he himself, to spare his friends an embarrassment, had offered to resign, their bargain with Plekhanov could not but irk him. Sulkily he left Geneva and for a few months disappeared from Menshevik circles. The personal resentment was mixed up with incipient political differences. The Mensheviks, as they tried to rationalize their motives in the feud with the

---

[1] *Iskra*, no. 62, 15 March 1904. See also Trotsky's half-apologetic comment in the Supplement to *Iskra* of June 1904.

[2] The incident is related on the basis of *Perepiska Plekhanova i Axelroda*, vol. ii, pp. 198–201; *Pisma Axelroda i Martova*, pp. 101–5, and of *Iskra*.

Bolsheviks, began to react away from the views to which they had been committed before the split. The reaction spread from matters of organization to issues of policy. Zasulich was dreaming aloud about an alliance between socialism and middle-class liberalism. Theodore Dan, now gaining eminence, bluntly advocated that alliance. Even now, when Dan and Trotsky were the leaders of the same faction, they instinctively repelled each other. Dan was by temperament as solid and pedestrian as Trotsky was flamboyant and impetuous. The one could thrive best in a climate of political compromise, as his role under Kerensky's régime in 1917 would show; the other was made for revolution. While the Mensheviks were beginning to grope for more moderate formulas, Dan's influence among them was naturally rising and Trotsky's declining. Martov himself forebodingly watched his followers in their quest for moderation; but he was overpowered by the process he had initiated. The reaction against the spirit of the 'old' *Iskra* did not leave Trotsky unaffected. It could not be otherwise, for Lenin, whom he was opposing, embodied that spirit. Trotsky now found that the old *Iskra* had not been free from the *Narodnik*-like, conspiratorial attitude; that it had been unjust towards the Economists; and that it had falsely preached the supremacy of organization over the 'spontaneous' Labour movement. These were the stock conclusions which most Mensheviks reached as they reviewed their own recent past; and thus far Trotsky went along with them.[1] But at one point he balked and balked for good, the point at which they made the first attempt to bridge the gulf between socialism and liberalism. He stuck to the anti-liberal attitude which had, on the whole, prevailed in the old *Iskra*. In long arguments with the Mensheviks he began to realize how much, in this crucial issue, divided him from them, and how little from Lenin.

Yet, before parting with the Mensheviks he once again assailed Lenin with a hailstorm of his most hurtful invective, which made any reconciliation with him wellnigh impossible. In April 1904 Trotsky left *Iskra*. In August there appeared in Geneva his pamphlet *Our Political Tasks*, which he dedicated to 'My dear teacher Paul B. Axelrod'. The historical and bio-

---

[1] In this respect there was no difference between Trotsky (in *Nashi Politicheskye Zadachi*) and the most right-wing Menshevik Cherevanin (in *Organizatsionnyi Vopros*).

graphical interest of the pamphlet lies in the fact that this was the most strident bill of impeachment that any Socialist had ever drawn up against Lenin. Its interest also lies in the train of thought which it initiated and in the amazing flashes of historical intuition scattered over more than a hundred closely-printed pages of vituperation.

'Just at a time', so Trotsky began, referring to the Russo-Japanese war, 'when history has placed before us the enormous task of cutting the knot of world reaction, Russian social democrats do not seem to care for anything except a petty internal struggle.' What a 'heartrending tragedy' this was, and what a 'nightmarish atmosphere' it created! '. . . almost everybody was aware of the criminal character of the split, but nobody could free himself from the iron grip of history'. The deep cause of the division lay in the difficulty the party had had in reconciling its democratic and its socialist tasks. Russia had not yet gone through a bourgeois democratic revolution; and the party's immediate interest was to overthrow Tsarist absolutism. Yet its real but more remote objective was socialism. The party was constantly torn between the two pursuits. Whenever a controversy arose in its ranks, each side charged the other with abandoning the class interest of the proletariat in favour of bourgeois democracy. 'Every group representing a new trend excommunicates its predecessors. To those who come with new ideas the previous period seems to have been but a crude deviation from the correct road, an historical misunderstanding. . . .'[1]

Thus, he went on, had Lenin and the old *Iskra* as a whole treated the Economists, who, for all their limitations, had awakened the Russian working class. The Mensheviks were the first group 'trying to establish itself on the shoulders, not on the broken bones, of its predecessors'; and this alone was a sign of maturity. The Economists 'had appealed to the proletariat, but they did so not in the spirit of social democracy' but in that of non-political trade unionism. *Iskra*, on the other hand, had addressed its social democratic message to the intelligentsia, not to the workers. Lenin had bullied the revolutionary intelligentsia into a Marxist orthodoxy, into an unconditional surrender to Marx's authority, hoping that in this way he would train the

[1] N. Trotsky, *Nashi Politicheskye Zadachi*, p. 4.

men of the intelligentsia into reliable leaders of an immature and timid labour movement. But Lenin was merely trying to force the pace of history: for to be in possession of a proletarian doctrine, such as Marxism, 'was no substitute for a politically developed proletariat'.[1] Lenin distrusted the masses and adopted a haughty attitude towards their untutored activities, arguing that the workers by themselves could not rise from trade union-ism to revolutionary socialism, and that socialist ideology was brought into the Labour movement 'from outside', by the revolutionary intelligentsia. This, Trotsky wrote, was the theory of an 'orthodox theocracy'; and Lenin's scheme of organization was fit for a party which would '*substitute* itself for the working classes', act as proxy in their name and on their behalf, regard-less of what the workers felt and thought.

To this 'substitutism' (*zamestitelstvo*), as Trotsky called it, to this conception of a party acting as a *locum tenens* for the pro-letariat, he opposed Axelrod's plan for a 'broadly based party', modelled on European social democratic parties.[2] 'Lenin's methods lead to this: the party organization [the caucus] at first substitutes itself for the party as a whole; then the Central Committee substitutes itself for the organization; and finally a single "dictator" substitutes himself for the Central Com-mittee. . . .'[3] 'The party must seek the guarantee of its stability in its own base, in an active and self-reliant proletariat, and not in its top caucus, which the revolution . . . may suddenly sweep away with its wing. . . .' After an ironical travesty of Lenin's 'hideous, dissolute, and demagogical' style,[4] and after some ridicule directed at Lenin's attempt to impose discipline on the party, Trotsky asked: 'Is it so difficult to see that any serious group . . . when it is confronted by the dilemma whether it should, from a sense of discipline, silently efface itself, or, regardless of discipline, struggle for survival—will undoubtedly choose the latter course . . . and say: perish that "discipline", which suppresses the vital interests of the movement.' History will not say that discipline should have prevailed even if the world had to perish; it will eventually vindicate those who had 'the fuller and the deeper understanding of the tasks of revolution'.[5]

The most curious part of the pamphlet is its last chapter on

[1] N. Trotsky, *Nashi Politicheskye Zadachi*, p. 23.   [2] Ibid., p. 50.
[3] Ibid., p. 54.   [4] Ibid., p. 75.   [5] Ibid., p. 72.

'Jacobinism and Social Democracy'.[1] At the congress, Trotsky refuted the charge of Jacobinism when the Economists levelled it against *Iskra* as a whole. Now he turned the charge against Lenin. Lenin faced it almost with pride: 'A revolutionary Social Democrat', he rejoined, 'is precisely a Jacobin, but one who is inseparably connected with the organization of the proletariat and aware of its class interests.' Trotsky elaborated the charge in the light, as the pamphlet shows, of his recent detailed study of the French Revolution; and he pointed towards the future drama of the Russian Revolution. The characters of the Jacobin and of the Social Democrat, he stated, are mutually exclusive. The French Revolution, because of the limitations of its epoch, could establish only a bourgeois society with bourgeois property as its basis. Jacobinism (that 'maximum of radicalism of which bourgeois society has been capable') strove to perpetuate a fleeting, quasi-egalitarian climax of the revolution, which was incompatible with the fundamental trend of the time. This was a foredoomed Utopia: history would have had to stop in its course in order to save Jacobinism. The conflict between Jacobinism and its age explains the Jacobin mentality and method of action. Robespierre and his friends had their metaphysical idea of Truth, their *Verité*; but they could not trust that their *Verité* would win the hearts and the minds of the people. With morbid suspicion they looked round and saw enemies creeping from every crevice. They had to draw a sharp dividing line between themselves and the rest of the world, and they drew it with the edge of the guillotine. 'Every attempt to blur [this division] between Jacobinism and the rest of the world threatened to release inner centrifugal forces. . . .' His political instinct suggested to Robespierre that only through a permanent state of siege could he prolong the ephemeral climax of the revolution. 'They spared no human hecatomb to build the pedestal for their Truth. . . . The counterpart to their absolute faith in a metaphysical idea was their absolute distrust of living people.'

From the Jacobin, Trotsky went on, the Social Democrat differed in his optimism, for he was in harmony with the trend of his age. At the threshold of the twentieth century, with the growth of modern industry and of the working classes, socialism

[1] Ibid., pp. 97–107.

was no longer Utopia. The Social Democrat and the Jacobin stand for 'two opposed worlds, doctrines, tactics, mentalities. . . . They were Utopians; we aspire to express the objective trend. They were idealists . . . we are materialists . . . they were rationalists, we are dialectitians. . . . They chopped off heads, we enlighten them with class consciousness.'

Trotsky did not deny that there were similarities between the Jacobin and the Social Democrat. Both were irreconcilable: the Jacobin fought against *moderantisme*; the Socialist is opposed to reformist opportunism. But the Social Democrat had no use for the guillotine. 'A Jacobin tribunal would have tried under the charge of moderation the whole international Labour movement, and Marx's lion head would have been the first to roll under the guillotine.'[1] 'Robespierre used to say: "I know only two parties, the good and the evil citizens"; and this aphorism is engraved on the heart of Maximilian Lenin', whose 'malicious and morally repulsive suspiciousness is a flat caricature of the tragic Jacobin intolerance. . . .' (In the same passage he described Lenin as 'an adroit statistician and slovenly attorney'.)

A clear-cut choice—this was Trotsky's conclusion—must be made between Jacobinism and Marxism. In trying to combine them, Lenin was virtually abandoning socialism and setting himself up as the leader of a revolutionary wing of bourgeois democracy. This was the gravamen of Trotsky's accusation that Lenin was changing from a Socialist into a radical bourgeois politician, because only a bourgeois politician could distrust the working classes as intensely as Lenin did.[2] Lenin's followers went even farther and frankly envisaged their 'dictatorship over the proletariat' and when one read how some Bolsheviks (here Trotsky quoted their leaflets published in the Urals) were advocating the need for an absolutely uniform party, 'one felt a shiver running down one's spine'.

He wound up his argument with the following plea against uniformity:

The tasks of the new régime will be so complex that they cannot be

[1] N. Trotsky, *Nashi Politicheskye Zadachi*, p. 95.
[2] Trotsky here quoted Axelrod, who had compared Lenin's evolution to Struve's. In this pamphlet Trotsky also gave eulogistic sketches of the Menshevik leaders, especially of Axelrod and Martov, describing the former as 'a great Marxist and penetrating political mind' and the latter as the 'Dobrolyubov of his generation'.

solved otherwise than by way of a competition between various methods of economic and political construction, by way of long 'disputes', by way of a systematic struggle not only between the socialist and the capitalist worlds, but also between many trends inside socialism, trends which will inevitably emerge as soon as the proletarian dictatorship poses tens and hundreds of new . . . problems. No strong, 'domineering' organization . . . will be able to suppress these trends and controversies. . . . A proletariat capable of exercising its dictatorship over society will not tolerate any dictatorship over itself. . . . The working class . . . will undoubtedly have in its ranks quite a few political invalids . . . and much ballast of obsolescent ideas, which it will have to jettison. In the epoch of its dictatorship, as now, it will have to cleanse its mind of false theories and bourgeois experience and to purge its ranks from political phrasemongers and backward-looking revolutionaries. . . . But this intricate task cannot be solved by placing above the proletariat a few well-picked people . . . or one person invested with the power to liquidate and degrade.[1]

Among the writings that came from Trotsky's prolific pen in the course of four decades, this is perhaps the most amazing document, not least because it contains so odd an assortment of great ideas and petty polemical tricks, of subtle historical insights and fustian flourishes. Hardly any Menshevik writer attacked Lenin with so much personal venom. 'Hideous', 'dissolute', 'demagogical', 'slovenly attorney', 'malicious and morally repulsive', these were the epithets which Trotsky threw at the man who had so recently held out to him the hand of fellowship, who had brought him to western Europe, who had promoted him and defended him from Plekhanov's aspersions. Marxists, to be sure, especially the Russian ones, were wont to state their views with ruthless frankness. But, as a rule, they refrained from personal mud-slinging. Trotsky's offence against this rule cannot be explained merely by youthful ebullience—he now exhibited a characteristic of which he would never quite free himself: he could not separate ideas from men.

Nor did he support his accusations by any fact that would give them weight in the historian's eye. Lenin had so far not expelled a single member from the party. All he had done was to insist on the validity of the mandate which the congress had given him, and to warn the opposition that, if they persisted in

[1] Ibid., p. 105.

obstructing the formal decisions of the congress and boycotting the elected leadership, he would have to take action against them. In so doing, he behaved as any leader of any party would have behaved in the circumstances.[1] Since, through a series of accidents and personal shifts the Mensheviks had first recaptured *Iskra* and then virtually ousted Lenin from leadership, his formal predominance lasted a very short time, in the course of which he did nothing to implement his warnings to the opposition. Once the opposition was on top, its leaders confronted Lenin with exactly the same warning, although, as they had not been elected at a congress, they had less right to do so.[2]

Trotsky knew all this and he said as much in his pamphlet. His accusations were therefore based merely on inferences and on one point of theory. Lenin had argued that, historically, the revolutionary intelligentsia played a special role in the Labour movement, infusing it with the Marxist outlook, which the workers would not have attained by themselves. Trotsky saw in this view a denial of the revolutionary capacities of the working class and an aspiration of the intelligentsia, whose mouthpiece Lenin was, to keep the Labour movement under their tutelage. Implied in this he saw a design for a Jacobin-like, or, as we would now say, a totalitarian dictatorship. Yet many socialist writers had stressed the special role of the intelligentsia in the Labour movement; and Lenin had in fact drawn his view from Kautsky, the recognized authority on Marxist theory.[3] Both factions, Mensheviks as well as Bolsheviks, were led by intellectuals: at the recent congress only three workers had appeared

---

[1] When Rosa Luxemburg attacked Lenin in the *Neue Zeit* and then in *Iskra* (no. 69, 10 July 1904), she criticized him for transplanting European, German, and British (Fabian) models of organization to Russia. In the German Social Democratic Party centralism was upheld by the moderate leaders against the revolutionary wing. Karl Kautsky (*Iskra*, no. 66, 15 May 1904) criticized Lenin on the same ground, saying that what was meat for Europe was poison for Russia. The Russian Social-Revolutionaries, future enemies of Bolshevism, warmly approved Lenin's attitude (see 'Evolutsia Russkoi Sots. Mysli' in *Vestnik Russkoi Revolutsii*, no. 3). It can be seen from this how unhistorical is the view, held by both Bolsheviks and many of their critics, that the brand of centralism which Lenin represented in 1903 was the exclusive feature of Bolshevism, its exclusive virtue or its original sin.

[2] Parvus, who stood nearer to the Mensheviks than to the Bolsheviks (see next chapter), criticized the Mensheviks for adopting the dictatorial methods of organization which they attributed to Lenin. Parvus, *Rossya i Revolutsia*, pp. 182 ff.

[3] Lenin, *Sochinenya*, vol. v (*Chto Delat?*), pp. 354–5; K. Kautsky in *Neue Zeit*, no. 3, 1901.

among the several scores of delegates. There was no reason therefore why the odium of voicing the aspirations of the intellectuals should fall only on Lenin. In Lenin's conception of the revolutionary régime, as he had developed it so far, there was not a single point on which Trotsky could base his indictment. Now and for many years to come Lenin held that a revolutionary government in Russia would be formed by a coalition of parties, and that the Socialists could not even aspire to hold a majority of seats in it.[1] The idea of a monolithic state had not even occurred to him. Trotsky himself would presently come much nearer to this idea than Lenin: against Lenin he would soon begin to advocate the proletarian dictatorship as the direct objective of revolution in Russia, which need not necessarily have meant a monolithic state, but which inevitably implied an approximation to it. Briefly, neither in fact nor in theory could Trotsky find any important premiss for his anticipatory portrait of Lenin as the Russian Robespierre, drawing by the guillotine a line of division between his party and the world. It required a volatile and irresponsible imagination in the pamphleteer to show his adversary in so distorting a mirror.

And yet this was the faithful mirror of the future, although the Russian Robespierre shown in it was to be not so much Lenin as his successor, at this time still an unknown Caucasian Social Democrat. So faithful indeed was this mirror of the future that in it one finds, in confused assortment, all the elements of the drama of the Russian Revolution. There is, first of all, the dilemma between the bourgeois democratic and the socialist objectives of the revolution, a dilemma which was often to recur. There is further the conflict of the two souls, the Marxist and the Jacobin, in Bolshevism, a conflict never to be resolved either in Lenin, or in Bolshevism at large, or even in Trotsky himself. Much as Trotsky now pressed for a clear-cut choice between Marxism and Jacobinism, circumstances would not permit Lenin or Trotsky to make that choice. Moreover, the mirror showed in advance the stages through which, in its 'substitutism', the party of the revolution would move: 'The caucus substitutes itself for the party; then the Central Committee for the caucus; and finally a dictator substitutes himself for the Central Committee.' These are in fact headings for several

[1] Lenin, *Sochinenya*, vol. viii, pp. 262–3; see next chapter.

yet remote chapters in the annals of the revolution. Here again, Trotsky could have no inkling that one day he himself would go much farther than Lenin in preaching and glorifying that 'substitutism', before he would shrink in horror from its consummation. And then there is the grim picture of that consummation: the image of the morbidly suspicious dictator, 'invested with the power to degrade and liquidate', who sees enemies creeping from every crevice around him, and who, sparing no human hecatomb, struggles to perpetuate a climax of the revolution and hermetically separates the revolution from the rest of the world. And, as in the prelude to classical tragedy, the omens appear which seem to point to Trotsky's own fate: He makes the plea for the free competition of ideas and trends, a plea he will repeat, almost in the same words, before the tribunals of Bolshevism twenty years later. He now confidently believes that 'a working class capable of exercising its dictatorship over society will tolerate no dictator over itself'; and he is unaware that he begs the gravest question of all: what will happen if, after the revolution, the working class is not capable of exercising its dictatorship over society? He trusts that history will eventually vindicate those who have 'the fuller and the deeper understanding' of the needs of their epoch, an assurance which he will go on expressing all his life, up to the moment when the rusty axe of an assassin cleaves his brain. And, finally, as if in premonition of that moment, he feels 'a cold shiver running down his spine' at the mere thought of what might become of Lenin's party.

We cannot reconstruct in any detail the mental process by which he arrived at this view of the future. The circumstance that he had lacked any solid factual premiss for his conclusions indicates that the process was one of imaginative perception, not of reasoning. We can only trace some of the external stimuli to which his imagination responded. In a general manner, the comparison between Bolsheviks and Jacobins had already been made by some of the Mensheviks. Plekhanov, even while he was Lenin's ally, had said about the latter: 'Of such stuff the Robespierres are made.' The *obiter dictum* was repeated by others, first in whispers and then publicly. But hardly anybody, not even its author, meant it literally—it was received as one of Plekhanov's polemical *bon mots*. Trotsky took the saying literally, or at any rate seriously enough to plunge into the history of Jacobinism and to explore it avidly with an eye to the parallel. His imagination, inflamed by the Jacobin tragedy and overflowing with the freshly absorbed images, projected these upon the groups and individuals with whom he was in daily contact and—upon Russia's indefinite future. In the light of a strictly rational analysis, this projection may have been gratuitous and erratic. A cooler and better disciplined mind would not have lent itself to such visionary anticipations. But Trotsky was possessed of a sixth sense, as it were, an intuitive sense of history, which singled him out among the political thinkers of his generation, sometimes exposed him almost to derision, but more often found triumphant, if much delayed, vindication.

Behind his polemical pursuits and imaginative projections there was the pent-up emotion of the romantic revolutionary, who, much as he himself may have argued about the need for a closely-knit and disciplined party, broke into individualistic protest against the reality of that party as soon as he was confronted by it. His inclinations, his tastes, his temperament revolted against the prosaic and business-like determination with which Lenin was setting out to bring the party down from the clouds of abstraction to the firm ground of organization. Trotsky's present protest was little different from that which, as a boy of seventeen, he had, with so much ill temper, thrown at Sokolovskaya, the first Marxist he had met: 'A curse upon all of you who want to bring dryness and hardness into all the relations of life!' The cry into which he had burst at Shvigovsky's orchard on the last night of 1896, reverberated in his anti-Leninist philippic of 1904.

CHAPTER IV

An Intellectual Partnership

WHEN *Our Political Tasks* appeared in Geneva, in August 1904, the situation in the party was very different from what it had been the year before, immediately after the split. The Menshevik *Iskra* ceaselessly harassed Lenin, who for a time was not even in a position to counter the attacks: it was almost six months before he could publish his own paper, the *Vperyod* (*Forward*). Plekhanov was pouring ridicule upon his erstwhile ally and was confident that he was destroying Lenin's reputation for good and all. The authorities of European, especially of German, socialism who had long known and respected Plekhanov and the other veterans, joined in condemnation of Lenin, who in their eyes was an obscure young intruder. Even the Bolshevik Central Committee disregarded Lenin's attitude and came to terms with the Mensheviks. However, on the day when Trotsky's pamphlet appeared, Lenin gathered in Switzerland those Bolsheviks who were prepared to follow him and laid before them a plan for the convocation of a new congress, with or without Menshevik participation.

Trotsky's broadside seemed surpassed by events—the enemy appeared to have scattered before he had pressed home the attack. By way of afterthought he therefore wrote in the preface to *Our Political Tasks* that the crisis in the party was over, and that those who stood for unity could look to the future with confidence, because the extremists among both Bolsheviks and Mensheviks had been discredited and isolated. A more experienced politician, or one inclined to give more thought to the wounding effect of his words, might in the circumstances have either refrained from publishing the pamphlet or at least pruned its polemical extravagances. Trotsky was too much enamoured of his own words to do that. However, he tried in the preface to make allowance for the new situation: he called upon the Mensheviks to wind up their own separate organization, that party within the party, of which he himself had been one of the secret leaders. The Mensheviks, he wrote emphatically, should accept 'organizational death', that is, a merger of the hitherto opposed groups.[1] His call fell on deaf ears. The schism was beginning to acquire its own momentum. Its 'fanatics' were active in both groups. Among the Bolsheviks, Lenin's group considered the changes that had taken place since the congress as Menshevik usurpations, to which a new congress would put an end. The Mensheviks, having recaptured positions of influence, would not risk losing them at a new congress, let alone sharing them, through a merger, with their adversaries. Having with so much thunder pilloried Lenin as the 'disorganizer', Trotsky was shocked to find 'disorganizers' among his Menshevik friends. He began, mildly enough, to plead with them the need of reconciliation. He had joined the Mensheviks in order to make good the injury Lenin had inflicted on the founding fathers of the movement and through them on the movement itself. The injury had been made good with a vengeance. The Bolshevik Central Committee itself was anxious to make it good. All that was now needed to close the painful chapter was that the *ad hoc* arrangements which had been necessary in order to defeat Lenin be scrapped and that the men of good will in both sections of the party join hands. He did not realize that the *ad hoc* arrangements had come to stay.

In controversies like this the conciliator is unwelcome. He threatens to upset well-laid plans and to mix all the cards. His own friends look askance at him, considering him little better than a traitor. Thus did some Mensheviks now look upon Trotsky: his attitude was not stable; it was indistinguishable from that of the moderate Bolsheviks; and nobody could say where he would stand tomorrow. Indeed, Trotsky might easily have become one of the Bolshevik 'conciliators' had not his hurtful attacks on Lenin and Lenin's followers estranged him from all Bolsheviks. In their eyes he was one of the most vicious Mensheviks. And so he was breaking with his political friends without much chance of agreement with his adversaries.

In this situation he came under the influence of a man who was in a sense an outsider to the party and whose role in its affairs was that of a brilliant interloper. He was A. L. Helfand, a Russian Jew who had made his home in Germany and had won distinction as an economist, publicist, and author of

---

[1] N. Trotsky, *Nashi Politicheskye Zadachi*, p. viii.

scholarly Marxist books.[1] Under the pen-name Parvus he
contributed to Kautsky's *Neue Zeit*, the most important and
sophisticated Socialist periodical in Europe, and to many other
Socialist newspapers. He also published his own review *Aus der
Weltpolitik*, in which, as early as 1895, he forecast war between
Russia and Japan and foresaw that out of that war would develop
the Russian revolution—the prophesy was much quoted in
1904–5, when it came true. In the German party Parvus stood
on the extreme left, sharply opposed to the reformist trend and
disdainful of the pretences of Marxist orthodoxy with which
some of the leaders still covered their reconciliation with the
established order. Shrewd and militant, he searched for ways
and means to bring about the regeneration of the revolutionary
spirit in German socialism.

The reformist leaders viewed him with fear and that special
irony which is reserved for immigrants seeking to mend the
ways of their adopted country.[2] Parvus compensated himself
with more biting criticism and adopted, in his turn, a patronizing attitude towards his original countrymen: to the Russians
in exile he eagerly pointed out their eastern 'backwardness and
parochialism' and he tried to teach them western political
manners. Despite these droll postures, the Russians regarded
him as a sort of guide to world politics and economics. He
contributed to *Iskra*, first under the pen-name Molotov and
then as Parvus. His essays usually appeared on *Iskra's* front
page—the editors gladly relegated their own writings to make
room for him. They respected his massive knowledge, gifts, and
judgement. But they were also apprehensive of a streak of
unreliability in him. There was something Gargantuan or
Falstaffian about him and his (to quote Trotsky) 'fat, fleshy,
bulldog-like head'. For many years, however, nothing seemed
to justify the apprehension: there was no distinct instance of
misdemeanour on Parvus's part, nothing, at any rate, that

---

[1] His books were translated into Russian. One of them, *The World Economy and
the Agricultural Crisis*, was reviewed with great admiration by Lenin in 1899. 'Parvus
deals primarily with the development of the world market', Lenin wrote, 'and
describes . . . the recent phases of this development connected with the decline of
England's industrial predominance.' 'We strongly recommend . . . Parvus's book.'
Lenin, *Sochinenya*, vol. iv, pp. 51–52.

[2] The irony gave way to enormous respect as soon as the immigrant had begun
to conform. Towards the end of his life Parvus was the brain behind Ebert, the
President of the Weimar Republic.

would allow anybody to impugn his Socialist integrity and conviction. He was a somewhat erratic contributor, writing his essays in long serials and rarely delivering them on time; all the same his contributions were most welcome. He had somewhat brittle financial schemes: he had tried to set up a Socialist publishing house and had failed; and he laid plans for a great Socialist daily, to be issued simultaneously in several European languages, which was to shake European socialism from its reformist coma. But to found such a paper he needed enormous funds, and these he could not obtain, probably because he was not yet prepared to plunge into dubious financial ventures. Enough that, for one reason or another, the respect in which he was held was mingled with a little irony and distrust. His later fortunes were to show that hidden in him was a snob and a political impostor. Nevertheless, his was one of the boldest and most penetrating political minds of his generation; and the political thinker still overshadowed the impostor.

In the controversy among the Russians, Parvus at first showed sympathy for the Mensheviks but later kept himself decently aloof from both groups, as befitted a man who cast himself for the role of peacemaker. He had once tried to reconcile the *Iskra* men with the Economists; now he attempted to bring about a truce between the former *Iskra* men. His relations with both groups were, at any rate, unspoilt. When somewhat later he launched into criticism of both, the antagonists, though unpersuaded, took his intervention with grace and accorded him the treatment due to a well-wishing and reputable outsider.[1]

When Trotsky, barred from *Iskra* and at loggerheads with everybody, left Geneva, he went to Munich, where Parvus was living; he stayed in Parvus's home, and there Sedova, his second wife, later joined him. In Parvus he found a man viewing with detachment internal Russian alignments, capable of taking in the whole international scene of socialism, a master at Marxist analysis, unsurpassed at visualizing for himself and others the broad vistas of class struggle. Last but not least, Trotsky

---

[1] Parvus, *Rossya i Revolutsia*, pp. 182 ff.; *Iskra*, nos. 111 (24 September 1905) and 112 (8 October 1905). See also Martov, *Istorya Ross. Sots. Dem.*, pp. 112 ff. Lenin's reply to Parvus was in a tone of the highest respect (*Sochinenya*, vol. viii, p. 261).

admired in Parvus his 'virile, muscular style', which he was to remember hankeringly long after their break. In brief, Parvus still towered above Trotsky in erudition, experience, and literary taste. It is not easy, however, to define the extent of his influence on Trotsky. To this day Trotsky's detractors attribute the exclusive authorship of the theory of 'permanent revolution', the hallmark of Trotskyism, to Parvus, and suggest either that Trotsky copied or plagiarized it or that a theory coming from so contaminated a source must be worthless. Trotsky himself never denied his debt to Parvus, although the warmth with which he acknowledged it varied with times and circumstances. What they both wrote in the hey-day of their association reveals how many of the ideas and views first formulated by Parvus left a deep mark on Trotsky, and how many of them he was to repeat through his life in a form not very different from that in which his older friend had first put them.

But Trotsky was possessed of certain qualities which enabled him to be from the outset more than Parvus's mere disciple. He had the fresh experience of Russia and of the underground struggle, which Parvus had not. He had an incandescent political imagination, while Parvus's analyses and prognostications sprang from a bold but cold mind. He had the revolutionary fervour which gave wings to his ideas, while Parvus was the cynical type of revolutionary. Trotsky, then, had his own individual contribution to make to their common fund of ideas. As in most associations of this sort, the respective shares of the partners cannot be unscrambled, not even by the partners themselves. The thinking is done in common; and even if sometimes it is possible to say who has first formulated in print this or that part of a theory, the invisible, two-way traffic of suggestions and stimuli that has passed between the partners can never be traced. All that can be said of Parvus and Trotsky is that at first the older of the two was well ahead, leading with ideas and formulas. At the next stage both seemed to advance *pari passu*. In the end the junior leapt forward with a contribution which was distinctly his own, and which made and rounded off a new political doctrine; and with this doctrine he came to the fore on the vast and confused stage of the revolution. It should be added that the whole process developed and was concluded rapidly. It began in the summer of 1904. It was consummated

in 1906, when, awaiting trial in a Petersburg prison, Trotsky
expounded in writing the theory of the permanent revolution
in its finished form. The time of his apprenticeship with Parvus
was briefer still: it hardly lasted longer than till the beginning
of 1905, the opening of the first revolution. This was a time of
condensed and rapid thinking; and the young Trotsky, who
had already projected the image of Jacobinism on to the Russian
revolution, was a quick learner.

.   .   .   .

After the outbreak of the Russo-Japanese war, Parvus published a series of essays in *Iskra* on 'War and Revolution'.[1] Even
before that his contributions, which he used to sign as Molotov,
had strongly impressed Trotsky. But it was mainly the views
which he put forward in 'War and Revolution' that made the
lasting impression.

Parvus's central idea was that the nation-state, as it had
developed with capitalism, had outlived its day. This view had
belonged to the common stock of Marx's theory—it had been
stated by Marx in the *Communist Manifesto*. But to most Socialist
writers at the turn of the century this was one of the master's
sayings, fit to be repeated on festive occasions, but bearing little
relation to the realities of a late Victorian, nation-conscious, and
empire-proud Europe. Only a very remote future, it was
thought, might bring the eclipse of the nation-state. Parvus, on
the contrary, saw the eclipse coming, pointed to its symptoms,
forecast its cataclysmic intensification, and urged the Socialists
to adjust their attitudes and policies accordingly. He placed an
unusual emphasis on the interdependence of nations and states,
and this emphasis gave to his reasonings a broad, worldwide
sweep, rare in other Socialists. He saw the Russo-Japanese
conflict of 1904 as the start of a long sequence of wars, in which
the nation-states, impelled by capitalist competition, would fight
for their survival. The fate of continents had become intertwined. The opening up of the American west had sharpened the
competition for world markets between the agricultural producers. European, especially German, farming and industrial
interests joined hands in order to do away with free trade and to
impose a protectionist system on western Europe. 'The customs
walls have become an economic barrier to the historical process

[1] The series began in *Iskra*, no. 59, 10 February 1904.

of the cultural unification of nations; they have increased the
political conflicts between states . . . and enhanced the power of
states and governments . . .—the stronger the power of governments, the easier do the states clash in arms.' These ideas were
to become for Trotsky axioms from which he would argue all
his life.

Russia's expansion in Asia and conflict with Japan, Parvus
held, were partly brought about by domestic pressures: Tsardom was seeking in external conquest an escape from internal
weakness. But more important were the external pressures to
which Russia was subjected. In the worldwide struggle between
capitalist nation-states only the great modern powers acted with
independence; and even an empire as vast as the Tsar's, was,
because of its industrial backwardness, merely 'a pensioner of
the French Bourse'. 'The war has started over Manchuria and
Korea; but it has already grown into a conflict over leadership
in east Asia. At the next stage Russia's entire position in the
world will be at stake; and the war will end in a shift in the
political balance of the world.'

Parvus concluded his analysis as follows: 'The worldwide
process of capitalist development leads to a *political upheaval* in
Russia. This in its turn must have its impact on the political
development of all capitalist countries. The Russian revolution
will shake the bourgeois world. . . . And the Russian proletariat
may well play the role of the vanguard of social revolution.'[1]

Thus already in 1904 Parvus viewed the approaching revolution not as a purely Russian affair but as a reflection in Russia
of worldwide social tensions; and he saw in the coming Russian
upheaval a prelude to world revolution. Here were the main

---

[1] *Iskra*, no. 82, 1 January 1905. In the same series Parvus wrote: 'One must
reach the paradoxical conclusion that the most decisive subjective factor of historical
development is not political wisdom but political stupidity. Men have never yet
been able fully to benefit from the social conditions they themselves have created.
They always think that they are far ahead, whereas they are far behind the objective
historical process. . . . History has often led by the noses those who have thought
that they could keep her in check.' 'The capitalist order in Europe has long since
been an obstacle to Europe's economic, political, and cultural development. It
survives only because the popular masses have not yet become sufficiently aware
of their tragic condition. The political energy of the proletariat is not concentrated
enough, the socialist parties lack decision and courage. One can imagine such a
turn of events that the Social Democratic Party will bear the political guilt for the
survival of the capitalist order.' To contemporaries this seemed a far-fetched
prophesy.

elements for the theory of permanent revolution. Yet, Parvus had so far spoken only about a 'political upheaval' in Russia, not about a 'social' or Socialist revolution. He apparently still shared the view, then accepted by all Marxists, that the Russian revolution by itself would, because of the country's semi-feudal and backward outlook, be merely bourgeois in character. Trotsky would be the first to say that the revolution would of its own momentum pass from the bourgeois to the Socialist stage, and establish a proletarian dictatorship in Russia, even before the advent of revolution in the West.

Not only were Parvus's international ideas and revolutionary perspectives becoming part and parcel of Trotsky's thinking, but, also, some of Trotsky's views on Russian history, especially his conception of the Russian state, can be traced back to Parvus.[1] Parvus developed the view that the Russian state, a cross between Asian despotism and European absolutism, had formed itself not as the organ of any class in Russian society, but as a military bureaucratic machine designed primarily to resist pressure from the more highly civilized West.[2] It was for this purpose that Tsardom had introduced elements of European civilization into Russia, especially into the army. 'Thus came into existence the Russian state organism: an Asian absolutism buttressed by a European type of army.' It was enough, he remarked, to cast a glance at the line of Russian frontier fortresses to see that the Tsars had intended to separate Russia from the West by a sort of Chinese wall. Some of these theories, as they were developed and refined by Trotsky, became the objects of heated historical and political disputes twenty years later.

Parvus's influence on Trotsky is felt also in the style and manner of exposition, especially in the characteristic sweep of historical prognostication. This is not to say that Trotsky played the literary ape to Parvus. He absorbed the influence naturally and organically because of his intellectual and literary affinity with Parvus, an affinity which was not lessened by contrasts in character and temperament.

. . . .

During his first stay in Munich, towards the end of September

---

[1] In part, however, the original source of the views on Russian history held by both Trotsky and Parvus is the liberal historian P. Miliukov.

[2] *Iskra*, no. 61, 5 March 1904.

1904, Trotsky announced his break with the Mensheviks in an 'Open Letter to Comrades', which he sent for publication to *Iskra*. The letter was never published. We have only a Menshevik summary of it, which says that 'in a stilted and supercilious tone' Trotsky brought a number of charges against 'some comrades' and raised various demands. The gravamen of those charges was that the Menshevik group tended to place its sectional interests above those of the party. In addition, he wrote, the Mensheviks were reacting wrongly to Lenin's attitude in one important point: while Lenin was bent on giving the intelligentsia a privileged and dominant position in the party, the Mensheviks were inciting the workers against the Socialist intelligentsia. In a private letter to Martov and Zasulich, Trotsky explained that his criticisms were directed mainly against Theodore Dan, the politician of moderation; and that his intention was to promote the creation of a 'stable party centre' and an understanding with the Bolshevik Central Committee. He also complained that writers 'whom *Iskra* could not assimilate'—a hint at his having been squeezed out by Plekhanov—had no chance of reaching the Socialist public. Finally, he announced in a formal manner his secession from the Menshevik group.[1]

The Mensheviks responded with the anger of embarrassment. 'A very stormy correspondence' passed between Trotsky and Martov, which, so Martov wrote, 'if I had given him free rein would have ended in a complete breaking off of my relations with him.' Martov and other Mensheviks were anxious to prevent the breach, for if they became public the criticisms levelled against them by their most outspoken anti-Bolshevik controversialist, were likely to harm the group. A closed conference was arranged at Geneva, at which Trotsky's Open Letter was discussed in his presence. It was formally agreed that the further existence of the Menshevik émigré organization might become 'the source of new conflicts in the party', and that the organization should be disbanded, pending further instructions from Menshevik groups in Russia.[2]

This decision was clearly meant to appease Trotsky and to keep him quiet. It had no further repercussions: the Menshevik 'party within the party', just like the Bolshevik, was to function

[1] *Pisma Axelroda i Martova*, pp. 110–11.   [2] Ibid.

as before, although Trotsky may have consoled himself with the illusion that the Mensheviks had accepted his advice. At any rate, the formal decision to disband the Menshevik organization freed him from the group discipline by which he had been bound. Martov soon reported to Axelrod that Trotsky had at last 'calmed down', 'softened', and that he had resumed writing for *Iskra*—Trotsky's first contribution since the clash with Plekhanov did indeed soon appear in the paper.[1] As usual, personal resentments, pretensions, and political motives were so mixed up that it is well-nigh impossible to disentangle them. We cannot say whether Trotsky 'calmed down' because the Mensheviks seemed to yield to him on a matter of principle, or because they gave him some satisfaction for Plekhanov's rebuff, or for both these reasons. He was not now one of *Iskra's* policy-makers and editorial writers; he contributed a political note-book, which appeared on one of the back pages. But *Iskra* was still the Mensheviks' militant paper, and so to outsiders Trotsky remained a Menshevik.

. . . .

His differences with the Mensheviks were not really settled and news from Russia presently widened them. The Russo-Japanese war had taken a turn disastrous for Russia; and cracks were showing in the edifice of Tsardom. In July, the Minister Plehve, the inspirer of the Tsar's Far Eastern policy, was assassinated by Sazonov, a social revolutionary.[2] Plehve had banned and dispersed the *Zemstvos*, which were the strong-holds of the Liberal and semi-Liberal gentry. His successor, Svatopolk-Mirsky, tried to appease the opposition and allowed the *Zemstvos* to hold a national convention in November 1904. The convention was followed by a long sequence of political banquets held in many towns. At these the Liberal leaders of the gentry and of the middle classes voiced their demands; but side by side with them there also appeared, for the first time, workers and members of the Socialist underground. Although all of them still spoke in unison against the government, the banquets afforded a glimpse of a deep division in the

---

[1] *Iskra*, no. 75, 5 October 1904. (Trotsky's only contribution in the interval had appeared in a discussion sheet published in June as a supplement to *Iskra*.)

[2] Azev, the *agent-provocateur* whom Plehve himself had employed to disrupt the clandestine terrorist organization, helped in preparing the assassination.

opposition. The workers suspected that the purpose of the Liberal spokesmen was not to overthrow the Tsar but to strike a bargain with him.

The émigrés in western Europe watched with hopeful suspense the banqueting campaign, which went on till the end of the year. Events pressed the Socialists to clarify their attitude towards liberalism. The division between socialism and liberalism existed in the émigré circles as well. Since the middle of 1902, Peter Struve had been publishing his *Osvobozhdenie* (Liberation) first in Stuttgart and then in Paris. At the outset the paper advocated 'legal Marxism', a diluted version of the doctrine; it placed particular emphasis on that part of the Marxist argument which was directed against *Narodnik* terrorism and agrarian socialism and it insisted that capitalist industrialization would bring social progress to Russia. In this phase the old *Iskra* and *Osvobozhdenie* were not yet openly opposed to each other. But soon it became clear that Struve's group used the Marxist argument to dispose of one brand of socialism, the agrarian, not to advocate proletarian socialism. *Osvobozhdenie* evolved from 'legal Marxism' towards liberalism; and the evolution became very marked just when the cleavage between the Socialists was deepening. The Mensheviks inclined towards the Liberals; the Bolsheviks were turning against them. Over this issue, in the autumn of 1904, Trotsky again fell out with the Mensheviks.[1]

In November and December he wrote a brochure on the problems raised by the banqueting campaign, and he submitted it to the Menshevik publishers. The latter were reluctant to bring it out, delayed publication, and, according to Trotsky, intended to suppress it. This was hardly their set intention, for they did bring it out in the end. But the brochure contained so sweeping and devastating a diatribe against the Liberals that it could not but arouse misgivings in men who had begun to see their chance in joint Socialist-Liberal action against the Tsar. The crux of Trotsky's argument was that the Liberals, more afraid of the revolution than of the Tsar, were incapable of such action.[2]

[1] L. Martov, *Istorya Ross. Sots. Dem.*, p. 102; Trotsky, *Moya Zhizn*, vol. i, chapter xiii.

[2] The brochure *Do 9 Yanvara* (*The Period up to 9 January*) is reprinted in *Sochinenya*, vol. ii, book 1.

In the first instance he flayed the pathetic and insincere patriotism which the Liberals had displayed in the Russo-Japanese war. Struve, he wrote, 'sacrificed the last remnants of his spirit of opposition and of his political dignity not to "patriotic feeling" but to patriotic hypocrisy'.[1] Because of its military defeats, Tsardom was in an impasse. 'All the more sharply and energetically . . . should the opposition have revealed the gulf that yawns between Tsardom and the nation. All the more firmly should it have tried to push Tsardom, the nation's real enemy, into the gulf. Instead, the liberal *Zemstvo* . . . harnesses itself to the rickety war-chariot, removes the corpses and sweeps away the trail of blood.' At heart the Liberals prayed for the Tsar's defeat which might induce him to meet the opposition half-way. 'But what does the liberal Press do? That miserable, mumbling, slick, mendacious, wriggling, corrupted and corrupting liberal Press? . . . Not believing its own words and concealing a slavish yearning for the Tsar's destruction [it speaks about] '*our* Monarch and *our* war.' The Liberal opposition was seeking to 'deserve the gratitude and the trust of absolutism, to become indispensable to it, and finally to bribe it with the people's money,—tactics as old as Russian liberalism, which has become neither more sensible nor more dignified with the years'.[2] The new Minister, Prince Svatopolk-Mirsky had initiated an era of spurious concessions by expressing ('stupidly and insolently') his government's confidence in the people, 'as if the question was whether the Ministry trusted the people and not whether the people trusted the Ministry'. But this was enough, Trotsky went on, for the *Zemstvos* to omit from their statements the demand for universal suffrage and constitutional government. They were afraid of the foreign word 'constitution'; and 'behind the fear of the word was concealed the fear of the deed. . . '. 'He who wants to be understood by the masses and to have them on his side, should above all express his demands clearly and precisely, call things by their proper names, call constitution—constitution, republic—republic, universal suffrage—universal suffrage.'[3] By their timidity the Liberals were unwittingly restoring in rulers and ruled alike confidence in the future of absolutism. They pretended to be the party of

[1] L. Trotsky, *Sochinenya*, vol. ii, book 1, p. 6.
[2] Op. cit., p. 9.   [3] Op. cit., p. 15.

democracy; but they were betraying their own principle. 'We have no democratic traditions; these have to be created. Only the revolution can do that. The party of democracy cannot but be the party of the revolution.'[1] Neither the Liberal intelligentsia nor the middle classes but the Socialist factory workers would deal the decisive blow to Tsardom.

The whole brochure is permeated with a triumphant sense of the imminence of the revolution. 'Barristers are demonstrating in the streets, political exiles are protesting in newspapers against their banishment, . . . a naval officer opens a public campaign against the naval department. . . . The incredible becomes real, the impossible becomes probable.'[2] So close a premonition of approaching events can hardly be found in the writings of any other émigré. The others were so immersed in their internecine struggles and so engrossed in manœuvring against one another, with the intention, no doubt, of securing for the party the best possible vantage-point in a revolution, that they almost missed the advent of the revolution. Because he stood almost alone, Trotsky turned his undivided attention to developments in Russia. He was, as Lunacharsky put it, less of an émigré than were other Socialists, who had, in varying degrees, lost contact with their country.[3] His sceptical friends shrugged their shoulders at his triumphant heralding of the upheaval not less than at the vehemence of his anti-Liberalism.

He saw the revolution developing from a general strike. This was a novel concept: the labour conflicts in Russia had so far been on a local scale; and even the industrial countries in the West, with their old trade unions, had not yet any real experience of a general strike. In *My Life* he says that he had mooted this idea since 1903, although he finally adopted it only in 1904.[4] He now sketched a 'plan of action' which he summed up as follows:

Tear the workers away from the machines and workshops; lead them through the factory gate out into the street; direct them to neighbouring factories; proclaim a stoppage there; and carry new masses into the street. Thus, moving from factory to factory, from workshop to workshop, growing under way and sweeping away police

[1] L. Trotsky, *Sochinenya*, vol. ii, book 1, p. 30.   [2] Op. cit., p. 3.
[3] A. Lunacharsky, *Revolutsionnye Siluety*, pp. 20–25.
[4] L. Trotsky, *Moya Zhizn*, vol. i, chapter xiii; *Sochinenya*, vol. ii, book 1, p. 521.

obstacles, haranguing and attracting passers-by, absorbing groups that come from the opposite direction, filling the streets, taking possession of the first suitable buildings for public meetings, entrenching yourselves in those buildings, using them for uninterrupted revolutionary meetings with a permanently shifting and changing audience, you shall bring order into the movement of the masses, raise their confidence, explain to them the purpose and the sense of events; and thus you shall eventually transform the city into a revolutionary camp—this, by and large, is the plan of action.[1]

This was indeed the picture of the revolution which was to materialize both in October 1905 and in February 1917. The 'plan of action' was not modelled on any precedent: in the French Revolution the industrial-proletarian element had been absent. The picture sprang from a fervent revolutionary imagination, in which romanticism was curiously blended with realism. Some parts of this brochure read like passages from Trotsky's own histories of 1905 and 1917, only that the events are described here in the future tense; and even the watchwords are those that would resound in 1905 and 1917: 'End the war', and 'Convoke a constituent assembly!'[2]

Finally, he surveyed the social forces that were coming into action. 'The town will be the main arena of revolutionary events.'[3] But the urban proletariat alone will not decide the issue. The peasantry represented 'a major reservoir of potential revolutionary energy'.[4] It is 'necessary to carry the agitation into the countryside, without a day's delay and without missing a single opportunity'.[5] Far from calling the urban proletariat, as his later critics say, to brave Tsardom single-handedly and court defeat, he strongly underlined the dangers of isolation that threatened the working class.[6] He analysed the role of the army, composed of peasants, and urged Socialists to watch soberly what was going on in the barracks. When ordered to fire at crowds, soldiers preferred to shoot into the air; the morale of the army was under a strain:

Our ships are slow. Our guns do not fire far enough. Our soldiers are illiterate. Our N.C.O.s have neither map nor compass. Our soldiers go barefoot, naked and hungry. Our Red Cross steals. Our supply services steal. Rumours about this reach the army and

---

[1] L. Trotsky, *Sochinenya*, vol. ii, book 1, p. 51.
[2] Ibid. and *passim*.   [3] Op. cit., p. 50.
[4] Op. cit., p. 20 and *passim*.   [5] Op. cit., p. 52.   [6] Op. cit., p. 46.

are avidly absorbed. Every such rumour corrodes like a sharp acid the rust of official indoctrination. Years of our peaceful propaganda could not achieve what one day of war does.

On the decisive day the officers should not be able to rely on the soldiers. . . . The same soldier who yesterday fired his shots in the air, will tomorrow hand over his weapon to the worker. He will do so as soon as he has gained the confidence that the people is not out merely to riot, that the people knows what it wants and can fight for what it wants. . . . We must develop the most intense agitation among the troops so that at the moment of the [general] strike every soldier sent to suppress the 'rebels' should know that in front of him is the people demanding the convocation of the constituent assembly.[1]

The Menshevik publisher was still withholding Trotsky's brochure from the press when news arrived of the first act of revolution in Russia. On 9/23 January 1905 the workers of Petersburg marched in an enormous but peaceful procession to the Tsar's Winter Palace. They were led by Father Gapon, a prison chaplain and a protégé of Zubatov, the chief of the gendarmerie, who had set up his own Labour organization to combat clandestine socialism. The demonstrators, carrying the Tsar's portraits, holy icons, and church banners, hoped to submit to the Tsar a petition, in which they humbly and plain-tively begged him to redress their grievances. The Tsar refused to receive the petitioners and ordered the troops guarding the Winter Palace to fire into the crowd. Thus he ignited the revolu-tionary explosion.

The news found Trotsky in Geneva, whither he had just arrived from a lecturing tour. His forecasts, which he had in vain been trying to publish, began to come true. Full of hopeful excitement, he returned to Parvus in Munich, the galley proofs of the brochure in his pocket. Parvus read the proofs and was so impressed that he decided to put the weight of his authority behind Trotsky's views. He wrote a preface to the brochure and urged the Mensheviks to publish it. In his preface he stated a conclusion which Trotsky still hesitated to draw. 'The revolu-tionary Provisional Government of Russia', Parvus wrote, 'will be the government of a workers' democracy. . . . As the Social Democratic party is at the head of the revolutionary movement . . . this government will be social democratic . . . a coherent

---

[1] L. Trotsky, *Sochinenya*, vol. ii, book 1, p. 50.

government with a social democratic majority.' When the brochure at last appeared, it aroused much controversy, and it spurred on both Bolsheviks and Mensheviks to formulate their own anticipations. Disputation centred on Parvus's conclusion: both Mensheviks and Bolsheviks rejected it. The former advanced the view that as the revolution was bourgeois in character, directed against absolutism and residual feudalism, not aiming at socialism, the bourgeoisie, not the proletariat, was the legitimate heir to power. The Socialists, according to them, could not participate in any bourgeois government, even in one that emerged from a revolution. Their task was to guard, in opposition, the interests of the working class. Lenin agreed that the revolution was bourgeois in so far as it could not aim at socialism; but he did not believe in the revolutionary mission of the bourgeoisie. The Socialists, he held, were bound in duty to enter a revolutionary government. Yet he, too, contested Parvus's forecast about the Social-Democratic character of that government. 'This *cannot be*', Lenin wrote, 'if we have in mind not fleeting episodes but a halfway lasting revolutionary dictatorship, capable of leaving some mark on history. This cannot be, because only such a revolutionary dictatorship can have any stability . . . as is based on a great majority of the people. The Russian proletariat constitutes now a minority of Russia's population.' The revolutionary government would have to be formed by a coalition, in which 'petty bourgeois and semi-proletarian elements' would participate 'or even predominate. . . . It would be extremely harmful', Lenin added, 'to entertain any illusions whatsoever about this.'[1]

This was the first time that any group or individual laid, on behalf of Russian socialism, open claim to power, or to the major share in it. It was a curious freak that this claim should have been first made by Parvus, an outsider to the Russian revolution, and that it should have been repudiated almost in horror by Lenin. In Lenin's person the revolution seemed 'to shrink back appalled before the vague immensity of its own aims'. Yet even Parvus spoke about a 'workers' government', not a proletarian dictatorship. Nor did Trotsky yet question the common assumption that the revolution would be merely bourgeois, and that with the destruction of feudal and absolutist

[1] Lenin, *Sochinenya*, vol. viii, pp. 262–3.

institutions its role would be exhausted. At the same time it seemed to him as to Parvus irrefutable that if the urban proletariat was the chief driving-force of the revolution, then its representatives must, if the revolution succeeded, wield the major influence in the provisional government. No social class would be willing to bear the brunt of a revolution and then give up the fruits of its victory. The critics were incapable of effectively refuting this argument.   But both Bolsheviks and Mensheviks asked two pertinent questions: How could this prospect be reconciled with the bourgeois character of the revolution? And how could one envisage a government by a proletarian minority, without abandoning the principle of representative democratic government, which none of the disputants was willing to abandon? To these questions neither Trotsky nor Parvus had any answer yet.

In January 1905, at Parvus's home, Trotsky began to write another series of essays, which appeared later under the title *After the Petersburg Insurrection.* The series consisted of rather disparate segments: of new, sarcastic polemics against the Liberals, of intensely enthusiastic passages greeting the revolution, and of highly sober reflections on the techniques of revolution. In his strictures on the Liberals he dwelt on the point that only two days before the demonstration in Petersburg, Struve had stated that 'no revolutionary people exists in Russia'. 'These words', Trotsky commented, 'should be engraved on Mr. Struve's forehead, if, even without this, his head did not already look like a gravestone, under which are buried so many plans, slogans, and ideas—socialist, liberal, "patriotic", revolutionary, monarchist, democratic, and others.'[1] Trotsky's conclusion was: *'Our struggle for the revolution, our preparation for it, will go hand in hand with our ruthless struggle against liberalism for influence on the masses, for the leading role of the proletariat . . .'*

The tenor of the passages in which he greeted the revolution may be gauged from these words:

Yes, she has come. We have awaited her. We have never doubted her. For many years she was only a deduction from our 'doctrine', at which the nonentities of every political shade mocked. . . . With her first sweep, she has already uplifted society. . . . Before 9 January our demand for a republic seemed fantastic, doctrinaire, and dis-

[1] L. Trotsky, *Sochinenya*, vol. ii, book 1, pp. 57 ff.

gusting to all liberal pundits. One day of revolution was enough, one magnificent contact between the Tsar and the people was enough for the idea of constitutional monarchy to become fantastic, doctrinaire, and disgusting. The priest Gapon rose with his idea of the monarch against the real monarch. But, as behind him there stood not monarchist liberals but revolutionary proletarians, this limited 'insurrection' immediately manifested its rebellious content in barricade fighting and in the outcry: Down with the Tsar. The real monarch has destroyed the idea of the monarch. . . . The revolution has come and she has put an end to our political childhood.[1]

At this stage problems of revolutionary technique acquired 'colossal importance'. 'The proletarians of Petersburg have shown great heroism. But the unarmed heroism of the crowd could not face the armed idiocy of the barracks.' Henceforth scattered efforts would lead to nothing—the movement must culminate in an all-Russian insurrection. The revolution must arm itself. Some people held that insurgents had no chance against a government armed with modern weapons; an English writer, for instance, believed that if Louis XVI had had a few batteries of machine-guns the French Revolution would not have occurred. 'What pretentious nonsense it is', Trotsky observed, 'to measure the historical chances of revolution by the calibre of weapons and guns. As if weapons and guns had command of men, as if men did not wield the weapons and guns.'[2] He granted that workers by themselves, even if armed, could not conquer in a rising—they must bring the army over to their side. But to be able to achieve this, they must first arm themselves and impress by their own determination the Tsar's vacillating soldiers. He developed this idea in passages which were in part instructions on how the workers should arm themselves and in part descriptive images illustrating the process by which the Tsar's troops would go over to the insurgent people. These anticipatory scenes again read like pages from his own histories of the revolution, written after the event. He concluded with an appeal to his own comrades framed in Dantonesque style: All that you needed, he said, in order to rise to the opportunity, was 'a few very simple qualities: freedom from organizational routine and from the miserable

---

[1] Loc. cit.   [2] Op. cit., p. 60.

traditions of a clandestine movement; a broad view; courageous initiative; the ability to evaluate situations; and once again, courageous initiative'.

.   .   .   .

Between the lines of these writings one can still feel the fever that consumed the author. He was burning with impatience to return to Russia and to plunge into the vortex. Not for him the stale air of the émigré colonies, where he was at cross-purposes with almost everybody. Not for him an exile from which the revolution could be only dimly watched as a storm on the high seas is watched from a remote shore. The return to Russia was bound up with grave risks. A fugitive from Siberia, if caught by the police, was automatically treated as an outlaw and deported for hard labour, even if his original sentence had not provided for this. All the same, he made up his mind to return. Sedova went ahead of him to prepare secret lodgings. In February 1905 he himself was on his way back. He stopped in Vienna and called on Victor Adler, the Austrian leader, in whose home he shaved off his moustache and beard to make it difficult for the Russian police to recognize him.

It was at Adler's home that he had first called for help while he was on his way from Siberia to England. Only two and a half years had passed since, but how crowded and full of portent those years were.

CHAPTER V

Trotsky in 1905

In February Trotsky arrived in Kiev, and there, having assumed the identity of a retired ensign, Arbuzov, he hid for several weeks. Kiev was then the hub of the clandestine organization; but the police were less alert there than in Petersburg and Moscow. There Trotsky met Leonid Krasin, with whom he was to be closely associated for the rest of the year. An eminent technician and prosperous industrial manager, Krasin was also a member of the Central Committee second only to Lenin in the Bolshevik hierarchy, and the actual manager on the spot of the clandestine organization. He was, however, a 'conciliator', anxious to overcome the breach in the party and therefore at loggerheads with Lenin. This made it easier for Trotsky to co-operate with him. And to Krasin, Trotsky, the only prominent Socialist policy-maker and writer then in Russia, soon became indispensable. In the spring, Krasin took him to Petersburg.

The other Socialist leaders stayed in western Europe until late in the year. In normal times, when events moved slowly, the clandestine organization could well afford to consult the émigrés and to wait for their instructions. But now the range of its activities was expanding feverishly; more and more often the party had to act under the compulsion of events and on the spur of the moment; consequently, routine contacts with the émigrés became too cumbersome and slow.

Having returned to Russia so early, Trotsky found himself at once at the very centre of clandestine affairs. This was to make him loom much larger in the revolution of 1905 than did any of the older leaders. But he was to loom larger for yet another, more fundamental, reason: The two trends in the party had not yet crystallized sufficiently to become two separate and hostile forces. Yet the controversy had advanced enough to absorb the minds and energies of the leaders. The turmoil in Russia came too late for the party to be able to act with the immediate initiative and massive vigour of a single body. But it also came too early—before the two parties, Bolshevik and Menshevik, had disengaged from each other and gained a new

freedom of movement. More than anybody else Trotsky represented that mood of indecision and that horror of division
which was still common to both sections of the party. In a sense,
he embodied the 'immaturity' of the movement, while the
'fanatics of the schism' were more representative of its future.
He expressed the party's strongest sentiment against the even
stronger logic of its development. But he also embodied the
highest degree of 'maturity' the movement had so far attained
in its broader aspirations: in formulating the objectives of the
revolution, Trotsky went farther than either Martov or Lenin;
and he was therefore better equipped for an active role in the
upheaval. An unfailing political instinct led him at the right
moments to the sensitive spots and the foci of the revolution,
and guided his steps.

During the first months after his return, he could do little
more than write and inspire Krasin, and through him the
organization. The turmoil of January and February was over;
and in the spring the Labour movement was in the doldrums.
The strikes had fizzled out; police repression and executions
had intimidated the workers. The political initiative passed to
the Liberal middle class. A long series of congresses and conventions, held by industrialists, merchants, bankers, doctors,
lawyers, and others, raised the cry for constitutional government and reform. Only later in the year, after the defeat of
Tsushima, the revolt of the crew on the *Potemkin*, and the end
of the war with Japan, was the initiative to slip back from the
middle class to the workers.

In the meantime Trotsky could not appear in the open. Even
in the clandestine circles of Petersburg he moved warily as
'Peter Petrovich'. The ground was shaky—the *Okhrana* had its
agents provocateurs in the organization. But from his hiding-
places he watched the political scene and produced an unending
stream of essays, sociological studies, letters to *Iskra*, leaflets,
pamphlets, polemical broadsides, and writings on the strategy
and tactics of revolution. He became confirmed in the views
he had expounded together with Parvus; and he went farther.
Immediately after his return, he wrote in *Iskra* that apart from
the Social Democratic Party 'there is nobody on the battlefield of
the revolution' capable of organizing a nation-wide insurrection:

Other groups in the urban population will play their part in the revolution only in so far as they follow the proletariat. . . . Neither the peasantry, nor the middle class, nor the intelligentsia can play an independent revolutionary role in any way equivalent to the role of the proletariat. . . . Consequently, the composition of the Provisional Government will in the main depend on the proletariat. If the insurrection ends in a decisive victory, those who have led the working class in the rising will gain power.[1]

Abroad, Parvus, too, advocated armed insurrection; and Lenin, of course, did likewise. The Mensheviks bided their time, saying that an armed rising, like a revolution at large, could not be organized—it would come of its own accord with the growth of popular revolt. Behind this expectant Menshevik attitude was a hardening conviction that the leadership in the Russian revolution belonged not to socialism but to liberalism. In the issue of *Iskra* in which Trotsky wrote that 'apart from social democracy there is nobody on the battlefield of the revolution', capable of leadership, Martov insisted that it was the historical mission of the middle classes to bring about a radical democratization of Russian society. 'We have the right to expect', these were Martov's words, 'that sober political calculation will prompt our bourgeois democracy to act in the same way in which, in the past century, bourgeois democracy acted in western Europe, under the inspiration of revolutionary romanticism.'[2]

Trotsky countered Martov's view with a critique of the Liberal attitude as it was expressed by such bodies as the Association of Industrialists of Moscow, the Iron and Steel Industries of Petersburg, the provincial banks, the employers of the Urals, the sugar-mill owners of the Ukraine, the national congresses of surgeons, actors, criminologists, &c. He did not deny that the middle classes were constrained by autocratic rule, and that their interest in economic progress and free trade induced them to demand political freedom. He even said that 'the liberal régime becomes a class necessity for capital', and that 'the urban merchant has shown that in opposition he is not inferior to the "enlightened landlord" '.[3] But he added that in their demands the middle classes merely echoed the workers; and they were inhibited by the fear of revolution. 'For the proletariat

---

[1] *Iskra*, no. 93, 17 March 1905.   [2] Ibid.
[3] L. Trotsky, *Sochinenya*, vol. ii, book 1, pp. 71, 79.

democracy is in *all* circumstances a political necessity; for the capitalist bourgeoisie it is in *some* circumstances a political inevitability.'[1] Their gestures of opposition were creating for the middle classes a political prestige which was not without peril to the revolution. The intelligentsia had until recently looked down upon the industrialist and the merchant; now they were hailing them as the heroes of a popular cause; and to the Liberal spokesmen 'their own speeches sound so convincing that they await the enemy's [the Tsar's] immediate surrender. . . . But Jericho still stands, and, moreover, it is scheming evil.'[2]

'Jericho' was indeed scheming—on the initiative of Bulygin, the Tsar's minister—for the convocation of a pseudo-parliament, the so-called Bulygin Duma. On 6 August the Tsar announced the plan in a Manifesto. The Duma was to be his consultative council, not a legislature; in the election each Estate was to cast its vote separately; the vote was to be based on property; and the Tsar reserved the right to prorogue or disband the Duma. The working classes were virtually disfranchised. Yet the Manifesto threw the opposition into some confusion. Miliukov, the great historian, who was now assuming the leadership of liberalism, greeted the Manifesto and described it as the crossing by the nation of the rubicon of constitutional government.[3] The Liberal leader's readiness to content himself with the sop from the Tsar prompted Trotsky, who stood for boycotting the Duma, to write an 'Open Letter to Professor P. N. Miliukov'.[4] Of all his philippics against liberalism, this was the most biting and subtle; and it was widely circulated in semi-secrecy. 'An historical Rubicon', Trotsky wrote, 'is truly crossed only at the moment when the material means of government pass from the hands of absolutism into those of the people. Such things, Professor, are never achieved with the signing of a parchment; they take place on the street and are achieved through struggle.' He recalled how in the French Revolution the great turns came not with declarations of constitutional principle but with real shifts of power. He further recalled events in Germany in 1848—how middle-class liberalism had contented

---

[1] L. Trotsky, *Sochinenya*, vol. ii, book 1, p. 91.   [2] Ibid., pp. 98–99.
[3] The confusion cut across party lines: disagreeing with Miliukov, many Liberals were preparing to boycott the Duma, the Mensheviks were for a time against the boycott. The Bolsheviks were for it. See L. Martov, *Istorya Ross. Sots. Dem.*, p. 126.
[4] L. Trotsky, *Sochinenya*, vol. ii, book 1, pp. 196–205.

itself with the Prussian king's promise of freedom; how it had helped the autocrat to subdue the revolution; and how, in the end, on the ebb of the revolution, the autocrat had defeated and humiliated liberalism:

But history teaches the professors of history nothing. The mistakes and crimes of liberalism are international. You are repeating what your predecessors did in the same situation half a century ago. . . . You are afraid of breaking with the Duma, because to you this constitutional mirage seems real in the dry and barren desert through which Russian liberalism has been wading not for its first decade. . . . You, Professor, you will not tell the people this. But we shall. And if you try to debate with us not at liberal banquets but in front of the masses, we shall show that in our crude, harsh, revolùtionary idiom we can be irrefutably convincing and eloquent. . . . If the revolution does not ebb away, the bureaucracy will cling to you as to its bulwark; and if you really try to become its bulwark, the victorious revolution will throw you overboard . . . [if, on the other hand, the revolution is defeated, then Tsardom will have no use for liberalism]. You propose not to be disturbed by the voices from the right and the voices from the left. . . . The revolution has not yet said its last word. With powerful and broad thrusts it lowers the edge of its knife over the head of absolutism. Let the wiseacres of liberalism beware of putting their hands under the glittering steel blade. Let them beware.

The style was the whole man in this 'Open Letter', at once scholarly, rhetorical, and implacable. In his attitude towards liberalism he was akin to Lenin. But Lenin had little or no inclination to engage in a direct ideological dialogue with liberalism, while Trotsky felt the need for a constant confrontation between revolutionary socialism and liberalism. He conducted this dialogue now, and he would do so to the end of his life, not because he had broken less decisively than Lenin with bourgeois liberalism, but in part because he was more aware of its attraction. Lenin instructed and led his followers, and in a sense preached to the converted, while Trotsky addressed the Liberal spokesmen directly and dissected and countered their arguments before large and undecided audiences. The dialogue with the adversary also best suited his polemical temperament and his dialectical style. Not for nothing was the Open Letter his favourite form of expression.

He addressed thus directly the most diverse audiences, speaking to each social group in its own idiom, with an extraordinary ease and *élan*. In his diatribes against liberalism he turned towards the intelligentsia and the advanced workers. In his 'Open Letter to Miliukov' he spoke to an academic public. Soon after his return to Russia he wrote peasant proclamations, which Krasin published, putting under them the signature of the Central Committee. In these proclamations Trotsky had before his eyes a primitive, illiterate mass of farm labourers, such as he could remember from his father's farm, a crowd in which a few individuals might be able to read his words aloud to the rest. He framed his appeal in the simplest terms and in the rhythm of a Slavonic folk-rhapsody, with characteristic refrains and evocations. The words and the rhythm were as if designed for recital by a semi-agitator, semi-bard in a village. Yet, he spoke to the muzhiks with the same logic and sweep with which he addressed his academic adversary. In the whole revolutionary literature written for or by peasants, there are very few, if any, documents which could compare, in folk style and directness of appeal, with a proclamation in which Trotsky related to the peasants the January massacre in Petersburg. He described how the workers had marched 'peacefully and calmly' to the Tsar's palace with the Tsar's pictures, icons, and church banners:

'What did the Tsar do? How did he answer the toilers of St. Petersburg?

'Hearken, hearken peasants. . . .

'This is the way the Tsar talked with his people. . . .

'All the troops of Petersburg were raised to their feet. . . . Thus the Russian Tsar girded himself for the talk with his subjects. . . .

'200,000 workers moved to the palace.

'They were dressed in their Sunday best, the grey and old ones and the young; the women went along with their husbands. Fathers and mothers led their little children by their hands. Thus the people went to their Tsar.

'Hearken, hearken peasants!

'Let every word engrave itself on your hearts. . . .

'All the streets and squares, where the peaceful workers were to march, were occupied by troops.

' "Let us through to the Tsar!", the workers begged.

'The old ones fell on their knees.

'The women begged and the children begged.

' "Let us through to the Tsar!"——

'And then it happened!

'The guns went off with a thunder. . . . The snow reddened with workers' blood. . . .

'Tell all and sundry in what way the Tsar has dealt with the toilers of St. Petersburg! . . .

'Remember, Russian peasants, how every Russian Tsar has repeated with pride: "In my country, I am the first courtier and the first landlord." . . .

'Russian Tsars have made the peasants into an Estate of serfs; they have made of them, like of dogs, presents to their faithful servants. . . .

'Peasants, at your meetings tell the soldiers, the people's sons who live on the people's money, that they dare not shoot at the people.'

Thus, in plain words, without weakening for a moment his grasp on the muzhik's imagination, he explained the ends his party was pursuing and the means it would employ; and he translated the alien term 'revolution' into the peasants' idiom: 'Peasants, let this fire burst all over Russia at one and the same time, and no force will put it out. Such a nation-wide fire is called revolution.'[1]

In a different manner again he addressed urban workers—for instance when they failed to respond to the party's call and demonstrate on May Day: 'You have taken fright before the Tsar's soldiers. . . . But you are not afraid of delivering your brothers to the Tsar's army so that they may perish on the great, unwept-for Manchurian cemetery. . . . You did not come out yesterday, but you will come out tomorrow or the day after.'[2] A small masterpiece of revolutionary journalism was a very short article: 'Good morning, Petersburg *Dvornik*.'[3] He wrote it later in the year, after the Tsar had, in the so-called October Manifesto, promised a constitution and civil liberties. The *dvornik* (*concierge*) had usually served the political police as informer and stooge; but now he became infected with revolution. 'The Petersburg *dvornik* awakens from the police nightmare',

---

[1] *Iskra*, no. 90, 3 March 1905. *Sochinenya*, vol. ii, book 1, pp. 217–24. The manuscript of this proclamation was found, after 1917, in the archives of the gendarmerie of Kiev—it had been seized during a raid on Krasin's printing shop.

[2] L. Trotsky, *Sochinenya*, vol. ii, book 1, pp. 241–5. This proclamation, signed by the Central Committee was also found in the archives of the Kiev gendarmerie after 1917.

[3] *Russkaya Gazeta*, 15 November 1905; *Sochinenya*, vol. ii, book 1, pp. 300–1.

Trotsky wrote. '2500 *dvorniks* met to discuss their needs. The *dvorniks* do not wish to serve any longer as tools of police violence.' They put forward their demands and refused to sign a thanksgiving address to the Tsar, because in the Tsar's Manifesto 'freedom had been given but not yet proven'. 'Many sins and crimes', Trotsky wrote, 'weigh on the conscience of the Petersburg *dvorniks*. More than once have they, on police orders, manhandled honest workers and students. . . . The police have bullied them, and the people have come to hate them. But the hour of universal awakening has come. The Petersburg *dvornik* is opening his eyes. Good morning to you, Petersburg *dvornik*.'

Thus he spoke to every class of society, from the highest to the humblest, in its own language, but always in his own voice. The Russian Revolution never had, and never would have, another mouth-piece with such a variety of accent and tone.

.   .   .   .

During his stay in Kiev he shifted from one secret lodging to another, precariously concealing his identity under the mask of 'Ensign Arbuzov'. The 'ensign' looked respectable, even elegant; but he was strikingly busy, received odd visitors, was closeted with them for hours, or pored over piles of newspapers, books, and manuscripts. Some of his hosts took fright and he had to move out. Others sheltered him with courage and good humour. In *My Life* he describes how, posing as a patient, he found asylum in an ophthalmic hospital. The doctor in charge of the ward and some of his assistants were in the secret. An unsuspecting nurse conscientiously and tenderly struggled with the odd patient, urging him to take eye-drops and foot-baths and to stop reading and writing.

After he had moved to Petersburg, Krasin found him accommodation in the home of Colonel Littkens, the chief medical officer of the Imperial Military Academy, where Krasin, too, had his secret meeting-place with members of the underground. The colonel's sons were engaged in clandestine work, and he himself was a 'sympathizer'. In his home Trotsky and Sedova lived as the landowning family Vikentiev, escaping for a time the *Okhrana's* attention. Sedova, however, was arrested at a May Day demonstration; and the *agent provocateur* planted in the clandestine organization was on Trotsky's track. Trotsky hurriedly left for Finland, which was then part of the Tsarist empire but enjoyed much greater freedom than Russia. Amid the lakes and pine woods of the Finnish countryside, in a hotel called *Rauha* (Peace) he meditated, studied, wrote, and kept in touch with Krasin, until in the middle of October the news of a general strike in Petersburg broke into the quiet deserted hotel 'like a raging storm through an open window'. On 14 October, or at the latest on the 15th, he was back in the Russian capital.

.　.　.　.　.　.　.　.　.　.

The strike had begun with a printers' demand for shorter hours and higher wages; it then spread rapidly to other industries and from Petersburg to the provinces, assuming a markedly political character and taking by surprise the leaders of the Socialist underground. The workers clamoured for constitutional freedom as well as for better wages and shorter hours. As the strike developed there sprang into being an institution bred in the bone of the Russian Revolution: the first Council, or Soviet, of Workers' Deputies. The Soviet was not a Bolshevik invention. On the contrary, the Bolsheviks, led in Petersburg by Bogdanov and Knuniants-Radin, viewed it with suspicion as a rival to the party. Only in the first week of November (the third week, in the new-style calendar) when the Soviet was already at the peak of its strength and influence, did Lenin try from Stockholm to induce his followers to approach the Soviet in a more co-operative spirit.[1] The nucleus of the Soviet was set up by the strikers from fifty printing shops, who elected delegates and instructed them to form a council. These were soon joined by delegates of other trades. Paradoxically, the idea itself had, indirectly and unwittingly, been suggested by the Tsar who, after the events of January, had appointed a commission under a Senator Shydlovsky to investigate the causes of the trouble. The commission had ordered the workers to elect their representatives from the factories in order to voice grievances. The strikers in October followed this precedent. When the Soviet first met, on 13 October, only delegates of one district (the Neva district) attended. A stimulus was needed to induce other

---

[1] Lenin wrote a letter to this effect to the Bolshevik *Novaya Zhizn* (*New Life*), appearing in Petersburg, but the paper failed to publish the letter—it first saw the light in *Pravda* thirty-five years later—on 5 November 1940.

districts to join in. That stimulus was provided by the Mensheviks, who would one day bitterly oppose the institution to which they now acted as godfathers.

The Soviet instantaneously gained an extraordinary authority. This was the first elective body which represented the hitherto disfranchised working classes. Under a government which held in supreme contempt the very principle of popular representation, the first institution embodying that principle at once tended morally to overshadow the existing administration. The Soviet at once became a revolutionary factor of the first magnitude.

For the first time Trotsky appeared at the Soviet, assembled at the Technological Institute, on 15 October, the day of his return from Finland, or the day after. Deputies from several districts were present—about 200,000 people, nearly 50 per cent. of all workers in the capital, had taken part in the election. Later, after further elections, the number of deputies grew and varied from 400 to 560. The Soviet had just decided to publish its own paper, *Izvestya* (*Tidings*); and it negotiated with the municipal council for accommodation and facilities for work. In the halls and corridors of the Technological Institute there was an air of feverish agitation: strikers were coming and going, deliberating and waiting for instructions—a foretaste of the Soviet of 1917.

The Socialist parties and groups, however, were not yet agreed in their attitude towards the Soviet. The Mensheviks and Social Revolutionaries had decided to send their representatives immediately. The Bolsheviks were reluctant to follow suit and demanded that the Soviet should accept the party's guidance beforehand—only then were they prepared to join. Trotsky, invited by Krasin to a meeting of the Bolshevik Central Committee, urged its members to join the Soviet without any preliminary condition. No party or group, he pleaded, could aspire to exclusive leadership. The Soviet should be a broad representative body embracing all shades of working-class opinion, for only then would it be able to provide a united leadership in the general strike and in the revolutionary situation that might develop from it.

This wrangle was still on when on 17 October the Tsar, frightened by the general strike, issued a Manifesto promising a constitution, civil liberties, and universal suffrage. The Manifesto was composed by Count Witte, a semi-Liberal Prime Minister. The Bulygin Duma had been buried before it was born; and the Tsar appeared to be renouncing the absolutism that was as old as the dynasty itself. Petersburg was first stunned and then intoxicated with joy. Festive crowds filled the streets and read the Manifesto in amazement. In the government, however, the opponents of the reform continued to wield effective power. General Trepov, Minister of the Interior, gave the police the order: 'Spare no bullets!'; and this order was posted on the walls side by side with the Tsar's Manifesto, as if it had been intended to provide a malicious comment on the 'new era'. Just before the Tsar issued his proclamation, the police had made numerous arrests.

On the morning of the 17th Trotsky moved with a huge and excited crowd towards the Technological Institute, where the Soviet had sat the previous two days. Gendarmes on horseback rode into the crowd. Trepov's proclamation seemed to warn everybody that it was too early for exultation. All the same, the crowd, consisting of workers and middle-class people, gave itself up to common rejoicing. The workers, however, were the heroes of the day. It was their strike that had wrested from the Tsar the promise of a constitution and freedom. The houses were at first decorated with the white–red–blue flag of the dynasty, but young workers tore off the white and the blue strips of cloth, littered the pavements with them, and hoisted the narrow and ragged red flags. The procession reached the Technological Institute, but there it was halted by a barrier of police and gendarmerie.

The crowd moved on towards the University, where meetings were held. The swelling, good-humoured procession carried with it the young man who had so long waited for this moment, who had forecast it, and who was now full of misgivings and of an impatient desire to warn the multitude against too early rejoicing. The procession poured into the courtyard of the University. From a balcony speakers were already haranguing the crowds. Tense with his misgivings and with the emotion absorbed from the procession, Trotsky pushed his way through the vast and dense multitude up to the balcony: there was his place! The organizers of the meeting knew him as the man who, under the name Yanovsky (the man of Yanovka), had appeared at the Soviet to represent the Mensheviks; some knew him as the Trotsky of *Iskra*.[1] He eyed the mass of humanity, the like of which he had never seen before; and in a voice which seemed remote and strange to himself he exclaimed: 'Citizens! Now that we have put our foot on the neck of the ruling clique, they promise us freedom.'

He stopped, as if wondering whether the cold shower he was about to pour on the crowd's enthusiasm would not freeze them; and he searched for the words which would show the people that he was rejoicing with them but which would also warn them against their own credulity.

'It is this tireless hangman on the throne', he went on, whom we have compelled to promise us freedom. What a great triumph this is! But——do not hasten to celebrate victory: it is not yet complete. Does the promissory note weigh as much as pure gold? Is a promise of freedom the same as freedom? . . . Look round, citizens, has anything changed since yesterday? Are the gates of our prisons open? . . . Have our brothers returned to their homes from the Siberian wilderness? . . .'

'Amnesty! Amnesty!', the crowd responded. But this was not yet what he was driving at. He went on to suggest the next watchword:

'. . . if the government were honestly resolved to make peace with the people, they would first of all have granted an amnesty. But, citizens, is this all? Today hundreds of political fighters may be released, tomorrow thousands will be jailed. . . . Is not the order 'Spare no bullets' posted side by side with the freedom manifesto. . . . Is not the hangman Trepov the undisputed master of Petersburg?'

'Down with Trepov!' came the cry from the crowd.

'Down with Trepov!' Trotsky resumed; 'but is Trepov alone? . . . He dominates us by means of the army. His power and mainstay is in the Guards, stained by the blood of 9 January. Them he orders to spare no bullets for your bodies and your heads. We cannot, we will not and we shall not live under the gun barrels.'

The crowd replied with the demand for the removal of troops from Petersburg. Then the speaker, as if exasperated by

[1] *Pervaya Russkaya Revolutsia v Peterburge 1905*, vol. i, p. 63; vol. ii, p. 68.

the unreality of this people's victory and excited by the unfailing response of the crowd and his own unsuspected mastery over it, concluded:

'. . . citizens! Our strength is in ourselves. With sword in hand we must defend freedom. The Tsar's Manifesto, however, . . . see! it is only a scrap of paper.'

With a theatrical gesture he flourished the Manifesto in front of the crowd and angrily crumpled it in his fist:

'Today it has been given us and tomorrow it will be taken away and torn into pieces as I am now tearing it into pieces, this paper-liberty, before your very eyes.'[1]

Thus the capital of Russia first heard the orator of the revolution.

.   .   .   .

In this speech Trotsky pointed to all the fatal weaknesses which were to frustrate the revolution. The Tsar's self-confidence, but not his massive machine of power, had been shaken. There was a ferment in the armed forces, especially in the navy. But the Cossacks, the Guards, and the endless ranks of the muzhik infantry were gripped by the age-old habit of blind obedience. Behind the army lay rural Russia, its whole immensity steeped in apathy and despair. The revolution was still a purely urban affair. And even in the towns its triumph was mixed with fear. The middle classes and their Liberal spokesmen, wistfully believing in the Tsar's promise of freedom and uneasy at the thought that they owed that promise to the workers' general strike, were anxious to stop the revolution. They were haunted by the spectre of plebeian 'anarchy', and by the fear that, if the revolution went on, the Tsar would listen to those of his advisers who counselled suppression not concession. 'If you do not call off the struggle', so the Liberals argued with the Socialists, 'our newly-won freedom will prove illusory.' 'But it *is* illusory', the Socialists retorted. To the working class the October Manifesto gave a sense not so much of victory as of strength and an impatience to use that strength for further assaults. Each class intended different aims for the movement. The middle classes hoped to gain most from a constitutional monarchy. The workers were republicans. The former desired nothing but political freedom. The latter raised

[1] L. Trotsky, *Die Russische Revolution 1905*, pp. 93–96.

social demands as well, directed against the middle classes more than against Tsardom.

The fervour of the working class, hot and impulsive, out-stripped even that of the Socialist leaders. The leaders counted the ranks, laid plans, and marked time-tables. They expected the struggle to reach its climax by 9 January 1906, the anni-versary of the march to the Winter Palace.[1] But all phases and dates were unexpectedly advanced by the impetuous temper of the masses, easily inflamed by provocation and stampeded into action. Yet the helplessness of the masses was as great as their self-confidence; and the outcome could only be disastrous. The working class was unarmed; and it could not get arms, in sufficient quantity, until the army itself was in rebellion. Even in conditions ideal for a revolution, it takes time before the prevalent rebellious mood seeps through to the barracks. The mood in the Russian army depended on the state of mind of the peasantry. Only in 1906 did rural Russia become seriously restive. By that time the revolution in the towns had been reduced to cinders; and it had been put down by the uniformed sons of the peasants, who, if the urban movement had been less hasty, might have joined it. The revolution squandered its reserves piecemeal. The working class lacked experience in insurrection. The Socialist parties were too weak to curb the workers' im-patience. And the basic fact behind all this was that the old order was not yet quite at the end of its strength; it was still capable of dividing the forces that might have converged on it.

The Soviet of Petersburg, the hub of this foredoomed revolu-tion, was from the first placed in the very middle of all the cross currents; and it was constantly torn between courage and caution, between the volcanic heat of its surroundings and its political judgement. The Soviet elected its Executive on 17 October. On that Executive sat, among others, three repre-sentatives of the Bolsheviks, three of the Mensheviks, and three of the Social Revolutionaries. The chief Bolshevik spokesmen were Knuniants-Radin and Sverchkov. (Sverchkov later wrote

---

[1] In his letter from Stockholm, which was published by *Pravda* only in 1940, and which we have already quoted, Lenin wrote: 'On the anniversary of the great day of 9 January, let there not remain in Russia even a trace of the institutions of Tsardom.' Lenin, *Sochinenya*, vol. x, p. 11. Others hardly reckoned on such rapid and radical results. On another occasion Lenin wrote that it would be best to delay insurrection till spring 1906. (Ibid., vol. xxxiv, p. 311.)

a history of the Soviet.) Trotsky was the chief Menshevik representative, even though abroad he had resigned from the group. He had in the meantime come to sway the Menshevik organization in the capital and to turn it against the émigré leaders.[1] He was assisted by Zlydniev, a worker who had come to Petersburg from Nikolayev and who had earlier in the year represented his fellows on Senator Shydlovsky's commission. On Trotsky's initiative, the Bolshevik and Menshevik committees in Petersburg formed a Federal Council, which was to prepare the reunion of the two groups, and in the meantime to co-ordinate their activities in the Soviet.[2] The Social Revolutionaries were led by Avksentiev, who in 1917, as Minister of the Interior under Kerensky, was to order Trotsky's imprisonment. In 1905, however, all three parties co-operated harmoniously. None attempted to impose its will upon the other; and all agreed to elect as President of the Soviet Khrustalev-Nosar, a lawyer, who stood outside the parties and had gained the workers' confidence as their attorney in labour conflicts.[3] To the outside world, Khrustalev-Nosar represented the Soviet and momentarily he won great fame. The policies of the Soviet were, however, framed by the parties, mainly by the Social Democrats; and Khrustalev's role in the revolution was episodic. Politically, Trotsky, as the records and memoirs of participants testify, was the Soviet's moving spirit. On major occasions he spoke for both Bolsheviks and Mensheviks and for the whole Soviet. He wrote most of the Soviet's manifestoes and resolutions, and edited its *Izvestya*. Behind the scenes a silent rivalry developed between the formal President of the Soviet and its presiding spirit.[4]

On 19 October, two days after the Tsar had issued his

---

[1] L. Martov, *Istorya Russ. Sots. Dem.*, pp. 141–2.

[2] The agreement appeared under Trotsky's signature in *Izvestya*, no. 2. See also Martov, loc. cit.

[3] Khrustalev-Nosar later, however, joined the Social Democrats (Mensheviks).

[4] Khrustalev-Nosar's legend was cruelly dispelled when as an émigré he was arrested by the French police and charged with financial offences. In 1917 he turned up at the Soviet in Petersburg demanding admission, as a former President, but was disdainfully refused. During the civil war in 1918–19 he emerged as the head of a tiny republic, the so-called Khrustalev republic in one of the southern Russian provinces and was shortly thereafter killed. For Khrustalev's controversies with Trotsky see L. Trotsky, *Sochinenya*, vol. viii, pp. 190–7 and vol. ii, book 1, pp. 110–11, 508–9; N. Sukhanov, *Zapiski o Revolutsii*, vol. i, pp. 126, 129.

Manifesto, Trotsky urged the Soviet to call off the general strike. Its continuance offered no prospect of further success and might lead to more bloodshed. The Soviet unanimously accepted this view, and on 21 October the strike came to an end. The Soviet then announced that a solemn funeral of workers who had been killed during the strike would take place on 23 October. On the 22nd it was learned that General Trepov was preparing the gendarmerie to suppress the demonstration, and that the *Okhrana* was scheming a pogrom of Jews. The same night Trotsky stood before the Soviet, pleading for the cancellation of the funeral. 'The Soviet declares [ran a motion he submitted]: the proletariat of Petersburg will give the Tsarist government the last battle not on a day chosen by Trepov, but when this suits the armed and organized proletariat.'[1] The Soviet swallowed its pride and cancelled the funeral of its martyrs. There was anguish in this humiliation: would the proletariat be able to give battle on the day chosen by itself only if it had armed and organized itself? And how was it to be armed? On the same day the Soviet resolved to organize fighting squads, whose immediate task was to prevent the pogrom. Later, at the trial of the Soviet, conclusive evidence was to be produced that the pogrom had indeed been planned and that only the Soviet's action had averted it. But the fighting squads, even the one that guarded the Soviet, were at best armed with revolvers; and most had only sticks and pieces of iron. This call to arms was, nevertheless, to be one of the main counts in the indictment of the Soviet.[2]

The Soviet maintained a vigorous political initiative, however. The October Manifesto had promised freedom of the press; but the pseudo-liberal Prime Minister Witte ordered the censorship to function as before. In reply, the compositors and the printers, encouraged by the Soviet, declared that they would neither set nor print newspapers and books submitted to the censors; and, by forcing the hands of the government, the publishers, and the writers, they gave Russia her first taste of a free press. Then a clamour rose for the eight-hour day; and under the auspices of the Soviet the workers themselves began to introduce it in the workshops. Towards the end of October

[1] L. Trotsky, *Sochinenya*, vol. ii, book 1, p. 284.
[2] See Chapter VI, and Sverchkov, *Na Zarie Revolutsii*, p. 200.

the government proclaimed a state of siege in Poland; and the sentiment of revolutionary Petersburg was outraged. On 1 November the Soviet arranged a solemn reception for the 'delegates of oppressed Poland'. The assembly was disconcerted to find that the men who came to speak for Poland were Count Zamojski, Count Krasiński, Prince Lubomirski, a few Roman Catholic priests and merchants, and only one peasant and one worker. Trotsky, nevertheless, warmly welcomed the delegation, and solemnly proclaimed Poland's right to determine her own fate. The Soviet called for a new general strike in sympathy with Poland. The government at the same time announced that sailors of Kronstadt who had taken part in the October strike would be court martialled, and clamour for the release of the sailors merged with the cry for Poland's freedom.[1]

A mood so generous and heroic was not without its aggressive humour. The Prime Minister Witte issued an appeal to the strikers: '*Brother workers*, listen to the advice of a man who is well disposed towards you and wishes you well.' The appeal was brought to the Soviet in the middle of a stormy session and Trotsky proposed this immediate reply:[2]

'The proletarians are no relatives of Count Witte. . . . Count Witte calls us to have pity on our wives and children. The Soviet . . . calls upon . . . the workers to count how the number of widows and orphans has grown in the working class since the day when Witte took office. Count Witte speaks about the Tsar's gracious consideration for working people. The Soviet recalls . . . the Bloody Sunday of 9 January. Count Witte begs us to give him 'time' and promises to do 'everything possible'. . . . The Soviet knows that Witte has already found time to deliver Poland to military hangmen, and the Soviet has no doubt that he will do "everything possible" to strangle the revolutionary proletariat. Count Witte . . . wishes us well. The Soviet declares that it has no need for the good wishes of the Tsar's time-servers. It demands popular representation on the basis of universal, equal, direct, and secret suffrage.'[3]

The Liberals in their drawing-rooms, the students and professors in their lecture-halls, and the workers in their tea-shops

[1] Trotsky's speech of welcome to the Poles appeared in *Izvestya*, no. 5 (3 November).

[2] Sverchkov relates that the Soviet had commissioned him, Sverchkov, to draft the reply, but as nothing occurred to him, he asked Trotsky, who had just arrived, to write it. Trotsky produced the reply on the spot and read it out amid general applause. Sverchkov, *Na Zarie Revolutsii*, p. 28.   [3] Trotsky, op. cit., p. 287.

roared with laughter; and Witte himself was said to have suffered
a fit when he read the Soviet's riposte.[1]

On 5 November Trotsky, speaking at the Soviet for the whole
Executive, proposed to call an end to the second general strike.
The government had just announced that the sailors of Kronstadt would be tried by ordinary military courts, not courts
martial. The Soviet could withdraw not with victory indeed,
but with honour. Yet withdraw it had to, especially as strikers in
the provinces were growing weary. 'Events work for us and we
have no need to force their pace', Trotsky said. 'We must drag
out the period of preparation for decisive action as much as we
can, perhaps for a month or two, until we can come out as an
army as cohesive and organized as possible.' A general strike
could not be waged indefinitely. Its sequel ought to be insurrection, but for this the Soviet was not ready. One day, when the
railwaymen and the post and telegraph workers had joined in,
they would 'with the steel of rails and with telegraph wire bind
together all revolutionary bulwarks of the country into a single
whole. This would enable us to arouse when necessary the whole
of Russia within twenty four hours.'

Even while he tried to dam up the raging element of revolt,
he stood before the Soviet like defiance itself, passionate and
sombre. He related a conversation he had with an eminent
Liberal who had urged moderation:

I recalled to him an incident from the French revolution, when
the Convention voted that 'the French people will not parley with
the enemy on their own territory'. One of the members of the Convention interrupted: 'Have you signed a pact with victory?' They
answered him: 'No, we have signed a pact with death.' Comrades,
when the liberal bourgeoisie, as if boasting of its treachery, tells us:
'You are alone. Do you think you can go on fighting without us?
Have you signed a pact with victory?', we throw our answer in their
face: 'No, we have signed a pact with death.'[2]

[1] That Trotsky did not treat Count Witte unfairly Miliukov testifies. About this
time Miliukov visited Witte and expressed the view that the Tsar ought to promulgate a constitution at once, without waiting for the Duma. Witte answered that the
Tsar wanted no constitution, and that the October Manifesto had been issued in a
'fever'. Witte himself did not want a constitution either—he was interested only
in sham constitutionalism. Miliukov, *Istorya Vtoroi Russkoi Revolutsii*, vol. i, book 1,
pp. 18–19.
[2] The speech appeared in *Izvestya* no. 7, 7 November 1905; *Sochinenya*, vol. ii,
book 1, pp. 290–3.

A few days later he had again to impress upon the Soviet its own weakness and urge it to stop enforcing the eight-hour day: the employers had answered with the lockout of more than 100,000 workers. The Soviet was divided, a minority demanding a general strike; but Trotsky, supported by the metal workers, prevailed. These displays of weakness were becoming all too frequent, but the popular impulse to action made them inevitable. What was surprising was that the Soviet's weakness was not revealed with more disastrous results, especially as the Soviet's chief inspirer was a young man who had never led, or participated in, a mass movement of any size. When all the handicaps under which this revolution laboured are considered, the tactics of the Soviet, designed to harass the enemy without engaging him in general battle, appear almost faultless; and its results, the undiminished authority maintained by the Soviet and the concessions it contrived to wrest, must be judged impressive. It was not until twenty years later, during the struggle between Stalin and Trotsky, that Trotsky's 'moderation' in 1905 was held out against him. During the intervening years no such reproach was heard; and the Bolsheviks treated the Soviet's record as a proud chapter in the annals of the revolution.[1] Nor was any alternative line of conduct ever proposed by the Bolsheviks to the Soviet, or even as much as hinted at. In the political literature devoted to the subject, the failure of the revolution of 1905 was invariably attributed to the broad, 'objective' alignments in the country, never to the errors of any leader, least of all of Trotsky.[2]

The Soviet had with such breath-taking rapidity become the main focus of the revolution that the groups and factions did not even have time to ponder its significance or to adjust themselves to the new institution. By the middle of November all their leaders had at last returned from western Europe; and

[1] The Bolsheviks, however, cultivated with warmer sentiments the memory of the Moscow rising of December 1905, which had been led by members of their group.

[2] Lenin, *Sochinenya*, vol. xxiii, pp. 228–46; *Pervaya Russkaya Revolutsia v Peterburge 1905*, vols. i and ii. No differences over the Soviet's tactics came to light at the next congress of the party. See *Pyatyi Syezd RSDRP*; and Sverchkov, op. cit. Only about 1926 did the party historians (Lyadov and Pokrovsky) begin gradually to 'revise' this attitude until Stalin's *History of the C.P.S.U.*; *Short Course* (pp. 79–80) stated plainly that, under the influence of Trotsky and other Mensheviks, the Soviet was 'against preparations for an uprising'.

they watched in suspense and bewilderment this forum, which looked very much like the Russian Convention. But they had too much of the air of émigrés about them to gain a foothold in it—the Soviet had, in any case, constituted itself three or four weeks before their arrival. It was now Trotsky who, on behalf of the proletariat of Petersburg, paid a tribute in the Soviet to the martyrdom and heroism of the émigré elders.[1] When at the beginning of the year he had taken leave of the émigrés they still treated him with the mixture of admiration and condescension shown to the child prodigy. Now they viewed him with new respect, watched his dominating attitude on the platform and read in the rough and grave faces of the working men's assembly the authority and devotion he commanded. Lunacharsky recalls that when Lenin, after his return on 8 or 10 November, was told that 'the strong man in the Soviet is Trotsky', his face darkened somewhat but he said: 'Well, Trotsky has earned that with his fine and tireless work.' His face darkened, for the wounding epithets which Trotsky had flung at him must have flashed through Lenin's mind. The epithets rankled: only a short time before, Lenin had chided Parvus of all men for his partnership with Trotsky, that 'hollow bell', that 'phrase-monger' and 'Balalaykin'.[2] Yet he now acknowledged fairly Trotsky's merit and achievement.

For one further reason Trotsky seemed vindicated against his former adversaries. Both Lenin and Martov now admitted that their passionate controversies had been storms in so many émigré tea cups. The disputes over the prerogatives of the Central Committee and the conditions of membership had referred to the clandestine type of organization. The party had since emerged from the underground and it conducted its activities in broad daylight. For the first time its members could vote and elect their leading bodies without fear of the *Okhrana*. Lenin no less than Martov was anxious that the committees be elected from below and not appointed from above.[3] The Mensheviks, on the other hand, were shaken in their belief in the

---

[1] See the memoirs of F. Mikhailov in *Pervaya Russkaya Revolutsia v Peterburge, 1905*, vol. i, p. 128; L. Trotsky, *Moya Zhizn*, vol. i, chapter xiv.

[2] Balalaykin—a satirical character in Saltykov-Shchedrin, a calculating, complacent chatterbox, and a lawyer. This was Lenin's tit-for-tat for the epithet 'slovenly lawyer' Trotsky had thrown at him.

[3] Lenin, *Sochinenya*, vol. x, pp. 12-21.

revolutionary mission of the middle class, a belief which it was difficult to square with the facts. The Menshevik following in Petersburg had so strongly come under the sway of Trotsky's radicalism that the émigré leaders had to tolerate this. All differences seemed thus to have vanished; and before the year was out the reunion of the two factions, complete with the merger of their Central Committees, was taking place. The fanatics of the schism, so it seemed, had been proven wrong, and the preacher of unity right.[1]

The force of Trotsky's personality and ideas was felt in those days far beyond the Soviet and the Socialist parties. In 1906, when the revolution was already on the wane, Miliukov thus defended himself against attacks from the right: 'Those who now charge our party [the Constitutional Democrats] that it did not then protest . . . against the revolutionary illusions of Trotskyism . . . simply do not understand or remember the mood which then prevailed among the democratic public at the meetings.' Those, Miliukov said, who would have tried in 1905 to protest against the 'illusions of Trotskyism' would have merely brought discredit upon themselves.[2] This is all the more significant as the 'democratic public' Miliukov had in mind, professional people and enlightened businessmen, was not directly within the orbit of Trotsky's activity. Only very rarely did he emerge from the plebeian Soviet to face a bourgeois public; and even then he did so as the Soviet's envoy. In his chronicle of 1905 Trotsky relates how, during the November strike, he appeared at the home of Baroness Uexküll von Hildebrandt to attend an important political gathering. 'The butler waited for my visiting card, but, woe is me, what visiting card shall a man with a cover name produce? . . . In the reception room there appeared first a student, then a radical lecturer, then the editor of a "solid" periodical, and at last the Baroness herself. They apparently expected a more awe inspiring personality to come "from the workers".' Incidentally, in this turbulent year Trotsky looked so very bourgeois and was so immaculately dressed that some of his Socialist friends were shocked.[3] At any rate, the people gathered at the Baroness's

---

[1] L. Martov, *Istorya Russ. Sots. Dem.* pp. 141–51.

[2] P. Miliukov, *Kak Proshli Vybory vo Vtoroyu Gos. Dumu*, pp. 91–92.

[3] A. Lunacharsky, *Revolutsionnye Siluety*; A. Ziv, op. cit., pp. 50–52.

home missed the thrill of rubbing shoulders with an uncouth revolutionary demagogue. 'I mentioned my name and I was most politely shown in. Drawing back the drapery, I saw a gathering of sixty or seventy persons . . . on one side of the passage—thirty senior military men, among them resplendent Guards officers; on the other side sat the ladies. In the forefront there was a group of black tailcoats', the leading lights of liberalism. Peter Struve, the ex-Marxist, was just urging the Guards officers to defend the Tsar's October Manifesto against attacks from right and left; and as he listened to Struve, Trotsky recalled the words written by Struve himself only seven years before: 'The farther we go to the east in Europe, the more slavish, cowardly and mean is the political conduct of the bourgeoisie.' Then it was Trotsky's turn to address the officers. He told them that the working class, and with it freedom itself, was unarmed. They, the officers, had the keys to the nation's arsenals. It was their duty at the decisive moment to hand these keys to whom they belonged by right, to the people.[1] That senior Guards officers should even have listened to such talk was a measure of the political unsettlement. All the same, his appeal must have sounded to them like a desperate joke. The pyramid of Tsardom could be destroyed, if at all, from its base, not from its top.

From the meetings he hurried to his editorial desks, for he edited and co-edited three papers. The Soviet's *Izvestya* appeared at irregular intervals and was produced with naïve bravado. Each copy was set in the printing shop of another extreme right-wing newspaper, which a Soviet squad raided and requisitioned for the occasion. Apart from this, Trotsky contrived, with the help of Parvus, who had come to Petersburg, to obtain control of a radical Liberal daily *Russkaya Gazeta* (*The Russian Gazette*), which he transformed into a popular organ of militant socialism. Somewhat later he founded, with Parvus and Martov, a great, solid daily *Nachalo* (*The Start*), which was nominally the mouthpiece of Menshevism. In fact, *Nachalo* was mainly Trotsky's paper, for he dictated his terms to the Mensheviks: the paper would advocate his and Parvus's 'permanent revolution'; and it would have no truck with the Constitutional Democrats (Liberals). 'We shall have to agree', so Martov wrote to Axel-

[1] L. Trotsky, *Sochinenya*, vol. ii, book 2, p. 73.

rod, 'to the propaganda of a fairly risky idea, without any counter criticism on our part.'[1] On the contributor's list were the great names of European socialism: Victor Adler, August Bebel, Karl Kautsky, Rosa Luxemburg, Franz Mehring, Klara Zetkin; and it was Trotsky's sweet revenge to open the columns of *Nachalo* to Plekhanov, who had only the year before found it 'morally repugnant' to be Trotsky's neighbour in *Iskra*. Trotsky's papers were much more successful than the Bolshevik *Novaya Zhizn*, edited by Lenin, Gorky, Lunacharsky, and Bogdanov. This is not surprising to anybody who looks through the files and compares them—Trotsky's dailies had far greater verve and pungency.[2] For all their journalistic rivalry, the papers supported one another politically and jointly backed the Soviet.

.   .   .   .

This flowering of plebeian freedom, with the Soviet and the Socialist parties and press working in the open, was soon to be nipped. The government succeeded in putting down sporadic revolts in the army. The working class began partly to succumb to attrition, and partly to be carried away by eagerness to take up arms. Count Witte reimposed press censorship. The Soviet resisted. 'Defend the free word!' Trotsky appealed. 'To the workers the free word is bread and air. The government fears it as one fears a sharp-edged knife.'[3] The next blow fell on the Soviet itself. On 22 November, Khrustalev-Nosar and a few other leaders were arrested. The government waited to see what the Soviet would do. Once again the Soviet was faced with the familiar dilemma. The Social Revolutionaries pressed for reprisals against the Tsar's ministers. Others preferred to retort by a general strike. The Social Democrats were on principle opposed to terroristic reprisals; and they were wary of calling another general strike. Once again it fell to the exuberant Trotsky to plead for cool-headedness and for a further postponement of

---

[1] *Pisma Axelroda i Martova*, pp. 145–6.

[2] Lenin himself later acknowledged this. In May 1917, even before Trotsky joined the Bolshevik party, he proposed that Trotsky be appointed Editor-in-Chief of the Bolshevik popular daily; and he recalled the excellent quality of Trotsky's *Russian Gazette* in 1905. Lenin's proposal was, however, rejected. *Krasnaya Letopis*, no. 3 (14), 1923.

[3] *Russkaya Gazeta*, 17 November 1905; L. Trotsky, *Sochinenya*, vol. ii, book 2, pp. 301–3.

the final trial of strength. He submitted a motion proposing that 'the Soviet of Workers' Deputies temporarily elect a new chairman and continue to prepare for an armed rising'. The Soviet accepted Trotsky's recommendation and elected a three-headed Presidium, consisting of Yanovsky (this was Trotsky's cover name), Sverchkov, and Zlydniev. The preparations for the rising which Trotsky had mentioned had so far been less than rudimentary: two delegates had been sent to establish contact with provincial Soviets. The sinews of insurrection were lacking. The government was determined not to leave the Soviet time for further preparation. Soon a police detachment was posted outside the doors of the Free Economic Society, where the Soviet held its sessions.

It was clear that the days of the Soviet were numbered, and henceforward its activity had mainly a demonstrative character. It was designed to impress on the people the principles and methods of revolution. When Trotsky proposed to the Soviet to stop the enforcement of the eight-hour day, he said: 'We have not won the eight-hour day for the working class, but we have succeeded in winning the working class for the eight-hour day.' And, indeed, a short time before the demand for the eight-hour day had seemed unreal to the Russian, and even to the western European, worker. Yet this claim was to head the list of the Russian workers' demands from now until 1917. Similarly, it was Trotsky's fate in 1905 not to win a proletarian insurrection but to win the proletariat for insurrection. On every occasion he explained why a general strike, which some expected miraculously to overthrow Tsardom, could achieve no fundamental change in society unless the strike led to insurrection; and he went on to explain what was needed to ensure the success of insurrection. He would expound this lesson even from the dock; and the events of the next few months and years would help to drive it home. Those who think of a revolution as a cleverly engineered conspiracy and fail to see behind it the long and slow accumulation of grievances, experiences, and tactical ideas in the minds of the people, may think little of such revolutionary pedagogics; they may regard the Soviet's insurrectionary resolutions as empty threats, which in the short run they were. But the test of the Soviet's and of Trotsky's method lay in the future. The revolution of February 1917 was to put into effect the idea bequeathed from 1905. Its first act was to be a combination of general strike and armed insurrection, carried to success by the same Petersburg workers whom Trotsky had addressed in 1905, and by their sons.

The Soviet's last gesture was the proclamation of a financial boycott of the Tsar. The Soviet called upon the people to stop payment of taxes; to accept only gold coins, no banknotes; and to withdraw deposits from the banks.[1] The 'Financial Manifesto', written by Parvus, denounced the corruptness of the administration, the bankruptcy of its finances, its faked balances, and above all, its unrepresentative character. 'The fear of popular control, which would expose to the whole world the financial insolvency of the government, prompts the government to shelve the convocation of a popular representation. . . . The government has never had the confidence of the people and has received no power from it. At present the government rules over its own country as over a conquered land.' The Manifesto declared that the Russian people would not pay the Tsar's debts, a warning of which the Soviet government was one day to remind the Tsar's western European creditors. The moral and political arguments of the Manifesto sounded convincing, yet as an act of practical policy the boycott merely served to precipitate the clash which the Soviet had been anxious to postpone. Both sides saw in it, not without reason, a substitute for insurrection. The Soviet resorted to it precisely because it was incapable of armed action. 'There is only one way out . . . one way to overthrow the government—to deny it . . . its revenue', the Manifesto declared, in obvious contradiction of the view so frequently expounded that the 'only way' to overthrow Tsardom was by an armed rising. The government, on the other hand, might have been hit almost as hard by a strike of tax-payers as by insurrection. It had to act instantaneously.[2]

[1] The initiative of this boycott came not from the Soviet but from the more moderate All-Russian Association of Peasants, with which the Soviet closely co-operated. The 'Financial Manifesto' was signed by the Soviet, the All-Russian Peasant Association, both factions of the Social Democratic party, the Social Revolutionary party, and the Polish Socialist Party (P.P.S.).

[2] Seven months later, when, after the defeat of the Socialists, the Tsar decided to settle accounts with the Liberals and dispersed the second Duma, in which the Liberals predominated, the latter also called in their famous Viborg Manifesto,

In the afternoon of 3 December, Trotsky presided over a meeting of the Executive which was to prepare the agenda for a plenary session of the Soviet, about to open. He reported on the government's latest strokes: the provincial governors had been given power to declare a state of siege; in some places they had already done so; strikers had been threatened with heavy penalties; the newspapers which had published the 'Financial Manifesto' had been seized; the Minister of the Interior was preparing to re-enforce the ban on the Socialist parties and to imprison their leaders. This time both Mensheviks and Bolsheviks proposed a general strike. In the middle of the debate word was brought that a police raid on the Soviet was imminent. The Executive resolved to go on with its business but to send away a few members who, if the Soviet were to be imprisoned, would continue to act on its behalf. Those so chosen went but came back: the building was already surrounded by Guards, Cossacks, gendarmerie, and police. The Executive then unanimously decided to stay put but to offer no armed resistance against the heavy odds. It continued to deliberate. The trampling of boots and the rattling of sabres came nearer. From the hall on the ground floor, where delegates had assembled for the plenary session, there rose voices of angry protest. From a balcony Trotsky shouted down to the delegates: 'Comrades, offer no resistance. We declare beforehand that only an *agent provocateur* or a policeman will fire a shot here!' He instructed the delegates to break the locks of their revolvers before surrendering them to the police. Then he resumed his chair at the Executive's conference table.

A trade-union spokesman was just declaring his union's readiness to join in the general strike, when a detachment of soldiers and police occupied the corridors. A police officer entered the room where the Executive was sitting and began to read a warrant of arrest. It was now only a question whether the Soviet would carry its own weakness and humiliation with dignity. Resistance was ruled out. But should they surrender meekly, gloomy-faced, without a sign of defiance? Trotsky's pride and his sense of stage effect would not permit him to

for a financial boycott. They did it in almost the same terms in which the Soviet had proclaimed its boycott, and equally without effect. The Viborg Manifesto also called upon the people to refuse recruits to the Tsar's army.

preside over so flat and disheartening a scene. But as he could not afford any serious act of defiance, he could relieve the gloom of the situation only with humour. And so he turned the last scene of this spectacle into a witty burlesque of a bold performance. As the police officer, facing the Executive, began to read the warrant of arrest, Trotsky sharply interrupted him: 'Please do not interfere with the speaker. If you wish to take the floor, you must give your name and I shall ask the meeting whether it wishes to listen to you.'

The perplexed officer, not knowing whether he was being mocked at or whether he should expect armed resistance, waited for the trade-union delegate to end his speech. Then Trotsky gravely asked the Executive whether he should allow the officer to make a statement 'for the sake of information'. The officer read the warrant, and Trotsky proposed that the Executive should acknowledge it and take up the next item on its agenda. Another speaker rose.

'Excuse me', the police officer, disconcerted by this unheard of behaviour, stammered and turned towards Trotsky, as if for help.

'Please do not interfere', Trotsky sharply rebuked him. 'You have had the floor; you have made your statement; we have acknowledged it. Does the meeting wish to have further dealings with the policeman?'

'No!'

'Then, please, leave the hall.'

The officer shuffled his feet, muttered a few words and left. Trotsky called upon the members of the Executive to destroy all documents and not to reveal their names to the police. From the hall below rose the clangour of broken revolver-locks—the delegates were carrying out Trotsky's order.

The police officer re-entered, this time leading a platoon of soldiers. A member of the Executive rose to address the soldiers: The Tsar, he said, was at this very moment breaking the promise of the October Manifesto; and they, the soldiers, were allowing themselves to be used as his tools against the people. The officer, afraid of the effect of the words, hurriedly led the soldiers out into the corridor and shut the door behind them. 'Even through closed doors', the speaker raised his voice, 'the brotherly call of the workers will reach the soldiers.'

At length a strong detachment of police entered, and Trotsky declared 'the meeting of the Executive closed'.

Thus after fifty days ended the epic of the first Soviet in history.[1]

[1] Sverchkov, *Na Zarie Revolutsii*, pp. 163–5; L. Trotsky, *Die Russische Revolution 1905*, pp. 177–9. Some material for this chapter has been derived *inter alia* from V. Voitinsky, *Gody Pobied i Porazhenii*, book 1, pp. 184, 222–3 and *passim*; Garvi, *Vospominanya Sotsial Demokrata*; and S. Yu. Witte, *Vospominanya*, vol. ii.

CHAPTER VI

'Permanent Revolution'

THE liquidation of the Soviet was a political event of the first magnitude; and the Soviet's chief spokesman was an important prisoner of state. Political uncertainty still filled the air. In the prisons, first in Kresty and then in the Peter-Paul fortress, the members of the Soviet were accorded every privilege. Nominally they were kept in isolation; but their cells not being locked, they were free to meet one another, to take walks in the court-yard, to receive books, and under the slightest disguise to engage in intensive political activity.[1]

It was not clear at first whether in its coup against the Soviet the government had not over-reached itself. Petersburg pro-tested through strikes, and Moscow through a general strike, which led to ten days fighting at the barricades. Even after the suppression of the rising in Moscow, the revolution seemed only half defeated. Throughout December and January revolts were flaring up in Siberia, in the Baltic provinces, in the Cau-casus; and punitive expeditions were busy quelling them. In March the elections to the first Duma, boycotted by the Socialists, brought a reverse to the government and striking success to the Constitutional Democrats. It was still doubtful whether the trial of the Soviet would take place at all. The authorities, at any rate, were in no hurry to fix its date. Later it was planned to open the trial on 12 June 1906. In the summer, however, the Tsar recovered confidence, dismissed the semi-Liberal Witte, stopped the talks on the formation of a Constitu-tional Democratic ministry which were in progress, dispersed the Duma, and appointed Stolypin as Prime Minister. The trial became the object of a tug-of-war in the administration; and it was adjourned from month to month till the end of September. The adherents of unmitigated autocracy planned to use the case in order to demonstrate to the Tsar that Witte's weak

[1] The usual prison discipline was so much relaxed that Rosa Luxemburg, herself just released from a prison in Warsaw, was able to pay a 'secret' visit to Parvus and Deutsch in the Peter-Paul fortress. She does not seem to have met Trotsky on this occasion.

policy had been undermining the throne. The quasi-Liberals in the administration were anxious to use the trial for the opposite purpose, and to show that the intrigues of the reactionaries had wrecked the policy of the October Manifesto.

In the meantime the prisoners carefully prepared their defence. At first there were differences over the line of conduct they were to adopt in the dock. On behalf of the Menshevik Central Committee (now about to give up its separate existence) Martov wrote to the prisoners urging them to plead their case with moderation, to base their defence on the October Manifesto, and to demonstrate to the court that the Soviet had acted within limits allowed by that Manifesto. The Soviet should, in particular, refute the charge that it had aimed at armed insurrection. Trotsky indignantly rejected the advice. From his cell he sent through his attorney a reply expressing the 'greatest surprise': 'Not one of the defendants takes this attitude. The programme of the October Manifesto has never been the programme of the Soviet.' The Soviet had met the Tsar's promises with a straight affirmation of its own republican attitude. It was 'a grave political error' on the part of the Central Committee to advise the defendants that they should dissociate themselves from insurrection. All they could and would deny before the Court was that they had engaged in *technical* preparations for a rising; but they must shoulder responsibility for *political* preparation.

The letter, written in a hurry while the attorney was waiting to smuggle it out, was an angry explosion, a retort to an affront. The men of the Soviet, Trotsky insisted, should state their principles, explain their motives, proclaim their objectives; they must use the dock as a political platform rather than defend themselves.[1] In this the Bolshevik Central Committee supported Trotsky; and this was probably why, to quote his old friend Ziv, now again imprisoned with Trotsky, 'his words were full of warm sympathy for the Bolsheviks, to whom he was spiritually akin, and of a hardly suppressed antipathy to the Mensheviks' with whom he was associated.[2] However, Trotsky succeeded in

---

[1] Trotsky's letter to Martov later fell into the hands of the police when Martov was arrested, and it was produced as part of the evidence for the prosecution. The letter is published in L. Trotsky, *Sochinenya*, vol. ii, book 1, pp. 459–60; see also ibid., p. 639, n. 338.   [2] A. Ziv, op. cit., p. 53.

persuading all the defendants to adopt the same defiant attitude, and all endorsed his letter to the Menshevik Central Committee. The only discord was caused by Khrustalev-Nosar, the Soviet's first President, who had behaved ambiguously in the preliminary investigation. The prisoners threatened to brand him publicly, in the dock, as a traitor. Yet despite his former rivalry with Khrustalev-Nosar, Trotsky was anxious to avoid a scandal, which would have lessened the political effect of the trial. He prevailed upon Khrustalev to behave in the dock like all the others and promised him that in return he would be spared the denunciation. Then the chief defendants agreed on their parts in the trial: Khrustalev was to give an account of the Soviet's work under his presidency; Sverchkov was to speak about the Soviet's last days; Knuniants was to describe the attitude of the Social Democratic party, and Avksentiev that of the Social Revolutionaries. Trotsky was to tackle the most dangerous topic: armed insurrection.

Having completed these arrangements, he gave himself to reading and writing. Even the preliminary investigation, conducted by General Ivanov of the gendarmerie, could not divert him: he refused to make any depositions and reserved all that he wanted to say for the public trial. 'Trotsky's prison cell', writes Sverchkov, 'soon became a sort of library. He received all the new books that deserved attention; he read everything; and all through the day, from morning till late night, he was busy with his literary work. "I feel extremely well", he used to say, "I sit and work and am quite sure that nobody can arrest me—in Tsarist Russia this is a rather unusual feeling".'[1] Ziv describes how eagerly Trotsky passed on his books and papers to other prisoners and with what inexhaustible verve he stimulated them intellectually.

A picture of Trotsky taken in his cell some time before the trial shows a man of handsome and cultivated appearance, strikingly 'highbrow'. The face, looking somewhat more regular than it really was, topped by an abundant thatch of black hair and tapering into a little pointed beard, has an air of pensive concentration and self-command. For all its calm, it seems to reflect an inner animation, an intense play of feeling and mood. The thatch of hair, the broad forehead, the raised and strongly

[1] Sverchkov, *Na Zarie Revolutsii*, p. 189.

marked eyebrows, the dark pince-nez, the well-cut moustache and the thrusting chin give to the face a variety of angles emphasizing its inner animation. The prisoner, lean and of average build, is dressed in black. The black suit, the stiff white collar, the white cuffs slightly protruding from the sleeves and the well-polished shoes give the impression of almost studious elegance. This might have been the picture of a prosperous western European *fin-de-siècle* intellectual, just about to attend a somewhat formal reception, rather than that of a revolutionary awaiting trial in the Peter-Paul fortress. Only the austerity of the bare wall and the peephole in the door offer a hint of the real background.

He spent much of his time reading the European classics. 'As I lay on my bunk I absorbed them with the same physical delight with which the gourmet sips choice wine or inhales the fragrant smoke of a fine cigar. . . . It was then that I first truly acquainted myself with the great masters of the French novel in their originals.'[1] This love of the French novel, classical and modern, was to remain with him for life. He had by now mastered French and German and he spoke both languages extremely well, although he used German more easily for economics and politics and preferred French as a literary language. He was now far from those days spent in the prisons of Kherson and Odessa, when he had groped laboriously towards Marx's theories. He was no longer learning Marxism—he was teaching it; and his mind was free to roam at large over the expanses of European literature.

. . . .

In the quietness of his cell he pondered the lessons of the last stormy months; and he set down his conclusions in essays and pamphlets, one of which was to become exceptionally important. Nearly all of his writings of this period are reproduced in his *Works*, except for a study on land rent, which was lost and never saw the light. In his autobiography he describes this as a 'tragic loss' to himself. How far his regret is justified we cannot say. His grasp of economics was sure; but, unlike Lenin or Bukharin, he did not distinguish himself as an abstract economic theorist, and it may be doubted whether he had an original contribution to make to so highly specialized a subject as the

[1] L. Trotsky, *Moya Zhizn*, vol. i, p. 216.

Marxian conception of land rent. Whatever the truth, some of his political writings of this year were of greater weight and originality than any work of his on land rent was likely to be. We may leave aside his *Mr. Struve in Politics*, a brochure, published under the pen-name N. Takhotsky, which gained great popularity. This was another broadside against liberalism, mordantly effective but adding little to a familiar stock of arguments. More important was the *History of the Soviet (Istorya Sovieta Rabochikh Deputatov)*, a work written by several hands and edited by Trotsky. He conceived the idea of it as soon as the doors of the prison had closed behind him; and he contributed a chapter summing up the Soviet's role:

> Urban Russia [so he concluded] was too narrow a base for the struggle. The Soviet tried to wage the struggle on a national scale, but it remained above all a Petersburg institution. . . . there is no doubt that in the next upsurge of revolution, such Councils of Workers will be formed all over the country. An All-Russian Soviet of Workers, organized by a national congress . . . will assume the leadership. . . History does not repeat itself. The new Soviet will not have to go through the experiences of these fifty days once again. Yet from these fifty days it will be able to deduce its entire programme of action. . .: revolutionary cooperation with the army, the peasantry, and the plebeian parts of the middle classes; abolition of absolutism; destruction of the military machine of absolutism; part disbandment and part overhaul of the army; abolition of the police and of the bureaucratic apparatus; the eight hour day; the arming of the people, above all, of the workers; the transformation of the Soviets into organs of revolutionary, urban self-government; the formation of Peasant Soviets to be in charge of the agrarian revolution on the spot; elections to the Constituent Assembly. . . . It is easier to formulate such a plan than to carry it out. But if victory is destined for the revolution, the proletariat cannot but assume this role. It will achieve a revolutionary performance, the like of which the world has never seen.
>
> The history of these fifty days will be a pale page in the great book of the proletariat's struggle and victory.[1]

This was indeed the programme for 1917. However, these writings were merely sketches and essays preparatory to his chief work of this period, *Itogi i Perspektivy—Dvizhushchie Sily Revolutsii (The Balance and the Prospects—the Moving Forces of the*

---

[1] L. Trotsky, *Sochinenya*, vol. ii, book 1, p. 206.

Revolution). As the fundamental statement of 'Trotskyism', this was to be for decades the object of a fierce controversy.[1] He wrote it as a long concluding chapter to his book *Nasha Revolutsia* (*Our Revolution*), which was a collection of essays and chronicles on 1905; and in it he gave a full, almost mathematically succinct formulation of the theory of permanent revolution. He reviewed recent critical events in the perspective of age-old trends in Russian history; and then, turning to the international scene, he defined the place of the Russian Revolution in modern European history; and he forecast, in broad outline, the impact of the Russian Revolution upon the world and the world's impact upon it. Within this framework he explicitly opposed his conception to the views then current among Marxists. This was the most radical restatement, if not revision, of the prognosis of Socialist revolution undertaken since Marx's *Communist Manifesto*, that is since 1847. For this reason alone, it deserves to be summarized in some detail.

Marxists, we know, generally viewed the Russian upheaval as a bourgeois revolution, whose purpose it was to overthrow Tsardom and to clear away its semi-feudal heritage. Only after the completion of this phase, it was held, could a modern industrial capitalist society develop fully in Russia; and only in such a society, after the wealth and the productive resources of the country had grown and expanded, would revolutionary socialism rise to power and begin to satisfy the egalitarian aspirations of the masses. Marxists took it for granted that in the old capitalist countries of the West the ground for Socialist revolution was ready. There, in the West, they expected socialism to win, while the East was still engaged in its bourgeois revolutions. These were axioms commonly held by western European Socialists and Russian Mensheviks and Bolsheviks. The controversy between the latter centred on the question which social class, the bourgeoisie or the workers, would play the leading part in the Russian 'bourgeois' revolution.

Trotsky questioned most of these assumptions. He agreed with the Bolsheviks that the Russian bourgeoisie was incapable of

---

[1] The summary and the quotations are taken from the Moscow (March 1919) reprint of this work. The author had the original 1906 edition (now a bibliographical rarity) in his library in Warsaw, which he lost during the Second World War. The 1919 edition is a faithful reprint of the original, prefaced by a special foreword.

revolutionary leadership, and that the industrial working class was cast for that role. He now went farther and argued that the working class would by its own political supremacy in the revolution be compelled to carry the Russian Revolution from the bourgeois to the Socialist phase, even before the Socialist upheaval had begun in the West. This would be one aspect of the 'permanence' of the revolution—it would be impossible to confine the upheaval to bourgeois limits.

What had destined Russia to become the pioneer of socialism? Why could the Russian middle classes not bring their revolution to a consummation, as the French had done in the eighteenth century? The answer lay in the peculiarities of Russian history. The Russian state, half-Asian, half-European, was based on a slowly evolving, undifferentiated, primitive society. The military pressure of superior European powers, not the impulses coming from Russian society, moulded that state. From its earliest days, when it struggled against Tartar domination and then against Polish-Lithuanian and Swedish invasions, the state exacted from the Russian people the most intense exertions; it absorbed a disproportionately high share of the social wealth produced. It thereby impeded the already slow formation of privileged classes and the even slower growth of productive resources. Yet the state needed a hierarchical organization, and to achieve it it had to stimulate social differentiation. Thus Tsardom curbed and at the same time fostered the development of Russian society. This fact had prompted Miliukov to say that whereas in the West the Estates had created the State, in Russia the State had brought into being the Estates. Trotsky dismissed this as a one-sided view, for 'state-power could not at will manufacture social groups and classes'. Nevertheless, so prodigious had been the rulers' initiative and so sluggish and torpid had been Russian society that in Russia even 'capitalism appeared as the child of the state'.[1] The state, and not private enterprise, had laid the foundations of modern industry. Even Russian thought and opinion appeared as the state's offspring. In modern times, fiscal and military protectionism and European financial assistance secured to Tsardom a degree of modernization which further increased its power over society. The Liberals held that this prodigious preponderance of the state

[1] L. Trotsky, *Itogi i Perspektivy*, p. 16.

made revolution impossible. On the contrary, it made it inevitable.

One outcome of this trend was that Russia entered the twentieth century with an extremely feeble urban middle class. The Russian town itself was the product of the last few decades. Under Peter the Great, the city dwellers were only 3 per cent. of the total population. After the Napoleonic wars they formed 4½ per cent., and even towards the end of the nineteenth century only 13 per cent. The old Russian town, unlike its European counterpart, had been not a centre of industry and commerce but a military administrative unit or a fortress. (Moscow had been the Tsar's village.) The Russian town—like the Asian— did not produce; it merely consumed. It neither accumulated wealth nor evolved a division of labour. Thus were aggravated all the cruel handicaps which Russia's severe climate and enormous spaces had imposed upon the growth of her civilization. In the middle of the nineteenth century, capitalism found in Russia not the urban handicraft from which, in the West, modern industry had sprung, but rural cottage craft. This fact had one striking political consequence, already noted by Parvus: Russia possessed no social class comparable to that concentrated mass of urban craftsmen who had formed the backbone of the French middle class and had made the great French Revolution. Russia's four million craftsmen (*kustari*) were scattered over the country-side.

Even the advance of modern industry did not significantly strengthen the middle class, because Russian industry was, in the main, fostered by foreign investment. In their own countries, the Western bourgeoisie had rallied to the banner of liberalism. In Russia, they were interested mainly in the security of their investments, which seemed best guaranteed by 'strong', that is absolutist, government. Thus, the economic preponderance of the state, the numerical weakness of the middle classes, the predominance of foreign capital in industry, the absence of a middle-class tradition—all combined to make Russian bourgeois liberalism stillborn. Yet modern industry, which did not significantly enhance the middle class, brought the proletariat to the fore. The more belatedly Russian industry expanded, the more readily did it adopt the most advanced forms of organization that had elsewhere been developed slowly and laboriously. The few modern factories that Russia did possess were larger and more concentrated than any western European or even American establishments. Consequently the political strength of the Russian proletariat, its capacity to organize itself and to act *en masse*, was all the more concentrated.

This alignment of the social classes entailed a radical change in the familiar patterns of revolution. European revolutionary history knew three landmarks: 1789, 1848, and 1905. In 1789 the French bourgeoisie, strong and confident, led the struggle against absolutism. True, it was often driven forward against its will by Jacobin plebeians, the *sans culottes*. But these were a shapeless, incoherent mass, lacking a consistent programme of their own. Only sporadically could they oppose themselves to the wealthy bourgeoisie, which, after the brief interval of Robespierre's dictatorship, regained ascendancy. No modern industrial working class was there to challenge its leadership.[1]

By 1848 the centre of bourgeois revolution had shifted to Germany and Austria. But the German middle class had neither the strength nor the self-confidence of the French. The courage which it needed to oppose absolutism was blighted by fear of the rising proletariat. The plebeian mass of 1848 was no longer an angry, confused lower middle class with a pauper-like fringe, but a class of factory workers, groping towards political independence and opposed to the employers even more directly than to the monarchy. However, the working class, already strong enough to inspire fear in the bourgeoisie, was still too feeble and timid to guide the nation. The revolution foundered because it lacked leadership: the bourgeoisie was *already* and the proletariat was *still* too weak to assume it.

Finally, in Russia in 1905 the wheel had turned full circle. The revolution was no longer leaderless. The bourgeoisie was both too feeble and too frightened of the proletariat to direct the war against autocracy. This mission had fallen to the industrial workers, who were much stronger than their German counterparts of 1848, and had avidly assimilated the last word in European socialism.[2]

It followed from this, Trotsky went on, that the revolution,

---

[1] Many years later Trotsky held that this view, which he had accepted from Marx, exaggerated the revolutionary virtues of the French bourgeoisie even in the eighteenth century.   [2] L. Trotsky, *Itogi i Perspektivy*, p. 33.

if it succeeded, would end in the seizure of power by the proletariat. 'Every political party deserving the name aims at
seizing governmental power in order to put the state at the
service of the class whose interests it expresses.'[1] The Mensheviks argued that in backward Russia, 'unripe' for socialism,
the workers must help the bourgeoisie to seize power. Against
this Trotsky boldly declared: 'In a country economically backward, the proletariat can take power earlier than in countries
where capitalism is advanced. . . . The Russian revolution
produces conditions, in which power may . . . pass into the
hands of the proletariat before the politicians of bourgeois
liberalism have had the chance to show their statesman-like
genius to the full.'[2] He brushed aside arguments based on familiar Marxist texts about the sequence of bourgeois and Socialist
revolutions: 'Marxism is above all a method of analysis of social
relations, not of texts.'

His critics were soon to accuse him of wanting Russia to
'jump over' the bourgeois phase of development, and of advocating a policy which would oppose the industrial workers, a
small minority, to the rest of the nation. Trotsky tried to forestall these criticisms. He did not gainsay, he stated, the bourgeois character of the Russian Revolution, in this sense at least,
that its immediate task was to free Russia from the dead weight
of her feudal past, to accomplish that is, what the bourgeoisie
had accomplished in England and France. But he insisted
—and in this he differed from other Socialists—that the revolution would not stop at this. Having uprooted the feudal institutions, it would proceed to break the backbone of capitalism and
to establish a proletarian dictatorship.[3] He did not rule out a
governmental coalition of Socialists and representatives of the
peasantry; but to the latter he assigned the role of junior
partners. The representatives of the workers 'will give content
to the policy of the government and will form a homogeneous
majority in it'.[4]

Was this, then, to be a dictatorship of a minority? More by
implication than explicitly, he envisaged that the revolution
itself would indeed be carried out by the workers alone. It was
in the towns that the old order must be overthrown; and there

---

[1] L. Trotsky, *Itogi i Perspektivy*, p. 34.   [2] Ibid., pp. 34–35.
[3] Ibid., pp. 39–40.   [4] Ibid., p. 40.

the industrial proletariat would be master. 'Many layers of the toiling mass, especially in the country, will be drawn into the revolution and for the first time obtain political organization only after . . . the urban proletariat has taken the helm of government.'[1] But even though the overthrow of the old order and the seizure of power would be the work of a minority, the revolution could not survive and consolidate itself unless it received the genuine support of the majority, i.e. of the peasants. '*The proletariat in power will appear before the peasantry as its liberator.*'[2] It would, among other things, sanction the seizure of the large estates by the peasants. The French peasant had followed Napoleon, because the latter guaranteed his small-holding against the émigré landlord. For the same reason the Russian peasant would back a proletarian government. That government, therefore, would and would not represent the rule of a minority. The proletarian minority would form its core and in all important matters hold the initiative. But it would rule in the interest, and enjoy the willing support, of an overwhelming majority.

His conception of the peasantry's place in the revolution—in a sense the crux of 'Trotskyism'—was to be the centre of many controversies. The stock accusation levelled against Trotsky is that he 'underrated' the revolutionary potentiality of the Russian peasantry, and denied the possibility of an 'alliance' between it and the proletariat. For this charge no support can be found in his own words. We have seen how emphatically he stated that 'the proletariat in power will appear before the peasantry as its liberator'. In insisting that the Socialists would not merely expropriate the landlords but sanction the seizure of their land by the peasants, he went farther than most Russian Socialists had so far gone. The Mensheviks held that the municipalities should take over the gentry's land. Most Bolsheviks, especially Lenin, advocated, in general terms, nationalization, but not partition of the land.[3] If the 'alliance' with the peasantry is to be understood as the

[1] Ibid., p. 41.
[2] Ibid., p. 42.
[3] Of the now known Bolshevik leaders only Stalin pleaded in 1906 that the party should pronounce itself in favour of the sharing out of the large estates among the peasants. J. Stalin, *Sochinenya*, vol. i, pp. 214–35, 236–8. See also I. Deutscher, *Stalin, a Political Biography*, pp. 82–83.

Bolsheviks understood it in and after 1917, then Trotsky certainly stood for it in 1906.

Yet it is true that he did not consider the peasants, any more than other small proprietors or the petty bourgeoisie at large, as an independent revolutionary force. He saw them as an amorphous, scattered mass, with narrow local interests, incapable of co-ordinated national action. It was the peasantry's fate that its rebellions, even in the rare cases when they were successful, led to the rise of new oppressive dynasties or were exploited by other classes. In modern society, the peasants were politically even more helpless than before: 'the history of capitalism is the history of the subordination of the country to the town.'[1] In the town there were only two poles of independent power, actual or potential: the big bourgeoisie, with its concentrated wealth, and the proletariat, with its concentrated capacity to produce wealth. The peasants, despite their far greater numerical strength, had to follow either the one or the other. On the scales of a parliamentary election, the vote of one peasant weighs as much as does the vote of one worker. In revolutionary situations this equality is illusory. A thousand railwaymen on strike are politically more effective than a million scattered villagers. The role of modern social classes is determined not by numbers, but by social function and specific weight. The proletariat must win the support of the peasantry— without this it cannot hold power. But the only way for it to attract the mass of small rural proprietors is to show vigour and determination in the contest for power. The weak are attracted by the strong.

This view, so explicitly stated, marked a radical departure from the then accepted Marxist notions, even though it had been strongly implied in Marx's own writings. (Trotsky's aversion to 'analysis of texts' prevented him from dabbling in helpful quotations.) It was a common Marxist notion that the working class could not and ought not to try to seize power before it had become a majority of the nation. It was also a deep-seated illusion of popular socialism that in modern countries the industrial working class would gradually expand into a majority, as it had done in England.[2] With this illusion Trotsky

[1] L. Trotsky, *Itogi i Perspektivy*, p. 43.
[2] In the foreword to his *Works*, written in 1946 (*Sochinenya*, vol. i, pp. xiv–xv),

broke radically: the revolution, he wrote, would conquer long before the majority of the nation had become transformed into proletarians.[1]

His appraisal of the peasantry was no less sharply opposed to current opinion. The Mensheviks tended to view the small rural proprietor as a prop of reaction. Their hope was in a coalition between the working class and the Liberal bourgeoisie. Lenin, on the contrary, reckoned with the muzhiks' revolutionary energy; but, unlike Trotsky, he would not prejudge its potentialities. He kept his mind open and waited to see whether the peasantry would not form its own revolutionary party, with whom the Socialists would have to deal as with an equal partner. At the beginning of 1905, to the amusement of Plekhanov, Trotsky, and Martov, Lenin approached with intense curiosity and exaggerated hope the enigmatic figure of Gapon. He wondered whether that priest, the son of a Cossack, who had led the workers of the capital to the Winter Palace and thereby helped to open the sluices for the revolution, was not the harbinger of an independent and radical peasant movement.[2] Lenin's formula of a 'democratic dictatorship of the proletariat and the peasantry' seemed broader and more cautious than Trotsky's 'proletarian dictatorship', and better suited for an association of Socialists and agrarian revolutionaries. In 1917 events in Russia were to confirm Trotsky's prognostication. In the twenties, however, the problem was to be posed anew in connexion with Communist policy in China; and nearly half a century after Trotsky had formulated his view, it would be posed over and over again by the revolutions in Asia, in which the relation between the urban and the rural elements would be more intricate and blurred than it was in Russia.

So far we have dealt with the domestic aspect of the revolution. Its international and domestic aspects were, in Trotsky's view, closely interwoven. Although the peasants would by

Stalin stated that in the era of 1905 he 'accepted the thesis familiar among Marxists, according to which one of the chief conditions for the victory of the socialist revolution was that the proletariat should become the majority of the population. Consequently in those countries in which the proletariat did not yet form the majority of the population, because capitalism had not sufficiently developed, the victory of socialism was impossible.'   [1] L. Trotsky, op. cit., p. 55.

[2] Lenin, *Sochinenya*, vol. viii, pp. 384–8; Trotsky, *Sochinenya*, vol. ii, book 1, pp. 54–57; see also Parvus on Gapon, *Iskra*, no. 85 (27 January 1905).

themselves be unable 'to squeeze out the workers',[1] a conflict
between the two classes was looming ahead, a conflict in
which the proletariat might forfeit the position of acknowledged
leader of the nation. As long as the revolution was engaged in
breaking the rule and the power of the landlord, it would have
the entire peasantry on its side. But after that—'two major
features of the proletarian policy, its *collectivism* and its *internationalism*, would meet with [the peasants'] opposition'.[2] Thus,
in spite of its initial strength the new régime would discover its
weakness as soon as it had carried the revolution, in the country
as well as in town, from the bourgeois to the socialist phase. It
would then be compelled to seek salvation in international
revolution. Russia's industrial poverty and backwardness would
anyhow prove formidable obstacles to the building of a Socialist
economy; and only with the help of the Socialist West could
these obstacles be broken and removed. Finally, the hostility of a
Conservative Europe would force the Russian revolution to
carry the struggle beyond Russia's frontiers.

Without the direct state support of the European proletariat, the
working class of Russia will not be able to remain in power and
transform its temporary rule into a stable and prolonged socialist
dictatorship. . . .[3]

This will from the very outset impart an international character
to the development of the events and open the broadest perspectives:
*the working class of Russia, by leading in the political emancipation will
rise to a height unknown in history, gather into its hands colossal forces and
means and become the initiator of the liquidation of capitalism on a global
scale. . . .*[4]

If the Russian proletariat, having temporarily gained power,
does not carry the revolution of its own initiative on to the ground of
Europe, then the feudal and bourgeois reaction will force it to do so.[5]

It will be precisely the fear of the proletarian rising which will
force the bourgeois parties, voting prodigious sums for military
expenditure, solemnly to demonstrate for peace, to dream of international chambers of conciliation and even of the organization of
the United States of Europe—all miserable declamation, which can
neither do away with the antagonism of the powers, nor with armed
conflicts. . . . European war inevitably means European revolution.[6]

[1] L. Trotsky, *Itogi i Perspektivy*, p. 42.   [2] Ibid., p. 46.
[3] Ibid., p. 71.   [4] Ibid., p. 73 (Trotsky's italics).
[5] Ibid., p. 74.   [6] Ibid., p. 77.

He went on to denounce the 'propagandist conservatism' of the Socialist parties, which could impede the struggle of the proletariat for power; and he expressed the hope that the Russian Revolution would shake up international socialism, just as the events of 1905 had already stimulated the Austrian and Prussian proletariat to claim universal suffrage by means of general strikes. 'The revolution in the east infects the western proletariat with revolutionary idealism and imparts to it the desire to speak Russian with its enemies.'[1] He concluded his argument as follows:

> The Russian proletariat . . . will meet with organized hostility on the part of world reaction and with readiness on the part of the world proletariat to lend the revolution organized assistance. Left to itself, the working class of Russia will inevitably be crushed by the counter-revolution at the moment when the peasantry turns its back upon the proletariat. Nothing will be left to the workers but to link the fate of their own political rule, and consequently the fate of the whole Russian revolution, with that of the socialist revolution in Europe. The Russian proletariat will throw into the scales of the class struggle of the entire capitalist world that colossal state-political power, which the temporary circumstances of the Russian bourgeois revolution will give it. With state power in its hands, with the counter-revolution behind its back, with the European reaction in front of it, it will address to its brothers all over the world the old appeal, which this time will be the call to the last onslaught: Proletarians of all lands, unite![2]

The tenor of Trotsky's argument suggests that he envisaged the European revolution as a single, continuous process. There was thus in his prognostication a fatal admixture of illusion, at least as regards the tempo of the whole process. Here Trotsky was paying his tribute to a belief then commonly accepted by European Socialists, and authoritatively voiced by Karl Kautsky, the intellectual guide of the International, that the European economy and society were already 'ripe' for socialism. Yet, even in 1906, Trotsky, for all the categorical tenor of his forecast, was cautious enough to write that it was impossible to prophesy in what manner the revolution would expand from Russia, whether it would strike out through Poland into Germany and Austria, or whether it would turn eastwards to Asia.[3]

[1] Ibid., p. 80.   [2] Ibid.
[3] Ibid., pp. 74–77.

Not for a moment did Trotsky imagine, however, that the Russian Revolution could survive in isolation for decades. It may therefore be said, as Stalin was to say twenty years later, that he 'underrated' the internal resources and vitality of revolutionary Russia. The miscalculation, obvious in retrospect, is less surprising when one considers that the view expressed by Trotsky in 1906 was to become the common property of all Bolshevik leaders, including Stalin, in the years between 1917 and 1924. Hindsight, naturally, dwells on this particular error so much that the error overshadows the forecast as a whole. True enough, Trotsky did not foresee that Soviet Russia would survive in isolation for decades. But who, apart from him, foresaw, in 1906, the existence of Soviet Russia? Moreover, Trotsky himself, indirectly and unknowingly, provided in advance the clue to his own error—it is found in his appraisal of the Russian peasantry. Its political helplessness and lack of independence best account for the survival of a collectivist régime in a country in which the individualistic peasantry formed the overwhelming majority, and also for the forcible and relatively successful imposition of collectivism upon it.

In apparent contradiction of his own view, Trotsky then stated that the proletarian régime would break down as soon as the muzhiks turned against it. This error, if an error it was, was intimately bound up with his conception of the revolution, as he stated it in 1905–6. It did not occur to him that a proletarian party would in the long run rule and govern an enormous country against the majority of the people. He did not foresee that the revolution would lead to the prolonged rule of a minority. The possibility of such a rule was implicit in his theory; but its actuality would still have appeared to him, as to nearly all his contemporaries, incompatible with socialism. In fact, he did not imagine, in spite of all he had written about Lenin's 'Jacobinism', that the revolution would seek to escape from its isolation and weakness into totalitarianism.

If the trend of his thought is considered as a whole, then it may be said that hardly ever has any political prophecy appeared to be alternately so brilliantly confirmed and so utterly confounded and then in a way confirmed again by the onrush of new historical cataclysms. This is especially true of that part of Trotsky's prognostication in which he spoke about the impulse Russia would give to world revolution. Over the decades events were to throw ever new light on this. In 1917 and after, amid the crumbling of thrones and the thunder of upheaval, his words seemed to be coming true with uncanny accuracy. Then came the reflux of communism in Europe; Bolshevik Russia withdrew within her shell; and Trotsky stood discredited and derided as the prophet of the utterly absurd, of 'the patently impossible and vain'. But then again, in the aftermath of the Second World War, his voice seems posthumously to reverberate in the clash of two worlds. More than ever Russia appears to the West as 'having risen to a height unknown in history, gathered into her hands colossal forces and means, and become the initiator of the liquidation of capitalism on a global scale'. We cannot run too much ahead of our story and consider here whether or to what an extent this is Russia's real role. Nor can we do more here than hint at the contrast between Trotsky's vision and its apparent materialization. He expected the new régime in Russia to become the initiator and inspirer, but not the master, of international revolution; and he saw the 'liquidation of capitalism' beyond Russia as the genuine achievement of the Western working classes rather than as the by-product of a victorious advance of Russian armies.

But no matter how the course of events has swayed and diverged from the route he had mapped out in 1904–6, by the middle of the present century he seemed once again to have grasped the 'main chance of things' correctly. Whether one reads his message with horror or hope, whether one views him as the inspired herald of a new age surpassing all history in achievement and grandeur, or as the oracle of ruin and woe, one cannot but be impressed by the sweep and boldness of his vision. He reconnoitred the future as one who surveys from a towering mountain top a new and immense horizon and points to vast, uncharted landmarks in the distance. True enough, from his coign of vantage, he could not take in the whole landscape below: patches of dense fog enveloped parts of it: and the play of distance and perspective looked different from what is seen in the valley. He misjudged the exact direction of a major road; he saw two or more separate landmarks merged into one; and he grievously overlooked one of the rocky ravines into which one day he himself would slip to his doom.

But his compensation was the unique magnitude of his horizon. Compared with this vision, which Trotsky drew in his cell in the fortress, the political predictions made by his most illustrious and wisest contemporaries, including Lenin and Plekhanov, were timid or muddle-headed.

In *Balance and Prospects* Trotsky reached a peak in his development. The months in prison, in the course of which he pondered and digested recent experience, were for him the transition from early to mature manhood, a transition as sudden and rapid as had been his jumps from childhood to adolescence and from adolescence to adult life. In this brochure of eighty pages was the sum and substance of the man. For the rest of his days, as leader of the revolution, as founder and head of an army, as protagonist of a new International· and then as hunted exile, he would defend and elaborate the ideas he had put in a nutshell in 1906. Similarly, Karl Marx spent his whole life developing and drawing conclusions from the ideas he had advanced in the *Communist Manifesto*, his early and brief statement of doctrine.

Trotsky's work might have been for the Russian party what the *Communist Manifesto* had, ever since 1848, been for European socialism: a grand prospectus of revolution and a stirring call to action. Yet the influence of Trotsky's work was almost negligible, despite the controversy it aroused. The reasons for this were in part adventitious, in part inherent in the author's attitude. No sooner had the book appeared, in 1906, than it was seized and confiscated by the police. The few copies that reached readers aroused little interest, even though the author was just then, about the time of the Soviet's trial, very much in the public eye. Most of the book was made up of reprints of old essays; and readers looking for new viewpoints easily missed the one new and important chapter in it.[1] It seems established that Lenin, for instance, never read this work before 1919, although once or twice he referred to it disparagingly on the basis of second-hand quotations.[2] By the time the book went to the printers, the revolution was fizzling out. From a practical standpoint, Socialists were more inclined to weigh the chances of triumphant reaction than to contemplate the vistas of victorious revolution.

---

[1] L. Trotsky, *Permanentnaya Revolutsia*, pp. 39–42.

[2] See Yoffe's farewell letter to Trotsky (16 November 1927) in *The Trotsky Archives* (Harvard).

Thus *Balance and Prospects* appeared either too soon or too late to make a stronger impression than it did. Finally, neither of the two main currents in the party wished to identify itself with the novel and provocative forecast. The Mensheviks had recovered from the radicalism of 1905; they were impatient to shake off Trotsky's influence; and they considered this new epitome of 'Trotskyism' as an exercise in day-dreaming. The Bolsheviks were not in a mood to give serious attention to any prospects of revolution drawn by the spokesman of Menshevism. A lone wolf within his own party, Trotsky was condemned to relative futility just when he might have been most effective. Nor was the accident of his age without effect. He had gained enormous popularity among the rank and file and among non-party workers; but in the eyes of active propagandists and organizers, to whom his doctrine was meant to appeal, he was still too young to be accepted as a prophet.[1]

Despite this lack of response, he was already strongly aware that he was taking his place among the makers of history; and it was with this awareness that, on 19 September 1906, he went into the dock.

.   .   .   .

The trial was full of fight and heat. It did not take place before a military tribunal, as had been expected; and so the shadow of death did not hang over the dock. But the defendants were prepared for long terms of hard labour. The court was surrounded by masses of Cossacks and soldiers. Within the precincts, where a state of siege had been declared, it swarmed with gendarmes with drawn sabres in their hands. Only a hundred persons, among them Trotsky's parents, were admitted to the proceedings. Two score attorneys conducted the defence. In the course of several weeks, 250 witnesses from every walk of life gave evidence on every detail of the Soviet's activity. From the first day the court was flooded by resolutions, signed by scores of thousands of workers, protesting against the trial. 'We, the workers of the Obukhov plant', ran a typical protest, 'declare ... that the Soviet does not consist of a handful of conspirators but of true representatives of the proletariat of Petersburg ... and that if our esteemed comrade P. A. Zlydniev is guilty, then we are all guilty, and we confirm this by our own signatures.'[2]

[1] A. Lunacharsky, *Revolutsionnye Siluety*.
[2] L. Trotsky, *Sochinenya*, vol. ii, book 2, pp. 142–3.

The sentiment of the anti-Tsarist public expressed itself in a thousand incidents. 'On the benches of the defendants there constantly appeared newspapers, letters, boxes with sweet-meats, and flowers. No end of flowers! In their buttonholes, in their hands, on their knees, and all over the dock—flowers. The presiding judge has not the courage to remove this fragrant disorder. In the end, even the officers of the gendarmerie and the clerks, altogether "demoralized" by the atmosphere in the hall, carry the flowers from the public to the dock.'[1] At one moment the defendants rose to pay homage to the memory of one of them who had been executed before the trial. The attorneys and the public, too, rose to their feet; and so did the embarrassed officers of the gendarmerie and the police. The aftermath of the revolution was still in the air.

'We have decided to take part in the present extraordinary trial only because we think it necessary . . . to explain publicly the truth about the activity and the significance of the Soviet.' Thus Zlydniev, on behalf of all accused, stated at the opening of the proceedings. The defendants so conducted themselves that they aroused respect, and at times a grudging sympathy, even among their enemies. The police brought against some of the members of the Soviet—Trotsky was not among them—the charge that they had embezzled funds collected from workers. The charge brought forth such a hail of protests from factories and was so effectively exploded in the court that the prosecution itself dismissed it as slanderous. So striking was the evidence that the Soviet had had overwhelming popular sup-port for the general strikes and demonstrations it had called, that the prosecution could not base its case on these activities and concentrated instead on the count of insurrection.[2]

On 4 October Trotsky rose to speak on this subject. He modelled his speech on the pleas which Marx and Lassalle had made when in 1848 they had been confronted with identical charges, but on this occasion he perhaps surpassed his masters. He began with the statement that the issues of republic and

---

[1] L. Trotsky, *Sochinenya*, vol. ii, book 2, p. 141.

[2] A contemporary correspondence from Petersburg in *The Times* stated: 'The remarkable feature about the revolutionary gathering [of October 1905] was its perfect organization. . . . On the other hand, the procession of the "Whites" was a mere rabble of butchers' boys, shopkeepers, beadles, and a few enthusiasts.' *The Times*, 1 November 1905.

insurrection had never figured on the Soviet agenda, so that in strict law the charge was groundless; but that this was so only because the Soviet had taken its own attitude in these matters for granted and had had no need to discuss them. He at once took the bull—the problem of political force—by the horns:

> Did the Soviet . . . consider itself justified in using force and repressive measures in certain instances? To this question, posed in this general form, my answer is: Yes. . . . In the conditions created by a political general strike, the essence of which was that it paralyzed the mechanism of government, the old governmental force that had long outlived its day and against which the political strike was directed, proved itself completely incapable of undertaking anything. Even with the barbarous means which alone were at its disposal, it was not in a position to maintain and regulate public order. In the meantime the strike had thrown hundreds of thousands of workers from the factories into the street and had awakened them to public political life. Who could take over the direction of those masses, who could carry discipline into their ranks? Which organ of the old governmental power? The police? The gendarmerie? . . . I find only one answer: nobody, except the Council of Workers' Deputies.'[1]

The Soviet could not but begin to assume quasi-governmental functions. It refrained from coercion, however, and preferred to act by persuasion. The prosecution had produced in its evidence only a few minute, comic rather than tragic, cases of violence. The defence might plead that the Soviet had acted within the limits permitted by the Tsar's own Manifesto; but it preferred frankly to proclaim its democratic, republican conviction. Let the court decide whether the freedom promised in the Manifesto was for monarchists only or for republicans and Socialists as well. 'Let the Manifesto now proclaim to us through the court's verdict: you have denied my reality, but I do exist for you as well as for the whole country.' Otherwise the defendants would be convicted for their beliefs not for their deeds.

Trotsky then went on to prove that, in certain circumstances, insurrection which the court considered illegal must develop from the general strike, which the court held to be legal. Insurrection had in a sense begun with the general strike. The strike had paralysed the existing government and required another

[1] L. Trotsky, op. cit., pp. 163–4.

government to step into its place. Something like dual power had come into existence. The prosecution professed to defend the existing order against the Soviet. Yet this order, in so far as it was expressed in the Tsar's Manifesto, had itself been the product of a general strike—it was in response to the October strike that the Tsar had proclaimed it. The legal as well as the real basis under the old order had been shattered. Two governments had in fact existed, each struggling to assert itself, each endeavouring to win the army for itself. Their collision was inevitable. 'Did the workers of Petersburg become aware of this? Yes. Did the proletariat, did the Soviet, believe the open clash of these two powers to be unavoidable? Yes.' And not only they—the middle classes, too, realized this and in many cases demonstrated their sympathy for the Soviet. It was the old government not the Soviet that represented anarchy and bloodshed. It was a requirement of order that the old government be overthrown; and only insurrection could overthrow it.

What was the nature of the insurrection? Trotsky asked. The Russian code, which was a hundred years old, had known only the notion of a conspiracy against the government, staged in secret by a handful of rebels. This had, indeed, been the only form of rising possible in bygone times. The new insurrection was a popular rising, never envisaged by the code. The law was lagging behind the times; and it did not give the prosecution even technical ground for the charge against the Soviet.

And yet our activity was revolutionary! And yet we did prepare ourselves for an armed rising! A rising of the masses is not made, gentlemen the judges. It makes itself of its own accord. It is the result of social relations and conditions and not of a scheme drawn up on paper. A popular insurrection cannot be staged. It can only be foreseen. For reasons that were as little dependent on us as on Tsardom, an open conflict had become inevitable. It came nearer with every day. To prepare for it meant for us to do everything possible to reduce to a minimum the number of victims of this unavoidable conflict.

The Soviet tried to organize the masses and to explain to them the meaning of events. It was not preparing an insurrection; it was preparing itself for an insurrection. True, the masses had no arms. But—'no matter how important weapons may be, it is not in them, gentlemen the judges, that great power resides.

No! Not the ability of the masses to kill others, but their great readiness themselves to die, this secures in the last instance the victory of the popular rising. . . .' For only when the masses show readiness to die on the barricades can they win over the army, on which the old régime relies. The barricade does not play in revolution the part which the fortress plays in regular warfare. It is mainly the physical and moral meeting-ground between people and army. 'It serves the insurrection, because, by hampering the movement of troops it brings these into close contact with the people. Here on the barricade, for the first time in his life, the soldier hears honest, courageous words, a fraternal appeal, the voice of the people's conscience; and, as a consequence of this contact between soldiers and citizens, in the atmosphere of revolutionary enthusiasm, the bonds of the old military discipline snap. . . .'

Having thus defined the place of insurrection in the revolution, he returned to the attack on the government. The rulers, he said, were trying to prolong their domination by means of assassination and pogroms; the hooligans of the Black Hundreds had been taking their cue from the police and gendarmerie; and the Tsar himself had been their protector.[1] Trotsky quoted revelations made in the first Duma by the Liberal Prince Urusov, who had related the following boast of one of the leaders of the gendarmerie: 'We can make a pogrom whenever it suits us, a pogrom of ten people, if we wish, or of ten thousand.'

The prosecution does not believe in all this. It cannot believe, for otherwise it would have to turn the accusation against those whom it now defends, and to acknowledge that the Russian citizen who arms himself with a revolver against the police acts in self-defence. . . . We had no doubt that behind the façade of the Black Hundreds was the powerful fist of the ruling clique. Gentlemen the judges! this sinister fist we see even now in front of us!

The prosecution is asking you to recognize that the Soviet armed the workers for the direct struggle against the existing 'form of

---

[1] The programme of the Black Hundreds ran:
'1. The good of the Fatherland lies in the unshakable conservation of Orthodoxy and of the unlimited Russian autocracy. . . .
'2. The Orthodox Christian Church must have the predominant and dominating position in the state.
'3. Russian autocracy has sprung from popular reason; it has been blessed by the Church and justified by history.'

government'. If I were asked categorically 'Was this so?', I would answer: Yes! . . . I am prepared to admit this charge, but on one condition only. I do not know whether the prosecution and the court will agree to this condition.

I am asking you: What exactly does the prosecution mean by 'form of government'? Do we live under any form of government at all? The government has long since broken with the nation. . . . What we possess is not a national governmental force but an automaton for mass murder. I can find no other name for the machine of government that cuts into pieces the living flesh of our people. And if you tell me that the pogroms, the arson, the violence . . ., if you tell me that all that has happened in Tver, Rostov, Kursk, Siedlce, . . . if you tell me that Kishinev, Odessa, Bialystok [the places where the pogroms had been staged] represent the form of government of the Russian Empire, then—yes, then I recognize, together with the prosecution, that in October and November we were arming ourselves against the form of government of the Russian Empire.[1]

Thus he faced his judges, addressing them in a sonorous, metallic voice, and casting fleeting glances at the public. There, amid the public, sat his parents; his father staring at him, proud and completely reconciled; his mother quietly weeping. His plea stirred so much emotion that counsel for the defence asked for an adjournment for cooling off; and the court granted the request. During the interval attorneys and the public crowded around the dock to compliment Trotsky; and he tried gently to prepare his mother for a harsh sentence; for she had become naïvely reassured by the respectful commotion around her son. When the proceedings were resumed, the chief prosecutor gleefully declared that the defendant had given him all the evidence required but he also paid homage to Trotsky's honesty and courage.

The cross-examination of witnesses became an entire exposure of the violence and corruption into which government and police had sunk. At one point Trotsky, questioning Ivanov, the general of the gendarmerie who had conducted the investigation, compelled him to say, amid hilarious laughter in court, that a brief-case containing documents had been stolen from him at the headquarters of the political police. It was careless, the general explained, to leave there any personal belongings unattended,

[1] L. Trotsky, *Sochinenya*, vol. ii, book 2, pp. 163-77.

even for a moment—they were invariably stolen. Then, on
13 October, something like a bombshell exploded in the courtroom. One of the defence counsel received a letter from Lopukhin, a recently dismissed director of the police department,
who asked to be called as witness. A semi-Liberal official,
Lopukhin had conducted a special inquiry into the obscure
activities of his own department; and he forwarded to the court
a copy of the report he had submitted to Stolypin, the new
Minister of the Interior. He wished to testify that the year before
Petersburg had escaped a bloody pogrom only thanks to
measures taken by the Soviet. He wished to bear witness that
the leaflets inciting to the pogrom had been printed at the
headquarters of the political police, in the offices of one of its
chiefs who had just testified before the court that he had never
seen them. He further revealed that the political police itself
had organized the gangs of the Black Hundreds, that General
Trepov was actually in command of those gangs; and that the
commandant of the Imperial Court personally submitted to the
Tsar regular reports on these activities. The defence asked that
Witte, the former Prime Minister, Durnovo, the former Minister
of the Interior as well as Lopukhin be summoned to the witness-
stand. The request was refused on the pretext that the cross-
examination had been concluded. To allow the erstwhile chief
of the police department to give evidence for the defendants and
to implicate the Imperial Court would have brought the Tsar's
wrath upon the magistrates. But their refusal to call the witnesses effectively exposed the political character of the trial and
much beside. The defendants and attorneys decided to boycott
further proceedings.

On 2 November the verdict was delivered before an empty
court-room. The members of the Soviet were declared not guilty
on the chief count, that of insurrection. But Trotsky and fourteen others were sentenced to deportation to Siberia for life and
loss of all civil rights.

.   .   .   .

The convicts, dressed in grey prison clothes, started on their
journey at dawn on 5 January 1907. They had been kept in
the dark about the date of their departure and about their
destination; and they were awakened for the journey just after
they had gone to sleep, having spent most of the night at a

'passionate game of chess'. Yet, before departing they had managed to smuggle out a 'Farewell Message' to the workers of Petersburg, thanking them for their solidarity with the Soviet and reaffirming hope in the eventual triumph of the revolution.

The party of deportees, some with their wives and small children, was hustled to the railway station through dark and empty streets, under a strong military escort. The government was still afraid of an attempt to rescue them; and so elaborate were the precautions that the military escort had been brought from Moscow—soldiers of the Petersburg garrison were not thought reliable. At the stations, *en route*, the car with the convicts was surrounded by a dense cordon of gendarmes; and not till very late in the journey were the convicts told the place of their deportation. Apart from this, however, they were treated with respect and consideration. The soldiers openly showed their sympathy; all of them had read the reports of the trial and were relieved to learn that they would escort the workers' delegates to a place of deportation, not of execution. On the way they secretly posted the prisoners' mail; and to this circumstance we owe a vivid description of the journey which Trotsky gave in his letters to Sedova.[1]

The route led from Petersburg through Vologda, Viatka, and Perm, across the Urals, to Tiumen, where the party left the train and the escort was changed. From there they travelled by sleigh northwards towards Tobolsk. The convoy of forty horse-driven sledges was on the move only between sunrise and sunset, so that it covered not more than twenty *versts* at a stretch. The precautions were tightened and the journey was interrupted long before dusk, to prevent any attempt at escape. The country traversed was dotted with deportees' settlements, where the convoy was often greeted with revolutionary songs and red flags. Among the native Siberian peasants rumour and legend ran ahead of the travellers: the unusually strong escort suggested that the deportees were men of great importance, dukes or governors in disgrace, or the deputies of the first dispersed Duma; and the peasants looked on them with reverence and awe.

---

[1] Trotsky later published these letters in a little book *There and Back*. Our quotations are taken from the German translation which appeared as an appendix in L. Trotsky, *Die Russische Revolution 1905*.

After more than three weeks, the convicts reached Tobolsk, where they were put up for a few days in the local prison. Here they were told that the goal of their journey was the penal colony at Obdorsk, lying in the mountains over the estuary of the river Ob, just on the Polar Circle, nearly 1,000 miles from any railway and 500 from a telegraph station. The route from Tobolsk to Obdorsk led northwards, along the river Ob, through Samarovo and Berezov, across barren, empty, snow- and ice-bound *tundra* and *taiga*, where for hundreds of miles there was no human settlement, except a few scattered Ostyak huts or tents. Horses could still be used on part of the road, but farther on the horse was replaced by the reindeer. Here the finality of his severance from civilization came upon the depor- tee with a shock. From the Tobolsk prison, on 29 January, Trotsky wrote to his wife about the sudden and sharp longing that had overcome him 'for the light of an electric street lamp, for the clangour of a tramway' and—characteristically—'for the loveliest thing the world can offer, the smell of the printing ink of a fresh newspaper'.

So far he had not yet thought of trying to escape, even though before departing from Petersburg he had prudently concealed a false passport and money in the sole of his boot. For one thing, political convicts now refrained from escaping *en route* so as not to get the escort into trouble. For another, he reflected whether, having been so much in the public eye, it was not too risky for him to make the attempt: the escaping deportee, if caught, was automatically punished with three years' hard labour. Enough that when he was writing to Sedova about the place of his deportation, he still expected her to join him there with their baby son, born while he was in prison awaiting trial. He attempted to cheer up Sedova and wrote that Obdorsk had a healthy climate, was inhabited by a thousand people, and that he would have chances of earning a living there. He also urged her to bring or send to Obdorsk books and papers, no end of books and papers. In this mood, bracing himself for a long wait beyond the Polar Circle, not without melancholy, he started out from Tobolsk towards Samarovo and Berezov, the next halting-places.

Galloping at full speed, the convoy traversed a vast area, where typhus was raging and Ostyaks in their huts were dying like flies. On 12 February the convicts were lodged at the prison of Berezov, but allowed to leave their cells in the daytime and to move about. This was the month of snow blizzards in the *tundra*, and the police did not think that anybody would try to get away.

At Berezov a set of favourable circumstances induced Trotsky to change his mind about escape. He met a deportee doctor, who taught him how to simulate sciatica so as to dodge the last lap of the journey and be left behind, under mild surveillance, in the local hospital. The malingering required much will-power; but, if effective, it could not be detected. If he continued the journey and then tried to get away from Obdorsk, he would have added to his road 500 *versts* across the northern desert; and so he made up his mind to apply the lesson the doctor had taught him and to stay behind at Berezov. He found a sympathetic peasant ready to help. He had to choose one of three routes: the Tobolsk road, by which he had come, was in some ways the most convenient, but on it he might easily be caught; the northernmost way across the Urals to Archangel and Finland was difficult as well as dangerous; and so he chose to cross the roadless *tundra* south-westward, across the river Sosva, to a gold-mining settlement in the Urals, which was the terminus of a small single-track railway connected with the Perm-Viatka line. His peasant friend found him a guide, a native Zyrian drunkard, who knew his way in the *tundra* and spoke Russian and the native dialects. They struck a bargain. The guide bought the reindeer and furs needed for the journey; and he was to keep them on completion of the trip.

As the day approached, Trotsky pretended to have recovered from the fit of sciatica. On the evening before the escape, he went to an amateur theatrical performance of a Chekhov play. During the interval, he met the chief of the local police and told him that he was feeling well enough to make the last lap of the journey north. The police officer was well pleased. At midnight, Trotsky, having uneasily put himself into the hands of the drunken guide, was heading southwards.

It took him a week—travelling mostly night and day—to traverse the *tundra* over distances 'which nobody had measured except the archangel Michael'. The guide had an instinctive, animal-like sense of direction and feeling for the *tundra*. Like nearly all Ostyaks and Zyrians he was constantly drunk and falling asleep, to the horror of the passenger who saw the sleigh running into deep snowdrifts and feared pursuit. Himself without food, drink, or sleep, Trotsky kept on thumping and kicking the driver, tearing off his headgear, exposing him to the frost and thus keeping him awake. As they passed by Ostyak huts, which were happily very few and very far between, the driver would stop and disappear; and the passenger would find him either indulging with the Ostyaks and their wives and children in wild bouts of drinking, or lying unconscious on the floor. On the way, the leading reindeer strained its leg, and the others were worn out. The animals had to be left behind and fresh ones bought. This happened again and again, and Trotsky had to join the Ostyaks in a hunt for reindeer.

Despite the discomfort and exasperation, he was happy to be on the move, and he watched with wide eyes the awe-inspiring beauty of the white desert and the ugliness and misery of life in Ostyak huts. Most of the time he fought off sleep; and when they halted in the open waste to make a fire and to melt the snow for tea, he sat by the fire to jot down his observations, which he was later to put into a book. Even the tension of this flight and the terror of the *tundra* could not subdue the inquirer and the man of letters in him. He took notes on the landscape; on the shape of the woods; on the variety of the trails left on the snow by the wolf, the fox, the ermine, the elk, and other beasts; on his conversations with his driver; on the customs and manners of the natives (who liked best to eat fish raw, while it was still fluttering in their hands); on the abject slavery of their women; on hunting for deer; on the behaviour of the hunters and the hunted; and on a thousand other points.

As they approached the Urals, human settlements became frequent, and the inquisitiveness of people encountered embarrassing. He posed alternately as a merchant and as a homebound member of a polar expedition. He had to use his wits to find plausible answers when goods were insistently offered to him for sale and when he ran into someone who had known one or two members of the polar expedition to which he claimed to belong. But nothing untoward happened, and at length he reached Bogoslovsk, the terminus of the single-track railway.

A day later a train carried him westward from Perm through

Viatka and Vologda to Petersburg. 'For the first few minutes', he later recollected, 'the large and almost empty compartment was too crowded and stuffy for me, and I went out on to the front platform, where the wind was blowing and it was dark. A loud cry burst out from me—a cry of joy and freedom.'[1] So flushed was he with joy that he did all that prudence should have counselled him not to do: he was heading for Petersburg, where every police agent knew him; and he cabled to his wife about his arrival, asking her to meet him *en route*. Sedova could hardly believe her eyes: when the cable arrived the newspapers of Petersburg were still carrying reports about the journey of the convicted Soviet leaders to the Polar Circle.

[1] Trotsky, *Moya Zhizn*, vol. i, p. 227.

CHAPTER VII

The Doldrums: 1907–1914

THE year 1907 was the year of the Tsar's revenge. With the *coup* of 3 June autocracy was fully re-established, and Stolypin's reign of terror began. The second Duma was dispersed. A new law disfranchised the bulk of the people; and only after that was a new Duma elected. The Social Democratic deputies to the second Duma were deported to Siberia. The revolutionary parties were crushed, their clubs and newspapers suppressed, and thousands of their members massacred. Courts martial and the gallows dominated the political scene. Even moderate Liberals, who only recently had hoped to come to terms with the Tsar, were victimized and humiliated. Miliukov complained bitterly: 'We were invited to assume office as long as we were thought to have the red forces behind us. . . . We were respected so long as we were regarded as revolutionaries. But since we have turned out to be a strictly constitutional party, we have been found useless.'

The influence of socialism, so recently still overwhelming, shrank and dwindled. In 1905 everybody seemed in sympathy with socialism; now nearly everybody abjured it. Those who stood by it were a mere handful; even they could not withstand the all-pervading disillusionment and confusion. The Socialists were being driven back into the underground from which they had so hopefully emerged. But how much easier it had been for them before 1905 to band together in small clandestine circles than now, with defeat in their hearts, to re-descend into the underground. They seemed back where they had started, but without the original faith and courage. Some were reluctant to resume the clandestine struggle and hoped to work in the open, within such limits as the régime of 3 June would permit. Others, disdainful of any adjustment to triumphant counter-revolution, made desperate attempts to continue a war *à outrance* from the underground, and most of these boycotted the few social and political institutions which existed precariously in the open. The first attitude, that of the so-called 'liquidators', was prevalent among the Mensheviks, although some

Menshevik leaders, especially Plekhanov and Martov, were convinced of the need for clandestine organization. The 'boy-cotters' were strong among the Bolsheviks; but they were opposed by Lenin, who endeavoured to combine clandestine and open forms of activity.

In the recovery of Tsardom Trotsky saw a mere interval between two revolutions. He insisted, as much as did Lenin, on the necessity for the movement to rebuild its clandestine organization; and he also urged the underground workers to 'infiltrate' every open institution, from the Duma to the trade unions, in order to preach their views inside. He was therefore opposed to both liquidators and boycotters and went on ex-pounding the idea of permanent revolution with an optimism and ardour uncommon in those years of depression.[1]

Nevertheless, the years between 1907 and 1914 form in his life a chapter singularly devoid of political achievement. 'During the years of reaction', he wrote later, 'the greater part of my work consisted in interpreting the revolution of 1905 and paving the way for the next revolution by means of theoretical research.'[2] He did indeed interpret the revolution of 1905, or rather he repeated his earlier interpretation. But of the new 'theoretical research' there is little evidence in his writings, which consisted of brilliant journalism and literary criticism, but did not include a single significant work on political theory. Yet even in this somewhat apologetic retrospect Trotsky does not claim any practical revolutionary achievement to his credit. In these years, however, Lenin, assisted by his followers, was forging his party, and men like Zinoviev, Kamenev, Bukharin and, later, Stalin were growing to a stature which enabled them to play leading parts within the party in 1917. To the stature which Trotsky had attained in 1904–6 the present period added little or nothing.

Stalin, in the days before he began opposing Trotsky with nothing but preposterous calumny, made a remark which offers a clue to this chapter. Trotsky's strength, Stalin said, reveals itself when the revolution gains momentum and ad-vances; his weakness comes to the fore when the revolution is

[1] See his editorial statements in the Viennese *Pravda*, nos. 1, 4, 5; 'Letter to Russian Workers—*Vivos Voco*' in no. 6; and '*Chto-zhe dalshe?*', Supplement to *Pravda*, no. 17. [2] L. Trotsky, *Moya Zhizn*, vol. i, p. 251.

defeated and must retreat.[1] There is some truth in this. Trotsky's mental and moral constitution was such that he received the strongest impulses from, and best mobilized his resources amid, the strains and stresses of actual upheaval. On a gigantic stage, which dwarfed others, he rose to the giant's stature. Amid the roar and din of battle, his voice attained full power; and when he faced multitudes in revolt, absorbing from them their despair and hope and imparting to them his own enthusiasm and faith, his personality dominated men and, within limits, events. When the revolution was on the wane, however, he was out of his element and his strength sagged. He was equal to herculean, not to lesser, labours.

. . . .

On his return from the far north, Trotsky stopped for a few days in Petersburg, and then, before the police were on his track, crossed into Finland. A new stream of revolutionary émigrés was moving westward, and Finland was their first halting-place. The chief of the police at Helsinki, a Finnish patriot, was only too glad to offer shelter to the Tsar's enemies. Lenin and Martov had already arrived there. They warmly welcomed Trotsky and congratulated him on his behaviour in the dock. His sojourn in Finland lasted a few weeks, during which he prepared for publication a description of his escape from the *tundra*. At the end of April, he was in London to attend a congress of the party.

This was in many respects a strange assembly. Attended by about 350 delegates—nearly ten times as many as in 1903—it was the last congress of the united party. The delegates, although they met on the eve of Stolypin's *coup d'état*, had no clear awareness that the revolution had suffered defeat. On the contrary, the party still seemed to them to be at the zenith of its strength. Its membership was still nominally very large, and not only did Bolsheviks and Mensheviks work together, but even the Polish and the Latvian parties had joined the Russian mother-party— hitherto they had kept aloof so as not to become identified with either of its two factions. The party was, however, so poor that it had to borrow money from a liberal English business man to enable the congress to proceed in a Brotherhood Church in London.

[1] Stalin, *Sochinenya*, vol. vi, pp. 329–31.

The great issues of the revolution—the economic trends, the alignment of the classes, and the historical perspectives—were thrown open to a prolonged and thorough debate, which lasted three weeks. 'The speeches of the leaders lasted for hours . . . it might have been a gathering of academicians. . . .'[1] For the first time Trotsky had the opportunity to expound the theory of permanent revolution before a gathering of this sort. He strongly criticized the Mensheviks for their inclination to coalesce with the Constitutional Democrats; and he advocated a bloc of workers and peasants.[2] Rosa Luxemburg, representing the Polish Social Democratic Party, endorsed the theory of permanent revolution. Lenin twice emphatically acknowledged that in advocating an alliance of workers and peasants Trotsky was on common ground with the Bolsheviks. Once again Lenin hoped to win Trotsky over, and once again he failed. For the moment Trotsky was keeping aloof from both factions, and to both he preached unity. 'Here comes', he said, 'Martov . . . and threatens to raise between the Bolsheviks and the Mensheviks a Marxist wall bristling with guns.' . . . 'We are not afraid . . .', replies the Bolshevik, and threatens to fortify himself behind a deep moat. 'Comrade Martov, you are going to build your wall with paper only, with your polemical literature —you have nothing else to build it with.'[3] In this Trotsky was, of course, wrong: the 'wall' separating the two factions was of much more solid stuff than he imagined, and Martov and Lenin had a prescience of the ultimate irreconcilability of their political methods. 'If you think', Trotsky further pleaded, 'that a schism is unavoidable, wait at least until events, and not merely resolutions, separate you. Do not run ahead of events.'

There was in his attitude towards both wings of the party a certain intellectual superciliousness, for he looked at both through the prism of his theory of permanent revolution. Both Lenin and Martov agreed that the Russian revolution would be merely bourgeois democratic; both were therefore in his eyes wrong, and the views of neither would withstand the test of events.[4] In strict theory, this was true enough; but the

---

[1] A. Balabanoff, *My Life as a Rebel*, p. 88.

[2] *Pyatyi Syezd RSDRP*, pp. 272–3, 417–18, 420–4.   [3] Ibid., pp. 54–55.

[4] Shortly after the congress, Trotsky wrote in the *Przegląd Socjal-Demokratyczny* (Rosa Luxemburg's Polish paper) that 'while the anti-revolutionary aspects of Menshevism are already revealing themselves fully, the anti-revolutionary features

strictly theoretical viewpoint was not necessarily the most realistic. Whatever the formulas, the party of the revolution was constituting itself under Lenin's inspiration and the potential party of reform under Martov's. With his gaze fixed on wide horizons, Trotsky failed to see this division taking place before his very eyes. His own theory should have prompted him to come closer to the Bolsheviks; but the ties of personal friendship and the dead weight of his old controversy with Lenin held him closer to the Mensheviks.

At the congress in London a new issue brought back the old exacerbation. In committee, delegates discussed the guerilla activities and 'expropriations' in which the Bolshevik fighting-squads had been engaged, especially in the Caucasus. The Mensheviks angrily denounced these activities as a relapse into the old *Narodnik* terrorism, if not outright banditry; and they persuaded the congress, at which Lenin otherwise commanded a majority, to ban them. Throughout this discussion Lenin's attitude was ambiguous. Apparently he still intended to use the fighting squads for a few raids on Russian treasury transports, in order to obtain the money the party needed for its work under the terror of counter-revolution. Throughout the congress, an unknown Caucasian delegate, closely connected with the Bolshevik fighting-squads, Djugashvili-Ivanovich—he had not yet assumed the cover name Stalin—sat in silence, waiting for the result of the controversy and for Lenin's instructions. The records of the congress say nothing about the course of this controversy; only fragmentary reminiscences, written many years after, are available. But there is no doubt that Trotsky was, with Martov, among those who sharply arraigned the Bolsheviks; and some time after the congress he went so far as to carry the denunciation into the columns of the Western European Socialist press. He must have vented his indignation in the lobbies of the congress or in committee. Thus Lenin's earlier acknowledgement of the *rapprochement* in their basic views and his renewed attempt to win over Trotsky led to nothing, and towards the end of the congress were succeeded by bitter invective. Trotsky

of Bolshevism strongly threaten to come to light only in the case of a revolutionary victory'. Trotsky hoped, however, that a new revolution would compel both factions to revise their views and would thus bring them closer together, just as the events of 1905 had done. See *Die Russische Revolution 1905*, p. 231.

still cast his vote now for a Bolshevik and now for a Menshevik motion; but on several occasions he burst out against Lenin with ill feeling for which the records offer no explanation.[1]

The quarrel over the fighting-squads was superseded by a wider controversy concerning the character of the movement. The so-called liquidators tried to justify their opposition to clandestine work as part of an endeavour to reform Russian socialism in a European spirit. European Socialist parties, they argued, worked in the open, and so should the Russian organization. The argument appealed to a sentiment which had been strong in all sections of the party because, since the days of the struggle against the *Narodniks*, all Marxists had seen their mission as the 'Europeanization' of Russian socialism. But now each faction gave a different meaning to the term. The liquidators saw the essence of European socialism in its democratic mass organizations, the open work of its growing parliamentary representations, the peaceful bargaining of the trade unions: briefly, in its reformist practice. To the Bolsheviks 'Europeanization' meant what at the beginning it had meant to the party as a whole: the transplantation to Russia of Marxist proletarian socialism, the combined product of German philosophy, French socialism, and English political economy. But they could not see how they could go beyond that and imitate the open and lawful methods of western socialism; the Russian police state, especially under Stolypin, refused to allow even a Liberal party to exist openly, let alone a Socialist. If socialism did no more than what the law allowed, the law dictated by triumphant autocracy, it would in effect efface itself.

Trotsky glorified the underground struggle, its heroism and its martyrdom, with all the romantic zest peculiar to him. But he also responded keenly to the watchword of Europeanization. What he meant by it he never made quite clear. For him it summed up an emotional and cultural attitude rather than a clear-cut political concept. It expressed in a positive form his dislike of the 'dryness and hardness' of the clandestine organization, as Lenin conceived it. He knew that under Tsardom a

[1] Shortly after the congress Lenin wrote to Maxim Gorky (who had been present at the congress and tried to reconcile Lenin with Trotsky), that Trotsky behaved 'like a poseur'. Lenin, *Sochinenya*, vol. xxxiv, p. 335. See also *Pyatyi Syezd, RSDRP*, pp. 506, 602, 619, and Medem, op. cit., vol. ii, pp. 187–9.

broadly based, open Labour movement was a castle in the air. But, yearning for the best of both worlds, he wanted to see the broad democratic and tolerant spirit of western socialism infused into the Russian underground. He wanted the clandestine organization to give that scope to the 'self-activity' (*samodeyatelnost*) of the rank and file, which the western Labour parties seemed to provide. Yet any clandestine movement is of necessity narrow and rigid in comparison with any party which works in the open. It cannot in truth be broadly based; it cannot really afford to relax the discipline which its leadership imposes on the members; it cannot leave to the rank and file that freedom of initiative and 'self-activity' which may exist (or merely appear to exist) in a normal party. Lenin had reason on his side when he insisted that to 'Europeanize' the Russian party, even in the sense in which Trotsky and not the liquidators wanted it, would have meant wrecking the party.

.   .   .   .

From nobody did the cry for Europeanization come more naturally than from Trotsky. More than any other émigré he was a 'European'. Most émigrés lived in their closed circles, immersed in Russian affairs, unaffected by life in the countries of their residence. Not so Trotsky. With the adaptability and mental receptiveness of the wandering Jew—although these are by no means exclusively Jewish qualities—he felt at home in most European countries, was passionately absorbed in their affairs, spoke and wrote in their languages, and participated in their Labour movements.

In the summer of 1907, after the congress, he went from London to Berlin, where Sedova with their baby son was waiting for him. There he was warmly welcomed by the intellectual *élite* of German socialism. His fame had gone ahead of him: his conduct in the Soviet and in the dock had aroused admiration, and his essays had been translated and published in German periodicals. Parvus, who had also escaped from Siberia, introduced him to Karl Kautsky, then at the height of his influence as the spiritual guide of European socialism, the 'Pope' of Marxism. Trotsky often recollected the exultation of this visit and the 'other-worldly impression' which the 'white-haired and bright-eyed' Kautsky made on him. It could not have entered his mind that one day Kautsky would be the most severe critic of the October Revolution and the butt for his own devastating attacks. For a few years more, Trotsky, like all Socialists, sat at Kautsky's feet, even though the master's 'dry, angular' mind, and a certain banality and lack of subtlety soon disappointed him. Kautsky's home became his port of call in Berlin, and he took part in the intimate gatherings of the 'Pope's' inner circle. There he met Bebel, the old pioneer who had stood up to Bismarck, and had led German socialism through years of persecution into its seemingly golden age. There he also met Ledebour, Haase, and other leaders. He turned these friendships and contacts to political advantage. In *Neue Zeit*, Kautsky's monthly, and in *Vorwärts*, the influential Socialist daily, he often presented the case of Russian socialism and explained, from his angle, its internal dissensions.[1] The fact that he stood outside the quarrelling Russian factions commended him to the Germans, who could not make head or tail of the intricate Russian controversy and were loth to become involved in it.[2] Trotsky's manner of writing was undogmatic, attractive, European; and he appealed to German readers as no other Russian Socialist did. His German friends, on the other hand, occasionally contributed to his Russian émigré paper, helping to boost it—the German Social Democratic Party was still 'mother, teacher and living example' to all Russian Socialists.

Curiously enough, Trotsky's closest ties were not with the radical wing of German socialism, led by Rosa Luxemburg, Karl Liebknecht, and Franz Mehring, the future founders of the Communist party, but with the men of the centre group, who maintained the appearances of Marxist orthodoxy, but were in fact leading the party to its surrender to the imperialist ambitions of the Hohenzollern empire. This was all the stranger since the German radicals were by no means the counterparts of the Bolsheviks. In most essentials their attitude coincided with

---

[1] In a letter to his followers Lenin once complained that 'Trotsky and Co. write, and the Germans believe. Generally speaking, Trotsky is master at *Vorwärts*.' Lenin, *Sochinenya*, vol. xxxv, p. 11.

[2] This was the attitude of nearly all European Socialists. Jaurès, for instance, warned his staff on *Humanité* not to publish anything from, or about, the Russian party, because otherwise the paper would be swamped by interminable and very obscure statements from the opposed factions. A. Morizet, *Chez Lénine et Trotski*, p. 101.

Trotsky's. They, too, cherished the party's unity; they, too, represented an intellectual and revolutionary brand of Marxism, opposed to the empirical reformism which emanated from the German trade unions. Of all the personalities of European socialism, nobody was in origin, temperament, and political and literary gifts more akin to Trotsky than Rosa Luxemburg— not for nothing was Stalin to denounce her posthumously, in 1932, as a 'Trotskyist'. They found themselves in agreement at the recent congress in London and again at the congress of the International at Stuttgart, where Luxemburg spoke for the anti-militarist left. Like Trotsky, she rejected the general Menshevik conception of the revolution, but viewed with suspicion the work of the Bolsheviks. Like Trotsky, she wanted to see the Russian movement 'Europeanized', while she herself tried to breathe into the German party something of the Russian revolutionary idealism. They sometimes met at Kautsky's home, but they remained aloof from each other, perhaps because of their extraordinary affinity. Agreeing so closely, they may have had little to say to each other. Nor did Karl Liebknecht's passionate and sincere yet unsophisticated idealism attract Trotsky, to his regret in later years. Franz Mehring, whose political temperament was to flare up during the First World War, was now immersed in historical and philosophical work which was a little remote from the issues agitating Trotsky.

For the next seven years, till the outbreak of the First World War, Trotsky settled in Vienna. 'His house in Vienna', writes a Russo-American Socialist who visited him there in 1912, 'was a poor man's house, poorer than that of an ordinary working man.... His three rooms in a ... working-class suburb contained less furniture than was necessary for comfort. His clothes were too cheap to make him appear "decent" in the eyes of a middle-class Viennese. When I visited his house, I found Mrs. Trotsky engaged in housework, while the two light-haired lovely boys were lending not inconsiderable assistance. The only things that cheered the house were loads of books in every corner.'[1] The visitor received perhaps an exaggerated impression of poverty. The Trotskys were better off than most émigrés, even though they lived very modestly and at times, as we shall see, did suffer

[1] See M. J. Olgin's 'Biographical Notes' in the American edition of Trotsky's *Our Revolution*, p. 18.

penury. Throughout these years Trotsky, writing under his old pen-name Antid Oto, was the Vienna correspondent of *Kievskaya Mysl (Kievan Thought)*, a widely-read radical Liberal daily; and he contributed frequently to at least half a dozen Russian, German, and Belgian papers.[1] His wealthy parents, who were helping to bring up the two daughters of his first marriage and who several times came abroad to meet him, almost certainly on occasion opened their purses to him. The two boys mentioned by the American visitor were Lev or Lyova, his older son of the second marriage, born in 1906, while Trotsky was in prison, and Sergei (Seryozha), born in Vienna in 1908.

By all accounts the family led a quiet and happy existence. The revolutionary lion was a devoted husband and warm-hearted father. Anxious to help his wife and to enable her to pursue her artistic interests and to follow the political life of the Russian colony, he lent a hand in domestic chores and in the upbringing of the children. Later, when the boys went to school, he regularly helped them in their homework, and he found time for this even in the fever of the war years, after the family had moved to Paris.[2] Sedova, for her part, resumed in Vienna her husband's artistic education, which she had begun in Paris without initial success in 1902. The couple spent many a day together amid the rich art collections in the Burgschloss and in Viennese galleries. His interest in the arts was growing appreciably: on his frequent visits to Paris, London, or Munich he would steal away from political conventicles to the Louvre, the Tate Gallery, and other collections; and his writings of this period, especially his reviews of the annual Viennese exhibitions, written for *Kievan Thought*, show a slightly more than dilettante appreciation of trends in European art. While politics and journalism claimed only part of his time, he also enlarged his already wide familiarity with the French and the Russian novel and with German poetry; and this, too, is reflected in his literary essays of the time.

He settled in Vienna reluctantly, after the German police had

---

[1] Apart from *Kievskaya Mysl*, he contributed in these years irregularly to the following papers: *Luch, Den, Odesskie Novosti* (of which his uncle Spentzer was the publisher), *Borba, Neue Zeit, Vorwärts, Le Peuple* (of Brussels).

[2] A. Rosmer, 'Trotsky during World War I', *The New International*, September–October 1950.

refused him domicile in Berlin. He was anxious to stay within the orbit of German socialism, and for this Vienna was second best. From Vienna he also watched the clash of German and Slav aspirations in the Balkans. Towards the close of Francis Joseph's rule Vienna, although already somewhat provincial, was still one of Europe's spiritual centres. In politics it prided itself on Austro-Marxism, which had broken the unchallenged domination of clericalism in the most Catholic of empires. In literature it had made, with Arthur Schnitzler, Peter Altenberg, Karl Krauss, and others, its contribution to the hypersensitive, sex- and death-conscious trend of the *fin de siècle*. In the arts, its secession revolted mildly against academic conservatism and bourgeois crudity. There was no lack of solid education and taste in the Viennese intelligentsia and its radical wing, although these virtues were not matched by strength of character or sense of purpose. Perhaps only in psychology did Vienna at that time produce anything epoch-making: Freud's great mind was beginning to dominate the field. For the rest, Court, Parliament, editorial offices, Socialist meetings, literary and artistic groups and cliques, were all reflected in the life and gossip of the cosy Viennese cafés, always astir with intelligent, witty, yet strangely futile conversation.

In *My Life* Trotsky describes this environment with disdainful irony. His writings at that time, however, strongly suggest that he enjoyed the mild effervescence of the Viennese atmosphere. He plunged into local life, joined the Austrian Social Democrats, visited their clubs and meetings, contributed to local Socialist papers, was stirred by local literary and artistic events, and occasionally gave way to the attraction of the cafés. Years later, as the leader of a victorious revolution and the implacable enemy of reformism he drew devastating portraits of the Austro-Marxist leaders. During his stay in Vienna, he was less hard on them and felt gratified by their friendship. He warmly admired Victor Adler, the founding father of the party, in whose home he was as welcome as he was at Kautsky's in Berlin and repeatedly for Russian readers he wrote of Victor Adler with gusto and love.[1] He was attached to Victor's son, Fritz, the rebellious Benjamin of the party and editor of *Kampf*, who would one day kill the Austrian Prime Minister Baron

[1] L. Trotsky, *Sochinenya*, vol. viii, pp. 10 ff.

Stürgkh, in protest against world war.[1] Ties of friendship also
bound him to Rudolf Hilferding, the master mind of Austro-
Marxism. Just as Trotsky was settling down in the Viennese
suburb of Hütteldorf, Hilferding was writing, or completing,
his monumental *Finanzkapital*, virtually the only ambitious
attempt made since Marx's death to bring the theory of *Das
Kapital* up to date. (Hilferding's work was used by Lenin to
justify his revolutionary policy, while its author became
Minister of Finance in the Weimar republic.) It was Hilferding
who introduced Trotsky to Karl Renner, the future Chancellor
and President of the Austrian republic, to Otto Bauer, foremost
Austro-Marxist theorist and expert on national minorities, and
future Foreign Minister, and to nearly all the other Austro-
Marxist leaders. 'They were well educated people', writes
Trotsky, 'who knew about various subjects more than I did.
I listened with intense and, one might say, reverent interest to
their conversation when I first saw them at the Central Café.'[2]

But Trotsky also grew aware of the difference between his
own Marxism and theirs; they were academic, over-sophisti-
cated sceptics, without mettle; and he sensed the politely concealed condescension with which they met his own revolutionary
ardour. Behind the thinkers and leaders he saw 'a phalanx of
young Austrian politicians, who have joined the party in the
firm conviction that an approximate familiarity with Roman
law gives a man the inalienable right to direct the fate of the
working class'.[3] But he believed that in critical times the bold
spirit of socialism would overcome the scepticism of the leaders
and the opportunism of the party officials, and that the revolution, when it came, would carry the Austro-Marxists with it,
as it would carry the Mensheviks. He obviously mistook his
friends for revolutionaries just as they liked to think of him as of
one who was at heart a mild reformist.[4]

[1] During the war Trotsky described Friedrich Adler as his 'comrade in ideas
and friend' (*Sochinenya*, vol. viii, pp. 33–36). In 1919, Trotsky and Lenin nominated
F. Adler Honorary Secretary of the Third International, and they were greatly disappointed when he turned his back on them. Later F. Adler became the secretary
of the Second International.   [2] *Moya Zhizn*, vol. i, p. 237.
[3] L. Trotsky, *Sochinenya*, vol. viii, pp. 12–13.
[4] The following incident offers an amusing illustration: towards the end of 1917
when Count Czernin, the Austrian Foreign Minister, was setting out for peace
negotiations with Trotsky at Brest Litovsk, he had a talk with Victor Adler. 'Adler
said to me in Vienna: "You will certainly get on all right with Trotsky", and when

Fortified by these friendships, Trotsky frequently appeared as the mouthpiece of Russian socialism before the congresses of the German and Austrian parties. He also became a familiar figure at the gatherings of the International, where he met the pioneers: Jaurès and Guesde, Keir Hardie and MacDonald, Vandervelde and Turati. He was spellbound by the personality of Jaurès, and this despite the latter's reformism, by 'the genius-like *naïveté* of Jaurès's enthusiasm' and his 'volcanic moral passion and gift of concentrated anger', and by Jaurès's oratorical genius, more classical, less soaring than his own, yet so much akin to it. At these gatherings, where all the talent of European socialism was assembled, he compared various styles of oratory, noting, for instance, the 'cool, exquisite finish of style and polish of gesture' in Vandervelde, whom he was later to mock as a mediocrity, or analysing the strong oratorical effect of Victor Adler, who 'could never control his [rather weak] voice, wasting it uneconomically, so that towards the end of his speeches he usually coughed and was hoarse'. But it was to Jaurès that, whether in full congress, in committee, or at public meetings, he listened 'each time as if it were the first', as 'he [Jaurès] moved rocks, thundered and exploded but never deafened himself. Like a heavy steel hammer, he could crush a rock or work with infinite precision on the thinnest gold plate.'[1] And once, portraying the great Frenchman, he characteristically remarked: 'Sometimes the man of the Russian black-soil steppe may find in Jaurès merely artificial technical training and pseudo-classical recitation. But in such an appraisal is revealed only the poverty of our own Russian culture.'

The more he steeped himself in this atmosphere of pre-1914 Europe, the more did the sense of the 'poverty and crudity' of Russian culture oppress him and the more emphatically did he insist that it was part of the mission of socialism, and of socialism alone, to transform the Scythian into a 'good European'. He best expressed this idea, with all its strength and weakness, in a superb essay on the Russian intelligentsia which he wrote for *Kievan Thought* in 1912. The editor hesitated long before he published it: even in a radical paper the essay seemed likely to

I asked him why he thought so, he answered: "Well, you and I get on quite well together, you know." ' Count O. Czernin, *In the World War*, p. 234.

[1] L. Trotsky, *Sochinenya*, vol. viii, pp. 13, 19, 30–31.

hurt Russian *amour propre* too strongly. The occasion was a celebrated book by Ivan Razumnik, which extolled the exceptional virtues and the historical role of the Russian intelligentsia. In his criticism of this book Trotsky elaborated some of the views on Russian history he had formulated earlier and tried to explain the peculiar role of the Russian intelligentsia against a wide historical background.

'We are poor', he wrote, 'with the accumulated poverty of over a thousand years. . . . History has shaken us out of her sleeve into a severe environment and scattered us thinly over a vast plain.' Only a Leviathan-like state could defend that plain against Asiatic invasion and withstand the pressure of wealthy and powerful Europe. To feed itself the Leviathan starved the nation, crippled the growth of its social classes and institutions and atrophied its civilization. 'The Russian people was not less heavily oppressed by nobility and Church than were the peoples of the West. But that complex and rounded-off way of life which, on the basis of feudal rule, grew up in Europe—that gothic lacework of feudalism—has not grown on our soil. We lacked the life-matter for it, we could not afford it. . . . A thousand years we have lived in a humble log cabin and filled its crevices with moss—did it become us to dream of vaulting arcs and gothic spires?'

'How miserable', he went on, '. . . was our gentry! Where were its castles, where were its tournaments? Its crusades, its shield bearers, its minstrels and pages? Its chivalrous love?' The Russian gentry was coarse, barbarous, vulgar. Nor did Russia go through the purifying experience of the Reformation; and so she had no inkling of the western burgher's 'human personality, which strove to establish more intimate relations between itself and its God'. In the medieval European town, that 'stone cradle of the third estate', there had grown up a striking diversity of cultural types, and a whole new epoch had been prepared there. 'In the crafts, guilds, municipalities, universities, academic assemblies, elections, processions, fêtes, and disputes there crystallized the precious habits of self-government; there grew the human personality—a bourgeois personality, of course, but still a personality, not a snout which every policeman could kick and punch.' All that the third estate, as it grew, needed to do was to transfer the new human relations and the habits of self-government from the corporations to the nation and the state as a whole. In contrast, the Russian towns, those 'military-feudal excrescences on the body of the Russian countryside', had created no starting-points for bourgeois progress. Under Peter the Great it was the police that sponsored crafts, but no genuine urban culture could grow out of police sponsorship. The misery of Russian bourgeois democracy supplemented the crudeness of the feudal tradition.

The state, however, needed men who were educated and therefore Europeanized; but it was afraid of them. The Tsars gave the intelligentsia compulsory education; but then they kept the . . . whip over them. 'No sooner had the young elements of the old estates . . . entered the sunlit zone of European ideology than they broke away irresistibly, almost without inner hesitation, from feudalism and inherited orthodoxy.' The Russian intelligentsia were compelled to defend their most elementary rights by the most extreme and wasteful means. 'It became their historical calling . . . to use watches for knocking nails into walls.' A Russian had to become a Darwinist in order to justify his decision to marry according to his choice; he had to invoke revolutionary ideas to excuse his craving for education; and he had to have recourse to socialism when all he wanted was a constitution. For all their radicalism, the Russian intelligentsia merely imitated the West, adopting from it ready-made systems, doctrines, and programmes. In a passage which did less than justice to Russian thought and literature of the nineteenth century, Trotsky dismissed these as backwater growths: '. . . the history of our social thought has so far failed to cut its way even with the thin edge into the development of universal human thought. This is a poor consolation for national *amour propre*? . . . Historical truth is not a lady-in-waiting on national pride. . . . Let us rather invest our *amour propre* in the future and not in the past.'

Throughout their severe struggle, the Russian intelligentsia stood alone in the nation, receiving no support from the main social classes. This shaped their character. They 'lived in a terrible moral tension, in concentrated asceticism. . .' They bought moral self-confidence and stability at the price of intellectual conceit and of 'fanaticism in ideas, ruthless self-limitation and self-demarcation, distrust and suspicion and

vigilant watching over their own purity. . .', at the price, that is,
of an orthodoxy in rebellion opposed to official orthodoxy.
Thus they came to develop 'that zeal for the letter, which can
sometimes be observed in our intellectuals of the most extreme
wing'. It was the misfortune of the intelligentsia that they had
always had to act as proxy for undeveloped and passive social
forces. Here Trotsky set in a long historical perspective the
phenomenon of 'substitutism' about which he had first written
in his polemics against Lenin in 1904.[1] He now saw the intelligentsia's 'substitutism' running like a thread through Russian
history. First, the leaders of the Decembrist rising of 1825
represented the ideas of an as yet unborn middle class. Then the
Narodniks tried to speak for a mute and dumb peasantry. Lastly
the Marxist intellectuals set themselves up as the spokesmen
of a weak, only just awakening industrial working class. To all
of them the idea of the class was more important than the class
itself. He rounded off this gloomy survey in a more hopeful
tone, saying that the revolution of 1905–6 had set in motion
the mass of the workers and that henceforward nobody could
act as their proxy: this was the end of substitutism.[2]

We shall see later whether or to what extent this optimistic
conclusion was justified; substitutism was to reassert itself with
unparalleled strength after the revolution, and the idea of the
class was then to become for a long time more important than
the class itself. Some of the other long trends of Russian history,
which Trotsky grasped here with such mastery, were also
to come overwhelmingly to the surface after the revolution.
What is at this stage of our narrative more relevant is the self-
revealing acuteness with which Trotsky contrasted the 'sunlit
zone of European ideology', 'the vaulting arcs' and 'the gothic
spires and lacework' of western civilization with the barbarous
'log cabin' of Russian history. This contrast was greatly overdrawn, not in historical perspective, where it was broadly true,
but in its concluding and contemporary part. The lacework
façade of European civilization before 1914 concealed processes
of self-destruction and inner decay which were presently to
manifest themselves in a succession of world wars, in the
paroxysms of Fascism and Nazism and in the impotence and
deterioration of the western European Labour movement. On

---

[1] See Chapter III.   [2] L. Trotsky, *Sochinenya*, vol. xx, pp. 327–42.

the other hand, Trotsky did not do justice to the creative energies with which nineteenth-century and contemporary Russia was boiling over, the energies with which his own personality and activity were merged. He sometimes seemed to view Russia's past and present almost as a vacuum. This was the weakness underlying his call for Europeanization and also the flaw in his attitude towards Bolshevism. It was Lenin's strength that he took Russian reality as it was, while he set out to change it. Lenin's party had its roots deep in Russian soil; and it absorbed all that that soil could yield in revolutionary strength and harshness, in world-shaking courage and in primitive crudity. Bolshevism had its thinkers, its Lenin and Bukharin and others, who drew from European socialism whatever could be transplanted to Russia; but it also had its tough committee-men, its Stalins, who worked in the depths of a semi-European and semi-Asiatic proletariat, and to whom Europeanization meant little.

.   .   .   .

Trotsky did not and could not really abandon the humble Russian 'log cabin'. In October 1908 he began to edit the so-called Viennese *Pravda*. An insignificant paper, published since 1905 by Spilka, a small Ukrainian Menshevik group, *Pravda* was completely run down, and its publishers hoped that Trotsky would put new life into it. The first few issues he edited still bore the imprint of the Ukrainian group; but at the end of 1908, the group disbanded itself and left Trotsky as *Pravda's* sole master. For lack of money, he published it very irregularly— only five issues appeared in the first year of his editorship.[1] But it was less difficult to bring out the paper than to transport it clandestinely to Russia. The editor often appealed to readers for help, complaining that 'several *poods*' of the paper got stuck on the Russian frontier and could not be forwarded because of the lack of fifty roubles; that manuscripts for a new issue had piled up on his desk and he could not send them to the printers; or that *Pravda* was compelled to stop correspondence with readers in Russia because it could not afford the postage.[2] Trotsky's

---

[1] At this time this was the lot of all émigré publications, and most of them appeared even more rarely. N. Popov, *Outline History of the C.P.S.U.*, vol. i, p. 233. Trotsky's *Pravda* is commonly referred to as the Viennese *Pravda*, to distinguish it from the Bolshevik *Pravda* which began to appear much later. The Viennese *Pravda* was at first published in Lvov, in Austrian Galicia, and only in November 1909, with its sixth issue, was it transferred to Vienna.   [2] *Pravda*, nos. 3 and 5.

journalistic fees, earned from other papers, went to finance the little sheet; he sold his books, and his wife trudged to a pawn-shop so that the few *poods* of *Pravda* should at last get across the frontier. Or the central committee of the mighty German Social Democratic Party would lend a thousand roubles; and so some of the debts would be paid, Mrs. Trotsky would recover a few of her pawned belongings; and for a couple of months *Pravda* would come out every fortnight. Then again the intervals be-tween one issue and another began to lengthen, the fortnightly became a monthly, then almost a quarterly, until its shaky finances were again temporarily restored by a modest grant from the Latvian Socialists or from some other well-wishers. Throughout 1909 Trotsky tried in vain to obtain assistance from the Russian Central Committee, in which the Bolsheviks were a majority. Lenin agreed to help, but only on condition that Trotsky admitted a delegate of the Central Committee as co-editor. Since Trotsky would not accept this condition, Lenin forbade his followers to produce *Pravda* at the Bolshevik printing shop at Geneva otherwise than on strictly commercial terms.[1] Despite these difficulties and the irregularity of its appearance, the paper evoked response in Russia and soon its 'wide circula-tion' was noted in the confidential reports of the *Okhrana's* agents.[2]

Pravda had a curious team of contributors. A young student Skobelev, at this time Trotsky's favoured pupil, acted as the paper's secretary—later Skobelev gained eminence as a Menshevik parliamentarian in the fourth Duma, and in 1917 he became Minister of Labour in Kerensky's government. Trotsky's assistant was another Menshevik, Semkovsky, whose name at this time frequently appeared in inner party con-troversy; Ryazanov, the future founder of the Marx–Engels Institute, an untameable rebel bowing to no authority and standing outside the two factions, was a regular contributor and Trotsky's close friend. In charge of the paper's contact with the Russian underground was Uritsky, a former Menshevik, already renowned for his cool courage in Tsarist prisons; in 1917 Uritsky was among the chief organizers of the October insurrection, and he then, as special Commissar, dispersed the

[1] Lenin, *Sochinenya*, vol. xxxiv, pp. 348–9.
[2] *Bolsheviki, Dokumenty Okhrannovo Otdelenia*, vol. i, p. 42.

Constituent Assembly. The team included the Menshevik Victor Kopp, one day to make his mark as a subtle and adventurous diplomat: in 1922 he prepared behind the scenes the Russo-German treaty of Rapallo; and in the 1930s he secretly explored for Stalin the chances of agreement with Hitler.

The most original character in this pléiade was Adolphe Yoffe. A young, able but neurotic intellectual of Karaite[1] origin, Yoffe was sharing his time between academic work, contributions to *Pravda*, and psychoanalysis. Through Yoffe, Trotsky met Alfred Adler (whose patient Yoffe was), became interested in psychoanalysis, and reached the conclusion that Marx and Freud had more in common than Marxists were prepared to admit.[2] In Vienna Yoffe struggled desperately with recurrent nervous breakdowns; and the contributions which he produced with painful effort needed much editorial rewriting. Trotsky did his best to befriend him and to boost his self-confidence. In 1917 Yoffe was one of the chief actors in the October insurrection and later in the peace negotiations of Brest Litovsk. (In his private papers Trotsky remarked that the revolution 'healed Yoffe better than psychoanalysis of all his complexes'.)[3] Yoffe was to repay Trotsky's friendship with boundless devotion, and in 1927 he committed suicide in protest against Trotsky's expulsion from the Bolshevik party.

On the whole, *Pravda* was not one of Trotsky's great journalistic ventures. He intended to address himself to 'plain workers' rather than to politically-minded party men, and to 'serve not to lead' his readers.[4] *Pravda*'s plain language and the fact that it preached the unity of the party secured to it a certain popularity but no lasting political influence. Those who state the case for a faction or group usually involve themselves in more or less complicated argument and address the upper and medium layers of their movement rather than the rank and file. Those who say, on the other hand, that, regardless of any differences, the party ought to close its ranks have, as Trotsky had, a simple case, easy to explain and sure of appeal. But more

---

[1] The Karaites were a sect which abandoned rabbinical Jewry in the middle ages to return to the pure Gospel.

[2] After the revolution Trotsky appealed to Bolshevik scholars to keep an open mind to what was new and revealing in Freud. *Sochinenya*, vol. xxi, pp. 423–32.

[3] *The Trotsky Archives.*

[4] *Pravda*, no. 1.

often than not this appeal is superficial. Their opponents who win the cadres of a party for their more involved argument are likely eventually to obtain the hearing of the rank and file as well; the cadres carry their argument, in simplified form, deeper down. Trotsky's calls for the solidarity of all Socialists were for the moment applauded by many—even the Bolsheviks in Petersburg reprinted his *Pravda*. But the same people who now applauded the call were eventually to disregard it, to follow the one or the other faction, and to leave the preacher of unity isolated. Apart from this, there was in Trotsky's popular posture, in his emphasis on plain talk and his promise to 'serve not to lead', more than a touch of demagogy, for the politician, especially the revolutionary, best serves those who listen to him by leading them.

More than anybody else Trotsky voiced the sentiment, still widespread in the party, which may best be described as a horror of final schism. In January 1910 the leaders of factions met in Paris and for the last time tried to patch up their differences. In both factions there were men determined to bring matters to a head and to part company. But in both the moderates prevailed for the moment. The conciliators who carried the day among the Bolsheviks were Rykov, Sokolnikov, Lozovsky, and Kamenev.[1] On the other side, Trotsky exerted himself for unity and kept in check Martov, who later admitted that he gave way only because the Mensheviks were too weak to risk an immediate break.[2] An agreement was reached; but, even on the face of it, it was too good to be true. Both factions consented to disband their separate organizations and to merge; and both agreed to eliminate the 'extremists' from their midst, the Mensheviks to expel their liquidators and the Bolsheviks their boycotters. Both further agreed to suspend their separate publications and to put their financial resources into a common pool, to be placed under the trusteeship of three German Socialists, Karl Kautsky, Franz Mehring, and Klara Zetkin. Trotsky received all the tributes that on such solemn occasions are paid to the successful matchmaker. The Central Committee formally acknowledged the services his *Pravda* had rendered to the whole party, 'regardless of faction', and it decided to place

[1] N. Popov, op. cit., vol. i, p.248.
[2] Martov, *Spasiteli ili Uprazdniteli*, p. 16.

its authority behind the paper, to pay Trotsky a regular subsidy (150 roubles a month) and to support him in every other way. Trotsky's Bolshevik brother-in-law, Kamenev, was delegated to serve on *Pravda* as the Central Committee's liaison officer. The appointment was calculated to smooth co-operation, for Kamenev had sincerely striven to overcome the division inside the party.

It is easy to imagine the jubilation with which Trotsky announced all this in *Pravda*.[1] A few weeks later, however, he had to record that the attempt at reconciliation had broken down, because—so he himself stated—the Mensheviks had refused to disband their faction. This could not have greatly surprised him; he had known all along their utter reluctance to come to terms with the Bolsheviks, who had in the meantime suspended their separate publication. This was the occasion on which Trotsky, the champion of unity, should have spared the offenders against unity no censure. Yet in *Pravda* he 'suspended judgement' and only mildly hinted at his disapproval of the Mensheviks' conduct.[2] In vain did Kamenev urge him to take a firmer attitude. Trotsky resented this as an infringement of his editorial independence and an attempt to use *Pravda* for Bolshevik purposes. There followed the inevitable bickerings, and in no time all the émigré colonies were seething with intrigue.

The Paris conference had resolved to disown the two extreme wings of the party, the liquidators and the boycotters. The Mensheviks had undertaken to have no truck with the former, the Bolsheviks with the latter. Lenin could easily keep his part of the undertaking. He had, anyhow, expelled the chief boycotters, Bogdanov and Lunacharsky, from his faction. The Mensheviks, on the other hand, found it almost impossible to live up to their obligation. The liquidators' attitude was too common in their ranks for them to dissociate themselves from it in earnest. If they were to expel those who had turned their backs on the underground struggle, they would merely have destroyed their own influence and helped Bolshevism to ascendancy. This they refused to do. The issue then presented itself in this form. Those who were opposed to clandestine work, argued the Bolsheviks, had no place in a party staking its future on that work. The Mensheviks—that is, the anti-liquidators

---

[1] *Pravda*, no. 10.   [2] *Pravda*, no. 12.

among them—replied that there should be room in the party for dissenters. The general principle that dissent was permissible was not questioned by Lenin. He merely argued that this particular dissent could not be tolerated, because the opponents of clandestine work could not be effective clandestine workers. Since, from one angle, this difference could be seen as a conflict between the upholders of discipline and the defenders of the right to dissent, Trotsky took his stand against the disciplinarians. Having done so, he involved himself in glaring inconsistencies. He, the fighter for unity, connived in the name of freedom of dissent at the new breach in the party brought about by the Mensheviks. He, who glorified the underground with zeal worthy of a Bolshevik, joined hands with those who longed to rid themselves of the underground as a dangerous embarrassment. Finally, the sworn enemy of bourgeois liberalism allied himself with those who stood for an alliance with liberalism against those who were fanatically opposed to such an alliance.

So self-contradictory an attitude brought him nothing but frustration. Once again to the Bolsheviks he appeared not just an opponent, but a treacherous enemy, while the Mensheviks, though delighted to oppose to Lenin a man of Trotsky's radicalism and record, regarded him as an unreliable ally. His long and close association with Martov made him turn a blind eye more than once on Menshevik moves which were repugnant to him. His long and bitter quarrel with Lenin made him seize captiously on every vulnerable detail of Bolshevik policy. His disapproval of Leninism he expressed publicly with the usual wounding sarcasm. His annoyance with the Mensheviks he vented mostly in private argument or in 'querulous' letters, with which he bombarded Martov and Axelrod. Consequently, he appeared in public not quite the same man as he was in private. The longer this state of affairs lasted, the more did he become Martov's political prisoner. Martov's correspondence throws an instructive light on this:

> I have answered him [Trotsky] with a more ironical than angry letter [Martov wrote on one occasion], although I admit that I have not spared his *amour propre*. I have written him that he can escape nowhere from the liquidators and ourselves, because it is not his magnanimity that compels him to defend the right of the liquidators to remain in the party . . . but the correct calculation that Lenin

wants to devour all independent people, including Trotsky, as well as the liquidators.[1]

The logic of things [Martov wrote to another correspondent] compels Trotsky to follow the Menshevik road, despite all his reasoned pleas for some 'synthesis' between Menshevism and Bolshevism . . . he has not only found himself in 'the camp of the liquidators', but he is compelled to take up there the most 'pugnacious' attitude towards Lenin. His pupils, however, . . . are fretful.[2]

In the summer of 1910 Trotsky's breach with the Central Committee was complete. Kamenev had left *Pravda*, after Trotsky had asked that the Central Committee should replace him by another liaison officer; and the Central Committee withdrew its subsidy.[3] By now the initiative in splitting the united movement had passed from Martov to Lenin; and Trotsky denounced 'the conspiracy of the [Bolshevik] émigré clique against the Russian Social Democratic Party,' adding that 'Lenin's circle, which wants to place itself above the party, will find itself outside it'.[4] He carried the campaign into the German Socialist press, where he wrote that none of the émigré leaders represented the real movement in Russia, which craved for unity and resented their intrigues. This was then, in fact, a common view among the underground workers: none other than Stalin wrote in a similar vein in the Caucasus.[5] Trotsky's articles, nevertheless, caused an uproar among the delegates of the party, who assembled in Copenhagen in October 1910 for a congress of the International. At a meeting of the Russian delegation, Plekhanov, seconded by Lenin, demanded disciplinary action, while Lunacharsky and Ryazanov acted as Trotsky's counsel for the defence. The offender was let off—even his accusers must have found it awkward to penalize him for an opinion expressed in 'fraternal' German papers.

The feud was not without its comic incidents, of which one at least may be related here. Both factions tried to recover the funds which they had deposited with the German trustees; but for some reason neither was able to establish a valid title. In the summer of 1911 Axelrod and Trotsky went to Jena, where a congress of the German Social Democrats was being held, in

[1] *Pisma Axelroda i Martova*, p. 230.   [2] Ibid., p. 233.
[3] *Pravda*, no. 20; Lenin, *Sochinenya*, vol. xvi, p. 360.   [4] *Pravda*, no. 21.
[5] Stalin, *Sochinenya*, vol. ii, pp. 146–58; I. Deutscher, *Stalin*, pp. 104–6.

order to approach, on behalf of the Mensheviks, the trustees of
the fund.[1] Trotsky certainly hoped to repair *Pravda*'s finances
should he succeed in helping the Mensheviks to repair theirs.
Kautsky apparently favoured the plan, but the attitude of the
other trustees was uncertain; and one of them, Zetkin, was
friendly to the Bolsheviks. In great secrecy, Axelrod and Trotsky
met Kautsky. 'Only on Tuesday', Axelrod reported to Martov,
'K[autsky] had an opportunity to suggest to me and T[rotsky]
that we meet him somewhere for a preliminary private talk. . . .
Haase chose as meeting place a restaurant, where one might
hope that we would not be detected by other delegates, especially
by those close to Zetkin and Luxemburg. . . . The next day,
after K[autsky] had talked with Z[etkin] about a joint meeting
with us, he and Haase asked me and T[rotsky] not to mention
our conversation to Z[etkin]. . . .'[2] Ironically, most of the money
deposited had been obtained by the Bolsheviks through the
raids and expropriations which Trotsky and the Mensheviks
had so indignantly denounced. But the delicate manipulation
designed to expropriate the Bolsheviks with the assistance of the
senior German trustee, yielded nothing, and the envoys left
Germany without the golden fleece.

Early in 1912, the schism was brought to its conclusion. At
a conference in Prague Lenin proclaimed the Bolshevik faction
to be the Party.[3] The Mensheviks and a few Bolshevik splinter
groups coalesced against him under the so-called Organization
Committee. In *Pravda* Trotsky denounced Lenin's venture with
much sound and fury.[4] His anger rose to the highest pitch in
April, when the Bolsheviks began to publish in Petersburg a
daily called *Pravda*. This was an outrageous plagiarism, clearly
calculated to exploit for the Bolsheviks the goodwill of Trotsky's
paper. He thundered against the 'theft' and 'usurpation', committed by 'the circle whose interests are in conflict with the vital
needs of the party, the circle which lives and thrives only through

---

[1] In *My Life* Trotsky relates that he was to address the congress on the persecution
of the Finns by the Tsar. During the congress came the news of the assassination of
Stolypin in Kiev by Bagrov, an *agent-provocateur*. The Germans were afraid that the
appearance of a Russian revolutionary on their platform might provoke diplomatic
complications and repressive measures, and so Bebel induced Trotsky to give up
his intention of addressing the congress.

[2] *Pisma Axelroda i Martova*, p. 217; Lenin, *Sochinenya*, vol. xviii, pp. 193–4.

[3] Apart from the Bolsheviks, a Menshevik splinter group led by Plekhanov
participated in the conference.   [4] *Pravda*, no. 24.

chaos and confusion'. He called upon the editor of the Bolshevik paper to change its name within a given time; and he threatened meaningfully: 'We wait quietly for an answer before we undertake further steps.'[1] He apparently sent a similar ultimatum directly to the Bolshevik editorial offices. He had no inkling that the man who set up the rival paper in Petersburg and issued its first copy was the little-known Bolshevik Joseph Djugashvili, the man who would in the future similarly expropriate him of glories greater than the editorship of *Pravda*—of the titles of the leader of the revolution and the founder of the Red Army.

Yet it would be wrong to blame the plagiarism on to Stalin alone. Lenin wholeheartedly approved it; and in a letter to Petersburg he wrote: 'I advise you to answer Trotsky in the column "Answers to Readers" as follows: "To Trotsky in Vienna: We shall leave your quibbling and pettifogging letters without reply." '[2] One can easily guess how Lenin justified the plagiarism to himself: the Central Committee had subsidized *Pravda*; the title and the goodwill of the paper belonged to the party, not to Trotsky; and since the Bolsheviks were the party, they were entitled to appropriate the paper's name. This was a lame excuse, even though such quarrels over titles occurred in all émigré groups. Trotsky threatened to take further steps; but it seems that he took none, and he ceased to publish his *Pravda*, while the Bolshevik paper under its stolen name embarked on a long and famous career. In 1922, when *Pravda* celebrated its tenth anniversary, Trotsky took part in the celebration and contributed an article in which he did not even hint at the paper's origin.

.   .   .   .

The fact that Socialists could now openly publish dailies in Petersburg (the Mensheviks were publishing *Luch—The Torch*— which counted Trotsky among its contributors) showed a significant change in Russia. The years of reaction were over; the terror had spent itself; the Labour movement was experiencing a new revival; and, willy-nilly, Tsardom had to put up with it. A new generation of revolutionaries was coming of age and flocking into the few openly existing workers' clubs and trade unions and into the clandestine organizations. The new

---

[1] *Pravda*, no. 25. (From now on all references to *Pravda* are to the Bolshevik paper, unless it is stated otherwise.)   [2] Lenin, *Sochinenya*, vol. xxxv, p. 17.

situation provided the protagonists with new arguments. The liquidators pointed to the government's growing tolerance as proof that it was possible to Europeanize the party and to lead it out of the recesses of the underground. In the years of the terror their argument had sounded unreal; now it was based on facts. Yet the political revival also brought new vigour into the clandestine organization, and the young revolutionaries who were now entering it were not content with that cautious expression of opposition which the police tolerated in the legal clubs and trade unions. The government itself was the more inclined to put up with legal forms of opposition the more it was afraid of the illegal ones. This gave the Bolsheviks a powerful argument: we must, they said, intensify our clandestine efforts even if only to gain more elbow-room for open work.[1]

In these circumstances, Trotsky set out to pursue once again the will-o'-the-wisp of unity. He induced the Organization Committee to convene in Vienna a conference of all Social Democrats for August 1912. He hoped that the rise of the revolutionary temper in Russia would now, as in 1905, help to bring about a reconciliation. This was not to happen. In 1905 the strong tide of revolutionary events could still stop or delay incipient schism. In 1912 the cleavage had become so wide that the new political revival could only widen it further. Moreover, Lenin was now reaping the fruits of his labours: his men led the Social Democratic underground, while Menshevism was a farrago of weak and disconnected groups. The Leninists refused to attend the conference in Vienna; and so Mensheviks, ultra-left Bolsheviks, boycotters, the Jewish Bund, and Trotsky's group came together and formed a confederation, known in the annals of Russian socialism as the August Bloc. Trotsky was that bloc's chief mouthpiece, indefatigable at castigating Lenin's 'disruptive work'. There is no reason to doubt the sincerity of the apologia in which he claimed that he had never intended to turn the conference against the Bolsheviks, and that only Lenin's refusal to attend it or to countenance any attempt to re-establish unity had driven him into his anti-Bolshevik position. This apologia is amply borne out by the private correspondence of the Menshevik leaders; but it also shows how thoroughly Trotsky had misjudged the outcome of a decade of controversy.

[1] F. Dan, *Proiskhozhdenie Bolshevisma*, pp. 440–2.

His Menshevik friends did not share his illusions. They found it tactically convenient to place, once again with his help, the odium of the schism on Lenin; but they were no less determined than Lenin to carry the schism through to the end. The main difference was that while Lenin openly avowed his intention and almost shouted it from the house-tops, Martov, Axelrod, and Dan kept their design to themselves and sought to put it into effect through a subtle tactical game. It is enough to compare Lenin's utterances with the confidential correspondence of the Menshevik leaders, to see how strongly from their opposed angles they agreed on this one point that the split was both inevitable and desirable; and how they ridiculed, almost in the same terms, Trotsky's efforts to avert or to reverse it.[1]

.   .   .   .

The August Bloc left Trotsky galled and upset, despite, or perhaps because of, the 'pugnacity' he had displayed on its behalf. When, therefore, in September 1912 the editor of *Kievan Thought* asked him to go as the paper's correspondent to the Balkans, he eagerly seized this opportunity of getting away from émigré politics and changing from an actor playing an uncongenial part into an observer watching a storm centre of world politics. Early in October he left Vienna; and in a cab on the way to the station he learned of the outbreak of the first Balkan war, in which the southern Slavs joined hands against the Turkish empire.

From Vienna he had watched the Balkans and established connexions with Balkan Socialists. Two years before, in July 1910, he went to Sofia to expose and denounce a Pan-Slav congress taking place there under Miliukov's auspices. He addressed there a convention of the Bulgarian *Tesniaki* ('die-hards' of socialism), which assembled simultaneously with the Pan-Slav demonstration. Kolarov, the future Stalinist president of Bulgaria, introduced Trotsky to the congress and to crowds

[1] Trotsky was at this time on very friendly terms with the 'ultra-left' Bolshevik splinter groups, the boycotters and 'god-seekers'. In the summer of 1911 he lectured at their party school at Bologna, which Lunacharsky had set up with Gorky's help. A vivid description of the school is contained in a report by an *agent-provocateur* to the Okhrana. The report says *inter alia* that the lecturers (Lunacharsky, Menzhinsky, Kollontai, Pokrovsky) behaved towards their pupils, clandestine workers from Russia, in a haughty and patronizing manner. Trotsky, exceptionally, entertained friendly and private relations with his pupils. *Bolsheviki. Dokumenty Okhrannovo Otdelenia*, vol. i, p. 40.

in streets and squares as the legendary hero of the Petersburg Soviet; and Trotsky was enthusiastically acclaimed. He warned the southern Slavs that Tsarist diplomacy was trying to use them as pawns, and that the Russian Liberals were fostering Pan-Slavism because they were anxious to find common ground with Tsardom in foreign policy, while surrendering to it at home.[1] After that Trotsky often went on short trips to Belgrade and Sofia and kept in close touch with events there. As early as January 1909 he wrote in *Kievan Thought* that the Balkans were the Pandora's box of Europe.[2]

The Pandora's box had now begun to release its horrors; and the sight of them shook Trotsky. He had speculated abstractly on the problems of war; but now as he saw the castle in Belgrade floodlit by Austrian searchlights from across the frontier, as he watched the long queues of called-up reservists and learned that many of his friends, politicians, editors, university lecturers, were already in the front line, the first to kill and to die, a sense of tragedy overcame him, a 'feeling of helplessness before fate . . . and a pain for the human locusts carried to their destruction'.[3] 'The abstract, humanitarian, moralist view of history is barren —I know this very well. But this chaotic mass of material acquisitions, of habits, customs, and prejudices, which we call civilization, has hypnotized us all, giving us the false impression that we have already achieved the main thing. Now comes the war and shows us that we have not even crawled out on our bellies from the barbarous period of our history.'[4]

This sense of tragedy coloured all his Balkan correspondence, which was in the grand style of journalism, characteristic of the Liberal-radical press of pre-revolutionary Russia. Each article was a considerable essay, remarkable for the solidity of its background information, for the wealth of impression and local colour, for the excellence of its portraiture and analysis, and, last but not least, for imaginative and vivid language. Collected in his *Works*, these essays are still an invaluable chronicle of the Balkans before 1914. The essayist was also a

---

[1] L. Trotsky, *Sochinenya*, vol. ii, book 1, pp. 207–23; vol. vi, pp. 34, 46.

[2] 'Only a single state', Trotsky wrote then, 'of all Balkan nationalities, built on a democratic, federative basis—on the pattern of Switzerland or of the North American republic—can bring international peace to the Balkans and create conditions for a powerful development of productive forces.' Ibid., vol. vi, p. 10.

[3] Ibid., p. 66.   [4] Ibid., p. 141.

full-blooded journalist, keen to see things for himself, to interview people in all walks of life, and to supply his readers with hot topical matter. He loved the excitement and the drudgery of news gathering, and he mingled so freely with his colleagues from the European press—he worked in close partnership with the correspondents of the *Frankfurter Zeitung* and the *Daily Telegraph*—that for a time the ambitious politician and the tribune of the revolution seemed to disappear behind the newspaper man.[1] No sooner had he arrived in Belgrade than he interviewed nearly every member of the Serbian government and, with much wit and artistry, wrote character-sketches of them, showing how the personalities reflected recent history and the mentality of a small peasant nation. He delved into problems of supply, military training, and tactics, and revealed the atrocities and the primitive cruelty of the war. He visited and described with the same eagerness churches in Sofia where thanksgiving services were held for victories invented by propagandists; hospitals where he talked to wounded soldiers; dirty and overcrowded prisoners' cages where he learned about the experiences of Turkish infantrymen; comfortable hotels which served as prisoners' cages for Turkish officers; fashionable cafés in the spuriously European centres of the Balkan capitals; and wretched, almost Asiatic, suburbs—nests of destitution, horror, and degradation.

He had first approached the war of the southern Slavs against the Turkish empire with a certain sympathy, for he found the memory of Turkish oppression even more alive in the Balkans than was the memory of serfdom in Russia.[2] The Slav revolt in some respects reminded him of the Italian *Irredenta* of 1859. But he feared that the grievances of the Slavs would be abused by the great powers, especially by the Tsar, and that they would be used as pretexts for European war. Paraphrasing one of Bismarck's sayings, he wrote: 'If the leading Balkan parties . . . see no way of settling the fate of the Balkans other than by a new European intervention . . . then their political plans are truly not worth the bones of a single infantryman of the Kursk province. This may sound cruel, but only thus can an honest, democratic politician pose this tragic problem.'[3] The Balkan

[1] Ibid., pp. 283–92.
[2] Ibid., pp. 142–3, 187.   [3] Ibid., p. 144.

peasant leaders, who had in their youth imbibed the Russian revolutionary influence, were now paradoxically setting their hopes on the Tsar. This alone was enough to cool and to damp Trotsky's sympathy for their cause. The local contrasts of luxury and hunger, the corruption of the rulers, the needless atrocities inflicted on Turkish soldiers and civilians, the orgies of chauvinism, the bluff of the propagandists and the follies of the censorship evoked in Trotsky anger and disgust. He defended the weak and the defeated, the Turks.

The Bulgarian censorship pounced upon him, confiscated his articles and barred him from visiting the front. Curiously enough, the chief censor was a radical poet, Petko Todorov, who only two years before had, together with Trotsky, addressed in Sofia the meetings against Pan-Slavism. In an 'Open Letter to the Censor' Trotsky retorted with a scathing exposure of the sophisms and excuses with which military censorship is usually justified, and with an eloquent plea for freedom of information. The Letter, full of fire and thunder a little out of proportion to the object of the attack, made a considerable stir.[1] A more worthy object of attack presented itself soon. When Miliukov, as apostle of Pan-Slavism, arrived in Sofia, he flattered the Bulgarians and kept conveniently silent about their atrocities. Trotsky wrote another 'Open Letter' to Miliukov, which, when it appeared in a Petersburg daily,[2] opened a controversy which for many months filled the columns of the Russian press. Miliukov questioned the truthfulness of Trotsky's reports on atrocities; and Russian correspondents of Pan-Slav leanings joined in the affray. Trotsky, however, produced documentary evidence, collected by himself and the correspondents of the *Daily Telegraph* and *Frankfurter Zeitung*. These acrimonious exchanges were still in full swing when the whole situation suddenly changed: the first Balkan war ended with Slav victory; the victors, Serbs and Bulgarians, fell out over the spoils; official and Liberal Russian sympathies went to the Serbs; and the Bulgarians changed overnight from glorified heroes into atrocious villains, even in Miliukov's own paper.

Trotsky conducted part of this campaign from Vienna, where he also summed up the bearing of the first Balkan war upon

[1] L. Trotsky, *Sochinenya*, pp. 263–73.
[2] *Luch*, 13 January 1913 and *Sochinenya*, vol. vi, pp. 273–92.

European politics. Through the Balkan prism he saw the alignment of the great powers as it was to appear in 1914; and he saw it with great clarity, dimmed only by the wishful belief that the French, Austrian, and German Socialists, the latter with their 'eighty-six dailies and millions of readers', would defend to the end 'the cause of culture and peace against the onslaught of chauvinist barbarism'.[1]

Back in Vienna, he was soon again engrossed by the party cabal, protesting in private letters against the undisguised relish of his Menshevik friends at their separation from the Bolsheviks and against the ascendancy of the liquidators in the August Bloc. He quietly resigned from one Menshevik paper and growled against another, to which he continued to contribute. He was too much attached to the Mensheviks to part company and too restive to stay with them. 'Trotsky', Martov sneered in a private letter, 'while he was in the Balkans missed the evolution of the entire [August] Bloc'; the Mensheviks had in the meantime finished with talk of unity and with that 'empty, verbal conciliationism' which had been in vogue in the dubious hey-day of the Bloc. 'I think', Martov added, and he repeated this advice right and left, 'that we ought to show him [Trotsky] our "teeth" (of course, in the softest and politest manner).'[2]

It was therefore without regret that Trotsky again left Vienna to watch the second Balkan war. This time Serbia and Greece defeated Bulgaria, and Trotsky, the supposed enemy of the Bulgarians, turned into their defender. He described the plunder and violence of which the new victors were guilty; he visited the territories they annexed, and depicted the political unsettlement, the human misery, and the ethnographical nonsense entailed by hostilities 'conducted in the manner of the Thirty Years War' and by the shifting of frontiers and populations. He wrote a study of Romania, a classic of descriptive reporting, reprinted many times after 1917. 'Whereas Bulgaria and Serbia', he summed up, 'emerged from Turkish domination as primitive peasant democracies, without any survivals of serfdom and feudalism, Romania, in spite of decades of spurious constitutionalism, even now keeps its peasantry in the grip of

[1] L. Trotsky, *Sochinenya*, vol. vi, p. 302.
[2] *Pisma Axelroda i Martova*, pp. 262 ff. and 274.

strictly feudal relations.'[1] Romania was the 'jackal' in this war, and without having fired a shot, shared in the victors' spoils and annexed southern Dobrudja. Trotsky toured the province while its rural areas were afflicted by an epidemic of cholera and by a plundering *soldateska*, to the total indifference of the new Romanian rulers. He described how whole villages were dying out from lack of food and medicine; and how doctors, belonging to landed families, examined—from afar through binoculars—the cholera-stricken peasants, not deigning to approach them.

His descriptions of these scenes were oddly shot through with intimate flashes of a peculiarly Russian nostalgia. He travelled in a cab over land very similar to his native steppe. The landscape of the Dobrudja swept by breezes from the Black Sea, the burial mounds scattered over the steppe, the heat, and the sleepy pace of the journey brought back memories of his childhood at Gromokla and Yanovka and the picture of his recently deceased mother.

The road is so Russian, dusty like our Kherson road. The hens flee from under the horses' hoofs in a somewhat Russian way, and around the necks of little Russian horses are tied Russian harness ropes; even the back of Kozlenko [the cabman] is Russian. . . . Oh, how Russian his back is: you may travel round the world and you will not find such a back. . . . It is growing dusky. There is a smell of grass and road dust, Kozlenko's back darkens, and it is calm all around. Holding on to each other, we doze off. Phrrr!! Kozlenko stops his horses, patiently waits and thoughtfully whistles at them. Quiet. The blood itches in the feet, and it seems that we are travelling for our holidays from the station Novyi Bug to the village Yanovka.[2]

His homesickness became even more nagging when he visited Russian settlements scattered over the Dobrudja. The settlements were inhabited by Skoptsy. It was with members of this strange sect, the 'holy eunuchs', that he had travelled on barges down the Lena river during his first deportation to Siberia in 1901. The colonies and orchards of the Skoptsy in Dobrudja shone with cleanliness and neatness; but, Trotsky noted, 'somehow it is boring here, lonesome and dull. Something is lacking. Life is lacking; children are lacking; mothers are lacking.

[1] L. Trotsky, *Sochinenya*, vol. vi, p. 348.   [2] Ibid., pp. 415–20.

Faces are bloated, and, despite honest looks, unpleasant.' And he copied with approval a remark made by a 'doctor friend', who was his guide through the Dobrudja: 'Watching the life of the Skoptsy you become convinced . . . that sex is a social principle, the source of altruism and of every sort of human nobility.'[1]

The 'doctor friend' and guide was Christian Rakovsky, whom Trotsky had met many times before in western Europe and in the Balkans. Their friendship now acquired an intimacy which was to outlast war, revolution, triumph and defeat, exile, and even purges—this was perhaps the only lasting and intimate friendship in Trotsky's life. Six or seven years older than Trotsky, Rakovsky was to play in the Russian Revolution a role reminiscent of that played by Anacharsis Cloots in the French. Like Cloots, he was an aristocrat, a thinker, and a citizen of the world; and, also like Cloots, he adopted the country of the revolution as his own and sided with the radical wing in the revolution. Even now, in 1913, he had behind him an astonishing career. The scion of a great Bulgarian landed family of northern Dobrudja, he had become a Romanian citizen when his native land was annexed by Romania in 1878. At the age of fifteen he was, as a Socialist, expelled and barred from all schools in Bulgaria. His family sent him abroad to study medicine. He graduated at the University of Montpellier; and his doctorial thesis on 'The Causes of Crime and Degeneration' earned him high repute in the medical profession. Then he studied law at another French university. In 1893, when he was twenty, he represented the Bulgarian Socialists at the congress of the International in Zürich, where he came under Plekhanov's influence and was befriended by Jules Guesde, the eminent French Marxist, and by Rosa Luxemburg. In the next year he engaged in Socialist activity in Berlin, which was still living in the aftermath of Bismarck's draconian anti-Socialist laws, and he was expelled from Germany. Thereafter he appeared at every important Labour gathering on the Continent. In 1905 he returned to Romania. As a defender of the peasants he drew upon himself the landlords' hatred, and was persecuted and finally expelled on the ground that he was a Bulgarian citizen, although he had in the meantime served as medical officer in

[1] Loc. cit.

the Romanian army. For five years the Socialist party and the trade unions waged a campaign for his return. The government refused to admit him, denouncing him alternately as an agent of the Russian General Staff and as a dangerous anti-Tsarist conspirator.

In exile Rakovsky published several books, one, *Russia in the East*, exposing Tsarist expansion in Asia, and another, *The Rumania of the Boyars*. In his spare time, the pamphleteer, propagandist, and doctor devoted himself to historical research, the fruit of which was *Metternich and his Age*. Writing with equal ease in Bulgarian, French, Russian, German, and Romanian, he contributed to political, medical, and historical periodicals in all these languages. Repeatedly he returned to Bucharest, but each time the expulsion order was re-enforced despite stormy parliamentary protests and street demonstrations. Once the French government, prompted by Jaurès, intervened to release him from a Balkan jail, for he was also the Balkan correspondent of Jaurès's *Humanité*. Just before the first Balkan war he was allowed to return to Bucharest; and he became the acknowledged leader of the Romanian Socialist party, editor of its daily, expounder of the idea of a Balkan federation, and the most effective mouthpiece of anti-militarism in the Balkans. At the same time he managed his family estate in the Dobrudja, where he freed his peasants from feudal servitude and served them as doctor. Constantly on the move between parliament, party headquarters, and editorial offices in Bucharest and his native estate in the country, constantly struggling against some injustice, great or small, he would also follow the plough, often in the tailcoat in which he had just arrived from the capital. It was while thus inspecting his fields, the tails of his coat flapping in the wind, in the intervals between talks with his peasants and visits to patients, that he initiated Trotsky into the intricacies of Romania's economics and politics.

During this trip Trotsky also entered into friendship with Dobrodjanu Gerea, the old founder of Romanian socialism, from whom Rakovsky had just taken over the leadership of the party. Gerea was an enchanting and picturesque character. A Russian Jew—his original name was Katz—one of the early *Narodniks*, he had escaped from Russia and settled in Romania, where he discovered for the Romanians their own history and became their most important historian and literary critic and the inspirer of Romania's so-called literary renaissance. A whole generation of Romanian intellectuals learned to think politically from his book *Neo-Serfdom*; and his pupils later led the Conservative and Liberal parties as well as the Socialist. Dobrodjanu Gerea kept a restaurant at the railway station of Ploesti, and this was a place of pilgrimage for Romanian men of letters and politicians. At the counter of that restaurant Trotsky spent many an hour, picking the brains of the eccentric old sage.[1]

It was towards the end of January or the beginning of February 1913, during Trotsky's short stay in Vienna between the two Balkan wars, that Stalin's figure flitted past like a shadow on a screen. Curiously enough, Trotsky described the incident in detail only in the last year of his life.[2] One day he visited the Menshevik Skobelev, his former assistant on *Pravda*, who had just been elected a deputy to the Duma. They were sitting by a *samovar* and talking when suddenly, without knocking at the door, there entered from another room a man of middle height, haggard, with a swarthy greyish face, showing marks of smallpox. The stranger, as if surprised by Trotsky's presence, stopped a moment at the door and gave a guttural growl, which might have been taken for a greeting. Then, with an empty glass in his hand, he went to the *samovar*, filled the glass with tea, and went out without saying a word. Skobelev explained that this was a Caucasian, Djugashvili, who had just become a member of the Bolshevik Central Committee and seemed to be acquiring some importance in it. Trotsky, so he himself asserted, retained a vivid memory of this first glimpse of his future adversary and of the perturbing impression Stalin then made on him. He noticed the Caucasian's 'dim but not commonplace' appearance, 'a morose concentration' in his face, and an expression of set hostility in his 'yellow' eyes. It was his silence and the weird look of the man that engraved the casual scene on Trotsky's

---

[1] L. Trotsky, *Sochinenya*, vol. vi, pp. 386–402.

[2] This description of the meeting between Stalin and Trotsky is based on Trotsky's own memoir (written on 22 September 1939), which I found in the *Archives* at Harvard. In my *Stalin* I wrote mistakenly that 'neither Trotsky nor Stalin has described their meeting in Vienna'. Trotsky, at any rate, did not describe it before the last year of his life.

memory, enabling him to describe it with a retrospective shudder twenty-seven years later.

On internal evidence, Trotsky's description seems truthful, and not necessarily coloured by after-knowledge. The haggard, grim, inwardly concentrated and somewhat uncouth Bolshevik appears true to character: this was the Stalin of those days, after years of clandestine work, of hiding among Tartar oil-workers at Baku, and after repeated imprisonments, deportations, and escapes. Nor does Trotsky's impression of the set hostility in Stalin's looks seem unfounded; that hostility reflected the attitude of the Bolshevik Committee man towards the inspirer of the August Bloc. Stalin had seen Trotsky before, at the party congress in the Brotherhood Church in London, although Trotsky had not noticed him then. He had certainly remembered Trotsky's agitation against the Bolshevik raids and expropriations, with which Stalin had been closely concerned; and even in 1907, in his report on the congress, Stalin had already written of Trotsky's 'beautiful uselessness'. Trotsky did not know who edited the first issue of the Bolshevik paper which appropriated the name of his *Pravda*. Stalin knew. Only a fortnight or so before this silent meeting he had described Trotsky in the *Social Democrat* as a 'noisy champion with faked muscles', and under these words he had placed, for the first time, the signature Stalin.[1]

The rough growl with which he had met Trotsky came as if from the depth of the Russian log cabin.

[1] Stalin, *Sochinenya*, vol. vii, pp. 271–84; see also chapter iv in Deutscher, op. cit.

CHAPTER VIII

War and the International

THE outbreak of the First World War brought to an abrupt end the golden age of European Liberal capitalism, parliamentarianism, and reformist socialism which had flourished together in nearly half a century of peace, interrupted only by minor wars in the colonies and on the Balkan fringe. Two generations of Europeans had grown up in the optimistic belief that man had progressed far enough to secure ascendancy over nature and to change and perfect his social environment through argument, conciliation, and the majority vote. They had also been inclined to view war as a relic of a barbarous past, to which mankind would surely not revert. The accumulation of wealth in Europe as a whole had been so impressive and so rapid that it appeared to guarantee growing prosperity to all classes of society and to rule out violent social conflict.

Nowhere were these illusions more deeply seated than in the Labour movement, especially in the Second International. The International had inherited its ideology, its watchwords, and its symbols from the revolutionary periods of the past century, from the upheavals of 1848, from the Paris Commune of 1871, and from the underground struggle of German socialism against Bismarck. The watchwords and symbols spoke of the workers' international solidarity and of their irreconcilable class struggle, culminating in the overthrow of bourgeois government. The practical work of the Socialist parties had long since ceased to have much in common with these traditions. Irreconcilable class struggle had given way to peaceful bargaining and parliamentary reformism. The more successful these methods, the closer grew the connexion between the formerly outlawed Socialist parties and trade unions on the one hand and governments and associations of employers on the other; and the more effectively did national interests and viewpoints prevail over the inherited watchwords of internationalism. Up to 1914 the Socialist parties still managed, on the whole, to explain and justify their reformist work in customary revolutionary terms. Their leaders continued to profess Marxism, internationalism, and anti-militarism until the first day of war, when the International crumbled.

Of the great European nations, Russia was the only one that had participated but little in the peaceful progress of the preceding era. Her economic advance, indubitable though it had been, was insignificant in comparison with the accumulation of wealth in western Europe. It had, at any rate, been insufficient to implant in the nation habits of peaceful bargaining and compromise and to foster belief in a gradual progress from which all classes would benefit. Parliamentarianism, and all the institutions for social conciliation and arbitration which usually cluster around it, had taken no roots in Russian soil. Class struggle, in its most violent and undisguised form, had been raging from one end of the empire to the other; and Tsardom had not left the workers and peasants even the illusion that it was allowing them any influence on the nation's destinies. In the Socialist International, the Russian party had been almost the only one to treat the revolutionary traditions and watchwords with passionate seriousness and not as a matter of mere decorum.

In 1914 the Russian émigrés, with few exceptions, watched with horror the cataclysm engulfing the International; and they could hardly believe their eyes when they saw the leaders of European socialism throwing to the winds all their solemn anti-militarist resolutions and internationalist oaths and calling their working classes to fight for their emperors and to hate and kill the 'enemy'. At first, most Russian émigrés—Bolsheviks, Mensheviks, and Social Revolutionaries alike—denounced this conduct as a betrayal of socialism. Later many of them had second thoughts, but many went even farther: the slaughter of the next few years, in which millions of people laid down their lives to wrest a few yards of land from the enemy, taught them to despise and hate the humanitarian façades and shams of the European body politic. They concluded that if civilized governments in pursuit of their national power-politics found it possible to exterminate millions of people and to maim scores of millions, then it was surely the Socialists' duty to shrink from no sacrifice in the struggle for a new social order that would free mankind from such folly. The old order was giving them a lesson in ruthlessness. The 'Gothic lace-work' of European civilization had been torn to pieces and was being trampled into the mud and blood of the trenches.

. . . .

The outbreak of war found Trotsky in Vienna—he had just returned from Brussels where, together with Martov and Plekhanov, he had made a last appeal to the Bureau of the International asking it to intervene in the internal feud of the Russian party. In the morning of 3 August he went to the editorial offices of the Viennese *Arbeiterzeitung*. The news of the assassination of Jaurès by a French chauvinist had just reached Vienna. The diplomatic chancelleries were exchanging the last notes, designed to shift the blame for the war on to the enemy. General mobilization was on foot. On his way to the Socialist editorial offices, Trotsky watched vast crowds carried away by warlike hysteria and demonstrating in the fashionable centre of the city. At the *Arbeiterzeitung* he found confusion. Some editors were ready to support war. His friend Friedrich Adler spoke with disgust about the rising flood of chauvinism. On Adler's desk lay a pile of xenophobe pamphlets and next to it another pile of jubilee badges prepared for a congress of the Socialist International convened to meet in Vienna on 15 August—the International was to celebrate the twenty-fifth anniversary of its foundation. The congress was now cancelled, and the treasurer of the Austrian party was lamenting the 20,000 crowns he had wasted on preparations. The old Victor Adler despised the chauvinist mood invading his own entourage, but he was too sceptical to resist. He took Trotsky to the chief of the political police to inquire how, in view of the expected state of war between Austro-Hungary and Russia, he proposed to treat the Russian émigrés. The chief of the police answered that he was preparing to intern them. A few hours later, Trotsky and his family boarded a train for Zürich.

Neutral Switzerland became the refuge of Russian revolutionaries who had lived in Germany and Austria. To Zürich went Karl Radek, expelled from Germany for anti-militarist propaganda; Bukharin, who had been detained for a short time in Vienna; while Lenin, still jailed by the Austrians in Galicia, was to arrive a little later. The country's neutrality allowed the Swiss Socialist party to view with tolerance and even friendliness the internationalist propaganda of the Russians. In a workers' educational association Trotsky found an eager audience for his denunciations of the war and of the Socialists who supported it. 'With Trotsky's arrival in Zürich', recollects a well-known Swiss writer, 'life returned to the Labour movement, or at least to one sector of it. He brought with him the belief . . . that from this war would arise revolution. . . . With Trotsky these were not merely words but his innermost conviction.'[1] So strongly did he sway his new audience that almost at once he was elected delegate to a national convention of the Socialist party of Switzerland. It gave the leaders of the party some trouble to explain to the rank and file that it was impolitic to give voting rights at the congress to a foreigner and a citizen of a belligerent country.

During this stay in Zürich, which lasted only a little more than two months, Trotsky wrote *The War and the International*, the first extensive statement of anti-war policy by a Russian Socialist. Its polemical edge was turned primarily against the German Social Democrats, who were arguing that in fighting Tsardom, the 'gendarme of Europe', Hohenzollern Germany was pursuing a progressive historical mission. 'In our struggle against Tsardom', Trotsky retorted, 'in which we know no truce, we have not sought and are not seeking assistance from the militarism of the Habsburgs or the Hohenzollerns. . . . We have owed a lot to the German Social Democratic Party. We have all gone through its school and learned from its successes and mistakes. It was for us not one of the parties of the International but *the* party.' All the keener was the indignation with which he now repudiated the attitude of the German Social Democrats. It was the Socialists' duty, he insisted, to stand for peace, but not for a peace that would mean a return to the *status quo* or a new balance between the imperialist powers. The Socialists' objective must be a democratic peace, without annexation and indemnities, and one allowing for the self-determination of the subject nations. Only a rising of the belligerent peoples against their rulers could achieve such a peace. This part of his argument anticipated by more than three years President Wilson's Fourteen Points; and Trotsky's pamphlet, when it appeared in the United States, had a direct influence on Wilson. Yet, 'self-determination of the nations',

[1] F. Brupbacher, *60 Jahre Ketzer*, pp. 188–9.

as Trotsky advocated it, had little in common with its Wilsonian interpretation. Its purpose was not to set up new nation-states— Trotsky, we know, had long since considered the nation-state an anachronism. The small and oppressed nations should be enabled to obtain independence in order that they might, of their free will, join in the building of an international Socialist body politic. 'In the present historical conditions', he wrote, 'the proletariat is not interested in defending an anachronistic national "Fatherland", which has become the main impediment to economic advance, but in the creation of a new, more powerful and stable fatherland, the republican United States of Europe, as the foundation for the United States of the World. To the imperialist blind alley of capitalism the proletariat can oppose only the socialist organization of world economy as the practical programme of the day.'[1] This bold conclusion seemed unreal to many. Trotsky relates that Radek criticized it there and then on the ground that the 'productive forces' of the world, or even of Europe, had not developed sufficiently to allow of their organization on an international Socialist basis. Lenin, on his arrival in Switzerland, criticized the phrase 'the United States of Europe', because it suggested to him that Trotsky envisaged the Russian Revolution only as part of a simultaneous Europe-wide insurrection. To this controversy we shall return.

In November 1914 the pamphlet was brought out in a German translation and with the help of Swiss Socialists dispatched to Germany. German anti-militarists who distributed it were prosecuted, and Trotsky himself was indicted *in absentia* for *lèse majesté* and sentenced to several months of prison by a German court—he learned this from reports in French newspapers. The German Social Democrats insinuated that he had written his pamphlet in the interest of Russia and her allies. But, as he had not hesitated to criticize the allied Socialists who supported the war, they in their turn charged him with whitewashing the German 'social-patriots'.[2]

Late in November Trotsky left Switzerland for France. *Kievan Thought* appointed him correspondent in Paris, and he eagerly seized the opportunity of watching the war from this

---

[1] *War and the International* was first published in Russian serially in the Parisian *Golos*, in November 1914, beginning with no. 59.

[2] *Golos*, no. 63, 25 November 1914.

excellent vantage-point. He was also anxious to join Martov, who was then editing in a spirit of undiluted opposition to war a Russian paper in Paris, *Golos* (*The Voice*). He had last seen Martov in Brussels, in the middle of July, where they went together to obtain from the Executive of the International a verdict against Lenin's schismatic activities; and jointly with Plekhanov they had then composed a manifesto to Russian Socialists. How remote and irrelevant all this seemed only a few months later! The leaders of the International, whom, as the highest authorities in socialism, they had solicited to intervene against Lenin, were now branded as 'social-chauvinists and traitors' by Martov and Trotsky as well as by Lenin. Plekhanov had in the meantime patriotically extolled the war on the ground that the Hohenzollerns and the Habsburgs, not the Romanovs, were the arch-enemies of progress and socialism. It seemed that the old divisions had been effaced and super-seded by new ones. Lenin, who had never abandoned a secret yearning for political reunion with Martov, the friend of his youth, stated: 'The Parisian *Golos* is at present the best socialist newspaper in Europe. The more often and the more strongly I dissented from Martov, the more categorically must I say that he is now doing exactly what a social democrat ought to do.'[1] The founder of Menshevism warmly reciprocated: he welcomed the appearance of Lenin's *Social Democrat* and agreed that the old controversies had lost all significance.[2] Events were to show that this was not so and that a reunion was, after all, impossible. But at the moment Trotsky rejoiced at its prospect.

In Paris he divided his time between work for Martov's paper and *Kievan Thought* and contacts with anti-militarist groups in the French Socialist party and trade unions. Almost from the day of his arrival he had to defend himself against charges of pro-Germanism, which emanated mostly from Alexinsky, a former Bolshevik deputy to the Duma, now a violent anti-Bolshevik and supporter of war. (The same ex-Bolshevik was in 1917 to spread the accusation that Lenin was a German spy.) A curious circumstance gave colour to the insinuations: a man bearing the name Nicholas Trotsky stood at the head of an Austrian-sponsored Union for the Liberation of the Ukraine,

[1] Lenin, *Sochinenya*, vol. xxi, p. 21, and *Golos*, no. 38, 27 October 1914.
[2] *Golos*, no. 52, 12 November 1914.

the prototype of the Ukrainian agencies that Germany was later to launch. It was easy to attribute the pro-Austrian and pro-German statements of the one Trotsky to the other, even after the author of *War and the International*, convicted in his absence by a German court, had publicly explained the confusion.[1]

Golos continued to appear for only six or seven weeks after Trotsky's arrival in Paris. Harassed by the censorship it ceased publication in the middle of January 1915. In these few weeks Trotsky gave even more definite expression to his views. The future, he wrote, held out only one set of alternatives: 'permanent war or proletarian revolution'. The war was 'a blind rebellion' of Europe's outgrown productive forces against the tight and constraining framework of the capitalist nation-states. Capitalist imperialism could break down the national barriers only by force; it was therefore incapable of breaking them down for good; and as long as it ruled the world it would plunge mankind into war after war, slaughter on slaughter, and drive civilization to its doom. Socialist reformism had no future, for it had become an integral element of the old order and an accomplice in its crimes. Those who were hoping to rebuild the old International, imagining that its leaders could by a mutual amnesty wipe out their betrayal of internationalism, were impeding the rebirth of the Labour movement.[2]

In one of the last issues of *Golos* he carried the argument even farther, saying that the struggle against 'the chauvinist falsifiers of Marxism' was only the negative side of the task ahead. The positive, constructive side was 'to gather the forces of the Third International'. This trend of thought ran parallel to Lenin's and was almost certainly inspired by it, for Lenin had formulated the same idea a little earlier.[3]

Martov had at first eagerly concurred in these views. But even before *Golos* had ceased publication, he was beset by doubts and second thoughts. The émigré Mensheviks who had, like himself, been opposed to the war, were reluctant to draw such sweeping conclusions. They held that the Socialist parties, in

[1] Ibid., nos. 62 and 63, 24 and 25 November 1914. Incidentally, in 1903–4, Leon Trotsky used to sign his writings *N.* Trotsky.

[2] Ibid., no. 66, 28 November 1914; no. 79, 13 December 1914.

[3] Ibid., no. 100, 8 January 1915; Lenin, *Sochinenya*, vol. xxi, p. 24.

supporting the war, had committed a grave error; but that they could still expunge it; and that the working classes, quite as much as their leaders, had been carried away by the social-patriotic mood. A new, 'purified' International had no chance of rallying the working classes; it would be a sect incapable of superseding the old organization. Some Mensheviks were opposed to war from pacifist rather than revolutionary conviction. Most were opposed to the Tsar, who on behalf of their nation conducted the war, rather than to war itself. And, inside Russia, some Mensheviks had committed themselves to a more patriotic attitude. All this could not but influence Martov. He was torn between his own conviction and the pull that the party he had founded exercised on him. He slid backwards and forwards, tried to patch up differences, and escaped from his dilemmas into the soothing atmosphere of the Parisian cafés.

Before the year 1914 was out, the pre-war divisions began to reimpose themselves on the recent 'solidarity of the internationalists'. Lenin insisted that his party as a whole had remained true to internationalism, while those of the Mensheviks who did so, Martov and Axelrod, were in discord with their own followers. Martov soon confided to Axelrod that Trotsky, too, was charging him, Martov, with Machiavellian tactics and with grinding the Menshevik axe. In reply Martov resorted to a well-tested stratagem: he tried to 'frighten' Trotsky (as Martov himself put it), telling him that if he were to break with the Mensheviks he would place himself at the mercy of the Bolsheviks and 'deliver himself into the hands of Grisha Zinoviev', now Lenin's chief assistant in Switzerland. But the bogy was not as effective as it used to be; and Martov related that he had to approach Trotsky with smooth diplomacy and to treat him 'like a little china statuette'.[1]

Trotsky, although as yet unwilling 'to deliver himself into the hands of Grisha Zinoviev', was nevertheless anxious to disentangle himself at last from the old alignment, dating back to the August.Bloc. On 14 February 1915 he published a statement in *Nashe Slovo* (*Our Word*), the paper that had replaced *Golos*, in which for the first time he recounted publicly the inner story of his disagreements with the Mensheviks, revealing that even

[1] *Pisma Axelroda i Martova*, p. 309. Martov wrote this letter to Axelrod on 9 January 1915.

two years before he had refused to contribute to their papers and to speak for them at the Bureau of the Socialist International; and that he was now refusing to represent them at a planned conference of allied Socialists in London. This repudiation of the August Bloc was Trotsky's first and decisive step on the road that was to lead him into the Bolshevik party.[1]

Other ties of old political connexions and friendship were snapping as well. The most painful to Trotsky personally was his break with Parvus, who had just declared his solidarity with the official German Socialist leaders in support of the war and was, in addition, engaged in vast commercial operations in the Balkans to his own and the German government's profit. The metamorphosis of this Marxist writer, who had so brilliantly analysed the obsolescence of the nation-state and expounded internationalism, into a 'Hohenzollern socialist' and a vulgar war-profiteer, was indeed one of the most startling changes that men were undergoing in those days. To Trotsky this was a severe blow: his and Parvus's names had been coupled in the joint authorship of the 'permanent revolution'; and since 1904 Parvus had participated in most of Trotsky's journalistic and political ventures. On Parvus Trosky must have fixed his fondest expectations, hoping that alongside Rosa Luxemburg and Karl Liebknecht, he would defy the chauvinism triumphant in the German party.

More in grief than in anger, Trotsky wrote 'An Obituary on a Living Friend', in which, even across the gulf now yawning between them, he paid sad homage to Parvus's wasted greatness.

To turn away for a moment from the figure which now appears under so well merited a pseudonym in the Balkans, the author of these lines considers it a matter of personal honour to render what is due to the man to whom he has been indebted for his ideas and intellectual development more than to any other person of the older generation of European social democrats. . . . Even now, I see less reason than ever to renounce that diagnosis and prognosis, the lion's share of which was contributed by Parvus.

Trotsky generously recalled how much he and others had

---

[1] *Nashe Slovo*, no. 13, 14 February 1915; *Pisma Axelroda i Martova*, pp. 315–17. The occasion of Trotsky's statement was a speech which Larin, still a Menshevik, made at a national convention of the Swedish Socialist party. Larin had referred to Trotsky, Plekhanov, and Axelrod as the three leaders of the so-called Organizational Committee.

learned from Parvus and how proud they had been of him. He acknowledged that Parvus had taught him, among other things, 'to express plain thoughts in plain words'. But—'Parvus is no longer. A political Falstaff is now roaming the Balkans, and he slanders his own deceased double.'[1] When presently Parvus set up at Copenhagen a 'sociological institute', suspected of being a German propagandist agency, Trotsky publicly warned Socialists against entering into any contact with it.[2] When Parvus sent an apologia, in the form of a Letter to the Editor, Trotsky first intended to publish it, but then changed his mind.[3] Once for all he put an end to relations with his former friend; and when, after the revolution, Parvus tried to approach him and to offer his services to the Soviet government, Trotsky left these approaches without an answer. Even so, the shadow of this association was to haunt him more than once: in July 1917, the 'month of the great slander', and again during his struggle against Stalin in the years of the great slander.[4]

Nashe Slovo began to appear on 29 January 1915. This was a modest sheet of two, rarely four, pages abundantly strewn with white spaces marking the censor's deletions, and yet packed with news and comment. The paper was constantly in danger of being killed by the censor and by its own poverty. Editors and contributors received no salaries or fees. Wages of the compositors and printers were usually many months in arrears; but the half-starved workers, political émigrés like the editors, went on producing the daily without a murmur. Every now and then collections were made in shabby émigré centres such as the Russian Library in the Avenue des Gobelins, the Club of the Russian Émigrés in Montmartre, or the Library of Jewish Workers in the rue Ferdinand Duval. The donations were in *centimes* and *sous* rather than francs, and the money went to pay

---

[1] *Nashe Slovo*, no. 15, 14 February 1915.

[2] Ibid., no. 208, 5 October 1915. Yet, when Alexinsky used Trotsky's warning to brand Parvus as a German *agent-provocateur*, Trotsky wrote a letter to *Humanité*, explaining that he had charged Parvus with being a social-patriot, but he did not believe him to be an *agent-provocateur*. Ibid.

[3] Martov revealed this when he himself resigned from *Nashe Slovo*. Martov, 'Letter to the Editor', *Nashe Slovo*, no. 235, 9 November 1915.

[4] Rich, and enjoying great influence in the Weimar Republic, Parvus nevertheless felt frustrated and repeated his advances to the Bolsheviks, until Lenin curtly dismissed him, saying that 'the Soviets certainly need clever brains, but above all clean hands'. M. Beer, *Fifty Years of International Socialism*, p. 197.

for the meagre supply of paper. Yet, *Nashe Slovo* had a remark-able circle of contributors, nearly every one of whom was to inscribe his name prominently in the annals of the revolution; and as a journalistic venture it was much superior to the Viennese *Pravda*, and much more influential. If a Parisian journalist or politician had been told that this obscure Russian daily was politically weightier than all the French boulevard press, he would have taken this as a joke. Yet in less than three years the ideas expounded in *Nashe Slovo* would resound from Petrograd and Brest Litovsk throughout the world.

The chief organizer of the paper was Antonov-Ovseenko, a Menshevik of long standing and a former officer in the Tsarist army, who had rebelled in 1905 at the head of his detachment, had been sentenced to death, but escaped and joined in the clandestine struggle. In October 1917 he was to lead the Red Guards in the attack on the Winter Palace, arrest Kerensky's ministers, and thus bring the Bolshevik insurrection to success. Small, lean, short-sighted, of mercurial temper and imagina-tion, the future Commissar now used his inventiveness to secure, against all odds, the existence of the paper. He 'showed a tenacity and an optimism which astonished even Trotsky, who was by no means devoid of these qualities'.[1] This was one of the new ties of friendship which were replacing the old ones in Trotsky's life: between 1923 and 1925 Antonov-Ovseenko was to be one of the leaders of the Trotskyist opposition.

It was apparently Antonov-Ovseenko who invited Trotsky and Martov to be joint editors of *Nashe Slovo*. Trotsky at first refused, suspecting that the paper was meant to serve a narrowly Menshevik purpose.[2] But eventually he assumed the co-editor-ship and, in constant controversy with Martov, so strongly impressed his own outlook on *Nashe Slovo* that the paper came to be considered his personal domain. Lunacharsky, the God-seek-ing Bolshevik, who had broken away from Lenin and who was to become the revolution's great Commissar of Education, worked for the daily and sometimes acted as peacemaker between Trotsky and Martov. Ryazanov, who had also come from Vienna to Paris, was one of the pillars of *Nashe Slovo*. Lozovsky, the future chief of the Red trade unions' International,

[1] A. Rosmer, *Le Mouvement ouvrier pendant la guerre*, pp. 244–9.
[2] *Pisma Axelroda i Martova*, p. 319.

now leader of a small trade union of Jewish hat-makers in Paris, surveyed French political and syndicalist developments. Manuilsky, the Bolshevik boycotter, future chief of the Stalinist Comintern and Foreign Minister of the Ukraine, contributed under the pen-name *Bezrabotnyi*—the Jobless. His only 'job' at the moment was that of the *gérant* of *Nashe Slovo*, the figure-head editor, legally responsible to the authorities. He regaled the editorial staff with witty anecdotes, which he composed and narrated with the *élan* of a first-rate comedian. Angelica Balabanov, the half-Russian, half-Italian Socialist, exposed in *Nashe Slovo* her old friend and protégé Mussolini, whom she had once lifted from the gutter to prominence in the Italian party and who was now urging neutral Italy to join in the war. Balabanov also translated into many languages, but especially into Italian, Trotsky's more important articles, helping thereby to keep the bulk of the Italian Socialist party in opposition to war. The editorial team further included men like Sokolnikov, later one of the chief organizers of the October insurrection, signatory to the peace of Brest Litovsk, Commissar of Finance, and diplomat; Pokrovsky the historian, and a few eminent Polish Socialists.

Of the outside contributors Chicherin, correspondent in London, should be mentioned first. Descendant of one of the first families of the Russian aristocracy, former Secretary of a Tsarist Embassy, he had thrown away his diplomatic career to cultivate in obscurity the great passions of his life: revolution, music, and history. For years he was a familiar figure in Paris at the Montparnasse branch of the French Socialist party. He used to appear there before midnight, wrapped in a vast Spanish cloak, the pockets of which were bulging with an incredible number of books, pamphlets, and periodicals: and there for many an hour of the night he would develop his ideas in leisurely fashion to those who would listen, supporting his arguments with quotations from his pocket reference library. These bat-like habits and this taste for keen but unhurried argument he was to retain as Foreign Secretary of the Soviet republic. In Paris, Chicherin was still a Menshevik, but he was too aloof and wayward to involve himself in émigré politics, and so nobody even guessed the talents hidden in him. The war had caught him in London. In a memoir, which does not seem to have been published, Trotsky says that Chicherin's correspondence from London was written in a vaguely social-patriotic spirit, but was so uncommonly subtle and original that he, Trotsky, was glad to have it in the paper.[1] Later in the war Chicherin was interned in Britain as an anti-war propagandist.

From Sweden and Denmark Alexandra Kollontai and Moissei Uritsky, both former Mensheviks, disgusted with 'social-patriotism' and rapidly evolving towards Bolshevism, contributed more or less regularly. Kollontai was to be Commissar of Social Welfare in Lenin's first government, while Uritsky—he had worked for the Viennese *Pravda* too—was to become one of the foremost Bolshevik leaders in 1917. The list of contributors included Theodore Rothstein, the Anglo-Russian historian of Chartism and future Soviet Ambassador in Persia; Radek, Rakovsky, and Maisky the future Soviet Ambassador in London. Rarely has any paper had so brilliant a galaxy of contributors.

The members of the editorial team were at one in their opposition to war and 'social-patriotism'; but, apart from this, they represented various shades of opinion. The editorial conferences, which took place every morning in the printing shop, developed into lively disputes which in their turn were reflected in the columns of the paper. As is usual in cases in which outward agreement conceals differences in frame of mind and approach, the controversies were involved and seemingly irrelevant; and often they degenerated into bitter wrangling. We might well ignore these wranglings were it not for the fact that they manifested the re-alignment of groups and individuals who were soon to come forward as leaders of great parties and mass movements. Next to Lenin's *Social Democrat*, Trotsky's paper was at this juncture the most important laboratory of the revolution. The issue passionately debated in it concerned the demarcation line that was to be drawn between the internationalists and the social-patriots. Where, how firmly, with what degree of finality should it be drawn? In their attempts to answer this question groups and individuals either drew closer to, or drifted away from, one another, until eventually some of those who at first seemed of one mind found themselves on different sides of that line.

[1] *The Trotsky Archives.*

Broadly speaking, three groups tried to influence *Nashe Slovo*. Martov exerted himself to reconcile his loyalties to Socialist internationalism and to Menshevism; and gradually he transferred his old distrust of Bolshevism to the single-minded 'angular' internationalism which Lenin preached. At the other extreme were the prodigal sons of Bolshevism, Manuilsky and Lozovsky, and to a lesser extent Lunacharsky, whom the impulse of war was driving back towards Lenin. Trotsky held an intermediate position; he tried to curb the pro-Bolshevik group and also to persuade Martov that he should dissociate himself from Menshevik social-patriots. 'The editorial conferences', Lunacharsky relates, 'dragged on in long debates, in the course of which Martov evaded with amazing elasticity of mind and almost sophistic slyness a clear answer. . . . Trotsky often attacked him very angrily.'[1] In the first issue of the paper Martov had, in fact, denounced some of his followers;[2] but after a few weeks he argued that it was wrong to charge the 'social-patriots' with treason to socialism.[3] The pro-Bolshevik group then indignantly turned against Martov; but Trotsky, for all his anger in debate, still shrank from a break with him.

Nevertheless, recent events and the continued débâcle of European socialism impelled him to review in his thoughts past controversies, and, as he himself put it, 'to see Lenin in a new light'. This revision, in all its gradualism and minute twists and turns can be followed through his writings in *Nashe Slovo*. In July 1915 he admitted, for instance, that the pre-war divisions in the Russian party had a close bearing on the current controversy, and that the Bolsheviks formed the core of the internationalist sector in Russian socialism. But he was still afraid that they were out to dominate the non-Bolshevik internationalists.[4] Martov protested against this and similar statements, refused to bear responsibility for the direction Trotsky was giving to the paper, and threatened to resign. At the same time, Lenin subjected Trotsky to relentless criticism, saying that Trotsky's internationalism was purely verbal, for it did not prevent him from co-operating with Menshevik social-patriots.

[1] A. Lunacharsky, *Revolutsionnye Siluety*, pp. 23–26, 68.
[2] *Nashe Slovo*, no. 1, 29 January 1915. Martov repudiated there the Menshevik periodical *Nasha Zarya*, published in Petrograd.
[3] Ibid., no. 31, 5 March 1915.
[4] Ibid., no. 146, 23 July 1915.

In the middle of this dispute there occurred the one great event of those days in which Trotsky played a central part. On 5 September 1915 there assembled at Zimmerwald, a little village in the Swiss mountains outside Berne, an international conference of Socialists, the first to take place since the outbreak of war. The initiative came from Italian Socialists who had had no intention of convening the gathering in defiance of the pre-war International. Earlier in the year an Italian Socialist deputy, Ordino Morgari, went to Paris to request the president of the International, the Belgian Socialist Vandervelde, to convene a session of the Executive. 'As long as German soldiers are billeted in the homes of Belgian workers', Vandervelde replied, 'there can be no talk of convening the Executive.' 'Is the International then a hostage in the hands of the Entente?' asked Morgari. 'Yes, a hostage!' replied Vandervelde. Morgari then asked for a conference at least of the Socialist parties of neutral countries. When Vandervelde rejected this suggestion too, the Italian deputy approached Martov, Trotsky, and Swiss Socialists with the proposal to convene a conference independently of the old International. Thus came into being the movement which was to become the forerunner of the Third International.[1]

Thirty-eight delegates from eleven countries, belligerent and neutral, assembled at Zimmerwald to reassert their international solidarity.[2] The German delegation was headed by several influential deputies of the Reichstag and brought greetings from the imprisoned Karl Liebknecht. The French delegation was less impressive, for the anti-militarist groups in the French party were weak and only a few syndicalist leaders arrived. Lenin represented the Bolsheviks, Axelrod the Mensheviks. Rakovsky and Kolarov came from the Balkans, and there were Polish, Swiss, Dutch, Italian, and other delegates. In normal times a gathering of this sort would not have been considered very representative; but in the days when it was a crime for

---

[1] Trotsky described the preliminaries to the Zimmerwald conference in *Nashe Slovo*, no. 109, 10 May 1916.

[2] Before the opening of the conference the Russians met to discuss their representation. *Nashe Slovo* sent three delegates: Martov, Trotsky, and Manuilsky, representing the three attitudes among the editorial staff. Lenin questioned their credentials and Martov and Manuilsky resigned in favour of Trotsky. The conference admitted Trotsky and accorded him full voting rights, but only against Lenin's protests. Trotsky related this with mild resentment in *Nashe Slovo*, no. 212, 9 October 1915.

citizens of belligerent countries to be in contact with one another,
the mere fact that well-known labour leaders 'shook hands
across the barbed wire and bleeding trenches' was an unheard-
off challenge to all warring governments.

The participants in the conference were, however, less united
in purpose than their resolutions implied. The majority were
pacifists, eager to reassert their faith, but not inclined to go
farther. A minority, grouped around Lenin, who for the first
time now came forward as the protagonist of an international
and not merely of a Russian trend in socialism, urged the conference to adopt a defeatist attitude towards all warring governments, to call upon the peoples to 'turn the imperialist war into
civil war', and to proclaim the need of a new International. This
the majority refused to do. On most points Trotsky was in
agreement with the minority, although he would not endorse
Lenin's revolutionary defeatism. (It was, he wrote, in the interest
of socialism that the war should end 'without victors and vanquished'.) He held, moreover, that these differences should be
transcended so as to enable the conference unanimously to
condemn the war. In this everybody concurred, and Trotsky was
asked to draw up a statement of principles, which was soon to
become famous as the Zimmerwald Manifesto. In it he stirringly
described the plight of embattled Europe, placing the responsibility on the capitalist order, the governments, and the self-
betrayed Socialist parties; and he called upon the working
people to recover from their intoxication with chauvinism and
to put an end to the slaughter. Rousing though it was, the
Manifesto was vague in its conclusions. It did not call for civil
war that would put an end to the imperialist war; and it did not
envisage the new International. The conference adopted the
Manifesto unanimously, but Lenin's group placed its reservations
on record. Finally, an international committee was elected which,
although it was not yet nominally opposed to the second International, was nevertheless to become the nucleus of the third.

Only good luck enabled Trotsky safely to return to France.
On the frontier his luggage was opened for examination, and in
it he carried all the Zimmerwald documents. An inspector picked
them up, but seeing on top of them a sheet of paper with a conspicuous, patriotic inscription *Vive le Tsar!*, he did not bother to
examine them further. At Zimmerwald during the sessions,

while he had been covering sheets of paper with doodles, Trotsky had copied those words from an article by Gustave Hervé, the French semi-anarchist turned patriot. In Paris the censorship suppressed reports of the conference. 'All the same, the conference has taken place; and this is a momentous fact, Mr. Censor', Trotsky wrote in *Nashe Slovo*. 'The French press has written more than once that Karl Liebknecht has saved Germany's honour. The Zimmerwald conference has saved the honour of Europe.' 'An obtuse professor', Trotsky went on, 'had written in *Journal des Debats* that the conference had no significance and that it gave comfort to Germany; an equally obtuse professor across the Rhine had written that it was of no significance and that it gave comfort to the Entente. If the conference was so impotent and insignificant, why have your superiors banned every mention of it? And why, despite all the banning, have you yourselves had to begin to discuss it? You shall still discuss it, gentlemen. . . . No force will delete it from the political life of Europe.'[1] The article was more than usually mutilated by the censor, the white gaps taking more space than the printed matter.

Almost since the beginning of his stay in Paris, Trotsky, at first jointly with Martov and then alone, kept in touch with small French anti-militarist groups, mainly syndicalist, headed by Alfred Rosmer, Pierre Monatte, Bourderon, and Merrheim, who were later to found the French Communist party. Trotsky attended regularly the weekly meetings of these groups, which were closely watched by the police. He gave them the benefit of his political experience, and explained to them the background of the war and the developments in foreign Labour movements; he inspired their policy and brought them into the Zimmerwald movement. He thus acted as godfather to the French Communist party, with which he was to maintain close ties in later years.

In addition to these activities he kept up his correspondence for *Kievan Thought*, which earned him his livelihood. *Kievan Thought* supported the war, and so in his articles he had to tack about cautiously to avoid a breach with the paper. The Kievan editor was only too glad to publish the Paris correspondent's denunciations of German imperialism, but his criticisms of the

[1] *Nashe Slovo*, no. 218, 19 October 1915.

Entente were unwelcome. Trotsky could tell his readers in Russia only half the truth as he saw it, that half which somehow fitted in with official Russian policy. He tried on occasion to tell it in such a manner that the shrewd reader should guess the suppressed half of the story. To the author of the Zimmerwald Manifesto this was a most embarrassing position; and so he confined himself more and more to reportage and strictly military surveys.

The man who from Zimmerwald had defied the mighty of the world and whose Manifesto resounded throughout Europe did not spurn the chores of journalism. He travelled to the south of France and to the Channel ports to gather impressions and to gauge the moods behind the fighting lines. As he had done during the Balkan wars, he visited the hospitals to talk to the wounded, and mingled with French and British soldiers in the cafés and market places of small French towns. With never-flagging curiosity he listened to the harrowing tales of wartime refugees, Belgian, French, and Serbian, and filled his notebooks with their stories. Back in Paris, he would read some twenty European newspapers a day at the Café Rotonde, where Martov could be found at almost any time of the day. From the Rotonde he rushed to a library to study serious military periodicals and literature, French, English, Italian, German, Austrian, and Swiss. In these journeys and studies he found relaxation and refreshment; and they also prepared him for a great job ahead. As the experience of a Captain of the Hampshire Grenadiers had not been useless to Gibbon as historian of the Roman Empire, so the experience of a conscientious military correspondent would one day be of use to the founder of the Red Army.

His military correspondence, reprinted in his *Works*, has been altogether forgotten since his political eclipse; yet, together with his writings of the years of the civil war, it should have earned him a place in the history of military thought. Like nearly all Marxists who seriously delve into military matters, he was greatly influenced by Clausewitz's classical strategic conceptions. Amateur though he was, he had this advantage over contemporary military experts, Clausewitzian and anti-Clausewitzian, that he saw behind the clash of arms a contest of economic powers and political régimes; and that he had a shrewder eye for the morale of the embattled nations.

Almost from the first weeks of hostilities he forecast, against prevailing expert opinion, the prolonged and bloody stalemate of trench warfare, and ridiculed the hopes which Clausewitz's German epigones were placing on the offensive power of their army.[1] He did not share, however, the characteristically French illusions of a purely defensive strategy and a war of attrition. He pointed out that their conception of defence would impel the French repeatedly to undertake the most costly and futile offensives, and that a war of attrition would be more, not less, bloody than ordinary warfare. He explained the military stalemate as the result of an equilibrium between the economic resources of the hostile coalitions. This approach, which we can only baldly summarize here, enabled him over the first three years of the war to forecast with rare accuracy the course of successive military operations. With the prospect of a relentless strategic deadlock he connected the vistas of revolution, for he expected that the stalemate of trench warfare would drag on almost indefinitely, sap the foundations of the old society, and drive the peoples to despair and revolt. Sometimes, it is true, he expected a development of strategy and technology which would break the stalemate, but not before very late in the war; and he came close to adumbrating the invention of the tank.[2] Yet, on the whole, the nightmare, for so long only too real, of the self-perpetuating mutual slaughter of equally balanced forces overshadowed his military thinking; and it would still do so even in the last year of the war, when, as we shall see later, it would cause him to make important errors of judgement.

Even while he was surveying with detachment the course of hostilities and eagerly absorbing military theories, his mind was gripped by the tragedy of Europe, bleeding and distraught.

[1] L. Trotsky, *Sochinenya*, vol. ix, pp. 7–15.

[2] On one occasion he forecast that after the war the military leaders would forget or neglect this new weapon which would decide the outcome of the war. He thus came very near to predicting the neglect of the tank by the British and French General Staffs on the eve of World War II. Ibid., p. 190. In a sarcastic aside he dismissed in advance the illusion of a Maginot Line as it was beginning to emerge from the French experience in World War I. 'The triumph of the French [in defence] is so evident that not only military experts bow to it, but also . . . pacifists. One of them . . . has reached the happy conclusion that war can be eliminated altogether if the boundaries of states are reinforced by continuous trenches and demarcated by a powerful electric current. Poor, scrofulous pacifist who seeks a shelter in the trenches.' Loc. cit.

This preoccupation with the 'human factor' in war lifts his military writings far above the professional level. For example, his essay 'Barbed Wire and Scissors' is a technical study of trench warfare and, at the same time, an intuitive and imaginative reconstruction of its psychological impact on the huge armies involved in it. It is almost incredible that the author of this essay had never even seen a trench—so intimately did he penetrate its strange atmosphere, foreshadowing much of what writers like Remarque, Zweig, Hasek, Sherriff, Barbusse, Gläser, and others were to write after the war in autobiographical novels and plays.

If the fate of Trotsky's writings, we repeat, and the extent to which they are read or ignored had not been so inseparably bound up with his political fortunes and with the sympathies and antipathies that his mere name evokes, he would have had his niche in literature on the strength of these writings alone. This is especially true of his descriptive pieces. In these he usually narrates the adventures of a single soldier, revealing through them some significant aspect of the war. In 'The Seventh Infantry Regiment in the Belgian Epic', for instance, which he wrote at Calais in February 1915, he describes the experiences of De Baer, a student of law at the University of Louvain, in whom he focuses the whole drama of invaded and occupied Belgium. He follows the young lawyer from the outbreak of the war through the confusion of mobilization, through battles, retreats, encirclements, and escapes, through a sequence of strange yet quite normal scenes, in which we see and feel the elemental upsurge of patriotism in the invaded people, their sufferings, their unwitting, often accidental heroism, a heroism in which the tragic and the comic are intertwined, and, above all, the boundless absurdity of war. The student De Baer goes through appalling torments in the trenches; then he is detailed to a court martial to act as defending counsel for fellow soldiers; he returns to the trenches and unknowingly distinguishes himself in battle and is decorated with much pomp and solemnity. After that, almost alone of his encircled company, he survives without a scratch, and loses only his spectacles in the fray. Sent to a hospital in France, he is found to be too short-sighted to be a soldier, and is released. Thrown out by the military machine in a foreign country, he finds no employment; and, when the author meets him, he is starving and in rags. Because of its great realistic simplicity, the story reads like a modernized fragment of *War and Peace*. The author makes no propaganda; his hero is no proletarian; the patriotic feelings of the invaded Belgians, in seeming contradiction with the writer's political views, are described with such warm sympathy that the story might fit excellently into a patriotic anthology of Belgian martyrdom; all the more effectively does he expose the absurdity of war.

'From a Notebook of a Serb' is written in a similar vein. There the epic of another small nation, first flattered, then exploited, and then trampled on by the great powers, is brought into focus in the adventures of Todor Todorovich, a Serbian peasant from the Austrian-ruled Banat who has deserted from the Austrian army. Todor Todorovich plods alongside the retreating Serbian army, through burning villages and ice-bound mountains. Frequently he is in danger of being shot either as a deserter and Serbian traitor by the Austrians or as an Austrian spy by the Serbs. Each time he has a tragi-comic escape and trudges on to stare at scenes of Dantesque horror, until he becomes almost a symbol of man, forlorn amid the primordial savagery which has burst through the thin crust of civilization.[1]

In other essays such as 'The Psychological Puzzles of War' Trotsky tried to feel himself into the condition in which the European mind would emerge from the holocaust. He guessed that the man of the trenches would not easily adjust himself to 'normal' society:

. . . the present disaster will, in the course of years, decades, and centuries, emit a sanguinary radiation, in the light of which future generations will view their own fate, just as Europe has hitherto sensed the radiation of the great French Revolution and of the Napoleonic wars. Yet how small were those events . . . in comparison with what we are performing or experiencing now, and especially with what we are heading for. The human mind tends to banality; only slowly and reluctantly does it clamber up to the height of these colossal events . . . it strives unwittingly to belittle for itself their

[1] Op. cit., pp. 87–112. 'Where is the modern Swift to place before bourgeois Europe his satirical mirror?' Trotsky asked in *Nashe Slovo* (16 May 1916), describing satirically how the embassies, general staffs, and academies of Germany and France tried to exploit, each for its own patriotic purposes, an anniversary of Cervantes.

import so that it can more easily assimilate them. . . . It is not our mind that masters the great events; on the contrary the events, arising from a combination, interplay, and concatenation of great objective historical forces, compel our sluggish, lazy mind, waddlingly and limpingly to adjust itself. About this fact, so hurtful to our megalomania, our second nature, there cries out, in the merged thunder of all the guns and weapons, the present fate of the civilized nations.[1]

.   .   .   .

Towards the turn of the year 1915 the cleavage in the Zimmerwald movement became accentuated. The minority, led by Lenin, was more and more emphatically dissociating itself from the pacifist Socialists and from those 'centrists' who tried to hold a middle position. The controversy grew in bitterness as the belligerent governments, supported by the 'social-patriots', proceeded to repress the Zimmerwald movement, to imprison its leaders and adherents or to send them to the trenches. Among the Russian émigrés feelings were incensed by the conduct of the Menshevik deputies in the Duma—the Bolshevik deputies had already been tried and deported to Siberia. The leader of the Menshevik deputies, the Georgian Chkheidze, had spoken in the Duma about Zimmerwald, defending it in so ambiguous and half-hearted a manner that the defence amounted to repudiation. Lenin at once denounced Chkheidze and insisted that every Russian member of the Zimmerwald movement should do the same.

The bitterness was aggravated when, in Russia, Vera Zasulich and Potresov, like Plekhanov, came out in support of the war. To Trotsky this was a new blow and disillusionment. He had first embroiled himself with Lenin from devotion to the veterans of the party; and although he had in the meantime outgrown the veterans and had had his differences with them, his devotion to them had remained undiminished. Now he saw all of them, with the partial exception of the émigré Axelrod, 'deserting the cause'. With Chkheidze, too, he had been politically associated before the war: it was to Chkheidze that in 1913 he had written in a letter about that 'master squabbler Lenin . . . that professional exploiter of the backwardness

---

[1] L. Trotsky, *Sochinenya*, vol. ix, pp. 244–8. These words were written in September 1915.

of the Russian labour movement . . . '.[1] Now Trotsky still tried to find mitigating circumstances for Chkheidze's behaviour; but with Vera Zasulich he broke with a heavy heart as he had broken with Parvus.[2] More than once he had to ask himself what had caused the old guard to abandon their principles, and whether Lenin had not been right all along in spurning them and going his way.

In his autobiography Trotsky describes his evolution towards Bolshevism as a process in which of his own accord he was drawing closer and closer to Lenin, and he does no justice to the influence which some of his contributors had on him. The truth which emerges from the pages of *Nashe Slovo* is that he was prodded and pushed that way by the pro-Bolsheviks on his staff, who, although they were men of much smaller stature, were quicker in grasping the trend of the realignment and urged him to abandon his old loyalties and to draw conclusions from the new situation.[3]

One ought not to and one need not (wrote one of them) share the sectarian narrow-mindedness of [Lenin's group] . . . but it cannot be denied that . . . in Russia, in the thick of political action, so-called Leninism is freeing itself from its sectarian features . . . and that the workers' groups connected with *Social Democrat* (Lenin's paper) are now in Russia the only active and consistently internationalist force. . . . For those internationalists who belong to no faction there is no way out but to merge with the Leninists, which in most cases means joining the Leninist organization. . . . There exists, of course, the danger that through such a merger we shall forfeit some valuable features . . . but the spirit of the class struggle, which lives not in literary laboratories but in the dust and tension of mass political strife, will brace itself and boldly develop.[4]

Another writer, himself a former Menshevik, tried to explain why the founding fathers of Russian socialism had turned into

---

[1] This letter to Chkheidze was found in the archives of the Russian police in 1921. Olminsky, who was in charge of the party archives, wrote to Trotsky asking him whether the letter should be published. Trotsky advised against publication, saying that it was impolitic to revive old controversies, especially as he did not think that he was always wrong in what he had written against the Bolsheviks. See Trotsky's letter to Olminsky of 6 December 1921 in the *Trotsky Archives*.

[2] *Nashe Slovo*, no. 58, 9 March 1916.

[3] When Trotsky was writing his autobiography, in 1929, most of his former pro-Bolshevik contributors to *Nashe Slovo* had sided with Stalin against him.

[4] *Nashe Slovo*, no. 15, 19 January 1916.

'social-patriotic opportunists'. They had begun their political and literary careers with a critique of the voluntarist Utopias of the *Narodniks*; and this left a lasting impression on their outlook. In their polemics against the *Narodniks* they had concentrated so exclusively on 'objective conditions', on what was and what was not historically possible in Russia, that they became the slaves of their own determinism. The Mensheviks had indubitable merits in analysing the social conditions of Russia and in attempting to Europeanize the movement (merits, the writer added, which Trotsky's *Pravda* shared with them). But they completely neglected to cultivate the revolutionary will, which changes the social conditions within which it works. The principle of will and action was as much essential to the Marxist doctrine as was its determinism; and this principle, so the writer concluded, was embodied in Lenin's group. That was why the Mensheviks had floated with the tide of events to their social-patriotic débâcle, while the Bolsheviks had the strength to resist the tide.[1]

Manuilsky and Lozovsky, especially the former, argued along the same lines. Still refusing to accept Leninism as the 'ready made and rounded off form of the new internationalist ideology', still criticizing its 'national narrow-mindedness and angular crudity', Manuilsky, nevertheless, insisted that Bolshevism, because of its emphasis on will and action, had legitimately become the core of the Russian revolutionary movement. 'History', he wrote, 'has placed the Russian working class in a position more favourable for revolutionary initiative than that in which the western proletariat has found itself. . . . It has imposed higher duties and obligations on us than on European labour.' All the more urgent was it to find a common language with Lenin's group. Discreetly, Manuilsky criticized Trotsky, without mentioning him by name, for his attempts to excuse the ambiguous conduct of Chkheidze and of the other Menshevik deputies.[2]

Quite perceptibly these influences worked on Trotsky. If a distaste for the 'sectarian' and distinctly Russian side of

---

[1] The author of this article was K. Zalewski, a Polish Socialist, who had before the war sided with the Menshevik liquidators. *Nashe Slovo*, nos. 35, 36, 11 and 12 February 1916.

[2] *Nashe Slovo*, nos. 75–78, 29 March–1 April 1916. In the same issues Trotsky went on defending Chkheidze in unsigned editorials.

Bolshevism lingered on in a man like Manuilsky, it was all the stronger in Trotsky. But he, too, preached close co-operation with 'the very active and influential group of Leninists', although he was still afraid of remaining tête-à-tête with it.[1] When he made the *rapprochement* with the Bolsheviks a principle of editorial policy, Martov, after many 'ultimatums and counter-ultimatums', at last resentfully resigned from *Nashe Slovo*.[2] Thus snapped another old friendship, and thus Trotsky made another step towards Lenin and the Third International.

However, neither Trotsky nor even Lenin had yet made up his mind to secede at once, come what might, from the Second International. In the spring of 1916 the leaders of that International, alarmed by the response which the Zimmerwald movement had evoked, at last convened at the Hague a session of their International Bureau. In *Nashe Slovo*, Lozovsky urged the Russian Socialists to boycott the conference or to attend it only in order to declare demonstratively that they would not rejoin the pre-war organization. In a reply which is of considerable interest to the historian of the Third International, Trotsky pleaded for a more cautious attitude: '. . . it is possible that we, the left, may be in a position not to attend The Hague conference, if we have the masses behind us. We might then go there only in order to make a demonstration . . . as Lozovsky, pre-judging the issue, one-sidedly counsels us to do. But it is also possible that the alignment inside the labour movement may compel us to take up for a time the position of a left wing in *their* [i.e. the Second] International.'[3] He recalled that the Zimmerwald movement had not arisen as an explicit attempt to set up a new International. Trotsky's attitude in this matter was a shade less definite than Lenin's. At the end of April 1916 Lenin carried with him the second conference of the Zimmerwald movement, which assembled at Kienthal, in Switzerland. Trotsky did not attend—this time the French authorities did not permit him to cross the frontier. But in defiance of the raging censorship, he stated in *Nashe Slovo* his solidarity with the Kienthal resolutions.[4]

[1] Ibid., no. 89, 14 April 1916.   [2] Ibid., no. 93, 19 April 1916.
[3] Ibid., no. 97, 23 April 1916. In support of his attitude Trotsky quoted *The Communist*, a Bolshevik paper, edited by Bukharin, which had expressed a similar view.
[4] Ibid., nos. 111, 115, 12 and 17 May 1916. See also issue of 2 September 1916.

Differences on broader issues still separated Trotsky from Lenin. There was, first, the disagreement over revolutionary defeatism. 'The revolution is not interested in any further accumulation of defeats', Trotsky wrote, while Lenin expounded the view that Russia's military defeat would favour revolution. On the face of it, two extremely opposed views seem to clash here; and so the Stalinist historians present the story. Actually the difference was one of propagandist emphasis, not of policy. Both Lenin and Trotsky urged Socialists to turn the war into a revolution and to spread their ideas and views among workers and in the armed forces, even if this should weaken their country militarily. Both agreed that the fear of national defeat should not deflect the Socialist from doing his duty. For all the provocative emphasis which Lenin gave to his defeatism, he did not ask his followers to engage, or to encourage others to engage, in sabotage, desertion, or other strictly defeatist activities. He merely argued that although revolutionary agitation would weaken Russia's military strength, Russian Socialists were bound in duty and honour to take this risk in the hope that German revolutionaries would do the same so that in the end all the imperialist governments would be vanquished by the joint efforts of the internationalists. The defeat of any one country would thus prove only an incident in the revolution's advance from country to country. Trotsky, and with him many of Lenin's own followers, refused to tie the fortunes of revolution so exclusively to defeat.[1] It was enough, Trotsky argued, to preach and prepare revolution, no matter what the military situation. Each attitude had, from the viewpoint of those who held it, its advantages and disadvantages. Trotsky's non-defeatism did not in advance expose the internationalist to the charge that he was giving aid and comfort to the enemy. Lenin's attitude, for all its obvious tactical inconvenience, was better calculated to make the revolutionary immune from warlike patriotism and to erect an insurmountable barrier between him and his adversaries. In 1917 these two shades of opposition to war merged without controversy or friction in the policy of the Bolshevik party.

Another controversy concerned the 'United States of Europe'. Although this has come to be regarded as a hallmark of Trotskyism, Lenin had included it in his own theses on Socialist war

[1] *Nashe Slovo*, no. 68, 21 March 1916; *Sotsial-Demokrat*, no. 50.

policy as early as September 1914.[1] 'The United States of Europe' epitomized the unshakeable hope of both Lenin and Trotsky that at the end of the war the whole of Europe would be engulfed by proletarian revolution. Lenin, nevertheless, raised objections to the manner in which Trotsky advanced the idea, because at one moment Trotsky seemed to imply that revolution could break out in Russia only simultaneously with a European upheaval. Such a view, Lenin pointed out, might be an excuse for quietism and might lead the Socialists of any country to wait passively until 'the others begin'. Or it might contain the pacifist illusion that the United States of Europe could be erected on a capitalist, instead of a Socialist, foundation. The revolution, Lenin wrote, might well develop and succeed in Russia before it did so in the rest of Europe, because 'the unevenness of economic and political development is an ineluctable law of capitalism'. For this criticism Trotsky had given some grounds when, carried away by the grandiose vista of a unified Socialist continent, he had argued that the war 'breaking up the nation-state, was also destroying the national basis for revolution'.[2] If the whole trend of Trotsky's reasoning is kept in mind, the interpretation which Lenin gave to these words appears incorrect, since Trotsky had argued all along that the Russian revolution would be the first to conquer and that it would then stimulate revolutions elsewhere.

To Lenin's criticism Trotsky replied: 'That no country should in its struggle idly wait for the others to begin is a basic idea which it is useful to repeat. . . . Without waiting for the others we have to begin the struggle on our national ground, fully confident that our initiative would give a fillip . . . to other countries.'[3] He went on to develop an argument which contained the seeds of a controversy not with Lenin but with Lenin's successor. It was true, Trotsky wrote, that capitalism had developed 'unevenly'; and so the revolution was likely to win in a single country first. Yet 'the unevenness of the development is itself uneven.' Some European countries had advanced, economically and culturally, more than others; but Europe, as a whole, had progressed further than Africa or Asia and was riper for Socialist revolution. There was, therefore, no

---

[1] Lenin, *Sochinenya*, vol. xxi, p. 4.   [2] *Nashe Slovo*, no. 23, 24 February 1915.
[3] Ibid., no. 87, 12 April 1916.

need to contemplate the prospects of a revolution permanently
or for long isolated in a single country. There was no need to
fall into 'that national revolutionary Messianic mood which
prompts one to see one's own nation-state as destined to lead
mankind to socialism. If a victorious social revolution were
really conceivable within the boundaries of a single . . . nation,
then this Messianic attitude . . . would have its relative historic
justification.' 'To fight for the preservation of the national base
for social revolution by methods which threaten to cut the
international ties of the proletariat, means to sap the foundations of the revolution. *The revolution must begin on a national basis
but, in view of the economic and military-political interdependence of the
European states, it cannot be concluded on that basis.*'[1]

With this attitude Lenin had no quarrel. What strikes us now
about Trotsky's words is his prescience, negatively expressed,
of the 'national revolutionary Messianic mood', which views
'its own nation-state as destined to lead mankind to socialism'.
Of this mood Stalin, in his later years, was to become the
exponent.[2]

.   .   .   .

The second year of Trotsky's stay in Paris was drawing to a
close when, on 15 September 1916, the French police banned
Nashe Slovo. The next day Trotsky himself was ordered to leave
the country. Socialist deputies protested to the Prime Minister,
Aristide Briand, and obtained a delay in the enforcement of the
order. Legally there was no ground for the expulsion. *Nashe
Slovo* had not been able to say more than the censorship had
allowed it to say; and although Trotsky had often wrangled
with and poked fun at the censor, he had scrupulously complied
with his directions. Nor did the French government take a
grave view of Trotsky's contacts with the still feeble French
anti-war groups. But the Tsarist Embassy intrigued against the
revolutionary émigrés, and the French complied, willy-nilly,

---

[1] Loc. cit.

[2] Trotsky took it for granted, of course, that the prospect of a capitalist United
States of Europe was Utopian. German imperialism, he wrote, was striving to
unify the old continent under its domination; but even if it succeeded, it would
merely produce a compulsory military alliance and customs union, 'a parody of the
United States of Europe, written in fire and by the sword of German militarism'.
Only Socialist revolution could bring about a voluntary union of the peoples.
Nashe Slovo, no. 29, 4 February 1916.

with the wishes of their allies. An accident assisted the embassy's intrigue. A mutiny, partly provoked by a secret agent of the Russian police, had broken out among Russian soldiers disembarked at Marseilles; and it was claimed that the mutineers had acted under the influence of *Nashe Slovo*. Trotsky feared that the French intended to extradite him to Russia. For six weeks he tried in vain to obtain permission to enter Switzerland or Italy or to travel through England to Scandinavia until, on 30 October, he was detained by two police agents and deported to the Spanish frontier.

Before the expulsion he addressed an 'Open Letter' to Jules Guesde, the pioneer of French Marxism who had become Minister of War:

Is it possible for an honest socialist not to fight against you? In an epoch when bourgeois society—whose mortal enemy you, Jules Guesde, once were—has disclosed its true nature through and through, you have transformed the Socialist Party into a docile chorus accompanying the coryphaei of capitalist banditry. . . . The socialism of Babeuf, Saint-Simon, Fourier, Blanqui, the Commune, Jaurés, and Jules Guesde—yes, of Jules Guesde, too—has finally found its Albert Thomas to deliberate with the Tsar on the surest way of seizing Constantinople. . . . Step down, Jules Guesde, from your military automobile, get out of the cage, where the capitalist state has shut you up, and look around a little. Perhaps fate will for once, and for the last time, have pity on your sorry old age, and you will hear the muted sound of approaching events. We await them; we summon them; we prepare them.[1]

He entered Spain, hoping to proceed from there to Italy and Switzerland—his Italian friends were still trying to obtain the entry permits. But while the French had compelled him to cross the Spanish border, they had warned the Spanish police that a 'dangerous anarchist' had sneaked into their country. He stayed for a day at San Sebastian, and with rueful irony contemplated in his hotel a picture 'La Muerte del Pecador' ('The Death of a Sinner') hung over his bed. From there he went to Madrid, and, in expectation of news from Italy, loitered for ten days, mingling with gay and noisy crowds, watching picturesque ceremonies and taking notes. He knew no Spanish and had no acquaintance

---

[1] Quoted by Alfred Rosmer in 'Trotsky during World War I' in *The New International*, September–October 1950.

in Madrid, except a French Socialist who worked there as manager of the Spanish branch of a French insurance company. The day of 7 November—next year on this very day he would lead the Bolshevik insurrection—he spent at the Prado and jotted in his note-book reflections on the 'eternal' element in Spanish classical paintings, contrasting it with the less majestic but more intimate and subtle appeal of French impressionistic art.

Two days later, while he was attending a sporting event, he was spotted by a police agent and arrested. Fearing that the Spanish police might put him on board a ship bound for Russia, he dispatched cables and letters of protest right and left. In a letter to the Spanish Minister of Home Affairs he explained, with the usual flourish and irony, that he knew no Spanish, had met not a single Spanish citizen, had published not a single line in Spain, and had only visited museums and churches. The only reason for his arrest, given to him by the chief of the police of Madrid, was that his 'views were a little too advanced for Spain'. The Socialist and republican press began to clamour for his release. After three days he was ordered to proceed under escort to Cadiz. There he was allowed to remain at large, under mild, almost farcical police surveillance, to await the arrival of the first boat in which he could leave the country.[1]

At Cadiz Trotsky spent six weeks, bombarding the Spanish government with protests and killing time in the company of a police agent at an ancient library, where, in a quietness such that 'one could hear the bookworm eating his way through the folios', he pored over old French and English books, took notes and copied excerpts on Spanish revolutions and counter-revolutions, on their effect on bullfights, on the failures of Spanish liberalism and on the intrigues of the great powers in the Peninsula.[2] At last a boat bound for Cuba came in. He

---

[1] In the Madrid prison he made long entries in his diary, describing humorously the prison, its administration, its inmates, and his own wranglings with his jailors. One of the inmates was a 'Thieves' King', who had 'operated' in half the world and was treated with reverence by the prisoners and the guards. The 'King' wanted to learn from Trotsky what chances Canada offered to an enterprising thief—surely, a multilingual pacifist and anarchist should be able to tell that. ' "Canada?" I answered hesitatingly, "you know, there are many farmers there, and a young bourgeoisie, who, like the Swiss, should have a strongly developed sense of property!" '

[2] After a visit to the old harbour of Cadiz, where he had watched a brutal brawl,

refused to board it, and, after new protests and a few anxious moments, was allowed to stay until the arrival of a ship bound for the United States. His Italian friends now wrote him that they hoped soon to obtain the Italian and Swiss visas. 'When I am already at Cadiz', he remarked, 'the whole of Europe becomes hospitable to me.' On 20 December he was allowed to leave, again under police escort, for Barcelona whither his wife and two sons had arrived from Paris. From Barcelona he sailed with his family on a ramshackle Spanish ship, crowded with well-to-do deserters and destitute 'undesirables' from all European countries. The neutral flag of the ship at least offered some protection from German submarines. On the last day of the year, the ship passed Gibraltar.

'This is the last time', Trotsky wrote to Alfred Rosmer, 'that I cast a glance on that old *canaille* Europe.'

. . . .

On a cold, rainy Sunday morning, 13 January 1917, he disembarked in New York harbour. The colony of Russian Socialists enthusiastically welcomed the author of the Zimmerwald Manifesto; and there was no end to greetings and ovations.[1]

Trotsky 'looked haggard; he had grown older; and there was fatigue in his face', says the Russo-American Communist M. Olgin, who had visited him in Vienna five years before. 'His conversation hinged around the collapse of international socialism.' This was also the theme of the lectures which, shortly after his arrival, he delivered to Russian, Finnish, Latvian, German, and Jewish Socialists in New York, Philadelphia, and other cities.

With his family he settled in a lodging rented (for 18 dollars a month) in the Bronx, 164th Street. The cheap apartment offered the family unaccustomed luxuries: for the first time in his life, the future leader of the revolution had a telephone in his home. Various American writers have given highly coloured descriptions of Trotsky's life in New York: one remembered him as a starving tailor, another as a dish-washer in a restaurant, and still another as a film actor. Trotsky denied these stories; and the memoirs of people like Ziv and Olgin who were at the

he noted in his diary: 'Gigantic screwjacks will be needed in order to raise the culture of the masses.'   [1] A. Ziv, op. cit., pp. 68–69.

time close to him, offer no foundation for them. He earned his living from journalism and lecturing.[1]

The Russian émigrés published in New York a daily, *Novyi Mir* (*New World*), edited by Bukharin, Kollontai, and Volodarsky. Of this paper Trotsky at once became the mainstay. This was his first close association with any Bolshevik circle. Bukharin had lived in Vienna while Trotsky was editing his *Pravda* there, but the bitterness of factional strife had separated them. Now they drew together in a friendship which was to dissolve, though not entirely, only eight years later, after Bukharin had become Stalin's partner. Kollontai had from a Menshevik become one of Lenin's most fanatical adherents. Volodarsky, a Russo-American who described himself as 'an American worker by origin and way of life' was also strongly attracted by Bolshevism—he was to bring something of the American *élan* and organization into the Bolshevik revolution. With this group, though not yet with the Bolshevik party, Trotsky identified himself.

During his sojourn in the States, which lasted little more than two months, he had only a slender chance to acquaint himself with American life, and he had, as he himself put it, 'only a peep into the foundry in which the fate of men is to be forged'. He was fascinated by New York and impressed by the statistical evidence of American wealth, which had grown rapidly since the war. But his mind and heart were with that 'old *canaille* Europe': 'It is a fact', he said at a meeting, 'that the economic life of Europe is being shattered to its very foundations, while American wealth is growing. As I look enviously at New York— I who have not ceased to feel like a European—I wonder anxiously: "Will Europe be able to stand all this? Will it not decay and become little better than a graveyard? And will not the world's economic and cultural centres of gravity shift to America?" '[2] Now and through the rest of his life he dreamt about the great and original contribution which the United States would make to Marxism and socialism, a contribution surpassing in scale and momentum the one it had made and

[1] An amusing 'memoir' which appeared in the *New York Herald Tribune* (14 February 1932), depicts Trotsky as acting the part of a station-master in a film 'My Official Wife'. As an actor, says the writer, Trotsky was a 'washout', without personality and sex appeal, a 'shy, retiring man' who never talked about politics or socialism.   [2] L. Trotsky, *Moya Zhizn*, vol. i, p. 308.

was making to the development of capitalism. For the time being, however, the American Socialist sects appeared to him narrow, timid, ludicrously parochial, and led by a quaint Socialist variety of Babbitt, who 'supplements his commercial activities with dull Sunday meditations on the future of humanity'. A 'Babbitt of Babbitts', so he described, for instance, Hillquit, that 'ideal socialist spokesman for successful dentists'. The only exception was Eugene Debs, the pioneer and martyr, who, although a poor Marxist, had in him the 'quenchless inner flame of his socialist idealism. . . . Whenever we met, he embraced and kissed me. . . .'[1]

Before the middle of March 1917 came the first confused news about 'disturbances' in the Russian capital. Because of a break in communications the telegraph agencies still reported mere 'bread riots'. But already on 13 March Trotsky was writing in *Novyi Mir*: 'We are the witnesses of the beginning of the second Russian revolution. Let us hope that many of us will be its participants.' A fever of excitement took hold of the Russian colony; and meeting followed upon meeting. 'At all those meetings', wrote Dr. Ziv, now a Menshevik and a 'social-patriot', 'Trotsky's speech was the main event and the natural climax. Meetings were sometimes delayed for hours because Trotsky was taking part in many gatherings convened simultaneously . . . but the public patiently waited for him, thirsting for the words that would throw a light on the momentous event that had occurred in Russia.'[2] From the beginning, so Ziv relates resentfully, Trotsky assailed the Provisional Government of Prince Lvov, which had just constituted itself. Was it not a shame, he exclaimed at the meetings, that the first Foreign Minister of the revolution should be Miliukov, who had called the Red Flag a red rag, and its first Minister of War should be Guchkov, who had kowtowed to Stolypin? Kerensky, the only man of the left in this government, was merely its hostage. 'What has happened to Trotsky? What does he want?' Ziv's friends asked in amazement.

How Trotsky received the revolution and what he expected from it can be seen from his writings in *Novyi Mir*. Within the fortnight that passed between the first news of the 'bread riots'

---

[1] Ibid., vol. i, p. 313.   [2] A. Ziv, op. cit., p. 80.

in Petrograd and his departure from New York, he stated fully and clearly the main ideas he was to expound in the course of the year. When the composition of Prince Lvov's government became known and when that government called for a return to order, he wrote: 'The powerful avalanche of the revolution is in full swing, and no human force will stem it.' The Liberals were afraid that the popular movement which had given them power would swamp them. So they were calling for an end to the revolution 'as if its iron broom had already cleared to the end all the reactionary litter that had over the centuries piled up' around the Tsar's throne. 'The nation will now rise, layer after layer, all those who have been oppressed, disinherited, deceived. . . . At the head of the popular masses of Russia the revolutionary proletariat will carry out its historical work: it will expel monarchist reaction from wherever it tries to shelter; and it will stretch out its hand to the proletariat of Germany and of the whole of Europe. It is necessary to liquidate not only Tsardom but the war as well.'[1]

He accused the first government of the revolution of inheriting from Tsardom its imperialism and its designs on the Balkans and the Dardanelles; and he greeted hopefully the emergence of the Soviet of Petrograd as the potential government bound to assert itself against the old administration, now headed by the Cadets (Constitutional Democrats). When it became evident that the Soviet, guided by the Mensheviks and presided over by Chkheidze, had given its support to Prince Lvov's government and endorsed its foreign policy, Trotsky vehemently attacked Chkheidze, whom he had so recently defended from the Bolsheviks, and Kerensky, that 'young lawyer of Saratov . . . who has no great weight on the scales of revolution'. The Mensheviks and the Social Revolutionaries were evoking the patriotism of the peasantry to justify their support of the war. But, Trotsky wrote, it was not the alleged patriotism of the peasantry but its hunger for land that was of real importance. Tsardom, the landlords, and the bourgeoisie had done their best to divert the peasantry from agrarian revolution to imperialist war. It was the task of socialism to lead the peasants back from war to agrarian revolution. 'The landlords' land and not Constantinople', thus the soldier–proletarian will say to the soldier–

[1] L. Trotsky, *Sochinenya*, vol. iii, part i, pp. 5–7.

peasant.[1] In an essay written for *Zukunft*, an American-Jewish Socialist monthly, Trotsky made this point even more explicit: 'The peasant masses will rise in the villages and, not waiting for a decision of the Constituent Assembly, they will begin to expel the big landlords from their estates. All efforts to put an end to class warfare . . . will lead to nothing. The philistine thinks that it is the revolutionaries who make a revolution and who can call it off at any point as they wish.'[2]

Thus, separated by an ocean and a continent from the scene of events, through the haze of confused and contradictory reports, he firmly grasped the direction in which things were moving, formulated the problems of the revolution, and un-hesitatingly pointed to those whom he now considered to be its enemies, even if only yesterday they had been his friends. The question which he still had to answer was: Which was the real party of the revolution, *his* party?

Having drawn with so much foresight and precision the image of the revolution, he threw over that image, however, a veil of dream and fantasy. He fondly cherished his hope for the insur-rection of the European proletariat, and he saw the Petrograd rising as a mere prelude to it. This hope underlay all his ideas; it was to give him wings in his ascendancy; and its frustration was subsequently to break and crush him. Through the pages of *Novyi Mir* we can watch Trotsky in the first of his many wrestlings with illusion. Just before he left New York he tried to answer critics who fervently held that Russia, even while she was governed by Prince Lvov, must be defended against invasion by the Kaiser's troops. Trotsky, even now, persisted in opposition to war:

'The Russian revolution [so he answered the critics] represents an infinitely greater danger to the Hohenzollern than do the appetites and designs of imperialist Russia. The sooner the revolution throws off the chauvinist mask, which the Guchkovs and Miliukovs have forced upon her, and the sooner she reveals her true proletarian face, the more powerful will be the response she meets in Germany and the less will be the Hohenzollern's desire and capacity to strangle the Russian revolution, the more will he have of his own domestic trouble.

'But what will happen [the critic asks] if the German proletariat fails to rise? What are you going to do then?

[1] Op. cit., pp. 17–20.   [2] Op. cit., pp. 27–28.

'You suppose, then, that the Russian revolution can take place without affecting Germany . . .? But this is altogether improbable.

'Still, what if this were nevertheless to be the case?

'Really, we need not rack our brains over so implausible a supposition. The war has transformed the whole of Europe into a powder magazine of social revolution. The Russian proletariat is now throwing a flaming torch into that powder magazine. To suppose that this will cause no explosion is to think against the laws of historical logic and psychology. Yet if the improbable were to happen, if the conservative, social-patriotic organization were to prevent the German working class from rising against its ruling classes in the nearest future, then, of course, the Russian working class would defend the revolution arms in hand . . . and wage war against the Hohenzollern, and call upon the fraternal German proletariat to rise against the common enemy. . . . The task would be to defend not the fatherland but the revolution and to carry it to other countries.'[1]

Thus, every time he tried to answer the question: 'What happens if there is no revolution in Germany?' he actually dodged it. He seemed to be getting away from his dream only to plunge back into it, and to throw away his hope only in order to embrace it again. He saw no prospect, no hope, no life beyond European revolution.

.   .   .   .

On 27 March Trotsky, his family, and a small group of other émigrés, having the day before been given a boisterous farewell by a multilingual gathering of Socialists, sailed from New York on board the Norwegian ship *Christianiafjord*. For the first time in his life he travelled 'respectably', having obtained without difficulty all the necessary documents, the Russian entry permit and the British transit visa; and he expected plain sailing. All the greater was the surprise, when, on 3 April, the *Christiania-fjord* dropped anchor at Halifax, Nova Scotia, and the British naval police forcibly removed him and his family from the ship, carried him away to a camp for German prisoners of war at Amherst, and placed his wife and children under close surveillance. The other Russian émigrés who had accompanied him were also prevented from continuing the voyage. They had all refused to tell the British interrogating officer what were their political views and what they intended to do in Russia. This, they claimed, was no business of the British naval police.

From the camp, Trotsky cabled protests to the Russian government and to the British Prime Minister; but his messages, confiscated on the spot, never reached their destination. All the same, the internment became a political scandal. The Menshevik Executive of the Petrograd Soviet demanded Trotsky's release: 'The revolutionary democracy of Russia', it stated, 'impatiently awaits the return of its fighters for freedom and calls to its banners those who, by their lifelong efforts, have prepared the overthrow of Tsardom. Yet, the English authorities allow some émigrés to pass and hold up others. . . . The English government thereby intervenes intolerably in Russia's domestic affairs and insults the Russian revolution by robbing her of her most faithful sons.' Meetings of protest were held all over Russia; and Miliukov, the Foreign Minister, asked the British Ambassador that Trotsky be released. Two days later, however, he cancelled the request, knowing full well that he had nothing to expect from Trotsky but enmity.[1] Meanwhile, as the internment dragged on for nearly a month, Trotsky raged, protested, and hurled insults at the camp administration. There were at Amherst 800 German prisoners, sailors of sunken submarines. Trotsky addressed them, explaining to them the ideas of Zimmerwald, and telling them of the fight against the Kaiser and the war, which Karl Liebknecht had been waging in Germany. The camp resounded with his speeches, and life in it changed into a 'perpetual meeting'.[2] On the insistence of the German officers, the commandant of the camp forbade Trotsky to address the prisoners. 'Thus', Trotsky mocked, 'the English colonel immediately sided with Hohenzollern patriotism.' More than 500 sailors signed a protest against the ban. Finally, after much bungling and intrigue, Miliukov was compelled to renew the demand for Trotsky's release. On 29 April Trotsky left Amherst, followed to the gates of the camp by cheering German sailors and by the sounds of the *Internationale* played by their orchestra.

[1] Sir George Buchanan, *My Mission to Russia*, vol. ii, p. 121; Trotsky, *Sochinenya*, vol. iii, book 1, pp. 35 ff.
[2] Trotsky described his experience in a brochure *V Plenu u Anglichan* which he published immediately after his return to Petrograd (*Sochinenya*, vol. iii).

After a sea voyage of nearly three weeks, on 17 May (4 May in the old Russian calendar) he travelled by train across Finland to Petrograd. By the same train, and in the same compartment, went Vandervelde, the president of the Second International, and De Man, another eminent Belgian Socialist, both intent on infusing a warlike and patriotic spirit into their Russian comrades. Trotsky and Vandervelde have given two different accounts of this meeting, the former claiming that he refused to talk with the 'social patriots', the latter describing their long, polite, but rather unfriendly conversation.[1] Whatever the truth, the gulf between the Second and the Third Internationals ran for a few hours across that railway compartment.

At the Russian frontier a delegation of internationalists from Petrograd waited to welcome Trotsky. The Bolshevik Central Committee also greeted him, but not without reserve: the Bolshevik delegate who came to the frontier was not one of the party's well-known leaders. In Petrograd a crowd, demonstrating with red banners, carried Trotsky on its shoulders from the train; and to that crowd he made at once his call for a new revolution.

[1] Trotsky, *Moya Zhizn*, vol. ii, pp. 5–6. E. Vandervelde, *Souvenirs d'un Militant Socialiste*, p. 230.

CHAPTER IX

Trotsky in the October Revolution

TROTSKY arrived in Petrograd on 4 May. The revolution was then ten weeks old; and during those weeks events had thronged so thick and fast that the capital presented a dream-like picture even to the man who had cherished the memory of its streets and crowds ever since 1905.[1] The revolution had begun where it had stopped in 1905; but it had already left its recent starting-point far behind. The Tsar and his ministers were still prisoners of state, but to most of their former subjects they were like ghosts of a remote past. The age-old splendours, terrors, and fetishes of the monarchy seemed to have vanished with last winter's snow.

Lenin, who had returned exactly a month before Trotsky, described the Russia he found as the freest country in the world.[2] Her freedom, to be sure, was only that of expression; but of this the people availed themselves to the full, as if hoping to discover through passionate debate a new mode of existence, since the old had led to the brink of the abyss. That tense search for new principles, new forms, and a new content of social life, a search in which the mass of the humbled and the downtrodden participated with impressive dignity, characterized the moral climate of Petrograd in this spring of 1917. No authority and no truth was taken for granted. Only a vague belief prevailed that good was what promoted the revolution and helped to right the wrongs of the oppressed. The social character of the upheaval was reflected even in the city's appearance. The streets and squares in the fashionable centre were constantly crowded with dwellers from suburban slums. Multitudes of workers and soldiers attended the meetings, which took place day and night there and in the factories and barracks on the outskirts. The red flag, until recently the forbidden standard of rebellion, dominated the neo-classical architecture of the buildings on the Neva. The predominance of the worker and the soldier in the revolution could be guessed from every casual scene and incident in

---

[1] Trotsky, *Moya Zhizn*, vol. ii, p. 7.   [2] Lenin, *Sochinenya*, vol. xxiv, p. 4.

the street. The newcomer had only to glance at the capital to see how incongruous it was that Prince Lvov should still be the revolution's first minister.

Trotsky had hardly deposited his family and its few belongings in a lodging-house when he made for the Smolny Institute, the seat of the Petrograd Soviet.[1] Its Executive, the successor to the body of which he had been the presiding spirit in 1905, was just in session. The man who now presided was Chkheidze, his former associate whom he had just attacked in *Novyi Mir*. Chkheidze rose to welcome Trotsky, but the welcome was lukewarm.[2] A moment of embarrassment followed. The Mensheviks and Social Revolutionaries, who were in a majority, did not know whether the newcomer was their friend or their foe—from a friend of long standing he seemed to have turned into a foe. The Bolshevik members of the Executive pointed out that the leader of the Soviet of 1905 ought to be invited to take a seat on the Executive of the present Soviet. The Mensheviks and Social Revolutionaries consulted each other in perplexed whispers. They agreed to admit Trotsky as an associate member, without the right to vote. He wished for nothing more: what mattered to him was not the right to vote, but the opportunity to make himself heard from the chief platform of the revolution.

Nevertheless, the cool reception could not but irk him. Angelica Balabanov, the secretary of the Zimmerwald movement, wrote that he even suspected that the party leaders had not pressed energetically enough for his release from British internment, because they had not been eager to see him on the scene. 'Both Mensheviks and Bolsheviks regarded him with rancour and distrust . . . partly out of fear of competition. . . .'[3] Whatever the truth, the fact was that between February and May the political alignments had become defined; the parties and groups had formed their ranks and clarified their attitudes, and the leaders had assumed their roles and taken up their positions. In 1905 Trotsky had been the first of the émigrés to return. Now he was the last. And no appropriate vacancy seemed to be open for a man of his gifts and ambition.

[1] From now on 'the Soviet' (in the singular) denotes the Soviet of Petrograd, unless it is stated otherwise.

[2] L. Trotsky, *Moya Zhizn*, loc. cit.; N. Sukhanov, *Zapiski o Revolutsii*, vol. iii, pp. 440–1.

[3] A. Balabanoff, *My Life as a Rebel*, p. 176.

The moment was such that all parties, except the Bolsheviks, had reason to fear any new and incalculable influence. For the first time, the régime that sprang from the February insurrection had lost its unstable balance; and it was trying to regain that balance through delicate combinations and manœuvres. Prince Lvov's first government had ceased to exist. In that government only the gentry and the upper middle class had been represented, the former by the Conservatives who followed Guchkov, the latter by Miliukov's Cadets. The Mensheviks and Social Revolutionaries, who dominated the Soviet, had pledged their support to the government but had not joined it. Yet the government could not have existed a single day without the backing of the Soviet, the *de facto* power created by the revolution. The point had now been reached where the moderate Socialist parties in the Soviet could no longer support the government without joining it.

The parties which had formed Prince Lvov's first government strove to limit the revolution to the overthrow of Tsar Nicholas II and to save, if possible, the monarchy; to continue the war, and to restore the social and military discipline without which it could not be continued.[1] The workers and soldiers who followed the Soviets hoped, on the contrary, for a 'deepening' of the revolution and for an early 'democratic peace without annexations and indemnities'. The moderate Socialists tried to reconcile the conflicting policies and demands. Inevitably they involved themselves in blatant contradictions. They tried to assist the government in prosecuting the war and at the same time to soothe the popular longing for peace. They told their followers that the government had discarded the Tsar's rapacious war aims—Russian domination over the Balkans, the conquest of Galicia and Constantinople—and that it was seeking to achieve a just and democratic peace.[2] Prince Lvov tried to put into operation the old administrative machinery inherited from Tsardom, while the workers and soldiers regarded the Soviets as the real administration. The Mensheviks and Social Revolutionaries hoped that the new system of government would

---

[1] P. Miliukov, *Istorya Russkoi Revolutsii*, vol. i, book 1, pp. 54–76 and *passim*.

[2] 'Miliukov . . . held that the acquisition of Constantinople was a matter of vital moment for Russia', wrote Sir George Buchanan the British Ambassador in Russia in *My Mission to Russia*, vol. ii, p. 108.

incorporate both the old administration and the Soviets. The government exerted itself to re-establish discipline in the war-weary and revolutionized army, in which the soldiers refused to obey their officers and listened only to their own elected committees. The moderate Socialists pledged themselves to help the government in restoring discipline; yet they called upon the soldiers to defend their newly won rights embodied in the Soviet's famous Order No. 1 against Tsarist generals and officers. The government wished to create security for landed property, while the peasantry clamoured for a sharing out of the gentry's estates. The Mensheviks and Social Revolutionaries tried to postpone the solution of this vital problem until the convocation of the Constituent Assembly, which in its turn was indefinitely postponed.[1]

It was inevitable that this tall structure, built of equivocation and delusion, should one day crumble over the heads of those who erected it. The first tremor shook it in April. Guchkov, unable to restore military discipline, resigned from the Ministry of War. Soon afterwards Miliukov had to resign from the Ministry of Foreign Affairs. He had declared in a note to Russia's western allies that the new government would faith-fully pursue the war aims of its Tsarist predecessor. This pro-voked such an outburst of popular indignation that Prince Lvov's first government could no longer carry on.

The ruthless logic of revolution began to show itself. Within two months the revolution had discredited and used up its first government and the parties that had formed it. Only a short time before, in the last days of the Tsarist régime, Doumergue, the President of the French Republic, on a state visit to Petro-grad, had urged the Cadet leaders to compose patiently their differences with the Tsar. 'At the very word "patience" Miliukov and Maklakov jumped up: "Enough of patience! We have exhausted all our patience! Anyhow, if we do not act soon, the masses will not listen to us any longer. . . ." '[2] These words were to become one of the revolution's favourite refrains; and now they recoiled upon Miliukov. The moderate Socialist major-ity of the Soviet had no intention of unseating him. But when

[1] Miliukov, op. cit., vol. i, book 1, pp. 101–15, 125–38 and *passim*; L. Trotsky, *The History of the Russian Revolution*, vol. i, chapters xi–xiii.
[2] M. Paléologue, *La Russie des Tsars pendant la Grande Guerre*, vol. iii, p. 188.

he openly pledged government and country to the pursuit of the Tsarist war aims, the Mensheviks and Social Revolutionaries jumped up: 'Enough of patience! We have exhausted all our patience! And, anyhow, if we do not act soon, the masses will not listen to us any longer.' The masses would not have listened to them any longer if they had left the whole business of government to the leaders of those classes that had used the February Revolution but not made it.

The first coalition between the Cadets and the moderate Socialists thus came into being. When Trotsky appeared at the session of the Soviet Executive, the new partners were just sharing out the governmental seats. There were to be 'ten capitalist and six socialist ministers'. The Cadets were the senior partners; and so the programme of the new government was in essentials indistinguishable from that of its predecessor. The six Socialist ministers could only dilute it to make it more palatable to the Soviet. Kerensky, who had a connexion with the Social Revolutionary party, succeeded Guchkov as Minister of War. Tseretelli, the most eminent Menshevik leader of this period, a former deputy and hard-labour convict, became Minister of Posts and Telegraphs. Chernov, chief of the Social Revolutionaries and a participant in the Zimmerwald conference, was appointed Minister of Agriculture. Skobelev, Trotsky's former pupil and editorial assistant, was Minister of Labour.

On 5 May, the day after Trotsky's arrival, the Socialist ministers stood before the Soviet, asking it to support the coalition. When Trotsky appeared he was greeted with loud applause, and Skobelev addressed him as 'dear and beloved teacher'. From the floor Trotsky was asked to state his view on the day's event. He 'was visibly nervous over the début, under the . . . stare of an unknown mass and the hostile glances . . . of "social traitors" '.[2] Cautiously he felt his way. He began by extolling the grandeur of the revolution, and he so described the impression it had made upon the world that by implication he at once reduced that day's event to modest proportions. If only, he said, they could see and gauge, as he had done abroad, the impact of the revolution upon the world, they would know that Russia 'had opened a new epoch, an epoch of blood and iron, a struggle no longer of nation against nation, but of the suffering and

---

[1] N. Sukhanov, op. cit., vol. iii, pp. 440–2.

oppressed classes against their rulers'.[1] These words jarred on the ears of the Socialist ministers, who had committed themselves to continuing the war and calming the raging elements of revolution. 'I cannot conceal', Trotsky went on, 'that I disagree with much that is going on here. I consider this participation in the Ministry to be dangerous. . . . The coalition government will not save us from the existing dualism of power; it will merely transfer that dualism into the Ministry itself.' This was indistinguishable from what the Bolsheviks were saying—they, too, dwelt on the division of power between the Soviets and the government. As if wary of hurting his old friends, Trotsky then struck a more conciliatory note: 'The revolution will not perish from a coalition Ministry. But we must remember three commands: distrust the bourgeoisie; control our own leaders; and rely on our own revolutionary strength. . . .' He spoke in the first person plural—'we must', 'our strength'—as if to identify himself, in his manner, with his former comrades. But in the matter of his speech he was irreconcilable: 'I think that our next move will be to transfer the whole power into the hands of the Soviets. Only a single power can save Russia.' This again sounded like Lenin's slogan. He concluded a long and brilliant argument with the exclamation 'Long live the Russian revolution, the prologue to world revolution', and the audience was captivated if not by his ideas then by the sincerity and eloquence with which he expounded them.[2]

One after another the ministers rose to reply. Chernov promised that the Socialists would make their influence felt in the government, but for this they needed the Soviet's wholehearted support. Tseretelli dwelt on the dangers to which the Soviets would be exposed if they refused to share power with the bourgeoisie. Skobelev admonished his 'dear teacher': in the middle of a revolution 'cool reason was needed as much as a warm heart'. The Soviet voted confidence in the new ministry. Only the extreme left minority voted against it.

The political group which greeted Trotsky as its proper chief was the Inter-Borough Organization, the *Mezhrayonka* as it was briefly called. He had inspired this group from abroad since its formation in 1913 and contributed to its publications. The group did not aspire to form a party. It was a temporary association

[1] L. Trotsky, *Sochinenya*, vol. iii, book i, pp. 45–46.   [2] Sukhanov, loc. cit.

of neither-Bolsheviks-nor-Mensheviks, who persisted in opposition to war, Prince Lvov, and the 'social patriots'. Its influence
was confined to a few working-class districts in Petrograd only;
and even there it was swamped by the rapid growth of Bolshevism. To this small group adhered, however, men who had
in the past been eminent either as Mensheviks or as Bolsheviks
and who were presently to rise again. Most of them, Lunacharsky, Ryazanov, Manuilsky, Pokrovsky, Yoffe, Uritsky, Volodarsky, had written for Trotsky's papers. A few others, like
Karakhan and Yureniev, later became leading Soviet diplomats.
Together they formed a brilliant political *élite*, but their organization was too weak and narrow to serve as a base for independent action. When Trotsky arrived, the group was discussing
its future and contemplating a merger with the Bolsheviks and
other Left groups. At public meetings its agitators were insistently asked in what they differed from the Bolsheviks and why
they did not join hands with them. To this question they had,
in truth, no satisfactory answer. Their separation from the
Bolsheviks had resulted from the long and involved feud in the
old party; it reflected past not present differences.[1]

On 7 May the Bolsheviks and the Inter-Borough Organization arranged a special welcome for Trotsky; and on 10 May
they met to consider the proposed merger. Lenin arrived,
accompanied by Zinoviev and Kamenev; and here Trotsky
saw him for the first time since their not very friendly meeting
at Zimmerwald. Of this conference we have only a fragmentary
but informative record in Lenin's private notes. Trotsky
repeated what he had said at the reception in his honour: he
had abandoned his old attitude and no longer stood for unity
between Bolsheviks and Mensheviks. Only those who had
completely broken with social patriotism should now unite
under the flag of a new International. Then he apparently asked
whether Lenin still held that the Russian Revolution was merely
bourgeois in character and that its outcome would be 'a
democratic dictatorship of the proletariat and the peasantry',
not proletarian dictatorship.[2] It seems that he was not clearly
aware of the radical re-orientation which Lenin had just carried

[1] Sukhanov, op. cit., vol. iv, p. 365; Trotsky, *Sochinenya*, vol. iii, book 1, p. 47;
See also Yureniev's report in *6 Syezd RSDRP*.
[2] *Leninskii Sbornik*, vol. iv, pp. 300–3.

through in the Bolshevik party. Lenin had spent the month before Trotsky's arrival in an intense controversy with the right wing of his party, headed by Kamenev; and he had persuaded the party to abandon the 'old Bolshevik' view on the prospects of the revolution. It may be assumed that this was explained to Trotsky there and then. If nobody else, then his brother-in-law Kamenev must have told him that Lenin's Bolshevik opponents, indeed Kamenev himself, had reproached Lenin with having taken over lock, stock, and barrel the theory of 'permanent revolution', and with having abandoned Bolshevism for Trotskyism.

In truth, the roads of Lenin and Trotsky, so long divergent, had now met. Each of them had reached certain conclusions to which the other had come much earlier and which he had long and bitterly contested. But neither had consciously adopted the other's point of view. From different starting-points and through different processes their minds had moved towards their present meeting. We have seen how the events of the war had gradually driven Trotsky to take the view that the breach in the Labour movement could not be healed; that it was wrong and even pernicious to try to heal it; and that it was the duty of the revolutionary internationalists to form new parties. Long before the war, Lenin had arrived at this conclusion, but only for the Russian party. The war had induced him to generalize it and to apply it to the international Labour movement. In Lenin's reasonings and instinctive reactions his Russian experience was the primary factor, although it alone did not determine his attitude. Trotsky had, on the contrary, proceeded from the international generalization to the application of the principle to Russia. Whatever the processes by which they arrived at the common conclusion, the practical implications were the same.

A similar difference in approach and identity in conclusion can be seen in their evaluation of prospects. In 1905–6 Trotsky had foreseen the combination of anti-feudal and anti-capitalist revolutions in Russia and had described the Russian upheaval as a prelude to international socialist revolution. Lenin had then refused to see in Russia the pioneer of collectivist socialism. He deduced the character and the prospects of the revolution from Russia's historic stage of development and from her social structure, in which the individualistic peasantry was the largest element. During the war, however, he came to reckon

with Socialist revolution in the advanced European countries
and to place the Russian Revolution in this international perspective. What now seemed decisive to him was not that Russia
was not ripe for socialism, but that she was part of Europe
which he thought to be ripe for it. Consequently, he no longer
saw any reason why the Russian Revolution should confine
itself to its so-called bourgeois objectives. The experience of the
February régime further demonstrated to him that it would be
impossible to break the power of the landlords without breaking
and eventually dispossessing the capitalist class as well; and this
meant 'proletarian dictatorship'.[1]

Although the old differences between Lenin and Trotsky had
evaporated, the position of the two men was very different.
Lenin was the recognized leader of a great party, which, even
though a minority in the Soviets, had already become the rallying ground for all proletarian opposition to the February régime.
Trotsky and his friends were a pleiade of brilliant generals
without an army. As an individual, Trotsky could make his
voice heard from the platforms of the revolution; but only a
massive and well-disciplined party could now transform words
into lasting deeds. Each side needed the other, though in
different degrees. Nothing suited Lenin better than to be able
to introduce the pleiade of gifted propagandists, agitators,
tacticians, and orators, headed by Trotsky, into the 'general
staff' of his party. But he was proud of the party he had built
and aware of the advantages it held. He was determined that
Trotsky and Trotsky's friends should join *his* party. Inside it,
he was willing to accord them every democratic right, to share
with them his influence, and, as the record shows, to allow
himself to be outvoted on important occasions. But he was
not prepared to scrap his party and to merge it with minor
groups into a new body. To do so he would have had either to
indulge in make-believe or to pay a needless tribute to the
vanity of others.

At the meeting of 10 May he asked Trotsky and Trotsky's
friends to join the Bolshevik party immediately. He offered
them positions on the leading bodies and on the editorial staff
of *Pravda*.[2] He put no conditions to them. He did not ask Trotsky

---

[1] Lenin, *Sochinenya*, vol. xxiv, pp. 214–16, 274–5, 276–9, and *passim*.
[2] Even earlier, Lenin had proposed to the Bolshevik Central Committee that

to renounce anything of his past; he did not even mention past controversies. He himself had put these out of his mind and expected Trotsky to do likewise—so anxious was he to join hands with anybody who could promote the common cause. At this time he even hoped for a reunion with Martov, who had detached himself from the Mensheviks, remained faithful to the programme of Zimmerwald, and opposed the coalition government.[1]

Trotsky would have had to be much more free from pride than he was to accept Lenin's proposals immediately. He also had to consider objections raised by some of his associates who spoke about the lack of democracy in Lenin's party and the 'sectarian practices' of the Bolshevik committees and conventicles. Trotsky, who had so long criticized Lenin's party in the same terms, now saw little substance in these misgivings. In his reply to Lenin he dwelt on the recent change in the Bolshevik party, which, he said, 'had acquired an internationalist outlook' and become 'de-bolshevized'. Politically, he was therefore in complete agreement with Lenin; and he also accepted most of Lenin's technical proposals for immediate co-operation. But, precisely because the Bolshevik party had changed so strikingly and to such advantage, he and his friends should not be asked to call themselves Bolsheviks. 'I cannot describe myself as a Bolshevik. It is undesirable to stick to the old labels.'[2] They ought to join hands in a new party, with a new name, at a joint congress of their organizations. Trotsky must have been aware that at such a congress, the Bolsheviks would in any case enjoy an absolute preponderance; and so the whole difference reduced itself to the 'label'. This was too slight a matter to justify him and his associates in clinging to their political isolation. But for the moment the issue was shelved.

When about this time Lenin was asked what, despite their complete agreement, still kept him and Trotsky apart, he

Trotsky be invited to edit the party's popular daily, but this proposal had been rejected by the Committee. *Krasnaya Letopis*, no. 3, 1923.

[1] Lunacharsky (*Revolutsionnye Siluety*, p. 69) writes: 'In May and June of 1917 Lenin desired an alliance with Martov.' Lunacharsky himself hoped even much later that Martov might yet become the leader of a right wing within the Bolshevik party and he expressed this hope in his book, which was published in 1923. Ibid., p. 70.

[2] *Leninskii Sbornik*, vol. iv, loc. cit.

replied: 'Now don't you know? Ambition, ambition, ambition.'[1]
For Trotsky to declare himself a Bolshevik was a tacit surrender,
not to the Lenin of the present, but to the Lenin of the past;
and at this he balked. Yet the surrender was in part inevitable,
for it was the Lenin of the past, the émigré, who had been the
master architect of what turned out to be *the* party of revolution.
On the other hand, the present programme of the party embodied what used to be Trotsky's rather than Lenin's point of
view. For this Trotsky received no recognition and no acknowledgement. Much as this may have hurt Trotsky, Lenin was
almost certainly unaware of it; and it was practically impossible
for him to make the acknowledgement in any form, even if he
had been willing to make it. A revolutionary party, in the middle
of a revolution, has no time for fine scruples over the copyright
of political ideas. Later in the year, Lenin unstintingly paid
tribute to Trotsky, saying that since he had broken with the
Mensheviks there was no better Bolshevik.[2] Trotsky on his part
had far too much political sense not to see that it would be
laughable to insist at this time on his superior foresight. For him,
too, the practical politics of the revolution were infinitely more
important than old theoretical prognostications. His hesitancy
was merely the last flicker of his opposition to Lenin.

For the moment he remained a political free-lance. Looking
round for contacts he stopped at the editorial offices of Maxim
Gorky's *Novaya Zhizn* (*New Life*). He and Gorky had known and
admired each other for a long time past. The differences in their
ages, temperaments, and modes of thinking were such as to
preclude intimate friendship; but they had occasionally co-
operated, especially when Gorky moved away from Lenin. At
present Gorky stood half-way between Bolsheviks and Mensheviks; and in his great daily he remonstrated with both and
preached revolutionary morals to both. He hoped for Trotsky's
accession, believing that like himself Trotsky would try to
conciliate the adversaries in the Socialist camp. Trotsky's first
utterances in Petrograd had caused him forebodings, and his
contributors whispered that 'Trotsky was even worse than
Lenin'. Nevertheless, Gorky arranged a meeting between his
editorial staff and Trotsky. At once it became clear that they

[1] Balabanoff, op. cit., pp. 175–6.
[2] Trotsky, *The Stalin School of Falsification*, p. 105.

were at cross purposes. Apart from this, Gorky's influence was strictly literary. His paper, for all its journalistic merits, had no serious ties with the bodies of opinion and the organizations that mattered in the revolution. In Marxist politics, the great novelist was childishly naïve. Yet with the lack of modesty characteristic of a famous self-made man, he assumed the posture of political oracle. Nothing would have been more incongruous than that Trotsky should associate himself with Gorky, let alone accept him as a political guide. Trotsky was in search of a firm framework of organization, of a solid anchorage in the realities of the revolution; and this Gorky could not offer him. Their exchange of views was rather sour, and Trotsky concluded it by saying that nothing was left to him but to join hands with Lenin.[1]

In the meantime he founded *Vperyod* (*Forward*), the paper of the Inter-Borough Organization. *Vperyod*, although it had many brilliant contributors, was not successful. At this time only such papers gained wide currency as could rely on strong financial backing or on the disinterested services of a widely ramified organization. *Vperyod* had neither. It began as a weekly; but it came from the presses irregularly; altogether only sixteen issues appeared before the Inter-Borough Organization joined the Bolshevik party.

It was through the spoken rather than the written word that Trotsky made his impact on the political life in the capital. He addressed, usually with Lunacharsky, innumerable meetings. Within only two or three weeks of his arrival, both he and Lunacharsky had gained enormous popularity as the most eloquent agitators of the Soviet Left.[2] The naval base of Kronstadt, situated just outside the capital, was his favourite stumping-ground; and Kronstadt proved extremely important in his further political fortunes. The navy was in utter rebellion. The base formed a sort of red republic bowing to no authority. The sailors violently resisted attempts to reimpose discipline on them. The ministry appointed commissars, some of whom had been discredited by their association with the old régime and even with the Black Hundred gangs. The sailors refused to admit them on board ship and manhandled some of them. Trotsky

---

[1] Sukhanov, op. cit., vol. iv, p. 191; Trotsky, *History of the Russian Revolution*, vol. i, pp. 486–7.   [2] Sukhanov, op. cit., vol. iv, pp. 164–7.

urged the sailors to keep their tempers and to refrain from vengeance; but he also did his best to kindle their revolutionary ardour.

Towards the end of May the Socialist ministers indicted the sailors before the Soviet, and Trotsky came out to defend them. He did not condone their excesses, but he pleaded that these could have been avoided if the government had not appointed as commissars discredited and hated men. 'Our socialist ministers', he exclaimed, 'refuse to fight against the danger of the Black Hundreds. Instead, they declare war on the sailors and soldiers of Kronstadt. Yet should reaction rise and should a counter-revolutionary general try to throw a noose around the neck of the revolution, your Black Hundred commissars will soap the rope for all of us, while the Kronstadt sailors will come and fight and die with us.'[1] This phrase was much quoted later when the sailors of Kronstadt actually defended Kerensky's government against General Kornilov's mutiny. Trotsky also wrote for the sailors the fiery manifesto in which they appealed against the Ministry of War to the country—this was Kerensky's first setback since he had become Minister of War. Henceforward the sailors faithfully followed Trotsky, guarded him, almost idolized him, and obeyed him whether he called them to action or exhorted them to curb their tempers.[2]

In these days, too, he established his platform in the Cirque Moderne, where almost every night he addressed enormous crowds. The amphitheatre was so densely packed that Trotsky was usually shuffled towards the platform over the heads of the audience, and from his elevation he would catch the excited eyes of the daughters of his first marriage, who attended the meetings. He spoke on the topics of the day and the aims of the revolution with his usual piercing logic; but he also absorbed the spirit of the crowd, its harsh sense of justice, its desire to see things in sharp and clear outline, its suspense, and its great expectations. Later he recollected how at the mere sight of the multitude words and arguments he had prepared well in advance receded and dispersed in his mind and other words and arguments, unexpected by himself but meeting a need in his listeners, rushed up as if from his subconscious. He then listened

[1] Trotsky, *Sochinenya*, vol. iii, book 1, pp. 52 ff.
[2] F. F. Raskolnikov, *Kronstadt i Piter v 1917 godu*, p. 77.

to his own voice as to that of a stranger, trying to keep pace with
the tumultuous rush of his own ideas and phrases and afraid lest
like a sleepwalker he might suddenly wake and break down.
Here his politics ceased to be the distillation of individual
reflection or of debates in small circles of professional politicians.
He merged emotionally with the warm dark human mass in
front of him, and became its medium. He became so identified
with the Cirque Moderne that when he went back to the Tauride
Palace or the Smolny Institute, where the Soviet sat, and assailed
his opponents or argued with them, they shouted at him: 'This
is not your Cirque Moderne', or 'At the Cirque Moderne you
speak differently.'[1]

.   .   .   .

At the beginning of June the first All-Russian Congress of the
Soviets assembled in Petrograd; and it was in session for three
weeks. For the first time the parties and their leaders confronted
one another in a national forum, the only national elected body
then existing in Russia. The moderate Socialists commanded
about five-sixths of the votes. They were led by civilian intellectuals, but in their ranks military uniforms and peasant
rubakhas were most conspicuous. On the extreme left, among the
120 members of the opposition, workers from the great industrial centres were predominant. The Congress reflected a
division between the military and rural elements of the provinces and the proletarian elements of the cities. A few days
before, a municipal election in Petrograd had revealed a significant shift. The Cadets, dominant in the government, had
suffered a crushing defeat in their 'safest' boroughs. The Mensheviks had polled half the votes. The working-class suburbs
had solidly voted for the Bolsheviks. The Mensheviks came to
the Congress as the hopeful victors of the day. The Bolsheviks
brought with them a new confidence in their future victory.[2]

The spokesmen of the Left opposition used against the
majority the latter's own success. Prince Lvov and the Cadets,
they said, had a negligible following. The moderate Socialists
represented the nation's overwhelming majority. Why then did
they content themselves with the roles of ministerial hewers
of wood and drawers of water for the Cadets? Why did they

[1] Trotsky, *Moya Zhizn*, vol. ii, pp. 15–16; John Reed, *Ten Days that Shook the World*, p. 17.   [2] Sukhanov, op. cit., vol. iv, pp. 204–5.

not form their own government, as they were democratically entitled and in honour bound to do? This was the tenor of Lenin's speech.[1] This was also Trotsky's main theme.[2] Although his argument was in parts more trenchant than Lenin's, he appealed to the majority in a more friendly tone, invoking common interests and destinies. He tried to open the eyes of the Mensheviks and Social Revolutionaries to their own humiliating position and to persuade them to break up their partnership with the bourgeois parties. It was, he said, no use trying to turn the government into a chamber of conciliation between social classes. 'A chamber of conciliation cannot exercise power in a revolutionary epoch.' Prince Lvov and his friends represented classes accustomed to rule and dominate; and the Socialist ministers, with their sense of inferiority, all too easily allowed themselves to be browbeaten. He made, however, a few friendly references to Peshekhonov, the least known of the Socialist ministers, which brought him applause from the benches of the majority. And he argued that a government consisting only of such Peshekhonovs would be 'a serious step forward'. 'You see, comrades, that in this issue I am starting not from the angle of any faction or party, but from a broader view. . . .' He agreed with the Socialist ministers that the working classes should be disciplined; but they could not be disciplined by a capitalist ministry and for the sake of capitalist policies. This was the source of all the agitation on the extreme Left, about which the majority complained.

'The so-called Left agitators', he pleaded, 'prepare the future of the Russian revolution. I venture to say that we, with our work, do not undermine your authority—we are an indispensable element in preparing the future.' 'Comrades, I am not hoping to convince you to-day, for this would be too bold a hope. What I would like to achieve to-day is to make you aware that if we oppose you, we do so not from any hostile . . . motives of a selfish faction, but because, together with you, we are suffering all the pangs and agonies of the revolution. We see solutions different from those which you see, and we are firmly convinced

---

[1] Lenin, *Sochinenya*, vol. xxv, pp. 3–14.

[2] *Pervyi Vseros. Syezd Sovietov*, vol. i, pp. 142–9. The summary of Trotsky's speech is based on this source—in later reprints the friendly references to the Mensheviks were retouched.

that while you are consolidating the present of the revolution, we prepare its future for you.'[1] At this stage, Lenin no longer granted his adversaries the credit Trotsky still gave them, although he agreed with Trotsky that a 'Ministry of twelve Peshekhonovs' would be an advance upon the present coalition.

These debates were exacerbated by the 'Grimm incident'. Grimm was a Swiss parliamentarian, a Socialist, and a pacifist, who had taken part in the Zimmerwald conference. There he had belonged to the 'centre' and disagreed with Lenin's revolutionary tactics. Later he helped to arrange Lenin's journey from Switzerland to Russia, via Germany. In May Grimm conveyed to leaders of the ruling parties in Petrograd a message from the German government sounding Russia on the possibility of peace. The Russian government expelled him as a German agent, but it did not reveal its reasons.

Grimm was not, strictly speaking, a German agent. As a pacifist of not much sophistication, he found it quite natural to convey a peace feeler. Not well versed in the intricacies of Russian revolutionary politics, he could not see why Russian Socialists, whether those who, like the Bolsheviks and Trotsky, clamoured for peace or those who, like the Mensheviks, merely kept on promising an early peace, should object to his action.[2] Lenin and Trotsky were not informed about his doings. The fact, however, that the government had denounced Grimm as a German agent was at once used to discredit the Russian participants of the Zimmerwald movement. Miliukov made a speech in which he was reported to have branded Lenin and Trotsky, too, as German agents. Trotsky rose in Congress to defend Grimm. He did not believe that the government was right in expelling Grimm, and he saw in the incident Miliukov's sinister intrigue. Referring to Miliukov's charges against himself and Lenin, he said, turning to the journalists' bench: 'From this platform of revolutionary democracy, I am appealing to the honest Russian press with the request that they should reproduce my words: As long as Miliukov does not withdraw his charges, he is branded as a dishonest slanderer.'[3]

'Trotsky's statement', so Gorky's paper reported the scene, 'made with *élan* and dignity, met with the unanimous applause

---

[1] *Pervyi Vseros. Syezd Sovietov*, vol. i, p. 149.   [2] Balabanoff, op. cit., p. 178.
[3] *Pervyi Vseros. Syezd Sovietov*, p. 158.

of the whole assembly. The whole Congress, without difference of faction, stormily acclaimed Trotsky for several minutes.'[1] On the next day Miliukov declared that he had not described Lenin or Trotsky as German agents—he had merely said that the government ought to imprison them for their subversive activity.[2]

This was the last occasion on which the Congress so unanimously acclaimed Trotsky. As the debates went on, the gulf between the parties became fixed. Tempers rose during a controversy over the last Duma. That Duma had been elected in 1912 on a very limited franchise; it had functioned as the Tsar's consultative assembly, not as a real parliament; and its great majority had consisted of the Tsar's underlings. The Cadets pressed for the revival of the Duma, which they hoped to use as a quasi-parliamentary base for their government. The Mensheviks and Social Revolutionaries laid before the Soviet a vague resolution, which Martov wittily paraphrased as follows: 'The Duma no longer exists, but a warning is hereby issued against any attempts to put it out of existence.'[3] Lunacharsky moved that the Duma should be buried as a relic of a shameful past. Trotsky seconded him with a scathing speech. When at one of the next sittings he rose again and as usual began his address with the word 'Comrades', he was interrupted by an outcry: 'What sort of comrades are we to you?' and 'Stop calling us comrades!' He stopped, and he moved closer to the Bolsheviks.[4]

The main issue which occupied the Congress was the condition of the army. Since the overthrow of Tsardom the Russian fronts had been inactive. Pressed by the western allies, the government and the General Staff were preparing a new offensive for which they were anxious to obtain the Soviets' approval. The General Staff was also pressing for a revision of the famous Order No. 1, the Magna Charta of the soldiers' freedom. In this debate Trotsky made his chief speech, in which he warned the government that after the prodigious losses the army had suffered and after the disruption of its supply services by inefficiency, profiteering, and corruption, the army was incapable of further fighting. The offensive would end in disaster; the attempt to reimpose the old discipline would lead

[1] *Novaya Zhizn*, 6 June 1917.
[2] *Rech*, 7 June 1917.
[3] *Pervyi Vseros. Syezd Sovietov*, pp. 295–8.
[4] Ibid., p. 352.

nowhere. 'Fortunately for Russia's whole history, our revolutionary army has done away with the old outlook of the Russian army, the outlook of the locust . . . when hundreds of thousands used to die passively . . . without ever being aware of the purpose of their sacrifice. . . . Let this historical period which we have left behind be damned! What we now value is not the elemental, unconscious heroism of the mass, but a heroism which refracts itself through every individual consciousness.'[1] At present the army had no idea to fight for. 'I repeat, that in this same army, as it has emerged from the revolution . . . there exist and there will exist ideas, watchwords, purposes capable of rallying it and of imparting to this our army unity and enthusiasm. . . . The army of the great French revolution consciously responded to calls for an offensive. What is the crux of the matter? It is this: no such purpose that would rally the army exists now. . . . Every thinking soldier asks himself: for every five drops of blood which I am going to shed today will not one drop only be shed in the interest of the Russian revolution, and four in the interest of the French Stock Exchange and of English imperialism?'[2] If only Russia disentangled herself from the imperialist alignments, if only the power of the old ruling classes was destroyed and a new democratic government established by the Soviets, then 'we should be able to summon all European peoples and tell them that now a citadel of revolution has risen on the map of Europe'.[3]

He then resumed his ever-recurring dialogue with the sceptic who did not believe that 'the revolution would spread and that the Russian revolutionary army and Russian democracy would find allies in Europe': 'My answer is that history has given no guarantee to us, to the Russian revolution, that we shall not be crushed altogether, that our revolutionary will is not going to be strangled by a coalition of world capital, that world imperialism will not crucify us.' The Russian Revolution represented so great a danger to the propertied classes of all countries that they would try to destroy it and to transform Russia into a colony of European or, what was more probable, of American capital. But this trial of strength was still ahead, and the Soviets were in duty bound to be ready for it. 'If . . . [revolutionary] Germany does not rise, or if she rises too feebly, then we shall move

[1] *Pervyi Vseros. Syezd Sovietov*, p. 353.   [2] Ibid., p. 354.   [3] Ibid., pp. 356 ff.

our regiments . . . not in order to defend ourselves but in order to undertake a revolutionary offensive.' At this point the powerful peroration was interrupted by an anonymous voice from the floor: 'It will be too late, then'. Before the year was out, the anonymous voice was proved right. But in the Trotsky who addressed the Congress the features can be clearly discerned of the man who was not only to confront, without any armed strength behind him, the diplomacy of the Hohenzollerns and the Habsburgs, but also to create the Red Army.

At this Congress he had his last clash with Plekhanov. They addressed each other frigidly as 'Citizens', not 'Comrades'. Plekhanov had reached the extreme of his warlike mood, and even the Mensheviks were so embarrassed by his chauvinist outbursts that they kept aloof from him. But the Congress paid a warm tribute to Plekhanov's past merits, only to be treated by him to a hackneyed patriotic sermon. Trotsky aggressively reproached him for this, and Plekhanov replied haughtily, comparing himself now with Danton and now with Lassalle and contrasting the disheartened and dejected armies of the Russian Revolution with the armies of Cromwell and of the Jacobins, whose 'spirits soared when they drank the sap of revolution'. Little did the sick veteran imagine that it was his younger and much snubbed opponent who was destined for the role of the Russian Danton, destined to make the Russian armies 'drink the sap of revolution'.

Through the greater part of the proceedings, the majority treated lightly the Bolsheviks and their associates. When Tseretelli, pleading for the coalition government, challenged the delegates to say whether there was a single party in Russia prepared alone to shoulder responsibility for government, Lenin interrupted from the floor to say that his party was prepared for that. The majority drowned Lenin's words in hilarious laughter. The delegates from the provinces were not aware that in Petrograd the opposition's influence was already growing like an avalanche. Lenin was eager to impress them and to show them that Petrograd demanded an end to the coalition and the formation of a Socialist ministry, that is of a ministry consisting only of the moderate Socialists. Despite his statement from the floor of the Congress, which was a declaration of principle, not of immediate purpose, Lenin did not yet aim at the overthrow

of the government. Still less did he favour a coalition between
the moderate Socialists and his own party. As long as the Bolsheviks were a minority in the Soviets, he urged his followers not
to play at seizing power but 'patiently to explain their attitude
to the masses', until they gained the majority. This was the
crux of his Soviet constitutionalism. In the meantime, the Bolshevik slogan was not 'Down with the government', but 'Down
with the ten capitalist ministers!' Overcoming the forebodings
in his own Central Committee, Lenin was in great secrecy preparing a monster demonstration under this slogan for 10 June.
Trotsky, dispelling his friends' misgivings, induced the Inter-
Borough Organization to join in the demonstration. But on 9
June, when *Pravda* made an open call to the workers and the
garrison, the Executive of the Congress banned the demonstration.

Neither Lenin nor Trotsky wished to defy the ban. They
decided to submit to the decision of the majority, to cancel the
demonstration, and to explain their attitude in a special manifesto. This was an anxious moment. Would the workers and
soldiers take note of the cancellation? If so, would they not
misunderstand the party's attitude? Would their urge for action
not be chilled? Lenin drafted an explanatory statement, but as
his followers and he himself were not pleased with it he gladly
adopted another text, submitted by Trotsky; and this was
read out at the Congress in the name of the entire opposition.
Trotsky, not yet a member of the party, also composed for the
Bolshevik Central Committee a manifesto on the subject.[1]

On 10 June Petrograd remained calm. But the leaders of
the Soviet majority decided to call another monster demonstration on 18 June, hoping to turn it into a manifestation in favour
of their policies. On the appointed day, 500,000 workers and
soldiers marched past the stands on which the Congress had
assembled *in corpore*. To the dismay of the moderate Socialists,
all the banners in the procession had Bolshevik slogans inscribed on them: 'Down with the ten capitalist ministers!',
'Down with the war!', and 'All power to the Soviets!' The
march-past was concluded peacefully. There were no riots and
no clashes, but for the first time the anti-Bolshevik parties

[1] Lenin, *Sochinenya*, vol. xxv, pp. 60–61; Trotsky, *Sochinenya*, vol. iii, book 1, p.
137; and *Lénine*, pp. 66–69.

gauged the impression which Bolshevik policies and slogans had made on the masses.

In this early period of his activity—it was only the second month after his return—Trotsky's personality had already acquired a fresh and immense lustre. Lunacharsky writes that 'under the influence of Trotsky's dazzling success, and of the enormous scope of his personality many people who were close to Trotsky were even inclined to see in him the genuine first leader of the Russian revolution. Uritsky . . . said once to me and, it seems, to Manuilsky: "Well, the great revolution has come, and you see that, although Lenin has so much wisdom, he begins to grow dim beside the genius of Trotsky."' This opinion, Lunacharsky goes on, was incorrect, not because it exaggerated Trotsky's gifts and his power, but because the scope of Lenin's political genius had not yet revealed itself. 'It is true that in this period . . . Lenin was dimmed a little. He did not speak publicly very often and he did not write very much. He directed mainly the work of organization in the Bolshevik camp, while Trotsky thundered at the meetings.' In 1917, however, the revolution was made as much at mass meetings as within the narrower compass of the party.[1]

.   .   .   .

For the beginning of July the Bolsheviks convened the sixth national congress of their party. This was to be the occasion on which the Inter-Borough Organization was to join their ranks. There was no longer any talk about changing the party's 'label'. For a time the majority of the Inter-Borough Organization resisted; and on its behalf Yureniev still warned members against 'the bad organizational manners' of the Bolsheviks and their inclination to work through narrow secretive caucuses. Trotsky headed the minority which was impatient for the merger. He pleaded that with their emergence from the twilight of clandestinity and the awakening of the broad popular movement, the Bolsheviks had largely rid themselves of their old habits, and that what was left of these would best be overcome in a common, openly working party. Assisted by Lunacharsky, he converted the majority to this view.[2] But before the merger had taken place, the country was shaken by the crisis of the July days.

[1] Lunacharsky, op. cit., pp. 25–28.
[2] Trotsky, *Sochinenya*, vol. iii, book 1, pp. 145–9.

This was one of those violent convulsions which occur unexpectedly in every revolution, upset the plans of all leaders,
accelerate the rhythm of events, and press the polarization of
hostile forces to the utter limit. The patience of the garrison and
of the working population of Petrograd was exhausted. Bread
queues grew interminably. Money, of which ten times more
than before the war was in circulation, was depreciated.
Profiteering was rampant. The masses saw that since the revolution the conditions of their daily existence had become worse,
and they felt that they had been cheated. On top of all this came
the costly offensive, now in progress. But there was still a
discrepancy between the mood of the capital and that of the
provinces. Petrograd clamoured for immediate change and for
the resignation of Prince Lvov's second government. In the
provinces, however, the February régime was by no means
discredited.

Trotsky and Lenin, as they surveyed the balance of strength
in the country as a whole, knew that the hour had not yet come
for them to strike. But their following in the capital, seething
with restlessness, began to view with distrust their tactics. The
Anarchists denounced the waiting game and the treachery of
the Bolsheviks, as the Bolsheviks had denounced the hesitations
and the treachery of the Mensheviks and Social Revolutionaries.
Finally, a number of regiments confronted Bolshevik headquarters with an accomplished fact and called an armed demonstration for 3 July. The sailors of Kronstadt and the civilian
workers in the capital, stirred by rank-and-file Bolshevik
agitators, eagerly responded to the call. As in most such situations, when a risky political initiative springs directly from the
impulsive anger of the masses, the purpose of the initiative was
not clear. Those who called the demonstration did not know
whether they were out to overthrow the government or merely
to demonstrate in a peaceful manner. Bolshevik headquarters
made an attempt to cancel the demonstration as they had done
on 10 June. But this time popular passion could not be dammed.[1]

Lenin then tried to place his party at the head of the move-

[1] Trotsky, *History of the Russian Revolution*, vol. ii, chapters i–iii; Zinoviev,
Sochinenya, vol. xv, p. 41; Lenin, *Sochinenya*, vol. xxv, pp. 142–3. Stalin, who was very
active in the opening phase of the July events, gave a full account of them to the
sixth Congress of the party. Stalin, *Sochinenya*, vol. iii, pp. 156–68. (His account is
summarized in Deutscher, *Stalin*, pp. 148–9.) Raskolnikov, op. cit., pp. 116 ff.

ment in order to keep the movement within the limits of a peaceful demonstration, the purpose of which would be once again to urge the moderate Socialists to form their own Ministry based on the Soviets. With this demand enormous crowds appeared in the centre of the city, filling the streets, marching, and holding meetings in the course of two days and nights. Bolshevik speakers, including Lenin, addressed them, inveighing against the ruling coalition but also appealing for calm and discipline.

The greatest and the angriest crowd besieged the Tauride Palace, where the central Executive of the Soviets had its offices. The crowd sent delegations to the Palace to declare that they would not disperse until the moderate Socialists broke up their coalition with the Cadets. Some Mensheviks and Social Revolutionaries were convinced that Lenin had staged the spectacle and intended it as an armed insurrection. True, for leaders of an insurrection, the Bolsheviks behaved strangely: they harangued the masses, restraining them and warning them against acts of violence. There were, nevertheless, some appearances of premeditated Bolshevik action. It was known that Bolshevik rankers had led the agitation, and the sailors of Kronstadt were most prominent in the commotion.[1] The moderate Socialists sat in the besieged Palace in terror of their lives. They appealed to military headquarters for help. As almost the entire garrison was on the side of the Bolsheviks, reliable detachments were called from the front. While the Mensheviks and Social Revolutionaries waited to be rescued, word came that the crowd outside had seized Chernov, the Minister of Agriculture, and was about to lynch him. Trotsky, who had spent the whole night and the morning in the Palace, now pleading with the demonstrators outside and now with the Executive inside, rushed out to the scene of the riot.

---

[1] Thirty-five years after the event, R. Abramovich, the Menshevik leader wrote: 'The anti-war mood began to rise feverishly after the ill-starred June offensive. The hostile reaction to this attempt to revive a war which in the mind of the masses was already dead was so strong that my own feeling at the time was that already during the July days the Bolsheviks could have seized power by means of their semi-coup, if Lenin and his friends had shown greater determination.' (*Sotsialisticheskii Vestnik*, March 1952: 'The Tragedy of a Belated Revolution'.) During the events, however, and afterwards, Abramovich charged the Bolsheviks with outright conspiracy to seize power. Trotsky, *History of the Russian Revolution*, vol. ii, p. 39.

What followed has been described many times, but nowhere as vividly as in Sukhanov's *Notes on the Revolution*:

As far as the eye could see, the crowd was raging. Around one car, a group of sailors with quite ugly faces behaved in an exceptionally rowdy manner. On a back seat in that car sat Chernov who had quite visibly lost control of himself. The whole of Kronstadt knew Trotsky and seemed to trust him. But the crowd failed to calm down when Trotsky began his speech. If a provocative shot had at this moment been fired anywhere in the neighbourhood, a terrible bloodbath would have followed: they would have torn to pieces all of us, including Trotsky. Excited, with difficulty finding his words, . . . Trotsky just managed to compel the attention of those who stood nearest to him. [He began by extolling the revolutionary virtues of Kronstadt in a manner which seemed to Sukhanov to smack of unworthy flattery.] 'You have come here, you, red men of Kronstadt, as soon as you heard about the danger threatening the revolution. . . . Long live red Kronstadt, the glory and the pride of the revolution!'

But they listened to Trotsky in a sullen mood. When he tried to talk to them about Chernov, the people surrounding the car were again in a fury.

'You have come here to state your will [Trotsky went on] and to show the Soviet that the working class does not wish to see the bourgeoisie in power. But why should you harm your own cause? Why should you obscure and blot your record by mean violence over random individuals? . . . Every one of you has shown his devotion to the revolution. Every one of you is prepared to lay down his head for the revolution. I know this. . . . Give me your hand, comrade! . . . Give me a hand, my brother. . . .'

Trotsky stretched down his arm to a sailor who was violently protesting against his words. The sailor grasped a rifle in one hand and withdrew the other from Trotsky. It seemed to me that he must have listened to Trotsky more than once at Kronstadt, and that he was now really under the impression that Trotsky had betrayed the cause.[1]

Finally, Trotsky defied the crowd and asked those who wanted violence to be done to Chernov openly to raise their hands. Not a hand went up. Amid silence, he took Chernov, half-

[1] Sukhanov, op. cit., vol. iv, pp. 423–5. See also V. Chernov, *The Great Russian Revolution*, pp. 422–6. Trotsky later claimed that those who had seized Chernov were *agent-provocateurs* who had nothing in common with the sailors. (*Sochinenya*, vol. iii, book 1, pp. 193 ff.) On internal evidence, Sukhanov's version appears more credible, and it is shared by Raskolnikov, the leader of Kronstadt (op. cit., pp. 128–30).

fainting by now, by the arm and led him into the Palace.
Trotsky's own face, as he returned with his rescued enemy, was
of a deadly pallor and covered with cold perspiration.

In various parts of the city minor disturbances and affrays
occurred, which could easily have led to profuse bloodshed
had it not been for the restraining influence of the Bolsheviks.
At length the demonstrators became tired and their energy
sagged. They were on the point of dispersing when the troops
from the front arrived. A violent reaction set in at once. Secret
and half-secret right-wing organizations, which had hitherto
lain low, descended upon the streets. After a few clashes, the
pro-Bolshevik crowds, craving for sleep and rest, dispersed.
Just then the papers broke the news of the collapse of the
offensive on the front. This added fuel to the anti-Bolshevik
reaction. The right-wing parties, the generals, and the officers'
leagues blamed the Bolsheviks; it was their agitation, they said,
that had destroyed the army's morale and prepared the defeat.[1]

This charge alone would have been enough to bring a storm
on the heads of the Bolshevik party. Added to it was another,
even more inflammatory, accusation. A popular right-wing
newspaper published 'documents' alleging that Lenin had been
in the pay of the German General Staff; and writs were issued
for the arrest of Lenin, Zinoviev, and Kamenev. The documents
could be recognized at a glance as a clumsy fabrication. The
witness who produced them, a certain Yermolenko, turned out
to be a former stool-pigeon, now in the service of military
counter-intelligence.[2] But at first the impression made by the
accusation was devastating. Appearances spoke against Lenin;
and for the moment appearances were decisive. The non-
political citizen, no initiate in the history and habits of revolutionary parties, asked: Did Lenin not in fact return via *Germany*,

[1] A week before these events, on 28 June, Trotsky wrote in *Vperyod*: 'And if after
three years of war and four months of revolution not all the soldiers are persuaded
by the evasively cautious resolution of the Congress [of the Soviets, which approved
the offensive] or by the cheap oratorical fanfaronade of semi-socialist semi-
ministers, then the 'loyal' press can always resort to a tested device: it can call
"society" to a crusade against the revolutionary socialists at large and the Bolsheviks in particular.'

[2] A detailed account and analysis of this affair will be given in my *Life of
Lenin*. Kerensky's version is in *Crucifixion of Liberty*, pp. 285–94 and its refutation is
in M. N. Pokrovsky, *Oktyabr'skaya Revolutsia*, pp. 115–36. See also Trotsky, *History*,
vol. ii, pp. 96–123.

by agreement with the German government? Did he not agitate against the war? Did he not foment upheaval? It was no use replying that Lenin had resolved to travel through Germany only after all other routes, via France and England, had been denied to him, and that many of his Menshevik adversaries had returned together with him, or somewhat later, by the same route.[1] It was no use pointing out that Lenin hoped that the revolution would destroy the Hohenzollerns and the Habsburgs as it had destroyed the Romanovs. In the stampede which followed the July days such subtleties were overlooked. The upper classes were mad with fear and hatred of revolution. The middle classes were blind with despair. The General Staff needed a face-saving explanation of the latest military disaster. And the moderate Socialists felt the earth opening beneath their feet. The need for a scapegoat and a spectacular sin-offering was overwhelming.

In the middle of this turmoil Trotsky saw Lenin. 'They have chosen this moment to shoot us all', Lenin said.[2] He reckoned with the probability of a successful counter-revolution; he believed that the Soviets, emasculated by the Mensheviks and Social Revolutionaries, had played out their role; and he was preparing his party for a return to clandestinity. After a little hesitation, he made up his mind that he would not allow himself to be imprisoned but would go into hiding, together with Zinoviev. Trotsky took a less grave view and Lenin's decision seemed to him unfortunate. Such behaviour was altogether against the grain of Trotsky's own habits. He thought that Lenin had nothing to hide, that, on the contrary, he had every interest in laying his record before the public, and that in this way he could serve his cause better than by flight, which would merely add to any adverse appearances by which people might judge him.[3] Kamenev shared Trotsky's feelings and decided to submit to imprisonment. But Lenin stuck to his decision. He did not expect to be given a fair trial by a government which heaped false accusations on him and circulated faked documents in the press.

---

[1] During the official investigation on the July days it was ascertained that about 500 Russian émigrés had returned from Switzerland via Germany. Of these 400 were anti-Bolsheviks and 'social patriots'. Pokrovsky, op. cit., p. 123.

[2] Trotsky, *Lénine*, p. 69.

[3] See Trotsky's deposition which he later made in prison. *Sochinenya*, vol. iii, book 1, p. 193 *passim*; *History*, vol. ii, pp. 240–1.

The atmosphere was tense. The Bolshevik party was virtually ostracized. *Pravda* had been banned and its offices demolished. Bolshevik headquarters in several districts had been wrecked. Nothing was easier for the thugs of the old Okhrana, who were still entrenched in the police, or for fanatics of the counter-revolution than to assassinate a hated leader of the revolution on the way to or from prison. Lenin was too well aware of his importance to the party to take this risk, and, disregarding all conventional considerations, went into hiding.[1]

In public attacks, Trotsky's name was most often coupled with Lenin's, but no writ of arrest was issued against him. There were obvious reasons: he was not nominally a member of the Bolshevik party; the circumstances of his return to Russia were so different from those in which Lenin had travelled that it was not easy to tack on to him the label of German agent; and the incident with Chernov, the political enemy whom he had so courageously rescued, was still fresh in everybody's mind. But he was not spared for long. *Ryech*, Miliukov's paper, published a story that before his departure from New York Trotsky had received 10,000 dollars from German-Americans, which he was to use for defeatist agitation in Russia. In less respectable newspapers the German General Staff figured as the source of the money. Trotsky at once replied with an Open Letter which appeared in Gorky's paper and deflated Miliukov's revelations with much comic effect. He remarked ironically that the German-Americans or the German General Staff apparently considered the overthrow of a régime in an enemy country an extremely cheap affair, costing only 10,000 dollars. He attacked the sources from which the story emanated, saying that it had come from Sir George Buchanan, the British Ambassador. The Ambassador denied the charge, but this did not prevent Miliukov from claiming that he had the story from that source. Then Trotsky related what had really happened before his departure from New York: Russian, American, Latvian, Jewish, Finnish, and German-American Socialists arranged a farewell meeting for him and three other Russian émigrés who were

---

[1] This step embarrassed quite a few of Lenin's followers. Only much later, when during the German revolution Rosa Luxemburg and Karl Liebknecht were assassinated in such a way, did Lenin's behaviour acquire full justification in the eyes of those who were at first uneasy about it.

about to leave with him. A collection was made on the spot which yielded 310 dollars to which the German-American part of the audience contributed 100. The sum was handed to Trotsky, and he divided it equally among the returning émigrés. The meeting and the collection were reported in American newspapers. He concluded with a good-humoured 'confession' which, as he knew, would discredit him in the eyes of the bourgeois public even more than being in the pay of the German General Staff: never in his life, he wrote, had he at one time possessed 10,000 dollars or even one-tenth of that sum.[1]

In another Open Letter he related the story of his friendship and break with Parvus, since this connexion was also brought up against him. He exposed Alexinsky, the former Bolshevik deputy turned renegade, as chief inspirer of the calumny. Alexinsky, he wrote, had been expelled as a slanderer from all journalistic organizations in Paris, and the Mensheviks had, on moral grounds, refused to admit him to the Petrograd Soviet. And this was the man now promoted to be the guardian of patriotic morality.[2]

This attempt at involving Trotsky having failed, intrigue was started from the opposite angle. The press was full of stories alleging that Trotsky had broken with Lenin, the German agent. On 10 July, four days after Lenin had gone into hiding, Trotsky therefore addressed the following Open Letter to the Provisional Government:

Citizen Ministers—I understand that you have decreed the arrest . . . of Comrades Lenin, Zinoviev, Kamenev, but that the writ of arrest does not concern me. I therefore think it necessary to bring these facts to your attention: 1. I share in principle the attitude of Lenin, Zinoviev, and Kamenev, and I have expounded it in the journal *Vperyod* and in all my public speeches. 2. My attitude towards the events of 3 and 4 July was uniform with that of the above-mentioned Comrades.[3]

He gave an account of those events and explained that the fact that he did not belong to the Bolshevik organization was due to outdated and now meaningless differences.

You can have no logical grounds for exempting me from the effect of the decree by dint of which Lenin, Zinoviev, and Kamenev are

[1] Trotsky, *Sochinenya*, vol. iii, book 1, pp. 150–4. [2] Ibid., pp. 155–9.
[3] Ibid., pp. 165–6.

subject to arrest. . . . You can have no reason to doubt that I am just as irreconcilable an opponent of the general policy of the Provisional Government as the above-mentioned Comrades. My exemption only underlines more graphically the counter-revolutionary and wanton character of the action you have taken against them.[1]

For two or three days, while the terror against the Bolsheviks was at its peak, Trotsky did not appear at the Soviet. He spent the nights at the home of Larin, the former Menshevik who was about to join the Bolsheviks. But after the publication of the 'Open Letter to the Provisional Government' Trotsky, full of fight and defiance, reappeared in the limelight. He defended Lenin and the Bolshevik party in the Soviet, on the Executive of the Soviets, and on the Executive of the peasant Soviets. Everywhere he spoke amid continuous uproar. 'Lenin', he exclaimed, 'has fought for the revolution thirty years. I have fought against the oppression of the popular masses twenty years. We cannot but hate German militarism. Only he who does not know what a revolutionary is can say otherwise. . . . Do not allow anybody in this hall to say that we are German mercenaries, for this is the voice . . . of villainy.'[2] He warned the Mensheviks, who were washing their hands of the affair, that this would be their own undoing. Chernov, the 'social patriot', had already been compelled to resign from the ministry, because he had participated in the Zimmerwald movement. The counter-revolution had chosen the Bolsheviks as its first targets; the moderate socialists would be its next victims.

Even in those days of hysteria and panic he was listened to with attention and respect. His appeals, however, had little or no effect. The moderate Socialists knew that it was preposterous to accuse Lenin and Zinoviev of being German agents; but they were convinced that the Bolshevik agitation against the war had gone too far; and they suspected that in the July days Lenin, or perhaps Lenin and Trotsky, had attempted to seize power;

[1] Loc. cit. At the same time Trotsky wrote a letter to Gorky. Gorky, who had been Lenin's close friend, behaved (in contrast to Martov, who defended Lenin) rather vaguely. Trotsky intended to urge him to come out strongly in Lenin's defence and to remind him of Zola's role in the Dreyfus affair. The letter, which Trotsky did not post, is reprinted in *Sochinenya*, vol. iii, book i, pp. 346–7.
[2] Sukhanov, op. cit., vol. v, pp. 52, 59–62.

and they refused to lift a finger for Lenin's rehabilitation. Only
Martov defended the honour of his old adversary.[1]

Trotsky remained at large for another fortnight. The ministry
was embarrassed by his challenge. It had no ground to order
his arrest, unless it declared as lawless the principles which
guided the Soviet as a whole, including its moderate majority,
for it was in terms of those principles that Trotsky had framed
his own activity. The ministry could not, on the other hand,
allow him to remain at large and make a mockery of its action
against the Bolsheviks. On the night of 23 July Trotsky and
Lunacharsky were arrested and transferred to the Kresty prison.
Sukhanov describes the impression which this made in Petrograd. The next day, Sukhanov himself addressed a Menshevik
meeting at the Cirque Moderne. 'My announcement about the
arrest of Trotsky and Lunacharsky . . . was met with such a
storm of indignation that for nearly a quarter of an hour it was
impossible to go on with the meeting. Shouts were heard that
the whole crowd, numbering many thousands, should at once
march and express its protest to the authorities. It was with
difficulty that Martov contrived to reduce the affair to an
improvised resolution of protest.'[2]

Thus in the middle of a revolution in which his former friends
and a former pupil had risen to power, Trotsky found himself in
the same prison in which the Tsarist government had locked
him up in 1905. The conditions inside the prison were worse
now. The cells were extremely overcrowded: the rounding up
of suspects continued, and large batches were brought in daily.
Criminal and political offenders were herded together, whereas
under the old régime the political offenders had enjoyed the
privilege of separation. All were kept on a near-starvation diet.
The criminals were incited against the 'German agents', robbed
them of their food and manhandled them. Prosecutors, examiners, and jailers were the same as under the Tsar. The contrast
between the pretensions of the new rulers and the inside aspect
of the judicial machinery was striking; and, as Trotsky watched

---

[1] Among the many versions of the July events one claimed that there had been a
plan for the dictatorship of a triumvirate, consisting of Lenin, Trotsky, and
Lunacharsky. How widely this version was believed can be judged from the circumstance that even Sukhanov was inclined to take it at face value. Sukhanov, op. cit.,
vol. iv, p. 511.

[2] Ibid., vol. v, p. 121.

it, he reflected that Lenin was not so mistaken when he decided to take refuge. Yet in this wild chaos, in which even the life of the prisoner was sometimes in peril, there was, just as under the old régime, still enough latitude for the prisoners' political and literary activity. With such debaters as Kamenev, Lunacharsky, Antonov-Ovseenko, and Krylenko, political debate flourished. Among the inmates were also Dybenko and Raskolnikov, the leaders of Kronstadt. Here were assembled nearly all the chief actors of the October insurrection and nearly the whole first Bolshevik Commissariat of War.

Trotsky himself took to the pen, and once again a cataract of his articles and pamphlets found its way to the outside world. Some of these, including a detailed description of life in the prison, appeared, under the pen-name P. Tanas, in Bolshevik papers, and others in Gorky's daily. In another of his 'Open Letters to the Provisional Government' Trotsky covered the legal proceedings with ridicule. He revealed that he was charged with having returned to Russia, together with Lenin, via Germany and with having been a member of the Bolshevik Central Committee. These charges testified to the wantonness and the lazy indolence of the prosecution.[1] It was, incidentally, only some weeks after Trotsky's arrest that the Inter-Borough Organization finally joined the Bolshevik party and Trotsky became a member of the Bolshevik Central Committee. His exposure of the proceedings had the effect of causing his prosecutor's dismissal. But the proceedings went on. 'The Dreyfus case and the Beyliss case are nothing compared with this deliberate attempt at moral assassination', Trotsky protested to Zarudny, the Minister of Justice who, by a strange freak, had been counsel for the defence in the Soviet's trial in 1906.[2]

As the weeks passed, events unexpectedly took a turn at once more hopeful and more menacing to the prosecuted men and their cause. The reaction against the July 'insurrection' was broadening into an impetuous movement against all the institutions and conditions which had their origin in the February Revolution: against the Soviets, the army committees, the land committees, the factory committees, and similar bodies which had wittingly and unwittingly disputed the authority of the old

---

[1] *Novaya Zhizn*, 30 July 1917.
[2] Trotsky, *Sochinenya*, vol. iii, book 1, p. 203; Raskolnikov, op. cit., pp. 170–9.

administrative machine. The reaction now hit the moderate
Socialists. The leaders of the right-wing argued, not without
reason, that the Bolsheviks were only the most consistent
advocates of a state of affairs to the defence of which the
moderate Socialists were in varying degrees also committed.[1]
The Bolshevik cry 'All power to the Soviets!' would not die
down as long as the Soviets were in existence; and the Mensheviks and Social Revolutionaries had a stake in their existence.
If the Bolsheviks did their utmost to stir up the opposition of
soldier against officer, the moderate Socialists, the initial mouthpieces of that opposition, had a vested interest at least in preventing the officers' corps from regaining its old status. The
leaders of the middle classes had hitherto hoped to tame the
revolution with the hands of the moderate Socialists; they now
cast around for a military dictator capable of taming or crushing
the moderate Socialists as well as the Bolsheviks. Only thus did
the right wing, which now included former Liberals, hope to
bring to an end what they regarded as the most shameful chapter
in Russian history.

The July days had shown that if any strength was left in
anti-Bolshevik Russia that strength resided in the officers' corps.
The picture of the moderate Soviet leaders, besieged in the
Tauride Palace, trembling for their lives and praying to be
rescued from Bolshevik crowds by loyal troops was not forgotten. Yet such was the illogical mechanism of the February
régime that the real relationship of power was now more than
ever masked by the political façade. Immediately after the July
days, a second coalition government was formed with Kerensky
as Premier, in which the moderate socialists assumed nominal
leadership. In their heyday they had been the junior partners
in the coalition; and only after their weakness had been so
devastatingly revealed did they assume the role of senior partners, at least in appearance. This paradox could not last.

The Conservative and anti-revolutionary forces rested their
hopes on General Kornilov, whom Kerensky had appointed
Commander-in-Chief. Feted and acclaimed by the upper and
middle classes, Kornilov began to feel and behave like a man of
Providence. His attitude towards Kerensky became ambiguous

---

[1] Miliukov, op. cit., vol. i, book 2, pp. 58–72; A. I. Denikin, *Ocherki Russkoi
Smuty*, vol. i, book 2, pp. 232–8.

and then provocative. Finally, on 24 August, he openly declared war on the government and ordered his troops to march on the capital. Confident of victory, he boasted in advance of the clean sweep he was going to make of the revolution.

Trotsky and his friends in Kresty received the news with mixed feelings. Kerensky kept them behind the bars, and if Kornilov were to win they would be delivered as virtual hostages to the victorious *soldateska*. They had no doubt that they would be slaughtered; and this was certainly not a figment of panicky imaginations. But the situation also offered new hope. The moderate Socialists could not save themselves from Kornilov without the help of the Bolsheviks, just as in the July days they could not save themselves from the Bolsheviks without the help of the generals. Soon the government itself was pressing rifles into the hands of the Red Guards, whom it had just disarmed. It begged the Bolshevik agitators, on whose destructive influence it had blamed all military disasters, to bring that influence to bear on Kornilov's troops and persuade them to disobey and desert their commanders. And, finally, Kerensky implored the sailors of Kronstadt, the villains of July, to rally to his defence.

A scene of almost whimsical fantasy took place in Trotsky's cell. The sailors of Kronstadt sent a delegation to ask him whether they ought to respond to Kerensky's call and defend Kerensky against Kornilov or whether they should try to settle accounts with both Kornilov and Kerensky. To the hot-headed sailors the latter course certainly appealed more. Trotsky argued with them, reminding them how in May he had defended them in the Soviet and had said that if a counter-revolutionary general were to try to throw a noose around the neck of the revolution then 'the sailors of Kronstadt would come and fight and die with us'. They must now honour this pledge and postpone the reckoning with Kerensky, which could not be far off anyhow. The sailors took his advice. While this was going on, the prosecution mechanically continued its job. The examination dragged on and Trotsky had to answer questions about his connexions with the German General Staff and the Bolsheviks. Antonov-Ovseenko and Krylenko, against whom no charges were brought after six weeks of imprisonment, threatened a hunger strike, but Trotsky tried to dissuade them. At length he decided to take no further part in the farce of interrogation. He refused to answer the examiner's questions and gave his reasons in a letter to the Central Executive of the Soviets. Three days later, on 4 September, he was released on bail.

Straight from the prison he went to the Smolny Institute to participate in a session of the Committee for Struggle against Counter-revolution, which had, with Kerensky's blessing, been formed by the Soviet. This body was to be the prototype of the Military Revolutionary Committee which led the October insurrection.

Kornilov was defeated not by force of arms, but by Bolshevik agitation. His troops deserted him, without firing a shot. From Kornilov's defeat started a new chain of events leading straight to the October insurrection. Just as the abortive revolution of 3–4 July had swung the balance in favour of counter-revolution, so this abortive counter-revolution had swung it much more powerfully in the opposite direction. The second coalition government broke down. The Cadet ministers resigned, because they did not favour Kerensky's action against Kornilov. The Socialist ministers withdrew, because they suspected Kerensky of having previously intrigued with Kornilov against the Soviet and encouraged his ambitions. For a month Kerensky, incapable of piecing together the broken fragments of the coalition, ruled through a so-called Directorate, a small and quite unrepresentative committee.

In the Soviet Trotsky and Kamenev asked for an investigation of the events that led to Kornilov's coup and of Kerensky's role in the preliminaries. With increased insistence they pressed the moderate Socialists to part company at last with the Cadets, many of whom had backed Kornilov. After the Kornilov affair the argument in favour of a purely Socialist government sounded irrefutable. When the Mensheviks and Social Revolutionaries still continued their attempts to revive the coalition, their followers deserted them *en masse*. Within a few days the moderate majority in the Soviet disintegrated. On 9 September Trotsky made one of his rousing speeches, demanding an unequivocal rehabilitation of himself and the Bolshevik leaders. He asked for the government's long-overdue report on the July events, and he tabled a motion of no confidence in the Menshevik 'Presidium' of the Soviet. To everybody's immense surprise, the motion was carried. For the first time the Bolsheviks obtained for their proposal a majority vote in the Soviet. The revolution had set up a new landmark.[1]

As they were losing ground in the Soviet, the Mensheviks and their associates made an attempt to rally outside the Soviet. For 14 September they convened the so-called Democratic Conference. This was not in any sense an elected assembly. Its composition was so devised as to secure in advance an anti-Bolshevik majority. A haphazard assortment of delegations from various non-political institutions, such as co-operatives and pre-revolutionary *Zemstvos*, was to pronounce on all the burning political issues. Such was the paradox of the situation that, regardless of what was to happen later, at this stage it was the Bolsheviks who appeared to stand firmly by the principle of representative and elected government, while the moderate Socialists sought to negate that principle. The Soviets, elected in the factories and barracks, did not represent the bourgeoisie; but they fully represented the working classes, the army, and important sections of the peasantry. Their authority and popular appeal were in part due to the absence of any truly national parliamentary institutions. To create such institutions, so it might seem, was a vital interest of the anti-Bolshevik parties. Yet the coalition governments kept on postponing the promised elections to the Constituent Assembly, and the Bolsheviks clamoured for the elections. In their own minds they were not yet clear about the future relationship between a Constituent Assembly and the Soviets. They did not foresee that by investing all power in the Soviets they would make a Constituent Assembly impossible; and that they themselves would convoke it only in order to disperse it. The moderate Socialists, on the other hand, complied with the repeated postponement of elections in deference to the wishes of the Cadets, who feared that a national poll now taken would produce too radical a legislature.[2] In the meantime the moderate Socialists tried to concoct a substitute

[1] At the same sitting, Trotsky proposed the election of a new Presidium on the basis of proportional representation. This brought an angry comment from Lenin, who argued that the Mensheviks and Social Revolutionaries had not adopted proportionate representation when they were the majority—why should the Bolsheviks accord them this privilege? However, Trotsky's conciliatory gesture met with a rebuff from the Mensheviks too: they refused to sit with the Bolsheviks in the Presidium.
[2] Miliukov, op. cit., vol. i, book 2, pp. 91–2.

for a parliament in the form of the Democratic Conference and the so-called pre-Parliament which issued from it.

The Conference offered a spectacle of disarray in the ruling groups. The moderate Socialists came forward with bitter recriminations against the Cadets. Kerensky's own supporters openly aired their distrust of him, saying that his role in the Kornilov affair had been ambiguous and that he had tried to place himself above the parties that had sent him to the government and to establish his personal rule. Kerensky attempted to refute the charges and to persuade the conference of the need to revive the governmental coalition. But his performance was so grotesquely melodramatic that he filled his friends with despair and achieved none of his objectives. It was on this occasion that Trotsky for the first time appeared as the chief Bolshevik spokesman. The impression of his speech is thus described by the Menshevik chronicler of the revolution:[1]

This was undoubtedly one of this amazing orator's most brilliant speeches, and I cannot suppress the desire to adorn the pages of my book with an almost full reproduction of this magnificent oration. If in the future my book finds a reader as Lamartine's not very imaginative book still finds readers today, let that reader judge from this page the oratorical art and the political thought of our days. He will draw the conclusion that mankind has not lived in vain this last century and a half, and that the heroes of our revolution relegate far to the background the famous leaders of 1789.

The audience at the Alexandrinsky theatre was electrified at the very sound of Trotsky's name. . . . Trotsky had prepared himself well. Standing on the stage a few steps behind him, I saw on the pulpit in front of him a closely written sheet, with underlined phrases, footnotes, and arrows drawn with a blue pencil. . . . He spoke quite plainly, without any rhetorical art (though he can rise to its heights whenever he needs to), without the slightest posturing or trickery. This time he talked with the audience, sometimes advancing towards it a step or two and then leaning his elbow on the pulpit. The metallic clarity of speech and the polish of the phrase, which are so characteristic of Trotsky, were not there in this performance.

We need not summarize this speech, which reproduced the main lines of Bolshevik policy; only a few points illustrating his polemical manner will suffice. 'Comrades and Citizens,' he began very quietly, 'the socialist ministers have just spoken to

[1] Sukhanov, op. cit., vol. v, pp. 125-6. See also Chernov, op. cit., pp. 306-7.

you. Ministers are supposed to appear before representative bodies to give an account of their work. Our ministers have preferred to give us advice rather than an account. For the advice we are grateful, but we still demand an account. Not advice, but an account, Citizen Ministers', the speaker repeats very quietly, tapping the pulpit. Summing up the preceding debate, he remarked that not a single speaker had defended Kerensky, and so the Prime Minister stood condemned by his own friends and followers. This struck the opposing camp at its most vulnerable point, and an angry tumult rose from the floor. One of the issues most hotly debated was a recent decree reintroducing the death penalty. 'You may curse me if I ever sign a single death sentence', Kerensky, anxious to appease his own resentful followers, exclaimed at the conference. To this Trotsky retorted: 'If the death penalty is necessary, how can Kerensky take it upon himself to say that he will make no use of it? If he thinks that he can commit himself in front of the whole of democratic opinion and say that he will not apply the death penalty, then I tell you that he is turning its reintroduction into an act of lightmindedness which transcends the limits of criminality.'

The supporters of the coalition had said that the whole Cadet party should not be blamed for Kornilov's mutiny; and that the Bolsheviks who protested when their party was denounced as responsible for the July days, should be the last to blame the Cadets wholesale. 'In this comparison', Trotsky replied, 'there is one small inaccuracy. When the Bolsheviks were charged with . . . having brought about or provoked the movement of 3–5 July, there was no question of your inviting them into the Ministry— they were being invited to the Kresty prison. There is, comrades, a certain difference here. . . . We say: if in connexion with the Kornilov movement you want to drag the Cadets to prison, then, please, do not act indiscriminately. Examine the case of every Cadet individually, examine it from every possible angle!' The hostile audience was convulsed with laughter; and even the most pompous among the ministers and the leaders on the platform could not suppress a giggle. But this note of jollity was quickly silenced by one of grim gravity. Trotsky urged that the Red Guards be armed. 'What for? What for?' the cry came from the Menshevik benches. 'Firstly, in order that we may build up a genuine rampart against counter-revolution', he answered, 'against a new and more powerful Kornilov movement. Secondly, if a government of genuine dictatorship by the revolutionary democracy is established, if that new government offers an honest peace and its offer is rejected, then, I am telling you this on behalf of our party . . ., the armed workers of Petrograd and of the whole of Russia will defend the land of revolution from the troops of imperialism with a heroism such as Russian history has never known.' He concluded by denouncing the unrepresentative character of the Conference; and he led the Bolshevik delegates out of the assembly.[1]

Even after this exodus, the Conference failed to meet Kerensky's expectations. It ended, as it had begun, in confusion. A slight majority voted for a new coalition; but then a solid majority emphatically decided against any accommodation with the Cadets, the only partners available for a coalition. When, on 21 September, Kerensky, disregarding the view of his own pseudo-parliament, did set up a new government with the Cadets, the government was in the air from the outset. This was the fifth cabinet formed in seven months. The life-span which Trotsky and Lenin were to leave to it was one month.

In the Soviets, the Bolsheviks went from strength to strength. At the beginning of September they had a majority in Petrograd, Moscow, and other industrial cities. They confidently expected to emerge as the dominant party at the forthcoming national Congress of Soviets. The body entitled to convene the Congress was the Central Executive of the Soviets, which had been elected in June and was still controlled by the moderate Socialists. The latter did their best to postpone what for them was a leap in the dark, and the Bolsheviks pressed, of course, for early convocation. Trotsky pleaded with the moderate leaders and threatened them: 'Do not play with this Congress. The local Soviets, those of Petrograd and Moscow in the first instance, demand it; and if you do not convene it in a constitutional manner, it will be convened in a revolutionary manner.'[2]

On 23 September the Petrograd Soviet elected Trotsky as its President. As he mounted the dais, 'a hurricane of applause went up . . . everything changed in the Soviet!' In contrast to the disheartened assembly of the July days, 'this was now once

<hr/>

[1] Trotsky, *Sochinenya,* vol. iii, book 1, pp. 287–93.   [2] Ibid., p. 320.

again a revolutionary army. . . . This was now Trotsky's guard, ready at a wink from him to storm the coalition, the Winter Palace and all the fortresses of the bourgeoisie. . . . The only question was whither Trotsky would lead them.'[1] In his presidential address, he recalled 1905 and expressed the hope that this time he would lead the Soviet towards a different destiny. He gave a solemn and emphatic pledge, on which later events were to throw a melancholy shadow: 'We are all party men, and more than once we shall clash with one another. But we shall conduct the work of the Petrograd Soviet in a spirit of lawfulness and of full freedom for all parties. The hand of the Presidium will never lend itself to the suppression of a minority.'[2] On behalf of the new Soviet he sounded the first summons to the second revolution, calling for Kerensky's resignation and the transfer of governmental power to the Congress of Soviets. He argued against the Mensheviks and Social Revolutionaries as trenchantly as ever, but without ill feeling, without a trace of the craving for revenge which might have been expected from a leader of a party so recently proscribed.[3]

Despite Lenin's objections, all parties were represented in the new Presidium of the Soviet in proportion to their strength.[4] Was this display of scrupulous respect for the rights of the minority merely a tactical stratagem, designed to deceive the minority's vigilance? Hardly so. Sukhanov relates that three years later, after the Bolsheviks had banned all the parties of the opposition, he reminded Trotsky of his pledge not to lend himself to the suppression of any minority. Trotsky lapsed into silence, reflected for a while, and then said wistfully: 'Those were good days.'[5] They were indeed. The revolution was still taking seriously its own assurance that it would widen and make real the freedoms which bourgeois democracy only promised or which it granted with a niggardly hand.

Trotsky now referred to himself in public without inhibition as a Bolshevik. He accepted the label he had so long considered as little better than a slur. While in prison he had been elected to the Central Committee of the party. In the seven weeks that

---

[1] Sukhanov, op. cit., vol. vi, pp. 188 ff.
[2] Loc. cit.   [3] Ibid., p. 194.
[4] Even a group like Gorky's which was too small to claim representation, was allocated seats.   [5] Sukhanov, ibid., p. 190.

passed between his release and the October insurrection, his name became not merely identified with Bolshevism, but to the outside world it came to symbolize the aspirations of Bolshevism even more strongly than did the name of Lenin, who had withdrawn from the public eye.[1] These were weeks so charged with history that they crowded from men's minds the events of preceding months and years. Trotsky's feud with Lenin for nearly fifteen years seemed insignificant in comparison with the things he would do in fifteen minutes for the Bolshevik party nowadays. Yet in the inner circle of the party there were, naturally, men from whose memories nothing could efface the past feud. They viewed his sudden ascendancy in the party with well-concealed pique. They had to acknowledge the proud courage with which he had stood by their party in recent adversity, when he was not yet a member of it. Nor could they deny that in Lenin's absence none of them could speak for the party with Trotsky's firmness, clarity, and authority; and that not even Lenin could act as its mouthpiece with comparable brilliance.

Trotsky's ascendancy in the party was therefore undisputed. But it is enough to scan the records of the Central Committee to glimpse the feelings below the surface. Earlier in the year Lenin had tried in vain to prevail upon his colleagues to accord Trotsky a prominent role in the direction of the Bolshevik press. As late as 4 August the Central Committee elected a chief editorial board for Bolshevik newspapers. The board consisted of Stalin, Sokolnikov, and Miliutin. A proposal that Trotsky, when released from prison, should join the board was defeated by eleven votes to ten.[2] On 6 September, however, two days after his release, when he first appeared at the Central Committee, he was appointed unopposed as one of the party's chief editors.[3] The Central Committee was now composed of twenty-one regular and eight deputy members. Some of these had been familiar figures in the émigré colonies, and some had come from the Inter-Borough Organization. Others, like Miliutin, Nogin, Rykov, Sverdlov, Stalin, and Shaumian were home-bred com-

---

[1] Jacques Sadoul, later an ardent Stalinist, wrote at the time: 'Trotsky dominates the insurrection, being its soul of steel, while Lenin remains rather its theoretician.' *Notes sur la Révolution*, p. 76.

[2] *Protokoly Tsentralnovo Komiteta*, p. 5.   [3] Ibid., p. 56.

mittee men, who had known almost no life outside their austere, clandestine party, who felt that they had been the real moles of revolution, and who looked with instinctive distrust upon the former émigrés, especially the one who was the most proud, colourful, and eloquent of all. But this antagonism was suppressed almost to the depth of the unconscious.

In the Central Committee Trotsky at first behaved with the discretion and tact of a newcomer. On the day of his first appearance there, differences between the old Bolsheviks came to light which bore directly upon the party's fundamental attitude. These were the preliminaries to the great controversy over the insurrection: from his refuge, Lenin had just posed the problem before the Central Committee. Zinoviev, who shared Lenin's hiding place, had already applied to the Committee for permission to come into the open and dissociate himself from Lenin. The Committee had refused permission; but it was uneasy about the continued concealment of its two leaders; and it allowed Kamenev to negotiate with the moderate Socialists an arrangement which would make it possible for both of them to come into the open. In this prelude to the controversy over insurrection and for some time later, Trotsky said little or nothing, although he held strong views.

Lenin was already prodding his party to insurrection. In his letters to the Central Committee he dwelt on the change in the mood of the Soviets, the rising tide of peasant revolt, and the impatience of the army, to urge that the party should at once pass from revolutionary declarations and promises to armed action. He was confident that if the party seized the opportunity it would gain the support of an immense majority of the people. But history offered a fleeting opportunity only: if the Bolsheviks missed it, another Kornilov would soon be ready with a *pronunciamento* and crush the Soviets and the revolution. In view of this danger, Lenin wrote, no constitutional niceties, not even the niceties of Soviet constitutionalism, deserved attention. The party ought to stage the insurrection in its own name and on its own responsibility. It need not necessarily start in Petrograd: the beginning might be made in Moscow or even in Finland, and from there the insurgent movements could later converge upon the capital.[1] On 15 September the Central Committee

[1] Lenin, *Sochinenya*, vol. xxvi, pp. 1–9.

debated these proposals for the first time. Kamenev came out in categorical opposition and asked the Committee to warn all organizations against any move of an insurrectionist character. The Committee did not accept Kamenev's advice, nor did it accept Lenin's proposals.[1]

In the meantime Trotsky was approaching the problem from his new point of vantage as President of the Petrograd Soviet. He agreed with Lenin on the chances and the urgency of insurrection. But he disagreed with him over method, especially over the idea that the party should stage the insurrection in its own name and on its own responsibility. He took less seriously than Lenin the threat of an immediate counter-revolution.[2] Unlike Lenin, he was confident that the pressure of the Bolshevik majority in the Soviets would not allow the old Central Executive to delay much longer the All-Russian Congress. He reasoned that since the Bolsheviks had conducted their whole agitation under the slogan 'all power to the Soviets', they should stage the rising in such a manner that it would appear to everyone as the direct conclusion of this agitation. The rising should therefore be timed to coincide with, or slightly precede, the Congress of the Soviets, in whose hands the insurgents should then lay the power seized. Furthermore, he wanted the insurrection to be conducted in the name of the Petrograd Soviet and through its machinery, all the components of which were in Bolshevik hands, and of the whole of which he was in personal command. The rising would then appear to the world not as the business of one party only but as a much broader undertaking.[3]

It would be a mistake to read into this difference any deeper conflict over principles, and to deduce from it that, while Trotsky wished to seize power for the Soviets, Lenin aimed at placing power in the hands of his party alone. Both were in a sense Soviet constitutionalists. Lenin, too, envisaged that the insurgents would convene an All-Russian Congress of the Soviets and place power in its hands. He refused to let insurrection wait until the Congress convened, because he was convinced that the Menshevik Executive would delay the Congress to

---

[1] *Protokoly Tsen. Kom.*, p. 65.
[2] This difference can be traced back to the July days. Raskolnikov, op. cit., p. 171; Trotsky, *History*, vol. ii, pp. 315–19.　　　[3] Ibid., vol. iii, chapters v and vi.

the Greek Calends, and thus the insurrection would never take place as it would be forestalled by a successful counter-revolution. But he, too, saw the Congress of the Soviets as the constitutional source of power. Trotsky, on the other hand, took it for granted that the Bolsheviks, constituting a majority in the Soviets, would actually be the ruling party. Neither of them at this stage saw any conflict between Soviet constitutionalism and a Bolshevik dictatorship, just as, *mutatis mutandis*, no British democrat sees any conflict between parliamentary rule and the cabinet system based on the majority party.

The difference between Lenin and Trotsky centred on a much narrower issue: namely, on whether the rising itself ought to be conceived in terms of Soviet constitutionalism. The tactical risk inherent in Trotsky's attitude was that it imposed certain delays upon the whole plan of action. The political disadvantage of Lenin's approach was that it was likely to narrow the popular appeal of insurrection. Lenin concentrated exclusively on the end to be attained. Trotsky paid more regard to its political context, to the moods of the masses, and to the need to win over the hesitant elements, who might respond to the Soviet's but not to the party's call. The one in hiding had the bare and changeable realities of power before his eyes. The other weighed, in addition, the moral and political imponderables; and he did so with the confidence that comes from being at the centre of events and dominating them.

This difference was incidental to the main controversy between the adherents and the opponents of insurrection. Zinoviev and Kamenev held that Lenin and Trotsky were plunging the party and the revolution into a suicidal adventure. This was one of the greatest and most stirring arguments that had ever rent a party, an argument the basic pros and cons of which were to reappear, in different combinations, in innumerable future controversies; an argument about which, regardless of its immediate conclusion, history has perhaps not yet said its last word. After the event, it is easy and natural to say that the advocates of the insurrection were right, and its opponents wrong. In truth, each side presented its case in such a way that the rights were strangely blended with the wrongs and the realistic assessment of historical prospects was offset by momentous errors. Lenin and Trotsky assessed Russia's national situation and the balance of the forces inside the country with penetrating clear-sightedness. They detected the illusion in the appearance of strength with which the Kerensky régime was endowed by the mere fact of its existence; and they based their optimism about the outcome of the insurrection on an almost mathematically accurate survey of the forces arrayed against each other. Against this optimism, Zinoviev and Kamenev placed on record this warning: 'Before history, before the international proletariat, before the Russian revolution and Russian working class, we have no right to stake the whole future on the card of an armed uprising. . . . There are historical situations when an oppressed class must recognize that it is better to go forward to defeat than to give up without battle. Does the Russian working class find itself at present in such a situation? No, and a thousand times no!!!'[1]

Zinoviev and Kamenev saw nothing ahead but débâcle; and for the rest of their tragic lives they were to burn with shame whenever they were reminded of these words. But the advocates of the rising, in the first instance Lenin and Trotsky, based their arguments not merely and not even mainly on their view of the balance of strength inside Russia. Even more emphatically they pointed to the imminence of European revolution, to which the Russian insurrection would be the prelude, as Trotsky had maintained since 1905–6. In the motion which Lenin submitted to the Central Committee on 10 October, he put first among the motives for insurrection: 'the international position of the Russian revolution (the revolt in the German navy, which is an extreme manifestation of the growth throughout Europe of the world socialist revolution).'[2] He repeated this in almost every subsequent statement, public and private. 'The ripening and inevitability of world socialist revolution can be under no doubt.'[3] 'We stand on the threshold of world proletarian revolution.'[4] 'We shall be genuine traitors to the International', he wrote in a letter to party members, 'if, at such a moment, under such propitious conditions, we answer such a summons from the German revolutionaries [i.e. the revolt in the German navy]

[1] *Protokoly Tsen. Kom.*, pp. 102–8. The English version of this statement is in Lenin, *Collected Works*, vol. xxi, book 2, pp. 328–32.

[2] Lenin, *Sochinenya*, vol. xxvi, p. 162.

[3] Ibid., p. 21.   [4] Ibid., p. 55.

only by verbal resolutions.'[1] 'The international situation', he argued on another occasion, 'gives us a number of objective data showing that if we act now we shall have on our side the whole of proletarian Europe.'[2] This belief governed not only Trotsky's but also Lenin's entire view of the situation, and Lenin insisted that a Soviet government ought to be prepared to wage a revolutionary war to help the German proletariat in its rising.

Zinoviev and Kamenev, on the other hand, said: 'If we should come to the conclusion . . . that it is necessary to wage a revolutionary war, the masses of the soldiers will rush away from us.' This was a precise anticipation of the developments which led to the peace of Brest Litovsk. 'And here we come', they argued further, 'to the second assertion—that the majority of the international proletariat is, allegedly, already with us. Unfortunately, this is not so. The revolt in the German navy has immense symptomatic significance. . . . But it is a far cry from that to any sort of active support of the proletarian revolution in Russia, which is challenging the entire bourgeois world. It is extremely harmful to overestimate [our] forces.'

Thus those who were supreme realists when summing up the Russian situation became illusionists when they turned towards the broader international scene; and those who saw Russia only dimly through a mist of timid scepticism became then the realists. To be sure, the advocates of insurrection embodied the energy and the indomitable courage of the revolution, while their opponents voiced the revolution's faint doubt of itself. Yet it may be wondered whether Lenin and Trotsky would have acted as they did, or whether they would have acted with the same determination, if they had taken a soberer view of international revolution and foreseen that in the course of decades their example would not be imitated in any other country. A speculative question of this sort cannot be answered. The fact was that the whole dynamic of Russian history was impelling them, their party, and their country towards this revolution, and that they needed a world-embracing hope to accomplish the world-shaking deed. History produced the great illusion and planted and cultivated it in the brains of the most soberly realistic leaders when she needed the motive power of

[1] Ibid., pp. 154-5.   [2] Ibid., p. 164.

illusion to further her own work. In the same way she once inspired the leaders of the French Revolution with a belief in the imminence of a universal republic of the peoples.

.   .   .   .

While the controversy was unresolved in the Central Committee, the party was naturally incapable of initiative. Towards the end of September Kerensky opened the pre-Parliament, the new substitute for an elected assembly. The Bolsheviks had to decide whether they would participate. The question was related to that of the insurrection. Those who were opposed to the rising and those who hesitated were for participation: they wished the Bolshevik party to act as a regular opposition in the pre-Parliament, despite the fact that this body could not claim to be a national representation. The advocates of the insurrection held that the time for their party to act as an opposition had passed—otherwise they would not have contemplated the immediate overthrow of the existing government. They argued that as long as the Bolsheviks were a minority in the Soviets they could only urge the moderate majority to transfer all power to the Soviets; they themselves could not effect the transfer. But having become the majority, they had to effect it, if they were not to prove themselves mere phrasemongers. By their presence in the pre-Parliament they would merely give the latter the appearance of a real parliament and divert their own energy from direct action.

In this debate, Trotsky and Stalin—this was the first time they appeared together—spoke in unison for a boycott of the pre-parliament. Kamenev and Rykov pleaded for participation. The Bolshevik delegates, who had arrived from all over the country for the opening of the pre-Parliament, voted by a majority for participation. Lenin pressed for a revision of this attitude. In a letter to the Central Committee he wrote: 'Trotsky has spoken for the boycott—bravo, comrade Trotsky! The boycott has been defeated inside the group of the Bolshevik delegates. . . . We are still for the boycott.'[1] The incident showed that the party was mentally not yet in a condition to lead in an insurrection.

It was with evident relief that Lenin penned the words: 'Trotsky has spoken for the boycott—bravo, comrade Trotsky!'

[1] Lenin, *Sochinenya*, vol. xxvi, p. 37.

He viewed Trotsky's attitude in the matter of insurrection with uneasiness, and even suspicion. He wondered whether, by insisting that the rising should be linked with the Congress of the Soviets, Trotsky was not biding his time and delaying action until it would be too late. If this had been the case, then Trotsky would have been, from Lenin's viewpoint, an even more dangerous opponent than Kamenev and Zinoviev, whose attitude had at least the negative merit that it was unequivocal and that it flatly contradicted the whole trend of Bolshevik policy. Trotsky's attitude, on the contrary, seemed to follow from the party's policy and therefore carried more conviction with the Bolsheviks; the Central Committee was in fact inclined to adopt it. In his letters, Lenin therefore sometimes controverted Trotsky's view almost as strongly as Zinoviev's and Kamenev's, without, however, mentioning Trotsky by name. To wait for the rising until the Congress of the Soviets, he wrote, was just as treasonable as to wait for Kerensky to convoke the Constituent Assembly, as Zinoviev and Kamenev wanted to do.

Much later Trotsky excused Lenin's behaviour: 'If it were not', he wrote, 'for this Leninist anxiety, this pressure, this criticism, this tense and passionate revolutionary distrust, the party might not have straightened its front at the decisive moment, because the resistance at the top was very strong. . . .'[1] It may be added that it was natural that Lenin's 'tense and passionate revolutionary distrust' should include Trotsky himself, the lover of words and gestures, the 'empty bell' and 'Balalaykin' of the past, the former Menshevik helpmeet, who had only just become a Bolshevik and was now by the fortuitous circumstance of Lenin's absence placed at the head of the party. True enough, he had behaved with impressive dignity and courage in the July days. But Lenin had never doubted Trotsky's dignity and personal courage, not even in the days of their most bitter quarrelling. Martov, too, had bravely defended Lenin in July. Yet it was one thing to defend a comrade, even an opponent, baited by counter-revolutionaries, but quite another to lead in a revolution. Would Trotsky be equal to that? Would he know when to pass from tirades to deeds? Up to the moment of the rising, and even during it, doubt was gnawing at Lenin's mind.

[1] See *Uroki Oktyabrya* in *Sochinenya*, vol. iii, book 2, pp. xlviii–xlix.

In the meantime Trotsky was working on the preliminaries to the insurrection. He was doing this with so much psychological subtlety and tactical acumen that although he made his moves in broad daylight, neither friend nor foe could be sure what he was aiming at. He did not try to impose from outside a scheme of insurrection upon the course of events. He developed the insurrection out of the situations as they arose. He was therefore able to justify each step he took by some urgent and in a sense real need of the moment, which ostensibly had nothing to do with insurrection. Everything he did had an aspect of innocence; and although his moves were connected with one another in a single design, their connexion, too, was perfectly camouflaged. Not a single one of the trained political and military observers who watched the scene for the government, the General Staff, the allied embassies and military missions, saw through the camouflage. And even Lenin was in part misled by it.

By the beginning of October the crisis had reached a new height. Economic chaos was mounting. The provisioning of the cities broke down. Over wide stretches of the country peasants were seizing the gentry's estates and burning the mansions. The army suffered fresh defeats. The German navy was active in the Gulf of Finland. For a moment Petrograd itself seemed exposed to German attack. Government departments and military and business circles mooted the evacuation of the capital and the transfer of the government to Moscow. A reversal of attitudes took place, for which parallels can be found in the annals of war and revolution. Some of those who longed for a counter-revolution but were themselves too weak to bring it about, came to contemplate with pleasure, despite their habitual profession of patriotism, the prospect that an invading enemy might do the job for them. Rodzianko, the ex-President of the Duma, was imprudent enough to state publicly that he would rejoice if the German army re-established law and order in Petrograd. Dismay spread in the working class and in the 'defeatist' Soviet. On 6 October, in the presence of delegates from all regiments stationed in the capital, Trotsky addressed the soldiers' section of the Soviet and presented the following resolution: 'If the Provisional Government is incapable of defending Petrograd, then it ought either to conclude peace or to make room for another government. The transfer of the government to Moscow would be a desertion from a responsible battle position.'[1] The resolution was carried without a single dissentient vote. The garrison gave notice of its interest in organizing the defence of the city, if need be without and even against the government.

On the next day Trotsky sounded the alarm from the platform of the pre-Parliament: 'The idea of surrendering the revolutionary capital to German troops', he said, 'was a natural link in a general policy designed to promote . . . counter-revolutionary conspiracy.'[2] A flood of abuse broke loose against the speaker, but this was the last time he addressed the pre-Parliament—on Lenin's insistent promptings, the party had, after all, decided to boycott the assembly. Overcoming the tumult, Trotsky announced the Bolshevik exodus: 'With this government of treason to the people and with this Council of counter-revolutionary connivance we have nothing in common. . . . In withdrawing from the Council, we summon the workers, soldiers, and peasants of all Russia to be on their guard and to be courageous. Petrograd is in danger! The revolution is in danger! The people is in danger!' From now on almost every day the insurgents took a long stride towards their goal.

Both sides, Kerensky and his General Staff on the one hand, Trotsky and the Soviet on the other, were engaged in a series of manœuvres designed to set the stage for civil war; but both pretended to act in the broader interest of national defence. Kerensky was preparing a redistribution of troops, ostensibly designed to strengthen the front. In the process the most revolutionary regiments were to be sent out of Petrograd, as a prelude to a showdown with the Soviet. Trotsky had to frustrate Kerensky's plan and to prevent the departure of the pro-Bolshevik regiments. He did so on the ground that the depletion of the garrison would expose the capital to German invasion, which was not untrue. The government had in the meantime denied that it proposed to evacuate Petrograd. But mistrust of its intentions had been aroused; and when it became known that Kerensky was bent on reshuffling the troops the suspicion was confirmed and strengthened. On 9 October the Soviet was in a state of extraordinary agitation. Trotsky urged its plenary session

[1] Trotsky, *Sochinenya*, vol. iii, book 1, p. 321.   [2] Ibid., pp. 321–3.

and its sections to intervene in the matter of the redistribution of troops. Since the Soviet had already assumed responsibility for the defence of Petrograd, it could not look on idly at the dismantling of the garrison. Trotsky did not yet explicitly propose that the Soviet should veto Kerensky's plan—the first step he proposed was that the Soviet should find out what was the significance of the plan and that it should 'keep a check' on the condition of the garrison. Implicitly, however, he had already posed the question who was to be the master of the garrison.[1]

On the same day, the Military Revolutionary Committee was formed at a session of the Executive of the Soviet. This committee, eventually the supreme organ of insurrection, appeared at the time only to assume on behalf of the Soviet the responsibility for the city's defence. The proposal for setting it up was made by one Lazimir, a boy of eighteen, a Left Social Revolutionary, who had no premonition of the consequences. The Menshevik members of the Executive were opposed to the idea, but, when it was pointed out to them that this Committee would be a replica and a continuation of a body they themselves had formed at the time of Kornilov's coup, they had no effective answer. In its Menshevik period, the Soviet had, indeed, repeatedly vetoed moves contemplated by the government— the practice was inherent in the 'dual power' of the February régime—and these precedents, when they were now cited, disarmed the opposition. Trotsky *ex officio* headed the Military Revolutionary Committee. The task of the Committee was to establish the size of the garrison needed for the defence of the capital; to keep in touch with the commands of the northern front, the Baltic fleet, the Finnish garrison, &c.; to assess the man-power and the stocks of munitions available; to work out a plan of defence; and to maintain discipline in the civilian population. Among the members of the Committee there were, apart from its youthful and uncomprehending initiator, Podvoisky, Antonov-Ovseenko, and Lashevich, the future operational commanders of the insurrection. The Committee split into seven sections, which were to be in charge of defence, supplies, liaison, information, workers' militias, and so on. Again in conformity with precedents, the Committee appointed

[1] Trotsky, *Sochinenya*, vol. iii, book 1, pp. 324 ff.

commissars who were to represent it with all detachments of the garrison.[1]

While, partly by design and partly by the spur of great events and trivial accidents, Trotsky was forging the machinery of insurrection, the Central Committee of the party had not yet taken any final decision. On 3 October it listened to the report of an envoy from Moscow, Lomov-Oppokov, who spoke for insurrection and demanded an end to irresolution. 'It was decided', says the record of the Central Committee, 'not to discuss this report' but to ask Lenin to come to Petrograd and to put his arguments before the Central Committee.[2] On 7 October a Bureau was appointed to 'collect information on the struggle against counter-revolution'. Its members were Trotsky, Sverdlov, and Bubnov.[3] Only on 10 October, the day after the formation of the Military Revolutionary Committee, did that historic session take place at which Lenin was present and at which, after grave debate, the leaders of the party took by ten votes to two the decision in favour of the rising. At this session, also, the first Political Bureau was elected —Lenin, Zinoviev, Kamenev, Trotsky, Stalin, Sokolnikov, and Bubnov—to offer the party day-to-day guidance on the insurrection.[4] But the next day Zinoviev and Kamenev appealed to the lower grades of the organization against the decision of the Central Committee, and the party's attitude was again in flux. In any case, the newly-elected Politbureau was incapable of offering guidance. Lenin returned to his refuge in Finland. Zinoviev and Kamenev were opposed to the rising. Stalin was almost completely absorbed by editorial work. Sokolnikov's views were a shade more cautious than Trotsky's. Lenin, however, still distrustful of Trotsky's plan, urged the party to take on itself alone the initiative of armed action. All members of the Politbureau who were not in principle opposed to such action preferred the rising to be conducted through the Soviet.

During the following week, Trotsky, assisted by the most effective agitators, Lunacharsky, Kollontai, and Volodarsky, was mustering the forces of the revolution. On 10 October he addressed a city conference of factory committees. On 11 and

---

[1] See the memoirs of the participants given on the third anniversary of the insurrection in *Proletarskaya Revolutsia*, no. 10, 1922.

[2] *Protokoly Tsen. Kom.*, p. 87.   [3] Ibid., p. 94.   [4] Ibid., pp. 98–101.

12 October he called upon a conference of northern Russian Soviets to be ready for great events. 'Our government', he stated, 'may flee from Petrograd. But the revolutionary people will not leave the city—it will defend it to the end.'[1] At the same time he did his utmost to force the hands of the Menshevik Central Executive and to compel it to convene the second Congress of the Soviets. On 13 October, over the heads of that Executive and on behalf of the Soviets of northern Russia, he sent out a radio message 'To All, To All, To All', calling all Soviets and the army to send delegates to the Congress. 'At the famous Cirque Moderne', writes Sukhanov, 'where Trotsky, Lunacharsky, and Volodarsky took the platform, there were endless queues and crowds, whom the enormous amphitheatre could not contain. . . . Trotsky, breaking away from his work at the revolutionary headquarters, ran from the Obukhovsky to the Trubochnyi, from the Putilovsky to the Baltiisky [the largest industrial plants], from the Manege to the barracks; and it seemed that he spoke everywhere simultaneously. Every worker and soldier of Petrograd knew him and listened to him. His influence on the masses and the leaders alike was overwhelming. He was the central figure of those days, and the chief hero of this remarkable chapter of history.'[2]

On 16 October the regiments of the garrison declared that they would disobey Kerensky's marching orders and remain in Petrograd. This was, as Trotsky later put it, the silent rising which in advance decided the outcome of the contest.[3] Until now Trotsky himself had been somewhat uneasy about the risk he had taken by linking the insurrection with the Congress of the Soviets. Now he was reassured: in the short run, Kerensky would not be able to alter the balance of strength in his favour. On the same day, Trotsky signed an order to the arsenals that 5,000 rifles be issued to the civilian Red Guards. This was a way of checking whether the writ of the Military Revolutionary Committee ran in the garrison. It did.

During this 'silent rising', the Central Committee met once again in the presence of important local Bolshevik leaders.[4]

---

[1] Trotsky, *Sochinenya*, vol. iii, book 2, p. 5.
[2] Sukhanov, op. cit., vol. vii, pp. 44, 76.
[3] Trotsky, *Sochinenya*, vol. iii, book 2, p. 1.
[4] *Protokoly Tsen. Kom.*, pp. 110–25.

Lenin who had arrived, heavily disguised, moved that the conference should confirm the decision on insurrection, and that the Central Committee should at once issue a call to action. The representative of the Petrograd Committee spoke about apathy in the masses, but declared that the call for insurrection, if it came from the Soviet, not from the party, would stir up the masses and meet with response. Krylenko, leader of the party's military branch, on which the execution of Lenin's plan entirely depended, declared that only a minority of the branch was for insurrection, but even this minority favoured initiative by the Soviet, not by the party. Volodarsky spoke in the same vein. Zinoviev and Kamenev emphatically restated their objections to armed action in any form. Stalin reproached them with lack of faith in European revolution, and remarked that while the party leaders were engaged in confused argument, the Soviet was already 'on the road to insurrection'. Miliutin, for Moscow, spoke ambiguously. Sokolnikov held that the rising ought to be started only after the opening of the Congress of the Soviets. From all sides there came anxious voices about the apathy and the weariness of the masses. Lenin recapitulated his arguments, but he made a concession to the adherents of Trotsky's plan and submitted that 'the Central Committee *and* the Soviet should in due time indicate the right moment and the practical methods of attack'.[1] Tentatively 20 October was fixed as the day of action.

The Central Committee had fixed this date because it was the eve of the expected opening of the Congress. Only three or four days were left for preparations. Yet no sooner had the Central Committee confirmed its decision on insurrection than Zinoviev and Kamenev made a vigorous attempt to frustrate it. They denounced the plan, this time not within the Bolshevik caucus but in the pages of Gorky's newspaper. Thus, from the men supposed to act as members of the General Staff of the insurrection, the outside world received a warning about what was pending. Lenin, beside himself with indignation, demanded

[1] Loc. cit., and Lenin, *Sochinenya*, vol. xxvi, p. 165. At this session a 'Military Centre' was appointed, consisting of Sverdlov, Stalin, Bubnov, Uritsky, and Dzerzhinsky. It was to 'become part of the Military Revolutionary Committee of the Soviet', i.e. to serve under Trotsky. On his membership of this 'Centre', which throughout the rising never acted as a separate body, Stalin and the Stalinist historians later based the claim that Stalin had been the actual leader of the rising.

the immediate expulsion from the party of the two 'strike-breakers of the revolution'. His demand fell on deaf ears. In the Bolshevik newspaper Stalin tried to reconcile the adversaries, although this was a matter in which reconciliation was impossible: an insurrection either is or is not made.[1]

Trotsky utilized even the confusion among the Bolshevik leaders to further his plan. On 17 October he received with well concealed relief the news that the Menshevik Central Executive had again postponed the Congress of the Soviets for a few days. This gave him a little more time for the last preparations. But the other camp might also have benefited from the delay; and Zinoviev's and Kamenev's disclosures threatened to arouse its vigilance. On 18 October two embarrassing questions were put to Trotsky in the Soviet, one about the widespread rumours on insurrection, and the other about his order to the arsenals for the issue of rifles to Red Guards. His answer was a masterpiece of diplomatic camouflage: 'The decisions of the Petrograd Soviet are published', he said. 'The Soviet is an elected institution, every deputy is responsible to the workers and soldiers who have elected him. This revolutionary parliament . . . can have no decisions which are unknown to the workers. We conceal nothing. I declare on behalf of the Soviet: we have not decided on any armed action.' This was literally true: the *Soviet* had decided nothing of the sort. As its President he was expected to give an account only of the Soviet's work. He was under no obligation to make a public confession of a confidential decision taken by a private body such as the Central Committee of the party.

But he did not stop at this denial, which might have confounded friends as well as foes. Nor did he tie his hands. 'If the course of events', he added, 'compels the Soviet to decide on armed action, then the workers and the soldiers will come out in response to its appeal like one man.' He admitted that he had ordered rifles for the Red Guards, but he covered himself by the familiar precedent: the Menshevik Soviet had done the same. 'The Petrograd Soviet', he added defiantly, 'will go on organizing and arming workers' guards. . . . We must be ready. We have entered a period of more acute struggle. We must be constantly prepared for attack by the counter-revolution.

[1] *Protokoly Tsen. Kom.*, pp. 127–9.

But to the first counter-revolutionary attempt to break up the Congress of the Soviets, to the first attempt of an attack on us, we shall retort with a counter-attack which will be merciless and which we shall press to the very end.'[1] Thus he stirred the militancy of the insurgents and of their friends while he was obfuscating their enemies. With meticulous care he brought to the fore the defensive aspect of the insurgents' activity, and kept the offensive aspect in the background. On the spot Kamenev rose to declare his complete solidarity with Trotsky, and Zinoviev did the same in a letter to the editor of *Rabochyi Put*. The two opponents of the rising hoped thereby to tie down their party to a strictly defensive attitude, and so to make it renounce insurrection in a roundabout way. But their demonstrative expression of solidarity with Trotsky had a quite different effect. The anti-Bolshevik parties, seeing that the known opponents of the coup declared their agreement with Trotsky, assumed that he was also in agreement with them. 'There will be no insurrection, then', the Mensheviks and Social Revolutionaries consoled themselves.

Immediately after this incident, Trotsky had a secret meeting with Lenin, the only one, it seems, that they had in these weeks. He wondered whether Lenin had not misunderstood his statement and the appearance of agreement between himself and Zinoviev and Kamenev; and he was anxious to dispel Lenin's misapprehension.[2] But on this point his fears were groundless. Lenin had just written to the Central Committee: 'Kamenev's trick at the session of the Petrograd Soviet is something simply mean. He, you see, is in full agreement with Trotsky. But is it difficult to understand that Trotsky could not and should not have said more than he did in the face of enemies.'[3] At this meeting, Trotsky wrote later, Lenin was 'more calm and confident, I would say, less suspicious. . . . All the same, now and again he shook his head and asked: "And will they not forestall us? Will they not catch us napping?" I argued that from now on everything would develop almost automatically.'[4]

Lenin was not quite reassured. That his reiterated demand for the immediate expulsion of Zinoviev and Kamenev met with

[1] Trotsky, *Sochinenya*, vol. iii, book 2, pp. 31–32.
[2] Trotsky, *Lénine*, p. 86.
[3] Lenin, *Sochinenya*, vol. xxvi, p. 192.   [4] Trotsky, *Lénine*, loc. cit.

no response from Trotsky and the Central Committee as a whole made him bristle with suspicion again. Zinoviev's and Kamenev's indiscretion would be regarded as treacherous by any party in similar circumstances. And so Lenin saw in the consideration shown to them by the Central Committee a sign of the latter's irresolute attitude in the matter of insurrection.[1]

The preliminaries to the rising came to a close when the Soviet instructed the garrison to carry out only such official orders as were endorsed by the Military Revolutionary Committee or its commissars. On 21 October Trotsky conveyed this instruction to a general meeting of regimental committees; and he appealed to the Cossacks, the former praetorian guards of the Tsars, to stand by the revolution. The regimental committees adopted Trotsky's resolution, which stated *inter alia*:

Endorsing all political decisions of the Petrograd Soviet, the garrison declares: the time for words has passed. The country is on the brink of doom. The army demands peace, the peasants demand land, the workers demand employment and bread. The coalition government is against the people, an instrument in the hands of the people's enemies. The time for words has passed. The All-Russian Congress of Soviets ought to take power in its hands and secure peace, land, and bread to the people. . . . The Petrograd garrison solemnly

[1] Characteristic of the relations inside the Bolshevik party at the time is the fact that not a single voice in the Central Committee supported Lenin's demand. Kamenev had of his own accord announced his resignation from the Committee. Lenin, nevertheless demanded his and Zinoviev's expulsion as an exemplary punishment not for their dissent but for the unheard-of breach of discipline they had committed. The record of the sitting of the Central Committee of 20 October makes instructive reading. Dzerzhinsky expressed the opinion that Kamenev should be advised to withdraw from political activity; but he did not advocate expulsion. It was not worth while bothering, he added, about Zinoviev, who was in hiding anyhow. Stalin and Miliutin advised shelving the question until a plenary session of the Central Committee. Stalin had in the party's paper defended the motives of Zinoviev and Kamenev, and he himself now came under fire. Uritsky was for postponing the matter. Sverdlov spoke strongly against Kamenev, but held that the Central Committee had no right to expel anybody. Trotsky was for accepting Kamenev's resignation, but not for expulsion. He attacked Stalin's editorial conduct, saying that the ambiguous attitude of the party's paper created 'an intolerable situation'. Yoffe spoke in the same vein. Stalin once again defended Zinoviev and Kamenev, saying that they should remain on the Central Committee: 'Expulsion from the party is no remedy—unity must be preserved.' Kamenev's resignation was accepted by five votes to three. Then Stalin announced that he was resigning as editor of the party's paper. But this was not accepted. It is quite impossible to square this and many similar episodes with the view that monolithic or totalitarian uniformity had reigned in the Bolshevik party ever since its inception. *Protokoly Tsen. Kom.*, pp. 127–9.

pledges itself to put at the disposal of the All-Russian Congress all its
forces, to the last man, to fight for these demands. Rely on us. . . .
We are at our posts, ready to conquer or die.[1]

Events showed that this last assurance was more solemn than
true. The civilian workers were in fact 'ready to conquer or
die'; but the garrison supported the Soviet because it was
confident in an easy victory over Kerensky, a victory which was
expected to end the war. Whatever its motives, the fact was that
the garrison placed itself under the orders of the Soviet.

Inevitably this gave rise to a conflict between the regular
military command and the Military Revolutionary Committee.
Even now, Trotsky did not claim on behalf of that Committee
that it was superseding the military command. Commissars of
the Committee were attached to the General Staff, ostensibly
in order to co-ordinate activities and eliminate friction; and
on the very day of the rising Trotsky inspired reports that the
negotiations were proceeding satisfactorily.[2] At the same time
as he made these military preparations, Trotsky put the Red
Guards and the civilian organizations on the alert. On 22
October he addressed a monster meeting at the *Narodnyi Dom*
(People's House). 'Around me', the eyewitness whom we have
often quoted describes the scene, 'the crowds were in an almost
ecstatic mood.' Trotsky asked them to repeat after him the
words of an oath. 'A numberless multitude lifted up their hands.
Trotsky hammered out the words: "Let this your vote be your
oath with all your might and power of sacrifice to support the
Soviet, which has taken on itself the great burden of bringing
the victory of the revolution to completion and of giving the
people land, bread, and peace." The numberless multitude
keep their hands up. They agree. They take the oath. . . .
Trotsky has finished. Somebody else is taking the platform. But
it is not worth while to wait and look any more.'[3]

The theatrical quality of Trotsky's appearances and the
almost poetic loftiness of his speech did no less than his *ruses de
guerre* to mislead the anti-Bolshevik leaders. The latter were too
well accustomed to the bright fireworks of his oratory to suspect
that this time it was real fire. Trotsky seemed to them, and not
only to them, too voluble for a commander of a successful

[1] Trotsky, *Sochinenya*, vol. iii, book 2, p. 37.
[2] Trotsky, *Lénine*, p. 87.   [3] Sukhanov, op. cit., vol. vii, p. 91.

insurrection. Yet in this revolution words, great idealistic words, were in fact more effective than regiments and divisions, and inspired tirades did the work of pitched battles. Up to a certain moment they relieved the revolution of the need to fight battles at all. The revolution worked mainly through its titanic power of persuasion, and it seemed to have vested the greater part of that power in a single person.

By 23 October the Military Revolutionary Committee had a detailed plan of operations in hand. It was as simple as it was carefully laid. It provided for a rapid occupation by picked detachments of all strategic positions in the capital. Liaison between insurgent headquarters and the garrison functioned infallibly. The picked units were ready for the signal. As the members of the Military Revolutionary Committee surveyed for the last time the disposition of forces, they were confident that they could knock the government over by a slight push— so overwhelming was the superiority of the forces arrayed behind the Soviet. Only one important position was uncertain: the Peter-Paul fortress on the Neva, the garrison of which was reported to stand for Kerensky or at least to waver. Antonov-Ovseenko prepared a plan to assault the fortress, the only important engagement which was expected. Trotsky, however, decided to try to storm it with words. In the afternoon of the 23rd, accompanied by a non-Bolshevik commander of the Soviet guard, he went on a lorry into what was supposed to be the enemy's camp. He addressed the garrison of the fortress and induced it to repeat after him the oath of allegiance to the Soviet.[1]

All that Trotsky was now waiting for was provocation from Kerensky, which would allow him to launch the insurrection as a defensive operation. He had no doubt that Kerensky was bound to give the provocation—he himself had provoked him sufficiently into giving it.[2] And indeed, on the 23rd, Kerensky

[1] *Proletarskaya Revolutsia*, no. 10, 1922; Sukhanov, op. cit., vol. vii, p. 113.

[2] There can be no doubt, however, that Kerensky had always regarded the Soviets as an embarrassment to be got rid of. He did so even when Bolshevik influence in the Soviets was slight and when he himself owed his position entirely to the Soviets. As early as 27 March (9 April in the new calendar) Sir George Buchanan noted in his diary: 'Kerensky, with whom I had a long conversation yesterday, does not favour the idea of taking strong measures at present either against the Soviet or the Socialist propaganda in the army. On my telling him that the government would never be masters of the situation as long as they allowed

attempted to strike a blow from the vacuum in which he and his government were suspended. He banned *Rabochyi Put* (*Workers' Road*), under which title *Pravda* had appeared since the July days, and he ordered the closing of its editorial offices and printing-press. A working girl and a man from the press rushed to the Military Revolutionary Committee, saying that they were prepared to break the seals on the premises of *Rabochyi Put* and to go on producing the paper if the Committee gave them an effective military escort. This suggestion, breathlessly made by an unknown working girl, came to Trotsky like a flash. 'A piece of official sealing wax', he wrote later, 'on the door of the Bolshevik editorial room as a military measure—that was not much. But what a superb signal for battle!'[1] On the spot he signed an order sending a company of riflemen and a few platoons of sappers to guard the Bolshevik offices and printing-press. The order was carried out instantaneously.

This was a tentative gambit. It was made on the dawn of 24 October. Next morning the papers were full of reports about Kerensky's plan to suppress the Soviet and the Bolshevik party. The Military Revolutionary Committee was working out the last details of the rising, which, as was now clear, could not be delayed a single day. The Smolny Institute, hitherto guarded with insouciant slackness, was rapidly transformed into a fortress, bristling with cannon and machine-guns. In the early morning, the Central Committee of the party met for the last time before the decisive event. All members present in Petrograd had arrived, with the exception of Lenin and Zinoviev, who had not yet come into the open, and Stalin who was unaccountably absent.[2] Kamenev, who had resigned from the Committee to oppose the insurrection, placed himself at the service of the insurgents once the action had started; and he displayed surprising initiative. It was he who proposed, *inter alia*, that no member of the Committee should leave Smolny during the day. On Trotsky's initiative, each was given a specific assignment in liaison and organization. Dzerzhinsky kept in touch with the posts and telegraphs; Bubnov with the railwaymen; Nogin and Lomov with Moscow. Sverdlov was to watch the movements

themselves to be dictated to by a rival organization, he said that the Soviet would die a natural death. . . .' Sir George Buchanan, *My Mission to Russia*, vol. ii, p. 11.
    [1] Trotsky, *History*, vol. iii, p. 205.   [2] *Protokoly Tsen. Kom.*, pp. 141–3.

of the Provisional Government, while Miliutin was to take charge of the city's food supplies. Kamenev and Berzin were to win over the Left Social Revolutionaries, who were breaking away from their mother party. Finally, Trotsky proposed that, in case the Bolsheviks were routed at the Smolny, the headquarters of the insurrection should move to the Peter-Paul fortress, the garrison of which he had just won over for the cause.[1]

While this was taking place, Kerensky addressed the pre-Parliament and indulged in belated threats. He announced that he had ordered the prosecution of the entire Military Revolutionary Committee, a new search for Lenin, the arrest of Trotsky and other Bolshevik leaders released on bail, and that he was taking action against the sailors of Kronstadt.[2] Trotsky convened an extraordinary session of the Petrograd Soviet and reported on the steps just taken by the Military Revolutionary Committee. Even now he did not proclaim the rising:

> We are not afraid to shoulder responsibility for maintaining revolutionary order in the city. . . . Our principle is—all power to the Soviets. . . . At the forthcoming sessions of the All-Russian Congress of the Soviets, this principle ought to be put into effect. Whether this will lead to an insurrection or to any other form of action depends not only and not so much on the Soviets as on those who, in defiance of the people's unanimous will, still hold governmental power. [He reported the incident with *Rabochyi Put* and asked:] Is this an insurrection? We have a semi-government in which the people has no confidence and which has no confidence in itself, because it is dead within. This semi-government only awaits the sweep of history's broom. . . .

He announced that he had countermanded Kerensky's action against the Kronstadt sailors and ordered the cruiser *Aurora* to lie in readiness on the Neva:

> To-morrow the Congress of the Soviets opens. It is the task of the

[1] Loc. cit., Kamenev proposed that reserve headquarters be established on board the cruiser *Aurora*, with the crew and the radio station of which he kept liaison.

[2] The day before, Major General Sir Alfred Knox, the British Military Attaché, knew about the plan. 'To-day Bagratuni told me', runs an entry in his note-book, 'that Kerensky had decided to arrest Trotsky and the members of the Military Revolutionary Committee. . . . I asked if we were strong enough to carry out this programme, and Bagratuni said we were. Podryelov said: "We can take the risk." ' *With the Russian Army*, vol. ii, p. 705.

garrison and of the proletariat to put at its disposal the power they have gathered, a power on which any governmental provocation will founder. It is our task to carry this power, undiminished and unimpaired, to the Congress. If the illusory government makes a hazardous attempt to revive its own corpse, the popular masses will strike a decisive counter-blow. And the blow will be the more powerful the stronger the attack. If the government tries to use the twenty-four or forty-eight hours still left to it in order to stab the revolution, then we declare that the vanguard of the revolution will meet attack with attack and iron with steel.[1]

When a delegation from the city council approached him to inquire about the Soviet's intentions, he answered cryptically that the Soviet was prepared to co-ordinate the defence of the revolutionary order with the city council; and, tongue in cheek, he invited the council to participate in the Military Revolutionary Committee.

Late in the evening the Menshevik Central Executive called a meeting of the delegates who had assembled for the Congress. For the last time Dan spoke on behalf of the old leadership of the Soviets. He warned the delegates against bloodshed. 'The counter-revolution is only waiting for the Bolsheviks to begin riots and massacres—this will be the end of the revolution. . . . The masses are sick and exhausted. They have no interest in the revolution. . . . It is inadmissible . . . that the Petrograd garrison should not submit to the orders of the Staff. . . . All power to the Soviets means death. . . . We are not afraid of bayonets. . . . The old Executive will defend the revolution with its body. . . .'[2] Amid uproar and cries of derision, Dan promised immediate peace negotiations and land reform, thereby unwittingly admitting that the Bolsheviks had all along been right in their demands. ('Russia' he declared, 'could no longer afford to wage the war.') From the floor came cries: 'Too late!'

Then Trotsky mounted the tribune, borne on a wave of roaring applause . . . a rising house, thunderous. His thin, pointed face was positively Mephistophelian in its expression of malicious irony.

'Dan's tactics proved that the masses—the great, dull, indifferent masses—are absolutely with him!' (Titanic mirth.) He turned towards the Chairman, dramatically. 'When we spoke of giving the land to the peasants you were against it. We told the peasants, "If they don't

[1] Trotsky, *Sochinenya*, vol. iii, book 2, pp. 51–53.
[2] John Reed, *Ten Days that Shook the World*, pp. 58–60.

give it to you, take it yourselves!" and the peasants followed our advice. And now you advocate what we did six months ago. . . . The time may come when Dan will say that the flower of the revolution participated in the rising of the July days. . . . No. The history of the last seven months shows that the masses have left the Mensheviks. . . . Dan tells you that you have no right to make an insurrection. Insurrection is the right of all revolutionaries! When the downtrodden masses revolt it is their right. . . . If you maintain complete confidence, there will be no civil war. Our enemies will surrender at once and you will take the place which is legitimately yours, that of the masters of the Russian land.'[1]

Dan, deceived by the vague manner in which Trotsky still spoke about the rising, and perhaps also hoping that the Bolsheviks might not obtain a majority at the Congress, rushed off to Kerensky to assure him that there would be no Bolshevik coup and to implore him to refrain from repressive action.[2]

The rising was already in progress. Trotsky issued his famous Order No. 1: 'The Petrograd Soviet is in imminent danger. Last night the counter-revolutionary conspirators tried to call the Junkers and the shock battalions into Petrograd. You are hereby ordered to prepare your regiment for action. Await further orders. All procrastination and hesitation will be regarded as treason to the revolution.' The firmness of his tone inspired the insurgents with confidence. During the night of 24–25 October Red Guards and regular regiments occupied with lightning speed, almost noiselessly, the Tauride Palace, the post-offices and the railway stations, the national bank, the telephone exchanges, the power-stations, and other strategic points. While the movement which overthrew Tsardom in February lasted nearly a week, the overthrow of Kerensky's government took a few hours only. In the morning of 25 October Kerensky had already escaped from the capital in the car of a foreign embassy. His Ministers were vainly waiting for him in the Winter Palace, when at noon they were already besieged there, just as the Tsarist government had been in the final phase of the February Revolution. Without bloodshed, the Bolsheviks had become the masters of the capital.[3] By mid-day

---

[1] Loc. cit.   [2] Kerensky, *Iz Daleka*, pp. 197–8; *Crucifixion of Liberty*, p. 346.
[3] Major-General Sir Alfred Knox, a most hostile observer of the Bolshevik success, gives the total number of the casualties as 'about ten'. *With the Russian Army*, vol. ii, p. 711.

Trotsky reported to the Petrograd Soviet, almost stunned with incredulity, on further developments: some Ministers had been placed under arrest; the pre-Parliament had been disbanded; the whole city was under control. The enemy now held only the Winter Palace, which Antonov-Ovseenko was preparing to storm.

On the evening of the 24th Lenin, still heavily disguised, arrived in the Smolny. Reports in the newspapers about friendly negotiations between the General Staff and the Military Revolutionary Committee had stirred his mistrust afresh. He still suspected that the rising was being bungled. As he made his way stealthily from the Vyborg suburb, where he had been hiding for the last few days, to the Smolny, he did not realize that the city he walked through was virtually in his party's hands. He bombarded Trotsky and the other leaders with questions: Were they really on the point of coming to terms with the General Staff? And why was the city so calm?[1] But as he listened to the answers, as he watched the tense staff work in the room of the Military Revolutionary Committee, the reports coming in ceaselessly and the instructions going out, as he eyed the leaders of the rising themselves, almost exhausted, unshaven, dirty, with eyes inflamed from sleeplessness, yet confident and composed, he realized that they had crossed the Rubicon without him, and his suspicion melted away. Somewhat shyly and apologetically, he remarked that the rising could, of course, be conducted in their manner as well—the main thing was that it should succeed.

He behaved like a commander-in-chief who, watching the decisive battle from afar and knowing that the operational commander has ideas at variance with his, is inclined to exaggerate the importance of the difference and fears that without his intervention things might go wrong; who then rushes to the battlefield while the battle is in progress and then, without a trace of offended vanity, reconciles himself to the course of action taken and acknowledges his junior's achievement. Although Trotsky had been in charge of the operation and had conducted it entirely according to his own lights, Lenin's influence was a decisive factor in the success. Trotsky had more than any single man moulded the mind of the broad

[1] *Proletarskaya Revolutsia*, no. 10, 1922.

mass of workers and soldiers, on whose attitude the issue depended. But the active insurgents had come from the cadres and the ranks of the Bolshevik party; and on their minds, Lenin, the founder and unrivalled leader of the party, had even from his hiding-place exercised by far the greater influence. Without his sustained and stubborn promptings, without his alarming warnings, they might not have followed Trotsky's orders and instructions as they did. He had inspired them with the idea of the rising before they carried out Trotsky's scheme of the rising. But it was only when he actually saw the insurrection in progress that Lenin finally and unreservedly acknowledged in Trotsky his monumental partner in the monumental game.

On the evening of 25 October, the two men were resting on the floor of a dark and empty room adjoining the great hall of Smolny, where the Congress of the Soviets was about to open. The night before, Trotsky had fainted from fatigue, and now he tried to get a little sleep. But sleep would not come. Ceaseless telephone calls in the next room roused him. Assistants and messengers knocked at the doors. One message reported a hitch in the attack on the Winter Palace; and Trotsky ordered the cruiser *Aurora* into action: Let them bombard the Winter Palace with blanks—this should be enough to bring about the government's surrender. He went back to lie on the floor by Lenin's side. There were fleeting moments of somnolence, new messages, rapid whispers along the floor. Soon they would have to go to the large and brightly lit hall and face the Congress. They would, of course, declare that the Congress was the only source of power, that the land belonged to the peasants, and they would offer immediate peace to Russia and the world; and tomorrow they would present the new government to the world. The thought that he or any of his comrades, the professional revolutionaries, should assume titles of ministers seemed incongruous to Lenin. Shreds of historical reminiscences—as always, reminiscences from the great French Revolution— floated through Trotsky's somnolent mind: perhaps they would call themselves *Commissaires*, People's Commissars—a Council of People's Commissars?[1]

The Congress opened to the accompaniment of the *Aurora's*

---

[1] Trotsky proposed these titles at a session of the Central Committee next day. *Moya Zhizn*, vol. ii, pp. 48–49, 59–60.

bombardment of the Winter Palace—with blanks. The Bolsheviks alone commanded a majority of nearly two-thirds; with the Left Social Revolutionaries they had about three-quarters of the votes. Fourteen Bolsheviks, seven Social Revolutionaries, Right and Left, three Mensheviks, and one representative of Gorky's group, took their seats at the table of the new 'Presidium'. The defeated parties at once raised an outcry against the rising and the storming of the Winter Palace. In the name of the most irreconcilable group of Mensheviks, Khinchuk, Stalin's future Ambassador in Berlin, declared that they were leaving the Congress. Amid cries: 'Deserters! Go to Kornilov!' the group left the hall. The Mensheviks of the Centre and of the Left stayed behind and demanded the formation of a coalition government of Bolsheviks, Mensheviks, and Social Revolutionaries. When the Bolsheviks rejected this demand, these groups, too, declared a boycott of the Congress and of its decisions. As Trotsky watched their exodus, led by Martov and Abramovich, his mind may have flashed back to the scene at the second congress of the party, in 1903, when Martov declared a boycott of the Bolshevik Central Committee. He himself was then among the boycotters. How similar in a way these two scenes appeared: the leading men were the same, the 'soft' and the 'hard' ones; most of the recriminations of 1903 echoed in the declaration Martov had just made: even the words 'conspiracy', 'usurpation', and 'state of siege' came back. But how different was the scale of the spectacle and the intensity of the struggle. And how different was his own place in it, after all the years of side-slipping and straying, from which he had returned to Lenin.

As Trotsky rose to answer Martov, while the latter was still standing opposite him on the platform, he could find in himself no softness, no lenity, not even charity for the vanquished— only gravity, exasperation, and angry contempt. 'The rising of popular masses', he began, 'needs no justification. What has taken place is an insurrection not a conspiracy. We have hardened the revolutionary energy of the workers and soldiers of Petrograd. We have openly steeled the will of the masses for a rising, not a conspiracy. . . .' Politically this was true, although militarily the insurrection had in fact been conducted like a conspiracy, and could not have been conducted otherwise.

'Our rising', he went on, 'has been victorious. Now they tell us: Renounce your victory, yield, make a compromise. With whom? With whom, I am asking, shall we make this compromise? With those miserable little groups that have left or with those that make these proposals? But we have seen them in their full stature. Nobody in the whole of Russia follows them any more, and is it with them as with equal partners that the millions of workers and peasants . . . should conclude an agreement? . . . You are miserable, isolated individuals. You are bankrupt. You have played out your role. Go where you belong: to the dustheap of history!'[1] This *Vae Victis!* pierced the ears of Martov and of his followers as they made their way out of the hall, through the serried ranks of soldiers and workers, who indignantly reminded them of all the misdeeds of the Provisional Government, of the people's hunger and cold, of the senseless and bloody offensives, of the July days, of the proscription of the Bolsheviks, and of the peasants' craving for land. Pent-up emotion burst from the victors.

Nemesis stalked the halls of the Smolny. She was only beginning her work.

. . . .

Never before had any body of men seizing power assumed so prodigious a burden of commitments as that which the Bolshevik leaders shouldered when they read out to the Congress their first hastily scribbled decrees. They promised to give the people Peace, Land, and Bread. The distance from promise to fulfilment was immeasurable. The peace was to be just and democratic. It was to admit no annexations or indemnities, none of the injuries and insults which victors impose upon vanquished. Lenin and Trotsky had said over and over again that such a peace could not be expected from the absolutist or even the bourgeois parliamentary governments—it could only be achieved by proletarian revolutions in the belligerent countries. Yet the armies of the Hohenzollerns and Habsburgs stood on lands wrested from the Russian empire; and as long as they had not renounced their emperors and their rulers and had not disavowed their rapacious ambitions, the Bolsheviks were in a sense committed to go on waging war, the revolutionary war for a just peace. But they were also, and in the popular mind even

[1] Sukhanov, op. cit., vol. vii, pp. 202–4. John Reed, op. cit., p. 79.

more strongly, committed to achieve an *immediate* peace, which could be neither just nor democratic. This was their first dilemma. Its solution would be dictated to them by weary peasant–soldiers, who were all the more eager to turn their guns into ploughs now that all the land to plough was at last theirs. But the tenuous peace, attained under their pressure, would not avert from Russia the long ordeal of foreign intervention and civil war.

The Bolsheviks shared the land among the peasants, or, rather, they sanctioned the share-out accomplished by the peasantry itself. No great country can go through an agrarian revolution of this scale and momentum without its entire economy being shaken and weakened, if only temporarily. The old links between town and country were loosened or broken; the old channels of exchange shrank and became clogged; the old obsolete and inadequate yet automatic, and in its way effective, manner of running the body politic was rendered impossible. In the most favourable circumstances, even without a civil war, it would have taken time before new links, new channels, and a new way of managing the nation's existence replaced the old ones. Before that happened, so elementary a process as the flow of food from country to town, the pre-condition of modern civilization, was bound to be disrupted. The demands for land and bread were not quite compatible. After the large estates had been split, less, not more, bread was available to urban workers. To the peasants the agrarian revolution was a boon at first. It not only gave them land— it relieved them of the burdens of age-old servitude and debt. But to the nation as a whole the prospect looked less promising. Rural Russia was now broken up into 25,000,000 smallholdings, most of which were tiny and worked with ante-diluvian tools. The Bolshevik leaders knew that in the long run this spelt economic and social stagnation. They had to encourage and then to sanction the share-out of the land, because this was preferable to the old semi-feudal system of tenure, and because otherwise they would have suffered the fate of their predecessors in government. But they were from the beginning broadly committed to foster collective ownership in land, to regroup and merge the 25,000,000 smallholdings into relatively few large, modern, and efficient farms. They could not say when, how, or by means of what industrial resources they would be able to do this. They only knew that they had embarked upon a complex, paradoxical, and dangerous course: they had made one agrarian revolution with the avowed purpose of undoing it by means of another.

'Bread' means to the industrial worker and the city dweller at large the growth and the development of industry. To the Russian worker in 1917 it also implied the elimination from industry of private ownership and control. In the theoretical conception of socialism, which the leaders of the revolution had imbibed from early youth, national and ultimately international ownership and central planning of production and distribution held a crucial place. Russia's industry, as the Bolsheviks found it, even if it had not been further destroyed through civil war, was too small and poor to serve as a basis for socialism. It provided only a starting-point for evolution towards socialism. Despite the fact that they had proclaimed the Socialist purpose of their revolution, the Bolsheviks could ill afford an attempt to bring Russian industry under public ownership or management at once. The resources, the administrators, the technicians, and the techniques needed were not available. They hoped to be able to seek an unhurried solution of the problem by trial and error. They were at first as reluctant to dispossess the industrialists and merchants as they had been eager to dispossess the landlords.

But in the course of 1917 a state of affairs had spontaneously come to prevail, under which the owners of factories had already been more than half dispossessed. Just as in the barracks the elective soldiers' committees had deprived the commissioned officers of all authority and function, even before they tore off their epaulettes, so in the factories and mines the elected works committees had appropriated most of the rights and privileges of owners and managers, even before the latter were dispossessed or dismissed. The duality of power which, from February to October, ran through Russia's system of government ran also through Russian industry, even after October. The popular instinct was a mixture of anarchism and socialism. In part naturally and in part because of the prevalent chaos, it tended to destroy the national coherence of industry, without which there could be no evolution towards socialism. Each works committee tended to become a closed community and a law unto itself. Not only the capitalists but also the nation itself was in danger of being expropriated of its industrial resources.

Such a state of affairs forced the hands of the Bolsheviks. The revolutionary government, which seized power on behalf of the working class, could not re-establish the authority of the old industrialists, even if for economic reasons it had wanted to do so. It was compelled to put an end to the dual power in industry in the same way as it put an end to it elsewhere—by destroying the old power. Only after that could it strive to over-come the centrifugal trends in the nation's economy. The half-dispossessed bourgeoisie, knowing that it could expect nothing good from the revolution, could not help defending itself by the only means at its immediate disposal: economic resistance and sabotage. This again impelled the Bolsheviks to press dispossession through to the end. When the economic and political struggle culminated in civil war, all these trends became focused in the sudden and premature nationalization of all industry, which was decreed in June 1918. The revolution was permanent, according to the forecast of the chief character of this book. More firmly than other Bolsheviks, Trotsky had reckoned with this prospect. But its realization meant that from the outset the Russian Revolution had to build on extremely shaky economic foundations. The result was that over the years now this and now that part of the structure was bound to collapse over the heads of the Russian people or to be pulled down in panicky haste.

The Bolsheviks, nevertheless, believed that they were capable of fulfilling the three great and simple promises—Peace, Land, Bread—to which they owed their victory. They ardently believed that the bleeding and maimed peoples of Europe would very soon follow the Russian example and help the Russian revolution to solve its staggering problems. Russia would then enter the international Socialist community, within which the wealth and civilization of western Europe would outweigh Russian poverty and backwardness, just as the many millions of enlightened German, French, and perhaps also British proletarians would outweigh, if not outnumber, the millions of benighted muzhiks. Russia had opened to the West the road of Socialist revolution; and now the West would tow

Russia along that road, helping her to obtain access to the blessings of real civilization. Each phrase uttered by the Bolsheviks breathed this passionate, almost Messianic, belief. The dazzling blaze of this great vision brightened in their eyes even the darkest aspects of the legacy they were taking over.

Similar hope glowed through their ideas on their intended system of government. Theirs was to be a state without a standing army, without police, without bureaucracy. For the first time in history, the business of government was to cease to be the professional secret and privilege of small groups of people, elevated above society. It was to become the daily concern of the ordinary citizen. After the July days, while he was hunted as a German spy and expected to be assassinated at any moment, Lenin wrote his *State and Revolution*, a sort of political testament, in which he revived the half-forgotten Marxist idea about the withering away of the state, the idea of a government which in a classless society would cease to be government, because it would administer 'things' instead of governing human beings and so would no longer wield the instruments of coercion (prisons, courts, &c.). To be sure, this was the ideal state of the future, not the Russian state of 1917. But the Soviet republic, as it emerged from the revolution, was to be directly related to the ideal. Trotsky's conception of the state was less crystallized than Lenin's, though this did not prevent him from accepting Lenin's view when he became familiar with it. In their ideas on the Soviet republic, which were of more immediate consequence, there was no difference between them.

In the Soviets the propertied classes were not represented: they were to be disfranchised in the way in which old ruling classes are disfranchised in any revolution. (This did not necessarily imply that they should also be deprived of freedom of expression.) The Soviets were to combine legislative and executive powers, and the government was to be responsible to them. The electors were entitled to revoke, to change their deputies at any time, not merely during periodic polls; and the Soviets could at any time depose the government through a vote of no confidence. The existence of opposition and the continued contest of parties within the Soviets were taken for granted. That the ruling party alone should be entitled to form public opinion did not yet enter anybody's mind. Of course, the Soviet republic was to be a 'proletarian dictatorship'. By this was meant the social and political preponderance of the working class; but the means by which this preponderance was to be established were not fixed in advance. The Bolsheviks, and Socialists of other schools as well, were wont to describe the parliamentary democracies of the West as 'bourgeois dictatorships', in the sense that they embodied the social preponderance of the bourgeoisie, not that they were actually ruled in a dictatorial manner. The Bolsheviks at first described their own system of government as a dictatorship in that broad sense, expecting in all sincerity that by comparison with the bourgeois democracies the republic of the Soviets would bring to the vast majority of the nation more, not less, liberty; more, not less, freedom of expression and association.

The plebeian democracy of the Soviets did not at first think of itself as a monolithic or totalitarian state, because its leaders were confident that the bulk of the Russian people shared their aspirations. It did not soon occur to them to consider what they would do if this hopeful assumption proved wrong. They took it for granted that if they came in conflict with the majority of the nation, then they, their party, and their revolution would be doomed, and that all that would be left to them would be to perish with honour. But in 1917 this danger seemed to them no more real than the threat of a cosmic catastrophe.

How did the Russian people view the Bolsheviks and their objectives? A mere handful participated directly in the October insurrection—'hardly more', says Trotsky, 'than 25,000 or 30,000 at the most'.[1] In this sense, the revolution was the work of a tiny minority, unlike the February insurrection during which the great, overflowing, unguided energy of the masses had swept away the monarchy. But in the last fortnight before the October rising, in Petrograd alone 'hundreds of thousands of workers and soldiers took direct action, defensive in form but aggressive in essence'.[2] Many more facilitated the Bolshevik victory through their friendly attitude, active and passive; and many others did so by adopting all possible shades of neutrality. The second Congress of the Soviets represented about 20,000,000 electors, perhaps rather fewer. Of these the great majority voted for the Bolsheviks. Even in the elections to the Constituent

[1] Trotsky, *History of the Russian Revolution*, vol. iii, p. 290.   [2] Loc. cit.

Assembly, held after the revolution, nearly 10,000,000 votes were cast for the Bolsheviks alone without their Left Social Revolutionary associates. These 10,000,000 included the bulk of the urban working class, proletarianized elements of the peasantry, and a very large section of the army—at any rate the most energetic elements in the nation, on whose continued active support the revolution depended for its survival. But the electorate represented by the Constituent Assembly was nearly twice as large as that represented in the Soviets; and in the poll for the Assembly the Bolsheviks obtained only a large minority of the votes.

Rural Russia, vast, illiterate, boiling over with revolt and revenge, had little grasp of the involved disputes between the urban parties. It would be futile to try to put the attitude of that Russia into a clear-cut formula: it was confused, changeable, self-contradictory. Nothing characterizes that attitude better than the following scene described by historians: In one rural area a large body of peasants concluded a meeting with a religious vow that they would no longer wait for any land reform; that they would at once seize the land and smoke out the landlords; and that they would consider as their mortal enemy anybody trying to dissuade them. They would not rest, the peasants proceeded to swear, until the government concluded an immediate peace and released their sons from the army and until 'that criminal and German spy' Lenin had received exemplary punishment. In the election to the Constituent Assembly, peasants like these undoubtedly cast their votes for a Social Revolutionary. But they did so because they attributed to the Social Revolutionaries, the party which had had its roots in the country, the firm intention of carrying out the programme to which the Bolsheviks alone were determined to give effect. That is why each of these two parties, the only broad movements left after the débâcle of the Cadets and the Mensheviks, could claim, each with some reason, to enjoy the peasantry's support. 'Do not the peasants abhor Lenin, the German spy?' the Social Revolutionary said with self-confidence. 'But do they not declare those who, like you, delay the dispossession of the landlords and prolong the war as their mortal enemies?' the Bolshevik retorted triumphantly.

The abhorrence in which many peasants held the Bolsheviks

was due to the fact that the Bolsheviks were the avowed enemies of property. This feeling, however, was largely dispelled as soon as the Bolsheviks appeared in the countryside as the ruling party, and proclaimed the end of the war, and sanctioned or regulated the share-out of the land. In the civil war, the peasants further discovered that, by and large, only the Red Army stood between them and the return of the landlord. As the only effective opponents of restoration and defenders of the agrarian revolution, the Bolsheviks did in fact enjoy the support of the nation's overwhelming majority. But in the countryside this support was often reluctant, and it changed into its opposite when the figure of the returning landlord had ceased to cast its shadow and when Bolshevik squads went on rummaging the villages for food. Even at the height of Bolshevik popularity only the urban proletarian minority whole-heartedly identified itself with the cause of the revolution. It was to that minority that the Bolsheviks appealed in every predicament. To it they preached their transcendent ideals. From its ranks they drew the new administrators, commanders, and leaders.

The Russian working class of 1917 was one of history's wonders. Small in numbers, young, inexperienced, uneducated, it was rich in political passion, generosity, idealism, and rare heroic qualities. It had the gift of dreaming great dreams about the future and for dying a stoic death in battle. With its semi-illiterate thoughts it embraced the idea of the republic of the philosophers, not its Platonic version in which an oligarchy of pundits rules the herd, but the idea of a republic wealthy and wise enough to make of every citizen a philosopher and a worker. From the depth of its misery, the Russian working class set out to build that republic.

But side by side with the dreamer and the hero there lived in the Russian worker the slave; the lazy, cursing, squalid slave, bearing the stigmata of his past. The leaders of the revolution addressed themselves to the dreamer and the hero, but the slave rudely reminded them of his presence. During the civil war, and still more after it, Trotsky in his military speeches repeatedly complained that the Russian Communist and Red Army man would sacrifice his life for the sake of the revolution sooner than clean his rifle or polish his boots. This paradox reflected the lack in the Russian people of those innumerable small habits of self-disciplined and civilized life on which socialism had hoped to base itself. Such was the human material with which the Bolsheviks set out to build their new state, the proletarian democracy, in which 'every cook' should be able to perform the business of government. And this was perhaps the gravest of all the grave contradictions with which the revolution had to contend.

History gave the Bolshevik leaders a first warning of this problem almost immediately after she had given them her most gracious smile; and she did so with that malignant taste for anti-climax which she so often exhibits. The grotesque sequel to the October insurrection, a sequel to which historians rarely give attention, was a prodigious, truly elemental orgy of mass drunkenness with which the freed underdog celebrated his victory. The orgy lasted many weeks and at one time threatened to bring the revolution to a standstill and to paralyze it. Drunkenness reached its height just when the new government was confronted with the boycott of the entire civil service and with the first stirrings of civil war, when the government had no administrative organs of its own and when its fate depended entirely on the vigilance, discipline, and energy of its supporters. The orgy was also of some importance in the events which set the stage for the peace of Brest Litovsk, for in the course of it much of the old Russian army dissolved into nothingness. Contemporary sources abound in descriptions of these strange saturnalia. A most striking account is found in the memoirs of Antonov-Ovseenko, who at the time was one of the two chief Commissars of the Army and commander of the Petrograd garrison:

> The garrison, which began completely to disintegrate, gave me personally much more trouble than did the adherents of the Constituent Assembly. . . . A wild and unexampled orgy spread over Petrograd; and until now it has not been plausibly explained whether or not this was due to any surreptitious provocation. Now here and now there, crowds of ruffians appeared, mostly soldiers, broke into wine cellars and sometimes pillaged wine shops. The few soldiers who had preserved discipline and the Red Guards were worn out by guard duty. Exhortations were of no avail.
> The cellars of the Winter Palace [the former residence of the Tsar] presented the most awkward problem. . . . The Preobrazhensky

regiment, which had hitherto kept its discipline, got completely drunk while it was doing guard duty at the Palace. The Pavlovsky regiment, our revolutionary rampart, did not withstand the temptation either. Mixed guards, picked from different detachments were then sent there; They, too, got drunk. Members of the [regimental] committees [i.e. the revolutionary leaders of the garrison] were then assigned to do guard duty. These, too, succumbed. Men of the armoured brigades were ordered to disperse the crowds—they paraded a little to and fro, and then began to sway suspiciously on their feet.

At dusk the mad bacchanals would spread. 'Let us finish off these Tsarist remnants!' This gay slogan took hold of the crowd. We tried to stop them by walling up the entrances. The crowd penetrated through the windows, forced out the bars and grabbed the stocks. An attempt was made to flood the cellars with water. The fire brigades sent to do this themselves got drunk.

Only the sailors from Helsingfors managed to render the cellars of the Winter Palace harmless. This was in its way a titanic struggle. The sailors stood firm, because they were bound by a severe comradely vow: 'Death to anyone who breaks the oath'; and, although they themselves were at other times magnificent tipplers, they came off with flying colours. . . .

This was not yet the end of the struggle. The whole city was infected by the drinking madness. At last the Council of the People's Commissars appointed a special commissar, endowed him with emergency powers, and gave him a strong escort. But the commissar, too, proved unreliable. . . . A bitter struggle was in progress at the Vassilevsky Island. The Finnish regiment, led by men with anarcho-syndicalist leanings, declared a state of siege on the island and announced that they would blow up the wine cellars and shoot plunderers at sight. Only after an intense effort was this alcoholic lunacy overcome. . . .[1]

Trotsky again and again addressed the Soviet on this matter, for the first time on 29 October, four days after the rising, and for the last time on 2 December. 'Vodka is just as much a political factor as the word', he said. 'The revolutionary word awakens the people and enthuses it to fight against its oppressors; vodka . . . puts the people to sleep again. . . .'[2] More than anybody Trotsky had appealed to the dreamer and the hero in the working man and had spread before his eyes the grand

[1] Antonov-Ovseenko, *Zapiski o Grazhdanskoi Voinie*, vol. i, pp. 19–20.
[2] Trotsky, *Sochinenya*, vol. iii, book 2, pp. 139–40.

vision of socialism. Now this vision seemed blurred by alcoholic vapours. At length the Council of the People's Commissars ordered the contents of the wine cellars to be pumped into the waters of the Neva.

In the course of the orgy, the great Petrograd garrison, which had played so important a role in the revolutions of February and October, ultimately disintegrated and ceased to exist. After Petrograd came the provinces' turn. 'Comrade Berzin [a well-known member of the Central Committee] reports his great difficulties', Antonov-Ovseenko notes further in his memoirs. 'He also notices mass consignments of spirits and wine on the railways. . . . Echelons of soldiers break into the wagons and get drunk. Detachments disintegrate. Plunder goes on. . . .'[1]

Under this grotesque omen, which seemed to mock at its high and noble aspirations, the Soviet republic started its first year.

[1] Antonov-Ovseenko, op. cit., vol. i, p. 31. A vivid description of the orgy and of its tragi-comic consequences by a foreign, pro-Bolshevik eye-witness is in Bessie Beatty, *The Red Heart of Russia*, pp. 329–34.

CHAPTER X

The People's Commissar

THE first Soviet Government was in its composition purely Bolshevik. It was out of the question that the parties which had refused to acknowledge the Congress of the Soviets as the only constitutional source of power, and had then declared a boycott on the Congress, should join the government. Only one non-Bolshevik group, the Left Social Revolutionaries, who had broken away from their mother-party, were inclined to share with the Bolsheviks the responsibilities of government. To them Lenin offered seats in the Council of the People's Commissars. But the Left Social Revolutionaries still hoped to mediate between the Bolsheviks and their adversaries and, in order not to spoil the chance of this, they preferred to stay outside the government.[1]

Trotsky relates that, when the composition of the government was first discussed, Lenin proposed that Trotsky should be placed at its head, since he had led the insurrection of which this government was born. Out of deference to Lenin's political seniority, Trotsky refused.[2] This version has never been denied by any source; and it is indirectly confirmed by what Lunacharsky, a member of this government, related to Sukhanov, his intimate friend. Lenin, Lunacharsky said, was reluctant to preside over the Council of the People's Commissars or even to join it; he preferred to give undivided attention to the management of the party's affairs. But those Bolshevik leaders who had been opposed to the insurrection and those who had vacillated, including Lunacharsky himself, saw in this an attempt by Lenin to evade his responsibilities and insisted that he should preside over the government. Lenin was the last man to shrink from the consequences of his actions, and he agreed to head the *Sovnarkom*.[3]

He then proposed that Trotsky be appointed Commissar of Home Affairs.[4] This Commissariat was to direct the struggle against the counter-revolution, and a firm hand was needed there. Trotsky objected to this appointment, too, partly be-

---

[1] John Reed, op. cit., p. 116. [2] Trotsky, *Moya Zhizn*, vol. ii.
[3] Sukhanov, op. cit., vol. vii, p. 266. *Sovnarkom*, abbreviation for the Council of the People's Commissars. [4] Trotsky, op. cit., vol. ii, pp. 62–63.

cause he had been tired by the exertions of the last months and partly because he feared that in this office his Jewish origin might be a liability: the counter-revolution would whip up anti-Semitic feeling and turn it against the Bolsheviks. This consideration seemed irrelevant to Lenin. But Sverdlov, another Jew among the Bolshevik leaders, shared Trotsky's apprehension, and Lenin gave way.

This was a curious episode. In the Socialist parties and the Soviets, racial prejudice had never made itself felt; if it had, it would not have been countenanced. Jews, Poles, and Georgians had been prominent in all radical and revolutionary movements for the simple reason that they had been members of oppressed minorities. There were even more Jews among the Mensheviks and Social Revolutionaries than among the Bolsheviks. Despite his origin, Trotsky had been the leader of the insurrection. But, so far, the revolution had been an urban affair, and Russia's most advanced city its main scene. Now the Bolsheviks had to feel themselves into new roles, those of the rulers of rural Russia, which was still wrapped up in Greek Orthodoxy, distrust of the cities, and racial prejudice. In a few months Trotsky would call the sons of that Russia to defend the revolution on a dozen fronts; and his origin would not handicap him. But in those few months the Soviet régime had acquired some sense of stability and so could defy inveterate prejudice. On the day after the insurrection, Trotsky may have felt that it would be imprudent for the victors to offer too strong a provocation.

It is possible, however, that he had other and unavowable motives. The job of the revolution's chief policeman may not have suited his inclinations and tastes. True, he would presently be among the strongest advocates of repressive measures against incipient counter-revolution; and he would not shun the Red Terror when the time for it came. But it was one thing to justify and even direct the red terror in a civil war, in an atmosphere of high drama; and it was quite another to accept the office of chief policeman on the very day of the revolution. This may have seemed to him too flat a sequel. The internationalist may have been unattracted by an office in which he would have had to turn his mind mainly to domestic preoccupations.

Whatever the truth, he readily agreed to become the revolution's first Foreign Secretary. It was on Sverdlov's initiative that he was invited to assume this office. Next to the leadership of the government this was the most important appointment. Trotsky himself played it down. The revolution, he said, had no need for diplomacy: 'I shall publish a few revolutionary proclamations and then close shop.' There was a little affectation in his assumption of the back seat. Sverdlov proposed his appointment on the ground that he was the right man 'to confront Europe' on behalf of the revolution; and this assignment was as important as it was congenial to Trotsky. It is true, however, that he did not intend to 'confront Europe' in the manner of the conventional diplomat.[1]

The government was formed, but few believed it would last. To the anti-Bolsheviks, and to many Bolsheviks as well, the insurrection and its outcome looked quite unreal. Most of them expected a bloody suppression. The day after the formation of the government, the capital was astir with rumours that Lenin and Trotsky had already fled.[2] From Gatchina, less than twenty miles south-west of Petrograd, Kerensky self-confidently announced his imminent return at the head of General Krasnov's loyal Cossacks. The Commissar for Foreign Affairs, resuming his functions as chief of the Military Revolutionary Committee, had to gather an armed force in order to stop the advance of Kerensky's troops. This proved to be more difficult in some respects than it had been to make the insurrection. The garrison was in no fighting mood. It had gladly helped Trotsky to overthrow Kerensky when the latter threatened to send the rebellious regiments to the front. But when Trotsky ordered these same regiments to leave their barracks and to take up positions on the heights outside the capital, it was with much grumbling and discontent that they carried out his order. They did not expect any fighting, and when suddenly they found themselves under fire, their hearts sank. The Red Guards of the civilian workers were the only militant force available. But, like any such militia, while they acted with self-reliance and boldness as long as they moved within the walls of their city—where they were familiar with every street, passage, and recess—they were little suited to meet an enemy in the open field.[3]

[1] Trotsky, loc. cit.; *Proletarskaya Revolutsia*, nr. 10, 1922.
[2] Sadoul, *Notes sur la Révolution*, p. 63.
[3] Trotsky, *Sochinenya*, vol. iii, book 2, pp. 86–90.

At this moment Kerensky might have re-entered Petrograd if he had mustered a few reliable and disciplined detachments, though it is doubtful whether he would have been able to re-assert his authority. But, like the troops which Trotsky sent against him, his Cossacks were by no means prepared to shed their blood. They had been told that their job was to suppress a revolt staged by a handful of German spies; and they were surprised to find the regiments of the capital and the Red Guards arrayed against them. For a moment the fate of a great country, indeed the fate of the world, depended on the encounter of a few small dispirited brigades. That side which could evoke a flicker of spirit in its troops and act with the more purpose and speed was bound to win. Victory lay in a very narrow margin of superiority, as it sometimes does even when numerous, well-equipped, tenaciously fighting but equally strong armies are locked in battle.

Trotsky was confident that words of persuasion rather than bullets would disperse Krasnov's Cossacks.[1] But, before Bolshevik propagandists could approach the Cossacks, guns had to shake their self-assurance. At this stage already Trotsky had to look round for experienced and skilled commanders. On the day after the insurrection, he and Lenin turned for help to the regular officers, hitherto the target of Bolshevik attacks. But the officers who were persuaded to appear at the Smolny cautiously refused co-operation. Only a few desperados and careerists were ready to serve under the 'illegitimate' government. One of these, Colonel Muraviev, was chosen to command in the battle on the Pulkovo Heights; and subsequently he played a conspicuous part in the first phase of the civil war. A braggart, posing as a Left Social Revolutionary, he seems to have been moved less by sympathy with the Bolsheviks than by a grudge against Kerensky. Trotsky first received him with suspicion. But the Colonel was mettlesome, resourceful, and eager to win a prize in a seemingly hopeless assignment; and so Trotsky was captivated by his initiative and courage. Colonel Valden, another officer of this small group, commanded the artillery, which decided the outcome of the Pulkovo battle in favour of the Bolsheviks.

The employment of these officers aroused much indignation in the Soviet. Bolsheviks and Left Social Revolutionaries were

[1] Sadoul, op. cit., pp. 68–69.

horrified to see, as they thought, the fate of the revolution placed in the hands of disreputable climbers—Muraviev was said to have been especially zealous in the suppression of the Bolsheviks in July. Boycotted by the entire officer corps, the Bolsheviks could not, however, afford to scrutinize too closely the credentials of those few who were willing to serve. In the party's military branch there were men skilled in the arts of insurrection, but almost none competent in regular warfare. The garrison was in complete chaos; and Trotsky was incapable even of tracing the stocks of ammunition and food in its possession. At that moment he was ready to employ the devil himself, provided he could keep a pistol at the devil's head and watch the way he went. In these improvisations one may discern in miniature the main elements of Trotsky's military policy in the civil war.

On 28 October Trotsky arrived at the head of the Red Guards at Gatchina, where a battle was fought for the approaches to the capital. At Gatchina Kerensky's troops suffered their first reverse; and Trotsky hoped to bring back the former Premier as the Soviet's prisoner. But Kerensky escaped him.[1]

While the fighting outside Petrograd was still on, inside the city the cadets of the officers' schools staged a revolt. They had some initial success, and among the prisoners they captured was Antonov-Ovseenko, the Commissar of War. Speaking to the Soviet on the steps taken to suppress this revolt, Trotsky declared among other things:

> The prisoners we have taken are hostages in our hands. If our enemies happen to take prisoners from us, let them know that we shall exchange each worker and peasant for five military cadets. . . . We have shown them to-day that our hesitations have come to an end. We do not joke when the fundamental interests of the workers and peasants are at stake. We know how the landlords and capitalists have fought . . ., how they have treated insurgent soldiers, workers

---

[1] Sukhanov, op. cit., vol. vii, p. 305. The atmosphere which prevailed in the Soviet is well conveyed by a scene described by John Reed (op. cit., pp. 178–9): Trotsky was reporting on the progress of the fighting. 'The cruisers *Oleg*, *Aurora*, and *Respublika*', he said, 'are anchored in the Neva, their guns trained on the approaches to the city. . . .'

'Why aren't you out there, with the Red Guards?' shouted a rough voice.

'I'm going now!' answered Trotsky and left the platform. The rough plebeian anger of the masses did not spare even the leaders of the revolution and often dictated their steps.

and peasants, how much blood they have shed, how much life they have destroyed. . . .[1]

These words, liable to be taken as a signal for indiscriminate executions, provoked angry protests.[2] During a later sitting, Trotsky took advantage of a question put to him from the floor to explain what he meant. It was a matter of course, he said, that the life of prisoners was inviolable 'for humanitarian reasons and because the living are worth more to us than the dead'. He had previously referred to the 'exchange', not the shooting of prisoners.[3] The incident, nevertheless, gave a foretaste of the ferocity of the civil war. At the same session, reporting on the difficulties of supplying the Red Guards, Trotsky announced that the Soviet would not respect the sanctity of private property: 'The organizations of workers and soldiers can obtain from the Military Revolutionary Committee authorization for requisitions.' He also reported that the government was preparing a decree which would give it power to ban newspapers backing the other side in the civil war.

On 31 October Kerensky's Cossacks surrendered at Pulkovo. Their commander General Krasnov was taken prisoner, but Kerensky escaped once again. From the battlefield Trotsky reported victory in an eloquent message to the Soviet. He released Krasnov on parole, which did not prevent the general from taking up arms against the Soviets soon afterwards. At the same time, after protracted and bloody fighting, the Bolsheviks obtained control in Moscow. The ascendancy of the Soviets was reported from most other cities as well. Lenin's government was no longer isolated in Petrograd, and some time was to elapse before the civil war flared up for good.

The first armed threat to Lenin's government had hardly been warded off when that government was in danger of being undone by the scruples and second thoughts of its own members. The moderate Bolsheviks were anxious to reconcile the Mensheviks and Social Revolutionaries and to invite them to participate in the government. The leaders of the railwaymen's union threatened to stop traffic on the railways if a coalition government of all Socialist parties was not formed. On 29 October

---

[1] Trotsky, op. cit., vol. iii, book 2, p. 71.
[2] Lozovsky, for instance, reproached Trotsky with 'imitating the methods of Hindenburg'.   [3] Loc. cit.

the Bolshevik Central Committee, in the absence of Lenin, Trotsky, and Stalin, resolved to open negotiations.[1] The Mensheviks and Social Revolutionaries then put forward the following conditions for their entry into the coalition: the new government was to be responsible not to the Soviets but to 'the broad circles of revolutionary democracy'; it was to disarm the Bolshevik detachments; and Lenin and Trotsky were to be debarred from it.[2] These conditions amounted to a demand that the Bolsheviks should declare the October Revolution null and void; that they should disarm themselves in the face of their enemies; and that they themselves should ostracize the inspirer and the leader of the insurrection. Addressed by parties defeated in a revolution to victors seeking reconciliation, these were bold demands. The Bolshevik negotiators, Kamenev, Ryazanov, and Sokolnikov, especially the former two, stood on the right wing of their party and desired nothing more than to be able to return to the party with a practicable compromise which it would be hard for Lenin and Trotsky to reject. So anxious were the Bolshevik negotiators to meet the Mensheviks and Social Revolutionaries half-way that, while the battle at Pulkovo was still undecided, they signed a joint appeal for a cease-fire, an appeal implicitly directed against their own party and the government. Yet even the most moderate Bolsheviks could not accept the Menshevik terms. They could not return to their party with the advice that it should commit suicide.

Straight from the Pulkovo battle, Trotsky rushed to a conference which the Central Committee held with the Petrograd committee and the leaders of the military branch in order to take a decision on the negotiations. He was the first to assail Kamenev and Ryazanov. 'There was no need for us to stage the rising', he said, 'if we were not to obtain a majority in the government. . . . We ought to obtain three-quarters of all the seats.' He added that Lenin must in any circumstances continue to preside over the government.[3] Lenin went even farther and asked that the negotiations be broken off. At the other extreme Ryazanov (and Lunacharsky) was inclined to agree to the exclusion of Lenin and Trotsky from the government, saying that the party should insist on principles,

---

[1] *Protokoly Tsen. Kom.*, pp. 144–7.
[2] Ibid., p. 156.   [3] Ibid., p. 149.

not on personalities. The conference decided to carry on the negotiations, but only on conditions guaranteeing the party's preponderance in the proposed coalition.

This controversy was a prolongation of that which had preceded the insurrection. On the face of it, all Bolsheviks agreed that the Soviets should form the constitutional basis and framework of government. All seemed to agree also on the advisability of a coalition with any party or group prepared to endorse this principle. On 2 November the Central Committee solemnly reiterated that the Bolsheviks were still willing to form a government with the parties which had declared a boycott on the Soviets, provided that those parties retraced their steps and accepted Soviet constitutionalism. The Mensheviks and Social Revolutionaries could not agree to this without disavowing everything they had done since February. If the terms the Mensheviks had laid down were an implicit demand that the Bolsheviks should commit political suicide, then Lenin's party, in its turn, invited its would-be partners to commit an act of moral self-effacement. Lenin had no doubt that they would not agree and so he saw no use in further parleying. At best, he said, this could only serve as a *ruse de guerre*, designed to confound Kerensky's supporters while the struggle against Kerensky lasted.

Neither Lenin nor Trotsky saw any reason why their party should not form an administration consisting solely of its own members. There was nothing, they argued, to prevent the Soviet majority from shouldering exclusive responsibility. In no democratic system can the minority claim the right to participate in the government. What is vital for the minority is that it should be unhampered in its activity as an opposition, on the understanding that that activity remains within a constitutional framework accepted by both government and opposition. No such commonly accepted framework existed after the October revolution. One party had proclaimed a new constitutional principle, which was inherently unconstitutional in the view of nearly all other parties. Emphatically denying the sovereignty of the Soviets, the Mensheviks and their associates could not even become a loyal opposition within the Soviets (even though some groups of them occasionally tried to do so). Still less could they become the Bolsheviks' partners. The opposed parties were all Socialist in name; yet all that connected them now were fading reminiscences of a common past.

The large and influential body of Bolshevik leaders who still sought to bridge the gulf, was in part moved by these reminiscences. Many of the Bolshevik conciliators also felt that their party had driven into a blind alley and that to get out it ought to grasp the helping hands of its adversaries. Kamenev, Rykov, Zinoviev, and others argued in alarm that Petrograd was without food supplies, that the Bolsheviks could not rule the country if the railways were stopped, and that they had no chance of surviving a protracted civil war. Lenin and Trotsky, ardently supported by Sverdlov and Dzerzhinsky, did not deny the risks and dangers; but they believed that they could hold their ground if they acted with determination. To sue for coalition was to show weakness; and, anyhow, the would-be partners had stretched out hands not to help but to strangle.

On 2 November the issue was discussed by the Central Executive of the Soviets; and the Bolshevik 'conciliators', together with anti-Bolshevik members, voted against their own party. This open split was most embarrassing; all the more so as the 'conciliators' were headed by Kamenev who, despite his recent quarrel with the party, had been elected Chairman of the Central Executive of the Soviets, an office equivalent to that of President of the republic. Briefly, the Bolshevik President openly asked for the dismissal of the Bolshevik government and for its replacement by a coalition. Kamenev had behind him most important members of the government itself: Rykov, Commissar of Interior; Miliutin, Commissar of Agriculture; Nogin, Commissar of Industry and Trade; Lunacharsky, Commissar of Education; Teodorovich, Commissar of Supplies; and outside the government Zinoviev, Lozovsky, Ryazanov, and Yureniev, to mention only the most influential.

There could be no graver crisis in both government and party. The rule that the members of a party should act in office on the party's instructions and be bound by its discipline was generally accepted not only by the Bolsheviks but by most Russian and indeed European parties, although the rule was more often honoured in the breach than in the observance. Lenin and Trotsky set out to enforce observance. They persuaded the Central Committee to reaffirm its view: 'To yield to ultimatums

and threats from a minority in the Soviets would amount to
a complete renunciation [by us] not only of government based
on the Soviets but of the democratic attitude. Such yielding
would testify to the majority's fear of using its majority; it
would amount to submission to anarchy; and it would encourage any minority to confront us with ever-new ultimatums.'[1]
On 3 November the majority of the Central Committee presented the 'conciliators' with its own 'ultimatum' demanding
disciplined behaviour and threatening to convoke an emergency
Congress of the party, which would be asked either to endorse
the 'conciliators' ' policy or to expel them.[2] The 'conciliators'
replied with collective resignation from the Central Committee
and the government. They justified their step in strongly
worded protests against the party's insistence on a purely Bolshevik government. Such a government, Nogin declared on their
behalf, 'can be kept in power only by means of political terror'.
It would lead to an 'irresponsible régime'; and it would 'eliminate the mass organizations of the proletariat from leadership
in political life'.[3]

As in Trotsky's controversy with Lenin in 1904 and as in
recent debates on insurrection, so here the wrongs and the rights
of the issue were inextricably confused. From the Bolshevik viewpoint, the considerations which Lenin and Trotsky adduced to
justify their policy were irrefutable. The negotiations for a
broad coalition were futile. The Mensheviks and the Right
Social Revolutionaries were trying in a roundabout way to
wrest power from the Bolsheviks, not to share it with them. For
all his anxiety to bring about agreement with the Mensheviks,
Kamenev could not accept their terms. At the same session of
the Central Executive of the Soviets where he virtually demanded the resignation of Lenin's government, he also declared
that without Lenin and Trotsky the party would be 'decapitated'.[4] The other side insisted on the 'decapitation' because it
could not eliminate the Bolsheviks from power without first
breaking their self-reliance. Nothing was better calculated to
achieve this than the demand that the Bolshevik party should
allow outsiders to dictate whom it was to delegate to the government and to insist that it should disavow its two chiefs.

---

[1] *Protokoly Tsen. Kom.*, p. 161.   [2] Ibid., pp. 162–4.
[3] Ibid., pp. 169–70.   [4] Ibid., p. 166.

As in October, so now, Lenin did not question the right of Kamenev and his friends to dissent. But he denied them the right to act against the party's declared policy beyond the confines of the party. When they demonstratively left office, he branded them once again as 'deserters'. Kamenev and his friends eventually surrendered, as they had done in October. Their roles had been played out when it became clear that neither of the opposed parties was in a mood for conciliation. Zinoviev was the first to change sides and to declare that the Mensheviks had made a compromise impossible.[1] In words foreshadowing his future and more tragic surrenders, he appealed to his friends: 'We remain with the party; we prefer to err with the millions of workers and to die with them than to stand aside in this decisive, historical moment.' Within a few days the 'conciliators' were routed. Kamenev was deposed from his high office on the Executive of the Soviets; and at a session of the Executive Trotsky sponsored Sverdlov as Kamenev's successor. The only positive outcome of the negotiations was that the Left Social Revolutionaries, resentful at the attitude of the anti-Bolshevik parties, joined Lenin's government.

Yet Lenin's and Trotsky's opponents in the party were not quite as wrong as they presently professed. Their forecast that 'a purely Bolshevik government could be maintained only by means of political terror' and that it would result in an 'irresponsible régime', was eventually to come true. For the moment, Lenin and Trotsky repudiated this forecast with sincere indignation, reiterating the assurance that the Soviets could overthrow the government by a simple majority vote.[2] But history was to justify the warning though, when it was made, no basis for it was apparent. Lenin, Trotsky and the other Bolshevik leaders undoubtedly had every intention of governing the country in a spirit of genuine responsibility to the Soviet electorate. But the fact that their party alone was to embrace Soviet constitutionalism wholeheartedly could not but lead them to identify the policies of their party with Soviet constitutionalism, then to substitute the party's wishes and desires for the principles of that constitutionalism, and in the end to abandon those principles altogether. To put it more broadly, the circumstance that the Bolsheviks were *the* party of the revolution impelled them

[1] Ibid., p. 177.   [2] Ibid., pp. 171–5.

first to identify the revolution with themselves, and then to reduce the revolution to being exclusively an affair of their party. Eleven years later Bukharin, surveying the sequence of events that led to the perversion of Soviet democracy and to Stalin's ascendancy, traced back these 'disasters' to a 'single mistake': the identification of the party with the state.[1] The force of circumstances began to drive the party on to this road in the first week of the revolution; and the moderate Bolsheviks expressed an instinctive dread of the road. Nobody imagined the length, the direction, or the tragic character of the journey.

Next to Lenin, Trotsky was the most outspoken and tenacious advocate of an exclusively or predominantly Bolshevik government. He had proudly sent the Mensheviks and the Social Revolutionaries to the 'dustheap of history'; and he was in no mood to recall them as partners and allies. Yet neither he nor any of his colleagues intended to suppress these parties. When, on the day after the Menshevik exodus from the Congress of the Soviets, Martov returned to intercede with the Bolsheviks for the arrested Socialist ministers, as he had in July interceded with these ministers for the arrested Bolsheviks, the Bolsheviks softened. Trotsky released the ministers from prison, placing them first under house arrest and then freeing them altogether. This was at any rate more generous than the treatment the ministers had so recently meted out to himself and Lenin.[2] In the Soviets the Bolsheviks kept the doors wide open for the return of the Mensheviks and Social Revolutionaries; and on the Central Executive they kept vacant a number of seats proportionate to their adversaries' strength at the Congress. Both Lenin and Trotsky, even though they had no desire to share the government with the Mensheviks and Social Revolutionaries, wished to see them fairly represented in the 'proletarian parliament' and its agencies.

Trotsky opposed the Bolshevik 'conciliators' without showing any sign of hesitation. Yet we have reliable testimony to his inner misgivings. Sadoul relates that three days after the insurrection Trotsky confided to him his worry about the Mensheviks, who were likely by their pretensions and obstructiveness

---

[1] This is quoted from Bukharin's conversation with Kamenev in 1928, of which *The Trotsky Archives* contain the fullest summary.

[2] Sukhanov, op. cit., vol. vii, p. 243.

to compel the Bolsheviks to treat them roughly and so to widen the gulf between the parties. This, Trotsky said, caused him more anxiety than the advance of Krasnov's Cossacks and the reports about the formation of White Guards.[1] Somewhat later he expressed to Sadoul his hope that, after the Bolsheviks had carried out the most essential points of their programme, they would invite the Mensheviks to join the government.

The talks about coalition came to an abrupt end on 3 November, when Martov and Abramovich declared that they would engage in no negotiations as long as the arrests then taking place continued and the newspapers just banned were not allowed to reappear.[2] The Bolsheviks had arrested a few right-wing politicians and banned some newspapers which had openly called for armed resistance. In the Soviet Trotsky thus justified these measures: 'The demand to stop all repression at the time of civil war amounts to a demand that we stop the civil war. . . . Our adversaries have not proposed peace to us. . . . In conditions of civil war it is legitimate to ban hostile papers.'[3] He emphatically assured the Soviet that the government had no intention of setting up its own press monopoly. It was, however, in duty bound to destroy the press monopoly of the propertied classes, as every Socialist party had promised to do. The printing presses and the paper-mills would be nationalized; and then the government would allocate printing facilities and paper to all parties and groups in proportion to their strength in elections. Thus genuine freedom of the press would be established for the first time in history. The capacity of people to spread their views would depend on their real influence in social and political life, not on their financial resources.[4]

A month after the revolution, the first White Guards, under the command of Kornilov, Kaledin, Alexeev, and Denikin,

---

[1] Sadoul, op. cit., pp. 68–69.   [2] *Protokoly Tsen. Kom.*, p. 174.
[3] Trotsky, *Sochinenya*, vol. iii, book, 2 pp. 104–5.
[4] Some time later Trotsky addressed the Grenadier Regiment on the same subject. 'What do the advocates of the bourgeoisie mean by the freedom of the press? The same as they mean by freedom of trade. Every man who has some capital has the right, because he has the means, to open a factory, a shop, a brothel, or a newspaper, according to his personal tastes. . . . But do the millions of peasants, workers, and soldiers enjoy freedom of the press? They do not have the essential condition of freedom, the means, the actual and genuine means of publishing a newspaper.' On this occasion, too, he defended the principle of proportional allocation of newsprint and other facilities to the political parties. Ibid., pp. 125–7.

moved into action on the Don; and the Cossacks of Orenburg rose under their *Ataman* Dutov. The White generals did not even pretend to fight for the restoration of Kerensky's government. They aimed frankly either at the restoration of Tsardom or at their own dictatorship. Simultaneously with this opening of actual civil war in remote provinces, the Cadets and some Right Social Revolutionaries staged a semi-insurrection in the capital. On 28 November Trotsky announced that the Cadet party was outlawed. The Central Committee of that party, he said, was the political headquarters of the White Guards; and it directed the recruiting of officers for Kornilov and Kaledin.[1] The Cadets would therefore be barred from the Constituent Assembly which the government was about to convene. 'We have made', Trotsky added, 'a modest beginning. We have arrested the chiefs of the Cadets and ordered that a watch be kept on their followers in the provinces. At the time of the French Revolution, the Jacobins guillotined men more honest than these for obstructing the people's will. We have executed nobody and we have no intention of doing so. But there are moments of popular anger, and the Cadets themselves have been looking for trouble.'[2]

The words 'we have made a modest beginning' had an ominous ring. Having accomplished a revolution, the Bolsheviks could not renounce revolutionary terror; and the terror has its own momentum. Every revolutionary party at first imagines that its task is simple: it has to suppress a 'handful' of tyrants or exploiters. It is true that usually the tyrants and exploiters form an insignificant minority. But the old ruling class has not lived in isolation from the rest of society. In the course of its long domination it has surrounded itself by a network of institutions embracing groups and individuals of many classes; and it has brought to life many attachments and loyalties which even a revolution does not destroy altogether. The anatomy of society is never so simple that it is possible surgically to separate one of the limbs from the rest of the body. Every social class is connected with its immediate neighbour by many almost impercep-

---

[1] That this was literally true can be seen from as authoritative a source as Denikin who describes in great detail the connexions between the White Guards and the headquarters of the Cadets. *Ocherki Russkoi Smuty*, vol. ii, pp. 35, 186–94.

[2] Trotsky, *Sochinenya*, vol. iii, book 2, p. 138.

tible gradations. The aristocracy shades off into the upper middle class; the latter into the lower layers of the bourgeoisie; the lower middle class branches off into the working class; and the proletariat, especially in Russia, is bound by innumerable filiations to the peasantry. The political parties are similarly interconnected. The revolution cannot deal a blow at the party most hostile and dangerous to it without forcing not only that party but its immediate neighbour to answer with a counter-blow. The revolution therefore treats its enemy's immediate neighbour as its enemy. When it hits this secondary enemy, the latter's neighbour, too, is aroused and drawn into the struggle. The process goes on like a chain reaction until the party of the revolution arouses against itself and suppresses all the parties which until recently crowded the political scene.

The generals who led the White Guards were monarchists *tout court*. They had been brought up to be the servants of Tsarist absolutism; and they viewed the revolution in all its phases, Bolshevik and pre-Bolshevik, with bitter hatred and a yearning for revenge. The Cadets had been constitutional monarchists. Under the Tsar, the main body of the defenders of absolutism and the main body of the constitutional monarchists had confronted one another in hostility and mutual contempt. But the two parties had also overlapped. Since the downfall of the monarchy their disagreements had become largely irrelevant—they all aimed at the overthrow of the 'socialist republic'. After the October Revolution, they finally sank their differences and fought under the same banner. But a large section of the constitutional monarchists was closely connected with the semi-Socialist republicans, who had been the pillars of the February régime. Within the Menshevik and Social Revolutionary parties all shades of opinion, from bourgeois republicanism to quasi-revolutionary socialism, could be found; and in their extreme left wings these parties overlapped with the Bolsheviks. If it had been possible for the Bolsheviks to isolate the White Guards, their most active and dangerous enemies, as the sole targets for attack, the revolution and the civil war might have developed in a different way. The natural alliance between the constitutional monarchists and the White Guards made this impossible. To deprive the White Guards of their political supply services, the Bolsheviks were compelled to outlaw the Cadets.

The main body of the Mensheviks and Social Revolutionaries would never have dreamt of defending Kornilov, Denikin, or Kolchak. But they could not remain indifferent when the Cadets were declared 'enemies of the people', if only because their own right wing had lived with the Cadets in a sort of political symbiosis, hatching common political plans and plots. A Left Menshevik like Martov would hardly have stood up for the Cadets alone. But he was well aware that after the Cadets, the scourge of the revolution would chastise the right wing of the Social Revolutionaries and of his own party; and this he was anxious to avert.

Trotsky's assurance that the Bolsheviks had no intention of installing the guillotine testified to his awareness that the terror might run away with the revolution. The anxiety to prevent this was widespread among the Bolsheviks. On the day after the rising they abolished the death penalty; and Lenin was alone in protesting.[1] But even Lenin, when he argued against the moderate Bolsheviks, said: 'In Paris, they [the Jacobins] used the guillotine, while we only take away the food cards of those who fail to obtain them from the trade unions.'[2] The party as a whole tried, in part instinctively and in part consciously, to avoid the slope, slippery with blood, down which the Jacobins had rushed. Having, of necessity, put one foot on the top of the slope the party resisted the downward pull hard and long. The government outlawed the Cadets, but not the right wing of the Social Revolutionaries, who had taken part in the semi-insurrection of 28 November. It decreed elections to the Constituent Assembly, and it was still half-unaware of the inevitable conflict between government by Soviets and a Constituent Assembly. Towards the end of November, Bukharin still urged the Central Committee to postpone the settling of accounts with the Cadets till the opening of the Constituent Assembly. Invoking precedents from French and English history, he proposed that the Cadets be expelled from the Constituent Assembly, and that the rump Assembly should then declare itself a revolutionary Convention. He hoped that in the Assembly the Bolsheviks and Left Social Revolutionaries would command an overwhelming majority, and that this would give the revolution the advantage

[1] Trotsky, *Lénine*, pp. 116–17.
[2] Trotsky, *The Stalin School of Falsification*, p. 110.

of formal legitimacy. Trotsky broadly supported Bukharin's plan of action. Stalin alone seems to have had, at this stage, a clearer idea of the trend of events, probably because he did not believe that the Bolsheviks and the Social Revolutionaries commanded a majority in the country. Bukharin's proposal, he declared, had come too late; the suppression of the Cadets had already begun and could not be delayed. He expected a split in the Assembly and a struggle between two rival assemblies. As yet nobody mooted the dispersal of the Constituante. In the records of even the most confidential discussions not a trace can be found of any suggestion for the suppression of other parties.[1]

. . . .

It was little more than two months since Trotsky had joined the Bolshevik party, and his leading position in its inner councils was firmly established. The first Politbureau, elected before the insurrection, never came to life. It was replaced by a smaller body, 'the Bureau of the Central Committee', an Executive in permanent session, which consisted of four men: Lenin, Trotsky, Stalin, and Sverdlov.[2] When the coalition with the Left Social Revolutionaries was consummated, the Council of the People's Commissars elected an inner cabinet in which the Bolsheviks were represented by the same men, with the exception of Sverdlov who held no office in the government. Lenin and Trotsky were generally recognized as the party's chief policy-makers and supreme authorities in matters of doctrine. Stalin and Sverdlov were the chief organizers.

The relationship between Lenin and Trotsky was one of mutual confidence, cordiality, and respect, though not of personal intimacy. Their common struggle against the moderate Bolsheviks, before and especially after the insurrection, the hatred with which their enemies honoured both of them, demanding the exclusion of both from any coalition government, their agreement on all major issues—all this bound the two men with the strongest of ties. Underneath this concord there was still a discord in temperament and habit. Lenin's manner was unassuming and almost impersonal, even in the exercise of power. He mistrusted the colourful gesture and word. For about two decades he had been surrounded by many devoted followers, whom he had led by the sheer strength of his intellect

[1] *Protokoly Tsen. Kom.*, pp. 180–91.　　　[2] Ibid., p. 189.

and character. He had acquired a mastery in judging the merits and the faults of his colleagues and subordinates and in handling them with the greatest advantage to the party. Blunt and even ruthless in serious controversy, he was otherwise reserved, tactful, and careful to spare his followers' susceptibilities and weaknesses, and open-minded to their ideas and suggestions.

Trotsky's volcanic passion and his mighty language stirred the souls of the people in a way in which Lenin's incisive didactic prose never did. Now, when they were once again united in a common cause, Lenin listened to Trotsky's overflowing tirades with approval and even with admiration, but also with something of that uneasiness with which the muzhik listened to urban grandiloquence. The contrast in their temperaments extended to other qualities as well. The many years of political free-lancing had left their traces on Trotsky. He did not possess the habits of free and easy teamwork which make the strength of a real leader of men. Lunacharsky, even when he still looked up to Trotsky with intense admiration, dwelt emphatically on this feature, saying that Trotsky had never succeeded in organizing any stable group of followers.[1] He was imperious and wrapped up in himself. It is all the more remarkable that in the next few years he proved himself so great and brilliant an administrator. His administrative achievement, however, was due not to his management of men but to the clarity and precision of his schemes, to his drive and will-power, and to his systematic method of work. The capacity for systematic work, in which he surpassed Lenin, was rare in a country where people attached little value to time or to steady effort. His present close partnership with Lenin was based on certain personal adjustments as well as on common purpose. With indubitable sincerity he acknowledged Lenin's leadership. He did so without a hint of sycophancy and without renouncing his own independence, but with distinct remorse for his past mistake in underrating Lenin as a revolutionary and leader. Lenin, on his part, did his best to make Trotsky feel in the party as if he had always been in it and of it. In the course of the six years of their partnership, years which brought a number of new disputes, Lenin made not a single allusion to their past controversies, except to say privately that in some respects Trotsky had

[1] Lunacharsky, *Politicheskye Siluety*, pp. 25–30.

been right and to warn the party, in his will, that it ought not to hold his non-Bolshevik past against Trotsky.

The two other men in the 'Bureau of the Central Committee' were of quite different stuff. Sverdlov was Stalin's actual predecessor as the party's General Secretary—nominally the office had not yet been created. Like Stalin, he had spent all his political life in the underground. He had the same gift for organization, the same flair for handling men, the same empirical mind, and the same firmness of character.[1] More happy than Stalin in his role of organizer, cherishing no ambition to shine as an authority in matters of doctrine, Sverdlov possessed, however, if one may judge from his few writings and speeches, an intellect broader, more cultivated and flexible than Stalin's; and he was vastly more articulate.[2] It was he who, in Lenin's absence, had introduced Trotsky to the inner life of the party, had made him *au fait* with its military organization and facilitated Trotsky's co-operation with the various grades of the Bolshevik caucus. Sverdlov, we know, had also proposed Trotsky's appointment as Commissar of Foreign Affairs. While Trotsky's relations with Sverdlov were those of an easy comradeship, his first closer contacts with Stalin were quite different. He himself wrote later that he was hardly aware of Stalin's existence until after the October Revolution.[3] Yet Stalin had been the editor of the party's paper and one of the most important members of the Central Committee. If it was true that Trotsky overlooked him, as it were, this would point not so much to the unimportance of Stalin's role, which Trotsky was out to prove, as to Trotsky's own lack of interest in the personal influences that were at work in the party he had joined. Stalin was not a spectacular personality. Reserved, inarticulate, at times vulgar, he did not catch Trotsky's eye, because Trotsky was inclined to look in other people for the qualities which distinguished himself. With more excuse he repeated a mistake he had once made about Lenin: Stalin's 'greyness' concealed from him Stalin's strength. He continued to treat his future rival with an unintentional yet all the more hurtful haughtiness, even after Stalin

[1] Sadoul mentions that the Bolsheviks nicknamed Sverdlov '*la ferme gueule*', op. cit., p. 266.

[2] This emerges clearly from Sverdlov's private correspondence published in *Pechat i Revolutsia*, vol. ii, 1924.

[3] Trotsky, *Stalin*, pp. 242–3 and *passim*.

had become his colleague in the smallest group which managed the party's and the government's affairs. It is hardly surprising that Stalin's pride was stung.

Personal feelings and barely incipient jealousies were as yet of no importance. Amid the turmoil and the raptures of these months, the Bolshevik leaders lived as if in an ecstatic dream which might suddenly and tragically fade. They held on to, and tried to consolidate, positions of power in which for the time being there seemed to be no power at all; but they half-expected that in the process they themselves might go under and that the revolution would then roll over their dead bodies to ultimate triumph. 'If we both are killed by the White Guards', Lenin once said to Trotsky, 'do you think that Sverdlov and Bukharin will be able to carry on?'[1] In the meantime they were issuing proclamations, decrees, and laws, more for the historical record than for immediate execution. If the worst came to the worst, they thought and said, they would at least bequeath to their successors a set of ideas, a restatement of revolutionary policy, which would inspire others as the message of the Commune of Paris had inspired two generations of Socialists. In this seemingly impractical manner, the Bolshevik leaders were actually laying the foundations of the Soviet republic.

The external circumstances in which they carried out this task conformed to the idealistic purpose. It would be an understatement to say that the founders of the new state had around them none of the paraphernalia and nothing of the pomp of power. They did not possess even the simple facilities for work which could be found in the most modest of business offices. At the Smolny a typewriter was a rarity, stenographers a myth, and the telephone a delightful technical amenity. The new rulers wrote their momentous proclamations and decrees with their own hands. They ran to one another's offices through a maze of corridors. They lunched and supped at the Smolny's canteen on thin cabbage soup and black bread. And most of them lived and slept in their tiny offices, amid the endless tumult, the comings and goings of messengers and agitators, the trampling of soldiers' boots, the alarums, the panics, the enthusiasms, the *Tohu-wabohu* of dying and nascent worlds. Their offices were already guarded by volunteers from the Red

---

[1] Trotsky, *Moya Zhizn*, vol. ii, p. 60.

Guards; but they were always accessible to the humblest worker, sailor, and journalist. To this circumstance we owe innumerable descriptions of the Trotsky of the Smolny period. Here is a typical impression, given by an American journalist:

During the first days of the Bolshevik revolt, I used to go every morning to Smolny to get the latest news. Trotsky and his pretty little wife, who hardly ever spoke anything but French [to foreign journalists], lived in one room on the top floor. The room was partitioned off like a poor artist's attic studio. In one end were two cots and a cheap little dresser and in the other a desk and two or three cheap wooden chairs. . . . Trotsky occupied this office all the time he was Minister of Foreign Affairs and many dignitaries found it necessary to call upon him there. . . . every little difficulty under the sun was brought to Trotsky. He worked hard and was often on the verge of a nervous breakdown: he became irritable and flew into rages.[1]

Before the insurrection Trotsky had lived as a sub-tenant in a middle-class block of flats, where he and his family were surrounded by intense hatred. 'Trotsky appears tired, nervous . . .', writes Sadoul. 'Since 20 October he has not been in his home. His wife, nice, small, militant, fresh, vivacious and charming, says that their neighbours threatened to kill her husband. . . . Is it not amusing to think that this pitiless dictator, this master of all the Russias, dare not sleep in his home for fear of the broom of his concierge?'[2]

[1] Louise Bryant, *Six Red Months in Russia*, p. 145.
[2] Sadoul, op. cit., p. 94.

CHAPTER XI

The Drama of Brest Litovsk

'THIS government would consider it the greatest crime against humanity if the war were to be continued solely in order to decide which of the strong and wealthy nations should dominate the weak ones.... This government solemnly declares its resolution to conclude at once a peace ... equally just to all nations and nationalities without exception.'[1] In these words Lenin's peace decree, adopted on 26 October by the Congress of the Soviets, formulated the essence of Bolshevik foreign policy. Only that peace would be just that allowed all occupied and subject peoples, whether in Europe or on other continents, to determine their own fate in free votes, taking place after the withdrawal of all occupation armies. Having put forward this bold peace aim, which could be attained only through the overthrow of all colonial empires, Lenin cautiously added that the Soviets were prepared to join in peace talks even if their programme was not accepted—they were willing to consider any alternative terms. For itself, the Bolshevik government stood for open covenants openly arrived at; and it would therefore publish and declare null and void the secret imperialist treaties concluded by previous Russian governments. This message, as Lenin explained to the Congress, appealed to the governments as well as the peoples of the belligerent countries. Implicitly, it called on the peoples to rise against the existing governments, and expressly it urged those governments to arrange an immediate armistice. The central dilemma of Bolshevik foreign policy and the germ of the Brest Litovsk tragedy were contained in this double appeal.

War-weary Russia received the decree on peace with a gasp of relief. The governments and the patriotic opinion of France and Britain replied with an outcry of indignation. The allied ambassadors and the heads of allied military missions in Russia had been more or less aware of Russia's incapacity to wage war.[2]

---

[1] Lenin, *Sochinenya*, vol. xxvi, p. 218.

[2] M. Paléologue, *La Russie des Tsars*, vol. iii, pp. 265, 280, and *passim*, Sir George Buchanan, *My Mission to Russia*, vol. ii, p. 228 and *passim*. As early as on 1 April 1917, i.e. before Lenin's arrival in Russia, Paléologue watched a parade in which

The Bolshevik peace propaganda, as an American observer put it, 'was indeed urgent and active, but . . . it was much the case of a man blowing with his breath in the same direction with a full grown natural tornado'.[1] Yet in their desire to avert Russia's 'defection', the allied envoys almost persuaded themselves that the tornado would die down if only the Bolsheviks stopped blowing. Almost from the beginning of the February Revolution the British and the French ambassadors urged Prince Lvov, Miliukov, and Kerensky to suppress Lenin's party.[2] The heads of their military missions hopefully encouraged Kornilov to stage his coup against Kerensky and the Menshevik Soviets.[3] Two days before the October insurrection, the British Ambassador in quite undiplomatic language pressed the Russian Ministers for Trotsky's immediate arrest.[4] Now when the Bolsheviks were in power, their revolutionary appeals, their disregard of diplomatic form, and their threat to publish and declare null and void the secret treaties and to withdraw Russia from the war, brought the hostility of the allies to a head. Their envoys were so bewildered by the upheaval they had witnessed and at such a loss to account for it that they were inclined to accept any crime story purporting to offer an explanation. They were half-convinced that Lenin and Trotsky were in fact Germany's bought agents and that it was German officers who had so efficiently and smoothly directed the October insurrection.[5] One consolation was left—that the Bolsheviks would soon be overthrown; and that it was the duty of the allied powers to speed up that moment.[6]

only the least revolutionized troops took part, and he noted in his diary that even these most loyal detachments were completely unwilling to fight. Even earlier, in March 1917, Paléologue sent a report to Ribot, the French Foreign Minister, which he concluded with the following significant sentence: 'In the present phase of the revolution Russia can make neither peace nor war.' Thus the French Ambassador anticipated Trotsky's formula by nearly a year.

[1] W. Hard, *Raymond Robins' Own Story*, p. 29. Later, when they were in exile, most leaders of the anti-Bolshevik parties agreed with this view.

[2] Paléologue, op. cit., vol. iii, pp. 245–7, and *passim*. Buchanan, op. cit., vol. ii, p. 11, 119 and *passim*.

[3] Major General Sir Alfred Knox, *With the Russian Army 1914–1917*, vol. ii, p. 692; A. Kerensky, *The Crucifixion of Liberty*, pp. 295–319.   [4] Buchanan, ibid., p. 203.

[5] Sir George Buchanan wrote in his diary: 'Information has now reached me, though I am unable to vouch for its accuracy, to the effect that there are six of their officers [i.e. German officers] attached to Lenin's staff in the Smolny Institute.' Ibid., p. 232; Knox, op. cit., vol. ii, p. 718.

[6] Sadoul claims that it was under the inspiration of allied diplomatic circles that

Despite their revolutionary appeals, the Bolsheviks were anxious to enter into diplomatic contact with the allies. No sooner had they routed Kerensky's troops than Trotsky suggested the resumption of normal relations to the British and the French.[1] The Bolsheviks, and Trotsky more than others, reckoned with the possibility that the Germans might, by dictating unacceptable peace terms, force Russia back into the war and into the Entente. Trotsky's suggestion fell on deaf ears. The allied embassies ignored him. Only the Belgian Minister paid him a reconnoitring visit in that little partitioned room in the Smolny. Trotsky's manner, as he was explaining his government's peace aims to the incredulous envoy, was 'a little firm, a a little haughty', but courteous. The Belgian Minister went away impressed by Trotsky's personality and by his sincerity, but also convinced that the revolution's Foreign Secretary was an ideologue and dreamer, not to be taken seriously; and thus he described him to colleagues.[2]

Not only the foreign embassies but also the staff of the Russian Ministry of Foreign Affairs met Trotsky with a boycott. It was only a week after his appointment, the week taken up by the fighting against Kerensky's troops, that he first appeared at the ministry, accompanied by Markin, a sailor from Kronstadt. He was eager above all to get hold of the secret treaties and the diplomatic correspondence of his predecessors. But the offices and the corridors of the ministry were deserted—there was not a soul to answer his questions. At length, his sailor friend found the permanent head of the ministry, Count Tatishchev, descendant of a long line of diplomats. The Count declared that the employees of the ministry had failed to come to work. Trotsky threateningly ordered him to assemble at once the whole staff, and in no time a crowd of officials came to report. Trotsky briefly introduced himself as their new chief, told them that no force on earth could undo the revolution and that those of them who wanted honestly to serve the new government could do so. But the officials refused to hand over the secret documents and the keys to the safes containing them. Trotsky left the ministry. A little later his sailor friend returned and ordered Tatishchev and

the Mensheviks made the exclusion of Lenin and Trotsky a condition for the formation of a coalition government, op. cit., p. 74.

[1] Sadoul, op. cit., p. 77.   [2] Ibid., pp. 77–80.

the heads of the departments to follow him to the Smolny—where he placed them under arrest. Two days later the Count conducted Trotsky over the ministry, opened all safes, and sorted out and handed over the secret treaties and the diplomatic correspondence. To the alarm of the diplomatic chancelleries, the treaties soon began to appear in print. They confirmed all too clearly the Bolshevik accusations: Russia had been fighting the war in order to conquer Galicia and Constantinople and to dominate the Balkans.[1]

On 7 November, Lenin, Stalin, and Krylenko ordered General Dukhonin, Kerensky's last Chief of Staff, to propose an immediate cease fire to the German command. Trotsky addressed his first formal message to the allied ambassadors, asking them to consider the decree on peace, which he enclosed, as a formal proposal for the immediate opening of peace negotiations. 'Accept, Mr. Ambassador', he concluded, 'assurances of the Soviet Government's profound respect for the people of your country, which cannot but strive for peace, as do all the other peoples, exhausted and bled white by the unparalleled slaughter.'[2] On the same day he reviewed for the first time the diplomatic scene at the Central Executive of the Soviets. 'The routine-ridden mind of bourgeois Europe', startled by the decree on peace, treated it as a statement of party policy rather than an act of statesmanship. The first reaction of the Germans was ambivalent: as Germans they rejoiced at the offer of peace; as Conservatives they were afraid of the revolution which was making the offer. Official Britain was unmistakably hostile. The French were war-weary, but 'the *petite bourgeoisie* of France considers us as a government allied to the German Kaiser'. Italy responded enthusiastically; the United States tolerantly. Far from lumping together all shades of foreign opinion, Trotsky drew careful and precise distinctions between them. Then he announced the publication of the secret treaties. He granted that the central powers would try to benefit from the disclosures, but the Soviets had to give an example to others, especially the German working class, of how to treat the secret bargains and compacts of their ruling classes. He hoped that when the German Social Democrats obtained access to the diplomatic safes of their governments and published their secret treaties, the world would

[1] Trotsky, *Sochinenya*, vol. iii, book 2, pp. 97–99.   [2] Ibid., p. 157.

see that 'German imperialism, in its cynicism and banditry, was in no way inferior to the banditry of the allies'.[1] 'The peoples of Europe', thus he inaugurated the publication of the secret treaties on the next day, 'have paid with numberless sacrifices and universal impoverishment for the right to know this truth. The elimination of secret diplomacy is the very first condition for an honest, popular, truly democratic foreign policy.'[2]

The allied ambassadors held a conference at which they decided to ignore Trotsky's message and to advise their governments to leave it unanswered on the ground that the Soviet régime was illegitimate. The allied governments accepted the advice and decided to establish formal relations only with the Supreme Command of the Russian army, that is with General Dukhonin, who had his headquarters at Moghilev. By this act they elevated, as it were, Army Headquarters to the status of a rival government. They also warned Dukhonin against any parleying for a cease fire; and they clearly hinted that if Russia withdrew from the war, they would retaliate by a Japanese attack on Siberia.[3] Trotsky at once protested against these moves and threatened to arrest any allied diplomats who might try to leave Petrograd in order to attach themselves to anti-Bolshevik forces in the provinces; and he appealed to the neutral diplomats to use their influence for peace. On the same day, General Dukhonin, who had in any case refused to carry out the cease fire order, was deposed—he was brutally murdered later by his own soldiers when they learned that he was bent on continuing the war. The Bolshevik Krylenko, who had been an ensign in the Tsarist army and one of the leaders of the party's military branch, was appointed Commander in Chief.

The relations between Russia and the Entente at once assumed the bitterness which foreshadowed the wars of intervention. It could not have been otherwise. Given the determination of the allied powers to continue the war, their ambassadors could not but use their influence against a government which threatened to withdraw Russia from the war. This alone inevitably led to their interference in Russia's domestic affairs. The fundamental hostility of the old school of diplomats and

<hr />

[1] Trotsky, *Sochinenya*, vol. iii, book 2, p. 161.   [2] Ibid., pp. 164–5.
[3] J. Noulens, *Mon Ambassade en Russie Soviétique*, vol. i, p. 145; John W. Wheeler-Bennett, *The Forgotten Peace*, p. 71.

soldiers towards the revolution gave to that interference an unscrupulous and spiteful appearance. In the circumstances the allied embassies and military missions tended from the beginning to become participants in the Russian civil war.[1] Trotsky tried to counteract this trend and to prevent the British, the French, and the Americans from committing themselves irrevocably. With Lenin's consent he did what he could to impress on them that it was in their interest that Russia should not feel completely abandoned and driven to sign any peace with Germany, regardless of terms. To this consideration the Entente paid little or no attention. Its ambassadors maintained unofficial contacts with Trotsky through junior members of their staffs, Captain Sadoul of the French military mission and Bruce Lockhart of the British Embassy. It was to these officials, and to Colonel Robins of the American Red Cross, that Trotsky made his proposals and protests; and through them he kept the allies informed about the preliminary armistice talks. Each of the allied officials in touch with him was converted to Trotsky's view and hopefully went to convert his superiors; but nothing came of it. 'We persist in denying that the earth turns,' so Sadoul, at this time still an unrepentant 'social patriot', wrote to Albert Thomas, one of the chief exponents of French 'social patriotism', 'we go on claiming that the Bolshevik government does not exist.' Bruce Lockhart was reprimanded from London for treating Trotsky as seriously as if he were 'another Talleyrand'.[2]

On 14 November the German High Command agreed to negotiate an armistice. Krylenko ordered the cease fire and 'fraternization on the fronts', hoping that through contact with the Russian troops the German army would become infected with revolution. On the same day Trotsky notified the western powers:

Ensign Krylenko, the Supreme Commander of the armies of the republic, has proposed delaying the opening of the armistice talks for five days until 18 November/1 December so that it may once

[1] In the Second World War the western powers, confronted by the defection of France, also intervened in French domestic affairs. While Russia's withdrawal from the war in 1917–18 was inspired by revolutionary elements, it was under Conservative, right-wing leadership that France withdrew in 1940. A comparative study of allied policy in these two cases would reveal striking similarities and differences. It would also show more clearly to what extent the anti-Bolshevik policy of the Entente was a reaction against the defection of an ally and to what extent it was prompted by class antagonism.

[2] Sadoul, op. cit., p. 127; Lockhart, *Memoirs of a British Agent*, pp. 197, 226–31.

again be proposed to the allied governments to define their attitude. . . . We, the Council of the People's Commissars, put this question to the governments of our allies . . . we are asking them in the face of their own peoples, in the face of the whole world: do they agree to join us in the peace talks on 1 December? We . . . appeal to the allied peoples and above all to their working masses: do they agree to drag on this senseless and purposeless slaughter and to rush blindly towards the doom of European civilization? . . . The answer should be given now, in deeds not words. The Russian army and the Russian people neither can nor will wait any longer. . . . If the allied peoples do not send their representatives, we alone shall negotiate with the Germans. We desire a universal peace, but if the bourgeoisie of the allied countries compels us to conclude a separate peace, the responsibility for this will rest totally on the bourgeoisie. Finally, we appeal to the soldiers of the allied countries to act and not to lose a single hour: Down with the winter campaign! Down with the war![1]

In a report to the Petrograd Soviet, Trotsky added: 'We shall in no case allow the principles of universal peace, proclaimed by the Russian revolution, to be distorted. . . . Under popular pressure, the German and Austrian governments have already agreed to place themselves in the dock. You may rest assured that the prosecutor, in the person of the Russian revolutionary peace delegation, will be equal to his task and in due time pronounce the thunderous accusation of the diplomacy of all imperialists.'[2]

Such was the unprecedented style which he introduced into diplomacy. Even as Foreign Secretary he remained the revolution's chief agitator. He staked almost everything on the potential or actual antagonism between the rulers and the ruled; and he spoke to the former so that the latter might hear him. But, since he did not exclude the possibility of an understanding with the existing governments, he combined his revolutionary appeals with extremely flexible and subtle diplomacy. Irreconcilable and mordantly aggressive when confronted with hostility, he responded to any conciliatory gesture with tact and politeness. When General Judson, head of the American military mission, breaking the allied boycott, paid him a visit and expressed the hope that the allies would use no more threats against the Soviets, Trotsky answered that he had no desire to quarrel over bygones, that he was satisfied with the general's

---

[1] Trotsky, *Sochinenya*, vol. iii, book 2, pp. 173–5.   [2] Ibid., p. 179.

declaration; and he repeated the assurance that he would conduct the peace negotiations openly and publicly so that the allies
could watch them closely and join in later, if they so desired.[1] But
when General Niessel, head of the French military mission, who
had been accustomed to talk down to Russian ministers and
generals in their palatial offices—France had been Russia's chief
creditor and political inspirer—appeared in the 'poor artist's
attic' at the Smolny, confident that here he could afford to speak
even more haughtily, Trotsky quite unceremoniously turned
him out. He ordered the French Embassy to close down its
press bureau, which published bulletins offensive to the Soviet
government.[2] When Noulens, the French Ambassador, came to
the Smolny to smoothe out the conflict, Trotsky was all politeness and helpfulness. His first business with the British was to
demand the immediate release of Chicherin, the former correspondent of *Nashe Slovo*, and of other Russian revolutionaries
imprisoned in Britain for anti-war propaganda. When the
British continued to keep Chicherin in jail, he notified them
that until his demand was satisfied no British citizen would be
allowed to leave Russia.[3] With firmness and dignity quite unknown to recent Russian governments, Trotsky insisted on
Russia's equality with other powers, and answered insult with
insult, although even his insults took the form of reasoned and
persuasive argument.

On 19 November the armistice delegations met, and the
Germans at once proposed a preliminary truce of one month.
The Soviet delegation refused this and asked instead for the
prolongation of the cease fire for one week only so as to give the
western powers time to consider the situation. Once again
Trotsky turned to the allied embassies; and once again he met
with icy silence. Yet he instructed the Soviet negotiators to
sign no truce unless the central powers undertook not to transfer
any troops from the Russian to the western fronts, and—this was
a quite extraordinary condition—unless they expressly allowed
the Soviets to conduct revolutionary agitation among German

[1] Ibid., p. 185.   [2] Noulens, op. cit., vol. ii, p. 27.
[3] 'There is, after all', the British Ambassador noted in his diary, 'something in
Trotsky's argument that, if we claim the right to arrest Russians for making
pacifist propaganda in a country bent on continuing the war, he has an equal right
to arrest British subjects who are conducting war propaganda in a country bent on
peace.' Buchanan, op. cit., vol. ii, p. 228.

and Austrian troops. General Hoffmann, German Supreme Commander on the Russian front, rejected both demands. For a moment it seemed that the negotiations were breaking down and that Russia was back in the war. Facing once again his old audience at the Cirque Moderne, Trotsky declared that the Soviets would go on demanding an armistice on all fronts. 'But if we are compelled alone to sign the armistice, then we shall tell Germany that the transfer of troops from the Russian to other fronts is impermissible, because we are proposing an honest armistice and because England and France must not be crushed. . . . And if, because of these open, direct and honest statements the Kaiser refuses to sign a peace . . . the peoples will see who is right, and . . . we shall feel like victors not like vanquished, for there are victories other than the military ones . . . If France and Germany . . . do not join us in the peace talks, their peoples will drive their governments to join us, they will drive them with sticks.'[1]

On the same day, 3 December, he reported to the All-Russian Congress of Peasant Soviets: 'There was another point giving rise to serious conflict: the condition that no troops must be transferred to the western front. General Hoffmann declared that this was inacceptable. The problem of peace was on a knife edge. In the course of the night we instructed our delegates: make no concession. Oh, I shall never forget that night! Then Germany made the concession and committed herself not to transfer any troops, except those already under way. . . . We have our representatives with the staffs of the German army who will watch whether these terms are observed.' Displaying a map showing German troop movements in the two months preceding the revolution, he went on: 'While Kerensky was still in office and dragged on the war, the German General Staff could well afford to switch troops. . . . Now, thanks to us, the allies are in a more advantageous position.'[2] The German command no doubt treated this condition as make-believe and had no intention of observing it; but events were to show that Trotsky's words were not an empty boast.[3]

[1] Trotsky, *Sochinenya*, vol. iii, book 2, pp. 185–9.
[2] Ibid., p. 199.
[3] Mr. Wheeler-Bennett, in his excellent history of the Brest Litovsk peace, written from the Entente's viewpoint, thus sums up its results: 'But a victor's peace must be enforced. A million troops immobilized in the east was the price of German

So far all the great issues arising from the armistice had been left open. The Bolsheviks and the Left Social Revolutionaries had made up their minds in favour of separate peace talks, but not of a separate peace. And even those who, like Lenin, already inclined towards a separate peace were not yet prepared to have it at any price. The main purpose of the Soviet government was to gain time, to proclaim loudly its peace aims amid the sudden stillness on the front; to gauge the intensity of the revolutionary ferment in Europe; and to test the attitude of allied and enemy governments.

The Bolsheviks had no doubt about the proximity of social upheaval in Europe. But they began to wonder whether the road to peace would lead through revolution or whether, on the contrary, the road to revolution did not lead through peace. In the first case, the war would be brought to an end by revolutionary governments. In the second, the Russian Revolution would have to come to terms for the time being with capitalist rulers. Only time could show which way events were moving and to what extent the revolutionary impulse from Russia determined or failed to determine their direction. So far the soundings had produced no clear results. The German and the Austrian working classes were unmistakably restless; but it could not be said whether this pointed to the enemy's immediate collapse or towards a crisis in a more remote future. The peace delegations of the central powers had shown a surprising readiness to yield. Their attitude might reflect the desperate position of the central powers; but it might also conceal a trap. On the other hand, the hostility of the Entente seemed to relax for a moment. While still refusing to recognize the Soviets, the allied powers, at the beginning of December, consented to exchange certain diplomatic privileges which are usually granted to recognized governments. Soviet diplomatic couriers were allowed to move between Russia and western Europe; diplomatic passports were mutually recognized; Chicherin was at last released and returned to Russia; and Trotsky exchanged diplomatic visits with some western envoys. Was the Entente perhaps changing its mind about peace? In *Pravda*, Trotsky wishfully commented on these

aggrandizement, and half that number might well have turned the scale in the early stages of the battle of giants which was raging in the west.' Op. cit., p. 327.

events as 'symptoms pointing to the possibility of a general armistice and universal peace'.[1]

That he should have drawn such far-fetched conclusions from what were, after all, details of the diplomatic game, must be explained by a basic mistake in his reading of the strategic prospects. Early in the war, when governments and general staffs were taking an early conclusion of hostilities for granted, he had rightly forecast the protracted stalemate of trench warfare.[2] He had been inclined to believe that neither camp could break the stalemate resulting from the equilibrium of opposed forces. The events of more than three years had so strikingly confirmed this forecast that he clung to it even now, when the premiss for it was about to vanish. The United States had entered the war. But this did not cause Trotsky to modify his view; and after the revolution, as before, he reiterated that neither of the hostile camps could hope to win. From this rigid assumption it seemed logical to conclude that at length the belligerent governments might realize the futility of further fighting, acknowledge the deadlock, and agree to open peace negotiations. This was the reasoning which made him jump to a conclusion about the possibility of an imminent 'general armistice and universal peace'.

At the same time, however, the Bolsheviks feared that the Entente might conclude a separate peace with Germany and Austria and strike jointly at the Russian Revolution. More than anybody, Lenin voiced this apprehension in public and private. The inner story of the war, when it was revealed, showed that this was not quite groundless. Germany and Austria had repeatedly and secretly, jointly and separately put out peace feelers to their enemies in the West.[3] In the ruling classes of France and Britain the fear of revolution was mounting; and the possibility of an accommodation between the Entente and the central powers, an accommodation prompted by that fear, could not be ruled out in advance. This was a potential threat only; but it was enough to drive Lenin to the conclusion that only separate peace in the East could forestall separate peace in the West.

---

[1] Trotsky, *Sochinenya*, vol. iii, book 2, pp. 210–11.
[2] See Chapter viii, p. 229.
[3] D. Lloyd George, *War Memoirs*, vol. ii, chapter lxx; Richard von Kühlmann, *Erinnerungen*, pp. 475–87.

To sum up, the Bolsheviks were enmeshed in the following intertwined dilemmas: They had to resolve whether they could wait for peace until the revolution had spread; or whether they would try to spread the revolution by concluding peace? If the road to European revolution were to lead through peace, would it be universal or separate peace? And if the terms of a separate peace were to prove so onerous and humiliating as to be unacceptable, could they wage a revolutionary war against Germany? If driven to war, could they, as a matter of principle, accept assistance from the Entente? And would the Entente be willing to grant them assistance? If not, should they strive for separate peace at any price? Or was there perhaps some way of escaping these dilemmas?

On 8 December, the day before the inauguration of the actual peace talks at Brest Litovsk, Trotsky addressed a joint session of the government, the Central Executive of the Soviets, the Soviet and town council of Petrograd, and leaders of trade unions. This was one of his most remarkable speeches, not only because of its rhetorical excellence and its soaring revolutionary humanitarian ethos, but also because it vibrated with his own mental wrestlings:

Truly this war has demonstrated man's power and resilience, which enables him to endure unheard of sufferings. But it has also shown how much barbarity is still preserved in contemporary man. . . . He, king of nature, has descended into the trench-cave, and there, peeping out through narrow holes, as from a prison cell, he is lurking for his fellow man, his future prey. . . . So low has mankind fallen. . . . One is oppressed by a feeling of shame for man, his flesh, his spirit, his blood, when one thinks that people who have gone through so many phases of civilization—Christianity, absolutism, and parliamentary democracy—people who have imbibed the ideas of socialism, kill each other like miserable slaves under the whip of the ruling classes. Should the war have this outcome only that people return to their mangers, to pick the miserable crumbs thrown from the tables of the propertied classes, should this war finish with the triumph of imperialism, then mankind would prove itself unworthy of its own sufferings and of its own prodigious mental effort, which it has sustained over thousands of years. But this will not happen—it cannot happen.

Having risen in the land of Europe's former gendarme, the Russian people declares that it desires to speak to its brothers under arms . . .

not in the language of guns, but in that of international solidarity of the toilers. . . . This fact cannot be eliminated from the mind of the popular masses . . . of all countries. Sooner or later they will hear our voice, they will come to us and stretch out a helpful hand. But even if . . . the enemies of the people were to conquer us and we were to perish . . . our memory would still pass from generation to generation and awaken posterity to a new struggle. To be sure, our position would have been much easier if the peoples of Europe had risen together with us, if we had to parley not with General Hoffmann and Count Czernin but with Karl Liebknecht, Klara Zetkin, and Rosa Luxemburg. This has not happened. And we cannot be blamed for that. Our brothers in Germany cannot accuse us of having communed with the Kaiser, their sworn enemy, behind their backs. We are talking to him as to an enemy—we do not soften our irreconcilable hostility to the tyrant.

The truce has brought a pause in hostilities. The booming of guns has been silenced, and everybody is anxiously waiting to hear in what voice the Soviet government will talk with the Hohenzollerns and Habsburgs. You must support us in this that we should talk with them as with freedom's enemies . . . and that not a single atom of freedom should be sacrificed to imperialism. Only then will the genuine meaning of our strivings penetrate deeply into the consciousness of the German and Austrian peoples.

This appeal was followed by a curious passage in which he was thinking aloud before his large audience and gave free rein to his hesitation and indecision. 'If the voice of the German working class . . . does not exercise a powerful and decisive influence . . . peace will be impossible', he stated abruptly. Then came a second thought: 'But if it should turn out that we had been mistaken, if this dead silence were to reign in Europe much longer, if this silence were to give the Kaiser the chance to attack us and to dictate terms insulting to the revolutionary dignity of our country, then I do not know whether—with this disrupted economy and universal chaos entailed by war and internal convulsions—whether we could go on fighting.' As if feeling that his audience was stunned by his cry of despair, he turned abruptly and exclaimed: 'Yes, we could.' This brought forth stormy applause. Spurred on by the response, he added: 'For our life, for our revolutionary honour, we would fight to the last drop of our blood.' Here the verbatim report records 'a new outburst of applause'. The audience, which consisted of the leading groups of the two governmental parties, thus demonstrated its emotional opposition to separate peace.

'The weary and the old ones', Trotsky continued, 'would step aside . . . and we would create a powerful army of soldiers and Red Guards, strong with revolutionary enthusiasm. . . . We have not overthrown the Tsar and the bourgeoisie in order to kneel down before the German Kaiser.' If the Germans were to offer an unjust and undemocratic peace, then 'we should present these terms to the Constituent Assembly and we should say to it: make up your mind. If the Constituent Assembly accepts such terms, the Bolshevik party will step aside and say: Look for another party willing to sign such terms. We, the Bolsheviks, and I hope the Left Social Revolutionaries too, would summon all peoples to a holy war against the militarists of all countries.' It hardly entered his mind that one day the Left Social Revolutionaries would rise against the Bolsheviks with the cry for this 'holy war,' and that he himself would then suppress them. 'If in view of the economic chaos', he concluded, 'we should not be able to fight . . . the struggle would not be at an end: it would only be postponed, as it was in 1905, when Tsardom crushed us but we lived to fight another day. That is why we have joined in the peace negotiations without pessimism and without black thoughts. . . .'[1] His speech worked up his audience into an exalted state similar to that in which before the insurrection the crowds of Petrograd repeated after him the words of the revolutionary oath.

The negotiations at Brest Litovsk began on 9 December. The representatives of the central powers let it be known that they 'agreed to conclude immediately a general peace, without annexations and indemnities'.[2] Yoffe, who headed the Soviet delegation, asked for another pause of ten days to give the western powers once again time to change their minds. During the pause, only the commissions of the peace conference were in session, and their work proceeded with strange smoothness. The real negotiations were not to begin till 27 December, when Trotsky arrived. In the meantime the Council of the People's Commissars took a number of demonstrative steps. It intensified its propaganda against German imperialism; and Trotsky,

---

[1] Trotsky, *Sochinenya*, vol. iii, book 2, pp. 211-17.
[2] *Mirnye Peregovory v Brest Litovske*, p. 9.

assisted by Karl Radek who had just arrived in Russia, edited
Die Fackel (*The Torch*), which was distributed in the German
trenches. On 13 December the government allocated two million
roubles for revolutionary propaganda abroad, and it publicized
the fact. On the 19th it started the demobilization of the Russian
army. It also freed German and Austrian prisoners of war from
compulsory labour, allowing them to leave the camps and to
organize and work as free citizens. It declared null and void
the Russo-British treaty of 1907, under which Persia had been
partitioned between the two powers; and on 23 December it
ordered Russian troops to evacuate northern Persia. Finally,
Trotsky instructed Yoffe to demand that the peace negotiations
be transferred from Brest Litovsk to Stockholm, or any other
place in a neutral country.

Exactly two months after the insurrection, on 24 or 25 December, Trotsky set out for Brest Litovsk. On the way, especially
in the area of the front, he was greeted by delegations from local
Soviets and trade unions which urged him to speed up the
negotiations and to return with a peace treaty. He was astounded
to find that the trenches on the Russian side of the front were
almost empty: the soldiers who had manned them had dispersed.
A German liaison officer who conducted him across the front
noticed the fact and reported to his superiors that Trotsky 'grew
ever more and more depressed'.[1] He did indeed become acutely
and painfully aware that it was without any armed strength
behind him that he would have to confront the enemy. He was
all the more determined to wield his 'weapons of criticism'.
With him travelled Karl Radek, whose luggage bags were packed
with revolutionary pamphlets and leaflets, and as soon as their
train stopped at Brest Litovsk, Radek, before the eyes of the
diplomats and officers assembled on the platform to greet them,
began to distribute the pamphlets among German soldiers.
A Polish Jew, nominally an Austro-Hungarian subject, Radek
had gained fame as a radical, sharp-witted pamphleteer in the
German Social Democratic party. His appearance at Brest, as
a member of the Russian delegation, could not but scandalize
the German and Austrian diplomats. It was intended to demonstrate that the revolution championed the cause of a class, not
of a nation, and that the mere notion of an 'enemy national'

[1] Count Ottokar Czernin, *In the World War*, p. 232.

was alien to it. Trotsky had asked Radek to accompany him, because, as he told Sadoul, 'he had confidence in his very lively intelligence and political loyalty and was convinced that the intransigence and *élan* of this energetic, passionate man would act as a tonic for the Yoffes, Kamenevs, and other softer Russian delegates'.[1]

The scene of the meeting was desolate and grim. The town of Brest Litovsk had early in the war been burnt and razed to the ground by retreating Russian troops. Only the old military fortress was intact; and in it was the general headquarters of the eastern German armies. The peace delegations were housed in drab blocks and huts within the compound. The officers' mess served as the conference hall. The place had the air of a Prussian barrack transferred to the Polish-Ukrainian plain. Enclosed by barbed wire, surrounded by sentries, amid the routine bustle of a military establishment, the Russian delegates might have felt like inmates of an internment camp. The Germans had insisted that the negotiations should be held there, partly for their own convenience and partly in order to humble the Soviet envoys. But they had also put on several layers of velvet glove. Before Trotsky's arrival, the delegations had supped and dined together; had been received by Prince Leopold of Bavaria, the nominal Commander in Chief; and had exchanged various other courtesies. It was ironical that those who exchanged the courtesies were, on the one hand, titled members of the German and Austrian aristocracies, and, on the other, professional agitators, recent convicts, among them a Left Social Revolutionary woman-terrorist, Bitsenko, who had assassinated a Tsarist Minister of War and had served a sentence of forced labour. The insinuating sociability of the Germans and Austrians did not fail to disconcert even the leading Bolshevik delegates. Yoffe, Kamenev, Pokrovsky, Karakhan, seasoned and well educated revolutionaries, showed at the conference table something of the awkwardness natural in novices to diplomacy. Throughout the first phase of the parleys, when Yoffe acted as chief Soviet delegate, the conference was completely dominated by Kühlmann, the German Foreign Minister.

Trotsky arrived dissatisfied with this state of affairs. On Lenin's insistence, he had undertaken this mission in order to

[1] Sadoul, op. cit., p. 176.

give quite a different aspect to the conference. At the outset, he frigidly rejected an invitation to meet Prince Leopold, and he put a stop to all hobnobbing. 'With Trotsky's appearance here', General Hoffmann remarked, 'the easy social intercourse outside the conference hall has ceased. Trotsky has requested that the delegations be served their meals at their quarters and has generally forbidden any private contact and entertainment.'[1] 'The wind seems to blow in a very different direction than it did until now', Czernin, the Austrian Foreign Minister, noted in his diary.[2] A diplomat of the other side had only to approach Trotsky with jovial flattery or a gesture of familiarity to make him stiffen and bristle. Appearances had to conform to the realities: he had come to negotiate with enemies, not with friends.

The first session, at which he replaced Yoffe as chief of the Russian delegation, was held on 27 December. Kühlmann opened it with a statement that the principle to which the central powers had agreed—'peace without annexations and indemnities'—had been intended for a general peace only. As the western powers had refused to join in the negotiations and only a separate peace was on the agenda, Germany and her allies were no longer bound by that principle.[3] He rejected the Soviet demand for negotiations in a neutral country; and he assailed Soviet propaganda against German imperialism, which, he said, raised doubts whether the Soviets sincerely desired peace; but he wound up on a conciliatory tone. Then General Hoffmann, a pile of Soviet proclamations to German soldiers in front of him, repeated the protest on behalf of the German Supreme Command. The Austrian, Turkish, and Bulgarian diplomats spoke in the same vein. Trotsky, taking the measure of his adversaries, listened with a faintly ironical smile; and, without answering the charges, asked for a day's break.

Among his adversaries three figures stood out. Kühlmann, a Bavarian Catholic and traditionalist, one of the shrewdest diplomats of Imperial Germany, was not devoid of personal charm, some open-mindedness, and courage. Earlier than the Kaiser's other servants, he had come to reckon with Germany's defeat in a war on two fronts; and he was anxious to obtain in

---

[1] *Die Aufzeichnungen des Generalmajors Max Hoffmann*, vol. ii, pp. 206–7.
[2] Czernin, op. cit., p. 232.   [3] *Mirnye Peregovory*, p. 45.

the East a peace profitable to his government but not too obviously imposed on Russia. Perhaps alone among Germany's rulers, he realized that a dictated peace would amount to a defeat for Germany: it would forewarn other nations what they had to expect from German victory and would stiffen their resistance. The Supreme Command bitterly opposed Kühlmann's policy. In the eyes of Hindenburg and Ludendorff he was little better than a traitor; and they did their utmost to discredit him. He was therefore compelled to defend himself behind the scenes against the military, while he was engaged in his open duel with Trotsky. Both the military and he appealed to the Kaiser as supreme arbiter. The Kaiser backed now his diplomat and now his generals, but at heart he was with the latter, allowing them to overrule his civilian government. Kühlmann had enough character not only to defy Ludendorff, but to disregard, on one occasion, the Kaiser's blunt order to break off the negotiations. His differences with the military, nevertheless, concerned the manner rather than the matter: he was at one with them in wishing to secure for Germany the Polish and Baltic lands conquered from Russia. But he was anxious to obtain the appearance of Russian consent; and the weakness of his position, as it revealed itself later, was that he could not obtain it. He also wished to disguise the German annexation of those lands as their liberation. The generals had neither the time nor the patience for such subtleties.

General Hoffmann was supposed to be the Supreme Command's eye, ear, and strong arm at the conference table. It was his business to bring the talks to a speedy conclusion and to release the eastern armies of the central powers for the last, all-out offensive in the West. Every now and then he voiced his irritation and impatience with Kühlmann's method. But more sophisticated than his superiors and more in touch with the impact of the revolution, he could not gainsay that Kühlmann's method had its merits. He sometimes yielded to Kühlmann and then brought Ludendorff's thunders upon his own head.[1]

Count Czernin, the Austrian Foreign Minister, acted Kühlmann's brilliant second. Even more acutely than his German

---

[1] Trotsky mistakenly treated Hoffmann as the authentic voice of the German Supreme Command, and this may have contributed to his underrating later the German readiness to renew hostilities against Russia.

colleague, he was aware of the catastrophe which hung over the central powers. From the secret treaties which Trotsky had published, he knew that the allies had marked down the Austro-Hungarian empire for dismemberment. With starvation in Vienna and revolt among the subject nations, the empire had begun to crumble already; only by draining strength from Germany did it prolong its days. Czernin was therefore in a real panic whenever it seemed to him that Hoffmann's blunt intervention lessened the chances of peace. At first he threatened his German colleagues with separate negotiations, but, as his government was becoming every day more dependent on German help, he abandoned the threat. He still tried to act the soft-spoken mediator although he was more than a little frightened by the 'clever and very dangerous adversary [as he described Trotsky] . . . exceptionally gifted, with a swiftness and adroitness in retort which I have rarely seen'.[1] In his spare hours, Czernin read memoirs on the French Revolution, trying to find a historical yardstick for the 'dangerous adversary'; and he wondered whether a Russian Charlotte Corday was not already lurking for Trotsky.

Czernin, it seems, was alone in indulging in such meditations and looking for historical parallels. His colleagues at first viewed Trotsky and the other Russian delegates as petty adventurers, obscure upstarts or, at best, quixotic creatures, whom a quirk of destiny had thrown on the stage to act a very brief, grotesque episode in the world's drama, in which they, the great servants of two illustrious dynasties, were among the chief characters. They were sure that they would buy the Russian delegates with small favours; but they wanted first to put them in their places. This they tried to do at their first meeting with Trotsky; and they adopted the same tactics at the next session. They set against the Soviet delegation the Ukrainians, who claimed to represent independent Ukraine and denied Petrograd's right to speak for all the Russias.

Such was the interplay of interests, personalities, and ambitions into which Trotsky wedged himself, when, on 28 December, he addressed the conference for the first time. He brushed aside the Ukrainian intrigue. The Soviets, he declared, had no objection to the Ukraine's participation in the parleys; they had proclaimed

[1] Czernin, op. cit., pp. 234–5.

the right of all nationalities to self-determination; and they meant to respect that right. Nor did he question the credentials of the Ukrainian delegates, who represented the *Rada*—a provincial replica or rather parody of the Kerensky régime. Kühlmann once again tried to provoke an open quarrel between the Russians and the Ukrainians, which would have allowed him to become the *tertius gaudens*, but once again Trotsky avoided the pitfall. Turning to the charges and protests of the previous day, he refused to make any apology for the revolutionary propaganda which the Soviets conducted among German troops. He had come in order to discuss peace terms, Trotsky said, not in order to limit his government's freedom to express its views. The Soviets raised no objection to the counter-revolutionary propaganda which the Germans spread among Russian citizens. The revolution was so confident of its case and of the appeal of its ideals that it welcomed an open argument. This gave the Germans no ground to question Russia's desire for peace. It was Germany's sincerity that must be doubted, especially when the German delegation declared that it was no longer bound by the principle of a peace without annexations and indemnities. 'We, on our part, think it necessary to state that the principles of a democratic peace which we have proclaimed have not, in our eyes, become null and void after ten days . . . For us they are the only conceivable basis for the co-existence and co-operation of peoples.'

He renewed the protest against holding the conference in the artificial isolation of the Brest fortress. The German Chancellor had told the Reichstag that in a neutral country the conference would be exposed to allied machinations. 'The job of protecting the Russian government from hostile machinations', Trotsky remarked, 'belongs exclusively to the Russian government.' 'We are confronted by an ultimatum: either parleys at Brest Litovsk or no parleys at all', an ultimatum prompted by the German sense of power and conviction of Russia's weakness. 'We neither can deny nor intend to try to deny that our country has been weakened by the policy of its recent ruling classes. But the place of a country in the world is determined not only by the present condition of its technical apparatus, but also by the potentialities inherent in it.' He was not going to measure the economic strength of Germany, whose population was starving, by the present state of Germany's food stocks. The central powers tended to base the peace not 'on agreement between the peoples, but on the so-called war map. This tendency is equally perni- cious to the German and to the Russian peoples, because the war maps change and the peoples remain.' Yet—'we stay here, at Brest Litovsk, in order not to leave unexplored a single chance of peace . . . in order to learn, here at the headquarters of the eastern front, clearly and precisely whether a peace . . . is now possible without violence towards the Poles, Lithuanians, Lat- vians, Estonians, Armenians, and other peoples, to whom the Russian revolution has guaranteed the full right of self-deter- mination'. But the conference could continue on one condition only, namely that the negotiations should be held in public throughout; and Trotsky refused to engage in private talks, for which Kühlmann had asked, believing that Trotsky's defiant statement was merely meant as face-saving.[1]

Two days later the delegations discussed a German draft of the peace treaty. At the outset a little incident seemed to trans- fer the sedate diplomats of the central powers into the atmo- sphere of a Shavian comedy. A preamble to the treaty contained the respectable cliché that the contracting parties desired to live in peace and friendship. The authors of the draft could not expect this to give rise to objections. They were mistaken. 'I would take the liberty', Trotsky said, 'to propose that the second phrase [about friendship between the contracting pow- ers] be deleted. Its thoroughly conventional, ornamental style does not correspond, so it seems, to the dry business-like sense of the document.'[2] Half-amused and half-scandalized, the pro- fessional diplomats could not see the point: Was Trotsky speaking seriously? And how could he dismiss so lofty a state- ment as ornamental and conventional? 'But such declarations', Trotsky pertly went on, 'copied from one diplomatic document into another, have never yet characterized the real relations between states'; he could only hope that more serious factors would shape these relations in the future. For a moment the diplomats felt as if they had been told that their emperors and they themselves were naked. What were those 'more serious factors'? And what formula would Trotsky propose? He could give them his formula, Trotsky said, but they would not accept

[1] *Mirnye Peregovory*, pp. 52–60. [2] Ibid., p. 66.

it anyhow. The comic wrangle went on for a while, and the words about friendship disappeared from the draft.

Then followed a dramatic argument, centred on the principle of self-determination and dealing with the fate of the nations situated between Russia and Germany. The argument, mainly between Trotsky and Kühlmann, occupied many sessions and took the form of a conflict between two interpretations of self-determination. Both sides pursued the argument in the tone of a seemingly dispassionate, academic debate on legal, sociological, and historical themes; but behind these themes loomed the realities of war and revolution, occupation and annexation. Convinced that Trotsky was merely seeking to dress up Russia's surrender, Kühlmann seemed anxious to provide Trotsky, and himself even more, with decorous formulas, and to present the German annexation of Poland and the Baltic States as self-determination for these. To his perplexity, Trotsky thrust aside all attempts at face-saving and insisted on the facts of annexation. Kühlmann made his case with a systematic, relentless, yet subtle logic, the only defect of which was that it summed up the wisdom of a Conservative statesman in the face of the ungovernable phenomenon of revolution. Trotsky stood before the conference as the embodiment of that phenomenon, endowed with a logic even more relentless and subtle and with a quick and deadly wit from which there was no escape. He himself obviously revelled in his own wry and sardonic humour which made General Hoffmann growl and sent him into a huff, while the rest of the delegates quivered with suppressed laughter. Trotsky once begged the general to remember that the differences in their views were due to deeper discrepancies in their outlooks: he, the head of the Russian delegation, was still under the prison sentence which a German court had passed on him for anti-war propaganda. The general suddenly saw himself in the role of a jail-bird's partner, and, feeling as if all his medals had been torn off his chest, he withdrew from the exchange. When Kühlmann asked him whether he had anything more to say, Hoffmann angrily snapped back: 'No, enough.'

Almost every paragraph in the draft treaty contained the statement of a noble principle and also its negation. One of the first clauses provided for the evacuation of the occupied territories. This did not prevent Kühlmann from declaring that

Germany intended to occupy the territories seized from Russia until a general peace, and indefinitely even after it. Kühlmann also argued that Poland and the other German-occupied countries had achieved self-determination, because the Germans had installed native governments everywhere. No country, Trotsky retorted, can determine its fate while it is held by foreign troops—'as a preliminary foreign troops must clear out of the territories in question'. Politely, and without calling anyone names, yet unmistakably, he made it clear that what the Germans had installed were puppet administrations.

As the argument became involved and apparently abstract, Trotsky switched from Russian to German. Kühlmann was in his element with juridical-diplomatic formulas and imprudently provoked further debate. 'When, according to the Chairman of the Russian delegation', he asked, 'does a nation come into existence as a single entity?' If it cannot come into existence under foreign occupation, then when and how does the moment of birth arise? Grateful for the new opportunity to restate his case, Trotsky began to answer the puzzling question by the method of elimination. What is certain is that no nation is independent as long as it is occupied and possesses only an administration whose title to govern rests on the presence of foreign troops. The final criterion is the will of the people, freely and democratically expressed in a referendum. Finland, evacuated by Russian troops, was a case in point. In the Ukraine 'the process of self-determination was still in progress'. But, Kühlmann pointed out, a government so created meant a break in legal continuity; and to the Conservative way of thinking legal continuity is alpha and omega. Trotsky reminded the German Minister, that any occupying power breaks legal continuity and does so without the justification with which a revolution does it. Kühlmann adroitly retorted that, if revolution claims for itself no basis in law, then it is based solely on force and accomplished fact. This seemed to knock the bottom out of Trotsky's argument: if he admitted the point, he had no ground for protest against the accomplished facts of German annexation. The crux of Trotsky's answer lay in the distinction which he drew between a force emerging from inside a nation to determine its fate and an outside force imposing its will.

The controversy had thus developed into a clash of *Weltan-*

schaungen, a contest of opposed moral and historical philosophies. Every phase of this contest was reported and misreported all over the world. The occupied nations whose future was at stake listened with bated breath. At one point Kamenev prompted Trotsky to explain that in denying so forcefully Germany's right to keep these nations in subjection, he was not claiming that right for Russia, as any traditionalist Russian diplomat would have done. 'We undertake the obligation', Trotsky declared, 'not to coerce these countries directly or indirectly into accepting this or that form of government, not to infringe their independence by any customs or military conventions. . . . And I should like to know whether the German and the Austro-Hungarian delegations are in a position to make statements to the same effect. . .?'

This brought the debate back to the burning issues. Kühlmann answered that the governments of the German-occupied countries had the right to conclude any agreement they wished; they were even entitled to cede territory to the occupying powers. On Kühlmann's part this was an act of self-exposure, into which Trotsky had skilfully enticed him. 'The assertion of the Chairman of the German delegation', said Trotsky, clinching the argument, 'that these people [the puppet governments] are entitled to conclude pacts and agreements and to cede territories is a full and categorical denial of the principle of self-determination.' The central powers had not invited the governments of the occupied countries to Brest; and this alone revealed that they treated them as dependencies with no will of their own. 'In the conventional language which we use in such cases this is described, not as self-determination of the peoples, but by quite a different expression . . . annexation. . . .'[1]

Trotsky had undoubtedly out-argued his adversary. Yet the argument was somewhat inconclusive, and precisely because of its subtlety it had less effect upon German opinion than Trotsky was inclined to believe. It could not, at any rate, greatly appeal to the German workers and soldiers whom he was out to revolutionize; and therein consisted the weakness of this part of his performance. Only when General Hoffmann, eager to clothe himself in the spoils of Achilles, intervened, did the debate become at once more popular and, from the Bolshevik

---

[1] *Mirnye Peregovory*, pp. 84–85; Kühlmann, op. cit., pp. 524–32.

standpoint, politically fruitful. 'The Russian delegation', the general, freeing himself from Kühlmann's restraints, burst out, 'has spoken as if it represented a victorious invader of our country. I should like to remind its members that the facts point to the contrary: victorious German troops are on Russian soil. I should further like to say that the Russian delegation demands that we should recognize the right to self-determination in a form and on a scale which its own government does not recognize. . . . The German Supreme Command thinks it necessary to repudiate its interference in the affairs of the occupied areas.' Hoffmann refused to enter into any discussion on evacuation.

This was Trotsky's field day. Ironically he asked Hoffmann whether he represented the Supreme Command only or the German government; and the allusion was received with a great deal of *Schadenfreude* by Kühlmann and Czernin. If, as the general claimed, the most important fact was where whose troops stood, then the Russians, who held Austrian and Turkish territory, should talk with the Austrians and the Turks in a tone different from the one they used with the Germans; but they were not going to do so. Trotsky welcomed Hoffmann's brutal remarks about Bolshevik domestic policy, for he himself had invited his adversaries to speak on this without inhibition. 'The General was quite right when he said that our government based itself on force. In history hitherto we have known no government dispensing with force. . . . I must, however, categorically pro-test against the completely untrue statement that we have outlawed all those who do not think as we do. I should be very happy to know that the Social Democratic press in Germany enjoys the freedom which our adversaries and the counter-revolutionary press enjoy in our country.' (At this stage this comparison did in fact still work in favour of the Soviets.) 'What in our conduct strikes and antagonizes other governments is the fact that we place under arrest not workers who come out on strike but capitalists who declare lock-outs on workers, that we do not shoot peasants demanding land, but arrest the landlords and the officers who try to shoot the peasants.'[1] He pointed to a contradiction between Kühlmann's and Hoffmann's arguments. The former had claimed that the German-occupied lands already had more or less independent governments, while

[1] *Mirnye Peregovory*, p. 102.

the latter tried to justify indefinite German occupation by the fact that they had no administration of their own. Yet from their different arguments both the general and the *Staatssekretar* drew the same conclusion, which went to show that 'legal philosophy had quite a subordinate place in their decisions on the fate of living peoples'.[1]

The effect of this exposure was devastating. Hoffmann noted in his diary: 'My speech actually made a smaller impression than I expected.'[2] Kühlmann lost his temper and regretted that he had allowed himself to be tempted into open diplomacy.[3] Later he tried to efface the aftertaste of Hoffmann's intervention and to excuse the latter's 'soldierly bluntness'. The excuse, Trotsky remarked, confirmed that the differences between the military and the civilians in the enemy camp were a matter of form, not of substance. 'As for ourselves, members of the Russian delegation, our record is there to show that we do not belong to the diplomatic school. We ought rather to be considered as soldiers of the revolution. We prefer—I shall admit this frankly —statements which are definite and clear in every respect.'[4]

On 5 January, Trotsky asked for a break in the conference so that he might acquaint his government with the German demands. The conference had already lasted nearly a month. Much time had been gained; and now party and government had to take a decision. As he travelled back to Petrograd, Trotsky stared again at the Russian trenches, the very emptiness of which seemed to cry out for peace. But now he knew better than ever that the price of peace was Russia's and the revolution's utter prostration and discredit. At Brest, reading the German and Austrian Socialist newspapers, he had been shocked to see that some of these treated the peace conference as a prearranged spectacle, the outcome of which was in no doubt. Some German Socialists believed that the Bolsheviks were in fact the Kaiser's agents, and even those who did not doubt Lenin's and Trotsky's integrity viewed their policy as a 'psychological puzzle'. The desire to lift the stigma from the

---

[1] In an aside, Trotsky turned to Kühlmann, who had quoted in his support a decision of the Supreme Court of the United States after the War of Independence. Herr *Staatssekretar*, Trotsky said, would have been truer to character if he drew inspiration from the jurisdiction of George III rather than from that of George Washington.   [2] Hoffmann, op. cit., vol. ii, p. 209.
[3] *Mirnye Peregovory*, pp. 100–4.   [4] Ibid., pp. 133–4.

party was among the most important motives which guided Trotsky's conduct at the conference table.[1] It now seemed as if his efforts had not been quite fruitless. Peace demonstrations and strikes had at last begun in the enemy countries; and from Berlin and Vienna came loud protests against Hoffmann's attempt to dictate terms. The Soviets, so Trotsky concluded, must not accept these terms. They must go on biding their time and try to establish between themselves and the central powers a state which would be neither war nor peace. With this conclusion he reached the Smolny, where he had been eagerly and tensely awaited.

His return coincided with the conflict between the Soviet government and the Constituent Assembly, at last convoked. Against the expectations of the Bolsheviks and their associates, the Right Social Revolutionaries commanded a majority. The Bolsheviks and the Left Social Revolutionaries decided to disperse the Assembly; and they did so after the latter had refused to ratify Lenin's decrees on land, peace, and the transfer of power to the Soviets. The dispersal was at first justified by the specious argument that the elections had been held under an obsolete law, so construed under Kerensky as to give undue weight to the well-to-do minority of the peasantry. The paradox which made it possible for the Bolsheviks to emerge as the majority in the Soviets and remain a minority in the Assembly has been discussed in a previous chapter. The real reason for the dispersal was that the rule of the Assembly was incompatible with the rule of the Soviets. Either the Assembly or the October Revolution had to be undone. Trotsky was wholeheartedly for the dispersal, and he repeatedly defended the deed in speech and writing, assuming unqualified moral responsibility for it.[2] Since 1905–6 he had stood for proletarian dictatorship in Soviet form, and when he had to choose between that dictatorship and parliamentarianism he knew no hesitation. In the event itself, however, he played no role. The Assembly was dispersed on 6 January before his return to Petrograd. When he arrived, on the 7th, he and Lenin had a moment of anxiety

[1] See Trotsky's preface to *Mirnye Peregovory v Brest Litovske*.
[2] See the chapter on the Constituent Assembly in *The Defence of Terrorism*, pp. 41–45. Also *Tretii Vseross. Syezd Sovietov*, pp. 17, 69–70.

because the adherents of the Assembly seemed on the point of organizing a strong popular protest against the dispersal. But the protest fizzled out inconsequentially—only much later, during the civil war, was a 'movement for the Constituante' started on the Volga.[1]

On 8 January, two days after the dispersal of the Assembly, the Central Committee was completely absorbed in the debate on war and peace; and in order to sound the party's mood it conducted the debate in the presence of Bolshevik delegates who had arrived from the provinces for the third Congress of Soviets. Trotsky reported on his mission and presented his conclusion: neither war nor peace. Lenin urged the acceptance of the German terms. Bukharin spoke for 'revolutionary war' against the Hohenzollerns and Habsburgs. The vote brought striking success to the adherents of revolutionary war, the Left Communists as they were called. Lenin's motion for immediate peace received only fifteen votes. Trotsky's resolution obtained sixteen. Thirty-two votes were cast in favour of Bukharin's call for war.[2] Since outsiders had taken part, however, the vote was not binding on the Central Committee.

The whole Bolshevik party was soon rent between those who advocated peace and those who stood for war. The latter had behind them a large but confused majority and they were powerfully reinforced by the Left Social Revolutionaries, none of whom favoured peace. But the war faction was not sure of its case. It was stronger in voicing opposition to the peace than in urging resumption of hostilities.

At the next session of the Central Committee, on 11 January, the war faction bitterly attacked Lenin. Dzerzhinsky reproached him with timidly surrendering the whole programme of the revolution, as Zinoviev and Kamenev had surrendered it in October. To accept the Kaiser's *Diktat*, Bukharin argued, would

---

[1] Antonov-Ovseenko describes this incident almost humorously. Lenin had received a report that the Right Social Revolutionaries were leading a demonstration 100,000 strong to the Tauride Palace. Trotsky's wife had seen the demonstrators and estimated their number at 20,000. Lenin and Trotsky nervously ordered Antonov-Ovseenko to disperse the demonstration if need be. Antonov led a regiment to the Tauride Palace but found nobody to disperse. 'The adherents of the Assembly had come, had made a glorious noise, and had disappeared like Chinese shadows. There had been no more than 5,000 demonstrators in all.' Antonov-Ovseenko, *Zapiski o Grazhdanskoi Voinie*, vol. i, pp. 18–19.

[2] *Protokoly Tsen. Kom.*, p. 200.

be to stab in the back the German and Austrian proletariat—
in Vienna a general strike against the war was just in progress.
In Uritsky's view, Lenin approached the problem 'from a
narrow Russian and not from an international standpoint', an
error of which he had been guilty in the past. On behalf of the
Petrograd organization, Kossior repudiated Lenin's attitude.
The most determined advocates of peace were Zinoviev, Stalin,
and Sokolnikov. As in October, so now, Zinoviev saw no ground
for expecting revolution in the West; he held that Trotsky had
wasted time at Brest; and he warned the Central Committee
that Germany would later dictate even more onerous terms.
More cautiously, Stalin expressed the same view. Sokolnikov,
arguing that the salvation of the Russian Revolution was the
overriding consideration, foreshadowed in a curious epigram a
distant future change in the party's outlook. 'History clearly
shows', he said, 'that the salt of the earth is gradually shifting
eastwards. In the eighteenth century, France was the salt of the
earth, and in the nineteenth—Germany. Now it is Russia.'[1]

Lenin was sceptical about the outcome of the general strike
in Austria, to which Trotsky and the war faction attached so
much importance; and he drew a graphic picture of Russia's
military impotence. He admitted that what he advocated was
a 'shameful' peace, implying the betrayal of Poland. But he was
convinced that, if his government refused that peace and tried
to wage war, it would be wiped out and another government
would accept even worse terms. He disavowed, however, the
cruder arguments of Stalin and Zinoviev about the sacred
egoism of the Russian Revolution. He did not ignore the revolutionary potentialities of the West, but he believed that the peace
would hasten their development. The West was merely pregnant with revolution, while the Russian Revolution was already 'a healthy and loudly crying infant' whose life must be
safeguarded.

For the time being, Trotsky's formula provided a meeting
point for the opposed factions, although each at heart accepted
only that part of the formula that suited its purpose. The war
faction adopted it because it made peace impossible, while
Lenin and his group saw in it a means of keeping the war faction
at bay. Lenin was willing to let Trotsky try his hand once again

[1] *Protokoly Tsen. Kom.*, p. 206.

and play for time, especially as Trotsky was doing his best to impress the Left Communists with the unreality of revolutionary war. On Lenin's proposal, against Zinoviev's solitary vote, the Central Committee authorized Trotsky to delay by every possible means the signature of the peace. Trotsky then submitted his own resolution: 'We interrupt the war and do not sign the peace—we demobilize the army.' Nine members voted for this, seven against. Thus the party formally authorized Trotsky to pursue his policy at Brest.[1]

During this interval Trotsky also presented his report to the third Congress of Soviets. The mood of the Congress was so overwhelmingly in favour of war that Lenin kept in the background. Even Trotsky spoke more emphatically about his opposition to peace than about his opposition to war. 'The great speech of the evening', writes a British eye-witness, 'was made by Trotsky, whose report . . . was listened to with rapt attention. All eyes were upon him, for he was at the zenith of his influence . . . the man who incorporated the revolutionary will of Russia, speaking to the outer world. . . . When Trotsky had ended his great speech, the immense assembly of Russian workmen, soldiers and peasants rose and . . . solemnly sang the *Internationale*. The outburst [was] as spontaneous as it was soul-stirring to those who, like the writer, witnessed it. . . .'[2] The Congress unanimously approved Trotsky's report, but it took no decision and left the government a free hand.

Before Trotsky set out on his return journey to Brest, he made a private arrangement with Lenin which, in one point, modified essentially the decisions of the Central Committee and of the government. He promised that in certain circumstances he would abandon his own policy in favour of Lenin's. His tactics made sense as long as the Germans were willing to allow him to evade the choice between war and peace. What would happen, Lenin anxiously asked, if they chose to resume hostilities? Lenin was rightly convinced that this was bound to happen. Trotsky treated this danger lightly, but he agreed to sign the peace if Lenin's fears proved justified. That he and Lenin should have found it permissible so to depart from the formal decision of the Central Committee and of the government was due to the

[1] *Protokoly Tsen. Kom.*, pp. 199–207.
[2] M. Philips Price, *My Reminiscences of the Russian Revolution*, pp. 224–5.

ambiguity of that decision: the vote for 'neither war nor peace' had made no provision for the contingency which was uppermost in Lenin's mind. But their private arrangement, too, was ambiguous, as it turned out later. Lenin was under the impression that Trotsky had promised to sign the peace as soon as he was confronted with an ultimatum or a threat of a renewed German offensive. Trotsky held that he had obliged himself to accept the peace terms only after the Germans had actually launched a new offensive; and that even then he had committed himself to accept such terms only as the Central powers had so far offered, not the even worse terms which they dictated later.

By the middle of January Trotsky was back at the conference table in Brest. In the meantime the strikes and peace demonstrations in Austria and Germany had been suppressed or had come to a standstill; and his adversaries met him with new self-confidence. In vain did he, discarding formality, ask that German and Austrian Socialists be invited to Brest.[1] In vain did he ask for permission for himself to go to Vienna to contact Victor Adler, who had protested in the Austrian parliament against General Hoffmann's conduct at Brest. He was allowed, however, to pay a brief visit to Warsaw, where he was warmly acclaimed for his defence of Poland's independence.

Ukraine and Poland came to the fore in this part of the discussions. Behind the scenes Kühlmann and Czernin prepared a separate peace with the Ukrainian *Rada*. At the same time the Bolsheviks strenuously fostered a Soviet revolution in the Ukraine: the *Rada*'s writ still ran in Kiev, but Kharkov was already under a Soviet government; and a representative of the latter accompanied Trotsky on his return to Brest. Among the Ukrainian parties a curious reversal of attitudes occurred. Those who, under the Tsar and Kerensky, had stood for union or federation with Russia were now bent on separation. The Bolsheviks who had encouraged separatism now called for federation. Separatists became federalists and vice versa, not from motives of Ukrainian or Russian patriotism, but because they desired to separate from, or to federate with, the system of government prevalent in Russia. From this reversal of atti-

[1] The German government had just refused the Social Democratic leaders permission to go to Stockholm, whence they had intended to get in touch with the leaders of the Russian Revolution.

tudes the central powers hoped to benefit. By appearing as the protectors of Ukrainian separatism, they hoped to lay hands on the Ukraine's food and raw materials, of which they stood in desperate need; and also to turn the argument about self-determination against Russia. The *Rada*, weak, lacking self-confidence, on the verge of collapse, tried to lean on the central powers, despite the oath of loyalty it had sworn to the Entente. The *Rada*'s delegation consisted of very young, half-baked politicians—'*Bürschchen*', to quote Kühlmann[1]—who had just emerged from the backwoods and were intoxicated by the roles assigned to them in the great diplomatic game.

Even at this stage, Trotsky did not object to the *Rada*'s participation, but he served notice that Russia would recognize no separate agreements between it and the central powers. He also warned Kühlmann and Czernin that they overrated the strength of Ukrainian separatism. Then Lubinsky, the *Rada*'s delegate, launched a violent attack against Trotsky and the Soviet government, accusing them of trampling on the rights of the Ukraine and forcibly installing their own government in Kharkov and Kiev. 'Trotsky was so upset that it was painful to see', Czernin noted in his diary. 'Unusually pale, he stared fixedly in front of him. . . . Heavy drops of sweat trickled down his forehead. Evidently he felt deeply the disgrace of being abused by his fellow citizens in the presence of the enemy.'[2] Trotsky later denied that he was so greatly embarrassed, but Czernin's account seems credible. Trotsky certainly realized that his adversaries had succeeded up to a point in confusing the issue of self-determination. At heart he may have wondered whether the *Rada*'s spokesman was not justified in claiming that the Ukrainian Soviets were not representative of the Ukrainian people.[3] Not that Trotsky himself would have scrupled greatly about imposing Soviet rule on the Ukraine: the revolution could not be consolidated in Russia without its being extended to the Ukraine, which was wedged in deeply between northern and southern Russia. But here for the first time the interest of

---

[1] *Erinnerungen*, p. 531. [2] Czernin, op. cit., p. 246.

[3] This is inferred from a private message from Trotsky to Lenin, found in the *Trotsky Archives* at Harvard and written towards the end of the civil war. In that message Trotsky bluntly stated that the Soviet administration in the Ukraine had from the beginning been based on people sent from Russia and not on local elements. He then asked for a radical break with this method of government.

the revolution clashed with the principle of self-determination; and Trotsky could no longer evoke that principle with quite the same clear conscience with which he had evoked it hitherto.

He returned to the attack with the question of Poland, and asked why Poland was not yet represented at Brest. Kühlmann made the appearance of a Polish delegation dependent on Russia's prior recognition of the existing Polish administration. 'We have been asked again', Trotsky said, 'whether or not we acknowledge Poland's independence. . . . The question so posed is ambiguous. Do we acknowledge Ireland's independence? Our government does . . . but for the time being Ireland is still occupied by the British. We recognize that every human being has the right to food . . . which is not the same as recognizing the hungry man as sated.'[1] The recognition of Poland's right to independence did not imply the admission that she was independent under German-Austrian tutelage. Then Radek came forward with a telling indictment of German-Austrian domination of his native country: he spoke of the forced deportation of hundreds of thousands of Polish labourers to Germany; the appalling conditions in which this had taken place; political oppression; the imprisonment or internment of Polish political leaders of all parties, including the internment of Radek's old adversary Pilsudski, then commander of a Polish legion which had fought on Germany's and Austria's side, and Poland's future dictator.

In the middle of these exchanges, on 21 January, Trotsky received a message from Lenin about the downfall of the *Rada* and proclamation of the Soviet government all over the Ukraine.[2] He himself got in touch with Kiev, checked the facts, and notified the central powers that he no longer recognized the *Rada*'s right to be represented at the conference.

These were his last days at Brest. The mutual charges and recriminations had reached a point where the negotiations became barren and could not be much prolonged. In the intervals between the sessions he refreshed himself by writing *From February to Brest Litovsk*, one of his minor classics, a preliminary sketch for the monumental *History of the Russian Revolution* which he was to produce fifteen years later during his exile on Prinkipo Island. At last he sent a letter to Lenin in which he wrote: 'We

---

[1] *Mirnye Peregovory*, p. 162.   [2] Lenin, *Sochinenya*, vol. xxvi, p. 464.

shall declare that we end [the negotiations] but do not sign a peace. They will be unable to make an offensive against us. If they attack us, our position will be no worse than now. . . . We must have your decision. We can still drag on negotiations for one or two or three or four days. Afterward they must be broken off.'[1] Events did not allow him to wait for any new decision from Petrograd; and the vote taken before his departure had in any case given him enough latitude for the action he contemplated. Count Czernin still offered his services as mediator and even visited Trotsky in his lodging, warning him about the imminence of a new German offensive and begging him to state his final terms. Trotsky replied that he was prepared to bow to force, but would not give the Germans a testimonial of good moral conduct. Let them, if they so desired, annex foreign countries, but let them not expect the Russian Revolution to exonerate or embellish their acts of violence.

On the last day before the break, the central powers produced a *fait accompli*: they signed a separate peace with the *Rada*. 'We have officially informed the other side about the downfall of the *Rada*', Trotsky remonstrated. 'Nevertheless, the negotiations with a non-existing government continued. We then proposed to the Austro-Hungarian delegation—we did it in a private talk but in quite a formal manner—that they should send a representative to the Ukraine who would see for himself the *Rada*'s collapse . . . but we have been told that the signature of the treaty could not be delayed.'[2] General Hoffmann noted in his diary that Trotsky said that they were concluding a peace with a government whose territory extended no farther than its rooms at Brest Litovsk. Kühlmann self-righteously declared that German reports, 'the reliability of which was subject to no doubt, sharply contradicted this communication'.[3] This did not prevent General Hoffmann from remarking in his diary that 'according to reports that lay before me . . . there was unfortunately ground for regarding Trotsky's statement as not unfounded'.[4] The separate peace with the Ukraine served the central powers merely as a pretext for spreading their control to the Ukraine; and so in their eyes the credentials of their

---

[1] Trotsky confirmed to Mr. Wheeler-Bennett the authenticity of this letter. See *The Forgotten Peace*, pp. 185–6.   [2] *Mirnye Peregovory*, pp. 178–81.
[3] Ibid., p. 182.   [4] Hoffmann, op. cit., vol. ii, p. 213.

Ukrainian partners were irrelevant. It was precisely for this reason that Trotsky felt that he could not go on with the negotiations, for to do so would have meant to connive at the *coup* and at all that it entailed: the overthrow of the Ukrainian Soviets and the separation of the Ukraine.

On the next day, at a sub-commission, took place the famous scene at which General Hoffmann displayed a great map showing the full extent of the proposed German annexations. As Trotsky had said that he was 'prepared to bow to force' but would not help the Germans to keep up appearances, the general evidently believed that a blunt statement of German claims might be the short-cut to peace. When, on the same day, 28 January/10 February, the political commission reassembled, Trotsky rose to make his final statement:

> The task of the sub-commission . . . was to say to what extent the frontier proposed by the opposite side was capable of securing, be it in the slightest degree, the self-determination of the Russian people. We have heard the reports of our representatives and . . . the time for decision has come. The peoples wait with impatience for the results of the peace talks at Brest Litovsk. They ask when this unparalleled self-annihilation of mankind, provoked by the selfishness and lust for power of the ruling classes, is going to end? If either of the two camps has ever fought this war in self-defence, this has long since ceased to be true. When Great Britain seizes African colonies, Baghdad, and Jerusalem, she is not waging a defensive war. When Germany occupies Serbia, Belgium, Poland, Lithuania, and Rumania and seizes the Monsoon Islands, this is not a defensive war either. This is a struggle for the partitioning of the world. Now this is clear, clearer than ever.
>
> We do not want to take part any longer in this purely imperialist war, in which the claims of the possessing classes are openly paid for in human blood. . . .
>
> In expectation of the approaching hour when the working classes of all countries seize power . . . we are withdrawing our army and our people from the war. Our soldier, the tiller of the land, should go back to his land to till it this spring, the land which the revolution has taken from the landlord and given to the peasant. Our soldier, the worker, should return to the factory bench to turn out not tools of destruction but tools of construction and to build, together with the tiller of the land, a new socialist economy.

As they listened to these impassioned words, the delegates of the central powers were still ready to applaud Trotsky with a 'well roared, lion'. This, they hoped even now, was Trotsky's final roar, after which would come the whimper of surrender. Only gradually did the import of his statement dawn upon them, and then they became breathlessly aware that they were witnessing an act which in its tragic pathos, was unique in history.[1]

We are withdrawing from the war [Trotsky went on]. We announce this to all peoples and governments. We are issuing an order for the full demobilization of our army. . . . At the same time we declare that the terms proposed to us by the governments of Germany and Austro-Hungary are in fundamental conflict with the interest of all peoples. They are repudiated by the toiling masses of all countries, including the Austro-Hungarian and the German peoples. The peoples of Poland, Ukraine, Lithuania, Kurland, and Estonia feel in them the violence inflicted upon their aspirations. To the Russian people these terms are a permanent threat. The popular masses of the whole world, guided by political consciousness or moral instinct, repudiate them. . . . We refuse to endorse terms which German and Austro-Hungarian imperialism is writing with the sword on the flesh of living nations. We cannot put the signature of the Russian revolution under a peace treaty which brings oppression, woe, and misfortune to millions of human beings.[2]

'When the echoes of Trotsky's powerful voice died away', writes the historian of Brest Litovsk, 'no one spoke. The whole conference sat speechless, dumbfounded before the audacity of this *coup de théâtre*. The amazed silence was shattered by an ejaculation of Hoffmann: "*Unerhört*", he exclaimed, scandalized. The spell was broken. Kühlmann said something about the necessity of calling a plenary session of the conference, but this Trotsky refused, saying that there remained nothing to discuss. With that the Bolsheviks left the room, and in gloomy silence, still scarcely believing what they had heard and wholly at a loss as to what to make of it, the delegates of the Central Powers dispersed.'[3]

However, before the delegations had dispersed, something

---

[1] On the next day, Krüge, the chief German legal expert, told Yoffe that he had looked for historical precedents and found only one—in the remote antiquity of the wars between Persia and Greece. See Yoffe's memoir appended to *Mirnye Peregovory*, p. 262.

[2] *Mirnye Peregovory*, pp. 207–8.   [3] Wheeler-Bennett, op. cit., pp. 227–8.

happened, the full significance of which Trotsky missed—something which confirmed Lenin's worst fears. Kühlmann declared that in view of what had taken place, hostilities would be resumed, because Russia's demobilization was of no legal consequence—only her rejection of the peace mattered. Trotsky treated this as an empty threat; he did not believe, he replied, that the German and Austrian peoples would allow their governments to continue a war so obviously devoid of any defensive pretext. Kühlmann himself gave Trotsky some reason for dismissing the threat when he inquired whether the Soviet government was at least prepared to enter into legal and commercial relations with the central powers and in what way they could keep in touch with Russia. Instead of answering the query, as, from his own standpoint he ought to have done—this might have entailed a commitment by the central powers to respect the state of 'neither war nor peace'—Trotsky haughtily refused to discuss it.

He stayed on at Brest for another day and got wind of a quarrel between Hoffmann, who insisted on the resumption of hostilities, and the civilian diplomats, who preferred to accept the state of neither war nor peace. On the spot the civilians seemed to have carried the day. Trotsky was therefore returning to Petrograd confident and proud of his achievement. At this moment, the man stands before our eyes in all his strength and weakness. 'Single-handed, with nothing behind him save a country in chaos and a régime scarce established, [he] . . . who a year before had been an inconspicuous journalist exiled in New York, [had fought] successfully the united diplomatic talent of half Europe.'[1] He had given mankind the first great lesson in genuinely open diplomacy. But at the same time he allowed himself to be carried away by his optimism. He underrated his enemy and even refused to listen to his warning. Great artist that he was, he was so wrapped up in himself and in his ideal and so fascinated by the formidable appeal of his own work that he lightly overlooked its deficiencies. While Trotsky was still on his way to Petrograd, General Hoffmann, backed by Ludendorff, Hindenburg, and the Kaiser, was already issuing marching orders to the German troops.

The German offensive began on 17 February, and it met with

[1] Wheeler-Bennett, op. cit., p. 166.

no resistance.[1] 'This is the most comic war I have ever experienced', Hoffmann wrote, 'It is waged almost exclusively in
trains and cars. One puts on the train a handful of infantry-men
with machine guns and one gun, and one rushes to the next
railway station. One seizes that station, arrests the Bolsheviks,
entrains another detachment and travels farther.'[2] When the
news of the offensive reached Smolny, the Central Committee
of the party, after eight votes, failed to agree on a way out of the
situation. The Committee was equally divided between the
adherents of peace and the advocates of war. Trotsky's single
vote could resolve the deadlock. Indeed, during this and the
next day, 17 and 18 February, he and he alone could make the
momentous decision. But he refused to join either faction.

His position was extraordinarily complex. He had so behaved
and spoken that many identified him with the war faction; and
politically and morally he did in fact stand closer to it than to
Lenin's faction. But he had also made the private promise to
Lenin that he would support peace, if and when the Germans
resumed military operations. He still refused to believe that this
moment had arrived. On 17 February he voted with the adherents of war against Lenin's proposal for an immediate request for new peace negotiations. He then voted with the peace
faction against revolutionary war. And finally he submitted his
own motion, advising the government to hold up new negotiations
until the military and political results of the German offensive
had become clear. As the war faction voted with him, his motion
was passed by a majority of one vote, his own. Lenin then posed
the question whether peace should be concluded if it turned out
that the German offensive was a fact and if no revolutionary
opposition to it developed in Germany and Austria. The Central
Committee answered the question in the affirmative.[3]

Early next morning, Trotsky opened a session of the Central
Committee with a survey of the latest events. Prince Leopold
of Bavaria had just broadcast to the world that Germany was
defending all nations, including her western enemies, from the
infection of Bolshevism. German divisions from the western front
were reported to have appeared in Russia. German aviation

---

[1] From now on all dates are given according to the European calendar, which
was adopted in Russia on 14 February 1918.
[2] Hoffmann, op. cit., vol. i, p. 187.   [3] *Protokoly Tsen. Kom.*, pp. 226–9.

was active over Dvinsk. An attack on Revel was anticipated. All this pointed towards a full-scale offensive, but the facts were not yet established. Prince Leopold's broadcast indicated a possibility of collusion between Germany and the Entente, but no more than a possibility. Lenin urgently renewed his proposal for an immediate approach to Germany. 'We must act', he said, 'we have no time to lose. It is either war, revolutionary war, or peace.' Trotsky, wondering whether 'the offensive might not bring about a serious explosion in Germany', still held that it was too early to sue for peace. Once again Lenin's proposal was rejected by the majority of one vote.

Between the morning and the evening of this day, 18 February, a dramatic change occurred. When Trotsky opened the evening session of the Central Committee, he reported that the Germans had already seized Dvinsk and that there were widespread rumours of an imminent offensive in the Ukraine. Still hesitant, he proposed to sound the central powers about their demands but not to request peace negotiations. 'People will not understand this', Lenin answered, 'If there is war we should not have demobilized'. This was 'joking with war', which might lead to the collapse of the revolution. 'We are writing papers and in the meantime they [the Germans] are seizing rolling stock. . . . History will say that you have delivered the revolution [to the enemy]. We could have signed a peace which was not at all dangerous to the revolution.' Sverdlov and Stalin spoke in the same vein. 'If they open a hurricane fire for five minutes', Stalin said, 'we shall not be left with a single soldier on the front. . . . I disagree with Trotsky. To pose the question as he does is all right in literature.' Yet Zinoviev, the most extreme advocate of peace, now had his qualms. Lenin was for peace even if it entailed the loss of the Ukraine, but Zinoviev would not go as far as that.[1]

Thrice Trotsky spoke against suing for peace, and thrice he proposed only tentative soundings. But when Lenin once again presented his motion, Trotsky to everybody's surprise voted not

---

[1] Of this session two records are available. According to one, Zinoviev argued for peace, saying that the Bismarck tradition of co-operation with Russia was not yet dead in Germany and that the Germans had just as vital an interest in the peace as the Russians. It is curious to see how many of the future *leitmotifs* of Soviet foreign policy appear fleetingly and inchoately in these hurried debates. *Protokoly Tsen. Kom.*, p. 242.

for his own proposal, but for Lenin's. With the majority of one vote the peace faction won. The new majority asked Trotsky and Lenin to frame the message to the enemy governments. Later that night the Central Committees of the two ruling parties, the Bolshevik and the Left Social Revolutionary, met; and at this meeting the war faction once again had the upper hand. But in the government the Bolsheviks outvoted their partners; and on the next day, 19 February, the government formally sued for peace.

Four days of suspense and panic passed before the German answer reached Petrograd. In the meantime nobody could say whether or on what terms the central powers would agree to reopen negotiations. Their armies were on the move. Petrograd was exposed. A committee of revolutionary defence was formed in the city, and Trotsky headed it. Even while they were suing for peace, the Soviets had to prepare for war. Trotsky turned to the allied embassies and military missions to inquire whether, if the Soviets re-entered the war, the western governments would help them. He had made such soundings before, but without effect.[1] But this time the British and the French seemed more responsive. Three days after he had sent off the request for peace, Trotsky reported to the Central Committee (in Lenin's absence) an Anglo-French suggestion for military co-operation. To his mortification, the Central Committee rejected this out of hand and so repudiated his action. Both factions turned against him: the adherents of peace—because they feared lest the acceptance of allied help compromise the chances of separate peace; and the adherents of war—because the same motives of revolutionary morality, by which they were actuated in opposing a compact with Germany, militated also against co-operation with 'the Anglo-French imperialists'. Trotsky then declared that he was resigning from the Commissariat of Foreign Affairs. He could not stay in office if the party did not see that a Socialist government

[1] Colonel Robins relates that in January Trotsky proposed that American officers should go to the front and help to stop the leakage of Russian goods to Germany and to remove stocks of raw materials to the interior of the country. Trotsky then said that even if they signed a separate peace, the Soviets had no interest in strengthening Germany. Hard, *Raymond Robins' Own Story*, pp. 64–65. 'The Allied and American Governments', this is Robins's comment, 'rather than admit the existence of Trotsky, let the Germans do all the grabbing of Russian raw materials on the Russian frontier.' Ibid., pp. 70–71.

had the right to accept assistance from bourgeois powers, provided it maintained complete independence.[1] Eventually he converted the Central Committee to his view, and Lenin firmly supported him.

The German answer, when it at last arrived, came as a shock. It allowed the Soviets only forty-eight hours for a reply and only three days for negotiations. The terms were much worse than those offered at Brest: Russia was to carry out complete demobilization; to cede Latvia and Estonia; and to evacuate the Ukraine and Finland. When, on 23 February, the Central Committee met, it had less than a day to make up its mind. It was again on Trotsky's single vote that the outcome hung. He had yielded to Lenin on the point that a new request for peace be made, but he was not committed to accept the new, much harsher, terms. He did not agree with Lenin that the Soviets were utterly incapable of defending themselves. On the contrary, more distinctly than hitherto, he now leaned towards the war faction. 'Lenin's arguments', he said, 'are far from convincing. If only we had unanimity in our midst we could shoulder the task of organizing the defence, we could cope with this. We would not act a bad role even if we were compelled to give up Petrograd and Moscow. We would keep the whole world in tension. If we sign this German ultimatum to-day, we may be confronted by another to-morrow. . . . We may gain peace but we shall lose the support of the advanced elements of the proletariat. We shall, in any case, lead the proletariat to disintegration.'[2]

And yet, despite his forebodings about the peace, despite his confidence in the capacity of the Soviets to defend themselves, he once again ensured, by his single vote, the ascendancy of the peace faction.

His puzzling conduct cannot be explained without a closer look at the alignment of the groups, their arguments and motives. Lenin strove to obtain for the Soviets a 'respite', which would enable them to put their house into some order and to build up a new army. He was prepared to pay almost any price for the respite, to withdraw from the Ukraine and the Baltic lands and to discharge any indemnity. He did not accept this 'shameful' peace as final. He, too, held that revolutionary war

---

[1] *Protokoly Tsen. Kom.*, pp. 243–6.   [2] Ibid., p. 248.

was inescapable; and more than once he recalled the peace of Tilsit which Napoleon had dictated to Prussia in 1807 and which the progressive Prussian statesmen, von Stein and Gneisenau, had used to modernize their country and army and to prepare revenge. He was following their example; and he also hoped that during the respite revolution might mature in Germany and renounce and annul the Kaiser's conquests.

Against this the war faction argued that the central powers would not permit Lenin so to use the respite: they would cut off Russia from the grain and coal of the Ukraine and the petrol of the Caucasus; they would bring under their control half the Russian population; they would sponsor and support counter-revolutionary movements and throttle the revolution. Nor would the Soviets be able to build up a new army during any respite. They had to create their armed strength in the very process of the fighting; and only so could they create it. True, the Soviets might be forced to evacuate Petrograd and even Moscow; but they had enough space into which to retreat and gather strength. Even if the people were to prove as unwilling to fight for the revolution as they were to fight for the old régime—and the leaders of the war faction refused to take this for granted—then every German advance, with all the accompanying terror and pillage, would shake the people from weariness and torpor, force them to resist, and finally generate a broad and truly popular enthusiasm for revolutionary war. On the tide of this enthusiasm a new and formidable army would rise. The revolution, unshamed by sordid surrender, would achieve its renaissance; it would stir the souls of the working classes abroad; and it would finally dispel the nightmare of imperialism.

Each faction was convinced that the policy proposed by the other was pernicious, and the debates were charged with emotional tension. Trotsky, it seems, was alone in holding that much could be said from a realistic standpoint for and against each of the proposed courses of action, and that neither was inadmissible on grounds of principle and revolutionary morality.

It has since become the historian's commonplace, a commonplace which after the event Trotsky himself did much to establish, that Lenin's policy had all the merits of realism and that the war faction represented an utterly quixotic aspect of

Bolshevism. This view does not do full justice to the leaders of
the war faction. It is true that Lenin's political originality and
courage rose in those days to the height of genius and that
events—the crumbling of the Hohenzollern and Habsburg
dynasties and the annulment of the treaty of Brest before the
end of the year—vindicated him. It is also true that the war
faction often acted under confused emotional impulses and presented no consistent policy. But at their best its leaders argued
their case very strongly and realistically; and much of their
argument, too, was confirmed by events. The 'respite' which
Lenin obtained was, in truth, half-illusory. After the signing of
the peace, the Kaiser's government did all it could to strangle
the Soviets. It could not, however, do more than its involvement
in the gigantic struggle on the western front allowed it to do.
Without a separate peace in the West it could not have done
much more even if the Soviets had not accepted the *Diktat* of
Brest. Bukharin and Radek, when they argued against Russia's
surrender, pointed to this circumstance as to one which
severely restricted Germany's freedom of action. In this respect
the inner story of the war, when it was revealed, proved their
judgement to have been more correct than Lenin's. The occupation of the Ukraine and of parts of southern Russia alone
tied down a million German and Austrian troops. If Russia had
refused to sign the peace, the Germans might, at the most, have
tried to seize Petrograd. They could hardly have risked a
march on Moscow.[1] If they had seized both Petrograd and
Moscow, the Soviets, whose chief strength lay in the two capitals, would have found themselves in an extremely dangerous,
perhaps fatal, crisis. But this was not the point at issue between
Lenin and the war faction, for Lenin, too, repeatedly stated,
with curious confidence, that the loss of the one or the two
capitals would not be a mortal blow to the revolution.[2]

The other argument advanced by the leaders of the war
faction that the Soviets would have to build up a new army on
the battlefields, in the process of the fighting, and not in the

[1] Ludendorff states that a deep German offensive was 'out of the question'—
only 'a short energetic thrust' had been planned. *Meine Kriegserinnerungen*,
p. 447.
[2] Stalin alone held that the surrender of any capital would mean the decay, the
'rotting' of the revolution; and in this, as an advocate of peace, he was in a way
more consistent than Lenin. *Protokoly Tsen. Kom.*, p. 248.

barracks during a calm respite, was, paradoxically, realistic. This was how the Red Army was eventually built up; and Bukharin's and Radek's speeches at the seventh congress of the party anticipated on this point the military policy which Trotsky and Lenin were to adopt and pursue in the coming years.[1] Precisely because Russia was so extremely war weary, she could not raise a new army in relatively calm times. Only severe shocks and the ineluctable necessity to fight, and to fight at once, could stimulate the energies hidden in the Soviet régime and bring them into play. Only thus could it happen that a nation which had under the Tsar, Prince Lvov, and Kerensky been too exhausted to fight, went on fighting under Lenin and Trotsky in civil wars and wars of intervention for nearly three years.

The weakness of the war faction lay not so much in its case as in its lack of leadership. Its chiefs were Bukharin, Dzerzhinsky, Radek, Yoffe, Uritsky, Kollontai, Lomov-Oppokov, Bubnov, Pyatakov, Smirnov, and Ryazanov. All were eminent members of the party. Some of them had great intellectual gifts and were brilliant spokesmen and pamphleteers. Others were courageous men of action. Yet none of them possessed the indomitable will, the moral authority, the political and strategic talents, the tactical flexibility, and the administrative capacity required of a leader in a revolutionary war. As long as the war faction had no such leader, it represented merely a state of mind, a moral ferment, a literary cry of despair, not a policy, even though at first a majority of the party was drawn into the ferment and echoed the cry of despair. The leadership of the war faction was vacant, and the faction cast inviting glances at Trotsky. Incidentally, in their ranks were many of his old friends who had joined the Bolshevik party together with him. On the face of it, there was little to prevent him from responding to their expectations. Although he held that Lenin's policy, like that of the adherents of war, had its justification, he did not conceal his inner revulsion against it. All the more astounding was it that at the most critical moments he threw the weight of his influence behind Lenin.

He shrank from assuming the leadership of the war faction because he realized that this would have transformed at a

[1] *Sedmoi Syezd RKP*, pp. 32–50, 69–73 and *passim*.

stroke the cleavage among the Bolsheviks into an irretrievable split and, probably, into a bloody conflict. He and Lenin would have confronted each other as the leaders of hostile parties, divided not over ordinary differences but over a matter of life and death. Lenin had already warned the Central Committee that if they outvoted him once again in the matter of peace, he would resign from the Committee and the government and appeal against them to the rank and file.[1] At this time Trotsky was Lenin's only possible successor as the chief of the government. But as chief of a government committed to wage a most dangerous war in desperate conditions, he would have had to suppress the opposition to war, and almost certainly to take repressive action against Lenin. Both factions, aware of these implications, refrained from uttering plain threats. But the unspoken threats were there—in the undertones of the debate. It was in order to stop the party drifting towards a civil war in its own ranks that at the crucial moments Trotsky cast his vote for Lenin.[2]

Some analogy to the situation which was likely to arise if Trotsky had acted otherwise may be found in the three-cornered struggle which developed between the Commune of Paris, Danton and Robespierre during the French Revolution. In 1793 the Commune (and Anacharsis Cloots) stood, as Bukharin and the Left Communists were to do, for war against all the anti-revolutionary governments of Europe. Danton advocated

---

[1] *Protokoly Tsen. Kom.*, pp. 247–8.

[2] Twenty years later, during the purge trials, Bukharin was charged with having attempted at the time of the Brest crisis to stage a coup against Lenin and to arrest him. This version, designed to make credible the charge about Bukharin's plot against Stalin, must be dismissed. But the leaders of the war faction must have considered at one point what they would do if they obtained a majority in the Central Committee. They would then have had to form a government without Lenin and, if Lenin persisted in opposing war, they might have had to arrest him. In 1923 Zinoviev claimed that Bukharin and Radek seriously discussed this with the Left Social Revolutionaries. Radek denied the allegation, saying that they had only joked about Lenin's arrest. Col. Robins, a completely disinterested witness, who kept in close touch with the Bolshevik leaders, described, as early as in 1920, a scene between Radek and Lenin, in which Radek is alleged to have said that if there were 500 courageous men in Petrograd, they would imprison Lenin and make possible a revolutionary war. Lenin replied that he would first imprison his interlocutor (Hard, *Raymond Robins' Own Story*, p. 94). If any serious conspiracy against Lenin had been afoot, Radek would hardly have hastened to give Lenin advance notice of it. But although this dialogue was in fact jocular, the logic of the situation gave it a serious undertone.

war against Prussia and agreement with England, where he hoped that Fox would replace Pitt in office. Robespierre urged the Convention to wage war against England; and he strove for an agreement with Prussia. Danton and Robespierre joined hands against the Commune, but, after they suppressed it they fell out. The guillotine settled their controversy.

Trotsky, who so often looked at the Russian Revolution through the prism of the French, must have been aware of this analogy. He may have remembered Engels's remarkable letter to Victor Adler, explaining all the 'pulsations' of the French Revolution by the fortunes of war and the disagreements engendered by it.[1] He must have seen himself as acting a role potentially reminiscent of Danton's, while Lenin's part was similar to Robespierre's. It was as if the shadow of the guillotine had for a moment interposed itself between him and Lenin. This is not to say that, if the conflict had developed, Trotsky, like Danton, would necessarily have played a losing game; or that Lenin was, like Robespierre, inclined to settle by the guillotine an inner party controversy. Here the analogy ceases to apply. It was evident that the war party, if it won, would be driven to suppress its opponents—otherwise it could not cope with its task. A peaceable solution of the crisis in the party was possible only under the rule of the adherents of peace, who could better afford to tolerate opposition. This consideration was decisive in Trotsky's eyes. In order to banish the shadow of the guillotine he made an extraordinary sacrifice of principle and personal ambition.

To Lenin's threat of resignation he replied, addressing himself more to the advocates of war than to Lenin: 'We cannot wage revolutionary war with a split in the party. . . . Under these conditions our party is not in a position to wage war, especially as those who stand for war do not want to accept the material means for waging it [i.e. assistance from the western powers].'[2] 'I shall not take upon myself the responsibility of voting for war.' Later he added: 'There is a lot of subjectivism in Lenin's attitude. I am not sure that he is right, but I do not want to do anything that would interfere with the party's unity. On the contrary, I shall help as much as I can. But I

[1] K. Marx and F. Engels, *Selected Correspondence*, pp. 457–8.
[2] *Protokoly Tsen. Kom.*, p. 248.

cannot stay in office and bear personal responsibility for the conduct of foreign affairs.'[1]

The leaders of the war faction did not share Trotsky's fears. Dzerzhinsky, already the head of *Cheka*,[2] held that the party was strong enough to stand the split and Lenin's resignation. Lomov-Oppokov, leader of the Bolsheviks in Moscow, appealed to Trotsky not to let himself be 'intimidated' by Lenin's ultimatums—they could take power without Lenin.[3] In the course of the debate, however, the gravity and urgency of Trotsky's argument so impressed some of the advocates of war, Dzerzhinsky and Yoffe, that they retraced their steps. Lenin obtained seven votes for peace. This was still a minority of the Central Committee. But as Trotsky and three leaders of the war faction abstained, and only four voted against Lenin, the peace terms were accepted. The three leaders of the war faction who abstained, Yoffe, Dzerzhinsky, and Krestinsky, issued a solemn statement saying that they could not contemplate 'a war to be fought simultaneously against German imperialism, the Russian bourgeoisie, and a section of the proletariat headed by Lenin'; and that a split would be such an unmitigated disaster that the worst peace was preferable.[4] But the irreconcilable adherents of war, Bukharin, Uritsky, Lomov, Bubnov (and Pyatakov and Smirnov, who were present at the session) denounced the decision in favour of peace as a minority opinion; and in protest against it they resigned from all responsible offices in party and government. In vain did Lenin try to dissuade them from taking this step. Trotsky, having brought about the defeat of the Left Communists, now showed them his sympathy and affection, and wistfully remarked that he would have voted differently had he known that they were going to resign.[5]

The peace faction had won, but its conscience was troubled. No sooner had the Central Committee, on 23 February, decided to accept the German terms than it voted unanimously to

---

[1] *Protokoly Tsen. Kom.*, p. 251.

[2] *Cheka*—Extraordinary Commission for Struggle against the Counter-revolution, the predecessor of G.P.U.   [3] Ibid., p. 250.   [4] Ibid., p. 253.

[5] At the same session, a curious scene took place. Lenin assured his defeated opponents that they had every right to conduct an agitation against the peace. Against this Stalin remarked that since they had been so undisciplined as to resign from their posts, the leaders of the war faction automatically placed themselves outside the party. Both Lenin and Trotsky strongly protested against Stalin's statement, and Stalin had to withdraw it. Ibid., pp. 254–5.

start immediate preparations for future war. When it came to the appointment of a new delegation for Brest Litovsk, a tragi-comic scene took place: every member of the Committee dodged the dubious honour; none, not even the most ardent advocate of peace, was eager to place his signature under the treaty. Sokolnikov, who eventually headed the new delegation, threatened to resign from the Central Committee when his candidature was proposed; and only Lenin's good-tempered persuasion induced him to yield.[1] This matter having been settled, Trotsky asked—amid Stalin's sneers, for which Stalin later apologized—that the Central Committee take cognizance of his resignation from the Commissariat of Foreign Affairs, which was already virtually under Chicherin's management. The Central Committee appealed to Trotsky to stay in office until the peace was signed. He only agreed not to make public his resignation until then and declared that he would not appear any more in any governmental institution. Prompted by Lenin, the Committee obliged him to attend at least those sessions of the government at which foreign affairs were not under debate.[2]

After all the recent exertions, triumphs, and frustrations Trotsky's nerves were frayed. It looked as if his performance at Brest had been wholly wasted; and this was indeed what many thought and said. Not without reason, he was blamed for having lulled the party into false security by his repeated assurances that the Germans would not dare to attack. Overnight the idol became almost a culprit. 'On the evening of 27 February', writes M. Philips Price, 'the Central Soviet Executive met at the Tauride Palace, and Trotsky addressed them. . . . He had dis-appeared for some days, and no one seemed to know what had happened to him. That night, however, he came to the Palace . . . hurled the darts of eloquent scorn against the Imperialisms of the central powers and of the allies, upon whose altar the Russian Revolution was being sacrificed. When he had finished, he retired again. Rumour had it that he was so overcome with mortification that he broke down and wept.'[3]

.   .   .   .

On 3 March Sokolnikov, making it abundantly clear that the

---

[1] Ibid., pp. 259–66.   [2] Ibid., p. 268.
[3] M. Philips Price, op. cit., p. 251. See also I. Steinberg, *Als ich Volkskommissar war*, pp. 208–13.

Soviets were acting under duress, signed the treaty of Brest Litovsk. In less than a fortnight, the Germans seized Kiev and vast parts of the Ukraine, the Austrians entered Odessa, and the Turks Trebizond. In the Ukraine the occupying powers crushed the Soviets and reinstalled the *Rada*, only to overpower shortly thereafter the *Rada* too, and to place *Hetman* Skoropadsky at the head of their puppet administration. The momentary victors showered upon Lenin's government demands and ultimatums, each more humiliating than the preceding. Most galling was the ultimatum demanding that the Soviets sign an immediate peace with 'independent Ukraine'. In the Ukraine the people, especially the peasants, were putting up a desperate resistance to the occupying forces and their Ukrainian tools. By signing a separate treaty with the latter, the Soviets could not but appear to disavow the whole Ukrainian resistance. At the Central Committee Trotsky demanded the rejection of the German ultimatum. Lenin, always with the idea of future revenge in his mind, was determined to drain the cup of humiliation. But at every German provocation the opposition to peace rose again in the party and in the Soviets. The treaty of Brest had not yet been ratified and ratification was still uncertain.

On 6 March an emergency congress of the party met at the Tauride Palace to decide whether to recommend ratification to the forthcoming Congress of the Soviets. The proceedings were held in strict secrecy, and the records were published only in 1925. The atmosphere was heavy with dejection. The delegates from the provinces found that, in expectation of a German attack, governmental offices were preparing to evacuate Petrograd, a move from which Kerensky's government had shrunk. The Commissars were already 'sitting on their bags and cases' —only Trotsky was to stay behind to organize the defence. The delegates reported a general slump in the party's popularity.[1] Only recently the clamour for peace had been so powerful as to destroy the February régime and to lift the Bolsheviks to power. But now, when the peace had come, the party responsible for it was the first to be blamed.

At the congress, Trotsky's activity was inevitably the pivot of

---

[1] 'The local organizations', says the official record, 'were weak and disorganized, and the congress reflected the condition of our entire party, of the entire working class, of the whole of Russia.' *Sedmoi Syezd RKP*, pp. 4–5.

debate. In a most incisive speech Lenin urged ratification of the peace. The main burden of his argument was against the war faction, but he also castigated Trotsky's 'great mistake' and wishful belief that the Germans would not attack, the belief which had underlain 'neither war nor peace'.[1] The war faction jumped to Trotsky's defence. 'Even the chauvinist German press', Radek said, 'had to admit that the proletariat of Germany was against Hindenburg and for Trotsky. Our policy at Brest Litovsk has not failed; it has not been an illusion but a policy of revolutionary realism.'[2] It was much better for the Soviets to have concluded peace only after the German offensive, because nobody could doubt that they acted under external compulsion. But then Radek voiced the war faction's disappointment with Trotsky: 'One may reproach Trotsky only for this, that having achieved so much at Brest he then joined the other side. . . . For this we have a right to reproach him; and we do so.'[3]

Trotsky once again, and more explicitly, justified his behaviour. Bukharin, Radek, and their friends, he said, saw in war the only salvation and so they were 'obliged, infringing upon formal party considerations, to pose the issue on a knife-edge. . . . With a weak country behind us, with a passive peasantry, with a sombre mood in the proletariat, we were further threatened by a split in our own ranks. . . . Very much was at stake on my vote. . . . I could not assume responsibility for the split. I had thought that we ought to retreat [before the German army] rather than sign peace for the sake of an illusory respite. But I could not take upon myself the responsibility for the leadership of the party. . . .'[4]

This, as far as the records show, was the only time he openly stated that he had shrunk from superseding Lenin as the leader of the party. 'The danger of the split', he added, 'will have neither disappeared nor lessened if European revolution is further delayed.'[5] He admitted that he had misjudged German intentions, but he reminded Lenin that they had both agreed on breaking off the negotiations. He had, he said, a profound respect for Lenin's policy, but not for the manner in which Lenin's faction was putting its case before the country. They fostered apathy and defeatism, which were demoralizing the working

[1] Ibid., p. 22.   [2] Ibid., p. 71.   [3] Ibid., p. 72.   [4] Ibid., p. 83.   [5] Ibid., p. 84.

class, and amid which it was extremely difficult to build up the
new army they all wanted. He did not urge the congress to
refuse ratification; but there ought to be a limit to surrenders:
they must not give in to Lenin and sign a treaty with Germany's
Ukrainian puppets.[1] And here he made a remark hinting at a
most ominous contingency. If, he said, the party was so power-
less that it had to let down the Ukrainian workers and peasants,
then it might be its duty to declare: '. . . *we have come before
our time*, we withdraw into the underground, and we let
Chernov, Guchkov, and Miliukov settle accounts with . . . the
Ukraine. . . . But I think that even if we should be compelled so
to withdraw, we must still act as a revolutionary party and fight
for every position to the last drop of our blood.'[2] This was his
strongest intimation so far that the Russian Revolution might
have been a false spring; and to Marxist ears his words carried
the grimmest connotation: Marx and Engels had repeatedly
written about the tragic fate which overtakes revolutionaries
who 'come before their time'.[3] Finally, recalling Dzerzhinsky's,
Yoffe's, Krestinsky's, and his own 'great act of self-restraint'
and his 'sacrifice of the Ego' on the altar of Bolshevik unity, he
told Lenin that there were as many dangers as opportunities in
Lenin's policy, and that the peace faction might be 'sacrificing
life's only end for the sake of mere living'.[4]

Lenin once again used the threat of resignation: he would
resign, he said, if the congress limited his freedom of action with
regard to the Ukraine. There is, he pleaded, no treason in the
behaviour of soldiers who refuse to come to the rescue of surrounded comrades in arms, when they know that they are too
weak to rescue those surrounded and that they themselves will
perish in the attempt. Such was the position of the Soviets in relation to the Ukraine. This time a large majority agreed with Lenin.

---

[1] 'Lenin knows no limit to surrender and retreat, even though Trotsky tries to
catch him by his coat-tails and stop him', Ryazanov said in the debate. *Sedmoi
Syezd RKP*, p. 9.   [2] Ibid., p. 85.
    [3] 'The worst thing that can befall a leader of an extreme party is to be compelled
to take over a Government in an epoch when the movement is not yet ripe for the
domination of the class which he represents and for the realization of the measures
which that domination would imply . . . he necessarily finds himself in a dilemma.
What he *can* do is in contrast to all his previous actions, to all his principles and
to the present interests of his party; what he *ought* to do cannot be achieved. . . .
Whoever puts himself in this awkward position is irrevocably lost.' Engels, *The
Peasant War in Germany*, pp. 135–6.   [4] *Sedmoi Syezd RKP*, p. 86.

Trotsky, nevertheless, tabled an amendment to Lenin's motion affirming that peace was 'necessary'—he proposed to replace 'necessary' by 'permissible'. From the platform of the congress, he could not fully explain why, after all he had done to promote Lenin's policy, he vacillated again. Behind the scenes he and Lenin, in perfect concord, were sounding the Entente once again on whether they would get assistance if they refused to ratify the peace. In expectation of the answer Lenin was even delaying the Congress of the Soviets which was to vote on ratification. He very nearly committed himself with President Wilson to renouncing the treaty of Brest if the President gave a binding promise of help.[1] At the congress of the party, Lenin cryptically remarked that the situation was changing so rapidly that in two days he himself might speak against ratification.[2] Trotsky was therefore anxious that the congress should not frame its resolution in terms which were too rigid. Lenin, however, did not at heart expect any encouraging answer from the Entente; and once again he was right. He had agreed, on Trotsky's prompting, to make the soundings in order to have a clear conscience in the matter. But in the meantime he wished the congress to approve peace without qualification. This the congress did.

In the debate Trotsky had recalled his 'great act of self-restraint' and his 'suppression of the Ego'. These words bring to mind the remark of a friend of his early youth: 'Trotsky's entire behaviour is dominated by his Ego, but his Ego is dominated by the revolution.'[3] This trait of the boy of eighteen was still there in the great and famous man of thirty-eight. His conduct during this drama testified to his subordination of personal ambition and inclination to the interests of the party. But now, when Lenin's triumph was complete, Trotsky's Ego chafed; and from the platform of this grim congress it cried out for compensation. The great debate over peace was followed by a grotesque wrangle over Trotsky's faults and merits. His friends and followers, Krestinsky, Yoffe, and Ryazanov, tabled a formal motion justifying his policy at Brest. It was, from every point of view, preposterous to press such a motion at this moment.

---

[1] Hard, *Raymond Robins' Own Story*, pp. 135–9; Wheeler-Bennett, *The Forgotten Peace*, pp. 290–301.

[2] *Sedmoi Syezd RKP*, p. 140.   [3] See Chapter II, p. 35.

The congress had just decided that peace was an absolute
necessity, and it should not have been expected to give now its
retrospective blessing to 'neither war nor peace'. The circumstance that Trotsky's defenders came from the war faction made
this demonstration appear a last sally from a defeated minority.
The congress had been in no mood to rebuff Trotsky for what
he had done at Brest; it preferred to let bygones be bygones.
But, having been expressly asked to declare itself, it could not
but administer a rebuff. It rejected the motion; and this wounded
Trotsky's pride and ambition. He exclaimed that he had
become the man most hated by the imperialists of the central
powers, the man blamed for the continuation of war, and now,
wittingly or unwittingly, the party had lent its authority to the
enemy's charges against him. He therefore resigned from all
responsible offices with which the party had entrusted him.

By this time Trotsky's appointment as Commissar of War
was either mooted or decided upon in the inner councils of
the party; and the congress was anxious to give him at least
partial satisfaction. Amid much uproar and confusion, several
resolutions were tabled and many votes were taken, the result
of which was not clear. During this undignified wrangle, Lenin
kept silent. In the name of Lenin's faction, Zinoviev assured
Trotsky that the whole party warmly appreciated his brilliant
efforts from Brest to arouse the German working class and considered this part of his work as 'fully correct'. But Trotsky ought
to appreciate that the party had changed its attitude, and that
it was pointless to argue over the formula 'neither war nor
peace'. The congress first adopted Zinoviev's resolution. Then
it voted for Radek's motion which contradicted it, and then it
passed still another text which contradicted Radek's. 'It is an
event unheard of in history', Trotsky complained, 'that in the
face of the enemy a party should repudiate the policy of its
representatives.' In pique he submitted an ironical resolution
roundly condemning his own policy. The congress, of course,
rejected it, and he withdrew from the fray. When it came to the
election of the Central Committee, he and Lenin obtained the
highest number of votes. Abandoning his policy, the party
nevertheless gave him its unreserved confidence.

Four crowded months had passed since the Soviets had

ratified the peace. The Council of the People's Commissars had moved from Petrograd and had installed itself at the Kremlin in Moscow. The allied diplomatic missions had also left Petrograd; but in protest against the peace they went to Vologda, a small provincial town. Trotsky had become Commissar of War and had begun to 'arm the revolution'. The Japanese had attacked Siberia and occupied Vladivostok. The Germans had suppressed the Finnish revolution and forced the Russian navy to withdraw from the Bay of Finland. They had also occupied the whole of the Ukraine, the Crimea, and the coasts of the Black and the Azov Seas. The British and the French had landed at Murmansk. The Czech Legion had risen against the Soviets. Encouraged by foreign interventions, the Russian anti-revolutionary forces had resumed the life-and-death struggle, subordinating to it all principles and scruples. Many of those who had only recently accused the Bolsheviks of being German agents, Miliukov and his followers in the first instance, had come to rely on German assistance in their fight against the Bolsheviks.[1] Hunger had visited Moscow and the cities of northern Russia, cut off from their granaries. Lenin had decreed wholesale nationalization of industry and called on the Committees of Poor Peasants to requisition food from wealthier farmers in order to feed the urban workers. Several real risings and several phantom conspiracies had been suppressed.

Never yet had any peace brought so much suffering and humiliation as the 'peace' of Brest had brought to Russia. But Lenin nursed his 'child'—the revolution—through all these trials and disappointments. He would not renounce the treaty of Brest, although in more than one respect he disregarded its stipulations. He had not ceased to call on the German and Austrian workers to rise in revolt. He had, despite the clause about Russia's disarmament, authorized the formation of the Red Army. But in no circumstances did he permit his followers to rise in arms against Germany. He had recalled to Moscow the Bolsheviks who had directed the Ukrainian Soviets and who had been tempted to strike from the underground at the occupying power.[2] All over the Ukraine, the German war machine crushed anti-German guerillas. Russian Red Guards

---

[1] Denikin, *Ocherki Russkoi Smuty*, vol. iii, pp. 72–90.
[2] Antonov-Ovseenko, *Zapiski o Grazhdanskoi Voinie*, vol. i, pp. 294–5.

watched their agony from across the frontier and yearned to go to their rescue; but Lenin held the Red Guards unyieldingly in check.

Trotsky had long since given up his opposition to the peace. He had accepted the party's final decision and its consequences. Cabinet solidarity and party discipline alike obliged him to stand by Lenin's policy. He did so with complete loyalty and devotion, although he must have paid for that loyalty with many an inner conflict and many moments of acute anguish. The Bolshevik war faction, leaderless and confused, had lapsed into silence. All the more loudly and impatiently did the Left Social Revolutionaries voice their opposition to the peace. In March, immediately after the ratification, they had withdrawn from the Council of the People's Commissars. They still sat in nearly all departments of the government, including the *Cheka*, and in the executive organs of the Soviets. But, exasperated by all that had happened, they could not for long remain half in opposition to the government and half responsible for it.

Such was the situation when the fifth Congress of the Soviets assembled in Moscow at the beginning of July 1918. The Left Social Revolutionaries resolved to bring matters to a head and to break with the Bolsheviks. The outcry against the peace went up once more. Delegates from the Ukraine mounted the platform to describe the desperate struggle of the Ukrainian guerillas and to beg for help. The leaders of the Left Social Revolutionaries, Kamkov and Spiridonova, denounced the 'Bolshevik betrayal' and clamoured for a war of liberation.

Both Kamkov and Spiridonova were great revolutionaries of the old *Narodnik* type. They had fought bomb in hand against Tsardom and had paid for their courage with many years of solitary confinement and hard labour. They spoke with the authority of heroes and martyrs rather than that of leaders and politicians. They refused to weigh pros and cons. They demanded from the victorious revolution the heroism and the martyrdom to which they themselves had risen. The Bolsheviks as a body were far removed from such unreasoning ardour. Yet Spiridonova's and Kamkov's appeals still struck a chord in many a Bolshevik, and certainly in Trotsky. When, at the Congress, Kamkov walked across the platform towards the diplomatic box where Count Mirbach, the German Ambassador, was listening to the debates and, pointing at the Ambassador, poured out his detestation of the Kaiser and of German imperialism, the Congress applauded his courage. At heart Trotsky must have done the same. Kamkov was, after all, only repeating what he himself had done at Brest; and from the lips of Kamkov and Spiridonova the echoes of his own voice seemed to come back to him. It was only a few months since he had publicly, solemnly, and confidently vowed that the Bolsheviks would defend the honour of the revolution 'to the last drop of blood', and expressed the hope that the Left Social Revolutionaries would do likewise. It was an even shorter time since he had begged his comrades rather to declare that they had come before their time and go under in unequal struggle than wash their hands of the fate of the Ukraine. He had in the meantime followed Lenin, hoping that this might be the way to save the revolution. But at heart he could not condemn those who did not do so.

He was therefore acting a grimly paradoxical part when, on 4 July, he asked the Congress to authorize an emergency order which, as Commissar of War, he was about to issue.[1] The order was designed to impose severe discipline on Russian partisan detachments which threatened to disrupt the peace by self-willed attacks on German troops. The text ran as follows: 'These are my orders: all agitators who, after the publication of this order, continue to urge insubordination to the Soviet government are to be arrested, brought to Moscow, and tried by the Extraordinary Tribunal. All agents of foreign imperialism who call for offensive action [against Germany] and offer armed resistance to Soviet authorities are to be shot.'

He argued the need for this order with perfect logic. He was not going to discuss, he said, which was the right policy: peace or war. On this the previous Congress of Soviets, constitutionally the supreme authority in the state, had spoken the last word. What he was arguing was that nobody had the right to arrogate to himself the functions of the government and take war into his own hands. The agitation against peace, conducted among Red Guards and partisans, had assumed dangerous forms. Commissars who had stood for peace had been assassinated; commissions of inquiry sent from Moscow had been fired

[1] Trotsky, *Kak Vooruzhalas Revolutsia*, vol. i, pp. 266–74.

at; his friend Rakovsky, who at one time headed the delegation negotiating with the *Rada*, had been threatened with bombs. 'You understand, comrades, that there can be no joking in such matters. As the person at present responsible for the conduct of the Red Army. . . .'

At this moment, Kamkov interrupted him with the cry: 'Kerensky!' 'You think yourself the new Napoleon', another Left Social Revolutionary shouted. 'Kerensky!' Trotsky replied, 'Kerensky obeyed the bourgeois classes, and I here am responsible to you, representatives of Russian workers and peasants. If you pass censure upon me and adopt a different decision, one with which I may or may not agree, then, as a soldier of the revolution, I shall submit to your decision and carry it out.' He thus made it clear that he was acting in solidarity with the government of which he was a member rather than from fundamental disagreement with the opposition. But he also warned the opposition that at this stage the disruption of peace could only benefit either the Entente or the extreme German militarists who were not satisfied even with the Brest *Diktat*. Despite their bitter attacks on him, he still addressed the Left Social Revolutionaries with mild persuasiveness, not accusing them yet of any responsibility for incitement to war.[1] When Spiridonova scolded him for his 'militarist, Bonapartist style', he replied half-apologetically: 'I myself, comrades, am by no means a lover of military style. I have been accustomed to use the publicist's language, which I prefer to any other style. But every sort of activity has its consequences, even stylistic ones. As the People's Commissar of War who has to stop hooligans shooting our representatives, I am not a publicist, and I cannot express myself in that lyrical tone in which comrade Spiridonova has spoken here.'

By now Spiridonova, too, had abandoned the 'lyrical tone'. The small, frail woman mounted the platform to accuse Lenin and Trotsky of treason and to threaten them. 'I shall grasp in my hand the revolver and the bomb, as I once used to do', she exclaimed. This was advance notice of an insurrection which

---

[1] Only towards the end of the debate did Trotsky accuse the Left Social Revolutionaries, but even then he made it clear that his accusations were directed against individuals, not against the party as a whole. In truth, the party as a whole was engaged in a desperate attempt to disrupt the peace. Op. cit., p. 275.

was only two days off. Sadoul has left a graphic description of the scene and of the different ways in which Lenin and Trotsky reacted to the threat:

Lenin rises. His strange, faun-like face is, as always, calm and mocking. He has not ceased and will not cease to laugh under the insults, attacks, and direct threats showered upon him. In these tragic circumstances, when he knows what is at stake, his work, his idea, his life, this vast laughter, broad and sincere, which some find out of place, gives me the impression of extraordinary strength. Every now and then . . . a sharper affront just for a second manages to freeze this laughter, which is so insulting and exasperating to the adversary. . . .

By Lenin's side, Trotsky, too, tries to laugh. But anger, emotion, agitation change his laughter into a painful grimace. Then his animated, expressive face becomes extinguished . . . and disappears under a Mephistophelian, terrifying mask. He does not have the master's sovereign will, his cool head, his absolute self-control. Yet he is . . . less implacable.[1]

It was, of course, easier for Lenin so self-confidently to face his opponents: he had all the time been firmly convinced that peace was the revolution's only salvation. The contortion of Trotsky's face reflected the conflict in his mind.

These tumultuous debates were interrupted on 6 July by the assassination of Count Mirbach, the German Ambassador. The assassins, two Left Social Revolutionaries, high officials of the *Cheka*, Blumkin and Andreev, acted on Spiridonova's order, hoping to provoke war between Germany and Russia.[2] Immediately afterwards the Left Social Revolutionaries staged their insurrection against the Bolsheviks. They succeeded in arresting Dzerzhinsky and other chiefs of the *Cheka*, who had gone without any guard to the insurgents' headquarters; and they occupied the Posts and Telegraphs and announced to the country the overthrow of Lenin's government. But they had no

---

[1] Sadoul, *Notes sur la révolution Russe*, p. 396.

[2] Blumkin later repented his deed, joined the Bolshevik party, won distinction in the civil war, and rejoined the *Cheka*. In the 1920s he was in sympathy with the Trotskyist opposition, but, on Trotsky's advice, continued to serve with the G.P.U. When Trotsky was an exile on Prinkipo Island, Blumkin secretly visited him there and returned to Moscow with a message from Trotsky to the opposition. Before he managed to deliver the message, however, he was arrested and shot. (*The Trotsky Archives*, Harvard.)

leadership and no plan of action; and after two days of skir-
mishing they surrendered.

On 9 July the Congress of the Soviets reassembled and Trotsky
reported the suppression of the rising. He said that the government had been surprised by the attack. It had denuded the
capital of the few reliable detachments it had possessed, sending
them to fight against the Czechoslovak Legion in the east. For
its own security the government had relied mainly on that same
Red Guard, consisting of Left Social Revolutionaries, which
staged the rising. All that Trotsky could oppose to the insurgents
was a Latvian rifle regiment commanded by Vatzetis, a former
Colonel of the General Staff, who was presently to become
Commander-in-Chief of the Red Army; and a detachment of
revolutionized Austro-Hungarian prisoners of war, led by Bela
Kun, the future founder of the Communist party of Hungary.
But the rising had an almost farcical character, from the
military if not from the political viewpoint. The insurgents were
a band of brave but undisciplined partisans. They failed to
co-ordinate their attacks; and eventually they yielded more to
Bolshevik persuasion than to force. Trotsky, who was just then
disciplining the Red Guards and guerillas into a centralized
Red Army, used the rising as an object lesson demonstrating
the correctness of his military policy. Even now he spoke of the
insurgents half-pityingly saying that he and others had defended
them in the government as 'children who had run amok'; but
he added that there could be 'no room for such children'.[1] The
leaders of the rising were arrested; but they were amnestied a
few months later. Only some of those who had abused positions
of trust inside the *Cheka* were executed.

Thus, with Trotsky hurling back the stubborn echo of his
own passionate protests against the peace, ended the great controversy over Brest Litovsk.

[1] Trotsky, *Kak Vooruzhalas Revolutsia*, vol. i, pp. 276 ff.

CHAPTER XII

Arming the Republic

'WAR is an instrument of Policy; it must necessarily bear its character, it must measure with its scale: the conduct of War, in its great features, is therefore Policy itself, which takes up the sword in place of the pen, but does not on that account cease to think according to its own laws.' This Clausewitzian phrase described war between nations, in which the identity of strategy and politics is often obscured and far from obvious. In civil war it is direct and undisguised. It is the laws of politics that dominate every phase, dictate to the belligerents nine-tenths of their moves, and produce the final verdict on the battlefields. When in the middle of March 1918 Trotsky was appointed Commissar of War and President of the Supreme War Council, he did not even put down his pen to take up his sword—he used both.

He undertook to conjure an army out of an apparent void. The armed forces of the old régime had vanished. On the Don and in the Northern Caucasus a few pro-Bolshevik detachments of the old army still confronted the first White Guards. But they too were militarily so worthless that the government preferred to disband them rather than try to salvage them for the new army: so strong was its fear that the remnants of the old army might infect the new with anarchic vices. Thus the once gigantic military power was completely scrapped; all that survived of it and was still battleworthy was a single division of Latvian riflemen, commanded by Colonel Vatzetis. Apart from this there were the workers' Red Guards and bands of partisans inspired by enthusiasm and sometimes not lacking self-discipline, but with little or no training or organization. Their numbers were far from impressive. In October 1917 the Red Guards of Petrograd had no more than 4,000 and those of Moscow no more than 3,000 fully trained and armed members.[1] Since October their numerical strength had not grown appreciably. From such slender beginnings sprang into being the Red Army which, after two and a half years, had five million men under arms.

[1] *Pyat Let Vlasti Sovietov*, pp. 154–5.

Numbers alone give only a faint idea of the difficulties. The greatest obstacles were moral and political. When he set out to found the Red Army, Trotsky seemed to be burning all that he had worshipped and worshipping all that he had burned. The Bolsheviks had denounced militarism and encouraged the soldier to revolt against discipline and to see in .the officer his enemy. They had done this not from enmity towards the army as such, but because they had seen in that army the tool of hostile interests. So overwhelmingly successful had their agitation been that it rebounded upon them. They were therefore compelled to break down the frame of mind which they themselves had built up before they could create the army which was a condition of their self-preservation. The popular mood was compounded of various strains: pacifist abhorrence of war; conviction that the revolution could rely on Red Guards and partisans and needed no regular army; and belief that it was the inalienable right of soldiers to elect their commanders and soldiers' committees. When Trotsky first came forward to say that soldiers' committees could not lead regiments into battle and that an army needed centralization and formal discipline, his words sounded like a profanation of a revolutionary taboo.

Moreover, all the machinery of government had broken down so completely that the attempt to create a new army seemed hopelessly unreal. Trotsky took over his department from an ineffective Collegium of three Commissars—Podvoysky, Antonov-Ovseenko, and Dybenko. Since November he had nominally headed the 'All-Russian Collegium for the Administration of the War Department Affairs'; but the Brest crisis had prevented him from giving much attention to this office. This Collegium prepared the decree of 15 January 1918 about the creation of an army of volunteers. Like most laws and ordinances of this period, this too was a statement of principle, on which the government was as yet unable to act. There were no administrative agencies to recruit the men, to put them into barracks, to clothe and feed them. There were no officers and sergeants to train the recruits. Only in April, a month after he had assumed his new office, did Trotsky begin to form regional and local offices of his Commissariat, i.e. recruiting centres; but still there was a gulf between decree and execution. All that had been achieved five months after the October insurrection was that in a few cities several hundred members of the Red Guards had begun to train for positions of command.

The first pronouncements which Trotsky made in his new office contained the main elements of his military policy.[1] He appealed primarily to the members of the party and of the Soviets: only with their support could he hope to carry out his task. He impressed upon them the need for the revolution to pass from its first, destructive, to its next, constructive, phase; and his text was: 'Work, Discipline, and Order will save the Soviet Republic.' It was in the military field that the transition had to be made first, for on it depended the revolution's survival. He did not opportunistically decry the first destructive phase, which, he said, had brought 'the great awakening of the personality in Russia'. Therein lay the historical significance and greatness of the first phase of the revolution. But the 'awakened personality', reacting against its former suppression, revealed its self-centred and anti-social features: 'Yesterday the man of the mass was still a nobody, a slave of the Tsar, of the gentry, of the bureaucracy, an appendage to the... machine ... a beast of burden.... Having freed himself, he is now most acutely aware of his own identity and begins to think of himself as of ... the centre of the world.'[2] It was the party's duty to inure the awakened personality to a new, conscious social discipline. For this the party itself must overcome its own anti-militarist bias: too many of its members still viewed any army as an instrument of counter-revolution. It was not yet the immediate task to create a fully fledged army; it was rather to gather a nucleus for it. The government decreed universal obligatory military training, in principle; but only volunteers would be immediately drafted and trained. The party must also overcome the crude bias in favour of elected commanders and soldiers' committees, for these were not of the essence of revolutionary democracy. The democratic principle required that the government should be elected and controlled by the masses, not that the masses should arrogate its functions and deprive it of the powers of appointment. The Red Army must use the services of the former Tsarist officers. In matters of defence, courage, revolutionary

---

[1] See his speech of 19 March to the Moscow Soviet, his statement of 21 March, and his speech of 28 March at the Moscow conference of the party. *Kak Vooruzhalas Revolutsia*, vol. i.   [2] Ibid., p. 39.

enthusiasm, and readiness for sacrifice were not enough. 'As industry needs engineers, as farming needs qualified agronomists, so military specialists are indispensable to defence.'[1]

While those who had made the revolution were utterly reluctant to take orders from the generals and colonels of the old régime, the generals and colonels were not less reluctant to place their skill and experience at the disposal of the Bolsheviks. There were only a few exceptions. The first military man of stature who volunteered for service was General Bonch-Bruevich, former commander of the northern front, who was won over by his brother, a well-known Bolshevik writer. Trotsky entrusted the general with organizing the General Staff, a task which had been quite beyond the ensign Krylenko, the Commander-in-Chief appointed in the first days of the revolution. But very few officers followed Bonch-Bruevich. Those who did so approached their task with all the mental habits of the regular soldier, accustomed to work within the rigid and well-ordered framework of a normal army and ill at ease in the climate of revolution. Radek describes Trotsky's first conferences with these officers in April 1918. In the course of many days the officers put forward and discussed their ideas, while Trotsky listened in silence. All sorts of schemes for galvanizing the old army were advanced; and none took account of the recent psychological upheavals. Then Trotsky outlined his scheme for recruiting volunteers. The only answer he obtained was an embarrassed silence and a shrugging of shoulders. The officers attributed the collapse of the old army to lack of discipline, and they were sure that there would be no discipline in an army of volunteers. Trotsky's project struck them as the fancy of a revolutionary dilettante.[2]

But in Trotsky's scheme of things politics dictated the military course of action. He had to enlist the enthusiasts of the revolution first, for only they would serve with complete self-discipline and could be counted upon later to impose discipline upon others. Even the drafting of volunteers was no easy matter. Adventurers and pot-hunters flocked to the recruiting centres, and they had to be carefully eliminated. Only in the late summer of 1918 did Trotsky proceed to experiment with conscription; he called up a small number of industrial workers in

[1] *Kak Vooruzhalas Revolutsia*, vol. i., p. 29.   [2] K. Radek, *Portrety i Pamflety*, pp. 31–32.

Petrograd and Moscow. When the first 10,000 workers had been drafted, this was hailed as a feat. Gradually more were recruited although, as conscription widened, the workers' reluctance to enrol began to show itself. But persuasion and appeals to class solidarity were, for the most part, effective. Only when the proletarian core of the army had been firmly established, did Trotsky begin to call up the peasants, first the poor and then the *serednyaks* (the middle peasants). These often deserted *en masse* and their morale fluctuated violently with the ups and downs of the civil war.[1]

As armies were lost and raised periodically with the frequent and sudden contraction and expansion of Soviet-held territory, the process had to be repeated in various provinces at different times. Until very late in the civil war, the Red Army had therefore little uniform outlook. Various stages in its organization constantly overlapped. Hardened and well-disciplined divisions fought side by side with units which were little better than a half-armed rabble. This increased the instability and nervousness peculiar to a revolutionary army, formed amid universal unsettlement. If, in spite of this, and in spite of a chronic shortage of munitions, uniforms, and boots, and also in spite of hunger and epidemics, the Red Army stood the test, this was due to the fact that it was set up in a number of concentric and gradually widening rings, each from a different social stratum and each representing a different degree of loyalty to the revolution. In every division and regiment the inner core of Bolsheviks carried with it the proletarian elements, and through them also the doubtful and shaky peasant mass.

On 22 April 1918 Trotsky laid his scheme before the Central Executive of the Soviets.[2] When he came to his point about the

---

[1] The *kulaks* were, like the urban bourgeoisie, drafted only for auxiliary services and labour detachments. Conscientious objectors, who refused service on religious grounds, were granted exemption.

[2] The decree which Trotsky laid before the Executive began as follows: 'Socialism has as one of its basic tasks to free mankind from militarism and from the barbarism of bloody contests between peoples. The goal of socialism is general disarmament, permanent peace, and fraternal co-operation of all the peoples inhabiting the earth.' *Kak Vooruzhalas Revolutsia*, vol. i, pp. 123–4. On this occasion the Executive also approved the text of the Red Army oath written by Trotsky:

'I, a son of the toiling people and a citizen of the Soviet Republic, assume the title of a soldier of the Workers' and Peasants' Army.

'Before the working classes of Russia and of the whole world I undertake to bear this title with honour, to learn conscientiously to wield arms. . . .

employment of officers, the Mensheviks raised an outcry. 'Thus the Napoleons make their appearance!' Dan exclaimed. Martov accused Trotsky of paving the way for a new Kornilov. These charges carried little conviction when they came from a party which had all but delivered the revolution to Kornilov.[1] More serious were the objections of the Left Social Revolutionaries, to whom this was no mere debating point. But the most persistent and influential opposition arose within the Bolshevik party itself. This opposition was actuated by the most diverse motives. Most of the Left Communists, who had opposed the peace of Brest, repudiated Trotsky's policy in the name of the revolution's libertarian spirit. They refused to countenance a centralized standing army, let alone one officered by Tsarist generals and colonels. Led by I. N. Smirnov, Bukharin, Pyatakov, and Bubnov, the Left Communists came out against Trotsky as frankly and bitterly as they had come out against Lenin in the controversy over Brest; they saw in their present opposition a continuation of their previous struggle: they refused to accept any compromise with forces of the old régime, whether in foreign or in domestic policy.

The other element in the opposition was formed by men who belonged to the inner Bolshevik hierarchy. As a rule these men stood for centralized authority and strict discipline and they viewed the Left Communists as irresponsible trouble-makers. They were not fundamentally opposed to Trotsky's idea of the new army; but they viewed with suspicion his solicitations of the former officers' corps. They suspected, not quite without reason, that the officers would enlist in order to betray the Red Army from within; and some were jealous for newly-acquired positions of power which they were now being asked to share in the

'I undertake to observe revolutionary discipline strictly and unflaggingly. . . .

'I undertake to abstain and to restrain other comrades from deeds which might harm and lower the dignity of a citizen of the Soviet Republic, and to direct all my actions and thoughts towards the great goal of the emancipation of all working people.

'I undertake to come forward on the first call of the Workers' and Peasants' Government to defend the Soviet Republic . . . in the struggle for the Russian Soviet Republic and for the cause of socialism and of the brotherhood of the peoples I shall spare neither my own strength nor my own life.

'If by evil design I should depart from this my solemn promise, let general contempt be my lot and let the severe hand of the revolutionary law punish me.' Ibid., p. 125.   [1] Ibid., p. 117.

army with erstwhile enemies. The jealousy and the suspicion were blended into a strong sentiment, which found expression in the Central Committee of the party. Even those Bolsheviks who agreed that the officers should be employed did so with strong mental reservations; and every now and then they gave vent to suppressed feeling. They opposed Trotsky's policy deviously, attacking it not in principle but in detail and execution.

These two trends of opposition overlapped and formed an ambiguous alliance. They enlisted the support of the commissars and commanders of the Red Guards and partisan groups, ordinary workers and non-commissioned officers, who had distinguished themselves in the first weeks of the upheaval, were surrounded by a halo of heroism, and bitterly resented subordination to Tsarist generals or any other military authority.

Implied in the immediate issue was a wider question concerning the attitude of the new state towards the positive values of the pre-revolutionary civilization and towards the intelligentsia which represented the sum total of the ideas, knowledge, and higher skills bequeathed by the old order. In the military field this question was most acute; but it was of vital significance to every aspect of Soviet life. Among Bolsheviks and ordinary workers there was an intense dislike of the professional men who had enjoyed freedom and privileges while the revolutionaries had spent their best years in banishment and prison. They were stunned when they were told that the revolution should restore the Tsar's 'flunkeys' and the 'bourgeois philistines' to respectability and influence. Yet this was what the revolution was beginning to do, because it could not wreak vengeance upon the intelligentsia without shattering the basis of its own future. Without its doctors, scientists, research workers, and technicians, of which it had none too many, and without its writers and artists, the nation would have sunk finally to the level of primitive barbarism, to which it was anyhow dangerously close. The disputes over the 'specialists' were therefore implicitly a struggle over the level of civilization from which the 'building of socialism' was to begin. Trotsky repeatedly posed the issue in this wider context, and not merely as a matter of military expediency. He argued that the 'cultural heritage' of which the revolution had taken possession must be saved, cultivated, and developed; and as long as the revolution had to defend itself,

military skill and knowledge must be considered as part of that
heritage. His exhortations to this effect make up many pages in
the volumes of his military writings and they belong to the
cultural as well as to the military history of the Soviet régime.

The combination of the groups opposed to Trotsky's policy
was all the more formidable as Lenin for a long time reserved
judgement on the employment of the officers, although he himself most emphatically insisted on a considerate and tactful
treatment of the civilian 'specialists'. The military branch of the
party, on whose co-operation so much depended, was firmly
against Trotsky's policy. The conflict came into the open when
Lashevich, the leader of that branch, a member of the Central
Committee and Zinoviev's close friend, publicly boasted that
the party would use the old generals only to 'squeeze them like
lemons and then throw them away'. Zinoviev spoke in the
same manner, as if setting out to wound the officers' self-respect
and to obstruct Trotsky's attempts to enlist them.[1] A General
Novitsky who had of his own accord declared his readiness to
serve under the Bolsheviks wrote an open letter to Trotsky, in
which he refused co-operation, saying that he had no desire to
be 'squeezed and thrown away like a lemon'. Trotsky countered
this with an emphatic repudiation of the attacks on the officers:
'Those former generals', he wrote, 'who work conscientiously
in the present difficult conditions, deserve, even if they are of
a conservative outlook, infinitely more respect from the working
class than pseudo-socialists who engage in intrigue. . . .'[2]

Trotsky was not merely anxious to reassure the officers. He
was sincerely indignant about Zinoviev's and Lashevich's crude
and offensive language. Even after the civil war, when the need
to employ the old officers was less pressing, he continued to
demand that they should be treated with consideration. He
held that they should be employed even after a new officers'
corps had been raised up, because no civilized and rationally
governed society can waste men of skill, knowledge, and merit.
He also spoke from his own faith in the moral greatness of the
revolution by which even men of conservative upbringing must

---

[1] A. F. Ilin-Zhenevskii, *Bolsheviki u Vlasti*, pp. 87–89.

[2] Trotsky, *Kak Vooruzhalas Revolutsia*, vol. i, p. 135; Ilin-Zhenevskii, op. cit., pp.
89–90. Trotsky's words were ostensibly directed against the non-Bolshevik opposition, but they actually aimed at Zinoviev and Lashevich. He explicitly repudiated
the talk about 'squeezing them like a lemon'.

be impressed; and he bitterly reproached with pusillanimity those Bolsheviks who thought that once a man had been a Tsarist officer he must for ever remain insensitive to the appeal of socialism.

He himself strove to impress upon the officers the moral grandeur of the revolution, obscured by its miseries. Some of his pleadings with the officers therefore belong among the most stirring apologias for the revolution. This, for instance, is a passage from an inaugural address he gave at the Military Academy in 1918. The address was devoted largely to the Academy's curriculum, but it also contained words the like of which had hardly ever resounded within the walls of a Military Academy:

People unaccustomed to the revolution and its psychology . . . may, of course, view with some horror . . . that riotous, self-willed, and violent anarchy which appeared on the surface of revolutionary events. Yet in that riotous anarchy, even in its most negative manifestations, when the soldier, the slave of yesterday, all of a sudden found himself in a first-class railway carriage and tore off the velvet upholstery to make puttees for himself, even in such a destructive act there manifested itself the awakening of the personality. The ill-treated, down-trodden Russian peasant, accustomed to be slapped in the face and abused with the worst curses, all of a sudden found himself, perhaps for the first time in his life, in a first-class carriage; he saw the velvet upholstery; in his own boots he had stinking rags; he tore off the velvet, saying that he, too, had the right to something good. After two or three days, after a month, after a year—no, after a month, he has understood the ugliness of his behaviour. But his awakened personality . . . the human personality will remain alive in him for ever. Our task is to adjust this personality to the community, to induce it to feel itself not a number, not a slave, as it had felt before, and not merely an Ivanov or a Petrov, but Ivanov the Personality.[1]

Supremely self-confident in his own intellectual power, Trotsky often castigated the generals he had enlisted for their attachment to routine, narrowness, and sometimes ignorance. For all his insistence on the need to employ the old officers, he showed the utmost vigour and initiative in educating former N.C.O.s and ordinary workers into a new officers' corps. He appealed to the N.C.O.s as the future 'unbreakable cadre of the

[1] Trotsky, op. cit., p. 165.

officers' corps of the Soviet Republic', telling them that in the
Russian Revolution as in the French, it was they who carried
the marshal's batons in their knapsacks.[1] By the end of the
civil war, the 'Tsarist' officers made up only one-third of
the commanding staffs—two-thirds had been promoted from the
ranks; and among those so promoted were many of the future
marshals of the Second World War. But in 1918 more than
three-quarters of the commanding and administrative staffs of
the Red Army consisted of officers of the old régime; and in
the highest commands the proportion was even greater.[2]

Among the officers there were, of course, traitors and would-
be traitors. Some waited for an opportunity to join the White
Guards; others deployed their troops so as to expose them to
loss and defeat; still others passed important secrets to enemy
headquarters. Soon after he became Commissar of War, Trotsky
appeared as chief witness in the trial of Admiral Shchastny,
whom he charged with sabotage. The admiral was condemned
to death on the strength of Trotsky's deposition. The trial was
designed to implant in the mind of the nascent army the idea,
taken for granted in any established army, that certain actions
must be regarded and punished as treason; and it was meant to
intimidate the officers who were in sympathy with the White
Guards. In civil war any penalty milder than death rarely has
a deterrent effect. The fear of prison does not deter the would-be
traitor, because he hopes in any case for the victory of the other
side which will free him, honour him, and reward him; or he
may hope at least for an amnesty after the end of the civil war.
Trotsky's orders of the day bristled with dire threats to the
agents of the White Guards. But even the threat of capital
punishment was no grave deterrent to officers in the fighting
lines. Trotsky then ordered that a register of their families be
kept so that the would-be traitor should know that if he went
over to the enemy, his wife and children would stay behind as
hostages. This was a cruel measure, and Trotsky employed all
his dramatic eloquence to make the threat as awe-inspiring as
possible. He justified it on the ground that without it the
revolution would be defeated and the classes that stood for the

---

[1] Trotsky, *Kak Vooruzhalas Revolutsia*, vol. i, pp. 174–85.
[2] Trotsky, *Stalin*, p. 279. See also *Voprosy Istorii*, no. 2, 1952; Yu. P. Petrov,
'*Voennye Komissary.*'

revolution be exposed to the vengeance of the White Guards. Amid the panics, the intense suspicions, and the violent passions of civil war, there were many innocent victims; and all too often Trotsky had to remind his over-zealous subordinates that the purpose of the terror was not to destroy potential enemies but to compel them to serve the revolutionary state.

He placed the commissar by the officer's side. For this, as for many other institutions, precedents could be found in the French Revolution, and Kerensky had already appointed commissars with the army. But hitherto the commissars had been attached only to the highest commands, and their role had been vague. Trotsky placed them at every level of the military ladder, from company commander to Commander-in-Chief. He also tried clearly to define the duties and responsibilities of commander and commissar. The former was responsible for military training and the conduct of operations, the latter for the commander's loyal behaviour and the morale of the troops.[1] No military order was valid unless it was signed by both. But no matter how clearly duties were assigned in theory, military authority was split. Rivalry and jealousy were inevitable. The officer resented the commissar's control; the commissar refused to reconcile himself to an arrangement which placed a colonel or a general under him politically and above him militarily. Trotsky tried to keep the balance between the two hierarchies. He sometimes appeared to the commissars as the protector of the officers and to the officers as the chief instigator of the commissars; and as he acted without regard for persons, he made many enemies. But he gained many devoted adherents among the officers, who were grateful to him for their rehabilitation, and also among the commissars, who held that the Red Army owed its political cohesion and power to his scheme. On the whole the system worked, though not without friction; and no alternative to it could be devised. Under the uncontrolled leadership of the former officers the Red Army would have collapsed politically. Under the command of Bolshevik dilettantes it would have been doomed on the battlefields. And nobody paid the effectiveness of this system a fuller, though reluctant, tribute than Denikin, its victim: 'The Soviet Govern-

---

[1] See the speech which Trotsky gave at the first congress of commissars in Moscow, in June 1918. *Kak Vooruzhalas Revolutsia*, vol. i, pp. 130 ff.

ment may be proud of the artfulness with which it has enslaved the will and the brains of the Russian generals and officers and made of them its unwilling but obedient tool. . . ."[1]

The task still to be accomplished was to centralize the Red Army and to establish single command. Trotsky went on to disband the Red Guards and the partisan detachments. The incorporation of partisan units proved unsatisfactory, because it infected the regular detachments with the 'guerilla spirit'. In the end Trotsky demanded the complete disbandment of partisan units and threatened with severe punishment commanders and commissars willing to incorporate such units. He insisted on the organization of the entire army into uniformly constituted divisions and regiments. This led to innumerable conflicts with guerillas, especially with the anarchist partisan army led by Makhno.[2] But even in divisions which were led by Bolsheviks often only lip service was paid to centralization and uniform organization. To many a Bolshevik the enforcement of centralization was all the more odious when it entailed subordination to a 'Tsarist' general. The Left Communists continued frankly to voice their opposition. A less open but all the more effective focus of the opposition was in the Tenth Army, which, under Voroshilov's command, stood at Tsaritsyn, the future Stalingrad.

.   .   .   .

In the middle of 1918 the Soviet republic was still virtually without an army. If foreign intervention had developed then on its later scale, or if the White Guards had been ready, the position of the Soviets would have been desperate. But the course of events somehow favoured the Bolsheviks: it imparted approximately the same rhythm and tempo to the efforts of both camps to gather and marshal their armed strength. Like the Red Army, the White Guards were only beginning to form. The German advance was confined to the southern fringe, and the troops of the Entente landed only at the remote outposts of

---

[1] Denikin, *Ocherki Russkoi Smuty*, vol. iii, p. 146.

[2] Several vain attempts were made to achieve reconciliation with Makhno's partisans. In the course of one such attempt Trotsky publicly stated that the accusation that Makhno had collaborated with the White Guards was false, but he emphatically denounced the conduct of Makhno's partisans on military and political grounds. In the end, Budienny's cavalry dispersed and destroyed Makhno's detachments. See *Kak Vooruzhalas Revolutsia*, vol. ii, book 2, pp. 210–12, 216–17; and P. Arschinoff, *Geschichte der Machno-Bewegung*.

Murmansk, Archangel, and Vladivostok. In central Russia the Bolsheviks consolidated their power in comparative safety. This circumstance accounted in part for the relatively slow progress they had so far made in the military field. It needed an imminent and mortal threat to speed up the process. That threat came suddenly from the Czechoslovak Legion, formed earlier in the war by prisoners of war eager to fight against Austro-Hungary.

Under the treaty of Brest the Soviet government was obliged to disarm the Legion. The disarming was carried out so reluctantly and perfunctorily that the Legion remained in possession of most of its arms. The British and the French at first proposed to evacuate the Legion from a Russian harbour; and to this the Soviet government agreed. Subsequently, however, the Entente failed to supply the ships and resolved to leave the Legion in Russia, where it might be used against either the Bolsheviks or the Germans, or against both. Trotsky guaranteed the Legion full security; and he offered its members the right to settle and work in Russia, if they so desired. While the Legion was aimlessly shifted across the Urals and Siberia, it was aroused by a rumour that the Bolsheviks were about to extradite it to the Germans. The Legion took up arms. In the military vacuum of Asian Russia, it rapidly occupied a vast area, overthrew the Soviets and made common cause with Kolchak's White Guards.[1]

When the Czechs seized Samara on the Volga, Trotsky ordered the first compulsory call-up of workers. From Moscow he hastily dispatched the conscripts against the Czechs. Most of them had had almost no preliminary training and were armed only *en route*. During the Czech advance the Left Social Revolutionaries rose against the Bolsheviks. The latter, we know, had at their disposal in Moscow only the Lettish troops commanded by Vatzetis and a detachment of revolutionized prisoners of war under Bela Kun. After the suppression of the rising in Moscow, the Lettish troops, too, were sent to fight the Czechs. The situation on the Volga was aggravated by the alleged treason of Muraviev, the colonel who had defeated

---

[1] '. . . I succeeded in securing Trotsky's good-will, and but for the folly of the French I am convinced that the Czechs would have been safely evacuated without incident', writes R. H. Bruce Lockhart, op. cit., pp. 272, 285.

Kerensky's attempt to recapture Petrograd, who had then distinguished himself fighting in the south and who had been appointed commander of the eastern front. Muraviev was, or claimed to be, in sympathy with the Left Social Revolutionaries; and the Bolsheviks accused him of collusion with the Czechs and Kolchak. According to one version, he committed suicide after he had been unmasked; according to another, he was executed. In the meantime the Czechs seized Ufa, Simbirsk, and Ekaterinburg.

In Ekaterinburg the Bolsheviks had kept in internment the Tsar and his family: they had intended to let a revolutionary tribunal try the Tsar, as Charles I and Louis XVI had been tried; and Trotsky had chosen for himself the role of the Tsar's Chief Prosecutor. But the advance of the Czechs and of Kolchak had so surprised the Bolsheviks on the spot that, so they claimed, they had no time to arrange for the safe evacuation of the Tsar and his family. They feared that the Tsar might be rescued by the Whites and rally all the forces of the counter-revolution, hitherto divided because of the lack of any unifying authority. Remembering perhaps Marat's dictum: 'Woe to the revolution which has not enough courage to behead the symbol of the *ancien régime*', the Bolsheviks, before their hasty withdrawal, executed the Tsar and his whole family. The official Bolshevik version claims that the execution was decided upon by the local Bolsheviks but approved after the event by Moscow. There are reasons to doubt the veracity of this version. It seems that the local Bolsheviks first asked the Politbureau for a decision, that Trotsky still counselled evacuation so that the Tsar might be placed in the dock; but that the Politbureau refused to take any risk and ordered the execution. Thus the world was deprived of the spectacle of a most dramatic trial, in which Trotsky and the Tsar would have faced each other.

The advance of the Czechs and of the White Guards continued. On 6 August the Red Army withdrew in panicky haste from Kazan, the last important town on the eastern bank of the upper Volga. If the Czechs succeeded in crossing the river at this point, they could surge across the open plain towards Moscow; and they would have found no obstacle in their way.

The Central Executive of the Soviets declared the Republic in danger. Trotsky ordered the first compulsory call-up of commissioned and non-commissioned officers, and stern measures against easy-going or privilege-seeking Communists in the army.[1] Two days after the fall of Kazan, he himself left for the front in the train which was to serve as his abode and mobile headquarters during two and a half years. In an order of the day issued before his departure, he wrote:

Leaving for the Czechoslovak front, I send my greetings to all those . . . who honestly and bravely defend the freedom and independence of the working class. . . .
Honour and glory to the valiant fighters!
At the same time I am issuing this warning: no quarter will be given to the enemies of the people, the agents of foreign imperialism, the mercenaries of the bourgeoisie. In the train of the People's Commissar for War, where this order is being written, a Military Revolutionary Tribunal is in session . . . [which] has unlimited powers within the zone of this railway line. A state of siege is proclaimed over this zone. Comrade Kamenshchikov, whom I have charged with the defence of the Moscow-Kazan line, has ordered concentration camps to be set up at Murom, Arzamas, and Svyazhsk. . . . I am warning responsible Soviet officials in all regions of military operation that we shall be doubly exacting towards them. The Soviet Republic will punish its sluggish and criminal servants no less severely than its enemies. . . . The Republic is in peril! Woe to those who directly or indirectly aggravate the peril.[2]

Trotsky arrived at Svyazhsk, a little town on the western bank of the Volga, opposite Kazan. This was the most advanced position of the Reds, after their retreat across the river. He found the front in a state of virtual collapse: mass desertion from the ranks, prostration among commanders and commissars. From his train, which stood within the reach of enemy fire, he descended into panic-stricken crowds of soldiers, poured out on them torrents of passionate eloquence, rallied them and, on occasion, personally led them back to the fighting line. At an especially critical moment, his own escort joined in the battle, leaving him almost alone on his train. The local commissars proposed that he should move to a safer place on a steamboat on the Volga; but fearing the effect this might have on the troops, he refused. On a ramshackle torpedo boat he went with

[1] Trotsky, *Kak Vooruzhalas Revolutsia*, vol. i, pp. 174–85.   [2] Ibid., p. 233.

sailors of Kronstadt, who had brought over a tiny flotilla to the Volga, on an adventurous night raid to Kazan. Most of the flotilla was destroyed but it managed to silence the enemy batteries on the banks of the river; and Trotsky returned safely to his base.

The forces engaged in this fighting were extremely small.[1] As at the opening of every civil war, so here the fortunes of a great revolution swayed on minute scales. In a battle of this sort the leader is constantly before the eyes of the men: his faith, his presence of mind, and his courage may work wonders. He has to establish his military authority also by personal example, which the leader of a normal army is rarely expected to give. In such a battle, on the other hand, the local commanders are constantly before his eyes; and the reputation which they gain on the spot helps them to undreamt-of promotion and fame. From Svyazhsk dated Trotsky's friendship for Vatzetis, whom he presently promoted to Commander-in-Chief of the Red Army. There, too, the young Tukhachevsky caught his eye. There the ties of comradeship with Raskolnikov, the commander of the Kronstadt sailors, and with the commissars I. N. Smirnov and Arkadi Rosengoltz grew close. At Svyazhsk he also conceived a high regard for V. Mezhlauk's organizing ability, and throughout the civil war he promoted Mezhlauk, who later became his enemy and vice-Premier under Stalin. These men— the veterans of the Fifth Army—remained close to Trotsky during the civil war; and they formed something like a counterpart to the Tsaritsyn group, whom Stalin befriended.

Lavish in praise for those who distinguished themselves by courage and talent, Trotsky dealt implacably with those who failed in their duties. He brought before a court martial the commander and the commissar of a regiment—the commissar's name was Panteleev—who at the height of the battle had taken themselves and their men away from the front line. Both the commander and the commissar were shot. 'The soldiers of the Red Army . . .', Trotsky commented on the event, 'are neither cowards nor scoundrels. They want to fight for the freedom of the working class. If they retreat or fight poorly, commanders

---

[1] Even after their victory, when their ranks grew considerably, the Reds numbered only 25,000 men. When Trotsky arrived their strength must have been much smaller.

and commissars are guilty. I issue this warning: if any detachment retreats without orders, the first to be shot will be the commissar, the next the commander. . . . Cowards, scoundrels, and traitors will not escape the bullet—for this I vouch before the whole Red Army.'[1]

Trotsky's unpublished correspondence with Lenin shows what meticulous attention he gave to the details of battle. In one message he insistently demands reinforcements; in another he asks that disciplined Communists 'ready to die' be sent to the Volga—'light-weight agitators are not needed here'. In still another message he asks for a supply of pistols and for a good military band. Eager to appeal to the soldiers' imagination and pride, he asked that the popular satirical poet Demian Bednyi be sent to the front and that the government should establish medals for bravery. The shyness which, after the abolition of all medals, the Bolsheviks felt about this last proposal can be guessed from the fact that Trotsky repeated it three times with increasing impatience. The correspondence also reveals a curious instance of Trotsky's ruthlessness. On 17 August Lenin communicated to him that the Red Cross, supported by the French and American Consuls, asked for permission to transport food from Nizhnii Novgorod, which was held by the Bolsheviks, to Samara which was occupied by the Whites. Lenin saw no objection to the expedition. But Trotsky refused to allow the Red Cross to move across the fighting lines. 'Fools and charlatans', he answered Lenin, would start talking about the possibility of conciliation with the Whites. He did not, he added, wish the Red Cross to witness the bombardment ('the burning and the scorching') of the 'bourgeois quarters' of Kazan. Before the bombardment, however, he issued a public warning to the working people of Kazan: 'Our artillerymen . . . will do their utmost to avoid damaging the dwellings and living quarters of the poor. But in a savage battle accidents may occur. We warn you about the imminent danger. . . . Remove your children from the town . . . seek refuge on Soviet territory—we offer fraternal hospitality to all toiling and needy people.'[2]

On 10 September the Reds stormed and seized Kazan. Two

---

[1] Trotsky, *Kak Vooruzhalas Revolutsia*, vol. i, p. 235.

[2] Ibid., p. 244: Lenin's message about the Red Cross was published in *Leninskii Sbornik*, vol. xviii, p. 186; Trotsky's answer is in *The Archives*.

days later Tukhachevsky captured Simbirsk and announced this in a laconic message to Trotsky: 'Order carried out. Simbirsk taken.' At the beginning of October the whole of the Volga region was again under Soviet rule.

This victory had an electrifying effect, especially because it coincided with a grave political crisis. In Moscow, a Social Revolutionary, F. Kaplan, had just made an attempt on Lenin's life. Another Social Revolutionary assassinated Uritsky in Petrograd. In retaliation, the Bolsheviks proclaimed the Red Terror and ordered the shooting of hostages. During these events Trotsky was recalled to Moscow. He found Lenin recovering from his wound; and, having reassured Lenin and the Executive of the Soviets about the prospects of the campaign, he returned to the front. About the same time the Right Social Revolutionaries tried to reassemble the dispersed Constituent Assembly and to form a rival government at Samara, under the protection of the Czechs and Kolchak. The Social Revolutionaries wielded considerable influence among the Volga peasants; and even a mere symbolic revival of the Constituent Assembly threatened to embarrass the Bolsheviks. By recapturing the Volga region, the Red Army eliminated this threat. The movement for the Constituante, cut off from its peasant following, was reduced to impotence. The Social Revolutionaries found themselves at the mercy of Kolchak, who presently proclaimed himself dictator ('Supreme Ruler'), dispersed the rump Assembly, executed some of its leaders, and compelled others to seek refuge in Soviet territory. Thus the adherents of the Assembly were crushed between the millstones of the Soviets and the White Guards.[1]

Finally, the victory on the Volga gave a powerful stimulus to the growth of the Red Army. Peril had shaken the Soviets from complacent indolence; victory gave them confidence in their own strength. The work of preliminary organization carried on in the Commissariat of War began to yield results: commanding staffs had been set up; recruiting centres were functioning; a rough framework for an army was ready.

At the end of September Trotsky returned to Moscow and reorganized the Supreme War Council into the Revolutionary War Council of the Republic. The body had to decide on

[1] V. Tchernov, *Mes Tribulations en Russie.*

matters of military policy.[1] Under it were the Revolutionary War Councils of fourteen armies, each Council consisting of the commander of the army and two or three commissars. Trotsky himself presided over the War Council of the Republic. His deputy, who managed the Council's day-to-day work while Trotsky was inspecting the fronts, was E. M. Sklyansky. Trotsky himself paid generous tribute to the talents, energy, and industry of his deputy, describing him as the Carnot of the Russian Revolution. The histories of the civil war written during the Stalin era hardly ever mention Sklyansky, even though he had not been involved in the struggle between Trotsky and Stalin and died in 1925. But Lenin's published correspondence and, even more, the unpublished records leave no doubt about Sklyansky's crucial role in the conduct of military affairs. His was one of the extraordinary careers of the time. As a young graduate of the medical faculty of Kiev, he had been drafted before the revolution into the army as a doctor and soon became prominent in the clandestine military organization of the Bolsheviks. Trotsky met him only in the autumn of 1917; and he was so impressed by Sklyansky's 'great creative *élan* combined with concentrated attention to detail' that he appointed him as his deputy.[2]

The other members of the Council were Vatzetis, who had just been appointed Commander-in-Chief; I. N. Smirnov and A. Rosengoltz, the commissars who had served with Vatzetis on the Volga; Raskolnikov who commanded the Red flotilla at Kazan; and Muralov and Yureniev. Thus the victors of Kazan were now placed at the head of military affairs.

With their help Trotsky set out to overhaul and centralize the southern front. It was in the south that the White Guards now had their main strongholds. The strongest Bolshevik force in the south was Voroshilov's Tenth Army. But Voroshilov was refusing to overhaul his troops according to Trotsky's uniform pattern. The conflict had been brewing for some time. Stalin had spent most of the summer at Voroshilov's headquarters at Tsaritsyn and had lent his support to Voroshilov. Somewhat

---

[1] The Revolutionary War Council should not be confused with the Council of Workers' and Peasants' Defence (where Lenin presided, with Trotsky as his deputy), which co-ordinated military and civilian policies.

[2] Trotsky, *Sochinenya*, vol. viii, pp. 272–81.

later, in September, Stalin acted as chief political commissar to
the whole southern front; and there was constant friction between the front and headquarters in Moscow. Trotsky was resolved to put an end to this. At the beginning of October, he
appointed Sytin, a general of the old army, as commander of
the southern front; and he demanded subordination from
Voroshilov. He also appointed a new Revolutionary War
Council for the southern front, on which Shlyapnikov, a prominent Bolshevik, replaced Stalin as chief commissar. Trotsky
accompanied these appointments by a threat: 'Commanders
and commissars who dare to infringe on rules of discipline, will,
regardless of past merit, be immediately committed to trial
before the Revolutionary Military Tribunal of the southern
front.'[1] At the same time, Trotsky proposed the appointment of
Stalin to the War Council of the Republic, hoping either to
appease him or to tie his hands—Stalin had already repeatedly
protested to Lenin against Trotsky's handling of the southern
front.

Stalin returned to Moscow, and a superficial reconciliation
between the adversaries took place. But Voroshilov, confident
in Stalin's protection, continued to defy higher authority and
ignored the orders of the new commander. Soon afterwards
Stalin returned to Tsaritsyn. But as the conflict was getting
worse, Lenin diplomatically recalled him to Moscow, and
Trotsky set out to inspect the front. The story of Trotsky's visit
to Tsaritsyn has been described many times by Trotsky himself
and others. He threatened to court martial Voroshilov. In a
public order of the day, he castigated his command for putting
its own ambitions above the interests of the entire front.[2] Confronted with the threat, Voroshilov promised obedience; and
Trotsky took no further action, except that he placed a man
whom he trusted, Okulov, in the command of the Tenth Army
in order to keep Voroshilov in check.[3] He gave further publicity
to the conflict when, on the first anniversary of the revolution, he
reported on the military situation to a Congress of Soviets and
spared no black paint in depicting the condition of the Tenth

---

[1] Trotsky, *Kak Vooruzhalas Revolutsia*, vol. i, pp. 347–8.
[2] See Trotsky's order of the day dated Tsaritsyn, 5 November 1918, *Kak Vooruzhalas Revolutsia*, vol. i, pp. 250–1.
[3] Trotsky's message to Lenin of 14 December 1918 in *The Trotsky Archives*.

Army. The Tsaritsyn group did not forgive Trotsky this humiliation.[1]

Trotsky spent the rest of the autumn and the beginning of the
winter at the southern front. In the meantime, his opponents
in Moscow, especially Stalin and Zinoviev, worked against
him and tried, not without some success, to influence Lenin.
Trotsky later recounted that, while he was at the front, Menzhinsky, the future chief of the G.P.U., warned him about the
'intrigue'. Menzhinsky said that Stalin tried to persuade Lenin
that Trotsky was gathering around him elements hostile to
Lenin. Trotsky frankly put the question to Lenin; and he relates
that Lenin, embarrassed, did not deny the fact of the intrigue,
but assured Trotsky of his complete confidence in Trotsky's
loyalty. All the same, Lenin refused to become involved in the
quarrel and exerted himself to compose it. Some time later he
suggested that Okulov, the man whom Trotsky had left at
Tsaritsyn to keep an eye on Voroshilov, should be recalled.
Trotsky refused and this time brought matters to a head: he
asked that Voroshilov be deposed from his command and transferred to the Ukraine, and that new commissars should be
appointed to the Tenth Army. Lenin yielded, and Voroshilov
had to go.

The Tsaritsyn group sought to revenge itself. It whispered
that Trotsky was the friend of Tsarist generals and the persecutor of Bolsheviks in the army. The accusation found its way into
the columns of *Pravda*, which was under Bukharin's editorship.
On 25 December 1918 *Pravda* published a scathing attack on
Trotsky by a member of Voroshilov's staff.[2] This coincided with
a new attempt of the Left Communists to achieve a revision of
military policy. Having failed in their opposition to the employment of officers, the Left Communists shifted their ground and
demanded that the commissars should hold all commanding
posts and that the officers should serve under them as mere
consultants. The whispering campaign against Trotsky became

[1] In the anniversary report, mainly devoted to argument against the critics of
centralization, Trotsky gave a deliberately exaggerated account of the Red Army's
strength, saying that *The Times* of London, which estimated the army's establishment at half a million men, greatly underrated it. In truth, the establishment was
still only 350,000 men. *Kak Vooruzhalas Revolutsia*, vol. i, pp. 332–41; *Pyat Let Vlasti
Sovietov*, p. 156.

[2] The article bore the title: 'It's High Time!' and was signed by Kamensky.

even deadlier: it was said that he delivered Communists and commissars to the firing squad. The accusation was brought before the Politbureau and the Central Committee by Smilga and Lashevich, two members of the Committee, who held important political posts in the army. (Lashevich, it will be remembered, had been in conflict with Trotsky because of the speech about 'squeezing the officers like lemons'.) The cases of the commissar Panteleev, who had been court martialled and shot at Svyazhsk, and of two other commissars, Zalutsky and Bakaev, who were said to have narrowly escaped execution, were brought to the notice of the Central Committee.

Trotsky replied to these charges in a confidential letter to the Committee.[1] He made no apology for the shooting of Panteleev, who had been court martialled for plain desertion; but he added that as far as he knew this was the only case of the sort which had occurred. More recently there was a misunderstanding in con-nexion with his order that the commissars should keep a register of officers' families in order that officers should know that if they committed treason their relatives might be victimized. On one occasion several officers went over to the White Guards; and it turned out that the commissars had not bothered to keep a register of their families. Trotsky then wrote that Communists guilty of such neglect deserved to be shot. Smilga and Lashevich apparently thought that it was at them that Trotsky had aimed his threat. Trotsky explained that this was preposterous. Smilga and Lashevich knew that he valued them as the best commissars in the army. He had uttered the threat 'as a general remark', aimed at nobody in particular.

On internal evidence, Trotsky's explanation seems to be true. His opponents did not support their charges by any specific instances, except the case of Panteleev. Nevertheless, Trotsky's orders were full of such blood-curdling threats; and although he may have uttered them merely to discipline his subordinates, they blotted his reputation; and the charges connected with them were levelled against him by Stalin's followers long after the civil war.

Trotsky asked the Central Committee to define its attitude towards his military policy and to remonstrate with *Pravda* for

---

[1] The letter bears no date but from inner evidence it is clear that it was written towards the end of December 1918. It has not been published. *The Trotsky Archives.*

having printed the accusation without prior investigation. He himself replied in *Pravda* with an attack on 'conceited, semi-educated party quacks', who spread distrust and hostility towards the officers. 'The general public knows almost every case of treason . . . but even in narrower party circles all too little is known about those professional officers who have honestly and willingly given their lives for the cause of the Russia of workers and peasants.'[1] The public should, of course, be informed about the instances of treason; but it should also know how often entire regiments perished because they were commanded by amateurs incapable of understanding an order or reading a map. He firmly rejected the new proposals that the officers should be mere consultants to the commissars. The idea was militarily worthless; and it was 'calculated to satisfy vindictive cravings'. The purpose of the Red Terror was not to exterminate or to degrade the intelligentsia, but at the most to intimidate it and so to induce it to serve the workers' state.

He took up this subject in a 'Letter to a Friend', which appeared in *Voennoe Delo* (*Military Affairs*) in February 1919.[2] The letter reveals the bitterness of the controversy. He wrote with scorn about the 'new Soviet bureaucrat', 'trembling over his job', who looked with envy and hatred at anybody superior to him in education or skill. Unwilling to learn, he would never see the cause of his failings in himself, but was always on the look-out for a scapegoat, and always ready to cry treason. Conservative, sluggish, and resenting any reminder that he ought to learn, this bureaucrat was already a baleful 'ballast' in the new state. 'This is the genuine menace to the cause of communist revolution. These are the genuine accomplices of counter-revolution, even though they are not guilty of any conspiracy.' The revolution would be an absurdity if its only result were to be that a few thousand workers should get government jobs and become rulers. 'Our revolution will fully justify itself only when every toiling man and woman feels that his or her life has become easier, freer, cleaner, and more dignified. This has not yet been achieved. A difficult road lies between us and this our essential and only goal.'[2]

This in a nutshell is the *leitmotif* of Trotsky's later struggle

---

[1] *Pravda*, 31 December 1918; *Kak Vooruzhalas Revolutsia*, vol. i, pp. 154–61.
[2] Trotsky, op. cit., vol. i, pp. 170–2.

against Stalin; and it first appears as early as one year after the October insurrection.

. . . .

In November 1918 the Austro-Hungarian and German empires crumbled under the impact of defeat and revolution. The treaty of Brest was annulled. The armies of the central powers withdrew from Russia and the Ukraine, leaving a military vacuum. Into this vacuum Trotsky was anxious to move the Red Army. But the bulk of the army was tied down by Kolchak in the Urals and by Denikin and Krasnov in southern Russia and on the Don. On the western and south-western fronts the situation was much the same as it had been on other fronts shortly after the revolution: the Bolsheviks there could rely only on Red Guards and partisan units. Even these were desperately short of ammunition; their guns rusted because lubricants could not be obtained; and their horses died for lack of fodder. The railways carried military transport at only a mile an hour. The rigours of the Bolshevik rural policy—the requisitioning of food—adversely affected the temper of the troops.[1]

In such circumstances Lenin was not very anxious to press on with the occupation of the Ukraine. He attached more importance to clearing the Don and the northern Caucasus of anti-Bolshevik forces. Trotsky was inclined to give priority to the occupation of the Ukraine. He expected allied expeditionary forces to land on the coast of the Black Sea; and, by bringing the Ukraine under Soviet control, he wanted to keep them as far from Moscow as possible. In the meantime, Kolchak's Guards had struck once again and seized Ufa and Perm. Fearing that Kolchak, Denikin, and Krasnov might effect a juncture on the Volga, Lenin warned Trotsky not to allow himself 'to be carried away' by his Ukrainian plans at the expense of other fronts. Soon, however, Kolchak's advance was stopped; and the danger which was uppermost in Lenin's mind did not arise. On the other hand, the French landed at Odessa and Nikolaev, as Trotsky had feared. The Bolshevik guerrillas in the Ukraine proved, after all, strong enough to defeat Petlura, to seize

[1] This description is based on the messages exchanged between Lenin and Trotsky in November, December, and January. Throughout this time Trotsky alarmed Moscow about the conditions prevailing in the Ukraine, and he urged an easing of the party's policy towards the peasants. *The Trotsky Archives.*

Kharkov, and to carry the revolution into most of the country. But in the meantime Denikin was gathering strength in the steppe of the northern Caucasus.

With the beginning of the winter a lull set in in the fighting; and for a moment it seemed that the lull might end in a formal armistice. The French intervention was collapsing. Stirred by Bolshevik agitation, the French garrison of Odessa revolted; and some time afterwards the whole French expeditionary force was withdrawn from Russia, to the disappointment of the White Guards. But Clemenceau and Foch did not give up the policy of intervention. In opposition to them, President Wilson proposed an armistice between the warring Russian parties and governments and a conference on Prinkipo Island. The Soviet government accepted the proposal. On 24 January 1919 Lenin cabled Trotsky: 'I am sorry but you will have to go to Wilson.'[1] He urged Trotsky to seize a few more cities so as to strengthen his bargaining position at the Prinkipo conference, which indicates that he seriously contemplated the armistice. Trotsky agreed to speed up military operations, but refused the diplomatic assignment, perhaps because of the still fresh and bitter aftertaste of Brest; and he proposed that Chicherin and Rakovsky be sent. The incident had no sequel. The chiefs of the White Guards, encouraged by the French, refused to meet the Bolsheviks, and so President Wilson's attempt at mediation foundered.

The new campaigning season was approaching, but even now, a year after Trotsky had become Commissar of War, his military policy had not yet received the party's blessing—he carried it out as if on his own responsibility. His opponents feverishly prepared to challenge his policy at the forthcoming eighth congress of the party, convened for March. Lenin stood at least as firmly as Trotsky for centralization and strict discipline, but he had not yet made up his mind on the employment of officers. Treason occurred all too frequently; and the opposition made the most of it. Shortly before the congress Lenin suggested to Trotsky the wholesale dismissal of the officers and the appointment of Lashevich, who had been a sergeant in the Tsarist army, as Commander-in-Chief. He was intensely surprised when Trotsky told him that more than 30,000 officers were already serving with the Red Army. Only now did Lenin realize the

[1] *The Trotsky Archives.*

magnitude of the problem and admit that, in comparison with
the number of the officers employed, the instances of treason were
few. He agreed at last that it was impossible to dismiss the
officers; and he publicly spoke with admiration of the originality with which Trotsky was 'building communism' with the
bricks left over from the destroyed edifice of the old order.[1]

Assured of Lenin's support, Trotsky confidently looked forward to the debate. The opposition marshalled its adherents
in the army and brought to the congress as many of them as
could be elected. However, before the congress opened, Kolchak
launched a new full-scale offensive. Once again the eastern
front was convulsed. It seemed preposterous that at such a
moment the head of the War Department should waste time
defending his policy in prolonged debate, and that hosts of
commissars should leave the fighting line to attend the congress.
The Central Committee therefore decided that Trotsky should
at once leave for the eastern front and that the military delegates should return to the front. The opposition protested,
saying that Trotsky was using the emergency to silence its
adherents and to evade a critical scrutiny of his policy. The
Central Committee then reversed its decision and allowed the
military delegates of the opposition to stay in Moscow. But
Trotsky himself and his adherents from the army immediately
departed for the front. He left behind 'Theses' explaining the
main aspects of his policy; and on his behalf Sokolnikov presented these to the congress.

The main debate on military affairs took place in secret
sessions of the military section of the congress. The records are
not available, but the broad lines of the debate and its outcome

---

[1] Lenin, *Sobranie Sochineniy* (First edition, 1920–6), vol. xvi, p. 73. The fact
that a year after the controversy had begun, Lenin had not been aware of the
scale on which officers had been drafted, shows that, absorbed in the conduct of
political and economic affairs, he took only a remote and general interest in the
direction of military affairs. Under the fresh impression of what Trotsky had
revealed to him, he thus argued with Gorky, whom he was trying to win back for
Bolshevism: 'Show me another man able to organize almost a model army within
a single year and win the respect of military experts. We have such a man. We have
everything. And we shall work wonders.' M. Gorky, *Lénine et le Paysan Russe*,
pp. 95–96. Gorky wrote this after Lenin's death, when the campaign against Trotsky was already in full swing. In a later edition, published after Trotsky's expulsion,
Gorky toned down the eulogistic words about Trotsky in a way which only confirms the authenticity of his own first version. See Gorky, *Days with Lenin*, pp. 56–
57. Lenin's eulogy of Trotsky is omitted from later editions of Lenin's works.

are clear from the papers of the Politbureau and from messages exchanged between Trotsky, Zinoviev, and Stalin.[1] The Left Communists and Voroshilov subjected Trotsky to severe criticism; and even the charges about his shooting of commissars were brought up again. Lenin made a strong plea in defence of Trotsky and left to attend to other business. The debate was then conducted by Zinoviev and Stalin. The defeat of the opposition was a foregone conclusion after Lenin's intervention. Both Zinoviev and Stalin were careful to give the impression that their views were identical with Lenin's; but they supported Trotsky's policy rather half-heartedly; and they made a few minor concessions to the opposition which were just enough to sully Trotsky's triumph. The opposition mustered about one-third of the votes; and it may be that the concessions helped to reduce its strength, as Zinoviev later reported to the Politbureau. In a public vote the congress fully approved Trotsky's activity and adopted his 'Theses'. But the approval was qualified by an instruction, passed in secret by the military section, which demanded that Trotsky pay more attention to Communist opinion in the army, hold regular monthly meetings with the important commissars, and so on. Thus, while the general public learned that the party had fully endorsed Trotsky's policy, his opponents in the Bolshevik hierarchy had the satisfaction that not all the charges against him had been unequivocally dismissed. Something of the accusation that he was the enemy of the party man in uniform had indeed stuck to Trotsky.[2]

Trotsky first learned that the congress had fully approved his policy from a telegram, signed by Stalin, which reached him at the front on 22 or 23 of March. Soon afterwards he received a message from the Central Committee, written by Zinoviev, who informed him about the concessions made to the opposition and urged him to treat this as a 'warning'. Trotsky refused to accept the 'warning'. He replied in writing that he could not recall commissars from the front every month to hold conferences with them. The 'warning' was in any case dictated by 'a shameful, crude, plebeian bias', which permeated all of

[1] *The Trotsky Archives.* Also *Vosmoi Syezd RKP*, pp. 337–8.

[2] In later controversy Trotsky dwelt on the public vote of the congress, while Stalinist sources spoke about the rebuff which the congress had administered to him in secret. Both versions are true, but each gives a different part of the truth.

Voroshilov's attacks. He reproached himself for having treated Voroshilov too leniently, for 'every discontent in the army is armed discontent'. Even in the civilian Bolshevik organization, he wrote, the margin of permissible controversy was narrow, from the moment when the party had passed from debate to action. The margin must be even narrower in the army; he must exact formal discipline. With much warmth he then recounted some of his conflicts with commanders and commissars, whom he had had to arrest and punish for breaches of discipline, but who, he hoped, would realize the need for this and would face him without bitterness in the future. Finally, he demanded a formal inquiry into the charges about the shooting of commissars.[1] He implied that Lenin and Zinoviev were not fully aware of the appalling conditions at the front. The attitude of the opposition resulted from weariness and strained nerves; and he was afraid that the party leadership, too, might succumb to this mood.

For the moment the matter was closed. The Left Communists, defeated at the congress, could not repeat their challenge. Their resentment still simmered; but in the subsequent crises of the civil war the need for discipline, centralization, and expert military leadership was generally accepted as a matter of course. However, the opposition in the party hierarchy, led by Stalin and Zinoviev, was as strong as ever—it merely shifted its ground from the issues hitherto debated to strategy and operational plans.

.   .   .   .

The strategy of the civil war was determined by the fact that the Red Army fought on fronts with a circumference of more than 5,000 miles. Even a numerous, well-equipped, and superbly trained army could not hold all these fronts simultaneously. The war consisted of a series of deep thrusts by the White Guards now from this and now from that part of the outer fringe into the interior and of corresponding, even deeper, Red counter-thrusts. After the defeat of the Czech Legion, three major campaigns formed the climaxes of the civil war in 1919: Kolchak's offensive, undertaken from Siberian bases, towards the Volga and Moscow, in the spring; Denikin's advance from

[1] A commission of inquiry was formed, but apart from the notorious case of Panteleev, no evidence was brought to support the charges. It seems that the commission's verdict was made public, but I have not been able to trace it.

the south, also aiming at Moscow, in the summer; and Yudenich's attempt to capture Petrograd, in the autumn. Had all
these offensives converged simultaneously on the centres of
Soviet power, the counter-revolution might have won. But the
White Guards operated on 'external lines'; and they were
separated from each other by thousands of miles. Each White
Army grew up independently and at a different pace; and the
commander of each was eager to win laurels exclusively for
himself. The Red Army, on the contrary, benefited from operating on 'internal lines'. It shifted its strength from one front to
another to secure local superiority. Its operations were eventually planned and its resources controlled from a single centre.
But it was natural that the fixing of strategic priorities should
give rise to friction and controversy, especially as almost every
decision involved a choice between political as well as strategic
alternatives.

In March and April Kolchak's troops once again advanced
on a broad front towards the Volga and renewed the threat to
Moscow so narrowly averted in the previous summer. The Red
Army in the east was depleted: its best troops had been sent
against Denikin in the south. Trotsky spent two months on the
eastern front, during which he stiffened the retreating army
and prepared the counter-thrust. This time he could view the
prospects with greater confidence than during the campaign
against the Czechs. He already had more than half a million
men under arms; and as the trade unions called up 50 per cent.
of their members, the army's establishment rose to one and a
half million men before the close of this campaign.[1] Towards
the end of April the commander of the eastern front, S. Kamenev, a former colonel of the Tsarist General Staff, carried out a
bold outflanking manœuvre against Kolchak's southern flank
and struck at the over-extended lines. Soon the White troops
began to fall back in disorder towards the Urals.

At this point a controversy ensued between Vatzetis, the
Commander-in-Chief, and Kamenev, the commander of the
front. The latter was eager to exploit his victory and to pursue
Kolchak into Siberia. He was confident that he could inflict a
final defeat on Kolchak even though with only a part of his
forces, which were again to be depleted in order to strengthen

[1] *Pyat Let Vlasti Sovietov*, pp. 156–7.

the southern front. Vatzetis, however, vetoed Kamenev's plan. He supposed that Kolchak had strong reserves in Siberia, and, considering the risk of a deep pursuit to be too great, he ordered Kamenev to stop at the Urals. Trotsky backed the Commander-in-Chief. He, too, feared that the eastern armies might march into a trap set for them by Kolchak.[1] At the moment Trotsky was also more eager to clear European Russia of the White Guards than to extend Soviet rule to Siberia. New commitments also appeared: Hungary and Bavaria had just been proclaimed Soviet republics, and Lenin urged the Red Army to establish liaison with Soviet Hungary, even though Polish troops in eastern Galicia barred access to Hungary.[2] For all these reasons Trotsky was anxious to reduce the commitments on the eastern front. As Kamenev would not give up his plan to pursue Kolchak, Trotsky removed him from the command. But now the commissars of the eastern front, Lashevich, Smilga, and Gusev, declared their solidarity with the removed commander and asked that he should be reinstated and given a free hand. The commissars had Stalin's ear, then Lenin's; and they achieved a reversal of Trotsky's and Vatzetis's decision. Kamenev pressed the pursuit beyond the Urals and presently crushed Kolchak, who, it turned out, had no strategic reserve in Siberia. Thus Trotsky's opponents scored a notable advantage.

Trotsky had in the meantime gone to the southern front, and there he spent most of the summer. Just as Kolchak's retreat was beginning, Denikin had advanced into the Ukraine, meeting only negligible resistance. The Ukraine, having only recently and superficially come under Soviet control, had no regular army. Red Guards and partisan bands roamed the country, looting and spreading anarchy. Makhno's anarchist detachments held part of the country under their sway. The Left Communists, defeated in Russia, had found refuge on the Ukrainian front which, being in an early phase of revolutionary ferment, was congenial ground to them. Trotsky himself had placed Antonov-Ovseenko, Podvoysky, and Bubnov in charge of military affairs in the Ukraine: but Bubnov was one of the leaders of the Left Communists and Antonov-Ovseenko was also inclined to give free

---

[1] Trotsky, *Sochinenya*, vol. xvii, book 2, p. 587.
[2] See messages exchanged between Vatzetis and Lenin on 21, 22 April 1919. *The Trotsky Archives*.

rein to Red Guards and partisans. At first Trotsky proposed firm action, and suggested to Moscow that the three commissars be removed from the Ukraine and replaced by convinced disciplinarians. He even complained about the 'softness' of his friend Rakovsky, who headed the Soviet Ukrainian government; and he asked that either S. Kamenev or Voroshilov should be appointed commander of the Ukrainian front, with a categorical assignment to subdue the guerrillas.[1]

From Moscow no reply came at first. The longer Trotsky stayed in the Ukraine, however, the more he felt himself overwhelmed by the prevalent chaos. He came to think that the military disorder could not be overcome before the economic and political condition of the country had become more normal. He could not, he reported to Moscow, centralize and discipline troops whom he was unable to feed, clothe, and arm. 'Neither agitation nor repression can make battleworthy a barefoot, naked, hungry, lice-ridden army.'[2] He asked for supplies from Russia, but in vain. In addition, the Ukrainian peasantry showed utter hostility towards the Soviets; and the Bolshevik leaders on the spot were half-resigned to defeat. The reshuffling of commanders he himself had proposed could not remedy these conditions. In the meantime Lenin began to urge him with increasing impatience to carry out the proposed change in the Ukrainian command.

At the beginning of July Trotsky returned to Moscow. This was the lowest point in his fortunes during the civil war. He admitted that he had misjudged the position on the eastern front when he opposed the pursuit of Kolchak. Now he had to answer strictures on his management of the Ukrainian front. In addition, the Commander-in-Chief whom he had promoted and backed had become the victim of scathing attacks. Stalin pressed for Vatzetis's dismissal and even charged him with treason. He proposed that Kamenev, the victor over Kolchak, whom Trotsky had so recently demoted, should be appointed Commander-in-Chief. Stalin himself, incidentally, had just successfully directed the defence of Petrograd against Yudenich;

[1] Trotsky believed that Voroshilov had in the meantime become a convinced adherent of his policy (cable of 17 May sent from Kharkov to the Central Committee. *The Trotsky Archives*). Now it was Lenin who denounced Voroshilov for 'pilfering' army stocks, &c. (Lenin's cable to Trotsky of 2 June).

[2] Message of 1 July 1919.

and he walked in the fresh glory of that victory. On 3 July the Central Committee resolved to act on Stalin's advice: Vatzetis was dismissed with honours, and Kamenev was appointed Commander-in-Chief. Trotsky resisted the change and sulked; but Kamenev's 'success on the eastern front', as he himself wrote later, 'bribed Lenin and broke down my resistance'.[1] This reverse was bitter enough, but yet another followed. The Central Committee also decided to overhaul the Revolutionary War Council of the Republic. Trotsky was to remain its Chairman, but his friends (Smirnov, Rosengoltz, Raskolnikov) were removed, and their places were taken by Smilga and Gusev, the commissars who had defended the new Commander-in-Chief against Trotsky and whose candidatures Stalin favoured.

The double reproof was so hurtful to Trotsky that he resigned on the spot from the Politbureau, the Commissariat of War, and the Council of War. But the Politbureau could not permit the conflict to come into the open. No matter with what Trotsky may have been taunted in the inner councils of the Kremlin, to the country he remained the leader of the October insurrection, the founder of the army, the artisan of its victories. His resignation in the middle of a new emergency would have dismayed the army and the party. And Lenin, at any rate, was genuinely anxious that his government should not forfeit Trotsky's services. On Lenin's proposal, the Politbureau rejected Trotsky's resignation, and it adopted unanimously a resolution solemnly assuring Trotsky of its deep respect and complete confidence and urging him to continue his 'extremely difficult, dangerous and important' work on the southern front. It was also on this occasion that Lenin, obviously perturbed by the incident, handed to Trotsky as a token of his confidence an endorsement in blank of any order which Trotsky might issue.[2] On these terms Trotsky stayed in office.

Another tug-of-war arose at once over the campaign against Denikin; and in this, too, Trotsky's adversaries worsted him. By this time Denikin had seized Tsaritsyn, the coal basin of the Donetz, and Kharkov. The anti-Bolshevik front spread from the

---

[1] Trotsky, *Stalin*, p. 313.

[2] The endorsement, under Lenin's official stamp, runs as follows: 'Knowing the stern character of Comrade Trotsky's orders, I am so convinced, so absolutely convinced, of the correctness, expediency, and necessity for the success of the cause of Comrade Trotsky's order that I endorse it without reservation.' *The Archives.*

Volga and the Don to the western steppe of the Ukraine. Its eastern sector between the Volga and the Don was held by the Don Cossacks, while the White Guards proper advanced on the central and western sectors. The question to resolve was at which sector the Red Army should direct a counterstroke. The new Commander-in-Chief proposed to direct it at the eastern sector, along the Don valley, towards Tsaritsyn and Denikin's bases in the northern Caucasus. On strictly military grounds this was a sound plan. It was designed to outflank Denikin's forces and to cut them off from their main bases. It was also calculated to separate Denikin's army from Kolchak's so that even if Kolchak were to regain the initiative and advance once again, he could not join hands with Denikin. The offensive was to be carried out by Red armies withdrawn from the Urals; and it was easier to throw these armies against Denikin's eastern flank than to shift them farther to the west.

To this scheme Trotsky objected. Denikin, he argued, was weakened by a dissension between the White Guards proper and the Don Cossacks. The White Guards consisted mainly of Russian officers impatient to overthrow the Bolsheviks in Moscow and Petrograd. The Cossacks, indulging in particularism, wished merely to keep the Bolsheviks out of their *stanitsas*, and were reluctant to stick out their necks beyond the Don valley. Denikin's plans for an offensive on Moscow left them lukewarm. Trotsky held that if the Red Army were to throw its main force into the Don valley, it would arouse the Cossacks, force them into a bitter fight, and thus unwittingly help to close the breach in the enemy's camp. Even after an initial success, the Red Army would have to advance across land with poor communications and amid a hostile population. In the meantime, Denikin would strike at the weak central sector, for there was the shortest route to Moscow. Trotsky proposed that the main force of the Red Army should be shifted to the central sector, with Kharkov and the Donetz Basin as its chief objectives. In an advance along this line the Reds could split Denikin's army, separate the Cossacks from the White Guards and neutralize them. The attackers would enjoy the advantage of operating in a highly industrialized area, the population of which favoured the Soviets; and they would also have at their disposal a dense network of roads and railways.

The social and political lie of the land should therefore determine the direction of the offensive. Kamenev's plan, though correct from an abstract strategic standpoint, failed to make allowance for the close interplay of politics and strategy in civil war.

When the controversy between the Commissar of War and the Commander-in-Chief was brought before the Politbureau, the arguments of the Commander-in-Chief carried the day. The Politbureau authorized the main offensive on the eastern sector.

This continuous succession of personal reverses for Trotsky had a strange sequel. In a somewhat sullen mood Trotsky returned to the southern front. He had hardly arrived at his field headquarters at Kozlov before he received an enigmatic message, bearing the signatures of Dzerzhinsky, Krestinsky, Lenin, and Sklyansky, informing him that the Commander-in-Chief (i.e. Vatzetis) had been charged with treason and imprisoned. The message did not specify the charges—it merely stated that they were based on depositions made by another arrested officer. The blow was deadly. It originated with Stalin who had already denounced Vatzetis as a traitor and it was unmistakably aimed at Trotsky. We do not know exactly how Trotsky reacted to this blow. Almost certainly he strongly defended the imprisoned man and personally vouched for his integrity, for this is how he acted in similar cases, when less important officers were implicated.[1] Enough that after a few days Vatzetis was released and rehabilitated. Trotsky himself later gave two versions of the charges: according to one, Vatzetis had not shown enough vigilance in dealing with counter-revolutionary officers in his entourage: according to the other, he nourished hopes of a future Napoleonic career.[2] Neither lack of vigilance nor a privately cherished ambition amounted to treason or justified the imprisonment; and, after his release, Vatzetis continued to hold high posts in the army

[1] Earlier in the year, for instance, Trotsky categorically protested against the arrest of General Zagin, who, he wrote, had done more to help the Soviets than those who kept him behind bars. The arbitrary treatment of such men had a disastrous effect on the officers' morale, Trotsky wrote; he asked for the General's release and personally vouched for him until his conviction in court should take place. *The Trotsky Archives* (correspondence of January 1919).

[2] Trotsky, *Stalin*, pp. 310–16.

until late in the Stalin era. His arrest in 1919 was therefore intended to add humiliation to the setbacks Trotsky had already suffered.

These were weeks of exceptional tension between Trotsky and Lenin, as their correspondence testifies. In part this was due to the disagreement over strategy and in part to the fact, connected with it, that Trotsky's assignment to hold the Ukraine against Denikin was a Sisyphean labour. Lenin also suspected that Trotsky was seeking to discredit the new Commander-in-Chief in the eyes of the officers on the southern front. From the south Trotsky reported that Yegoriev, the commander of the front, took a highly critical view of Kamenev's plan for the offensive; and that he carried out Kamenev's orders without conviction. Regardless of the rights and wrongs of the issue, Trotsky wrote, this was an abnormal state of affairs; and he proposed the appointment of a new commander of the front who would share the views of the Commander-in-Chief. This proposal, which actually testified to Trotsky's loyalty, stirred suspicion in the Kremlin. The Politbureau changed the commander of the front, but also detailed to the Ukraine Smilga and Lashevich, who were at loggerheads with Trotsky; and, further, it meaningfully reminded Trotsky that he ought to do all he could to strengthen the authority of the new Commander-in-Chief. Against the insinuation Trotsky vigorously protested. Repeatedly he expostulated with Lenin and the Politbureau for their 'unbusinesslike' replies to his messages. Lenin, in his turn, showered upon him admonitions and reproaches: why had he so little achievement to report? Where were the offensives that were to be mounted in the Ukraine?

In truth the unsettlement prevalent in the Ukraine afforded Trotsky little or no scope for military action. The Red Army had invested its main strength in the eastern sector of the front; and the Ukraine, which formed the central and western sectors, was left to fend for itself. Trotsky ceaselessly alarmed Moscow about the insufficiency of the Ukrainian forces, still utterly disorganized; and he demanded reinforcements and supplies. The Politbureau almost certainly suspected that Trotsky made these demands in order to achieve by a roundabout way a revision of Kamenev's operational plan and a different distribution of the troops.

A glimpse of the situation on the spot may be gained from an angrily aggressive message which Trotsky addressed to the Politbureau on 11 August. The Red Army men in the Ukraine, he wrote, were starving. Half of them had neither boots nor underwear, and very few had coats. It was no better with rifles and ammunition. Everybody was armed except the soldiers. The *kulaks* had vast stocks of weapons bought from deserters. Hungry and unarmed, the Red Army man lost confidence when he came face to face with the well-fed village usurer. The *kulaks* must be taken severely to task and disarmed. Two or three thousand well-equipped and reliable communists could stiffen the front; but Moscow refused to dispatch them. The Ukrainian Bolsheviks were in a defeatist mood. They held that it might not be a bad idea to let the Ukraine experience White rule for a short time—this would cure the people of illusions and turn them back towards the Bolsheviks. He assured the Politbureau that he firmly resisted this mood. But the Ukrainian divisions needed a respite, a chance 'to wash, to dress, and to prepare for the offensive'.[1]

Denikin, however, did not allow them the respite. A fortnight later he seized Kiev and nearly the whole of the Ukraine; and he pressed at the Red Army's weak centre, towards Voronezh and Kursk, along the shortest line to Moscow.

At this moment Trotsky demanded a revision of the operational plan. He urged that the reserves of the Supreme Command be shifted from the eastern sector towards Voronezh and Kursk. Over and over again he repeated this demand; and over and over again the Politbureau and the General Staff rejected it. Meanwhile the Red Army failed to make any decisive progress on the Don, and Denikin seized Kursk, Voronezh, and Orel. Only when the threat to Moscow became imminent, at the beginning of October, did the Commander-in-Chief change his mind and begin to mass reserves on the central sector. But by now Denikin's forces had broken through towards Tula, the last important town in front of Moscow. And simultaneously, Yudenich, armed by the British and supported by the British Navy, rapidly advanced from Estonia towards Petrograd and reached the outskirts of the city.

If it were not for the extreme gravity of the situation, Trotsky

[1] *The Trotsky Archives.*

might have rejoiced at the completeness with which events had vindicated him and converted all his opponents to his view. Now even Stalin pressed for the final abandonment of Kamenev's operational plan, and sparing Kamenev no insult, he repeated word by word Trotsky's arguments.[1]

At this moment of general depression Trotsky's optimism and energy knew no bounds. He was convinced that the regrouping of forces at last undertaken would soon yield results. The front was virtually overhauled, the reserves built up; and, with communication lines so radically shortened, abundant supplies reached the troops. The enemy was over-extended; and the power of the Red Army was like a compressed spring ready for the recoil. Trotsky confidently assessed the material and moral resources the Soviets could still marshal. Like no other member of the Politbureau, he had constantly stared at the inferno of the civil war. He was haunted by the image of half-naked soldiers trembling in the frost and of the wounded dying *en masse* for lack of medical attention. He had also fully gauged the army's nervous instability. But at moments of mortal peril he believed in the army's capacity for sudden bursts of enthusiasm, in its readiness for sacrifice, and in the spirited initiative of its commanders and men, which triumphed over the chaos into which the revolution seemed periodically to dissolve.

He now rose to his full height not merely as the chief manager and organizer of the army but as its inspirer, as the prophet of an idea. He boldly tapped the hidden moral resources of the revolution. The quality of his appeal may be gauged, for instance, from an address he gave at a congress of the Comsomol, the Communist Youth, which met just when Moscow and Petrograd had come within reach of the White Guards. He spoke to juveniles about the duties they had to perform 'within the shrinking area left to the Red Army'. They should assist in the mobilization; they should help to maintain liaison between units in combat; they should steal through the enemy's lines to reconnoitre his dispositions; and so on. But before they went on

---

[1] It is on this basis that latter-day Soviet historians attribute to Stalin the authorship of Trotsky's scheme for the offensive. But Stalin's letter to Lenin in which he urged a concentration of striking-power on the central sector is dated 15 October 1919 (see Stalin, *Sochinenya*, vol. iv, pp. 275-7) while Trotsky wrote his memorandum on this issue in September. Trotsky, *Sochinenya*, vol. xvii, book 2, pp. 556-9; Voroshilov, *Stalin i Krasnaya Armia*, pp. 21-22.

their perilous assignments, they ought to know the place they occupied in the affairs of the world. Lucidly, simply, without a trace of condescension, he surveyed the international scene. They should also see their own role against the background of world history, in the long perspective of mankind's slow, painfully slow, yet inspiring progress 'from the dark animal realm' to undreamt-of summits of civilization, towards which socialism was leading them. He turned his listeners' minds back to primitive man, who 'hobbling and limping, wandered through sleepy forests and who, gripped by superstition, created for himself little gods and tsars and princes'. Then man 'replaced the many gods by one God and the many little tsars and princes by one Tsar'. 'But he has not stopped at this. He has renounced tsars and gods and has made an attempt to become free master of his own life. . . . We are participants in this unprecedented historic attempt.' 'These hundreds of thousands of years of man's development and struggle would be a mockery if we were not to attain . . . a new society, in which all human relations will be based on . . . co-operation and man will be man's brother, not his enemy.' He then spoke about 'history's enormous furnace', in which the Russian national character was remoulded and freed from its langour and sluggishness. 'This furnace is cruel . . . tongues of flame lick and scorch us, but [they also] . . . steel our national character.' 'Happy is he', Trotsky exclaimed, 'who in his mind and heart feels the electrical current of our great epoch.'[1]

It was in the grimmest of moods that the Politbureau met on 15 October. At Orel the battle still swayed; and on its outcome hung Moscow's fate. There seemed to be little hope for Petrograd's defence. Under so gloomy an aspect did the situation present itself to Lenin that he proposed to abandon Petrograd and to gather all available strength around Moscow. He reckoned even with the possibility of Moscow's fall and with a Bolshevik withdrawal to the Urals.

Against this proposal Trotsky vigorously protested: Petrograd, the cradle of the revolution, must not be abandoned to the White Guards. The surrender of that city might have a disastrous effect on the rest of the country. He proposed that he himself should go to Petrograd to take charge of its defence.

[1] Trotsky, *Pokolenie Oktyabrya*, pp. 157-67.

He submitted to the Politbureau a series of emergency decrees aiming at total mobilization: Let them disband the multiple and now useless government departments and agencies in Moscow and call everybody to arms. He would rush reinforcements to Petrograd from the dead ends of the front, from the coast of the White Sea and the Polish marches.

This time his habitual antagonist supported him. Stalin, too, demanded the defence of both capitals.[1] In their attitude there was that concord which may unite enemies on a sinking ship when they are bent on rescuing it. While Trotsky volunteered to go to Petrograd, Stalin replaced him on the southern front. The Politbureau adopted the decrees submitted by Trotsky; and it elected a commission of four (Lenin, Trotsky, Kamenev, Krestinsky) which was to give effect to them. It also authorized Trotsky to leave for Petrograd, but it still reserved judgement on his plan to defend the city.

On 16 October, in his train *en route* to Petrograd, Trotsky dictated his reflections on the situation. He mocked at Churchill's recent proclamation of the anti-Soviet crusade of fourteen nations. These, he wrote, were nothing but 'fourteen geographic notions'—Kolchak and Denikin would have been happier to be succoured by fourteen Anglo-French divisions. The loud rejoicing of the bourgeois West over the imminent downfall of the Soviets was premature. Even if the Red Army were not to succeed in halting Yudenich outside Petrograd, it would crush him within the walls of the city. He sketched something like a plan for a battle inside Petrograd, which curiously resembles the tactics of the battle of Stalingrad in the Second World War.

Having broken through this gigantic city, the White Guards would get lost in this labyrinth of stone, where every house will present them with an enigma, a threat or a deadly danger. From where should they expect a blow? From a window? From a loft? From a cellar? From behind a corner? From everywhere! . . . We can surround some streets with barbed wire, leave other streets open and transform them into traps. All that is needed is that a few thousand people should be firmly resolved not to surrender. . . . Two or three days of such street fighting would transform the

---

[1] This is based on Trotsky's own account. From the records it does not appear that Stalin was present at this session of the Politbureau. On 15 October he sent a letter to Lenin from the southern front. He probably communicated his opinion before his departure.

invaders into a frightened and terrified flock of cowards, surrendering in groups or individually to unarmed passers-by and women. . . .
But street fighting causes accidental casualties and it results in the
destruction of cultural values. This is one of the reasons why the
field command is obliged to take every step not to allow the enemy
to approach Petrograd.[1]

In Petrograd bad news awaited him: Yudenich had seized
Krasnoe Selo, at the approaches to the city. The defences had
been depleted by a transfer of troops to the southern front and
disorganized by treason among high staff officers. Zinoviev,
chief of the 'Commune of the North', was in a mood of prostration; and his irresolution infected his subordinates. But from
Moscow came Lenin's notification that the Politbureau had
approved Trotsky's plan and authorized him to wage the battle,
if need be, inside the city. Lenin still prudently insisted that he
should prepare for a retreat, evacuate official documents and
arrange for the blowing up of power-stations and for the scuttling of the Baltic fleet. Trotsky replied with a confident report;
and as if to give to his confidence a peculiarly defiant twist, he
inquired whether he would be allowed to pursue Yudenich
into Estonia, Yudenich's jumping-off ground.[2]

He addressed once again the Petrograd Soviet he had led in
1905 and 1917. He described frankly the threatening disaster
and, calling for a supreme effort, he gave vent to his personal
feeling for the city:

In these dark, cold, hungry, anxious, bad autumn days Petrograd
presents to us again the grand picture of rallying self-confidence,
enthusiasm, and heroism. The city which has suffered so much,
which has burned with so strong an inward flame and has braved
so many dangers, the city which has never spared itself, which has

---

[1] Trotsky, *Sochinenya*, vol. xvii, book 2, pp. 266–7.

[2] This question led to a long exchange between Lenin, Trotsky, and Chicherin.
The Commissar of Foreign Affairs, fearing international complications, strongly
protested against pursuit into Estonia. Trotsky then contented himself with a mere
threat that the Red Army would cross the frontier if the Estonian government
failed to disarm the White Guards retreating into its territory. The attitude of the
Baltic states gave the Politbureau and Trotsky some anxiety. Trotsky publicly
threatened the Finnish government that he would let loose Bashkirian divisions
upon Helsinki if the Finns made any move against Petrograd. The governments of
the Entente secretly urged the Baltic governments to join in Yudenich's offensive;
but impressed by Trotsky's threats the Baltic states adopted an attitude of wait and
see.

inflicted on itself so much devastation, this beautiful Red Petrograd remains what it has been—the torch of revolution. . . .[1]

Of the effect of Trotsky's intervention we have many eye-witness accounts. The following comes from Lashevich, who at this time was, as we know, anything but friendly towards Trotsky and himself played an eminent role in these events:

Like fresh reinforcements arriving . . . Trotsky's presence on the spot at once showed itself: proper discipline was restored and the military and administrative agencies rose to their task. Whoever was inefficient was demoted. The higher and the middle commanding personnel were changed. Trotsky's orders, clear and precise, sparing nobody and exacting from everybody the utmost exertion and accurate, rapid execution of combat orders, at once showed that there was a firm directing hand. . . . The inward rallying had begun. The staffs got into working order. Liaison, hitherto defective, became satisfactory. The supply departments began to function without a hitch. Desertion from the front was radically reduced. In all detachments field tribunals were in session. . . . Everybody began to realize that only one road was left—forward. All avenues of retreat had been cut. Trotsky penetrated into every detail, applying to every item of business his seething, restless energy and his amazing perseverance.[2]

For a few days Yudenich's advance continued. The appearance of British tanks on the outskirts of the city caused a panic. On horseback Trotsky gathered terror-stricken and retreating men and led them back into the fighting-line. In a spurt of improvisation factories, working within the range of Yudenich's artillery, began to turn out tank-like vehicles; and the panic was over. Regular troops, hastily formed Red Guards, even detachments of women, fought back, as Yudenich put it, with 'heroic madness'. A week after Trotsky's arrival, the defenders passed to the offensive. On the second anniversary of the revolution, which was also his fortieth birthday, Trotsky was back in Moscow to report victory to the Central Executive of the Soviets.

The last act of the civil war had begun. On the southern front, too, the White Guards were reeling back and disintegrating.[3] The Red Army pressed forwards towards Kharkov, Kiev,

---

[1] Trotsky, *Sochinenya*, vol. xvii, book 2, p. 287.

[2] *Borba za Petrograd*, pp. 52–53.

[3] The reasons for the collapse of the White armies have by nobody been stated more bluntly and truthfully than by Denikin himself: 'The liberation by ourselves of enormous areas should have brought about . . . a rising of all elements hostile to

and Poltava. In Siberia Kolchak was utterly defeated. So rapidly did the tide turn that only three weeks after that critical session at which defeat had stared the Politbureau full in the face, Red Moscow gloried in triumph. At the ceremonial anniversary session of the Executive of the Soviets, Trotsky was acclaimed as father of victory and awarded the Order of the Red Banner.[1]

He was now at the summit of his political and military achievement. He had led a revolution, he had founded a great army and had guided it to victory. He had won the adoration of the broad mass of the revolution's well-wishers and the grudging admiration as well as the unforgiving hatred of its enemies. Like other Bolshevik leaders, he hoped that the horrors and terrors of the civil war were over and that the era of peaceful Socialist reconstruction was about to begin. In this he expected to play a part as pre-eminent as the one he had played in military affairs. In December 1919, at the seventh Congress of the Soviets, he drew up a balance-sheet of the civil war; for, although the fighting was still on, its outcome was in no doubt.[2] He paid a high-minded tribute to those who had borne the crushing burden of the last years. He eulogized the commissars,

Soviet power. . . . The question was only whether the popular masses had lived down Bolshevism . . . ? Will the people go with us . . . ? Life has given an answer which was at first indefinite and then negative.' Denikin, *Ocherki Russkoi Smuty*, vol. v, p. 118. 'The troops of the army of the south did not avoid the general malady and they blotted their reputation by pogroms of Jews. . . . The inner sores festered in the atmosphere of hatred. The pogroms brought suffering to the Jewish people, but they also affected the spirit of the troops, warped their mind and destroyed discipline. . . .' Ibid., p. 146. And this is how Wrangel drew the moral balance of the campaign: 'The Volunteer Army has discredited itself by pillage and violence. Here we have lost everything. We cannot even try to march once again along the same roads, under the same flag.' Ibid., p. 263. Writing about corruption in his army, Denikin goes on to say: 'This feast at a time of pestilence aroused anger and disgust in outside observers. . . .' And finally: 'English munitions and Kuban bread still reached us from our supply bases, but the moral bases had already been destroyed.' Ibid., p. 314.

[1] The same Order was awarded to the city of Petrograd and to Stalin, who did not even attend the ceremony. Trotsky later recounted that those present were surprised by the honour bestowed upon Stalin and that nobody applauded it. Be that as it may, Trotsky was certainly annoyed, for soon afterwards he wrote: 'Petrograd has been awarded the Order of the Red Banner. And it is Petrograd which has really and honestly deserved it. When rewards are given to individuals, mistakes and accidental privileges are always possible. But when the distinction goes to Petrograd there is no mistake and no bias.' *Sochinenya*, vol. xvii, book 2, p. 310.   [2] Ibid., pp. 325–55.

whose enemy he had been supposed to be: 'In our commissars
. . . we have a new communist order of Samurais, the members
of which have enjoyed no caste privileges and could die and
teach others to die for the cause of the working class.' He
praised lavishly the commanders of the victorious armies, those
who had been Tsarist generals and those who had risen from
the ranks and had in civilian life been metal-workers or barbers.
With especial warmth he spoke of the achievements of three
army commanders: Frunze, the worker, Tukhachevsky, the
Guard officer, and Sokolnikov, the revolutionary journalist.
Then he outlined the prospect of the abolition of the standing
army and of its transformation into a democratic militia
inspired by the Socialist ideal, the militia of which Jaurès had
once dreamt.[1] He had a few friendly words even for the Mensheviks who had, in the last emergency, rallied to the defence
of the Soviets and were present at this congress. 'We appreciate
very highly', he said, 'the fact that other parties, too, parties
belonging to the opposition . . . have mobilized a certain
number of their workers for the army. They have been received
there as brothers.' A few months earlier he had threatened the
Mensheviks that they would be 'crushed to dust' if they obstructed defence. But now he addressed himself to Martov, who
had congratulated the Bolsheviks on their military and diplomatic successes. He expressed 'real joy . . . without any *arrière
pensée* and without a trace of irony', because 'Martov has spoken
about *our* army and *our* international struggle—he has used the
word *we*, and in so doing he has added political and moral
strength to our cause.'

Like other Bolsheviks, Trotsky looked forward to appeasement
in domestic policy, which would allow the parties at least of the
Socialist opposition to resume open activity. The curtailment of
the powers of the *Cheka* and the abolition of the death penalty
in January 1920 were intended as first steps in that direction.
But these sanguine hopes were not to materialize.

The horrors of war had not yet receded into the past.[2]

[1] See 'Note on Trotsky's Military Writings', pp. 477 ff.
[2] Material for this and the next chapter has been drawn, *inter alia*, from
Bubnov, Kamenev, Eideman, *Grazhdanskaya Voina*, vols. i–iii; Kakurin, *Kak
Srazhalas Revolutsia*, vols. i–ii; and Frunze, *Sobranie Sochineniy*, vols. i–iii.

CHAPTER XIII

Revolution and Conquest

THROUGHOUT these years the leaders of Bolshevism anxiously watched for the omens of revolution in Europe. Every phase in the social and political struggles of Europe reacted directly upon the course of the civil war. The downfall of the Hohenzollerns and Habsburgs allowed the Soviets to regain ground lost under the Peace of Brest Litovsk. But soon afterwards the victorious Entente proclaimed the blockade of Russia and this was followed by the 'crusade of fourteen nations'. The mere threat of Allied intervention profoundly affected the situation in Russia. Since the revolution the old ruling classes had been in a state of utter depression, terrified by the abyss which separated them from the mass of the people. They lacked organization and faith in their own cause; they were divided against themselves; they were incapable of producing any plan of action.[1] The promise of intervention put courage into their hearts. It was only after the promise had been made, after British, French, and American liaison officers had appeared at the headquarters of the White generals and the first foreign cargoes of guns and munitions had reached Russian shores that the ranks of the White Guards began to swell and the civil war flared up in earnest. The Bolsheviks thought that only intense revolutionary ferment abroad could paralyse the intervention. They were compelled to carry the struggle into the enemy's camp; and they were all the more inclined to do so as they had persistently predicted that Europe's ruling classes would not reconcile themselves to the Russian Revolution and that for its self-preservation the revolution would be forced to assail the European capitalist order, which was anyhow about to crumble under the blows of the European working classes. Half of this prediction had come true: the ruling classes of the Entente had declared war on Bolshevism; and there were moments when

[1] One of the first leaders of the White Guards, General Kaledin, said before he committed suicide early in 1918: 'Our situation is hopeless. The population not only does not support us—it is definitely hostile. We have no strength, and resistance is useless.' Denikin, op. cit., vol. ii, p. 220.

the other half, too, foreshadowing the rising of the European proletariat, seemed close to fulfilment.

Since November 1918 Germany and most of central Europe had been in the throes of upheaval. In Berlin, Vienna, and Warsaw councils of workers' deputies existed side by side with Social Democratic governments. The Bolsheviks, who looked at things through the prism of their own recent experience, saw in this an exact reproduction of that 'dual régime' which had, in Russia, sprung from the February Revolution. They spoke about the 'German February'; and they expected a rapid disintegration of the dual régime, an ascendancy of the Councils of Workers' Deputies, a 'German October'.

It was an extremely simple-minded notion that history could so precisely and so rapidly repeat itself in country after country. But the mechanics of all the classical popular revolutions have very many features in common. Each begins with a partial collapse of the established system of government; each passes through the transitory phase of a dual régime; and in each the conservative, moderate, and conciliatory parties, at loggerheads with one another, successively exhaust and discredit themselves. It was this broad succession of phases that the Bolsheviks expected to recur in other countries. What was wrong in their expectations was not merely the calendar of revolutionary events but the fundamental assumption that European capitalism was at the end of its tether. They grossly underrated its staying power, its adaptability, and the hold it had on the loyalty of the working classes. The revolutionary ferment in Europe was strong enough for a minority of the working class to be determined to follow in Bolshevik footsteps. The majority exerted themselves to wrest reforms from their governments and propertied classes. But even when they exhibited sympathy for the Russian Revolution, they were in no mood to embark upon the road of revolution and civil war at home and to sacrifice in the process the standards of living, the personal security, the reforms they had already attained, and those which they hoped to attain.

The historic tragedy of Bolshevism in its heroic period was its refusal not merely to reconcile itself to this fact but even to make full allowance for it. The Bolshevik leaders viewed the relative conservatism of European labour as the deceptive surface of politics, beneath which pulsated all the revolutionary instincts of the proletariat. What was needed was to break through the thin crust and to release the hidden anti-capitalist energies. This picture of the world resulted from something more than an error of political judgement. It reflected the psychological incapacity of early Bolshevism to acknowledge its own isolation in the world, an incapacity which was common to all leaders of the revolution, but which was in nobody as strong and as complete as in Trotsky. An instinctive horror of the revolution's isolation permeated the whole of his being, his brain and his heart. None of the Bolshevik leaders had as yet even the faintest premonition of 'socialism in one country'. But to Trotsky the isolation of Bolshevism was already a nightmare too terrible to contemplate, for it meant that the first and so far the only attempt to build socialism would have to be undertaken in the worst possible conditions, without the advantages of an intensive international division of labour, without the fertilizing influence of old and complex cultural traditions, in an environment of such staggering material and cultural poverty, primitiveness, and crudity as would tend to mar or warp the very striving for socialism. Sooner or later this horror of isolation was bound to clash with reality; and the clash was to compel Bolshevism to wrestle convulsively with its own mental image of the world.

After Brest, when this dilemma had first upset his inner confidence, Trotsky found a sort of escape in the herculean exertions of the civil war. For the time being his horror of isolation found inverted expression in violent bursts of confidence in the imminent expansion of the revolution. In January 1919, when the streets of Berlin were littered with barricades, he wrote: 'It is no longer the spectre of communism that is haunting Europe . . .—communism in flesh and blood is now stalking the continent.'[1] It was the ideas and the hopes of the bourgeoisie that had assumed an air of utter unreality in his eyes. He saw something ghost-like in the appearance in Europe of President Wilson, 'that Tartuffe brought up on a Quaker fasting diet, who roams bleeding Europe as the supreme representative of morality, the Messiah of the American dollar, and punishes and pardons the nations and settles their fate'. Europe

[1] Trotsky, *Sochinenya*, vol. xiii, pp. 6–14.

could not fail to see that its only salvation was a continent-wide federation of Soviet republics; and once Germany had acceded to that federation 'Soviet Italy and Soviet France will join a month earlier or a month later'.[1]

In the first week of March 1919 a significant event occurred within the walls of the Kremlin. In an old, imperial court of justice, Lenin opened a meeting of about two score of delegates from various foreign Left Socialist groups. The arrival of those delegates was in a sense the first breach in the blockade. Most of them had had to steal across frontiers: some of the expected delegates had been prevented by their governments from leaving their countries; others had been arrested *en route*. Having for a long time been completely cut off from the West, the Bolsheviks listened eagerly to what the delegates reported on the state of affairs abroad. The reports were confused and contradictory; but on balance they seemed to justify the expectation of early revolution.

The purpose of the conference was not quite clear. It was either to proclaim the foundation of the Third International or to make preliminary arrangements for this. The Bolsheviks were inclined to form the new International there and then, but they waited to hear the opinion of foreign delegates. The most important of these, the Germans, held that the groups represented at the conference were, apart from the Russian party, too weak to constitute themselves as a fully fledged International. However, an Austrian delegate who, after an adventurous journey, arrived in the middle of the debate, gave a startling description of Europe seething with revolution; and he passionately called on the conference to raise at once the banner of the new International. The conference responded: it constituted itself as the foundation congress of the Communist International. Thus, fathered by wish, mothered by confusion, and assisted by accident, the great institution came into being.

Its birth coincided with the ebbing away of revolution in Europe. The January rising in Berlin had been crushed; its reluctant leaders Rosa Luxemburg and Karl Liebknecht had been assassinated. This was a turning-point in European history, for none of the waves of revolution that came in the following

[1] Loc. cit.

years equalled in impetus and impact the wave of 1918. The Bolshevik leaders failed to recognize the turning-point for what it was. The defeat of the January rising in Berlin seemed to them an episodic reverse, very much like their own setback in July 1917, to be followed by an aggravation of social strife. Greeting the foreign delegates in the Kremlin, Lenin told them: 'Not only in Russia, but even in the most advanced capitalist countries of Europe as, for instance, in Germany, civil war has become a fact. . . . Revolution has begun and is gaining strength in all countries. . . . The Soviet system has won not merely in backward Russia, but even in Germany, the most developed country of Europe, and also in England, the oldest capitalist country.'[1] Lenin was given to this illusion not less than Trotsky, although Trotsky, with his foible for indulging in breath-taking predictions, made the blunder appear even more egregious.

It is doubtful whether Lenin and Trotsky would have founded the International at this stage if they had had a clearer perception of the condition of Europe. They would, in any case, have gone on advocating the idea of the new International, as they had done since 1914. But it is a far cry from advancing an idea to imagining that it has become reality. In the period of Zimmerwald and Kienthal both Trotsky and Lenin had contemplated the new International not as a body representing a revolutionary minority and competing with the old 'social patriotic' International, but as an organization leading the majority of workers and replacing the old International. Trotsky had explicitly argued that, if they remained in a minority, the revolutionary Marxists might have to return to the old International and act as its left wing.[2] Nothing had been further from his thoughts or Lenin's than the intention of giving an assortment of small political sects the high-sounding label of the International.

And yet this was what they did in March 1919. Most of the delegates who constituted themselves the founding fathers of the Comintern represented small Marxist or pacifist sects nesting in the nooks and crannies of the European Labour movements. This might not have mattered in a truly revolutionary situation, for, in such a situation the extreme 'sect' as a rule, rises rapidly to influence and leadership. The Bolsheviks were not quite

[1] Lenin, *Sochinenya*, vol. xxviii, pp. 433-4.   [2] See above, p. 235.

aware of the weakness of their foreign associates; but even if they had been aware of it they could still hope that with the progress of international revolution these associates would gain strength, as it had been gained by the Bolsheviks, who had themselves been little more than a 'sect' early in 1917. The hope seemed all the more justified as the Second International had fallen into such disrepute that it appeared to be dead beyond resurrection. The workers' widespread opposition to the old International sprang, however, not from any positive revolutionary attitude, but from a revulsion against war and social patriotism. The Bolsheviks, naturally, confused the motives. Even so, their expectations were not altogether groundless: within a year the new International did, in fact, gain a formidable hold on the European Labour movement.

Trotsky made only a brief appearance at the founding congress. Kolchak's spring offensive had just begun and Trotsky, interrupting an inspection of the battlefields, came to the conference hall straight from his train, in full uniform, bringing with him a breath of the civil war. The delegates who had known him as the spokesman of Zimmerwald eyed with thrilled curiosity the passionate anti-militarist transfigured into the leader of an army.[1] He gave the conference a hurried explanation of the main lines of his military policy and then presented a manifesto he had written to introduce the new International to the world. The manifesto began with a rapid incisive survey of the changes which capitalism had recently undergone. The war had brought the twilight of *laissez faire*. The state now tended to dominate economic life. Which state would dominate it, the bourgeois or the proletarian? This was the question. The reformists and social patriots evaded the issue and preached conciliation. 'If these preachings were to find acceptance among the working classes, capitalist development in new, much more concentrated and monstrous forms, would be restored on the bones of several generations, with the inevitable prospect of new world war. Luckily for mankind, this is impossible.'[2] Socialism, if it won in Europe, would also free the colonial nations, and assist them with its technology, organization, and spiritual influence so as to speed up their transition to an organized Socialist economy.

[1] Arthur Ransome, *Six Weeks in Russia*, p. 143.
[2] Trotsky, *Sochinenya*, vol. xiii, pp. 38–49.

'Colonial slaves of Africa and Asia! The hour of proletarian dictatorship in Europe will strike for you as the hour of your own emancipation.' From earlier classical statements of Marxist policy, the manifesto differed mainly in its emphasis on proletarian dictatorship, on the role of a revolutionary party, and in its aggressive opposition to bourgeois democracy. But if these were differences of emphasis rather than principle the idea of an alliance between Socialist revolution in the West and the colonial peoples of the East was quite new; it bore the hallmark of the Third International. Nevertheless, the manifesto was addressed primarily to Europe:

The whole bourgeois world charges the communists with the destruction of freedom and political democracy. The charge is untrue. Assuming power, the proletariat only discovers the full impossibility of the application of . . . bourgeois democracy, and it creates the conditions and the forms of a new and higher workers' democracy. . . . The wailings of the bourgeois world against civil war and Red Terror are the most prodigious hypocrisy known in history. . . . There would have been no civil war if cliques of exploiters, who had brought mankind to the brink of perdition, had not resisted every step forward made by the toilers, if they had not organized conspiracies and assassinations and called in armed assistance from outside. . . . Never artificially provoking civil war, the Communist Parties strive to shorten as much as possible the duration of such war . . ., to diminish the number of its victims and, above all, to secure victory to the working class.

Far from forming a group of conspirators or from renouncing the patrimony of European socialism, the International prided itself on inheriting 'the heroic efforts and the martyrdom of a long line of revolutionary generations from Babeuf to Karl Liebknecht and Rosa Luxemburg'.[1]

Not a month passed from the issue of this manifesto before revolution had gained important footholds in central Europe: Hungary and Bavaria were proclaimed Soviet republics. Bolshevik hopes soared: from Munich and Budapest the revolution would surely spread at once to Berlin and Vienna. The news reached Trotsky while he was mounting an offensive in the foothills of the Urals; and there, on the marches of Asia, he greeted the promise of the revolution's salvation coming from

[1] Trotsky, *Sochinenya*, vol. xiii, pp. 38–49.

the West. In 'Reflections on the Course of the Proletarian Revolution', written under the fresh impression of these events, he remarked: 'Once the Church used to say: *Ex Oriente Lux*. . . . In our epoch, indeed, the revolution has begun in the east'; but 'the revolution which we live through is a proletarian one, and the proletariat is strongest, most organized, most enlightened in the old capitalist countries'. Yet he had a foreboding about the strange course of events. Hungary had been the most backward land in the Austro-Hungarian empire. Bavaria was the most retrograde province of Germany. In both countries the peasants, not the workers, predominated; and both had traditionally been regarded as ramparts of reaction. Why was it that the revolution obtained footholds there and not in the centres of proletarian socialism?

He answered his own question, saying that although the proletariat was weak in the backward countries, the ruling classes there were weaker still. 'History has moved along the line of least resistance. The revolutionary epoch has made its incursion through the least barricaded gates.' The suggestive metaphor suggested more than Trotsky himself intended. He had no doubt that the revolution would advance to the heart of the fortress: 'To-day Moscow is the centre of the Third International. To-morrow—this is our profound conviction—the centre will shift westwards, to Berlin, Paris, London. The Russian proletariat has welcomed with joy the envoys of the world's working classes within the walls of the Kremlin. With even greater joy will it send its own envoys to the second congress of the Communist International to one of the western European capitals. An international congress in Berlin or in Paris will mean the full triumph of proletarian revolution in Europe and consequently all over the world. . . . What happiness it is to live and fight in such times!'[1]

Barely three months later the great prospects and hopes had gone with the wind. Soviet Bavaria had succumbed to the troops of General Hoffmann, Trotsky's adversary at Brest. White Terror reigned over the ruins of Soviet Hungary. The workers of Berlin and Vienna viewed with apathy the suppression of the two Communes. Germany and Austria, indeed the whole of Europe, seemed to be finding a new conservative

Op. cit., pp. 14–30.

balance under the Peace of Versailles, just concluded. These events coincided with the worst predicament of the civil war: British and French intervention reached its height, and Denikin seized the Ukraine and advanced towards Moscow.

This was a strange moment in the history of Bolshevism. Not only did the anti-Soviet intervention gather strength and momentarily meet with little or no effective counteraction from the western working classes. Not only had the revolution lost its footholds in central Europe. Even in Russia it stood in the gravest danger of forfeiting the relatively wealthy and civilized western and central provinces and of having to draw back into the wastes of the east, for only there did the course of the war favour the Red Army. But while fortune frowned upon the Bolsheviks from the West, it enticed them with new opportunities in the East. Not only did the wild mountain ranges of the Urals offer hospitality and security to the Soviets. Beyond the Urals and Siberia, Asia stirred in rebellion against the bourgeois West. In India these were the days of Amritsar, when Gandhi's campaign of civil disobedience all but transformed itself into a nation-wide anti-British rising. This concatenation of events set in motion Trotsky's political imagination and impelled it in a curious direction.

On 5 August 1919 Trotsky sent from the front a secret memorandum to the Central Committee, urging a radical 'reorientation' in international affairs. He argued that the revolution had been thrown back eastward and—eastward it must face. He still assumed that the delay in European revolution would last from one to five years only; and he did not believe that Denikin would consolidate his hold on the Ukraine. Yet for the time being, he wrote, the Red Army could play only a minor part in Europe, whether as an offensive or a defensive force. But the gates to Asia were open before it! There the Red Army would have to contend only with Japanese forces which were too small for Siberian spaces and which would be hampered by American jealousy of Japanese expansion.[1] The weight of the Soviet régime in Asia was such that the Bolsheviks were in a position

[1] Trotsky remarked that the United States was so frightened of Japanese domination in Siberia that the 'Washington wretches' (although they were still using Kolchak as their agent) might yet resolve to back the Soviets against Japan. Some time later Lenin similarly set store by the rivalry between America and Japan. Lenin, *Sochinenva*, vol. xxxi, pp. 433–40.

not merely to wait there for new developments in Europe, but to embark upon an intense activity in the east.

In a tone of disillusionment with the recently formed International, Trotsky suggested that a body directing the revolution in Asia might soon be of much greater importance than the Executive of the Comintern. The Red Army might find the road to India much shorter and easier than the road to Soviet Hungary. A 'serious military man' had suggested to him a plan for the formation of an expeditionary cavalry corps to be used in India. Trotsky repeated that the revolution's road to Paris and London might lead through Kabul, Calcutta, and Bombay. With the utmost urgency he made the following proposals: an industrial base should be built up in the Urals to make the Soviets independent of the strategically vulnerable Donetz Basin; a revolutionary academy should be opened in the Urals or in Turkestan; political and military staffs should be set up to direct the struggle in Asia; technicians, planners, linguists, and other specialists should be mobilized for this work, particularly from the Ukrainian Communists, who, having lost the Ukraine, should now help the revolution to establish itself in Siberia.[1]

These proposals bore little relation to what could and had to be done immediately to ward off a military débâcle. Together with this memorandum Trotsky forwarded two other messages with detailed proposals for the overhaul of the southern front. To these, it may be surmised, the Politbureau immediately devoted closer attention than to the suggested 'Asian reorientation'.[2] Nor was this train of thought firmly rooted in Trotsky's own mind. It came as an impetuous reflex of his own brain in response to an exceptional set of circumstances; and the reflex ran counter to the principal, European, direction of his thought. It is, nevertheless, instructive as a pointer towards the future. In milder form the circumstances which gave rise to these suggestions—Russia's severance from the West and the abeyance of revolution in Europe—would persist after the end of intervention and civil war; and the reaction to them would follow broadly the lines suggested by Trotsky. The centres of

[1] *The Trotsky Archives.*
[2] The influence of Trotsky's ideas may, of course, be traced in the work of the second congress of the Comintern and in the congress of the eastern peoples at Baku which took place a year later.

Soviet power would shift eastwards, to the Urals and beyond. Only Stalin, not Trotsky, was to become the chief agent and executor of this momentous shift, which could not but entail an 'orientalization' of the revolution's mental and political climate, an orientalization to which Trotsky was not assimilable. The road of the revolution to Peking and Shanghai, if not to Calcutta and Bombay, was to prove shorter than that to Paris and London and certainly easier than the road to Berlin or even to Budapest. It is a tribute to the fertility of Trotsky's mind that in a single side-flash it opened vistas upon the future which far surpassed the comprehension of most contemporaries.

Before the year 1919 was out, the Bolsheviks again hopefully faced west. The Ukraine and the southern provinces of European Russia were again under their control. The White Armies awaited the *coup de grâce*. The opposition of western European labour was at last seriously hampering British and French intervention. Only relations with Poland were in suspense. Poland was egged on by France to act as the spearhead of the anti-Soviet crusade. But Pilsudski, who already ruled Poland but not yet as dictator, adopted an ambiguous attitude. He cherished the ambition of conquering the Ukraine, where the Polish landed gentry had possessed vast domains, and setting up a Polish-Ukrainian federation under Polish aegis. But he hung fire as long as the Bolshevik forces were engaged against the White Guards, for he knew that Denikin's or Yudenich's victory would mean an end to Poland's independence. In strict secrecy from the French, who were arming and equipping his army, he concluded an informal cease-fire with the Bolsheviks. For a moment it seemed that the cease-fire would lead to an armistice and peace. In November 1919 the Politbureau deliberated over the terms of a settlement proposed by the Poles. It found the terms acceptable, and it commissioned Trotsky and Chicherin to work out the details.[1]

So confident were the Bolshevik leaders in the approach of peace that they put on a peace footing those of their armies which were not engaged in combat and transformed them into labour armies. On 16 January 1920 the Entente lifted the block-

[1] See the excerpts from the records of the Politbureau, session of 14 November 1919, in *The Trotsky Archives*.

ade from Russia; and immediately the Central Executive of the Soviets decreed the reforms already mentioned—the abolition of the death penalty and the curtailment of the *Cheka*'s powers. A few days later, however, on 22 January, Trotsky communicated to the Politbureau his apprehension that Pilsudski was preparing for war.[1] With Lenin's encouragement, he proceeded to strengthen the Red Armies on the Polish front.[2]

At the beginning of March the Poles struck. From the Urals, where he had been inspecting the labour armies, Trotsky rushed to Moscow. The peace reforms were stopped or annulled. The country was once again in a warlike spirit.

In view of what happened later, it ought to be underlined that at this juncture Trotsky stood for a policy of the strong arm towards Poland. For many months Chicherin had in vain addressed secret peace offers to Warsaw, urging a settlement of frontier disputes extremely favourable to Poland. Pilsudski ignored the advances and kept Polish opinion in the dark about them. Chicherin continued to make conciliatory proposals even after the beginning of the Polish offensive. His policy, however, aroused opposition within the Commissariat of Foreign Affairs, especially from Litvinov, his deputy. Trotsky intervened and firmly sided with Litvinov. He urged the Politbureau to stop the overtures. Pilsudski saw in them merely signs of Soviet weakness; and, as they had been made secretly, they failed to move Polish opinion towards peace. Trotsky demanded a return to open diplomacy which should enable the Polish people to see who was responsible for the outbreak of hostilities. Pilsudski settled this controversy, for shortly thereafter he found a pretext for breaking off negotiations, invaded the Ukraine, and seized Kiev. On 1 May 1920 Trotsky appealed to the Red Army to inflict upon the invader a blow 'which would resound in the streets of Warsaw and throughout the world'.

The Polish invasion stirred Russia deeply. For the first time the Bolsheviks now called for national not for civil war. To be sure, to them this was a struggle against 'Polish landlords and capitalists', a civil war in the guise of national war. But whatever their motives, the conflict let loose patriotic instincts and chauvinist emotions beyond their control. To the Conservative

---

[1] Trotsky's message to Zinoviev, Lenin, and Krestinsky in *The Archives*.
[2] Messages from the second half of February in *The Archives*.

elements in Russia this was a war against a hereditary enemy, with whose re-emergence as an independent nation they could not reconcile themselves—a truly Russian war, even though waged by Bolshevik internationalists. To the Greek Orthodox this was a fight against a people incorrigible in its loyalty to Roman Catholicism, a Christian crusade even though led by godless Communists. Some of those Conservative elements had at heart been in sympathy with the White Guards. But now that the White Guards had gone down in ruin, they were on the look-out for a pretext which would allow them to climb on the Soviet band-wagon without loss of patriotic and Greek Orthodox 'face'. The Polish invasion provided it. General Brusilov, Commander-in-Chief under the old régime, headed the movement of conversion. He placed himself at Trotsky's services and called upon all good Russians to follow in his footsteps. Thus, in addition to its revolutionary overtones, the war acquired its nationalist undertones. Pilsudski's troops did much to whip up the anti-Polish sentiment. Their behaviour in occupied Ukraine was overbearing; they began to establish the Polish landlords on their former domains; and they marked their victories by the shooting of prisoners of war and by pogroms.

To be carried on a tide of national unity was for the Bolsheviks a novel and embarrassing experience. Trotsky exerted himself to assert the party's internationalist outlook. He welcomed Brusilov's demonstration of solidarity with the Red Army; but he publicly repudiated Brusilov's chauvinist and anti-Catholic tone.[1] When the rumour spread that Brusilov would lead the Red armies against the Poles, Trotsky denied this and emphasized that the Polish front was under the command of Tukhachevsky and Yegorov, whose loyalty to the internationalist idea of the revolution had been tested in the civil war. At the height of hostilities, he publicly ordered the closing down of *Voennoe Delo* (*Military Affairs*), the periodical of the General Staff, because in an article on Pilsudski it had used language 'insulting the national dignity of the Polish people'. He further ordered an inquiry into the matter, so that the culprits 'should never again be entrusted with any work enabling them to influence the mind of the Red Army'.[2] (The incident has re-

---

[1] Trotsky, *Sochinenya* vol. xvii, book 2, pp. 407–8.
[2] *Kak Vooruzhalas Revolutsia*, vol. ii, book 2, p. 153.

mained something of a noble curiosity in an age v.hen during war 'civilized' statesmen and men of letters brand without scruple the national character of an enemy as Hun-like, beast-like, or subhuman.) On his visits to the front, he kept in check the angry passion aroused in the army by reports about Polish shootings of prisoners of war. Even an enemy, he argued at meetings of front-line soldiers, must not be slandered. He emphatically forbade retaliation on Polish prisoners: 'Let the hand be cut off of any Red Army man who lifts his knife on a prisoner of war, on the disarmed, the sick and wounded', he wrote in an order of the day. Ruthless in battle, the Red Army man must show magnanimity towards the captive and helpless enemy.[1]

Pilsudski's victory in the Ukraine was short-lived. A few weeks of Polish occupation were enough to arouse the Ukrainian peasantry against the invaders. Tukhachevsky's armies on the northern sector of the front and Yegorov's on the southern were reinforced by divisions released from fighting against Denikin and Kolchak. The Red Army, although poorly equipped, was now at the peak of its strength—before the end of the campaign it had five million men under colours. On 12 June the Bolsheviks recaptured Kiev; and presently Pilsudski's troops retreated in panic towards the boundaries of ethnographic Poland.

At this point important political issues intervened to complicate the conduct of the war. Some of these concerned Russia's relations with Britain; others bore on her attitude towards Poland; and the two sets of problems were at some points interconnected.

The opposition of British Labour to intervention and the defeat of the White Guards had weakened the interventionist party, led by Winston Churchill. The government was divided against itself, the Prime Minister (Lloyd George) being inclined to withdraw from intervention and to resume trade with Russia. At the end of May 1920 a Soviet trade mission, headed by Krasin, left Moscow for London. In the meantime, however, the interventionist party was momentarily strengthened by Pilsudski's victories. The Politbureau was under the impression that the British government, like the French, wholeheartedly backed Pilsudski. The Commissariat of Foreign Affairs and the

[1] Trotsky, *Sochinenya*, vol. xvii, book 2, pp. 403–5.

Comintern tried to hit back at British positions in Asia, especially in Persia and Afghanistan, as Trotsky had suggested in the previous year. But before long British official policy wavered again: Labour's opposition to intervention had risen to a high pitch; and the Red Army's pursuit of the Poles had in any case exposed once more the futility of intervention. On 11 July Lord Curzon, the British Foreign Secretary, offered his government's mediation between the Soviets and Poland and also between the Soviets and that remnant of Denikin's army which, under Baron Wrangel, had entrenched itself in the Crimea.

Throughout June and July the Politbureau and the Commissariat of Foreign Affairs tried to grasp the trend of British policy. Trotsky repeatedly intervened in the debate and found himself in opposition to the majority view. Of this controversy there is a vivid account in Trotsky's confidential messages to Chicherin, Lenin, and other members of the Politbureau, and in Lenin's laconic remarks, in his own handwriting, found in *The Trotsky Archives*. In a memorandum of 4 June, Trotsky insistently urged the adoption of a conciliatory attitude towards Britain. He argued that British policy by no means followed a single line set on intervention, and that it was in the Soviet interest to keep it fluctuating. Soviet attempts to stage anti-British revolts in the Middle East, let alone a Soviet expedition to the Middle East, would tend to consolidate British policy in extreme hostility towards the Soviets. Last August he himself had set great store by the revolutionary movements in Asia; but now, in the light of fresh information, he argued that in the Middle East, at any rate, these movements lacked inherent strength.[1] The Bolsheviks ought to further revolutionary propaganda and clandestine organization, but avoid any steps which might involve them in risky military commitments. At best they could use the threat of revolution in the Middle East as a bargaining counter in diplomatic exchanges with Britain. But they ought to use every opportunity to impress the British with their desire to reach agreement over the East.

On the margin of this document Lenin remarked with some irony that Trotsky, like Krasin, was mistaken about British

---

[1] Trotsky added that even in Soviet Azerbaijan, in the Caucasus, which had a numerous industrial working class and old ties with Russia, the Soviet régime did not stand on its own feet.

REVOLUTION AND CONQUEST 473

policy: its line was firmly set; it was 'absolutely clear' that England helped and would continue to help both the Poles and Wrangel.[1]

In July, after Lord Curzon's offer of mediation, the issue was once again under discussion. Lenin communicated the offer to Trotsky, who was at the front. On the same day, 13 July, Trotsky replied in two messages, urging the Politbureau and Chicherin to accept British mediation between Russia and Poland, and to aim at an armistice which would lead to peace with the Entente as well as with Poland.[2] He once again advised the Politbureau to pay more careful attention to divergent trends in British opinion and policy.[3]

The Politbureau rejected Trotsky's proposals and, of course, the British offer. Oddly enough, it asked Trotsky to administer the rebuff to Lord Curzon. Actuated by the principle of Cabinet solidarity, he did so. In a scintillating sarcastic manifesto, from which nobody could even remotely guess his mental reservations, he explained that the British government, with its record of intervention, was a party to the conflict and could not aspire to render service as an impartial conciliator.[4]

This difference, after all, concerned only diplomatic tactics. But it was connected with another and fundamental controversy. Rejecting Curzon's proposal, Lenin demanded 'a furious speeding up of the offensive on Poland'. To this, too, Trotsky was opposed. By now the Red Army had reconquered all Ukrainian and Byelorussian lands and stood roughly along a line which Lord Curzon, when he still reckoned with Denikin's victory, had proposed as the frontier between Russia and Poland. At this line Trotsky intended to halt the Red Army and to make a public offer of peace. Lenin and the majority of the Politbureau were bent on continuing the pursuit of the Poles into Warsaw and beyond.

Once again the interplay of politics and strategy dominated the dispute. There was a military risk in Trotsky's proposal.

---

[1] A resolution of the Politbureau, also dated 4 June, shows that the Politbureau believed that Pilsudski acted in collusion with the German government as well.

[2] Trotsky was, however, against any mediation in the conflict between the Soviets and Wrangel, which was a domestic Russian affair.

[3] *Inter alia* Trotsky asked that Theodore Rothstein, the eminent Russo-British Marxist, should be consulted about the state of British opinion.

[4] Trotsky, *Sochinenya*, vol. xvii, book 2, pp. 426 ff.

Pilsudski was not likely to accept the 'Curzon line' as a frontier and he might have used the respite of an armistice to prepare a come-back. Trotsky was willing to take this risk. He set his mind on the political and moral advantages of the course of action he advocated and on the dangers which would attend Lenin's policy. He held that a straightforward public peace offer, making it clear that the Soviets had no designs on Poland's independence and coveted no truly Polish territory, would favourably impress the Polish people. If Pilsudski accepted the offer, well and good. If not, the Polish people and the world would know whom to blame for the continuation of war. Trotsky argued that the Red Army's advance towards Warsaw, without a preliminary offer of peace, would destroy the Russian Revolution's goodwill with the Polish people and play into Pilsudski's hands. For nearly a century and a half the greater part of Poland had been subjugated by the Tsars. It was less than two years since the Poles had regained independence, solemnly guaranteed to them by the Russian Revolution. A Russian army invading Polish soil, even though under provocation from Pilsudski and even though marching under the Red Flag, would seem to them the direct successor to those Tsarist armies which had kept them, their fathers, and their forefathers in bondage. The Poles would then defend their native soil tooth and nail.[1]

Lenin did not share these scruples and forebodings. It was Pilsudski who had, deliberately and conspicuously, played the aggressor's part, while Lenin had made every effort to avert the war. Now, when the fortunes of battle favoured the Red Army, it was, in Lenin's view, its right and duty to grasp the fruits of victory—no victorious soundly led army stops halfway in the pursuit of an almost routed enemy; and no moral, political, or strategic principle forbids an army to invade the aggressor's territory in the course of a pursuit.

Nor was this all. Lenin believed that the workers and peasants of Poland would greet the invaders as their liberators. All the Bolshevik leaders, including Trotsky, had only a dim idea of the facts of the situation: they had as a result of the blockade lost

[1] The feelings of the small Baltic nations were similar. Throughout the year Trotsky urged the Politbureau to conclude peace with all of them. This was done (*The Trotsky Archives*).

contact with Poland as completely as if that country had been many thousands of miles away. They knew that there had been Soviets in Poland, in which the communists had wielded a very strong influence; and they believed them to be still in existence. Their information was more than a year out of date. In the meantime, in Poland as in the rest of central Europe, the tide had turned: Pilsudski had dispersed the Soviets and severely suppressed the Communist party.[1] A group of eminent Polish Socialists, who had joined the Bolsheviks, lived in Moscow; and to them the Politbureau turned for advice. They were strangely divided: Radek, Markhlevsky, and (it seems) Dzerzhinsky, who had belonged to the internationalist wing of Polish socialism and had not believed in the resurrection of Poland as a nation-state, now warned the Politbureau that the Red Army's invasion would be foiled by a powerful upsurge of Polish patriotic sentiment. It was in part as an effect of this warning that Trotsky adopted his attitude. Lenin appears to have been more impressed by a report of Lapinsky, who had come from the more patriotic wing of Polish socialism, and who greatly exaggerated the strength of Polish communism. Swept by optimism, believing that the Red Army's advance would be a signal for the outbreak of revolution in Poland, Lenin swayed the Politbureau. Even Stalin, who had soberly dismissed the idea of a march on Warsaw, changed sides; and Trotsky was alone in opposing it.

Lenin played for even higher stakes. Poland was the bridge between Russia and Germany; and across it Lenin hoped to establish contact with Germany. He imagined that Germany, too, was in intense revolutionary ferment. There was some fire behind the smoke of illusion. In March 1920 a section of the German army carried out a *coup d'état* in Berlin, with the intention of crushing the parliamentary régime and establishing a military dictatorship. Within two days, the coup, the so-called Kapp *Putsch*, was undone by a general strike of the German workers. This was a signal demonstration of the strength of German Labour. The initiative for the strike had come from the trade unions, not from the communists; but shortly thereafter German communism was vigorously making headway,

---

[1] In 1920 even Trotsky still spoke about the significance of the Polish Soviets, assuming that they were still in existence. See his *Sochinenya*, vol. xv, p. 301.

although it still failed to carry the bulk of the working class. Enough that Lenin mooted the idea that the appearance of the Red Army at Germany's frontier might stimulate and intensify the processes of revolution. He intended to 'probe Europe with the bayonet of the Red Army'. At a session of the Revolutionary War Council, which took place at the height of the offensive, he passed a note to Sklyansky, saying that 'Warsaw must be taken within three to five days at any cost'. He insistently inquired whether the Red Army, which had already entered the Pomeranian 'corridor', could cut that corridor so as to deny the Poles access to Danzig. Danzig was the port through which Poland received munitions from the West; but it was also a point of contact with Germany.[1]

Despite his premonition of disaster, Trotsky submitted to the decision of the majority. He stayed in office, issued the marching orders, and carried on with routine jobs—only his visits to the front seem to have ceased. As the offensives progressed, a Revolutionary War Council of Poland was appointed, virtually a Provisional Government, headed by those Polish Bolsheviks who had been opposed to the venture. The farther the Red Army advanced, the more uneasy were the Council's reports to Moscow. The Polish workers and peasants met the invaders as conquerors, not liberators. But now the Red Army was irresistibly carried forward by its own impetus, extending its lines of communication and exhausting itself. A dangerous gap also arose between the northern armies, which, under Tukhachevsky, were approaching Warsaw, and the southern ones, which, under Yegorov and Budienny, had veered south-westwards towards Lvov. The chief political commissar to the southern armies, appointed on Trotsky's insistence,[2] was Stalin, who was keen on emulating Tukhachevsky and on getting Lvov as his prize while Tukhachevsky was entering Warsaw. Into this gap in the centre Pilsudski would presently spring to strike at Tukhachevsky's flank and rear. For a moment the gap worried Lenin;[3] and the General Staff began, somewhat late in the day, to urge the commanders of the southern armies to close it.

---

[1] The note is in *The Trotsky Archives*.

[2] Trotsky's message to the Central Committee of 11 May 1920. *The Archives*.

[3] *The Trotsky Archives* contain an undated note from Lenin to Sklyansky, in which Lenin expressed his misgivings.

But the Red Army still rolled on; and Moscow was all exultation.

At this stage of the campaign, from the middle of July to 7 August, the second congress of the Communist International was in session in Petrograd and Moscow. During the past year the European Labour movements had swung towards the International: leaders of great and old Socialist parties now almost humbly knocked at its doors. The congress discussed the terms of membership, the famous '21 Points', formulated by Lenin and Zinoviev, the tasks of the Communist parties, the fate of the colonial nations, and so on. But the debates were dominated by the thrilling expectation of the military *denouement* in Poland which would give a new and mighty impulse to European revolution. In front of a large war map Lenin daily gave the foreign delegates his optimistic comment on Tukhachevsky's advance.

At the beginning of the congress, Trotsky made a brief appearance in order to endorse the '21 Points' in the debate. He came back just before the end of the congress—the Red Army now stood at the very gates of Warsaw—to present the Manifesto he had written on behalf of the International. The delegates greeted him with a tributary roar of applause. In a crescendo of resounding phrases and images he surveyed the international scene in the first year of the Versailles Peace. He angrily denounced the 'Babylon' of decaying capitalism and tore the 'mask of democracy' from its face. 'German parliamentary democracy', he stated, 'is nothing but a void between two dictatorships.'[1] The delegates listened to him in breathless suspense; and the magic of his words and images was heightened as the battle, of which they thought him to be the inspirer, mounted to its climax. Yet Trotsky refrained from boasting, and in the manifesto he made no reference to the Red Army's victories. The delegates did not even notice his reticence. They could not guess what tense apprehension was hidden behind his self-confident appearance and resounding language. In this assembly, where even the most prudent men were carried away by joyous excitement, he alone refused to celebrate the victory, as the architect of which he was being acclaimed.[2]

[1] Trotsky, *Pyat Let Kominterna*, p. 89.
[2] Addressing the party cells of the Military Academy and of other schools,

A week later the battle of the Vistula began. It lasted only three days. It did not change the course of history, as its contemporaries believed—it only delayed it by a quarter of a century. But at the end of the battle the Red Army was in full retreat. While the battle was at its height, the Politbureau asked Trotsky to go to the front and try to retrieve the situation. He refused. He did not deceive himself, he replied, that he could now stave off defeat by any brisk personal intervention on the spot.[1]

For the moment the débâcle seemed even worse than it was, because Wrangel's Guards, seeing the Red Army tied down by the Poles, had broken out of the Crimea and invaded the Caucasus. Two days after the battle of the Vistula, on 19 August, Trotsky and Stalin jointly reported to the Politbureau on the military situation; and the Politbureau, apparently acknowledging defeat in Poland, resolved to give first priority to the campaign against Wrangel. Both Stalin and Trotsky were put in charge of a new mobilization of party members. Most of those mobilized were to be sent to the Crimea; and the bulk of Budienny's cavalry was to be diverted from the Polish front. Stalin was also instructed to work out measures to be taken in case of Wrangel's further advance. However, Wrangel's troops, although excellently equipped, were too weak in numbers and too disheartened to create a serious threat. They soon withdrew into the Crimea, hoping to hold out behind the fortified narrow neck of the Perekop Isthmus. After an epic and savage battle, directed by Frunze and Stalin, the Red Army broke through the Isthmus and drove Wrangel into the sea. This was the epilogue of the civil war.[2]

On 12 October the Soviets signed a provisional peace with Poland. But for a time war was still in the air. In Poland the ruling parties were divided. The Peasant Party—its leader Witos headed the government—pressed for peace, while

Trotsky said soon after the war that he did not believe for a moment that the Red Army would seize Warsaw—he did not even expect it to advance as far as it did. On this and other occasions he spoke quite frankly about the disagreements over the march on Warsaw, and his version was not contradicted from any source. (*Kak Vooruzhalas Revolutsia*, vol. iii, book 1, p. 91.)

[1] Trotsky's message to the Politbureau of 17 August. (*The Trotsky Archives.*) The battle lasted from 14 to 17 August.

[2] *The Trotsky Archives.*

Pilsudski's military party did its utmost to disrupt the parleys with Russia.[1] In Moscow, too, views were divided. The majority of the Politbureau favoured a renewal of hostilities. Some of those who did so expected that Pilsudski would not keep the peace anyhow; others craved for revenge. The General Staff discussed a new offensive. Tukhachevsky was confident that next time he would hold his victory parade in Warsaw. Trotsky relates that Lenin was at first inclined towards war, but only half-heartedly. At any rate, Trotsky insisted on peace and on the loyal observance of the provisional treaty with Poland; and once again he found himself in danger of being outvoted and reduced to dutiful execution of a policy he abhorred. From this he at last shrank. He declared that the differences went so deep that this time he would not feel bound by any majority decision or by Politbureau solidarity, and that, if outvoted, he would appeal to the party against its leadership. He used a threat similar to that which Lenin had, with overwhelming effect, used in the controversy over Brest; and he, too, achieved his purpose. In comparison with that controversy the roles were indeed curiously reversed. But the sequel was in a way similar, for now Lenin deserted the war faction and shifted his influence to back Trotsky. Peace was saved.[2]

The differences had gone deep. Yet it is doubtful whether any single Bolshevik leader, including Trotsky, was or could be aware of their full historic import, on which only the events of the middle of this century have thrown back a sharp, illuminating light.

It had been a canon of Marxist politics that revolution cannot and must not be carried on the point of bayonets into foreign countries. The canon was based on the experience of the French Revolution which had found its fulfilment and also its undoing in Napoleonic conquest. The canon also followed from the fundamental attitude of Marxism which looked to the working classes of all nations as to the sovereign agents of socialism and certainly did not expect socialism to be imposed upon peoples from outside. The Bolsheviks, and Trotsky, had often said that the Red Army might intervene in a neighbouring country, but

[1] An authoritative description of this tug-of-war was given by J. Dabski, the chief of the Polish peace delegation at Riga, in his memoirs.

[2] Trotsky, *Moya Zhizn*, vol. ii, pp. 193–4.

only as the ally and auxiliary of actual popular revolution, not as an independent, decisive agent. In this auxiliary role Lenin wished the Red Army to help the Soviet revolution in Hungary, for instance. In this role, too, the Red Army or the Red Guards had sporadically intervened in Finland and Latvia to assist actual Soviet revolutions which enjoyed popular backing and which were defeated primarily by foreign, mostly German, intervention. In none of these instances did the Red Army carry the revolution abroad. In the Polish war the Bolsheviks went a step farther. Even now Lenin had not become plainly converted to revolution by conquest. He saw the Polish working classes in potential revolt; and he expected that the Red Army's advance would act as a catalyst. But this was not the same as assisting an actual revolution. Whatever Lenin's private beliefs and motives, the Polish war was Bolshevism's first important essay in revolution by conquest. True, the Politbureau embarked on it in the heat of war, under abundant provocation, without grasping all the implications of its own decision. But this is the way in which great fateful turns in history occur: those who initiate them are often unconscious of what it is they initiate. This in particular is the manner in which revolutionary parties begin to throw over-board their hallowed principles and to transform their own character. If the Red Army had seized Warsaw, it would have proceeded to act as the chief agent of social upheaval, as a substitute, as it were, for the Polish working class. It will be remembered that in his youthful writings Trotsky had berated Lenin for 'substitutism', i.e. for a propensity to see in the party a *locum tenens* of the working class.[1] And here was indeed an instance of that substitutism, projected on the international scene, except that an army rather than a party was to act as proxy for a foreign proletariat.

This was all the more strange as in the course of two decades Lenin had fervently inculcated into his disciples and followers an almost dogmatic respect for the right of every nation, but more especially of Poland, to full self-determination. He had parted with comrades and friends who had been less dogmatic about this. He had filled reams with incisive argument against those Poles—Rosa Luxemburg, Radek, and Dzerzhinsky— who, as internationalists, had refused to promote the idea of a

[1] See above, pp. 90–7.

Polish nation-state, while Poland was still partitioned. Now Lenin himself appeared to obliterate his own efforts and to absolve the violation of any nation's independence, if committed in the name of revolution.

Lenin grew aware of the incongruity of his role. He admitted his error.[1] He spoke out against carrying the revolution abroad on the point of bayonets. He joined hands with Trotsky in striving for peace. The great revolutionary prevailed in him over the revolutionary gambler.

However, the 'error' was neither fortuitous nor inconsequential. It had had its origin in the Bolshevik horror of isolation in the world, a horror shared by all leaders of the party but affecting their actions differently. The march on Warsaw had been a desperate attempt to break out of that isolation. Although it had failed it was to have a deep influence on the party's outlook. The idea of revolution by conquest had been injected into the Bolshevik mind; and it went on to ferment and fester. Some Bolsheviks, reflecting on the experience, naturally reached the conclusion that it was not the attempt itself to carry revolution abroad by force of arms but merely its failure that was deplorable. If only the Red Army had captured Warsaw, it could have established a proletarian dictatorship there, whether the Polish workers liked it or not. It was a petty bourgeois prejudice that only that revolution rested on solid foundations which corresponded to the wishes and desires of the people. The main thing was to be better armed and better prepared for the next venture of this kind.[2]

We shall discuss in the next chapter the domestic experiences of the Bolsheviks which fed and reinforced this trend of thought. Here it is enough to say that the trend showed itself in the attitude of those members of the Politbureau who favoured a renewal of hostilities with Poland. Yet the old Bolsheviks could develop such views only privately and tentatively. They were not in a

[1] Klara Zetkin, *Reminiscences of Lenin*, pp. 19–21.

[2] The party historian N. Popov writes: 'Trotsky was opposed to the advance on Warsaw, not because he considered our forces insufficient . . . but because of a Social-Democratic prejudice that it was wrong to carry revolution into a country from the outside. For these same reasons Trotsky was opposed to the Red Army aiding the rebels in Georgia in February 1921. Trotsky's anti-Bolshevik, Kautskyist reasoning was emphatically rejected by the Central Committee, both in July 1920 in the case of Poland and in February 1921 in the case of . . . Georgia.' (*Outline History of the C.P.S.U.*, vol. ii, p. 101.)

position to state them in a more formal manner or elevate them to a principle. It was in the nature of such views that they did not lend themselves to public statement; and the Marxist tradition could not be openly flouted. That tradition was so much alive in all Bolshevik leaders that it inhibited the working of their own minds and prevented them from pursuing the new line of thought to its conclusion. Even three decades later Stalin would never admit that he favoured revolution by conquest, even though he had already practised it on a vast scale. How much more difficult was it for Bolsheviks to admit the fact even to themselves in 1920!

Yet an idea which is in the air soon finds a mouthpiece. Shortly after the Polish war, Tukhachevsky came forward as the advocate of revolution by conquest. He had not lived down the defeat on the Vistula, the only setback—and what a setback—he had suffered since his meteoric rise. He had come to Bolshevism only in 1918 as a young officer, and now, at the age of twenty-six, he was the most brilliant and famous general of the Red Army. He was unquestionably devoted to the Soviets, but he was the revolution's soldier, not a revolutionary. He was not inhibited by the party's traditions; and he drew his inspiration from Napoleon rather than from Marx. He did not understand why the Bolsheviks should go on mouthing anathemas against carrying revolution on the point of bayonets. He expounded his views in essays and lectures at the Military Academy and argued that it was both possible and legitimate for the Red Army to impose revolution on a capitalist country 'from without'.[1] Somewhat later he even proposed the formation of an international General Staff of the Red Army, which would direct revolutionary military activities in all countries. Intellectually impulsive, original, and courageous, he openly attacked the party's taboo. But he presented his case in so extreme a form that it did not gain much support. Other leaders of the civil war were inclined to accept his argument, properly diluted. There was, at any rate, a logical link between Tukhachevsky's view and their insistence that the Red Army should adopt an expressly offensive military doctrine.[2]

Trotsky struggled against this new mood. In the aftermath of

---

[1] M. Tukhachevsky, *Voina Klasov*, see, in particular, his essay 'Revolution from Without', pp. 50–60.   [2] See the 'Note on Trotsky's Military Writings'.

the Polish war, he warned against the temptation to carry revolution abroad by force of arms. The warning runs indeed like a red thread through his writings and speeches of this period.[1] His rational opposition to revolution by conquest was in a sense merely the obverse side of his almost irrational belief in the craving of the western working classes for revolution and in their ability to make it. He was so unshakably confident that the proletarians of Europe and America were already impelled by their own circumstances to follow in the footsteps of Bolshevism that he was firmly convinced of the absolute harm latent in any attempt to make the revolution for them or to probe and prod them with bayonets. He saw the world pregnant with socialism; he believed that the pregnancy could not last long; and he feared that impatient tampering with it would result in abortion. The solidarity which the Russian Revolution owed to the working classes of other countries, he maintained, should express itself mainly in helping them to understand and interpret their own social and political experience and their own tasks, not in trying to solve those tasks for them. In one controversy he angrily remarked of anyone who thought of replacing revolution abroad by the Red Army's operations that 'it were better for him that a millstone were hanged about his neck and he cast into the sea'.[2]

Yet such was the strength of the new Bolshevik proclivity that it could not be altogether suppressed. It soon manifested itself again in the Red Army's invasion of Georgia.

Up to February 1921 Georgia had been ruled by a Menshevik government, with which the Soviets had signed a treaty during the Polish war. Nearly the whole of the Caucasus was already under Soviet control; and Menshevik Georgia was a thorn in its flesh. The claim of the Georgian Mensheviks to independent nationhood was rather spurious: before the October Revolution they themselves had ardently advocated Georgia's unity with Russia and had asked only for a degree of local autonomy. Their present separatism was a convenient pretext. The mere existence of Menshevik Georgia made it more difficult for the Bolsheviks to consolidate their régime in the rest of the Caucasus; and the Bolsheviks had not forgotten that the Georgian

[1] *Kak Vooruzhalas Revolutsia*, vol. iii, book 2, pp. 114, 124, 142–3, 206, 225–7 and *passim*.   [2] Trotsky, op. cit., p. 225.

Mensheviks had meekly submitted to the successive occupation of their country by the Germans and then by the British, and had severely suppressed the Georgian Bolsheviks. Nevertheless the Soviet government had solemnly committed itself to respect Georgia's independence, and it had recognized the Menshevik government. The Politbureau hoped that Georgia would eventually find the pull of the Soviet Caucasus irresistible, that its Menshevik rulers would not be able to govern the country in opposition to all its neighbours, and that the scene would thus be set for their overthrow by native revolutionary forces. Consequently, the Politbureau was inclined to wait patiently until the experiment had run its course.

Trotsky was therefore greatly surprised when, in the middle of February 1921, during an inspection in the Urals, he learned that the Red Army had marched into Georgia. He was on the point of leaving for Moscow to attend a session of the Central Committee; and before his departure he got in touch with Sklyansky and inquired who had issued the marching orders and why. It turned out that the invasion was a bolt from the blue to the Commander-in-Chief as well. Trotsky suspected that the adventure had been irresponsibly staged behind the back of the General Staff and of the Politbureau; and he intended 'to raise the matter in full session of the Central Committee' and to bring to book the presumed adventurer.[1] But the marching orders had been issued, with the Politbureau's approval, by the Revolutionary War Council of the Caucasus, on which Ordjonikidze, Stalin's friend and himself a Georgian, served as chief commissar. The Politbureau had considered the matter in Trotsky's absence. Stalin and Ordjonikidze had reported that a Bolshevik insurrection had, with strong popular backing, broken out in Georgia; that the outcome was in no doubt; and that the Red Army would merely shorten the struggle. The Politbureau, which naturally treated Stalin and Ordjonikidze as experts on Georgian affairs, accepted their advice.

The rising in Georgia did not, however, enjoy the popular backing claimed for it; and it took the Red Army a fortnight of heavy fighting to enter Tiflis, the Georgian capital. Like the other small border nations, the Georgians had long memories of

[1] The Trotsky Archives.

Tsarist oppression. The forcible re-annexation aroused fierce resentment. The grievance rankled long after, and it was indirectly reflected in the opposition of Georgian Bolsheviks to Moscow's centralizing policies. This was to become one of the major points at issue between Stalin and Trotsky in the last year of Lenin's leadership. For the time being, however, Trotsky accepted the accomplished fact. The invasion could not be called off. It was only possible to try to soften its shock. This Lenin was doing of his own accord. He warned Ordjonikidze and the other Caucasian commissars 'to behave with especial respect towards the sovereign organs of Georgia and to show special attentiveness and caution in dealing with the Georgian population'. He asked to be informed of any offence against his instruction and of the slightest instances of friction with the Georgians. He further urged Ordjonikidze to strive for a reconciliation with the Mensheviks, even with Jordania, the head of the Menshevik government, who had not been absolutely hostile towards the Soviet régime.[1] There was little else that Trotsky himself could do or could wish to be done at the moment. Lenin's injunctions, however, produced little effect, because the invaders, having violated Georgia's sovereignty wholesale, were in no mood to respect it in detail. But it took time before this became clear.

Trotsky went on to disclaim and denounce in general the idea of revolution by conquest. But he did not feel justified in discussing publicly the specific differences over Georgia and once again flouting the Politbureau's collective responsibility. Moreover, when the Social Democratic leaders of the West, Kautsky, MacDonald, Henderson, and others, raised an outcry for the evacuation of Georgia by the Red Army, Trotsky rejoined with a *tu quoque*: he wrote a pamphlet in which he devoted only a brief passage to the invasion. He reasserted the right of the Red Army to assist a fully fledged revolution abroad; but he evaded the question whether such a revolution had occurred in Georgia. Instead, he concentrated on an acute exposure of the inconsistencies in the attitude of the Social Democratic critics towards the Russian Revolution, the fate of the colonial peoples, &c.[2] With all his fiery temperament he defended the Soviets, right or wrong, against their enemies and lukewarm friends. In

[1] Lenin, *Sochinenya*, vol. xxxii, p. 137. [2] Trotsky, *Between Red and White*.

the eyes of the world he therefore bore a major share of responsibility for the invasion of Georgia.

In the Politbureau's behaviour over Poland and Georgia Trotsky saw mistakes, into which the party had blundered as if in a fit of absent-mindedness. He set his face against both 'mistakes', but he saw no inner connexion and no deeper significance in them. Up to a point he was right, because the party as a whole had entered the road of revolutionary conquest neither consciously nor deliberately. The invasion of Georgia was its only successful step on that road, and there was no lack of mitigating circumstances. Georgia had, after all, been part of Russia: it could not survive as a little 'bourgeois island' in the Soviet Caucasus. Yet there was an inner connexion between the Polish and the Georgian ventures, for both marked the initiation of a new current in Bolshevism.

The revolutionary cycle, which the First World War had set in motion, was coming to a close. At the beginning of that cycle Bolshevism had risen on the crest of a genuine revolution; towards its end Bolshevism began to spread revolution by conquest. A long interval, lasting nearly a quarter of a century, separates this cycle of revolution from the next, which the Second World War set in motion. During the interval Bolshevism did not expand. When the next cycle opened, it started where the first had ended, with revolution by conquest. It is a commonplace in military history that there exists a continuity between the closing phase of one war and the opening phase of the next: the weapons and the ideas on warfare invented or formed towards the end of one armed conflict dominate the first stage of the next conflict. A similar continuity may be seen to exist between the two cycles of revolution. In 1945–6 and partly even in 1939–40 Stalin began where he, and in a sense he and Lenin, had left off in 1920–1. Trotsky did not live to witness the momentous chapter which Stalin's revolutionary conquest has since written in modern history. His attitude towards the early symptoms of the trend was inconclusive. He was for revolution and against conquest; but when revolution led to conquest and conquest promoted revolution, he was confronted with a dilemma which, from his viewpoint, admitted no satisfactory solution. He did not press his opposition to revolutionary conquest to the point of an open breach. On the other hand, he left behind this suggestive half-warning, half-curse: 'He who wants to carry revolution abroad on the point of bayonets, it were better for him that a millstone were hanged about his neck. . . .'

Note

A SUMMARY of Trotsky's military activities cannot be concluded without a reference to his military writings. As founder and leader of an army, he remained a man of letters with the urge to give form and expression to his experiences and ideas, even in the smoke of battle. The many volumes of his military essays, speeches, and orders are distinguished by such contrasting qualities as romantic *élan*, and practical realism and at times by an almost philosophical depth.

Radek relates that Trotsky, when he became Commissar of War, had read only a few books on military affairs: Jaurès's *L'Armée Nouvelle*, a large *History of War* by Schulz, a German Socialist, and Franz Mehring's writings on Frederick the Great. Radek undoubtedly belittles Trotsky's theoretical preparation in order to emphasize all the more strongly his achievement. During the Balkan wars and in the first years of the World War Trotsky had studied current military literature. He was certainly familiar, as Lenin was, with the work of Clausewitz, whom he quoted and in whose spirit he often approached his own problems. But Radek is right in holding that Trotsky was most strongly impressed by Jaurès's *L'Armée Nouvelle*, the work of a great historian and democratic Socialist, not a military expert.

Jaurès tried to reconcile two aspects of his own policy: his struggle against the reactionary French officers' corps, whose influence on domestic politics had shown itself in the Dreyfus affair; and his patriotic desire to see the French Republic armed and ready for defence. He conceived a reform of the army which, he hoped, would fit in with the economic and political reforms which were to transform bourgeois France into a 'social republic'. He advocated the replacement of the standing army by militias. The standing army, confined and trained within the rigid framework of the barracks, in artificial isolation from and latent opposition to civilian society, had been the officers' corps' main source of political strength. Militias were to be set up on the basis of productive units, factories, and village communities; the militiamen were to receive their training locally and were to continue to live and work as normal citizens, devoting themselves part-time or intermittently to the art and craft of war. The militias should therefore be so organically integrated into the civilian community that no ambitious general or military clique could use them as a political instrument.[1]

Trotsky borrowed Jaurès's idea but put it in a different context. Jaurès believed that it would be possible to democratize the army into a militia system even under the capitalist system. To Trotsky this belief was a reformist illusion. The virtual or actual opposition of a standing army to civilian society reflected, in his view, the clash between the interests of the propertied classes, which that army defended in the last instance, and those of the working classes. Only after the interest of the working classes had become paramount, he argued, could the army become submerged in the people and identified with it. The abolition of the standing army fitted the state which was to wither away gradually, as the proletarian state was expected to do.

Nevertheless, Trotsky built the Red Army as a standing army. The militia system, he argued, could be fully effective only against the background of a highly industrialized, organized, and civilized society. The Russian environment dictated to the Red Army the principles of its organization, which were very much the same as those that had underlain the structure of the Tsarist army. The difference between the two armies lay in their political and social outlook, not in their strictly military features.

Trotsky excused this as a temporary necessity and insisted that party and government should commit themselves to the militia system as their ultimate objective. He argued the case in the 'Theses' which he submitted to the eighth party congress in March 1919 and which, in his absence, Sokolnikov defended before the congress.[2] He looked forward to the time when men would receive their military training not in barracks but in conditions closely approximating to the workaday life of workers and peasants. The transition could not begin in earnest before a revival of industry; but even now, Trotsky insisted, a barracks must be made to resemble a military and general school, not a mere drilling-place. In the Red Army the commanding staffs were appointed, not elected; but Trotsky envisaged a return to the elective principle in the future. The eighth congress adopted Trotsky's 'Theses', and the ninth endorsed them again.

The programme aroused considerable criticism towards the end of the civil war, when Trotsky made the first attempt to put it into effect. The old professional officers were surprised that he, who had so severely centralized the army and extirpated the guerrilla spirit,

[1] Poles apart from Jaurès's conception is the idea of a wholly professional army, to be used as a decisive weapon in civil war, the idea expounded by General de Gaulle in *Vers l'Armée de Metier* before 1939.

[2] Trotsky, *Kak Vooruzhalas Revolutsia*, vol. i, pp. 185–95.

should advocate a military organization which in their eyes looked suspiciously like the old Red Guards. They could not seriously entertain the idea that an army could be trained, disciplined, and inured to collective action otherwise than in the barracks. One of Trotsky's critics was General Svechin, the author of a standard work on strategy and professor at the Military Academy. Against this critic Trotsky defended 'the dreamer Jaurès':

> If Professor Svechin thinks that the Communist Party has taken power in order to replace the three-coloured [Tsarist] barracks by a red one, he is gravely mistaken. . . . The objection that under a militia system the command would not enjoy proper authority strikes one with its political blindness. Has perhaps the authority of the present leadership of the Red Army been established in the barracks? . . . That authority is based not on the salutary hypnosis of the barracks but on the appeal of the Soviet régime and of the Communist Party. Professor Svechin has simply overlooked the revolution and the enormous spiritual upheaval it has brought about. . . . To him the ignorant, drunken mercenary, syphilis-ridden and numbed by Catholicism, who served in Wallenstein's camp, the artisan-apprentice of Paris, who, led by journalists and lawyers, destroyed the Bastille, the Saxon worker and member of the Social Democratic Party of 1914–18, and the Russian proletarian who first in world history took power—all these are to him approximately the same cannon fodder to be delicately processed in the barracks. Is this not a mockery of history?
>
> The development of the communist order will run parallel to the growth in the spiritual stature of the broadest popular masses. What the party has so far given mainly to advanced workers, the new society will increasingly give to the people as a whole. . . . For its members the party has hitherto in a sense 'replaced' the barracks: it has given them the necessary inner solidarity, made them capable of self-sacrifice and collective struggle. Communist society will be able to do this on an incomparably vaster scale. . . . The spirit of co-operation in the broadest sense is the spirit of collectivism. It can be fostered not merely in the barracks, but in a well-arranged school, especially one which combines education with physical labour; it can be fostered by the co-operative principle of labour; it can be fostered by broad and purposeful sporting activities. If the militias are based on the natural, occupational-productive groupings of the new society, the village communes, the municipal collectives, industrial associations . . . inwardly unified by school, sports association, and circumstances of labour,

then the militia will be much richer in the 'corporate' spirit, in a spirit of much higher quality, than are barracks-bred regiments.[1]

The idea of the militias was also criticized in the party, and a demand arose for the revision of the resolutions adopted in its favour. At a congress of army commissars at the end of 1920 Smilga made a convincing case against the militias. He argued that under this system most regiments and divisions would consist almost exclusively of muzhiks; the industrial, proletarian units would be very few and isolated from the rest of the army. This might spell danger to the proletarian dictatorship. It was vital for the Bolsheviks to distribute the proletarian elements over the whole army; but this was incompatible with the territorial-productive principle of organization. On military grounds, Smilga argued, the militias would also be inadequate. With defective and sparse railways, Russia would not be able at the outbreak of war to mobilize in time and concentrate the militias at strategic points. Under this system, Russia might not be able to fight before an invader had reached the Volga. Militias were defensive in character. Jaurès had been prejudiced in their favour because he had started from an unrealistic distinction between defensive and offensive warfare. For their success militias required: a very high degree of industrialization; a numerous, technically advanced, and relatively educated working class; and a dense network of communication lines. It followed that Russia could not dispense with a standing army.[2]

Trotsky acknowledged the validity of much of this criticism, but he continued to point to the militias as the ultimate goal of military policy. In 1921 he set up three militia divisions—in Petrograd, in Moscow, and in the Urals—by way of experiment. But he himself urged caution. This was a time of much trouble and popular discontent. 'If the workers of the Urals were to starve', he said, 'the experiment would break down.' 'One cannot say in the abstract which system is preferable, one should not try to solve this like a mathematical problem. It is necessary to work this out as a political and social task, in accordance with prevailing circumstances.'[3] In later years, however, nearly three-quarters of the Red Army was reorganized into territorial units, and only one-quarter remained on the footing of a standing army. The experiment went farther than Russia could afford. In the middle 1930s, under the threat of the Second World War, the whole Red Army was overhauled and restored as a standing army. The reasons for this counter-reform,

---

[1] Trotsky, op. cit., vol. ii, book 1, pp. 115–21.
[2] I. Smilga, *Ocherednye Voprosy Stroitelstva Krasnoi Armii*, pp. 8–12.
[3] Trotsky, op. cit., vol. iii, book 1, p. 12.

carried out by Stalin and Tukhachevsky, were those which Smilga had stated in 1920. The counter-reform also harmonized with the general authoritarian trend of the time.

The problem of military doctrine occupies an important place in Trotsky's writings. He himself claimed no originality in this field. But he brought to the discussion of the issues a broad view of history and a freshness of approach which, if they were not enough to make a new philosophy of war, did much to guard the Red Army from pitfalls of one-sided doctrines. He had to contend against the old generals on the one hand, and against young revolutionary officers on the other. To the former he spoke as an innovator, attacking their conservative habits of thought. To the latter he appeared almost as an advocate of military orthodoxy.

He was the presiding spirit of Moscow's Military Academy, where the old generals were professors and lecturers. He strove to modernize the Academy's curriculum, to free it from pedantry, and to bring it close to the fresh experiences of warfare. Once, for instance, he expostulated with the writers of the Academy for their lifeless pseudo-historical style and urged them to emulate French military writers who, he said, knew how to combine historical research with an interest in contemporary warfare and in its sociological background. The academicians viewed the civil war rather contemptuously, as a bastard of grand strategy. Trotsky retorted irritably:

> It is said among you that in the present civil or small war . . . military science has no role, in any case. I am telling you, Messieurs the military specialists, that this is an altogether ignorant statement. . . . Civil war, with its highly mobile and elastic fronts, affords enormous scope to genuine initiative and military art. The task is just the same here as elsewhere: To obtain the maximum result through a minimum expenditure of strength. . . . It was precisely the last [world] war . . . that offered relatively little scope to strategic art. After the gigantic front from the Belgian coast to Switzerland had become fixed, the war became automatic. Strategic art was reduced to a minimum; everything was staked on mutual attrition. Our war, on the contrary, has been full of mobility and manœuvre which allowed the greatest talents to reveal themselves. . . .[1]

While the old generals refused to learn the lessons of the civil war, the young ones were often reluctant to learn anything else. Their ambition was to construct a brand-new 'proletarian military

[1] Trotsky, op. cit., vol. iii, book 1, p. 156.

doctrine'. That doctrine, they held, should meet the needs of the revolutionary class and suit its mentality: It must disdain defence and static warfare and favour mobility and the offensive. Only decaying classes, retreating in all fields, favoured the defensive attitude. The 'proletarian style of warfare' appealed to commanders who had risen from the ranks. Its most gifted expounders were Tukhachevsky and Frunze, while Voroshilov and Budienny also counted among its adherents. With Tukhachevsky the offensive doctrine logically supplemented 'revolution from without'; and in advocating both he remained within the Napoleonic tradition. But being of a more modern outlook than his colleagues, he saw the future offensive warfare as conducted by means of mass formations of tanks and armoured vehicles co-operating with air forces. (He was also the originator of parachute troops, whom he intended to use far behind the enemy lines, in areas engulfed by civil war.)

Trotsky's polemic against this school of thought is perhaps the most instructive part of his military writings. He dismissed 'pro-letarian strategy', just as in another field he disavowed 'proletarian culture' and 'proletarian literature'. 'War bases itself on many sciences', he wrote, 'but war itself is no science—it is a practical art, a skill . . . a savage and bloody art. . . . To try to formulate a new military doctrine with the help of Marxism is like trying to create with the help of Marxism a new theory of architecture or a new veterinary text-book.'[1] He protested, often with biting derision, against the treatment of Marxist dialectics as the philosopher's stone; and he demanded respect for a certain continuity of experience and cultural tradition. He saw in the 'proletarian' innovations a cover for intellectual crudity and conceit. He constantly drew the attention of his military audiences to the barbarous poverty, uncouthness, and dirt of the Red Army, to be mitigated only by hard work and attention to detail, from which the Russian only too frequently sought to escape into the realm of abstract doctrine.

The adherents of the 'proletarian doctrine of the offensive' theorized from their own experience in the civil war, in which rapid manoeuvre predominated. Trotsky replied that the Red Army had learned manoeuvrability, allegedly the exclusive virtue of a rising social class, from the White Guards, just as the latter had borrowed methods of propaganda from the Red Army. Whites and Reds had become mutually assimilated in military matters: 'Fighting one another over a long time, enemies come to learn from one another.'[2]

---

[1] From a speech to the military delegates at the eleventh party congress. Op. cit., vol. iii, book 2, p. 244.

[2] Trotsky, op. cit., vol. ii, book 1, pp. 61–62.

Trotsky himself had issued his famous order 'Proletarians, to horse!', the signal for the formation of Budienny's cavalry corps, only at the height of Denikin's offensive when the White cavalry, led by Mamontov, threatened to disrupt the Bolshevik interior by its deep and swift raids behind Bolshevik lines.[1]

But the high mobility peculiar to the civil war reflected (according to Trotsky) the primitive conditions in which the war was fought over vast, sparsely populated areas. He drew an analogy between the American Civil War and the Russian. In both, the opposed forces operated over thinly populated continents, with extremely poor lines of communication and means of transport. In both, cavalry had exceptionally wide scope. In both, the Whites were the traditional horsemen; and the armies both of the Northern States and of the Soviets had to wrest the initiative and form their own cavalries. It did not follow that high mobility was the 'style' of civil war at large. On the Scheldte, the Seine, or the Thames civil war would be fought much more statically than in steppes or prairies.[2]

The civil war had been fought in Russia in quasi-Napoleonic style, because of the country's low level of civilization. But it was foolish and unhistorical, Trotsky argued, to try to adopt the Napoleonic offensive doctrine for the Red Army, as Tukhachevsky tried to do. Trotsky sharply contrasted the position of revolutionary France in Europe with that of revolutionary Russia. At the beginning of the nineteenth century France was the most civilized and technically advanced nation on the Continent—this enabled Napoleon to pursue the offensive strategy. Russia was technically one of the most backward nations in Europe; Napoleonic strategy would bear no relation whatever to her social and military potentialities. He pointed out that the French General Staff, especially Foch, had in vain cultivated the Napoleonic strategy—France's position in

---

[1] Trotsky at first viewed Budienny's plan for a cavalry corps with reluctance, in part because the typical cavalryman was the reactionary Cossack, and in part because, thinking characteristically in terms of western technique, Trotsky was inclined to assume that the day of the horseman had gone. When he finally changed his mind, he wrote in September 1919: 'This most conservative service, largely withering away, has suddenly, as it were, revived. It has become the most important means of defence and offence in the hands of the most conservative and decaying classes. We must wrest this weapon from their hands and make it our own.' Op. cit., vol. ii, book 1, pp. 287–8. Budienny had a justified grievance against Trotsky for his initial, contemptuous dismissal of the idea.

[2] To illustrate his reasoning Trotsky discussed the hypothetical problem of defence which 'proletarian Britain' would have to solve if confronted by a threat of invasion. He sketched an imaginative picture of that defence: fortified shores; defence of the beaches; trenches, bunkers, barbed wire, and road blocks along the roads leading to the interior of the island, &c., a picture strangely familiar in Britain in 1940–1. Op. cit., vol. iii, book 2, p. 268.

Europe could not and did not allow for its application in 1914–18. And Trotsky poked fun at the brand-new 'proletarian doctrine' which on a closer view was merely a plagiarism of French pre-1914 text-books.

Attempts to define the 'essence' of warfare in general and of proletarian warfare in particular were, according to Trotsky, metaphysical doctrine-mongering.[1] He himself argued the need for a certain eclecticism in military theory. 'In practical arts', he approvingly quoted Clausewitz, 'one should not drive the flowers and the foliage of theory too high—one should rather keep them close to the soil of experience.' He spoke with qualified respect about the empirical methods of the English imperialists, 'who think in centuries and continents' and slightingly about the German epigones of Clausewitz. None of the 'national' doctrines of war offered or could offer any 'final truth' about war. Each school of thought merely reflected temporary conditions of national existence. The English doctrine of balance of power and naval supremacy; the cautious military thought of Bismarck's Germany, which went hand in hand with diplomatic aggressiveness; the exclusively offensive doctrine of latter-day German imperialism, which, carried away by its own momentum, threw all caution to the winds; the Bonapartist offensive doctrine of pre-1914 France (and, one might add, the reaction from it in the form of the Maginot mood before 1940); all these doctrines merely isolate and exaggerate certain moments and aspects of military experience. The Marxist way of thinking is averse to military doctrinairism of any sort. 'Only the traitor renounces attack; only the simpleton reduces all strategy to attack.'[2]

Scattered in these essays and speeches are noteworthy suggestions and anticipations, thrown out in the course of argument, of which only a few can be adduced here. Thus, discussing the strategy of a second world war, nearly twenty years before its outbreak, Trotsky remarked that it would greatly differ from that of the first, both in western Europe and in Russia. In western Europe, trench warfare would become less prominent or would disappear altogether. In Russia, on the contrary, there would be more position fighting than

[1] 'If we check the inventory of the 'eternal truths' of military science, we obtain not much more than a few logical axioms and Euclidean postulates. Defend your flank; secure your lines of communications and retreat; strike at the enemy's least defended point; and so on, and so on. Such principles . . . may well be applied even to matters very remote from the art of warfare. The donkey that steals oats from a hole in a torn sack ('the enemy's least defended point') and vigilantly turns its croup in the direction opposite to that from which danger threatens, certainly behaves according to the eternal principles of military science.' Op. cit., vol. iii, book 2, essay on 'Military Doctrine and Pseudo-Military Doctrinairism'.

[2] Ibid., p. 222.

there was in the civil war.[1] In a polemic against Frunze and Voroshilov he argued that if Russia were attacked from the west by a
technically stronger capitalist power, the Red Army's task in the
first phase of hostilities would be not to attack but to behave defen-
sively, because Russia would be slower in mobilization, and the
defensive operations should give her time to complete it. It was
therefore absolutely wrong to inculcate in the army the notion about
the attacker's invariable moral superiority. 'Having space and
numbers on our side, we may calmly and confidently mark the line
at which mobilization, secured by our stubborn defence, will allow
us to gather sufficient striking-power to pass to the counter-offensive.'[2]
The Red Army may be forced to retreat, but the depth of the
retreat should be dictated solely by the needs of mobilization.

If [however] I am the first to attack and my attack is not sufficiently supported by mobilization and I am compelled to retreat,
then I lose tempo and I may lose it irretrievably. If, on the contrary, my plan envisages a preliminary retreat, if the plan is clear
to the senior commanding staffs, if the latter have confidence in
the near future and convey this confidence downwards, if their
confidence does not founder on the prejudice that one ought
invariably to be the first to attack—then I have every chance of
regaining tempo and winning.[3]

Trotsky found, of course, no use for Tukhachevsky's International
General Staff. The time, he maintained, for the setting up of such a
staff would come only when, in the process of genuine revolution
abroad, new Red armies would come into being. But he himself
insisted on the need for rules and regulations of civil war, in which
the experiences of the revolutions and risings in various countries
would be utilized and evaluated; and he drew up a conspectus for
such rules and regulations.

In the aftermath of the civil war, the educational problems of
the army, the technological complications of warfare and its ever
closer connexion with politics occupied Trotsky. 'In the education of
our Red commanding officer', he said, 'the development of his
capacity for a synthetic evaluation of the co-operation and mutual
interaction of all kinds of modern weapons ought to go hand in
hand with the acquisition of a correct social-political orientation.
. . .'[4] At the Military Academy he urged the commanding staffs to
learn foreign languages, to get out of their national shell, to broaden
their horizon and to 'participate in mankind's world-wide experience'.

[1] Ibid., p. 268.   [2] Ibid., p. 256.   [3] Loc. cit.   [4] Op. cit., vol. i, p. xi.

CHAPTER XIV

Defeat in Victory

AT the very pinnacle of power Trotsky, like the protagonist of a classical tragedy, stumbled. He acted against his own principle and in disregard of a most solemn moral commitment. Circumstances, the preservation of the revolution, and his own pride drove him into this predicament. Placed as he was he could hardly have avoided it. His steps followed almost inevitably from all that he had done before; and only one step now separated the sublime from the sinister—even his denial of principle was still dictated by principle. Yet in acting as he did he shattered the ground on which he stood.

Towards the end of the civil war he initiated courses of action which he and the Bolshevik party could carry through only against the resistance of the social classes which had made or supported the revolution. The Bolsheviks had denounced bourgeois democracy as a sham concealing the inequality of the social classes and the predominance of the bourgeoisie. But they had pledged themselves to uphold proletarian democracy, guaranteeing freedom of expression and organization to the working class and the poor peasantry. No Bolshevik leader had repeated that pledge so often and so ardently as Trotsky. None repudiated it now as plainly. The paradox is all the more striking because at the same time he was unaffectedly opposed to carrying revolution abroad on the bayonet's point. Such opposition was consistent with the principle of proletarian democracy. If the working class of any country was to be its own master, then it was preposterous and even criminal to try to impose on it any social order 'from without'. But this argument applied *a fortiori* to the Russian working class: it, too, should have been master in its own country. Yet the policies which Trotsky now framed were incompatible with that *samodeyatelnost*, that political self-determination of the working class, which he had indefatigably preached for twenty years and which he was to preach again during the seventeen years of his open struggle against Stalin.

He promoted the new policies at first with Lenin's consent.

But as he proceeded, he found Lenin and most of the Bolsheviks arrayed against him and invoking the principle of proletarian democracy. His own ideas now bore the clear hallmark of that 'substitutism', which he himself had once denounced as the chief vice of Bolshevism, indeed, as the hereditary vice of Russian revolutionary politics. For, in his view, the party, informed by the proper understanding of the 'tasks of the epoch' and of its own 'historic mission', was to substitute that understanding and that mission for the wishes and strivings of the broad social forces which it had led in the revolution. Thus Trotsky now began to resemble that caricature of Lenin which he himself had once drawn.[1]

What accounted for this extraordinary transformation? What was it that made the armed and victorious prophet of revolution contradict the tenor of his own prophecy? Before an answer can be attempted, the economic and social condition of Russia must be briefly surveyed, for it was to that plane that the drama had now shifted.

.   .   .   .

From the end of 1919 Trotsky devoted only a minor part of his attention to military affairs. The issue of the civil war was no longer in doubt; and in the latter part of 1920 he kept somewhat aloof from the conduct of military policy because of his differences with the Politbureau over the Polish war. But even earlier he had become absorbed in the problems of economic reconstruction. He entered this new field with the impetuous self-confidence which success at the Commissariat of War had given him; and he was inclined to apply there the methods and solutions which he had worked out and tested in the military field. On 16 December 1919 he submitted to the Central Committee a set of propositions ('Theses') on the economic transition from war to peace. Among the measures which he proposed, militarization of labour was the most essential. He had written this paper only for the members of the Central Committee, hoping to start a discussion in their closed circle. By mistake Bukharin at once published the paper in *Pravda*. The indiscretion gave rise to an extremely tense public controversy which lasted until the spring of 1921.[2]

The years of world war, revolution, civil war, and intervention

---

[1] See above, pp. 90–7.   [2] Trotsky, *Sochinenya*, vol. xv, pp. 10–14, 36.

had resulted in the utter ruin of Russia's economy and the disintegration of her social fabric. From a ruined economy the Bolsheviks had had to wrest the means of civil war. In 1919, the Red Army had already used up all stocks of munitions and other supplies. The industries under Soviet control could not replace them by more than a fraction. Normally southern Russia supplied fuel, iron, steel, and raw materials to the industries of central and northern Russia. But southern Russia, occupied first by the Germans and then by Denikin, was only intermittently and during brief spells under Soviet control. When at last, at the end of 1919, the Bolsheviks returned there for good, they found that the coal-mines of the Donetz valley were flooded and the other industries destroyed. Deprived of fuel and raw materials, the industrial centres of the rest of the country were paralysed. Even towards the end of 1920, the coal-mines produced less than one-tenth and the iron- and steel-works less than one-twentieth of their pre-war output. The production of consumer goods was about one-quarter of normal. The disaster was made even worse by the destruction of transport. All over the country railway tracks and bridges had been blown up. Rolling stock had not been renewed, and it had only rarely been kept in proper repair, since 1914. Inexorably transport was coming to a standstill. (This, incidentally, was one of the contributory causes of the Red Army's defeat in Poland. The Soviets had enlisted five million men, but of these less than 300,000 were actually engaged in the last stages of the Polish campaign. As the armies rolled onward, the railways were less and less capable of carrying reinforcements and supplies over the lengthening distances.) Farming, too, was ruined. For six years the peasants had not been able to renew their equipment. Retreating and advancing armies trampled their fields and requisitioned their horses. However, because of its technically primitive character, farming was more resilient than industry. The muzhik worked with the wooden *sokha*, which he was able to make or repair by himself.

The Bolsheviks strove to exercise the strictest control over scarce resources; and out of this striving grew their War Communism. They nationalized all industry. They prohibited private trade. They dispatched workers' detachments to the countryside to requisition food for the army and the town-dwellers. The government was incapable of collecting normal taxes; it possessed no machinery for doing so. To cover government expenses, the printing-presses produced banknotes day and night. Money became so worthless that wages and salaries had to be paid in kind. The meagre food ration formed the basic wage. The worker was also paid with part of his own produce, a pair of shoes or a few pieces of clothing, which he usually bartered away for food.

This set of desperate shifts and expedients looked to the party like an unexpectedly rapid realization of its own programme. Socialization of industry would have been carried out more slowly and cautiously if there had been no civil war; but it was, in any case, one of the major purposes of the revolution. The requisitioning of food, the prohibition of private trade, the payment of wages in kind, the insignificance of money, the government's aspiration to control the economic resources of the nation, all this looked, superficially, like the abolition of that market economy which was the breeding-ground of capitalism. The fully grown Communist economy about which Marxist text-books had speculated, was to have been a natural economy, in which socially planned production and distribution should take the place of production for the market and of distribution through the medium of money. The Bolshevik was therefore inclined to see the essential features of fully fledged communism embodied in the war economy of 1919–20. He was confirmed in this inclination by the stern egalitarianism which his party preached and practised and which gave to war communism a romantic and heroic aspect.

In truth, war communism was a tragic travesty of the Marxist vision of the society of the future. That society was to have as its background highly developed and organized productive resources and a superabundance of goods and services. It was to organize and develop the social wealth which capitalism at its best produced only fitfully and could not rationally control, distribute, and promote. Communism was to abolish economic inequality once for all by levelling up the standards of living. War communism had, on the contrary, resulted from social disintegration, from the destruction and disorganization of productive resources, from an unparalleled scarcity of goods and services. It did indeed try to abolish inequality; but of necessity it did so by levelling down the standards of living and making poverty universal.[1]

The system could not work for long. The requisitioning of food and the prohibition of private trade for the time being helped the government to tide over the direst emergencies. But in the longer run these policies aggravated and accelerated the shrinkage and disintegration of the economy. The peasant began to till only as much of his land as was necessary to keep his family alive. He refused to produce the surplus for which the requisitioning squads were on the look-out. When the countryside refuses to produce food for the town, even the rudiments of urban civilization go to pieces. The cities of Russia became depopulated. Workers went to the countryside to escape famine. Those who stayed behind fainted at the factory benches, produced very little,. and often stole what they produced to barter it for food. The old, normal market had indeed been abolished. But its bastard, the black market, despoiled the country, revengefully perverting and degrading human relations. This could go on for another year or so; but, inevitably the end would be the breakdown of all government and the dissolution of society.

Such was the situation to which Trotsky bent his mind towards the end of 1919. To cope with it one of two courses of action had to be taken. The government could stop the requisitioning of food from the peasant and introduce an agricultural tax, in kind or money. Having paid his taxes, the peasant could then be permitted to dispose of his crop as he pleased, to consume it, sell it, or barter it. This would have induced him to grow the surpluses for urban consumption. With the flow of food from country to town restored, the activity of the state-owned industries could be expected to revive. This indeed would have been the only real solution. But a reform of this kind implied the revival of private trade; and it could not but explode the whole edifice of war communism, in the erection of which the Bolsheviks took so much pride.

The alternative was to look for a solution within the vicious circle of war communism. If the government was to go on requisitioning food and enforcing the ban on trade, it had to

[1] The reader will find a detailed and instructive account of war communism in E. H. Carr, *The Bolshevik Revolution*, vol. ii.

increase the pressure on the peasantry first in making it produce more food and then in requisitioning the food. It might also offer special rewards to food growers—clothing, footwear, agricultural implements. It could not do so, however, before the famished workers had repaired and set in motion the destroyed and dilapidated industrial plant and begun to turn out the goods for which the peasantry craved. The government was therefore compelled to press for more industrial production. Unable to offer incentives to the workers, it had to apply more force to them as well as to the peasants. It was a sure sign of the Utopian character of war communism that it went on ignoring realities until it drove itself into an impasse and could maintain itself only by ever-increasing doses of violence.

Trotsky did not at first go beyond the framework of accepted policy. He was preoccupied with the means by which the dispersed working class could be reassembled and brought back to industry. There were the workers who had fled to the countryside; there were those who in search of food had abandoned skilled jobs for unskilled ones; and there were those *declassés* who were completely engulfed in the black market and lost to industry. How could they all be brought back to a normal environment and reintegrated into the nation's productive apparatus? As they could not be attracted by a promise of better living, so Trotsky concluded, they must be recruited to the factories in the same way as soldiers. Thus, empirically, Trotsky arrived at the idea of militarization of labour. The revolution had loudly proclaimed the duty of every citizen to work and declared that 'he who does not work shall not eat'. The time had now come, Trotsky argued, to enforce that duty. The revolution had sent hundreds of thousands to die on the battlefields. Surely it had the moral right to send people into workshops and mines, where the new battle for survival must be waged.

In those 'Theses' which *Pravda* published prematurely on 17 December 1919, Trotsky characteristically linked this scheme with the military reform he envisaged, the transition of the army to the militia system. He proposed that the machinery for military mobilization should be employed for the mobilization of civilian labour. It is strange how his aspiration to carry out a most democratic reform in the army was combined with his attempt to introduce this extreme form of compulsion of labour. The army was to become permeated with the spirit of civilian citizenship. Its detachments were to be organized on the basis of productive units. On the other hand, civilian labour was to be subjected to military discipline; and the military administration was to supply manpower to industrial units. The Commissariat of War was to assume the functions of the Commissariat of Labour.[1]

Lenin wholeheartedly supported Trotsky's policy. He clung to war communism, which could be made to work, if at all, only on condition that the measures proposed by Trotsky were successful. Nor did Lenin object to the assumption by the Commissariat of War of the responsibility for the supply of industrial labour. Lenin had had to build up the civilian branches of his administration from scratch; and, after the years of civil war, most of them were still in a rudimentary stage. The Commissariat of War had absorbed the best men; it had had first claim on the government's resources; it was directed by the most clear-headed administrator. Its machinery, formidable and highly efficient, was the most solid part of Lenin's administration, its real hub. It seemed a matter of administrative convenience to switch the Commissariat to civilian work.

No sooner had these proposals become known than they let loose an avalanche of protests. At conferences of party members, administrators, and trade unionists, Trotsky was shouted down as the 'new Arakcheev', the imitator of that ill-famed general and Minister of War who, under Alexander I and Nicholas I, had set up military farming colonies and ruled them with a rod of iron. *Arakcheevshchina* had ever since been the by-word for grotesque flights of military-bureaucratic fancy over the field of economic and social policies. The cry of protest rose in the Bolshevik newspapers. It came from Trotsky's old associates, Ryazanov and Larin, from the eminent Bolsheviks Rykov, Miliutin, Nogin, Goltzman, and from others. Weariness of civil war and impatience with the architect of victory mingled in these protests. As usually happens in a time of reaction from the tensions and sacrifices of war, people were willing to cover with

---

[1] On 27 December 1919 it was announced that the government had formed a Commission on Labour Duty, over which Trotsky presided.

laurels the man responsible for victory. But they were even more eager to get rid of the rigours of wartime discipline; and they looked for guidance to men who were of less fiery temperament and less splendid talents, but who were willing to pursue milder courses of action. Old, battle-hardened Bolsheviks were heard to declare that they had had enough of the army's impositions, that the Commissariat of War had long enough kept the country under terror and sucked its blood, and that they would not countenance Trotsky's new ambitions.

Matters came to a head on 12 January 1920, when Lenin and Trotsky appeared before the Bolshevik leaders of the trade unions and urged them to accept militarization. Trotsky defended his own record. If his Commissariat, he said, had 'pillaged' the country and exacted severe discipline, it had done so to win the war. It was a disgrace and a 'sin against the spirit of the revolution' that this should now be held against him, and that the working class should be incited against the army. His opponents were complacent about the country's economic condition. The newspapers concealed the real state of affairs. 'It is necessary to state openly and frankly in the hearing of the whole country, that our economic condition is a hundred times worse than our military situation ever was. . . . Just as we once issued the order "Proletarians, to horse!", so now we must raise the cry "Proletarians, back to the factory bench! Proletarians, back to production!" '[1] The nation's labour force continued to shrink and degenerate. It could not be saved, reconstituted, and rehabilitated without the application of coercive measures. Lenin spoke in the same vein. Yet the conference almost unanimously rejected the resolution which he and Trotsky jointly submitted. Of more than three score Bolshevik leaders only two men voted for it. Never before had Trotsky or Lenin met with so striking a rebuff.

Trotsky's strictures on the complacency of his critics were not unjustified. The critics did not and could not propose any practical alternative. They, too, clung to war communism and disavowed only the conclusion Trotsky had drawn from it. He had little difficulty therefore in exposing their inconsistency. Yet there was a certain realism and valuable scruple in their very lack of consistency. Trotsky's opponents refused to believe

[1] Trotsky, op. cit., pp. 27–52.

that the wheels of the economy could be set in motion by word of military command, and they were convinced that it was wrong for a workers' state to act as a press gang towards its own working class.[1]

In the meantime the first labour army came into being, not by the militarization of civilian labour but by the transformation of a regular army into a labour force. The initiative came from the Revolutionary War Council of the Third Army, which was stationed in the Urals. After its victory over Kolchak, that army frittered away its time and energy in idleness. It could not release and send home its men, primarily because of the lack of transport. Its Revolutionary War Council proposed that meanwhile the army should be employed in timber felling, farming, and other work. Lenin and Trotsky welcomed the suggestion, which gave them a chance to put their policy into effect virtually without opposition: the trade unions did not object to the productive employment of idle regiments.[2]

Trotsky hoped to use this experiment as a starting-point for the conscription and direction of civilian labour. Nothing could be simpler than that the army, before releasing its men, should take a census of their productive skills, mark every soldier's trade in his service-book, and then direct him straight from the demobilization point to the working place where he was wanted. Trotsky planned to combine the soldier's service-book with the worker's labour-book, a device which should also facilitate the formation of militias on the basis of productive units. This was an imaginative idea. Its flaw was that the released soldier, anxious to reunite with his family or to look for a better living, was likely to abandon the working place to which he had been directed. Trotsky drew blueprints for the organization of communal feeding-centres to attract workers; but such schemes could not be put into effect amid the famines and disorders of the time. He displayed astounding originality and inventiveness, but his imagination worked feverishly in a vacuum; and his ideas were out of joint with reality.

After the army of the Urals, the armies of the Caucasus and of the Ukraine were put to work in mines, forests, and fields. Trotsky headed the entire organization. General Bonch-Bruevich

---

[1] This controversy filled the pages of *Ekonomicheskaya Zhizn* and *Pravda* throughout January 1920. [2] *The Trotsky Archives.*

was his Chief of Staff; Pyatakov was his representative in the Urals; and Stalin was chief commissar of the Ukrainian labour army. The organization maintained military discipline; and each labour army regularly reported its successes and failures on the 'fronts'. (It was Trotsky who first systematically applied military terms, symbols, and metaphors to civilian economic matters and thus introduced a fresh, vivid style in the Russian language, a style which later became ossified into a bureaucratic mannerism and spread to other languages.) Views about the economic efficiency of the labour armies were divided—it could, at any rate, not have been lower than that of civilian labour at the time. The Bolsheviks acclaimed the labour armies, especially after Trotsky had gone to some length to mollify the trade unions and had appealed to the labour armies for friendly co-operation with them.

He brought to this work his moral passion and theatrical *élan*, which led him, however, to exaggerate the significance of what he did and to cast a false glamour over what were at best sad expedients. This, for instance, is how he wrote in one of his Orders to the Labour Armies:

Display untiring energy in your work, as if you were on the march or in battle. . . . Commanders and commissars are responsible for their detachments at work as in battle. . . . The political departments must cultivate the spirit of the worker in the soldier and preserve the soldier in the worker. . . . A deserter from labour is as contemptible and despicable as a deserter from the battlefield. Severe punishment to both! . . . Begin and complete your work, wherever possible, to the sound of socialist hymns and songs. Your work is not slave labour but high service to the socialist fatherland.[1]

On 8 February he departed with his staff for the Urals, on the first inspection of the labour armies. In *En Route*, the paper published on his train, he thus addressed his staff:

The old capitalist organization of labour has been destroyed irrevocably and for ever. The new socialist organization is only beginning to take shape. We must become conscious, self-sacrificing builders of the socialist economy. Only on this road shall we find a way out, salvation, warmth, and contentment. We must begin from the foundations. . . . Our train is proceeding to the northern

[1] *Pravda*, 16 January 1920.

Urals, where we shall devote all our strength to the organization of labour in which the Ural workers, the Ural peasants, and the Red Army men . . . will participate hand in hand. Bread for the starving! Fuel for the freezing! This is the slogan of our team this time.[1]

He had just written these words when, in the middle of the night, he was shaken by a violent concussion. His train became derailed in a severe snowstorm. Throughout the night and the whole of the next day the train lay in snowdrifts almost within sight of a small station. Not a soul came to inquire what had happened. The station-masters had ceased to signal the passage of trains; even the train of the President of the Supreme War Council had passed through unnoticed. Despite the threat of court martial, nobody bothered to clear away the snowdrifts from the tracks. The accident unexpectedly revealed to Trotsky the void which grew around governmental policies and plans. A fathomless apathy shrouded the people. Trotsky raged, conducted an investigation on the spot, and ordered a military tribunal into action. But he could not help reflecting that repression alone could not remedy the people's numb insensibility. His forebodings grew darker during his sojourn in the countryside of the Urals. He became acutely aware that the nation's energy and vitality was drying up at its very source—on the farmstead.

He now searched for remedies beyond war communism. He returned to Moscow with the conclusion that a measure of economic freedom should be restored to the peasantry. In clear and precise terms he outlined the reform which alone could lead the nation out of the impasse. There must be an end to the requisitioning of crops. The peasant must be encouraged to grow and sell surpluses and to make a profit on them. The government and the party were not aware of the magnitude of the disaster, because the last forcible collection had yielded more food than the previous one. This, he argued, was because after the retreat of the White Guards, the requisitions had been carried out over a much wider area than before. 'In general, however, the food reserves are in danger of drying up, and against this no improvement in the requisitioning machinery

---

[1] Trotsky, *Sochinenya*, vol. xv, pp. 324-5.

can help.' That way lay further disruption, further shrinkage of the labour force and final economic and political degradation.[1]

At the Central Committee his arguments carried no conviction. Lenin was not prepared to stop the requisitions. The reform
Trotsky proposed looked to him like a leap in the dark. The
government, he held, had already shown too much haste in
preparing the transition to peace: Trotsky himself had just
warned the Central Committee that Poland was about to attack.
It seemed safer to stick to an established policy rather than
tamper with the army's food supplies, which had, after all, been
secured by the requisitions. Nor was that all. Lenin and the
Central Committee had not yet lived down the illusions of war
communism. They still hoped that the system, having rendered
valuable service in war, would be even more useful in peace.
Trotsky proposed to throw the economy back on to the treacherous tides of a free market. This was what the Mensheviks
demanded. Did Trotsky agree with them? had he become a
free trader? he was asked.[2] He was told that the party had advanced towards an organized and controlled economy and that
it would not allow itself to be dragged back.

The Central Committee rejected his proposals. Only more
than a year later, after the failure of war communism had been
demonstrated with tragic conclusiveness, did Lenin take up the
same proposals and put them into effect as the New Economic
Policy (N.E.P.). This was then and still is hailed as a stroke
of Lenin's genius, a rare feat of courageous, undogmatic
statesmanship. In the light of the facts it seems that the feat
was at least overpraised; and that when Trotsky later reproached Lenin and the Central Committee for initiating
the most important changes in economic policy when these
were overdue by a year or two, the stricture was not quite

---

[1] Trotsky, *Sochinenya*, vol. xvii, book 2, pp. 543–4. It is not clear, however,
whether Trotsky was aware that his proposals, if accepted, would necessarily lead
to the winding up of the policies of war communism, including those he himself
advocated. In later years he argued that he had stood for militarization of labour
only in the context of war communism. At the tenth congress of the party, however,
when N.E.P. was introduced, he insisted that his labour policies retained their
validity and that they were not necessarily connected with war communism. See
Desyatyi Syezd RKP, p. 191, and *Moya Zhizn*, vol. ii, chapter xxxviii.

[2] *Desyatyi Syezd RKP*, loc. cit.

undeserved.[1] The incident also shows how unreal is the juxtaposition, in Stalinist versions, of Lenin the friend and Trotsky the
enemy of the peasantry: Lenin's reputation as the well-wisher
of the muzhik rests primarily on the New Economic Policy.

Yoffe, whom we know as Trotsky's close friend, remarked in
the letter he wrote before his suicide in 1927, that it was
Trotsky's major weakness that he did not persist in his wisdom,
especially when to be wise was to be alone.[2] One might add that
on this occasion Trotsky, rebuked for his wisdom, plunged back
into the accepted folly and persisted in it with an ardour which
even the fools thought too foolish. After the Central Committee
rejected his proposals, he dropped the matter. He did not raise
it again or even hint at it at the ninth congress of the party,
which met a month later, at the end of March 1920. Instead he
appeared as the government's chief economic policy-maker and
expounded a master plan for the next phase of war communism. Did he become convinced that the revision of policy
he had suggested was unseasonable? Did he consider it impolitic
to advocate a reform for which the Mensheviks, too, clamoured?
Did he fear that the party as a whole was not in a receptive
mood? Probably all these motives had their part in inducing
him to act as he did.

The nation's economy continued to decay. The need for
radical action became more pressing. As the party had refused
to ease the rigours of war communism it had to aggravate
them. Trotsky consented to bear the onus and the odium of the
job. The Politbureau urgently requested him to take charge of
the wrecked transport system and offered to back him to the
hilt in any course of action he might take, no matter how severe.
Trotsky pleaded incompetence, but agreed to take over temporarily the department of transport in addition to that of war.[3]
With increased confidence he returned to the theme of militarization of labour. This, he said at the congress, was indispensable for the integration and development of the nation's
resources under a single economic plan. Planned economy was
still far off; but the party and the nation should not expect to

[1] See Trotsky's messages to the Central Committee and the Politbureau of 7
August 1921 and 22 August 1922. *The Archives.*
[2] *The Trotsky Archives.*
[3] See the correspondence between Lenin and Trotsky (1 February and 9 March
1920), ibid.

move towards it by cautious, well-measured steps. In the past Russia had always advanced by violent leaps and bounds; she would continue to do so. Compulsion of labour was, of course, unthinkable under fully fledged socialism; but it *'would reach the highest degree of intensity during the transition from capitalism to socialism'*. He urged the congress to approve disciplinary measures, 'the severity of which must correspond to the tragic character of our economic situation': 'deserters from labour' ought to be formed into punitive battalions or put into concentration camps.[1] He also advocated incentive wages for efficient workers and 'Socialist emulation'; and he spoke of the need to adopt the progressive essence of 'Taylorism', the American conception of scientific management and organization of labour, which had been abused by capitalism and rightly hated by the workers, but of which socialism could and should make rational use. These were then startling ideas. At the congress a minority denounced them and indignantly resisted the disciplinarian trend of Trotsky's policy. That minority consisted of the 'libertarians', the 'ultra-lefts', the 'democratic centralists', led by Osinsky, Sapronov, and Preobrazhensky, men with whom Trotsky would one day join hands against Stalin. Now he was their chief antagonist, and he swayed the congress.[2]

Soon afterwards he again expounded and elaborated his policy at a congress of trade unions. He demanded that the unions should discipline the workers and teach them to place the interest of production above their own needs and demands. The Central Council of trade unions was already split into two groups: one supported his 'productionist' attitude; the other, led by Tomsky, felt that the trade unions could not help defending the 'consumptionist' claims of the workers. Trotsky argued that the workers must first produce the resources from which their claims could be met; and that they should remember that they were working for the workers' state, not for the old possessing classes. Most Bolshevik trade unionists knew from experience that such exhortations did not impress hungry men. But since the party had endorsed Trotsky's policy, they could not oppose him in public. At the congress the Mensheviks became the mouthpieces of discontent. They attacked the labour armies. They denied the government the right to conscript

[1] Trotsky, *Sochinenya*, vol. xv, p. 126.   [2] *Devyatyi Syezd RKP*, pp. 81–4, 123–36.

workers and deprive them of the freedom to defend their
interests. They argued that compulsory labour was inefficient.
'You cannot build a planned economy', exclaimed Abramovich, the Menshevik, 'in the way the Pharaohs built their
pyramids.'[1] Abramovich thus coined the phrase, which years
later Trotsky was to repeat against Stalin. The Mensheviks
were on strong ground; and the fact that their record in the
revolution had been poor, even odious, could not detract from
the logic and truth of their argument. Trotsky himself could not
at heart contradict them when they argued that the wastage
of the industrial labour force could not be stopped as long as the
peasants were not allowed to sell their crops freely.[2]

His answer to the criticisms was little better than a piece of
brilliant sophistry. Its historical interest lies in the fact that this
has been perhaps the only frank attempt made in modern times
to give a logical justification of forced labour—the actual task-
masters and whippers-in do not bother to produce such justi-
fications. The crux of Trotsky's argument was that under any
social order 'man must work in order not to die'; that labour
was therefore always compulsory; and that Communists should
approach the matter without cant, because they were the first
to organize labour for the benefit of society as a whole. He came
to deny by implication the significance of the differences in
form and degree in which the natural compulsion of labour
manifested itself under different social systems. Man had worked
as slave, serf, free artisan, independent peasant, and free wage-
earner. The natural compulsion of labour had been aggravated
or softened by social relations. Man had fought against slavery,
serfdom, and capitalism in order to ease it. The Russian Revolution had promised to ease it radically by means of rational
economic organization. It was not the revolution's fault that,
because of inherited poverty and the devastation of several
wars and of blockade, it could not honour its promise. But the
Bolsheviks need not have expressly repudiated that promise.
This was what Trotsky appeared to do when he told the trade
unions that coercion, regimentation, and militarization of labour
were no mere emergency measures, and that the workers' state

---

[1] *Tretii Vserossiskii Syezd Profsoyuzov*, p. 97.
[2] The case for a change in policy which anticipated the N.E.P. was made at the
congress by the Menshevik Dallin. Ibid., p. 8.

normally had the right to coerce any citizen to perform any work at any place of its choosing.

> We are now heading towards the type of labour [he stated] that is socially regulated on the basis of an economic plan, obligatory for the whole country, compulsory for every worker. This is the basis of socialism. . . . The militarization of labour, in this fundamental sense of which I have spoken, is the indispensable basic method for the organization of our labour forces. . . . Is it true that compulsory labour is always unproductive? . . . This is the most wretched and miserable liberal prejudice: chattel slavery, too, was productive. . . . Compulsory serf labour did not grow out of the feudal lords' ill-will. It was [in its time] a progressive phenomenon.[1]

Carried away by his desire to justify the measures he sponsored, he, the rebel *par excellence*, the expounder of permanent revolution, came very near to talking like an apologist for past systems of coercion and exploitation.

For a time the Polish war blunted the edge of this controversy. Peril from without once again induced people to accept without murmur policies which, before, had aroused their intense resentment. At the height of the war, Trotsky, surrounded by a team of technicians, made a determined effort to set the railways in motion. By this time the stock of locomotives had been almost entirely wasted. Engineers forecast the exact date— only a few months ahead—when not a single railway in Russia would be working. Trotsky placed the railway men and the personnel of the repair workshops under martial law; and he organized systematic and rapid rehabilitation of the rolling-stock. He went into the repair workshops to tell the workers that the country was paying for their slackness in blood: the paralysis of transport had encouraged the Poles to attack. 'The situation of the worker', he declared, 'is grievous in every respect . . . it is worse than ever. I would deceive you if I were to say that it will be better to-morrow. No, ahead of us are months of heavy struggle until we can lift our country out of this terrible misery and utter exhaustion, until we can stop weighing our bread ration on the chemist's scales.'[2] When the railwaymen's trade union raised objections to his action, he

---

[1] Ibid., pp. 87–96.
[2] See his speech at the Muromsk workshops of 21 June 1920 in *Sochinenya*, vol. xv, p. 368.

dismissed its leaders and appointed others who were willing to do his bidding. He repeated this procedure in unions of other transport workers. Early in September he formed the *Tsektran*, the Central Transport Commission, through which he brought the whole field of transport under his control. The Politbureau backed him to the hilt as it had promised. To observe electoral rights and voting procedures in the unions seemed at that moment as irrelevant as it might seem in a city stricken with pestilence. He produced results and surpassed expectations: the railways were rehabilitated well ahead of schedule—'the blood circulation of the economic organism was revived'—and he was acclaimed for the feat.[1]

But no sooner had the Polish war been concluded than the grievances and dissensions exploded anew and with greater force than before. He himself provoked the explosion. Flushed with success, he threatened to 'shake up' various trade unions as he had 'shaken up' those of the transport workers. He threatened, that is, to dismiss the elected leaders of the unions and to replace them by nominees who would place the nation's economic interest above the sectional interests of the workers. He grossly overstepped the mark. Lenin now bluntly dissociated himself from Trotsky and persuaded the Central Committee to do likewise. The Committee openly called the party to resist energetically 'militarized and bureaucratic forms of work': and it castigated that 'degenerated centralism' which rode roughshod over the workers' elected representatives. It called on the party to re-establish proletarian democracy in the trade unions and to subordinate all other considerations to this task.[2] A special commission was formed to watch that these decisions were carried out. Zinoviev presided over it, and, although Trotsky sat on it, nearly all its members were his opponents.[3] As a finishing stroke, the Central Committee forbade Trotsky to speak

[1] For the famous Order no. 1042 concerning the railways see op. cit., pp. 345–7. Later in the year Trotsky was placed at the head of special commissions which took emergency action to rehabilitate the industries of the Donetz valley and of the Urals.

[2] See the report of the Central Committee in *Izvestya Tsentralnovo Komiteta RKP*, no. 26, 1920, and G. Zinoviev, *Sochinenya*, vol. vi, pp. 600 ff.

[3] The Commission consisted of Zinoviev, Tomsky, Rudzutak, Rykov, and Trotsky. Later Shlyapnikov, Lutovinov, Lozovsky, and Andreev were co-opted. Of these only Andreev, who thirty years later was still a member of Stalin's last Politbureau, shared Trotsky's view.

in public on the relationship between the trade unions and the state.

Trotsky, unrepentant, sulked. At the beginning of December, at a closed session of the *Tsektran*, he returned to the attack on trade unionists who, as he said, had been good at conducting strikes in the old days but showed little understanding of the needs of a Socialist economy. He defended his practice of overruling them, made light of the demand for elections in the trade unions, and castigated those who cried out that a new bureaucracy was reviving Tsarist methods of government. 'Bureaucracy . . .', he replied, 'was not a discovery of Tsardom. It has represented a whole epoch in the development of mankind', an epoch by no means closed. A competent, hierarchically organized civil service had its merits; and Russia suffered not from the excess but from the lack of an efficient bureaucracy. He made this point repeatedly, arguing that for the sake of efficiency it was necessary to grant certain limited privileges to the bureaucracy. He thus made himself the spokesman of the managerial groups, and this later enabled Stalin to taunt him plausibly with being the 'patriarch of the bureaucrats'.[1] He was confident, Trotsky said, that he could win popular support for his policy; but the economic and social breakdown left no time for the application of the democratic process, which worked with unbearable slowness, because of the low cultural and political level of the Russian masses. 'What you call bossing and working through nominees is in inverse proportion to the enlightenment of the masses, to their cultural standards, political consciousness, and the strength of our administrative machinery.'[2]

Once again the Central Committee rebuffed him. Trotsky fretfully reminded Lenin and the other members of how often they had privately urged him, the 'trouble-shooter', to act ruthlessly and disregard considerations of democracy. It was disloyal of them, he remarked, to pretend in public that they defended the democratic principle against him.[3]

The deeper ill which afflicted the whole system of government, and of which this tug-of-war was merely a symptom, lay in the

[1] Stalin, *Sochinenya*, vol. vi, p. 29.
[2] Trotsky, *Sochinenya*, vol. xv, p. 422.   [3] *Desyatyi Syezd RKP*, p. 215.

frustration of the popular hopes aroused by the revolution. For the first time since 1917 the bulk of the working class, not to speak of the peasantry, unmistakably turned against the Bolsheviks. A sense of isolation began to haunt the ruling group. To be sure, the working class had not come to regret the revolution. It went on to identify itself with it; and it received with intense hostility any openly counter-revolutionary agitation. 'October' had so deeply sunk into the popular mind that Mensheviks and Social Revolutionaries now had to preface their criticisms of the government with an explicit acceptance of the 'achievements of October'. Yet the opposition to current Bolshevik policies was just as intense and widespread. The Mensheviks and Social Revolutionaries, who in the course of three years had been completely eclipsed and had hardly dared to raise their heads, were now regaining some popular favour. People listened even more sympathetically to anarchist agitators violently denouncing the Bolshevik régime. If the Bolsheviks had now permitted free elections to the Soviets, they would almost certainly have been swept from power.[1]

The Bolsheviks were firmly resolved not to let things come to that pass. It would be wrong to maintain that they clung to power for its own sake. The party as a whole was still animated by that revolutionary idealism of which it had given such abundant proof in its underground struggle and in the civil war. It clung to power because it identified the fate of the republic with its own fate and saw in itself the only force capable of safeguarding the revolution. It was lucky for the revolution—and it was also its misfortune—that in this belief the Bolsheviks were profoundly justified. The revolution would hardly have survived without a party as fanatically devoted to it as the Bolsheviks were. But had there existed another party equally devoted and equally vigorous in action, that party might, in consequence of an election, have displaced Lenin's government without convulsing the young state. No such party existed. The return of Mensheviks and Social Revolutionaries would have entailed the undoing of the October Revolution. At the very

---

[1] Many Bolshevik leaders explicitly or implicitly admitted this. See Lenin, *Sochinenya*, vol. xxxii, pp. 160, 176, 230 and *passim*; Zinoviev in *Desyatyi Syezd RKP*, p. 190. In a private letter to Lunacharsky (of 14 April 1926) Trotsky describes the 'menacing discontent' of the working class as the background to the controversy of 1920-1. *The Trotsky Archives.*

least it would have encouraged the White Guards to try their luck once again and rise in arms. From sheer self-preservation as well as from broader motives the Bolsheviks could not even contemplate such a prospect. They could not accept it as a requirement of democracy that they should, by retreating, plunge the country into a new series of civil wars just after one series had been concluded.

Nor was it by any means likely that a free election to the Soviets would return any clear-cut majority. Those who had supported Kerensky in 1917 had not really recovered from their eclipse. Anarchists and anarcho-syndicalists, preaching a 'Third Revolution', seemed far more popular among the working class. But they gave no effective focus to the opposition; and they were in no sense pretenders to office. Strong in criticism, they possessed no positive political programme, no serious organization, national or even local, no real desire to rule a vast country. In their ranks honest revolutionaries, cranks, and plain bandits rubbed shoulders. The Bolshevik régime could be succeeded only by utter confusion followed by open counter-revolution. Lenin's party refused to allow the famished and emotionally unhinged country to vote their party out of power and itself into a bloody chaos.

For this strange sequel to their victory the Bolsheviks were mentally quite unprepared. They had always tacitly assumed that the majority of the working class, having backed them in the revolution, would go on to support them unswervingly until they had carried out the full programme of socialism. Naïve as the assumption was, it sprang from the notion that socialism was the proletarian idea *par excellence* and that the proletariat, having once adhered to it, would not abandon it. That notion had underlain the reasoning of all European schools of Socialist thought. In the vast political literature produced by those schools the question of what Socialists in office should do if they lost the confidence of the workers had hardly ever been pondered. It had never occurred to Marxists to reflect whether it was possible or admissible to try to establish socialism regardless of the will of the working class. They simply took that will for granted. For the same reason it had seemed to the Bolsheviks as clear as daylight that the proletarian dictatorship and proletarian (or Soviet) democracy were only two complementary and inseparable aspects of the same thing: the dictatorship was there to suppress the resistance of the propertied classes; and it derived its strength and historic legitimacy from the freely and democratically expressed opinion of the working classes. Now a conflict arose between the two aspects of the Soviet system. If the working classes were to be allowed to speak and vote freely they would destroy the dictatorship. If the dictatorship, on the other hand, frankly abolished proletarian democracy it would deprive itself of historic legitimacy, even in its own eyes. It would cease to be a proletarian dictatorship in the strict sense. Its use of that title would henceforth be based on the claim that it pursued a policy with which the working class, in its own interest, ought and eventually must identify itself, but with which it did not as yet identify itself. The dictatorship would then at best represent the idea of the class, not the class itself.

The revolution had now reached that cross-roads, well known to Machiavelli, at which it found it difficult or impossible to fix the people in their revolutionary persuasion and was driven 'to take such measures that, when they believed no longer, it might be possible to make them believe by force'. For the Bolshevik party this involved a conflict of loyalties, which was in some respects deeper than any it had known so far, a conflict bearing the seeds of all the turbulent controversies and sombre purges of the next decades.

At this cross-roads Bolshevism suffered a moral agony the like of which is hardly to be found in the history of less intense and impassioned movements. Later Lenin recalled the 'fever' and 'mortal illness' which consumed the party in the winter of 1920–1, during the tumultuous debate over the place of the trade unions in the state. This was an important yet only a secondary matter. It could not be settled before an answer had been given to the fundamental question concerning the very nature of the state. The party was wholly absorbed in the controversy over the secondary issue, because it was not altogether clearly aware of the primary question and was afraid to formulate it frankly in its own mind. But as the protagonists went on arguing they struck the great underlying issue again and again and were compelled to define their attitudes.

It is not necessary here to go into the involved and somewhat technical differences over the trade unions, although the fact that the drama of the revolution revealed itself in a seemingly dry economic argument significantly corresponded to the spirit of the age.[1] Suffice it to say that, broadly speaking, three attitudes crystallized. The faction led by Trotsky (and later by Trotsky and Bukharin) wanted the trade unions to be deprived of their autonomy and absorbed into the machinery of government. This was the final conclusion which Trotsky drew from his conflicts with the trade unions. Under the new dispensation, the leaders of the unions would, as servants of the state, speak for the state to the workers rather than for the workers to the state. They would raise the productivity and maintain the discipline of labour; they would train workers for industrial management; and they would participate in the direction of the country's economy.

At the other extreme the Workers' Opposition, led by Shlyapnikov and Kollontai, protested against the government's and the party's tutelage over the unions. They denounced Trotsky and Lenin as militarizers of labour and promoters of inequality. In quasi-syndicalist fashion they demanded that trade unions, factory committees, and a National Producers' Congress should assume control over the entire economy. While Trotsky argued that the trade unions could not in logic defend the workers against the workers' state, Shlyapnikov and Kollontai already branded the Soviet state as the rampart of a new privileged bureaucracy.

Between these two extremes, Lenin, Zinoviev, and Kamenev spoke for the main body of Bolshevik opinion and tried to strike a balance. They, too, insisted that it was the duty of the trade unions to restrain the workers and to cultivate in them a sense of responsibility for the state and the nationalized economy. They emphasized the party's right to control the unions. But they also wished to preserve them as autonomous mass organizations, capable of exerting pressure on government and industrial management.

Implied in these attitudes were different conceptions of state and society. The Workers' Opposition and the so-called *Decemists* (the Group of Democratic Centralism) were the stalwart defenders of 'proletarian democracy' *vis-à-vis* the dictatorship.

[1] A detailed account of the debate can be found in Deutscher, *Soviet Trade Unions* (*Their place in Soviet labour policy*), pp. 42–59.

They were the first Bolshevik dissenters to protest against the
method of government designed 'to make the people believe by
force'. They implored the party to 'trust its fate' to the working
class which had raised it to power. They spoke the language
which the whole party had spoken in 1917. They were the real
Levellers of this revolution, its high-minded, Utopian dreamers.
The party could not listen to them if it was not prepared to
commit noble yet unpardonable suicide. It could not trust its
own and the republic's fate to a working class whittled down,
exhausted, and demoralized by civil war, famine, and the black
market. The quixotic spirit of the Workers' Opposition was
apparent in its economic demands. The Opposition clamoured
for the immediate satisfaction of the workers' needs, for equal
wages and rewards for all, for the supply, without payment, of
food, clothing, and lodging to workers, for free medical attention, free travelling facilities, and free education.[1] They wanted
to see fulfilled nothing less than the programme of full communism, which was theoretically designed for an economy of
great plenty. They did not even try to say how the government
of the day could meet their demands. They urged the party to
place industry, or what was left of it, once again under the control of those factory committees which had shown soon after the
October Revolution that they could merely dissipate and squan-
der the nation's wealth. It was a sad omen that the people
enveloped in such fumes of fancy were almost the only ones to
advocate a full revival of proletarian democracy.

Against them, Trotsky prompted the party to cease for the
time being the advocacy and practice of proletarian democracy
and instead to concentrate on building up a Producers' Democracy. The party, to put it more plainly, was to deny the workers
their political rights and compensate them by giving them scope
and managerial responsibility in economic reconstruction. At
the tenth congress (March 1921), when this controversy reached
its culmination, Trotsky argued:

The Workers' Opposition has come out with dangerous slogans.
They have made a fetish of democratic principles. They have placed
the workers' right to elect representatives above the party, as it
were, as if the party were not entitled to assert its dictatorship even
if that dictatorship temporarily clashed with the passing moods of

[1] *Desyatyi Syezd RKP*, p. 363; A. M. Kollontai, *The Workers' Opposition in Russia*.

the workers' democracy. . . . It is necessary to create among us the awareness of the revolutionary historical birthright of the party. The party is obliged to maintain its dictatorship, regardless of temporary wavering in the spontaneous moods of the masses, regardless of the temporary vacillations even in the working class. This awareness is for us the indispensable unifying element. The dictatorship does not base itself at every given moment on the formal principle of a workers' democracy, although the workers' democracy is, of course, the only method by which the masses can be drawn more and more into political life.[1]

The days had long passed when Trotsky argued that the Soviet system of government was superior to bourgeois parliamentarianism because under it the electors enjoyed, among other things, the right to re-elect their representatives at any time and not merely at regular intervals; and that this enabled the Soviets to reflect any change in the popular mood closely and instantaneously, as no parliament was able to do. His general professions of faith in proletarian democracy now sounded like mere saving clauses. What was essential was 'the historical birthright of the party' and the party's awareness of it as the 'indispensable unifying element'. Euphemistically yet eloquently enough he now extolled the collective solidarity of the ruling group in the face of a hostile or apathetic nation.

Lenin refused to proclaim the divorce between the dictatorship and proletarian democracy. He, too, was aware that government and party were in conflict with the people; but he was afraid that Trotsky's policy would perpetuate the conflict. The party had had to override trade unions, to dismiss their recalcitrant leaders, to break or obviate popular resistance, and to prevent the free formation of opinion inside the Soviets. Only thus, Lenin held, could the revolution be saved. But he hoped that these practices would give his government a breathing space—his whole policy had become a single struggle for breathing spaces—during which it might modify its policies, make headway with the rehabilitation of the country, ease the plight of the working people, and win them back for Bolshevism. The dictatorship could then gradually revert to proletarian democracy. If this was the aim, as Trotsky agreed, then the party must reassert the idea of that democracy at once and

[1] *Desyatyi Syezd RKP*, p. 192. See also p. 215.

initiate no sweeping measures suggesting its abandonment. Even though the régime had so often had recourse to coercion, Lenin pleaded, coercion must be its last and persuasion its first resort.[1] The trade unions ought therefore not to be turned into appendages of the state. They must retain a measure of autonomy; they must speak for the workers, if need be against the government; and they ought to become the schools, not the drill-halls, of communism. The administrator—and it was from his angle that Trotsky viewed the problem—might be annoyed and inconvenienced by the demands of the unions; he might be right against them in specific instances; but on balance it was sound that he should be so inconvenienced and exposed to genuine social pressures and influences. It was no use telling the workers that they must not oppose the workers' state. That state was an abstraction. In reality, Lenin pointed out, his own administration had to consider the interests of the peasants as well as of the workers; and its work was marred by muddle, by grave 'bureaucratic distortions', and by arbitrary exercise of power. The working class ought therefore to defend itself, albeit with self-restraint, and to press its claims on the administration. The state, as Lenin saw it, had to give scope to a plurality of interests and influences. Trotsky's state was implicitly monolithic.

The tenth congress voted by an overwhelming majority for Lenin's resolutions. Bolshevism had already departed from proletarian democracy; but it was not yet prepared to embrace its alternative, the monolithic state.

. . . .

While the congress was in session the strangest of all Russian insurrections flared up at the naval fortress of Kronstadt, an insurrection which, in Lenin's words, like a lightning flash illumined reality.

The insurgents, sailors of the Red Navy, were led by anarchists. Since the end of February they had been extremely restless. There had been strikes in nearby Petrograd; a general strike was expected; and Kronstadt was astir with rumours of alleged clashes between Petrograd workers and troops. The crews of the warships were seized by a political fever reminiscent of the excitement of 1917. At meetings they passed resolutions demanding freedom for the workers, a new deal for the peas-

[1] *Desyatyi Syezd RKP.*, pp. 208 ff.

ants, and free elections to the Soviets. The call for the Third Revolution began to dominate the meetings, the revolution which was to overthrow the Bolsheviks and establish Soviet democracy. Kalinin, President of the Soviet Republic, made a flat-footed appearance at the naval base; he denounced the sailors as 'disloyal and irresponsible' and demanded obedience. A delegation of the sailors sent to Petrograd was arrested there.

Soon the cry 'Down with Bolshevik tyranny!' resounded throughout Kronstadt. The Bolshevik commissars on the spot were demoted and imprisoned. An anarchist committee assumed command; and amid the sailors' enthusiasm the flag of revolt was hoisted. 'The heroic and generous Kronstadt', writes the anarchist historian of the insurrection, 'dreamt of the liberation of Russia. . . . No clear-cut programme was formulated. Freedom and the brotherhood of the peoples of the world were the watchwords. The Third Revolution was seen as a gradual transition towards final emancipation; and free elections to independent Soviets as the first step in this direction. The Soviets were, of course, to be independent of any political party—a free expression of the will and the interests of the people.'[1]

The Bolsheviks denounced the men of Kronstadt as counter-revolutionary mutineers led by a White general. The denunciation appears to have been groundless. Having for so long fought against mutiny after mutiny, each sponsored or encouraged by the White Guards, the Bolsheviks could not bring themselves to believe that the White Guards had no hand in this revolt. Some time before the event, the White émigré press had indeed darkly hinted at trouble brewing in Kronstadt; and this lent colour to the suspicion. The Politbureau, at first inclined to open negotiations, finally resolved to quell the revolt. It could not tolerate the challenge from the Navy; and it was afraid that the revolt, although it had no chance of growing into a revolution, would aggravate the prevailing chaos. Even after the defeat of the White Guards, numerous bands of rebels and marauders roamed the land from the northern coasts down to the Caspian Sea, raiding and pillaging towns and slaughtering the agents of the government. With the call for a new revolution bands of famished Volga peasants had overrun the *gubernia* of Saratov, and later in the year Tukhachevsky had to

[1] Alexander Berkman, *Der Aufstand von Kronstadt*, pp. 10–11.

employ twenty-seven rifle divisions to subdue them.[1] Such was
the turmoil that leniency towards the insurgents of Kronstadt
was certain to be taken as a sign of weakness and to make matters
worse.

On 5 March Trotsky arrived in Petrograd and ordered the
rebels to surrender unconditionally. 'Only those who do so',
he stated, 'can count on the mercy of the Soviet Republic.
Simultaneously with this warning I am issuing instructions that
everything be prepared for the suppression of the mutiny by
armed force. . . . This is the last warning.'[2] That it should have
fallen to Trotsky to address such words to the sailors was another of history's ironies. This had been his Kronstadt, the
Kronstadt he had called 'the pride and the glory of the revolution'. How many times had he not stumped the naval base
during the hot days of 1917! How many times had not the
sailors lifted him on their shoulders and wildly acclaimed him
as their friend and leader! How devotedly they had followed him
to the Tauride Palace, to his prison cell at Kresty, to the walls
of Kazan on the Volga, always taking his advice, always almost
blindly following his orders! How many anxieties they had
shared, how many dangers they had braved together! True, of
the veterans few had survived; and even fewer were still at
Kronstadt. The crews of the *Aurora*, the *Petropavlovsk*, and other
famous warships now consisted of fresh recruits drafted from
Ukrainian peasants. They lacked—so Trotsky told himself—
the selfless revolutionary spirit of the older classes. Yet even this
was in a way symbolic of the situation in which the revolution
found itself. The ordinary men and women who had made it
were no longer what they had been or where they had been. The
best of them had perished; others had become absorbed in the
administration; still others had dispersed and become disheartened and embittered. And what the rebels of Kronstadt
demanded was only what Trotsky had promised their elder

[1] See the correspondence between S. Kamenev, Shaposhnikov, and Smidovich
with the commander of the Saratov area, and Tukhachevsky's report to Lenin of
16 July 1921. *The Trotsky Archives*. And here is a characteristic message sent to
Lenin from Communists in the sub-Polar region on 25 March 1921: 'The Communists of the Tobolsk region in the North are bleeding white and sending their fiery
farewell greetings to the invincible Russian Communist Party, to our dear comrades and our leader Lenin. Perishing here, we carry out our duty towards the
party and the Republic in the firm belief in our eventual triumph.' Ibid.

[2] Trotsky, *Sochinenya*, vol. xvii, book 2, p. 518.

brothers and what he and the party had been unable to give. Once again, as after Brest, a bitter and hostile echo of his own voice came back to him from the lips of other people; and once again he had to suppress it.

The rebels ignored his warning and hoped to gain time. This was the middle of March. The Bay of Finland was still ice-bound. In a few days, however, a thaw might set in; and then the fortress, bristling with guns, defended by the whole Red Navy of the Baltic, assured of supplies from Finland or other Baltic countries, would become inaccessible, almost invincible. In the meantime even Communists joined in the revolt, announcing that they had left 'the party of the hangman Trotsky'. The fortress, so Trotsky (or was it Tukhachevsky?) resolved, must be seized before ice floes barred the approach. In feverish haste picked regiments and shock troops were dispatched to reinforce the garrison of Petrograd. When the news of the mutiny reached the tenth congress, it aroused so much alarm and anger that most of the able-bodied delegates rushed straight from the conference hall in the Kremlin to place themselves at the head of the shock troops which were to storm the fortress across the Bay of Finland. Even leaders of the Workers' Opposition and *Decemists* who, at the congress, had just raised demands not very different from those the rebels voiced, went into battle. They, too, held that the sailors had no right to dictate, hands on triggers, even the justest of demands.

White sheets over their uniforms, the Bolshevik troops, under Tukhachevsky's command, advanced across the Bay. They were met by hurricane fire from Kronstadt's bastions. The ice broke under their feet; and wave after wave of white-shrouded attackers collapsed into the glacial Valhalla. The death march went on. From three directions fresh columns stumped and fumbled and slipped and crawled over the glassy surface until they too vanished in fire, ice, and water. As the successive swarms and lines of attackers drowned, it seemed to the men of Kronstadt that the perverted Bolshevik revolution drowned with them and that the triumph of their own pure, unadulterated revolution was approaching. Such was the lot of these rebels, who had denounced the Bolsheviks for their harshness and whose only aim it was to allow the revolution to imbibe the milk of human kindness, that for their survival they fought a battle which in cruelty was unequalled throughout the civil war. The bitterness and the rage of the attackers mounted accordingly. On 17 March, after a night-long advance in a snowstorm, the Bolsheviks at last succeeded in climbing the walls. When they broke into the fortress, they fell upon its defenders like revengeful furies.

On 3 April Trotsky took a parade of the victors. 'We waited as long as possible', he said, 'for our blinded sailor-comrades to see with their own eyes where the mutiny led. But we were confronted by the danger that the ice would melt away and we were compelled to carry out . . . the attack.'[1] Describing the crushed rebels as 'comrades', he unwittingly intimated that what he celebrated was morally a Pyrrhic victory. Foreign Communists who visited Moscow some months later and believed that Kronstadt had been one of the ordinary incidents of the civil war, were 'astonished and troubled' to find that the leading Bolsheviks spoke of the rebels without any of the anger and hatred which they felt for the White Guards and interventionists. Their talk was full of 'sympathetic reticences' and sad, enigmatic allusions, which to the outsider betrayed the party's troubled conscience.[2]

.   .   .   .

The rising had not yet been defeated when, on 15 March, Lenin introduced the New Economic Policy to the tenth congress. Almost without debate the congress accepted it. Silently, with a heavy heart, Bolshevism parted with its dream of war communism. It retreated, as Lenin said, in order to be in a better position to advance. The controversy over the trade unions and the underlying issue at once died down. The cannonade in the Bay of Finland and the strikes in Petrograd and elsewhere had demonstrated beyond doubt the unreality of Trotsky's ideas: and in the milder policies based on the mixed economy of subsequent years there was, anyhow, no room for the militarization of labour.

The controversy had not been mere sound and fury, however. Its significance for the future was greater than the protagonists

[1] Trotsky, *Sochinenya*, vol. xvii, book 2, p. 523.
[2] André Morizet, *Chez Lénine et Trotski*, pp. 78–84 and V. Serge, *Mémoires d'un Révolutionnaire*, chapter iv, describe the Kronstadt period from the standpoint of foreign Communists in Russia. Both writers accepted the party's case, although both sympathized with the rebels.

themselves could suppose. A decade later Stalin, who in 1920–1 had supported Lenin's 'liberal' policy, was to adopt Trotsky's ideas in all but name. Neither Stalin nor Trotsky, nor the adherents of either, then admitted the fact: Stalin—because he could not acknowledge that he was abandoning Lenin's attitude for Trotsky's; Trotsky—because he shrank in horror from his own ideas when he saw them remorselessly carried into execution by his enemy. There was hardly a single plank in Trotsky's programme of 1920–1 which Stalin did not use during the industrial revolution of the thirties. He introduced conscription and direction of labour; he insisted that the trade unions should adopt a 'productionist' policy instead of defending the consumer interests of the workers; he deprived the trade unions of the last vestige of autonomy and transformed them into tools of the state. He set himself up as the protector of the managerial groups, on whom he bestowed privileges of which Trotsky had not even dreamt. He ordered 'Socialist emulation' in the factories and mines; and he did so in words unceremoniously and literally taken from Trotsky.[1] He put into effect his own ruthless version of that 'Soviet Taylorism' which Trotsky had advocated. And, finally, he passed from Trotsky's intellectual and historical arguments ambiguously justifying forced labour to its mass application.

In the previous chapter we traced the thread of unconscious historic continuity which led from Lenin's hesitant and shamefaced essays in revolution by conquest to the revolutions contrived by Stalin the conqueror. A similar subtle thread connects Trotsky's domestic policy of these years with the later practices of his antagonist. Both Trotsky and Lenin appear, each in a different field, as Stalin's unwitting inspirers and prompters. Both were driven by circumstances beyond their control and by their own illusions to assume certain attitudes in which circumstances and their own scruples did not allow them to persevere—attitudes which were ahead of their time, out of tune with the current Bolshevik mentality, and discordant with the main themes of their own lives.

[1] At the beginning of 1929, a few weeks after Trotsky's expulsion from Russia, the sixteenth party conference proclaimed 'Socialist emulation', quoting *in extenso* the resolution written by Trotsky and adopted by the party in 1920. The author's name was not mentioned, of course.

It was only under the threat of the total decomposition of the revolution and of the Russian body politic that Trotsky advanced the idea of complete state control over the working classes. His alert, restless, experimenting mind boldly sought a way out in contradictory directions. In each direction it moved to the ultimate limit, while the main body of Bolshevik opinion marked time. He proposed the New Economic Policy when the party was still rigidly committed to war communism. Then his thought switched in the opposite direction, explored it to the end and reached the alternative conclusion: that the only remedy for the ills of war communism was cast iron discipline of labour. By now the main current of Bolshevik opinion had slowly moved towards the New Economic Policy, which it had compelled him to abandon. It was his clear, consistent, and swift logic—the logic of the great administrator impatient of confusion and bungling—that defeated Trotsky. His mind fixed on his objective, he rushed headlong into controversy, impetuously produced arguments and generalizations, and ignored the movement of opinion until he overreached himself and aroused angry resentment. The self-confident administrator in him got the better of the sensitive political thinker and blinded him to the implications of his schemes. What was only one of many facets in Trotsky's experimental thinking was to become Stalin's alpha and omega.[1]

In his aberration Trotsky remained intellectually honest— honest to the point of futility. He made no attempt to conceal his policy. He called things by their names, no matter how unpalatable. Accustomed to sway people by force of argument and appeal to reason he went on appealing to reason in a most unreasonable cause. He publicly advocated government by coercion, that government which can never be publicly advocated and is practised only *sub silentio*. He hoped to *persuade* people that they needed no government by persuasion. He told them that the workers' state had the right to use forced labour; and he was sincerely disappointed that they did not rush to enrol in the labour camps.[2] He behaved thus absurdly because before

---

[1] It was probably with these incidents in his mind that Lenin in his last will remarked on Trotsky's 'too far-reaching self-confidence and a disposition to be too much attracted by the purely administrative side of affairs'.

[2] It is a moot point to what extent Trotsky was led astray by his habit of applying European standards to Russia. It was one thing for a government to direct labour

his mind's eye he had no cold machine of coercion slowly and remorselessly grinding its human material, but the monumental and evanescent outlines of a 'Proletarian Sparta', the austere rigours of which were part of the pioneering adventure in socialism. The very absurdity of his behaviour contained its own antidote. In his candour he gave the people ample notice of the danger threatening them. He indicated the limits to which he was prepared to go. He submitted his policies to public control. He himself did everything in his power to provoke the resistance that frustrated him. To keep politically alive he needed broad daylight. It took Stalin's bat-like character to carry his ideas into execution.

The Bolshevik party still defended the principle of proletarian democracy against Trotsky; but it continued to depart from it in practice.

It was only in 1921 that Lenin's government proceeded to ban all organized opposition within the Soviets. Throughout the civil war the Bolsheviks had harassed the Mensheviks and Social Revolutionaries, now outlawing them, now allowing them to come into the open, and then again suppressing them. The harsher and the milder courses were dictated by circumstances and by the vacillations of those parties in which some groups leaned towards the Bolsheviks and others towards the White Guards. The idea, however, that those parties should be suppressed on principle had not taken root before the end of the civil war. Even during the spells of repression, those opposition groups which did not plainly call for armed resistance to the Bolsheviks still carried on all sorts of activities, open and clandestine. The Bolsheviks often eliminated them from the Soviets or reduced their representation by force or guile. It was through the machinery of the Soviets that Lenin's government organized the civil war; and in that machinery it was not prepared to countenance hostile or neutral elements. But the government still looked forward to the end of hostilities when it would be able to respect the rules of Soviet constitutionalism and to readmit

in an industrialized country and to shift workers, say, from Manchester to Birmingham or from Stuttgart to Essen, and quite another to direct Ukrainian peasants or Petrograd workers to factories and mines in the Urals and in Siberia, or in the Far North. Direction of labour in a more or less uniform industrial environment may involve a minimum of compulsion. It required a maximum in Russia.

regular opposition. This the Bolsheviks now thought themselves unable to do. All opposition parties had hailed the Kronstadt rising; and so the Bolsheviks knew what they could expect from them. The more isolated they themselves were in the nation the more terrified were they of their opponents. They had half-suppressed them in order to win the civil war; having won the civil war they went on to suppress them for good.

Paradoxically, the Bolsheviks were driven to establish their own political monopoly by the very fact that they had liberalized their economic policy. The New Economic Policy gave free scope to the interests of the individualistic peasantry and of the urban bourgeoisie. It was to be expected that as those interests came into play they would seek to create their own means of political expression or try to use such anti-Bolshevik organizations as existed. The Bolsheviks were determined that none should exist. 'We might have a two-party system, but one of the two parties would be in office and the other in prison'—this dictum, attributed to Bukharin, expressed a view widespread in the party. Some Bolsheviks felt uneasy about their own political monopoly; but they were even more afraid of the alternative. Trotsky later wrote that he and Lenin had intended to lift the ban on the opposition parties as soon as the economic and social condition of the country had become more stable. This may have been so. In the meantime, however, the Bolsheviks hardened in the conviction, which was to play so important a part in the struggles of the Stalinist era, that any opposition must inevitably become the vehicle of counter-revolution. They were haunted by the fear that the new urban bourgeoise (which soon flourished under the N.E.P.), the intelligentsia, and the peasantry might join hands against them in a coalition of over-whelming strength; and they shrank from no measure that could prevent such a coalition. Thus, after its victory in the civil war, the revolution was beginning to escape from its weakness into totalitarianism.

Almost at once it became necessary to suppress opposition in Bolshevik ranks as well. The Workers' Opposition (and up to a point the *Decemists* too) expressed much of the frustration and discontent which had led to the Kronstadt rising. The cleavages tended to become fixed; and the contending groups were inclined to behave like so many parties within the party. It would have been preposterous to establish the rule of a single party and then to allow that party to split into fragments. If Bolshevism were to break up into two or more hostile movements, as the old Social Democratic party had done, would not one of them —it was asked—become the vehicle of counter-revolution?

In the temper of the party congress of 1921 there was indeed something of that seemingly irrational tension which had characterized the congress of 1903. A split similarly cast its shadow ahead—only the real divisions were even more inchoate and confused than in 1903. Now as then Trotsky was not on the side of the controversy to which he would eventually belong. And now as then he was anxious to prevent the split. He there-fore raised no objection when Lenin proposed that the congress should prohibit organized groups or factions within the party; and he himself disbanded the faction he had formed during the recent controversy.[1] This was not yet strictly a ban on inner party opposition. Lenin encouraged dissenters to express dissent. He liberally invited them to state their views in the Bolshevik newspapers, in special discussion pages and discussion sheets. He asked the congress to elect the leaders of all shades of opposi-tion to the new Central Committee. But he insisted that opposition should remain diffuse and that the dissenters should not form themselves into solid leagues. He submitted a resolu-tion, one clause of which (kept secret) empowered the Central Committee to expel offenders, no matter how high their stand-ing in the party. Trotsky supported the clause, or, at any rate, raised no objection to it; and the congress passed it. It was against Shlyapnikov, Trotsky's most immitigable opponent, that the punitive clause was immediately directed; and against him it was presently invoked. It did not occur to Trotsky that one day it would be invoked against himself.

The arrangement under which opposition was permitted pro-vided it remained dispersed could work as long as members of the party disagreed over secondary or transient issues. But when the differences were serious and prolonged it was inevitable that members of the same mind should band together. Those who, like the Workers' Opposition, charged the ruling group with being

---

[1] Among the leaders of the faction were, apart from Trotsky and Bukharin, Dzerzhinsky, Andreev, Krestinsky, Preobrazhensky, Rakovsky, Serebriakov, Pyatakov and Sokolnikov.

animated by 'bureaucratic and bourgeois hostility towards the masses' could hardly refrain from concerting their efforts against what they considered to be a sinister and formidably organized influence within the party. The ban on factions could thus at first delay a split only to accelerate it later.

Barely two years were to elapse before Trotsky was to take up and give a powerful resonance to many of the criticisms and demands made by the less articulate leaders of the Workers' Opposition and of the *Decemists*, whom he now helped to defeat, and before he, too, was to cry out for a return to proletarian democracy.

It was only a few years since Trotsky had, as an émigré in Vienna, drawn that impressive vista of Russia's past, in which he showed how history had thrown the Russian people into a 'severe environment', exposed them to pressures from wealthy and powerful Europe and to invasions from all directions, and let a Leviathan-like state mould their destinies for them. To feed itself, he then wrote, the Leviathan starved the nation, retarded or accelerated the growth of its social classes, and atrophied its civilization.[1] The revolution was in one of its aspects the people's triumph over the Leviathan. The triumph had seemed complete, for the old state had been reduced to dust and ashes.

Yet the revolution, too, had to draw its nourishment and its vitality from that same 'severe environment'. From this it absorbed all its severity. Rich in world-embracing ideas and aspirations, the new republic was 'poor with the accumulated poverty of over a thousand years'. It mortally hated that poverty. But that poverty was its own flesh and blood and breath.

Trotsky had contrasted 'the spires and the vaulting arches and the gothic lacework' of western European feudalism with the coarse and barbarous vulgarity of Russian feudalism, which could only fill the crevices of its log cabin with moss. He had juxtaposed the rich and complex growth of the Third Estate in Europe with the Russian police-sponsored crafts; the free and cultivated 'bourgeois personality' of the West with the 'snout which every policeman could kick and punch'. Yet from that same log cabin, shattered by revolution and war, he set out with the Bolshevik party to pioneer for socialism. Against all ex-

[1] See above, chapter VII.

pectations, the 'advanced, civilized' West had turned its back on the revolution; and for decades Bolshevism had to entrench itself in its native environment in order to transform it. The brand of socialism which it then produced could not but show the marks of its historic heritage. That socialism, too, was to rise rough and crude, without the vaulting arches and spires and lacework of which Socialists had dreamt. Hemmed in by superior hostile forces, it soon delivered itself up to the new Leviathan-state—rising as if from the ashes of the old. The new state, like the old, was to protect and starve the nation, retard and accelerate its growth, and efface the human personality, the revolutionary-proletarian personality. It was another of history's ironies that Trotsky, the hater of the Leviathan, should have become the first harbinger of its resurrection.

When he was still at the threshold of his career, Trotsky wrote: 'A working class capable of exercizing its dictatorship over society will tolerate no dictator over itself.'[1] By 1921 the Russian working class had proved itself incapable of exercising its own dictatorship. It could not even exercise control over those who ruled in its name. Having exhausted itself in the revolution and the civil war, it had almost ceased to exist as a political factor. Trotsky then proclaimed the party's 'historical birthright', its right to establish a stern trusteeship over the proletariat as well as the rest of society. This was the old 'Jacobin' idea that a small virtuous and enlightened minority was justified in 'substituting' itself for an immature people and bringing reason and happiness to it, the idea which Trotsky had abjured as the hereditary obsession of the *Decembrists*, the *Narodniks*, and the Bolsheviks. This 'obsession', he himself had argued, had reflected the atrophy or the apathy of all social classes in Russia. He had been convinced that with the appearance of a modern, Socialist working class that atrophy had been overcome. The revolution proved him right. Yet after their paroxysms of energy and their titanic struggles of 1917–21 all classes of Russian society seemed to relapse into a deep coma. The political stage, so crowded in recent years, became deserted and only a single group was left on it to speak boisterously on behalf of the people. And even its circle was to grow more and more narrow.

[1] See above, p. 96.

When Trotsky now urged the Bolshevik party to 'substitute' itself for the working classes, he did not, in the rush of work and controversy, think of the next phases of the process, although he himself had long since predicted them with uncanny clear-sightedness. 'The party organization would then substitute itself for the party as a whole; then the Central Committee would substitute itself for the organization; and finally a single dictator would substitute himself for the Central Committee.'

The dictator was already waiting in the wings.

VOLUME II

THE PROPHET UNARMED

1921–1929

Trotsky in exile, on a hunting trip

PREFACE

CARLYLE once wrote that as Cromwell's biographer he had to drag out the Lord Protector from under a mountain of dead dogs, a huge load of calumny and oblivion. My job, as Trotsky's biographer, has been somewhat similar, with this difference, however, that when I set out to assail my mountain of dead dogs great events were about to strike at it with immense force. I had concluded *The Prophet Armed*, the first part of my study of Trotsky, while Stalin was still alive, and while his 'cult' appeared as indestructible as the stigma attached to Trotsky seemed indelible. Most reviewers of *The Prophet Armed* agreed with a British critic who wrote that 'that single book undoes three decades of Stalinist denigration'; but, of course, neither the book nor its documentation brought forth a single word of comment from the Soviet historians and critics, who usually devote an unconscionable amount of attention to every piece of 'Sovietology', no matter how trashy, that appears in the West. Then came Stalin's death, the Twentieth Congress, and Khrushchev's 'secret' speech. An earthquake shook the mountain of dead dogs, scattering half of it far and wide; and for a moment it looked as if the other half too was about to be blown away. Historically truthful references to Trotsky's part in the Russian Revolution began to appear in Soviet periodicals for the first time in three decades, although the paucity and timidity of the references suggested how close the connexion between history and politics still was in this case, and how delicate the problem.

When Stalin's idol was being smashed and the Stalinist falsification of history was being officially and emphatically denounced, the shade of Stalin's chief antagonist inevitably aroused fresh and lively, though bewildered, interest. In Moscow, Peking, Warsaw, and East Berlin people wondered anew what had been the significance and the moral of Trotsky's struggle against Stalin. Young historians, to whom the archives, hitherto kept under lock and key, had suddenly been thrown open, avidly looked for an answer in the unfamiliar records of Bolshevism. Khrushchev having declared that Stalin had destroyed his inner party critics by means of false and monstrous accusations, the historians naturally expected an explicit rehabilitation of the victims of the Great Purges. Here and there the rehabilitation was already taken for granted. In Poland, for instance, the writings of Trotsky and Bukharin, Rakovsky and Radek, were quoted, and even reprinted, as offering much needed illumination of the enigma of the Stalin era (and so were my own books and essays).

Soon thereafter, however, the assault on the 'mountain of dead dogs' was halted in its tracks. Towards the end of 1956, or early in 1957, during the reaction against the Hungarian turmoil, a halt was called in Moscow to the restitution of historical truth. The dilemmas and fluctuations of current policy became once again reflected in the writing of history, and were focused, as it were, in the treatment of Trotsky. Since then Stalin's discredited *Short Course of the History of the C.P.S.U.* has been replaced by a new official compendium of party history which attempts to reimpose, though in a modified and softened version, the anathema on Trotsky; and in Soviet periodicals the volume of writings designed surreptitiously to defame Trotsky has grown much larger than it ever was in the last decade or so of the Stalin era.

However, what was once a drama has now become sheer farce. The Stalinist anathema, absurd though it was, had its 'logic' and consistency: Stalin knew that he could not maintain it effectively without gross, unscrupulous, and systematic falsification of the past. Khrushchev tries to ban the truth about Trotsky without resorting to outright falsification—he contents himself with a 'moderate' dose of distortion; and by this alone he renders the anathema ludicrous. Thus, the authors of the new party-history extol the work of the Military Revolutionary Committee of 1917 and of the Commissariat of War of the civil war period, without mentioning in this connexion that Trotsky stood at the head of both these bodies; but almost in the same breath they do mention this fact when they have to find fault with the work of the same Committee or the same Commissariat. (It is as if one watched a child, who has not yet learned the meaning of hide-and-seek, pull at his mother's skirt and shout: '*Here* I am, look for me.') The Khrushchevite historians evidently assume that Soviet readers will not be intelligent enough to see that the praise and the blame are both directed alike at the same person. In his own, perverse way Stalin took a far higher view of the perspicacity of his subjects; and he preferred to give them no facts that might stimulate heretical guesswork, and to leave no scope for such guesswork. The new versions of party history also dwell one-sidedly on disagreements between Lenin and Trotsky; but by publishing Lenin's suppressed writings and throwing open the archives, the new party leaders have in fact done virtually everything that was needed for Trotsky's rehabilitation. Now all their attempts to banish him once again from the annals of the revolution are vain.

. . . .

Trotsky's ghost is evidently still haunting Stalin's successors. I trust that in these pages readers will find at least part of the explanation of this apparently bizarre fact. Despite all the great changes that have occurred in Soviet society since the 1920's, or rather because of these changes, some of the crucial issues of the controversy between Stalin and Trotsky are as alive today as ever. Trotsky denounced the 'bureaucratic degeneration' of the workers' state; and he confronted Stalin's 'monolithic' and 'infallibly' led party with the demand for freedom of expression, debate, and criticism, believing that on these alone could and should voluntary and genuine communist discipline be based. His voice was smothered in the Russia of the 1920's; but with the many-sided, industrial, educational, and social progress of the Soviet Union this his idea has come back to life, gaining possession of many communist minds. In their brief hour of truth, Khrushchev and Mikoyan, Mao and Gomulka, Kadar and Togliatti, not to speak of Tito and Nagy, had to pay their tribute to it. A substratum of 'Trotskyism' could be found in the contributions, however half-hearted and fragmentary, which each of them then made to 'de-Stalinization'. Indeed, in this hour of truth Trotsky appeared as the giant forebear of all of them, for none of them approached Stalinism with anything like the depth, the sweep, and the vigour of his critical thought. Since then, frightened by their own bravado, they have retraced their steps; and the Soviet régime and the Communist party, moving two steps forward and one step back, are still far from having overcome their 'bureaucratic deformation'.

The fact that as yet the issues posed by Trotsky have, at best, been only half resolved makes the story of his opposition to Stalinism more, not less, topical. Nor is Trotsky's antagonism to Stalinist bureaucracy the only aspect of his struggle which has a bearing on our times. A large part of this narrative centres on the conflict between his internationalism and the isolationist self-sufficiency of latter-day Bolshevism embodied in Stalin. This conflict reappeared and grew acute even before the close of the Stalin era; and since then the balance has begun to tilt towards internationalism. This is yet another unresolved issue lending fresh interest to the controversy of the 1920's.

Stalin's successors live in such grotesque horror of Trotsky's shade because they are afraid of coming to grips with the issues with which he, so much ahead of his time, did come to grips. Their behaviour may be explained in part by objective circumstances and in part by inertia, for Khrushchev and his associates, even in their rebellion against Stalinism, are still Stalin's epigones. But they act also from the narrowest motives of self-defence. The following incident, which occurred during a session of the Central Committee in June 1957, illustrates the nature of their predicament. At that session Khrushchev, speaking on the motion for the expulsion of Molotov, Kaganovich, and Malenkov, recalled the Great Purges, the subject invariably recurring in all the secret debates since Stalin's death. Pointing at Molotov and Kaganovich, he exclaimed: 'Your hands are stained with the blood of our party leaders and of innumerable innocent Bolsheviks!' 'So are yours!', Molotov and Kaganovich shouted back at him. 'Yes, so are mine', Khrushchev replied. 'I admit this. But during the Great Purges I only carried out your orders. I was not then a member of the Politbureau and I am not responsible for its decisions. You were.' When Mikoyan later reported the incident to the Comsomol in Moscow, he was asked why the accomplices of Stalin's crimes were not tried in court. 'We cannot try them', Mikoyan is said to have answered, 'because if we start putting such people in the dock, there is no knowing where we should be able to stop. We have all had some share in conducting the purges.' Thus, if only in order to safeguard their own immunity, Stalin's successors must still keep in the dock the ghosts of some of Stalin's victims. As to Trotsky, is it not safer indeed to leave him where he lies, under the half-shattered pyramid of slander, rather than transfer him to the Pantheon of the revolution?

.   .   .   .

I do not believe and have never believed that Trotsky's memory is in any need of rehabilitation by rulers or party leaders. (It is, I think, rather they who, if they can, ought to work for their exculpation!) Nothing, however, is farther from my intention than to indulge in any cult of Trotsky.

I do indeed consider Trotsky as one of the most outstanding revolutionary leaders of all times, outstanding as fighter, thinker, and martyr. But I am not seeking to present here the glorifying image of a man without blemish or blur. I have endeavoured to portray him as he was, in his real stature and strength but with all his weaknesses; I have tried to show the extraordinary power, fertility, and originality of his mind, but also his fallibility. In discussing the ideas which form his distinctive contribution to Marxism and modern thought, I have attempted to disentangle what in my view is, and for a long time is likely to remain, of objective and lasting value from that which reflected merely transient situations, subjective emotions, or errors of judgement. I have done my best to do justice to Trotsky's heroic character to which I find only very few equals in history. But I have also shown him in his many moments of irresolution and indecision: I describe the embattled Titan as he falters, and boggles, and yet goes out to meet his destiny. I see him as the representative figure of pre-Stalinist communism and the precursor of post-Stalinist communism. Yet I do not imagine that the future of communism lies in Trotskyism. I am inclined to think that the historic development is transcending both Stalinism and Trotskyism and is tending towards something broader than either of them. But each of them will probably be 'transcended' in a different manner. What the Soviet Union and communism take over from Stalinism is mainly its practical achievement; in other respects, as regards methods of government and political action, ideas, and 'moral climate', the legacy of the Stalin era is worse than empty; the sooner it is disposed of

the better. But precisely in these respects Trotsky has still much
to offer; and the political development can hardly transcend
him otherwise than by absorbing all that is vital in his thought
and applying it to realities which are far more advanced,
varied, and complex than those he knew.

. . . .

In the preface to *The Prophet Armed*, I indicated that I
intended to tell the whole story of Trotsky's life and work from
1921 onwards in a single volume entitled *The Prophet Unarmed*.[1]
A reviewer, writing in *The Times Literary Supplement*, doubted
whether the story could be told, on the appropriate scale, in
one volume. His doubt has proved justified. *The Prophet
Unarmed* ends with Trotsky's banishment from the Soviet
Union in January 1929; another volume, *The Prophet Outcast*,
is to cover the stormy twelve years of Trotsky's last exile and
to give the final assessment of his role. These three volumes
form part of a larger trilogy, of which one section, *Stalin, A
Political Biography*, appeared in 1949, and another, a two-
volumed *Life of Lenin*, is still in an early stage of preparation.
(I also intend to supplement my biography of Stalin by a book
Stalin's Last Years, if and when sufficient historical documentation becomes available.)

The three volumes of the present work are, of course, interconnected, as are also, more loosely, all the parts of the entire
trilogy. But I have so planned them that each volume is as
far as possible self-contained and can be read as an independent work. The narrative of this volume covers the
years which were in many respects the formative period of
the Soviet Union. It begins with 1921 and the aftermath of the
civil war, with Trotsky still at the height of power; it ends in
1929, with Trotsky *en route* to Constantinople, and the Soviet
Union entering the epoch of forced industrialization and collectivization. Between these years there unfolds the drama of
the Bolshevik party which, after Lenin's death, found itself
plunged into what was probably the fiercest and the most
momentous political controversy of modern times, uncertain of
its policies and groping for direction, caught in extraordinary

---

[1] It will be remembered that both these titles allude to Machiavelli's dictum
that 'all armed prophets have conquered, and the unarmed ones have been
destroyed'. (See the text from *The Prince* quoted in *The Prophet Armed*, p. xii.)

social and political tensions and in the logic of the single-party system, and succumbing to Stalin's autocracy. Throughout, Trotsky is at the centre of the struggle as Stalin's chief adversary, the only alternative candidate to the Bolshevik leadership, the 'premature' advocate of industrialization and planned economy, the critic of Socialism in One Country, and the champion of 'proletarian democracy'.

Much of the documentation on which this narrative is based has hitherto been unknown. I have drawn heavily on Trotsky's Archives, which offer rich insights into the proceedings of the Politbureau and the Central Committee and into the work of all the factions of the Bolshevik party; on the voluminous and revealing correspondence between Trotsky, Radek, Rakovsky, Preobrazhensky, Sosnovsky, and many other eminent Bolsheviks; on the records of party congresses and conferences, on files of contemporary Russian and non-Russian newspapers and periodicals; and on published and unpublished eye-witness accounts. I have benefited from personal contact with Natalya Sedova, Trotsky's widow, Heinrich Brandler, Alfred Rosmer, Max Eastman, and other participants and survivors of the struggle who have been good enough to answer my queries and sometimes to submit to prolonged and repeated questioning. In my attempt to reproduce the background and the 'climate' of the time, my own experience may have been of some value. From the middle 1920's I was active in the Polish Communist party which stood closer to Bolshevism than did any other party; soon thereafter I was leading spokesman of an inner-party opposition strongly influenced by Trotsky's ideas; and in 1932 I had the somewhat curious distinction of being the first member ever to be expelled from the Polish party for his anti-Stalinism.

Access to untapped sources has, I think, enabled me to give either wholly or partly new versions of many crucial events and episodes. The relations between Lenin and Trotsky in Lenin's last years; the vicissitudes of the subsequent struggles; the relations between Trotsky, Bukharin, Zinoviev, Kamenev, Radek, and other leaders; the formation and the defeat of the various anti-Stalinist oppositions; the events of Trotsky's first year of exile near the Soviet-Chinese frontier, especially the divisions which had already appeared in the Trotskyist Opposition, foreshadowing its collapse many years before the Moscow trials—nearly all of these are narrated or interpreted in the light of some hitherto unknown facts. I have also, as in the previous volume, paid special attention to Trotsky the man of letters and devoted many pages to his views on science, literature, and the arts, in particular to his work as Russia's leading literary critic in the early 1920's. That work, remarkable for the largeness of his views and his clear-sighted rejection of any party tutelage over science and art, has also a special relevance to the present situation: such progress in these fields as was achieved in the Soviet Union during the post-Stalinist 'thaw' went in the direction of Trotsky's ideas, although it will probably still take a long time before views as undogmatic and bold as his make their appearance again in the Soviet Union.

Much as I have been concerned with the restoration of the various features and details of the historic drama, I have never been able to dismiss from my thoughts the tragic theme that runs through it from beginning to end and affects nearly all the characters involved. Here is modern tragedy in the sense in which Trotsky himself has defined it (see Chapter III, p. 193): 'As long as man is not yet master of his social organization, that organization towers above him like Fate itself. . . . The stuff of contemporary tragedy is found in the clash between the individual and a collective, or between hostile collectives represented by individuals.' Trotsky found it 'difficult to foresee whether the dramatist of the revolution will create "high" tragedy'. The Soviet dramatist has certainly not yet created it; but what modern Sophocles or Aeschylus could possibly produce tragedy as high as Trotsky's own life? Is it too much to hope that this is nevertheless an 'optimistic tragedy', one in which not all the suffering and sacrifice have been in vain?

. . . .

I am greatly indebted to Mr. Donald Tyerman who has read in manuscript this volume as well as all my previous books and has been a constant source of encouragement to me; and my thanks are due to Mr. Dan Davin and Mr. John Bell for most valuable stylistical criticisms and suggestions. My wife has as ever been my only research assistant and also my first, the most severe and the most indulgent, critic. I. D.

CHAPTER I

The Power and the Dream

THE Bolsheviks made their October Revolution of 1917 in the conviction that what they had begun was mankind's 'leap from the realm of necessity to the realm of freedom'. They saw the bourgeois order dissolving and class society crumbling all over the world, not merely in Russia. They believed that everywhere the peoples were at last in revolt against being the playthings of socially unorganized productive forces, and against the anarchy of their own existence. They imagined that the world was fully ready to free itself from the necessity to slave and sweat for the means of its subsistence—and ready also to put an end to man's domination by man. They greeted the dawn of the new age in which the human being, all his energies and capacities released, would achieve self-fulfilment. They were proud to have opened for humanity 'the passage from pre-history to history'.

This brilliant vision inspired the minds and hearts not only of the leaders, ideologues, and dreamers of Bolshevism. It sustained the hope and ardour of the mass of their followers as well. They fought in the civil war with no mercy for their enemies and no pity for themselves because they believed that by doing so they were ensuring for Russia and the world the chance of accomplishing the great leap from necessity to freedom.

When victory was theirs at last they found that revolutionary Russia had overreached herself and was hurled down to the bottom of a horrible pit. No other nation had followed her revolutionary example. Surrounded by a hostile or, at best, indifferent world Russia stood alone, bled white, starving, shivering with cold, consumed by disease, and overcome with gloom. In the stench of blood and death her people scrambled wildly for a breath of air, a faint gleam of light, a crust of bread. 'Is this', they asked, 'the realm of freedom? Is this where the great leap has taken us?'

What answer could the leaders give? They replied that the

great and celebrated revolutions of earlier ages had suffered similar cruel setbacks but had nevertheless justified themselves and their work in the eyes of posterity; and that the Russian Revolution too would emerge triumphant. Nobody argued thus with greater power of conviction than did the chief character of this book. Before the hungry crowds of Petrograd and Moscow Trotsky recalled the privations and the distress which revolutionary France endured many years after the destruction of the Bastille; and he told them how the First Consul of the Republic every morning visited in person the *Halles* of Paris, anxiously watched the few peasant carts bringing food from the country, and went away every morning knowing that the people of Paris would continue to starve.[1] The analogy was all too real; but consoling historical parallels, no matter how true and relevant, could not fill Russia's empty stomach.

Nobody was able to gauge the depth to which the nation had slumped. Down below hands and feet fumblingly searched for solid points of support, for something to lean on and something to grasp at—in order to climb up. Once revolutionary Russia had climbed up she would surely resume the leap from necessity to freedom. But how was the ascent to be accomplished? How was the pandemonium at the bottom to be calmed? How were the desperate multitudes to be disciplined and led for the ascent? How could the Soviet republic overcome its appalling misery and chaos and then go on to fulfil the promise of socialism?

At first the Bolshevik leaders did not try to belittle or embellish the predicament or deceive their followers. They attempted to uphold their courage and hope with words of truth. But the truth, unvarnished, was too harsh to mitigate misery and allay despair. And so it began to make room for the soothing lie which at first sought merely to conceal the chasm between dream and reality but soon insisted that the realm of freedom had already been reached—and that it lay there at the bottom of the pit. 'If people refused to believe, they had to be made to believe by force.' The lie grew by degrees until it became elaborate, complex, and vast—as vast as the chasm it was designed to cover up. It found among the Bolshevik leaders its mouthpieces and dedicated supporters, who felt that without the lie and the force which supported it the nation could not be

[1] Trotsky, *Sochinenya*, vol. xii, pp. 318–29.

dragged out of the mire. The salutary lie, however, could bear no confrontation with the original message of the revolution. Nor as the lie grew could its expounders stand face to face or side by side with the genuine leaders of the October Revolution to whom the revolution's message was and remained inviolable.

The latter did not at once raise their voices in protest. They did not even at once recognize the falsehood for what it was, for it insinuated itself slowly and imperceptibly. The leaders of the revolution could not help being entangled in it at the outset; but then, one after another, hesitantly and falteringly, they rose to expose and denounce the lie and to invoke against it the revolution's broken promise. Their voices, however, once so powerful and inspiring, sounded hollow at the bottom of the pit and brought forth no response from hungry, weary, and cowed multitudes. Of all these voices none vibrated with such deep and angry conviction as did that of Trotsky. He now began to rise to his height as the revolution's prophet unarmed, who, instead of imposing his faith by force, could rely only on the force of his faith.

. . . .

The year 1921 at length brought peace to Bolshevik Russia. The last shots died down on the battlefields of the civil war. The White Armies had dissolved and vanished. The armies of intervention had withdrawn. Peace was concluded with Poland. The European frontiers of the Soviet Federation were drawn and fixed.

Amid the silence which had fallen on the battlefields Bolshevik Russia listened intently to sounds from the outside world and was becoming poignantly aware of her isolation. Since the summer of 1920, when the Red Army was defeated at the gates of Warsaw, the revolutionary fever in Europe had subsided. The old order there found some balance, unstable yet real enough to allow the conservative forces to recover from disarray and panic. Communists could not hope for imminent revolutionary developments; and attempts to provoke such developments could result only in costly failures. This was demonstrated in March 1921, when a desperate and ill-prepared communist rising broke out in central Germany. The rising had been encouraged and in part instigated by Zinoviev, the President of the Communist International, and Bela Kun, the luckless leader of the Hungarian Revolution of 1919, who believed that the rising might 'electrify' and spur to action the apathetic mass of the German working class.[1] The mass failed to respond, however; and the German government suppressed the rising without much difficulty. The fiasco threw German communism into confusion; and amid bitter recriminations the leader of the German Communist party, Paul Levy, broke with the International. The March rising thus weakened even further the forces of communism in Europe and deepened the sense of isolation in Bolshevik Russia.

The nation ruled by Lenin's party was in a state of near dissolution. The material foundations of its existence were shattered. It will be enough to recall that by the end of the civil war Russia's national income amounted to only one-third of her income in 1913, that industry produced less than one-fifth of the goods produced before the war, that the coal-mines turned out less than one-tenth and the iron foundries only one-fortieth of their normal output, that the railways were destroyed, that all stocks and reserves on which any economy depends for its work were utterly exhausted, that the exchange of goods between town and country had come to a standstill, that Russia's cities and towns had become so depopulated that in 1921 Moscow had only one-half and Petrograd one-third of its former inhabitants, and that the people of the two capitals had for many months lived on a food ration of two ounces of bread and a few frozen potatoes and had heated their dwellings with the wood of their furniture—and we shall obtain some idea of the condition in which the nation found itself in the fourth year of the revolution.[2]

The Bolsheviks were in no mood to celebrate victory. The Kronstadt rising had finally compelled them to give up war communism and to promulgate N.E.P.—the New Economic Policy. Their immediate purpose was to induce peasants to sell food and private merchants to bring the food from country to town, from producer to consumer. This was the beginning of

---

[1] Trotsky, *Pyat Let Kominterna*, pp. 284–7; Radek, *Pyat Let Kominterna*, vol. ii, pp. 464–5; *Tretii Vsemirnyi Kongress Kominterna*, pp. 58 ff., 308 ff; Lenin, *Sochinenya*, vol. xxxii, pp. 444–50 *passim*.

[2] Kritsman, *Geroicheskii Period Velikoi Russkoi Revolutsii*, pp. 150 ff.; *3 Syezd Profsoyuzov*, pp. 79–86 and Miliutin's report in *4 Syezd Profsoyuzov*, pp. 72–77.

a long series of concessions to private farming and trade, the beginning of that 'forced retreat' which Lenin avowed his government was compelled to beat before the anarchic elements of small property which were predominant in the country.

Presently calamity struck the nation. One of the worst famines in history visited the populous farming land on the Volga. Already in the spring of 1921, just after the Kronstadt rising, Moscow had been alarmed by reports about droughts, sand blizzards, and an invasion of locusts in the southern and south-eastern provinces. The government swallowed its pride and appealed for help to bourgeois charitable organizations abroad. In July it was feared that 10 million peasants would be hit by the famine. By the end of the year the number of sufferers had risen to 36 million.[1] Uncounted multitudes fled before the sand blizzards and the locust and wandered in aimless despair over the vast plains. Cannibalism reappeared, a ghastly mockery of the high socialist ideals and aspirations emanating from the capital cities.

Seven years of world war, revolution, civil war, intervention, and war communism had wrought such changes in society that customary political notions, ideas, and slogans became almost meaningless. Russia's social structure had been not merely over-turned; it was smashed and destroyed. The social classes which had so implacably and furiously wrestled with one another in the civil war were all, with the partial exception of the peasantry, either exhausted and prostrate or pulverized. The landed gentry had perished in their burning mansions and on the battlefields of the civil war; survivors escaped abroad with remnants of the White Armies which scattered to the winds. Of the bourgeoisie, never very numerous or politically confident, many had also perished or emigrated. Those who saved their skins, stayed in Russia, and attempted to adjust themselves to the new régime, were merely the wreckage of their class. The old intelligentsia, and to a lesser degree the bureaucracy, shared the fate of the bourgeoisie proper: some ate the émigré's bread in the West; others served Russia's new masters as 'specialists'. With the revival of private trade, a new upstart middle class made its appearance. Its members, contemptuously labelled N.E.P.-men, were bent on exploiting quickly the opportunities N.E.P.

[1] See Kalinin's report in 9 *Vserossiiskii Syezd Sovietov*, pp. 23–26.

offered them, amassed mushroom-fortunes, and enjoyed their day with the feeling that one deluge was behind them and another ahead of them. Despised even by the survivors of the old bourgeoisie, this new middle class did not aspire to develop a political mind of its own. *Sukharevka*, Moscow's sprawling and squalid black market, was the symbol of its social existence and morality.

It was a grim and paradoxical outcome of the struggle that the industrial working class, which was supposed now to exercise its dictatorship, was also pulverized. The most courageous and politically minded workers had either laid down their lives in the civil war or occupied responsible posts in the new administration, the army, the police, the industrial managements, and a host of newly created institutions and public bodies. Proudly conscious of their origin, these proletarians turned Commissars did not in fact belong to the working class any longer. With the passage of time many of them became estranged from the workers and assimilated with the bureaucratic environment. The bulk of the proletariat too became *déclassé*. Masses of workers fled from town to country during the hungry years; and being mostly town dwellers in the first generation and not having lost roots in the country, they were easily reabsorbed by the peasantry. In the early years of N.E.P. there started a migration in the opposite direction, an exodus from country to town. Some old workers returned to the cities; but most of the new-comers were raw and illiterate peasants, without any political, let alone cultural, tradition. However, in 1921 and 1922 the migration from country to town was only a trickle.

The dispersal of the old working class created a vacuum in urban Russia. The old, self-reliant, and class-conscious labour movement with its many institutions and organizations, trade unions, co-operatives, and educational clubs, which used to resound with loud and passionate debate and seethe with political activity—that movement was now an empty shell. Here and there small groups of veterans of the class struggle met and argued about the prospects of the revolution. They had once formed the real 'vanguard' of the working class. Now they were a mere handful; and they could not see behind them the main force of their class which had once listened to them, taken its cue from them, and followed them into the thick of social struggle.[1]

The proletarian dictatorship was triumphant but the proletariat had nearly vanished. It had never been more than a small minority of the nation; and it had played a decisive part in three revolutions not because of its numbers but because of the extraordinary strength of its political mind, initiative, and organization. At the best of times Russia's large-scale industry employed not much more than three million workers. After the end of the civil war only about half that number remained in employment. Even of these many were in fact idle because the plant was idle. The government kept them on industrial payrolls as a matter of social policy, in order to save a nucleus of the working class for the future. These workers were, in fact, paupers. If a worker received his wage in money, the wage was worthless because of the catastrophic depreciation of the rouble. He made his living, such as it was, by doing odd jobs, trading on black markets, and scouring nearby villages for food. If he received his wage in kind, especially in the produce of his factory, he rushed from the bench to the black market to barter away a pair of shoes or a piece of cloth for bread and potatoes. Left with nothing to barter, he would return to the factory to steal a tool, a few nails, or a sack of coal, and he went back to the black market. Theft in factories was so common that it was estimated that half the workers normally stole the things they themselves produced.[2] It may be imagined what effect the hunger, the cold, the terrifying idleness at the factory bench and the hurly-burly of the black markets, the cheating and the stealing—the almost zoological struggle for survival—had on the morale of the people who were supposed to be the ruling class of the new state.

As a social class the peasantry alone emerged unbroken. World war, civil war, and famine had, of course, taken their toll; but they had not cracked the mainsprings of the peasantry's life. They had not reduced its resilience and powers of regeneration. Not even the worst calamity could disperse the heavy bulk

---

[1] See *4 Syezd Profsoyuzov*, Bukharin's, Lozovsky's, and Miliutin's reports.

[2] Lozovsky claimed that 50 per cent. of the produce was stolen in some factories; and it was estimated that wages covered only one-fifth of a worker's cost of living. Ibid., p. 119.

of the peasantry which, indestructible almost like nature itself, needed to work in contact only with nature in order to keep alive, while the industrial workers dispersed when the artificial industrial machinery on which their existence depended had collapsed. The peasantry had preserved its character and its place in society. It had enhanced its position at the expense of the landed gentry. It could now afford to count the gains as well as the losses the revolution had brought it. The requisitions having ceased, the peasants hoped to gather in at last the full harvest from their enlarged possessions. True, they lived in utter poverty. But this and the backwardness which went with it were part and parcel of their social heritage. Freed from seignoral overlordship, the peasants preferred poverty on their own small-holdings to the incomprehensible vistas of abundance under communism which the urban agitators unfolded before them. The muzhiks were no longer greatly disturbed by the agitators' talk. They noticed that of late these had become chary of offending them and even sought to befriend them and to flatter them. For the time being, the muzhik was indeed the Benjamin of the Bolshevik government which was anxious to re-establish the 'link' between town and country and the 'alliance between workers and peasants'. Since the working class could not make its weight felt, the peasantry's weight was all the heavier. Every month, every week, brought the farmer a thousand fresh proofs of his new importance; and his self-confidence was heightened accordingly.

Yet this social class which alone had preserved its character and place in society was by its very nature politically impotent. Karl Marx once described in a striking image the 'idiocy of rural life' which in the last century prevented the French peasantry from 'asserting their class interests in their own name'; and his image fits well the Russian peasantry of the 1920's:

Throughout the country they live in almost identical conditions, but enter very little into relationships with one another. Their mode of production isolates them, instead of bringing them into mutual contact. The isolation is intensified by the inadequacy of the means of communication . . . and poverty. Their farms are so small that there is practically no scope for division of labour. . . . Among the peasantry therefore there can be no diversity of development, no differentiation of talents, no wealth of social relationship. Each family is almost self-sufficient, producing on its own plot of land the greater part of its requirements, and thus providing itself with the necessaries of life through an interchange with nature rather than by means of intercourse with society. Here is a small plot of land, with the peasant-farmer and his family; there is another plot of land, another peasant with wife and children. A score or two of these atoms make up a village, and a few scores of villages make up a *département*. In this way, the great mass of the French nation is formed by the simple addition of like entities, much as a sack of potatoes consists of a lot of potatoes huddled into a sack.[1]

The huge sack of potatoes that was rural Russia also proved quite incapable of asserting itself 'in its own name'. Once the Populist, or Social Revolutionary intelligentsia represented it, and spoke on its behalf. But the Social Revolutionary party, discredited by its own refusal to countenance the agrarian revolution and then driven underground and destroyed by the Bolsheviks, had played out its role. The sack of potatoes lay vast, formidable, and mute. Nobody could take his eyes off it; nobody could ignore it, or trample on it with impunity: it had already hit urban Russia on the head; and the Bolshevik rulers had to bow to it. But the sack of potatoes could not give backbone, form, will, and voice to a shapeless and disintegrated society.

.   .   .   .

Thus a few years after the revolution the nation was incapable of managing its own affairs and of asserting itself through its own authentic representatives. The old ruling classes were crushed; and the new ruling class, the proletariat, was only a shadow of its former self. No party could claim to represent the dispersed working class; and the workers could not control the party which claimed to speak for them and to rule the country on their behalf.

Whom then did the Bolshevik party represent? It represented only itself, that is, its past association with the working class, its present aspiration to act as the guardian of the proletarian class interest, and its intention to reassemble in the course of economic reconstruction a new working class which should be able in due time to take the country's destinies into its hands. In the meantime, the Bolshevik party maintained itself in power

[1] Marx, *18 Brumaire of Louis Bonaparte.*

by usurpation. Not only its enemies saw it as a usurper—the party appeared as a usurper even in the light of its own standards and its own conception of the revolutionary state.

The enemies of Bolshevism, we remember, had from the outset denounced the October Revolution and then the dispersal of the Constituent Assembly in 1918 as acts of usurpation. The Bolsheviks did not take this accusation to heart: they replied that the government from which they seized power in October had not been based on any elective representative body; and that the revolution vested power in a government backed by the overwhelming majority of the elected and representative Councils of Workers' and Soldiers' Deputies. The Soviets had been a class representation and· by definition an organ of proletarian dictatorship. They had not been elected on the basis of universal suffrage. The gentry and the bourgeoisie had been disfranchised; and the peasantry was represented only in such a proportion as was compatible with the predominance of the urban workers. The workers cast their votes not as individuals in traditional constituencies but in factories and workshops as members of those productive units of which their class consisted. It was only this class representation that the Bolsheviks had since 1917 considered as valid and legitimate.[1]

Yet it was precisely in the terms of the Bolshevik conception of the workers' state that Lenin's government had gradually ceased to be representative. Nominally, it was still based on the Soviets. But the Soviets of 1921–2, unlike those of 1917, were not and could not be representative—they could not possibly represent a virtually non-existent working class. They were the creatures of the Bolshevik party; and so when Lenin's government claimed to derive its prerogatives from the Soviets, it was in fact deriving them from itself.

The Bolshevik party had the usurper's role thrust upon it. It had become impossible for it to live up to its principle once the working class had disintegrated. What could or should the party have done under these circumstances? Should it have thrown up its hands and surrendered power? A revolutionary government which has waged a cruel and devastating civil war does not abdicate on the day after its victory and does not surrender to its defeated enemies and to their revenge even if it

[1] Lenin, *Sochinenya*, vol. xxvi, pp. 396–400; Trotsky, *Kommunizm i Terrorizm*.

discovers that it cannot rule in accordance with its own ideas and that it no longer enjoys the support it commanded when it entered the civil war. The Bolsheviks lost that support not because of any clear-cut change in the minds of their erstwhile followers, but because of the latters' dispersal. They knew that their mandate to rule the republic had not been properly renewed by the working class—not to speak of the peasantry. But they also knew that they were surrounded by a vacuum; that the vacuum could be filled only slowly over the years, and that for the time being nobody could either prolong or invalidate their mandate. A social catastrophe, a *force majeure*, had turned them into usurpers; and so they refused to consider themselves as such.

The disappearance in so short a time of a vigorous and militant social class from the political stage and the atrophy of society consequent upon civil war formed a strange but not a unique historic phenomenon. In other great revolutions, too, society broke down exhausted, and revolutionary government was similarly transformed. The English Puritan Revolution and the French Great Revolution had each first upheld a new principle of representative government against the *ancien régime*. The Puritans asserted the rights of Parliament against the Crown. The leaders of the French Third Estate did likewise when they constituted themselves as the National Assembly. Upheaval and civil strife followed, in consequence of which the forces of the *ancien régime* were no longer able to dominate society while the classes which had supported the revolution were too strongly divided against themselves and too exhausted to exercise power. No representative government was therefore possible. The army was the only body with enough unity of will, organization, and discipline to master the chaos. It proclaimed itself the guardian of society; and it established the rule of the sword, a nakedly usurpatory form of government. In England the two broad phases of the revolution were embodied in the same person: Cromwell first led the Commons against the Crown and then as Lord Protector usurped the prerogatives of both Crown and Commons. In France there was a definite break between the two phases; and in each different men came to the fore: the usurper Bonaparte played no significant part in the early acts of the revolution.

In Russia the Bolshevik party provided that closely knit and disciplined body of men, inspired by a single will, which was capable of ruling and unifying the disintegrated nation. No such party had existed in previous revolutions. The main strength of the Puritans lay in Cromwell's army; and so they came to be dominated by the army. The Jacobin party came into being only in the course of the upheaval. It was part of the fluctuating revolutionary tide. It broke up and vanished at the ebb of the tide. The Bolshevik party, on the contrary, formed a solid and centralized organization long before 1917. This enabled it to assume leadership in the revolution and, after the ebb of the tide, to play for many decades the part the army had played in revolutionary England and France, to secure stable government and to work towards the integration and remodelling of the national life.

By its cast of mind and political tradition the Bolshevik party was extremely well prepared and yet peculiarly ill adapted for the usurper's part. Lenin had trained his disciples as the 'vanguard' and the *élite* of the Labour movement. The Bolsheviks had never contented themselves with giving expression to the actual moods or aspirations of the working class. They regarded it as their mission to shape those moods and to prompt and develop those aspirations. They looked upon themselves as political tutors of the working class and were convinced that as consistent Marxists they knew better than the oppressed and unenlightened working class could know what was its real historic interest and what should be done to promote it. It was because of this, we remember, that the young Trotsky had charged them with the inclination to 'substitute' their own party for the working class and to disregard the workers' genuine wishes and desires.[1] The charge, when Trotsky first levelled it, in 1904, ran far ahead of the facts. In 1917 as in 1905 the Bolsheviks made their own intervention in the revolution wholly dependent on the degree of proletarian mass support they could muster. Lenin and his staff scrutinized with cold and sober eyes even the most minute fluctuations in the workers' political temper; and to these they carefully related their own policies. It never then occurred to them that they could seize or hold power without the approval of the majority of the

[1] See *The Prophet Armed*, pp. 89–97 and *passim*.

workers or of the workers and the peasants. Up to the revolution, during it, and for some time afterwards, they were always willing to submit their own policies to the 'verdict of proletarian democracy', i.e. to the vote of the working class.

Towards the end of the civil war, however, the 'verdict of proletarian democracy' had become a meaningless phrase. How could that verdict express itself when the working class was scattered and *déclassé*? Through elections to the Soviets? Through 'normal' procedures of Soviet democracy? The Bolsheviks thought that it would be the height of folly on their part to be guided in their actions by the vote of a desperate remnant of the working class and by the moods of accidental majorities which might form themselves within the shadowy Soviets. At last they —and Trotsky with them—did in fact substitute their own party for the working class. They identified their own will and ideas with what they believed would have been the will and the ideas of a full-blooded working class, if such a working class had existed. Their habit of regarding themselves as *the* interpreters of the proletarian-class interest made that substitution all the easier. As the old vanguard, the party found it natural for itself to act as the *locum tenens* for the working class during that strange and, it hoped, short interval when that class was in a state of dissolution. Thus the Bolsheviks drew a moral justification for their usurpatory role from their own tradition as well as from the actual state of society.

The Bolshevik tradition, however, was a subtle combination of diverse elements. The party's moral self-reliance, its superiority, its sense of revolutionary mission, its inner discipline, and its deeply ingrained conviction that authority was indispensable to proletarian revolution—all these qualities had formed the authoritarian strands in Bolshevism. These, however, had been held in check by the party's intimate closeness to the real, and not merely to the theoretical, working class, by its genuine devotion to it, by its burning belief that the weal of the exploited and the oppressed was the beginning and the end of the revolution and that the worker should eventually be the real master in the new state, because in the end History would through his mouth pronounce a severe and just verdict on all parties, including the Bolsheviks, and all their deeds. The idea of proletarian democracy was inseparable from this attitude.

When the Bolshevik evoked it he expressed his contempt for the formal and deceptive democracy of the bourgeoisie, his readiness to ride roughshod, if need be, over all the non-proletarian classes, but also his feeling that he was bound in duty to respect the will of the working class even when momentarily he dissented from it.

In the early stages of the revolution the proletarian-democratic strand was pre-eminent in the Bolshevik character. Now the bent towards authoritarian leadership was on top of it. Acting without the normal working class in the background, the Bolshevik from long habit still invoked the will of that class in order to justify whatever he did. But he invoked it only as a theoretical surmise and an ideal standard of behaviour, in short, something of a myth. He began to see in his party the repository not only of the ideal of socialism in the abstract, but also of the desires of the working class in the concrete. When a Bolshevik, from the Politbureau member to the humblest man in a cell, declaimed that 'the proletariat insists' or 'demands' or 'would never agree' to this or that, he meant that his party or its leaders 'insisted', 'demanded', and 'would never agree'. Without this half-conscious mystification the Bolshevik mind could not work. The party could not admit even to itself that it had no longer any basis in proletarian democracy. True, at intervals of cruel lucidity the Bolshevik leaders themselves spoke frankly about their predicament. But they hoped that time, economic recovery, and the reconstitution of the working class would solve it; and they went on to speak and to act as if the predicament had never arisen and as if they still acted on a clear and valid mandate from the working class.[1]

.   .   .   .

[1] At a congress of Soviets in December 1921 Lenin arguing against those who all too often referred to themselves as 'representatives of the proletariat' said: 'Excuse me, but what do you describe as proletariat? That class of labourers which is employed in large-scale industry. But where is [your] large-scale industry? What sort of a proletariat is this? Where is your industry? Why is it idle?' (*Sochinenya*, vol. xxxiii, p. 148.) In March 1922, at the eleventh party congress, Lenin again argued: 'Since the war it is not at all working-class people but malingerers that have gone to the factories. And are our social and economic conditions at present such that genuine proletarians go to the factories? No. They should go, according to Marx. But Marx wrote not about Russia—he wrote about capitalism in general, capitalism as it has developed since the fifteenth century. All this has been correct for 600 years, but is incorrect in present-day Russia.' (Op. cit., p. 268.) Shlyapnikov, speaking on behalf of the Workers' Opposition, thus replied

The Bolsheviks had by now finally suppressed all other parties and established their own political monopoly. They saw that only at the gravest peril to themselves and the revolution could they allow their adversaries to express themselves freely and to appeal to the Soviet electorate. An organized opposition could turn the chaos and discontent to its advantage all the more easily because the Bolsheviks were unable to mobilize the energies of the working class. They refused to expose themselves and the revolution to this peril. As the party substituted itself for the proletariat it also substituted its own dictatorship for that of the proletariat. 'Proletarian dictatorship' was no longer the rule of the working class which, organized in Soviets, had delegated power to the Bolsheviks but was constitutionally entitled to depose them or 'revoke' them from office. Proletarian dictatorship had now become synonymous with the exclusive rule of the Bolshevik party. The proletariat could 'revoke' or depose the Bolsheviks as little as it could 'revoke' or depose itself.

In suppressing all parties, the Bolsheviks wrought so radical a change in their political environment that they themselves could not remain unaffected. They had grown up under the Tsarist régime within a half-open and half-clandestine multiparty system, in an atmosphere of intense controversy and political competition. Although as a combatant body of revolutionaries they had had their own doctrine and discipline which even then set them apart from all other parties, they nevertheless breathed the air of their environment; and the multiparty system determined the inner life of their own party. Constantly engaged in controversy with their adversaries, the Bolsheviks cultivated controversy in their own ranks as well. Before a party member took the platform in order to oppose a Cadet or a Menshevik, he thrashed out within his own party cell or committee the issues which occupied him, the adversary's case, the reply to it, and the party's attitude and tactical moves. If he thought that the party was wrong on any point or its leadership inadequate, he said so without fear or favour, and tried to convert his comrades to his view. As long as the party fought for the

to Lenin: 'Vladimir Ilyich said yesterday that the proletariat as a class, in the Marxian sense, did not exist [in Russia]. Permit me to congratulate you on being the vanguard of a non-existing class.' *11 Syezd RKP (b)*, p. 109. The taunt expressed a bitter truth. See also Zinoviev's speech, ibid., pp. 408–9.

workers' democratic rights, it could not refuse those rights to its own members within its own organization.[1]

Destroying the multiparty system the Bolsheviks had no inkling of the consequences to themselves. They imagined that outside that system they would still remain what they had always been: a disciplined but free association of militant Marxists. They took it for granted that the collective mind of the party would continue to be shaped by the customary exchange of opinion, the give and take of theoretical and political argument. They did not realize that they could not ban all controversy outside their ranks and keep it alive within their ranks: they could not abolish democratic rights for society at large and preserve those rights for themselves alone.

The single-party system was a contradiction in terms: the single party itself could not remain a party in the accepted sense. Its inner life was bound to shrink and wither. Of 'democratic centralism', the master principle of Bolshevik organization, only centralism survived. The party maintained its discipline, not its democratic freedom. It could not be otherwise. If the Bolsheviks were now to engage freely in controversy, if their leaders were to thrash out their differences in public, and if the rank and file were to criticize the leaders and their policy, they would set an example to non-Bolsheviks who could not then be expected to refrain from argument and criticism. If members of the ruling party were to be permitted to form factions and groups in order to advance specific views within the party, how could people outside the party be forbidden to form their own associations and formulate their own political programmes? No body politic can be nine-tenths mute and one-tenth vocal. Having imposed silence on non-Bolshevik Russia, Lenin's party had in the end to impose silence on itself as well.

The party could not easily reconcile itself to this. Revolutionaries accustomed to take no authority for granted, to question accepted truth, and to examine critically their own party, could not suddenly bow to authority with unquestioning obedience.

---

[1] How unreconciled to their own single-party system the Bolsheviks were even in the fifth year of the revolution can be seen *inter alia* from this passage of Zinoviev's speech at the eleventh congress: '. . . we are the only party which exists legally . . . we have, so to speak, a monopoly. . . . *This jars on the ears of our party patriotism* . . . we have denied our adversaries political freedom . . . but we could not act otherwise. . . .' Ibid., pp. 412–13. (My italics, I.D.)

Even while they obeyed they continued to question. After the tenth congress had, in 1921, declared the ban on inner party factions, Bolshevik assemblies still resounded with controversy. Like-minded members still formed themselves into leagues, produced their 'platforms' and 'theses', and made scathing attacks on the leaders. In so doing, they threatened to undermine the basis of the single-party system. Having suppressed all its enemies and adversaries, the Bolshevik party could not continue to exist otherwise than by a process of permanent self-suppression.

The very circumstances of its own growth and success drove the party to adopt this course. Early in 1917 it had no more than 23,000 members in the whole of Russia. During the revolution the membership trebled and quadrupled. At the height of the civil war, in 1919, a quarter of a million people had joined its ranks. This growth reflected the party's genuine pull on the working class. Between 1919 and 1922 the membership trebled once again, rising from 250,000 to 700,000. Most of this growth, however, was already spurious. By now the rush to the victors' bandwagon was in full progress. The party had to fill innumerable posts in the government, in industry, in trade unions, and so on; and it was an advantage to fill them with people who accepted party discipline. In this mass of new-comers the authentic Bolsheviks were reduced to a small minority.[1] They felt that they were swamped by alien elements; and they were alarmed and anxious to winnow the chaff from the wheat.

But how was this to be done? It was difficult enough to tell those who joined the party for the sake of a disinterested conviction from the turncoats and pot-hunters. It was more difficult still to determine whether even those who sought membership from no disreputable motive grasped the party's aims and aspirations and were ready to fight for them. As long as several parties expounded their programmes and recruited followers, their perpetual contest secured the proper selection of the human material and its distribution between the parties. The new-comer to politics had then every opportunity to compare the competing programmes, methods of action, and slogans. If he joined the Bolsheviks he did so by an act of conscious choice. But those who entered politics in the years 1921-2 could make

---

[1] According to Zinoviev, Bolsheviks who had fought in the underground before February 1917 formed only 2 per cent. of the membership in 1922. Ibid., p. 420.

no such choice. They knew the Bolshevik party only. In other circumstances their inclinations might have led them to join the Mensheviks, the Social Revolutionaries, or any other group. Now their urge for political action led them to the only party in existence, the only one which offered an outlet to their energy and ardour. Many of the new entrants were, as Zinoviev called them, 'unconscious Mensheviks' or 'unconscious Social Revolutionaries',[1] who sincerely thought of themselves as 'good Bolsheviks'. The influx of such elements threatened to falsify the party's character and to dilute its tradition. Indeed, at the eleventh party congress, in 1922, Zinoviev claimed that there were already within the Bolshevik organization two or more potential parties formed by those who honestly mistook themselves for Bolsheviks. Thus by the mere fact that it was the single party, the party was losing its single mind; and inchoate substitutes for the parties it had banned began to appear in its own midst. The social background with all its repressed diversity of interest and political mentality reasserted itself and pressed on the only existing political organization and infiltrated it from all sides.

The leaders resolved to defend the party against this infiltration. They began a purge. The demand for a purge had come from the Workers' Opposition at the tenth congress; and the first purge was carried out in 1921. Police and the courts had nothing to do with the procedure. At public meetings the Control Commissions, i.e. party tribunals, examined the record and the morals of every party member, high or low. Every man and woman in the audience could come forward and testify for or against the investigated individual, whom the Control Commission then declared either worthy or unworthy of continued membership. The unworthy bore no punishment; but the loss of membership in the ruling party was likely to deprive him of chances of promotion or of a responsible post.

Within a short time 200,000 members, about one-third of the total membership, were thus expelled. The Control Commission classified those expelled into several categories: vulgar careerists; former members of anti-Bolshevik parties, especially former Mensheviks, who joined after the end of the civil war; Bolsheviks corrupted by power and privilege; and, finally, the politically

[1] Ibid., pp. 413–14.

immature who lacked an elementary grasp of the party's principles.[1] It seems that people whose only fault was that they had criticized the party's policy or its leaders were not expelled. But it soon became clear that the purge, needed though it was, was a double-edged weapon. It provided the unscrupulous with opportunities for intimidation and with pretexts for settling private accounts. The rank and file applauded the expulsion of turncoats and corrupt commissars, but were bewildered by the scope of the purge. It was known that purges would be repeated periodically; and so people wondered what, if a third of the membership could be expelled in a single year, would happen next year or the year after. The humble and the cautious began to think twice before they ventured to make a risky remark or take a step which at the next purge might bring upon them the reproach of political immaturity or backwardness. Initiated as a means of cleansing the party and safeguarding its character, the purge was destined to serve the party as the most deadly instrument of self-suppression.

We have seen that, when the working class had vanished as an effective social force, the party in all its formidable reality substituted itself for the class. But now the party too appeared to turn into an entity as elusive and phantom-like as that for which it had substituted itself. Was there any real substance, and could there be any autonomous life, in a party which in a single year declared a full third of its members unworthy and expelled them? The 200,000 purged men and women had presumably taken part in all normal procedures of party life up till now, voted for resolutions, elected delegates to congresses, and had thus had a large formal share in determining the party's policy. Yet their expulsion brought about no perceptible change or modification of policy. Not even a trace could be found in the party's outlook of the great surgical operation by which one third of its body had been slashed off. This fact alone proved that for some time past the mass of members had had no influence whatsoever on the conduct of affairs. Bolshevik policy was determined by a small section of the party which substituted itself for the whole.

Who constituted that section? Lenin himself answered the question in no uncertain terms. In March 1922 he wrote to Molotov who was then secretary to the Central Committee: 'If one

[1] *Izvestya Ts. K.* of 15 November 1921 (Nr. 34). Popov, N. *Outline History of the CPSU (b)*, vol. ii, p. 150.

does not wish to shut one's eyes to reality, one ought to admit that at present the proletarian character of the party's policy is determined not by the class composition of the membership but by the enormous and undivided authority of that very thin stratum of members who might be described as the party's old guard.'[1] In that Guard Lenin now saw the only repository of the ideal of socialism, the party's trustee, and ultimately the *locum tenens* of the working class. The Guard consisted in all of a few thousand authentic veterans of revolution. The bulk of the party was, in Lenin's present view, a mushroom growth exposed to all the corrupting influences of a deranged and anarchic society. Even the best of the young members needed patient training and political education before they could become 'real Bolsheviks'. Thus, the identification of proletariat and party turned out to be an even more narrow identification of the proletariat with the Old Guard.

Yet even that Guard could not easily maintain itself on the dizzy height to which it had risen; it too might not be able to withstand the debasing influences of time, weariness, corruption by power, and the pressures of the social environment. Already there were cracks in the unity of the Old Guard. In his letter to Molotov Lenin remarked: 'Even a slight dissension in this stratum may be enough to weaken . . . its authority to such an extent that [the Old Guard] should forfeit its power of decision' and become unable to control events. At all costs, therefore, it was necessary to maintain the solidarity of the Old Guard, to keep alive in it the sense of its high mission, and to secure its political supremacy. Periodic purges of the party were not enough. Severe restrictions were to be placed on the admission of members; and new entrants were to be subjected to the most exacting tests. Finally, inside the party, Lenin suggested, it was necessary to establish a special hierarchy based on merit and length of revolutionary service. Certain important offices could be held only by people who had joined the party at least early in the civil war. Other posts involving still higher responsibility were to be available to those only who had served the party since the beginning of the revolution, while top positions were to be reserved for veterans of the clandestine struggle against Tsardom.[2]

---

[1] Lenin, *Sochinenya*, vol. xxxiii, pp. 228–30.
[2] See the resolutions of the eleventh party conference and the eleventh congress in *KPSS v Rezolutsyakh*, vol. i, pp. 595–6, 612, 628–30.

There was as yet no flavour of vulgar patronage about these rules. The Old Guard still lived by its austere code of revolutionary morality. Under the *partmaximum* a party member, even one who held the highest office, was not allowed to earn more than the wages of a skilled factory worker. True, some dignitaries were already availing themselves of loopholes and supplemented meagre earnings by all kinds of benefits. But such evasions were still the exception. The new regulations about the distribution of offices were designed not to bribe the Old Guard but to make sure that party and state should remain in its hands unfailing instruments for the building of socialism.

The Old Guard was a formidable body of men. They were bound together by the memory of heroic struggles fought in common, by an unshakeable belief in socialism, and by the conviction that, amid universal dissolution and apathy, the chances of socialism depended on them and almost on them alone. They acted with authority but often also with arrogance. They were selfless yet ambitious. They were animated by the loftiest sentiments and were capable of unscrupulous ruthlessness. They identified themselves with the revolution's historic destiny but they also identified that destiny with themselves. In their intense devotion to socialism they came to regard the struggle for it as their exclusive affair and almost private business; and they were inclined to justify their behaviour and even their private ambitions in the theoretical terms of socialism.

Amid the tribulations of these years the moral strength of the Old Guard was an invaluable asset to Bolshevism. The revival of private trade and the partial rehabilitation of property spread despondency in party ranks. Many a communist wondered uneasily where the 'retreat' Lenin had ordered would take the revolution: Lenin seemed ready to go to any length to encourage the merchant and the private farmer. Since the peasant refused to sell food for worthless bank-notes, money, despised under War Communism as a relic of the old society, was 'rehabilitated' and then stabilized. Nothing was to be had without it. The government cut down the subsidies it had paid to state-owned concerns; and workers who had clung to the factory bench through the worst times lost employment. The state banks used their scanty resources to encourage private enterprise with credits. The Central Committee assured the party that, nevertheless, by holding the 'commanding heights' of large-scale industry, the state would in any event be able to control the national economy. But these 'commanding heights' had a sad and unpromising look: state-owned industry was at a standstill while private trade began to flourish. Then Lenin invited the old concessionaires and foreign investors to return to Russia and do business; and only because the investors did not respond did an important element of capitalism fail to reappear. But what would happen, Bolsheviks wondered, if the concessionaires were to respond after all? In the meantime the N.E.P.-man grew self-confident, feasted in famished towns, and mocked at the revolution. In the country, the kulak tried to get the farm labourer under his thumb once again; and here and there he and his dependants began to dominate the rural Soviet, while his son became ringleader in the local branch of the Communist Youth. At universities teachers and students staged anti-communist demonstrations and strikes, and communists were man-handled for singing the *Internationale*, the revolution's anthem. Where was the retreat going to end? The Workers' Opposition threw the question at Lenin during the sessions of the Central Committee and at public assemblies. Repeatedly he promised to halt the retreat; and repeatedly events compelled him to retreat even farther. The idealists were shocked. Cries of 'betrayal' came from the ranks. Often a worker, a veteran of the Red Guards, appeared before his party committee, tore in disgust his member card and threw it in the face of the party secretary. So much was this a sign of the times that the description of such scenes can be found in many a contemporary novel and party chiefs spoke about them with undisguised anxiety.[1]

Amid all this dejection it seemed that the revolution could rely only on the Old Guard, on its steadfast faith and iron will. But could it?

.   .   .   .

At the end of the civil war Trotsky descended from the military train which had served him as field headquarters and in

---

[1] Manuilsky, for instance, protested at the eleventh congress against the fact that the veteran of the civil war who tore his party card was surrounded by a halo of heroism, whereas he should be treated as a traitor. He compared the prevalent mood to the depression which followed the defeats of revolution in 1849 and 1907. *11 Syezd RKP (b)*, pp. 461–3.

which he had, for three fateful years, rushed from danger spot to danger spot along a frontline of 5,000 miles, interrupting his journeys only for brief consultations and public appearances in Moscow. The military train was placed in a museum; its crew of drivers, mechanics, machine-gunners, and secretaries was disbanded; and Trotsky took his first holiday since the revolution. He spent it in the country not far from Moscow—hunting, fishing, writing, and preparing for a new chapter in his life. When he returned to Moscow, as whose voice he had spoken all these years, he was almost a stranger there. He had his first glimpse of the old capital at the turn of the century when he was brought to Butyrki prison to await deportation to Siberia; and so it was from behind the bars of a prison van that he first viewed the city of his future triumphs and defeats. He did not return to Moscow until twenty years later, in March 1918, during the Brest Litovsk crisis, after the Bolshevik government had evacuated Petrograd and established itself in the Kremlin. Presently he left for the fronts. Whenever he returned he felt as if out of place in the sprawling 'village of the Tsars', the Third Rome of the Slavophiles, with its Byzantine churches and Asiatic bazaars and its listless oriental fatalism. His revolutionary associations both in 1905 and in 1917 had been with Petrograd, Moscow's rival and Russia's window to Europe; and he always felt more at ease with the engineers, shipbuilders, and electrical workers of Petrograd than with the workers of Moscow who, employed mostly in textile mills, still looked and behaved more like muzhiks than like city dwellers.

He felt even more out of place within the walls and towers of the Kremlin, in the narrow tortuous streets of the old fortress, in the shade of its battlements reverberating with ancient bells, amid its cathedrals, arsenals, barracks, prison towers, and belfries, in the gilded halls of its palaces, surrounded by innumerable miraculous ikons the Tsars had assembled from all their conquered lands. With his wife and children he occupied four small rooms in the Kavalersky building, the former quarters of Court officials. Across the corridor lived Lenin and Krupskaya; the two families shared the dining-room and bath-room—in the corridor or in the bath-room Lenin might often be caught playing with the Trotsky children. Now and then an old friend, Rakovsky, Manuilsky, or someone else, arriving from the provinces on government business, stayed with the family. The Trotskys' domestic life was still as modest as it was when as exiles they lived in a garret in Paris or in a tenement block in Vienna. It was perhaps poorer, for food was scarce even in the Kremlin.[1] The children—Lyova was fifteen and Seryozha thirteen in 1921 —enjoyed little parental care: they saw even their mother for brief moments only; she spent her days at the Commissariat of Education and headed its Arts Department.

The magnificent setting of the Kremlin contrasted strangely with the way of life of its new inhabitants. Trotsky describes the family's amused embarrassment when they were first attended by an old Court butler who served meals on plates bearing the Tsar's coat of arms and carefully turned and manipulated the plates in front of the grown-ups and the children so that the Tsar's eagles should never, God forbid, be placed upside down.[2] From every corner 'the heavy barbarism of Moscow' stared at the Bolshevik leaders; and when the chimes of the old bells intruded in their conversation, Trotsky and Lenin 'looked at each other as if we had both caught ourselves thinking the same thing; we were being overheard by the past . . .'. They were not merely being overheard—the past was fighting back against them. In any case, Trotsky, as he confesses, never merged with the Kremlin background. He kept his distance from it; and only his sense of historic irony was tickled by the revolution's intrusion into Muscovy's holy of holies.

He had a gnawing feeling that the end of the civil war was an anticlimax in his fortunes. He repressed this feeling by an effort of conscious optimism, the optimism which should never abandon the revolutionary; and he looked forward to new triumphs for his cause and for himself. But scattered in his speeches and writings there were already nostalgic notes about the heroic era of revolution and civil war now closed. It was not that he idealized that era during which, as he put it, the muzhik's club served the revolution as its 'finest tool', that primordial club with which the peasants had once driven Napoleon and with which they had now driven the landlord

[1] Arthur Ransome relates that when, in 1919, he gave Bukharin a little saccharine for tea, this was quite a treat; a meal at Zinoviev's headquarters consisted of 'soup with shreds of horseflesh . . . a little *kasha* . . . tea and a lump of sugar'. *Six Weeks in Russia*, pp. 13, 56.

[2] *Moya Zhizn*, vol. ii, p. 77.

PLATE I

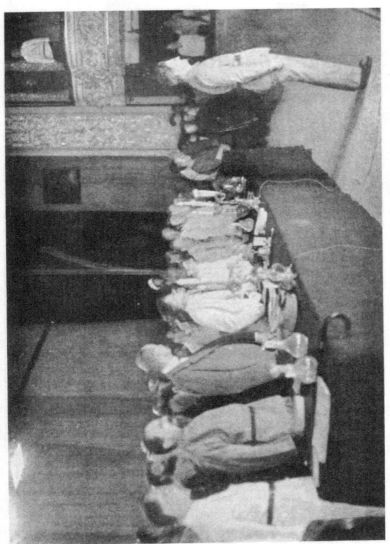

Trotsky addresses a Congress of the Communist International (Moscow, 1920)

PLATE II

(*a*) Trotsky as Commissar of War

(*b*) Inspecting troops in Moscow in 1921, after the end of the civil war

from Russia. Nor did he overlook the heavy legacy of that era—the destructive furies let loose by civil war which were revenging themselves on the Soviet Republic as it turned towards its constructive tasks. But for all their miseries, squalor, and cruelty, the years of destruction had also been years of creation; and he harked back to their mighty sweep, courage, and soaring hope; and he sensed the gap they left behind.[1]

His brain and energy were now only half occupied. The Commissariat of War was no longer the hub of government. The army was demobilized. By the beginning of 1922 it had been reduced to one-third of its establishment. It was also losing its revolutionary idealism and fervour. The veterans of the civil war had left; and the freshly mobilized age-groups in the barracks seemed as listless and apathetic as had been the peasant sons who came to the same barracks in the days of the Tsar. Circumstances compelled the Commissar of War to shelve his cherished plans for transforming the army into a modern, democratic, and socialist militia, and imposed on him the humdrum routine of administration and training. He spent his time delousing the army, teaching it to grease its boots, and clean its rifles, and entreating the best commanders and commissars to stay on in their jobs. He urged the Central Committee to arrest the mass exodus of Communists from the army; and the Central Committee tried formal prohibitions and bans. But these were ineffective. At national conferences Trotsky again and again implored political commissars to resist the 'infectious pacifist mood' and he lamented the Red Army's sagging morale. He struggled to keep the army uncontaminated by the 'spirit of Sukharevka' and to use it as an instrument of a Marxist *Kulturkampf* against the filth, backwardness, and superstition of Mother Russia, and above all, to keep alive in it revolutionary tradition and internationalist awareness.[2]

This was the time when the young commanders of the civil war, among them the future marshals of the Second World War, obtained serious training, and the Red Army received its rules and regulations. Of these Trotsky was the inspirer and part

[1] See, for instance, Trotsky's address to the commanding officers and commissars of the Moscow garrison of 25 October and his speech at the end of army manœuvres in September 1921, *Kak Vooruzhalas Revolutsia*, vol. iii, book 1.

[2] See Annual Report of C.C. in Appendix to *11 Syezd RKP* (*b*), pp. 637–64; *Pyat Let Sovietskoi Vlasti*; and *Kak Vooruzhalas Revolutsia*, vol. iii, *passim*.

author. It is curious, for instance, to note the affinity between Trotsky's 'Infantry Regulations' and the Cromwellian Soldier's Catechism. 'You are an equal among comrades', the Infantry Regulations instructed the Red Army man, 'Your superiors are your more experienced and better educated brothers. In combat, during training, in the barracks, or at work you must obey them. Once you have left the barracks you are absolutely free. . . .' 'If you are asked in what way you fight, you answer: "I fight with the rifle, the bayonet, and the machine-gun. But I also fight with the word of truth. I address that to the enemy's soldiers who are themselves workers and peasants so that they should know that in truth I am their brother, not their enemy."'

His love of words, the simple words as well as the rich, and his sense of form and colour went into the making of a new pageantry with which he sought to appeal to the recruit's imagination and to develop in the army the feeling that it was not merely regimented cannon-fodder. On May Day and on the anniversaries of the revolution, flanked by the commanders of the Moscow garrison, he rode out on horseback, through the Kremlin's Spasky gates to the Red Square to review the massed columns of the garrison. To his greeting 'Salute, Comrades!' the troops replied: 'We Serve the Revolution!'; and the echo thundered against the spires of the Vassily Cathedral and over the graves of the revolution's martyrs along the Kremlin wall. There was as yet no mechanical pomp or ceremony. After the review the Commissar of War joined the other members of the Central Committee who from a wooden ramshackle stand or from a crowded army lorry took the parade of soldiers and workers.[1]

Trotsky's appearance and speech still thrilled the crowds. But he no longer seemed to find the intimate contact with his audiences which he found unerringly during the civil war, the contact which Lenin invariably established by his unobtrusive appearance and simple expression. Trotsky on the platform

---

[1] Morizet, *Chez Lénine et Trotski*, pp. 108–11. Serge and Rosmer give in their writings vivid and friendly descriptions of Trotsky in these years. Of the many eye-witness accounts and character-sketches, friendly and hostile, only a few will be mentioned here: L.-O. Frossard, *Sous le Signe de Jaurès* and *De Jaurès à Lénine*; B. Bajanov, *Avec Staline dans le Kremlin*; R. Fischer, *Stalin and German Communism*; F. Brupbacher, *60 Jahre Ketzer*; Clare Sheridan, *Russian Portraits*, the early writings of Radek, Bukharin, Sadoul, Eastman, Holitscher, L. Fischer.

appeared more than life-size; and his speech resounded with all its old heroic tones. Yet the country was tired of heroism, of great vistas, high hopes, and sweeping gestures; and Trotsky still suffered from the slump in his popularity caused by his recent attempts to militarize labour. His oratorical genius still cast its spell on any assembly. But the spell was already shot through with doubt and even suspicion. His greatness and revolutionary merits were not doubted; but was he not too spectacular, too flamboyant, and perhaps too ambitious?

His theatrical manner and heroic style had not struck people as odd in earlier years when they accorded with the drama of the time. Now they carried with them a suggestion of histrionics. Yet he behaved as he did because he could not behave otherwise. He did not posture to appear more than life-size—he could not help appearing it. He spoke an intense and dramatic language not from affectation or craving for stage effect, but because this was his most natural language, best suited to express his dramatic thought and intense emotion. One might apply to him the words in which Hazlitt described a man as different from him as Burke. He 'gave a hold to his antagonists by mixing up sentiment and imagery with his reasoning', and 'being unused to such a sight in the region of politics' people 'were deceived, and could not discern the fruit from the flowers . . .'. 'The generality of the world' was as always 'concerned in discouraging any example of unnecessary brilliancy.' But 'his gold was not the less valuable for being wrought into elegant shapes'; and 'the strength of a man's understanding is not always to be estimated in exact proportion to his want of imagination. His understanding was not the less real because it was not the only faculty he possessed.'

Like Burke, Trotsky was 'communicative, diffuse, magnificent'. He too conversed in private as he spoke in public, and addressed his family and friends in the same images, with the same wit, and even in the same rhythmical cadences which he used on the platform and in his writings. If he was an actor, then he was one to whom it made no difference whether he found himself on the proscenium, in the green-room, or at his home—one to whom theatre and life were one. He was indeed the heroic character in historic action; and because of this he must appear unreal and unnatural to a prosy or jaundiced generation; and because of this he seemed out of place—a stranger—in the unheroic atmosphere of the early N.E.P.

There is no need, however, to overdraw the romantic aspect of Trotsky's character. He remained as strong in his realism as ever. In any case, he was not the veteran 'superfluously lagging on the stage'. He threw himself with zest upon the new economic and social issues posed by N.E.P.; and he did not by any means view N.E.P. through the prism of revolutionary fundamentalism. Absorbed in problems of finance, industry, trade, and agriculture, he placed before the Politbureau and the Central Committee specific proposals of policy about which more will be said later. He used all his inspiring eloquence to defend the uninspiring 'retreat'; and he appeared as the expounder of N.E.P. before the Communist International at its third and fourth congresses in 1921 and 1922.[1] He gave more of his time and energy than before to the International, on the Executive of which he resisted Zinoviev's and Bukharin's inclination to encourage untimely and reckless risings abroad, such as the German *Märzaktion*. He presided over the French Commission of the Comintern and intervened in the conduct of affairs of every major section of the International.

However, the Commissariat of War, domestic economic preoccupations, and the Comintern, did not absorb his whole energy. He was busy with a host of other assignments each of which would have made a full-time job for any man of less vitality and ability. He led, for instance, the Society of the Godless before Yaroslavsky took over its direction. He led it in a spirit of philosophical enlightenment which was least likely to produce those excesses, offensive to the sentiment of the believers, which marred the Society's work under Yaroslavsky. (He even headed a secret Commission for the confiscation and collection of ecclesiastical treasures which were to be used as payment for food imported from abroad to alleviate the famine on the Volga.[2]) He was at this time Russia's chief intellectual inspirer and leading literary critic. He frequently addressed audiences of scientists, doctors, librarians, journalists, and men of other professions, explaining to them where Marxism stood in relation to the issues which occupied them. At the same time he

---

[1] *Chetvertyi Vsemirnyi Kongress Kominterna*, pp. 74–111; and Trotsky, *Pyat Let Kominterna*, pp. 233–40, 460–510.   [2] *The Trotsky Archives.*

resisted within the party the tendency which was already becoming apparent to impose a deadly uniformity upon the country's cultural life.[1] In many articles and speeches he insisted in a more popular vein on the need to civilize the uncouth Russian way of life, to cultivate manners, to raise hygiene, to improve the spoken and written language which had been debased since the revolution, to widen and to humanize the interests of party members, and so on, and so on. With Lenin already somewhat withdrawn from the public eye, he was the party's chief and most authoritative spokesman in these, the last years of the Lenin era.

Nor did his romantic temperament revolt as yet against the harsh realism with which the party, or rather the Old Guard, established and consolidated its political monopoly. After as before the promulgation of N.E.P., he was indeed one of the sternest disciplinarians, although his call for discipline was based on persuasive argument and appeal to reason. He still extolled the party's 'historic birthright';[2] and he argued that the procedures of proletarian democracy could not be observed in conditions of social unsettlement and chaos, that the fate of the revolution should not be made dependent on the unstable moods of a shrunken and demoralized working class, and that it was the Bolsheviks' duty towards socialism to maintain their 'iron dictatorship' by every means at their disposal. He had once intimated that the party's political monopoly was an emergency measure to be revoked as soon as the emergency was over; but this was not what he said now. More than a year after the Kronstadt rising, writing in *Pravda* on the signs of economic recovery and on the 'upward movement' noticeable in all fields, he posed the question whether the time had not come to put an end to the single-party system and to lift the ban at least on the Mensheviks. His answer was a categorical No.[3] He now justified the monopoly not so much by the republic's internal difficulties as by the fact that the republic was a 'besieged fortress' within which no opposition, not even a feeble one, could be tolerated. He pleaded for the enforcement of the single-party system during the whole period of Russia's international isolation, which he did not, however, expect to last as long as it was to last. Recalling

[1] See Chapter III.   [2] See *The Prophet Armed*, pp. 508–9.
[3] *Pravda*, 10 May 1922; and *Pyat Let Kominterna*, pp. 373–4.

that he himself had once ridiculed attempts made by governments to suppress political opposition and had demonstrated their ultimate inefficacy, he excused his apparent change of attitude with the following argument which would be flung back at him one day: 'Repressive measures', he wrote, 'fail to achieve their aim when an anachronistic government and régime applies them against new and progressive historic forces. But in the hands of a historically progressive government they may serve as very real means for a rapid cleansing of the arena from forces which have outlived their day.'

He reasserted this view in June 1922, during the famous trial of the Social Revolutionaries. He produced a brilliant and ferocious exposure of the defendants, holding them to be politically responsible for Dora Kaplan's attempt on Lenin's life and for other terroristic acts. The trial took place at the time of the 'conference of three Internationals' in Berlin. At that conference, which aimed at establishing a 'united front' between Communist and Socialist parties in the west, Bukharin and Radek represented the Bolsheviks. Western Social Democratic leaders protested against the trial; and to smooth negotiations Bukharin and Radek promised that the defendants would not be sentenced to death. Lenin was indignant at Bukharin's and Radek's 'yielding to blackmail' and at their allowing European reformists to interfere with domestic Soviet affairs. Trotsky was not less indignant. But in order to avoid a breach of the undertaking he proposed a compromise by which death sentence was pronounced but then suspended on the express condition that the Social Revolutionary party refrained from committing and encouraging further terroristic attempts.[1]

Trotsky's disciplinarian attitude showed itself inside the party as well. On behalf of the Central Committee he indicted the Workers' Opposition before the party and Communist International. Since the tenth congress, at which its activity and views had been condemned, the Workers' Opposition had continued to attack the party leadership with increasing bitterness. Shlyapnikov and Kollontai charged the government with promoting the interests of the new bourgeoisie and of the kulaks,

---

[1] *Pravda*, 16, 18 May and 18 June 1922; Lenin, *Sochinenya*, vol. xxxiii, pp. 294–8; *The Second and Third International and the Vienna Union*; Trotsky, *Moya Zhizn*, vol. ii, pp. 211–12.

with trampling upon the workers' rights, and with the gross betrayal of the revolution. Defeated in the party and threatened by Lenin with expulsion, they appealed against Lenin to the Communist International. At the Executive of the International Trotsky presented the case against them and obtained the dismissal of their appeal.[1] Then, at the eleventh congress of the Russian party, in the spring of 1922, which was again called upon to pronounce itself on the matter, Trotsky once again acted as counsel for the prosecution.[2] He spoke without ill will or rancour and even with a certain warmth of sympathy for the Opposition; but he nevertheless firmly upheld the indictment. The Workers' Opposition, he said, acted within its rights when it took the unprecedented step of appealing against the Russian party to the International. What he held against Shlyapnikov and Kollontai was that they had introduced an intolerably violent tone into the dispute and that they spoke of themselves and the party in terms of 'we' and 'they', as if Shlyapnikov and Kollontai 'had already another party in reserve'. Such an attitude, he said, led to schism and provided grist to the mills of the enemies of the revolution. He defended the government, its rural policy, its concessions to private property, and also its view, equally strongly attacked, that ahead lay 'a long period of peaceful coexistence and of business-like cooperation with bourgeois countries'.[3]

The Workers' Opposition was not alone in voicing disillusionment. At the eleventh congress, the last attended by Lenin, Trotsky saw himself and Lenin attacked by old and intimate friends: Antonov-Ovseenko, who spoke about the party's surrender to the kulak and foreign capitalism;[4] Ryazanov, who thundered against the prevalent political demoralization and the arbitrary manner in which the Politbureau ruled the party;[5] Lozovsky and Skrypnik, the Ukrainian commissar, who protested against the over-centralistic method of government, which, he said, was all too reminiscent of the 'one and indivisible' Russia of old;[6] Bubnov, still the Decemist, who spoke about the danger of the party's 'petty bourgeois degeneration';[7] and Preobrazhensky, one of the leading economic theorists and former

[1] *11 Syezd RKP (b)*, appendix.　　　[2] Ibid., pp. 138–57.
[3] Ibid., p. 144.　　　[4] Ibid., pp. 80–83.　　　[5] Ibid., pp. 83–87.
[6] Ibid., pp. 77–79.　　　[7] Ibid., pp. 458–60.

secretary of the Central Committee.[1] One day most of the critics would be eminent members of the 'Trotskyist' Opposition; and one day Trotsky himself would appeal, as Shlyapnikov and Kollontai had done, against the Russian Central Committee to the International. But for the time being, heartily applauded by Lenin, he confronted the Opposition as mouthpiece of the Bolshevik Old Guard, demanding discipline, discipline, and once again discipline.

And yet he remained a stranger in the Old Guard as well—in it but not of it. Even at this Congress of 1922 Mikoyan, then still a young Armenian delegate, stated this from the platform without being contradicted. In the course of the debate Lenin, Zinoviev, and Trotsky had expressed uneasiness over the merger of party and state, and had spoken about the need to separate in some measure their respective functions. Mikoyan then remarked that he was not surprised to hear this view from Trotsky who was 'a man of the state but not of the party'; but how could Lenin and Zinoviev propound such ideas?[2] Mikoyan did not speak from his own inspiration. He summed up what many members of the Old Guard thought but did not yet utter in public: in their eyes Trotsky was the man of the state but not of the party.

Now, when the Old Guard found itself elevated to an un-dreamt-of height, above the people, the working class, and the party, it began to cultivate its own past, and also the legends about it, with a pietism which is never quite absent from any group of veterans with memories of great battles fought and great victories won in common. The nation had known little or nothing about the men who, having risen from the obscurity of an underground movement, stood at its head. It was time to tell the people who those men were and what they had done. The party historians dug up the archives and set out to reconstruct their epic story. The tale they told was one of almost super-human heroism, wisdom, and devotion to the cause. They did not by any means concoct the tale in cold blood. Much of it was true; and they sincerely believed even in that which was not quite true. As the members of the Old Guard viewed themselves in the dim mirror of the past, they inevitably saw that mirror brightened up and their own reflections in it enlarged by the

---

[1] Ibid., pp. 89–90.　　　　　　　　　　　　[2] Ibid., pp. 453–7.

PLATE III

Trotsky leaving his 'military train'

PLATE IV

Trotsky and General Muralov, Army Inspector and Commander of Moscow

retrospective glare of the victorious revolution. But as they looked into that mirror they invariably saw in it Trotsky as their antagonist, the Menshevik, the ally of the Mensheviks, the leader of the August bloc, and the bitter polemicist who had been dangerous to them even when he stood alone. They re-read all the excoriating epithets he and Lenin had once exchanged in open controversy; and the archives, which contained unknown manuscripts and letters, yielded many other rough remarks the two men had made about each other. Every document bearing on the party's past, no matter how trivial, was treasured and published with reverence. The question arose whether Trotsky's old anti-Bolshevik tirades should be withheld from publication. Olminsky, the comptroller of the party archives, put the question to him, when Trotsky's letter to Chkheidze, written in 1912, and describing Lenin as 'intriguer', 'disorganizer', and 'exploiter of Russian backwardness', was discovered in the files of the Tsarist gendarmerie.[1] Trotsky objected to publication: it would be foolish, he said, to draw attention to disagreements which had long since been lived down; besides, he did not think that he had been wrong in all that he had ever said against the Bolsheviks, but he was not inclined to go into involved historical explanations. The offensive document did not appear in print; but its contents were too piquant for copies not to be circulated among old and trusted party men. So this, they commented, is how Trotsky denigrated Lenin in a letter. And to whom?— To Chkheidze, the old traitor; and he still says that he was not altogether wrong! True, Trotsky had since made ample amends, if these were at all needed; in 1920, when Lenin was fifty years old, Trotsky paid his tribute to Lenin and wrote a character sketch of him, which was as incisive in its psychological truth as it was full of admiration.[2] All the same, the odd episodes from the past reminded those who had never felt anything but adoration for the party's founder how relatively recent was Trotsky's conversion to Bolshevism.

Not only memories of old feuds prevented the Old Guard from acknowledging Trotsky as its man. His strong personality had not become submerged in the Old Guard or taken on its protective colouring. He towered above the old 'Leninists' by

---

[1] *The Trotsky Archives.* Trotsky's letter to Olminsky is dated 6 December 1921.
[2] *Pravda,* 23 April 1920.

sheer strength of mind and vigour of will. He usually arrived at his conclusions, even when they coincided with those of others, from his own premises, in his own way, and without reference to the axioms consecrated by party tradition. He stated his opinion with an ease and freedom which contrasted strikingly with the laboured style of orthodox formulas in which most of Lenin's disciples expressed themselves. He spoke with authority, not as one of the scribes. The very width and variety of his intellectual interests aroused a sneaking suspicion in men who, from necessity, self-denial, or inclination, had accustomed themselves to concentrate narrowly on politics and organization and who prided themselves on their narrowness as on their virtue.

Thus, almost everything in him, his fertile mind, his oratorical boldness, his literary originality, his administrative ability and drive, his precise methods of work, the exacting demands he made on associates and subordinates, his aloofness, the absence of triviality in him, and even his incapacity for small talk—all this induced in the members of the Old Guard a sense of inferiority. He never bothered to stoop down to them and he was not even aware that he might do so. Not only did he not suffer fools gladly—he always made them feel that they were fools. The men of the Old Guard were much more at ease with Lenin whose leadership they had always accepted and who usually spared their susceptibilities. When Lenin, for instance, attacked a political attitude which he knew that some of his followers shared, he was careful not to attribute that attitude to those whom he hoped to wean from it; and so he always allowed them to retreat without losing face. When he was intent on converting anyone to his view, he conversed with the man in such a manner that the latter went away convinced that he had himself, by his own reasoning and not under Lenin's pressure, arrived at a new viewpoint. There was little of that subtlety in Trotsky, who could rarely withstand the temptation to remind others of their errors and to insist on his superiority and foresight.

His very foresight, not less real because of its ostentatiousness, was offensive. His restless and inventive mind perpetually startled, disturbed, and irritated. He did not allow his colleagues and subordinates to abandon themselves to the inertia of circumstances and ideas. No sooner had the party decided

upon a new policy than he laid bare its 'dialectical contradictions', seized its consequences, anticipated new problems and
difficulties, and urged new decisions. He was the born trouble-
maker. His judgement, even though it turned out to be correct
in most cases, inevitably aroused resistance. The rapidity with
which his mind worked left others breathless, exhausted, resentful, and estranged.

And yet, almost a stranger in Moscow, in the Kremlin, and
within the Old Guard, by Lenin's side he still dominated the
stage of the revolution.

.   .   .   .

In April 1922 an incident occurred which did much to
cloud relations between Lenin and Trotsky. On 11 April, at
a session of the Politbureau, Lenin proposed that Trotsky
should be appointed deputy chairman of the Council of People's
Commissars. Categorically and somewhat haughtily Trotsky
declined to fill this office. The refusal and the manner in which
it was made annoyed Lenin; and much was made of this in the
new controversies which, added to old animosities, divided the
Politbureau.[1]

Lenin had hoped that Trotsky would consent to act as his
deputy at the head of the government. He made the proposal
a week after Stalin had become the party's General Secretary.
Even though the General Secretary was supposed only to give
effect to the Politbureau's and the Central Committee's decisions, Stalin's appointment was calculated to enhance discipline
in the ranks. Lenin, we know, had already demanded the
expulsion of the leaders of the Workers' Opposition; and at the
Central Committee he failed by only one vote to obtain for this
the necessary two-thirds majority.[2] He expected that Stalin
would enforce the ban on organized inner party opposition
which the tenth congress had declared in a secret session. In
these circumstances it was almost inevitable that the General
Secretary should assume wide discretionary powers.

Lenin had had his misgivings about Stalin's appointment;
but having brought it about he apparently sought to counter-
vail it by placing Trotsky in a post of comparable influence and

---

[1] *The Archives.*
[2] This was on 9 August 1921—the fact was frequently referred to at the eleventh
congress, *11 Syezd RKP (b)*, pp. 605–8 and *passim*.

responsibility at the Council of Commissars. He may have designed this distribution of offices between Stalin and Trotsky as a means towards that separation of party and state on the need for which he had insisted at the Congress. For the separation to be effective it was necessary, so it seemed, that the work of the government machine should be directed by a man as strong-minded as the one who would manage the party machine.

In Lenin's scheme, however, Trotsky was not to be the only vice-Premier. Rykov, who was also chief of the Supreme Council of the National Economy, and Tsurupa, the Commissar of Supplies, already held the same title. Later Lenin proposed that Kamenev too should fill a parallel post.[1] Each vice-Premier supervised certain branches of the administration or groups of Commissariats. But although nominally Trotsky was to be only one of three or four vice-Premiers, there can be little doubt that it was Lenin's intention that he should act as his real second in command. Without any formal title Trotsky had acted in this capacity in any case by the sheer force of his initiative in every field of government; and Lenin's proposal was calculated to regularize and enhance his status.

How anxious Lenin was that Trotsky should occupy the post can be seen from the fact that he returned to the question over and over again and that he made the same proposal several times in the course of nine months. When he first put it forward in April, he was not yet ill; and the thought of the succession to his leadership had probably not yet crossed his mind. But he was overworked and tired. He suffered from long spells of insomnia and was compelled to try to lighten his own burden of office. Before the end of May he was struck down by the first attack of paralysis, and he did not return to work until October. Yet, on the 11 September, still ill and warned by doctors to take an absolute rest, he telephoned Stalin asking that the question of Trotsky's appointment should be placed again in the most formal and urgent manner before the Politbureau. Finally, early in December, when the problem of the succession was already causing Lenin grave anxiety, he took up the matter once again, this time directly with Trotsky and in private.

Why did Trotsky refuse? His pride may have been hurt by

[1] Lenin, *Sochinenya*, vol. xxxiii, pp. 299–306, 316–18.

an arrangement which would have placed him formally on the same footing as the other vice-Premiers who were only Lenin's inferior assistants. He said that he saw no reason for so many vice-Premiers; and he commented sarcastically on their ill-defined and overlapping functions.[1] He also made a distinction between the substance and the shadow of political influence and held that Lenin had offered him the shadow. All levers of the government were in the hands of the party's Secretariat, i.e. in Stalin's hands. The antagonism between him and Stalin had outlasted the civil war. It was ever present in the differences over policy and the bickerings over appointments that went on at the Politbureau. Trotsky had no doubt that even as Lenin's deputy he would depend at every step on decisions taken by the General Secretariat which selected the Bolshevik personnel for the various government departments and by this alone effectively controlled them. On this point his attitude, like Lenin's, was self-contradictory: he wanted the party, or rather the Old Guard, to be in exclusive command of the government; yet he sought to prevent the party machine from interfering with the government's work. The two things could not be had simultaneously, if only because the Old Guard and the party machine were largely, though not altogether, identical. Having rejected Lenin's proposal, Trotsky at first canvassed his own scheme for an overhaul of the administration; but then he formed the conviction that no such scheme would produce the results desired as long as the powers of the General Secretariat (and of the Orgbureau) were not curtailed.

Personal animosities and administrative disagreements were, as usual, mixed up with wider differences over policy.

The Politbureau's chief concern was now with the conduct of economic affairs. The broad outlines of the New Economic Policy were not under debate. All agreed that war communism had failed and that it had to be replaced by a mixed economy, within which the private and the socialist (i.e. the state-owned) 'sectors' would coexist and in a sense compete with one another. All saw in N.E.P. not merely a temporary expedient but a long-term policy, a policy providing the setting for a gradual transition to socialism. Everybody took it for granted that N.E.P. had a dual purpose: the immediate aim was the revival

[1] See Trotsky's comments to the Politbureau of 18 April 1922 in *The Archives*.

of the economy with the help of private enterprise; and the basic purpose was to promote the socialist sector and to ensure its gradual extension over the whole field of the economy. But if in these general terms the policy commanded common assent, differences arose when the general principles had to be translated into specific measures. Some Bolshevik leaders saw primarily the need to encourage private enterprise; while others, without denying this need, were above all eager to promote the socialist sector.

In the first years of N.E.P. the prevalent mood was that of an extreme reaction against war communism. The Bolsheviks were anxious to convince the country that it need not be afraid of any relapse into war communism; and they themselves were convinced that such a relapse would be impermissible (except in war). Nothing was more important than to save the economy from utter ruin; and they saw that only the farmer and the private trader could *begin* to save it. They regarded therefore no incentive offered to the farmer and the trader as too liberal. The results were not long in showing themselves. Already in 1922 the farmers harvested about three-quarters of a normal pre-war crop. This brought about a radical change in the country's condition, for in a primitive agricultural country one good harvest can work wonders. Famine and pestilence were overcome. But this first success of N.E.P. at once threw into relief the dangers of the situation. Industry recovered very slowly. In 1922 it produced only one-quarter of its pre-war output; but even this slight advance on previous years occurred mainly in light industry, especially in the textile mills. Heavy industry remained paralysed. The country was without steel, coal, and machines. This threatened once again to bring to a standstill light industry which could not repair or renew its machinery and lacked fuel. Prices of industrial goods soared out of the consumers' reach. The rise was due to vast unsatisfied demand, underemployment of plant, scarcity of raw materials, and so on; and the situation was made even worse by the Bolsheviks' lack of experience in industrial management and by bureaucratic inefficiency. Stagnation in industry threatened to react adversely upon farming and to break once again the still tenuous 'link' between town and country. The peasant was reluctant to sell food when he was unable to buy industrial goods for his money. Concessions to private farming and trading, necessary though these had been, could not by themselves solve the problem. Nor could 'the market' be expected to take care of it and to resolve it rapidly, through the spontaneous action of supply and demand, without detriment to the government's socialist aspirations.

The government did not see clearly how to deal with the situation. It lived from hand to mouth. It applied palliatives; and the choice of these was dictated by the prevalent reaction against war communism. The Bolshevik leaders had burned their fingers in a reckless attempt to abolish all market economy; and so they were now wary of interfering with the market. Under war communism they had allowed no scruple to hold them back from extracting food and raw materials from the peasant; and so they were now above all anxious to appease the peasant. They hoped that the continued intense demand for consumer goods would keep the wheels of industry turning, and that heavy industry would somehow muddle through to recovery. The same attitude showed itself in financial policy. Under war communism money and credit, despised as relics of the old order, were supposed to be withering away. Then the Commissariat of Finance and the State Bank rediscovered the importance of money and credit and invested their resources in enterprises which were immediately profitable rather than in those that were of national importance. They pumped credit into light industry and neglected heavy industry. Up to a point this reaction against war communism was natural and even useful. But party leaders like Rykov and Sokolnikov, who were in charge of the economic and financial departments, tended to carry the reaction to an extreme.

It should be recalled that no differences over the promulgation of N.E.P. had divided Trotsky from the other leaders. He had himself advocated the principle underlying N.E.P. a year before the Central Committee came to adopt it; and so it was not for nothing that he reproached Lenin privately that the government tackled urgent economic matters with a delay of two years or a year and a half.[1] But having been the first to advocate N.E.P., Trotsky did not succumb to the extreme

[1] Trotsky's statements to the Politbureau of 7 August 1921 and of 22 August 1922 in *The Archives*.

reaction to war communism. He was less inclined than were his colleagues at the Politbureau to believe that further concessions to farmers and traders would suffice to ensure recovery, or that the automatic work of the market would restore the balance between farming and industry and between heavy and light industry. Nor did he share Sokolnikov's and Rykov's fresh enthusiasm for the rediscovered virtues of financial orthodoxy.

These differences were of little or no importance in 1921 and early in 1922, before farming and private trade had got into their stride. But later a major controversy began to develop. Trotsky held that the first successes of N.E.P. necessitated an urgent revision of industrial policy, and that it was imperative to quicken the pace of industrial recovery. The 'boom' in light industry was superficial and narrowly based; and it could not go on for long unless light industry was enabled to repair and renew machinery. (Farming too needed tools to maintain progress.) A concentrated effort was therefore necessary to break the deadlock in heavy industry: the government must work out a 'comprehensive plan' for industry as a whole, instead of relying on the work of the market and the spontaneous play of supply and demand. A schedule of economic priorities should be fixed and heavy industry should have first claim. Resources and manpower should be rationally concentrated in those state-owned concerns which were of basic importance to the national economy, while establishments which could not contribute effectively and rapidly towards recovery should be closed down, even if this exposed their workers to temporary unemployment. Financial policy should be subordinated to the needs of industrial policy and guided by the national interest rather than by profitability. Credits should be directed into heavy industry; and the State Bank should make long-term investments in its re-equipment. Such a reorientation of policy, Trotsky argued, was all the more urgent because of the lack of balance between the private and the socialist sectors. Private business was already making profits, accumulating capital and expanding while the bulk of state-owned industry worked at a loss. The contrast between the two sectors created a threat to the socialist objectives of the government's policy.

These ideas, which thirty and forty years later were to become truisms, seemed far-fetched at first. Even more far-fetched appeared to be Trotsky's insistence on the need for planning. That planning was essential to a socialist economy was a Marxist axiom with which the Bolsheviks were, of course, familiar and which they had always accepted in general terms. Under war communism they imagined that they were in a position to establish immediately a fully fledged planned economy; and Trotsky then met with no opposition when he spoke of the need for a 'single plan' to assure balanced economic reconstruction.[1] Just before the end of war communism, on 22 February 1921, the government decided to form the State Planning Commission, the *Gosplan*. But after the introduction of N.E.P., when all efforts were directed towards reviving the market economy, the idea of planning suffered eclipse. So much had the idea been associated in people's thoughts with war communism that a reminder of it appeared to be out of season. True, just after the promulgation of N.E.P., on 1 April 1921, the State Planning Commission was constituted and Kzhizhanovsky was appointed as its chief. But the new institution led a shadowy existence. Its prerogatives were ill defined; few were eager to define them; and it had no power to devise long-term policy, and to plan or carry plans into operation. It merely advised industrial managements on their day-to-day administrative troubles.[2]

Almost from the first Trotsky criticized this state of affairs. He held that with the transition to N.E.P. the need for planning had become more and not less urgent, and that the government was wrong in treating it as a marginal or merely theoretical issue. Precisely because they lived again under a market economy, he argued, the government must seek to control the market and to equip itself for control. He renewed the demand for a 'single plan', without which, he said, it was impossible to rationalize production, to concentrate resources in heavy industry, and to redress the balance between the various sectors of the economy. Finally, he asked that the prerogatives of the Gosplan be clearly defined so that it should become a fully fledged planning authority, empowered to assess productive capacities, manpower, and stocks of raw materials, to fix targets of production

[1] Trotsky, *Sochinenya*, vol. xv, pp. 215–32. Even then, however, Lenin wrote in a short and expressive note to Kzhizhanovsky: 'We are paupers. Starving, destitute paupers. A comprehensive . . . plan for us = "bureaucratic Utopia".' Lenin, *Sochinenya*, vol. xxxv, p. 405.

[2] *Pyat Let Sovietskoi Vlasti*, pp. 150–2.

for years ahead, and to ensure 'the necessary proportionality between various branches of the national economy'. As early as on 3 May 1921, Trotsky was already writing to Lenin: 'Unfortunately, our work continues to be carried out planlessly and without any understanding of the need for a plan. The State Planning Commission represents a more or less planned negation of the necessity to work out a practical and business-like economic plan for the immediate future.'[1]

He found no response at the Politbureau. Lenin was against him. In accordance with classical Marxist theory, Lenin held that planning could be effective only in a highly developed and concentrated economy, not in a country with 20-odd million scattered small farms, a disintegrated industry, and barbarously primitive forms of private trade. It was not that Lenin denied the need for long-term development schemes. He himself jointly with Kzhizhanovsky had put forward a scheme for Russia's electrification and had introduced it with the famous dictum that 'Soviets plus electrification equal Socialism'. But he considered the idea of a 'comprehensive' plan, covering the whole of the nationalized industry, as premature and futile. Trotsky rejoined that even Lenin's electrification scheme was suspended in a void as long as it was not based on a comprehensive plan. How, he asked, could electrification be planned when the output of the industries which were to produce the power plants was not? He too was aware that under present conditions the type of planning which classical Marxist theory had expected was impracticable, because that theory presupposed a modern society with highly developed and fully socialized productive forces. But the comprehensive plan he asked for was to embrace only the state-owned industries, not the private sector; and it was not, he thought, too early to apply it. He saw a contradiction between the fact of state-ownership and the government's inclination to let sundry state-owned enterprises run their affairs in an unco-ordinated manner. National ownership, he argued, had transformed the whole of industry into a single concern which could not be run efficiently without a single plan.[2]

[1] Trotsky's letter to Lenin ('*Po povodu knizhki I. Shatunovskovo*') is in *The Archives*. See also *Leninskii Sbornik*, vol. xx, pp. 208-9. In a note to Zinoviev Lenin remarked: 'Trotsky is in a doubly aggressive mood.'

[2] Trotsky had argued on these lines even on the eve of NEP. See *Sochinenya*, vol. xv, pp. 215-32, 233-5.

This was a bold view at the time. Even bolder was the idea of 'primitive socialist accumulation' which Trotsky began to expound in 1922.[1] This was an adaptation of one of Marx's historical notions to the conditions of a socialist revolution in an under-developed country. Marx had described as the era of primitive accumulation the initial phase in the development of modern capitalism when normal accumulation of capital had hardly begun or was still too feeble to allow industry to expand from its own resources, that is from its own profits. The early bourgeoisie shrank from no violent, 'extra-economic' method in its striving to concentrate in its hands the means of production; and it went on using those methods until capitalist industry was strong and profitable enough to plough large profits back into production and to acquire a self-perpetuating and expanding basis within its own structure. Expropriation of the yeoman peasantry, plunder of colonies, piracy, and later also the underpayment of wages had been the main sources of that primitive accumulation, which in England, the classical country of capitalism, lasted over centuries. Only when this process was relatively far advanced did the era of normal accumulation set in and 'legitimate' profits formed the main, though not the only, basis for large-scale investment and continued industrialization.

What then was primitive socialist accumulation to be? Marxists had never imagined that socialism too might have to go through a phase of development comparable to the primitive accumulation of capitalism. They had always taken it for granted that a socialist economy would rise on the foundations of modern industrial wealth accumulated by bourgeois society and then nationalized. But there had not been enough of that wealth in Russia; and still less was left after the ravages of recent years. Having proclaimed socialism as their objective, the Bolsheviks now found that the material foundations for socialism were lacking in Russia. They had to lay these first. They had, Trotsky argued, to embark upon primitive accumulation which would differ from its predecessors in that it would be carried out on the basis of social ownership.

He had no intention of suggesting that a socialist government should or could adopt the 'bloody and disgraceful' methods of

[1] See his address at the fifth congress of the Communist Youth on 11 October 1922. *Sochinenya*, vol. xxi, pp. 294–317.

exploitation and plunder which Marx had associated with bourgeois primitive accumulation, or that socialism could come into
the world as capitalism had come 'dripping from head to foot,
from every pore, with blood and dirt'. But intensive and rapid
capital formation was necessary. Soviet industry could not yet
expand by the normal process of ploughing profits back into
production. Most of it still worked at a loss; and even if it did
not, it would still be incapable of producing surpluses large
enough to sustain rapid industrialization, that *conditio sine qua
non* of socialism. The nation's accumulation fund could be
increased either at the expense of the earnings of private business
and farming or of the nation's wages bill. Only some time later
did Trotsky begin to urge heavier taxation on the N.E.P.-men
and the wealthier peasants. At present, in 1922, he merely
pointed out with much force that the economy was run and
could be reconstructed and expanded only at the workers'
expense. He said, for instance, at a congress of the Comsomol in
October: 'We have taken over a ruined country. The proletariat,
the ruling class in our state, is compelled to embark upon a
phase which may be described as that of primitive socialist
accumulation. We cannot content ourselves with using our pre-
1914 industrial plant. This has been destroyed and must be
reconstructed step by step by way of a colossal exertion on the
part of our labour force.' And again: the working class 'can
approach socialism only through the greatest sacrifices, by
straining all its strength and giving its blood and nerves . . .'.[1]

His pleas at once aroused resistance. Men of the Workers'
Opposition had already said that N.E.P. stood for the New
Exploitation of the Proletariat; and the quip had become something of a slogan. Trotsky's argument came as if to illustrate the
truth of the charge and to give point to it. Was he not in fact
trying to argue the workers into submission to the new exploitation? He retorted that of exploitation it was proper to speak
only when one social class was made to toil and slave for the
benefit of another. He asked the workers to toil for their own
benefit. At the worst, he said, he might be accused of trying to
argue them into 'self-exploitation', for he called the workers to
make 'sacrifices' and to give their 'blood and nerves' for their
own proletarian state and their own socialist industry.[2]

[1] Loc. cit.   [2] Loc. cit.

This was not the first time that Trotsky rested his case on the identification of the working class with the state. In 1920 and 1921 he had argued in the same terms against the autonomy of the trade unions. The workers, he had said, had no interests of their own to defend against their own state. Lenin then replied that the proletarian state invoked by Trotsky was still an abstraction: it was not yet a workers' state proper, it often had to strike a balance between workers and peasants and, worse still, it was bureaucratically deformed. The workers were bound in duty to defend their state, but they should also defend themselves against it.[1] When Trotsky now again claimed that the interests of the working class and of its state were identical he laid himself open to the same criticism. Was it not in the name of an abstract idea that he urged the workers to shoulder the main burden of primitive socialist accumulation? Would not the bureaucracy and perhaps even the kulak and the N.E.P.-man be the chief beneficiaries? And how could primitive socialist accumulation be pursued if the working class refused to bear the brunt? These questions were to loom large in coming years. Immediately Trotsky replied that the policy he advocated could not and should not be imposed upon the workers—only with their consent could it be pursued. The chief difficulty was therefore of an 'educational character': the workers should be made aware of what was necessary and what was demanded of them, for without their willingness and socialist enthusiasm nothing could be achieved.[2] Once again he attempted to strike the heroic chord in the working class, as he had done, with overwhelming success, in 1919 when the White Armies threatened Moscow and Petrograd; and as he had again tried and utterly failed to do in the winter of 1920-1, before the Kronstadt revolt. It should be added that his advocacy of primitive socialist accumulation did not at this stage meet with objections within the Politbureau, although most of its members preferred not to compromise their popularity and face the workers with the frank demand for their 'blood and nerves'.

Such were the main economic ideas which Trotsky expounded in the early years of N.E.P., when he acted in effect as the fore-runner of the Soviet planned economy. He was not their sole

[1] *10 Syezd RKP (b)*, pp. 208 ff.; *The Prophet Armed*, pp. 509-10.
[2] *Sochinenya*, vol. xxi, loc. cit.

originator. What he said represented the collective thought of a small circle of theorists and administrators who were close to Trotsky even though some of them did not approve of his disciplinarian attitudes. According to Trotsky himself, Vladimir Smirnov, the leader of the Decemists, who served on the Supreme Council of the National Economy, first coined the term 'primitive socialist accumulation'.[1] Evgenii Preobrazhensky must be regarded as the chief theorist of the idea: his work *The New Economics*, which appeared in 1925, is distinguished by a greater depth of strictly theoretical argument than can be found in Trotsky's writings; and he undoubtedly mooted his theses in 1922–3. Yuri Pyatakov, who was the moving spirit of the Council of the National Economy, and also argued for a single economic plan, was disturbed by the condition of heavy industry, and criticized the credit policy of the Commissariat of Finance and of the State Bank.[2] No doubt, Trotsky made borrowings from these men, and perhaps from others also. But they were too absorbed in theorizing or too immersed in administration to produce more than either abstract treatises or fragmentary empirical conclusions. Trotsky alone transformed their ideas and conclusions into a programme of policy which he defended before the Politbureau and expounded before a nation-wide audience.

Lenin continued to show little enthusiasm for the 'single plan' and for the 'enlargement of the Gosplan's powers'. He described his electrification plan as the 'only serious work on the question' and dismissed the 'idle chatter' about a 'comprehensive' plan. Stalin did likewise; and he did his utmost to widen the breach between Lenin and Trotsky.[3] The lesser leaders, Rykov and Sokolnikov, saw Trotsky's policy as an encroachment upon their own responsibilities. They were sceptical of planning; and they were opposed to investing the Gosplan with wide powers. In their own circle they commented—presently they were to make the charge in public—that Trotsky demanded such wide powers for the Gosplan because he hoped to assume its direction, and that having ceased to be the country's military

---

[1] *12 Syezd RKP (b)*, p. 321; E. A. Preobrazhensky, *Novaya Ekonomika*, vol. i, part 1, p. 57.   [2] *The Trotsky Archives.*
[3] See Stalin's *Sochinenya*, vol. v, pp. 50–51, where, in a letter to Lenin, he describes Trotsky's ideas on planning as those of 'a medieval artisan who imagines himself an Ibsenite hero destined to save Russia . . .'.

dictator he aspired to become its economic master. We do not know whether Trotsky did indeed wish to become the head of the Gosplan. Even if he did, the aspiration was hardly reprehensible. He criticized Kzhizhanovsky, the actual head of Gosplan, as inefficient;[1] but he never put forward his own candidature; and he argued the case on its merits. However, personal ambitions and departmental jealousies again and again intruded. Thus his opponents suggested that an enhanced Gosplan would compete with the Council of Labour and Defence over which Lenin presided, with Trotsky as his deputy. At a session of the Central Committee, on 7 August 1921, Trotsky replied that in his view the Council should remain in charge of high policy, but that Gosplan should translate that policy into specific economic plans and supervise their execution. He failed to carry the Central Committee with him.[2]

Parallel with these controversies there dragged on a conflict over the Rabkrin, the Workers' and Peasants Inspectorate. Stalin had been the chief of Rabkrin, from 1919 till the spring of 1922, when he was appointed Secretary General; but he exercised a strong influence on it even later. The Inspectorate had wide and manifold functions: it was entitled to audit the morals of the civil service; to inspect without warning the work of any Commissariat; to watch over the efficiency of the entire administration, and to prescribe measures for raising it. Lenin intended that Rabkrin should act as a sort of super-commissariat through which the administration, which was not controlled democratically, was to control itself and maintain stern self-discipline. In reality, Stalin transformed the Inspectorate into his private police within the government. As early as 1920 Trotsky attacked Rabkrin, claiming that its methods of inspection were muddled and ineffective, and that all that it did was to throw spanners into the machinery of government. 'You cannot', he said, 'create a special department endowed with all the wisdom of government and able to audit all the other departments. . . . In every branch of government it is well known that whenever the need arises for any change of policy or for any serious reform in organization it is useless to look to Rabkrin for guidance. Rabkrin itself provides striking illustration

---

[1] Lenin referred to this criticism in his letter to the Politbureau of 5 May 1922. See his *Sochinenya*, vol. xxxiii, pp. 316–18.   [2] *The Trotsky Archives*.

of the lack of correspondence between governmental decree and governmental machinery, and is itself becoming a powerful factor of muddle and wantonness.' In any case, what was needed in a body like Rabkrin was a 'broad horizon, a broad view on matters of the state and of the economy, a view much broader than that possessed by those carrying out this work'. He described Rabkrin as the refuge and haven for frustrated misfits who had been rejected by all other commissariats and were 'utterly cut off from any genuine, creative, and constructive work'. He did not even once mention Stalin in whom he saw the super-misfit risen to eminence.[1]

Lenin defended Stalin and Rabkrin. Exasperated by the inefficiency and the corruption of the civil service, he pinned great hopes on the Inspectorate and was irritated by what he considered to be Trotsky's private vendetta.[2] Trotsky argued that the muddle, at least in the economic departments, was the result of faulty organization which, in its turn, reflected the lack of any guiding principle in economic policy. Inspections by Rabkrin could not change this—the remedy could be found in planning and in a reformed Gosplan. Nor could incompetence be cured by the shock treatment and intimidation to which Stalin's commissariat subjected the civil service. In a backward country, with the worst traditions of uncivilized and corrupt government, Trotsky said, the main task was to educate the government personnel systematically and to train it in civilized methods of work.

All these differences considered, Trotsky's refusal to become vice-Premier is less surprising. He could not, without contradicting himself, accept a post in which he would have had to give effect to an economic policy which in his view lacked focus, and to guide an administrative machinery which he held to be faultily constructed. When, in the summer of 1922, Lenin urged him to use the post for a drive against bureaucratic abuses of power, he replied that the worst abuses had their source at the very top of the party hierarchy. He complained that the Politbureau and the Orgbureau meddled intolerably with the affairs of the government and took decisions concerning various commissariats without deigning to consult even the

[1] Trotsky, *Sochinenya*, vol. xv, p. 223.
[2] Lenin, *Sochinenya*, vol. xxxiii, loc. cit. and *passim*.

heads of those commissariats. It was therefore vain to struggle against wantonness in the administration as long as this evil flourished unopposed in the party.[1] Lenin did not take Trotsky's hint. He relied on Stalin as the party's General Secretary not less than he relied on him as chief of Rabkrin.

In the summer of 1922 further disagreement arose over the manner in which Moscow controlled the non-Russian republics and provinces of the Soviet Federation. The Bolsheviks had guaranteed to those republics the right of self-determination, which included expressly the right to secede from the Soviet Federation; the guarantee had been enshrined in the 1918 Constitution. At the same time they insisted on strictly centralized government and in practice overruled the autonomy of the non-Russian republics. Early in 1921, it will be remembered, Trotsky protested against the conquest of Georgia, of which Stalin had been the chief prompter. Then Trotsky reconciled himself to the accomplished fact and even defended the conquest in a special pamphlet.[2] Later still, in the spring of 1922, he remained silent when at the eleventh congress eminent Bolsheviks accused Lenin's government of forsaking the principle of self-determination and restoring the 'one and indivisible' Russia of old. Shortly thereafter, however, he himself voiced the same accusation behind the closed doors of the Politbureau; and it was again over Georgia and Stalin's activities there that the conflict came to a head.

As Commissar of Nationalities, Stalin had just ordered the suppression of the Menshevik party in Georgia. When leading Georgian Bolsheviks, Mdivani and Makharadze, protested against this he sought to intimidate them and to quell their protests.[3] His action was up to a point consistent with the general trend of Bolshevik policy, for if it was right to ban the Menshevik party in Moscow, there was no apparent reason why the same should not be done at Tiflis. Trotsky had endorsed the ban in Russia, but attacked its extension to Georgia. He pointed out that the Russian Mensheviks had, because of their counter-

[1] See Trotsky's letters to the Politbureau of 22 August 1922, and of 15, 20, and 25 January 1923 in *The Archives*. Also *Moya Zhizn*, vol. ii, p. 216.

[2] *The Prophet Armed*, pp. 474–5.

[3] Mdivani, Makharadze, Ordjonikidze, Yenukidze, Stalin, and Bukharin gave accounts of the conflict in *12 Syezd RKP (b)*, pp. 150–76, 540–65. See also Deutscher, *Stalin, a Political Biography*, pp. 236–46.

revolutionary attitude, discredited themselves while the Georgian ones still enjoyed strong popular support. This was true
enough; but the argument might have carried conviction only
if the Bolsheviks had still based their rule on proletarian democracy. It sounded somewhat hollow once the view was accepted,
as it was by Trotsky, that the Bolsheviks were entitled, in the
interest of the revolution, to maintain their political monopoly
regardless of whether they did or did not enjoy popular support.
It was only a step from the establishment of the single-party
system to the persecution of those Georgian Bolsheviks who
opposed it, although this was a step from consistency to absurdity. Stalin for the first time now applied repression to
members of the Bolshevik party when he tried to intimidate
Mdivani and Makharadze. He also gravely compromised the
Bolshevik policy towards the non-Russian nationalities, the policy
of which he himself had been an inspirer and in the broad-
mindedness of which the Bolsheviks had taken great pride.

Defending themselves, Mdivani and Makharadze turned
against the ultra-centralistic principle of Stalin's policy. What
right, they asked, had any Commissariat in Moscow to take
decisions concerning the political life of Tiflis? Where was self-
determination? Were not the small nationalities being forced
back into the Russian empire, 'one and indivisible'? These were
pertinent questions. All the more so as at the same time Stalin
was preparing a new constitution which was to be much more
centralistic than its 1918 predecessor and was to curtail and
abrogate the rights of the non-Russian nationalities and to transform the Soviet *Federation* of republics into the Soviet *Union*.
Against this constitution, too, the Georgians, the Ukrainians,
and others raised protests.

When these protests came before the Politbureau Trotsky upheld them. He was now confirmed in the misgivings which had
caused him to oppose in the first instance the annexation of
Georgia. He saw in Stalin's behaviour a scandalous and flagrant
abuse of power, which carried centralism to a dangerous excess,
offended the dignity of the non-Russian nationalities, and suggested to them that 'self-determination' was a fraud. Stalin and
Ordjonikidze prepared an indictment of Mdivani and Makharadze and alleged that these 'national deviationists' opposed
the introduction of the Soviet currency in Georgia, refused to

co-operate with neighbouring Caucasian republics and to share with them scarce provisions, and that they generally acted in a spirit of nationalist selfishness and to the detriment of the Soviet Federation as a whole. Such behaviour, if the charges had been true, could not be tolerated in party members. Trotsky did not believe the charges to be true. Lenin and most members of the Politbureau viewed the conflict as a family quarrel between two sets of Georgian Bolsheviks; and they thought that the most prudent course for the Politbureau was to accept Stalin's views. Stalin was the Politbureau's expert on these matters; and Lenin saw no reason to suspect that Stalin, of all men, the author of the celebrated treatise on *Marxism and the Nationalities*, the party's classical plea for self-determination, would malignantly offend the national dignity of his own countrymen. Again Trotsky appeared to Lenin to be acting from personal animosity or from that 'individualism' which had led him to oppose the Politbureau on so many other questions. One of Lenin's first moves after his return to office, in October 1922, was to rebuke Mdivani and Makharadze and uphold Stalin's authority.

. . . .

As we follow these dissensions in the Politbureau and consider Trotsky's part in them, we are struck by the change which had occurred in Trotsky himself in about a year. In the first half of 1922 Trotsky still spoke primarily as the Bolshevik disciplinarian; in the second he was already in conflict with the disciplinarians. The contrast shows itself in many of his attitudes; but it becomes most apparent when it is recalled that at the beginning of the year he indicted, on behalf of the Politbureau, the Workers' Opposition before the party and the International. Yet towards its end he himself appeared to air views hitherto voiced by that Opposition (and by the Decemists). It was the Workers' Opposition which had first confusedly expressed the discontent of the Bolshevik rank and file with N.E.P. and had spoken of the need to give the policies of N.E.P. a socialist perspective. It was the Workers' Opposition which had first attacked the new bureaucracy, protested against abuses of power, and denounced new privileges. It was that Opposition and the Decemists who had begun the revolt against the excessive powers of the party machine and had clamoured for

the restitution of inner-party democracy. Trotsky at first castigated them and warned them that Bolsheviks must under no
circumstances oppose themselves to the party leaders in terms
of 'we' and 'they'. Yet, in the course of 1922, he appeared to
have adopted most of their ideas and to have taken up an attitude from which he was bound to argue against the majority
of the Politbureau in terms of 'we' and 'they'. It looked, indeed,
as if in the process of taming the Workers' Opposition he had
been converted to its views and become its most eminent
recruit.

In truth he was grappling all this time with a dilemma
which occupied the party as whole—only he grappled with it
more intensely than others. It was the dilemma between authority
and freedom. Trotsky was almost equally sensitive to the claims
of both. As long as the revolution was struggling for bare survival, he put authority first. He centralized the Red Army,
militarized labour, strove to absorb the trade unions in the
state, preached the need for a strong but civilized bureaucracy,
overruled proletarian democracy, and helped to subdue inner-
party opposition. Yet even in this phase the socialist 'libertarian' was alive and awake in him; and through his sternest
calls for discipline there reverberated, like a counterpoint, a
powerful note of socialist freedom. In his most ruthless deeds
and most severe words there still glowed a warm humanity
which distinguished him from most other disciplinarians. In
the very first phase of the revolution he was already pointing
an accusatory finger at the 'new bureaucrat', uneducated,
suspicious, and arrogant, who was a baneful 'ballast', and a
'genuine menace to the cause of communist revolution', the
cause which would 'fully justify itself only when every toiling
man and woman feels that his or her life has become easier,
freer, cleaner, and more dignified'.[1]

The end of armed hostilities sharpened the tension between
authority and freedom within Bolshevism; and within Trotsky
too. The Workers' Opposition and the groups close to it represented a revulsion against authority. What set Trotsky against
them was his deep grasp of the realities of the situation. He
could not easily dismiss those claims of authority which were
rooted in realities. Nor could he keep his peace of mind when

[1] *The Prophet Armed*, p. 427.

he saw that freedom—socialist freedom—was being uprooted. He wrestled with a real dilemma, whereas the Workers' Opposition seized only one of its horns and clung to it. He sought to strike a balance between Bolshevik discipline and proletarian democracy; and the more the balance was tipped in favour of the former, the more was he inclined to uphold the latter. The decisive shifts which upset the balance occurred in the years 1921–3; and in these years he gradually came to put the claims of inner-party democracy against those of discipline.

Yet he did not become a mere 'libertarian', resentful at the encroachments of authority. He remained the Bolshevik *statesman*, as convinced as ever of the need for a centralized state and a strong party leadership, and as mindful as ever of their prerogatives. He attacked the abuse, not the principle, of those prerogatives. Through his most angry broadsides against bureaucracy and his most spirited pleas for inner-party democracy there would still resound a strong disciplinarian counterpoint. Conscious that 'bureaucracy represented a whole epoch, not yet closed, in mankind's development', and that its evils appeared 'in inverse proportion to the enlightenment, the cultural standards, and the political consciousness of the masses',[1] he was careful not to induce the illusion that it was possible to sweep away those evils at a stroke. As yet he did not even turn against bureaucracy at large—he rather appealed to its progressive and enlightened men against its backward and despotic elements, and hoped that the former, together with the advanced workers, would be able to curb, to re-educate, and if need be to eliminate the latter. He had indeed shifted his ground, come closer to the Workers' Opposition and kindred groups, and implicitly acknowledged the rational side of their revulsion against authority; but, unlike them, he was not carried away by the revulsion. He did not simply 'reject' bureaucracy. He still grappled with a real dilemma, but he did it in a different manner than before and from the opposite end.

It is for this reason that it is impossible to pinpoint the change in Trotsky's attitude and to define more precisely what brought it about and when it occurred. No single event brought it about; and there was no single moment at which it was brought about. The policy of the Politbureau drifted over many issues

[1] Trotsky, *Sochinenya*, vol. xv, pp. 218–21; *The Prophet Armed*, p. 503.

from a workers' democracy to the totalitarian state. Trotsky's
ideas drifted with the drift of Bolshevik policy—but in the
opposite direction. He began to protest against the excesses of
centralism as these made themselves felt. He began to defend the
rights of the small nations as these rights were being violated.
He clashed with the party 'apparatus' as the apparatus grew
independent of the party and subjected party and state to itself. Because the processes against which he reacted developed
piecemeal and in an ambiguous manner, his reactions, too, were
piecemeal and vague. At no point did he feel the need for any
drastic revision of his views because what he said now, in his
anti-bureaucratic phase, he had also said in his disciplinarian
phase, although he had said it with less emphasis and in a
different context. He passed from one phase into the other
almost without noticing it.

Amid the drift of policies one relatively stable issue stood out
—the rivalry between Stalin and Trotsky. It had, we remember,
intruded itself even in the conduct of the civil war; and it had
sprung from an almost instinctive antagonism of temperaments,
backgrounds, political inclinations, and personal ambitions. In
this rivalry Stalin played the active and offensive part—he
was offended by the inferiority of the place he occupied. Only
slowly did Trotsky take cognizance of the rivalry; and only
reluctantly did he begin to react and to get involved in it. So
far the rivalry had remained in the background, where Lenin's
strong personality kept it; and it had not assumed any broader
significance, for it was not yet identified with any clear conflict
of policies and interests. In 1922 this identification began. As
manager of the party machine, Stalin, supported for the time
being by Lenin, came to represent authority at its extreme, to
enforce its claims and to exact obedience. A deep conflict of
policies and interests began to take shape, to absorb the personal
antagonism, and even to focus itself on it, until the personal
antagonism was thus at once overshadowed and yet magnified
by the wider conflict.

.   .   .   .

An account of the disagreements in which Trotsky was
opposed to Lenin, Stalin, and the majority of the Politbureau,
may leave a one-sided impression of his actual position in the

Bolshevik leadership. The biographer is bound to throw into relief the events and situations out of which grew Trotsky's later struggles with Stalin and which were therefore of the greatest consequence to his fortunes. These events and situations did not, however, appear in the same bold relief to contemporaries. Nor were the discords related here of the greatest importance in determining Trotsky's place among the Bolshevik leaders, especially his relationship with Lenin. The controversies were confined to the Politbureau. The party and the country had no inkling of them. The public voice still coupled Trotsky's name with Lenin's; and in the eyes of the world he was one of the chief inspirers of Bolshevik policy. And in truth, his disagreements with Lenin did not, in the balance of their common work, outweigh their solid and close agreement on an incomparably wider range of domestic and foreign issues.

As Commissar of War Trotsky continued to enjoy Lenin's full support. Even after the civil war he had to contend with the 'military opposition' which had challenged his policy in earlier years. Tukhachevsky still sought to win the party's support for his pet idea of an International General Staff of the Red Army. Frunze and Voroshilov, encouraged by Zinoviev and Stalin, still tried to obtain official sanction for their conceptions of 'proletarian strategy' and for their 'offensive military doctrine'. These issues were important enough to be thrashed out at the eleventh congress at a special session held in secret.[1] Trotsky obtained the final disavowal of the demands of his opponents; and he was assisted by the fact that he had Lenin's authority behind him. Lenin had learned to value his military work so much that he accepted almost automatically his judgement in that field. A curious incident may be cited as illustration. After the Kronstadt rising Lenin suggested to Trotsky that the Baltic Navy be scuttled or 'closed down'. The sailors, he held, were unreliable; the navy was useless; it consumed coal, food, and clothing, of which the country was desperately short; and so its disbandment would be a pure gain. Trotsky objected. He was determined to preserve the navy and was confident that he could reorganize it and bring about a change in its morale. The matter was settled in a most informal manner, through

[1] Trotsky's speech made at that session is in *Kak Vooruzhalas Revolutsia*, vol. iii, book 2, pp. 244 ff. See *The Prophet Armed*, pp. 484-5.

little private notes which Trotsky and Lenin scribbled to each other during a session of the Politbureau. Lenin accepted Trotsky's assurances, and the navy was saved.[1]

Lenin also repeatedly indicated to the party and the International his regard for Trotsky as interpreter of Marxism; and he lent wholehearted support to the outstanding influence Trotsky exercised on Russia's cultural life. (This aspect of Trotsky's activity is discussed in a later chapter.) Both rejected the ambition of clamorous groups of writers and artists, especially of the *Proletkult*, to sponsor a 'proletarian culture' and 'proletarian literature'. In educational affairs which since the civil war both considered to be of paramount importance, and in all matters relating to the advocacy of Marxism, both counselled caution and tolerance; and both discouraged firmly the crudity of approach, the conceit, and the fanaticism, which influential party members began to exhibit.

Trotsky showed also a highly active and constant initiative in the conduct of foreign policy. Important issues of diplomacy were decided upon by a small committee which consisted of Lenin, Trotsky, and Kamenev, who invited Chicherin, the Foreign Commissar, and often also Radek, to take part in deliberations. The present efforts of Soviet diplomacy were directed towards the consolidation of peace and the establishment of relations with bourgeois Europe. Trotsky, we remember, had used all his influence to secure the final conclusion of peace with Poland in 1921, a peace for which Lenin had not been so eager. He had similarly exerted himself to obtain the Politbureau's consent to the demarcation of frontiers and to the conclusion of peace with the small Baltic republics.[2] As early as 1920 Trotsky had urged Lenin to conciliate Great Britain; but it was only some time later that this advice was acted upon. But his most important initiative in the diplomatic field came early in 1921, when he set afoot a number of bold and highly delicate moves which eventually led to the conclusion of the Rapallo Treaty with Germany, by far the most outstanding feat of Soviet diplomacy in the two decades that lay between the Brest Litovsk Treaty and the Soviet-German agreement of 1939.

---

[1] This happened at the session of 21 March 1921. *The Trotsky Archives*. Some months later Trotsky mentioned the incident in a public speech. *Kak Vooruzhalas Revolutsia*, vol. iii, book 1, p. 81.   [2] See *The Prophet Armed*, pp. 463–70.

As Commissar of War Trotsky was anxious to equip the Red Army with modern weapons. The Soviet armament industry, primitive and run down, could not supply them. Through his agents abroad he purchased munitions wherever he could, even as far as the United States. But the purchases were haphazard and the Red Army was dangerously dependent on foreign supplies. Trotsky was bent on building up with foreign assistance a modern armament industry in Russia. But where, the question arose, could such assistance be obtained? Which bourgeoisie would consent to help in the building up of the military power of a communist government? There was only one country to which he could turn with a prospect of success; and that was Germany. Under the Versailles Treaty Germany had been forbidden to manufacture munitions. Her armament factories, the most modern in Europe, stood idle. Could not their owners be tempted to supply equipment and technological advice, if the enterprise was made sufficiently attractive? At the beginning of 1921 Victor Kopp, the former Menshevik who had once worked for the Viennese *Pravda*, established, on Trotsky's behalf, secret contacts with the great concerns of Krupp, Blohm und Voss, and Albatross Werke. As early on as 7 April 1921 he reported that these concerns were prepared to co-operate and to supply equipment and technological assistance needed for the manufacture in Russia of planes, submarines, artillery, and other munitions. Throughout the year envoys travelled between Moscow and Berlin; and Trotsky kept Lenin and Chicherin informed about every phase. The Politbureau authorized him to pursue the negotiations in the strictest secrecy; and he held their threads in his hands during all these preliminaries to the Rapallo Treaty, until the moment came for the diplomats to act.[1]

As the negotiations proceeded, the scope of transactions widened. Not only the armament industries were idle in Germany. The old and splendid officers' corps was also unemployed. Its members were therefore glad to undertake to instruct Russian soldiers and airmen; and in exchange they were allowed to train secretly in Russia German military cadres, whom they could not train at home. Thus the groundwork was laid for that long co-operation between the Reichswehr and the Red Army

[1] Kopp's report and Trotsky's and Lenin's notes are in *The Trotsky Archives*.

which was to outlast Trotsky's tenure of office by a full decade
and which contributed greatly to the modernization of the
Soviet armed forces before the Second World War.

However, till the spring of 1922 all these moves were still
tentative; and there was hesitation in both Moscow and Berlin,
for here and there diplomacy still hoped for a *rapprochement* with
the powers of the Entente at the forthcoming Genoa conference, the first international gathering to which both Germany and Soviet Russia, hitherto the outcasts of diplomacy, were
invited. Only when these hopes failed was the Rapallo Treaty
concluded. The Treaty was a 'sober and business-like' bargain
rather than a genuine alliance. Anxious to obtain for themselves
through give and take as much advantage as possible, the Bolsheviks were as a rule careful not to encourage revisionism and
a movement of revenge in the Reich, although they themselves
had, as a matter of principle, denounced the Versailles Treaty
from the outset, when their government was not even recognized by Germany and when the memories of the Brest Litovsk
Diktat were still fresh.

Trotsky in particular worked to prevent any entanglement of
Soviet policy with German nationalism. After as before Rapallo
he sought to improve Russia's relations with France. In the
autumn of 1922 he received in the Kremlin Edouard Herriot,
who, as leader of the *Cartel de Gauche*, was presently to become
French Prime Minister. Herriot describes the visit in detail and
recalls the strength of conviction with which Trotsky argued for
an improvement of relations between their countries. He assured
Herriot that it was only the Entente's blind hostility that had
driven Russia to come to terms with Germany first at Brest
Litovsk and then at Rapallo; and that the Rapallo Treaty contained no clauses directed against France. He evoked the Jacobin tradition of France and appealed to French statesmen and
French opinion for a greater understanding of the Russian
Revolution. As he spoke about the affinity of Jacobinism and
Bolshevism, Herriot recalls, a detachment of Red Army men
marched past singing the *Marseillaise* in French and through the
open window the words *Nous saurons mourir pour la liberté* burst
into the conference room.[1]

---

[1] E. Herriot, *La Russie nouvelle*, pp. 157–8.

The importance which diplomacy had by now assumed in Soviet affairs was connected with the defeats of communism outside Russia. In Europe the tide of revolution had ebbed, and the Communist International had run aground. Its parties led only a minority of the European working class and they were not in a position to undertake with any chance of success a frontal attack on the bourgeois order. Yet, most Communist parties refused to acknowledge defeat and were inclined to rely on their own strength and to go on staging revolts and coups in the hope that if they tried persistently enough they would carry the majority of the workers with them. A reorientation of the International was overdue; and this was the joint work of Lenin and Trotsky. With regard to the International they acted in a close and intimate partnership which, as far as can be ascertained, was not even once disturbed by the slightest discord.[1]

Neither Trotsky nor Lenin had abandoned their fundamental belief that the October upheaval in Russia had opened an era of international proletarian revolution; and Trotsky was to cling to this conviction throughout the next two decades, to the end of his life. But he now came to realize that the class struggle outside Russia was more complicated and protracted than he and others had at first imagined. He no longer took its outcome for granted; and he was anxious to dispel complacency about this and 'ultra-left' illusions in the International. Thus, in July 1921, he made a striking criticism of those Communists who held that the advent of socialism was 'inevitable'.[2] Such a belief in the predetermined progress of society, he said, was based on a 'mechanistic' misinterpretation of the Marxist approach to history.

Mankind has not always and not invariably moved upwards. . . . It has known in history long spells of stagnation. It has known relapses into barbarism. There have been instances . . . when society, having reached a certain height of development, was incapable of maintaining itself on that height. . . . Mankind can never be at a standstill. Any equilibrium, which it may attain in consequence of struggles between classes and nations, is unstable by its very nature. A society which does not rise must decline. A society from which no

---

[1] Lenin and Trotsky were the only two Soviet leaders elected Honorary Presidents at the third congress of the International. *Tretii Vsemirnyi Kongress Kominterna*, p. 16.　　　　[2] *Pyat Let Kominterna*, pp. 266–305.

class emerges capable of securing its ascendancy disintegrates. The road is then open to barbarism.

Such had been the main cause of the breakdown of the antique civilizations: the upper classes of Rome and Greece had decayed; and the exploited classes, the slaves, had been inherently incapable of revolutionary action and political leadership. This was a warning for our age. The decay of the bourgeois order was undeniable. True, American capitalism was still a dynamic and expansive force, although even in the United States socialism could already develop the nation's resources more rationally and with greater benefit to society than capitalism did. But European capitalism was historically at the end of its tether. It did not significantly develop its productive forces. It had no progressive role to play. It could open up no new vistas. If this were not so all thought of proletarian revolution in our time would be quixotic. But although European capitalism was decaying, the bourgeois order did not and would not collapse by itself. It had to be overthrown, and only the working class could overthrow it in revolutionary action. If the working class were to fail in this, then Oswald Spengler's gloomy prediction of the *Untergang des Abendlandes* would come true. History confronted the workers with a challenge as if saying to them: 'You ought to know that if you do not overthrow the bourgeoisie, you will perish under the ruins of civilization. Try and carry out your task!'[1]

Meanwhile European capitalism had withstood the shocks of world war and post-war crises. The possessing classes of Western Europe had learned their lessons from the Russian revolution: they did not allow themselves to be taken by surprise as Tsardom did; and they mobilized all their resources and strategic ideas. The appearance of fascism—Trotsky said this in 1922, the year of Mussolini's march on Rome—was a symptom of that mobilization; and there was the danger, he added, that 'a German Mussolini' might also rise to power.[2]

All this was of grave omen to the further course of socialist revolution. The whole development, with its peculiar sequence of phases unforeseen by earlier Marxists, might put socialism at a disadvantage. Proletarian revolution would have produced

[1] Loc. cit.   [2] Op. cit., p. 563.

the best results if it had occurred first in the United States or, as a second best, in Britain, against the background of highly developed productive resources. Instead the revolution had won in Russia, where it found only limited possibilities to demonstrate its advantages. It would find itself placed under even worse handicaps in the countries of Asia and Africa which were more backward than Russia. This led Trotsky to make the melancholy remark that *'History seems to be unwinding her skein from the other end'*, that is from the countries which are least mature.[1]

He did not cease to hope that 'the skein' would still unwind from the Western, the European, end as well. The delays of revolution, the mobilization of counter-revolution, the prospect of a stalemate in the class struggle, and of the decadence of European civilization were for him not certainties to be accepted fatalistically, but dangers to be acted against and averted. The chances were still overwhelmingly in favour of revolution; but much depended on the attitude of the Communist parties. It was their duty to lead European society out of the impasse. They had to struggle for leadership. They could succeed in this only if they became militant and conscious parties, versed in the strategy and tactics of revolution, and accustomed to concert their efforts under strict international discipline. They were bound to fail if they remained only a radical variety of the old Social Democratic parties, if they cherished illusions about bourgeois parliamentarianism, and if they worked only within the framework of their national politics. But they would fail just as surely if, reacting against the Social Democratic tradition, they were to become narrow, self-centred sects, rigid in outlook and tactics; if they contented themselves with purely negative and arid boycott of the institutions of bourgeois society instead of promoting the revolutionary idea even from within those institutions; and if they went on trying to storm the bastions of capitalism without paying due regard to the circumstances and the balance of forces.

The Communist parties were not immediately confronted with revolutionary opportunities. Their job was to gather strength and to win over the majority of the workers without whose support no revolution could ever succeed.

Together with Lenin, Trotsky worked out the tactics of the

[1] Op. cit., pp. 429–30.

'united front'.[1] The gist of it was this: the Communist parties, still too weak to overthrow the established order, should be the most active participants in the 'day-to-day' struggles of the workers for higher wages, shorter hours, and democratic freedoms. They should not change the idea of socialism into the small coin of trade unionism and parliamentary reform, but carry into the struggle for 'partial demands' their own revolutionary spirit and purpose. They should make the workers realize how tenuous were all the gains they could win under capitalism and so rally them, even through the fight for such gains, for the last battle. The Social Democrats directed the struggle for 'partial demands' in such a way as to contain the workers' militant energy within the framework of capitalism; and they used reform as the diversion from revolution. The Communists, on the contrary, should use it as the spring-board of revolution.

But since Communists had to fight for partial gains and reforms they had some common ground, however narrow, with the Social Democrats and the moderate trade unionists. They should try to concert action with them within a united front. This should remove at least one dangerous consequence of the fundamental and irremediable cleavage between reformism and communism: it should overcome the division of the working class and prevent the dispersal of its energies. Marching separately, Communists and reformists should strike jointly at the bourgeoisie whenever they were threatened by it or could wrest concessions from it. Common action should extend to parliaments and elections, in which Communists must be prepared to support Social Democrats. But the main arena of the united front lay outside parliaments, in trade unions, in industry, and 'in the street'. The Communists had to pursue a double objective: they should seek to secure the immediate success of the united front; and at the same time assert their own viewpoint within the united front in order to wean Social Democratic workers from reformist habits of mind and to develop in them a revolutionary consciousness.

Lenin had expounded these ideas as early as 1920 in the

[1] Trotsky presented the 'Report on the World Crisis and the Tasks of the International' at the second session of the congress on 23 June 1921. Radek presented the 'Report on Tactics', in place of Zinoviev who was inclined towards the 'ultra-left' opposition. *Tretii Vsemirnyi Kongress Kominterna.*

Infantile Disease of 'Leftishness' in Communism, where he dwelt on the harm done to communism by unreasoning ultra-radical sectarians. The need for a firm and formal disavowal of 'ultra-radicalism' became pressing after the German March rising of 1921. It was then that Lenin placed proposals for the united front before the Executive of the International. He met with strong opposition from Zinoviev, Bukharin, Bela Kun, and others. For a moment it seemed that the ultra-radicals would prevail. It was only after animated debates in the course of which Lenin and Trotsky jointly faced the opposition that the Executive was persuaded to authorize the policy of the united front and to instruct both Lenin and Trotsky to expound it at the forthcoming congress of the International.[1]

At the congress, in July 1921, the ultra-radicals made a stand. They exercised a strong influence on the German, Italian, and Dutch parties and they drew their strength from a powerful emotional current in the whole International. The Communist parties had come into existence in a desperate struggle against the leaders of the old Socialist parties whom they blamed for supporting the 'imperialist slaughter' of 1914–18, for the subsequent suppression of revolution in Europe, for the assassination of Rosa Luxemburg and Karl Liebknecht, and for an ambiguous attitude towards European intervention in Russia. No wonder that many Communists were bewildered and indignant when they now heard Lenin and Trotsky urging them to acknowledge defeat, be it temporarily, and to co-operate with the hated 'social imperialists' and 'social traitors'. This to the ultra-radicals was surrender or even betrayal. At the congress, as earlier on the Executive, Trotsky and Lenin had to use all their influence and eloquence to prevent the opposition from

[1] Alfred Rosmer gives an informative account of these days in *Moscou sous Lenine*, pp. 172–88. Radek, *Pyat Let Kominterna*, vol. ii, preface. At the Executive Lenin made a speech in which he declared his full solidarity with Trotsky and strongly attacked Bela Kun, the spokesman of the ultra-left, repeatedly describing Kun as a 'fool'. The full text of the speech, which I read many years ago, was not available at the time of writing. Trotsky published excerpts from it in his *Bulleten Oppozitsii* (December 1932). Lenin said: 'I have come here in order to protest against Bela Kun's speech who came out against comrade Trotsky instead of defending him— which he should have done if he had wished to act as a genuine Marxist. . . . Comrade Trotsky was a thousand times right. . . . I have considered it my duty to support in all essentials everything comrade Trotsky has said. . . .' Lenin backed Trotsky also against Cachin and Frossard who at the congress represented the extreme right wing. (Ibid.)

gaining the upper hand—they even threatened to split the International if it backed the ultra-radicals.

The congress voted for the united front. But it did so with mental reservations and without a clear grasp of the issues involved. Lenin and Trotsky had set the Communist parties the dual task of fighting arm in arm with the reformists against the bourgeoisie and of wresting from the reformists influence over the working class. The idea of the united front embodied the whole tactical experience of the Bolsheviks who had indeed fought first against Tsardom, then the Cadets, and then Kornilov, in a sort of a united front with the Mensheviks and Social Revolutionaries until, in the end, they gained ascendancy over the latter too. The Bolshevik success was secured not merely by the resourcefulness of the Bolshevik leaders, but by the breakdown of a whole social order and by the subsequent shift *from right to left* typical of all classical revolution. Could such tactics, even if no other tactics were, from the communist viewpoint, realistic, be applied outside Russia with comparable chance of success? In Europe the old order had regained a measure of stability which produced a confused but distinct shift *from left to right*. This alone tended to secure the ascendancy of the reformists within any united front. Nor was there among European Communists a single leader with a mastery of tactics comparable to Lenin's or Trotsky's. And so the European Communists were to prove incapable of applying the united front in both its aspects. Some took to heart their duty to co-operate in all earnestness with the Social Democrats. Others were above all eager to discredit the Social Democrats. Some saw the united front as a serious endeavour to unify the working class in the struggle for partial demands. Others saw it merely as a clever trick. Still others wavered between the opposed views. And so the International began to split into right and left wings and intermediate and extreme groups, 'centrists' and 'ultra-lefts'.

At the congress Trotsky and Lenin contended mainly with opposition from the ultra-radicals; and so at times they appeared to encourage the right wing. Trotsky in particular spoke scathingly and disdainfully about the ultra-radicals, for instance, Arkadi Maslov and Ruth Fischer, the leaders of the communist organization of Berlin, describing them as empty-headed emotionalists, who had little in common with Marxism and might be expected to switch over to the most unprincipled opportunism.[1] He was enthusiastically applauded by all the moderate elements at the congress; and the applause rose to an ovation when on behalf of the majority of the delegates Klara Zetkin, the famous veteran of German communism, paid him a solemn and stirring tribute.[2]

At the next, the fourth, congress Lenin, already ill, spoke only briefly and with great difficulty; and Trotsky came to the fore as the chief expounder of the International's strategy and tactics. He advocated once again the united front. He went a step farther and urged the Communist parties to support, on conditions, Social Democratic governments and even, under special circumstances, in pre-revolutionary situations, when such coalitions could pave the way for proletarian dictatorship, to participate in them.[3] The opposition was outraged. From the first day of its existence the International had declared it an axiom of its policy that a Communist party must never enter any coalition government: its task was to destroy the bourgeois state machine, not to try and capture it from within. However, the congress accepted the tactical innovation; and the Communist parties were instructed to watch for opportunities to form government coalitions with the Social Democrats. This decision was to assume a crucial importance in the crisis of German communism in the autumn of 1923.

Such were the tactical efforts through which Trotsky (and Lenin) still hoped to 'unwind the skein of revolution' from its 'proper', that is from its European, end.

. . . .

Throughout the summer of 1922 the disagreements in the Politbureau over domestic issues dragged on inconclusively. The dissension between Lenin and Trotsky persisted. On 11 September from his retreat in Gorki, outside Moscow, Lenin made contact with Stalin and asked him to place before the Politbureau once again and with the utmost urgency a motion proposing Trotsky's appointment as deputy Premier. Stalin communicated the motion by telephone to those members and

---

[1] Trotsky, *Pyat Let Kominterna*, pp. 288 ff.
[2] *Tretii Vsemirnyi Kongres Kominterna*, p. 58.
[3] See Trotsky's report on the fourth congress in his *Pyat Let Kominterna*.

alternate members of the Politbureau who were present in Moscow. He himself and Rykov voted for the appointment; Kalinin declared that he had no objection, while Tomsky and Kamenev abstained. No one voted against. Trotsky once again refused the post.[1] Since Lenin had insisted that the appointment was urgent because Rykov was about to take leave, Trotsky replied that he, too, was on the point of taking his holiday and that his hands were, anyhow, full of work for the forthcoming congress of the International. These were irrelevant excuses, because Lenin had not intended the appointment to be only a stopgap for the holiday season. Without waiting for the Politbureau's decision, Trotsky left Moscow. On 14 September the Politbureau met and Stalin put before it a resolution which was highly damaging to Trotsky; it censured him in effect for dereliction of duty.[2] The circumstances of the case indicate that Lenin must have prompted Stalin to frame this resolution or that Stalin at least had his consent for it.

Less than a month later an unexpected event put an end to the sparrings between Lenin and Trotsky. At the beginning of October the Central Committee adopted certain decisions concerning the monopoly of foreign trade. The Soviet government had reserved for itself the exclusive right to engage in trade with foreign countries; and it had centralized all foreign commercial transactions. This was a decisive measure of 'socialist protectionism'—the term was coined by Trotsky[3]—designed to defend the weak Soviet economy from hostile pressures and unpredictable fluctuations of the world market. The monopoly also prevented private business from overlapping into foreign trade, exporting essential goods, importing inessential ones, and disrupting even further the country's economic balance. The new decisions of the Central Committee, taken in Trotsky's and Lenin's absence, did not go so far as to admit private business to foreign trade; but they did loosen central control over Soviet trade agencies abroad. This might have enabled individual state concerns working on foreign markets to act independently with a view primarily to their sectional advantage and thus to make a breach in 'socialist protectionism'. In time private business might have benefited from the breach.[4]

---

[1] *The Trotsky Archives.*   [2] Ibid.   [3] Preobrazhensky, op. cit., p. 79.
[4] Lenin, *Sochinenya*, vol. xxxiii, pp. 338–40.

Lenin at once objected to the decision, describing it as a grave threat to the Soviet economy. He was alarmed, irritated, and—paralysed. In brief moments, snatched from his doctors and nurses, he dictated notes and memoranda, protests, and exhortations; but he could not intervene personally with the Central Committee. Then, to his relief, he learned that Trotsky adopted a view identical with his. In the course of nearly two months the issue hung in the balance. On 13 December Lenin wrote to Trotsky: 'I earnestly beg you to take it upon yourself to defend at the forthcoming plenary session [of the Central Committee] our common view about the imperative need to preserve and reinforce the monopoly of foreign trade.' Trotsky readily agreed. But having repeatedly warned Lenin and the Politbureau that their policy encouraged the administration to submit passively to the uncontrolled forces of the market economy, he pointed out that the Central Committee's latest decision showed that his warnings had been all too justified. Once again he urged the need for co-ordination and planning and for vesting wide powers in Gosplan. Lenin still tried to shelve the issue of Gosplan and entreated Trotsky to concentrate on the trade monopoly. 'I think we have arrived at a full agreement', he wrote to Trotsky again, 'and I am asking you to announce our solidarity at the plenary session.' Should they both be outvoted there, then Trotsky should announce that they would both go to any length to nullify the vote: they would both attack the Central Committee in public.[1]

There was no need for them to resort to such drastic action. Contrary to Lenin's fears, when the Central Committee came to review the issue in the second half of December, Trotsky easily persuaded it to reverse its decision. Lenin was all exultation. 'We have captured the position without firing a shot . . .', he commented to Trotsky in a note written 'with Professor Forster's permission',[2] 'I propose that we do not stop but press on with the attack. . . .'[3]

[1] See the correspondence between Lenin and Trotsky of 12–27 December 1922 in *The Trotsky Archives*, and Trotsky, *The Stalin School of Falsification*, pp. 58–63.

[2] Professor Forster was one of Lenin's doctors.

[3] I wrote the first two chapters of this volume in 1954, basing the documentation largely on *The Trotsky Archives*. Only two years later, after Khrushchev's disclosures at the twentieth congress of the Soviet Communist party, were some of these important documents published in Moscow for the first time; and they have

The incident brought the two men closer together than they had been for some time. In the next few days Lenin reflected further over the criticisms of economic policy Trotsky had made in the last two years. He communicated the result of his reflections to the Politbureau in a letter of 27 December:

Comrade Trotsky, it seems, advanced this idea [about the Gosplan's prerogatives] long ago. I opposed it . . . but having attentively reconsidered it I find that there is an essential and sound idea here: Gosplan does stand somewhat apart from our legislative institutions . . . although it possesses the best possible data for a correct judgment of [economic] matters. . . . In this, I think, one could and should go some way to meet Comrade Trotsky. . . .[1]

He realized that this would be a disappointment to members of the Politbureau—hence his apologetic undertone. The Politbureau was indeed annoyed by his sudden conversion and, despite Trotsky's protests, it resolved not to publish Lenin's remarks.[2]

In the last weeks and days of the year Lenin went a very long way to 'meet Comrade Trotsky' on further issues which had separated them. At the beginning of December he once again urged Trotsky to accept the post of vice-Premier.[3] This time he did it in a private talk, not amid the formalities of Politbureau proceedings. The question of the succession was already uppermost in his mind—presently he was to write his will. But he gave no hint of this to Trotsky. Instead he spoke in a tone of grave anxiety about the abuses of power which he saw were getting worse and worse and about the need to curb them. Trotsky did not this time reject the offer outright. He repeated that a drive against bureaucratic abuses in the government would yield little or no result as long as such abuses were

since been included in a special volume (vol. xxxvi) added to the fourth edition of Lenin's *Works.* Comparing the texts I have not had the need to alter a single comma in the quotations taken from *The Trotsky Archives.* Even now, however, only a fraction of the Lenin correspondence which these *Archives* contain, not to speak of other documents, has been published.

[1] *The Archives*; Lenin, *Sochinenya*, vol. xxxvi, pp. 548-9. Lenin in fact completely accepted Trotsky's basic idea, but not his allegation about Kzhizhanovsky's incompetence as head of Gosplan.

[2] *The Archives.* Stalin observed evasively: 'I suppose there is no necessity to print this, especially as we do not have Lenin's authorization.'

[3] Trotsky, *Moya Zhizn*, vol. ii, pp. 215-17.

tolerated in the party's leading bodies. Lenin replied that he was ready for a 'bloc' with Trotsky, that is for joint action against bureaucracy in the party as well as in the state. There was no need for either of them to mention names. Such action could be directed only against Stalin. They did not have the time to pursue the matter and to discuss any plan of action. A few days afterwards Lenin suffered another stroke.

In their last conversation Lenin gave Trotsky no indication that he had also pondered anew the other major issue over which they had differed: Stalin's policy in Georgia. On this, too, he was at last going to 'meet Comrade Trotsky'. He was in the mood of a man who, with one foot in the grave, uneasily looks back on his life's work and is seized by a poignant awareness of its flaws. Some months earlier, at the eleventh congress, he said that often he had the uncanny sensation which a driver has when he suddenly feels that his vehicle is not moving in the direction in which he steers it. Powerful forces diverted the Soviet state from its proper road: the semi-barbarous peasant individualism of Russia, pressure from capitalist surroundings, and above all, the deep-seated native traditions of uncivilized absolutist government.[1] After every spell of illness, when he returned to watch anew the movements of the state machine, Lenin's alarm grew; and with pathetic determination he struggled to grip the steering wheel in his paralysed hands.

The 'vehicle', he discovered, had run into the rut—oh, how familiar—of Great Russian chauvinism. In the second half of December he re-examined the circumstances of the conflict with the Georgian Bolsheviks, the conflict in which he had sided with Stalin. He carefully collected, sifted, and collated the facts. He learned about the brutality with which Stalin and Ordjonikidze, Stalin's subordinate, had behaved in Tiflis; he found that the accusations they levelled against the Georgian 'deviationists' were false, and he grew angry with himself for having allowed Stalin to abuse his confidence and to cloud his judgement.

In this mood, on 23 and 25 December, Lenin dictated that letter to his followers which became in effect his last will and testament. He intended to offer the party guidance about those who would presently be called upon to lead it. He characterized briefly the men of the leading team, so that the party should

[1] Lenin, *Sochinenya*, vol. xxxiii, pp. 235–76.

know which, in his view, were the merits and the faults of each. He contained his emotion and weighed his words so as to convey a judgement based on observation of many years and not a view formed on the spur of the moment.

The party, he wrote, should beware of the danger of a split in which Stalin and Trotsky 'the two most eminent leaders of the present Central Committee', would confront each other as the chief antagonists. Their antagonism reflected as yet no basic conflict of class interest or principle: it still was, he suggested, merely a clash of personalities. Trotsky was 'the most able' of all the party leaders; but he was possessed of 'excessive self-confidence', a 'disposition to be too much attracted by the purely administrative aspect of affairs', and an inclination to oppose himself individualistically to the Central Committee. In a Bolshevik leader these were, of course, important faults, impairing his capacity for teamwork and his judgement. Yet, Lenin added, the party ought not to hold against Trotsky his pre-revolutionary disagreements with Bolshevism. The warning implied that the disagreements had long since been lived down; but Lenin was aware that this was not necessarily the view taken by his disciples.

About Stalin he had only this to say: 'Having become General Secretary, Stalin has concentrated immeasurable power in his hands; and I am not sure that he will always know how to use that power with sufficient caution.' The warning was suggestive but inconclusive. Lenin refrained from offering explicit advice and stating personal preferences. He seemed to place somewhat stronger emphasis on Trotsky's faults than on Stalin's, if only because with Trotsky's qualities he dealt in greater detail. Soon, however, he had afterthoughts; and on 4 January 1923 he wrote that brief and pregnant postscript in which he stated that Stalin's rudeness was already 'becoming unbearable in the office of the General Secretary' and in which he advised his followers to 'remove Stalin' from that office and to appoint to it 'another man . . . more patient, more loyal, more polite, more attentive to comrades, less capricious, etc.'. If this were not to be done, the conflict between Stalin and Trotsky would grow more bitter with dangerous consequences to the party as a whole.[1] Lenin had no doubt that his advice to 'remove' Stalin could only establish Trotsky in the leadership.

[1] Lenin, *Sochinenya*, vol. xxxvi, pp. 545–6.

The understatements of the will and even of the postscript give no idea of the full force of Lenin's fresh fury against Stalin and of his fixed resolve to discredit him once and for all. It was between 25 December and 1 January that Lenin formed this resolution. The Congress of the Soviets had just assembled at which Stalin proclaimed the *Union* of Soviet Socialist Republics in place of the *Federation* established under the 1918 constitution.[1] Having supported this constitutional change, Lenin now suspected that it would do away completely with the autonomy of the non-Russian Republics and indeed re-establish Russia 'one and indivisible'. He formed the opinion that Stalin had used the need for centralized government to screen the oppression of the small nationalities. The suspicion hardened into a certainty when Lenin had a new insight into Stalin's character: he saw him as churlish, sly, and false. On 30 December, just when Stalin was proclaiming the Union, Lenin, cheating once again his doctors and his health, began to dictate a series of notes about policy towards the small nations. This was in effect his last message on the subject; and it was full of heart-searching, passionate remorse, and holy anger.[2]

He wrote that he felt 'strongly guilty before the workers of Russia for not having intervened vigorously and drastically enough in this notorious issue . . .'. Illness had prevented him from doing so, even though he had confided his fears and doubts to Zinoviev. But only now, after he had heard Dzerzhinsky's report on Georgia, did it become quite clear to him 'in what sort of a swamp' the party had landed. All that had happened in Georgia and elsewhere was being justified on the ground that the government must possess a single and integrated administrative machine or 'apparatus'. 'Where do such statements emanate from?' Lenin asked. 'Do they not come from that same Russian apparatus . . . [we had] borrowed from Tsardom and only just covered with a Soviet veneer?' To the small nations 'freedom of secession' from the Union was becoming an empty promise. They were in fact exposed to 'the irruption of that truly Russian man, the Great Russian chauvinist, who is essentially a scoundrel and an oppressor as is the typical

---

[1] Stalin, *Sochinenya*, vol. v, pp. 145–59.

[2] Lenin, op. cit., pp. 553–9. See also L. A. Fotieva's memoirs published in *Voprosy Istorii KPSS*, Nr. 4, 1957.

Russian bureaucrat'. It was high time to defend the non-Russian nationalities from that 'truly Russian *dzerzhymorda* [the great brutish bully of Gogol's satire]. . . . The rashness of Stalin's administrative zeal and his spite have played a fatal role. I fear that Dzerzhinsky too . . . has distinguished himself by his truly Russian state of mind (it is well known that Russified aliens are always much more Russian than the Russians themselves).'

On New Year's Eve Lenin continued:

. . . internationalism on the part of a . . . so called great nation (great only through its acts of oppression, great only in the sense in which the bully may claim to be great)—internationalism on the part of such a nation should consist not merely in respecting formal equality between nations. It is necessary to create such [real] equality as would reduce . . . the actual inequality which arises in life. The Georgian who treats this aspect of the matter with contempt and charges others with being 'social chauvinists' (that Georgian who himself is not merely a genuine social-chauvinist but a coarse brutish bully on behalf of a Great Power) that Georgian is offending against the interests of proletarian class solidarity. . . . Nothing hampers the growth and consolidation of such solidarity as much as does injustice towards smaller nationalities. . . . That is why it is better to show too much conciliation and softness towards national minorities, rather than too little.

The rights of the Georgians, Ukrainians, and others were more important than the need for administrative centralization which Stalin evoked in order to justify 'a quasi-imperialist attitude towards oppressed nationalities'. If need be, Lenin concluded, the new constitution sponsored by Stalin, together with the new centralistic organization of government, would have to be scrapped altogether.

Having expressed himself with so much anguish and merciless bluntness, Lenin apparently intended to turn the matter over in his thoughts and to consider what course of action to take. For over two months he did not communicate his notes to any member of the Politbureau.

.   .   .   .

The upheaval in Lenin's mind which caused him to reverse so many of his crucial policies may appear even more startling and more sudden than the change which had occurred in

Trotsky in 1921 and 1922. It, too, resulted from the intense conflict between the dream and the power of the revolution, a
conflict which was going on in Lenin's mind, and not only in
his. In its dream the Bolshevik party saw itself as a disciplined
yet inwardly free and dedicated body of revolutionaries, immune from corruption by power. It saw itself committed to
observe proletarian democracy and to respect the freedom of
the small nations, for without this there could be no genuine
advance to socialism. In pursuit of their dream the Bolsheviks
had built up an immense and centralized machine of power to
which they then gradually surrendered more and more of their
dream: proletarian democracy, the rights of the small nations,
and finally their own freedom. They could not dispense with
power if they were to strive for the fulfilment of their ideals;
but now their power came to oppress and overshadow their
ideals. The gravest dilemmas arose; and also a deep cleavage
between those who clung to the dream and those who clung to
the power.

The cleavage was not clear-cut, because dream and power
were up to a point inseparable. It was from attachment to the
revolution that the Bolsheviks had mounted and operated the
machine of power, which now functioned according to its
own laws and by its own momentum, and which demanded
from them all their attachment. Consequently those who
clung to the dream were by no means inclined to smash the
machine of power; and those who identified themselves with
power did not altogether abandon the dream. The same men
who at one moment stood for one aspect of Bolshevism at the
next moment rushed to embrace its opposite aspect. Nobody
had in 1920–1 gone farther than Trotsky in demanding that
every interest and aspiration should be wholly subordinated to
the 'iron dictatorship'. Yet he was the first of the Bolshevik
chiefs to turn against the machine of that dictatorship when it
began to devour the dream. When subsequently Trotsky became involved in the struggle over the succession to Lenin,
many of those who heard him invoke the revolution's ideals
doubted his sincerity, and wondered whether he did not use
them merely as pretexts in the contest for power. Lenin stood
above any such suspicion. He was the party's undisputed leader;
and he had and could have had no ulterior motive when in the

last weeks of his activity he confessed with a sense of guilt that he had not sufficiently resisted the new oppression of the weak by the strong, and when he used his last ounce of strength to strike a blow at the over-centralized machine of power. He invoked the purpose of the revolution for its own sake, from a deep, disinterested, and remorseful devotion to it. And when at last, a dying man, his mind ablaze, he moved to retrieve the revolution from its heavy encumbrance, it was to Trotsky that he turned as his ally.

CHAPTER II

The Anathema

FROM the beginning of the civil war the Politbureau acted as the party's brain and supreme authority although the party statutes contained no provision even for its existence. The annual congresses elected only a Central Committee which was endowed with the widest powers of determining policy and managing the organization and was accountable to the next congress. The Central Committee elected the Politbureau. At first, the Politbureau was to take decisions only on urgent matters arising during the weekly or fortnightly intervals between the sessions of the Central Committee. Then, as the scope of the affairs with which that Committee had to deal widened, including more and more of the business of government, and as the members of the Committee became increasingly absorbed in manifold departmental responsibilities and were often absent from Moscow, the Central Committee gradually and informally delegated some of its prerogatives to the Politbureau. The Central Committee once consisted only of a dozen or so members; but then it became too big and cumbersome to act effectively. In 1922 it met only once in two months, while the members of the Politbureau worked in close day-to-day contact. In their work they adhered strictly to democratic procedure. Where differences of opinion were marked, they decided by a simple majority. It was within this framework, as *primus inter pares*, that Lenin exercised supreme power.[1]

From December 1922 the problem of the succession to Lenin was uppermost in the Politbureau's mind. Yet in principle the problem could not even exist. With or without Lenin it was the Politbureau as a body (and through it the Central Committee) which was supposed to rule the party; and the will of the Politbureau was what its majority willed. The question therefore became not who would succeed Lenin, but how the alignments in the Politbureau would shape themselves without Lenin, and

[1] *KPSS v Rezolutsyakh*, vol. i, pp. 525, 576–7, 657–8.

what sort of a majority would form itself to provide stable leadership. Stability of leadership had so far rested, at least in part, on Lenin's unchallenged authority and on his powers of persuasion and tactical skill, which, as a rule, allowed him to secure in each matter as it arose majority votes for his proposals. Lenin had no need to form for this purpose any special faction of his own within the Politbureau. The change which occurred either in December 1922, or in January 1923 when Lenin finally ceased to take part in the Politbureau's work, was the creation of a special faction the sole purpose of which was to prevent Trotsky from having a majority which would enable him to take Lenin's place. That faction was the triumvirate of Stalin, Zinoviev, and Kamenev.

The motives which prompted Stalin to set his face against Trotsky are clear enough. Their antagonism dated back to the early Tsaritsyn battles of 1918;[1] and recently Trotsky's wounding criticisms of the Commissar of Rabkrin and of the General Secretary had exacerbated it. In December 1922 or in the following January Stalin could have had no knowledge of the 'bloc' against him which Lenin and Trotsky mooted, of Lenin's resolve to see him removed from the General Secretariat, or of the attack which Lenin was preparing against his policy in Georgia and his 'Great Russian chauvinism'. But he sensed danger.[2] He saw Lenin and Trotsky acting in unison over the trade monopoly and then over Gosplan. He heard Lenin inveighing against bureaucratic misrule; and he probably knew from Zinoviev that Lenin was disturbed by events in Georgia. As General Secretary, Stalin had already gained enormous power: the Secretariat (and the Organization Bureau) had taken over from the Politbureau most of its executive functions and left to it decisions on high policy. Nominally, however, the Politbureau exercised control over the Secretariat and the Orgbureau; and it could prolong or refuse to prolong Stalin's tenure of office. Stalin was convinced that he could expect no good for himself from a Politbureau swayed by Trotsky. At this stage he was anxious merely to preserve the influence he had acquired rather than to take Lenin's place. He was aware that the party saw in him only the supreme technician and

[1] *The Prophet Armed*, pp. 423–6.
[2] See Fotieva, '*Iz Vospominanii o Lenine*' in *Voprosy Istorii KPSS*, Nr. 4, 1957.

manipulator of its machine, but not a policy-maker and an expounder of Marxism such as it would expect Lenin's successor to be. No doubt Stalin's ambition was stung by this lack of appreciation, but his caution induced him to make allowance for it.

Next to Lenin and Trotsky, Zinoviev was by far the most popular member of the Politbureau. He was President of the Communist International; and in these years, when the Russian party had not yet come to use the International as a mere tool, but considered itself to be under its moral authority, the Presidency of the International was the most exalted position for any Bolshevik to occupy. Zinoviev was also the head of the Northern Commune, the Soviet of Petrograd. He was an agitator and speaker of tremendous power; and he was almost constantly before the party's eyes as one of the revolution's giants, an embodiment of Bolshevik virtue, indomitable and implacable. This popular image of his personality did not correspond to his real character, which was complex and shaky. His temper alternated between bursts of feverish energy and bouts of apathy, between flights of confidence and spells of dejection. He was usually attracted by bold ideas and policies which it needed the utmost courage and steadfastness to pursue. Yet his will was weak, vacillating, and even cowardly.[1] He was superb at picking Lenin's brain and acting as Lenin's loud and stormy mouthpiece; but he had no strong mind of his own. He was capable of the loftiest sentiments. In his best moments, in his idealistic vein, he impressed his listeners with such force that in a single speech lasting three hours and made in a foreign language, arguing against the most brilliant and authoritative men of European socialism, he persuaded a divided and hesitant congress of the German Independent Socialist party to join the Communist International.[2] His grip on the imagination of

---

[1] In a letter to Ivan Smirnov (written at Alma Ata in 1928) Trotsky relates this 'short talk' he had had with Lenin soon after the October Revolution: 'I told Lenin: "Who surprises me is Zinoviev. As to Kamenev, I have known him close enough to see where in him the revolutionary ends and the opportunist begins. But I did not know Zinoviev personally [before 1917]; and from accounts of him and appearances I imagined that this was the man who would stop at nothing and be afraid of nothing." To this Vladimir Ilyich replied: "If he is not afraid, it only means that there is nothing to be afraid of . . .".' *The Archives.*

[2] See *Protokoll über die Verhandlungen des Ausserordentlichen Parteitags zu Halle*, and Zinoviev, *Zwölf Tage in Deutschland.*

Russian crowds is described by eye-witnesses as 'demonic'.[1] Yet from the loftiest sentiments he could stoop at once to the meanest tricks and the demagogue's cheapest jokes. In the course of the many years which he had spent by Lenin's side in Western Europe, his quick mind had absorbed a considerable mass of knowledge about the world; yet it remained unrefined and unpolished. His temper was warm and affectionate; yet it was also savage and brutal. Genuinely attached to the principle of internationalism and a man of 'world outlook', he was at the same time a parochial politician inclined to settle the greatest issues by horse trading and petty manœuvre. He had risen to an undreamt-of height; and, devoured by ambition, he strove to rise even higher; but he laboured under inner uncertainty and doubt in himself.

It was Zinoviev's great pride that he had been Lenin's closest disciple in the ten years between 1907 and 1917, the years of reaction, isolation, and despair, when they were both struggling to keep the party in being and to prepare it for the great day, and when, at the time of the Zimmerwald and Kientahl conferences, together they launched on the world the idea of the Third International. But it was Zinoviev's great shame, or so he himself and his comrades thought, that he had failed at his test in October 1917, when he opposed the insurrection and Lenin branded him as 'strike-breaker of the revolution'. Between this shame and that pride his whole political life was torn. He did his best to get over the memories of 1917; and he was helped in this by Lenin, who even in his will begged the party not to remind Zinoviev and Kamenev of their 'historic error'. By 1923 most party members had almost forgotten the grave incident or were not inclined to delve into the past. The Old Guard preferred to let bygones be bygones, if only because the cleavage on the eve of the October Revolution had run right across it and many of its members were then on Zinoviev's side. All the more did the historians and the legend-mongers of the Old Guard turn the limelights on the earlier period, the one in which Zinoviev's great pride resided. If any man could in Lenin's absence speak for the Old Guard then it was surely Zinoviev.

It was unthinkable that he should now accept Trotsky's

[1] This is how Heinrich Brandler and Angelica Balabanoff, among others, have described it.

leadership. Not only was his memory crowded with the many incidents of their pre-revolutionary feud when, encouraged by Lenin, he had often vehemently inveighed against Trotsky.[1] Not only had his great shame been connected with the event on which rested Trotsky's chief title to glory, the October insurrection. Ever since 1917 he had been opposed to Trotsky at almost every crucial turn of Bolshevik policy. He was the most extreme advocate of the peace of Brest Litovsk; and he vaguely encouraged the military opposition to Trotsky during the civil war. In the spring of 1919 Trotsky arrived at Petrograd to organize its defences against Yudenich's offensive after Zinoviev, the city's official leader, had thrown up his hands in panic. During the Kronstadt rising Trotsky blamed Zinoviev for having needlessly provoked it. On the other hand, Zinoviev was one of Trotsky's most vocal critics in the debate over militarization of labour and trade unions.[2] Later, at the Politbureau, he cast his vote against Trotsky over economic policy and Gosplan only to find himself defeated when Lenin 'went over' to Trotsky. Even at the Executive of the International he was again defeated by Trotsky when the latter, together with Lenin, forced through the policy of the United Front. No wonder his attitude towards Trotsky was one of sneaking admiration mingled with envy and that sense of inferiority which Trotsky induced in so many members of the Old Guard.

Zinoviev's attitude was as a rule shared by Kamenev. The political partnership of these two men was so close that the Bolsheviks regarded them as their Castor and Pollux. Paradoxically, however, it was not the likeness but the contrast of their minds and temperaments that made of them political twins. Kamenev, although he headed the party organization of Moscow City, was far less popular than Zinoviev but far more respected in the inner circle of the leaders. Less self-confident on the public platform, not given to oratorical flourishes and heroic postures, he possessed a stronger and more cultivated intellect and a steadier character; but he lacked Zinoviev's fervour and imagination. He was a man of ideas rather than slogans. Unlike Zinoviev, he was as a rule attracted by moderate ideas and policies; but the strength of his Marxist convictions

---

[1] Zinoviev, *Sochinenya*, vols. i, ii, and v; and *Gegen den Strom*.
[2] *The Prophet Armed*, chapters x–xiii.

inhibited him in his moderation—his theoretical thinking was at loggerheads with his political inclination. His conciliatory character suited him well for the part of the negotiator; and in the early days Lenin often used him as the party's chief representative in contacts with other parties, especially when Lenin was anxious for agreement. (In inner-party controversy, too, Kamenev acted as the edge-blunter and the seeker for common ground between opposed viewpoints.) But his moderation repeatedly brought him into conflict with Lenin. During the 'treason' trial of the Bolshevik deputies to the Duma, early in the First World War, Kamenev declared from the dock that he was no adherent of Lenin's 'revolutionary defeatism'; in March and April 1917, before Lenin's return to Russia, he steered the party towards conciliation with the Mensheviks; and in October he was an opponent of the insurrection. Yet it was not courage that he lacked. Nor was he a mere trimmer. Cool and reserved, free from excessive vanity and ambition, he hid behind his phlegmatic appearance an infinite loyalty to the party. His character showed itself on the very day of the October Revolution: having publicly opposed the insurrection, he appeared at the insurgents' headquarters right at the very beginning, put himself at their disposal and wholeheartedly co-operated with them, thus assuming responsibility for the policy he had opposed and courting all the political and personal risks involved.[1]

What attracted him so strongly to Zinoviev was probably the very contrast of their characters. In each of them impulses were active which should have driven them wide apart; but in each strong inhibitions were also at work which kept their conflicting impulses in check, with the result that the two men usually met half-way between the opposed extremes towards which they gravitated.

Kamenev felt none of Zinoviev's and Stalin's intense hostility towards Trotsky, his former brother-in-law; and he might have put up with his leadership more easily than they. It was from sheer devotion to the Old Guard and friendship to Zinoviev that he turned against Trotsky. Whatever his private inclinations and tastes, he was extremely sensitive to the mood which prevailed among the Old Bolsheviks and by it he was swayed. When that mood went against Trotsky, Kamenev, full of mis-

[1] *Protokoly Tsentralnovo Komiteta*, pp. 141–3; *The Prophet Armed*, p. 307.

givings and heartbroken, went with it. He did not and could not hope to gain anything for himself by joining the triumvirate: he had no ambition to become Lenin's successor. But he supported and encouraged the restless ambition of his political twin, in part because he was convinced that it was harmless, that Zinoviev could not take Lenin's place anyhow, and that the triumvirs would in fact rule the party collectively; and partly, because in his moderation Kamenev was genuinely afraid of Trotsky's dominant and imperious personality and of his risky ideas and policies.

Zinoviev, Stalin, and Kamenev, however they differed in their characters and motives, were flesh and blood of the Old Guard; and between them they seemed to embody every aspect of the party's life and tradition. In Zinoviev were found the *élan* and the popular appeal of Bolshevism; in Kamenev its more serious doctrinal aspirations and its sophistication; and in Stalin the self-assurance and the practical sense of its solid and battle-hardened caucus. When they joined hands to debar Trotsky from the leadership they expressed a distrust and instinctive aversion felt by many members of the Old Guard. As yet they had no intention of eliminating him from the party, or even from its leading bodies. They acknowledged his merits. They wished him to occupy a prominent place in the Politbureau. But they did not consider him worthy of occupying Lenin's place; and they were horrified at the thought that, if nothing was undertaken against him, he might do so.

The triumvirs pledged themselves to concert their moves and act in unison.[1] In doing so they automatically swayed the Politbureau. In Lenin's absence the Politbureau consisted of only six members: the triumvirs, Trotsky, Tomsky, and Bukharin. Even if Trotsky had won over Tomsky and Bukharin, the vote would still have been divided equally. But as long as he, Bukharin, and Tomsky, formed no faction and voted each in his own way, it was enough that one of them should vote with the triumvirs, or abstain, to give them a majority. The triumvirs knew beforehand that Tomsky would not make common cause with Trotsky. An upright worker, a veteran Bolshevik,

[1] Stalin made the first public admission of the existence of the triumvirate at the twelfth congress in April 1923. See his *Sochinenya*, vol. v, p. 227, and also my *Stalin*, pp. 257–8.

and a trade-union leader in the first instance, Tomsky was the most modest member of the Politbureau. He was eager to defend, within limits and with caution, the demands and wage claims of the workers; and so in 1920 he was the first to oppose Trotsky over the militarization of labour and to raise a storm when Trotsky threatened to 'shake up' the trade unions. Trotsky criticized him harshly as an old-fashioned type of the trade unionist who from pre-revolutionary habit encouraged the 'consumptionist' attitude in the workers and showed no understanding for the 'productionist' outlook of the socialist state. For some time Tomsky led the trade unions in virtual revolt against the party. He was deposed from their Central Council and sent 'on an assignment', which was a barely veiled form of exile, to Turkestan. After the promulgation of N.E.P. he returned to the Kremlin and was promoted to membership of the Politbureau. But the wound inflicted on him rankled; and his attitude reflected the hostility towards Trotsky, the militarizer of labour, which many Bolshevik trade unionists had felt since 1920.

Bukharin was the only member of the Politbureau who was still friendly towards Trotsky. In his early thirties, yet an 'old' Bolshevik, he was the party's leading theorist, brilliant and profoundly educated. Lenin criticized his inclination to scholasticism and the doctrinaire angularity of his ideas. These ideas, however, exercised a strong influence even on Lenin who often adopted them and gave them a more realistic and supple expression.[1] Bukharin's was indeed an angular mind, fascinated more by the logical neatness of abstract propositions than by confused and confusing realities. Yet angularity of intellect was combined in him with an artistic sensitivity and impulsiveness, a delicacy of character, and a gay, at times almost schoolboyish, sense of humour. His rigidly deductive logic and his striving for abstraction and symmetry induced him to take up extreme positions: for years he had been the leader of the 'left Communists'—and by a process of radical reversal he was to become the leader of the party's right wing.

Bukharin had been in conflict with Trotsky as often as in agreement. During the Brest Litovsk crisis he led the war party

[1] Bukharin's intellectual relationship with Lenin will be discussed in my *Life* of Lenin.

and opposed the 'shameful peace'. During the civil war he was in sympathy with those who opposed the discipline and the centralistic organization which Trotsky gave to the Red Army. Then in the debate over trade unions he drew close to Trotsky. Like Trotsky, and even more passionately, he defended the rights of the non-Russian nationalities and stood up for the Georgian 'deviationists'. But whether he saw eye to eye with Trotsky or not, he was attracted to him by a strong affection and was spellbound by his personality.[1] Trotsky describes how in 1922, when he himself was laid up with a minor illness, Bukharin visited him and told him about Lenin's first stroke of paralysis.

At that time Bukharin was attached to me in his characteristic manner, half-hysterically, half-childishly. He finished his account of Lenin's illness and dropped down on my bed and muttered, as he gripped me through the blanket: 'Don't you fall ill too, I implore you, don't. . . . There are two men of whose death I always think with horror, Lenin and you.'

Another time he sobbed on Trotsky's shoulder: 'What are they doing with the party, they are turning it into a gutter.'[2] But with only this one friend in the Politbureau, Trotsky could not do much: Bukharin's sobs and sighs were of little assistance to him when he was confronted by the triumvirs.

Apart from these full members of the Politbureau, there were two alternate members: Rykov, chief of the Supreme Council of National Economy, and Kalinin, nominal Head of the State. Both were 'moderate' Bolsheviks. Both were of peasant origin and both retained much of the muzhik's character and outlook. In both, receptiveness to the moods of rural Russia, to the peasantry's hopes and fears, and also to some of its prejudices was stronger than in perhaps any other leader. Both embodied the element of nativeness in the party—'genuine Russianness'—and all that it implied: a distinct anti-intellectual bias, a distrust of the European element, a pride in social roots, and a certain stolidity of outlook. All this predisposed them against Trotsky. The peasantry, we know, cherished the regained freedom of private property and trade and was afraid of nothing more than of a

---

[1] 'Trotsky, the brilliant and heroic tribune of the October insurrection, the tireless and fiery preacher of revolution . . .' wrote Bukharin in his account of the events of 1917.   [2] Trotsky, *Moya Zhizn*, vol. ii, p. 207.

relapse into war communism. Of that fear Rykov and Kalinin were the mouthpieces within the party. More than anyone else they sensed a danger of such a relapse in Trotsky's ideas on planning. When Trotsky spoke of the lack of any guiding idea in the Supreme Council of the National Economy and of its inclination towards a Soviet variety of *laissez faire* he had Rykov in mind. Rykov, for his part, saw in Trotsky's scheme for a new Gosplan an encroachment upon his own prerogatives and more than that—an encroachment upon the basic principle of N.E.P. He was now the first to level against Trotsky the charge of hostility towards the peasant, the charge which was to resound through all the campaigns against Trotsky in coming years.[1]

Kalinin, on the contrary, had a deep respect for Trotsky and a friendly feeling, which he was to express even at the height of the drive against Trotskyism. The circumstance that in 1919 it was Trotsky who sponsored Kalinin's candidature for the office of Head of State, because of Kalinin's exceptional appeal to the peasants, had perhaps something to do with this.[2] Yet, when Rykov began to speak of Trotsky's hostility towards the peasantry, Kalinin was undoubtedly impressed. He had no strong views about Trotsky's proposals for policy, of which, in any case, he understood little; but he concluded, without rancour, that nothing could be safer and sounder than to keep in check Trotsky's influence, an influence which might endanger the 'alliance between workers and peasants'.

Two other men, Dzerzhinsky and Molotov, were at this time closely associated with the Politbureau, although they were not members. Dzerzhinsky, chief of Cheka and G.P.U., was the only one in this group of leaders who did not belong to the Old Guard. He had come from the Social Democratic party of the Kingdom of Poland and Lithuania, the party founded by Rosa Luxemburg; and he had adhered to the Bolsheviks only in 1917, about the same time as Trotsky. His original party had, under Rosa Luxemburg's inspiration, adopted towards the Bolsheviks an attitude indistinguishable from Trotsky's: it was usually critical of both Bolsheviks and Mensheviks; and it was the only party in the Socialist International to agree with

[1] *13 Konferentsya RKP*, pp. 6–7; *8 Vserossiiski Syezd Sovetov*, pp. 100–2.
[2] Trotsky, *Sochinenya*, vol. xvii, book 2, p. 542.

Trotsky's theory of permanent revolution. Dzerzhinsky, even after he had joined the Bolsheviks, remained opposed to Lenin over the self-determination of the non-Russian nationalities; and, again following Luxemburg, he argued that socialism should overcome, not encourage, separatist tendencies among the small nations. Paradoxically, this internationalist reasoning led him, the Pole of noble origin, to back Stalin's ultra-centralistic policy and to act *vis-à-vis* the Georgians as a spokesman of the new 'indivisible' Russia.

Dzerzhinsky's views, however, had not hitherto counted for much within the party. Important as the revolution's chief security officer, he was not a political leader. When the Bolsheviks decided to set up the Extraordinary Commission for the Struggle against Counter-revolution, as their political police were first called, they looked for a man with absolutely clean hands to do the 'dirty work'; and they found such a man in Dzerzhinsky. He was incorruptible, selfless, and intrepid—a soul of deep poetic sensibility, constantly stirred to compassion for the weak and the suffering.[1] At the same time his devotion to his cause was so intense that it made him a fanatic who would shrink from no act of terror as long as he was convinced that it was necessary for the cause. Living in permanent tension between his lofty idealism and the butchery which was his daily job, high-strung, his life force burning itself out like a flame, he was regarded by his comrades as the strange 'saint of the revolution' of the Savonarola breed. It was his misfortune that his incorruptible character was not allied to a strong and discriminating mind. His need was to serve the cause; and he came to identify the cause with the party of his adoption and then to identify that party with its leaders, with Lenin and Trotsky until lately, and now with the triumvirs behind whom he saw the Old Guard. Not being himself one of the Old Guard, he was all the more eager to promote its interest; and so he became more Bolshevik than the old Bolsheviks themselves just as he was, according to Lenin, more Great Russian than the Russians themselves.

For sheer lack of colour Molotov forms a striking contrast to Dzerzhinsky. In his late twenties, he already occupied a high

---

[1] Dzerzhinsky's private correspondence, published in *Z Pola Walki* and other Polish periodicals, gives a good insight into his character.

position in the hierarchy: he had been secretary to the Central Committee before Stalin became General Secretary, and then he served under Stalin as his chief aide. Even at this stage his narrowness and slow-mindedness were already bywords in Bolshevik circles; he appeared to be devoid of any political talent and incapable of any initiative. He usually spoke at party conferences as *rapporteur* on a second- or third-rate point; and his speech was always as dull as dishwater. The descendant of an intellectual family, a relative of Scriabin, the great musician, he seemed the very opposite of the intellectual—a man without ideas of his own. He could not have been altogether without his spark—the spark had shown itself in 1917—but it was now quite extinguished.

Molotov was the almost perfect example of the revolutionary turned official; and he owed his promotion to the completeness of this conversion. He possessed a few peculiar virtues which helped him along: infinite patience, imperturbable endurance, meekness towards superiors, and a tireless, almost mechanical industry which in the eyes of his superiors compensated for his mediocrity and incompetence. Very early he attached himself like a shadow to Stalin; and very early, too, he conceived an intense dislike, mingled with fear, of Trotsky. The story is told that Trotsky once appeared at the Secretariat, dissatisfied with something that had been done there, and all but pointing at Molotov taunted the dull-witted bureaucrats of the Secretariat. 'Comrade Trotsky', Molotov stammered out, 'Comrade Trotsky, not everyone can be a genius.'[1]

.   .   .   .

Thus even before the beginning of the struggle for the succession Trotsky stood almost alone in the Politbureau. He had the first inkling of a concerted action against him in the early weeks of 1923—a full year before Lenin's death—when at sessions of the Politbureau he found himself attacked by Stalin with quite unwonted ferocity and venom.[2] Stalin assailed him for his persistence in declining to be vice-Premier. He questioned Trotsky's motives and insinuated that Trotsky refused to respond to the call of duty because in his craving for power he would not content himself with being one of Lenin's deputies.

[1] Bajanov, *Avec Staline dans le Kremlin*, p. 139.   [2] *The Trotsky Archives.*

Then he heaped on Trotsky accusations of pessimism, bad faith, and even of defeatism, all on the flimsiest of grounds. Thus, to show up Trotsky's 'defeatism' he made much play of a remark Trotsky had once made to Lenin in private, saying that the 'cuckoo would soon sound the death knell for the Soviet Republic'.[1]

Stalin had several purposes in mind. He still reckoned with the possibility of Lenin's return to office; and so he took up the issue of the appointment Lenin had proposed hoping that he might drive this wedge between Lenin and Trotsky. He knew that nothing could embarrass Trotsky more than the insinuation that he craved to inherit Lenin's position. The calculation was shrewd. Trotsky was touched to the quick. He had sounder reasons than Stalin had to hope for Lenin's return, which would bring into action their 'bloc'. Even apart from this, he was so confident of his own position in the party and the country and of his superiority to his adversaries, that he had no inclination to fight for the succession. He did not try to recruit partners and associates; and it did not even occur to him to manœuvre for position. Yet Stalin's charges and insinuations were such that it was as absurd for Trotsky to refute them as it was dangerous to ignore them. Their effect was to drag him down and to extract from him those denials and excuses of which it is said *qui s'excuse s'accuse*. Once a man in a position comparable to Trotsky's is charged with craving for power, no denial on his part can dispel the suspicion aroused, unless he resigns all office on the spot, goes out into the wilderness, and ceases even to voice his views. This Trotsky was, of course, not prepared to do. Time and again he had explained that he could not see what useful role he could perform as one of the vice-Premiers whose functions overlapped; and that the division of labour in the government was faulty because 'every Commissar was doing too many jobs and every job was done by too many Commissars'. He now added that as vice-Premier he would have no machinery through which to work and no real influence. 'My appointment to such a work would, in my view, efface me politically.' He denied the imputation of pessimism and defeatism: he had indeed made the remark about the 'cuckoo sounding the death knell for the Soviet Republic' when he tried

[1] In Slavonic folk-lore the cuckoo is a bird of omen.

to impress on Lenin the ruinous effects of economic waste and
red tape; but his purpose—was there any need to say it?—
was to remedy those ills, not to sow panic.[1] To such irrelevancies
had the bickering in the Politbureau sunk; and it dragged on
for weeks during which Trotsky, waiting for Lenin's return,
held his fire.

He had some reason for waiting. The medical reports on
Lenin's health were encouraging. Even from his sick-bed Lenin
dealt blow after blow at Stalin with a relentless resolve which
surprised Trotsky. It was only proper, Trotsky held, that he
should leave to Lenin the initiative in this matter. At the beginning of February Lenin produced *inter alia* a severe criticism of
Rabkrin and communicated it to the Politbureau. Although
Stalin had already withdrawn from Rabkrin, Lenin's attack
affected him personally, because Lenin left no doubt that he
considered the Commissariat to have been an utter failure
during Stalin's tenure of office. He spoke of the vices of the
Commissariat in almost the same terms that Trotsky had used:
'lack of culture', 'muddle', 'bureaucratic misrule and wantonness', &c.; and he inserted barbed remarks against 'bureaucracy
in the party as well'. He concluded with proposals for an overhaul of Rabkrin, a reduction of its staff, and for the setting up of
a Central Control Commission, which was to take over many of
Rabkrin's functions. For several weeks Trotsky demanded that
Lenin's criticism be published, but the Politbureau refused.[2]

At the same time Trotsky submitted a scheme for a radical
reorganization of the Central Committee and of its various
agencies; and he supported this by a critical survey of the
party's condition. The Central Committee, he said with emphasis, had lost touch with the lower ranks and had become
transformed into a self-sufficient bureaucratic machine. This
was the issue over which the controversy was to burst into the
open next autumn; but already in January and February
Trotsky posed it before the Politbureau with even greater
bluntness than that which he was to allow himself in the public
debate later. In some details, such as the size of the Central

---

[1] See the papers of January 1923 in *The Archives*.
[2] Lenin, *Sochinenya*, vol. xxxiii, pp. 440 ff. Trotsky's letter to all members of the
Central Committee of 23 February 1923 in *The Archives*. (See also Fotieva's
memoirs in *Voprosy Istorii KPSS*, 4, 1957.)

Committee and its relationship with the Central Control Commission, his scheme differed from Lenin's. The triumvirs made the most of these differences, saying that Trotsky not only snubbed Lenin by refusing to become his deputy but also tried to divert the party from Lenin's ideas of organization. At this stage the upper ranks of the hierarchy were becoming initiated into the Politbureau dispute; and nothing could do more to damage Trotsky's position in their eyes as Lenin's presumed successor than a whispering campaign in which he was depicted as resisting Lenin on almost every issue. The words of the triumvirs were calculated to feed such a campaign. Their charges were recorded in the Politbureau minutes and opened for inspection to members of the Central Committee who were not slow in divulging their secrets to friends and subordinates.

The campaign had been afoot for some time already when Trotsky first reacted to it. On 23 February 1923 he addressed a letter to the Central Committee in which he said: 'Some members . . . have expressed the opinion that Comrade Lenin's scheme aims at preserving the party's unity while the purpose of my project is to create a split.' This insinuation was concocted and canvassed by a clique which in fact concealed Lenin's writings from party members. He disclosed what had happened at the Politbureau: 'While the majority . . . held it impossible even to publish Lenin's letter, I . . . not only insisted on publication, but defended the essential ideas of the letter, or, to put it more accurately, those of its ideas which seemed essential to me.' 'I reserve', he concluded, 'the right to expose these facts before the entire party, should this become necessary, in order to refute an insinuation [the authors of which] have enjoyed all too great an impunity because I have almost never reacted to insinuation.'[1] The occasion for the 'exposure' was to be the twelfth party congress convened for April. The threat was characteristic of Trotsky: he felt that he was by the unwritten code of inner party loyalty bound to give his antagonists due notice of any move against them which he might contemplate. He thereby deprived himself of the advantage of surprise and gave them time to parry the blow—this was the exact opposite of Stalin's tactics. Trotsky did not even intend to carry out his threat, however. His aim was merely to curb Stalin and to gain

[1] *The Archives.*

time while waiting for Lenin's recovery. He obtained one immediate result: on 4 March *Pravda* at last published Lenin's attack on Rabkrin.

On 5 March, while he, too, was confined to bed with illness, Trotsky received from Lenin a message of the utmost importance and urgency.[1] Lenin begged him to speak out in defence of the Georgian 'deviationists' at the forthcoming session of the Central Committee. This was Trotsky's first contact with Lenin since their talk about the 'bloc' in December, and the first intimation he had of Lenin's changed attitude in the Georgian affair. 'At present', Lenin wrote, 'their case [i.e. the case of the "deviationists"] is under *"prosecution"* by Stalin and Dzerzhinsky, and I cannot rely on Stalin's and Dzerzhinsky's impartiality. Quite the contrary. If you would agree to undertake the defence, my mind would be at rest.' Lenin attached a copy of his notes on Stalin's policy towards the nationalities (which are summarized in the previous chapter). These notes for the first time gave Trotsky a full idea of the relentlessness with which Lenin intended to press home the attack—by comparison Lenin's criticism of Rabkrin seemed mild. Lenin's secretaries added that Lenin had prepared, to use his own word, a 'bombshell' against Stalin to be exploded at the congress. Moreover, in a last moment of an exhausting tension of mind and will he urged Trotsky to show no weakness or vacillation, to trust no 'rotten compromise' Stalin might propose, and, last but not least, to give Stalin and his associates no warning of the attack. The next day he himself sent a message to the Georgian 'deviationists', conveying his warm sympathy and promising to speak up. About the same time Trotsky learned from Kamenev that Lenin had written a letter to Stalin threatening to 'break off all personal relations'.[2] Stalin had behaved in an offensive manner towards Krupskaya when she was collecting information for Lenin on the Georgian affair; and when Lenin learned about this, he could hardly contain his indignation. He decided, Krupskaya told Kamenev, 'to crush Stalin politically'.

What a moment of moral satisfaction and triumph this was

---

[1] *Moya Zhizn*, vol. ii, pp. 220–1; *The Stalin School of Falsification*, pp. 69–70.

[2] This letter was read out by Khrushchev at the twentieth congress and is included in the text of his speech published in the U.S.A. and Great Britain, but not in vol. xxxvi of Lenin's *Sochinenya*—nor in *Kommunist*, No. 9, 1956. Fotieva only hints at the existence of this letter.

for Trotsky. As on so many previous occasions Lenin at last acknowledged that Trotsky had been right all along. As so often before, Trotsky's bold foresight had condemned him for a time to political solitude and had caused dissension between him and Lenin; and just as events had vindicated him and led Lenin to conclusions identical with his, first over Gosplan, then over Rabkrin and 'party bureaucracy', so now they vindicated him over Georgia. Trotsky was confident that the triumvirate. was ruined and Stalin beaten. He was the victor and could dictate his terms. His adversaries thought likewise. When on their behalf Kamenev came to see Trotsky on 6 March, he was crestfallen, ready for chastisement, and anxious to mollify Trotsky.[1]

Not much mollifying was needed. Trotsky's revenge was to display magnanimity and forgiveness. Forgetting Lenin's warning, he jumped at a 'rotten compromise'. Lenin intended to demote Stalin and Dzerzhinsky and even to expel from the party 'for at least two years' Ordjonikidze (once his favourite disciple) because of the latter's brutal behaviour at Tiflis. Trotsky at once reassured Kamenev that he himself would propose no such severe reprisals. 'I am', he said, 'against removing Stalin and against expelling Ordjonikidze and displacing Dzerzhinsky . . . but I do agree with Lenin in substance.'[2] All he asked of Stalin was that he should mend his ways: let him behave loyally towards his colleagues; let him apologize to Krupskaya; and let him stop bullying the Georgians. Stalin had just prepared 'theses', to be submitted to the party congress, on policy towards the non-Russian nationalities—he was to address the congress on this point as the Central Committee's *rapporteur*. Anxious to justify his own behaviour, he had placed strong emphasis on the condemnation of 'local nationalisms'. Trotsky proposed that Stalin should reword his resolution, insert a denunciation of Great Russian chauvinism and of Russia 'one and indivisible', and give the Georgians and Ukrainians a firm assurance that henceforth their rights would be respected. This was all he demanded of Stalin—no breast-beating and no personal apologies. On these terms he was prepared to let Stalin continue as General Secretary.

On these terms Stalin was, of course, ready to surrender or at

[1] Trotsky, *Moya Zhizn*, vol. ii, pp. 223–4.   [2] Loc. cit.

least to feign surrender. To find himself threatened with political ruin, to feel Lenin's anger bursting over his head, and at this very moment to see Trotsky stretching out to him a forgiving hand was a quirk of fortune for which he could not but be grateful. He accepted Trotsky's terms at once. He rephrased his 'theses' and inserted all of Trotsky's amendments. As to the other 'conditions', well, all the offence he had given and all the hurts he had caused had sprung, he said, from misunderstandings and he was only too anxious to clear these up.

While Kamenev was still acting as go-between, Lenin succumbed to another stroke. He was to survive it by ten months, but paralysed, speechless most of the time, and suffering from spells of unconsciousness, the torment of which was all the greater because in the intervals he was acutely and helplessly aware of the intrigue in the background. The news of Lenin's relapse at once relieved the triumvirs. A few days after they had meekly submitted to Trotsky, they were once again working with redoubled energy but greater discretion to eliminate him from the succession. He still felt on top. He did not abandon the hope that Lenin would recover. In any case, he had in his hands Lenin's messages and manuscripts; and if he were to come out with these at the congress, especially with the notes on the Georgian affair, the party would have not a shadow of doubt where Lenin stood. Surely, he concluded, the triumvirs must know this and, fearing exposure, they must adhere to the compromise.

The triumvirs knew that Trotsky had promised Lenin to take up the case of the Georgian deviationists and to acquaint the congress with Lenin's views. (Kamenev had already read the notes on Georgia.) Stalin's chief preoccupation was now to prevail upon Trotsky not to act on this promise. Had he, Stalin, not done everything Trotsky demanded of him? He had, indeed; and so Trotsky consented to submit Lenin's notes to the Politbureau and to leave it to the Politbureau to decide whether or in what form they should be communicated to the congress. The Politbureau resolved that the notes should in no case be published, and that only chosen delegates should be acquainted in strict confidence with their content. This was not how Lenin had expected Trotsky to behave when he urged him to remain adamant, to address the congress with complete bluntness, and to allow no patching up of differences. But all these urgings and warnings were lost on Trotsky, who in his magnanimous mood helped the triumvirs to conceal from the world Lenin's death-bed confession of shame and guilt at the revival of the Tsarist spirit in the Bolshevik state. Lenin's notes on policy towards the non-Russian nationalities were to remain unknown to the party for thirty-three years.[1]

Hindsight makes Trotsky's behaviour appear incredibly foolish. This was the moment when his adversaries were taking up positions; and every one of his steps was as if calculated to smooth their way. Years later he remarked wistfully that if he had spoken up at the twelfth congress, with Lenin's authority behind him, he would probably have defeated Stalin there and then, but that in the long run Stalin might still have won.[2] The truth is that Trotsky refrained from attacking Stalin because he felt secure. No contemporary, and he least of all, saw in the Stalin of 1923 the menacing and towering figure he was to become. It seemed to Trotsky almost a bad joke that Stalin, the wilful and sly but shabby and inarticulate man in the background, should be his rival. He was not going to be bothered about him, he was not going to stoop to him or even to Zinoviev; and, above all, he was not going to give the party the impression that he, too, participated in the undignified game played by Lenin's disciples over Lenin's still empty coffin. Trotsky's conduct was as awkward and as preposterous as must be the behaviour of any character from high drama suddenly involved in low farce.

Of farce there was indeed no lack. When the Politbureau met on the eve of the congress, Stalin proposed that Trotsky should address the congress as the Central Committee's political *rapporteur*, that is in the role hitherto always reserved for Lenin. Trotsky refused saying that as General Secretary Stalin should be *rapporteur ex officio*. Stalin, all modesty and meekness, replied: 'No, the party would not understand it . . . the report must be made by the most popular member of the Central Committee.'[3] The 'most popular member', who only a few weeks earlier had been charged with craving for power, now leaned over backwards to show that the charge was baseless; and so he made it all

---

[1] They were first published in *Kommunist* in June 1956.
[2] *Moya Zhizn*, vol. ii, p. 219.   [3] Trotsky, *Stalin*, p. 366.

the easier for the triumvirs to overthrow him. The Politbureau decided that Zinoviev should deliver the address the party had been accustomed to hear from Lenin.

When the twelfth congress at last assembled, in the middle of April, its opening provided an occasion for a spontaneous display of homage to Trotsky. As usual, the chairman read out the greetings to the congress which poured in from party cells, trade unions, and groups of workers and students all over the country. In almost every message tributes were paid to Lenin and Trotsky. Only now and then did the greetings refer to Zinoviev and Kamenev, and Stalin's name was hardly mentioned. The reading of the messages went on during several sessions; and it left no doubt whom, if the party had now been asked to choose, it would have chosen as Lenin's successor.[1]

The triumvirs were surprised and annoyed; but they had little to fear. Lenin was not there to explode his 'bombshell'; and Trotsky, having promised not to explode it either, honoured his promise. He did not give the congress even the slightest hint of any disagreement between him and the triumvirs; and he kept himself well to the background. In the meantime the triumvirs acted behind the scenes. Their agents initiated delegates into the crisis in the leadership and turned against Trotsky even the homage just paid to him. They did their best to impress upon provincial delegates the dangers which they alleged were inherent in Trotsky's extraordinary popularity: had not Bonaparte, the 'grave-digger' of the French Revolution, risen to power on such acclaim? Could the imperious and ambitious Trotsky be trusted not to abuse his popularity? Was not, in Lenin's absence, the 'collective leadership' of smaller men, but men whom the party knew and trusted, preferable to his preeminence? Such questions, uttered in worried whispers, made many a delegate apprehensive. The Bolsheviks had been accustomed to look back to the great French precedent and to think in historical analogies. Occasionally, they cast round for that unpredictable character among their leaders, the potential Danton or the would-be Bonaparte, who might spring a dangerous surprise upon their revolution. Among all the leaders none seemed to have as much affinity with Danton as Trotsky; and none, it also seemed, would the mask of a Bonaparte fit as well

[1] *12 Syezd RKP (b)*, pp. 89, 488, 496, 502–3.

as him. In the eyes of many an old Bolshevik Trotsky's pre-eminence was a liability; and on reflection it seemed, indeed, safer that the party should be run by a team of less brilliant but reliable comrades.[1]

The triumvirs behaved with studious modesty. They declared that the only claim they had on the party's confidence was that they were Lenin's loyal and tested disciples. It was at this congress that Zinoviev and Kamenev initiated the exalted glorification of Lenin which was later to become a state cult.[2] No doubt the exaltation was in part sincere: this was the first Bolshevik congress without Lenin; and the party already felt bereft. The triumvirs played upon this mood, knowing that the glorification of Lenin would reflect glory upon those whom the party had known as his oldest disciples. Yet they had to work hard to convince the congress that they spoke with Lenin's voice. Delegates were uneasy. They received Zinoviev with sullen silence, when he came forward as *rapporteur*. His exaggerated and even ridiculous expressions of adoration of Lenin disgusted the sophisticated and the critically minded; but these were in a minority, and they did not protest lest they be misunderstood.

The triumvirs followed this up by calls for discipline, unity, and unanimity. When the party was leaderless it would have to close its ranks. 'Every criticism of the party line', Zinoviev exclaimed, 'even a so-called "left" criticism, is now objectively a

---

[1] A critic of my *Stalin*, where I mentioned this whispering campaign (p. 273), writes: 'That he [Trotsky] was viewed by some communists as a potential Bonaparte is a discovery made only quite recently by writers like Mr. Deutscher. . . . It was not appreciated at the time.' (G. L. Arnold in *Twentieth Century*, July 1951.) It is not always that a writer can give chapter and verse for a 'whispering campaign'; and in *Stalin* I referred to this particular campaign on the basis of what I had heard about it in Moscow, when the memory of it was still fairly fresh. In the meantime Alfred Rosmer, who in 1923 was in Moscow as member of the Executive of the Comintern and was extremely well informed about matters concerning Trotsky's person, has published his memoirs; and this is what he says: 'But now [in 1923] a rumour into which one ran everywhere indicated a well-prepared manœuvre . . .: "Trotsky imagines himself a Bonaparte", or "Trotsky wants to act a Bonaparte". The rumour circulated in every corner of the country. Communists arriving in Moscow came to tell me about it; they understood that something was afoot against Trotsky and urged me: "You should warn him about it." ' Rosmer, *Moscou sous Lénine*, p. 283. References to this 'whispering campaign' occur also in contemporary literature. In Eastman's *Since Lenin Died* there is a whole chapter about it under the title 'The anti-Bonaparte fraction'.

[2] See Kamenev's and Zinoviev's opening speeches in *12 Syezd RKP (b)*.

Menshevik criticism.'[1] He flung this warning at Kollontai, Shlyapnikov, and their followers; and, working himself up as he went, he told them that they were even more obnoxious than the Mensheviks. Ostensibly directed only against the Workers' Opposition, his words carried wider implications: they intimated to every potential critic with what sort of a denunciation he would be met. The maxim that *every* criticism was to be regarded *a priori* as a Menshevik heresy was novel—nothing like it had been pronounced before. Yet the maxim could be deduced from the argument Zinoviev had presented at the previous congress, when he said that in consequence of their political monopoly the Bolsheviks found that there were two or more potential parties within their party and that one of these consisted of the 'unconscious Mensheviks'. Concerned only with the immediate circumstances of the struggle for power and flushed with self-confidence, Zinoviev now went a step farther and described every opponent of the leading group as a virtual mouthpiece for those 'unconscious' and inarticulate Mensheviks. It followed that the leaders, whoever they were, had the right and even the duty to suppress opponents within the party as they had suppressed the real Mensheviks. In this way Zinoviev came to formulate what was to be the canon of Bolshevik self-suppression.

This call for discipline and the new view of unity did not pass unchallenged. The members of the Workers' Opposition and other dissenters mounted the platform to denounce the triumvirate and demand its disbandment. Lutovinov, a prominent party worker, protested against the 'papal infallibility' and immunity from criticism Zinoviev had claimed for the Politbureau.[2] Kossior, another old Bolshevik, maintained that the party was ruled by a clique, that the General Secretariat persecuted critics, that Stalin had during his first year in that office demoted and victimized the leaders of such important organizations as those of the Urals and of Petrograd; and that the talk about collective leadership was a fraud. Amid uproar Kossior demanded that the congress should revoke the 1921 ban on inner party groupings.[3]

---

[1] *12 Syezd RKP* (*b*), pp. 46–47.   [2] Ibid., pp. 105–6.

[3] Ibid., pp. 92–95. Another speaker referred to an anonymous leaflet circulated at the time of the congress and demanding the removal of the triumvirate from the Central Committee. He suggested that the Workers' Opposition was responsible for the leaflet. Ibid., p. 136.

The triumvirs, however, dominated the congress: Kamenev presided over it, Zinoviev enunciated policy, and Stalin manipulated the party machine. They made no bones about their partnership any longer: in reply to the challenge from the Workers' Opposition they defiantly acknowledged the existence of the triumvirate.[1] But within the triumvirate a shift was making itself felt: Zinoviev was losing his position as senior triumvir. He had overreached himself, antagonized many delegates, and drawn upon himself most of the attacks from the floor. Stalin's more discreet conduct gained him credit. The eyes of the delegates turned appreciatively on him when Nogin, an old influential and moderate member of the Central Committee, made his eulogy, praising the unobtrusive but vital work of direction he had done at the General Secretariat. 'Essentially', Nogin said, 'the Central Committee constitutes that basic apparatus which sets in motion all political activity in our country. The Bureau of the Secretariat is the most important part of the apparatus.'[2] Even some of the malcontents appealed from Zinoviev's flamboyance and demagoguery to Stalin's common sense.

Stalin's position was further enhanced in the debate over policy towards non-Russian nationalities, the debate which might have brought his undoing. The Georgians had come to Moscow expecting to get that strong support Lenin had promised them.[3] They did not obtain it. Rakovsky, who was the head of the Ukrainian government but had not enough influence in Moscow, took up their case. Was Moscow out to russify the small nationalities as the Tsarist gendarmes had done? he asked.[4] The Georgians were perplexed and confounded when they heard Stalin himself speaking with righteous indignation against the bullying of non-Russian nationalities, and when they found that their own denunciations of Great Russian chauvinism were inserted into the text of Stalin's 'theses'. This spectacle, the result of Trotsky's compromise with Stalin, seemed to them a mockery of all their complaints and protests. In vain did they demand that at least Lenin's notes should be read out. The members of the Politbureau were enigmatically reticent. Only one of them, Bukharin, broke the conspiracy of silence and in a great and stirring speech—this was to be the swan-song

[1] Stalin, *Sochinenya*, vol. v, p. 227.   [2] *12 Syezd RKP (b)*, p. 63.
[3] Ibid., pp. 150–1.   [4] Ibid., pp. 528–34.

of Bukharin the leader of Left Communism—he defended the small nationalities and exposed Stalin's pretences. He exclaimed that Stalin's disavowal of Great Russian chauvinism was sheer hypocrisy and that the atmosphere at the congress, where the party's *élite* was assembled, proved it: every word uttered from the platform against Georgian or Ukrainian nationalism aroused stormy applause, while even the mildest allusion to Great Russian chauvinism was received with irony or with icy silence.[1] It was with icy silence that the delegates received Bukharin's own speech. Stalin, emboldened by the attitude of the congress, could now permit himself to play down the meaning and import of Lenin's attack on his policy and to rout the 'deviationists'.

Trotsky followed the proceedings impassively or absented himself. He observed scrupulously the terms of his compromise with the triumvirs and the principle of the Politbureau's 'Cabinet solidarity'. This principle did not prevent Zinoviev from treating Trotsky to allusive pinpricks about his 'obsession with planning'.[2] Trotsky did not react. He showed a blank face to the speakers of the Workers' Opposition when they demanded the disbandment of the triumvirate and attacked the General Secretariat. He gave not a nod of encouragement to the disheartened Georgians; and when the debate over nationalities opened he left the assembly, excusing himself on the ground that he would be busy preparing his own report to the congress.[3]

When at last, on 20 April, Trotsky addressed the congress he turned away from the issues that had aroused so much heat and passion and spoke strictly on economic policy.[4] This, no doubt, was a great subject and the one in which he saw the key to all other problems; and at last he had the opportunity to present fully and before a nation-wide audience the ideas he had so far developed only loosely or only within the closed circle of the leaders. It was part of his bargain with the triumvirs that he was authorized to present his views as a statement of official policy, although the Politbureau agreed with his views no more than he

[1] *12 Syezd RKP* (*b*), pp. 561–5.   [2] Ibid., pp. 45–46.

[3] Ibid., p. 577. Yet only a month later Trotsky once again attacked in *Pravda* Stalin's policy in Georgia without mentioning Stalin. He wrote that if Great Russian chauvinism were to have its way in the Caucasus, then the Soviet invasion of the Caucasus would turn out to have been 'the greatest crime'. *Sochinenya*, vol. xxi, pp. 317–26.   [4] *12 Syezd RKP* (*b*), pp. 282–322.

agreed with Stalin's policy towards the non-Russian nationalities. He attached the greatest importance to his being able to launch his economic policy as the party's official 'line'; and this in his eyes probably justified in part his concessions to the triumvirs. And in fact no member of the Politbureau contradicted him openly while the congress debated his address.

He appealed to the party to master the country's economic destiny and to tackle the great and difficult task of primitive socialist accumulation. He surveyed the experience of two years of the New Economic Policy and redefined its principles. The twin purpose of N.E.P., he argued, was to develop Russia's economic resources and to direct that development into socialist channels. The rise in industrial production was still slow; it lagged behind the recovery of private farming. Thus a discrepancy arose between the two sectors of the economy; and it was reflected in the 'scissors' that opened between high industrial and low agricultural prices. (This metaphorical term which Trotsky coined soon entered the economists' idiom all over the world.)[1] Since the peasants could not afford to buy industrial goods and had no real incentive for selling their produce, the 'scissors' threatened to cut once again the economic ties between town and country and to destroy the political alliance between worker and peasant. The 'scissors' should be closed by lowering industrial prices rather than by raising agricultural ones. It was necessary to rationalize, modernize, and concentrate industry; and this required planning.

Planning was his main theme. He did not, as his adversaries later claimed, advocate that N.E.P. should be abandoned in favour of planning. He urged the party to pass from the 'retreat' to a socialist offensive within the framework of N.E.P. 'The New Economic Policy', he said, 'is the arena which we ourselves have set up for the struggle between ourselves and private capital. We have set it up, we have legalized it, and within it we intend to wage the struggle seriously and for a long time.'[2] Lenin had said that N.E.P. had been conceived 'seriously and for long'; and the opponents of planning often quoted the saying. 'Yes, seriously and for a long time', Trotsky retorted, 'but not for ever. We have introduced N.E.P. in order to defeat it on its own ground and largely by its own methods. In what way?

[1] Ibid., pp. 292–3.　　　　　　　　[2] Ibid., p. 285.

By making effective use of the laws of the market economy . . .
and also by intervening through our state-owned industry in the
play of those laws and by systematically broadening the scope
of planning. *Eventually* we shall extend planning to the entire
scope of the market, thereby absorbing and abolishing the
market.'[1]

Bolshevik views on the relationship between planning and a
market economy were still extremely vague. Most Bolsheviks
considered N.E.P. almost incompatible with planning. They
saw in N.E.P. an act of appeasement of private property to
which they had been driven by weakness. They thought that
the need for such appeasement would remain for years, and so
it was necessary to stress the stability of N.E.P. and to strengthen
the peasants' and the merchants' confidence in it. Only in a
more or less remote future would the party be able to withdraw
the concessions it had made to private property and to abolish
N.E.P.; and only then would it be possible to set up a planned
economy. This view was to underlie Stalin's policies throughout
the decade, in the course of which he first resisted planning in the
name of N.E.P. and then for the sake of planning decreed the
'abolition' of N.E.P., 'liquidated' private trade, and destroyed
private farming.

In Trotsky's conception N.E.P. was designed not merely to
appease private property. It had set the framework for long-term
co-operation, competition, and struggle between the socialist
and the private sectors of the economy. Co-operation and
struggle appeared to him dialectically opposed aspects of a
single process. Consequently he called on the party to protect
and expand the socialist sector, even while it conciliated and
helped to develop the private sector. Socialist planning would
not one day supersede N.E.P. at a stroke. Planning should
develop within the mixed economy until the socialist sector had
by its growing preponderance gradually absorbed, transformed,
or eliminated the private sector and outgrown the framework of
N.E.P. There was thus in Trotsky's scheme of things no room
for any sudden 'abolition' of N.E.P., for prohibition of private
trade by decree and for the violent destruction of private farming, just as there was no room for any administrative proclamation of the 'transition to socialism'. This difference between

[1] *12 Syezd RKP (b)*, p. 331.

Trotsky's and Stalin's approach was to show itself most strikingly only at the turn of the decade. Immediately, however, because of his insistence on the need for an offensive socialist policy, Trotsky seemed to many people basically opposed to N.E.P.

There is no need to go here into the economic detail of Trotsky's argument or into the case he made for primitive socialist accumulation—his ideas on this are summarized in the previous chapter. Suffice it to say that his address and the 'Theses' he presented are among the most crucial documents on Soviet economic history; and that he drew there a perspective on the Soviet economy for several decades ahead, the decades during which the evolution of the Soviet Union was to be determined by the processes of forced capital formation in an underdeveloped but largely nationalized economy. The Marxist historian may indeed describe and analyse those decades, the Stalinist decades, as the era of primitive socialist accumulation; and he may do so in terms borrowed from Trotsky's exposition of the idea in 1923.[1]

But whatever were the historic merits of Trotsky's performance at the twelfth congress and of whatever interest that performance may be to any study of Marxist ideas, it did not improve Trotsky's position for the struggle which awaited him. His central idea was, on the whole, beyond the understanding of his audience. The congress was as usual impressed, but this time it was impressed by the *élan* of his speech rather than by its content. The few implications of his thought that the mass of delegates could grasp were such as to arouse apprehension and even suspicion. Some could not help wondering whether he was not, after all, calling on the party to abandon N.E.P. and to return to the disastrous policies of war communism. When he demanded that industrial output should be concentrated in a small number of large and efficient concerns, the question arose what would happen to the workers who lost employment through the closing down of inefficient factories. When he argued that the working class would have to shoulder the main burden of industrial reconstruction, he made not the slightest attempt to soften the harsh impact of his words. On the contrary, he gave

[1] In later years Trotsky himself rarely, if ever, spoke of 'primitive socialist accumulation'.

his thought an overemphasis which was bound to startle and shock many workers. 'There may be moments', he said, 'when the government pays you no wages, or when it pays you only half your wage and when you, the worker, have to lend [the other half] to the state.'[1] It was in this way, by 'taking away half the worker's wage', that Stalin later promoted accumulation; but then he told the workers that the state paid them two or three times the wages they had earned before. When Trotsky put this issue before the congress with all his bluntness and merciless honesty, the workers were struck by his mercilessness rather than by his honesty. Is he again telling us, they could not help reflecting, as he told us when he formed the Labour Armies, that we must take the producer's, not the consumer's view? Nothing would be easier for the agents of the triumvirs than to confirm the workers in this suspicion.

And how, asked others, would Trotsky's policy affect the peasantry? Would it not drive the party to a collision with the muzhik? It would, Rykov and Sokolnikov had already said at the Politbureau and at the Central Committee. A significant incident at the congress gave new point to the question. In the debate Krasin, Trotsky's old comrade, addressed himself directly to Trotsky and asked whether he had thought out to the end the implications of primitive socialist accumulation? Early capitalism, Krasin pointed out, did not merely underpay workers or rely on the entrepreneur's 'abstinence' to promote accumulation. It exploited colonies; it 'pillaged entire continents'; it destroyed the yeomanry of England; it ruined the cottage weavers of India and on their bones, which 'whitened the plains of India', rose the modern textile industry. Did Trotsky carry the analogy to its logical conclusion?[2]

Krasin put the question without hostile intent. He approached it from his particular angle: as Commissar of Foreign Trade he had tried to persuade the Central Committee of the need for more foreign trade—and of the need to make more concessions to foreign capital. He wished to impress on the congress that since as Bolsheviks they could not expropriate peasants and plunder colonies—everyone took this for granted—they must seek to attract foreign loans; and that foreign capital might help Russia to proceed with primitive accumulation and to

[1] *12 Syezd RKP (b)*, p. 315.   [2] Ibid., pp. 351–2.

avoid the horrors that had accompanied such accumulation in the West. The Bolsheviks, however, had found out by now that they had little chance of attracting foreign credits on acceptable terms; and so the question which Krasin posed retained its full force: where would the resources needed for rapid accumulation come from? When Krasin spoke of the plunder of the peasantry and the 'white bones' of the Hindu cottage weavers, Trotsky jumped to his feet to protest that he had 'proposed nothing of the sort'.[1] This was true enough. Still, did not the logic of his attitude lead, after all, to 'plundering the peasantry'? That Trotsky jumped to his feet to deny it indicates that he felt a cloud of suspicion not yet larger than a man's hand gathering over his head.

Having said so much that was likely to antagonize the workers and to stir in the party the fear of a collision with the peasantry, Trotsky then incurred the enmity of the industrial managers and administrators. He could not help saying the most unpopular things once he was convinced that what he had to say was of vital importance and that it was his duty to say it. And so he drew the picture of the condition of industry in such dark colours and flayed the new economic bureaucracy so pitilessly for complacency, conceit, and inefficiency that it smarted under his lash and sought to work off the grudge. Trotsky, the managers replied, saw the economy in such dark colours and was so displeased with their work because he would content himself with nothing less than the Utopia of a planned economy.[2]

Thus slowly but inexorably the circumstances which eventually led to Trotsky's defeat began to unfold and agglomerate. He missed the opportunity of confounding the triumvirs and discrediting Stalin. He let down his allies. He failed to act as Lenin's mouthpiece with the resolution Lenin had expected of him. He failed to support before the entire party the Georgians and the Ukrainians for whom he had stood up in the Politbureau. He kept silent when the cry for inner-party democracy rose from the floor. He expounded economic ideas the historic portent of which escaped his audience but which his adversaries could easily twist so as to impress presently upon workers, peasants, and bureaucrats alike that Trotsky was not their

[1] Loc. cit.   [2] Ibid., pp. 322–50 and *passim*.

well-wisher, and that every social class and group ought to tremble at the mere thought that he might become Lenin's successor. At the same time the triumvirs sought assiduously to please everybody, promising something to every social class and group, pandering to every kind of complacency, and flattering every imaginable conceit.

Finally, Trotsky directly strengthened the triumvirs when he declared his 'unshaken' solidarity with the Politbureau and the Central Committee and called the rank and file to exercise 'at this critical juncture' the strictest self-restraint and the utmost vigilance. Speaking on a motion appealing for unity and discipline in Lenin's absence, he stated: 'I shall not be the last in our midst to defend [this motion], to put it into effect, and to fight ruthlessly against all who may try to infringe it.'[1] 'If in the present mood', he went on, 'the party warns you emphatically about things which seem dangerous to it, the party is right, even if it exaggerates, because what might not be dangerous in other circumstances must appear doubly and trebly suspect at present.' In this state of alarm and heightened suspicion the triumvirs would, of course, find it easy to assert themselves and stifle opposition. Trotsky shared their anxiety over the shock to which Lenin's death might expose the party; and in his eagerness to strengthen the party he weakened his own position in it. No doubt he counted on the triumvirs' loyalty. Little though he thought of them, he treated them as comrades whom he expected to behave towards him with a certain propriety. He did not imagine that they would turn his unselfish gestures to their immediate and private advantage.

.   .   .   .

The enlarged Central Committee elected at the twelfth congress reappointed Stalin as General Secretary. Trotsky made no attempt to prevent this—at any rate, he did not propose any other candidate, as he knew Lenin would have done. In Lenin's absence he had no chance of displacing Stalin anyhow. The triumvirs swayed the Politbureau and through it the Central Committee as before. They also dominated the new Central Control Commission elected to act as the party's supreme disciplinary Court. The man appointed to preside over it was Kuibyshev, Stalin's close associate.

[1] *12 Syezd RKP* (*b*), p. 320.

The triumvirs had no reason to precipitate a showdown with Trotsky. He offered no provocation; and they were not yet sure how the party would behave if the conflict came into the open. Yet Stalin lost no time in setting the stage. He used his wide powers of appointment to eliminate from important posts, in the centre and in the provinces, members who might be expected to follow Trotsky; and he filled the vacancies with adherents of the triumvirate or preferably of himself. He took great care to justify the promotions and demotions on the apparent merits of each case; and he was greatly assisted by the rule, which Lenin had established, that appointments should be made with reference to the number of years a member had served the party. This rule automatically favoured the Old Guard, especially its caucus.

It was in the course of this year, the year 1923, that Stalin, making full use of this system of patronage, imperceptibly became the party's master. The officials whom he nominated as regional or local secretaries knew that their positions and confirmation in office did not depend on the members of the organization on the spot but on the General Secretariat. Naturally they listened much more attentively to the tune called by the General Secretary than to views expressed in local party branches. The phalanx of these secretaries now came to 'substitute' itself for the party, and even for the Old Guard of which they formed an important section. The more they grew accustomed to act uniformly under the orders of the General Secretariat, the more it was the latter which virtually substituted itself for the party as a whole. In theory the party was still governed by the Central Committee and by decisions of party congresses. But henceforth a party congress could only be a sham: as a rule only nominees of the General Secretariat had any chance of being elected as delegates.

Trotsky watched this change in the party, grasped its significance, but could do nothing to arrest it. There was only one way in which he might have tried to counteract it: by appealing openly to the rank and file and calling on them to resist the impositions of the General Secretariat. But as Stalin was backed by the Politbureau and the majority of the Central Committee, this would have been incitement against the newly elected and regularly constituted leadership. No single member of the

Politbureau, not even one enjoying the highest authority, could risk such a step. Least of all could Trotsky risk it now, after he had concealed from the party his differences with the triumvirs, after he had solemnly declared his full solidarity with them, and pledged himself to act as the most zealous and vigilant guardian of discipline. If he were to try to arouse the party against the triumvirs, he would appear to act hypocritically, from a private grudge, or from the ambition to take Lenin's place.

For the time being he could resist Stalin only within the Politbureau and the Central Committee. But there he was isolated and his words counted for little. Even Bukharin was inclining ever more towards the triumvirs. (Among the forty members of the new Central Committee Trotsky had no more than three political friends: Rakovsky, Radek, and Pyatakov.) The sessions of the Politbureau held in his presence were becoming mere formalities: all the cards were stacked against him; and the real Politbureau worked in his absence. Thus shortly after the twelfth congress he began to pay the penalty of procrastination. He was already the political prisoner of the triumvirs. Unable to achieve anything against them within the leading party bodies, and unable to undertake any action against them from without, he could only bide his time and wait for some event to open a new prospect.

.   .   .   .

In the summer of 1923 Moscow and Petrograd were suddenly shaken by a political fever. Throughout July and August there was a great deal of industrial unrest. Workers felt that they were made to carry too much of the burden of industrial recovery. Their wages were a mere pittance; and often they did not receive even this. Industrial managers, running concerns at a loss and deprived of state subsidies and credits, had been unable to pay the men, had been in arrears to them for long months, and resorted to painful frauds and tricks to cut wage bills. Trade unions, reluctant to disturb the industrial revival, refused to press claims. Finally, 'wild' strikes broke out in many factories, spread, and were accompanied by violent explosions of discontent. The trade unions were caught by surprise; and so were the party leaders. The threat of a general strike was in the air; and the movement seemed on the point of turning into a political revolt. Not since the Kronstadt rising had there been so much tension in the working class and so much alarm in ruling circles.

The shock was all the more severe because it was unexpected. The ruling circles had viewed the economic situation with smugness and had boasted of continuous improvement. They had not received timely signals of the approaching trouble; or, if any warning had reached them, they ignored it. Rudely awakened, they began to look for the culprits who had incited the workers. Lower down, in the party branches, the commotion led people to inquire more seriously how it was that more than two years after the promulgation of N.E.P. there was still so much bitter discontent. What was the worth, they asked, of the official progress reports? Had not the party leaders been too complacent and had they not lost contact with the working class? There was not much use in looking for culprits if these questions remained unanswered.

The culprits were not easy to find. The agitation for strikes could not be traced to any source such as the remnants of the anti-Bolshevik parties—these, thoroughly suppressed, had been inactive. Official suspicion turned on the Workers' Opposition. But the leaders of the latter, too, had been surprised by the strikes. Intimidated by constant threats of expulsion, the Workers' Opposition had lain low and was breaking up. Its splinter groups, however, had to some extent been involved in the strike agitation, which was spontaneous in the main. The most important of these was the Workers' Group, led by three labourers, Myasnikov, Kuznetsov, and Moiseev, all party members at least since 1905. In April and May, immediately after the twelfth congress, they circulated a manifesto denouncing the New Exploitation of the Proletariat and urging the workers to fight for Soviet democracy.[1] In May Myasnikov was arrested. But his followers went on propagating his views. When the strikes broke out they wondered whether they should not go to the factories with the call for a general strike. They were still arguing about this when the G.P.U. arrested them, about twenty persons in all.[2]

[1] The manifesto was published by German sympathizers of the group in Berlin in 1924. *Das Manifest der Arbeitergruppe der Russischen Kommunistischen Partei.*

[2] V. Sorin, *Rabochaya Gruppa*, pp. 97–112. The group apparently had 200 members in Moscow.

The discovery that this and similar groups, like the Workers' Truth, had been active in the factories caused among party leaders a dismay which seemed quite out of proportion to its cause. But small as these groups were, they had many contacts in party and trade unions. Rank-and-file Bolsheviks listened to their arguments with open or sneaking sympathy. As the trade unions did not voice, and as the party paid all too little attention to, the workers' grievances, small political sects, had they not been stopped, might have rapidly acquired a broad influence and placed themselves at the head of the discontent. The instigators of the Kronstadt revolt had not been more numerous or influential; and where there is much inflammable material a few sparks may produce a conflagration. The party leaders sought to stamp out the sparks. They determined to suppress the Workers' Group and the Workers' Truth on the ground that the members of these organizations no longer considered themselves bound by party discipline and conducted half-clandestinely an agitation against the government. Dzerzhinsky was charged with the business of suppression. As he investigated the activities of the presumed culprits, he found that even party members of unquestioned loyalty regarded them as comrades and refused to testify against them. He then turned to the Politbureau and asked it to declare that it was the duty of any party member to denounce to the G.P.U. people who inside the party engaged in aggressive action against the official leaders.

The issue came before the Politbureau just after Trotsky had had several clashes with the triumvirs which had envenomed their relations; and Dzerzhinsky's demand was more than he could stomach. He was not at all eager to defend the Workers' Group and kindred sets of dissenters. He did not protest when their adherents were thrown into prison. Although he held that much of their discontent was justified and that many of their criticisms were well founded, he had no sympathy with their crude and anarchic tub-thumping. Nor was he inclined to countenance industrial unrest. He did not see how the government could meet the workers' demands when industrial output was still negligible: it was no use paying higher wages when wages could buy no goods. He saw that the strikes by delaying recovery only made matters worse; and he refused to seek popularity by bandying promises that could not be honoured or by exploiting grievances. Instead, he urged again the long over-due change in economic policy. Nor was he at all eager to support the demand for Soviet democracy in that extreme form in which the Workers' Opposition and its splinter groups had raised it. But he took exception to the manner in which the triumvirs and Dzerzhinsky proposed to deal with the trouble and to the obstinacy with which they dwelt on the symptoms of the discontent instead of turning to the underlying cause. When he saw that the Politbureau was on the point of ordering party members to spy upon and to denounce one another, he was seized with disgust.

Dzerzhinsky's demand had raised a delicate issue, because the attitude of the Bolsheviks to the G.P.U. had in it nothing of that haughty distaste with which the good bourgeois democrat normally views any political police. The G.P.U. was the 'sword of the revolution'; and every Bolshevik had been proud to assist it in work directed against the revolution's enemies. But after the civil war, when the reaction against the terror set in, many of those who had volunteered to serve in the G.P.U. were glad to leave its ranks. 'Only saints or scoundrels can serve in the G.P.U.', Dzerzhinsky complained to Radek and Brandler about this time, 'but now the saints are running away from me, and I am left with the scoundrels.'[1] Yet this debased G.P.U. was still the guardian of the Bolshevik monopoly of power. Hitherto it had defended it only against external enemies, White Guards, Mensheviks, Social Revolutionaries, and Anarchists. The question was whether the G.P.U. should also defend the monopoly against its supposed Bolshevik enemies? If so, then it could not do it otherwise than by operating within the party itself.

Trotsky did not tell the Politbureau plainly that it should reject Dzerzhinsky's demand. He evaded the question and dwelt on the underlying issue. 'It would seem', he wrote in a letter to the Central Committee on 8 October 1923, 'that to inform the party organization of the fact that its branches are being used by elements hostile to it is an obligation of members so elementary that it ought not to be necessary to introduce a special resolution to that effect six years after the October Revolution. The very demand for such a resolution is an

[1] This has been related to the writer by Brandler.

extremely startling symptom alongside of others no less clear.
. . .'[1] It pointed to the gulf that now separated the leaders
from the rank and file, the gulf which had grown especially
wide since the twelfth congress and was deepened by Stalin's
system of patronage.

When Trotsky stated this, the triumvirs reminded him that
he himself had under war communism ruled the trade unions
through his nominees. He replied that even at the height of the
civil war 'the system of appointment within the party did not
have one-tenth of the extent that it has now. Appointment of
the secretaries of provincial committees is now the rule. That
creates for the Secretary a position essentially independent of
the local organization. . . .' Trotsky did not explicitly question
the General Secretary's prerogatives—he merely urged him to
make moderate and prudent use of them. He confessed that at
the last congress, when he listened to the pleas made there for
proletarian democracy, many of these 'seemed to me exaggerated and to a considerable extent demagoguish, because a
fully developed workers' democracy is incompatible with the
régime of dictatorship'. However, the party ought not to go on
living under the high pressure of civil war discipline. This 'ought
to give place to a livelier and broader party responsibility. The
present régime . . . is much further from any workers' democracy
than was the régime of the fiercest period of war communism.'
'Secretarial selection' was responsible for 'unheard-of bureau-
cratization of the party apparatus.' The hierarchy of secretaries
'created party opinion', discouraged members from expressing
or even possessing views of their own, and addressed the rank
and file only in words of command and summons. No wonder
that discontent which could not 'dissipate itself through open
exchange of opinions at party meetings and through the exercise of influence upon the party organization by the mass of
members . . . accumulated in secret and gave rise to strains and
stresses'.[2]

Trotsky also renewed his attack on the triumvirs' economic
policy. The ferment within the party, he argued, was intensified
by industrial unrest; and this had been brought about by lack
of economic foresight. He had found out by now that the only
gain the triumvirs had allowed him to score at the twelfth

---

[1] Max Eastman, *Since Lenin Died*, pp. 142–3.   [2] Ibid.

congress, the gain for the sake of which he had yielded so much ground to them, was spurious: the congress had adopted his resolutions on industrial policy, but these had remained a dead letter. Now as before the economic administration bungled and muddled. Nothing had been done to make Gosplan the guiding centre of the economy. The Politbureau set up a number of committees to investigate symptoms of the crisis instead of going to its root. Trotsky himself had been invited to serve on a committee which was to inquire into prices; but he refused to do so. He had no wish, he declared, to participate in an activity designed to dodge issues and to postpone decisions.

Just before Trotsky made these criticisms he had his clashes with the triumvirs, already mentioned. Some of these occurred in deliberations over the situation in Germany, where, Trotsky held, the turmoil provoked by the French occupation of the Ruhr offered the German communists a unique chance. Other collisions developed when the triumvirs proposed changes in the Military Revolutionary Council over which Trotsky presided. Zinoviev was bent on introducing into that Council either Stalin himself or at least Voroshilov and Lashevich. It is not quite clear what induced him to make this proposal, and whether he acted in agreement with Stalin from an anxiety to gain for the triumvirs a decisive share in the control of military affairs; or whether he was already engaged in a subtle move against Stalin designed to oust him from the General Secretariat.[1] Enough that when Zinoviev tabled his motion, Trotsky, hurt and indignant, declared that he was resigning in protest from every office he held, the Commissariat of War, the Military Revolutionary Council, the Politbureau, and the Central Committee. He asked to be sent abroad 'as a soldier of the revolution' to help the German Communist party to prepare its revolution. The idea had not come out of the blue. The leader of the German party, Heinrich Brandler, had just arrived in Moscow; and doubting his own and his comrades' capacity to lead an insurrection, had inquired in all earnestness from Trotsky and Zinoviev whether Trotsky could not come *incognito* to Berlin or Saxony to take charge of revolutionary operations.[2] The idea stirred Trotsky; and the danger of the mission excited his courage. Disillusioned by the turn events had taken in

---

[1] See further, p. 241.   [2] The source for this statement is Brandler.

Russia, disgusted with the Politbureau cabal, and perhaps already tired of it, he asked for the assignment. To contribute once more to the victory of a fighting revolution suited him better than to taste the maggoty fruit of a victorious one.

The triumvirs could not let him go. In Germany he might have become doubly dangerous. If he went, succeeded, and returned in triumph, he would have dwarfed them as the acknowledged leader of both the Russian and the German revolutions. But if something untoward were to happen to him, if he were to fall into the hands of the class enemy or to die fighting, the party would suspect that they had sent him on a hopeless mission to get rid of him; and neither Stalin nor his partners could as yet risk such a suspicion. They could not permit Trotsky to win either the laurels of a new revolutionary victory or even the martyr's crown. They got out of the difficulty by turning the painful scene into a farce. Zinoviev replied that he himself, the President of the Communist International, would go to Germany 'as a soldier of the revolution' instead of Trotsky. Then Stalin intervened, and with a display of bonhomie and common sense said that the Politbureau could not possibly dispense with the services of either of its two most eminent and well-beloved members. Nor could it accept Trotsky's resignation from the Commissariat of War and the Central Committee, which would create a scandal of the first magnitude. As for himself, he, Stalin, would be content to remain excluded from the Military Revolutionary Committee if this could restore harmony. The Politbureau accepted Stalin's 'solution'; and Trotsky, feeling the grotesqueness of the situation, left the hall in the middle of the meeting 'banging the door behind him.'[1]

Such was the state of affairs in the Politbureau just before Dzerzhinsky made his proposal and Trotsky wrote the letter of 8 October, in which he confronted the triumvirs with a definite

[1] Stalin's ex-secretary thus underlines the grotesqueness of the incident: 'The scene took place in the Throne Hall. The door of the Hall is enormous and massive. Trotsky ran towards it, pulled it with all his strength, but it was dead slow to open. Some doors do not lend themselves to banging. In his fury, however, he failed to notice this; and he made yet another violent effort to close the door. Alas, the door was as slow to close as it was to open. Thus, instead of witnessing a dramatic gesture, indicating a historic break, we watched a sorry and helpless figure struggling with a door. . . .' Bajanov, *Avec Staline dans le Kremlin*, pp. 76–77.

PLATE V

(*a*) Lenin during his illness

(*b*) Lenin in his family circle with his wife Krupskaya next to him and his
sister Elizarova

PLATE VI

(*a*) Stalin during the struggle for the
succession

(*b*) Zinoviev

(*c*) Kamenev

THE TRIUMVIRATE

challenge. The latter were not yet unduly disturbed, because he did not carry the controversy into the open: his letter was addressed only to the members of the Central Committee who were entitled to know the Politbureau's secrets.

However, a week later, on 15 October, forty-six prominent party members issued a solemn statement directed against the official leadership and criticizing its policy in terms almost identical with those Trotsky had employed. They declared that the country was threatened with economic ruin because the 'majority of the Politbureau' had no policy and did not see the need of purposeful direction and planning of industry. They did not demand any definite change in the leadership; they only urged the Politbureau to awaken to its task. They, too, protested against the rule of the hierarchy of secretaries and against the stifling of discussion, alleging that the regular party congresses and conferences, packed by nominees, had ceased to be representative. Then, going farther than Trotsky, the Forty Six demanded that the ban on inner party groupings should be abolished or relaxed because it served one faction as a screen for its dictatorship over the party, drove disgruntled members to form clandestine groups, and strained their loyalty towards the party. 'The inner party struggle is waged all the more savagely the more it is waged in silence and secrecy.' Finally, the signatories of the statement asked that the Central Committee should call an emergency conference to review the situation.[1]

The Forty Six echoed Trotsky's criticisms so faithfully that the triumvirs could not but suspect that he was their direct inspirer, if not the organizer of their protest.[2] They assumed that the Forty Six had come together to form a solid faction. Trotsky's attitude was in fact more reserved than the triumvirs believed. True, among the Forty Six were his close political friends: Yuri Pyatakov, the most able and enlightened of the industrial administrators, Evgenii Preobrazhensky, the economist and former Secretary of the Central Committee, Lev Sosnovsky, *Pravda*'s gifted contributor, Ivan Smirnov, the victor over Kolchak, Antonov-Ovseenko, hero of the October insurrection, now chief political commissar of the Red Army, Muralov,

---

[1] *The Trotsky Archives.*

[2] Trotsky's responsibility for the action of the Forty Six was in the centre of the debate at the thirteenth party conference in January 1924.

commander of the Moscow garrison, and others. To these men Trotsky had confided his thoughts and anxieties; and he kept some of them informed even of his intimate talks with Lenin.[1] They formed the leading circle of the so-called 1923 Opposition and represented the 'Trotskyist' element in it. But the Forty Six were not a uniform group. There were among them also adherents of the Workers' Opposition and Decemists like V. Smirnov, Sapronov, Kossior, Bubnov, and Ossinsky, whose views diverged from those of the Trotskyists. Many of the signatories appended to the common statement strong reservations on special points or plain expressions of dissent. The statement dwelt with equal emphasis on two issues: economic planning and inner-party democracy. But some signatories were primarily interested in the former while others took the latter more to heart. Men like Preobrazhensky and Pyatakov demanded freedom of criticism and debate primarily because they were opposed to specific economic policies and hoped through debate to convert others to their views; while members like Sapronov and Sosnovsky were in opposition chiefly because they cherished inner-party freedom for its own sake. The former voiced the aspirations of the advanced and educated *élite* of the Bolshevik bureaucracy itself while the latter expressed a revulsion against bureaucracy at large. Far from forming a solid faction, the Forty Six were a loose coalition of groups and individuals united only on a vaguely common denominator of discontents and strivings.

Whether or to what extent Trotsky should be regarded as the direct sponsor of this coalition is not certain. He himself denied this while his adversaries claimed that his denial was a *ruse de guerre* to which he resorted in order to avoid the blame for organizing a faction.[2] However, they offered no specific proof; and the Forty Six did not act as a coherent faction with a distinct line of conduct and discipline. Even many years after Trotsky's death those who had stood close to him claimed that he observed the rules of discipline so strictly that he could not have acted as the sponsor of this particular demonstration of protest. In the light of all that is known about Trotsky's conduct in such matters, this may be accepted as true. However, it is

---

[1] *Moya Zhizn*, vol. ii, p. 215.

[2] *13 Konferentsya RKP (b)*, pp. 46, 92–102, 104–13; *13 Syezd RKP (b)*, pp. 156 ff.

doubtful that he had, as is also claimed, no foreknowledge of the action of the Forty Six or that he was surprised by it. Preobrazhensky, Muralov, or Antonov-Ovseenko undoubtedly kept him informed about what they were doing, and would not have done what they were doing without some encouragement from him. And so even if Trotsky was not formally responsible for their action, he must be regarded as its actual prompter.

The Forty Six addressed their protest to the Central Committee with the request that the Committee should, in accordance with long-established custom, bring it to the party's knowledge. The triumvirs refused the request. Moreover, they threatened to apply disciplinary sanctions if the signatories themselves were to circulate the document among party members. At the same time agents of the Central Committee were sent to the cells to denounce the authors of the unpublished protest. Then a special enlarged session of the Central Committee was held to deal with the statement of the Forty Six and with Trotsky's letter of 8 October.[1] Replying to Trotsky, the triumvirs repeated the charges which Stalin had brought against him at the Politbureau meetings of January and February. Trotsky, they alleged, was actuated by lust of power, and, sticking to the maxim 'all or nothing', he refused not merely to serve as Lenin's deputy, but even to attend to his normal duties. Then they enumerated all the issues over which he had in recent years dissented from Lenin; but they passed over in silence the fact that on nearly all these issues Lenin had in the end found himself in agreement with Trotsky. The Central Committee endorsed the charges and censured Trotsky. It also reprimanded the Forty Six, qualifying their joint protest as an infringement of the 1921 ban on factions. As to Trotsky, it did not charge him plainly with organizing the faction but held him morally responsible for the offence of which it found the Forty Six guilty.

The condemnation threw into relief the vicious circle in which any incipient opposition found itself under the disciplinary rules of 1921. The Forty Six had come forward precisely in order to demand that those rules be revoked or relaxed. But it was enough of them to speak up for a revision of the rules to lay themselves open to the accusation that they had already violated them. The ban on inner-party groupings was self-perpetuating

[1] *KPSS v Rezolutsyakh*, vol. i, pp. 766–8.

and irreversible: under it no movement for its revision could be set afoot. It established within the party that barrack discipline which may be meat for an army but is poison for a political organization—the discipline which allows a single man to vent a grievance but treats the joint expression of the same grievance by several men as mutiny.

The triumvirs could not easily suppress this particular 'mutiny'. The mutineers were not ordinary rankers—they were forty-six generals of revolution. Every one of them had held important positions in government and party. Most had a heroic civil-war record. Many had been members of the Central Committee. Some had joined the Bolsheviks in 1917, together with Trotsky; others had been Bolsheviks since 1904. Their protest could not be concealed. By denouncing it to the cells and calling upon the cells to join in the denunciation but refusing to show the condemned statement, the triumvirs aroused intense suspicion. The party was astir with alarming rumours. The triumvirs had to open at least a safety valve. On 7 November, the sixth anniversary of the revolution, Zinoviev made a solemn statement promising to restore democracy within the party. As a token, *Pravda* and other newspapers opened their pages for discussion and invited members to write frankly on all issues which troubled them.

To initiate a debate after 'three years of silence' was a risky undertaking.[1] The triumvirs knew it. They opened the discussion in Moscow and delayed it in the provinces. But no sooner had they lifted a safety valve than they were hit by pressure of unsuspected force. Moscow's party cells were in revolt. They received official leaders with hostility and acclaimed spokesmen of the opposition. At some meetings in large factories the triumvirs themselves were met with derision and were heavily outvoted.[2] The discussion was at once focused on the statement of the Forty Six who were now free to expound their views to the rank and file. Pyatakov was their most aggressive and effective spokesman; wherever he went he easily obtained large majorities for bluntly worded resolutions. Antonov-Ovseenko addressed

---

[1] At the thirteenth party conference Radek spoke of 'three years of silence' which preceded the discussion. *13 Konferentsya RKP (b)*, pp. 135–7.

[2] This was admitted by Rykov. Ibid., pp. 83–91. See also Preobrazhensky's description of the crisis in the party. Ibid., pp. 104–13.

the party organizations of the garrison; and shortly after the debate had begun at least one-third of those organizations had sided with the opposition. The Central Committee of the Communist Youth and most of the Comsomol cells in Moscow did likewise. The universities were seized with excitement; and a large majority of student cells declared enthusiastic support for the Forty Six. The leaders of the opposition were in a buoyant mood. According to one version, they were so self-confident that they discussed among themselves in what proportion they would be willing to share with the triumvirs control over the party machine.

The triumvirs took fright. When they saw which way the vote in the garrison cells went, they resolved that these cells must not be permitted to proceed with the vote. They at once dismissed Antonov-Ovseenko from his post as the Red Army's chief political commissar, alleging that he had threatened the Central Committee that the armed forces would stand up 'like one man' for Trotsky, 'the leader, organizer, and inspirer of the revolution's victories'.[1] Antonov-Ovseenko had not in fact threatened any military revolt. What he had meant and said was that the military party cells were 'like one man' behind Trotsky. This, no doubt, was an impulsive overstatement, but it was not very far from the truth. Nor had Antonov-Ovseenko acted illegitimately in carrying the discussion to the military cells. These had the same right as had the civilian cells to take part in any debate and to vote on policy; and they had never before been denied this right. But whether Antonov's behaviour was or was not beyond reproach—Trotsky held that he might have exercised more prudence in a delicate situation—the triumvirs decided that they could not leave him at the head of the army's political department. Demotions of other critics followed. The General Secretariat, violating the statutes, disbanded the Central Committee of the Comsomol and replaced it by nominees.[2] Disciplinary reprisals were applied to other supporters of the opposition as well, and every imaginable device was used to obstruct the further progress of controversy.

All this, however, did not relieve the tension. The triumvirs then decided to confound the opposition by taking a leaf from its book. They framed a special resolution bluntly denouncing

[1] Ibid., p. 124. [2] *14 Syezd VKP (b)*, p. 459.

the 'bureaucratic régime within the party' in terms which sounded like a plagiarism from Trotsky and the Forty Six; and they proclaimed the opening of a New Course which was to guarantee full freedom of expression and criticism for party members.

Throughout November, when Moscow was all excitement, Trotsky did not take part in the public controversy. An accident of ill health reduced him to silence. Late in October, during a week-end hunting trip to the marshy country outside Moscow, he had contracted a malarial infection; and he was bedridden with fever during these decisive months. It is curious to note how such accidents—first Lenin's illness and then his own—contributed to the trend of events which was more solidly determined by the basic factors of the situation. 'One can foresee a revolution or a war', Trotsky remarks in *My Life*, 'but it is impossible to foresee the consequences of an autumn shooting trip for wild ducks.'[1] It was certainly no mean disadvantage to Trotsky that at this crucial stage the use of his live voice and direct appeal to an audience was denied him.

Those were hard days [his wife writes], days of tense fighting for Lev Davidovich at the Politbureau against the rest of its members. He was alone and ill and had to fight them all. Because of his illness the Politbureau held its meetings in our apartment; I sat in the adjoining bedroom and heard his speeches. He spoke with his whole being; it seemed as if with every such speech he lost some of his health—he spoke with so much 'blood'. And in reply I heard cold and indifferent answers. . . . After each of these meetings L.D.'s temperature rose. He came out of his study soaked through, and undressed and went to bed. His linen and clothes had to be dried as if he had been drenched in a rain storm.[2]

When the triumvirs decided to confound the opposition by a resounding proclamation of the New Course, they were anxious that Trotsky should endorse the proclamation. They asked him to put his signature next to theirs under the text they had plagiarized from him. He could not refuse without giving the party the impression that it was he who stood in the way of its freedom; and he hoped that the formal inauguration of a public debate would at least enable him to bring into the open the issues over which he had wrestled with the triumvirs in the

[1] *Moya Zhizn*, vol. ii, pp. 234 ff.   [2] Op. cit., vol. ii, p. 240.

secrecy of the Politbureau. Yet he could not but suspect that he was being asked to endorse an empty promise. Only a few weeks later one of the leaders of the opposition compared this proclamation to the October Manifesto of 1905, that promise of constitutional freedoms which the last Tsar had made in a moment of weakness and which he withdrew as soon as his strength returned.[1] In October 1905 the young Trotsky, when he appeared for the first time before the revolutionary crowds of St. Petersburg, crumpled in his hand the Tsar's Manifesto and warned the people: 'To-day it has been given us and to-morrow it will be taken away and torn into pieces as I am now tearing it into pieces, this paper-liberty, before your very eyes.'[2] Now, in 1923, he could not go out to the crowds and tear to pieces the 'new October Manifesto' in front of them. It was to be proclaimed in the name of the Politbureau of which he was a member; and he was striving to reform, not to subvert, the established government. So, when the Politbureau brought the motion on the New Course to his bedside, he could only seek to introduce amendments designed to make the promise of inner-party freedom as plain and emphatic as possible and thereby to commit the triumvirs. The Politbureau accepted all his amendments; and on 5 December it voted unanimously for the motion.[3] Yet, although he had voted in favour, Trotsky could not help repeating after a fashion his gesture of 1905.

He did this in a few brief articles which he wrote for *Pravda* and which later appeared in his pamphlet *The New Course*.[4] These articles contain in a nutshell most of the ideas which at once became the hallmark of 'Trotskyism'. He began with an essay which appeared on 4 December, the day before the Politbureau voted on the New Course. This was a somewhat cryptic attack on 'officialdom' in his own department, the army, 'and —elsewhere'. The vices of officialdom, he wrote, show themselves when people 'cease to think things through; when they smugly employ conventional phrases without reflecting on what they mean; when they give the customary orders without asking

---

[1] See Sapronov's speech in *13 Konferentsya RKP (b)*, pp. 131-3.

[2] *The Prophet Armed*, pp. 128-9.

[3] The text appeared in *Pravda* on 7 December 1923.

[4] The quotations in the following pages are from the American edition of the pamphlet; but the text of the translation has been occasionally rephrased• after comparison with the original.

if they are rational; when they take fright at every new word, every criticism, every initiative, every sign of independence....'[1] The 'soul-uplifting' lie was the daily bread of officialdom. It could be found in histories of the Red Army and of the civil war, where truth was sacrificed to bureaucratic legend. 'To read it, you would think that there are only heroes in our ranks; that every soldier burns with the desire to fight; that the enemy is always superior in numbers; that all our orders are reasonable and appropriate to the occasion; that the execution is always brilliant; and so on.' The edifying effect of such legends is itself a legend. The Red soldier would listen to them as 'his father listened to the *Lives of Saints*: just as magnificent and uplifting, but not true to life'.

Supreme heroism, in military art as in revolution, consists of truthfulness and a sense of responsibility. We speak for truthfulness not from the standpoint of the abstract moralist who teaches that man must never lie or deceive his neighbour. Such idealistic talk is sheer hypocrisy in a class society where there are antagonistic interests, struggle, and war. Military art in particular includes, as it must, *ruse*, dissimulation, surprise, and deception. But it is one thing to deceive the enemy consciously and deliberately and to do so in the name of a cause for which life itself is given; and another—to spread injurious false information and assurances that 'all goes well' . . . from a spirit of sheer sycophancy.

Then he drew a parallel between army and party, especially between their attitudes towards tradition. The young communist stood in the same relation to the Old Guard as that in which the military subaltern stood to his superiors. In both the party and the army the young enter a ready-made organization which their elders had to build from scratch. Here and there tradition is therefore of 'vast importance'—without it there can be no steady progress.

But tradition is not a rigid canon or an official manual; it cannot be learned by heart or accepted as gospel; not everything the old generation says can be believed merely 'upon its word of honour'. On the contrary, tradition must, so to speak, be conquered by internal travail; it must be worked out by oneself in a critical manner and in that way assimilated. Otherwise the whole structure will be built on sand. I have already spoken of the representatives of the

---

[1] L. Trotsky, *The New Course*, pp. 99–105.

'Old Guard' . . . who impart tradition to the young in the manner of Famusov [a character from classical Russian comedy] : 'Learn by looking at the elders: at us, for example, or at our deceased uncle.' But neither from the uncle nor from his nephews is there anything worth while learning.

It is incontestable that our old cadres which have rendered immortal services to the revolution enjoy very great authority in the eyes of the young military men. And that is excellent because it assures the indissoluble bond between the higher and lower commands and their link with the ranks. But on one condition: that the authority of the old does not efface the personality of the young and most certainly that it does not terrorize them. . . . Any man trained merely to say 'Yes, Sir' is a nobody. Of such people the old satirist Saltykov said: 'They keep saying yes, yes, yes, till they get you in a mess.'[1]

This was Trotsky's first attack on the Old Guard. But it was couched in terms so general and allusive that very few grasped its meaning. The party and the country still had no inkling of his differences with the Politbureau and held him to be responsible for official policy. So much was this the case that when the Forty Six, addressing the cells, claimed that they had Trotsky's support, Stalin could reply that they had no right to do so because Trotsky, far from agreeing with the opposition, was one of the most determined disciplinarians among the leaders.[2] This, it seems, was the last straw which broke Trotsky's patience. On 8 December he wrote an Open Letter to party meetings in which he made clear his position.[3] He described the New Course as a historic turning-point; but he warned the rank and file that some of the leaders were already having second thoughts and trying to nullify the New Course in practice. It was, he said, the party's task and duty to free itself from the tyranny of its own machine. The rank and file must rely solely upon themselves, their own understanding, and their own initiative and courage. True, the party could not dispense with its machine; and the machine had to work in a centralized manner. But it must be the party's tool, and not its master; and the needs of centralism must be harmonized and balanced with the demands of democracy. 'During this last period there was no such balance.'

[1] Ibid., p. 104. [2] Stalin, *Sochinenya*, vol. v, pp. 369–70.
[3] *The New Course*, pp. 89–98.

'The idea or at the very least the feeling that bureaucratism is threatening to get the party into a blind alley has become pretty general. Voices have been raised to point out the danger. The resolution on the New Course is the first official expression of the change that has taken place in the party. It will be effective only to the degree that the party, that is its 400,000 members, want to make it effective and succeed in this.' Some leaders, afraid of this, were already arguing that the mass of members was not mature enough to enable the party to govern itself democratically. But it was precisely the bureaucratic tutelage that prevented the mass from growing politically mature. It was right 'to make astringent demands upon those who want to enter the party and stay in it'; but once they have been admitted they must be free to exercise all rights reserved for members. He then explicitly appealed to the young to assert themselves and not to regard the Old Guard's authority as absolute. 'It is only by constant active collaboration with the young, within the framework of democracy, that the Old Guard can preserve the Old Guard as a revolutionary factor.' Otherwise it will ossify and degenerate into a bureaucracy.

This was the first time that Trotsky confronted the Old Guard with the charge, still strongly qualified, of 'bureaucratic degeneration'. He supported the charge by a telling analogy; he recalled the process by which the Old Guard of the Second International had become transformed from a revolutionary into a reformist force and surrendered its greatness and historic mission to its own party machines. But Bolshevism was threatened not only by a divorce between generations. Even more menacing was the divorce between the party and the working class. Only 15 or 16 per cent. of the entire membership consisted of factory workers. He demanded 'an increasingly large flow into the party of working-class elements'; and he concluded his Letter with this tempestuous war cry:

Away with passive obedience, with mechanical levelling by the authorities, with suppression of personality, with servility, and with careerism! A Bolshevik is not merely a disciplined man: he is a man who in each case and on each question forges a firm opinion of his own and defends it courageously and independently not only against his enemies but inside his own party. To-day perhaps he will be in a minority . . . he will submit . . . but this does not always signify that he is in the wrong. Perhaps he has seen or has understood a new task or the necessity of a turn earlier than others have done. He will persistently raise the question a second, a third, a tenth time, if need be. Thereby he will render his party a service helping it to meet the new task fully armed, or to carry out the necessary turn without organic upheaval and without factional convulsions.[1]

This was the crux of the matter. He put forward the idea of a party which allowed the freedom of various trends of thought in its midst as long as these were compatible with its programme; and he opposed this idea to the conception of the monolithic party which the triumvirs had already advanced as belonging to the essence of Bolshevism. Of course, the party must not be 'chopped up into factions'; but 'factionalism' was only an extreme and morbid reaction against the excessive centralism and the domineering attitude of the bureaucracy. It could not be uprooted as long as its cause persisted. And so it was necessary to 'renew the party apparatus', to 'replace the mummified bureaucrats by fresh elements who are in close touch with the life of the party as a whole', and, above all, to remove from the leading posts 'those who, at the first word of criticism, of objection, or of protest, brandish the thunderbolts of penalties . . . the New Course must begin by making every one feel that from now on nobody will dare terrorize the party'.

Thus, after a delay of nearly nine months, he threw at last, alone, the bombshell he had hoped to explode together with Lenin at the twelfth congress. The delay was fatal. Stalin had already carried out the overhaul of the party machine and had placed his and to a lesser extent Zinoviev's subordinates at every sensitive spot, in every branch of the organization. By insinuation, obloquy, and stage-whisper he had prepared them thoroughly for the expected clash with Trotsky. And now he moved the phalanx of his secretaries into action.

When Trotsky's Letter was read out at the party meetings, pandemonium broke loose. Many received the Letter as the message for which they had long waited, the inspiring call from the great revolutionary who had at last turned his back upon the Pharisees and placed himself once again at the head of the humble and the humiliated. Even members of the opposition groups against whom he had only recently acted as counsel for

[1] *The New Course,* p. 94.

the prosecution responded with fervour, and acknowledged that even in his severity towards them he had been guided only by pure and high-minded motives. 'We address ourselves to you, Comrade Trotsky', wrote one of them, 'as to the leader of the Russian Communist Party and of the Communist International whose revolutionary thought has remained alien to caste exclusiveness and narrow-mindedness.' 'I approach you, Comrade Trotsky', wrote another, 'as one of the leaders of Soviet Russia to whom considerations of political revenge are alien.'[1] But many a Bolshevik was stunned by the sombre picture of the party he had drawn and by his harsh language; and some were outraged by what they considered to be an unprovoked insult to the party, if not a stab in its back. Everywhere, the secretaries led and organized this latter section of Bolshevik opinion, exacerbated it, excited it to the utmost, and gave to it a weight which was out of proportion to its real strength, placing at its disposal all means of expression, most of the time reserved for debates at meetings, and most of the discussion columns in leading newspapers and in local bulletins and sheets which played an enormous part in forming opinion in the provinces.

At the branch meetings the opposition's adherents often overwhelmed the party machine by their numbers and articulateness. But when the branch meetings with all their sound and fury were over, it was the secretaries who spoke on behalf of the branches, who handled the resolutions adopted, and who decided whether to suppress them or not, and, if not, how much currency to give them. Once a secretary had been confronted with the unmanageable temper of one meeting he prepared carefully for the next meeting, packed it with his men, and ruled out or silenced the opposition.

The debate was to be concluded by the holding of the thirteenth party conference. The preparations for the conference were also in the hands of the secretaries. The election of delegates was indirect and proceeded through several stages. At every stage the secretaries checked how many of the sympathizers of the opposition were elected; and they saw to it that they were eliminated at the next stage. It was never disclosed how many votes were cast for the opposition in the primary

---

[1] Yaroslavsky quoted these letters at the thirteenth party conference with the intention to discredit Trotsky. *13 Konferentsya RKP (b)*, p. 125.

cells of Moscow. The Forty Six claimed, without meeting with denial, that at the regional conference, which was the tier above the primary cells, they had obtained not less than 36 per cent. of the vote; yet at the *gubernia* conference, the next tier, that percentage dwindled to 18. The opposition concluded that, if its representation had been whittled down in the same proportion all the way from the primary to the final elections, then the opposition had behind it the great majority of the Moscow organization.[1] This was almost certainly true, but the secretaries were on top of the majority.

The triumvirs were anxious to bring the contest to a speedy conclusion. They replied to Trotsky's Letter with a deafening barrage of counter-accusations. It was, they said, disloyal on Trotsky's part to vote with the whole of the Politbureau for the New Course and then to cast aspersion upon the Politbureau's intentions. It was criminal to incite the young against the Old Guard, the repository of revolutionary virtue and tradition. It was wicked of him to try and turn the mass of the party against the machine, for every good old Bolshevik was aware how much importance the party had always attached to its machine and with how much care and devotion it had surrounded it. He equivocated over the ban on factions: he knew that the ban was essential to the party's unity and did not dare to demand plainly that it be revoked; but he sought to sap it surreptitiously. He played false when he described the party régime as bureaucratic; and he played with fire when he aroused an exaggerated and dangerous appetite for democracy in the masses. He pretended to speak for the workers, but played up to the students and the intelligentsia, that is to the petty bourgeois gallery. He spoke about the rights and responsibility of the rank and file only to cover up his own irresponsibility, *folie de grandeur*, and frustrated dictatorial ambition. His hatred of the party machine, his contumelious attitude towards the Old Guard, his reckless individualism, his disrespect for Bolshevik tradition, yes, and his notorious 'underestimation' of the peasantry—all this clearly indicated that at heart he had remained something of a stranger in the party, an alien to Leninism, an unreformed semi-Menshevik. Agreeing to become the mouthpiece of all the disparate opposition groups, he had set himself up as the chief, even if

[1] Ibid., pp. 131–3.

unconscious, agent of all the petty bourgeois elements which pressed upon the party from all sides, seeking to breach its unity and to inject into it their own moods, prejudices, and pretensions.[1]

. . . .

In the long history of inner-party oppositions none had been weighed down by so heavy a load of accusations and none had been ground down so remorselessly by the party machine as was the 1923 Opposition. By comparison the Workers' Opposition had been treated fairly, almost generously; and the oppositions which had been active before 1921 had as a rule enjoyed unrestricted freedom of expression and organization. What accounted for the vehemence and fury with which the party machine now bore down upon its chief critic?

The triumvirs were not able to meet Trotsky on his own ground, in fair argument. His attack was all too dangerous: his Open Letter and his few articles on the New Course rang out like powerful bells arousing alarm, anger, and militancy. Yet, the triumvirs resorted not merely to falsification and suppression. They also exposed and made the most of the weaknesses and inconsistencies, real or apparent, in Trotsky's attitude. Throughout he took his stand on the Bolshevik monopoly of power; and much more persuasively than the triumvirs did he call on the party to guard it as the sole guarantee of the revolution's survival; and he reaffirmed his own desire to defend it and to consolidate it. He objected only to the monopoly of power which the Old Guard obtained within the party and exercised through the machine. It was not difficult for his adversaries to demonstrate that the latter was the necessary sequel to the former, and that the party could maintain its monopoly only by delegating it to the Old Guard. Trotsky argued that the 400,000 members should be trusted to exercise their judgement and allowed to have their full share in shaping policy. Why then, his adversaries asked, had the party, under Lenin's inspiration and with Trotsky's consent, denied the mass of members that trust in recent years? Was it not because the party had been infiltrated by alien elements, ex-Mensheviks, turncoats, and even N.E.P. men? Had not even some authentic Bolsheviks become

[1] See, for instance, Stalin's replies in *Sochinenya*, vol. v, pp. 383–7, and vol. vi, pp. 5–40.

alienated from their comrades and corrupted by power and privilege? Trotsky stated that the purge in which hundreds of thousands had been expelled should have sufficiently purified the party and restored its integrity. But had not Lenin and the Central Committee stated repeatedly that this was not so? Had they not foreshadowed new and periodical purges? Had they all not agreed with Zinoviev that it was inevitable that the party should, because of its monopoly, comprise 'unconscious Mensheviks' and 'unconscious Social Revolutionaries'? No single purge could eliminate these alien elements, let alone the immature ones. Expelled, they were bound to reappear: they entered the party in good faith and bad with every group of new entrants. After it had been found necessary to expel one third of the membership in one year, how could 'the party' trust the judgement of the mass and allow it to exercise full rights?

Trotsky protested against the irrational self-suppression of Bolshevism which, however, followed ineluctably from the suppression by Bolshevism of all its enemies. If free competition of political trends within the party were to be tolerated, would that not allow the 'unconscious Mensheviks' to become articulate, to form a definite body of opinion, and to split the party? The monolithic system kept the heterogeneous mass unconscious of its heterogeneity and inarticulate; and thus it mechanically assured unity. Some of the more sophisticated adherents of the triumvirs saw that the dangers to which Trotsky pointed were real enough: the Old Guard might degenerate; and the monolithic system was bound to breed discontent and arouse sporadic revulsion which might also lead to schisms. But the party had to face perils whichever road it chose. Under monolithic control at least no schismatic movement could spread as easily as it could in a democratically ruled organization. The party machine would spot it in time, nip it in the bud, and keep the rest of the party more or less immune.

In other words, the party was in danger of losing its pro-letarian-socialist outlook, in danger of 'degeneration', no matter whether it entrusted its future to the mass of members or to the Old Guard. The predicament arose from the fact that the majority of the nation did not share the socialist outlook, that the working class was still disintegrated, and that, the revolution having failed to spread to the West, Russia had to fall back, materially and spiritually, on her own resources. The possibility of 'degeneration' was inherent in this situation; and what remained to be determined was whether its chief source lay in the heterogeneous mass of members or in the Old Guard. It was only natural that the Old Guard, or rather its majority, should trust its own socialist tradition and character infinitely more than it trusted the judgement and the political instincts of the 400,000 nominal party members. True, Trotsky did not ask the Old Guard to efface itself—he urged it to maintain its authority by democratic methods. But the Old Guard did not feel—and it was probably right in this—that it could do this. It was afraid of taking the risk; and it had a vested interest in preserving its acquired political privileges.

The reform within the party which Trotsky advocated could be upheld as the first act in the restoration of those free Soviet institutions which the party had sought to establish in 1917, as the beginning, that is, of a return to a workers' democracy and of the gradual dismantling of the single-party system. This idea was not far from Trotsky's mind;[1] but he did not voice it—either because he took it for granted but did not believe that the time had come to question and to weaken the single-party system; or because he did not wish to lay himself open to fresh and damaging charges and to complicate the controversy needlessly. Probably both these motives played their part. In effect, however, he claimed for the Bolsheviks a twofold privilege: the monopoly of freedom as well as the monopoly of power. These two privileges were incompatible. If the Bolsheviks wished to preserve their power they had to sacrifice their freedom.

There was a further weakness in Trotsky's attitude. He urged the party to preserve its proletarian-socialist outlook. At the same time he pointed out that workers from the bench formed only a small minority—one-sixth —of the party's membership. The majority consisted of industrial managers, civil servants, army officers, commissars, party officials, &c. (Some of these were of proletarian origin, but they were becoming more and more assimilated to the professional bureaucracy which the Soviets had inherited from Tsardom.) It was thus precisely under the rule of inner-party democracy that the influence of the

[1] See Trotsky's remarks on the secret vote in the USSR in a 'Letter to Friends' of 21 October 1928. *The Archives.*

workers was bound to be negligible and that the bureaucratic elements were bound to retain the upper hand. Trotsky therefore urged the party to recruit more workers and to 'strengthen its proletarian cells'. But he also insisted that the party should proceed cautiously and regulate carefully the admission of new members from the working class lest it be swamped by a politically raw and uncivilized mass.[1] This state of affairs appeared highly paradoxical from whichever angle it was approached. The application of democratic rules could not render the party democratic because it could only strengthen its bureaucracy; and the party could not become more enlightened and socialist in spirit by opening the doors widely to the working class.

In what then did the party's proletarian outlook consist? It would be easy to conclude that the Bolshevik leaders, including Trotsky, dealt in a mythology which bore no relation to the party's social composition and to its real attitude to the working classes. Inner Bolshevik controversy was indeed conducted, at least in part, in quasi-mythological terms, reflecting that substitutism which had led the party (and then the Old Guard) to consider itself as the *locum tenens* of the working class. Neither side to the controversy could frankly and fully admit the substitution. Neither could say that they were condemned to pursue the proletarian ideal of socialism without the support of the proletariat—such an avowal would have been incompatible with the whole tradition of Marxism and Bolshevism. They had to construct elaborate arguments and a peculiar and ambiguous idiom with its own conventions designed to veil and to explain away this sad state of affairs. The triumvirs were the worse sinners in this respect: and the mythology of substitutism finally congealed into the rigid cults of latter-day Stalinism. But even Trotsky, while he sought to reverse in part the process of substitution and struggled to tear to shreds the thickening fabric of the new mythology, could not help being entangled in it.[2]

[1] *The New Course*, pp. 20–21.

[2] Thus, referring to analogies between Bolshevism and Jacobinism, made by Mensheviks and liberals, as 'superficial and inconsistent', Trotsky wrote that the fall of the Jacobins had been caused by the social immaturity of their following and that the situation of the Bolsheviks was 'incomparably more favourable' in this respect. 'The proletariat forms the nucleus as well as the left wing of the [Russian] revolution. . . . *The proletariat is politically so strong* that while permitting, within limits, a new bourgeoisie to form itself . . . *it enables the peasantry to participate . . . directly . . . in the exercize of state power.*' Ibid., p. 40. (My italics, I. D.)

In truth, the Bolshevik bureaucracy was already the only organized and politically active force in society and state alike. It had appropriated the political power which had slipped from the hands of the working class; and it stood above all social classes and was *politically* independent of them all. And yet the party's socialist outlook was not a mere myth. It was not only that the Bolshevik bureaucracy subjectively saw itself as the exponent of socialism and that it cultivated, in its own manner, the tradition of proletarian revolution. Objectively, too, by the force of circumstances, it had to work as the chief agent and promoter of the country's development towards collectivism. What ultimately governed the behaviour and the policies of the bureaucracy was the fact that it was in charge of the publicly owned industrial resources of the Soviet Union. It represented the interests of the 'socialist sector' of the economy against those of the 'private sector', rather than the specific interests of any social class; and only to the extent to which the general interest of the 'socialist sector' coincided with the general or 'historic' interest of the working class, could the Bolshevik bureaucracy claim to act on behalf of that class.

The 'socialist sector' had its own claims and its own logic of development. Its first claim was that it should be made secure against wholesale restoration of capitalism and even against a partial but massive reintrusion of private enterprise. Its logic of development required planning and coordination of all the publicly owned branches of the economy and their rapid expansion. The alternative was contraction and decay. Expansion had to proceed, at least in part, at the cost of the 'private sector', through the absorption of its resources. This was to lead to conflict between the state and private property; and in this conflict the Bolshevik bureaucracy could not but side ultimately with the 'socialist sector'. True, even then it could not achieve socialism; for that presupposed economic abundance, high popular standards of living, of education, and of general civilization, the disappearance of striking social contrasts, the cessation of domination of man by man, and a spiritual climate corresponding to this general transformation of society. But to the Marxist the nationalized economy was the essential prerequisite of socialism, its genuine foundation. It was quite conceivable that even on that foundation the edifice of socialism might not rise; but it was unthinkable that it should rise without it. It was this foundation of socialism that the Bolshevik bureaucracy could not but defend.

At the point our narrative has reached, in the years 1923–4, the Bolshevik bureaucracy was only dimly aware of the nature of the interest to which it was tied. It was embarrassed and puzzled, as it were, by its own unprecedented command over the nation's industrial resources; and it did not quite know how to exercise it. It regarded uneasily, even fearfully, the property-loving peasantry; and it was momentarily even inclined to give more weight to the claims of the latter than to those of the 'socialist sector'. Only after a series of shocks and internal struggles was the Bolshevik bureaucracy to be driven to identify itself exclusively and irrevocably with the 'socialist sector' and its needs.

It was Trotsky's peculiar fate that even while he declared war on the political pretensions and the arrogance of the bureaucracy, he had to try and awaken it to its 'historic mission'. His advocacy of primitive socialist accumulation aimed at this. Yet such accumulation, in the circumstances under which it was to take place, could hardly be reconciled with the workers' democracy. The workers could not be expected to surrender voluntarily 'half their wages' to the state, as Trotsky urged them to do, in order to promote national investment. The state could take 'half their wages' only by force; and to do this it had to deprive them of every means of protest and to destroy the last vestiges of a workers' democracy. The two aspects of the programme which Trotsky expounded in 1923 were to prove incompatible in the near future; and therein lay the fundamental weakness of his position. The bureaucracy raged furiously against one part of his programme, the one which claimed a workers' democracy; but after much resistance, hesitation, and delay, it was to carry out the other part which spoke of primitive socialist accumulation.

.   .   .   .

At the turn of the year, while preparations for the thirteenth conference and the drive against the opposition were in full swing, Trotsky's health deteriorated. His fever persisted and he suffered from physical exhaustion and depression. He began to be overcome by a sense of approaching defeat. The campaign against him with its relentless barrage of accusations, distortions, and tricks, still seemed to him almost unreal; yet it induced in him a feeling of helplessness. He could only argue his case, but his argument was drowned in the hubbub. (Even the publication of *The New Course* was delayed by the public presses so that the pamphlet could not reach the cells before the opening of the thirteenth conference.) His mood alternated between tension and apathy. And so when his doctors told him to leave frost-bound Moscow—the winter was exceptionally severe that year —and to take a cure on the Caucasian coast of the Black Sea, this was for him an opportunity of escaping the oppressive atmosphere of the capital.[1]

He was getting ready for the journey when, on 16 January 1924, the thirteenth conference was opened. The triumvirs prepared a resolution blusteringly denouncing Trotsky and the Forty Six as guilty of a 'petty bourgeois deviation from Leninism'. The proceedings were taken up almost wholly by this question. In Trotsky's absence, Pyatakov, Preobrazhensky, V. Smirnov, and Radek argued the opposition's case. The triumvirs and their adherents replied with much venom; and their replies filled the newspapers. The outcome was a foregone conclusion. So thoroughly had the General Secretariat manipulated the elections that only three votes were cast against the motion condemning Trotsky. Even in the light of the accounts of the opposition's influence which Zinoviev's and Stalin's adherents gave at the conference, this vote was so ludicrously false that it should have had the effect of a bad and insolent joke.[2] But the triumvirs deliberately disregarded all the proprieties of normal political behaviour. Their purpose was to impress upon the party that they would stop at nothing and that all resistance was useless. The cells now knew that no matter how much they

[1] A bulletin on Trotsky's health, signed by Semashko, the Commissar of Health, and five Kremlin doctors, spoke of influenza, catarrh in the upper respiratory organs, enlargement of bronchial glands, persistent fever (not exceeding 38° C.), loss of weight and appetite, and reduced capacity for work. The doctors considered it necessary to release the patient from all duties, and to advise him to leave Moscow and take a 'climatic cure for at least two months'. The bulletin, signed on 21 December 1923, appeared in *Pravda* on 8 January 1924.

[2] According to Rykov, Pyatakov obtained a majority vote for the Opposition's motions at all party cells in Moscow which he addressed. (*13 Konferentsya RKP (b)*, pp. 83–91.) Yaroslavsky stated that one-third of the military party cells of Moscow had voted for the Opposition before the discussion in the garrison was stopped, and that the majority of student cells had done the same. Ibid., pp. 123–6.

stormed or protested, they had no chance of making the slightest imprint on official decisions. This alone was enough to show up the impotence of the opposition and to spread despondency in its ranks.

On 18 January, without waiting for the verdict, Trotsky set off on a slow journey to the south. Three days later his train halted at Tiflis. There, while the train was being shunted, he received a code message from Stalin informing him of Lenin's death. The blow hit Trotsky as if it had come suddenly—to the end Lenin's doctors, and Trotsky even more than they, had believed that they would save Lenin's life. With difficulty he jotted down for the newspapers a brief message mourning the deceased leader. 'Lenin is no more. These words fall upon our mind as heavily as a giant rock falls into the sea.'[1] The last flicker of the hope that Lenin would return, undo the triumvirs' work, and tear up their denunciatory resolutions, was extinguished.

For a moment Trotsky wondered whether he should not return to Moscow.[2] He got in touch with Stalin and asked for advice. Stalin told him that he would not be back in time for the funeral next day and counselled him to stay and proceed with the cure. In fact, Lenin's funeral took place several days later, on 27 January. Stalin had, of course, his reasons for keeping Trotsky away during the elaborate ceremonies in the course of which the triumvirs presented themselves to the world as Lenin's successors. From Tiflis, Trotsky, his head spinning with fever, proceeded to the sea-side resort of Sukhum. There, in semi-tropical sunshine, amid palms, flowering mimosas, and camellias, he lay many a long day on the veranda of a sanatorium and recollected in solitude the strange fortunes of his association with Lenin, the friendship with which Lenin first received him in London in 1902, their subsequent sharp disagreements, their eventual reunion, and the stormy and triumphant years during which they stood together at the helm of the revolution. It was as if the triumphant part of himself had together with Lenin gone down to the grave.

More recollections, fever, darkness, loneliness. A warm message from Lenin's weak and disconsolate widow now brought a crumb of comfort to the man whose prowess and power had only so recently amazed the world: she wrote that, just before he

[1] Trotsky, *O Lenine*, pp. 166–8.   [2] *Moya Zhizn*, vol. ii, p. 250.

died, Lenin had reread the character sketch of him Trotsky had written and was visibly moved by it, especially by the comparison Trotsky had drawn between him and Marx; and she wished Trotsky to know that Lenin had preserved to the end the friendly sentiment which he had shown him at their first meeting in London.[1]

Then gloom returned; and the sick man's imagination fed again on recollections, until a letter from his son Lyova jerked him back to the troubles of the day. Lyova described the great theatrically staged funeral in Moscow and the procession of huge crowds to Lenin's bier; and he expressed anguished astonishment at his father's absence.

Only now, it seems, as he read the disheartened letter from his adolescent son did it occur to Trotsky that he might have made a mistake when he did not return to Moscow. The multitudes which marched past Lenin's bier watched tensely the members of the Politbureau who stood guard over it and noted Trotsky's absence. Their imagination had been fired by the symbolism of the ceremonies; and in this mood they wondered why he was not there. Was it perhaps because of the difference which, according to the triumvirs, had separated him from the deceased man and because of his 'petty bourgeois deviation from Leninism'?

Trotsky's absence did not merely breed rumour and gossip in Moscow. It left the field free to his adversaries. This was a time of intense activity in the Kremlin and of important decisions. The succession to Lenin in government as well as party was being settled in the most formal manner. Rykov took Lenin's place as *Predsovnarkom*, chairman of the Council of the People's Commissars; and Rykov's place at the Supreme Council of the National Economy was taken by Dzerzhinsky. (Rykov was appointed *Predsovnarkom* because he had been Lenin's deputy—had Trotsky accepted the deputy's post, it would have been difficult to promote Rykov over his head.) Then the triumvirs made a new and more determined attempt to obtain control of the Commissariat of War. They dismissed from

[1] Many years later, after Trotsky had been exiled, Krupskaya told Count M. Károlyi and his wife: 'He [Trotsky] loved Vladimir Ilyich very deeply; on learning of his death he fainted and did not recover for two hours'. *Memoirs of Michael Károlyi*, p. 265.

the Commissariat Sklyansky, Trotsky's devoted assistant, and sent a special delegation to Sukhum to inform Trotsky that Frunze, who was Zinoviev's adherent, would take Sklyansky's place—a year later Frunze was to succeed Trotsky himself as Commissar of War. The Politbureau and the Central Committee were also giving effect to the decisions of the thirteenth conference directed against the opposition: still more adherents of the opposition were dismissed, demoted, or reprimanded. The propaganda department worked full blast to establish that cult of Lenin under which Lenin's writings were to be quoted as Gospel against all dissent and criticism, the cult which was designed primarily as an 'ideological weapon' against Trotskyism.

And, last but not least, the triumvirs stole yet more of Trotsky's thunder. He had dwelt on the weakness of the 'proletarian cells' as the chief cause of the party's bureaucratic deformation and had urged the party to recruit more members from the working class. This demand had undoubtedly gained him sympathy among workers. The triumvirs resolved to open at once a spectacular recruiting drive in the factories. But while Trotsky had advised a careful selection, they decided to recruit en masse, to accept any worker who cared to join, and to waive all customary tests and conditions. At the thirteenth conference they recommended the recruitment at a stroke of 100,000 workers. After Lenin's death they threw open the doors of the party even wider: between February and May 1924, 240,000 workers were inscribed.[1] This was a mockery of the Bolshevik principle of organization which required that, as the élite and vanguard of the proletariat, the party should accept only the politically advanced and the battle hardened. Among the mass of new entrants, the politically immature, the backward, the dullminded and the docile, the climbers, and the nest-featherers, formed a considerable proportion. The triumvirs hectically motioned the newcomers on to the band wagon, patted them on the back, flattered them, and exalted the keen and infallible class instinct and class consciousness that had brought them into the party.

This recruitment—the 'Lenin levy'—was presented as the spontaneous homage of the working class to Lenin and as the party's rejuvenation. The triumvirs were in effect saying to

[1] See Molotov's report on the 'Lenin Levy' in *13 Syezd RKP* (*b*), pp. 516 ff.

Trotsky: 'you thought you would endear yourself to the workers
by playing them against the bureaucrats and by arguing that
the proletarian element in the party should be strengthened.
We have strengthened it, and we have done so without any of
your scruples—we have wheedled a quarter of a million workers
into the party. And what is the result? Has the party thereby
become ennobled, more democratic, or more proletarian-
socialist in outlook? Has bureaucracy been weakened?' The
'Lenin levy' in fact supplied the triumvirs with a devoted
clientèle to which they presently appealed in the struggle against
the opposition. Trotsky was aware what this demagogic exploitation of his idea meant; but he could not utter a word
against the 'Lenin levy'. Had he done so, he would have been
howled down as the enemy of the workers and as the hypocrite
who at first pretended that he longed to see more proletarians in
the party, but who now betrayed his fear of them and his true
petty bourgeois nature. He made *une bonne mine au mauvais jeu*;
and he even chimed in with the official eulogies for the Lenin
levy.[1]

Trotsky's moody aloofness at a moment so critical for his and
the party's fortunes was, of course, in some measure caused by
his illness. Yet even more debilitating was his feeling that the
tide was running against him. This was an unfathomed tide,
and he tried to gauge and assess it in Marxist terms. He concluded that the revolution was on the ebb and that he and his
friends were being hit by a groundswell of reaction. The nature
of the reaction was confused and confusing: it looked like, and
up to a point it was, a prolongation of the revolution. He was
convinced that it was his duty to resist; but he did not see clearly
by what means to resist and what were the prospects. It was a
turbid and a slimy tide that threw him back. None of the great

[1] In a speech at Tiflis (on 11 April 1924) Trotsky said: 'The most important
political fact of the last few months . . . has been the influx of factory workers into
the ranks of our party. This is the best form in which [the working class] . . . demonstrates its will . . . and votes confidence in the Russian Communist Party. . . . This
is a true, reliable, and infallible test . . . far more genuine than any parliamentary
election.' (Quoted from Trotsky, *Zapad i Vostok*, p. 27.) Looking back on this 'test'
twelve years later, Trotsky wrote: 'Availing itself of the death of Lenin, the ruling
group announced a "Leninist levy". . . . The political aim of this manoeuvre was
to dissolve the revolutionary vanguard in raw [inexperienced and meek] human
material. . . . The scheme was successful . . . the "Leninist levy" was a death blow
to the party of Lenin.' *The Revolution Betrayed*, pp. 97–98.

PLATE VII

(*a*) Lenin's body brought to Moscow for the funeral

Carrying the coffin is Dzherzhinsky, head of the G.P.U. (in front) and at the right
Sapronov (bare-headed), a leader of the Workers' Opposition

(*b*) Molotov and Bukharin in 1921 or 1922

PLATE VIII

Trotsky resting in the Caucasus in 1924

issues over which they wrestled at the Politbureau could be made to stand out in clear outline. Everything was blurred. The greatest issues were dragged down to the level of sordid intrigue. Had he, as his adversaries claimed, coveted personal power, he would have behaved quite differently, of course. But in his whole being he shrunk from the scramble; and half-consciously perhaps he was glad to escape from it into his melancholy lonesomeness in the Caucasus.

In the spring his health was improved and he was back in Moscow. The party was just getting ready for the thirteenth congress convened in May. The Central Committee and senior delegates met on 22 May to acquaint themselves with Lenin's will which had hitherto been in Krupskaya's keeping. The reading of the will had the effect of a bolt from the blue. Those present listened in utter perplexity to the passage in which Lenin castigated Stalin's rudeness and disloyalty and urged the party to remove him from the General Secretariat. Stalin seemed crushed. Once again his fortunes trembled in the balance. Amid all the worshipping of Lenin's memory, amid the endless genuflexions and vows to 'hold Lenin's word sacred', it seemed inconceivable that the party should disregard Lenin's advice.

But once again Stalin was saved by the trustfulness of his future victims. Zinoviev and Kamenev, who held his fate in their hands, rushed to his rescue. They implored their comrades to leave him in his post. They used all their zeal and histrionic talents to persuade them that whatever Lenin held Stalin guilty of, the offence was not grave and that Stalin had made ample amends. Lenin's word was sacred, Zinoviev exclaimed, but Lenin himself, if he could have witnessed, as they all had, Stalin's sincere efforts to mend his ways, would not have urged the party to remove him. (In fact, Stalin's embarrassment suited Zinoviev who was already afraid of him, but did not dare to break the partnership. Zinoviev hoped to earn Stalin's gratitude and to put himself back into the position of the senior triumvir.)

All eyes were now fixed on Trotsky: would he rise, expose the farce, and demand that Lenin's will be respected? He did not utter a word. He conveyed his contempt and disgust at the spectacle only through expressive grimaces and shoulder shrugging. He could not bring himself to speak out on a matter in which his own standing was so obviously involved. It was resolved to disregard Lenin's advice on Stalin. But if so, then Lenin's will could not be published; for it would show up and render ridiculous all the mummeries of the Lenin cult. Against Krupskaya's protest the Central Committee voted by an over-whelming majority for the suppression of the will. To the end Trotsky, as though numb and frozen with detestation, kept his silence.[1]

In the last week of May the thirteenth congress assembled. The triumvirs asked it to repeat with bell, book, and candle the anathema on Trotsky which the less authoritative conference had pronounced in January. The congress turned into an orgy of denunciation. Zinoviev fumed and fulminated: 'It was now a thousand times more necessary than ever that the party should be monolithic.'[2] Months before he had urged his part-ners to order Trotsky's expulsion from the party and even arrest; but Stalin cool-headedly refused to comply and hastened to declare in *Pravda* that no action was contemplated against Trotsky, and that a party leadership without Trotsky was 'un-thinkable'.[3] At the congress Zinoviev struck out again; and in a moment of fatal recklessness he demanded that Trotsky should not merely 'lay down arms' but appear before the congress and recant. Not before Trotsky had done so, Zinoviev stated, would there be peace in the party.[4] This was the first time in the party's experience that a member had been confronted with the demand for recantation. Even this congress, zealous as it was to pronounce anathema on Trotsky, was shocked. The mass of delegates rose to give an ovation to Krupskaya when she, with-out supporting Trotsky, made a strong and dignified protest against Zinoviev's 'psychologically impossible demand'.[5]

Once only did Trotsky defend himself.[6] He spoke calmly and persuasively, with an undertone of resigned acceptance of de-feat; but he refused adamantly to retract a single one of his criticisms. He was anxious not to pour oil on the flames and not

[1] Bajanov, who acted as secretary at this meeting, gives an eye-witness descrip-tion of the scene (op. cit., pp. 43–47). Trotsky acknowledges implicitly the authen-ticity of Bajanov's account. (Trotsky, *Stalin*, p. 376.) In *The Suppressed Testament of Lenin* Trotsky adds this detail: 'Radek . . . sat beside me during the reading . . . and leaned to me with the words: "Now they won't dare go against you." I answered: "On the contrary, they will have to go the limit, and moreover as quickly as possible." ' p. 17.

[2] *13 Syezd RKP* (*b*), p. 112.

[3] *Pravda*, 18 December 1923.

[4] *13 Syezd RKP* (*b*), p. 113.

[5] Ibid., pp. 235–7.

[6] Ibid., pp. 153–68.

to burn his boats. He pleaded that he had framed all his criticisms in the terms of the Politbureau's resolution on the New Course, and that there was nothing in what he had said and written which had not been said or written in one form or another by his adversaries also. He even dissociated himself from some of the Forty Six who had demanded freedom for inner-party groupings. 'The allegation that I am in favour of permitting groupings is incorrect', he said. 'True, I did make the mistake of falling ill at the critical moment and did not have the opportunity . . . of denying this and many other allegations. . . . It is impossible to make any distinction between a faction and a grouping.' He repeated, however, that it was because of wrong policies and of the faulty inner-party régime that differences of opinion, which should have been only transient, became fixed and hardened and led to 'factionalism'. To Zinoviev's call for a recantation he replied:

Nothing could be simpler or easier, morally and politically, than to admit before one's own party that one had erred. . . . No great moral heroism is needed for that. . . . Comrades, none of us wishes to be or can be right against the party. In the last instance the party is always right, because it is *the only historic instrument which the working class possesses for the solution of its fundamental tasks*. I have said already that nothing would be easier than to say before the party that all these criticisms and all these declarations, warnings, and protests were mistaken from beginning to end. I cannot say so, however, because, comrades, I do not think so. I know that one ought not to be right against the party. One can be right only with the party and through the party because history has not created any other way for the realization of one's rightness. The English have the saying 'My country, right or wrong'. With much greater justification we can say: My party, right or wrong—wrong on certain partial, specific issues or at certain moments. . . . It would be ridiculous perhaps, almost indecent, to make any personal statements here, but I do hope that in case of need I shall not prove the meanest soldier on the meanest of Bolshevik barricades.[1]

He ended his plea by saying that he would accept the party's verdict even if it were unjust. But acceptance meant for him submission to discipline in action, not in thought. 'I cannot say so, comrades, because I do not think so', these words stood out in their stark simplicity and unyieldingness amid all the subtle

[1] Ibid., pp. 165–6. (My italics. I.D.)

reasonings, incisive arguments, and imaginative appeals in which his speech abounded. His calm and restraint infuriated the party secretaries. Bent but unbroken, disciplined but unrepentant, he seemed to them all the more defiant. His voice sounded in their ears like the cry of their own uneasy conscience; and they tried to blast it with insult. They drew from him no rejoinder. Only at the end of the congress he went out to the Red Square to address a meeting of Moscow's 'communist' children, the 'pioneers'. He greeted them as the 'new shift' who would one day come into the workshop of the revolution to replace those who had grown old, weary, and corrupt.[1]

.   .   .   .

By this time the whole Communist International had been drawn into the controversy. The triumvirs had to explain and justify their attitude to the foreign communists, from whom they were anxious to obtain a clear endorsement of Trotsky's condemnation in order to produce it to the Russian party. Yet the European communists—and in these years the influence of the International was still virtually confined to Europe—were alarmed by what was going on in Moscow and shocked by the violence of the attacks on Trotsky. To them Trotsky had been the embodiment of the Russian revolution, of its heroic legend, and of international communism. Because of his European manner of expression, he had appealed to them more than any other Russian leader. He had been the author of the International's stirring manifestoes, which in ideas, language and *éclat*, recalled the *Communist Manifesto* of Marx and Engels. He had been the International's strategist and tactician as well as inspirer. European communists could not see what it was that set Zinoviev, the International's President, and the other Russian leaders, against Trotsky; and they feared the consequences of the conflict for Russia and international communism. Their first impulse was therefore to defend Trotsky.

Before the end of the year 1923 the Central Committees of two important Communist parties, the French and the Polish,

---

[1] The speech is appended to the record of the congress. Ibid. Max Eastman, who was present at the congress, relates that he urged Trotsky to take a more militant attitude and to read from the platform Lenin's testament, but Trotsky would not listen. Eastman's account is confirmed by Trotsky himself, in a letter to Muralov, written from his exile at Alma Ata in 1928 (*The Archives*).

protested to Moscow against the defamation of Trotsky and appealed to the antagonists to compose their differences in a comradely spirit.[1] This happened shortly after Brandler had, on behalf of his party, asked that Trotsky should assume the leadership of the planned communist insurrection in Germany. The triumvirs resented the protests and feared that Trotsky, defeated in the Russian party, might yet turn the International against them. Zinoviev saw in the action of the three parties a challenge to his presidential authority.

At this time the International was agitated by the defeat it had just suffered in Germany. The questions connected with the defeat, the crisis which led up to it, and the policy of the German party, questions which in themselves provided enough ground for controversy, at once became entangled with the contention in the Russian party.[2]

The German crisis began when the French occupied the Ruhr early in 1923. The Ruhr was aflame with German resistance; and soon the whole of the Reich was embraced by a strong nationalist movement of protest against the Versailles Treaty and its consequences. At first the bourgeois parties led the movement; and the communists were swept aside. But then these parties, uncertain of the outcome, began to vacillate and withdraw, especially when social strife threatened to deepen the political turmoil. Germany's economy was thrown out of balance. Depreciation of money developed with catastrophic speed. The workers, whom inflation cheated of wages, were furious and impatient for action. The communists, who had lain low since the March rising of 1921, felt a strong wind in their sails. In July their Central Committee called upon the working class to prepare for a revolutionary decision. Its confidence in

[1] Souvarine spoke of the French protest at the thirteenth congress of the Russian party (*13 Syezd RKP (b)*, pp. 371–3). The Polish protest is in the archives of the Polish Communist party. (Deutscher, 'La Tragedie du communisme polonais entre deux guerres' in *Les Temps modernes*, March 1958.)

[2] The sources used for this account of the German crisis are: Trotsky's numerous essays, Brandler's reminiscences and explanations given to the author, Ruth Fischer, *Stalin and German Communism*, Thalheimer, *1923, Eine verpasste Revolution?*, Radek's, Zinoviev's, and Bukharin's analyses, Kuusinen's essay in *Za Leninizm, The Lessons of the German Events* (a record of the January 1924 session of the Executive of the Comintern devoted to the debate over Germany); the records of the congresses and conferences of the Comintern, and the Soviet and German Communist parties, at which the issue was thrashed out; and, finally, the extensive discussion that went on in the international communist press for over ten years after 1924.

its strength and capacity for revolutionary action, however, did
not go deep; nor was it shared by all those concerned with its
policy. Radek, who was in Germany as representative of the
International's Executive, warned Moscow that the German
party took too hopeful a view and that it might be heading for
another abortive insurrection. Zinoviev and Bukharin spurred
the Germans on, yet without proposing any definite course of
action. At this stage, in July, Trotsky said that he was not sufficiently informed about conditions in Germany to express an
opinion.

Presently, Trotsky arrived at the conclusion that Germany
was indeed about to enter an acutely revolutionary situation
and that the German party should not merely be encouraged
to take a bold line but assisted in the working out of a clear plan
of revolutionary action culminating in armed insurrection. The
date of the insurrection should be fixed in advance so that the
German party could conduct the struggle through the preliminary phases, prepare the working class, and deploy its forces
with a view to the *dénouement*. The Executive hesitated. Not only
Radek—Stalin, too, doubted the reality of the 'revolutionary
situation' and held that the Germans should be restrained.[1]
Zinoviev went on prodding them but balked at the plan for
insurrection. The Politbureau, absorbed in its domestic preoccupations, discussed the matter casually; and Zinoviev conveyed its broad view to the leaders of the International.
Somewhat half-heartedly it was decided to give the German
party the cue for revolution, to assist it in military preparations,
and, in the end, even to fix a date for the rising. The date was
to be as close as possible to the anniversary of the Bolshevik insurrection—it was to be 'the German October'.

In September Heinrich Brandler, the leader of the German
party, arrived in Moscow to consult the Executive. A bricklayer
in his earlier years and a disciple of Rosa Luxemburg, a shrewd
and cautious tactician and able organizer, he was not convinced
that circumstances favoured revolution. When he expressed his
doubts to Zinoviev—doubts very similar to those Zinoviev himself had entertained on the eve of the Russian October—the
latter, torn between hesitation and the desire to act resolutely,
sought to overrule Brandler's objections with heated argument

---

[1] See my *Stalin*, pp. 393–4.

and table-thumping. Brandler yielded. In his own party, especially in its Berlin branch which was led by Ruth Fischer and Arkadi Maslov, impatience for action and confidence had mounted high. He thought that he had found the same confidence in Moscow, for he assumed that Zinoviev spoke for the whole Politbureau. He diffidently concluded that if the leaders of the only victorious Communist party thought, as the Berliners did, that the hour had struck, then he ought to waive his objections.

It was at this point, feeling, as he himself put it, that he was not 'a German Lenin', that Brandler asked the Politbureau to assign Trotsky to lead the insurrection. Instead of Trotsky the Politbureau delegated Radek and Pyatakov. A plan of action was laid down, which centred on Saxony, Brandler's homeland where communist influence was strong, the Social Democrats headed the provincial government, and where they and the Communists already acted in a united front. Brandler and some of his comrades were to join the government of Saxony and use their influence in order to arm the workers. From Saxony the rising was to spread to Berlin, Hamburg, central Germany, and the Ruhr. According to Brandler—and his testimony on this point is confirmed by other sources—both Zinoviev and Trotsky pressed this plan on him.[1] Moreover, Zinoviev through his agents in Germany forced the pace of events so much that the coalition government in Saxony was formed on orders sent by telegram from Moscow; it was *en route*, while he was returning to Germany, that Brandler learned from a newspaper bought at a railway station in Warsaw that he was a Minister.[2]

Even if conditions in Germany had favoured revolution, the artificiality and the clumsiness of the plan and the remoteness of its direction and control would have been enough to produce a failure. The conditions were probably less favourable than they were assumed to be, and the social crisis in Germany less deep. Since the summer the economy had begun to recover, the Mark was stabilized, and the political atmosphere had become calmer. The Central Committee failed to arouse the mass of workers and to prepare them for insurrection. The scheme for arming the

---

[1] Ruth Fischer, op. cit., pp. 311–18; Zinoviev's speech in *The Lessons of the German Events*, pp. 36–37 ff. and in *13 Konferentsya RKP (b)*, pp. 158–78; and Trotsky, *Uroki Oktyabrya*.   [2] This has been related to the writer by Brandler himself.

workers miscarried: the Communists found the arsenals in
Saxony empty. From Berlin the central government sent a military expedition against the Red province. And so when the
moment of rising arrived, Brandler, supported by Radek and
Pyatakov, cancelled the battle orders. Only through a fault in
liaison did insurgents move into action at Hamburg. They
fought alone and, after a hopeless combat lasting several days,
were routed.

These events were to have a powerful impact on the Soviet
Union. They destroyed the chances of revolution in Germany
and Europe for many years ahead. They demoralized and
divided the German party and, coinciding with similar setbacks in Poland and Bulgaria, they had this effect on the International as a whole. They imparted to Russian communism a
deep and definite sense of isolation, a disbelief in the revolutionary capacity of the European working classes—even a disdain
for them. Out of this mood there developed gradually an attitude of Russian revolutionary self-sufficiency and self-centredness which was to find its expression in the doctrine of Socialism
in One Country. Immediately, the German débâcle became an
issue in the Russian contest for power. Communists both in
Russia and Germany delved into the causes of the defeat and
were eager to fix the responsibilities. In the Politbureau the
triumvirs and Trotsky laid the blame on each other.

On the face of it, there existed no connexion between the
German fiasco and the Russian controversy. The lines of division
were different and they even cut across one another. Radek and
Pyatakov, the two 'Trotskyists', had been from the outset at
least as sceptical as Stalin was about the chances in Germany; it
was they who advised Brandler to cancel the orders for insurrection. On the other hand, Zinoviev had, after hesitation,
sanctioned the plan for the rising, of which Trotsky was the
initiator; but he also sanctioned the cancellation of the marching
orders. Trotsky was convinced that the German party and the
International had missed a unique opportunity; and he held
that Zinoviev and Stalin were at least as much responsible for
that as Brandler. The triumvirs replied that the rising had been
bungled on the spot by the two Trotskyists; and they insisted
on Brandler's 'opportunism' and on the necessity to depose him
as leader of the German party.

Vis-à-vis Brandler the triumvirs were actuated by mixed motives. The rank and file of the German party had turned bitterly against him; and the organization of Berlin clamoured for his dismissal. Zinoviev was eager to appease the clamour and to save his own and the International's prestige by making a scapegoat of Brandler. In deposing him and installing Fischer and Maslov in the leadership of the German party, Zinoviev made of that party his fief. He had yet another reason for insisting on Brandler's exemplary punishment: he suspected Brandler and his friends in the German Central Committee of sympathy with Trotsky. In denouncing Brandler as Trotsky's follower Zinoviev also sought to burden Trotsky with the blame for Brandler's 'capitulation'. At last Brandler, unable to make head or tail of the rivalries, anxious to disentangle the German question from the Russian issues, and eager to save his position, declared his support to the official Russian leadership, that is to the triumvirs. This, however, did not save him.

Such was the situation in January 1924, when the Executive of the International met to hold a formal inquest on the German defeat. The meeting was preceded by much wire-pulling and many shifts in the Central Committees of foreign parties, designed to secure in advance the Executive's support for Zinoviev. When the Executive met, Trotsky was ill in a village not far from Moscow. He did not state his views, but asked Radek to convey their joint protest against Brandler's demotion and the changes in the German Central Committee. Radek conveyed the protest, but being mainly interested in defending his own and Brandler's policy, he gave the Executive the impression that Trotsky associated himself with that policy; and this enabled the triumvirs to link Trotsky once again with the 'right wing' in the German party.[1] In truth, Trotsky never ceased to be critical of Brandler's conduct; and the fact that Brandler had now declared his support for the triumvirs could not have commended him to Trotsky. Nevertheless, Trotsky objected on principle to the installation in Moscow of a 'guillotine' for foreign communist leaders. Foreign parties, he held, must be allowed to learn from their own experience and mistakes, to

---

[1] *The Lessons of the German Events*, p. 14. See also Trotsky's letters about this to A. Treint and A. Neurath, written in 1931 and 1932, and published in *The New International* (February 1938).

manage their own affairs, and to elect their own leaders. Brandler's demotion established a pernicious precedent.

Thus Trotsky demanded for the International the same inner freedom which he claimed for the Russian party; and he did it with the same result. Zinoviev had by now complete mastery over the International. He had deposed some of those foreign leaders who had appealed to the Politbureau to restrain its vehemence against Trotsky. Others allowed themselves to be browbeaten and apologized for their *faux pas*. Consequently, the Executive, although it failed to carry its inquest on Germany to a clear conclusion, left Zinoviev with his reputation untarnished; and it endorsed the demotions and promotions he had ordered. This allowed him presently to obtain from the International an endorsement of the triumvirs' action against Trotsky and the Forty Six.

In May, at the thirteenth congress of the Russian party, the leaders, old and new, of all the European parties appeared on the platform to echo the anathema on Trotsky. Only one foreign delegate, Boris Souvarine, Editor of *L'Humanité*, himself half-Russian and half-French, raised his voice against it, declaring that the French Central Committee had decided by twenty-two votes against only two to protest against the attacks on Trotsky, without necessarily declaring thereby its solidarity with the opposition; but that he, personally, shared Trotsky's views and would not abjure them. Souvarine's lonely voice only stressed Trotsky's defeat.[1]

A month later, the fifth congress of the International—the so-called 'congress of Bolshevization'—met in Moscow to put its seal under the excommunication of Trotsky, to which a denunciation of Radek and Brandler was added. Characteristic of the mood of the congress was a speech by Ruth Fischer, the new leader of the German party. A young, trumpet-tongued woman, without any revolutionary experience or merit, yet idolized by the communists of Berlin, she railed against Trotsky, Radek, and Brandler, those Mensheviks, opportunists, and 'liquidators of revolutionary principle' who had 'lost faith in the German and European revolution'. She called for a monolithic International, modelled on the Russian party, from which dissent and contest of opinion would be banished. 'This world

[1] *13 Syezd RKP (b)*, pp. 371-3.

congress should not allow the International to be transformed into an agglomeration of all sorts of trends; it should forge ahead and embark upon the road which leads to a single Bolshevik world party.'[1] Spokesmen of the French, English, and American delegations followed suit; and, shrinking from no abuse or insult, they challenged Trotsky to appear before the congress and state his views.[2] Trotsky refused to enter into any disputation. For one thing, he felt that all disputation was now useless. For another, having already been threatened with expulsion from the party if he indulged in any further controversy, he may have suspected that the challenge was a trap. And so he declared that he accepted the verdict of the Russian party and had no intention of appealing against it to the International. Even his silence, however, was received as proof of his malfeasance: echoing Zinoviev, delegates demanded from him nothing less than recantation.[3] He turned a deaf ear; and in the course of the full three weeks the congress heard nothing but foul-mouthed vituperation against the man to whom the previous four congresses had listened with deep respect and adoration. This time not a single voice rose to vindicate him. (Souvarine had by now been expelled from the French party for having translated and published Trotsky's *New Course*.)[4] Yet Trotsky still wrote the last of his great Comintern manifestoes for this congress. But he was not re-elected as full member of the Executive; Stalin took his place.

What accounted for the change that had come over the International? Only a few months earlier its three greatest parties had enough courage and dignity to rebuke the triumvirs. Now all gave a spectacle of submission and self-abasement. Zinoviev, we know, had in the meantime shuffled, displaced, or broken up at will the German, French, and Polish Central Committees. But why did these Committees and the parties behind them accept his dictates? Most of the deposed leaders had guided their parties from the day of foundation and had enjoyed high moral authority; yet nowhere did the rank and file stand up for them and refuse to accept the Executive's orders and to acknowledge Zinoviev's nominees as leaders. It took Zinoviev only a few weeks or at the most a few months to bring

---

[1] *5 Vsemirnyi Kongress Kominterna*, vol. i, pp. 175–92.
[2] Ibid., pp. 550–9. [3] Ibid., vol. ii, pp. 156–7. [4] Ibid., p. 181.

about what appeared to be a complete upheaval in the entire communist movement. But the ease with which he brought it about indicated a deep-seated weakness in the International. Only a diseased body could be thus subverted at a stroke.

Lenin and Trotsky had founded the International in the expectation that it would soon rally to its banners the majority of at least the European labour movement.[1] They expected it to become what its name said it was: a world party, transcending national boundaries and interests, not a decorous and platonic association of national parties in the style of the Second International. They believed in the basic unity of the revolutionary processes in the world; and this unity made it essential in their view that the new organization should possess a strong international leadership and discipline. The Twenty One Conditions of membership, which the second congress adopted in 1920, were designed to give the International a constitution appropriate to this purpose, and to establish, among other things, a centralized and strong leadership in the Executive. Trotsky had supported that constitution wholeheartedly.[2] By itself it was not calculated to assure the preponderance of the Russian party in the International. All parties were represented on the Executive in a democratic manner. Its few Russian members enjoyed in principle no privilege. Internationalism implied the subordination of national viewpoints to the broader interest of the entire movement but certainly not to any national-Russian viewpoint. Had revolution won in any of the important European countries or had at least the Communist parties there grown in strength and confidence, such international leadership and discipline might have become real. But the ebb of revolution in Europe tended to transform the International into an adjunct to the Russian party. The self-assurance of its European sections was weak; and it dwindled from year to year. The defeated parties developed a sense of inferiority; and they came to look to the Bolsheviks, the only successful practitioners of revolution, to tackle their problems, to solve their dilemmas, and to make their decisions for them. The Bolsheviks responded, first from a sense of solidarity, then from habit, and finally from self-interest, until they were only too eager to handle the leading strings in which the foreign parties had so willingly put themselves. International

---

[1] *The Prophet Armed*, p. 452.   [2] Ibid., p. 467.

leadership and discipline became in fact Russian leadership and discipline; and all the wide prerogatives which the Twenty One Points had vested in the international Executive of Lenin's and Trotsky's expectations passed almost imperceptibly to the Russian members of the Executive.

Lenin was disturbed by this state of affairs. He recalled Engels's forebodings about the preponderance of the German party in the Second International and pointed out that the supremacy of the Russian party might be not less harmful.[1] He tried to give foreign communists more self-reliance and even suggested that the Executive should be transferred from Moscow to Berlin or another European capital in order to remove it from the constant pressure of Russian interests and preoccupations. However, most foreign communists preferred to see the hub of their International placed in the safety of Red Moscow rather than expose it to persecution and police raids in bourgeois capitals.

Lenin's misgivings proved all too justified. As the years passed the intervention of the Russian members of the Executive in the affairs of foreign communism grew ever more meddlesome. Zinoviev ruled the International with relish, flamboyance, lack of tact and scruple. But even Trotsky found himself, as member of the Executive, involved in the exercise of a tutelage which was inherent in the situation. As chairman of the French commission of the Comintern, he supervised with plenary power the day-to-day work of the French communists. The German, the Italian, the Spanish, and the British parties eagerly sought his advice on every major issue and even on the detail of their activity; and he gave his advice freely.

This led him to make pronouncements and to engage in a voluminous correspondence which in themselves form a running commentary on the history of these crucial years, a commentary rich in thought, sparkling with wit, and often astonishingly far-sighted.[2] But parts of the correspondence also reflect the tutelage. Here, for instance, he summons peremptorily Frossard, the French leader, to face grave but not unjustified charges at the

[1] Lenin, *Sochinenya*, vol. xxxiii, pp. 392–4. More explicit remarks to this effect are in Lenin's, still unpublished, statements made at the Executive of the International.

[2] See his *Pyat Let Kominterna*, published also in English under the title *The First Five Years of the Communist International*, vols. i and ii.

International's assizes in Moscow. There he censures communist
editors and prescribes the tactical line and even the topics and
the style for their newspapers. Here he chides *L'Humanité* for
publishing the writings of dubious contributors. There again he
lays down a date by which the French party must expel, as it
had undertaken to do, all Free Masons and 'all careerists'. On
several occasions he acts as umpire to rival groups and lays
down the law for them.[1] These, it is true, are extreme and exceptional instances. He never hectored or cajoled his subordinates in the Comintern, as Zinoviev and then Stalin did; and he
always expected them to speak their mind on the affairs of the
Russian party as frankly as he expressed himself on the conduct
of their parties. It was not his fault if foreign communists rarely
felt self-confident enough to speak their mind. He still treated
the Executive as a truly international body and acted on its
behalf from the general principles of communism and not from
any peculiarly Russian angle. It was in this spirit that he used
the wide powers which the Twenty One Points had vested in the
Executive.

The actual preponderance of the Russian party, however,
made it all too easy to use the Twenty One Points as the constitutional framework for the establishment of a Russian *de facto*
dictatorship. This was what Zinoviev did even before 1923,
when he was still curbed by Lenin and Trotsky. Later all restraints had gone. Moreover, inner democracy could not survive
in the International after it had withered in the Russian party.
The habits of 'substitutism' spread to the entire movement; and
the chiefs of the Bolshevik Old Guard came to look upon themselves as the trustees not merely of the Russian working class but
of the working classes of the world.

In 1923–4 Zinoviev and Stalin indeed set out to refashion the
European movement after the new Russian image. They could
not tolerate in the International the opposition which they were
bent on suppressing in their own party. Just as they had used the
Russian 1921 ban on inner-party factions to destroy Trotsky's
influence at home, so they used the wide powers they wielded
under the Twenty One Points to destroy his influence abroad.
Trotsky had endorsed both the 1921 ban and the Twenty

[1] Ibid., vol. ii, pp. 124–84; Rosmer, *Moscou sous Lénine*, pp. 236–60; Frossard,
De Jaurès à Lénine.

One Points. His adversaries planned their moves so that every step they made appeared as a plain application of the principles and precedents laid down with Trotsky's consent, if not on his initiative. They struck him down with his own weapons— only that he had never used these weapons for any comparable purpose or with comparable brutality. He had occasionally threatened foreign communists with disciplinary sanctions; they demoted, dismissed, and denounced them wholesale. He had demanded that the Comintern should, in accordance with its programme, tolerate no bourgeois pacifism, no Free Masonry, and no 'social-patriotism'. They purged it of 'Trotskyism' which had hitherto been almost synonymous with communism.

. . . .

In May the thirteenth congress of the Russian party closed the debate which had started with the proclamation of the New Course. Trotsky could not reopen the controversy without incurring the charge of a breach of discipline; and he made no attempt to reopen it. He once described admiringly the self-discipline which had induced Jaurès to put, when necessary, 'his bovine neck under the yoke of party discipline'. He now put his own neck under a much harder yoke and refrained from discussing in public the party's economic policy and inner régime which had been declared taboo. Yet he could not reconcile himself to being branded as a semi-Menshevik guilty of a 'petty bourgeois deviation from Leninism'. Debarred from discussing the crucial and topical issues of policy, he fell back on history to vindicate himself. The opportunity offered itself when the State Publishers, carrying out an earlier decision of the Central Committee to produce a many-volumed edition of Trotsky's *Works*, prepared for the presses the book which contained his speeches and writings of 1917. He prefaced it with a long essay entitled 'The Lessons of October'. The volume appeared in the autumn of 1924; and at once it stirred up a storm.

Trotsky's speeches and writings of 1917 provided a strong reply to the obloquy about him as the unreformed Menshevik, for they reminded the party of his role in the revolution and of the unswerving militancy with which he then confronted the Mensheviks. Such a reminder was needed. The historical memory of nations, social classes, and parties is short, especially in times of great upheaval when the breathtaking events of one year crowd out of peoples' minds the events of preceding years, when in political life generations or age groups succeed one another at a furious pace, when the veterans of early struggles rapidly dwindle in numbers, disperse, or grow exhausted and weary, and when the young plunge into new struggles more or less unaware of what has gone before. In 1924 those who had belonged to the Bolshevik party since the early days of 1917 already formed less than 1 per cent. of the membership. To the mass of young members the revolution was already a myth as vague as it was heroic. The earlier political struggles with all their tangled alignments appeared even more remote and unreal. The young communist took it for granted, for instance, that Bolsheviks and Mensheviks had always opposed one another in irreducible enmity as they had done within his memory. It was almost inconceivable to him that they should have formed, in the course of many years, two factions of the same party, evoking common principles, quarrelling and breaking with one another, but also repeatedly trying to heal the breach. It was even more inconceivable that many Bolshevik leaders should have sought to make peace with the Mensheviks as late as 1917.

The young were therefore shocked when they learned that the Commissar of War had once been a Menshevik or semi-Menshevik; and many were inclined to believe the triumvirs when they maintained that once a Menshevik always a Menshevik. Nothing could shake that belief more severely than the perusal of Trotsky's speeches and writings of 1917, which showed up the recent anti-Trotskyist campaign as mendacious. Thus Trotsky, merely by republishing his old texts, called out his adversaries; but he challenged them directly in the 'Lessons of October'.

Trotsky advanced in this essay his own interpretation of the party's history and tradition, an interpretation which not merely vindicated him but also impugned the records of most of his assailants. The party's history, he wrote, fell into three distinct periods: the years of preparation for 1917; the decisive trial of 1917; and the post-revolutionary era. Each of these periods had problems, peculiarities, and a significance of its own. But it was in the second period that Bolshevism rose to its climax. A revolutionary party is tested in actual revolution just as an army is tested in actual battle. Its leaders and members are ultimately judged according to their conduct under this trial; compared with this their behaviour during the preparatory period is of little importance. A Bolshevik should not be judged by what he said or did before 1917, in the course of the confused and in part 'irrelevant manœuvres of émigré politics', but by what he said and did in 1917. The argument, although Trotsky gave it the impersonal form of historical narrative, was *pro domo sua*: his own pre-revolutionary associations with Menshevism belonged to the 'irrelevant manœuvres of émigré politics', but his position as leader of the October insurrection was unassailable. By the same criterion the record of his adversaries was against them: they may have been good 'Leninists' during the years of preparation, but they were found wanting in 1917.

He related the two major crises the party had gone through in 1917: in April, when Lenin had to overcome the resistance of the party's right wing, the 'old Bolsheviks', as Lenin himself called them, before he could persuade the party to set its course for socialist revolution; and on the eve of the October Revolution, when the same right wing balked at insurrection. The hesitancy and the errors of some of the leaders, Trotsky argued, did not detract from the Bolshevik achievement. The party was a living organism with its frictions and divergencies of opinion. However, Bolsheviks should be aware of the facts: even a revolutionary party of necessity includes conservative elements which hamper its progress, especially when the party faces a sharp turn and must take bold decisions. The edge of this argument was turned in the first instance against Zinoviev and Kamenev, the 'strike-breakers of revolution', but also against Rykov, Kalinin, and other leaders of the Old Guard who had opposed Lenin's policy in 1917. In effect, Trotsky called into question the triumvirs' right to speak as the only authentic interpreters of Bolshevik doctrine and, more broadly, the Old Guard's pretension to represent the Leninist tradition in its purity. The implied but obvious moral of his story was that this tradition was by no means as simple and constant as people were made to believe: the Old Guard represented that 'old Bolshevism' which Lenin had abjured because it clung to outdated slogans and irrelevant recollections, while Trotsky's attitude was in full harmony with the Bolshevism of 1917 under the sign of which the party had won.

From history and topical allusion Trotsky then passed to the latest critical event, the failure of communism in Germany. His main themes in the 'Lessons of October' were the role of leadership in a revolutionary situation and the strategy and tactics of insurrection. No Communist party, he argued, can create at will revolutionary opportunities, for these arise only as the result of a relatively slow decay of a social order; but a party can miss its opportunity through lack of determined leadership. In the affairs of revolution, too, there is a tide which must be 'taken at the flood'; missed, it may not return for decades. No society can live long in the tension of acute social crisis. If it finds no relief from that tension in revolution, it finds it in counter-revolution. It may take only a few weeks or even days for the scales to turn one way or the other. If during these weeks or days communists shrink from insurrection and delay action, believing that the revolutionary situation will drag on and offer them new chances, then indeed 'all the voyage of their life is bound in shallows and in miseries'. Such would have been the voyage of the Bolsheviks if the opponents of insurrection had had their way; and so was German communism bound in shallows and in miseries in 1923. Russia had offered the positive proof for the decisive role of revolutionary leadership; Germany offered the negative evidence. The same conservative frame of mind which the Bolshevik right wing showed in 1917 was responsible for the defeat in Germany. It was obvious at whom this sting of Trotsky's conclusion was aimed: the man who had spoken for the Bolshevik right wing in October 1917 was now President of the Communist International.

The triumvirs returned a massive riposte; and they summoned hosts of propagandists and historians and even foreign communist writers for the counter-attack.[1] Throughout the autumn and the winter the country's political life was entirely overshadowed by this controversy which has entered Bolshevik annals under the odd name of 'the literary debate'. Since it was

[1] The most important replies to Trotsky were collected in a large volume *Za Leninizm*—the contributors were Stalin, Zinoviev, Kamenev, Bukharin, Rykov, Sokolnikov, Krupskaya, Molotov, Bubnov, Andreev, Kviring, Stepanov, Kuusinen, Kolarov, Gusev, and Melnichansky.

impossible to deny roundly Trotsky's assertions about Zinoviev's and Kamenev's attitude in 1917, their defenders replied that he had fantastically magnified their errors, that there had been only fortuitous and superficial dissensions between them and Lenin, and that no special right wing or conservative trend of opinion had ever existed in the party. Trotsky, they said, had invented this in order to discredit not merely the Old Guard but the whole body of the Leninist tradition, and in order to ascribe to himself and to Trotskyism wholly imaginary merits.

To prove the point, the triumvirs and their historians had to oppose to Trotsky's account their own versions of the events of 1917, versions designed to enhance their own prestige and to belittle the part Trotsky had played. This was done timidly at first, but then with growing boldness and disregard for truth. Thus, it was not denied at first that Trotsky had acted an outstanding part; but this, it was said, was not superior to that acted by his present adversaries. Then Stalin himself intervened with a version of his own. He declared that the Military Revolutionary Committee of the Petrograd Soviet, over which Trotsky presided, had not at all been the headquarters of the October insurrection, as all historical accounts, without a single exception, had maintained hitherto. He asserted that a more or less fictitious 'Centre', of which Trotsky was not even a member but on which Stalin sat, directed the rising.[1] This version was so crudely concocted that even the Stalinists received it at first with embarrassed irony. But once put out, the story began to crop up stubbornly in the new historical accounts until it found its way to the textbooks, where it was to remain as the only authorized version for about thirty years. Thus that prodigious falsification of history was started which was presently to descend like a destructive avalanche upon Russia's intellectual horizons: it began as a mere attempt to bolster the reputations of Zinoviev and Kamenev whom it was eventually to depict, as it was also to depict Bukharin, Rykov, Tomsky, and so many other Bolshevik leaders, as the saboteurs and traitors of the October Revolution and as foreign spies. In 1924 most of the future victims of the falsification were united in a frantic effort to cast Trotsky into the shade.

Yet, as long as Trotsky stood on the ground of the events of

[1] Stalin, *Sochinenya*, vol. vi, pp. 324–31.

1917, his position was formidable. The triumvirs did therefore their utmost to shift him from that ground back to the pre-revolutionary era, the era of his opposition to Bolshevism. They established a canon of rigid continuity in the party's policies and a canon of its virtual infallibility. Whoever, they said, had, like Trotsky, opposed Bolshevism consistently throughout a long period was fundamentally in the wrong; and this was bound to show itself even in his later attitudes. Making a parody of determinism, the canon-makers instilled into the party's mind the idea that no political error or deviation, whether collective or individual, could be treated as a casual occurrence. (The rule did not apply, of course, to the triumvirs' own errors.) Each error had its deep causes or 'roots' in the peculiar make-up, petty bourgeois or otherwise, of any given group or individual. A major error weighed on him who committed it with the fateful gravity of original sin. Trotsky's fall dated back to his early Menshevik days, not merely to the 'manœuvres of émigré politics' but to his fundamental attitude towards the major problems of the time. In the October interval his petty bourgeois soul struggled to achieve grace. The party hoped to help him and to 'assimilate' him. But again and again his stubborn Menshevik nature reasserted itself.

In this light the disagreements which Trotsky had had with Lenin since the revolution also acquired a hitherto unsuspected sinister meaning. He had had two such major disagreements: over the peace of Brest Litovsk and over policy towards the trade unions. (The other disagreements in which Lenin acknowledged his own mistakes were ignored.) Innumerable pamphlets and articles were published which dwelt on these two cases and gave new accounts of them to prove that in both Trotsky's ineradicable anti-Leninism had revealed itself, and to establish a straight connexion between his opposition to Lenin and his attack on Lenin's successors. The contexts of the old controversies, the real alignments, the motives, the hesitations, the self-contradictions, and the human virtues and failings of the actors, were all omitted from the new accounts. The party was shown a picture of itself and of its leaders which resembled those early medieval frescoes of the Last Judgement, where the virtuous, whose faces express nothing but piety, climb straight to heaven while the sinners, concentrated symbols of vice, rush to damnation.

As the controversy switched backward and forward and back again to the years 1905–6, the fount of all of Trotsky's errors and deviations was at last discovered in his theory of permanent revolution. This was declared to be his master-heresy. Yet ever since 1917 the party had had no quarrel with that theory; Trotsky's early essays on it had been republished in the original and in many translations as an authoritative statement of communist doctrine. Even now its two chief tenets—that the Russian Revolution had to pass from the bourgeois to the socialist phase; and that it would be the prologue to world revolution—were still the party's household ideas; and they could not be openly refuted. The polemicists dug up a few barbed remarks which Lenin made in 1906: himself still holding that the Russian Revolution would be only bourgeois in character, Lenin then said that Trotsky spoke of a socialist consummation because he 'jumped' over the bourgeois phase and 'underestimated' the importance of the peasantry. In view of what had happened in 1917 these remarks had lost all relevance. This did not now prevent the polemicists repeating in circles that Trotsky's characteristic propensity was to 'jump over necessary intermediate stages' and to 'underestimate the peasantry'. True enough, it was not easy to square this charge with the other accusation that he was an unreformed Menshevik—the Mensheviks, far from 'jumping' over the bourgeois phase of the revolution, refused to go beyond it—and it took a great deal of purely scholastic argument to cope with this logical difficulty. However, as in all disputations of this sort, it was not the logic or the historical truth of the argument that mattered, but its undertone, its bearing on current policy, and the impression it made on the uninitiated.

That the insistence on Trotsky's inclination to 'underestimate the peasantry' had a bearing on current policy is obvious: the triumvirs and Rykov had begun to label Trotsky as the muzhik's enemy even the year before. Now they gave that label retrospective validity and historical colouring. More significant still was the broader undertone. To the popular understanding Permanent Revolution suggested a prospect of continuous upheaval and of endless struggle, and the impossibility for the Russian Revolution to settle down and achieve a measure of stabilization. In denouncing Permanent Revolution, the triumvirs appealed to the popular longing for peace and stability.

In truth, Trotsky's theory did claim that the fortunes of Bolshevik Russia depended *ultimately* on the spread of revolution abroad. Yet the hopes for its spread had been dashed many times and had just suffered the most severe setback in Germany. The Bolsheviks felt more isolated than ever. They found a psychological defence in their complacent sense of Russia's revolutionary self-sufficiency. Trotsky's theory offended and mocked that sense. Hence the intense irritation which the mere mention of Permanent Revolution began to arouse among Bolshevik cadres. They felt a vehement emotional urge to deprive Trotsky's theory of all ideological respectability. It was no matter of chance that in the autumn of 1924 Stalin, revising his own earlier views, formulated the doctrine of Socialism in One Country, which became the counterpart to Permanent Revolution. Stalin extolled the self-sufficiency of the Russian Revolution and thereby he offered the party an ideological consolation for its frustrated internationalist hopes.[1]

It is easy to see why and how the 'literary debate' weakened Trotsky's position even further. It fixed in the public mind a contradictory image of Trotsky as, on the one hand, an inveterate semi-Menshevik and, on the other, an equally inveterate 'ultra radical' and extremist seeking to involve the party in dangerous ventures at home and abroad. At home, it was said, he strove to embroil the Bolsheviks with the peasants whom he had never understood. Abroad, he always saw revolutionary opportunities where none existed. The same aberration had led him to oppose the Brest Litovsk Peace and to blame Zinoviev for the defeat of revolution in Germany. That Trotsky had also criticized Zinoviev for encouraging abortive risings abroad, that he had been opposed to the march on Warsaw in 1920, that he had consistently striven to normalize relations with the capitalist countries, and that he had been the first to advocate the N.E.P. policy in order to pacify the peasants—these and similar facts which contradicted the image of the ultra radical adventurer did not matter. Fact, fiction, and scholastic quibble were so jumbled together that Trotsky became the Quixote of communism, pathetic perhaps, but also dangerous, whom only the wisdom and the statesmanship of the triumvirs could restrain and render harmless.

[1] See *Stalin, A Political Biography*, pp. 281–93.

Many a party member, even some of Trotsky's own adherents, held that in the 'Lessons of October' he had chosen his ground wrongly.[1] He should have concentrated, they said, on issues that mattered instead of digging up Zinoviev's and Kamenev's errors of 1917. True, he had done this in self-defence after the triumvirs had raked up all the long-forgotten incidents of his controversies with Lenin and after they had prevented him from discussing current affairs. But most people quickly forgot 'who had started it all'; and they reproached him with not letting bygones be bygones. Official writers quoted against him the excerpts from Lenin's suppressed will in which Lenin begged the party not to hold against Zinoviev and Kamenev their 'historic errors'. Even Krupskaya, mindful of that advice, was prevailed upon to rebuke Trotsky and to say that he had made too much of the disagreements between Lenin and his disciples, because the fate of the revolution depended on the attitude of the party and of the working class as a whole, not on dissensions within a narrow circle of leaders.[2] This was a telling criticism, directed as it was against the advocate of inner-party democracy. Bolshevik self-esteem had anyhow been wounded by Trotsky in whose recollections the party's leadership appeared as a sluggish, hesitant body of men who would never have done their duty if they had not been prodded and pushed into action by Lenin.

The debate had a further consequence which greatly embarrassed Trotsky. Some elements of the dispersed anti-Bolshevik opposition, who had hitherto hated him like death, began to pin their hopes on him.[3] This was inevitable. In a single-party system some of the suppressed enemies of the government, no longer able to fight under their own banners, will applaud any important dissenter even if he belongs to the ruling party and no matter what the reasons for his dissent. They tend to view as their hero any one whom the ruling group itself stigmatizes as its dangerous adversary. The circumstance that Trotsky demanded freedom of expression, if only within the party, commended him at least to some anti-Bolsheviks who saw

[1] Trotsky, *The Stalin School of Falsification*, p. 90.
[2] Krupskaya, 'K Voprosu ob Urokakh Oktyabrya' in *Za Leninizm*, pp. 152–6.
[3] M. Eastman, *Since Lenin Died*, pp. 128–9; Bajanov, *Avec Staline dans le Kremlin*, p. 86.

no future for themselves without any freedom of expression. This was by no means the prevalent attitude among the anti-Bolsheviks. Many or perhaps most of them viewed with glee the fall of the man on whom they placed the chief blame for their defeat in the civil war. But the triumvirs made the most of any sign of real or spurious sympathy for Trotsky which could be detected outside the party, while he was all the more anxious to say and do nothing that might encourage such sympathy. This accounted largely for his restraint and long silences, and for his constant and emphatic reiteration of his solidarity with the triumvirs in the face of common enemies.

Finally, the 'literary debate' had an important effect on the triumvirs themselves. Its result was to discredit all the chief controversialists with the sole exception of Stalin, whose prestige was, on the contrary, enhanced. Trotsky had concentrated his attack on Zinoviev and Kamenev who had clearly expressed and placed on record their objections to the October insurrection. Stalin, having been less articulate and much more elusive in 1917, was now far less vulnerable. Indeed, Zinoviev and Kamenev stood at present in need of his moral support; and they were glad to receive from him testimonials of good Bolshevism.[1] This helped Stalin to establish himself definitely as the senior triumvir. Thus, unwittingly, Trotsky helped to defeat his future allies and to promote his chief and most dangerous adversary.

. . . .

The storm raised by the 'Lessons of October' made Trotsky's position as Commissar of War untenable. The triumvirs had denounced him in such terms that they could not leave him in charge of the country's military affairs, although only a year earlier they were still afraid to accept his resignation. They now openly worked to remove him from the Commissariat.

In no phase of the struggle did Trotsky make the slightest attempt to appeal against them to the army. He restrained those of his followers who, like Antonov-Ovseenko, had been tempted to draw into the controversy the military cells which were, under

---

[1] Stalin, *Sochinenya*, vol. vi, pp. 326–7. (The text of Stalin's statement in defence of Zinoviev and Kamenev as 'good old Bolsheviks' is somewhat toned down in his *Works* (compared with the original published in *Za Leninizm*, pp. 88–89) but clear enough.)

the party's rules and regulations, entitled to have their say. Official spokesmen, it should be added, never reproached Antonov-Ovseenko with any offence graver than this—there was no question of any plot or preparations for a *coup*; and they repeatedly acknowledged Trotsky's restraining influence.[1] When hints were dropped about his Bonapartist ambition, this was done in private gossip only. Trotsky was not accused of making any single move designed to use his position as Commissar of War to his political advantage. He acknowledged as a matter of course, the Politbureau's jurisdiction over the army. Consequently, he accepted, though not without protest, the dismissal and demotion of his followers from the most influential posts in his Commissariat and the appointment to them of his adversaries.[2]

It would be futile to speculate whether Trotsky would have succeeded if he had attempted a military *coup*. Early in the conflict, before the General Secretariat had begun to shift and shuffle the party personnel in the army, his chances of success might have been high; they dwindled later. He never tried to test the chances. He was convinced that a military *pronunciamento* would be an irreparable setback for the revolution, even if he were to be associated with it. He had declared at the thirteenth congress that he saw in the party 'the only historic instrument which the working class possessed for the solution of its fundamental tasks'; and he could not try and smash that instrument with the army's hands. In any conflict with the party, he held, the army would have to rely on the support of counter-revolutionary forces and this would have condemned it to play a reactionary part. True, he saw 'degeneration' in the party. But this consisted in the breach between the leaders and the rank and file and in the party's loss of its democratic base. The task, as he saw it, was to reconstitute that base and to reconcile the leaders and the rank and file. Ultimately the revolution's salvation lay in a political revival 'down below', in the depth of society. Military action 'from above' could only usher in a régime even further removed from a workers' democracy than was the present government. Such was the 'logic of things'; and

---

[1] At the thirteenth conference even official speakers referred to Trotsky's restraining influence, see, e.g., Lominadze's speech in *13 Konferentsya RKP (b)*, p. 113.　　　　　　　　　　　　[2] *Moya Zhizn*, vol. ii, pp. 253-4.

he did not believe that he could stand against it. He placed his own person and action within the framework of the social forces which determined the course of events; he saw his own role as subordinate to those forces; and his aim, the revival of proletarian democracy, dictated to him the choice of his means.

In the course of the year 1924 the direction of the Commissariat of War slipped from his hands. Through Frunze and Unschlicht the triumvirs gradually extended their control over the whole body of the army's political commissars; and now they had no qualms about drawing the armed forces into the inner-party conflict. They submitted to the military cells resolutions condemning Trotsky for publishing the 'Lessons of October'; and they convened a national conference of the political commissars and placed before them a motion demanding Trotsky's dismissal from the Department of War. At this time Trotsky once again succumbed to an attack of malaria and he did not, it seems, even state his case to the commissars. The conference duly passed the motion demanding his dismissal. Then he suffered the same rebuff from the communist cell on the Military Revolutionary Council, the Council over which he had presided since the day it was formed. To crown it all, a plenary session of the Central Committee was called for 17 January 1925, and 'the Trotsky case' figured as the first item on the agenda.

On 15 January Trotsky addressed a letter to the Central Committee in which he excused, on grounds of illness, his absence from the forthcoming session; but he stated that he had delayed his planned departure from Moscow—he was to go to the Caucasus again—in order to answer questions and offer explanations which might be required of him. Concisely and with subdued anger, he replied to the main accusations levelled against him— this was his only reply to the critics of the 'Lessons of October'. Then he asked to be immediately relieved from his duties as President of the Revolutionary Military Council and declared: 'I am ready to carry out any work whatever assigned to me by the Central Committee, in whatever position or without any position and, it goes without saying, under any conditions whatever of party control.'[1]

At the Politbureau Zinoviev and Kamenev proposed to ask

[1] The full text of the letter is in Eastman, *Since Lenin Died*, pp. 155–8.

the Central Committee to expel Trotsky from the Politbureau and the Committee. Once again, to their irritation, Stalin refused to comply; and Zinoviev and Kamenev wondered whether he might not make peace with Trotsky at their expense. The Central Committee decided that Trotsky should continue to sit on the Committee and the Politbureau; but it threatened him once again with expulsion if he engaged in any new controversy.[1] The Central Committee then formally declared the 'literary debate' as closed; but in the same breath it instructed all propaganda departments to continue the campaign 'which would enlighten the whole party . . . about the anti-Bolshevik character of Trotskyism, beginning from the year 1903 and ending with the "Lessons of October"'. Another campaign was to make clear to the country at large, not only to party members, the danger to the 'alliance of workers and peasants' which Trotskyism carried with it. As Trotsky was not allowed to reply, this became a 'one-sided debate'. The Central Committee finally 'declared it impossible that he should continue to work on the Revolutionary Military Council'.

Thus, with the badges of infamy stuck over the badges of his fame, with cries of denunciation ringing in his ears, gagged and forbidden even to defend himself, he left the Commissariat and the army which he had led for seven long and fateful years.

[1] Popov, *Outline History of the CPSU*, vol. ii, p. 216; *KPSS v Rezolutsyakh*, vol. i, pp. 913–21.

CHAPTER III

'Not by Politics Alone . . .'

'NOT by politics alone doth man live . . .' was the title Trotsky gave to a short essay of his which appeared in *Pravda* in the summer of 1923.[1] Least of all could he himself live by politics alone. Even at the most vital moments of the struggle for power his literary and cultural activities took up a great part of his energy; and he became still more deeply absorbed in them when he left the Commissariat of War and the inner-party controversy slackened for a time. Not that he sought to escape from politics. His interest in literature, art, and education remained political in a wider sense. But he refused to dwell on the surface of public affairs. He turned the struggle for power into a struggle for the 'soul' of the revolution; and he thereby gave new dimensions and new depth to the conflict in which he was involved.

How intensely indeed he was engaged in literary work during the most crucial clashes in the Politbureau can be seen even from the following few facts. In the summer of 1922, when he refused to accept the office of Vice-Premier under Lenin and, incurring the Politbureau's censure, went on leave, he devoted the better part of his holiday to literary criticism. The State Publishers had collected his pre-revolutionary essays on literature for republication in a special volume of his *Works*; and he intended to write a preface surveying the condition of Russian letters since the revolution. The 'preface' grew in size and became an independent work. He gave to it nearly all his leisure but failed to conclude it. He resumed writing during his next summer holiday, in 1923, when his conflict with the triumvirs, complicated by the expectation of revolution in Germany, was mounting to a climax; and this time he returned to Moscow with the manuscript of a new book, *Literature and Revolution*, ready for the printer.

In the course of the same summer he wrote a series of articles

[1] *Pravda*, 10 July 1923; *Sochinenya*, vol. xxi, pp. 3-12.

on the manners and morals of post-revolutionary Russia which were later collected in *Problems of Everyday Life*. The topics he discussed were: family life under the new régime; bureaucracy 'enlightened and unenlightened'; 'civility and politeness'; 'vodka, the Church, and the cinema'; 'swearing in the Russian language'; and so on. He addressed many meetings of educationists, librarians, agitators, journalists, and 'worker-correspondents'; and in his speeches he dwelt on the dullness, shabbiness, and lifelessness to which the press had sunk, and insisted on the need to restore purity and force to the Russian language, now littered with party jargon and cliché. In the same summer and in the following autumn he worked on such diverse subjects as a comparative analysis of trade cycles in the nineteenth and the twentieth centuries (about which he published a short but weighty treatise in the *Vestnik* of the Socialist Academy)[1] and the controversy between two schools in psychology, Pavlov's and Freud's. He had long been familiar with Freud's theory; and he studied Pavlov's works and prepared himself to intervene in the controversy with a plea for freedom of research and experimentation and for tolerance towards the Freudian school. In 1924 he also wrote, and published in book form, the biographical sketches of Lenin in which, by presenting the founder of Bolshevism in all his humanity, he implicitly made his critique of the official 'icon' of Lenin and of the incipient Lenin cult.

In these writings he sought to strike at the root and not merely at the symptoms of the evils which beset the revolution: at the spiritual backwardness of Mother Russia which was no less important than her economic poverty. He spoke of the need for 'primitive cultural accumulation' as being at least as urgent as the need for industrial accumulation. He exposed the soil in which Stalinism was beginning to grow, and he sought to change the climate in which it was to flourish. Hence the importance he attached to manners and morals and to 'small matters' of everyday life: he showed how these affected the affairs of state. His treatment of such topics is best illustrated by what he wrote about the peculiarly Russian habits of swearing:

Abusive language and swearing are a legacy of slavery, humiliation, and disrespect for the dignity of man, one's own dignity and that of other people. . . . I should like to hear from our philologists,

[1] *Sochinenya*, vol. xii, pp. 357–63.

linguists, and folklore experts whether they know in any other language such dissolute, sticky, and low terms of abuse as those we have
in Russian. As far as I know, nothing or almost nothing of the kind
exists outside our country. Swearing in our lower classes was the
result of despair, embitterment, and above all, of slavery without
hope and escape. The swearing of our upper classes, the swearing
that came out of the throats of the gentry and of those in office, was
the outcome of class rule, of slave-owners' pride, and of unshakeable
power. . . . Two streams of Russian abuse—the swearing of masters,
officials, and police, full and fat, and the hungry, desperate, and
tormented swearing of the masses—have coloured the whole of
Russian life with despicable patterns. . . .

The revolution, however, is primarily the awakening of the human
personality in the masses, in those masses which were supposed to
possess no personality. In spite of occasional cruelty and the
sanguinary relentlessness of its methods, the revolution is . . . marked
by growing respect for the dignity of the individual and by an ever
increasing concern for the weak. A revolution does not deserve its
name if it does not help with all its might and all the means at its
disposal—if it does not help woman, twofold and threefold enslaved
in the past, to get on to the road of individual and social progress.
A revolution does not deserve its name if it does not take the greatest
possible care of the children . . . for whose benefit it has been made.
But how can one create . . . a new life based on mutual consideration,
on self-respect, on the real equality of women . . ., on the efficient
care for children—in an atmosphere poisoned with the roaring,
rolling, ringing, and resounding swearing of masters and slaves, that
swearing which spares no one and stops at nothing? The struggle
against 'foul language' is an essential condition of mental hygiene just as
the fight against filth and vermin is a condition of physical hygiene. . . .

Psychological habits, coming down from generation to generation
and permeating the whole climate of life, are extremely tenacious.
. . . How often do we in Russia make a violent rush forward, strain
our forces, and then let things drift in the old way? . . . This is true
not only of the uncivilized masses but also of the advanced and
so-called responsible elements in our present social order. There is
no denying that the old pre-revolutionary forms of foul language are
still in use now, six years after October, and that they are even
en vogue high up 'at the top'. . . . Our life is made up of the most
striking contrasts.[1]

In this struggle against the persistent and resurgent traditions
of a way of life which had been rooted in serfdom Trotsky was

[1] *Pravda*, 16 May 1923; *Sochinenya*, vol. xxi, pp. 26–31.

to suffer a defeat as cruel as that which he suffered in the political field. But he showed a deep historical insight into the nature of the forces by which he was to be overwhelmed. The 'two streams of Russian abuse' were to merge in Stalinism and to impose their 'despicable patterns' on the revolution itself. Fifteen years later, during the great purges, the two streams swelled into a flood: it was then possible for an Attorney-General to rail at men in the dock, who had occupied the most exalted positions in state and party, in such terms as 'you son of a bull and a pig'; and the highest magistrates wound up their obsessive perorations with the scream: 'shoot the mad dogs!' The cursing rolled on from the courtrooms to factories, farms, editorial offices, and university halls; and for several years its din deafened the whole of Russia. It was as if centuries of swearing had become condensed in a single moment, come to life in Stalinism, and burst upon the world.

.   .   .   .

The October Revolution had given fresh impulses to cultural life; but it had also thoroughly upset it and created enormous difficulties. This would have been the effect of any revolution, even in the most favourable circumstances, and even with the educated elements of the nation on its side. The effect was immensely aggravated when the chief moving force of the revolution was an oppressed, property-less, and of necessity uneducated class. True, the Bolshevik leaders were men of the intelligentsia; and some of them possessed wide and profound education. But they were a mere handful. The 'cadres' consisted mostly of self-educated workers and half-educated people of petty bourgeois descent. The party had trained them in politics, organization, and sometimes in the broad philosophy of Marxism. But all too often their approach to cultural affairs only showed that a little knowledge could be worse than complete ignorance.

The majority of the intelligentsia had met the October Revolution with hostility. Some died in the civil war. Many emigrated. Of those who had survived and stayed in Russia many came to serve the new régime as 'specialists'. A few even became enthusiastically converted to the revolution and did their best to raise the nation culturally. But most of the men of the intelligentsia were either too rigid in conservative habits of mind or else too intimidated or too mediocre and servile to exercise a large and fruitful intellectual influence. They took it ill when they were placed under the orders of self-educated or half-educated commissars. On the other hand, the commissars often lacked confidence in themselves, and were suspicious and inclined to disguise inner uncertainty by bluff and bluster. They were also fanatically convinced of the justice of their cause and sure that they had found in Marxism, in which, of necessity, they were also only half-educated, the master key to all problems of society, including those of science and art. All the stronger were the intelligentsia confirmed in their characteristic pre-judices, and in the supercilious conviction that Marxism could teach them nothing, that its *Weltanschauung* was a mere 'farrago of half-baked half-truths'. Thus a gulf was fixed between them and the new ruling groups.

Trotsky, like Lenin, Bukharin, Lunacharsky, Krasin, and a few others, did his utmost to bridge the gulf. He pleaded with the commissars and the party secretaries to treat the intelli-gentsia with consideration and respect; and he urged the intel-ligentsia to show greater understanding for the needs of the time and for Marxism. These pleadings had their effect, but the gulf, though narrowed, was still there. Then it again began to widen. As the party hierarchy began to free itself from all forms of public control and get accustomed to arbitrary government, it became more and more inclined to impose its dictates upon the scientist, the man of letters, and the artist as well. It also began to develop its own ambitions and to encourage 'cultural' aspirations which flattered its parvenu vanity and yet appeared to have the merits of revolutionary innovation. The slogans of 'proletarian culture', 'proletarian art', and 'proletarian litera-ture' were coined, soon acquiring the same kind of popularity that the 'proletarian strategic doctrine' had enjoyed in the army somewhat earlier.[1]

Trotsky saw it his task to curb intolerance and to expose the futility of the slogans about proletarian culture and art. This was not easy. The idea of proletarian culture appealed to some Bol-shevik intellectuals, and to young workers in whom the revolu-tion had awakened a craving for education but in whom it had also released iconoclastic instincts. In the background there was

[1] See *The Prophet Armed*, pp. 482–5.

the peasants' anarchic hostility towards all that had been associated with the gentry's way of life, including its 'cultural
values'. (When the muzhik set fire to his landlord's mansion he
often let go up in flames the library and the paintings—he saw
in them only part of the landlord's possessions.) Theorizing
Bolsheviks rationalized this iconoclastic mood into a pseudo-
Marxist rejection of the old 'class culture' which was to be
swept away. *Proletkult* proclaimed the advent of proletarian
science and art. The doctrinaires of this group of writers and
artists argued with some plausibility that just as there had been
feudal and bourgeois epochs in the history of civilization, so the
proletarian dictatorship ought to inaugurate a culture of its
own, permeated by Marxist class consciousness, militant internationalism, materialism, atheism, and so forth. Some maintained that Marxism by itself already constituted that new
culture. The originators and adherents of such views strove to
obtain for them the party's support and even to make of them
the guiding principles of educational policy.

Both Lenin and Trotsky repudiated the *Proletkult* theory.
Lenin, however, confined himself to a few brief and sharp
statements and left the field to Trotsky, to whom it was more
congenial. We shall presently see how Trotsky conducted the
argument against *Proletkult*. The pretensions of *Proletkult*, however, were only the most extreme expression of an inclination
which was widespread far beyond *Proletkult* circles, especially
among party men in charge of educational and cultural affairs—
an inclination to settle such affairs by word of command, to
lay down the law, and to intimidate those who were too well
educated, too intelligent, or too independent-minded to obey.
It was this frame of mind, from which the cultural policy of
Stalinism was to take its rise, that Trotsky untiringly sought
to overcome: 'The state is an organization of compulsion',
he said in an address to educationists, 'consequently Marxists
in office may feel tempted to arrange even their cultural
and educational work among the toiling masses on the principle: "here is truth revealed to you—go down on your knees
before it". Of course, ours is a stern government. The workers'
state has the right and the duty to apply compulsion. We turn
ruthless force against the enemies of the working class. But in
the education of the working class this "here-is-truth-down-on-

your-knees" method . . . contradicts the very essence of Marxism.'[1]

Such exhortations and warnings fill many pages in *The Culture of a Transition Period*, Volume XXI of Trotsky's *Works*. Words of command addressed to scientists and bans on their theories 'can bring us nothing except harm and shame', he insisted, anticipating the harm and the shame of Stalin's pronouncements on linguistic and biological, not to speak of sociological heresies. It should be added that Trotsky did not argue in this spirit only after he had been driven into opposition. As early as in January 1919 he wrote, for instance:

> Our party . . . never was and never can become a flatterer of the working class. . . . The conquest of power does not by itself transform the working class or invest it with all virtues: it only opens before it the opportunity of learning, developing its mind, and freeing itself of its inadequacies. By an intense effort the leading groups of the Russian working class have carried out work of gigantic historic significance. But even in these groups there is still too much half-knowledge and semi-competence.[2]

With this half-knowledge and semi-competence he came to blows again and again. Lenin, when he introduced N.E.P., told the Bolsheviks that they had 'to learn to trade'. It was not less important, Trotsky added, that they should 'learn to learn'.[3]

It was baneful, he reiterated, to approach the 'cultural heritage' of the past with nihilistic contempt. The working class had to take possession of that heritage and to guard it. The Marxist should not accept it all indiscriminately; he ought to view the cultural legacy dialectically and see its historically formed contradictions. The achievements of civilization had so far served a double purpose: they had assisted man in gaining knowledge and control of nature and in developing his own capacities; but they had also served to perpetuate society's division into classes and man's exploitation by man. Consequently, some elements of the heritage were of universal significance and validity while others were bound up with obsolete or obsolescent social sys-

---

[1] He delivered this address in June 1924, just after the thirteenth congress had denounced his 'deviation from Leninism'. *Sochinenya*, vol. xxi, pp. 133–63.

[2] *Sochinenya*, vol. xxi, pp. 97–98.   [3] Ibid., p. 260.

tems.[1] The communist approach to the cultural legacy should therefore be selective. As a rule, the main body of the strictly scientific thought of the past was relatively little distorted through the fact that it grew up in class society. It was in ideological creation, especially in notions on society itself, that man's domination by man was mirrored most directly. But even there elements which reflected class oppression and served to perpetuate it were intricately combined with other elements through which man took cognizance of himself, sharpened his mind, enlarged his intelligence, gained insight into his emotions, learned to control himself, and therefore to some extent surmounted the limitations of his social circumstances. That was why works of art created hundreds and even thousands of years ago still fascinated modern man and continued to strike a chord in him even while he was engaged in proletarian revolution or in building socialism. To be sure, the builder of socialism should review critically, using the criteria of dialectical materialism, all inherited values; but this could have nothing to do with flat rejection or pseudo-Marxist humbug. Before the cultural values of the past could be subjected to criticism they must be thoroughly assimilated; and before the Marxist decided to revise from his angle any field of knowledge, he must first master it 'from the inside'.

.   .   .   .

Addressing the old intelligentsia, Trotsky argued from the opposite angle: he sought to persuade them that they could not live by the cultural heritage alone, and that they should re-educate themselves and find their place in Soviet society. He was concerned in particular with the outlook of the scientists and technologists, whom he repeatedly addressed on the relation between Marxism and science. His own interest in the subject was stimulated when, after his departure from the Commissariat of War, he became head of the Board for Electro-technical Development and of the Committee for Industry and Technology. A new field of study opened before him—one which

---

[1] Trotsky spoke of the dual role of the machine which has raised the worker's productive power but has, under capitalism, also served as an instrument of exploitation. Yet socialism cannot and does not renounce the use of the machine. This is obvious to everyone, but the same reasoning applies to most achievements of civilization.

had attracted him in his early youth and which he then abandoned for the sake of revolutionary activity. He now became 'half-administrator and half-student'. 'I was especially interested', he writes,[1] 'in the Committee for Industry and Technology, which, because of the centralized character of Soviet industry, had developed on quite a large scale. I diligently visited many laboratories, watched experiments . . . and listened to explanations given by outstanding scientists. In my spare time I studied textbooks on chemistry and hydrodynamics. . . .' These interests are strongly reflected in his writings of the years 1925–6. Sitting at the feet of the scientists, he also acted as their tutor in the sociology and the Marxist philosophy of science. He was probably influenced by Engels's *Dialektik der Natur*, the first German and Russian editions of which appeared in Moscow in 1925. He made no explicit reference to that work, but it is unlikely that he should not have read it; and on some points he follows closely Engels's line of thought.

At least three of his excursions into the philosophy of science deserve to be mentioned here: an address on Mendeleev, delivered at an All-Russian Congress of Scientists in September 1925, on the occasion of an anniversary of the great chemist; a lecture on 'Culture and Socialism' given at the Red Square Club in February 1926; and a speech on 'Radio, Science, Technology, and Society' at the Congress for the promotion of radio held in March of the same year.

There was nothing of the professional philosopher about Trotsky. He never plumbed the depths of gnosiology as Lenin did in *Empiriocriticism and Materialism*. He attempted no systematic exposition of the principles of dialectics; he preferred to apply them in political and historical analyses rather than to expound them in the abstract. Yet it is difficult to read his works without becoming aware of the well-formed philosophy behind them, of the deep thought he had given to questions of method, and of his wide if not very systematic erudition. He carried this erudition lightly, avoided the pundit's ponderous pronouncements, and as if deliberately spoke the language of the dilettante. For all this, or perhaps because of it, his few essays on the dialectics of science belong to the most illuminating and lucid Marxist statements on the subject.

[1] Trotsky, *Moya Zhizn*, vol. ii, p. 262.

Nothing was further from Trotsky's mind than any attempt to impose politics upon science. He asserted the scientist's right and even duty to remain politically disinterested in the course of research and study. This, however, should not prevent the scientist from seeing the place of science in society. There was no contradiction between the disinterestedness of the individual scientist and the deep involvement of science as a whole in the social conflicts of its age. Similarly, an individual soldier or revolutionary may fight and give his life disinterestedly, but an army and a party must have definite interests and aspirations to defend.

Detachment and rigorous objectivity in research are necessary, but not enough. It is a most vital interest of science itself that the scientist should have a broad and up-to-date philosophical outlook. This, as a rule, he does not possess. Hence a characteristic cleavage in the scientist's mind. In his special field or in his laboratory he is implicitly a materialist but outside it his thinking is most often confused, unscientific, inclined to idealism or even to plainly reactionary views. In no great thinker was this cleavage more in evidence than in Mendeleev. As a scientist he was one of the greatest materialists of all times; yet he was caught up in all the conservative beliefs and prejudices of his time and was devoted to the decaying Tsardom. When he formulated his Periodic Law, he testified to the truth of that principle of dialectics which occupies a central place in Marxist thought and asserts that quantitative changes, whether in natural or social processes, at certain points turn into changes of quality. According to the Periodic Law quantitative alterations in atom weights result in qualitative differences between chemical elements. Yet Mendeleev could not envisage the approach of the one great qualitative change—the revolution—in Russian society.

'Know in order to be able to predict and act' was the maxim of the great discoverer, who compared scientific creation to the throwing of an iron bridge across a precipice: it is not necessary, Mendeleev said, to descend and to look for a support for the bridge at the bottom of the precipice; it is enough to find support on one of the banks and then to throw across a precisely weighted arch which will rest securely on the other bank.

The same is true of all scientific thought. It must base itself on the granite foundation of experience; but the generalization, like the arch of the bridge, detaches itself from the world of facts in order to intersect it again at another precisely anticipated point. . . .

That moment of scientific creation . . . when generalization transforms itself into prognostication and prognostication tests itself successfully through experience invariably gives the human mind the proudest and the truest satisfaction.[1]

Mendeleev the citizen, however, shunned all sociological generalization and political prediction. He viewed with utter lack of comprehension the emergence in Russia of the Marxist school of thought which formed itself in the course of a controversy with the Narodniks precisely over a prognostication about the way Russian society would develop.

Mendeleev's case then illustrates the predicament of the modern scientist: his lack of an integrated vision of the world and even of science. Of necessity science works empirically; and specialization and fragmentation of knowledge accompanies its progress. Yet the greater the specialization and fragmentation, the more urgent is the need for a unifying conception of the world—otherwise the thinker's mind becomes constricted within his speciality and even within it his progress is impeded. Lack of philosophical insight and distrust of generalizing thought have been responsible for much avoidable scientific confusion and groping in the dark. Marxism offers the scientist an integrated vision of nature and human society, a vision which, far from being an arbitrary concoction or a figment of the metaphysical mind, accords intimately with the varied empirical experience of science.[2]

---

[1] *Sochinenya*, vol. xxi, p. 276.

[2] Engels in *Dialektik der Natur* points out that Descartes anticipated by about 200 years the findings of science about the conservation of energy, when he asserted that the mass of movement in the universe does not change. Had scientists grasped Descartes's thought they might have arrived at their findings much earlier. This was *a fortiori* true of Kant's 'nebular hypothesis'. 'Had the great majority of students of nature had less aversion for [philosophical] thought, the aversion which Newton expressed in his warning: Physics Beware of Metaphysics—they would have necessarily drawn from Kant's . . . discovery conclusions which would have saved them endless detours. . . . Kant's discovery was the starting point for all further progress [i.e. for overcoming the static and adopting the dynamic view of nature as a whole]. Had inquiry at once proceeded in this direction, the science of nature would have been much more advanced by now than it is. But what good could come from philosophy? Kant's work had no immediate impact and it was only years later that Laplace and Herschel . . . vindicated it.' *Dialektik der Natur*, pp. 14, 62.

The unity and the diversity of man's thought was Trotsky's grand theme. Taking once again Mendeleev's work as his starting point, he surveyed the structure of modern science. Mendeleev had discovered that chemistry has its basis in physics and that chemical reactions are caused by the physical and mechanical qualities of particles. Physiology, Trotsky proceeded, stands in the same relation to chemistry as that in which chemistry stands to physics—not for nothing is it described as 'the applied chemistry of living organisms'. 'Scientific, i.e. materialistic, physiology has no use for any special supra-chemical Life Force (as conceived by Vitalists and Neo-vitalists) in order to explain the processes with which it is concerned. Psychology in its turn rests on the foundations of physiology. As the physiologist in his strict research can make no use of the concept of Life Force, so can the psychologist not cope with a single one of his specific problems by reference to the "soul". He has to relate psychical experiences to the phenomena of physiological existence.' This is what Freud's school does when it reveals that man's sexual urges underlie so many of his mental states; and this is *a fortiori* what the Pavlov school does when it treats the human soul as a complicated system of physiologically conditioned reflexes. Finally, the modern science of society is inseparable from the insight man has gained into the laws governing nature; it sees society as a peculiar part of nature.

Thus on the foundations laid by mechanics and physics rises the vast structure of contemporary science, all its varied parts interrelated and forming a single whole. Yet unity is not uniformity. The laws governing one science cannot be substituted for those ruling another. Even though Mendeleev has proved that chemical processes are in the last instance physical or mechanical, chemistry cannot be reduced directly to physics. Still less can physiology be reduced to chemistry, or psychology and biology to physiology. Nor can the laws governing the development of human society be simply deduced from the laws which apply to nature. In a sense it may remain the ultimate objective of science to explain the infinite variety of natural and social phenomena by a few general and elementary laws.[1] But

[1] Engels, in the work already quoted, expresses the view that, at least 'in the present state of knowledge', these general and elementary laws can be formulated only in philosophical terms, that is in the terms of dialectics, but not in those of natural science.

scientific thought is progressing towards that objective in such a way that it appears more and more removed from it, namely, by way of the division and specialization of knowledge and of the formulation and elaboration of ever new, particular, and detailed laws. The view, for instance, that chemical reactions are ultimately determined by the physical qualities of particles was the beginning of all chemical knowledge; but by itself it offered not a single clue to any single chemical reaction. 'Chemistry works with its own keys; and it finds those keys only in its own laboratories, through empirical experience and generalization, hypothesis and theory.' Physiology, connected though it is through the solid channels of organic and physiological chemistry with chemistry at large, has methods and laws of its own. So has biology; and so has psychology. Every science seeks support in the rules of another only 'in the last instance'; and every science applies itself to so particular a sphere, in which elementary phenomena appear in such complex combinations, that every such sphere requires an approach, methods of inquiry, and hypotheses which are peculiar to it alone. It is through diversity that the unity of science asserts itself.

In the study of nature the autonomy of every sphere of research is taken for granted; no serious student permits himself to confound the laws prevailing in one sphere with those valid in another. Only in reasonings on society, in history, economics, and politics, is such confusion and arbitrariness of method still endemic. Here no law need be acknowledged; or else the laws of natural science are crudely projected into the study of society, as they are, for instance, by Darwinists who dabble in sociology and by the neo-Malthusians.[1]

[1] Trotsky illustrated this point by quoting J. M. Keynes who, on a visit to Moscow, in 1925, in the course of a lecture at the Supreme Council of the National Economy explained unemployment in Great Britain by the rate of the increase of the British population. Keynes (according to a report in *Ekonomicheskaya Zhizn* of 15 September 1925) went on to say: 'I suppose that Russia's poverty before the war was caused largely by an excessive growth of population. At present, too, a considerable excess of the birth rate over the death rate is noticeable. This is the greatest danger for Russia's economic future.' At that time there was still unemployment in Russia. But already three years later, when planned economy was established, and for decades afterwards, one of the 'greatest dangers' was shortage of manpower and too slow a growth of population, a fact which strikingly demonstrates the impropriety of applying the Malthusian or neo-Malthusian concept of the 'pressure of population upon means of subsistence' to the economics of an industrially expanding society.

Trotsky then surveyed broadly the advance of science and technology 'in the last few decades' and its philosophical implications. That advance, he asserted, constituted an almost uninterrupted triumph for dialectical materialism, a triumph which, paradoxically, the philosophers and even the scientists were reluctant to acknowledge. 'The successes of science in mastering matter are, on the contrary, accompanied by a philosophical struggle against materialism.' The discovery of radioactivity in particular had encouraged philosophers to draw anti-materialistic conclusions. Yet their arguments were effective only in criticism of the old physics and of the mechanistic variety of philosophical materialism connected with it. Dialectical materialism had never tied itself to the old physics—indeed, it had philosophically transcended it in the middle of the nineteenth century, well ahead of the scientists. Insisting only on the primacy of being—'matter'—in relation to thought, dialectical materialism identifies itself with no particular conception of the structure of matter and treats every such conception as being only of relative validity—a stage in the progress of empirical knowledge. The scientists, on the other hand, find it difficult to dissociate philosophical materialism from this or that phase of their inquiry into the nature of matter. If only they learned to approach the issues in a larger spirit, to combine inductive and deductive reasoning, and empirical and abstract thought—they would be able to see their own discoveries in better perspective, avoid attributing to them absolute philosophical significance, and even anticipate more clearly the transitions from one phase of science to another. Many scientists dwelling on the allegedly anti-materialistic implications of radio-activity could not even see whither the discovery of radio-activity led them; and they viewed sceptically the possibility of splitting the atom. Criticizing this attitude, Trotsky went on record with this prediction:

The phenomena of radio-activity lead us straight to the problem of releasing the inner energy of the atom. . . . The greatest task of contemporary physics is to extract from the atom its latent energy—to tear open a plug so that that energy should well up with all its might. Then it will become possible to replace coal and petrol by atomic energy which will become our basic fuel and motive power.

Countering the sceptics, he exclaimed:

This is by no means a hopeless task, and what vistas its solution will open up! . . . *scientific and technological thought is approaching the point of a great upheaval; and so the social revolution of our time coincides with a revolution in man's inquiry into the nature of matter and in his mastery of matter.*[1]

Trotsky made this prophecy on 1 March 1926. He was not to live to see it come true; he was to die almost on the eve of its fulfilment.

Of his excursions into the philosophy of science one deserves to be especially recalled—his plea in defence of Freudian psycho-analysis. Already in the early 1920's the Freudian school of thought found itself under a ferocious attack which was to ban-ish it from the Soviet Union for many decades. To influential party men, who had hardly any first-hand knowledge of Freud's theory, the school with its over-emphasis on sex appeared sus-pect and incompatible with Marxism. However, intolerance of Freudism was not confined to Bolsheviks; it was, at least, just as strong in politically conservative academic circles, among Pavlov's followers who were bent on establishing a virtual mono-poly for their own teachings. They had this advantage over the Freudians that their school had grown up on Russian soil, and that to Marxist intellectuals it appealed as being the more ob-viously materialistic of the two. Thus party men and Academi-cians formed a curious alliance against psycho-analysis.

Trotsky, we know, was perturbed by this as early as 1922. In that year he wrote a letter to Pavlov in which he sought to vindicate Freudism and tactfully entreated Pavlov to exercise influence in favour of tolerance and freedom of research. Whether he sent the letter is not known; but he included it in volume XXI of his *Works*. Pavlov, it seems, ignored the plea. In the heat of the subsequent political crisis Trotsky could not pur-sue the matter. But he took it up again in 1926; and this time he protested in public against the sycophancy by which the Pavlov school was already surrounded. He spoke with proper respect and admiration about the teaching of Pavlov himself as being 'completely in harmony with dialectical materialism' and as 'destroying the partition between physiology and psychology'. Pavlov sees 'the basic reflexes as physiological and the system of reflexes as resulting in consciousness'; he also views 'the accumu-lation of physiological quantity as producing a new "psycho-

[1] *Sochinenya*, vol. xxi, p. 415. (My italics.)

logical" quality'. But Trotsky spoke with irony about the exaggerated pretensions of the Pavlov school, especially about its boast that it could explain the subtlest play of the human mind and even poetic creation as the work of conditioned reflexes only. Indeed, Trotsky remarked, Pavlov's method is 'experimental and painstaking: it approaches its generalizations step by step: it starts from the dog's saliva and advances towards poetry'; but 'the road to poetry can hardly be seen yet'.

He protested against the disparagement of Freudism all the more strongly because he held that Freud's teaching, like Pavlov's, was inherently materialistic. The two theories, he argued, differ in their methods of inquiry, not in philosophy.[1] Pavlov adopts the strictly empirical method and actually proceeds from physiology to psychology. Freud postulates in advance the physiological urge behind psychical processes; and his approach is more speculative. It is arguable that the Freudians give too much weight to sex at the expense of other factors; but a controversy over this would still remain within the framework of philosophical materialism. The psycho-analyst 'does not ascend from the lowest [physiological] to the highest [psychological] phenomena and from the basic to the complicated reflexes. Instead, he attempts to take all the intermediate stages at one jump, a jump from above downwards, from the religious myth, the lyrical poem, or the dream straight down to the physiological basis of the human psyche.' In a striking image Trotsky clinched the comparison:

The idealists tell us . . . that the 'soul' is a bottomless well. Both Pavlov and Freud think that physiology forms its bottom. Pavlov, like the diver, plunges down to the lowest depth and painstakingly investigates the well from there upwards. Freud stands over it and with a penetrating gaze attempts to pierce its ever shifting and troubled waters and to explore or guess the shape of things down below.

Pavlov's experimental method had, of course, a certain advantage over Freud's partly speculative approach which sometimes led the psycho-analyst to fantastic surmises. Yet,

[1] In his letter to Pavlov, Trotsky argued about the affinity of the two schools as follows: 'Your teaching about conditioned reflexes embraces, so it seems to me, Freud's theory as a particular instance. The sublimation of sexual energy . . . is nothing but the formation on a sexual basis of the conditioned reflexes n plus one, n plus two, and of the reflexes of further degrees.' Ibid., p. 260.

it would be too simple and crude to declare psycho-analysis as incompatible with Marxism and to turn one's back on it. In any case we are not obliged to adopt Freudism either. Freudism is a working hypothesis. It can produce, and it does produce deductions and surmises which point to a materialist psychology. In due time experimentation will provide the tests. Meantime we have neither reason nor right to declare a ban on a method which, even though it may be less reliable, tries to anticipate results towards which the experimental method advances only very slowly.[1]

Trotsky's plea fell on deaf ears. The psycho-analytical theory was presently banished from the universities. Less specifically but even more categorically he defended Einstein's theory of relativity;[2] but to the ecclesiastical 'materialism' of the Stalin era that theory, too, became anathema; and only after Stalin's death was it to be 'rehabilitated'.

.   .   .   .

In his essays on the philosophy of science, Trotsky, well informed and at times inspired though he was, was nevertheless something of an amateur. There was nothing amateurish, however, about his literary criticism. He was Russia's leading critic in these years. His *Literature and Revolution* influenced strongly the writers of *Krasnaya Nov*, the leading intellectual journal of the time, and especially its editor A. Voronsky, who was an avowed Trotskyist and a distinguished essayist. Even now, nearly four decades after it was written, the book is still unsurpassed not merely as a survey of the revolutionary *Sturm und Drang* in Russian letters and as an advance denunciation of the stifling of artistic creation by Stalinism, but more generally as an essay in Marxist literary criticism. The book is written with an intimate feeling for art and literature, with original insight, captivating verve and wit, and—in the closing pages—a power of vision which rises to rare heights of poetic sublimity.

In literature, too, Trotsky declared war on the iconoclastic attitude and on pseudo-revolutionary conceit and arrogance. He demanded freedom of expression for all artistic and literary schools, at least as long as they did not abuse it for plainly and

[1] Ibid., pp. 430–1. Whether Trotsky was right in saying that Pavlov's method yielded results more slowly than Freud's it is for the experts to judge. He underlined that his defence of Freudism should not be mistaken for indulgence towards the 'vulgar pseudo-Freudism', *en vogue* among the bourgeois public.

[2] *Pod Znamyenem Marksizma*, Nr. 1.

unmistakably counter-revolutionary purposes. Again, the iconoclastic attitude and intolerance were in evidence not only, and not even mainly, among party men. They were even more characteristic of various groups of young writers and artists. New rebellious schools proliferated in art and literature. In normal circumstances these schools, with their innovations and attacks on established artistic authorities, might have excited curiosity and caused a flurry within relatively narrow circles, and then they might have fought their way, as so many of their predecessors had done, from obscurity to recognition, without much political flag-waving *en route*. But, circumstances being what they were, the rivalries of the artistic coteries and their controversies transcended normal limits. The new schools claimed for themselves momentous political significance, advertised themselves as pioneers of the revolution, and sought to discredit the older schools as socially reactionary as well as artistically outdated.

Proletkult, we know, clamoured for the official acceptance of its 'school of thought' and even for a monopoly. Its writers, Lebedinsky, Pletnev, Tretyakov, and others, found a forum in two periodicals, *Kuznitsa* and *Oktyabr*, and later founded their own militant *Na Postu*. Since Bukharin, as *Pravda*'s editor, and Lunacharsky, as Commissar of Education, patronized *Proletkult*, it took Lenin's pronouncement to rebuff its pretensions. When the *Proletkult* writers, upset by the rebuke, turned to Trotsky, begging his protection, he replied that he would in any case defend their right to advocate their views freely, but that he was in complete agreement with Lenin on the harmfulness and inanity of all slogans about proletarian literature and art. Even the more modest clichés about a 'new socialist epoch in art' or a 'new revolutionary renaissance in literature' were worthless: 'The arts have revealed a terrible helplessness, as they always do at the beginning of a great epoch. . . . Like the owl, the bird of wisdom, so the singing bird of poetry makes itself heard only after sunset. In day-time things are done, and only at dusk do feeling and reason take in what has happened.'

It was wrong to blame the revolution for the artist's plight. The 'singing bird of poetry' made itself heard still less in the camp of the counter-revolution. In a scathing survey of the émigré literature Trotsky pointed out that although most of the famous

Russian writers had gone abroad they had not produced there
a single noteworthy work. Nor had the 'internal émigrés'—
those writers in Russia who thought and felt as the émigrés did
—much to boast of, writers like Zinaida Gippius, Evgenii
Zamyatin,[1] and even Andrey Belyi. For all their indubitable
gifts, these writers, engrossed in a callous egotism, were incapable of responding to the drama of their time—at best they
escaped into mysticism. Thus even Belyi, the most outstanding
among them, 'is always preoccupied with his own self, tells stories
about his own self, walks around his own self, sniffs at his own
self, and licks his own self'.[2] Gippius cultivated a lofty, other-
worldly, mystical and erotical Christianity; yet 'it was enough
that the nailed boot of a Red Guardman should step on her
lyrical toe and at once she burst into a scream by which one
could recognize the witch obsessed with sacrosant property'.
(But as she did not lack talent, there was indeed a poetic quality
in her witch's scream!) In their attachment to the spurious
values of a lapsed social system and in their alienation from their
time, these writers were to Trotsky repulsive and grotesque. He
saw them as expressing all that was worthless in the old intelligentsia. He drew a thumb-nail sketch of one of the types of that
intelligentsia, an 'internal émigré' *par excellence*:

When a certain Constitutional Democratic aesthete, having made
a long journey in a stove heated goods wagon, tells you, muttering
between his teeth, how he, a most refined European, with a set of
superb false teeth, the best in the world, and with a minute knowledge of Egyptian ballet techniques, was reduced by this boorish
revolution to travelling with despicable lice-ridden bagmen, then
you feel rising up in your throat a physical nausea with his dentures,
ballet techniques, and generally with all his 'culture' pilfered from
Europe's market stalls; and the conviction grows upon you that the
very last louse of the most uncouth of our bagmen is more important
in the mechanics of history and more, so to speak, necessary than
this thoroughly 'cultured' and in every respect sterile egotist.[3]

[1] Some of these writers later became émigrés. On Zamyatin's novel '*We*',
written in emigration, George Orwell modelled his '*1984*'.

[2] *Literatura i Revolutsia*, p. 36.

[3] 'Bagmen'—people who, during the civil war and the famine, travelled with their
bags over the country in search of food. Sometimes petty black-marketeers were
also described as bagmen. Because of the destruction of rolling stock, people
travelled mostly in goods wagons. Ibid., pp. 26–27.

Having disposed somewhat summarily of the 'internal émigrés', Trotsky went on to discuss the more creative trends in literature. He criticized and defended the *paputchiki* or 'fellow-travellers'. He coined this term to describe those writers who, without embracing communism, 'travelled a stretch of the road with the revolution', but were liable to part company with it and go their own way.[1] Such were, for instance, the 'Imagists', a literary school of which Yessenin and Kluyev were the outstanding poets. They had brought the muzhik's personality and imagination into poetry—Trotsky showed how they composed their colourful and crowded poetic images in the manner in which the muzhik liked to adorn his *izba*. In their poems one could feel both the attraction and the repulsion which the revolution exercised on the peasantry. The ambiguity of their attitude gave artistic tension and social significance to their work. They were the 'poetic Narodniks of the October era'. That this frame of mind should find a stirring expression was only natural in a peasant country—and it was found not only among the Imagists. Boris Pilniak, whose talent Trotsky valued highly, shared with them the attachment to Russia's primordial primitivism which the revolution had sapped. Consequently he 'accepted' Bolshevism and 'rejected' communism, conceiving the former as the elemental 'peculiarly Russian', and in part Asiatic aspect of the revolution and the latter as the modern, urban, proletarian, and predominantly European element. More harshly Trotsky wrote about Marietta Shaginyan who had 'reconciled' herself to the revolution only from a sort of fatalistic Christianity and utter artistic indifference to anything that lay, metaphorically speaking, 'outside her private drawing room'. (Shaginyan was one of the very few writers of this group to survive the Stalinist purges and emerge as a Stalin Prizewinner.)

Trotsky described Alexander Blok also as a *paputchik*, but placed him in a class of his own. Blok's poetry had received a first and mighty stimulus from the revolution of 1905. It was his misfortune that his best creative years fell in the doldrums between two revolutions, between 1907 and 1917; he could never make peace with the emptiness of those years. His poetry was then

---

[1] The term is used throughout the chapter in this its original sense, and not in the meaning it has since acquired in English usage.

romantic, symbolic, shapeless, unreal; but underneath it there was the assumption of a very real way of life. . . . Romantic symbolism is an escape from reality only in so far as it evades its concrete quality . . .; essentially, however, symbolism is a way of transforming and elevating life. . . . Blok's starry, snow-drifty, and formless lyricism reflects an environment and an epoch . . . beyond which it would, like a cloudy patch, be suspended in a vacuum. It will not survive its time and author.

But 1917 once again shook Blok and gave him 'a sense of movement, purpose, and significance. He was not the poet of the revolution. But having withered in the dull impasse of pre-revolutionary life and art, he now grasped with his hand the wheel of revolution. From that contact came "The Twelve", the most significant of all his poems, the only one which will survive into the centuries.' Unlike most later critics, Trotsky did not treat 'The Twelve' as an apotheosis of the revolution but as the 'swan song of that individualistic art which sought to join the revolution'. 'Essentially, this was a cry of despair over a perishing past; but so great was the cry and so intense the despair that it rose to a cry of hope for the future.'

The Futurists were the most vigorous and vociferous literary grouping in these years. They clamoured for a break with all that was *passé*, insisted on the allegedly basic connexion between art and technology, introduced technical-industrial terms into their poetic idiom, and identified themselves with Bolshevism and internationalism.[1] Trotsky devoted a detailed and discerning study to this trend. He dismissed the technological raptures of the Futurists as reflexes of Russian backwardness:

Except for architecture, art bases itself on technology . . . only in so far as the latter forms the basis of civilized activity at large. In practice the dependence of art, especially of verbal art, on material technology is negligible. One can write a poem about skyscrapers, *dirigibles*, and submarines even when one lives in the backwoods of the Ryazan gubernia; one can write it with a pencil stump on rough wrapping paper. The fact that there are skyscrapers, *dirigibles*, and submarines in America is enough to fire the fresh imagination of Ryazan—the poet's word is the most portable of all materials.

[1] 'Only "futurist art" is built on collectivism. Only futurist art represents the art of the proletariat in our times', wrote N. Altman, the 'theorist' of the group in *Iskusstvo Kommuny* in 1918.

The identification of Futurism with proletarian revolution was also questionable. It was not by chance that in Italy the same poetic school was absorbed by fascism.[1] In both countries the Futurists, when they made their first appearance, were artistic rebels without definite political leanings. They might have gone the way of all literary flesh, fought and gained recognition, and settled in respectability, had they not been caught up by violent political upheavals before they had had the time to mellow. Then their literary rebelliousness took a political colour from the upheaval around them, the Fascist upheaval in Italy, the Bolshevik in Russia. This was all the more natural as both fascism and bolshevism attacked, from their opposed angles, the political *passéism* of the bourgeoisie. The Russian Futurists had, no doubt, been genuinely attracted by the dynamic force of the October Revolution; and so they mistook their Bohemian rebellion for the genuine artistic counterpart of the revolution. Because they themselves had broken with certain artistic traditions, they flaunted their contempt for the past and imagined that together with them, the revolution, the working class, and the party stood for a break with 'ages of tradition' in every field. They took, Trotsky remarked, 'too cheap a view of the ages'. The cry against tradition had its justification as long as it was directed at a literary public and against the inertia of established styles and forms. But it sounded hollow when 're-addressed to the working class, which does not need to break and which cannot break with any literary tradition because it is not at all in the grip of any such tradition'. The all-out crusade against *passéism* was a storm in the intelligentsia's tea-cup, an outburst of Bohemian nihilism. 'We, Marxists, have always lived in tradition, and we have not, because of this, ceased to be revolutionaries.'

The Futurists further claimed that their art was collectivist, aggressive, atheistic, and therefore proletarian. 'Attempts', Trotsky retorted, 'to derive by way of deduction an artistic style from the nature of the proletariat, from its collectivism,

---

[1] In an appendix to *Literature and Revolution* Trotsky published a memorandum on the origins of Italian Futurism and its relation to fascism, written at his request by Antonio Gramsci, the Italian communist theorist and founder of *Ordine Nuovo*. Shortly afterwards Gramsci returned to Italy and spent the rest of his life in Mussolini's prisons. During his stay in Moscow Gramsci enjoyed Trotsky's confidence.

dynamism, atheism, etc., are pure idealism and can produce only clever philosophical home-spun, arbitrary allegories, and . . . provincial dilettantism.'

We are told that art is not a mirror but a hammer: it does not reflect things but transforms them. But nowadays they teach one to handle even a hammer by means of a 'mirror', by means, that is, of a sensitive film which fixes all phases of the movement. . . . How can we transform ourselves and our lives without looking into the 'mirror' of literature?

His critical view of the Futurists did not prevent Trotsky from acknowledging their literary merits; and he acknowledged these all the more generously because influential party men looked askance at their experimental obscurity and eccentricities. He warned Communists to beware of that 'hasty intolerance' which treats experimental art as a fraud or as the whim of a decadent intelligentsia.

The struggle against the old poetical vocabulary and syntax was, despite all its . . . extravagances, a progressive rebellion against the closed vocabulary . . ., against an impressionism which sips life through a straw, and against a symbolism lost in . . . heavenly emptiness. . . . The Futurist's work has in this respect been vital and progressive . . . it has eliminated from poetry many words and idioms which had become hollow; it has made other words and idioms full-blooded once again; and in some cases it has successfully created new words and idioms. . . . This applies not only to individual words, but also to the place of each word among other words, to syntax.

True enough, the Futurists had over-reached themselves in innovation; but 'the same has happened even with our revolution: such is the "sin" of every living movement. The excesses are and will be discarded, but the essential cleansing and the indubitable revolutionizing of the poetic language will have lasting effects.' The same should be said in favour of new techniques in rhythm and rhyme. These must not be approached in a narrowly rationalistic spirit; man's need for rhythm and rhyme is irrational; and 'the sound of the word forms the acoustic accompaniment to its meaning'. 'Of course, the overwhelming majority of the working class cannot yet be bothered with these issues. Even its vanguard has not yet had the time for them—

there are more urgent tasks. But we also have a future before us. And this demands from us a more attentive, a precise, a craftsman-like, an artistic attitude towards language, the essential tool of culture, not only in poetry but even more so in prose.' In handling and weighing words, their meanings and shadings and sounds, 'micrometrical instruments' are needed. Instead, uncouth banality and routine were rampant. 'In one of its aspects, the better aspect, Futurism is a protest against slapdashness, that most powerful literary school which has its very influential representatives in every field.' From this point of view Trotsky found something to say even for the 'formalist' school and the chief expounder of its ideas, Victor Shklovsky, although he criticized their exclusive concentration on form: while the formalist believes that at the beginning was the word, the Marxist thinks that at the beginning was the deed—'the word follows the deed as its sound-shadow'.

A special essay in *Literature and Revolution* deals with Mayakovsky, the most gifted Futurist who was later canonized as *the* bard of communism. Trotsky held that Mayakovsky was artistically at his worst precisely where as a Communist he was at his best. This was not surprising: Mayakovsky took pains to be a Communist; yet a poet's outlook depends not on his conscious thought and exertion but on his semi-conscious perception and sub-conscious feeling and on the stock of images and impressions the poet has absorbed in early childhood. The revolution was for Mayakovsky a 'genuine and profound experience' because it turned with its thunder and lightning against the obtuseness and inertia of the old society which Mayakovsky hated in his own way and with which he had not had the time to make peace. He adhered enthusiastically to the revolution but did not and could not merge with it. To this Mayakovsky's poetic style testifies:

The dynamic élan of the revolution and its stern courage appeal to Mayakovsky much more closely than do the mass character of its heroism and the collectivism of its affairs and experiences. As the Greek anthropomorphist naïvely assimilated the forces of nature to himself, so our poet, the Mayakomorphist, crowds with his own self the squares and streets and fields of the revolution. . . . His dramatic pathos rises frequently to extraordinary tension, but behind the tension there is not always real strength. The poet is too conspicuous

—he allows too little autonomy to events and facts. It is not the revolution which wrestles with obstacles but Mayakovsky who displays his athletics in the arena of words, sometimes performing genuine miracles, but frequently lifting with heroic effort notoriously empty weights. . . . About himself Mayakovsky speaks all the time in the first and third person. . . . To lift up man he raises him up to Mayakovsky. He adopts a tone of familiarity towards the most majestic historic phenomena. . . . He stands with one foot on Mont Blanc and with the other on the Elbrus. His voice out-thunders thunder. What is the wonder that . . . the proportions of earthly things vanish and that no difference is left between the small and the great? He speaks about love, the most intimate of feelings, as if it were the migration of peoples. . . . No doubt, this hyperbolic style reflects in some measure the frenzy of our time. But this does not provide it with an over-all artistic justification. It is impossible to out-clamour war and revolution, but it is easy to get hoarse in the attempt. . . . Mayakovsky shouts too often where one should speak; and so his cry, where cry is needed, sounds inadequate.

Mayakovsky's overloaded images, often beautiful in themselves, just as often destroy the unity of the whole and paralyse movement.

The excess of dynamic imagery leads to stand-still . . . every phrase, every idiom, and every metaphor is intended to yield the maximum and to reach the upper limit, the peak. That is why the thing as a whole has no maximum . . . [and] the poem has no peak. . . .

.   .   .   .

The refutation of the idea of 'proletarian culture' forms the central and most controversial part of *Literature and Revolution*. In the Preface Trotsky gives this succinct summary of his argument:

It is fundamentally wrong to oppose proletarian to bourgeois culture and art. Proletarian culture and art will never exist. The proletarian régime is temporary and transitory. Our revolution derives its historic significance and moral greatness from the fact that it lays the foundations for a classless society and for the first truly universal culture.

One should not reason, therefore, from historical analogy and conclude that since the bourgeoisie has created its own culture and art the proletariat will also do so. It is not merely the 'purpose' of proletarian revolution—its striving for classless culture

—that invalidates the parallel.[1] What militates against it even more strongly is a basic difference in the historic destinies of the two classes. The bourgeois way of life developed organically in the course of several centuries, whereas the proletarian dictatorship may last years or decades, but not longer; and its life span is filled with savage class struggles which allow little or no room for the organic growth of new culture.

We are still soldiers on the march. We have a day of rest. We must wash our shirts, cut and brush our hair, and first of all clean and grease our rifles. All our present economic and cultural work is nothing but an attempt to bring ourselves into some sort of order between two battles and two marches. . . . Our epoch is not the epoch of a new culture. We can only force open the gate to it. In the first instance we must acquire the most important elements of the old civilization. . . .

The bourgeoisie could create its own culture because even under feudalism and absolutism, even before it had gained political domination, it possessed wealth, social power, and education, and was present in almost every field of spiritual activity. The working class can gain in capitalist society at the most the ability to overthrow that society; but being a property-less, exploited, and uneducated class, it emerges from bourgeois rule in a condition of cultural pauperism; and so it cannot originate a new and significant phase in the development of the human mind.[2] It was in fact not the working class but small groups of party men and intellectuals (who in this field, too, 'substituted' themselves for the class) that aspired to bring proletarian culture into being. Yet no 'class culture can be created behind the back of a class'. Nor can it be manufactured in Communist laboratories. Those who maintain that they have already found the proletarian culture in Marxism argue from ignorance: Marxism has been the product as well as the negation of bourgeois thought; and it has so far applied its dialectics mainly to the study of economics and politics, whereas culture

---

[1] 'The proletariat has taken power precisely in order to put an end to class culture for ever and to pave the way for a universal human culture. Not rarely we seem to be forgetting this.'

[2] 'The bourgeoisie assumed power when it was fully armed with the culture of its time. The proletariat assumes power when it is fully armed only with its acute need to obtain access to culture.'

is 'the sum total of knowledge and skill which characterizes society as a whole, or at least its ruling class'.

The contribution of the working class to literature and art is negligible. It is preposterous to speak of proletarian poetry on the strength of the work of a few gifted worker-poets. Such artistic achievement as these poets can claim they owe to their apprenticeship with 'bourgeois' or even pre-bourgeois poets. Even if their writings are inferior, they are still valuable as human and social documents. But it is an insult to the prole-tariat—'a piece of populist demagogy'—to treat such writings as new and epoch-making art. 'Art for the proletariat cannot be second rate. The *Proletkult* writers declaim much about "the new, monumental, dynamic" literature and painting. But where, comrades, is that art "of the great canvas and great style", that "monumental" art? Where is it? Where?' So far it had all been big talk, boasting, and baiting the opponents of *Proletkult*, the Imagists, the Futurists, the Formalists, and the *paputchiki*, without whose works Soviet literature would be utterly impoverished and left only with *Proletkult*'s dubious 'promissory notes'.

As might have been expected, Trotsky was accused of eclecticism, kow-towing before bourgeois culture, encouraging bourgeois individualism, and denying the party the right and the duty of 'exercising leadership' in literature and art. He replied:

> Art must find its own road. . . . The methods of Marxism are not its methods. The party exercises leadership in the working class but not over the [entire] historical process. There are some fields in which it leads directly and imperiously. There are other fields in which it supervises . . . and still others where it can only offer its cooperation. There are finally fields where it can only orientate itself and keep abreast with what is going on. The field of art is not one in which the party is called on to command.

Exaggerated attacks against individualism were out of place: individualism has played a dual role: it has had its reactionary effects, but it has also had progressive and revolutionary ones. The working class has suffered not from the excess but from an atrophy of individualism. The worker's personality is not yet formed and differentiated strongly enough; and to form and develop it is just as important as it is to train him in industrial skills. It is absurd to fear that the art of bourgeois individualism may sap his sense of class solidarity. 'What the worker will absorb from Shakespeare, Pushkin, Goethe, and Dostoevsky is . . . a more complex idea about the human personality, its passions and its feelings.'[1]

In the closing chapter of the book Trotsky discussed 'certainties and hypotheses' about the prospects. The 'certainties' referred only to the 'art of the revolution'; about 'socialist art', which could come to life only in a classless society, it was possible to make only guesses. The art of revolution, throbbing with all the class conflicts and the political passions of the time, belongs to a transition era—to the 'realm of necessity', not to that of freedom. Only in a classless society can human solidarity come to full fruition; and only then 'will those feelings which we, revolutionaries, are shy of calling by their names because the hypocrite and the canaille have made the words threadbare—only in classless society will the feelings of disinterested friendship, love for our fellow being, and heartfelt compassion ring out powerfully in socialist poetry'.[2]

The literature of revolution was still only groping for expression. It was argued that it must be realistic. In the broad philosophical sense this was true: the art of our epoch could not achieve greatness unless it was deeply sensitive to social reality. But it was preposterous to try and foster realism in the narrower sense, as a literary school. It was not true that such a school would be inherently 'progressive': by itself realism is neither revolutionary nor reactionary. Its golden age in Russia fell in the epoch of aristocratic literature. As a reaction against it came the tendentious style of the Populist writers, which then gave way to pessimistic symbolism, against which the Futurists reacted in their turn. The mutation of styles occurred against a definite social background and reflected changes in the political climate; but it also followed its own artistic logic and its own laws. Any new style grows out of the old style, as its dialectical negation: it revives and develops some elements of the old and abandons others.

Every literary school is potentially contained in the past, but develops through a hostile break with it. The relationship between

---

[1] *Literatura i Revolutsia*, p. 166. [2] Ibid., p. 170.

form and content . . . is determined by the fact that the new form is discovered, proclaimed, and evolved, under the pressure of an inner need, of a collective psychological demand which, like everything else . . . has its social roots. Hence the duality of every literary trend: on the one hand, any trend contributes something new to the techniques of artistic creation . . ., and on the other it expresses definite social demands. . . . These include individual demands because the social class speaks through the individual; and national demands because the nation's outlook is determined by that of its dominant class which is dominant also in its literature.[1]

The indubitable fact that literature has served as a vehicle for social aspirations does not justify anyone in neglecting or falsifying its artistic logic and in trying either to canonize or to ban any style. Some critics reacted crudely against symbolism. Yet, 'it was not Russian symbolism that had invented the symbol. It had only absorbed it into the modernized Russian language. The art of the future will certainly not renounce the formal achievements of symbolism.' Nor will it renounce the traditional genres and forms, even though some critics rejected these as obsolete, saying that satire and comedy had outlived their time, and that tragedy was dead because it was incompatible with a materialistic and godless philosophy of life. The burial of the old genres was at least premature. There was still room for a 'Soviet Gogol' or 'Soviet Goncharov' who would mercilessly expose 'the old and the new filth', the old and new vices, and the dull-mindedness which could be found in Soviet society.[2]

Those who spoke of the extinction of tragedy argued that religion, fate, sin, and penance are at the centre of the tragic motif. Against this Trotsky pointed out that the essence of tragedy lies in the wider conflict between man's awakened mind and his constricting environment, a conflict which is inseparable from man's existence and manifests itself in different forms at different stages of history. The religious myth had not created tragedy but only expressed it 'in the imaginative language of mankind's childhood'. Fate, as conceived by the ancients, and the medieval Christian Passions were not to be found in Shakespeare's drama, the artistic product of the Reformation. Shake-

[1] *Literatura i Revolutsia*, pp. 172–3.

[2] The new satirist had to contend with the Soviet censorship. Trotsky promised to lend him a hand in this struggle as long as his satire attacked social evils in the interests of the revolution.

speare marks, therefore, a significant advance upon Greek tragedy: 'his art is more human': it shows man's earthly passions transcending man himself and transformed into a sort of Fate. The same is true of Goethe's drama. Yet, tragedy can rise even higher. Its hero may become man defeated not by *hubris*, the gods, or even his own passion, but by society:

As long as man is not yet master of his social organization, that organization towers above him like Fate itself. . . . The struggle for communism which Babeuf waged before his time, in an immature society, was like the struggle of the classical hero against Fate. . . . The tragedy of restricted personal passion is too flat for our time— we live in an epoch of social passion. The stuff of contemporary tragedy is found in the clash between the individual and a collective or between hostile collectives represented by individuals. Our time is once again a time of great purpose . . . man attempts to free himself from all mystical and ideological fog and to reconstruct society and himself. . . . This is larger than the childish play of the ancients . . . or the monastic ravings of the Middle Ages, or the presumption of an individualism which wrenches the human personality from its social environment, exhausts it utterly and then hurls it into a vacuum of pessimism. . . .[1]

[The new artist will] project the great purposes of our time into art. It is difficult to foresee whether the dramatist of the revolution will create 'high' tragedy. But socialist art will certainly give it a new birth . . . as it will also give fresh life to comedy, because the new man will want to laugh, to the novel and to lyrical poetry, because the new man's love will be more beautiful and larger . . . and he will brood anew over issues of birth and death. . . . The decline of the old forms is by no means absolute or final . . . they will all have their renascence. . . . What matters is that the poet of the coming epoch should muse man's musings anew and feel man's feelings anew.[2]

Hypothetical though all anticipations of Socialist art were, Trotsky thought that one could discern odd pointers towards it in the confused, sometimes even meaningless, innovations in which Soviet art abounded during these years. In the theatre Meyerhold searched for a new 'biomechanical' synthesis of drama, rhythm, sound, and colour; and Tairov tried to 'break down the barrier' between stage and audience, theatre and life. Painting and sculpture struggled to get out of the impasse in

---

[1] *Literatura i Revolutsia*, pp. 180–1. [2] Ibid., pp. 181–2.

which they had found themselves after the exhaustion of the representational styles. In architecture Tatlin's 'constructivist' school rejected the ornamental forms, advocated 'functionalism', and drew up ambitious blueprints for garden cities and public buildings worthy of a socialist society. These plans unfortunately took no account of material possibilities; but they contained, in Trotsky's opinion, rational elements and valuable intuitive premonitions:

We could not yet afford to give thought to architecture, the most monumental of all arts. . . . Large scale construction must still be delayed. The authors of these gigantic projects . . . have a breathing space for fresh reflection. . . . Tatlin, however, is unconditionally right when he discards the nationally limited style, allegorical sculpture, stucco moulding, arabesques, frippery and finery, and seeks to subordinate the whole design to the correct constructive use of building materials. . . . Whether he is also right in what appears to be his personal whim, the use of the revolving cube, the pyramid, and the glass cylinder, he has still to prove. . . . In the future such monumental tasks as the planning of garden cities, model housing estates, railways, and harbours will touch to the quick not only architects . . . but the broadest mass of the people. The antheap-like, imperceptible accumulation of town districts and streets, brick by brick, from generation to generation, will give place to titanic building . . . with map and compass in hand.

The wall between art and industry will crumble. The grand style of the future will aim at form creation, not ornamentation. . . . But it would be mistaken to see this as the . . . self-effacement of art before technology. . . . The gulf between art and nature may be expected to disappear, but it will do so not because art will go back, in Rousseau's sense, to man in his natural condition, but because it will bring nature nearer to itself, to art. The present location of mountains and rivers, fields and greens, steppe, forest, and maritime coasts, should by no means be considered as final. Man has already carried out some far from negligible changes in nature's map. But these are only school-boyish essays in comparison with what is to come. If faith could only promise to move mountains, technology, which takes nothing on faith, will really pull them down and shift them. Hitherto it has done this only for industrial commercial purposes (mines and tunnels). In the future it will do it on an incomparably wider scale, in accordance with comprehensive productive-artistic plans. Man will make a new inventory of mountains and rivers. He will seriously and more than once amend nature. He will eventually reshape the earth to his taste . . . and we have no reason to fear that his taste will be poor.

Here, at last, Trotsky unfolds his vision of man in the realm of freedom, an up-to-date, Marxist version of

> The loathsome mask has fallen, the man remains
> Sceptreless, free, uncircumscribed, but man
> Equal, unclassed, tribeless, and nationless,
> Exempt from awe, worship, degree, the king
> Over himself; just, gentle, wise; but man
> Passionless?—no, yet free from guilt or pain.

There were those who, with Nietzsche, argued that a classless society, if it ever came into being, would suffer from excess of solidarity and that it would lead a passive and herd-like existence in which man, his competitive and fighting instincts extinguished, would degenerate. Yet socialism, far from suppressing the human instinct for emulation, would redeem it by turning it towards higher purposes. In a society free from class antagonisms there would be no competition for profit and no struggle for political power; and man's energies and passions would concentrate on creative emulation in the fields of technology, science, and art. New 'parties' would spring into being and contest with one another over ideas, over the planning of human settlements, trends in education, styles in the theatre, in music, and in sport, over schemes for gigantic canals, over the fertilization of deserts, the regulation of climate, new chemical hypotheses, and so on. The contests, 'exciting, dramatic, passionate', would embrace society as a whole, and not merely priest-like coteries. 'Art will therefore not be starved of those varieties of nervous energy and collective psychological stimuli' which produce new ideas and images. People will divide into rival artistic 'parties' according to temperament and taste. The human personality will grow, refine itself, and develop that priceless quality inherent in it—'the quality of never contenting itself with what it has achieved'.

To be sure, these were remote prospects. Immediately ahead was an epoch of fierce class struggle and civil wars from which mankind would emerge impoverished and destitute. Then the conquest of poverty and penury in all their forms would take decades—and during this time the nascent socialist society would be gripped by a 'passion for what are today the better sides of Americanism', for industrial expansion, records of productivity, and material comfort. But this phase, too, would pass; and then vistas which the imagination could not yet even encompass would open:

The present dreams of some enthusiasts . . . about imparting a theatrical quality and a rhythmical harmony to man's existence fit in with this prospect well and coherently. . . . The drudgery of feeding and bringing up children . . . will be lifted from the individual family by social initiative. . . . Woman will at last emerge from semi-slavery. . . . Socio-educational experiments . . . will evolve with a now inconceivable élan. The communist way of life will not grow up blindly like coral reefs in the sea. It will be built consciously. It will be checked by critical thought. It will be directed and corrected. . . . Man will learn to shift rivers and mountains, to build people's palaces on the heights of Mont Blanc and at the bottom of the ocean; and he will impart to his existence not only wealth and colour and dramatic tension but also a highly dynamic character. No sooner will one crust begin to form itself on the human existence than it will burst under the pressure of new . . . inventions and achievements.

At last man will begin in earnest to harmonize his own being. He will aim at bringing higher precision, purposefulness, economy, and consequently beauty into the movements of his own body at work, on the march, and at play. He will desire to master the half-conscious and unconscious processes of his own organism: breathing, blood circulation, digestion, reproduction; and he will seek, within unavoidable limits, to subordinate them to control by reason and will. . . . *Homo sapiens*, now stagnating, . . . will treat himself as the object of the most complex methods of artificial selection and psycho-physical training.

These prospects follow from the whole of man's development. He begins with expelling darkness from production and ideology—with breaking, by means of technology, the barbarous routine of his work and defeating religion by means of science. . . . Then by means of socialist organization he eliminates blind, elemental spontaneity from economic relationships. . . . Lastly, in the deepest and dimmest recesses of the unconscious . . . there lurks the nature of man himself. On it, clearly, he will concentrate the supreme effort of his mind and of his creative initiative. Mankind will not have ceased to crawl before God, Tsar, and Capital only in order to surrender meekly to dark laws of heredity and blind sexual selection. . . . Man will strive to control his own feelings, to raise his instincts to the height of his conscious mind, and to bring clarity into them, to channel his willpower into his unconscious depths; and in this way he will lift himself to new eminence, grow into a superior biological and social type—into the superman, if you like.

It is as difficult to say beforehand what are the limits of self-mastery that man may be able to reach as it is to foresee how far he can develop his technical mastery of nature. Social constructiveness and psychophysical self-education will become the twin aspects of a single process. All the arts—literature, theatre, painting, sculpture, music, and architecture—will impart to that process a sublime form. . . . Man will grow incomparably stronger, wiser, subtler; his body will become more harmonious; his movements more rhythmical; his voice more musical. The forms of his existence will acquire a dynamic theatrical quality. The average man will rise to the stature of Aristotle, Goethe, Marx. And above these heights new peaks will rise.

It is doubtful whether Trotsky knew that Jefferson had similarly anticipated 'progress . . . physical or intellectual—until every man is potentially an athlete in body and an Aristotle in mind'. He was influenced rather by the French Utopians, from Condorcet to Saint Simon. Like Condorcet he also found in the contemplation of the future 'an asylum in which the thought about his persecutors could not haunt him, and where he lived in his mind with man restored to his rights and dignity and forgot man tormented and corrupted by greed, fear, or envy'. His vision of the classless society had, of course, been implicit in all Marxist thought influenced as it was by French Utopian socialism. But no Marxist writer before or after Trotsky has viewed the great prospect with so realistic an eye and so flaming an imagination.

.   .   .   .

The whole 'Trotskyist' conception of culture and art soon came under fire. It offended the half-educated party man by its very breadth and complexity. It outraged the bureaucrat to whom it denied the right to control and regiment intellectual life. It also antagonized the ultra-revolutionary literary sects whose pretensions it refused to accept. Thus, a fairly wide anti-Trotskyist 'front' formed itself in the cultural field; and it was kept in being, reinforced, and eventually absorbed by the political front. The struggle against Trotsky's influence as a literary critic became part of the endeavour to destroy his political authority; and so his opponents declared his views on art to be part and parcel of the wider Trotskyist heresy.[1] Their attack centred on his denial of the possibility of proletarian culture, for here he challenged most provocatively the vested interests that were forming themselves; and he was denounced for expounding a variety of bourgeois liberalism. Only very little of the great mass of the dogmatic argumentation produced in this connexion still retains interest. Most of it was virtually disavowed by its own inspirers, especially by Stalin himself when some time later he brutally disowned all the claims of the 'proletarian' writers and artists, disbanded their organizations and mercilessly persecuted them. In the middle 1920's, however, Stalin flattered every half-baked literary and cultural ambition in order to 'mobilize' on his side the intelligentsia and the semi-intelligentsia.

Of the arguments advanced against Trotsky one or two should be mentioned here, however. Thus Lunacharsky criticized Trotsky on the ground that, recognizing only the great feudal and bourgeois cultures of the past and the culture of socialism which was to emerge in the future, he treated the proletarian dictatorship as a cultural vacuum and viewed the present as a sterile hiatus between a creative past and a creative future. This was also the substance of a more specific criticism which Bukharin made at a conference on literary policy which the Central Committee convened in February 1925.[2] While agreeing that Trotsky had most impressively argued his case, that Lenin, too, had been extremely critical of 'proletarian culture', and that a revolutionary working class could exercise political

---

[1] Thirty-five years after the publication of *Literature and Revolution* the struggle against Trotsky's influence on Soviet literary criticism was still on. During the 'de-Stalinization' of the middle 1950's many of the writers who had been charged with Trotskyism and had perished during the great purges of the 1930's were rehabilitated; and soon the guardians of orthodoxy were confronted with a revival of 'Trotskyist' influence in literature. In May 1958 a writer in *Znamya* stated: 'A. Voronsky, critic and editor of *Krasnaya Nov*, well known in those years [the 1920's] was under the definite influence of Trotskyist views on literature. True, it has now been revealed that he was not connected with the Trotskyist underground. He has been rehabilitated in this respect, as have been other writers wrongly accused. All the same, his . . . theoretical principles were borrowed from bourgeois and idealistic aesthetics and merged with Trotskyist ideas.' The writer devoted several pages to the views on literature expounded by Trotsky himself in order to refute them anew, without, however, resorting to the extremes of Stalinist falsification and abuse. [2] *Krasnaya Nov*, May 1925.

but not cultural leadership, Bukharin nevertheless held that the proletariat would in time achieve cultural preponderance as well and impart its own character to the spiritual creation of the last epoch of class society. Trotsky's mistake, Bukharin maintained, was that he imagined that the proletarian dictatorship and the transition to socialism would be of so short a duration as not to allow any distinctive proletarian class-culture to arise. He did not take into account the 'unequal tempo' of social and political development in different countries, the probability or even the certainty that this would break up the process of international revolution into many separate phases, prolonging greatly the proletarian dictatorship and consequently allowing time for the formation of a culture and art peculiar to it.

There was some truth in Bukharin's argument (which formed part of his and Stalin's case for socialism in a single country). When Trotsky stated: 'We are soldiers on the march. We have a day of rest. Our present . . . cultural work is but an attempt to bring ourselves into some sort of order between two battles and two marches', he did indeed suggest a rapid succession of the main 'battles' of international revolution which should have radically shortened the era of proletarian dictatorship and the transition to socialism. This expectation was ever present in his political forecasts and also in the accents in which he had expounded his conception of permanent revolution, although it was not essential to the conception itself. Yet the 'day of rest' between the Bolshevik onslaught of 1917–20 and the next great 'battle' of revolution was to last not less than a quarter of a century; and the Marxist may well wonder how long the 'day of rest' which has followed the Chinese Revolution may yet last. Trotsky undoubtedly underrated the duration of the proletarian dictatorship and, what goes with it, the extent to which that dictatorship was to acquire a bureaucratic character.

However, his all too evident mistake about this does not invalidate his argument against 'proletarian culture'. On the contrary, it gives to it even greater strength. The fact that the dictatorship and the transition to socialism was to last far longer than he anticipated did not make the era of transition more fruitful culturally and more creative. It made it less so. Stalinism did not beget any proletarian culture. It was instead engaged in 'primitive cultural accumulation', that is, in an exceptionally rapid and extensive spread of mass education and in the assimilation of Western technology. That this took place within the framework of the social relations created by the revolution accounted for the tempo and the intensity of the process and gave to it immense historic significance. All the same, the accomplishment consisted almost entirely in the absorption by the Soviet Union of the heritage of bourgeois and pre-bourgeois civilization, not in the creation of a new culture. Even this achievement was marred by the Stalinist cult with its dogmatic despotism, fetishism, horror of any foreign influence, and fear of independent initiative. The 'cultural accumulation' was 'primitive' in more than one sense: it was accompanied by the suppression or distortion of those finer and more complex cultural values which Trotsky was anxious to preserve and develop under a proletarian dictatorship. When he asserted: 'Our epoch is not the epoch of a new culture—we can only force open the gate to it', he unknowingly epitomized beforehand the cultural history of the entire Stalin era and even of its sequel. Throughout that era the Soviet Union, with bloody head and hands, could only batter at the gate to a new culture—the gate it has now half-forced.

CHAPTER IV

An Interval

AFTER Trotsky had left the Commissariat of War there followed a pause in his inner-party struggle; and it lasted throughout the year 1925 into the summer of 1926. During this time Trotsky did not express himself controversially in public on the issues that had been at the centre of the debates of 1923–4. Even behind the closed doors of the Central Committee and the Politbureau he did not attempt to keep up the discussion. He acknowledged his defeat and submitted to the restrictions which the Central Committee had imposed on him.

During this pause the '1923 Opposition' did not exist in any organized form. Trotsky had in effect disbanded it. 'We must not do anything at this moment', he advised his puzzled and bewildered followers, 'we must not come out into the open in any way. We should only maintain our contacts, preserve the cadres of the 1923 Opposition, and wait until Zinoviev has used himself up.'[1] Had he acted otherwise and initiated new protests or demonstrations of opposition, he and his adherents would at once have had to face the threat of expulsion from the party or at least from its leading bodies. He had every reason to assume that the triumvirs would not shrink from extreme reprisals.

How desperately Trotsky and his adherents were anxious at this time to avoid a renewal of the struggle can be seen from this incident: in 1925 Max Eastman, the American writer, published *Since Lenin Died*, a book in which he gave a true account, the first to see the light, of the struggle over the succession to Lenin and in which he quoted the substance of Lenin's testament. Eastman, who had also written a character sketch of Trotsky, *The Portrait of a Youth*, had been in Moscow, had become an adherent of the Opposition, had obtained from

---

[1] V. Serge, *Le Tournant obscure*, p. 97; *Mémoires d'un révolutionnaire*, p. 229. Serge attributes this 'directive' once to Trotsky himself and on a second occasion to Victor Elzin, Trotsky's assistant. Elzin, in any case, would have expressed Trotsky's view in this matter.

Trotsky himself the information about Lenin's last will and the contest over the succession; and had even begged Trotsky to act more aggressively and to read out the will at the thirteenth congress. He had submitted the manuscript of *Since Lenin Died* to Rakovsky in Paris and had received an indirect answer expressing full approval. He had therefore every reason to think that the work would meet with Trotsky's blessing as well.[1] Trotsky was indeed grateful to Eastman, with whom he remained in friendly relations until ten years later, when Eastman turned against Communism. However, he found Eastman's friendly service embarrassing: the triumvirs charged Trotsky with having committed a gross indiscretion, pressed him to issue a denial of Eastman's disclosures, and threatened him with disciplinary proceedings if he refused. Trotsky's closest associates, whom he consulted, were so reluctant to be forced into a fight over the Eastman incident, that they urged Trotsky to disclaim all responsibility for it. The Politbureau was not content with this, however. It demanded a straight denial of Eastman's story about the testament; it even dictated the terms of the denial. Once again, 'the leading group of the Opposition', as Trotsky puts it, asked him to yield for the sake of peace.[2] And so on 1 September 1925 there appeared in the *Bolshevik* a statement signed by Trotsky that 'all talk about [Lenin's] "testament", allegedly suppressed or violated, is a malicious invention and is directed wholly against Lenin's real will and the interests of the party of which he was the founder'. The statement was reproduced by all foreign communist newspapers and was later eagerly quoted by Stalin.[3] Although such denials made for tactical considerations are not rare in politics, this was particularly galling for Trotsky. After he had watched almost passively the suppression of the testament, his virtual title-deed to the succession, he had now to come forward as a witness bearing false testimony against himself and for Stalin—all in order to postpone a fresh outbreak of inner-party hostilities.

[1] 'I showed the manuscript to Rakovsky . . .', writes Eastman in a letter to the author, 'and told him I would publish it or not according as he decided. Madame Rakovsky sent it back with enthusiastic praise and that was, I thought, as much "authorization" as could be obtained under the circumstances.'

[2] Trotsky explained these circumstances in a letter to Muralov, written from his exile at Alma Ata on 11 September 1928. *The Archives.*

[3] Stalin, *Sochinenya*, vol. x, p. 175.

In such circumstances it was not easy to 'maintain contacts and preserve the cadres of the 1923 Opposition'. For any political group inaction, no matter how well justified by tactical considerations, is a most trying experience. A small band of intellectuals and very advanced workers may fill the interval with studying and arguing within its own circle. But for any larger group, especially if it is composed of factory workers, inactivity most often amounts to political suicide. It saps their faith in their cause; it deadens their fervour; it breeds indifference or despair. Such were the effects of waiting in most groups of the Opposition: they shrank and fell apart. Thus, in Leningrad there were, at the beginning of 1926, not more than about thirty Trotskyists who, grouped around Alexandra Bronstein-Sokolovskaya, Trotsky's first wife, still kept in close touch with one another and met regularly. Many hundreds of previously organized oppositionists had vanished into a political no man's land. In Moscow the Trotskyist 'cadres' were much more numerous and alive; but in the great provincial cities and towns, in Kharkov, Kiev, Odessa, and elsewhere the Opposition's strength declined as much as it did in Leningrad.

The chiefs of the Opposition, bound by ties of political and personal friendship, formed a close circle around Trotsky which often met and deliberated. In it were some of the strongest intellects and characters that could be found in the Bolshevik party. As to political ability, experience, and revolutionary achievement, this circle was certainly superior to the team which led Stalin's faction and ruled the party. Rakovsky, Radek, Preobrazhensky, Yoffe, Antonov-Ovseenko, Pyatakov, Serebriakov, Krestinsky, Ivan Smirnov, Muralov, Mrachkovsky, and Sosnovsky, had been prominent in the early years of the revolution and the civil war and had held offices of the highest responsibility.[1] Marxists of large views, unconventional, resourceful, and full of verve, they represented the most advanced and internationally minded elements in the party.

Of all these men Radek was by far the most famous, though not the most important. He was, next to Trotsky, the most brilliant and witty Bolshevik pamphleteer. Of mercurial temper, a shrewd and realistic student of men and politics, uncannily

[1] Rakovsky, Yoffe, and Krestinsky now held ambassadorial posts in London, Paris, Tokyo, and Berlin; but they remained in close relations with Trotsky.

sensitive to the moods of the most diverse social milieus, Radek
had prompted some of Lenin's most important initiatives in
diplomacy and Comintern policy. Europe was his home. Like
Dzerzhinsky, he had come to the Bolsheviks from the Social
Democratic Party of the Kingdom of Poland and Lithuania,
Rosa Luxemburg's party which had been strongly influenced
by Trotsky's views.[1] He also had behind him many years of a
stormy activity on the extreme left of German socialism; he had
been a forerunner and one of the founding fathers of the Communist International. When shortly after the October Revolution he arrived in Russia, he at once gained admittance into the
inner circle of the leaders; he accompanied Trotsky to Brest
Litovsk; and he led, together with Bukharin and Dzerzhinsky,
the Left Communists in their opposition to peace. After the collapse of the Hohenzollern monarchy, Lenin sent him on a clandestine mission to Germany, where he was to help to set afoot
the newly formed Communist party. He made a perilous and
adventurous journey across the 'cordon sanitaire' by which Russia
was surrounded and arrived in Berlin incognito just before Rosa
Luxemburg and Karl Liebknecht were assassinated. He was
seized by the police and thrown into prison. There, while Berlin
was swept by a White terror and his life hung by a thread, he
contrived a feat of extraordinary versatility: he managed to
make contact with leading German diplomats, industrialists,
and generals; and in his prison cell he conducted with them,
especially with Walter Rathenau, who was to be Foreign Minister
in the Rapallo era, talks designed to tear open the first breach
in the cordon sanitaire.[2] From his cell, too, he maintained clandestine contacts with the German Communist party and helped
to shape its policy.

A pioneer of revolutionary socialism, Radek had in him also
something of the gambler. He was as much in his element
weaving a diplomatic intrigue as when, a mole of revolution, he
tunnelled underground. Of observant eye and untrammelled
mind, he diagnosed the ebb of revolution in Europe before
other Bolshevik leaders saw it; and he advocated the united

---

[1] In that party, however, Radek and Dzerzhinsky had been Luxemburg's
antagonists and had stood closer than the rest of the party to the Bolsheviks.
[2] See Radek's memoirs in *Krasnaya Nov*, no. 10, October 1926; R. Fischer,
Stalin and German Communism, pp. 203–11.

front. When he returned to Germany in 1923, he still saw no flow and restrained Brandler from rushing into what he considered a hopeless attempt at revolution. His taste for the political gamble led him astray, however; and in his 'Schlagetter speech' he made an ambiguous appeal to the desperate extremists of German nationalism. On his return to Moscow he was made to bear the onus of the German defeat and of association with Trotsky. Barred from the European sections of the Comintern, he was, in 1925, appointed Principal of the Sun Yat-sen University in Moscow just at a time when the rumblings of the Chinese revolution made themselves heard—his job was to train propagandists and agitators for China's young Communist movement.[1] Restless, contemptuous of cant, Bohemian in appearance, sharp-tongued, and inclined to cynical postures, he was held by many to be an erratic and even a shady character. He was, however, the subject of much obloquy by adversaries who feared his disrespectful gaze, his banter and deadly pasquinade. The stuff of the man was certainly much more solid than it appeared, although it was to deteriorate dreadfully in later years, under the press of the Stalinist terror. His Bohemian exterior and cynical postures concealed a fervent faith which he was loath to exhibit; and even his snappy quips and jeers were hot with revolutionary passion.

Into the leading circle of the Opposition Radek discharged the electric shocks of his intellect and humour. He was greatly attached to Trotsky, with whom he had so much in common in range of international experience. Of that attachment he gave proof in his essay 'Trotsky, the Organizer of Victory', written in 1923.[2] Trotsky was somewhat wary of Radek's impulsive political improvizations but felt a warm affection for the man and admired his talent.[3] If he distrusted the gambler in Radek, he was nevertheless stimulated by his observations and ideas, and enjoyed the great jester and satirist.

Preobrazhensky's character stands out in stark contrast to Radek's. He was a theorist and probably the most original

[1] Before 1914 Radek had analysed revolutionary developments in the colonial and semi-colonial East in the Polish *Przegląd Socjal-Demokratyczny*, Rosa Luxemburg's theoretical paper.

[2] K. Radek, *Portrety i Pamflety*, pp. 29–34.

[3] See Trotsky's correspondence with Radek in *The Archives*, and 'Radek and the Opposition' in *Écrits*, vol. i, pp. 160–3.

Bolshevik economist. A Leninist since 1904, he had been co-author with Bukharin of the *ABC of Communism*, the once famous compendium on Bolshevik doctrine; and he had been secretary of the Leninist Central Committee. He left that office and made room for Molotov when the party's discipline had grown too rigid for him. As its critic he was Trotsky's forerunner—indeed he had criticized Trotsky's disciplinarian attitude at the eleventh congress, early in 1922. Later in the year, however, the two men drew together; Preobrazhensky was one of the few to whom Trotsky confided his plans and related his private talks with Lenin and their agreement to form the 'bloc' against Stalin. The author of important works on economic history, a man of rare erudition and analytical gifts, Preobrazhensky was primarily a scholar, pursuing his line of reasoning to no matter what unpopular conclusions it might lead him and no matter what damage it might do to his standing with the party. He thought in elaborate and massive theorems; and in his *New Economics* he made the first serious and still unequalled attempt to apply the 'categories' of Marx's *Das Kapital* to the Soviet economy. Only the introductory volume was allowed to appear and even that was suppressed soon thereafter and confined to oblivion. Yet the *New Economics* remains a landmark in Marxist thought. The anticipatory analysis it gave of the processes of primitive socialist accumulation will remain topical as long as there are under-developed countries in the world which strive to industrialize on a socialist basis. Many regarded Preobrazhensky rather than Trotsky as the author of the Opposition's economic programme—he created at any rate its theoretical groundwork. There were, however, implicit divergencies between his and Trotsky's views; but these did not become explicit and result in serious political conflict until 1928, the year when the two men were exiled from Moscow.

Pyatakov was the most outstanding industrial manager among the Bolsheviks. While Preobrazhensky supplied the Opposition with theorems, Pyatakov placed the theorems on the firm ground of practical experience. Lenin in his will describes Pyatakov as one of the two foremost leaders of the young generation—the other being Bukharin—and as an administrator of exceptional ability and drive but a man devoid of political judgement. This one-sidedness was characteristic of the Oppositionist as well: Pyatakov shared the Opposition's views on economic policy, but kept aloof from its 'battle of ideas' and quailed at its onslaughts on the party leadership. Yet he was far from being a timid character. Only a few years earlier he and his brother had led the Bolsheviks in the Ukraine when the Ukraine was occupied by Denikin; and there, behind enemy lines, he organized sabotage, set afoot partizan detachments, and directed the struggle. The White Guards seized the two brothers and put them, together with other Reds, before a firing squad. The execution was in progress and his brother had already been shot when the firing squad had to flee before the Reds who had captured the town and were converging on the spot where the massacre took place. Straight from the corpses of his brother and of his nearest comrades, Pyatakov went to assume command over the Red Guards. Such were the antecedents of the man who in and out of Opposition was to be the moving spirit and the chief organizer of the Soviet drive for industrialization for fifteen years, and who was to end in the dock, 'confessing' to having been a wrecker, a traitor, and a foreign spy.

Most of the other chiefs of the Opposition were men of heroic mould. Preobrazhensky had gone through fire and water when he led the Bolshevik underground movement in the Urals during the years of counter-revolution. Once, when caught by the Tsarist police and tried, he had Kerensky as his defence counsel. Kerensky, eager to save his client, declared in court that Preobrazhensky was not involved in any revolutionary movement. The defendant rose in the dock, disavowed his counsel, and proclaimed his revolutionary conviction. He led the Bolsheviks of the Urals in 1917 and during the early part of the civil war. Rakovsky, whose long and courageous struggle up to 1914 is related in *The Prophet Armed*,[1] directed the Communist forces during the civil war in Bessarabia, where the White Guards put a prize on his head. He returned to Russia and became Chairman of the Council of the People's Commissars in the Ukraine. Antonov-Ovseenko's part in the October insurrection and the civil war need not be recalled here.[2] Muralov had been, like Antonov, one of the legendary heroes of the 1905 revolution,

---

[1] *The Prophet Armed*, pp. 207–8.
[2] See op. cit., pp. 221, 298–301, 434–5.

and in October 1917 he led Moscow's Red Guards in their assault on the Kremlin. Afterwards he was commander of the military region of Moscow and Army Inspector. Trotsky describes him as a 'magnificent giant as fearless as kind'. An agronomist by education, he gave, in the intervals between battles, agricultural advice to peasants and 'medical treatment to men and cows'. Ivan Smirnov had led the army which defeated Kolchak in Siberia. Serebriakov was one of the most energetic political commissars on the fronts of the civil war. Sosnovsky had made his mark as an agitator in the fighting line and as vigilant observer and critic of morals and manners—his was one of the best pens in Bolshevik journalism.

For all their prowess and intelligence, these men did not for the time being see any clear road ahead. They were above all anxious to stay within the party; and they could stay in it only if they lay low. They watched events and the moves of their adversaries and waited for something to happen that would allow them to come to the fore.

.   .   .   .

Though he lay low, Trotsky did not lay down his arms. By hint and allusion he kept up his criticism of the official régime and its policy. Everything he said, even when he said it in a deliberately inoffensive manner, was a reflection on what his adversaries did, and even more so, on what they thought—no matter whether he spoke about the uncouthness of the Russian bureaucrat, the debased style of the newspapers, or the false starts the party was making in cultural affairs. And he never turned his attention from those major issues of policy, foreign and domestic, in which stuff for future controversy was piling up.

In May 1925, nearly five months after he had left the Commissariat of War, he was appointed to serve on the Supreme Council of the National Economy, under Dzerzhinsky. There was heavy irony in the appointment: Dzerzhinsky was neither economist nor policy-maker; and only to slight Trotsky did the triumvirs assign to him a post under Dzerzhinsky. They did not even consult Trotsky; but he could not easily refuse. When he resigned from the Commissariat of War he had declared that he was 'ready to carry out any assignment, under any conditions of party control'; and he could not go back on this pledge. Far off were the days when he had been able to decline the office of Lenin's deputy.

Within the Council of the National Economy Trotsky became chairman of three commissions: the Concessions Committee, the Board of Electrotechnical Development, and the Industrial-Technological Commission. The Concessions Committee had been set up in the early days of N.E.P. when Lenin hoped to reattract former concessionaires and other foreign investors to assist in Russia's economic recovery. These hopes had come to nothing. The Bolsheviks were too frightened of foreign capital to be able to attract it; and foreign investors were too frightened of the Bolsheviks to co-operate with them. The Concessions Committee was at a loose end. In his office, in a tiny one-floor hotel outside the Kremlin, Trotsky occasionally received a foreign visitor who inquired about the chances of gold prospecting in Siberia, or of manufacturing pencils in Russia.

Presently, however, Trotsky made a stronghold of the cage to which he was confined. Assisted by the secretaries who had served in his military train during the civil war, he opened an inquiry into the state of Concessions and of Russia's foreign trade. This led him to investigate costs of industrial production at home and abroad, and to make a comparative study of the productivity of Russian and Western labour. The inquiry threw into sharp relief the nation's industrial backwardness—it showed that the productivity of Russian labour was only one-tenth that of American. With graphic diagrams he illustrated the poverty of Russia's industrial equipment. Thus, while the United States possessed 14 million and Great Britain one million telephones, the Soviet Union possessed only 190,000. The length of its railway lines was 69,000 kilometres against 405,000 in the United States. The consumption of electricity per head was only 20 kilowatts compared with 500 kilowatts in the U.S.A.[1]

Obvious though the facts were, their emphatic presentation came as a shock. Official spokesmen dwelt smugly on the advance of Russia's industry since the civil war, when output had been close to nil; or they compared current production with that of 1913; and congratulated themselves on the results. Trotsky argued that new scales of comparison were needed and that the progress of recent years should be measured by the standards of

[1] *Sochinenya*, vol. xxi, pp. 419–20.

the industrial west rather than by those of native backwardness.[1] The nation could not rise unless it had a ruthlessly clear
awareness of the low level from which it started. 'It is often said
that we work "almost" like the Germans, or like the French. I
am ready to declare a holy war on this word "almost". Almost
means nothing. . . . We must compare costs of production, we
must find out what a pair of shoes costs here and abroad, we
must compare the quality of the goods, and the time it takes to
produce them—only then can we make comparisons with
foreign countries.'[2] 'We must not lag behind others', he concluded. 'Our first and essential watchword . . . is not to lag behind! Yes, we are extraordinarily far behind the advanced
capitalist countries. . . .'

In launching this watchword—'We must not lag behind'
—Trotsky was several years ahead of Stalin; but unlike Stalin
he strove to open Russia's eyes to the full length of the distance
to be made up. He realized that this involved political risks—
people viewing Russia's poverty soberly and gauging her misery
to its depth might become cynical or despondent. Stalin, when
he embarked on industrialization, preferred to keep the masses
unaware of the prodigious climb and the inhuman effort required of them. Trotsky relied on the people's courage and
maturity. 'Let us, comrades, neither mock at ourselves, nor take
fright. But let us firmly remember these figures: we must make
these measurements and comparisons in order to catch up with
the West at any price, and to surpass it.'[3] Thus he re-emerged
from the petty administrative technicalities under which the
triumvirs had intended to bury him; he found his way back to
the central issue of policy; and he took up the call for industrialization which he had raised in 1922–3.

As Chairman of the Board of Electrotechnical Development
he became engrossed in electrification. He travelled up and
down the country, investigated resources, examined schemes for
power plants, planned their location, and produced reports.
From one such journey he returned to urge the Politbureau to
adopt a project for the utilization of the rapids of the Dnieper,
the project which became famous as the Dnieprostroy, one of

---

[1] *Sochinenya*, vol. xxi, pp. 44–45. See Trotsky's speech of 7 December 1925.
Throughout most of the Stalin era official propagandists avoided making com
parisons between Russia and the West.   [2] Ibid., pp. 397–405.   [3] Ibid., p. 419.

the feats of industrial construction in the next decade. When he first canvassed the idea, early in 1926, the Politbureau made little of it. Stalin remarked that the planned power-station would be of no more use to Russia than a gramophone was to a muzhik who did not possess even a cow.[1] Trotsky then appealed to the enthusiasm and the imagination of the young. In a speech to the Comsomol he said:

Recently we opened the power station of Shatura, one of our best industrial installations, established on a turf bog. The distance from Moscow to Shatura is only a little over a hundred kilometres. A stone's throw, it would seem; and yet what a difference in conditions! Moscow is the capital of the Communist International. You travel a few scores of kilometres and—there is wilderness, snow, and fir, and frozen mud, and wild beasts. Blacklog cabin villages, drowsy under the snow. From the train one's eyes catch the wolf's foot-prints in the snow. Where Shatura station stands, elks roamed a few years ago. Now metal pylons of exquisite construction ran the whole way down from Moscow . . . and under these pylons she-foxes and she-wolves will lead out their cubs this spring. Such is our entire civilization—extreme contradictions: supreme achievements of technology and generalizing thought and primordial Siberian wilderness.

Shatura stands on marshes; we have many marshes, many more than power stations. We have many other sources of fuel which only wait to be transformed into power. In the south the Dnieper runs its course through the wealthiest industrial land; and it is wasting the prodigious weight of its pressure, playing over age-old rapids and waiting until we harness its stream, curb it with dams, and compel it to give light to cities, to drive factories, and to enrich ploughland. We shall compel it![2]

Industrialization was no end in itself, of course; it was part of 'the struggle for socialism with which the whole future of our civilization is inseparably bound up'. Again, in contrast to the Stalin of later years, Trotsky insisted that while struggling to catch up with the West the U.S.S.R. must not seek to isolate itself from the West. He had been a staunch defender of the monopoly of foreign trade and he had originated the idea of 'socialist protectionism'; but the purpose of that protectionism,

[1] Trotsky quoted Stalin's statement verbatim from the record of the April 1926 session of the Central Committee. See Trotsky's 'Personal Statement' of 14 April 1927 in *The Archives*.   [2] *Sochinenya*, vol. xxi, p. 437.

he argued, was not to cut off socialist industry, but, on the contrary, to enable it to establish close and many-sided links with the world economy. True enough, the 'world market' would press on Russia's socialist economy and subject it to severe and even dangerous tests. But these tests could not be avoided; they should be faced boldly. The dangers to which Russia was exposed by contact with the more advanced capitalist economy would be compensated by decisive advantages to be derived from international division of labour and from the assimilation of superior Western technology. In isolation, Russia's economic development must be distorted and retarded. In arguing thus, Trotsky was again in implicit conflict with official economic thought which was already becoming fixed in conceptions of national self-sufficiency: socialism in a single country presupposed a closed Soviet economy. Trotsky argued in effect against the essential premises of Stalin's doctrine even before the controversy over it had opened.

   .   .   .   .

After the 1923 débâcle in Germany, Trotsky endeavoured to reassess the international situation and the prospects of communism. The Comintern, anxious to save its face, belittled the importance of its setback, forecast a new revolutionary situation in Germany, and encouraged 'ultra-left' policies.[1] When, early in 1924, the first British Labour government was formed under Ramsay MacDonald and when Edouard Herriot, heading the Cartel de Gauche, became French Prime Minister, some of the communist leaders viewed these governments as 'Kerensky régimes' destined to pave the way for revolution. Against this Trotsky pointed out that it was necessary 'to distinguish the ebb of revolution from its flow', that it would take time for the German working class to recover from defeat, and that no rapid revolutionary developments should be expected in Britain and France.

Yet he still held that the capitalist world was unable to regain any enduring balance. He saw the greatest single factor of its instability, and the central issue of world politics at large, in the ascendancy of the United States. In the years 1924 and 1925 he analysed again and again the economic rise of the United States

[1] See Zinoviev's speech at the fifth Comintern congress (*Pyatyi Vsemirnyi Kongress Kom. Internatsionala*), pp. 64 ff.; also R. Fischer's statements, ibid., pp. 175–92.

and its impact upon the world. He predicted emphatically the emergence of the United States as the leading world power bound to involve itself in the affairs of all continents and to spread out its networks of military and naval bases over all oceans. He couched his conclusions in such forceful terms that most of what he said sounded far-fetched in the 1920's. This was the time of the 'Dawes Plan', of America's relatively timid and only tentative intervention in European affairs which, after 1929, was to be followed by a relapse into isolationism lasting over a decade. The world-wide expansion of American power, which Trotsky foreshadowed, could still be seen, if at all, only in embryo. He saw, as he so often did, the full-grown being in that embryo. The economic basis for expansion was there: the national income of the United States was already two and a half times as large as the combined incomes of Britain, France, Germany, and Japan. The United States' ascendancy was accompanied by Europe's impoverishment, 'Balkanization', and decline. He concluded, therefore, that 'the superiority which Britain in her heyday held *vis-à-vis* Europe is insignificant in comparison with the superiority which the U.S.A. has gained over the entire world, including Britain'.[1]

It was true that the ruling classes of both America and Europe were slow to grasp the full weight of this shift—they lagged mentally behind the events. 'The American is only beginning to grow aware of his international importance. . . . America has not yet learned to make its domination real. But it will presently learn to make it so, and it will learn on Europe's body and bones.'[2] The traditions of American isolationism and pacifism, rooted in geography and history, were brakes on expansion; but they were bound to give way to the dynamic force of the new facts. The United States would find itself compelled to assume the leadership of the capitalist world. The urge for expansion was inherent in its own economy; and it was intensified by the fact that European capitalism depended for its survival on American assistance. Here Trotsky made his celebrated and hotly contested forecast that the United States would 'put Europe on American rations' and then dictate to Europe its will. Having taken Britain's place as the world's industrial workshop and bank, the United States was also taking Britain's place

---

[1] *Europa und Amerika*, p. 22.   [2] Ibid., p. 36.

as the world's greatest maritime power and empire.[1] For this it need not burden itself with colonial possessions which had so often been a drain on the strength of British imperialism as well as a source of wealth. 'America will always find enough allies and helpers all over the world—the strongest power always finds them—and with the allies will be found also the necessary naval bases.'[2] Consequently 'we are entering an epoch of the aggressive unfolding of American militarism'.[3]

To those who, over-impressed by the strength of American isolationism and pacifism, doubted this prospect, Trotsky replied that the United States was following in Germany's footsteps. Like Germany, but incomparably more powerful, it was a latecomer among the great industrial nations. 'How long is it since the Germans were looked upon as starry eyed dreamers, as a "nation of poets and thinkers"? Yet a few decades of capitalist development were enough to transform the German bourgeoisie' into an exponent of the most brutal imperialism. Far less time was needed for a similar transformation in the United States. In vain did Britain's rulers console themselves that they would act as political and diplomatic tutors to the inexperienced Americans. They might do so, but only during a brief spell, until the Americans had learned the arts of imperialism and gained self-confidence. In the end the weight of American power would tell. Even now the 'inexperienced Yankee' enjoyed definite advantages over the sophisticated and subtle British imperialist: he could afford to pose as the liberator of the colonial peoples of Asia and Africa, helping to free from the British oppression the Indians, the Egyptians, and the Arabs; and the world believed in his pacifism and generosity.

It was beyond American power to arrest the decay of bourgeois Europe, however. American predominance was itself a source of instability for Germany, France, and Britain, for it was primarily at their expense that American power expanded. The economic disequilibrium between Europe and America would again and again be reflected in their trade and balances of payment, in financial crises, and in convulsions of the whole

---

[1] At the Washington Naval Conference of 1922 Great Britain had, in fact, given up the traditional forms of British naval supremacy.

[2] *Europa und Amerika*, p. 42.

[3] See Trotsky's speech of 25 October 1925 published in *Pravda* on 5 November 1925.

capitalist system. Nor was the United States immune: the more the world was dependent on it, the more did the transatlantic Republic become dependent on the world and involved in the world's menacing chaos.

The conclusion? 'Bolshevism has no enemy more fundamental and irreconcilable than American capitalism.'[1] These were 'the two basic and antagonistic forces of our age'. Wherever communism might advance, it would run into barriers set up by American capitalism; and in whatever part of the world the United States might seek to expand, it would be confronted by the threat of proletarian revolution: '. . . if and when American capital penetrates into China, . . . it will find there, among the masses of the Chinese people, not the religion of Americanism but the political programme of Bolshevism translated into Chinese.'

In this duel of giants American capitalism had all the material advantages. But Bolshevism would learn from America and assimilate its superior technology. It would be easier for the Bolsheviks to achieve this than for American capitalists to put the world on American rations. 'Americanized Bolshevism will defeat and crush imperialist Americanism.'[2] The United States might pose as 'liberator' of the colonial peoples and thereby contribute to the decomposition of the British empire; but it would not succeed in establishing its own supremacy over the coloured races. Nor would it in the long run succeed in banishing communism from Europe.

We do not in any way underrate the power of the United States. In evaluating the prospects of revolution we start from a clear realization of the facts. . . . However, we are of the opinion that American power itself . . . is the greatest lever of European revolution. We do not overlook the fact that this lever will turn, politically as well as militarily, with a terrible momentum against European revolution. . . . We know that American capital, once its existence is at stake, will unfold incalculable fighting energy. All that we know from history and our own experience about the struggle of privileged classes for their domination may pale into insignificance compared with the violence that American capital will let loose on revolutionary Europe.[3]

---

[1] *Europa und Amerika*, p. 47. Trotsky relates that shortly after the October Revolution he said half-jokingly to Lenin that two names, those of Lenin and Wilson, were the 'apocalyptic antipodes of our time'.

[2] Ibid., p. 49.   [3] Ibid., p. 91.

How then, Trotsky asked, would communism be able to hold its ground? He did not expect the clash between the two 'basic antagonistic forces' to develop while communism was entrenched only on Europe's eastern fringe and in parts of Asia. As always, he looked forward to revolution in Western Europe; and he was convinced that, to withstand American onslaught and blockades, the peoples of the Continent would have to form 'the United States of Socialist Europe'.

We, the peoples of Tsarist Russia, have held out through years of blockade and civil war. We have had to endure misery, privation, poverty, and epidemics. . . . Our very backwardness turned out to be our advantage. The revolution has survived because it could rely on its gigantic rural hinterland. . . . The outlook for industrialized Europe . . . would be different. A *disunited* Europe would not be able to hold out. . . . Proletarian revolution implies its integration. Bourgeois economists, pacifists, profiteers, cranks, and windbags like to chatter about the United States of Europe. But the bourgeoisie, divided against itself, cannot create it. Only the victorious working class will be able to unify Europe. . . . We shall serve socialist Europe as a bridge to Asia. . . . The United States of Socialist Europe together with our Soviet Union will exercise a tremendous magnetic attraction on the peoples of Asia. . . . And the gigantic bloc of the nations of Europe and Asia will then be unshakeably established, and it will stand up to the United States.[1]

The prospect of an Armageddon of global class struggle presently came under severe criticism as sheer fantasy.[2] No doubt, Trotsky threw into exaggerated relief what was at the time only one of the tendencies at work in world politics. In the following two decades other tendencies came to the fore: both the United States and Russia relapsed into relative isolation; Europe, with the Third Reich risen in its midst, became once again the world's storm centre; and Hitler's conquests and threats of domination made the U.S.A. and the U.S.S.R. temporary allies. However, Trotsky made his forecasts in the first

---

[1] *Europa und Amerika*, pp. 90–91.

[2] It will be remembered that both Trotsky and Lenin spoke for the United States of Socialist Europe as early as at the beginning of the First World War. (See *The Prophet Armed*, pp. 236–7.) The watchword was still included in the manifesto of the fifth congress of the Comintern which Trotsky wrote in 1924. Soon thereafter, however, the slogan and the idea of the United States of Socialist Europe were renounced by the Comintern as a Trotskyist day-dream.

years of the Versailles Peace, when Germany was still prostrate, when Hitler was merely an obscure provincial adventurer, and Germany's military power was incapable of asserting itself. Not more than a faint prelude had been enacted to the conflict of the two blocs, which was to unfold only after the Second World War. From the prelude Trotsky guessed the outline, the plot, and the ·eitmotif of the real drama. He ran so far ahead of his time that more than thirty years later much of his prediction still remains unconfirmed by events; but the truth of so much of it has since been demonstrated that few would venture to dismiss as chimerical the prophecy as a whole.

Against the general background of the changed relation between Europe and America Trotsky gave a more detailed prospect of a single country's future in *Where is Britain Going?* He wrote this book early in 1925, just when Moscow was beginning to attach great importance to a new link established between the Soviet and the British trade unions. In the previous November a delegation headed by A. A. Purcell, chairman of the British Trades Union Congress, had visited the Soviet capital and made a solemn pledge of friendship and solidarity with the Russian Revolution. The Soviet leaders eagerly responded, hoping that they had found solid allies in Purcell, Cooke, and other newly elected, leftish chiefs of the British trade unions; and they were all the more willing to cultivate the new 'friendship' because the Communist party of Great Britain was weak and insignificant. The Comintern's ultra-left policy was reaching a dead end; it was to be replaced by more moderate tactics. The question was mooted whether the revolution might not 'enter Britain through the broad gateway of the trade unions' rather than through the 'narrow path of the Communist party'. In May—Trotsky had just completed his book—Tomsky led a Soviet delegation to the annual Congress of the British unions and he formed, with the Politbureau's blessing, the Anglo-Soviet Trade Union Council, which was to occupy a large place in the inner party controversy of the following year.

In his book Trotsky spoke of the approach in Britain of a social crisis of the first magnitude. American predominance, the obsolescence of Britain's industrial equipment, and strains and stresses in the empire, all were combining to prepare it. Britain had emerged from the First World War victorious but battered and worn. Victory concealed her weakness, but not for long. British governments kept up the pretence of smooth and friendly co-operation with the United States, underneath which there was irreconcilable conflict. 'Peacefully' the British were surrendering their financial dominance, commercial privileges, and naval supremacy; but they could not go on doing this indefinitely, according to Trotsky,—at the end of the road was a clash of arms. Nor could the dissolution of the British empire, made inevitable by both the lapse of British rule on the seas and the rise of the colonial peoples, remain latent for any length of time. Lost to Britain were the strategic advantages of insularity. Finally, since 1918 the Versailles system and the disruption of the German economy had veiled Britain's industrial inferiority to Germany. But Germany, aided by the United States, was rapidly recovering strength and had already reappeared as Britain's most direct and dangerous competitor in the world market, upsetting her trade and payment balances and aggravating all the elements of British weakness. All this, Trotsky concluded, pointed to dangerous Anglo-American tensions, fraught with war, and to a violent flare-up of class struggle, indeed, to a revolutionary situation in the British Isles.

In retrospect both the realism of this analysis and the errors of perspective stand out clearly. Trotsky did not imagine that the British could escape an armed conflict with the United States, although he himself had shown convincingly that such a conflict would have been suicidal folly for bourgeois Britain. Although he was perhaps the first analyst to grasp all the implications of America's new superiority, his idea of the British empire had still an almost Victorian or Edwardian touch about it: he could not envisage that the British would 'peacefully' and 'to the end' surrender their supremacy to the United States. And he saw the decline of British power as a cataclysmic collapse, not as the chronic and long-drawn-out process it was to become.

Despite its errors of prognostication *Where is Britain Going?* is the most, or rather the only effective statement of the case for proletarian revolution and communism in Britain that has ever been made. This was Trotsky's encounter with Fabian socialism and its doctrine of the 'inevitability of gradualness'; and for a long time thereafter Fabianism could not recover intellectually from the assault.[1] With quick and sharp thrusts Trotsky stripped it of its socialist pretensions and showed up its dependence on Conservative and Liberal traditions, its staleness, its insularity, its parochial quaintness and empirical narrow-mindedness, its pacifist hypocrisy and national arrogance, its snobbery and meekness towards established opinion, its fetishistic attitude towards religion, monarchy and empire—in a word all the qualities which made MacDonald, Thomas, the Snowdens, and the other labour leaders of the time unfit to take the head of a militant socialist movement and which turned them into opponents of revolution glad to consume the fruit of past struggles, but shrinking in panic from new conflict and upheaval. Trotsky had no doubt that in the approaching crisis they would see their main task in keeping the working class mentally enthralled, morally disarmed and unable to act.

The ruthlessness of his argument was greatly enlivened but scarcely softened by the humour with which he conducted it:

British pigeon-fanciers, by means of artificial selection, achieve special varieties, with a continually shortening beak. But there comes a moment when the beak of a new stock is so short that the poor creature is unequal to breaking the egg shell and the young pigeon perishes, a sacrifice to compulsory restraint from revolutionary activities, and a stop is put to the further progress of varieties of short bills. If our memory is not at fault, MacDonald can read about this in Darwin. Having entered upon MacDonald's favourite course of analogies with the organic world, one can say that the political art of the British bourgeois consists in shortening the revolutionary beak of the proletariat, and so not allowing him to pierce the shell of the capitalist state. The beak of the proletariat is its party. If we look at MacDonald, Thomas, Mr. and Mrs. Snowden, we have to confess that the work of the bourgeoisie in selecting short-billed and soft-billed has been crowned with astonishing success. . . .[2]

The Fabian school prided itself on its peculiarly British tradition, which it refused to adulterate with alien Marxism. Trotsky retorted that the Fabians cultivated only the conservative patterns of their national tradition and neglected or suppressed its progressive strands.

---

[1] An American critic, writing in the *Baltimore Sun* (21 November 1925), remarked that the world had not heard anything like Trotsky's fiery invective since Luther's days.　　　　　　　　　　[2] *Where is Britain Going?* p. 67.

The MacDonalds inherited from Puritanism not its revolutionary strength, but its religious prejudices. From the Owenites they received not communistic fervour but Utopian hostility to the class struggle. From the past political history of Britain the Fabians borrowed only the mental dependence of the proletariat on the bourgeoisie. History turned its nether parts to these gentlemen; and the writings that they there read became their programme.[1]

For the benefit of young Marxists Trotsky recapitulated the two major British revolutionary traditions, the Cromwellian and the Chartist. He saw the Puritans as being beneath their biblical cloaks essentially political innovators, fighters, and promoters of definite class interests, who stood half-way between the German Reformation with its religious philosophy and the French Revolution with its secular ideology. Luther and Robespierre met in Cromwell's personality.[2] Obsolescent though much of Cromwell was, especially his bigotry, he was still a great master of revolution with whom British Communists might usefully serve an apprenticeship. A note of affinity crept into Trotsky's appreciation of the Commander of the Ironsides: '. . . it is impossible not to be struck by certain features which bring the existence and character of Cromwell's army into close association with the character of the Red Army . . . Cromwell's warriors regarded themselves as Puritans in the first instance and only in the second as soldiers just as our warriors recognize themselves to be revolutionaries and communists first and soldiers afterwards.'[3] For all his lack of reverence for Parliament, Cromwell set the stage for British parliamentarianism and democracy. This 'dead lion of the seventeenth century', this builder of a new society was still more alive politically than were the many living dogs of the Fabian kennel. So were the militant Chartists to whose heritage British Labour would turn afresh, once it had lost faith in the magic of gradualness. Chartist watchwords and methods of action were still greatly to be preferred to 'the saccharine eclecticism of MacDonald and the economist stupidity of the Webbs'. The Chartist movement was defeated because it was ahead of its time—'an historic overture'; but it would be 'resurrected on a new and immeasurably broader historic basis.'[4]

Trotsky saw in the Communist party, weak though it was, the

[1] *Where is Britain Going?* p. 47. [2] Ibid., p. 127.
[3] Op. cit., p. 126. [4] Op. cit., pp. 130–1.

sole legitimate successor to these traditions. He dismissed as a 'monstrous illusion' the hope that any leftish Fabians or trade union chiefs could give a revolutionary lead to the British workers. That the Communist party in Britain was of negligible size and that Fabianism appeared to be formidable and unshakeable was true. But had not British Liberalism also appeared to be powerful and invincible just before it collapsed as a party? When the Labour party came to occupy the place vacated by Liberalism, it was led by the men of the Independent Labour party which had been a small group. The shock of great events makes old and seemingly solid political structures crumble and brings about the emergence of new ones. This had happened after the shock of the First World War and it would happen again. The rise of Fabianism was 'only a brief stage in the revolutionary development of the working class'; and 'Macdonald has a still shakier seat than had Lloyd George'.

It was with subdued misgivings that Trotsky asked whether British communism would prove equal to its task. But once again revolutionary optimism led him astray as it had sometimes led Marx. 'We do not intend to prophesy', Trotsky wrote, 'what will be the tempo of this process [of revolution in Britain], but in any case it will be measured in terms of years, or at the most in terms of five years, not at all by decades.'[1] In later years Trotsky argued that at the decisive moment, in 1926, Stalin's and Bukharin's tactical prescriptions, the policy of the Anglo-Soviet Council, crippled British communism. The historian must doubt whether these prescriptions, inept though they were, were the basic cause of the prolonged impotence of British communism which thirty years later still vegetated as a sect on the outer fringe of British politics. However, the great social crisis which Trotsky forecast was indeed about to open with the strike of the British coal-miners, the longest and the most stubbornly fought in industrial history; and during the general strike Britain moved towards the brink of revolution.

Trotsky's book aroused much controversy in Britain. H. N. Brailsford initiated it in a preface to the English edition. Acknowledging Trotsky's exceptional merits as an analyst and writer and his familiarity with English history and politics,

[1] Op. cit., p. 14. 'The hive of revolution swarms too well this time!' Trotsky added, p. 52.

Brailsford wrote that Trotsky nevertheless failed to understand the democratic and nonconformist religious traditions of the British Labour movement and 'the instinct of obedience to the majority graven on the English mind'. Ramsay MacDonald,[1] George Lansbury,[2] and others, dismissed Trotsky's views as a foreigner's misconceptions. Bertrand Russell, on the other hand, held that 'Trotsky was perfectly familiar with the political peculiarities of the English Labour movement'; and he also agreed that socialism is incompatible with Church and Throne. Yet Russell could not see how anyone not an enemy of the British people could incite them to revolution, the sequel of which would be an American blockade or even a war in which Britain would be doomed to defeat.[3] Other writers resented the disrespect and derision with which Trotsky turned on MacDonald, although a few years later when MacDonald broke with the Labour party most of these critics tore the 'traitor' to shreds.

Trotsky answered his critics several times.[4] In a reply to Russell he denied any intention of inciting British workers to revolution in the interest of Soviet Russia. In no country, he wrote, should the workers undertake any steps in the interest of the Soviet Union which do not follow from their own interests. But he remained unconvinced by Russell's rationalistic pacifism:

Revolutions are as a rule not made arbitrarily. If it were possible to map out the revolutionary road beforehand and in a rationalistic manner, then it would probably also be possible to avoid revolution altogether. Revolution is an expression of the impossibility of reconstructing class society by rationalist methods. Logical arguments, even if Russell turns them into mathematical formulae, are impotent against material interests. The ruling classes will let civilization perish together with mathematics rather than give up their privileges. . . . You cannot get away from these irrational factors. Just as in mathematics we use irrational magnitudes in order to arrive at altogether realistic conclusions, so in revolutionary policy . . . one can bring a social system into rational order only when one makes frank allowance for the contradictions inherent in society so as to be able to overcome them by means of revolution. . . .[5]

[1] *The Nation*, 10 March 1926.
[2] Lansbury's *Labour Weekly*, 27 February 1926.
[3] *New Leader*, 26 February 1926.
[4] *Pravda*, 11 February and 14 March 1926.
[5] *Kuda Idet Angliya? (Vtoroi Vypusk)*, p. 59.

The British Communists at first received Trotsky's work with delight and enthusiasm—the giant had come to reinforce their puny ranks.[1] Later in the year, however, under the wing of the Anglo-Soviet Council, they had second thoughts, and began to feel embarrassed by Trotsky's attack on the leftish trade-union leaders. (Even earlier, in November 1925, he had already been criticized on this ground by the Russo-American Communist M. Olgin, until recently Trotsky's fervent admirer.[2]) In the spring of 1926 the British Communist party was already lodging a complaint with the Russian Politbureau about Trotsky's 'hostility' towards it; and Trotsky had to rebut the charge.[3]

.   .   .   .

It was during this interval in the struggle between Trotsky and his adversaries that a great regrouping of men and ideas occurred within the Bolshevik party and that a new and fundamental division appeared among its leaders and in its ranks—a division which forms the background to the political history of the following fifteen years.

The middle 1920's are often described as the halcyon time of N.E.P., as the only period between 1917 and the middle of the century when the Soviet people relaxed, enjoyed peace, and had a taste of well-being. This picture cannot be accepted at its face value. What gives the period a quasi-idyllic appearance is its contrast with the one that preceded it and the one that was to follow. The middle 1920's knew none of the bloody struggles and upheavals, and none of the famines, of the early 1920's and the early 1930's. The passage of time was healing the wounds the nation had suffered. Economic recovery was under way. The farmers tilled their land and reaped their harvest. The wheels of industry no longer stood still. Blown-up bridges and railways, burnt-out houses and bombshelled schools were rebuilt. Flooded coal-mines were restored. Links between town and country were re-established. Private trade flourished. Shoppers no longer carried sackfuls of depreciated bank-notes: the rouble, still somewhat shaky, reacquired the mysterious respectability of money.

---

[1] See, for instance, R. Palme Dutt's review in *Labour Monthly*, April 1926.
[2] *Die Freiheit*, 15 November 1925.
[3] *The Trotsky Archives*, excerpts concerning Politbureau sessions of the first days of June 1926.

There was even a bustle of prosperity about the central squares and thoroughfares of the cities.

Yet this bustle was largely deceptive. The great and now unified Soviet republic, extending from the Polish and Baltic frontiers over the whole area of the former empire, remained engulfed in cruel poverty and riddled with social tensions. Only one-sixth of the nation lived in the towns; and not even one-tenth of its manpower was employed in industry. Recovery was painfully slow. Mines and factories still turned out less than three-quarters of their pre-war output; they produced no engines, no machine tools, no motor-cars, no chemicals, no fertilizers, and no modern agricultural machinery. The Soviet Union did not yet possess most of the industries essential to modern society. The flourishing private trade, much of it barbarously primitive and fraudulent, covered the national misery as with bubbling froth.

It is true that the peasants consumed the produce of their enlarged fields and for the first time since ages ate their bread to the full. But this was 'prosperity' at the rock bottom of civilization. It was enjoyed in the absence of any higher needs and amenities, in squalor, darkness, and primeval rural idiocy. About a third of the rural population, not growing its own food, was excluded even from that kind of well-being. Because the peasants ate more than before, the town dwellers had to eat less: they consumed only two-thirds of the food and only half the meat they used to consume under Tsarist rule. Less produce was also left for export: Russia now sold abroad only about a quarter of the amount of grain she used to export. As of old most of her people were in rags and barefoot. Only in two significant respects, it seems, had there been a marked advance: in hygiene and education. The Russians used more soap and had more schools than ever before.

Of the social tensions the chronic antagonism between town and country was the most dangerous. The town dweller had the sense of being ill used by the farmer, who was indubitably the chief beneficiary of the revolution. The muzhik, on the other hand, felt that he was skinned by the town people. There was some ground for such feelings on both sides. The urban workers earned far less than before the revolution; and there were two million unemployed, almost as many as were employed in large-scale industry. The workers contrasted their own want with the ampleness of food in the country. The peasants resented the fact that they had to pay for industrial goods more than twice the prices they paid before 1914, while for their own produce they did not obtain much more than the pre-war price. Each of these two classes imagined that it was exploited by the other. In truth both were 'exploited' by the nation's poverty.

Neither town nor country represented, however, any uniform interest. Each was torn by its own contradictions. The urban worker knew that the N.E.P.-man, the middleman, and the bureaucrat cheated him of the fruit of his labour. He paid high prices for the food for which the peasant received so little—the middleman controlling nine-tenths of the retail trade cashed in on the difference. In the factory the worker was confronted by the manager who, acting on behalf of the employer-state, deprived him of his share in running the factory, kept down wages, and demanded more work and harder work.[1] By the manager's side stood the trade-union official and the secretary of the party cell, who were less and less inclined to side with the worker and often acted as arbitrators in industrial disputes. The employer-state could in fact rarely afford to meet the workers' claims. The national income was small, productivity low, and the need for capital investment desperately urgent. When the manager, the party secretary, and the trade-union official urged the worker to produce more, the latter cursed his new 'bosses'; but he did not dare to press his claims or down tools. Outside the factory gates there waited long queues of men anxious to get jobs. Once again, as under capitalism, the 'reserve army of the unemployed' helped to depress the wages and the conditions of the employed.

The cleavages in the peasantry were less marked but not less real. The muzhiks had benefited from the agrarian upheavals and from N.E.P. in unequal degrees. The middle layer of the peasantry was strengthened. There were many more small-holders now, more *serednyaks*, who lived on the yield of their land, without having to work on the land of wealthier farmers and without employing labour on their own farms. Of every ten peasants three or four belonged to this category. One or perhaps two were kulaks employing hired labour, enlarging their farms, and trading with the town. Five out of the ten were poor

[1] Only one in five or six workers was employed in privately owned industry.

peasants, *bednyaks*, who had carved out for themselves a few acres from the landlords' estates but only rarely possessed a horse or farm tools. They hired the horse and the tools from the kulak, from whom they also bought seed or food and borrowed money. To pay the debt, the *bednyak* worked on the kulak's field or let out to him part of his own tiny plot.

At every step the realities of rural life came into conflict with Bolshevik policy. Lenin's government had decreed the nationalization of the land together with the expropriation of the landlord. In theory and in law the peasants were in possession of the land without owning it. They were forbidden to sell and to rent it. The Bolsheviks had hoped to curb inequality in this way and to prevent the growth of rural capitalism. Slowly but surely life overlapped these barriers. In innumerable daily transactions, which no administration could trace, land passed from hand to hand; and capitalist relationships evolved: the rich grew richer and the poor poorer. True, this was only a rudimentary and extremely crude form of rural capitalism: by the standards of any advanced bourgeois society even the Russian kulak was a poor farmer. But such standards were irrelevant. That the new stratification of the peasantry developed on an extremely low economic level did not soften its impact; it sharpened it. The possession of a few horses and ploughs, of a stock of grain, and of a little cash gave to one man more direct power over another than the ownership of much more capital may give to anyone in a wealthy bourgeois society. Ten years after the revolution the wages of the landless farm labourers (who should not be confused with the poor peasants) were nearly 40 per cent. less than the wages the landed gentry had paid them. Their working day was much longer; and their conditions were little better than those of slave labour. The old landlord employed many hands on his estate whereas the kulak employed only a few; and so the labourers could not organize against him and defend themselves as effectively as they used to organize against the landlord. The *bednyak* was sometimes even more exploited and helpless than was the labourer.

In these relations there were the makings of a violent social conflict; but the conflict could not unfold itself and find expression. Much as the village poor may have resented the kulak's rapacity, they were utterly dependent on him and could rarely afford to stand up to him. More often than not the wealthy peasant led a submissive village community, diverted its resentment from himself, and turned it against the town, the workers, the party agitators and the commissars.

All these tensions within town and country and between them underlay the friction between the many nationalities of the Soviet Union. We have seen that friction at work in the transition from war communism to N.E.P. and have heard Lenin castigating the *dzerzhymorda*, the vile Russian bureaucrat, as the chief culprit. With the years matters grew worse. The ever stricter centralization of government automatically favoured the Russian against the Ukrainian, the Byelorussian, and the Georgian, not to speak of the more primitive nationalities and tribes of Soviet Asia. Great Russian chauvinism emanating from Moscow excited and exacerbated local nationalisms in the outlying republics. The kulak and the N.E.P.-men were nationalists by instinct. In Russia proper they were Great Russian chauvinists. In the other republics they were anti-Russian nationalists. The intelligentsia were extremely susceptible to the prevalent moods. Among industrial workers internationalism was on the wane. The working class was reconstituting itself and growing in size by absorbing fresh elements from the country, elements who brought with them into the factories all of the peasants' political inclinations, a distrust of things foreign and intense regional loyalties.

Every now and then the tensions snapped. In the autumn of 1924 a peasant rising swept Georgia and was quelled in blood. Less violent but more persistent signs of the peasantry's antagonism to the government showed themselves everywhere. In the elections to the Soviets which took place in March 1925 over two-thirds of the electorate abstained from voting in many rural districts; and the government had to order new elections. There was a sporadic agitation for independent peasant Soviets. Here and there energetic and politically minded kulaks furthered their interests and ambitions through the existing Soviets and even through the rural party cells. There were many scattered acts of terrorism in villages. Party agitators sent from the town were clubbed to death. 'Worker correspondents' reporting to newspapers on the exploitation of farm labourers were lynched. The strong farmer had used to the full the opportunities N.E.P.

had offered him; and now he felt constricted by its limitations and sought openly or surreptitiously to remove them. He pressed for higher food prices, for the licence to sell and rent land, for unrestricted freedom to hire labour, in a word for a 'neo-N.E.P.'.

All this foreshadowed a national crisis which might be delayed for a couple of years only to become more dangerous later on. The ruling party had to seek a solution. Yet the party itself was increasingly affected by the cleavages that rent the nation. Three major currents of Bolshevik opinion formed in 1925. The party and its Old Guard split into a right and a left wing and a centre. The division was in many respects new. In none of the many earlier factional struggles had there been anything like it. Never before had the dividing lines been so clear cut and stable. Factions and groups had sprung into being and vanished together with the issues which had given rise to their differences. Alignments had changed with controversies. Opponents in one dispute joined hands as friends in the next dispute, and vice versa. The factions and groups had not sought to perpetuate themselves and had had no rigid organization or discipline of their own. This state of affairs had begun to change since the Kronstadt rising; but it was only now that the change became complete and universal. From the Politbureau and the Central Committee down to the rank and file the party was torn, although lower down the differences remained unexpressed. Not only were the issues which caused the division largely new; new and fateful was above all its finality.

What was sometimes startling was the manner in which men regrouped themselves and took up new positions. As in any political movement, so among the Bolsheviks some people had always been inclined towards moderation; others had shown a propensity to radicalism, and still others had been habitual trimmers. In the present regroupment many remained true to character. Rykov and Tomsky, for instance, who had always been far from the Left Communists, quite naturally found their place at the head of the new right. Most of the trimmers, especially the professional managers of the party machine, took up positions in the centre. Of the persistent radicals some had already joined the Workers' Opposition, the Decemists, or the Trotskyists; others had still to decide where they stood. But strange and unexpected conversions also occurred. Under the pressure of new circumstances and difficulties and after much heart-searching, some Bolsheviks, among them the most eminent leaders, abandoned accustomed attitudes or postures and assumed new ones which appeared to negate all that they had hitherto stood for. Men burnt the things they had worshipped and worshipped the things they had burnt.

In part the new differences resulted from the fact that some of the groups and individuals exercised power while others did not. Many a Left Communist who had been in office for seven or eight years, had wielded great influence, and enjoyed the privileges of power, came to approach public affairs from the ruler's viewpoint, not from that of the ruled. On the other hand, a 'moderate' Bolshevik, who had lived all these years among the masses and shared their experiences, willy-nilly voiced their disillusionment and spoke like an 'ultra-left'. There were also other causes for realignment. Under the single-party system the broader class antagonisms which we have just surveyed could find no legitimate political expression; and so they found an illegitimate and indirect expression within the single party. Wealthy farmers could not send their representatives to Moscow to state claims and demands before any national assembly or to act as pressure groups. Workers could not hope that their nominal deputies would voice their grievances freely and fully. Yet every social class and group exercised its pressure in nonpolitical forms. The wealthy peasants controlled the stocks of grain on which the provisioning of the urban population depended: 6–10 per cent. of the farmers produced more than half of the marketable grain surpluses. This gave them a potent weapon: by withholding supplies they periodically created acute food shortages in the towns. Or else they refused to buy overpriced industrial goods; and stocks of unsold goods piled up in factory yards and warehouses. Symptoms of overproduction thus appeared in a country which really suffered from underproduction. The workers were sullen and inefficient and sought to quell their despair with vodka. Wild and widespread drunkenness made frightful ravages in popular health and morale. Hard as the party tried to neutralize the conflicting social pressures, and to isolate itself from them, it was not immune. Food shortages and stocks of unsold industrial goods rudely awakened its members to realities. Some Bolsheviks were more sensitive to the workers' demands; others were more susceptible to the pressure from the peasants. The great cleavage between town and country tended to reproduce itself within the party and within its ruling circle.

It was several years since Zinoviev had spoken of the 'unconscious Mensheviks' who could be found side by side with the 'genuine' Leninists within the Bolshevik party and who formed in its ranks a potential party of their own. Even more important, it now turned out, was the potential party of 'unconscious Social Revolutionaries'. The authentic Social Revolutionaries, like the Narodniks, their political forebears, had been distinguished by their bias in favour of the muzhiks, among whom they refused to make any class distinctions, whom they treated neither as kulaks nor as *bednyaks*, whom they glorified as land labourers at large, whose interests they refused to subordinate to those of the industrial workers, and in whose striving for private property they saw nothing incompatible with socialism. Woolly in their theories and addicted to sentimental generalities, the Social Revolutionaries had represented an agrarian antithesis to the collectivism of the urban proletariat, a quasi-physiocratic variety of socialism. It was only natural that such an ideology should exercise a powerful influence in a nation four-fifths of which lived on the land and by it. The Bolsheviks had suppressed the party that had expounded this ideology, but they had not destroyed the interests, the emotion, and the mood that had animated it. That emotion and that mood now invaded their own ranks. There, in an environment traditionally hostile to Narodnik ideas, the mood could not be expressed in customary terms. It refracted itself through the prism of the Marxist tradition and came to be voiced in Bolshevik terms. This trend had received a strong impulse from the anti-Trotskyist campaign, in the course of which the triumvirs sought to discredit Trotsky as the muzhik's enemy. The accusation was partly a cold-blooded invention; but it also summed up a real feeling. Subsequently the neo-Narodnik trend gained in strength until, during the present pause in the struggle against Trotskyism, it led to the emergence of the new right wing in the party.

The man who came forward as the inspirer, theorist, and ideologue of the right was Bukharin. His appearance in this role was something of a puzzle. Ever since the peace of Brest Litovsk he had been the chief spokesman of Left Communism, rigidly committed to a 'strictly proletarian' viewpoint. He had denounced aggressively Lenin's 'opportunism', opposed Trotsky's army discipline, and defended the non-Russian nationalities against Stalin. Then, early in 1923, he had sympathized with Trotsky's radical ideas. In the years 1924–5, however, his name became the symbol of moderation, 'opportunism', and of the penchant for the well-to-do peasant. The conversion was by no means fortuitous. Bukharin's Left Communism had been based on his expectation of early revolution in Europe, the prospect on which all Bolshevik leaders had staked much, but perhaps none as much as Bukharin. All had seen in European revolution Russia's escape from her poverty and backwardness. None had believed that with a small working class surrounded by many millions of property-loving peasants they could advance far towards the socialist goal. Least of all had Bukharin believed it. With eager enthusiasm he had looked to the Western workers to rise, overthrow their bourgeoisie, and stretch out helping hands to Russia. He had surrounded those Western workers with a halo of revolutionary idealization and exaggerated beyond all measure their class consciousness and militancy. He had rejected the Brest Litovsk peace with the utmost indignation, because he was afraid that the sight of Bolshevik Russia bowing to the Hohenzollerns might discourage and demoralize the European working classes, and that Bolshevism cut off from the latter and left alone with the Russian peasantry would find itself in an impasse.

Bukharin now found that Bolshevism was indeed left alone with the Russian peasantry. He ceased to count on revolution in the West. Together with Stalin he proclaimed 'socialism in a single country'. With the same assurance with which he had hitherto spoken of the imminent collapse of world capitalism, he now diagnosed its 'stabilization'. From this new angle he took a fresh look at the domestic scene. He could not humanly accept the conclusion to which his whole earlier reasoning pointed: that the Russian Revolution was in a blind alley. He concluded instead that, as the Western workers had failed as allies, Bolshevism must acknowledge that the muzhiks were its only true friends. He turned towards them with the same fervour, the same hope, and the same capacity for idealization with which he had hitherto looked to the European proletariat. It is true that under Lenin's inspiration the party had always cultivated 'the alliance of workers and peasants'. But never since 1917 had the Bolsheviks offered friendship to the wealthy farmer; and Lenin had always treated the middle and even the poor peasants as 'vacillating allies', whom the lure of property might turn into enemies. So difficult and uncertain an alliance now failed to reassure Bukharin. He wished to base the alliance on what seemed a wider and firmer foundation. He hoped to persuade his comrades that they ought to appeal to the peasantry at large and cease playing the poor muzhik against the rich, and that they ought even to stake their hopes on the 'strong farmer'. This amounted to the abandonment of class struggle in rural Russia. Bukharin himself, inhibited by old habits of mind or by tactical motives, shrank from drawing all these conclusions; but they were drawn for him and made explicit by his disciples, Maretsky, Stetsky, and other young 'red professors', who expounded the neo-Narodnik or neo-Populist ideas in the universities, the propaganda departments, and the press.

Bukharin was guided by more practical considerations as well. Within the framework of N.E.P., the Bolshevik 'alliance' with the poor peasants against the rich had yielded few, if any, positive results. The poor peasants, and even the middle ones, could not feed the towns. They produced, at best, just enough to feed themselves. The well-being and even the survival of the urban workers depended on the small minority of wealthy farmers. These were, of course, eager to sell their goods; but they sold in order to grow wealthier, not just to survive. Their bargaining position was extremely strong. Indeed, never before had the dependence of the town on the country been so one-sided, so brutal, so naked. Government and party could not improve matters by vexing and incommoding the kulaks and inciting the poor against them. Pestered with requisitions and price controls, fretful at the restrictions on the sale and renting of land and on the employment of labour, the kulak ploughed less, reaped less, and sold less. The government had either to break his strength or to allow him to accumulate wealth. Not a single group within the party suggested that the kulaks be dispossessed—to all groups the expropriation of millions of farmers was still inconceivable and from a Marxist viewpoint impermissible.[1]

There was therefore a peculiar realism and consistency in Bukharin's conclusion that the party must allow the wealthy farmer to grow wealthier. The purpose of N.E.P., he argued, was to use private enterprise in Russia'a reconstruction; but private enterprise could not be expected to play its part unless it obtained its rewards. The overriding interest of socialism lay in increasing national wealth; and that interest would not be harmed if groups and individuals grew wealthier together with the nation—on the contrary, by filling their own coffers they would enrich society as a whole. This was the reasoning which induced Bukharin to address to the peasants his famous appeal: 'Enrich yourselves!'

What Bukharin overlooked was that the wealthy peasant sought to enrich himself at the expense of other classes: he paid low wages to the labourers, squeezed the poor farmers, bought up their land, and tried to charge them and the urban workers higher prices for food. He dodged taxation and sought to pass its burden on to the poor.[2] He strove to accumulate capital at the expense of the state and thereby slowed down accumulation within the socialist sector of the economy. Bukharin dwelt on that part of the social picture in which the interests of the different classes and groups and of the various 'sectors' were seen as complementary and as according with one another so that kulak, *bednyak*, worker, factory manager, and even N.E.P.-man, all appeared as a happy band of brothers. This aspect of the picture was real enough, but it formed one part of it only. He overlooked the other part, where all was discord and conflict and where the band of brothers turned into a pack of enemies seeking to cut one another's throats. A Bolshevik Bastiat, he extolled

---

[1] Since at least 10 per cent. of the twenty-odd million farmsteads belonged to the kulaks, dispossession would have at once affected between two and three million holdings, even if the middle peasants had been spared. The upper layer of the middle peasantry was often indistinguishable from the kulaks and so the number of those affected would have been much larger in any case.

[2] The single agricultural tax then in force favoured the kulak. The *bednyak* who let out to the kulak part of his own holding, in order to obtain the horse and the tools with which to cultivate the other part, paid as a rule the land tax on the plot yielded to the kulak. Indirect taxation was becoming more and more important in the Soviet budget and, as always, it fell heavier on the poor than on the well-to-do.

les harmonies économiques of Soviet society under N.E.P. and prayed that nothing should disturb those harmonies. He prayed from the heart because he had a strong premonition of the furies that would descend upon the land with the 'liquidation of the kulaks as a class'.

The first major controversy in which Bukharin developed his ideas was one where Preobrazhensky, the Trotskyist, was his opponent. Trotskyism, with its purely Marxist emphasis on class conflict and class antagonism and on the primacy of the socialist interest *vis-à-vis* the private, was the obvious antithesis to the neo-Populist attitude; and within their respective groups the two co-authors of the *A.B.C. of Communism* represented the opposed poles of Bolshevik thought. The controversy developed before the end of the year 1924, when Preobrazhensky published fragments of his *New Economics*.

Preobrazhensky based his whole argument on the imperative need for rapid industrialization—on that hung the whole future of Russia's socialist régime. Because of its backwardness, the U.S.S.R. could industrialize only by means of primitive socialist accumulation. Contrary to Bukharin's assumptions this was by definition antagonistic to private accumulation. Internationally, the contest between capitalism and socialism would be decided by the relative wealth, efficiency, and cultural strength of the two systems. Russia had entered the contest with an antiquated, essentially pre-industrial structure. She could not afford any 'free competition' with Western 'monopoly capitalism'. She had to adopt a 'socialist monopolism' and stick to it until her productive forces had reached the level already attained by the strongest capitalist nation, the United States.[1] (Preobrazhensky argued that even if Russia had not stood alone and if the whole of Europe had overthrown capitalist rule, the whole of Europe would still have to engage, albeit far less forcibly and for a shorter time, in primitive socialist accumulation, because its productive resources would be inferior to those of American capitalism.)

What is the essence, he asked, of primitive socialist accumulation? In an underdeveloped country, socialist industry by itself cannot produce the sinews of rapid industrialization. Its profits or surpluses can make up only a part, and a small one at that, of

[1] E. A. Preobrazhensky, *Novaya Ekonomika*, vol. i, part 1, pp. 101–40.

the required accumulation fund. The rest must be obtained from what would otherwise have gone into the wages fund and from the profits and incomes earned in the private sector of the economy. (To put it in Keynesian terms, the savings of the nationalized industry are far too small in relation to investment needs and so private savings must provide the nationalized industry with the major portion of its investment capital.) The needs of accumulation in the socialist sector set therefore rather narrow limits to private accumulation; and the government must impose the limits. The workers' state is compelled in a sense to 'exploit' the peasantry during this period of transition. It cannot pander to consumer interests; it must press on with the development of heavy industry in the first instance. The resulting relative shortage of consumer goods implies different levels of consumption for various social groups, material privileges for administrators, technicians, scientists, skilled workers, and others. Repugnant though this inequality may be, it does not produce new class antagonisms. The privileged bureaucracy does not form a new social class. Discrepancies in the earnings of bureaucrats and workers are not different in kind and social import from 'normal' differences in the wages of skilled and unskilled workers. They amount to inequality within one and the same class, not to an antagonism between hostile classes. Such inequality must and can disappear only with the growth of social wealth and universal education which should blur and eventually abolish the distinction between skilled and unskilled labour, and between manual work and brain work. In the meantime 'we should take the productionist and not the consumptionist point of view. . . . We do not live yet in a socialist society with its production for the consumer. We are only in the period of primitive socialist accumulation—we live under the iron heel of the law of that accumulation.'[1]

In this transition era the workers' state has already forfeited advantages peculiar to capitalism but does not yet benefit from the advantages of socialism. This is 'the most critical era in the life of the socialist state. . . it is a matter of life and death that we should rush through this transition as quickly as possible and reach the point at which the socialist system works out all its advantages. . . .'[2] Preobrazhensky did not suggest that during

[1] Ibid., p. 240.   [2] Ibid., p. 63.

the transition industrial wages and peasant incomes should actually be depressed (as they were in the Stalin era). What he meant and said was that as a result of intensive accumulation the national income would grow rapidly and that with it should rise the earnings of workers and peasants; but these would rise less rapidly so that a high proportion of the national income could be earmarked for investment.

He maintained that the 'law' of accumulation asserted itself as an 'objective force', comparable in some respects to the 'laws' of capitalism which determined the economic behaviour of men regardless of whether they were aware or unaware of those laws and regardless also of their own ideas and intentions. The law of primitive socialist accumulation would eventually compel the managers of the nationalized industry, i.e. the party leaders, to embark upon intensive industrialization, no matter how reluctant they were to do so. For the time being many of them received with apprehension and even aversion the proposition that the state-owned industry must, in order to expand, absorb resources from the private sector, and gradually socialize it and transform many millions of scattered, tiny, and unproductive farmsteads into large-scale and mechanized producers' cooperatives. However, the 'subjective views' of those responsible for the conduct of economic affairs need not be of decisive importance: 'the present structure of our state-owned economy often proves itself to be more progressive than our entire system of economic leadership'.[1] The new bureaucracy might resist the logic of the transition epoch; but it would have to act on it. Preobrazhensky still assumed that revolution would spread to western Europe in not too remote a future. Even so, the problem of primitive accumulation 'would stand in the centre of our attention for two decades, at the very least'.[2] It has stood there for nearly four decades, and it still does so.

Trotsky did not share Preobrazhensky's views fully, although the basic idea was common to them both. He refrained, however, from engaging in any public discussion of the differences. He did not wish to embarrass Preobrazhensky who soon came under severe attack. At the moment their differences were of no political consequence—only four years later, after Trotsky's and Preobrazhensky's banishment from Moscow, were

[1] E. A. Preobrazhensky, *Novaya Ekonomika*, vol. i, part 1, p. 184. [2] Ibid., p. 254.

they to acquire significance and to contribute to a painful breach.

The very abstract manner in which Preobrazhensky presented his argument hardly appealed to Trotsky. He himself approached the same problem more empirically, though also less methodically. With the scholar's utter indifference to tactics, Preobrazhensky, when he dwelt on the necessity for the underdeveloped workers' state to 'exploit the peasantry', offered a handle to anti-Trotskyist propagandists. True, he spoke of exploitation only in the strictly theoretical sense in which the Marxist speaks of the exploitation by capitalism of even the best-paid workers on the ground that they produce more value than their wages represent. He argued that, in the exchange between the two sectors of the economy, the socialist sector would take out of the private one more value than it would put into it, although with the growth of the national income the mass of value would grow in the private sector too. Official critics, however, seized on the provocative phrase about exploitation, gave it the vulgar meaning, and so twisted it that Preobrazhensky was understood to say that the impoverishment and degradation of the peasantry were necessary concomitants of accumulation. He tried to correct himself and 'withdrew' the unfortunate phrase. The correction made matters worse: it suggested that the critics had not been quite wrong.

It will be remembered that at the twelfth congress, when Trotsky spoke about primitive socialist accumulation, Krasin asked whether this might not imply exploitation of the peasantry; and that Trotsky then jumped to his feet to deny it.[1] Preobrazhensky now posed the same question and answered it in the affirmative. On internal evidence, the answer was too blunt and too rigid for Trotsky. He, at any rate, refused to commit himself to the view that the peasantry would have, as a rule, to foot the bill of primitive accumulation from beginning to end.[2] Nor did Trotsky advocate a pace of industrialization as forced as that which Preobrazhensky expected. There were even deeper differences between them. Preobrazhensky, for all his

---

[1] See pp. 102–3.
[2] In the debate Bukharin underlined this difference between Trotsky and Preobrazhensky. Bukharin, *Kritika Ekonomicheskoi Platformy Oppozitsii*, p. 56.

references to international revolution, constructed his theorem in such a way that it implied that primitive socialist accumulation might be concluded by the Soviet Union alone or perhaps by the Soviet Union in association with other underdeveloped nations. This prospect appeared unreal to Trotsky, who did not see how the Soviet Union alone could raise itself to the industrial height attained by the West; and it was a prospect which created an opening for an intellectual reconciliation with 'socialism in a single country'. Nor could Trotsky agree with Preobrazhensky about the 'objective force' or logic of primitive accumulation which would impose itself on the party leaders and make them its agents, regardless of what they thought and intended. This was a view which must have appeared to Trotsky to be too rigidly deterministic, even fatalistic, and to rely too much on the automatic development of socialism and too little on the consciousness, the will, and the action of fighting men.

These were still platonic differences, however, containing only the seed of political disagreement. Even if Trotsky thought that Preobrazhensky had overstated the case for industrialization, it was still the same case that they were both defending. If he held that Preobrazhensky had shown too little political tact in dealing with the peasantry, he himself was just as critical as Preobrazhensky of the official pandering to the strong farmer. In abstraction, the theorem of the *New Economics* might have envisaged the transition to socialism within a single industrially underdeveloped nation-state. Yet, politically, Preobrazhensky held no brief for socialism in a single country. Finally, much though he trusted the laws of accumulation to prevail over the economic conservatism of the party leaders, he did not rely solely on the working of those laws—he was still a fighter calling on Bolsheviks to do their duty and not wait until necessity drove them to do it. Trotsky therefore watched Preobrazhensky's controversies sympathetically, if with reserve.

Bukharin attacked the whole of Preobrazhensky's conception as 'monstrous'.[1] He made the most of the dictum about the exploitation of the peasantry. If Bolsheviks were to act on Preobrazhensky's ideas, he stated, they would destroy the workers' alliance with the peasantry and would demonstrate that the proletariat (or those who ruled in its name) had become

[1] Bukharin, *Kritika Ekonomicheskoi Platformy Oppozitsii*, p. 21.

a new exploiting class, seeking to perpetuate its dictatorship.
State-owned industry could not and must not expand by
'devouring' the private sector of the economy—on the contrary,
only by leaning on it could it achieve any significant progress.[1]
In Preobrazhensky's scheme the peasant market played a
subordinate role: he saw the main outlet for the produce of the
state-owned industry within that industry itself, in its ever-
expanding demand for producer goods. Against this Bukharin
argued that in a country like Russia the peasant market must
form the basis of industrialization. It was primarily the rural
demand for goods that ought to dictate the pace of industrial
expansion. He was, as he said, afraid of, and alarmed by, the
'parasitically monopolistic tendencies' of a state-owned economy; and he saw in the peasantry's unfettered economic
activity the main, if not the only, counterbalance to such tendencies.

Here, however, Bukharin was caught in a fundamental
dilemma, for his argument turned against the very essence of
socialism. Where, he asked, if not in the peasant market, would
state-owned industry find 'the stimuli which would compel us to
move ahead, which would guarantee our progress and replace
the private economic stimulus, the stimulus of profit'?[2] As
peasant property was, in the Marxist view, incompatible with
fully fledged socialism, Bukharin in fact placed a question mark
over Marxist socialism at large. He implied that the socialist
sector could not find within itself any effective substitute for
the profit motive, and so it had ultimately to take the impulse
for its own progress from the profit motive which was active in
the private sector.[3] In quasi-Narodnik fashion Bukharin looked
to the peasant to save the nation from the monopolistic grip of
the state-owned economy. He pleaded that the peasant should

[1] Ibid., p. 16.

[2] Preobrazhensky replied that the pressure of workers defending their consumer
interests should provide the decisive counterbalance to the parasitic features of
a bureaucratically managed economy. Such pressure could make itself felt only
when the workers were free to defend their interests against the state, that is under
the conditions of a workers' democracy.

[3] The party as a whole, and Bukharin with it, remained committed to Lenin's
sketchy scheme for the development of co-operatives in farming. This commitment
did not affect practical policy, however. Preobrazhensky argued that even Lenin's
scheme was inadequate because its emphasis was not on producers' co-operatives,
but on other less important forms of co-operation.

not merely be allowed to thrive on his farm, but that the peasant's needs should determine the pace of the nation's advance towards socialism. Under such circumstances the advance would be slow, even very slow; but that could not be helped: '. . . we shall move ahead by tiny, tiny steps, pulling behind us our large peasant cart.'[1] There was perhaps more of Tolstoy than of Marx in this image of Russia's advance; and nothing could contrast with it more than Preobrazhensky's: 'We must go through this transition as quickly as possible. . . . We are under the iron heel of the law of primitive accumulation.' Here were two irreconcilable programmes.

As long as two theorists conducted the argument in more or less esoteric language, it did not generate much heat outside narrow circles. But it was inevitable that the issues should be taken up in more popular form and move into the centre of a wider political debate. It was not the Trotskyist Opposition, reduced to silence and dispersed as it was, that took them up in the first instance. The strongest reaction against Bukharin's neo-Populism, his 'wooing' of the strong farmer and his virtual reconciliation with Russia's industrial backwardness, came from Leningrad. It was mainly in the party organization of that city, led by Zinoviev, that a new left was forming itself as counterpart to the new right. Leningrad had remained the most proletarian of Soviet cities. It had the strongest Marxist and Leninist traditions. Its workers felt more acutely than anyone else the need for a bold industrial policy. The city's engineering plants and shipyards, starved of iron and steel, were idle. Less than anyone else could the Leningraders agree that the muzhiks should dictate the tempo of industrial reconstruction. Less than anyone could they reconcile themselves to the prospect that they were to move ahead only slowly and drowsily drag along the huge and heavy peasant cart. All the antagonism of urban Russia to the inert conservatism of rural Russia was focused in the old capital. The party organization, although it was managed in a bureaucratic manner and had long ceased to be representative of the workers, could not help reflecting in some measure the prevalent discontents. Its organizers and agitators had to deal with vast numbers of unemployed and became influenced by their resentments and impatience. The popular

[1] Bukharin, *Kritika Ekonomicheskoi Platformy Oppozitsii*, p. 9.

mood infected various grades of the party hierarchy on the spot and impelled them to make a stand against the new right. Throughout most of 1925 Zinoviev led the attack against Bukharin's school. The whole Northern Commune was aroused. The Comsomol passionately threw itself into the struggle; and the press of Leningrad opened a barrage.

At the same time a new rift appeared in the Politbureau. Once the triumvirs had defeated Trotsky and removed him from the Commissariat of War, the bonds of their solidarity snapped. Molotov related afterwards that the discord began in January 1925 when Kamenev proposed that Stalin should take Trotsky's place at the Commissariat of War. According to Molotov, Kamenev and Zinoviev hoped in this way to oust Stalin from the General Secretariat.[1] (Much earlier, as early as October 1923, Zinoviev and Kamenev had toyed with this idea and had even sounded Trotsky. He, however, saw no advantage then in joining hands with Zinoviev, whom he regarded as the most vicious of his adversaries.[2]) Stalin himself traces the beginning of this conflict to the end of the year 1924, when Zinoviev proposed Trotsky's expulsion from the party and Stalin replied that he was against 'chopping off heads and blood letting'.[3] When Trotsky left the Commissariat, Zinoviev proposed that he should be assigned to a minor job in the management of the leather industry; and Stalin persuaded the Politbureau to make a less humiliating appointment. In a pique, Zinoviev appealed to the Leningrad organization, charging Stalin and other Politbureau members with a leaning for Trotsky and with being 'semi-Trotskyists' themselves.

In these petty manœuvres, however, no divergencies over policy had as yet shown themselves. Only in the last week of April 1925 did members of the Central Committee notice signs of a political breach between the triumvirs. In the text of a resolution prepared for the forthcoming party conference, Stalin intended to proclaim socialism in a single country. He had

[1] See *14 Syezd VKP (b)*, p. 484.
[2] Voroshilov's disclosures about this made in Trotsky's presence did not meet with Trotsky's denial. Ibid., pp. 388–9. Zinoviev confirmed them in substance. Ibid., pp. 454–6.
[3] 'To-day they chop off one head, to-morrow another, the day after to-morrow still another—who, in the end, will be left with us in the party?' Stalin, *Sochinenya*, vol. vii, pp. 379–80.

formulated the idea some months earlier, but now for the first time he sought to obtain official sanction for it and to incorporate it in party doctrine. Zinoviev and Kamenev objected. None of the triumvirs, however, wished to scandalize the party by revealing their disunion so soon after their show-down with Trotsky. They hushed up the matter and agreed on an ambiguous motion which in its opening passages reminded the party that Lenin had never been a believer in socialism in a single country, and in its conclusion upbraided Trotsky for not having been a believer in it either.[1] With this incongruous text in their hands, the triumvirs presented a common front to the conference. They still maintained it over decisions of immediate practical importance. The conference voted for an enlargement of the freedom of private farming and trade, for a reduction in agricultural taxation, for the abolition of restrictions on the lease of land and on the hiring of farm labour. In these decisions there showed itself a marked influence of Bukharin's school of thought. None of the leaders objected to them, however, in part because all had been alarmed by a bad harvest and all recognized the need to offer new incentives to the farmers; and in part because these resolutions too were framed ambiguously so that any interpreter could make out of them whatever he wished.

For another four or five months, throughout the summer, the dissension among the triumvirs did not come into the open. Zinoviev and the Leningraders campaigned only against Bukharin and Rykov, and against the neo-Populist 'red professors'. By doing so they helped Stalin to consolidate his position. The Politbureau still consisted of these seven members: Stalin, Trotsky, Zinoviev, Kamenev, Bukharin, Rykov, and Tomsky. The leaders of the new right, Bukharin, Rykov, and Tomsky, allied themselves with Stalin and with him formed the majority. The arithmetic of the Politbureau vote was so plain that had Zinoviev and Kamenev been eager only to oust Stalin, they would have sought to make common cause with Bukharin rather than attack him. They acted as they did because in this situation matters of conviction and fundamental differences were more important to them than calculations of personal advantage.

Meantime the crisis in the country deepened. The concessions

[1] *KPSS v Rezolutsyakh*, vol. ii, pp. 46–50; Popov, op. cit., vol. ii, p. 239.

made to the strong farmers failed to appease them. In the summer the deliveries of grain fell far below expectation. The government was suddenly compelled to stop the export of grain and to cancel orders placed abroad for machinery and raw materials which were to be paid with the proceeds. Industrial recovery suffered a severe if temporary set-back. Food became scarce in the towns and the price of bread went up. The party leaders had to consider anew what should be done to ease the tension between town and country. Bukharin urged the Polit-bureau to offer the farmers further concessions and new in-centives—it was at this time that he wound up one of his appeals to the peasants with the call: 'Enrich yourselves!' He insisted on the need to do away at last with the restrictions that ham-pered the accumulation of capital in farming. To those who were outraged by his demand and afraid of the kulak, he replied: 'As long as we are in tatters, . . . the kulak may defeat us econo-mically. But he will not do so if we enable him to deposit his savings in our banks. We shall assist him, but he will also assist us. Eventually the kulak's grandson will be grateful to us for our having treated his grandfather in this way.'[1] Bukharin's disciples again dotted the i's, spoke of the advent of the neo-N.E.P., and elaborated the view that it should be possible to integrate peacefully the well-to-do farmer into socialism. One of them, Bogushevsky, argued in the *Bolshevik*, the Central Committee's policy paper, that the kulak was no longer a social force to be reckoned with—he was a mere bogy, a 'phantom', or a 'de-crepit social type of which only a few specimens have survived'.[2]

Leningrad replied with an outcry of indignation. Its workers were daily finding fresh proof of the kulak's strength and striking power—at their bakers'. At the Moscow Committee Kamenev, showing with fresh statistics how dependent the towns had be-come for the bare necessities of life on a small minority of the peasantry, sounded an alarm at the Central Committee's in-clination to accept this state of affairs and to yield even further to the clamour for a neo-N.E.P. The Leningraders demanded that the party should make a new appeal to the poor peasantry against the rich. They pointed out that by its attempts to pro-pitiate the kulak, the party had antagonized the great mass of the poor and middle peasants and enabled the kulaks to become

---

[1] *Bolshevik*, nr. 8, 1925. [2] *Bolshevik*, nrs. 9–10, 1925.

the virtual leaders of rural Russia. This was undoubtedly true.[1] But the weak point in the critics' argument was precisely that the poor and even the middle peasants did not produce the food surpluses the town needed. More than ever was the party hierarchy therefore afraid of 'fanning class struggle in the countryside' and incurring the kulaks' hostility. Rural committees became wary of organizing farm labourers and supporting their claims. There was much talk about an impending return of the nationalized land into private hands. In Georgia the Commissar of Agriculture published 'theses', i.e. the draft of a decree, to this effect; and similar decrees were expected to be promulgated in the rest of the Caucasus and in Siberia. Stalin himself saw no reason why the title-deeds to the land should not be handed over to the peasants 'even for the duration of forty years'. He, too, firmly discouraged 'incitement to class struggle in the country'.[2]

The controversy now turned from current policy to the larger underlying issues. Did we or did we not, the Leningraders asked, carry out a proletarian revolution? Are we going to sacrifice the vital interests of the workers to those of the strong farmers? What is happening to our party that makes it abandon class struggle in the country and turns it into a promoter of rural capitalism? What is it that impels our chief theoretician to cry out 'Enrich yourselves!'? Why are so many of our leaders resigned and ready to reconcile themselves to Russia's backwardness? Where is our revolutionary fervour of earlier years? The Leningraders concluded that all they had fought for was in jeopardy, that the party's ideals were being falsified and the Leninist principles abandoned. They wondered whether the revolution had not reached a point of exhaustion as other revolutions, especially the French, had done in their time. It was not Zinoviev or Trotsky or another of the illustrious intellectuals but Peter Zalutsky, a self-taught worker and secretary of the Leningrad organization, who first came out in a public speech with a significant analogy between the present state of Bolshevism and Jacobinism in decline, and who first

[1] Later in the year, at the fourteenth congress, the Stalinist spokesmen admitted the facts. Mikoyan, for instance, declared: 'We are making great efforts to regain the middle peasant who has become the kulak's political prisoner.' *14 Syezd VKP (b)*, pp. 188–9. More euphemistically Molotov stated: 'At present we do not as yet truly lead the middle peasant.' Ibid., p. 476.

[2] Stalin, *Sochinenya*, vol. vii, pp. 123, 173–81 and *passim*.

raised an alarm about the 'Thermidorian' danger that threatened the revolution—we shall presently find this idea in the very centre of all Trotsky's denunciations of Stalinism.[1]

Bolshevism, Zalutsky said, might decay through its own lassitude. Its destroyers might come from its own midst, from among those of its own leaders who succumbed to reactionary moods. A cry for the rehabilitation of the revolution came from Leningrad. Let our rulers remain loyal to the working class and the ideals of socialism! Let equality remain our ideal! The workers' state may be too poor to make our dream of equality come true, but let it not mock at the dream!

Of this mood Zinoviev made himself mouthpiece. Early in September he wrote an essay 'The Philosophy of the Epoch' which the Politbureau allowed him to publish only after he had deleted the most provocative parts. 'Do you want to know what the mass of the people is dreaming about in our days?' ran one of the censured passages,

It is dreaming about equality. . . . If we wish to be genuine mouthpieces for the people, we ought to place ourselves at the head of its struggle for equality. . . . In what name did the working class, and behind it the vast mass of the people, rise in the great days of October? In what name did they follow Lenin into the fire? In what name . . . did they follow his banner in the first difficult years? . . . In the name of equality. . . .[2]

About the same time Zinoviev also published his book *Leninism* which combined an interpretation of party doctrine with a critical survey of Soviet society. He exposed the conflicts and tensions between the private and the socialist sectors and pointed out that even in the socialist sector there were strong elements of 'state capitalism'. National ownership of industry represented the element of socialism there; but relations between the employer-state and the workers, bureaucratic management, and differential wages bore the marks of capitalism. For the first time Zinoviev here came out with an open critique of socialism in a single country. Even if the Soviet Union were to remain isolated for an indefinite time, he maintained, it could achieve much progress in building socialism; but, poor and

[1] *14 Syezd VKP (b)*, pp. 150–2.
[2] The censured passages were quoted by Uglanov at the fourteenth congress. Ibid., p. 195.

backward and exposed to dangers from without and within, it could not hope to achieve *full* socialism. It could not raise itself economically and culturally above the capitalist West, abolish class differences, and let the state wither away. The prospect of socialism in a single country was therefore unreal; and Bolsheviks had no need to place before the people such a *fata morgana*, especially as this would imply the abandonment of the hope for revolution abroad and a break with Leninist internationalism. Here was the crux of the new division. The new right framed its policies in strictly national and isolationist terms. The left adhered to the party's internationalist tradition, despite all the defeats that international communism had suffered.

At this stage, in the summer of 1925, Stalin and his followers defined their attitude as that of the centre. Partly from conviction and partly from opportunist calculation, because he depended on Bukharin's and Rykov's support, Stalin backed the pro-muzhik policy. But he curbed his right-wing allies and disavowed their most outspoken statements like Bukharin's 'Enrich yourselves!'[1] Cautious, cunning, and caring not a straw for logical and doctrinal niceties, he borrowed ideas and slogans from both right and left and combined them often quite incongruously. In this lay a great part of his strength. He managed to blur every issue and to confuse every debate. To critics who attacked him for any of his pronouncements he was always able to produce another statement of his which contained the exact opposite. His eclectic formulas were a boon to officialdom and to habitual sitters-on-the-fence; yet they also attracted many honest but timid or muddled minds. As in any 'centrist' faction, so among the Stalinists some leaned to the left and others to the right. Kalinin and Voroshilov were close to Bukharin and Rykov, while Molotov, Andreev, and Kaganovich were 'left Stalinists'. The differences among his own supporters also induced Stalin to keep his distance from the right. Only over one issue—socialism in a single country—was his solidarity with Bukharin complete.

Early in October the Central Committee considered arrangements for the fourteenth congress which was convened for the

---

[1] Stalin, op. cit., p. 159.

end of the year. Four members of the Committee, Zinoviev, Kamenev, Sokolnikov, and Krupskaya, came out with a joint statement demanding a free debate in which party members could speak their minds on all the controversial issues that had arisen. With this the two triumvirs gave notice of their intention to appeal against Stalin and Bukharin to the rank and file.

Sokolnikov did not share all of Zinoviev's and Kamenev's views. As Commissar of Finance he had in recent years done his utmost to encourage private enterprise; and many regarded him as a pillar of the right. But he too had become uneasy over the trend of policy and Stalin's growing power; and so he endorsed the demand for a debate. Krupskaya stood firmly behind Zinoviev and Kamenev and encouraged them to divulge to the entire party the differences in the Politbureau, without mincing matters. She had not yet reconciled herself to the fact that in defiance of her husband's will Stalin had remained General Secretary; and she viewed with hostility the growing influence of Bukharin's school of thought. She had tried to speak out against it, but the Politbureau had not allowed her to do so. Her voice carried weight with party members who knew how long and how closely she had been associated with Lenin, not only as wife but as secretary and co-thinker. She was now eager to testify in favour of Zinoviev's interpretation of Leninism and against socialism in one country.

In asking for an open debate, the four members acted in accordance with statute and custom: the party had never yet held a congress without a preliminary discussion. The Central Committee nevertheless refused to allow a debate; and it obliged Zinoviev and Kamenev to refrain from any public criticism of official policy. The two triumvirs were thus placed in the same quandary in which they had previously placed Trotsky. To speak up in public was to act against the principle of cabinet solidarity which bound them as members of the Central Committee and the Politbureau. But not to speak up was to act against their own political conscience and interest. While they were silent and their followers attacked only the Bukharinists, Stalin unremittingly worked to dislodge them from power. Kamenev had hitherto exercised the dominant influence over the Moscow committee. In the course of the summer the General Secretariat quietly removed his lieutenants from their posts, and filled the vacancies with reliable supporters of the new majority. In Leningrad, however, Zinoviev and his followers were firmly entrenched; and for the time being Stalin could do nothing against them. Zinoviev himself had to keep up the pretence of the Central Committee's unanimity; but his followers were free to speak. They were all anger and passion; and they were ready to carry their attack on official policy into full congress.

Between October and December Moscow and Leningrad were engaged in an intense, bitter, and barely concealed tug of war. In both capitals the elections of delegates to the congress were rigged; Moscow elected only Stalin's and Bukharin's nominees, while all of Leningrad's delegates turned out to be Zinoviev's followers. When three days before the opening of the congress the Central Committee met again, it was clear that nothing could avert an open conflict. Zinoviev and Kamenev had resolved to challenge publicly the official policy report and to present their own counter-report. On 18 December, the day the Congress assembled, Zinoviev opened the attack and in *Leningradskaya Pravda* thus branded his adversaries:

They bandy about loud phrases on international revolution; but they portray Lenin as the inspirer of a nationally limited socialist revolution. They fight against the kulak; but they offer the slogan 'Enrich yourselves!' They shout about socialism, but they proclaim the Russia of N.E.P. as a socialist country. They 'believe' in the working class; but they call the wealthy farmer to come to their aid.

. . . .

The exchanges between Bukharinists and Zinovievists had gone on for many months now and the conflict between the triumvirs had been simmering for nearly a year. This, it might have seemed, was the realignment for which Trotsky had waited, the opportunity to act. Yet throughout all this time he was aloof, silent about the issues over which the party divided, and as if unaware of them. Thirteen years later, when he stood before the Dewey Commission in Mexico, he confessed that at the fourteenth congress he was astonished to see Zinoviev, Kamenev, and Stalin clashing as enemies. 'The explosion was absolutely unexpected by me', he said. 'During the congress I waited in uncertainty, because the whole situation changed. It appeared absolutely unclear to me.'[1]

[1] *The Case of Leon Trotsky*, pp. 322–3.

This recollection, so many years after the event, may seem quite incredible; but it is fully borne out by what its author wrote in unpublished diary notes during the congress itself.[1] To the Dewey Commission he explained that he was taken by surprise because, although he was a member of the Politbureau, the triumvirs had carefully concealed their dissensions from him and had thrashed out their differences in his absence, within the secret caucus that acted as the real Politbureau. The explanation, although true, explains little. For one thing, the crucial controversy over socialism in a single country had already been conducted in public. Trotsky could not have missed its significance if he had followed it. He evidently failed to do so. For another, Zinoviev, Kamenev, Krupskaya, and Sokolnikov had raised the demand for an open debate not within a secret caucus but at the plenary session of the Central Committee, in October. But even if they had not done so, and even if the public controversy over socialism in a single country had given no indication of the new cleavage, it would still be something of a puzzle how an observer as close, as interested, and as acute as Trotsky could have remained unaware of the trend and blind to the many omens. How could he have been deaf to the rumblings that had for months been coming from Leningrad?

His surprise, we must conclude, resulted from a failure of observation, intuition, and analysis. Moreover, it is implausible that Radek, Preobrazhensky, Smirnov, and his other friends should not have noticed what was happening and that none of them tried to bring matters to Trotsky's attention. Evidently his mind remained closed. He lived as if in another world, wrapped up in himself and his ideas. He was up to his eyes in his scientific and industrial preoccupations and literary work, which protected him to some extent from the frustration to which he was exposed. He shunned inner-party affairs. Full of the sense of his superiority and contempt for his opponents, and disgusted with the polemical methods and tricks, he was not interested in their doings. He submitted to the discipline by which they had shackled him, but he held up his head and ignored them. A few years later his biographer was told in Moscow that he used to appear dutifully at the sessions of the Central Committee, take his seat, open a book—most often a French novel—and become

[1] See the summary of these notes on pp. 255–6. The text is in *The Archives*.

so engrossed as to take no notice of the deliberations. Even if this anecdote was invented, it was well invented: it conveys something of the man's temper. He could turn his back on his adversaries, but he could not view them with detachment. He was too close to them: he saw them as the small men, the rogues, and the sharpers that they sometimes were; and he half forgot that they were also the leaders of a great state and party and that what they said and did carried immense historic weight.

Had Trotsky kept his ears open to what the Leningraders were saying, he could not have failed to realize at once that they were defending the causes he himself had defended, and attacking the attitudes he himself had attacked. As oppositionists, they started where he had left off. They argued from his premises; they took up his arguments to carry them farther. He had criticized the Politbureau's lack of initiative, its neglect of industry, and its excessive solicitude for the private sector of the economy. So did the Leningraders. He had observed with apprehension the spirit of national narrow-mindedness which induced the party hierarchy to frame policy and think of the future in terms of self-sufficiency. Actuated by the same antagonism to 'national narrow-mindedness', Zinoviev and Kamenev were the first to come out with a critique of socialism in a single country. To Trotsky, Bukharin's and Stalin's ideas on this subject must have at first appeared as dull scholastic dogma-mongering, hardly worthy of his comment; and so he made no comment for nearly a year and a half, while socialism in a single country was becoming the new Bolshevik orthodoxy, the orthodoxy he was to fight to the end of his life. Zinoviev and Kamenev were more alive to the symptomatic meaning of the new doctrine. He could not but agree with their arguments against it for they drew them from the armoury of classical Marxist internationalism. Nor could the cry for equality that went up in Leningrad fail to strike a chord in him. Zinoviev, Kamenev, Sokolnikov, and Krupskaya had only echoed Trotsky when they protested against the stifling of party opinion. Like him, they spoke of the unholy alliance of N.E.P.-man, kulak, and bureaucrat; and like him, they called for the revival of proletarian democracy. He had warned the party against the 'degeneration' of its leadership; and now the same warning resounded even more poignantly and alarmingly in the Leningraders' outcry against the 'Thermidorian' danger. These were the ideas and the slogans that he was to take up presently and to expound in the years to come. Yet when he heard them expounded by his erstwhile adversaries, he 'waited in uncertainty' for several critical months; and his adherents waited together with him.

What contributed to his and his followers' confusion was that they had been accustomed to regard Zinoviev and Kamenev as the leaders of the party's right wing. No one had done more than Trotsky to spread this view. In *The Lessons of October* he had reminded the party of Zinoviev's and Kamenev's opposition to the October Revolution. He had argued that in 1923 Zinoviev had led the German Communists to 'capitulate' because his frame of mind had still been the same as in 1917. And when he told the party that its Old Guard might, like the hierarchy of the Second International, degenerate into a conservative, bureaucratic 'apparatus', he almost pointed an accusing finger at Zinoviev and Kamenev. No wonder that he looked at them incredulously when they appeared as the spokesmen of a new left. He suspected demagoguery. The suspicion, though not altogether groundless, made it difficult for him to grasp that the change of roles was real and that it formed part of that regroupment of men and ideas to which the extremely critical situation in the country had given rise. Zinoviev's and Kamenev's conversion was not less genuine and not less startling than that by which Bukharin, the ex-leader of the Left Communists, had become the ideologue of the new right—indeed, the two conversions supplemented each other. Official Bolshevik policy tended at present so strongly towards the right that some of those who only yesterday headed the right wing became frightened of the consequences and found themselves veering far to the left.

To be sure, personal ambitions and jealousies played their part: Zinoviev and Kamenev sought to strip Stalin of his power. But they might have had a better chance had they chosen to ride, with Bukharin, the mounting tide of isolationism and neo-Populism. Instead, they took their stand on the proletarian and internationalist traditions of Leninism which had become unpopular with the men of the party machine, on whom the outcome of the contest immediately depended. Zinoviev's and Kamenev's outlook and habits of mind as well as the moods among their followers set limits to their self-seeking. No matter how timidly or opportunistically they had behaved on important occasions, they had been Lenin's closest disciples; they were constitutionally incapable of shedding the influence that had moulded them. Others might turn their backs on the European working class and glorify, sincerely or not, the muzhik; they could not do so. Others might exalt Russia's self-sufficient socialism; to them the very thought was absurd and repugnant. The attitude to these issues, however, formed the watershed which now separated the various currents in Bolshevism.

There was yet another aspect of this change of roles. Like Trotsky and Lenin before them, Zinoviev and Kamenev grappled with the dilemma of authority and freedom, or of party discipline and proletarian democracy. They, too, felt the tension between the power and the dream of revolution. They had been the disciplinarians. Now they were tired and sick of the mechanical and rigid discipline they had enforced. Zinoviev had for years strutted the political stage, roared words of command, schemed and plotted, demoted and promoted people, built power for the revolution and for himself; he had been as if obsessed and drunken with authority. Now came the awakening, the bitter after-taste, and the yearning to find a way back to the irrecoverable clear spring of the revolution. Together with him many of the Old Guard had followed the same bents and suffered the same perplexities and disenchantments until, without knowing it, they took up attitudes indistinguishable from those of the Trotskyists whom they had just helped to defeat. Everything drove them to join hands with the men of the 1923 Opposition.

If Trotsky was to make common cause with Zinoviev and Kamenev, this was the time to do it. Till the beginning of 1926 the base from which the Leningraders operated was still intact. The administrative machinery of the city and the province was in Zinoviev's hands. He had a large body of ardent followers. He controlled influential newspapers. He possessed the material means for a long and sustained political struggle. In a word, he was still in his Northern Commune the master of a powerful fortress. He was also President of the Communist International, although Stalin was already active at its headquarters, sapping his influence. In some respects Zinoviev's position, when he came in conflict with Stalin, was much stronger than Trotsky's had ever been. Trotsky had never bothered to lay his hands on instruments of personal power; and so after his world-shaking career he began almost empty-handed the fight with the triumvirs. They found it all too easy to brand him as an alien to Bolshevism. It was far more difficult for Stalin and Bukharin to denounce Zinoviev, Kamenev, and Krupskaya as inveterate Mensheviks. The conflict was now clearly between two sections of the Bolshevik Old Guard. A coalition between Trotsky and Zinoviev, if it had come into being before Zinoviev's defeat, might have been formidable. Yet neither of them and neither of the two factions was ready. Their mutual grievances and hatreds and the memories of the knocks and insults exchanged were still too fresh to allow them to pull together.

One of the strangest moments in Trotsky's political life now followed. On 18 December the fourteenth congress, the last he was to attend, was opened. From first to last it was the scene of a political storm, the like of which the party had never witnessed in its long and stormy history. Before the eyes of the whole country the new antagonists wrestled and dealt each other mighty blows. The fate of the party and the revolution was in the balance. Nearly all the great issues which were to occupy Trotsky for the rest of his life were thrashed out. Each of the new antagonists had his eyes on Trotsky, wondering with whom he would join and waiting with bated breath for his word. Yet throughout the fortnight that the congress was in session Trotsky sat silent. He had nothing to say when to an audience convulsed with emotion Zinoviev recalled Lenin's testament and its warning against Stalin's abuse of power or when he dwelt on the danger that threatened socialism from the kulak, the N.E.P.-man, and the bureaucrat. Impassively Trotsky viewed the momentous scene when, after Kamenev had protested with great force against the establishment of autocratic rule over the party, the well-picked majority, foaming with rage and insulting the speaker, for the first time acclaimed Stalin as the Leader 'around whom the Leninist Central Committee was united'.

Nor did he rise and declare his solidarity with Krupskaya when she spoke about the stultifying effect of the Leninist cult, when she entreated the delegates to discuss the issues before them on their merits instead of swamping debates with meaningless quotations from the writings of her husband, and when, finally, she recalled by way of a warning how the campaign against Trotsky had degenerated into slander and persecution. He listened as though unconcerned to the controversy over socialism in one country, one of the greatest debates of the century. He was not provoked to make a single gesture of protest or disagreement when Bukharin built the case for socialism in one country on the party's previous rejection of Trotsky's permanent revolution, and went on to speak of building socialism at the 'snail's pace'. The triumvirs revealed the inner story of their disagreements in which Trotsky's person loomed so large: Stalin related how Zinoviev and Kamenev had asked for Trotsky's head and how he had resisted them. Zinoviev described how he and Stalin had, violating the statutes, dispersed the Central Committee of the Communist Youth after its overwhelming majority had declared for Trotsky. Speakers from all factions paid Trotsky compliments and made advances. While Krupskaya spoke, a cry: 'Lev Davidovich, you have gained new collaborators!' rose from the floor. Lashevich, hitherto one of his most embittered adversaries, acknowledged that Trotsky had not been altogether wrong in 1923. The Stalinists and Bukharinists were lavish with praise: Mikoyan held up to the new opposition the shining example of Trotsky who, when defeated, scrupulously observed party discipline. Yaroslavsky reproached the Leningraders with their rabid and still unabated anti-Trotskyism. Tomsky contrasted the 'crystal clear lucidity of Trotsky's views' and the integrity of his conduct with Zinoviev's and Kamenev's muddle-headedness and evasions. Kalinin spoke of the resentment and disgust he had always felt at their attempts to drag down Trotsky. When Zinoviev asserted his right to dissent from official policy, and complained that no opposition had ever been handled so roughly, Stalinists and Bukharinists showered on him derisive reminders of the things he had done to Trotsky. Then, winding up a great peroration, Zinoviev exhorted the congress to let bygones be bygones and to reform the party's leadership so that all sections of Bolshevik opinion should co-operate and unite. The eyes of the whole assembly were now on Trotsky: had the great and eloquent man nothing to say? His lips were sealed. He remained silent even when Andreev asked that new prerogatives be voted for the Central Committee to enable it to deal more effectively with dissenters—to enable it, that is, to break the back of the new Opposition. The latter had been heavily outvoted; but before its close the congress received with uproar and anger reports that in Leningrad turbulent demonstrations against its decisions were in progress: the Leningraders were fighting on within their fortress. And to the end not a word escaped from Trotsky's mouth.[1]

Trotsky's private papers offer us an insight into what was going on in his mind. In a note jotted down on 22 December, the fourth day of the congress, he remarked that there was 'a grain of truth'—but not more—in the view expressed by some that the Leningraders continued the work of the Trotskyist Opposition. The hue and cry, raised in 1923, about the enmity of Trotskyism towards the peasantry had paved the way for the neo-Populism which was now fashionable and against which the Leningraders reacted. It was natural that they should do so, although they had led in the drive against Trotskyism. The intense animosity of the congress towards Zinoviev's faction reflected *au fond* the hostility of the country to the town. This view, one might have thought, should have induced Trotsky to make common cause with the Leningraders at once. But the issues and the divisions did not yet seem to him as clear as they had so far appeared in his own analysis; and he entertained certain hopes which induced him to wait.

He wondered why Sokolnikov, of all people, the ultra-moderate who should have been on Bukharin's side, had joined the Leningraders. He was puzzled that the division was between Moscow and Leningrad. The artificially produced antagonism

---

[1] He made only one *Zwischenruf* in the debate. When Zinoviev explained that the year before he had asked for Trotsky's exclusion from the Politbureau because after all the accusations they had hurled at Trotsky, it was incongruous to re-elect him to the Politbureau, Trotsky interjected: 'Correct!'

Ruth Fischer, who was present in Moscow during the congress but was not admitted to it and was instead given daily reports by Bogrebinsky, Stalin's underling, 'a delegate from the G.P.U.', writes: 'Bogrebinsky was particularly interested in Trotsky. . . . Both groups feared him . . . and now both hoped to win him over; Trotsky's attitude might have been decisive among the wavering delegates from the provinces. Trotsky, Bogrebinsky noted each day, had looked well or badly; he had spoken with this person or that. "I saw Trotsky to-day in the corridors. He spoke with some of the delegates, and I could hear a little of the conversation. He said nothing on the decisive questions. He did not support the Opposition, even by hints and allusions. That is wonderful. Those dogs of Leningrad will get a thorough beating." ' R. Fischer, *Stalin and German Communism*, p. 494.

between them, he noted, veiled a deeper underlying conflict. He hoped that the organizations of the two capitals would draw together and reassert jointly the aspirations of the proletarian-socialist elements against the pro-muzhik right. He reckoned that all 'true Bolsheviks' would rise against the bureaucracy—nothing less could free the party organization of Moscow from Stalin's stranglehold. The situation was still in a state of flux. He expected something like a political landslide, of which the breach between the triumvirs was only the beginning, to shake the party and to bring about the final, far wider, and far more significant regrouping of forces. Then the lines of division would be less fortuitous and would correspond to the fundamental contradictions between town and country, worker and peasant, socialism and property. Meantime, he was not at all eager to throw in his lot with the 'vociferous, vulgar, and rightly dis-credited' leaders of the Leningrad Opposition. There is a whiff of *Schadenfreude* in these diary notes written as he watched Zino-viev's and Kamenev's discomfiture—as if he were saying: *Vous l'avez voulu, Vous l'avez voulu!*

Yet he could not give himself to *Schadenfreude* for any length of time; it was not in his nature to do so. Willy-nilly he had to rush to the rescue of the defeated. No sooner had the congress dis-persed than the Central Committee met to consider measures for taming Leningrad. Stalin proposed to dismiss in the first in-stance the editorial staff of *Leningradskaya Pravda* and to turn that newspaper into the mouthpiece of official policy. Next Zinoviev was to be deposed and Kirov was to take his place at the head of the Northern Commune. The whip was to come down on the Leningraders. At this point Trotsky broke his silence—he was against the reprisals.[1] He did not contemplate an alliance with Zinoviev and Kamenev, but by trying to shield them, he at once gave offence to Stalin who had walked around him gingerly seeking to mollify him.

There was a curious scene at the session. Bukharin spoke for the course of action proposed by Stalin. Kamenev protested. It was strange, he said, that Bukharin, who had always opposed drastic reprisals against the Trotskyists, should now call for the whip. 'Ah, but he has come to relish the whip', Trotsky inter-jected. Bukharin, as though caught off guard, cried back: 'You

---

[1] N. Popov, *Outline History of the CPSU*, vol. ii, p. 255.

think I have come to relish it, but this relishing makes me shudder from head to foot.'[1] In this cry of anguish were suddenly revealed the forebodings with which Bukharin backed Stalin. From this incident dates a 'private contact', which 'after a long interval' Trotsky resumed with Bukharin—a fairly friendly, but politically fruitless and shortlived affair, the traces of which are found in their correspondence.[2] Still 'shuddering from head to foot', Bukharin did his best to persuade Trotsky not to come to Zinoviev's aid. He tried to impress on him that the party's freedom was not at stake in this case and that Zinoviev, who himself brooked no opposition, was no defender of inner-party democracy. Trotsky did not deny this, but he argued that Stalin was surely no better; and that the evil lay in a monolithic discipline and the unanimous vote which both Stalin and Zinoviev enforced—this had made it possible that on the eve of the congress the two largest organizations, those of Moscow and Leningrad, should each carry its own resolutions in 'a hundred per cent. unanimity'. He held no brief for the Leningraders; but he could not but oppose the false discipline; and he appealed to Bukharin to join him in a common effort to restore 'a healthy inner-party régime'. Bukharin, however, was afraid that by asking for more freedom they would get less; and he concluded that those who demanded inner-party democracy were in effect its worst enemies, and that the only way to save what was left of it was not to use it.

While these pathetic 'confidential' exchanges went on, Stalin lost the hope of playing Trotsky against Zinoviev and Kamenev. Earlier perhaps than Trotsky himself he realized that the two oppositions would have to join hands. He therefore gave the signal for a new drive against Trotsky. He was anxious that Trotsky should not be able to address communist gatherings in working-class districts. Uglanov, who had replaced Kamenev as leader of the Moscow organization, saw to that. Under all sorts of pretexts Trotsky was refused admission to the cells. As he was just then addressing meetings of scientists and other intellectuals, the members of the proletarian cells were told that he preferred to speak to the bourgeoisie rather than face workers. Official agitators ceased to distinguish between Trotskyists and Zinovievists, incited the rank and file against both, and hinted

---

[1] *The Trotsky Archives.* [2] Ibid.

darkly that it was no matter of chance that the leaders of both were Jews—this was, they suggested, a struggle between native and genuine Russian socialism and aliens who sought to pervert it.

In another letter to Bukharin, dated 4 March, Trotsky described the vexations and the obloquy of which he had again become the object. Altogether against his inclination, he dwelt on the anti-Semitic undertones of the agitators' talk. 'I think', he wrote, attempting to arouse Bukharin, 'that what binds us, two Politbureau members, is still quite enough for us to try and check the facts calmly and conscientiously: is it true, is it possible that in *our party*, IN MOSCOW, in WORKERS' CELLS, anti-Semitic agitation should be carried on with impunity?!'[1] A fortnight later at a Politbureau meeting he asked the same astonished and indignant question. The Politbureau members shrugged, professed to know nothing, or pooh-poohed the matter. Bukharin blushed with embarrassment and shame; but he could not turn against his associates and allies. At any rate, at this stage his 'private contact' with Trotsky was coming to an end.

It was not by chance that the agitators struck the anti-Semitic note: they were briefed by Uglanov; and Uglanov took his cue from Stalin who was anything but fastidious in the choice of means. But there were means to which he could not have resorted even a year or two earlier; and playing on anti-Jewish prejudice was one of them. This had been the favourite occupation of the worst Tsarist reactionaries; and even in 1923–4 the party and its Old Guard were still too strongly imbued with internationalism to countenance such prejudice, let alone to exploit it. But the situation was changing. The new right appealed vaguely to nationalist emotions; and while these surged up, the political climate altered to such an extent that even Communists no longer frowned on anti-Semitic hints or allusions dropped in their midst. The distrust of the 'alien' was, after all, only a reflex of that Russian self-centredness, of which socialism in one country was the ideological abstract.

Jews were, in fact, conspicuous among the Opposition although they were there together with the flower of the non-

[1] *The Trotsky Archives.*

Jewish intelligentsia and workers. Trotsky, Zinoviev, Kamenev, Sokolnikov, Radek, were all Jews.[1] (There were, on the other hand, very few Jews among the Stalinists, and fewer still among the Bukharinists.) Thoroughly 'assimilated' and Russified though they were, and hostile to the Mosaic as to any other religion, and to Zionism, they were still marked by that 'Jewishness' which is the quintessence of the urban way of life in all its modernity, progressiveness, restlessness, and one-sidedness. To be sure, the allegations that they were politically hostile to the muzhik were false and, in Stalin's mouth, though perhaps not in Bukharin's, insincere. But the Bolsheviks of Jewish origin were least of all inclined to idealize rural Russia in her primitivism and barbarity and to drag along at a 'snail's pace' the native peasant cart. They were in a sense the 'rootless cosmopolitans' on whom Stalin was to turn his wrath openly in his old age. Not for them was the ideal of socialism in a single country. As a rule the progressive or revolutionary Jew, brought up on the border lines of various religions and national cultures, whether Spinoza or Marx, Heine or Freud, Rosa Luxemburg or Trotsky, was particularly apt to transcend in his mind religious and national limitations and to identify himself with a universal view of mankind. He was therefore also peculiarly vulnerable whenever either religious fanaticisms or nationalist emotions ran high. Spinoza and Marx, Heine and Freud, Rosa Luxemburg and Trotsky, all suffered excommunication, exile, and moral or physical assassination; and the writings of all were burned at the stake.

· · · · · · · · · ·

In the first weeks of 1926 the strength of the Leningrad

[1] In 1918, while the Ukraine was under German occupation and ruled by Skoropadsky, the rabbis of Odessa pronounced anathema on Trotsky and Zinoviev. (Zinoviev, *Sochinenya*, vol. xvi, p. 224.) The White Guards, on the other hand, made much of Trotsky's Jewishness and alleged that Lenin was also a Jew. Curious echoes of this can be found in Soviet folk-lore and fiction of the early twenties. In one of Seyfulina's stories a muzhik says: 'Trotsky is one of us, a Russian and a Bolshevik. Lenin is a Jew and a Communist.' In Babel's short story 'Salt' a peasant woman says to a Red Army man: 'You don't bother your heads about Russia; you just go about saving those dirty Jews Lenin and Trotsky.' The Red Army man replies: 'We aren't talking about Jews now, you harmful citizen. The Jews haven't got nothing to do with it. By the way, I won't say nothing about Lenin, but Trotsky was the desperate son of a Governor of Tambov and went over to the working class. . . . They work like niggers, Lenin and Trotsky do, to pull us up to the path of freedom. . . .'

Opposition was broken.[1] The Leningraders could not but submit to Stalin's orders. To defy them was to challenge the authority of the Central Committee, which backed Stalin, and the legality of the congress which had elected the Committee. This Zinoviev and Kamenev, who like Trotsky still sat on that Committee, were not prepared to do. They had openly declared that Stalin had rigged the elections to the congress and that the Central Committee represented the party machine, not the party. But it was one thing to state this, and quite another to proclaim that the decisions of the congress and of the Central Committee were invalid and to refuse to submit. For Zinoviev and Kamenev in particular it would have been a dangerous undertaking to question the legitimacy of the last congress: had they not, together with Stalin, rigged the elections and packed the thirteenth congress in the same way that Stalin packed the fourteenth? By challenging the authority of the Central Committee, the Leningraders would have virtually constituted themselves into a separate party, a rival to the official All-Union Communist party. It was unthinkable that they should do so. They had all accepted the single-party system as a *sine qua non*. Nobody had shown greater zeal in asserting this principle and drawing from it the most far-reaching and absurd conclusions than Zinoviev had. Leningrad's defiance of Moscow would have amounted almost to a declaration of civil war.

And so, when Kirov appeared in Leningrad as Stalin's envoy invested with plenary power and entitled to take command of the Northern Commune, there was nothing left for Zinoviev but to yield. Almost overnight all the local branches of the party, its editorial offices, its manifold organizations, and all the resources on which the opposition had hitherto drawn, passed into the hands of Stalin's and Kirov's nominees. Two of Zinoviev's lieutenants had controlled the armed forces of Leningrad: Lashevich, as political commissar of the garrison and the mili-

---

[1] After the fourteenth congress the Bukharinists and the Stalinists had an increased majority in the Central Committee. The new Politbureau consisted of nine instead of seven members: Stalin, Trotsky, Zinoviev, Bukharin, Rykov, Tomsky, Kalinin, Molotov, and Voroshilov. With Kalinin and Voroshilov vacillating between the right and the centre, Stalin's faction was somewhat weaker numerically than Bukharin's. Kamenev was now only an alternate member of the Politbureau. The other alternate members were Uglanov, Rudzutak, Dzerzhinsky, and Petrovsky.

tary region, and Bakaev as head of the G.P.U. Both surrendered
their offices, although Lashevich, being Vice-Commissar of
Defence, remained a member of the central government. This
was followed by a moral débâcle. As long as the leaders stood
in the full panoply of power it seemed that they had the whole
of Leningrad behind them. Now the great proletarian city appeared indifferent to their fate. The workers of Vyborg, that old
rampart of Bolshevism, were the first to desert them. For years
Zinoviev had bullied and browbeaten them; and so they were
not moved by his latest pleas on behalf of the workers and his
cry for equality, the pleas and the cry which they were to recall
nostalgically a few years hence when it was too late. Humble
men viewed the commotion as a brawl between bigwigs which
was of no concern to them. Even those who took a less cynical
view and felt with the opposition most often kept their feelings
to themselves: unemployment was rampant; and the punishment for 'disloyalty' might be the loss of one's job and starvation. Thus the active following of the Leningrad opposition
dwindled to a few hundred veterans of the revolution, a small
and closely knit band of men, who were devoted to their ideals
and leaders and who gradually found that all doors were shut
upon them.

The ease and speed with which Stalin overwhelmed the
Leningraders showed that the hopes to which Trotsky gave
himself in the days of the fourteenth congress were unfounded.
There was no sign of any further regroupment, no sign of that
rallying of the communist workers against the bureaucrats he
had expected. The Leningraders' struggle had caused no movement of sympathy, not even a ripple, in the cells of Moscow.
The party machine worked with deadly effectiveness, breaking
all resistance where it had shown itself or crushing it before it
had done so. This in itself indicated the weakness of the resistance. The working class was no longer dispersed and disintegrated as it had been a few years earlier, but it lacked political
consciousness, vigour, and the ability to assert itself. Yet it was
on a political revival in its midst that Trotsky had reckoned
when he assumed that Moscow and Leningrad would make a
common stand. Zinoviev and Kamenev too had hoped for this.
At the fourteenth congress they called for a return to proletarian
democracy and said that the working class was no longer as

splintered and demoralized as it was in the early 1920's, when the party leaders could not rely on the soundness of its political instincts and judgement. Bukharin then replied that Zinoviev and Kamenev were deluding themselves; that the working class had grown numerically by absorbing young and illiterate new-comers from the country, that consequently it was still politically immature, and that the time for a return to proletarian demo-cracy had not yet come. The void by which the Leningrad Opposition now found itself surrounded indicated that Bukharin was closer to the truth than Zinoviev and Kamenev. The work-ing class was apathetic and indifferent, although its apathy was due not merely to inherent immaturity but also to that bureau-cratic intimidation which Bukharin sought to justify. Whatever the truth of the matter, it must have become clear to Trotsky by now that he had nothing to gain by waiting. Yet, after the congress more than three months passed during which the Trotskyists and the Zinovievists did not move towards one another by one inch. Trotsky, Zinoviev, and Kamenev had not been on speaking terms since 1923; and they still said not a word to each other.

Only in April 1926 was the ice broken. At a session of the Central Committee Rykov presented a statement of economic policy. Kamenev tabled an amendment urging the Committee to take note of the ever sharper 'social differentiation of the peasantry' and to restrain the growth of capitalist farming. Trotsky tabled a separate amendment: he agreed with Kamenev's appraisal of rural conditions but added that the sluggish tempo of industrial development deprived the government of the means it needed to exercise a sufficiently strong influence on farming. In the discussion Kamenev, who as former head of the Council for Labour and Defence felt some responsibility for the in-dustrial policy which Trotsky criticized, made some barbed remarks about Trotsky. The Central Committee rejected Trot-sky's amendment. Kamenev and Zinoviev, it seems, abstained from voting. Then, when Kamenev's amendment was put to the vote, Trotsky supported it. This was the turning-point. As the session continued, they found themselves again on the same side. They unbent and moved towards each other until, at the end of the session, they acted virtually as political partners.

Only now did the three men meet in private for the first time in years. This was a strange meeting, full of heart-searchings, startling confessions, sighs of regret and of relief, forebodings, alarming warnings, and hopeful projects. Zinoviev and Kamenev were eager to make a clean breast of the past. They bemoaned the blindness which had led them to denounce Trotsky as the arch-enemy of Leninism. They admitted that they had concocted the charges against him to debar him from leadership. But had he not been mistaken also in attacking them, in reminding the party of their conflicts with Lenin in 1917, and in discrediting them rather than Stalin? They were relieved at having at last freed themselves from the net of a bizarre intrigue, the net they themselves had spun, and at having returned to serious and honest political thought and action.

As they related the various incidents of the intrigue, they made merry about Stalin, mimicking, to Trotsky's slight impatience, Stalin's behaviour and accents; but then they recalled their dealings with him with the shudder with which one remembers a nightmare. They described his slyness, perversity, and cruelty. They said that they had both written, and deposited in a safe place, letters to the effect that if they should perish suddenly and unaccountably, the world should know that this was Stalin's work; and they advised Trotsky to do the same.[1] Stalin, they maintained, had not taken Trotsky's life in 1923-4 only because he feared that some young, fervent Trotskyist might rise as an avenger. Doubtless, Zinoviev and Kamenev were eager to blacken Stalin and to advertise to Trotsky their own restraining influence on him. Trotsky himself did not take their revelations very seriously until many years later, when the Great Purges brought them back to his mind. It was indeed difficult to square what sounded like the story of a bloody court intrigue in the Kremlin of the early Tsars with the Kremlin of the Third International resounding with ideological disputes couched in Marxist terms. Had the Tsars' old fortress cast its evil spell upon Lenin's disciples? Stalin, so Zinoviev and Kamenev went on, was not interested in disputes over ideas—all he craved was power. What they failed to explain was how, if what they said was true, they could have remained in partnership with him for so long.

From these terrified and terrifying accounts and dark hints

[1] L. Trotsky, *Stalin*, p. 417.

the two men passed to plans for the future. They gave themselves to the wildest hopes. They had no doubt that all could
still be changed at a stroke. It would be enough, they said, for
the three of them appear together in public, reconciled and
reunited, to arouse enthusiasm among Bolsheviks and bring
the party back to the right road. Rarely has the blackest gloom
yielded so easily to the most cheerful innocence.

What accounted for their optimism? It was only a few months
since they had both enjoyed the fullness of power. It was only a
few weeks since Zinoviev had lost his fief in Leningrad, and he
was still President of the Communist International. Their fall
had been so rapid and sudden that they refused to believe it was
real. They had been accustomed to see a nod from either of
them swing into motion the massive wheels of party and state.
They still had in their ears the roar of popular acclaim, a false
acclaim, which had not come from the feelings of the people
but had been artificially produced by the party machine. Suddenly a deathlike stillness surrounded them. This seemed to
them to be a delusion, a misunderstanding, or a passing incident.
What brought it about was their breach with Stalin whom they
themselves had placed, or so it seemed to them, in command of
the party. Yet, who was Stalin? A coarse, half-educated, clumsy
manipulator, a misfit, whom they had repeatedly saved from
ruin because they had found him useful in their game against
Trotsky. They had never had any doubt that as man, leader,
and Bolshevik Stalin did not reach to Trotsky's ankles. Now
that they had made common cause with Trotsky, nothing would
surely be easier than to sweep Stalin out of their way and to
bring the party back under their joint leadership.[1]

Trotsky shook his head. He did not share their optimism.
He knew better the taste of defeat. He had for years felt the full
weight of the party machine as it ran against him and drove
him into the wilderness. He had a deeper insight into the pro-

[1] Ruth Fischer describes how Zinoviev in a talk with her 'broached, almost
timidly' the subject of his alliance with Trotsky. 'This is, he said, a fight for state
power. We need Trotsky, not only because without his brilliant brain and wide
support we will not win state power, but because after we have won we need a
strong hand to guide Russia and the International back to a socialist road. Moreover, no one else can organize the army. Stalin has opposed us not with manifestoes
but with power, and he can be met only with greater power, not with manifestoes.
Lashevich is with us, and if Trotsky and we join together, we shall win.' R. Fischer,
op. cit., pp. 547–8.

cesses which had deformed the party, into that 'bureaucratic degeneration' the progress of which he had watched in impotence since 1922. And behind the party machine he perceived more clearly than they did the abysmal barbarism of old Mother Russia, not to be conjured out of existence. He was also apprehensive of the fickleness and fecklessness of his new allies. He could not forget all that had passed between him and them. Yet he was unstinting in forgiveness; and he tried to steady their nerves for a long uphill struggle.

He himself was not unhopeful. He too believed that the party would be stirred by their reconciliation. Zinoviev and Kamenev volunteered to make a public admission that Trotsky had been right all along when he warned the party against its bureaucracy. In return he was prepared to say that he had been mistaken in assailing them as the leaders of that bureaucracy when he should have concentrated his fire on Stalin. He too hoped that by joining hands the two oppositions would not merely combine their followings but multiply them. The Old Guard had, after all, looked up to Zinoviev and Kamenev. It was known that Lenin's widow was in sympathy with them. In the team which led the Leningrad opposition, although it was less outstanding than the circle around Trotsky, there were such eminent men as Lashevich, still the Deputy Commissar of Defence, Smilga, one of the most able political commissars in the civil war and a distinguished economist, Sokolnikov, Bakaev, Evdokimov, and others. With such men and with Preobrazhensky, Radek, Rakovsky, Antonov-Ovseenko, Smirnov, Muralov, Krestinsky, Serebriakov, and Yoffe, to mention only these, the Joint Opposition would command far more talent and prestige than the factions of Stalin and Bukharin had at their disposal. And, despite everything, a political revival in the working class, though delayed, would still come and would put wind into the Opposition's sails.

The partners did not have the time to make precise plans or even to define clearly the points of their agreement. A day or two after their first private meeting, Trotsky had to leave Russia for medical treatment abroad. The malignant fever from which he had suffered in the last years still persisted, rising often to over 100° F., incapacitating him during the most critical moments of the struggle and compelling him to spend many months in the Caucasus. (There he spent the winters of 1924 and 1925, and the early months of the spring.) Russian doctors were unable to diagnose and urged him to consult German specialists. The Politbureau raised no objections to his journey abroad, but insisted that he undertook it on his own responsibility. About the middle of April, accompanied by his wife and a small bodyguard, he arrived in Berlin beardless and incognito, pretending to be a Ukrainian educationist by the name of Kuzmyenko. He spent most of his time in a private clinic undergoing treatment and a minor operation; but in the intervals he moved about freely, observing the depressed Berlin of those years, so different from the Imperial capital he had known, attending a May Day parade, watching a wine festival outside the city, and so on. He was thrilled to be able, for the first time since 1917, 'to move about in a crowd without attracting anyone's attention and feeling oneself part of the nameless listening and watching mass'.[1] But somehow his incognito was discovered later and the German police warned the director of the clinic that White Russian émigrés were about to make an attempt on the patient's life. Under heavy escort Trotsky moved to the Soviet Embassy, and shortly thereafter he returned home, his temperature as high as ever. It has never been discovered whether there was any ground for the alarm about the attempt on his life.[2]

During his stay in Berlin, which lasted about six weeks, he was agitated by two political events of unequal importance. In Poland, Marshal Pilsudski, supported by the Communist party, had just carried out a *coup d'état*, which established him as dictator. In Britain the protracted strike of the coal-miners had just led to the great general strike. The absurd behaviour of the

[1] 'Only once did our companions [at the May Day parade] say to me cautiously: "There they are selling your photographs." But from these photographs no one would have recognized . . . Kuzmyenko, the official of the Ukrainian Commissariat of Education.' *Moya Zhizn*, vol. ii, p. 269.

[2] While he stayed at the Berlin Embassy, Trotsky spent many hours in discussions with Krestinsky, the Ambassador, and E. Varga, the Comintern's leading economist. The subject of his discussions with Varga was socialism in a single country. Varga admitted that as an economic theory Stalin's doctrine was worthless, that socialism in one country was moonshine, but that it was nevertheless politically useful as a slogan capable of inspiring the backward masses. Recording the discussion in his private papers, Trotsky remarked of Varga that he was 'the Polonius of the Comintern'. *The Archives*.

Polish Communists resulted in part from the tangled conditions in their country, but in part from confusion in the Comintern generated by the anti-Trotskyist campaigns: the Polish party enacted on a small scale the policy which at the same time led the Chinese Communists to back General Chiang Kai-shek and the Kuomintang. The British general strike confirmed the forecasts which Trotsky had made in *Where is Britain Going?*;[1] and at once it subjected the Comintern to new strains. The British leaders of the Anglo-Soviet Council did their best to wind up the strike before it became a revolutionary explosion; and anxious to save their own respectability, they refused to accept the aid which the Soviet trade unions offered the strikers. The Anglo-Soviet Council was thus rendered ridiculous. The British trade-union leaders still derived some advantage, however, from its existence: at the critical stage of the general strike the Communists, anxious not to embarrass the Council, were extremely reticent in criticizing their conduct. Trotsky even before he was back in Moscow assailed in *Pravda* the policy of the Anglo-Soviet Council on which Stalin and Bukharin had placed great hopes.[2]

It was only after Trotsky's return that he and the two ex-triumvirs set out in earnest to unite their factions. This was not easy. For one thing, the Trotskyist faction had been dispersed and had to be reassembled. Its strength turned out to be far less than it had been in 1923. For another, the followers of the two factions were not at all eager to unite. Their old animosities had not yet evaporated. They still distrusted each other. Among Trotsky's associates some favoured the coalition; but others, Antonov-Ovseenko and Radek, would have allied themselves with Stalin rather than with Zinoviev. Still others wished a plague on both their houses: 'Stalin will betray us', Mrachkovsky said, 'and Zinoviev will sneak away'. The rank-and-file Trotskyists in Leningrad at first refused even to disclose themselves to the Zinovievists, at whose hands they had suffered

---

[1] In his autobiography Trotsky says that the confirmation came earlier than he had expected it. *Moya Zhizn*, vol. ii, p. 272.

[2] *Pravda*, 26 May 1926. Meantime Stalin eliminated Zinoviev's followers from the Executive of the Comintern. At a session in May the Executive voted for the demotion of Fischer and Maslov, Treint, Domski, and other Zinovievist leaders of the German, French, and Polish parties.

persecution and from whom they had been accustomed to conceal their comings and goings almost as much as they had once concealed them from the Tsarist *Okhrana*. What will happen, they asked, if the Zinovievists change their minds and make peace with Stalin? We shall then have delivered ourselves into the hands of our persecutors. Trotsky had to send Preobrazhensky to Leningrad to allay these fears and persuade his recalcitrant followers to accept the coalition. The Zinovievists were not less bewildered. When the news of the proposed coalition first reached Leningrad, they rushed to Moscow to remonstrate with their leaders for their 'surrender to Trotskyism'. Zinoviev and Lashevich had to explain that Trotskyism was a bogy which they themselves had invented; and that they had no use for it any longer. The admission could not but shock the unfortunate Leningraders who had taken Zinoviev's accusations against Trotsky seriously and had repeated them after him. But even when the mutual aversions were overcome or subdued and the two factions began to merge, the members of both still felt that they were entering a misalliance.[1]

Among the chiefs, too, the first elation had cooled off. Zinoviev and Kamenev began to look over their shoulders. They had no intention of pushing their differences with the ruling factions to the point of an irreparable breach. They felt uneasy at the charge that they 'surrendered to Trotskyism'. Having admitted that they had wronged Trotsky, they still had their record to defend; they were anxious to save for themselves the half-spurious glory of 'pure Leninism' in which they had walked. And so when on his return, surveying the events of the last weeks, Trotsky began to argue that the Polish Communists had supported Pilsudski's *coup* because the Comintern had instructed them to strive for that 'democratic dictatorship of the workers and the peasants' which Lenin had advocated in 1905, and not for proletarian dictatorship, Zinoviev and Kamenev could not agree. That 'democratic dictatorship' was a taboo of their 'old Bolshevism'; and although it was not very important in the case of Poland,[2] it was to crop up again and again in the

---

[1] V. Serge, *Le Tournant obscur*, p. 102.

[2] Even Bukharin and Stalin disavowed the action of the Polish Communists. See Deutscher, 'La Tragédie du Communisme Polonais' in *Les Temps Modernes*, March 1958.

controversy over China next year. They were also taken aback by the bluntness with which Trotsky attacked the Anglo-Soviet Council, saying that it had never served any useful purpose and that it should be disbanded. Zinoviev was willing to criticize the Politbureau and the British Communists for 'hob-nobbing' with the leaders of the British trade unions; but he would not 'wreck' the Council which he had helped to sponsor. Above all, he was wary of alienating those men of the Old Guard who either backed Stalin with reservations or vacillated and urged moderation on all factions. Briefly, the two ex-triumvirs were willing to join hands with Trotsky; but they were already shrinking from an all-out attack on Stalin and Bukharin. Thus Trotsky had no sooner made the alliance with them than he had to patch up differences and make concessions. He promised Zinoviev and Kamenev to respect the taboo of the 'democratic dictatorship of workers and peasants' and to waive his demand for the disbandment of the Anglo-Soviet Council. This allowed him to establish a fairly wide measure of agreement with them on other questions.

The battle was joined, partly on Stalin's initiative, in the first days of June. Immediately after Trotsky's return, Stalin met him at the Politbureau with two fresh, incongruous yet damaging, accusations: Trotsky allegedly exhibited an impermissible 'hostility towards the British Communist Party'; and in domestic matters he gave proof of ill will and perverse defeatism when he declared that he was 'afraid of a good harvest'.[1] Trotsky refuted these charges as best he could. Then, on 6 June, he addressed a challenging letter to the Politbureau, saying that unless the party was reformed thoroughly and honestly, it would awaken one day to find itself under the undisguised rule of an autocrat.

Thus he resumed his open struggle with Stalin. He had not chosen the moment all by himself—the action and the plight of the Leningrad Opposition induced him to re-enter the fray at this time. In any case, the years of his waiting in silence or

---

[1] The first charge was based on a complaint from the British Communist party; the second on a statement in which Trotsky had said that the problem of relations between country and town would remain acute no matter whether there was a good or a bad harvest this year. If the harvest was bad, there would be a shortage of food; if it was good, the kulak would be stronger, more self-confident, and would have greater bargaining power. *The Archives.*

reticence were over. He knew that they had given him nothing: all the 'rotten compromises' with Stalin, against which Lenin had warned him, had been in vain. He was willing to compromise with Zinoviev and Kamenev in order to keep them aligned against Stalin; but he was also ready to fight it out without them. He had sized up his implacable enemy, and he knew that there was no retreat. He had lived these last years to fight another day. Now the day had come and the die was cast.

CHAPTER V

The Decisive Contest: 1926–7

THE Joint Opposition contended with the Stalinists and the Bukharinists for about eighteen months. During this time Trotsky was engaged in a political battle so intense that by comparison his earlier encounters with all the triumvirs were mere skirmishes. Tireless, unrelenting, straining every nerve, marshalling matchless powers of argument and persuasion, ranging over an exceptionally wide compass of ideas and policies, and at last supported by a large section, probably the majority, of the Old Guard which had hitherto spurned him, he made a prodigious effort to arouse the Bolshevik party and to influence the further course of the revolution. As a fighter he may appear to posterity not smaller in the years 1926–7 than he was in 1917—even greater. The strength of his mind was the same. The flame of revolutionary passion burned in him as fierce and bright as ever. And he gave proof of a force of character superior to that which he had needed and had shown in 1917. He was fighting adversaries in the camp of the revolution, not class enemies; and for such a struggle courage not merely greater but of a different kind was required. Some years later even his adversaries, when they related privately the incidents of this strife and described his mighty thrusts and his conduct under the blows, conveyed the image of a fallen Titan—rejoicing over his fall, they still recollected in awe the greatness they had struck down.[1]

Of course, the other leaders, too, brought to the contest strong passions, the resources of their uncommon intellects steeped in Marxism, tactical ingenuity, and an energy and determination which even in the weakest of them were still well above the average. The issues over which they struggled were among the greatest and the gravest over which men had ever fought: the fate of 160 million people; and the destinies of communism in Europe and Asia.

[1] The reference is to accounts of the struggle given to the author by many party members in Moscow in 1931.

Yet this great contest took place in a frightful void. On either side only small groups were involved. The nation was mute. Nobody knew or could know what it thought; and even to guess how its sympathies were divided was difficult. The struggle was waged over matters of its life and death; but it was waged above its head. On the face of things, nothing that the nation felt or thought could affect the outcome—the mass of the people was deprived of all means of political expression. Yet not for a moment did the antagonists take their eyes off the workers and the peasants, for inarticulate though these were, in the last instance it was their attitude that decided the issue. To win, the ruling factions needed only the passivity of the masses, while the Opposition needed for its success their political awakening and activity. Consequently, the former had the easier task: it was much simpler to confuse the masses and to breed apathy in them than to make them see the issues at stake and arouse their spirit. Furthermore, the Opposition, in its attempts to appeal to the people, was from the beginning hampered by its own inhibitions. Considering itself a section of the ruling party and continuing to acknowledge the party's unique responsibility for the revolution, the Opposition could not with a clear conscience appeal against its adversaries to the working class, the bulk of which was outside the party. Yet, as the struggle went on, mounting in bitterness, the Opposition was driven to try and seek support precisely among that mass of workers. It then came to feel the full burden of the tame and torpid popular mood. Nobody suffered from this more severely than did Trotsky: he hurled all his thunder and lightning into the void.

Nor do all the disputed questions appear in historical retrospect as real as they were to the chief actors. Some of the major issues were to lose outline and to fade soon after the disputes were over; and together with them some of the divisions which had seemed deep and unbridgeable became blurred or vanished. With cold violence Stalin denounced Trotsky as the enemy of the peasant, while Trotsky arraigned Stalin as the friend of the kulak. The sound of these recriminations still filled the air when Stalin set out to annihilate the kulak. Similarly, Stalin warned the country against the 'super-industrialization' for which Trotsky allegedly stood; but then he himself embarked with breathless precipitancy upon the course of action he had just condemned as pernicious.

As the struggle proceeds a mist envelops also most of the characters. If following this narrative we keep in mind the ultimate fate that befell Zinoviev, Kamenev, Bukharin, Rykov, Tomsky, and many others, we are struck by the inconstancy and futility of their behaviour, even though we may discern their motives. Every one of these men is completely submerged in the business of the day or of the moment, and utterly incapable of looking beyond it and forestalling next day's evil. Not only Stalin and events drive them to their doom—they drive each other; and at various times they do so with an obsessive fury which distorts their characters and contorts their minds. The imposing figures of the leaders shrink and dwindle. They become helpless victims of circumstance. The giants turn into moths rushing blindly and chasing each other madly into the flame. Only two figures seem to confront each other in irreducible reality and fixed hostility to the end—Trotsky and Stalin.

.   .   .   .

In the summer of 1926 the Joint Opposition feverishly organized its adherents. It sent out its emissaries to party branches in Moscow and Leningrad to make contact there with members who had been known to hold critical views of official policy in order to form them into Opposition groups and induce them to speak with the Opposition's voice to their party cells. Anxious to spread the network of its groups, the Opposition sent out its emissaries to many provincial towns as well, furnishing them with instructions, papers, and 'theses', dealing with its attitudes.

Soon the comings and goings of the emissaries attracted the attention of the General Secretariat, which kept track of the movements of those suspected to be in sympathy with the Opposition. Trotskyists and Zinovievists were summoned to party headquarters to explain their doings. The party committees, whenever they learned of any gatherings of oppositionists, sent their representatives on the spot to disband the meetings as illegal. When this was of no avail, they dispatched squads of zealots and ruffians to break up the meetings. The Opposition was thus driven to organize more or less clandestinely. Its supporters met stealthily in the homes of humble workers in suburban tenement blocks. When the squads of disrupters traced them there too and dispersed them, they assembled in small groups at cemeteries, in woods on the outskirts, and so on; and they posted guards and sent out patrols to protect their meetings. The long hand of the General Secretariat reached to the remoteness of these odd assembly places as well. There was no lack of grotesque incidents. One day, for instance, the sleuths of the Moscow committee discovered a clandestine meeting in a wood outside the city. The meeting was presided over by a high official of the Executive of the Comintern, one of Zinoviev's lieutenants; and it was addressed by no less a person than Lashevich, the Deputy Commissar of War. Zinoviev, as President of the Communist International, used the facilities of his office for disseminating Opposition papers and contacting groups. The headquarters of the International became the hub, as it were, of the Opposition; and this fact, too, quickly attracted Stalin's attention.

Such were the circumstances under which the Opposition managed to recruit and organize several thousand regular adherents. The estimates of its actual membership, of which approximately one half were Trotskyists and the other Zinovievists, vary from 4,000 to 8,000.[1] The remnants of the Workers' Opposition, a few hundred men at the most, also declared their accession. The Joint Opposition was anxious to rally all who were willing to join, regardless of past differences; it aspired to become the great assemblage of all Bolshevik dissenters. It may therefore be held that it suffered a decisive initial defeat when it did not succeed in recruiting a larger following. Compared with the party's total membership, which amounted to about three-quarters of a million, a few thousand oppositionists formed a tiny minority.

The strength of the factions should not, however, be seen only in the light of these figures. The great majority of the party was a jelly-like mass; it consisted of meek and obedient members, without a mind and a will of their own. It was more than four years now since Lenin had declared that the party was virtually worthless as a policy-making body, and that only the Old Guard, that 'thin stratum' which counted no more than several thousand members, was the repository of Bolshevik

[1] The lower estimate comes from Stalinist sources, the higher from Trotskyist.

traditions and principles.[1] The result of the Opposition's recruiting drive ought to be judged in the light of this statement.
The Opposition drew its support not from the inert mass but
from the thoughtful, active, and energetic elements, mostly
from the Old Guard, and partly from young Communists.
Opportunists and careerists kept aloof. The sight of broken-up
meetings and the loud threats, to which Stalinist and Bukharinist
zealots treated the adherents of the Opposition, frightened away
the timid and the cautious. The few trimmers who in 1923
had still put their stakes on the wrong horse and had described
themselves as Trotskyists now had the chance to redeem themselves by joining the ruling factions. The several thousand
Trotskyists and Zinovievists were, like the professional revolutionaries of old, men and women who felt strongly about the
great issues and braved grave personal risks. Most of them had
been prominent among the Bolshevik cadres in the most critical
times and had had many political ties with the working class.
It is doubtful whether the core of the ruling factions was
stronger even numerically. For the time being the Bukharinists
seemed to be more popular than the Stalinists; yet, two years
hence they were to be defeated far more easily than the Joint
Opposition had been, although one of their leaders presided
over the Council of the People's Commissars, another over the
trade unions, and still another over the Communist International. As to the Stalinist faction, its strength lay not in its
size, but in its leader's complete mastery of the party machine.
This allowed him to draw on all the party's resources, to rig
elections, to manufacture majorities, to veil the sectional and
personal character of his policy—in a word, to identify his own
faction with the party. At the most, only about 20,000 people
were of their own choice, directly, and actively involved in the
momentous inner-party conflict.

The Joint Opposition officially proclaimed its existence at a
session of the Central Committee in the middle of July.[2] Shortly
after the opening of the session, Trotsky read a statement of

---

[1] See p. 20.

[2] This was a joint session of the Central Committee and the Central Contro
Commission; it lasted from 14 to 23 July. *The Trotsky Archives, KPSS v Rezolu-
tsyakh*, vol. ii, pp. 148–69. N. Popov, *Outline History of the CPSU*, vol. ii, pp. 274 ff.
L. Trotsky, *Moya Zhizn*, vol. ii, pp. 260–75. E. Yaroslavsky, *Aus der Geschichte der
Komm. Partei d. Sowjetunion*, vol. ii, pp. 394 ff.

policy in which he, Zinoviev, and Kamenev, expressing regret over their past quarrels, declared it as their common purpose to free the party from the tyranny of its 'apparatus' and to work for the restoration of inner-party democracy. The Opposition defined its attitude as that of the Bolshevik Left, defending the interests of the working class against the wealthy peasantry, the N.E.P. bourgeoisie, and the bureaucracy. The first of its desiderata was a demand for the up-grading of industrial wages. The government had decreed a wage stop, authorizing no increase in workers' earnings unless it was justified by a rise in productivity. Against this the Opposition held that the condition of the working class was so wretched—wages were still lower than before the revolution—that in order to achieve a rise in productivity it was necessary first to improve the workers' lot. They should be free to stake out claims through the trade unions and to bargain with the industrial administration, instead of being compelled to submit to dictates and of seeing the trade unions turned into the state's obedient tools. The Opposition also demanded a reform in taxation. The government drew its revenue increasingly from indirect taxes, the brunt of which was, as always, borne by the poor. This burden, the Opposition argued, ought to be lightened, and the N.E.P. bourgeoisie ought to be made to pay higher tax rates on profits.[1]

From a parallel viewpoint the Opposition approached rural affairs. There, too, it urged a reform of taxation, claiming that the single agricultural tax, which was then in force, benefited the rich. It urged that the great mass of *bednyaks*, 30–40 per cent. of all smallholders, be exempt from taxation, and that the rest of the peasantry pay a progressive tax which would fall heaviest on

[1] The Opposition regarded it as scandalous that the government should obtain a high proportion of revenue from the state monopoly of vodka and acquire thereby a vested interest in the drunkenness of the masses. What the government gained as producer of vodka it lost as industrial employer through the inefficiency of drunken workers and a high rate of accidents in industry. The government excused the vodka monopoly on the ground that it combated effectively the even more disastrous mass consumption of home-brewed alcohol. This was admittedly a difficult question. The Opposition proposed that the government should tentatively, as an experiment, suspend the vodka monopoly for a year or two. The majority rejected this proposal. Within the first week of the October Revolution, we remember, the Bolsheviks had to contend with the scourge of mass drunkenness which belonged to the heritage of Mother Russia. (*The Prophet Armed*, pp. 322–4.) Ten years later the scourge was still there; it was used by the rulers as a fiscal convenience and it kept the masses politically befuddled.

the kulaks. The Opposition further pressed for the collectivization of farming. It did not advocate forced or wholesale collectivization or the 'liquidation of the kulak as a class'. It envisaged a long-term reform to be carried out gradually, with the peasantry's consent, and to be furthered by the government's credit policy and the use of industrial resources. None of the Opposition's proposals went farther than the demands for a 50 per cent. rise in tax rates for kulaks and for virtually compulsory grain loans which would allow the government to step up exports and to proceed with the import of industrial machinery. In the face of strong official denials the Opposition maintained that the yield of new taxation and of the grain loans should enable the government to increase industrial investment funds, despite rises in wages and tax reliefs for poor peasants.

The Opposition's programme culminated in the demand for more rapid industrialization. Once again Trotsky, this time with Zinoviev's and Kamenev's support, charged the government with inability to think ahead and plan. So timid had official policy been and so resigned to the 'snail's pace' that as a rule industrial development ran ahead of official anticipations. In 1925 the iron and steel industries and transport reached the targets which the Supreme Council of the National Economy had not expected to be attained before 1930. How much more impetus could a far-sighted and vigorous direction impart to the economy! The fourteenth congress had declared itself in favour of raising the targets and accelerating the tempo. But these resolutions had had no practical effect: they were plainly ignored by a routine-ridden bureaucracy. To break the inertia nothing less would do than a comprehensive and specific plan covering five or even eight years ahead. 'Give us a real Five Year Plan' was the Opposition's watchword.

The more firmly the Opposition pressed for the development of the socialist sector of the economy, the more categorically did it reject socialism in a single country. This became the central 'ideological' issue. The Opposition repudiated the idea of a nationally self-sufficient socialism as incompatible with Leninist tradition and Marxist principle. It held that despite all the delays in the spread of international revolution, the party had no reason to view the future of the U.S.S.R. in isolation and to dismiss beforehand the prospect of revolutionary developments abroad. The building of socialism would in any case extend over many decades, and not just a few years—why then should it be assumed that the Soviet Union would all this time stand alone as a workers' state? This was what the Stalinists and Bukharinists assumed—otherwise they would not have insisted so stubbornly that the party must accept socialism in a single country as an article of faith.

Here then was the party's entire international orientation at stake. To assume beforehand that the Soviet Union would have to build socialism alone throughout was to abandon the prospect of international revolution; and to abandon it was to refuse to work for it, even to obstruct it. The Opposition maintained that by 'eliminating' international revolution from their theoretical conception, Stalin and Bukharin tended to eliminate it also from their practical policies. Already the Comintern's strategy was strongly coloured by Bukharin's views on the 'stabilization of capitalism'; and both Stalin and Bukharin, so Trotsky and Zinoviev pointed out, were steering European communism if not towards self-liquidation then at least towards an accommodation with the parties of the Second International and the reformist trade unions. This took the form of an 'opportunist' united front, in which the Communist parties followed the Social Democratic lead and adapted themselves to the reformist attitude. Of such tactics—the very negation of directives worked out at earlier congresses of the Communist International—the Anglo-Soviet Council was the outstanding example. It arose from a pact between the leaders of the trade unions in the two countries. At no point did it or could it bring Communists in contact with the reformist masses and enable them to influence the latter. At no point, therefore, did or could the pact further the class struggle in Britain. On the contrary, the Opposition argued, by cultivating friendship with the British trade-union leaders while these curbed industrial unrest and even broke a general strike, Soviet Communists contributed to the confusion of the British workers, who could not tell friend from foe. Trotsky and, to a lesser extent, Zinoviev and Kamenev concentrated their attack on the Anglo-Soviet Council as the epitome of that tacit abandonment of revolutionary purpose which they saw as the premiss and the corollary of socialism in a single country.

The statement which Trotsky read at the July session of the Central Committee contained little that either he or his partners had not said before. But this was the first time that they brought together the criticisms and proposals in a comprehensive declaration of policy and confronted the ruling factions with a joint challenge. The reaction was vehement. The debates were heated; and the exacerbation was heightened by a grim incident. Dzerzhinsky, highly strung and ill, delivered a long and violent speech denouncing the leaders of the Opposition, especially Kamenev. For two hours his high-pitched scream pierced the ears of the audience. Then, leaving the rostrum, he suffered a heart attack, collapsed, and died in the lobby before the eyes of the Central Committee.

Straightway the Central Committee rejected the Opposition's demand for a review of the wage scales. The leaders of the majority maintained that goods were scarce and that rises in wages, if unrelated to productivity, would cause inflation and worsen rather than improve the workers' lot. The Central Committee refused to exempt poor farmers from taxation and to impose heavier taxes on others. It resisted the demand for accelerated industrialization. It, finally, reaffirmed its support for Stalin's and Bukharin's Comintern policy and in particular for the Anglo-Soviet Council. But over all these matters the ruling factions were embarrassed and on the defensive; and it was not on grounds of policy but on those of party discipline that Stalin counter-attacked.

Stalin charged the chiefs of the Opposition with forming a regular faction within the party and thus violating the Leninist ban, now more than five years old. He aimed his blow at the weaker, the Zinovievist, section of the Opposition. He impeached Zinoviev for abusing his position as President of the Communist International and furthering the Opposition's activity from his headquarters; he arraigned Lashevich and a group of lesser oppositionists for holding the 'clandestine' meeting in the woods outside Moscow; and, finally, he brought up the case of one Ossovsky, who had expressed the view that the Opposition should constitute itself into an independent political movement and engage Stalin's and Bukharin's party in open hostility *from without* rather than act as a loyal opposition *within*. Trotsky dissociated himself and the Opposition from this view; but he pointed out that if some members came to despair of the party and saw no hope of reforming it from within, the blame lay with the leaders who had done their utmost to block every attempt at reform. The Central Committee resolved to expel Ossovsky from the party, to dismiss Lashevich from the Central Committee and the Commissariat of War, and to deprive Zinoviev of his seat in the Politbureau.[1]

Thus at this first formal encounter the Joint Opposition met with a severe reverse. The expulsion from the party of one of its adherents, even though he was a little-known 'extremist', was a menacing warning. With Lashevich's demotion the Opposition was cut off from the Commissariat of War. The worst shock was, of course, Zinoviev's dismissal from the Politbureau. As Kamenev had since the fourteenth congress been only an alternate member, both ex-triumvirs had already lost voting rights on the Politbureau; and of the chiefs of the Opposition Trotsky alone held his seat. It was because of his role in the Politbureau that Zinoviev had presided over the Communist International; it was now unthinkable that he should go on presiding. That Stalin had dared to depose the man whom only a short time ago many had considered as the senior triumvir was a sign of his extraordinary strength and self-confidence. He carried out the act with lightning dispatch and observing punctiliously all the statutory niceties. The proposal for Zinoviev's demotion had been duly tabled before the Central Committee, which alone was entitled to appoint and dismiss Politbureau members; and a massive majority voted for it.

Already at this stage there was in theory nothing to prevent Stalin from depriving Trotsky too of his Politbureau seat. He was not quite sure, however, that he would obtain the same massive majority for further reprisals; and he realized that a show of moderation could only strengthen his hand. By tackling the Opposition piecemeal he prepared party opinion all the better for the final show-down. Meantime he had little to fear from the Opposition's declarations of principle and statements of policy or from its demonstrations of protest staged at the Central Committee or the Politbureau. Little of what the

---

[1] N. Popov, *Outline History of the CPSU*, vol. ii, pp. 279–92; E. Yaroslavsky, op. cit., part ii, chapter 10; *The Trotsky Archives*; Stalin, *Sochinenya*, vol. viii, pp. 176–203; *KPSS v Rezolutsyakh*, vol. ii, pp. 160–6.

chiefs of the Opposition said there percolated to the cells down below and still less transpired in the press. As long as this was so and the ruling coalition maintained its solidarity, the verbal battles in the Politbureau and the Central Committee led the Opposition nowhere.

Precisely because of this there was nothing left for the Opposition to do but to appeal at last to the rank and file against the Politbureau and the Central Committee. In the summer of 1926 Trotsky and Zinoviev instructed their adherents to bring their common views to the notice of all party members, to disseminate policy statements, tracts, and 'theses', and to speak up in the cells. The chiefs of the Opposition themselves went into the factories and workshops to address gatherings. Trotsky made surprise appearances at large meetings held in Moscow's motor-car factory and railway workshops. But the leaders of the Opposition were no more fortunate in their efforts to shape party opinion from below than they had been in their attempts to influence policy from above. The party machine was ahead of them. Everywhere its agents, zealots and hecklers, met them with derisive booings, smothered their arguments in an infernal noise, intimidated audiences, broke up meetings, and made it physically impossible for the speakers to obtain a hearing. For the first time in nearly thirty years, for the first time since he had begun his career as revolutionary orator, Trotsky found himself facing a crowd helplessly. Against the scornful uproar with which he was met and the obsessive hissings and hootings, his most cogent arguments, his genius for persuasion, and his powerful and sonorous voice were of no avail. The insults to which other speakers were subjected were even more brutal. It was clear that the Opposition's first concerted appeal to party opinion had met with failure.

Stalin presently boasted that it was the good honest Bolshevik rank and file that had administered the Opposition the well-deserved rebuff. The Opposition replied that he had incited against it the worst elements, Lumpenproletarians and hooligans, who would not allow the decent rank and file to become acquainted with the Opposition's views. Stalin had indeed had no scruple; and the uproar with which his agents met Trotsky, Zinoviev, and their friends could hardly be mistaken for the 'voice of the people'. This, however, did not fully account for the Opposition's humiliating experience. Gangs of rowdies could disrupt the large meetings because the majority was either in sympathy or at least indifferent. An interested and self-disciplined audience usually knows how to eject or silence noisy individuals who try to prevent it from listening and collecting its thoughts. Behind the hooligans with their catcalls there were silent crowds, tame or unimpressionable enough not to think it worthwhile to exert themselves and assure order. At bottom it was the apathy of the rank and file that worsted the Opposition.

Yet the claims which the Opposition had raised on behalf of the workers, such as the demand for a rise in wages, were calculated to destroy apathy. Why then did they fail to evoke a response? On wages the ruling factions made a show of yielding. In July they had categorically refused to consider the claim, declaring that an increase in wages would greatly harm the national economy. But, in September, seeing that their adversaries were about to appeal to the rank and file, Stalin and Bukharin forestalled them and promised a rise to benefit the lowest paid and the most discontented groups of workers. The excuse for the change of policy was that the economic situation had radically improved, although no such improvement did or could occur within two months. The Opposition thus scored a partial success, but saw itself robbed of a most effective argument. Stalin further confounded it when he began to appropriate Trotsky's ideas on industrial policy. He was not by any means ready as yet for all-out industrialization; but in framing his resolutions and statements he borrowed many formulas and even entire passages from Trotsky.

The outlines of the party's rural policy were similarly blurred. Stalin insisted that the differences between the ruling factions and the Opposition were over the treatment not of the kulak, but of the middle peasant. The outcry against the kulak at the fourteenth congress had had its effect. It had aroused in the cadres a sneaking suspicion of the neo-Populist school. Bukharin could no longer afford to speak in public about the need to appease the strong farmer. The climate of Bolshevik opinion had changed: the kulak was once again recognized as *the* enemy of socialism. Although the government was still wary of antagonizing him and refused to burden him with higher taxes, it was in no mood to make new concessions either. There was now no question of any neo-N.E.P. Not that matters had improved. Caught between conflicting pressures, official policy was fixed in immobility. It had the worst of both worlds: it could count neither on the advantages which appeasement of the kulak might have yielded, nor on those which rigorous social and fiscal measures might have produced. The Opposition still had a strong case. Stalin, however, succeeded in diverting attention from it: he accused Trotsky and Zinoviev of trying to push the party to a conflict with the many millions of the middle peasants, those muzhiks *par excellence* who were no exploiters, whose attachment to private property was therefore harmless, and whose good will was essential to the alliance between proletariat and peasantry.

The Opposition had in truth no quarrel with the middle peasants.[1] It did not ask the party to turn the fiscal screws on them—and the mass of *serednyaks*, barely self-sufficient on their smallholdings, could not contribute much anyhow to the solution of the nation's food problem. However, the charge that the Opposition was out for the *serednyak*'s blood damaged its cause. Once again, as in 1923 and 1924, hosts of propagandists depicted Trotsky as the peasantry's arch-enemy; and they added that Zinoviev and Kamenev had become infected with Trotsky's hostility towards the muzhik. In the party cells people could no longer make head or tail of the charges and counter-charges. They had been apprehensive of Bukharin's pleas for the strong farmer; and now they became at least as distrustful of Trotsky's and Zinoviev's intentions. The last thing the workers, most of whom had their roots in the country, could look forward to was a conflict with the peasantry. They wished for safety first. As this was what Stalin seemed to offer them, they were wary of sticking out their necks for the Opposition.

Stalin's strength lay in the appeal he made to the popular craving for peace, safety, and stability. Trotsky once again appeared to go against that craving and to offend it. The weariness of the masses and their fear of risky experiments formed a constant background to the struggle. On that weariness and fear Stalin played even more strongly when he sought to justify his

[1] The Opposition claimed, however, that the Stalinists and the Bukharinists often played down the strength of capitalist farming by classifying the kulak as a *serednyak*.

foreign policy. Once again he depicted Trotsky as the Quixote of communism, who might involve the party in the most perilous ventures.

Trotsky's policy [he said, defending the Anglo-Soviet Council] is one of spectacular gestures . . . he takes as his starting point not real men, not real and living workers . . . but some ideal and airy creatures, revolutionaries from head to foot. . . . We saw him applying this policy for the first time during the negotiations at Brest Litovsk, when he refused to sign the peace between Russia and Germany and indulged instead in a spectacular gesture, assuming that this could arouse the workers of all countries against imperialism. . . . You know well, comrades, how dearly we paid for that. Into whose hands did Trotsky's spectacular gesture play? Into the hands of . . . all those who strove to strangle the still unconsolidated Soviet Republic. . . . No, comrades, we are not going to adopt this policy of spectacular gestures, we are not going to do it today any more than we did at the time of Brest . . . we do not want our party to become a plaything in the hands of our enemies.[1]

The juxtaposition of the Brest Litovsk Peace and the Anglo-Soviet Council was altogether incongruous: even a straight breach between Soviet and British trade-union leaders—and because of Zinoviev's objections the Opposition did not press for this—could not conceivably expose the Soviet Union to dangers remotely comparable with those it had had to face during the Brest Litovsk crisis. The charge sounded even more grotesque when Bukharin made it: in 1918 he led the war party which was defeated only when Trotsky, on whose vote the issue hung, cast his vote for peace.[2] But who knew and who remembered the details of that great drama? The memory of the Bolshevik party was short; all the easier was it to arouse it to fear of Trotsky's 'heroic gestures'.

This was also the mood in which the ordinary Bolshevik listened to the debates over socialism in a single country. It was extremely difficult for him to judge the issue on its merits. The controversy, in so far as it had not bogged down in distortions and sophistries, was between two schools of economists, one conceiving the 'building of socialism' within a nationally self-contained system and the other viewing it in the context of the

[1] Stalin, *Sochinenya*, vol. viii, pp. 190–1.
[2] See *The Prophet Armed*, chapter xi.

broadest international division of labour. Only the most educated party members could follow the argument on this level.
The rank and file could not grasp why Zinoviev and Kamenev
insisted that Russia's internal resources, although abundant
enough to allow much progress, would not be sufficient for the
establishment of fully fledged socialism. Still less could they
absorb Trotsky's reasoning which was rooted in deeper layers of
Marxist thought. He argued that although socialist revolution
might for a time be confined to the boundaries of a single state,
socialism could not be achieved within the framework of any
nation-state, not even one as vast as the Soviet Union or as the
United States. Marxism had always envisaged socialism in
terms of an international community, because it held that historically society tended towards integration on an ever larger
scale. In the transition from the feudal to the bourgeois order
Europe had overcome its medieval particularisms. The bourgeoisie had created the national market; and on its basis the
modern nation-state had taken shape. But the productive forces
and economic energies of the advanced nations could not settle
within national boundaries; they had outgrown these even
under capitalism with its international division of labour, the
outstanding feat of progress achieved by the bourgeois West.[1]
Marx, who on this point was Smith's and Ricardo's faithful
disciple, had written in the *Communist Manifesto*:

> Modern industry has established the world market . . . [which]
> has given an immense development to commerce, navigation, and
> communication by land. . . . The need of a constantly expanding
> market for its products chases the bourgeoisie over the whole surface
> of the globe. . . . The bourgeoisie has given . . . a cosmopolitan
> character to production and consumption in every country. *To the
> great chagrin of reactionaries, the bourgeoisie has drawn from under the feet
> of industry the national ground on which it stood. . . . In place of the old local
> and national seclusion and self-sufficiency we now have the many-sided inter-
> course of nations and their universal interdependence.*[2]

How then, Trotsky asked, could one see socialism as standing
only on its national ground, in seclusion and self-sufficiency?
The high level of technology, efficiency, and abundance which

---

[1] In the 1930's Trotsky accordingly saw in the relapse of the bourgeois West into
economic nationalism (especially in the autarchy of the Third Reich) the surest
sign of its decay.   [2] My italics.

socialism presupposed, a level superior to that achieved by capitalism, could not be attained within a closed and backward economy. Socialism was even more dependent than capitalism had been on the 'many-sided intercourse of nations'. It must carry international division of labour incomparably farther than the bourgeoisie had ever dreamt of carrying it; and while the latter developed it only fitfully and undesignedly, socialism would plan it systematically and rationally. The concept of socialism in one country was therefore not merely unreal—it was reactionary as well: it ignored the logic of historic develop-' ment and the structure of the modern world. Even more emphatically than before Trotsky advocated the idea of the United States of Europe as a preliminary to a socialist world community.

Whatever the merits or demerits of this reasoning, it was beyond the ken of the rank-and-file Bolshevik whose support the Opposition sought to enlist. Two years later, when he was already in exile, Radek, pondering over the reasons for the Opposition's defeat, wrote to Trotsky that they had approached their task as propagandists, dealing in great but abstract theories, not as political agitators seeking to arouse response for popular and practical ideas.[1] No doubt, Radek wrote this in a defeatist mood—he was presently to surrender to Stalin—and he did the Opposition less than justice. The practical ideas which the Opposition had advanced (its proposals about wages, taxation, industrial policy, proletarian democracy, and so forth) also failed to impress ordinary party members. There was, all the same, some truth in Radek's remark. The rank and file were weary, disillusioned, and prone to isolationism. Not for them were the sweeping historical prospects Trotsky unfolded. They craved, as Varga had put it, for a doctrine of consolation which would compensate them for the sacrifices they had made and were called upon to make. Socialism in one country was a feat of the myth-creation which was to mark the whole progress of Stalinism and which sought to conceal the gulf between Bolshevik promise and fulfilment. To Trotsky that myth-creation was a new opium for the people which the party should have refused to purvey.

[1] See Radek's memorandum 'Nado dodumat do kontsa', written in 1928 (no precise date), in *The Trotsky Archives*.

Our party [he wrote] in its heroic period looked forward un-reservedly to international revolution, not to socialism in one coun-try. Under this banner and with a programme which stated frankly that backward Russia alone . . . could not achieve socialism, our communist youth passed through the most strenuous years of civil war, enduring hunger, cold, and epidemics, worked of its own accord week-end shifts of hard labour (*subbotniki*), studied, and paid for every step forward with numberless sacrifices. Party members and *comsomoltsy* fought at the fronts and [on their rest days] volun-teered to load logs of wood at the railway stations, not because they hoped to build with these logs national socialism—they served the cause of international revolution, for which it was essential that the Soviet fortress should hold out; every log went to buttress that fortress. . . . The times have changed . . . but the principle still retains its full force. The worker, the poor peasant, the partisan, and the young communist have shown by their entire conduct up to 1925 that they have no need of the new gospel. It is the official who looks down on the masses, the petty administrator who does not wish to be disturbed, and the hanger-on of the party machine . . . who need it. It is they who think . . . that you cannot deal with the people without a doctrine of consolation. . . . The worker who understands that it is impossible to build a socialist paradise as an oasis amid the inferno of world capitalism and who realizes that the fate of the Soviet Republic and his own fate depend entirely on international revolution—that worker will fulfill his duties towards the Soviet Union much more energetically than the one who is told and believes that we already have 'a 90 percent socialism'.[1]

Unfortunately for the Opposition and for Trotsky, the weary and disillusioned mass, and not merely the 'petty official and the hanger-on', responded to the doctrine of consolation more readily than to the heroic evocation of permanent revolution. They deluded themselves that Stalin offered them the safer, the easier, the painless road.

Socialism in one country also stirred the people's national pride, while Trotsky's pleas for internationalism suggested to the simple-minded that he held that Russia could not rely on herself and so he maintained that her salvation would ultimately have to come from a revolutionized West. This could not but hurt the self-confidence of a people that had achieved the greatest of revolu-tions—a self-confidence which, despite all the miseries of daily

[1] Trotsky, *The Third International After Lenin*, p. 67. The English translation has been partly rephrased.

life, was real enough even though it was curiously blended with political apathy. Trotsky dwelt on the archaic outlook of Russia as a formidable obstacle to socialism. The Bolshevik-led masses sensed their backwardness; and the October Revolution had been their protest against it. But nations, classes, and parties, like individuals, cannot live indefinitely with an acute awareness of their own inferiority. Sooner or later they seek to suppress it. They begin to feel offended when they are reminded of it too frequently; and they are outraged when they suspect that someone is bent on reminding them of it. The apologists for socialism in one country made light of Russia's backwardness, explained it away, and even denied it.[1] They told the people that unaided they could achieve the consummation of socialism, the supreme miracle of history. It was not merely the easier and safer road that Stalin appeared to open up—it was the path of the chosen people of socialism, the path of Russia's peculiar revolutionary mission of which generations of Narodniks had dreamt. Indeed, two rival and quasi-Messianic beliefs seemed pitted against one another: Trotskyism with its faith in the revolutionary vocation of the proletariat of the West; and Stalinism with its glorification of Russia's socialist destiny. Since the impotence of Western communism had been repeatedly demonstrated, it was a foregone conclusion which of these beliefs would evoke the greater popular response.

However, for all his wishful belief in the proximity of revolution in the West, it was Trotsky rather than his adversaries who took as a rule the more sober view of current world affairs. His revolutionary idealism did not prevent him from approaching in a rigorously realistic manner specific situations either in the diplomatic field or in the communist movement. By its very nature, however, this side of his activity, his magisterial surveys and analyses of world events, could not make much impression on the rank and file, who grew or were made cynically aware of the aura of revolutionary romanticism which surrounded him.

The issues were further confused by the peculiar, scholastic style in which the controversies were conducted. For parallels

[1] This found a reflection even in Bolshevik history writing, especially in Pokrovsky's view of the evolution of capitalism and of the state in Russia. Pokrovsky was then the orthodox, Stalinist historian.

we should have to look to that medieval literature where theologians argued how many angels could sit on a pin-head or to the Talmudic disputes over which came first, the egg or the hen. When the ordinary Bolshevik heard Trotsky saying that the best way to advance socialism in Russia was to promote international revolution and Stalin replying that the best way to promote international revolution was to achieve socialism in Russia, the subtlety of the difference left him dizzy. Both sides argued from the canons of Leninist orthodoxy, canons which the triumvirs had first established in order to overwhelm Trotsky with them, and which they had succeeded in imposing upon him. Since then the orthodoxy had grown denser, harder, and more elaborate. Like so many orthodoxies, it served to exploit the moral authority of an inherited doctrine in the interest of the ruling group, to disguise the fact that that doctrine offered no clear answers to new problems, to reinterpret its tenets, to kill dissent or doubt, and to discipline the faithful. It was vain to search Lenin's writings for solutions to the problems of the day. A few years earlier most of the problems had not yet arisen or were only incipient; and even to the questions with which Lenin had dealt the most contradictory answers could be found for he had dealt with them in varying situations and contradictory circumstances. This did not prevent the party leaders from employing terms which with Lenin were political expressions as if they had been theological formulae. They quoted the lively epithets about his comrades which Lenin was wont to bandy about in controversy as if they had been Papal anathemas. The more independent-minded and capable of initiative any leading Bolshevik had been, the more such epithets about him could be culled from Lenin's writings or correspondence—only the trimmers and sycophants had nothing to fear from this kind of polemics. Lenin's shadow was thus conjured up to massacre his friends and disciples who now led the Opposition. The Opposition did its best to turn the shadow against the ruling factions. It alleged that it was its adversaries who were guilty of falsifying Lenin's teachings, while the Opposition strove to bring the party 'back to Leninism'.

It was true that on the central issue of the controversy—socialism in one country—the Opposition's claim to Leninist orthodoxy was extremely strong: Lenin had repeatedly spoken, as even Stalin and Bukharin had done up to 1924, about the impossibility of such a socialism.[1] If Stalin and Bukharin had been free to argue their case frankly, they might have said that in Lenin's lifetime the issue had not arisen in the form it had assumed now, that the isolation of the Russian Revolution had become much more evident since his death, that Lenin's pronouncements on this subject had therefore become irrelevant, and that they were entitled to advance their new doctrine without paying any regard to sacred texts. But Stalin and Bukharin were not free to argue thus. They, too, were swayed by the orthodoxy of their making. They could not afford to appear as the 'revisionists' of Leninism which they undoubtedly were. They had to present socialism in one country as a legitimate inference from Lenin's teachings, nay, as an idea developed by Lenin himself. Since the Leninist texts nevertheless bore strong witness in favour of the Opposition, Bukharin and Stalin had to divert the party's attention from them by turning the controversy into an endless and bizarre quibbling and hair-splitting which left the rank and file nonplussed, irritated, and finally bored to death. It is wellnigh impossible to convey in a historical narrative the obsessive repetitiveness and the unspeakable monotony of these scholastic performances. Yet the style of the controversy belongs to the very core of the events: its repetitiveness and monotony performed a definite function in the political drama. They killed in the average Bolshevik and worker every interest in the issues under debate. They gave them the feeling that those issues were of concern only to dogmatists dealing in abstruse questions, but not to ordinary people. This deprived the Opposition of its audience and enabled the ruling factions

[1] A detailed presentation and analysis of Lenin's attitude will be found in my *Life of Lenin*. Here a few brief quotations from Lenin will suffice: '. . . we put our stakes upon international revolution and were perfectly justified in doing this. . . . We have always emphasized that we look from an international viewpoint and *that in one country it is impossible to accomplish such a work as a socialist revolution.*' Lenin said this on the third anniversary of the October rising. Lenin, *Sochinenya*, vol. xxv, p. 474. (1928 edition—from later editions the italicized passage is omitted.) And again, after the final end of the civil war he declared: 'We have always and repeatedly told the workers that . . . the basic condition of our victory lies in the spread of the revolution at least to several of the more advanced countries.' At the sixth congress of the Soviets he said: 'The complete victory of the socialist revolution is unthinkable in one country, for it requires the most active co-operation of at least several advanced countries among which Russia cannot be classed. . . .' Lenin, *Sochinenya* (1950 ed.), vol. xxviii, p. 132.

to 'prove their doctrine orthodox by apostolic blows and knocks'.

The Opposition's call 'Back to Lenin!' fell similarly on deaf ears when the Opposition sought to remind the party of the freedom in which it had discussed and had managed its affairs in Lenin's time. Such reminders were double-edged, for although it was true that the Bolsheviks had enjoyed the fullest freedom of expression nearly to the end of the Lenin era, it was also true that at its end Lenin himself had severely curtailed that freedom by declaring the ban on factions and groups. Self-preservation, it might seem, should have induced the Opposition to denounce the ban as pernicious or at least obsolete and to demand its abolition. But the Opposition had by now become so entangled in the net of orthodoxy that it did not dare raise its voice against a ban which had behind it Lenin's authority. In 1924 Trotsky dissociated himself even from his friends when some of them tried to advocate freedom for inner-party groupings.[1] Two years later he still accepted the ban as valid, although he pointed out that it had been designed for a party enjoying freedom of expression and that in a muzzled party discontent and dissent tended of necessity to assume factional forms. Thus the Joint Opposition, having organized itself into a regular faction, did not have the courage to defend the act; and this half-heartedness made it doubly vulnerable. Only hypocrites, Stalin retorted, could call for a return to Lenin and flout that ban on factions and that monolithic discipline which were essential principles of Leninism. The Central Committee, he concluded, must not allow factional activity to go unpunished: there should be no room in Bolshevik ranks for those who rejected the Leninist conception of the party.

The rebuff the Opposition had received from the cells and the threat of expulsion which Stalin suspended over it caused disarray in its midst. Zinoviev and Kamenev, whose hopes had swelled with expectations of easy success, were crestfallen. Their sense of defeat was aggravated by remorse. They regretted that they had ever made the attempt to arouse the cells against the Central Committee. They were anxious to beat a retreat and to placate their adversaries. They were also uneasy over ideas that were becoming current on the ultra-radical fringe of the

[1] See p. 139.

Opposition, where many concluded that the party was completely under Stalin's and Bukharin's thumb, incapable of absorbing any independent view, and hopelessly ossified; and that the Opposition should learn the lesson of its defeat and at last constitute itself as an independent party. This view, commonly held by those who had originally come from the Workers' Opposition and the Decemists, began to spread also among Trotskyists—according to Trotsky's testimony even Radek was inclined to accept it.[1] The advocates of the 'new party' sought to justify their attitude on broader grounds: they argued that the old party was already in its 'post-Thermidorian' phase, that it had 'betrayed the revolution', that it no longer spoke for the working class, and that it had become the champion of the bureaucracy, the kulaks, and the N.E.P. bourgeoisie. Some held that the Soviet republic was not a workers' state any more because its bureaucracy was a new ruling and exploiting class, which had disinherited the toilers and appropriated the fruits of the revolution as the French bourgeoisie had done in 1794 and after. The Opposition must therefore seek to overthrow the bureaucracy just as Babeuf and his Conspiracy of Equals had sought to overthrow the post-Thermidorian bourgeoisie.

Neither Zinoviev and Kamenev nor Trotsky agreed with this. The 'Soviet Thermidor' was to them a danger to be averted, not an accomplished fact. The revolution, they held, had not yet come to a close. The bureaucracy was not a new ruling or possessing class, nor an independent social force, but merely a parasitic growth on the workers' state. Socially and politically heterogeneous, torn between socialism and property, the bureaucracy might eventually yield to the N.E.P. bourgeoisie and the capitalist farmers and in alliance with these destroy social ownership and restore capitalism. As long, however, as this had not happened, the basic conquests of the October Revolution were intact, the Soviet Union remained essentially a workers' state, and the old party was still in its own way the guardian of the revolution. Consequently, the Opposition must not sever its links with it, but must continue to regard itself as belonging to the party and defend with the utmost loyalty and determination the Bolshevik monopoly of power.

From this it followed that the Opposition must not seek to

[1] Trotsky, *Écrits*, vol. i, pp. 160–3.

recruit support outside the party. Yet it was not allowed to recruit it inside either. This was an insoluble dilemma. What was immediately clear was that in order to save for itself the chance of acting further within the party, especially after Stalin had thrown out hints about expulsion, the Opposition had to yield ground. Over this Trotskyists and Zinovievists did not see eye to eye. Zinoviev and Kamenev set loyalty to the old party above all else. They wondered how they could continue the struggle while Stalin was in complete mastery of the party machine. They desired a truce. They were willing to declare that henceforth they would respect the ban on factions. They were ready to disband the organized groups they had set up, ready, that is, to demobilize the Opposition as a faction. They were anxious to separate themselves from the adherents of a 'new party'. They would have no truck with those who questioned the Bolshevik political monopoly. Indeed, they were prepared to let the main issues between themselves and Stalin and Bukharin fall into abeyance, at least for a time. Most of their supporters seemed equally anxious to beat a retreat. The Trotskyists were of a more militant spirit; and the radicals among them listened sympathetically to arguments in favour of a new party.

Amid these cross currents, Trotsky attempted to save the Opposition. To prevent Zinoviev and Kamenev from prostrating themselves before Stalin, he was prepared to go with them some way in yielding ground. They agreed that they would jointly declare their willingness to demobilize the Opposition as a faction and to dissociate themselves from the advocates of a new party; but that they would also reassert firmly the Opposition's principles and criticisms; and that they would go on opposing the ruling factions within the Central Committee and within other committees on which they sat.

On 4 October 1926 Trotsky and Zinoviev approached the Politbureau with the proposal for a truce. Stalin consented, waived the threat of expulsion, but dictated the terms. Only after much haggling did the factions agree on the statement the Opposition was to make. Without retracting any of its criticisms, indeed, after having clearly restated them, the Opposition declared that it considered the decisions of the Central Committee as binding on itself, that it ceased all factional activity, and that it dissociated itself from Shlyapnikov and Medvedev, the former leaders of the Workers' Opposition, and from all those who stood for a 'new party'. On Stalin's insistence, Trotsky and Zinoviev further disavowed those foreign groups and individuals who had declared their solidarity with the Russian Opposition and had been expelled from their own Communist parties.[1]

The Opposition accepted these terms with a heavy heart. It knew that they were little short of surrender. Although it had reaffirmed its criticisms and saved its face, the Opposition was left without prospects and hope. Trotsky and Zinoviev had in effect resigned their right to appeal once again to the rank and file. They had undertaken to voice their views only within the party's leading bodies, knowing beforehand that there they would be regularly outvoted and that their views would have little or no chance of reaching the rank and file. They had made the round of a vicious circle. It was precisely because of their failure to make any impression on the Central Committee that they had tried to appeal to the cells; having failed to impress the cells they were driven back into the Central Committee; and they were trapped in it. They had weakened the Opposition by dissociating it, for whatever reason, from Shlyapnikov's and Medvedev's group, and by disavowing some of their own adherents abroad. By announcing the disbandment of their own organization, they acknowledged implicitly that Stalin and Bukharin had been justified in blaming them for forming it in the first instance; and by declaring that they recognized the ban on factions as valid and necessary, they blessed, as it were, the whip with which Stalin chastised them.

Having taken on themselves all these onerous obligations and demonstrated the Opposition's weakness, they failed to secure the truce for which they had asked. On 16 October their statement appeared in *Pravda*. Only a week later, on 23 October, not a trace was left of the truce. On that day the Central Committee met to discuss an agenda for the forthcoming (fifteenth) party conference. A more or less non-controversial agenda had already been prepared; but the Central Committee, no doubt on Stalin's prompting, suddenly decided to add a special report

[1] Stalin, *Sochinenya*, vol. viii, pp. 209–13. They disavowed in particular Ruth Fischer and Arkadi Maslov in Germany and Boris Souvarine in France.

on the Opposition, to be delivered by Stalin. This could not but reopen the wound. Trotsky protested and appealed to the majority to stand by the terms of the truce. The Central Committee nevertheless instructed Stalin to prepare his report.

Why did Stalin break the truce so soon after he had made it? He evidently wished to exploit his advantage and to rout the Opposition while it was in retreat. He was probably also provoked into fresh hostility by something that had happened two days after the truce had been announced. On 18 October the 'Trotskyist' Max Eastman published Lenin's last will in *The New York Times*—this was the first time that the full and authentic text saw the light. A year earlier he had published excerpts in *Since Lenin Died*; and Trotsky, we remember, disavowed him, and under the Politbureau's dictation denied the authenticity of the will. Stalin could not now seek to obtain another denial; but he must have suspected that Eastman had acted on Trotsky's direct or indirect inspiration. Such a suspicion was not groundless. Earlier in the year an emissary of the Opposition had indeed brought the text of Lenin's will to Paris and handed it to Souvarine who prompted Eastman to publish it. 'I think it was not only Souvarine's decision', Eastman writes, 'but the idea of the Opposition as a whole that I should be the one to publish it, one reason being that I had already got much publicity as a friend of Trotsky, another that a good many consciences in Moscow were troubled by Trotsky's disavowal of my book.'[1]

Eastman's surmise is undoubtedly correct. Among the 'troubled consciences in Moscow' none was more troubled than Trotsky's. He had denied the authenticity of the will and disavowed Eastman during that interval when neither Trotsky nor his friends wished to be drawn back into the struggle and to incur reprisals over this issue. But once he was back in the fray, after he had formed the Joint Opposition, he had every motive for trying to retrace the false step. Zinoviev and Kamenev could not but concur. It was they who had, at the fourteenth congress, raised anew the demand for the publication of the will and had repeated it at every subsequent opportunity. They, like Trotsky, would have preferred Lenin's will to be published in *Pravda*. But as this was out of the question, they could hardly have any scruple in arranging for its being broadcast by an important

[1] Quoted from Eastman's letter to the author.

bourgeois paper abroad—Lenin's will was in no sense a state secret or an 'anti-Soviet document'. Of course, they had to act with discretion because formally they were making themselves guilty of a breach of discipline. The copy of the document had been sent abroad in the heyday of the Joint Opposition, when it was hoped that the publication would assist Oppositions in foreign Communist parties and would have favourable repercussions in the Soviet Union as well. However, by the time the document was published, the situation had changed: the Opposition had already suffered discomfiture, had asked for the truce, and had dissociated itself from adherents abroad. When, on 23 October, the Central Committee met, the newspapers all over the world were full of the sensational disclosure; and this doubtlessly envenomed feelings in the Central Committee. The majority decided to disregard the truce and to give the Opposition a dressing-down.

Two days later there was a stormy scene at the Politbureau. Stalin had just submitted his 'theses' on the Opposition which he was to present at the fifteenth conference. He assailed the Opposition as a 'social-democratic deviation' and demanded that its leaders should admit the errors of their views and recant.[1] Trotsky once again protested against the breach of the truce, spoke of Stalin's faithlessness, warned the majority that they were embarking upon a course of action which, whether they wished it or not, must end in wholesale ostracism. In words charged with anger, he spoke of the fratricidal strife that would follow, the ultimate destruction of the party, and the mortal danger this would spell to the revolution. Then, facing Stalin and pointing to him, he exclaimed: 'The First Secretary poses his candidature to the post of the grave-digger of the revolution!' Stalin turned pale, rose, first contained himself with difficulty, and then rushed out of the hall, slamming the door. The meeting, at which many members of the Central Committee happened to be present, broke up in a hubbub. Next morning the Central Committee deprived Trotsky of his seat in the Politbureau and announced that Zinoviev would no longer represent the Soviet Communist party on the Executive of the Comintern, thus deposing him actually, though not

[1] Stalin's 'theses' appeared in *Pravda* on 22 October, the opening day of the conference. Stalin, *Sochinenya*, vol. viii, p. 233.

nominally, from the Presidency of the International. These events overshadowed the conference which opened on the same day.

The Opposition was thrown into utter perplexity. It had yielded so much ground and gained nothing. It had renounced co-thinkers and allies, admitted itself guilty of offending against the 1921 ban, called its organizations to disband—all in order to avoid an aggravation of the struggle. What it had achieved was to get itself involved in strife more bitter than ever and, after it had tied its own hands, to bring upon itself fresh blows. The discord in its own midst grew. Zinoviev and Kamenev reproached Trotsky with having needlessly insulted Stalin and exasperated the majority just at the moment when the Opposition was seeking to soothe tempers. Even some of the Trotskyists were horrified at the vehemence with which Trotsky had assailed Stalin. Trotsky's wife describes this scene:

Muralov, Ivan Smirnov and others came to our home in the Kremlin one afternoon and waited for Lev Davidovich to come back from a Politbureau meeting. Pyatakov was the first to return. He was very pale and shaken. He poured out a glass of water, gulped it down, and said: 'You know I have smelt gunpowder, but I have never seen anything like this! This was worse than anything! And why, why did Lev Davidovich say this? Stalin will never forgive him until the third and fourth generation!' Pyatakov was so upset that he was unable to relate clearly what had happened. When Lev Davidovich at last entered the dining-room, Pyatakov rushed at him asking: 'But why, why have you said this?' With a wave of his hand Lev Davidovich brushed the question aside. He was exhausted but calm. He had shouted at Stalin: 'Grave-digger of the revolution' . . . we understood that the breach was irreparable.[1]

The scene gives a foretaste of subsequent events: a year later Pyatakov was, together with Zinoviev and Kamenev, to desert the Opposition. Even now, so Sedova affirms, he was convinced that 'a long period of reaction had opened' within Russia and without, that the working class was politically exhausted, that the party was stifled, and that the Opposition had lost. He still

[1] Quoted from Serge, *Vie et mort de Trotsky*, pp. 180-1, of which considerable fragments were written by Sedova. She describes the incident as having taken place late in 1927; but she confuses the dates. At the fifteenth conference, in October 1926, Bukharin already referred to the incident ; and he quoted Trotsky's words about the 'grave-digger of the revolution'. *15 Konferentsya VKP (b)*, p. 578.

held out against Stalin but he did so from a sense of dignity and solidarity with his comrades rather than from conviction.

With such despondency taking hold of some of them, the leaders of the Opposition decided to make another attempt to retrieve the truce: they were to refrain from attacking the ruling factions at the conference, and to speak up only in self-defence. For seven of nine days the conference lasted they did not utter a single word in reply to adversaries, who exulted throughout in their defeat, mocked at them, and tried to draw them into debate. Finally, on the seventh day, Stalin delivered a full-blast attack which lasted many hours. He gave his version of the struggle, recalling all Zinoviev had said against Trotsky as arch-enemy of Leninism and all Trotsky's strictures on Zinoviev and Kamenev, 'the strike-breakers of October', and so ridiculing the 'mutual amnesty' they had granted each other. He described with glee the Opposition's discomfiture, and said that only this had led it to sue for a truce in order to gain time and postpone its own demise. But the party must give the Opposition no respite: 'it must wage . . . a resolute struggle against the Opposition's false views . . . no matter in what "revolutionary" phraseology these may be couched', until the Opposition renounced them. He raked interminably Trotsky's life story to prove for the nth time Trotsky's inveterate antagonism to Lenin's ideas and to taunt Zinoviev and Kamenev for their 'surrender to Trotskyism'. Finally, he denounced the Opposition for inciting the party against the peasantry and urging excessive industrialization which 'would condemn millions of workers and peasants to misery', and would therefore be no better than the capitalist method of industrialization. He and his associates, so the future author of forcible industrialization and collectivization declared, favoured only such forms of economic development as would contribute immediately to the people's well-being and spare the country social convulsions; and in the name of this he called the conference to give the Opposition a 'unanimous rebuff'.[1]

When the leaders of the Opposition at last came forward, delegates noticed the very different tones in which they answered Stalin. Kamenev, who spoke first, gave a thoughtful but rather timid exposition of his views, trying in vain to blunt the edges

[1] Stalin, *Sochinenya*, vol. viii, pp. 421–63.

of the controversy. He complained about Stalin's disloyalty in launching the ferocious attack less than a fortnight after the truce. He tried to exonerate himself and Zinoviev from the charge that they had 'surrendered to Trotskyism'. They had united with Trotsky, he said, only for a definite and limited purpose as Lenin had often done. He recalled once again Lenin's testament and Lenin's fear of a split in the party; but this brought forth a howl from the floor. Then he broke into these words, part warning and part self-consolation: 'You may accuse us, comrades, of what you like, but we do not live in the middle ages! Witch trials cannot be staged now! You cannot accuse [us] . . . who call for higher taxes on the kulak and wish to help the poor peasant and together with him to build socialism—you cannot charge [us] with wishing to rob the peasantry. You cannot burn us at the stake.'[1] Exactly ten years later Kamenev was to sit in the dock at a witch trial.

Then Trotsky rose to make one of his greatest speeches, moderate in tone, yet devastating in content, masterly in logical and artistic composition, gleaming with humour—yet revealing once again the main source of his immediate weakness: his unshakeable reliance on European revolution. He spoke for the Opposition as a whole; but he also pleaded *pro domo sua*, throwing off, as if with one heave, the mountain of misrepresentation and obloquy with which he had been freshly covered at the conference. He had been accused of panic-mongering, pessimism, defeatism, and 'social-democratic deviationism'. Yet he had argued only from facts and figures; and 'arithmetic knows neither pessimism nor optimism'. To speak of the shortage of industrial goods was panic-mongering; but was there no ground for concern in the fact that in the current year industry had underproduced by 25 per cent.? Stalin had dubbed him a defeatist and made much play of his 'fear of a good harvest' because he had argued that as long as the nation suffered from a deficit of industrial goods, tension between town and country would persist, no matter whether the harvest was good or bad. Unfortunately, the last harvest was worse than they had all expected. The social differentiation of the peasantry was growing apace. None of these difficulties were as yet disastrous; but the omens had to be noticed in time. The Opposition had asked

[1] *15 Konferentsya VKP (b)*, p. 486.

that the well-to-do pay higher taxes and that the poor be granted reliefs. This demand may have been justified or not; but 'what is there in it that is social-democratic?' The Opposition was against a credit policy which favoured the kulak—was this social-democratic? It favoured a modest rise in wages—was this social-democratic? It did not share Bukharin's view that capitalism had regained stability—was that social-democratic? Was the Opposition's criticism of the Anglo-Soviet Council perhaps 'social-democratic?'

He recalled his service in the Comintern, his intimate co-operation with Lenin, and especially the support he had given Lenin in the transition to N.E.P., the N.E.P. he allegedly wished to disrupt. He was charged with 'disbelief' in the building of socialism. Yet had he not written that 'the sum total of the advantages *vis-à-vis* capitalism which we possess gives us, if we use the advantages properly, the chance to raise the coefficient of industrial expansion in the next few years not only to twice but even three times the pre-war 6 per cent. per year and perhaps even higher'.[1] It was true that he did not believe in socialism in one country and that he had been the author of the theory of permanent revolution. However, permanent revolution had been dragged in artificially: he alone, not the Opposition, was responsible for that theory. As a sop to Zinoviev and Kamenev he added: 'and I myself consider this issue to have been deposited in the archives long, long ago.' But what had his critics to say? They held it against him that in 1906 he had forecast that after the revolution urban collectivism would inevitably clash with peasant individualism. Had they not lived to see that prediction come true? Had they not proclaimed N.E.P. precisely because of such a clash? Had not 'the middle peasants talked with the Soviet Government through naval guns' at Kronstadt and elsewhere in 1921? The critics held it against him that he had predicted a collision between revolutionary Russia and conservative Europe. Had they overslept the years of intervention? 'If we, comrades, are alive, this is because, after all, Europe has not remained what it was.'

---

[1] This was indeed the rate at which Soviet industry expanded later under the Five Year Plans. (Trotsky quoted here a passage from his booklet *Towards Socialism or Capitalism?* published in 1925.) In 1930 Stalin was to ask for an annual increase of 50 per cent.! See my *Stalin*, p. 321.

However, the fact that the revolution had survived did not guarantee it against a repetition of conflicts with the peasantry and the capitalist West; nor did it argue in favour of socialism in one country. Indeed, they would have to face new conflicts and face them in worse conditions if they were to advance only at a 'snail's pace' and turn their backs on international revolution. Bukharin had written that 'the controversy is over this: can we build socialism and complete the building if we leave aside international affairs . . ?'. 'If we leave aside international affairs', Trotsky retorted, 'we can; but the whole point is that we cannot leave them aside (laughter). You can go for a walk naked in the streets of Moscow in the month of January, if you leave aside the weather and the militia (laughter). But I am afraid, neither the weather nor the militia will leave you aside. . . . Since when has our revolution acquired this . . . self-sufficiency?'

Here Trotsky came to the 'core of the problem': What would happen in Europe while Russia would be building socialism? So far they had all agreed with Lenin in assuming that Russia would need 'a minimum of thirty to fifty years' to achieve socialism.[1] What would the world look like in the course of these years? If within that time revolution were to win in the West, the question over which they argued would lapse. The adherents of socialism in one country evidently presupposed that this would not happen. They must then be starting from one of the following three possible assumptions: Europe—this might be the first assumption—would economically and socially stagnate, its bourgeoisie and proletariat keeping each other in a precarious balance. But such a situation could hardly last forty or even twenty years. The next assumption might be that European capitalism was capable of a new ascendancy. In that case, 'if capitalism were to flourish and if its economy and culture were to be on the ascendant that would mean that we had come too early', that is that the Russian Revolution was doomed. '. . . an advancing capitalism will . . . have the appropriate military, technical, and other means to stifle and crush us. This dark prospect is, in my view, ruled out by the entire condition of the world economy.' In any case, one could not base on such an assumption the vista of socialism in Russia.

---

[1] Stalin denied that this had been Lenin's view (*Sochinenya*, vol. ix, p. 39), but he had little ground for the denial.

Finally, one might assume that in the course of thirty to fifty years European capitalism would decline but that the working class would prove incapable of overthrowing it. 'Can you imagine this?' Trotsky asked.

I am asking you why I should accept this assumption which is nothing but black and groundless pessimism about the European proletariat; and why should we at the same time cultivate an uncritical optimism about the building of socialism by the isolated forces of our country? In what sense is it my ... duty as a communist to assume that the European working class will not be able to take power in the course of forty or fifty years. ... I see no theoretical or political reason for thinking that we with our peasantry will find it easier to achieve socialism than the European proletariat will find it to seize power. ... Even to-day I believe that the victory of socialism in our country can be safeguarded only together with a victorious revolution of the European proletariat. This is not to say that what we are building is not socialism, or that we cannot or should not go ahead with it full steam. ... If we did not think that ours is a workers' state, even though it is bureaucratically deformed ...; if we did not think that we are building socialism; if we did not think that we have enough resources in our country to promote the socialist economy; if we were not convinced of our full and final victory, then, of course, there should be no place for us in the ranks of the Communist Party. ...

Then also the Opposition would have to build another party and seek to arouse the working class against the existing state. This, however, was not its purpose. But let them beware: Stalin's disloyal and unscrupulous methods, freshly exemplified by the manner in which he had turned the truce into a scrap of paper, might produce a real split in the party and lead to a struggle between two parties.[1]

The assembly listened to Trotsky in breathless suspense and respectful hostility, even though repeatedly he had to interrupt his speech at the most dramatic moments and beg to be allowed to go on; again and again the conference prolonged his speaking time. Restrained and persuasive, he showed no sign of vacillation or weakness. Larin, who took the platform immediately after Trotsky, thus expressed the mood of the majority:

---

[1] *15 Konferentsya VKP (b)*, pp. 505-35.

'This was one of the dramatic episodes of our revolution . . . the revolution is outgrowing some of its leaders.'[1]

It was in a very different mood that the delegates listened to Zinoviev as he made a plaintive apology and tried to ingratiate himself with them. They treated him with rough contempt and hatred, drove him from the platform, and did not allow him to speak even on the affairs of the Comintern, for which he had been responsible; and this despite the fact that they were about to vote on his 'withdrawal' from the Comintern's Executive.[2]

As one looks back upon these congresses and conferences and compares the tenor of their debates, one is struck by the venom and the violence with which the ruling factions treated the Opposition; and one senses almost palpably how, from assembly to assembly, the coarse brutality rises to an ever higher pitch and turns into a fury. An utterly grotesque effect is created by the fact that some of the most churlish and vindictive assaults on the Opposition and some of the most fulsome tributes to Stalin came from people who only a few years hence were to become disgusted with him, turn into his belated critics, and perish as his helpless victims. Among those who at this conference distinguished themselves by their zealotry were Gamarnik, the future chief Political Commissar of the Red Army, who was to be denounced as traitor and was to commit suicide on the eve of Tukhachevsky's trial; Syrtsov, Chubar, Uglanov, who

[1] Ibid., p. 535. Larin had stood on the extreme right wing of the Mensheviks up to 1914, joined the Bolsheviks in the summer of 1917, and was then in friendly relations with Trotsky. His attitude towards the 1923 Opposition was ambiguous; later he joined the Stalinists.

[2] This, according to the verbatim report, is the conclusion of Zinoviev's speech: 'Comrades, I would like to say a few words about the bloc [i.e. the Joint Opposition]. I would like to say (*interruptions: You have talked enough. . . . Enough! Noise.*) I would like to say a few words about the bloc and the Comintern . . . (*voices: enough, enough! You should have spoken about this earlier and not about other things!*) Now, this is not right. Would you say that the problem of socialism in one country [about which Zinoviev had spoken] is not an important one? Why then did Stalin speak about it for three hours . . .? (*Noise, protests.*) I am asking for ten to fifteen minutes, so that I may say something about the bloc and the problems of the Comintern. (*Noise, Voices: enough!*) You know, comrades, that the party is now deciding that I should cease to work in the Comintern. (*Exclamation from the floor: This has already been decided!*) Such a decision is absolutely inevitable in the present circumstances, but will it be fair on your part not to grant me five minutes to enable me to speak on Comintern problems? (*Noise. Shouts: Enough! The chairman rings the bell.*) I beg you, comrades, leave me another ten–fifteen minutes to cover these two points.' (*The chairman orders a vote; and an overwhelming majority is against prolonging Zinoviev's time by ten minutes.*) Ibid., p. 577.

were all to die as 'saboteurs and plotters'; and even Ossinsky, the former Decemist, who now professed his faith in socialism in one country, but was also to end as 'wrecker and enemy of the people'. None, however, excelled Bukharin. Only a few months earlier he still appeared to be in amicable intercourse with Trotsky. Now he stood by Stalin's side, as Zinoviev had stood there two years earlier, and assailed the Opposition with reckless virulence, exulting in its plight, bragging, threatening, inciting, sneering, and playing up to the worst elements in the party. The kindly scholar was as if transfigured suddenly, the thinker turned into a hooligan and the philosopher into a thug destitute of all scruple and foresight. He praised Stalin as the true friend of the peasant smallholder and the guardian of Leninism; and he challenged Trotsky to repeat before the conference what he had said at the Politbureau about Stalin 'the grave-digger of the revolution'.[1] He jeered at the restraint with which Trotsky had addressed the conference, a restraint due only to the fact that the party had 'seized the Opposition by the throat'. The Opposition, he said, appealed to them to avert the 'tragedy' that would result from a split. He, Bukharin, was only amused by the warning: 'Not more than three men will leave the party—this will be the whole split!', he exclaimed amid great laughter. 'This will be a farce not a tragedy.' He thus scoffed at Kamenev's apology:

When Kamenev comes here and . . . says: 'I, Kamenev, have joined hands with Trotsky as Lenin used to join hands with him and lean on him', one can only reply with homeric laughter: what sort of a Lenin have they discovered! We see very well that Kamenev and Zinoviev are leaning on Trotsky in a very odd manner. (*Prolonged laughter and applause.*) They 'lean' on him in such a way that he has saddled them completely (*giggling and applause*), and then Kamenev . . . squeals: 'I am leaning on Trotsky'. (*Mirth*) Yes, altogether like Lenin! (*Laughter*).

Within barely two years Bukharin would try to 'lean' on a broken and prostrate Kamenev and whisper in terror into his ears that Stalin was the new Genghiz Khan.[2] But now, self-assured and complacent, juggling and jingling with quotations from Lenin, he returned to the attack on permanent revolution, on Trotsky's 'heroic postures', hostility towards the muzhik, and

---

[1] *15 Konferentsya VKP (b)*, pp. 578–601.   [2] See pp. 440–3.

'fiscal theory of building socialism'; and again and again he extolled the steadfastness, the reliability, and the caution of his own and of Stalin's policies which secured the alliance with the peasantry. When the Opposition 'screamed' about the strength of the kulak and the danger of peasant strikes and of famine in the towns, it was trying to frighten the people with bogies. The party should not forgive them this and the 'chatter about the Soviet Thermidor', unless they came with their heads bowed, to repent, confess, and beg: 'Forgive us our sins against the spirit and the letter and the very essence of Leninism!' Amid frantic applause he went on:

> Say it, and say it honestly: Trotsky was wrong when he declared that ours was not a *fully* proletarian state! Why don't you have the plain courage to come out and say so? . . . Zinoviev has told us here how well Lenin treated oppositions. Lenin did not expel any opposition even when he was left with only two votes for himself in the Central Committee. . . . Yes, Lenin knew his job. Who would try and expel an opposition when he could muster two votes only? (*Laughter.*) But when you get all votes and you have only two against you and the two shriek about Thermidor, then you may well think about expulsion.

The conference was delighted with this display of cynicism and shook with merriment. From the floor Stalin shouted: 'Well done, Bukharin. Well done, well done. He does not argue with them, he slaughters them!'[1]

What accounted for Bukharin's strange, almost macabre performance? No doubt he was genuinely frightened of the policies advocated by the Opposition. He dreaded the collision with the peasantry which they might provoke; and he did not see that it was his and Stalin's policy that led to this. The Opposition, although far too weak to replace the ruling group, was strong enough to compel Stalin's faction to shift its ground. True, at this conference it looked as if the Bukharinists had gained the upper hand within the ruling coalition: Bukharin, Rykov, and Tomsky presented the three main reports on behalf of the Central Committee. However, even they had to reckon with the Opposition. Bukharin himself had now to tread cautiously in matters of rural policy—he could no longer appeal frankly to the strong farmer. He saw Stalin's faction increasingly

[1] *15 Konferentsya VKP (b)*, p. 601.

sensitive to Trotsky's and Zinoviev's criticisms and inclined to steal page after page from their book. Stalin was already yielding to the demands for more rapid industrialization; this showed itself even in the resolutions voted by this conference. Bukharin would have preferred the ruling coalition to stand fast and to defeat its adversaries without having to borrow their ideas and confuse the issues. He wondered how far the Opposition's pressure might not push the party. He 'shuddered from head to foot' at the thought that it might drive it to a bloody conflict with the peasantry. And so, he was, at this moment, even more anxious than Stalin to free official policy from the Opposition's indirect influence. He desperately clung to Stalin so as to keep him from yielding further ground; and he countenanced and instigated Stalin's violence and trickery hoping that the defeat of the Opposition would assure peace in the country. No sacrifice of tact, taste, and decency was for him too high a price to pay for this.

The ferocity of the attacks sprang also from embarrassment and perplexity. Stalin's faction shrank from the enormity of the step it was to take two years hence. Its speakers, too, imputed to Trotsky and Zinoviev that they were prompting the party to embark upon the forcible collectivization of the peasantry. Kaganovich, for instance, who was to play a very prominent part in the destruction of private farming, exclaimed: 'Theirs is the road of plundering the peasantry, a pernicious road, no matter how much Trotsky and Zinoviev may protest against this—such indeed are their slogans.'[1] Once more also the Opposition had run up against the wall of the single-party system. When it asked for freedom within that system, it was charged with jeopardizing the system itself: Bukharin and Stalin claimed that it tended to constitute itself into another party. Molotov, in his inarticulate manner, hit the mark: Opposition speakers, protesting against suppression, had recalled that even during the Brest Litovsk crisis Lenin had allowed the Left Communists to publish their own paper attacking him without fear or favour: and to this Molotov replied: 'But in 1918 . . . the Mensheviks and the Social Revolutionaries too had their newspapers. Even the Cadets had theirs. Somehow the present position is not at all like that.'[2] Once again: the Bolsheviks could not enjoy

[1] 15 Konferentsya VKP (b), p. 637.   [2] Ibid., p. 671.

the freedom they had denied to others. Kaganovich recalled the words Trotsky had spoken at the eleventh congress when he presented the case against the Workers' Opposition. It was inadmissible, Trotsky then said, for party members to speak about their comrades and leaders in terms of 'We' and 'They', for if they did, they would, whatever their intentions, oppose themselves to the party, seek to exploit its difficulties, and assist those who had raised the banner of Kronstadt. 'Why then', Kaganovich asked, 'did you, comrade Trotsky, have the right to say this to Medvedev and Shlyapnikov when they made a mistake (and these comrades had been old Bolsheviks), and why can we not tell you that you are going on the Kronstadt road? . . .'[1]

It was not only the ghosts of Kronstadt and of the Workers' Opposition that were pressed into the onslaught on Trotsky. Shlyapnikov and Medvedev joined it in their own persons. After the Opposition had, on Stalin's insistence, declared that it would have no truck with them, Stalin managed by threat and cajolery to persuade Shlyapnikov and Medvedev to admit the error of their ways, to repent, and to denounce the Opposition. With jubilation the Central Committee then broadcast their recantation and announced that it granted them a pardon. The two men had urged the Joint Opposition to give up allegiance to the single-party system, to form itself from a faction within the old party into a new party. But confronted with the threat of their own expulsion from the old party and incensed by the fact that the Joint Opposition had disavowed them, they surrendered to Stalin. Theirs was the first recantation Stalin succeeded in extorting—a precedent and an example for many others. Before the end of the conference, Stalin surprised the Opposition by yet another stroke: he announced that Krupskaya had severed her connexion with Trotsky and Zinoviev.[2] It was whispered in Moscow that Stalin had blackmailed her with hints of indiscretions about Lenin's private life—'I shall appoint', he allegedly said, 'someone else to be Lenin's widow'. It is more plausible that Krupskaya withdrew from the Opposition because she was horrified to see the party founded by her husband split and torn asunder. As she had been among Stalin's and Bukharin's most outspoken critics, her defection did the Opposition much harm.

[1] Ibid., p. 638.   [2] Ibid., pp. 754-5.

Finally, Stalin played against Trotsky and Zinoviev the leaders of foreign Communist parties. On their behalf Klara Zetkin, the veteran German Communist, who had at the Fourth Comintern Congress, when Lenin was already ill, paid in the name of the whole International a great and solemn tribute to Trotsky, now dissociated herself from him and Zinoviev, charging them with provoking a crisis in the International and supplying grist to the mills of all enemies of communism. '. . . even the lustre which attaches to the names of the leaders of the Opposition', she declared with a show of dignity, 'is not enough to redeem them. . . . The merits of these comrades . . . are imperishable. They will not be forgotten. Their deeds have entered into the history of the revolution. I am not forgetting them. However, . . . there exists something greater than deeds and merits of individuals.'[1]

The Opposition was routed; and the conference sanctioned the expulsion of the three chiefs of the Opposition from the Politbureau, threatening them with further reprisals if they dared to reopen the controversy.

Thus the Joint Opposition reached a point similar to that at which the 1923 Opposition had arrived after its defeat. The formal verdicts having gone against it, it had to decide what to do next: whether to go on with the struggle and risk wholesale and final expulsion, or accept defeat, at least temporarily? Each of the two sets of the Opposition reacted in a different manner. The Zinovievists were inclined to lie low. This was no easy matter, because the official attacks on them went on unabated, despite the formal closing of the controversy. The newspapers, purporting merely to comment on the resolutions of the conference, filled pages with the most virulent polemics, and gave the attacked no chance to answer. Rank-and-file Oppositionists paid for the courage of their convictions: they lost jobs, were subjected to ostracism, and were treated as little better than outcasts. Zinoviev and Kamenev resigned themselves to the mildest forms of passive resistance. Anxious to protect their adherents, they advised them to keep their views to themselves and, if need be, even to deny their association with the Opposition. Such advice could not but discredit the Opposition and demoralize those to whom it was given; they began to desert and recant.

[1] *15 Konferentsya VKP (b)*, pp. 698–707.

The Trotskyists, on the other hand, who had already gone through a similar trial, knew that they had nothing to gain from inaction and nothing to hope for from half measures. Trotsky himself reviewed the recent experience in diary notes written towards the end of November.[1] For himself he defined the Opposition's predicament with greater candour than he could afford to use in public or in the Central Committee. He acknowledged defeat. He attributed it not merely to Stalin's disloyalty and to bureaucratic intimidation, but to the lassitude and disillusionment of the masses, who had expected too much from the revolution, had found their hopes cruelly deceived, and reacted against the spirit and the idea of early Bolshevism. The young, finding themselves under a tutelage from the moment they entered politics, could not develop any critical faculties and political judgement. The ruling factions played on popular weariness and craving for security and frightened people with the bogy of permanent revolution. Speaking for the record, Trotsky usually dwelt on the antagonism between the ruling group and the rank and file. Off the record he admitted that the ideas and slogans of the ruling group met an emotional need in the rank and file, that this overlaid their antagonism, and that the Opposition was at variance with the popular temper.

What then was to be done? It is not the business of the Marxist revolutionary, Trotsky reflected, to bow to the reactionary mood of the masses. At times when their class consciousness is dimmed, he must be prepared to become isolated from them. The isolation need not last long, for the time was one of transition and crisis; and, within the Soviet Union and without, the forces of revolution might yet surge up. This was, in any case, no time for the Opposition to flag or waver, even if the odds were against it. The revolutionary has to fight no matter whether he is destined to end as Lenin did—to live and see his cause triumph—or to suffer Liebknecht's fate who served his cause through martyrdom. In his private notes and in talks with friends, Trotsky hinted at this alternative more than once; and although he did not give up hope that he might 'end like Lenin', he seemed already more and more resigned inwardly to 'Liebknecht's fate'.

[1] See his notes of 26 November 1926 in *The Archives*.

I did not believe in our victory [Victor Serge recollects] and at heart I was even sure that we would be defeated. When I was sent to Moscow with our group's messages for Lev Davidovich, I told him so. We talked in the spacious office of the Concessions Committee . . . he was suffering from a fit of malaria; his skin was yellow, his lips were almost livid. I told him that we were extremely weak, that we, in Leningrad, had not rallied more than a few hundred members, that our debates left the mass of workers cold. I felt that he knew all this better than I did. But he, as a leader, had to do his duty and we, as revolutionaries, had to do ours. If defeat was inevitable, what else could one do but meet it with courage . . . ?[1]

. . . .

The winter of 1926–7 passed in relative calm. The Opposition was debilitated by internal discord. Trotsky did his best to prevent his partnership with Zinoviev from dissolving; and as Zinoviev was in near panic, the Joint Opposition paid for its unity with irresolution. In December its leaders even protested to Stalin against attempts made in the party cells of Moscow to draw them into fresh debates.[2] In the same month the Executive of the Comintern discussed the situation in the Russian party; and willy-nilly the Opposition had to restate its attitude. Once again Trotsky had to defend his own record and, protesting against the 'biographical method' used in inner party controversy, he went through the story of his relations with Lenin in order to demonstrate to an audience whose mind was closed that the 'irreconcilable antagonism between Trotskyism and Leninism was but a myth'.[3] The Executive confirmed the expulsion from foreign Communist parties of Trotskyists and Zinovievists on the ground that they denied the proletarian character of the Soviet state. Trotsky declared that the Opposition would combat any of its supposed foreign supporters who

[1] V. Serge, *Le Tournant obscur*, p. 116.

[2] Trotsky's and Zinoviev's 'Letter' to Stalin and the Politbureau of 13 December 1926. *The Archives*.

[3] On this occasion Trotsky gave an illuminating account of his attitude towards Lenin up to 1917. He spoke of the 'inner resistance' with which he drew nearer and nearer to Lenin. All the more was his eventual acceptance of Leninism wholehearted and complete. He compared his case with that of Franz Mehring who had embraced Marxism only after he had struggled against it as a leading Liberal. In spite or rather because of this Mehring's conviction was unshakeable and in his old age he paid for it with his freedom and life, whereas Kautsky and Bernstein, and the other men of the 'old guard' of Marxism, deserted the banner. See *The Trotsky Archives* statement of 9 December. See also *The Stalin School of Falsification*, p. 85.

took such a view. Half resigned to Souvarine's expulsion, he stood up for Rosmer and Monatte, who had been his political friends since the First World War and had founded and led the French Communist party, from which they were now banished.[1] But apart from such minor political interventions, he spent the winter in reserve, editing volumes of his *Works* and 'carrying out a more thorough theoretical examination of many questions'.

The 'theoretical question' which, apart from the economic argument against socialism in one country, preoccupied him most strongly was the 'Soviet Thermidor'. In the ranks of the Opposition and among its sympathizers abroad there was a great deal of confusion over this. Some argued that the Russian Revolution had already passed into the Thermidorian phase. Those who held this view also spoke of the bureaucracy as of the new class which had destroyed the proletarian dictatorship and exploited and dominated the working class. Others, and Trotsky most of all, hotly contested this opinion. As often happens when an historical analogy becomes a political shibboleth, neither of the disputants had a clear view of the precedent to which they referred; and Trotsky was to revise repeatedly his own interpretation of it. At this stage he defined the 'Soviet Thermidor' as a decisive 'shift to the right' which might occur within the Bolshevik party against the background of general apathy and disillusionment with the revolution, and result in the destruction of Bolshevism and the restoration of capitalism. From this definition Trotsky concluded that it was at least premature to speak of a Soviet Thermidor, but that the Opposition was justified in raising an alarm. One element of a 'Thermidorian situation' had been in evidence all too strongly: the masses were weary and disillusioned. But the decisive 'shift to the right' leading to restoration had not occurred, although the 'Thermidorian forces' working towards it had gathered strength and momentum.

[1] *Inter alia* Trotsky intervened with the Politbureau when the latter planned to send Pyatakov on a trade mission to Canada. He pointed out that because of the presence of many Ukrainian émigrés in Canada such a mission might be dangerous for Pyatakov who had led the Bolsheviks in the Ukraine during the civil war. Pyatakov had just been refused admission to the U.S.A. as one 'who sentenced to death worthy citizens of Russia'. Trotsky's letter to Ordjonikidze, 21 February 1927. See *The Archives*.

There would be no compelling need to go here into this
rather abstruse argument if it were not that the view which
Trotsky now formulated determined in part his own behaviour
and the Opposition's fate in subsequent years and that the
controversy over it generated indescribable heat and passion
in all factions. This was indeed one of the seemingly most
irrational phenomena in the struggle. It was enough for an
Oppositionist to utter the word 'Thermidor' at any party meeting, and at once tempers flared up and the audience fumed and
raged, although many had only the faintest idea what it was
about. It was enough that they knew that the Thermidorians
had been the 'grave-diggers' of Jacobinism and that the Opposition charged the ruling group with being engaged in some
deep plot against the revolution. This curious historical slogan
enraged even educated Bukharinists and Stalinists, who knew
that its meaning was far less simple. The Opposition argued
that the men of the Thermidor had not been out to destroy
Jacobinism and to put an end to the First Republic—they had
done this unwittingly from weariness and confusion. In the
same manner the Soviet Thermidorians, not knowing what they
were doing, might do the same. The analogy preyed on the
thoughts of many a Stalinist and Bukharinist and sapped their
confidence. It brought to their minds the uncontrollable element in revolution, of which they were increasingly if dimly
aware; it made them feel that they were or might become playthings in the hands of vast, hostile, and unmanageable social
forces.

Uneasily many a Bolshevik felt that this might be true. To
whatever faction he belonged, he was terrified by the ghosts
which the Opposition had conjured up. This was a case of *le
mort saisit le vif*. When the Bukharinist or the Stalinist disclaimed
any affinity with the Thermidorian, he did so not with calm self-
assurance, but with that resentment, born of inner uncertainty,
with which Bukharin spoke at the fifteenth conference of the
Opposition's 'unforgivable chatter about Thermidor'.[1] His fury
against the Opposition helped him to smother his own fears.
The Oppositionist saw the ghost stalking the streets of Moscow,
hovering over the Kremlin, or standing among the Politbureau
members at the top of the Lenin Mausoleum on days of national

                         [1] See p. 305.

celebrations and parades. The uncannily violent passions which the bookish historical reminiscence aroused sprang from the irrationality of the political climate in which the single-party system had grown up and developed. The Bolshevik felt alienated from his own work—the revolution. His own state and his own party towered high above him. They appeared to have a mind and a will of their own which bore little relation to his mind and his will and to which he had to bow. State and party appeared to him as blind forces, convulsive and unpredictable. When the Bolsheviks made of the Soviets 'organs of power' they were convinced, with Trotsky, that they had established 'the most lucid and transparent political system' the world had ever seen, a system under which rulers and ruled would be closer to one another than ever before and under which the mass of the people would be able to express and enforce its will as directly as never before. Yet nothing was less 'transparent' than the single-party system after a few years. Society as a whole had lost all transparency. No social class was free to express its will. The will of any class was therefore unknown. The rulers and the political theorists had to guess it, only to be more and more often taught by events that they had guessed wrongly. The social classes therefore appeared to act, and up to a point did indeed act, as elemental forces, unpredictably pressing on the party from all sides. Groups and individuals within the party seemed to be unknowingly pushed in the most unexpected directions. On all sides cleavages arose or reappeared between what men thought (of themselves and others), what they willed, and what they did—cleavages between the 'objective' and the 'subjective' aspects of political activity. Nothing was now more difficult to define than who was the foe and who was the friend of the revolution. Both the ruling group and the Opposition moved in the dark, fighting against real dangers and against apparitions, and chasing one another and one another's shadows. They ceased to see one another as they were and saw each other as mysterious social entities with hidden and sinister potentialities which had to be deciphered and rendered harmless. It was this alienation from society and from one another that prompted the ruling factions to declare that the Opposition worked as an agency of alien social elements and the Opposition to claim that behind the ruling men stood Thermidorian forces.

Which then were those forces? The wealthy peasants, the N.E.P. bourgeoisie, and sections of the bureaucracy, Trotsky replied—briefly, all those classes and groups which were interested in a bourgeois restoration. The working class remained attached to the 'conquests of October' and was implicitly hostile to the Thermidorians. As for the bureaucracy, Trotsky expected that in a critical situation it would split: one section would back the counter-revolution; another would defend the revolution. He saw the divisions within the party as an indirect reflection of that cleavage. The right wing stood closest to the Thermidorians; but it was not necessarily identical with them. Bukharin's defence of the men of property savoured of a Thermidorian aspiration; but it was not clear whether the Bukharinists were the actual Thermidorians or merely their unwitting auxiliaries, who would in danger rally to the revolution. The left, i.e. the Joint Opposition, alone, according to this view, represented within the party the proletarian class interest and the undiluted programme of socialism; it acted as the vanguard of the anti-Thermidorians. The centre, the Stalinist faction, had no programme; and although it controlled the party machine, it had no broad social backing. It balanced between right and left and spawned on the programmes of both. As long as the centre was in coalition with the right, it helped to pave the way for the Thermidorians. But it had nothing to gain from a Thermidor which would be its own undoing; and so, when faced with the menace of counter-revolution, the centre or a large section of it would rally to the left in order to oppose, under the left's leadership, the Soviet Thermidor.

There is no need to run ahead of our story and to point out to what extent events confirmed or falsified this view.[1] Here it will be enough to indicate one important practical conclusion which Trotsky drew from it. This was, briefly, that under no conditions must he and his associates enter into an alliance with Bukharin's faction against Stalin. In certain circumstances and under certain conditions, Trotsky urged, the Opposition must even be prepared to form a united front with Stalin against Bukharin. The conditions were those that applied in any united front: the Opposition must not give up its independence, its

---

[1] A further analysis of the problem is found in chapter VI and in *The Prophet Outcast*.

right of criticism, and its insistence on inner-party freedom. According to a well-known tactical formula, left and centre should march separately and strike jointly. True, for the time being the Opposition had no opportunity to apply this rule: the Stalinists and the Bukharinists shared power and maintained unity. But Trotsky had no doubt that they would fall out presently. His tactical rule was designed to drive a wedge between them and assist in bringing about a realignment which would allow the Opposition to take command of all 'anti-Thermidorians', including the Stalinists. In the next few years the whole conduct of the Opposition was to be governed by this principle: 'With Stalin against Bukharin?—Yes. With Bukharin against Stalin?—Never!'

When this tactical decision, for which Trotsky was mainly responsible, is viewed in the grim light of the end which befell all anti-Stalinist factions and groups, it cannot but appear as an act of suicidal folly. The Thermidorian spirit which Trotsky saw as if embodied in the ineffectual Bukharin appears to have been the figment of an imagination overfed with history. And as one ponders, with the full knowledge of the after-events, Trotsky's many anxious alarms about the 'danger from the right', i.e. from Bukharin's faction, and his evident underestimation of Stalin's power, one may marvel at the short-sightedness or blindness which in this instance characterized the man so often distinguished by prophetic foresight. However, a view taken only from the angle of the *dénouement* would be one-sided. Trotsky's decision has to be seen also against the background of the circumstances in which he took it. N.E.P. was at its height, the forces interested in a bourgeois restoration were still alive and active, and nobody dreamt as yet of the forcible suppression of N.E.P. capitalism and of the 'liquidation of the kulaks as a class'. Trotsky could not take for granted the outcome of the contest between the antagonistic forces of Soviet society. The phantom of Thermidor, as he saw it, was still half real. Eight or even ten years after 1917 the possibility of a restoration could not be ruled out. As Marxist and Bolshevik, he naturally felt it to be his prime duty to strain all strength and to mobilize all energies against it. This determined his inner-party tactics. If anything at all could still pave the way for restoration, then it was Bukharin's rather than Stalin's policy. Within this context Trotsky could not but conclude that the Opposition must lend conditional support to the latter against the former. Such a conclusion was in line with Marxist tradition which approved alliances between left and centre against the right, but considered any combination of left and right directed against the centre as unprincipled and inadmissible. Thus, seen in its contemporary setting and judged in Marxist terms, Trotsky's attitude had its logic. It was his misfortune that subsequent events were to transcend that logic and to show it up as the logic of the Opposition's self-effacement. It was Trotsky's tragedy indeed that in the very process by which he defended the revolution he also committed political suicide.

. . . .

In the spring of 1927 the inner-party struggle flared up again in connexion with an issue which had hitherto played almost no part in it, but which was to remain at its centre to the end, until the final expulsion and the dissolution of the Joint Opposition.

That issue was the Chinese Revolution.

It was about this time that the Chinese Revolution entered upon a grave crisis which had been prepared by developments dating back to the close of the Lenin era. The Bolsheviks had very early set their eyes on the anti-imperialist movements among the colonial and semi-colonial nations, believing that these movements constituted a major 'strategic reserve' for proletarian revolution in Europe. Both Lenin and Trotsky were convinced that Western capitalism would be decisively weakened if it were cut off from the colonial hinterland which supplied it with cheap labour, raw materials, and opportunities for exceptionally profitable investment. In 1920 the Comintern proclaimed the alliance of Western communism and the emancipatory movements of the East. But it did not go beyond the enunciation of the principle. It left open the forms of the alliance and the methods by which it was to be promoted. It acknowledged the struggles of the nations of Asia for independence as the historic equivalent of bourgeois revolutions in Europe; and it recognized the peasantry and, up to a point, even the bourgeoisie of those nations as allies of the working class. But the Leninist Comintern did not yet attempt to define clearly the relationship between the anti-imperialist movements and the struggle for socialism in Asia itself, or the attitude of the Chinese and Indian Communist parties towards their own 'anti-imperialist' bourgeoisie.

It was too early to resolve these questions. The impact of the October Revolution on the East was still too fresh. Its strength and depth could not yet be gauged. In the most important countries of Asia the Communist parties were only beginning to constitute themselves; the working classes were numerically weak and lacked political tradition; even bourgeois anti-imperialism was still in a formative period. Only in 1921 did the Chinese Communist party, based on small propagandist circles, hold its first congress. But no sooner had it done so and set out to formulate its programme and shape its organization than Moscow began to urge it to seek a *rapprochement* with the Kuomintang. The Kuomintang basked in the moral authority of Sun Yat-sen which was then at its height. Sun Yat-sen himself was eager for an agreement with Russia which would strengthen his hands against Western imperialism; and in his vague, 'classless', Populist socialism, he was prepared to co-operate with the Chinese Communists as well, but only if they accepted his leadership unreservedly and supported the Kuomintang. He signed a pact of friendship with Lenin's government, but found it more difficult to get the Chinese Communists to co-operate with him on his terms.[1]

The Communists were led by Chen Tu-hsiu, one of the intellectual pioneers of Marxism in Asia, its first great propagandist in China, and the most outstanding figure of the Chinese Revolution up to the advent of Mao Tse-tung, to whom he was inferior as tactician, practical leader, and organizer, but superior, it seems, as thinker and theorist. Chen Tu-hsiu had been the initiator of the great campaign against the privileges the Western powers enjoyed in China: the campaign starting from Pekin University, of which Chen Tu-hsiu was a professor, assumed such power that under its pressure the Chinese government refused to sign the Versailles Treaty which sanctioned the privileges. It was largely under Chen Tu-hsiu's influence that

---

[1] The account given in these pages is based *inter alia* on Brandt, Schwartz, Fairbank, *A Documentary History of Chinese Communism*; Mao Tse-tung, *Selected Works*; M. N. Roy, *Revolution und Konterrevolution in China*; Chen Tu-hsiu, 'An Open Letter to the Party' (*Militant*, 1929); Stalin, *Works*; Trotsky, *Problems of the Chinese Revolution*; Isaacs, *The Tragedy of the Chinese Revolution*; Tang Leang-Li, *The Inner History of the Chinese Revolution*; files of *Bolshevik, Inprekor,* and *Revolutsionnyi Vostok*.

the Marxist propagandist circles had developed which formed the Communist party. He remained the party's undisputed leader from the moment of its foundation till late in 1927, throughout the crucial phases of the revolution. From the beginning he viewed with apprehension the political advice his party received from Moscow. He admitted the need for Communists to co-operate with the Kuomintang, but was afraid of too close an alliance which would prevent communism from establishing its own identity; he preferred his party to stand on its own feet before it marched with the Kuomintang. Moscow, however, insistently urged him to drop his scruples; and he possessed none of the strength of character and none of the slyness of Mao Tse-tung, who in similar situations never raised objections to Moscow's advice, always pretended to accept it, and then ignored it and acted according to his own lights, without ever provoking a genuine breach with Moscow. Chen Tu-hsiu was straightforward, soft, and lacked self-confidence; and these qualities made him a tragic figure. At every stage he frankly stated his objections to Moscow's policy; but he did not stick to them. When overruled, he submitted to the Comintern's authority, and against his better knowledge carried out Moscow's policy.

As early as in 1922–3 two men who were later prominent in the Trotskyist Opposition, Yoffe and Maring-Sneevliet,[1] played a crucial part in associating the young Chinese Communist party with the Kuomintang and in preparing the ground for the policy which Stalin and Bukharin were to pursue. Yoffe, as Ambassador of Lenin's government, negotiated the pact of friendship with Sun Yat-sen. Eager to facilitate his task and, no doubt, going beyond his terms of reference, he assured Sun Yat-sen that the Bolsheviks were not interested in promoting Chinese communism and that they would use their influence to ensure that the Chinese Communists co-operated with the Kuomintang on Sun Yat-sen's terms. Maring attended, as delegate of the Communist International, the second congress of the Chinese Communist party in 1922. It was on his initiative that the party

---

[1] Maring-Sneevliet, a Dutch Marxist, had been closely associated with the beginnings of communism in Indonesia, and represented the Dutch party in Moscow. In later years, especially throughout the 1930's, he was Trotsky's ardent follower. During the Second World War he led a resistance group in occupied Holland and was executed by the Nazis.

established contact with the Kuomintang and began to discuss the conditions of adherence to it. But Sun Yat-sen's terms were stiff; and the negotiations broke down.

Later in the year Maring returned to China and told Chen Tu-hsiu and his comrades that the Communist International firmly instructed them to join the Kuomintang, regardless of terms. Chen Tu-hsiu was reluctant to act on this instruction, but when Maring invoked the principle of international communist discipline, he and his comrades submitted. Sun Yat-sen insisted, like Chiang Kai-shek later, that the Communist party must refrain from criticizing openly the Kuomintang's policy and must observe its discipline—otherwise he would expel the Communists from the Kuomintang and consider his alliance with Russia null and void. By the beginning of 1924 the Communist party had joined the Kuomintang. It did not at first take Sun Yat-sen's terms to heart: it maintained its independence; and it pursued distinctly communist policies, incurring the Kuomintang's displeasure.

Communist influence grew rapidly. When in 1925 the great 'movement of 30 May' spread over southern China, the Communists were in its vanguard, inspiring the boycott of Western concessions and concerns and leading the general strike of Canton, the greatest so far in China's history. As the momentum of the movement increased, the Kuomintang leaders became frightened, tried to curb it, and clashed with the Communists. The latter sensed the approach of civil war, were anxious to untie their hands in time, and made representations to Moscow. In October 1925 Chen Tu-hsiu proposed to prepare his party's exodus from the Kuomintang. The Executive of the Communist International, however, vetoed the plan and admonished the Chinese party to do its utmost to avoid civil war. Soviet military and diplomatic advisers, Borodin, Blucher, and others, worked at Chiang Kai-shek's headquarters, arming and training his troops. Neither Bukharin nor Stalin, who by now effectively directed Soviet policy, believed that Chinese communism had any chance of seizing power in the near future; and both were anxious to maintain the Soviet alliance with the Kuomintang. The growth of communist influence threatened to disrupt that alliance and so they were determined to keep the Chinese party in its place.

Moscow thus urged Chen Tu-hsiu and his Central Committee to refrain from class struggle against the 'patriotic' bourgeoisie, from revolutionary-agrarian movements, and from criticism of Sun Yat-senism, which had since Sun Yat-sen's death become canonized as the ideology of the Kuomintang. To justify their attitude in Marxist terms, Bukharin and Stalin evolved the theory that the revolution which had begun in China, being bourgeois in character, could not set itself socialist objectives; that the anti-imperialist bourgeoisie behind the Kuomintang was playing a revolutionary role; and that it was consequently the duty of the Communist party to maintain unity with it, and do nothing that could antagonize it. Seeking further to substantiate their policy on doctrinal grounds, they invoked the view Lenin had expounded in 1905 that in the 'bourgeois' Russian Revolution, directed against Tsardom, socialists must aim at a 'democratic dictatorship of workers and peasants', not at a proletarian dictatorship. This precedent had little or no relevance to the situation in China: in 1905 Lenin and his party did not seek an alliance with the Liberal bourgeoisie against Tsardom—on the contrary, Lenin preached untiringly that the bourgeois revolution could conquer in Russia only under the leadership of the working class, in irreconcilable hostility to the Liberal bourgeoisie; and even the Mensheviks, who did seek an alliance with the bourgeoisie, did not dream of accepting the leadership and discipline of an organization dominated by it. Bukharin's and Stalin's policy was, as Trotsky later pointed out, a parody not merely of the Bolshevik but even of the Menshevik attitude in 1905.

However, these doctrinal sophistries served a purpose: they embellished Moscow's policy ideologically and soothed the conscience of Communists who felt uneasy over it. The opportunism of that policy showed itself startlingly when, early in 1926, the Kuomintang was admitted to the Communist International as an associate party and the Executive of the International elected with a flourish General Chiang Kai-shek as honorary member. With this gesture Stalin and Bukharin demonstrated their 'good will' to the Kuomintang and browbeat the Chinese Communists. On 20 March, only a few weeks after the 'General Staff of World Revolution' had elected him its honorary member, Chiang Kai-shek carried out his first anti-communist coup. He barred communists from all posts at the headquarters of the Kuomintang, banned their criticisms of Sun Yat-sen's political philosophy, and demanded from their Central Committee that it should submit a list of all party members who had joined the Kuomintang. Pressed by Soviet advisers, Chen Tu-hsiu and his comrades agreed. But, convinced that Chiang Kai-shek was preparing civil war against them, they were anxious to organize communist-led armed forces to match, if need be, his military strength; and they asked for Soviet assistance. The Soviet representatives at Canton categorically vetoed this plan and refused all assistance. Once again Chen Tu-hsiu bowed to the Comintern's authority.[1] The newspapers of Moscow made no comment on Chiang's coup—they did not even report the event. The Politbureau, fearing complications, sent Bubnov, the ex-Decemist, to China to enforce its policy and persuade the Chinese communists that it was their revolutionary duty to 'do coolie service' to the Kuomintang.[2]

During all these events the Chinese issue remained as if outside the Russian inner party controversy. The fact deserves to be underlined: it disposes of one of the legends of vulgar Trotskyism which maintains that the Opposition had from the beginning unremittingly resisted Stalin's and Bukharin's 'betrayal of the Chinese Revolution'. No doubt, Trotsky himself had had his misgivings as early as at the beginning of 1924. He had then expressed at the Politbureau a critical view of the adherence of the Chinese Communists to the Kuomintang; and in the following two years he restated his view on a few occasions. But he did it almost casually. He did not dwell on the matter and did not go to its heart. When he found that at the Politbureau he stood alone—all other members backed the Chinese policy—he did not try to repeat his objections before the wider forum of the Central Committee. Not once, it seems, in these years, 1924–6, did he speak about China in the Executive or the commissions of the Comintern. Not once, at any rate, did he allude in public to any difference of opinion in this matter. He appears to have given to it far less attention and far less weight than he

[1] Chen Tu-hsiu relates that the Chinese Central Committee requested the Soviet military advisers in Canton to supply from the munitions which had arrived for Chiang Kai-shek at least 5,000 rifles to the communists to enable them to arm insurgent Kwantung peasants. The request was refused.
[2] Quoted from Chen Tu-hsiu's 'Open Letter'.

gave British or even Polish communist policies. He was evidently not clearly aware of the force of the tempest breaking over China and of the magnitude and gravity of the approaching crisis in communist policy.

Early in 1926 he was still concerned more closely with the conduct of Soviet diplomacy towards China than with the direction of communist affairs there. He presided over a special commission—Chicherin, Dzerzhinsky, and Voroshilov were its members—which was to prepare recommendations for the Politbureau on the line that Soviet diplomacy ought to pursue in China. Of the commission's work little is known, apart from its report which Trotsky submitted to the Politbureau on 25 March 1926.[1] As he did not dissociate himself from the report, it must be assumed that he was in basic agreement with it. The commission made its recommendations in strictly diplomatic terms, without reference to the objectives of the Chinese Communist party. While that party strove, in co-operation with the Kuomintang, to abolish the *status quo* in China, the commission offered instructions for the Soviet diplomatic services on the attitudes they should adopt within the *status quo*. Both the Communist party and the Kuomintang called for the political unification of the country, that is for the overthrow of Chang Tso-lin's government, whose writ ran in the north, and for the spread of revolution from south to north. Trotsky's commission reckoned with China's continued division; and its recommendations were as if calculated to prolong it. At this time Chiang Kai-shek was already preparing his great military expedition against the north. Amid the confusion which reigned across the Soviet Far Eastern frontier, Trotsky's commission sought not to promote revolution but to secure every possible advantage for the Soviet government. Thus the commission suggested that Soviet diplomatic agencies should seek a *modus vivendi* and a division of spheres between Chiang Kai-shek's government in the south and Chang Tso-lin's in the north.

Trotsky later maintained that at the Politbureau, during the discussion on the report, Stalin tabled an amendment that Soviet military advisers should dissuade Chiang Kai-shek from undertaking his expedition. The commission rejected the amendment, but in more general terms it advised Soviet agencies in China to

[1] *The Archives.*

'urge moderation' on Chiang Kai-shek. The Politbureau's main concern was with safeguarding Russia's position in Manchuria against Japanese encroachments. The commission therefore advised that Russian envoys in northern China should encourage Chang Tso-lin to pursue a policy of balancing between Russia and Japan. Moscow, too weak to eliminate Japanese influence from Manchuria and not believing in the Kuomintang's ability to do so, was ready to reconcile itself to Japan's predominance in southern Manchuria, provided that Russia, remaining in possession of the North Eastern Chinese Railway, maintained her hold on the northern part of the province. The commission urged Soviet envoys to prepare public opinion 'carefully and tactfully' for this arrangement, which was likely to hurt patriotic feelings in China. The Politbureau's motives were mixed and tangled. It was concerned over Manchuria. But it also feared that Chiang Kai-shek's expedition against the north might provoke the Western powers to intervene in China more energetically than hitherto. And it also suspected that Chiang was planning the expedition as a diversion from revolution, a means to absorb and disperse the revolutionary energies of the south.

In April the Politbureau accepted the report of Trotsky's commission. At this point, however, Trotsky raised the problem of the strictly communist policy in China. This, he held, should remain independent of Soviet diplomatic considerations: it was the diplomats' business to make deals with existing bourgeois governments—even with old-time war-lords; but it was the revolutionaries' job to overthrow them. He protested against the admission of the Kuomintang to the Comintern. Sun Yatsenism, he said, extolled the harmony of all classes; and so it was incompatible with Marxism committed to class struggle. In electing Chiang Kai-shek an honorary member, the Executive of the Comintern had played a bad joke. Finally, he repeated his old objections to the adherence of the Chinese Communists to the Kuomintang.[1] Once more, all members of the Politbureau, including Zinoviev and Kamenev, who were now on the point of forming the Joint Opposition, defended the official conduct of Chinese communist affairs. This exchange, too, was incidental. It occurred within the closed doors of the Politbureau; and it had no consequences.

[1] Stalin, *Sochinenya,* vol. x, pp. 154-5.

Then, for a whole year, from April 1926 till the end of March 1927, neither Trotsky nor the other leaders of the Opposition took up the issue. (Only Radek, who since May 1925 had headed the Sun Yat-sen University in Moscow and had to expound party policy to perplexed Chinese students, 'pestered' the Politbureau for guidance. This he failed to obtain and he expressed mild misgivings.) Yet this was the most crucial and critical year in the history of the Chinese Revolution. On 26 July, four months after the Politbureau had discussed the report of Trotsky's commission, Chiang Kai-shek, ignoring Soviet 'counsels of moderation', issued his marching orders for the northern expedition. His troops advanced rapidly. Against Moscow's expectation, their appearance in central China acted as a tremendous stimulus to a nation-wide revolutionary movement. The northern and central provinces were astir with risings against Chang Tso-lin's administration and the corrupt war-lords who supported it. The urban workers were the most active element in the political movement. The Communist party was in the ascendant. It led and inspired the risings. Its members stood at the head of the trade unions, which had sprung into being overnight and found enthusiastic mass support in liberated cities and towns. All along the route of Chiang Kai-shek's advance the peasantry welcomed his troops and, counting on their support, rose against war-lords, landlords, and usurers, ready to dispossess them.

Chiang Kai-shek was frightened by the tide of revolution and sought to contain it. He forbade strikes and demonstrations, suppressed trade unions, and sent out punitive expeditions to subdue the peasants and to requisition food. Intense hostility developed between his headquarters and the Communist party. Chen Tu-hsiu, reporting these events to Moscow, demanded that his party should at last be authorized to make its exodus from the Kuomintang. He was still for a united front of Communists and Kuomintang against the northern war-lords and the agencies of the Western powers; but he held that it was imperative for his party to shake off the Kuomintang's discipline, regain freedom of manœuvre, encourage the proletarian movement in the towns, back the peasantry's struggle for land, and get ready for open conflict with Chiang Kai-shek. A rebuff was once again the answer Chen Tu-hsiu received from the

Executive of the International. Bukharin rejected his demand as dangerous 'ultra left' heresy. As the Central Committee's *rapporteur* at the party conference in October, Bukharin reasserted the need 'to maintain a single national revolutionary front' in China where 'the commercial industrial bourgeoisie was at present playing an objectively revolutionary role . . .'.[1] It might be difficult, he went on, for Communists to satisfy in these circumstances the peasantry's clamour for land. The Chinese party had to keep a balance between the interests of the peasantry and those of the anti-imperialist bourgeoisie which was opposed to agrarian upheaval. The Communists' overriding duty was to safeguard the unity of all anti-imperialist forces; and they must repudiate all attempts at disrupting the Kuomintang.[2] Patience and circumspection were the watchwords—all the more so as the revolutionary atmosphere was affecting the Kuomintang too, bringing about its 'radicalization', and 'reducing its right wing to impotence'.

Somewhat later Stalin also, speaking at the Comintern's Chinese commission, extolled Chiang Kai-shek's 'revolutionary armies', demanded from the Communists complete submission to the Kuomintang, and warned them against any attempts at setting up Soviets at the height of a 'bourgeois revolution'.[3]

On the face of it, Stalin's and Bukharin's predictions about a 'leftward shift in the Kuomintang' presently came true. In November the Kuomintang government was reconstructed into a broad coalition, in which leftish groupings led by Wang Ching-wei, Chiang's rival, came to the fore, and which included two Communist Ministers in charge of agriculture and labour. The new government moved from Canton to Wuhan. The Kuomintang right, however, was far from being 'reduced to impotence'. Chiang Kai-shek remained in supreme command of the armed forces and was busy setting the stage for his dictatorship. It was rather the Communists within the government who were reduced to impotence. The Minister of Agriculture exerted himself to stem the tide of agrarian revolt; and the Minister of Labour had to swallow Chiang Kai-shek's anti-labour

[1] *15 Konferentsya VKP (b)*, p. 27.
[2] Ibid., pp. 28-29.
[3] Stalin, *Sochinenya*, vol. viii, pp. 357-74.

decrees.[1] From Moscow ever new envoys arrived to calm the Communists: after Bubnov's departure, the eminent Indian communist leader M. N. Roy appeared with this mission at Wuhan towards the end of the year 1926.

The Politbureau was still preaching unity with the Kuomintang when in the spring of 1927 Chiang Kai-shek, still honorary member of the Executive of the Comintern, carried out another coup by which he initiated open counter-revolution. The scene was Shanghai, China's largest city and commercial centre, dominated by the extra-territorial enclaves of the Western powers and their warships anchored in the harbour. Shortly before Chiang Kai-shek's troops had entered, the workers of Shanghai rose, overthrew the old administration, and took control of the city. Once again the hapless Chen Tu-hsiu appealed to Comintern headquarters seeking to impress them with the significance of the event—the greatest proletarian rising Asia had seen—and to disentangle his party from its commitments to the Kuomintang. Once again he and his comrades were pressed to reaffirm their allegiance to the Kuomintang and also to yield control over Shanghai to Chiang Kai-shek. Bewildered but disciplined, rejecting assistance offered them by Chiang's own detachments, the Communists on the spot accepted these instructions, laid down arms, and surrendered. Then, on 12 April, only three weeks after their victorious rising, Chiang Kai-shek ordered a massacre in which tens of thousands of Communists and of workers who had followed them were slaughtered.

Thus the Chinese Communists were made to pay their tribute to the sacred egoism of the first workers' state, the egoism that the doctrine of socialism in one country had elevated to a principle. The hidden implications of the doctrine were brought out and written in blood on the pavements of Shanghai. Stalin and Bukharin considered themselves entitled to sacrifice the Chinese Revolution in what they believed to be the interest of the consolidation of the Soviet Union. They sought desperately to avoid any course of action which might turn the capitalist powers against the Soviet Union and disturb its hard-won and precarious peace and equilibrium. They conceived their Chinese

[1] M. N. Roy, *Revolution und Konterrevolution in China*, pp. 413 ff. Harold Isaacs, *The Tragedy of the Chinese Revolution*, chapters 14 and 15.

policy in the same mood in which they shaped their present domestic policies, believing that it was wisdom's first commandment to keep to the safe side and to proceed cautiously, step by step, in the conduct of all affairs of state. The same logic which had induced them to placate the 'strong farmer' at home led them to woo so excessively the Kuomintang. They had indeed expected the Chinese Revolution to develop at the snail's pace at which Bukharin thought that socialism could progress in Russia.

As so often in history, this kind of weary and seemingly practical realism was but a pipe-dream. It was impossible to ride the dragons of revolution and counter-revolution at the snail's pace. But the Bolsheviks had for years exerted themselves to gain a breathing space for the Soviet Union. Having gained it, they sought to draw it out indefinitely; and they reacted with sore resentment against anything which might conceivably interrupt it or shorten it. At home a policy risking conflict with the peasantry might interrupt it. Abroad a forward communist policy might interrupt it. The ruling factions were determined that this should not happen; and so, almost without turning a hair, they made the Chinese Revolution prolong with its dying breath the breathing space for the workers' first state.[1]

It was only on 31 March 1927, after a year's silence and barely a fortnight before the Shanghai massacre, that Trotsky attacked the Politbureau's Chinese policy.[2] That he had been implicitly opposed to that policy and its premisses cannot be doubted. His earlier protests against the entry of the Chinese party into the Kuomintang and against the honour the Comintern had bestowed on Chiang Kai-shek had shown it. His own conceptions, developed consistently over more than twenty years, made it impossible for him to accept even for a moment the ideological arguments with which Stalin and Bukharin endeavoured to justify their political strategy. Nothing was farther from the exponent of permanent revolution than their view that because the upheaval in China was bourgeois in character, the Communists

---

[1] Stalin attempted to treat the next Chinese Revolution (1947-9) in the same way, but the momentum of that revolution was too great for that; and Mao Tse-tung had learned his lesson from the experience of Chen Tu-hsiu.

[2] See his letter to the Politbureau and the Central Committee in *The Archives*.

there must forgo their socialist aspirations for the sake of an alliance with the Kuomintang bourgeoisie. It was inherent in Trotsky's whole way of thinking that he should take the view that the bourgeois and the socialist phases of the revolution would merge, as they had merged in Russia; that the working class would be the chief driving force throughout; and that the revolution would either win as a proletarian movement ushering in a proletarian dictatorship or would not win at all.

Why then did he keep silent during the decisive year? He was, of course, ill much of the time; he was up to his neck in domestic issues and the affairs of European communism; he was engaged in an unequal struggle; and he had to reckon with the Opposition's delicate tactical situation. His attention—so his private papers suggest—did not become focused on the Chinese problem before the early months of 1927. He had not been aware how far the Politbureau's opportunism and cynicism had gone. He had no knowledge of the reluctance with which the Chinese Communists had acted on its instructions. He had no inkling of Chen Tu-hsiu's many appeals and protests—Stalin and Bukharin had locked them up in secret files; nor was he acquainted with other confidential communications that had passed between Moscow and Canton or Wuhan. When at last, having little more to go by than news generally accessible, he became alarmed and raised the issue within the Opposition's leading circle, he found that even there he was almost isolated.

Up to the end of 1926 Zinoviev and Kamenev had had little with which to reproach official policy. Sticking to the 'old Bolshevik' ideas of 1905, they too held that the Chinese Revolution must of necessity limit itself to its bourgeois and anti-imperialist objectives. They approved the party's entry into the Kuomintang. In his heyday at the Comintern Zinoviev himself must have played his part in implementing this policy and in over-ruling Chen Tu-hsiu's objections. But even the most important Trotskyists, Preobrazhensky, Radek, and also, it seems, Pyatakov and Rakovsky, were taken aback when Trotsky applied the scheme of permanent revolution to China.[1] They did not think that proletarian dictatorship could be established and that the Communist party could seize power in a country even more

[1] See Trotsky's 1928 correspondence with Radek and Preobrazhensky in *The Archives*.

retarded socially than Russia had been. Only when Trotsky threatened to raise the issue on his own responsibility and virtually to split the Opposition over it, and only after it had become abundantly clear that the workers were in fact the 'chief driving force' of the Chinese Revolution and that in obstructing it Stalin and Bukharin had long since gone beyond the point at which 'old Bolshevik' theory and dogma had any meaning, did the leaders of the Opposition consent to open a controversy over China in the Central Committee. Even then they were prepared to turn against the official policy but not against its premises. They were willing to attack the excessive zeal with which Stalin and Bukharin had made of the Chinese party Chiang Kai-shek's accomplice in subduing strikes, demonstrations, and peasant risings; but they still held that the Communists should remain within the Kuomintang, and that this 'bourgeois' revolution could not usher in a proletarian dictatorship for China. This was a self-contradictory and self-defeating attitude, for once it had been conceded that the Communists must stay within the Kuomintang, it was inconsistent to expect them not to pay for it.

Trotsky contented himself with opening the new controversy inside the limits within which Zinoviev, Kamenev, Radek, Preobrazhensky, and Pyatakov were prepared to conduct it. In the early months of the year the chiefs of the Opposition were still seeking to adjust their differences; only towards the end of March did they define the common ground from which they would start the attack. They now embarked upon a new and dangerous venture. Trotsky was conscious of its bleak prospects. On 22 March, the very day when the workers of Shanghai were up in arms and Chiang Kai-shek's troops were entering the city, he remarked in his private papers that there was 'the danger that at the Central Committee they would turn the matter into a factional squabble instead of discussing it seriously'. Regardless of this, the issue had to be posed, for 'how can one keep silent when nothing less than the head of the Chinese proletariat is at stake?'[1]

The fact that the Opposition applied itself to China so late and with so many mental reservations weakened its stand from the beginning. The policy which was in the next few weeks to

[1] *The Trotsky Archives.*

produce the débâcle had been pursued for at least three long years. It could hardly have been reversed within two or three weeks. Even as Trotsky was resolving that he could not keep silent when 'the head of the Chinese proletariat was at stake' that head was already under Chiang Kai-shek's hammer-blow. When the Opposition then denounced Stalin and Bukharin as those responsible, they retorted by asking where the Opposition had been and why it had kept silent during three long years.[1] They plausibly suggested that the critics' indignation was spurious, that the Opposition had been on the look-out for a debating point, and that it grasped at the Chinese issue 'as a drowning man grasps at a straw'. The rejoinders were not wholly undeserved. Stalin further brought to light the inconsistencies in the Opposition's attitude and exploited to the utmost the differences between Trotsky and his colleagues. This does not alter the fact that the Opposition's criticisms, even if belated and half-hearted, were justified. As to Trotsky—throughout these fateful weeks, day after day he struggled with all his courage and energy for a last-minute revision of policy. His analyses of the situation were of crystalline clarity; his prognostications were faultless; and his warnings were like mighty alarm bells.

Posterity can only marvel at the malignant complacency and wilfulness with which the ruling factions shut their ears during these weeks, and throughout the rest of the year, when, amid many rapid shifts in China, Trotsky ceaselessly tried to induce them to salvage at least the wreckage of Chinese communism. At every stage they spurned his promptings, partly from political calculation and partly because they were bent on proving him wrong. When events proved him right and brought fresh disasters, they steered frantically and yet half-heartedly in the direction which he had favoured but which it was already too late to take; and invariably they sought to justify themselves by heaping denunciation and abuse upon Trotskyism.

It will not be out of place to survey here at least some of Trotsky's interventions. In his letter to the Politbureau, of 31 March, complaining that he had no access to reports from Soviet advisers and Comintern envoys, he pointed to the upsurge in China of the workers' movement and of communism as the dominant feature of this phase of the revolution. Why, he

---

[1] Stalin, *Sochinenya*, vol. x, pp. 17, 21, 25 and *passim*.

asked, did the party not call upon the workers to elect Soviets, at least in the main industrial centres such as Shanghai and Hankow? Why did it not encourage agrarian revolution? Why did it not seek to establish the closest co-operation between insurgent workers and peasants? This alone could save the revolution which, he insisted, was already confronted with the danger of a counter-revolutionary military coup.

Three days later, on 3 April, he came out against an editorial statement in the *Communist International* to the effect that the crucial issue in China was 'the further development of the Kuomintang'.[1] This was exactly what was not the crucial issue, he replied. The Kuomintang could not lead the revolution to victory. Workers and peasants must be urgently organized in Councils. Day in, day out, he protested against speeches by Kalinin, Rudzutak, and others, who asserted that all classes of Chinese society 'look upon the Kuomintang as upon *their* party and should give the Kuomintang government their whole-hearted support'. On 5 April, a week before the Shanghai crisis, he wrote emphatically that Chiang Kai-shek was preparing a quasi-Bonapartist or fascist coup and that only Workers' Councils could frustrate him. Such councils, Soviets, should first act as a counterbalance to the Kuomintang administration, and then, after a period of 'dual power', become the organs of insurrection and revolutionary government. On 12 April, the day of the Shanghai massacre, he wrote a scathing refutation of a eulogy of the Kuomintang which had appeared in *Pravda*—its author, Martynov, had for twenty years been the most right-wing Menshevik, had joined the Communist party only some years after the civil war, and was now a leading light in the Comintern. In the next few days Trotsky wrote to Stalin, once more asking in vain to be shown the confidential reports from China. Grotesquely, on 18 April, a week after the Shanghai massacre, the eastern secretariat of the Comintern invited him to autograph, as other Soviet leaders did, a picture for Chiang Kai-shek as a token of friendship. He refused and rebuked with angry contempt the Comintern officials and their inspirers.[2]

By this time reports about the Shanghai butchery had reached Moscow. Stalin's and Bukharin's pleadings were still fresh in

[1] *Kommunisticheskii Internatsional*, 18 March 1927.
[2] All this correspondence is quoted from *The Archives*.

everyone's memory. Fortunately for them the criticisms of the Opposition had not become public knowledge—only some party cadres, Comintern officials, and Chinese students in Moscow were aware of the controversy. Stalin and Bukharin did their best to belittle the events and presented them as an episodic set-back to the Chinese Revolution.[1] They were compelled, how-ever, to modify their policy. The 'alliance' with Chiang Kai-shek having lapsed, they instructed the Chinese Communists to attach themselves all the closer to the 'left Kuomintang', i.e. the Wuhan government, headed by Wang Ching-wei. The left Kuomintang was temporarily in conflict with Chiang Kai-shek and anxious to benefit from communist support. Moscow readily granted it and pledged that Chen Tu-hsiu and his comrades would refrain as before from 'provocative' revolutionary action and submit to Wang Ching-wei's discipline.[2]

Trotsky asserted that the new policy merely reproduced the old mistakes on a smaller scale. The Communists should be encouraged to adopt at last a forward policy, to form Workers' and Peasants' Councils, and to support with all their strength the rebellious peasantry in the south of China, where Chiang Kai-shek's writ did not run and they could still act. True, he saw the possibilities of revolutionary action as greatly reduced: Chiang Kai-shek's coup was, despite official attempts to belittle it, a 'basic shift' from revolution to counter-revolution and a 'crushing blow' to the urban revolutionary forces. But he as-sumed that Chiang Kai-shek had not succeeded in overwhelm-ing the scattered and elusive agrarian movements; that the peasants' struggle for the land would go on; and that it might in time provide the stimulus for a revival of revolution in the towns.[3] Communists should throw their full weight behind the agrarian movements; but to be able to do this they must at last break with the Kuomintang, 'left' as well as right, and pursue their own aims. On this point again the Zinovievists disagreed. They still preferred the Chinese party to remain within the left Kuomintang; but they wished it to pursue there an independent

---

[1] Stalin, *Sochinenya*, vol. ix, pp. 259–60 and *passim*.

[2] See Stalin's 'theses' in *Sochinenya*, vol. ix, p. 221. This attitude was reluctantly adopted by the Chinese Communist party during its congress at the end of April. See Chen Tu-hsiu's 'Open Letter'.

[3] See 'The Situation in China After Chiang's Coup and the Prospects' (written on 19 April 1927) in *The Archives*.

policy, in opposition to Wang Ching-wei. Along these lines the Opposition argued its case in many statements, none of which saw the light.

The Opposition's return to the attack over China threw the ruling factions into a fever. Their predicament was grave, for never before had the futility of their policy been so glaringly revealed and never before had their leaders so outrageously and ridiculously disgraced themselves. About the same time another setback, minor by comparison, added to their embarrassment. The Anglo-Soviet Council broke up: the leaders of the British trade unions contracted out. In the diplomatic field, there was high tension between Britain and the Soviet Union. Yet another of the great hopes of official policy had vanished into thin air. The ruling factions made the most of this circumstance, however, precisely to divert attention from China and to block all discussion. They raised an outcry about the danger of war and intervention and created a state of public nervousness and national alarm, in which it was all too easy to damn the Opposition as unpatriotic. Stalin cracked the whip, threw out fresh threats of expulsion, and used every means of moral pressure to silence his critics. At his prompting Krupskaya begged Zinoviev and Kamenev not to make a 'row over China' and to remember that they might find themselves 'criticizing the party from the outside'. The Opposition wished to avoid the 'row'. Trotsky and Zinoviev proposed that the Central Committee should meet and thrash out the differences in private so that the discussion should not be reported even in the confidential bulletin which the Central Committee issued for the 'activists'. Stalin, however, would have no debate even off the record, and the Politbureau refused to call the meeting.[1]

Then, in the last week of May, Trotsky forced a debate at a session of the Executive of the Comintern. He appealed from the

[1] On 7 May Trotsky wrote a letter to Krupskaya. Hurt by her talk about the 'row over China' he asked her not to evade a great issue. 'Who is right, we or Stalin?' He recounted all that the Opposition had done to secure an off-the-record discussion, and he reminded Krupskaya that until recently she had been with the Opposition against Stalin's 'brutality and disloyalty'. Had Stalin's régime become any better since? He wrote to Lenin's widow in grief and disappointment, mingled with a warm sentiment—this was in a way his farewell to her—and he hesitated over the conclusion of the letter: 'From all my heart I wish you good health and good ... confidence in the integrity of that line which ....' He deleted, rewrote, and deleted again the last two lines. The draft of the letter is in *The Archives*.

Russian party to the International. In doing so he acted within his rights. The Executive of the International was nominally the court of appeal before which any communist was entitled to lodge a complaint against his own party. *Pravda*, however, denounced the appeal beforehand as an act of disloyalty and a breach of discipline. The Opposition, nevertheless, used the opportunity to subject to criticism the whole of the official policy at home as well as abroad, in Asia as well as in Europe. To strengthen its hands and protect itself against reprisals, or, as Trotsky put it, 'to spread the expected blow over many shoulders', the Opposition staged a political demonstration similar to that the Forty Six had made in 1923: on the eve of the session a group of Eighty Four prominent party men declared their solidarity with Trotsky's and Zinoviev's views.[1] Stalin could not indeed apply disciplinary measures immediately against Trotsky and Zinoviev without applying them also to the Eighty Four and then to the Three Hundred, who signed the statement of solidarity. But their joint *démarche* enabled Stalin to claim that the Opposition had broken its pledge and reconstituted itself as a faction.[2]

On 24 May Trotsky addressed the Comintern Executive. Ironically, he had to begin with a protest against the Executive's treatment of Zinoviev, its erstwhile President who not so long ago had indicted him before this very Executive—Zinoviev was now not even admitted to the session. Trotsky spoke of the 'intellectual weakness and uncertainty' which led Stalin and Bukharin to conceal from the International the truth about China and to denounce the Opposition's appeal as a crime. The Executive should publish its proceedings—'the problems of the Chinese revolution could not be stuck in a bottle and sealed

---

[1] The document is sometimes referred to as the Statement of the Eighty Three and sometimes of the Eighty Four. It was presented to the Central Committee between 23 and 26 May. Later the number of signatories rose to 300.

[2] See Trotsky's letter of 12 July 1927 addressed to one of the leaders of the Opposition who held ambassadorial posts abroad (either to Krestinsky or to Antonov-Ovseenko). His correspondent thought that the *démarche* of the Eighty Four needlessly aggravated the struggle. Trotsky admitted that such doubts had been entertained by Oppositionists in Moscow as well, but said that they decided in favour of the *démarche* as a measure of self-protection. He did not believe that matters were aggravated because the Opposition spoke out. He thought that his correspondent had through a long absence become cut off from Russia and invited him to make a trip to Moscow to get the feeling of the atmosphere there. *The Archives.*

up'. It should beware of the grave dangers lurking in the 'régime' of the International modelled on that of the Russian party. Some foreign communist leaders were impatient with the Opposition and imagined that the Russian party and the International would resume normal life once Trotsky and Zinoviev had been disposed of. They were deluding themselves. 'The contrary will happen. . . . On this road there will be only further difficulties and further convulsions.' No one in the International trusted himself to speak up for fear that criticism might harm the Soviet Union. But nothing was as harmful as lack of criticism. The Chinese débâcle had proved it. Stalin and Bukharin were concerned mainly with self-justification and with covering up their disastrous mistakes. They claimed that they had foreseen it all and provided for all. Yet only a week before the crisis in Shanghai Stalin had boasted at a party meeting that 'we would use the Chinese bourgeoisie and then throw it away like a squeezed lemon'. 'This speech was never made public because a few days later the "squeezed lemon" seized power.' Soviet advisers and Comintern envoys, especially Borodin, behaved 'as if they represented some sort of a *Kuom*intern':

they hindered the independent policy of the proletariat, its independent organization and especially the arming of the workers. . . . Heaven forbid that arms in hand the workers should frighten away that great chimera of a national revolution which should embrace all classes of Chinese society. . . . The Communist Party of China is a shackled party. . . . Why has it not had and why does it not have to this day its own daily newspaper? Because the Kuomintang does not want it. . . . But in this way the working class has been kept politically disarmed.[1]

While the Executive was in session, the tension between Britain and the Soviet Union reached a critical point: the British police had raided the offices of the Soviet trade mission in London and the British government broke off relations with Russia. Stalin exploited this circumstance. 'I must state, comrades', he told the Executive, in conclusion of his speech, 'that Trotsky has chosen for his attacks . . . an all too inopportune moment. I have just received the news that the English Conservative government has resolved to break off relations with the U.S.S.R. There is no need to prove that what is intended is

[1] Trotsky, *Problems of the Chinese Revolution*, pp. 91–92.

a wholesale crusade against communists. The crusade has already started. Some threaten the party with war and intervention; others with a split. There comes into being something like a united front from Chamberlain to Trotsky. . . . You need not doubt that we shall be able to break up this new front.'[1] He staked everything on the left Kuomintang as confidently as he had previously staked it on the right Kuomintang: 'Only blind people can deny the left Kuomintang the role of the organ of revolutionary struggle, the role of the organ of insurrection against feudal survivals and imperialism in China.'[2] He demanded, in effect, that the Opposition should keep silent on pain of being charged with bringing aid and comfort to the enemy.

This was not the first time that Stalin had made hints about 'a united front from Chamberlain to Trotsky'. A few months earlier *Pravda* had done it anonymously.[3] But for the first time now vague and anonymous insinuation was replaced by direct accusation. Here is Trotsky's rejoinder:

> It would be manifestly absurd to believe that the Opposition will renounce its views. . . . Stalin has said that the Opposition stands in one front with Chamberlain and Mussolini. . . . To this I reply: Nothing has facilitated Chamberlain's work as much as Stalin's false policy, especially in China. . . . Not a single honest worker will believe the insane infamy about the united front of Chamberlain and Trotsky.

In reply to Stalin's appeal in favour of the left Kuomintang Trotsky said:

> Stalin assumes and wants the International to assume responsibility for the policy of the Kuomintang and of the Wuhan government as he repeatedly assumed responsibility for the policy of . . . Chiang Kai-shek. We have nothing in common with this. We do not want to assume even a shadow of responsibility for the conduct of the Wuhan government and the leadership of the Kuomintang; and we urgently advise the Comintern to reject this responsibility. We say directly to the Chinese peasants: the leaders of the left

---

[1] Stalin, *Sochinenya*, vol. ix, pp. 311–12.   [2] Ibid., p. 302.

[3] *The Archives* contain the draft of a sharp protest against this, written on 6 January 1927, addressed to the Politbureau. Zinoviev objected to its sharpness and produced another draft begging the Politbureau to protect the Opposition from slander.

Kuomintang . . . will inevitably betray you if you follow them . . . instead of forming your own independent Soviets. . . . [They] will unite ten times with Chiang Kai-shek against the workers and peasants.[1]

These exchanges were still going on in the Kremlin when in the remote south of China Trotsky's prediction was already coming true. In May there occurred the so-called Chan-Sha coup. The Wuhan government in its turn set out to suppress trade unions, sent out troops to quell peasant risings, and struck at the Communists. For almost a month the Soviet press kept silent about these events.[2] The resolutions of the Executive, dictated by Stalin and Bukharin, were grotesquely out of date even before they had come off the printing presses; and Stalin hastened to frame new instructions for the Chinese party. He still ordered it to remain within the left Kuomintang and go on supporting the Wuhan government; but he instructed it to protest against the employment of troops against the peasants and to advise the Wuhan government to seek the assistance of Peasant Councils in restraining the agrarian movement instead of resorting to arms. By now, however, the left Kuomintang was expelling Communists from its ranks. Throughout June and July the breach between them deepened; and the stage was set for a reconciliation between the left Kuomintang and Chiang Kai-shek.

At once the repercussions were felt in Moscow. Almost daily Trotsky protested against the suppression of information. Zinoviev asked that a party court should try Bukharin, who as Editor of *Pravda* was responsible for the suppression. At last Zinoviev and Radek agreed to demand with Trotsky that the Communists should contract out of the left Kuomintang. This was now pointless, for since the left Kuomintang had broken with the Communists, there was nothing that even Stalin could do but to advise them to . . . break with it.

Stalin was in fact already preparing to carry out one of his major turns of policy and switch over to that 'ultra left' course which, towards the end of the year, was to lead the Chinese Communists to stage, at the ebb of the revolution, the futile and

---

[1] *The Archives*; *Problems of the Chinese Revolution*, pp. 102–11.

[2] The chiefs of the Opposition learned about them from a confidential bulletin of the Soviet News Agency.

bloody rising of Canton. In July he withdrew Borodin and Roy from China and sent out Lominadze, a secretary of the Soviet Comsomol, and Heinz Neumann, a German communist, both without an inkling of Chinese affairs and both with a bent for 'putschism', to carry out a coup in the Chinese party. They branded Chen Tu-hsiu, the reluctant but loyal executor of Stalin's and Bukharin's orders, as the 'opportunist' villain of the piece and made him the scapegoat for all failures.

At home Stalin went on playing up the danger of war and of an anti-communist crusade; and he intensified the drive against the Opposition. He sent many chiefs of the Opposition abroad on the pretext that they were needed for various diplomatic missions. Pyatakov, Preobrazhensky, and Vladimir Kossior had joined Rakovsky at the Embassy in Paris. Kamenev was appointed Ambassador to Mussolini—there could be no more frustrating and humiliating assignment for the former Chairman of the Politbureau. Antonov-Ovseenko was in Prague; Safarov, the Zinovievist leader of the Comsomol, was posted to Constantinople; others were detailed to Austria, Germany, Persia, and Latin America. Thus the leading group of the Opposition was largely dispersed. One after another the Eighty Four were demoted, penalized, and, on the pretext of administrative appointments, shifted to remote provinces. Repression was all the less disguised and blunter the lower down it reached: men of the rank and file were sacked and dispatched into the wilderness without any pretext.

The Opposition was exasperated and tried to defend itself, protesting against the veiled forms of deportation and exile. This was of no avail. The ruling factions saw in every one of the Opposition's attempts at self-defence a new offence justifying fresh reprisals. Every complaint was received as another sign of malignant insubordination; and every cry or even whimper of protest as a call to revolt. So persistent were the Stalinists and Bukharinists in twisting the Opposition's intentions and in making even its most timorous gestures appear as acts of unheard of defiance that in the end every such gesture did become an act of defiance, that the Oppositionist had to be full of stubborn insubordination to lodge any complaint whatsoever, and that even a whimper of protest resounded like the clarion call of rebellion. Any incident, however trivial in itself, was now liable to arouse furious passions in the factions, to make their blood boil, and to shake party and government.

One such incident was 'the meeting at the Yaroslavl station'. About the middle of June Smilga was ordered to leave Moscow and to take up a post at Khabarovsk, on the Manchurian frontier. The leader of the Baltic Fleet in the October Revolution, a distinguished political commissar in the civil war, and an economist, Smilga was one of the most respected and popular chiefs of the Zinovievist faction. On the day of his departure from Moscow several thousand Oppositionists and their friends gathered at the Yaroslavl railway station to see him off and to demonstrate against the surreptitious victimization. The crowd was angry. The demonstration was unprecedented. It was staged in a public place, amid all the traffic normal at a great railway junction. Travellers and passers-by, non-party men, mingled with the demonstrators, overheard their unflattering remarks about the party leaders, and picked up their agitated exclamations. They also listened to Trotsky and Zinoviev who made speeches. Because of these circumstances, the farewell to Smilga became the Opposition's first public, though only half premeditated, demonstration against the ruling group. Trotsky, aware of the delicacy of the situation, addressed the crowd in a restrained manner. He made no reference to the inner-party conflict. He did not, it seems, even allude to the cause of the manifestation. Instead, he spoke gravely about the international tension and the threat of war and about the allegiance which all good Bolsheviks and citizens owed the party.

The ruling group nevertheless charged Trotsky and Zinoviev with making an attempt to carry the inner-party controversy beyond the party. Humble Oppositionists who were found to have been present at the Yaroslavl station were expelled from the cells without ado. The excitement over the incident lasted throughout the summer—against the background of a continuing war scare which led to a run on food shops.

'This is the worst crisis since the revolution', Trotsky declared in a letter to the Central Committee on 27 June.[1] He referred to the war scare and its adverse effects; and he pointed out that if the Central Committee believed the danger to be as imminent as its agitators made it out, then this was one reason more why

[1] *The Archives.*

the Committee should review its policy and restore normal relations, 'the Leninist régime', within the party. The opportunity for this, he pointed out, was close at hand: the Central Committee was preparing a new congress of the party—let it then open a free pre-congress debate and bring back all the virtually banished adherents of the Opposition and allow them to take part. Even before his appeal had reached its destination, the press spoke again about the Opposition's collusion with foreign imperialists. On the next day Trotsky again addressed himself to the Central Committee, saying *inter alia* that Stalin evidently aimed at the physical annihilation of the Opposition: 'The further road of the Stalinist group is mechanically predetermined. To-day they falsify our words, to-morrow they will falsify our deeds.' 'The Stalinist group will be compelled, and it will be compelled very soon, to use against the Opposition all those means that the class enemy used against the Bolsheviks in July 1917', during the 'month of the great slander', when Lenin had to flee from Petrograd—they would speak about 'sealed cars', 'foreign gold', conspiracies, &c. 'This is whither Stalin's course is leading—to this and all the consequences. Only the blind do not see it; only the Pharisee will not admit it.'[1]

Stalin indignantly denied that he was out to annihilate his critics. Shortly thereafter, however, he made up his mind to have the leaders of the Opposition arraigned before the Central Committee and the Central Control Commission—these two bodies acted jointly as the party's supreme tribunal. A demand for the exclusion of Zinoviev and Trotsky from the Central Committee was placed before them—this was to be the penultimate disciplinary measure before their expulsion from the party. In principle only a congress which elected the members of the Central Committee could deprive them of their seats; but the 1921 ban on factions gave that power also to the party's supreme tribunal, enabling it, in the intervals between congresses, to depose members who had infringed the ban. About the end of June the indictment of the two Opposition chiefs, by Yaroslavsky and Shkiryatov, had been lodged. It contained only two counts: Trotsky's and Zinoviev's appeal

---

[1] *The Archives.* The Zinovievists were so horrified at the idea of the guillotine descending upon them or so incredulous that they implored Trotsky to tone down his warning.

from the Russian party to the Executive of the International; and the demonstration at the Yaroslavl station. Both charges were so flimsy that in four months the tribunal, fervent Stalinists and Bukharinists to a man, could find no sufficient ground for a verdict.

As the proceedings dragged on, Stalin's impatience grew. He was bent on extracting a verdict of expulsion before he convened the fifteenth congress. As long as the chiefs of the Opposition sat on the Central Committee they were *ex officio* entitled to present to the congress full criticisms of official policy and even to offer formal counter reports, as Zinoviev and Kamenev had done at the last congress. They could therefore reveal the whole truth about China and place it in the centre of an open debate conducted in the hearing of the nation and the world. Stalin could not afford to take this risk. For this and for other reasons—events compelled him again to shift his ground in domestic policy as well and thus to admit implicitly his failures —Stalin had to do his utmost to deny Trotsky and Zinoviev the platform of the congress. For this he had first to expel them from the Central Committee. Once he had done so he could be sure that the excited attention of the congress would be absorbed by the inner party cabal rather than by the Chinese débâcle and other issues of policy, and that the chiefs of the Opposition would appear at the congress, if at all, only as defendants appealing against a degrading verdict. The congress was convened for November. He had to make the most of his time.

On 24 July Trotsky appeared for the first time before the Presidium of the Central Control Commission to answer the charges. It was five years since he himself had indicted the Workers' Opposition before the same body. The man who had then been in the chair—Solz, an old and respected Bolshevik, whom, in Lenin's days, some described as the 'party's conscience'—now sat as a Stalinist among Trotsky's judges. Presiding over the proceedings was the hot-tempered, yet in his way honest and even generous, Ordjonikidze, Stalin's countryman and friend, to whose expulsion from the party Trotsky had objected when Lenin insisted on it because of Ordjonikidze's behaviour in Georgia in 1922.[1] Yaroslavsky and Shkiryatov, Trotsky's accusers, were also among the members of the

[1] See p. 91.

Presidium. Another judge was one Yanson, whom the Control Commission had in the past censured for an excess of anti-Trotskyist zeal. The rest were likewise stalwarts of the ruling factions. Trotsky could not expect them to consider his case fairly. Indeed, he began his plea by denouncing their partiality and demanding that at least Yanson be disqualified. Yet even these men came to their job dispirited, their hearts in their mouths. They as well as the defendant went back in their thoughts to the French Revolution and were haunted by memories of Jacobin purges. Across 130 years the sepulchral cry of the condemned Danton: 'After me it will be your turn, Robespierre!' rang in their ears.

Shortly before the opening of the proceedings Solz, conversing with one of Trotsky's associates and trying to show him how pernicious was the Opposition's role, said: 'What does this lead to? You know the history of the French Revolution—and to what this led: to arrests and to the guillotine.' 'Is it your intention then to guillotine us?' the Oppositionist asked, to which Solz replied: 'Don't you think that Robespierre was sorry for Danton when he sent him to the guillotine? And then Robespierre had to go himself. . . . Do you think he was not sorry? Indeed he was, yet he had to do it. . . .'[1] Judges and defendants alike saw the giant and bloody blade above their heads; but as if gripped by fatality they were unable to avert what was coming; and each, hesitantly or even tremblingly, went on doing what he had to do to hasten its descent.

Trotsky replied briefly to the two formal charges laid against him. He denied the court the right to sit in judgement over him for a speech he had delivered before the Executive of the International. He would similarly deny any 'district commission' the right to try him for anything he had said at the Central Committee—his judges, the leading bodies of the party, acknowledged themselves to be subject to the International's authority. As to the second charge, the farewell demonstration for Smilga, the ruling group denied that it had intended to penalize Smilga. But 'if Smilga's assignment to Khabarovsk was a matter of administrative routine then how dare you say that our collective farewell to him was a collective demonstration against the Central Committee?' If, however, the assign-

---

[1] *The Archives*; Trotsky, *The Stalin School of Falsification*, pp. 126–48.

ment was a veiled form of banishment, then 'you are guilty of duplicity'. These trifling accusations were mere pretexts. The ruling group was determined 'to hound the Opposition and prepare its physical annihilation'. Hence the war scare produced in order to intimidate and silence critics. 'We declare that we shall continue to criticize the Stalinist régime as long as you have not physically sealed our lips.' That régime threatened to 'undermine all the conquests of the October Revolution'. The Oppositionists had nothing in common with those old-time 'patriots' for whom Tsar and Fatherland were one. Already they had been accused of giving aid and comfort to the British Tories. Yet they had every right to turn the accusation against the accusers. Stalin and Bukharin, by backing the Anglo-Soviet Council, had indeed indirectly helped Chamberlain; and their 'allies', the leaders of the British trade unions, had in all essentials backed Chamberlain's foreign policy, including the rupture of relations with the U.S.S.R. At the party cells official agitators asked suggestive questions, 'worthy of the Black Hundreds', about the sources from which the Opposition obtained means for carrying on with its activity. 'If you were really a Central Control Commission you would feel bound in duty to put an end to this dirty, abominable, contemptible, and characteristically Stalinist campaign. . . .' If the ruling group were genuinely concerned with the nation's security, they would not have dismissed the best military workers, Smilga, Mrachkovsky, Lashevich, Bakaev, and Muralov, only because they were adherents of the Opposition. This was a time to assuage the conflicts within the party, not to aggravate them. The drive against the Opposition had its origin in a rising tide of reaction.

Having surveyed the major questions at issue, Trotsky wound up with a forceful evocation of the French Revolution. He referred to the conversation, quoted above, between Solz and an Oppositionist. He said that he agreed with Solz that they all ought to consult anew the annals of the French Revolution; but it was necessary to use the historical analogy correctly:

During the great French Revolution many were guillotined. We, too, brought many people before the firing squad. But there were two great chapters in the French Revolution: one went like this (*the speaker points upwards*); the other like that (*he points downwards*). . . . In the first chapter, when the revolution moved upwards, the

Jacobins, the Bolsheviks of that time, guillotined the Royalists and Girondists. We, too, have gone through a similar great chapter when we, the Oppositionists, together with you shot the White Guards and exiled our Girondists. But then another chapter opened in France when . . . the Thermidorians and the Bonapartists, who had emerged from the right wing of the Jacobin party, began to exile and shoot the left Jacobins. . . . I would like Comrade Solz to think out his analogy to the end and to answer for himself first of all this question: which chapter is it in which Solz is preparing to have us shot? (*Commotion in the hall.*) This is no laughing matter; revolution is a serious business. None of us is scared of firing squads. We are all old revolutionaries. But we must know who it is that is to be shot and what chapter it is that we are in. When we did the shooting, we knew firmly what chapter we were in. But do you, Comrade Solz, see clearly in which chapter you are preparing to shoot us? I fear . . . that you are about to do so in . . . the Thermidorian chapter.

He went on to explain that his adversaries were mistaken in imagining that he called them names. The Thermidorians were not deliberate counter-revolutionaries—they were Jacobins, but Jacobins who had 'moved to the right'.

Do you think that on the very next day after 9 Thermidor they said to themselves: we have now transferred power into the hands of the bourgeoisie? Nothing of the kind. Look up the newspapers of that time. They said: We have destroyed a handful of people who disturbed the peace in the party, and now after their destruction the revolution will triumph completely. If comrade Solz has any doubts about it . . .

Solz: You are practically repeating my own words.

Trotsky: . . . I shall read to you what was said by Brival, a right Jacobin and Thermidorian, when he reported on that session of the Convention which had resolved to hand over Robespierre and his associates to the revolutionary tribunal: 'Intriguers and counter-revolutionaries draping themselves with the togas of patriotism, they had sought the destruction of liberty; and the Convention decreed to place them under arrest. They were: Robespierre, Couthon, St. Just, Lebas, and Robespierre the Younger. The Chairman asked what my opinion was. I replied: Those who had always voted in accordance with the principles of the Mountain . . . voted for imprisonment. I did more . . . I am one of those who proposed this measure. Moreover, as secretary, I hasten to sign and to transmit to you this decree of the Convention.' That is how the report was made by a Solz . . . of that time. Robespierre and his associates—these were the counter-revolutionaries. 'Those who had always voted in accordance with the principles of the Mountain' meant in the language of that time 'those who had always been Bolsheviks'. Brival considered himself an old Bolshevik. 'As secretary I hasten to sign and to transmit to you this decree of the Convention.' To-day, too, there are secretaries who hasten to 'sign and transmit'. To-day, too, there are such secretaries. . . .[1]

The Thermidorians too, Trotsky went on, had struck at the left Jacobins amid cries of *La Patrie en danger*! Convinced that Robespierre and his friends were only 'isolated individuals', they did not understand that they struck against 'the deepest revolutionary forces of their age', forces opposed to the Jacobin 'neo-N.E.P.' and Bonapartism. They branded Robespierre and his friends as aristocrats—'and did we not hear to-day this same cry "aristocrat" from the lips of Yanson addressed to me?' They stigmatized the left Jacobins as Pitt's agents just as the Stalinists denounced the Opposition as the agents of Chamberlain, 'that modern pocket edition of Pitt'.

The odour of the 'second chapter' now assails one's nostrils . . . the party régime stifles everyone who struggles against Thermidor. The worker, the man of the mass, has been stifled in the party. The rank and file is silent. [Such had also been the condition of the Jacobin Clubs in their decay.] An anonymous reign of terror was instituted there; silence was compulsory; the 100 per cent. vote and abstention from all criticism were demanded; it was obligatory to think in accordance with orders received from above; men were compelled to stop thinking that the party was a living and independent organism, not a self-sufficient machine of power. . . . The Jacobin Clubs, the crucibles of revolution, became the nurseries of Napoleon's future bureaucracy. We should learn from the French Revolution. But is it really necessary to repeat it? (*Shouts*.)

Not all was lost yet, however. Despite grave differences, a split could still be avoided. There was still 'a gigantic revolutionary potential in our party', the stock of ideas and traditions inherited from Lenin. 'You have squandered a great deal of this capital, you have replaced much of it with cheap substitutes . . . but a good deal of pure gold still remains.' This was an age of stupendous shifts, of sharp and rapid turns, and the scene might

[1] Loc. cit.

yet suddenly become transformed. 'But you dare not hide the
facts, for sooner or later they will become known anyway.
You cannot hide the victories and the defeats of the working
class.' If only the party were allowed to ponder the facts and to
form its opinion freely, the present crisis could be overcome. Let
the ruling group therefore take no rash and irreparable decision.
'Beware, lest you should find yourself saying later: we parted
company with those whom we should have preserved and we
preserved those from whom we should have parted.'

It is impossible to read these words without recalling the 'cold
shiver running down one's spine' of which the young Trotsky
spoke in 1904 when, at the threshold of his career, he thought of
the future of Lenin's party and compared it with the fate of the
Jacobins. The same cold shiver ran down his spine twenty-
three years later. In 1904 he had written that 'a Jacobin tribunal
would have tried under the charge of *modérantisme* the whole
international labour movement, and Marx's lion head would
have been the first to roll under the guillotine'. Now he himself
fought with a lion's courage for his own head before the Bolshevik tribunal. In 1904 he had been disgusted with Lenin's
'malicious and morally repulsive suspiciousness—a flat caricature of the tragic Jacobin intolerance'. Now he invoked Lenin's
ideas against the intolerance and the 'malicious and morally
repulsive suspiciousness' of Lenin's successors. But his view of
Jacobinism was almost diametrically opposed to the one he had
voiced in his youth. Then he saw Jacobinism as incompatible
with Marxist socialism—these were 'two opposed worlds, doctrines, tactics, mentalities . . .', for Jacobinism meant an 'absolute faith in a metaphysical idea and absolute distrust of living
people', while Marxism appealed in the first instance to the
class consciousness of the working masses. And so in 1904 he
demanded a clear choice between the two, because the Jacobin
method, if revived, would consist in 'placing above the proletariat a few well-picked people . . . or one person invested with
the power to liquidate and degrade'. Now he confronted these
few well-picked people and the one person acquiring the power
to liquidate and degrade. But his main charge against them was
not that they acted in the Jacobin spirit, but, on the contrary,
that they worked to destroy it. Now he dwelt on the affinity of
Marxism and Jacobinism; and he identified himself and his

adherents with Robespierre's group; and it was he who turned the charge of *modérantisme* against Stalin and Bukharin.

Thus the 'conflict of the two souls in Bolshevism, the Marxist and the Jacobin', a conflict which we first noticed in 1904,[1] and which underlay all Bolshevik affairs in recent years, now caused Trotsky to view Jacobinism from an angle altogether opposed to that from which he had first approached it. This conflict was in varying degrees characteristic for all Bolshevik factions. Curiously, they all appeared to identify themselves with the same aspect of Jacobinism. While Trotsky compared his own attitude with Robespierre's and saw his adversaries as 'moderantists', Solz and others with him saw Stalin as the new Robespierre and Trotsky as the new Danton. In truth, as events were to show, the alignments and divisions were far more complex and confused. What Jacobinism and Bolshevism had in common was—substitutism. Each of the two parties had placed itself at the head of society but could not rely for the realization of its programme on the willing support of society. Like the Jacobins, the Bolsheviks 'could not trust that their *Vérité* would win the hearts and the minds of the people'. They too looked around with morbid suspicion and 'saw enemies creeping from every crevice'. They too had to draw a sharp dividing line between themselves and the rest of the world because 'every attempt to blur the line threatened to release inner centrifugal forces'; and they too were drawing it 'with the edge of the guillotine', and having destroyed their enemies outside their own ranks began to see enemies in their own midst. Yet, as a Marxist Trotsky reiterated now what he had first said in 1904: 'The party must see the guarantee of its stability in its own base, in an active and self-reliant proletariat, and not in its top caucus, which the revolution . . . may suddenly sweep away with its wings. . . .' He cried out again that 'any serious group . . . when it is confronted by the dilemma whether it should, from a sense of discipline, silently efface itself, or, regardless of discipline, struggle for survival—will undoubtedly choose the latter course . . . and say: perish that "discipline" which suppresses the vital interests of the movement'.

.   .   .   .

---

[1] See *The Prophet Armed*, pp. 91-96.

Before the end of July the party tribunal dispersed without passing a verdict on Trotsky and Zinoviev. The majority of the judges still appeared to be as sorry for them as 'Robespierre had been sorry for Danton'. Stalin, however, pressed for a decision. With every day the consequences of his 'colossal blunders' were becoming clearer. The final collapse of the Chinese Revolution threatened to discredit him. The Anglo-Soviet Council had finally ceased to exist: its British members had not uttered even a word of protest against the rupture of relations between Britain and Russia. At home the war scare and the run on shops had led to another goods famine. The peasantry was restless. There was reason to fear that it would not deliver enough food to the towns in the autumn. So far Stalin had been able to conceal his responsibility: he had managed to suppress all the warnings and predictions made by his opponents. Almost every one of Trotsky's recent speeches might have exploded his laboriously acquired and still precarious authority; but he had not allowed Trotsky's voice to penetrate through the thick walls of the Kremlin and gain resonance outside. However, the date of the fifteenth congress was approaching; and with it Trotsky's and Zinoviev's opportunity to state their case. The whole country would listen. It would be impossible to suppress speeches made at a congress in the way criticisms uttered at the Central Committee were concealed. At any cost Stalin had to deprive them of this opportunity.

He had yet another reason for haste. He had to reckon with strains within the ruling coalition. The rightist policy of recent years was nearing exhaustion. It was increasingly difficult to maintain it abroad, in the Comintern. At home also everything pointed to the need for a change of policy; and although its possible scope was far from evident, it was clear that the change would require of the party a more radical attitude towards the peasantry and a bolder course in industry. On all these issues Stalinists and Bukharinists had hitherto patched up their differences so as to be able to present a common front to the Opposition. But the moment was drawing close when it might become difficult to patch them up any longer and a breach might follow. Yet Stalin could not turn against Bukharin, Rykov, and Tomsky as long as he had not concluded his struggle against Trotsky and Zinoviev. He could not confront two oppositions simultaneously, especially as a change of policy would appear to many a vindication of Trotsky's and Zinoviev's views. He had to crush the Joint Opposition and free his hands as soon as possible.

He lashed out with redoubled vehemence after Trotsky had made his so-called Clemenceau statements, first on 11 July, in a letter to Ordjonikidze, and then again, before the end of the month, in an article which he submitted to *Pravda*. Referring to the war scare, Trotsky had repeatedly declared that if war came the leaders of the ruling factions would prove themselves incompetent and unequal to their task and that the Opposition would in the interest of defence continue to oppose them and seek to take over the direction of the war. These declarations brought on Trotsky charges of disloyalty and defeatism. In refutation he explained that the Opposition stood for the 'unconditional defence' of the U.S.S.R. and that in war it would seek to replace the ruling factions precisely in order to pursue hostilities with the utmost vigour and clear-headedness which could not be expected from those who now led the party. Only 'ignoramuses and scoundrels' could from 'their rubbish heaps' blame this attitude as defeatist. This was, on the contrary, an attitude dictated by genuine concern over defence—'victory is not obtained from the rubbish heap'. And here came the much disputed 'Clemenceau statement':

One may find examples, and quite instructive ones, in the history of other social classes [Trotsky wrote to Ordjonikidze]. We shall cite only one: at the beginning of the imperialist war [i.e. of the First World War] the French bourgeoisie had at its head a blundering government, a government without rudder and sail. Clemenceau and his group were in opposition to it. Regardless of war and military censorship, regardless even of the fact that the Germans stood 80 kilometres from Paris (Clemenceau said: 'Precisely because of this'), he waged a furious struggle against the government's petty bourgeois irresolution and flabbiness—for the prosecution of the war with truly imperialist ferocity and ruthlessness. Clemenceau did not betray his class, the bourgeoisie; on the contrary, he served it more faithfully, firmly, resolutely, and wisely than did Viviani, Painlevé and company. The further course of events proved this. Clemenceau's group took office and by means of a more consistent policy—his was a policy of imperialist robbery—secured victory. ... Did any French journalistic scribes label Clemenceau's group defeatist? Of course, they did: fools and slanderers trail along in the camp of every social class. Not always, however, do they have the same opportunity to play important roles.[1]

This then was the example which Trotsky declared he would follow—an example, it may be added, which early in the Second World War Churchill followed in his opposition to Chamberlain. The retort came at once. The Stalinists and Bukharinists raised an outcry that Trotsky threatened to stage a *coup d'état* in the middle of war, while the enemy might be standing less than eighty kilometres from the Kremlin—what other proof of his disloyalty was needed? About the same time a group of army leaders addressed to the Politbureau a secret statement expressing solidarity with the Opposition and criticizing Voroshilov, the Commissar of War, for military incompetence. Among the signatories were, apart from Muralov, until recently chief Army Inspector, Putna, Yakir, and other generals, who were to perish in the Tukhachevsky purge ten years later.[2] The ruling factions took the *démarche* of the military as an earnest of the Opposition's intentions.

The hue and cry about the Clemenceau statement lasted till the end of the year, till Trotsky's banishment; and it was to echo for many years afterwards: it was cited whenever Trotsky's treachery was to be shown up. Very few were those party men who knew what the Clemenceau statement was about; most understood it in fact as Trotsky's threat to turn the next war into civil war, if not as an actual prelude to a *coup*. That he had meant to utter no such threat and that the precedent he invoked had not implied one did not matter. Few, very few, Bolsheviks had any idea what it was that the French 'Tiger' had done and by what means he had seized power. To Trotsky the reference to Clemenceau occurred naturally—it was in Paris he himself had watched Clemenceau's struggle ten years earlier. But the precedent was remote, obscure, and therefore sinister to the public, to the great majority of the Central Committee, and even to the members of the new Politbureau (among whom hardly any one, apart from Bukharin, had any knowledge of French affairs). This is how Trotsky himself describes satirically the

---

[1] Quoted *in extenso* by Stalin in *Sochinenya*, vol. x, p. 52.

[2] Tukhachevsky himself did not sign the statement, and he was at no time involved with the Joint Opposition.

dazed nescience with which the Central Committee received his analogy:

> From my article . . . Molotov had first learned many things which he then reported to the Central Committee as terrible *prima facie* evidence of these insurrectionist designs. And so Molotov learned that during the war there was in France a politician called Clemenceau, that that politician waged a struggle against the French government of the time in order to force a more determined and ruthless imperialist policy. . . . Stalin then explained to Molotov and Molotov expounded to us the real sense of that precedent: on the example set by Clemenceau's group the Opposition intends to fight for another policy of socialist defence—and that means an insurrectionist policy like that which the Left Social Revolutionaries adopted [in 1918].[1]

It was all too easy to frighten with the mysterious conundrum the cells, first in Moscow and then in the provinces, whence the clamour rose that it was time to render the Opposition harmless.

On 1 August the Central Control Commission and the Central Committee again considered the motion calling for Trotsky's expulsion. Once again Stalin, Bukharin, and others railed in good set terms and read out interminable indictments in which they brought up every detail of Trotsky's political past, beginning with 1903, and showed it in the darkest colours. Even the long-forgotten charges, made once, in 1919, by the Military Opposition, namely, that during the civil war Trotsky was the enemy of the Communists in the army and ordered brave and innocent commissars to be shot, were brought up afresh.[2] This time, however, the Clemenceau statement provided the gravamen of the indictment which was that the Opposition could not be depended upon to behave loyally in war and to contribute to the defence of the Soviet Union.

In reply Trotsky recalled the paramount responsibility he had

---

[1] See Trotsky's note 'Clemenceau' dated 2 August 1927, in *The Archives*.

[2] This particular charge was made by Yaroslavsky, but it shocked even Stalinists, and Ordjonikidze expressly dissociated himself from it. *The Archives*. Yaroslavsky belonged to the Military Opposition in 1919. The charges against Trotsky were then brought before the Politbureau by Smilga and Lashevich and the commissars whom Trotsky allegedly persecuted were Zalutsky and Bakaev—all four now prominent in the Opposition. For the account of the incident see *The Prophet Armed*, pp. 420–1, 425–6, 432.

borne over many years for the party's defence policy and for
formulating the Communist International's views on war and
peace. He attacked Stalin's and Bukharin's reliance for defence
on broken reeds, or, as he put it, on 'rotten ropes' and 'rotten
props'. Had they not hailed the Anglo-Soviet Council as a bulwark against intervention and war; and had this not turned out
a rotten prop? Was their alliance with the Kuomintang not a
rotten rope? Had they not weakened the Soviet Union by
sabotaging the Chinese Revolution? Voroshilov had stated that
'the peasant revolution [in China] might have interfered with
the northern expedition of the generals'. But this was precisely
how Chiang Kai-shek viewed the matter. 'For the sake of a
military expedition you have put a brake on the revolution . . .
as if the revolution were not . . . itself an expedition of the oppressed against the oppressors.' 'You came out against the
building of Soviets in the "army's rear"—as if the revolution
were the rear of an army!—and you did it in order not to dis-
organize the hinterland of the very same generals who two days
later crushed the workers and the peasants in their rear.' Such
a speech by Voroshilov, the Commissar of Defence and a member of the Politbureau, was in itself 'a catastrophe—equivalent
to a lost battle'. In case of war 'the rotten ropes will fall to
pieces in your hands'—and this was why the Opposition could
not forbear criticizing the Stalinist leadership.

But would criticism not weaken the moral standing of the
U.S.S.R.? To pose the question thus was 'worthy of the Papal
Church or of feudal generals. The Catholic Church demands
unquestioning recognition of its authority by the faithful. The
revolutionary gives his support while criticizing; and the more
undeniable his right to criticize the greater in time of struggle is
his devotion to the creative development and strengthening of
that in which he is a direct participant.' 'What we need is not a
hypocritical *union sacrée* but honest revolutionary unity.' Nor was
victory in war primarily a matter of arms. Men had to wield the
arms and men were inspired by ideas. What then was the idea
underlying Bolshevik defence policy? It might be possible to
secure victory in one of two ways: either by waging war in a
spirit of revolutionary internationalism, as the Opposition proposed to do, or by waging it in the Thermidorian style—but this
meant victory for the kulak, further suppression of the worker,

and 'capitalism on the instalment plan'. Stalin's policy was neither the one nor the other; he vacillated between the alternatives. But war would brook no irresolution. It would force the Stalinist group to make a choice. In any case, the Stalinist group, itself not knowing whither it was going, could not secure victory.

At this point of Trotsky's speech the record notes that an exclamation of eager assent came from Zinoviev, but that Trotsky stopped to correct himself: instead of saying that 'Stalin's leadership was *incapable* of assuring victory' he stated that it 'would make victory *more difficult*'. 'But where would the party be?' Molotov interjected. 'You have strangled the party'— Trotsky thundered back; and he repeated again with deliberation that under Stalin victory would prove 'more difficult'. The Opposition, therefore, could not identify the defence of the U.S.S.R. with the defence of Stalinism. 'Not a single Oppositionist will renounce his right and duty to fight for the correction of the party's course on the eve of war or during war . . . therein lies the most important prerequisite of victory. To sum up: for the socialist fatherland? Yes! For the Stalinist course? No!'[1]

After the Second World War these prophecies were as if lost in the blaze of Stalin's triumphs. Stalin did, after all, secure Russia's victory; and the sequel showed no similarity to 'capitalism on the instalment plan'. However, Trotsky spoke at the height of N.E.P. when Russia was still one of the industrially most backward nations; when private farming predominated in the country; when the kulak was growing in strength; and when the party was still a whirlpool of conflicting trends; and he spoke conditionally about a danger of war which the ruling factions claimed to be imminent. One can only speculate about the course which a war fought against this background might have taken and how Stalin might have fared in it. At any rate, against such a background Trotsky's assessment of the prospects was far more plausible than it appears when it is related to the Soviet Union of the years 1941-5. Yet, even after the Second World War, Stalinism endeavoured to overcome the tensions inside the Soviet Union by a forcible expansion of its rule into eastern and central Europe. It might be argued that the alterna-

[1] *The Archives*; *The Stalin School of Falsification*, pp. 161-77.

tive to expansion was precisely that 'capitalism on the instalment plan' inside the Soviet Union of which Trotsky had spoken.
And even in the light of victory, Trotsky's strictures on Stalin's
and Voroshilov's incompetence do not appear altogether groundless. In 1941, in the very first months of Russo-German hostilities, Voroshilov fumbled and bungled so badly that as a general
he could never raise his head again. As to Stalin, the General
Secretary of 1927 had as yet little of that empirical military
knowledge and experience that the dictator of the later period
had gathered in long years of absolute rule. And, although
Stalin's role in the Second World War is, and will for a long
time to come remain, the subject of historical controversy, it
seems nevertheless established that victory was indeed *more
difficult under Stalin* than it need perhaps have been, that under a
leadership more far-sighted than his the Soviet Union might not
have suffered as severe initial defeats as those of 1941–2, and
that it might not have needed to pay for its final triumph the
prodigious price in human life and wealth which it did pay.[1]

The weakness of Trotsky's attitude lay not in what he said
against his adversaries. It lay elsewhere—in the manner in
which he envisaged the Opposition's action in war. That there
was not a shred of defeatism in it is obvious. But how did he
imagine himself acting the Soviet Clemenceau? He returned to
this question on 6 August, when the Central Committee and the
Central Control Commission continued to debate the motion
for his expulsion. It was preposterous, he said, to charge him
with incitement to insurrection: Clemenceau had not staged
any insurrection or coup, or acted in any unconstitutional
manner; he overthrew the government he opposed and himself assumed office in a most lawful way, using for this purpose
the machinery of parliament. But the Soviet Union, it might be
said, had no such parliamentary machinery? 'Yes,' Trotsky rejoined, *'fortunately*, we do not have it.' How then could any
opposition overthrow any government constitutionally? 'But
we do have', Trotsky went on, 'we do have the machinery of
our party.' The Opposition, in other words, would act within
the party statutes and seek to overthrow Stalin by a vote at the
Central Committee or perhaps at a congress. But had not

[1] See the appraisal of Stalin's role in the war in my *Stalin, a Political Biography*,
pp. 456–60; and chapters xii–xiv, *passim*.

Trotsky himself repeatedly said and demonstrated that the party's nominal constitution was a sham and that its real constitution was Stalin's bureaucratic absolutism? Did not events daily prove this to be true? That, Trotsky replied, was why the Opposition strove to reform the inner-party régime: '. . . in case of war, too, the party ought to preserve or rather to restore a more supple, a sounder, and a healthier inner régime, which would make it possible to criticize in time, to warn in time, to change policy in time.' The ruling factions, however, made no bones about it: they would allow no such reform and permit no change in the leadership by any constitutional method. With this in mind they viewed Trotsky's declaration; and they concluded that as he would not be able to overthrow Stalin by means of any parliamentary procedure or vote, he would have to resort to a *coup d'état*. From their viewpoint they were in a sense consistent in regarding his Clemenceau statement as a proclamation of the Opposition's right to insurrection. Even though he had not in fact proclaimed that right—he was to do it in exile eight or nine years hence; and the ruling factions realized that it was inherent in the situation, which they had created, that he should proclaim it.

With even greater logic Trotsky charged that it was they who threatened to perpetuate their hold on the party and maintain themselves in power by measures of civil war; and that they were preparing to use such measures against the Opposition. And indeed, in raising the clamour against the Clemenceau statement, Stalin was out to establish indirectly the principle, which Bolshevik tradition did not allow him to proclaim openly, that his rule was inviolable and inalienable, and that any attempt to replace it was tantamount to counter-revolution. This was *the* issue which underlay the affair. The storm over the Clemenceau statement revealed the width, the depth, and the unbridgeability of the gulf between the ruling group and the Opposition: by force of circumstances the language in which they addressed each other was already the language of civil war.

Yet even now the party tribunal, deliberating for the second month over Trotsky's expulsion, still demurred at passing the verdict. For once Stalin had run ahead of his followers and associates. They were not yet quite ready to do his bidding.

Still entangled in shreds of old loyalties, still thinking of their adversaries as comrades, still worried about niceties of party statutes, and anxious to preserve appearances of Bolshevik decorum, they sought once again to come to terms with the Opposition. The latter were only too glad to meet them half-way; and so Trotsky and Zinoviev tried to calm the emotions aroused by the Clemenceau statement with a declaration of the Opposition's loyalty to party and state and of its commitment to the unconditional defence of the Soviet Union in any emergency. A new 'truce' was arranged; and on 8 August the Central Committee and the Central Control Commission concluded their deliberations, ignoring the motion for expulsion and content to pass no more than a vote of censure on the chiefs of the Opposition.

For the moment it looked as if the Opposition would be able to participate in the fifteenth congress and there make another appeal to the party. The leaders prepared a full and systematic statement of policy, a *Platform*, such as they had never before been able to present. The *Platform* was thrashed out in Opposition circles, carefully amended, and supplemented.[1] However, matters had long since gone beyond the point at which 'normalization' might have been possible. This was the last 'truce'; and it was even more shortlived than the previous one. The ruling factions had hesitantly agreed to it on the tacit understanding that the leaders of the Opposition, having narrowly escaped punishment, would hold their fire. This was not how the latter understood their obligation. They felt entitled to go on with what to them was normal expression of opinion and criticism, especially in the months preceding a congress, the season for an all-party debate. Stalin and his closest henchmen did what they could to nullify the truce. He exacerbated the Opposition by continuing, with and without pretext, to penalize and banish its adherents. He laid the blame at the Opposition's door, saying that it had broken the truce by preparing its *Platform*, by refusing to join in a condemnation of its sympathizers in Germany, &c. Seeing that he was behind schedule in his drive, he delayed the fifteenth congress by a month.

On 6 September Trotsky and his friends approached the

---

[1] The *Platform* is known under the title *The Real Situation in Russia* under which Trotsky published it later in exile.

Politbureau and the Central Committee and pointed out that the General Secretariat was pursuing its own policy, one which did not even accord with that of the Stalinist-Bukharinist majority; and they submitted a detailed report on the new persecution and a protest against the postponement of the congress. Trotsky asked once again for a loyal pre-congress debate with the participation of the banished Oppositionists. He also demanded that the Central Committee should, in accordance with a custom honoured in the past, publish the Opposition's *Platform* and circulate it, together with all the official documentation, among the party electorate. After fierce and relentless interventions by Stalin, the Central Committee rejected the Opposition's complaints and refused to publish the *Platform* as part of the papers for discussion. Moreover, it forbade the Opposition to circulate the document by its own means.

This was, of course, a new bone of contention. For the Opposition to observe the fresh ban was to surrender ignominiously, perhaps for ever. But to snap their fingers at it was also risky, for the *Platform* would then have to be produced and circulated clandestinely or semi-clandestinely. The Opposition resolved to take the risk. To protect itself against reprisals—to 'spread the blow' once again—and also to impress the congress, Trotsky and Zinoviev called on their adherents to sign the *Platform en masse*. The collection of signatures was to reveal the size of the Opposition's following; and so the campaign was from the outset a trial of strength in a form the Opposition had not hitherto dared to undertake.

Stalin could not allow this to go on undisturbed. On the night of 12–13 September the G.P.U. raided the Opposition's 'printing shop', arrested several men engaged in producing the *Platform*, and announced with a flourish that it had discovered a conspiracy. The G.P.U. maintained that they had caught the Oppositionists red-handed, working hand in glove with notorious counter-revolutionaries; and that a former officer of Wrangel's White Guards had set up the Opposition's printing shop. On the day of the raid Trotsky had left for the Caucasus; but several leaders of the Opposition, Preobrazhensky, Mrachkovsky, and Serebriakov, attempted to come forward with a refutation and declared that they assumed full responsibility for the 'printing shop' and the publication of the *Platform*. All three were immediately expelled from the party and one of them, Mrachkovsky, was imprisoned. This was the first time that such punishment was inflicted on prominent men of the Opposition.

The incident foreshadowed the 'amalgams' on which the great purges of the next decade were to be based. The G.P.U. revelations were calculated to impress all those who had listened incredulously to Stalin's asseverations about the 'united front from Chamberlain to Trotsky'. If the consciences of such people were uneasy and if they wondered whether that 'united front' was not a figment of Stalin's imagination, the story of the uncovered plot was there to reassure them. The native figure of the 'Wrangel officer' appeared as a link between the Opposition and the dark forces of world imperialism. The doubting and the confused received a clear warning. They were shown the net in which they might get entangled once they undertook or merely condoned any form of activity directed against the official leaders, no matter how innocent that activity appeared at first sight.

The blow was well aimed. By the time the Opposition managed to show up the G.P.U. revelations as a fake, the harm had been done. Zinoviev, Kamenev, and Trotsky—he had interrupted his stay in the Caucasus and returned to Moscow—intervened with Menzhinsky, the head of the G.P.U. since Dzerzhinsky's death, and cleared up the farcical circumstances of the plot. The G.P.U. had caught members of the Opposition duplicating typewritten copies of the *Platform*. The Opposition, it transpired, did not even possess a clandestine printing shop of the kind that every underground group had operated in Tsarist days. A few young men had volunteered to do the typing and duplicating. True, some of them were not party members; but this was their only fault—Stalin was later unable to find for them a label more damaging than 'bourgeois intellectuals'. A former Wrangel officer had indeed helped in the work and promised to assist in circulating the *Platform*; but Menzhinsky admitted, first to Trotsky and Kamenev and then to the Central Committee, that the G.P.U. had employed the officer as an *agent provocateur*; and that his particular job had been to spy on the Opposition. Stalin himself confirmed the disclosure and said: 'But what is wrong with this former Wrangel officer helping the Soviet government to unearth counter-revolutionary plots? Who can deny Soviet authorities the right to win over ex-officers and use them to uncover counter-revolutionary organizations?'[1] Thus Stalin first pointed to the Wrangel officer as proof positive of the counter-revolutionary character of the Opposition's activity, and then went on to say that he saw no reason why he should not have used the officer to provide the proof. The Opposition cried out: 'Our enemies, persecutors, and slanderers!' But it did not recover from the effects of the slander.

Trotsky had returned in haste to Moscow not only because of this affair. While he was in the Caucasus the Presidium of the Comintern unexpectedly announced that it was due to meet before the end of September and that it had placed on its agenda Trotsky's expulsion from the Executive of the International. He appeared before the Executive on 27 September to speak for the last time—with scorn and passion—to the envoys of all Communist parties. These were grotesque assizes. The foreign Communists who sat in judgement over one of the founding fathers of their International and denied him all the merits of a revolutionary, were almost to a man pathetic failures as revolutionaries: instigators of abortive risings, almost professional losers of revolution, or heads of insignificant sects all basking in the glory of that October in which the accused man had played so outstanding a part. Among them were Marcel Cachin, who had during the First World War, while Trotsky was being expelled from France as the author of the Zimmerwald Manifesto, gone as agent of the French government to Italy to back Mussolini's pro-war campaign; Doriot, the future fascist and Hitler's puppet;[2] Thälmann, who was to lead German communism in its capitulation to Hitler in 1933 and then perish in Hitler's concentration camp; and Roy, who had just returned from China where he had done his best to induce the Chinese party to lick the dust before Chiang Kai-shek. J. T. Murphy, an insignificant envoy of one of the most insignificant foreign Communist parties, the British, was chosen to table the motion of expulsion. The disdain which Trotsky hurled at this conventicle was proportionate to the insult they inflicted on him.

'You are accusing me', he told the Executive, 'of a breach of

[1] Stalin, *Sochinenya*, vol. x, p. 187.

[2] Doriot, it seems, was not present at the session; but he was an alternate member of the Executive and one of Trotsky's most vehement accusers,

discipline. I have no doubt that even your verdict is ready.'[1]
None of the members of the Executive dared to make up his
mind for himself—they were all only carrying out orders. Such
was their servility that the General Secretary of the Russian
party had the insolence to assign an envoy of a foreign Communist party to the job of a minor official in a remote Russian
province—the reference was to Vuyovich, the Yugoslav representative with the Comintern, a Zinovievist, who was now
also to be expelled. He, Trotsky, had been called to account for
having appealed from the Russian party to the International—
'just as in Tsarist days so now the *pristav* (the bailiff) still beats
up any one who dares to complain against him higher up'. The
supposed leaders of international communism did not even have
the dignity to try and save appearances: in their sycophancy
they had forgotten to expel Chiang Kai-shek and Wang Ching-
wei from their Executive, and the Kuomintang was still affiliated to the International; but they sat in judgement over
those who were of the flesh and the blood of the Russian
Revolution.[2]

In the course of four fateful years, Trotsky went on, they had
convened no congress of the International; in Lenin's days a
congress was held every year, even during civil war and blockade.
There had been no discussion of any of the grave issues that had
emerged, for all these issues were taboo—in all of them Stalin's
policy had suffered shipwreck. 'Why does the press of the
Communist parties keep silent? Why does the press of the International keep silent?' The Executive trampled almost daily
on the statutes of their organization; and then they charged the
Russian Opposition with breaches of discipline. 'The Opposition's . . . only guilt', he confessed, 'is that it has been too
amenable to the schemes of the Stalinist Secretariat which have
been calamitous to the revolution.' 'The manner in which the
congress of the Russian party is being prepared is a mockery . . .
Stalin's favourite weapon is slander.' 'Whoever knows history
knows that every step on the usurper's road is always marked
by such false accusations.' The Opposition could not give up
the right to speak out against a régime which was the deadliest

---

[1] *The Archives.*

[2] *L'Humanité* had hailed Chiang Kai-shek as the 'hero of the Shanghai commune', Trotsky said.

danger to the revolution: 'When a soldier's hands are tied, the chief danger is not the enemy but the rope which ties the soldier's hands.'

'He launched the attack', so Murphy, the author of the motion for expulsion, recollects, 'with all the vigour and power of which he was capable. He challenged us on every aspect of the problems that had been under discussion during the last three years . . . a forensic effort such as only he could make'; and, turning his back on the Executive of the organization on which he had once placed his highest hopes, he 'marched out with head erect'.[1] The Executive was not troubled even by such scruples as still beset the Russian Central Committee—its verdict had indeed been ready.

At this point the struggle in Moscow led to a diplomatic incident which aroused a flurry of international excitement. Since the breach between Britain and Russia Soviet relations with France had also deteriorated. The French government and press raised again the old clamour about the unpaid loans, the clamour which had been first heard after Lenin's government had repudiated all Tsarist debts to foreign creditors. The Politbureau and the Central Committee discussed the question on and off. In 1926 Trotsky was in favour of conciliating the French. Britain was then in the throes of industrial unrest; the Chinese Revolution was on the ascendant; France was labouring under the effects of inflation; and the Soviet Union was in a position of strength in which he held it to be advisable to make a concession to the French and remove a grievance of the small *rentiers*. At that time, however, Trotsky relates, Stalin was in an over-confident mood and would not hear of any settlement. Then, in the autumn of 1927, when the issue again became topical, Stalin was anxious to go some way to meet the French demands. Now, however, Trotsky and his friends were opposed to this. He argued that after the defeat of the Chinese Revolution, the breakdown of the Anglo-Soviet Council, and the

---

[1] J. T. Murphy, *New Horizon*, pp. 274–7. Murphy relates that before the sitting he met Trotsky in the corridor. 'Everybody had their heavy overcoats and fur hats, and the hat and coat rack in the hall was full. Trotsky was looking around, when . . . [Murphy's secretary] asked: "Can I help you, Comrade Trotsky?" Quick as thought he answered smartly: "I am afraid, not. I am looking for two things—a good communist and somewhere to hang my coat. They are not to be found here." ' The meeting lasted from 9.30 p.m. to 5 a.m.

rupture with Britain, the Soviet government was too weak to yield; and that any concession on its part would be taken as a further sign of weakness.

For the Opposition the situation was complicated by the fact that Rakovsky, as Ambassador, conducted the negotiations in Paris and became the butt of French attacks. Already in August the French envoy in Moscow had expressed his government's displeasure because of Rakovsky's connexion with the Trotskyist Opposition.[1] At the Central Committee, on the other hand, Stalin then made an attempt to play off Rakovsky against Trotsky: he asserted that it was Rakovsky, a 'loyal Oppositionist', who was urging Moscow to yield to the French. Trotsky wrote to Rakovsky and asked him to keep in mind that his role in Paris had become an issue in the inner-party struggle.[2] Rakovsky's devotion to the Opposition and to Trotsky personally was such that the reminder could not but impress him. But even before he had received it, he took a step which caused one of the great diplomatic scandals of the time. He put his signature to a Manifesto, calling workers and soldiers in capitalist countries to defend the Soviet Union in case of war. In these years of 'stabilization' and 'normalcy' in diplomatic relations with bourgeois governments, it was not customary for Soviet Ambassadors to make such revolutionary appeals. The French press fulminated. The French government declared Rakovsky *persona non grata*. Aristide Briand, the Foreign Minister, declared that the Soviet government should be all the more willing to recall its unruly Ambassador because it was anyhow improper that an adherent of the Opposition should represent it in Paris.

Moscow's reply was ambiguous. Chicherin, as Commissar of Foreign Affairs, defended his Ambassador, but the French ministry had reason to think that its attacks on Rakovsky were not altogether unwelcome to Chicherin's superiors. Trotsky maintained that Stalin played a disloyal game over Rakovsky's recall, and that the Soviet Foreign Office should have told Briand bluntly not to meddle in the inner affairs of the Bolshevik party. However, since the French government had declared Rakovsky *persona non grata*, Moscow had no choice but to

[1] See Degras (ed.), *Soviet Documents on Foreign Policy*, vol. ii, pp. 247–55.
[2] Trotsky's letter to Rakovsky of 30 September 1927 is in *The Archives*.

recall him. Rakovsky, distinguished though he was as diplomat, had chafed at his foreign assignments and was eager to plunge back, after an interval of four years, into the struggle at home. Trotsky, too, was glad to have his old friend back at his side. The Opposition derived some credit from the circumstances of Rakovsky's recall: the fact that one of its chiefs had drawn on himself the enmity of a bourgeois government, because he had appealed to foreign workers and soldiers to defend the Soviet Union, strikingly refuted the charges about the Opposition's defeatism and the 'united front from Chamberlain to Trotsky'.

Stalin, realizing that it was not enough to heap accusations on his adversaries, now endeavoured to enhance his popularity in a more positive way. The Opposition had, in its *Platform*, renewed the demands which it had made the year before and which the ruling factions then pretended to fulfil. It asked that wage increases be granted to poorly paid workers, that the eight-hour day be strictly observed, that tax reliefs be accorded to *bednyaks*, and so on. The *Platform* asserted that the ruling factions had honoured none of their promises; and that the conditions of the proletarian and semi-proletarian masses had gone from bad to worse. In reply to this Stalin made a startling move: he announced that the government would shortly introduce a seven-hour working day and a five-day week, and that the workers would receive the same wages as before. The occasion for the promulgation of the reform was to be the approaching tenth anniversary of the October Revolution, on which the Politbureau was to address the nation in a solemn Manifesto hailing the seven-hour day as the greatest achievement of socialism so far—the consummation of the first decade of revolution.

This was sheer duplicity. The Soviet Union was too poor to afford such a reform—even thirty years later, after it had become the world's second industrial power, its workers still worked eight hours a day and six days a week.[1] However, Stalin was not concerned with the economic realities of the case.

---

[1] The seven-hour day and five-day week were nominally in force for about thirteen years, but were not honoured in practice. At the beginning of the Second World War the return was decreed to the normal week and the eight-hour day and these remained obligatory for nearly two decades. Only in 1958 was a *gradual* return to the seven-hour day (but not yet to the five-day week) initiated.

He produced his sensational piece of legislation without discussing it beforehand with the trade unions, the Gosplan, and
even the Central Committee. The Bukharinists had misgivings.
Tomsky, who led the trade unions, did not hide his dislike of
the stunt. Stalin, nevertheless, forced it through; and for the
middle of October a special session of the Central Executive
Committee of the Soviets was convened to Leningrad to give its
formal and solemn sanction.

At the session, on 15 October, after Kirov had presented an
official report, Trotsky demonstrated the spuriousness of the
scheme. He recalled that when the Opposition had urged a
modest increase in wages, the claim had been indignantly rejected as threatening to strain the nation's economic resources.
How then could the economy now sustain a seven-hour day?
The Opposition maintained that even the eight-hour day was
not properly observed in state-owned industry—why then did
Stalin suddenly pull this grand reform out of his hat? Would it
not have been more honest to offer the workers some more
modest but real gains? It was a shame to commemorate the
revolution with such conjuring tricks. Trotsky pointed out that
none of the blueprints for the first Five Year Plan, which had
just been completed after years of preparation, contained as
much as a hint of the shorter working day. How then could they
genuinely shorten it when they had planned for years ahead on
the assumption of a longer working day? The whole reform,
he concluded, had one purpose only—to assist the ruling group
in its show-down with the Opposition.

In this dispute reason, truth, and honesty were all on Trotsky's side; and not for the first or the last time they led him
immediately into a trap. Nothing suited Stalin better than
Trotsky's protests. The Stalinists flocked to the factories to tell
the workers of Trotsky's latest indignity. He wanted, they said,
to rob the workers of the boon the party bestowed on them; he
was obstructing the epoch-making reform in which all could
see the dawn of socialism. What was the good of all his professions of Bolshevik loyalty and of all his posturing as a champion of the working class? To the men in the factories Trotsky's
arguments were unknown. Old and cool-headed workers may
have guessed them and have had their own thoughts about
Stalin's dubious gift. But the great credulous mass hailed it and

was impatient with the critics. The Opposition had mostly argued about issues which were high above the workers' head: Kuomintang, the Anglo-Soviet Council, permanent revolution, Thermidor, Clemenceau, &c. The one point at which the Opposition's language had not been abstruse was its demand for an improvement in the workers' lot. The demand had gained it wide, though passive, sympathy. Much of that sympathy was now dissipated. The wall of indifference and hostility closed around the Opposition.

Yet—so strong is sometimes in men 'the wish for that for which they only faintly hope'—precisely at this moment a freakish event brought the leaders of the Opposition solace and encouragement. During the session at which the seven-hour day was debated official demonstrations were staged in Leningrad to honour the event. There was the usual pomp and circumstance. Party leaders reviewed a parade and a march past of vast multitudes. Trotsky and Zinoviev were not to be seen among the leaders. By chance or choice, as if to demonstrate their divorce from officialdom, they stood on a lorry some distance away from the official stands, in a place where the demonstrators were due to pass on the way from the parade. Behind Trotsky's back was the Tauride Palace where ten years ago he had thundered against Kerensky and stirred the workers of the capital to enthusiasm, action, revolt. The columns of demonstrators, having marched past the official stands, approached. They recognized the two chiefs of the Opposition, halted, moved on, and halted again, stared mutely, raised hands, gesticulated, waved caps and handkerchiefs, moved on, and stopped again. The throngs around the lorry grew and traffic was blocked, while the space around the official stands became empty. It was as if an echo of the enthusiastic acclaim and clamour of the crowds of 1917 had come back. In truth, the crowd in front of Trotsky and Zinoviev, although visibly agitated, was subdued and timid. Its behaviour was ambiguous. If it intended to demonstrate sympathy with the Opposition, the demonstration was little more than a dumb show. It expressed the crowd's respect or pity for the defeated, not any readiness to fight on their side.

But the chiefs of the Opposition mistook the temper of the demonstrators. 'This was a silent, vanquished, stirring acclamation', so an eye-witness describes the scene. But 'Zinoviev and Trotsky received it with definite joy, as a manifestation of strength. "The masses are with us!" they said the same evening.'[1] The incident had a sequel quite out of proportion to its importance. It was largely under its impression, hoping that the masses were indeed with them at last, that the leaders of the Opposition decided to make a direct 'appeal to the masses' on the anniversary of the revolution, three weeks later. The ruling factions, on the other hand, saw in the ambiguous behaviour of the crowd a warning: they realized that they must take no chances with the temper of the people.

Stalin presently returned to the attack. On 23 October he once again asked for Trotsky's and Zinoviev's expulsion from the Central Committee. At length after four months he had worn down hesitation and resistance in the men who constituted the party's supreme tribunal. At last they were ready to do his bidding. But their fears and misgivings were still with them and showed in an extraordinary nervousness and the violence of the proceedings. There was a morbid tenseness in the air, such as might be felt at an execution where hangman and accomplices view their victim with deep hatred but also with deep awe and with gnawing uncertainty about the justice of the deed and the consequences. Whatever the victim says or does stirs in them these contradictory emotions which rise to a pitch of fury. All are convinced that the victim must die if they are to live; and all shudder at the thought of the horrors which may follow. They try to rout their own qualms by urging on the hangman, demanding haste, and hurling shameless abuse and heavy stones at the condemned. Such was the behaviour of the Stalinists and the Bukharinists at this session. They constantly interrupted Trotsky's last pleas with bursts of hatred and vulgar vituperation. They shut their ears to his arguments; and they urged the chairman to shut his mouth. From the chairman's table inkpots, heavy volumes, and a glass were flung at Trotsky's head while he spoke. Yaroslavsky, Shvernik, Petrovsky, President of the Ukraine, and others loudly incited Stalin and prompted him to get on with the job. There was no end to the

---

[1] Victor Serge, *Mémoires d'un Révolutionnaire*, p. 239. Trotsky's own description of the same scene in *Moya Zhizn*, vol. ii, p. 278, seems to reflect something of the wishfulness with which he first viewed the demonstration.

threats, gibes, and curses, which made this assembly look like a meeting of damned souls.[1]

Of the ruling group Stalin alone spoke with self-possession, with coarse and cold hatred, and without a trace of any qualm. He went over the familiar list of charges; and his speech—it was in it that he justified the employment of *agents provocateurs* (the 'Wrangel officer') against party members—was a feat of cynicism even for him.[2] Only Trotsky spoke with equal self-possession. His voice rose above the delirium for a last challenge before his departure. He warned the factions that Stalin's aim was nothing less than the extermination of all Opposition; and, amid cries of mockery, he forecast the long series of bloody purges in which not only his adherents but many Bukharinists and even Stalinists would be engulfed. He expressed the wishful assurance that Stalin's triumph would be shortlived and that the collapse of the Stalinist régime would come suddenly, with a crash. The victors of the moment, he said, relied on violence too much. True, the Bolsheviks had achieved 'gigantic results' when they had used violence against the old ruling classes and the Mensheviks and Social Revolutionaries who all stood for lost or reactionary causes. But they could not destroy in this way an Opposition which stood for historic progress. 'Expel us—you will not prevent our victory', these were the last words the party's supreme council heard from Trotsky's mouth.

.   .   .   .

Weeks of intensive activity followed. The Opposition still collected signatures for the *Platform* in the hope of impressing party opinion by the number of its adherents. Zinoviev was confident that 20,000 or 30,000 signatures would be obtained, that Stalin, confronted with evidence of such massive support, would have to stop short of further reprisals, and that the Opposition might even stage a come-back. The chiefs of the Opposition decided to make, on the anniversary of the revolution, that 'appeal to the masses' which had tempted them since the demonstration in Leningrad. It was not easy to determine the form of the appeal. Its purpose was to make the masses aware

---

[1] In a letter written to the Secretariat of the Central Committee on the next day Trotsky protested against the incomplete account of his speech in the official record and the omission of any reference to these scenes. *The Archives.*

[2] Stalin, *Sochinenya*, vol. x, pp. 172-205.

of the Opposition's demands and to stir them against the official leaders, without, however, giving the latter ground for charging the Opposition with a breach of discipline. The two things could hardly be reconciled; and the members of the Opposition spent days and nights deliberating and preparing for the trial of strength.

Trotsky, like his comrades, now spent most of his time in the suburban homes of humble workers, as he used to do when he was a young and unknown revolutionary, arguing, explaining principles and viewpoints, and instructing small groups of ardent and anxious adherents. At this moment he little resembled the Robespierre of the eve of Thermidor with whom he had compared himself. Two different characters seemed to have blended in him—Danton's and Babeuf's; but at this moment he looked more like the latter, the hunted leader of the Conspiracy of Equals, raising the cry for the regeneration of the revolution and defying the implacable builders of the new Leviathan state; and the tide of history ran against him as powerfully as it had run against Babeuf.

About fifty people filled a poor dining room [thus Victor Serge describes a typical meeting], listening to Zinoviev, who had grown fat, pale, dishevelled, and spoke with a low voice; there was about him something flabby yet also something very appealing. . . . At the other end of the table sat Trotsky. Ageing before our eyes, greying, great, stooping, his features drawn, he was friendly and always found the right answer. A woman worker, sitting cross-legged on the floor, asks him suddenly: 'And what if we are expelled from the party?' 'Nothing can prevent communist proletarians from being communists', Trotsky answers. 'Nothing can really cut us off from our party.' Half-smilingly, Zinoviev explains that we are entering an epoch when around the party there will be many expelled and semi-expelled people more worthy than the party secretaries of the name of a Bolshevik. It was simple and moving to see the men of proletarian dictatorship, yesterday still powerful, returning thus to the quarters of the poor and speaking here as men to men and looking for support and for comrades. On the staircase outside volunteers stood guard, watching passages and approaches; the G.P.U. might raid us any moment.

Once I accompanied Trotsky when he left such a meeting held in a dilapidated and poverty stricken dwelling. In the street Lev Davidovich put up the collar of his coat and pulled his cap over his

PLATE IX

Leaders of the Opposition after their expulsion from the party in 1927

Sitting from left to right: Serebryakov, Radek, Trotsky, Boguslavsky, Preobrazhensky

Standing: Rakovsky, Drobnis, Beloborodov, Sosnovsky

PLATE X

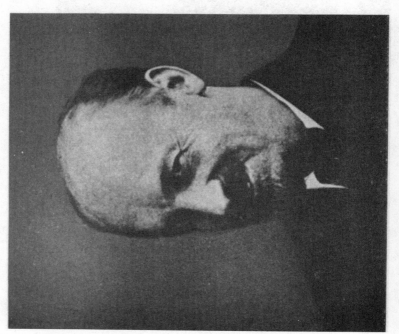

Radio Times Hulton Picture Library

(a) Bukharin as chief of the Communist International

(b) Rykov as Premier of the Soviet Union

eyes so that he should not be recognized. He now looked an old intellectual still erect after twenty years of wear and tear. We approached a cabman. 'Please do the bargaining over the fare', Lev Davidovich said to me, 'I have very little money on me.' The cabman, a bearded peasant of the old type, leaned towards him and said: 'There is no fare for you to pay. Come on, comrade. You're Trotsky, aren't you?' The cap had not concealed sufficiently the man of the battles of Svyazhsk, Kazan, Pulkovo, and Tsaritsyn. A faint cheerful smile lit Trotsky's face: 'Don't tell anyone about this. Everyone knows that cabmen belong to the petty bourgeoisie whose favour can only discredit us.'[1]

When he told the woman worker sitting cross-legged on the floor: 'Nothing can really cut us off from our party', Trotsky did not offer a mere half-hearted consolation. He reckoned, as Zinoviev did, with mass expulsion; but he hoped against hope that this would come as a salutary shock; that the party's conscience would be aroused; that people would wish to see the *Platform* in order to find out for themselves what the Opposition stood for; and that then the great debate for which the Opposition had so many times asked in vain would begin for good. He imagined that Stalin would overreach himself: if thousands of party members were to be expelled as counter-revolutionaries, they would also have to be imprisoned. This could not but 'dismay the party' and make it realize that such an act of suppression might well mean 'the end of the proletarian dictatorship'. For the moment, indeed, many Stalinists and Bukharinists were uneasy at the thought of becoming the persecutors and jailers of their own comrades and comrades-in-arms. Stalin and Molotov had to assure them that things would not come to such a pass and that there would be no need for wholesale expulsion, because the Politbureau would so handle the Opposition as to induce it to halt before it was too late and to surrender. On 2 November Trotsky, quoting these assurances, appealed to the Opposition to remain as aggressive as ever—only then would the mass of Stalinists and Bukharinists, seeing that their leaders' boasts were deceptive, exert themselves to stop the persecution, and force the persecutors themselves to falter and surrender.[2] However, Stalin's and Molotov's boasts were not at all groundless: they sized up the weakness of the Opposition and foresaw

---

[1] Victor Serge, *Le Tournant obscur*, pp. 113–14.   [2] *The Archives.*

that at the critical moment at least the Zinovievists would stumble. Meantime, the assurances that there would be no need for wholesale expulsion lulled disquiet and alarm and induced the party to await events passively and thus to reconcile itself to what was coming.

On the other hand, the torrents of abuse and threats let loose on the Opposition hampered the Opposition's efforts. Few were those who dared to put their signatures to the *Platform* daily denounced as a subversive document. Instead of the 20,000 or 30,000 signatures for which Zinoviev had hoped, the Opposition managed to collect only 5,000–6,000 at the most.[1] And the dread of the consequences for those who signed was such that, in order to protect their followers, the chiefs of the Opposition disclosed only several hundred names. The campaign over the *Platform* was thus yet another demonstration of the Opposition's weakness.

.   .   .   .

Trotsky was at this time, to quote Sedova, 'overworked, tense, and suffering from ill-health, fever, and sleeplessness'. To enemies he presented an unyielding front, and to followers he gave an example of self-control and heroic strength. But in domestic privacy human frailty came back into its own. In vain did he struggle with insomnia; drugs brought no relief. He complained more and more often of headaches and dizziness. He was depressed and disgusted. At moments his sensitivity was almost deadened by the stupendous venom and malignity that flooded in from all sides. 'At breakfast we would see him opening the newspapers', his wife writes, '. . . he glanced at them and disheartened scattered them over the table. All they contained was stupid lies, distortions of the plainest facts, the most vulgar abuse, hideous threats, and telegrams, from all over the world, repeating zealously and with boundless servility the same infamies. . . . "What have they made of the revolution, of the party, of Marxism, of the International!"'[2]

With Trotsky his next of kin drained the cup of defeat. Tense and expecting the worst, the whole family suffered from in-

---

[1] This was the figure given by the Opposition. V. Serge, *Mémoires d'un Révolutionnaire*, p. 243. Stalinist sources claimed that the Opposition collected 4,000 signatures. According to N. Popov, the Stalinist historian, the Opposition received 6,000 votes out of a total of 725,000 in the elections to the congress. (*Outline History of the CPSU*, vol. ii, p. 323.)

[2] *Vie et mort de Trotsky*, pp. 180–1.

somnia and through many a waking night awaited next day's blow—when day broke and friends came in, all put on a brave face and struggled on. Sedova, herself not very politically-minded, more at ease within the walls of museums and art galleries than amid arguing, scheming, and fighting party men, but moved by a woman's love and loyalty, was drawn completely into the cruel drama. Having given up her independent interests and placed herself in her husband's shadow, she lived with all her fibres his life, tried to think his thoughts, trembled with his anger, and shrank with worry and anxiety.

Their elder son, Lyova, now twenty-one, had spent his childhood and early youth, as he was to spend the rest of his short life, under the spell of his father's greatness. To be Trotsky's son, to share his ideas, and to follow in his footsteps had been for the adolescent and was for the young man a source of the greatest happiness. He had joined the Comsomol by subterfuge, before he had reached the age-limit, pretending to be older than he was, and he had tried to enlist in the Red Army too; he had left his parental home in the Kremlin to live in a commune-hostel, amid starving and tattered worker-students; and he had joined the Opposition the moment it had been formed. It was a galling experience for him to watch how the Comsomol, to whose members his father had so recently been a living legend and inspiration, was incited and turned against Trotskyism. With filial and revolutionary fervour he hated the men whom his father branded as bureaucrats corrupted by power. He spent years arguing and organizing Opposition groups, stumping party cells, and, side by side with such recognized leaders of the Opposition as Pyatakov and Preobrazhensky, addressing meetings in the provinces as far as the Urals. Youthful energy sustained his optimism and confidence; but in these weeks, amid rising bitterness and violence, he was seized with fear for his father's life, and became inseparable from him as assistant and body-guard, ready at any moment to jump at the throat of an assailant.

Unlike Lyova, Sergei, who was two years younger, had throughout adolescence rebelled against paternal authority and refused to be thrown in the shade by paternal greatness. The rebellion took the form of a revulsion against politics. He did not join the Comsomol; he would not hear of party affairs; and he would have nothing to do with the Opposition. Strong, brave, and adventurous, or, as his father and brother thought—light-minded, he revelled in games, sport, and the arts. Attracted by the circus (which in Russia then aspired to the dignity of an art in its own right), and, it seems, by a circus girl, he left his home in the Kremlin and spent a year or two with a troupe of performers. Having sown his wild oats, the prodigal was now back at home, still insisting on his independence and being sceptical about politics, but taking eagerly to mathematics and science for which he showed the outstanding ability that the father had shown at the same age. Yet a new sentiment began to break through the antagonism towards father and politics. The youth was moved by parental courage and sacrifice, outraged by the things done to father and his co-thinkers, and anxiously preoccupied with the uncertainties and dangers of the day.

The other branch of the family, the one which had sprung from Trotsky's first marriage, was also deeply involved. Alexandra Sokolovskaya, ageing, yet firm in conviction and still as unafraid of voicing it against all and sundry as she had been as a solitary Marxist at Nikolayev in the 1890's, continued to be the rallying centre of the Trotskyists in Leningrad. Her two daughters, Zina and Nina, both in their middle twenties, lived in Moscow and were ardent Oppositionists. Both were as thrilled to be their father's daughters as they were when they watched him during his rise in 1917, and both were heartbroken. Both had married; each had two children; and the husbands of both, active Trotskyists, had lost jobs and livelihood and were already either expelled or on the point of being expelled from the party and deported to Siberia. Sunk into poverty, helpless, and tormented by anxiety about children, husbands, and parents, both women were ill with consumption, and were marked to be the first victims of a fate which was to destroy all of Trotsky's children.

.   .   .   .

As the tenth anniversary of the revolution approached, the Opposition got ready to make the 'appeal to the masses'. It instructed its adherents to take part in the official celebrations of 7 November, but in such a way as to bring the Opposition's ideas and demands to the notice of the millions of people who would then fill the streets and squares of Soviet cities and towns. There was to be not a hint of incitement to insurrection or even disobedience. All that the members of the Opposition were to do was to march in closed ranks and as distinct groups within the official processions and to carry their own banners and slogans. These were so inoffensive outwardly, being directed against the ruling group merely by implication, that only the most politically minded of onlookers could distinguish them from the official slogans.

'Strike against the kulak, the N.E.P.-man, and the bureaucrat!', 'Down with opportunism!', 'Carry out Lenin's testament!', 'Beware of a split in the party!', 'Preserve Bolshevik unity!'—such were the Opposition's watchwords. They were designed to impress only party men and those outsiders who were intimately and sympathetically concerned with the trend of Bolshevik policy. One cannot therefore seriously describe the Opposition's action as any genuine 'appeal to the masses'—it was essentially an appeal to the party. But, driven from the party and denied access to its rank and file, the Opposition made the appeal from the outside, before the eyes of the nation and the world. Therein lay the weakness of the action. The Opposition tried to come into the open with a protest against the official conduct of party affairs and at the same time to demonstrate its own self-discipline and loyalty to the party. The protest, as it was planned, could therefore hardly become audible; and the show of self-discipline was to remain ineffective. On the dogmatically strictest interpretation of the rules—and no other interpretation could be expected from Stalin—a public demonstration against the party leaders did constitute a breach of discipline. In a word, the Opposition went either too far or not far enough. Yet such was its attitude and such were its circumstances that it had to go as far as it went and that it could go no farther.

The 7 November brought the Opposition a crushing defeat. Stalin had not been caught by surprise. He had issued strict orders for the swift suppression of any attempt at demonstration no matter how innocuous. No such attempt could from his viewpoint be innocuous, for if his adversaries succeeded this time, there was no saying whether they might not after all arouse now or later the brooding and disgruntled but cowed masses. Stalin knew

that even while he was nearing the pinnacle, he might still slip
and lose everything; and that, despite the crippling blows he
had inflicted on his adversaries, they could still overwhelm him
if he left them the slightest freedom of action. And so on
7 November squads of activists and police threw themselves on
any group of Oppositionists who tried to unfurl a banner, display a picture of Trotsky or Zinoviev, or shout an unauthorized
slogan. The Oppositionists were dispersed, abused, and beaten.
Bare-handed, they tried to defend themselves, to regroup, and
to demonstrate anew. The streets and squares became agitated
with scuffles and police charges, and with dispersing and
assembling crowds until even the least politically-minded person
in the festive mass of onlookers became aware that he or she was
witnessing a grave and critical event, that the inner-party
struggle had moved from the cells into the street, and that in
a way the contestants now appealed to all for support. It was
indeed suppression that turned the Opposition's action into
something like an appeal to the masses, and that surrounded it
with an air of scandal and made it appear a semi-insurrection.

Victor Serge has left a vivid description of the day in Leningrad.[1] Since 15 October the Opposition had pinned much hope
on the Leningraders, and Zinoviev had arrived there confident
in their response. But the party machine on the spot, forewarned by the events of 15 October, was ready. At first Opposition groups, together with all other demonstrators, marched
past the stands from which the official leaders took the parade;
and they raised their banners and slogans. These attracted little
attention. Then the police quietly surrounded the Oppositionists
and isolated them. Serge describes how he himself, prevented by
police barriers from joining the main demonstration, stopped to
watch a procession of workers advancing with their red flags towards the centre of the city. Every now and then activists turned
towards the marching men and women and shouted slogans.
The men and women took the cues apathetically. Then Serge
himself made a few steps towards the column and exclaimed:
'Long live Trotsky and Zinoviev!' or something to this effect.
An astonished silence was the demonstrators' only answer. Then
an activist, recovering his wits, shouted back in a voice charged
with threat and fury: 'To the dustbin with them!' The marching

[1] V. Serge, *Mémoires d'un Révolutionnaire*, pp. 246-7.

workers remained silent. Serge felt that he had exposed himself and 'was going to be torn to pieces'. Suddenly a void surrounded him—he found himself facing the column alone, with only a woman and a child a few steps behind him. Through the void a student rushed to him and whispered into his ear: 'Let's go away. This may turn out badly. I am coming with you so that nobody should hit you in the back.'

In another quarter of the city, outside the Ermitage, 'a few hundred Oppositionists struggled good-humouredly with the militia'. A tall man in military uniform—this was Bakaev, former chief of the G.P.U. in Leningrad—led a 'human wave' against mounted policemen, who tried to halt it. Every time it was pushed back, the 'wave' surged forward and returned. At another place a group of workers followed a small stocky man in an attack on mounted police. The stocky man dragged a policeman off the saddle, knocked him down, then helped him to get up, and in a loud confident voice 'accustomed to command', shouted: 'You should be ashamed of yourself. You should be ashamed of charging on Leningrad workers.' The man thus venting his comradely anger was Lashevich, the ex-deputy Commissar of War, who 'had once been in command of great armies'. Similar scuffles occurred all over the city and lasted many hours. Groups of spectators watched in 'dumb-founded silence'. In the evening, at meetings of Oppositionists, Serge saw again Bakaev and Lashevich—they had come, their uniforms torn, to discuss the events of the day.

In Moscow the disturbances and fights had a far less 'good-humoured' and 'comradely' aspect. Commandos of activists and police struck with cold and swift brutality. The city was tensely aware of a crisis; and it was alarmed. 'There were rumours on the eve of the anniversary', notes an eye-witness who, however, all too eagerly picked up rumours from official quarters, 'that the army massed in the Red Square for the annual parade would demonstrate against Stalin. Some courageous soldier or officer would cry out "Down with Stalin!" and others would echo the slogan.'[1] Nothing of the sort happened, the writer remarks. At first here and there bands of Oppositionists, marching towards the Lenin Mausoleum, managed to unfold a few banners; but before they reached the Red Square they were

[1] L. Fischer, *Men and Politics*, p. 92.

surrounded by commandos who tore the banners to shreds and made the Oppositionists move on with the official demonstration. Thus, hemmed in by their adversaries and awkwardly silent, keeping in step with the rest of the procession, the Oppositionists marched past the leaders and foreign guests assembled at the Red Square. Only 'the Chinese students of Moscow's Sun Yat-sen University . . . formed a long, sinuous dragon. In the middle of the Square they threw Trotsky's proclamations in the air.' Beyond the Square the Oppositionists were kicked out of the common ranks, attacked with truncheons, and dispersed or arrested. In various places Oppositionists had hung out of be-flagged windows portraits of Lenin and Trotsky. Everywhere these were torn down and those who had hung them out were maltreated. At the House of Soviets, Smilga, who had returned from Khabarovsk, decorated his balcony with such portraits and put out the slogan 'Carry out Lenin's testament!' A gang of toughs broke into his home, tore up the pictures and the banner, demolished the dwelling, and mauled the man who had ten years ago brought the Baltic Fleet into the Neva at Petrograd to assist in the October insurrection—his crime was to display the picture of the leader of that insurrection. Among others, Sedova, finding herself in a group of demonstrators, was beaten up.

Trotsky accompanied by Kamenev and Muralov spent the day touring the city by car. At Revolution Square he stopped and attempted to harangue a column of workers marching to-wards the Lenin Mausoleum. At once policemen and activists assailed him. Shots were fired. There were shouts: 'Down with Trotsky, the Jew, the traitor!' The windscreen of his car was smashed. The marching column watched the scene uneasily, but moved on.

What was going on in the minds of the multitudes which crowded the festive streets? Nobody knew, nobody could even guess. They marched obediently along the prescribed routes, shouted the prescribed slogans, and observed mechanically the prescribed discipline, without betraying their thoughts or vent-ing their feelings in a single flash of spontaneity. What a contrast they formed with the hungry, rough, warm-hearted, generous, enthusiastic, and drunken crowds of 1917! What a contrast there was between the present landscape of the cities and that of the revolution now commemorated! And what a contrast in the fortunes of the leaders! Ten years ago the workers of the two capitals were ready to give their lives at Trotsky's word of command. Now they would not even turn their heads to listen to him. Ten years ago Trotsky, as he watched Martov leading the Mensheviks in their exodus from the Soviets, shouted at him triumphantly: 'Go, go to the dustbin of history!'; and a thunder of Bolshevik applause covered his voice. 'To the dustbin with him!'—these words resounded now like a mocking echo through a square of Leningrad, when an Oppositionist tried to honour Trotsky's name. Had the wheel of history, so Oppositionists wondered, turned back or broken to pieces? Was this perhaps the Russian Thermidor?

These questions engaged Trotsky's thoughts also. He saw so many of the men who had led the Bolshevik revolution now aligned on his side. It seemed preposterous to assume that his and their defeat and humiliation had no deeper historic meaning, and that it did not mark that 'downward movement' of the revolution, that 'second chapter' of which he had spoken at the Central Committee a few months earlier. And yet he also saw that, changed as was the landscape of the revolution—its climate and colour—its broad and bare outline stood out as sharp as ever, unshaken and unaltered. It was still the Bolshevik party that ruled the republic, the party to which the Opposition still swore undying allegiance. He still regarded the republic, for all its 'bureaucratic degeneration', as a proletarian dictatorship; and he still resolutely dissociated himself and the Opposition from all those who branded it as a new police state, ruled by a 'new class' which had severed all ties with the working class and socialism. He refused to consider the bureaucracy as a new exploiting class—he viewed it as a 'morbid outgrowth on the body of the working class'. Public ownership, wherever Bolshevism had established it, was still intact. The kulak and the N.E.P.-man had not yet won. The antagonism between the workers' first state and world capitalism was unabated, even though it did not show itself in any clash of arms. So much had changed; and yet—so little. It was as if a hurricane had descended upon the scene, had flung the actors in opposite directions, had shifted all it could shift, had swayed the scene this way and that, but had left its frame solid and unimpaired. It seemed impossible that this should be the end—surely the hurricane portended an earthquake? Trotsky concluded that the 7 November was 'not yet the Soviet Thermidor', but that it was certainly 'the eve of Thermidor'.[1]

Serge relates that on the evening of 7 November, when the Oppositionists of Leningrad met, two voices could be heard: 'Nothing doing, we shall go on fighting', one voice repeated grimly. 'Against whom shall we fight?', asked another in anguish, 'Against our own people?' The same voices could be heard wherever Oppositionists met. As a rule it was the Trotskyists who asserted that they would go on fighting, and it was the Zinovievists who asked the awkward question. Zinoviev himself had returned from Leningrad in utter dejection; and he and Kamenev began to regret the luckless attempt to 'appeal to the masses' which they had undertaken with so much soaring confidence. Trotsky knew no regrets. The Opposition had done what it had to do; it could not undo what it had done: *Advienne que pourra*, he repeated. On the morrow of the fateful day he asked the Politbureau and the Presidium of the Central Control Commission for an official inquiry into the events; and he still took a rather sanguine view. He told his adherents that the up-shot of the demonstrations was not so bad: the Opposition had put on its banners the watchword 'Preserve Bolshevik unity' and had thereby shown where it stood and had at last wrested from Stalin a slogan from which he had sought to profit. Zinoviev and Kamenev replied that 7 November had brought them to the very brink of schism and that if the Opposition wished to preserve Bolshevik unity it had to retrace its steps.

For a few days they disputed what to do next. Trotsky soon abandoned his view of the consequences of the 7 November. Only five days after he had written how contented he was that the Opposition had 'wrested the slogan of unity' from Stalin, he argued that it was 'too late to talk about unity', because the party machine had become a will-less 'tool of Thermidorian forces' and was bent on routing the Opposition in the interest of kulak and N.E.P.-man.[2] Zinoviev and Kamenev were not sure of this: they noticed shifts of emphasis in Stalin's policy and

---

[1] See Trotsky's 'Balance of the Anniversary', written on 8 November, in *The Archives*.
[2] See his 'Zapiska' (Note) of 13 November in *The Archives*.

said that he was turning against the kulak and the N.E.P.-man. In any case they did not agree that it was 'too late to talk of unity'.

On 14 November the Central Committee and the Central Control Commission, convened for an extraordinary session, expelled from the party Trotsky and Zinoviev as guilty of incitement to counter-revolutionary demonstrations and virtually to insurrection.[1] Rakovsky, Kamenev, Smilga, and Evdokimov were expelled from the Central Committee; Bakaev, Muralov and others, from the Central Control Commission. From the party cells hundreds of members were ejected. Thus, after months and years in the course of which all factions hesitated and manœuvred, advanced, retreated, and went on contending, the schism was accomplished.

.   .   .   .

On the evening of 7 November Trotsky returned home and told his family that they must vacate their lodgings in the Kremlin. He himself moved out at once: he felt safer outside the Kremlin, and more than ever out of place in the residence of the ruling group. He took, provisionally, a tiny room at Granovsky Street 3, at the home of Beloborodov, an Oppositionist who was still Commissar of Home Affairs in the Russian Federal Republic, the man who, in 1918, had ordered the execution of Nicolas II at Ekaterinburg. For a few days Trotsky's whereabouts were unknown. The ruling group, somewhat alarmed, wondered what he might be up to and whether he had not 'gone underground'. He had no such intention; and for so well known a man it was impossible to go underground. On the day after his expulsion he gave his new address to the secretary of the Central Executive of the Soviets of which he was nominally still a member.[2] Leaving the Kremlin he saved himself a humiliation to which the other Opposition leaders were subjected: on 16 November they were all evicted. A friend describes their strange exodus from the Kremlin. Zinoviev left carrying only Lenin's death mask under his arm, a mask which was so depressing that the censorship had never allowed any reproduction

---

[1] *The Archives*; *KPSS v Rezolutsyakh*, vol. ii, pp. 368–70.

[2] He also notified the Executive that his wife and one of the sons were ill and unable to move, but that they would vacate their dwelling within a few days. *The Archives*.

of it to be published and so it remained Zinoviev's property. Then Kamenev came out, who in his early forties had grown suddenly white-haired and looked 'a handsome old man with very clear eyes'. Radek packed his books, with the intention of selling them; and handing out to those around him volumes of German poetry as souvenirs, muttered sarcastically: 'Haven't we been idiots! We are left penniless when we could have prepared a nice war chest. Lack of money is killing us. With our famous revolutionary probity we have been but feckless intellectuals full of scruples. . . .'[1]

Simultaneously another man made his exit in a different manner. In the evening of 16 November a revolver shot suddenly broke the stillness of the Kremlin. Adolf Abramovich Yoffe had committed suicide. He left a letter to Trotsky explaining that this was the only way in which he could protest against Trotsky's and Zinoviev's expulsion and express his horror at the indifference with which the party had received it. He had been Trotsky's disciple and friend since before 1910 when, a neurotic student, he helped Trotsky to edit the Viennese *Pravda*. With Trotsky he had joined the Bolshevik party in 1917, and was a member of the Central Committee at the time of the October insurrection. Soft-hearted, soft-smiling, and soft-spoken, he was one of the most determined advocates and organizers of the rising. He soon became one of the great Bolshevik diplomats: he led the first Soviet delegation to Brest Litovsk and was the first Soviet Ambassador in Berlin; he negotiated the peace treaty with Poland in 1921, and the pact of friendship between Lenin's and Sun Yat-sen's governments a year later; and he was Ambassador in Vienna and Tokyo. At the beginning of 1927 he returned from Tokyo, gravely ill with tuberculosis and polyneuritis, and was appointed Trotsky's deputy at the Concessions' Committee. In Moscow doctors held out no hope for him and urged him to take a cure abroad. Trotsky intervened on his behalf with the Commissar of Health and the Politbureau;[2] but the Politbureau refused to send him abroad on the ground that the cure would cost too much—1,000 dollars. An American publisher had just offered to pay Yoffe 20,000 dollars for

---

[1] V. Serge, *Le Tournant obscur*, p. 140.
[2] Trotsky's letters to Semashko, the Commissar of Health (20 January 1927), and to the Politbureau are in *The Archives*.

memoirs; and Yoffe asked to be allowed to leave at his own expense. Stalin then forbade him to publish memoirs, refused him an exit permit, deprived him of medical assistance, and harassed him with every kind of vexation. Bedridden, pain-stricken, penniless, and depressed by the savageness of the on-slaught on the Opposition, he blew out his brains.[1]

Yoffe's farewell letter is important not only for the light it throws on his attitude to Trotsky—it is also unique as a human and political document and a statement of revolutionary morality.

The letter begins with Yoffe's justification of his suicide, an act which revolutionary ethics normally condemned. In his youth, he recalled, he had stood up against Bebel in defence of Paul and Laura Lafargue, Marx's son-in-law and daughter, who had committed suicide when old age and infirmity had made them useless as fighters.

All my life I have been convinced that the revolutionary politician should know when to make his exit and that he should make it in time . . . when he becomes aware that he can no longer be useful to the cause he has served. It is more than thirty years since I embraced the view that human life has sense only in so far as it is spent in the service of the infinite—and for us mankind is the infinite. To work for any finite purpose—and everything else is finite—is meaningless. Even if mankind's life were to come to a close this would in any case happen at a time so remote that we may consider humanity as the absolute infinite. If one believes, as I do, in progress, one may assume that when the time comes for our planet to vanish, mankind will long before that have found the means to migrate and settle on other younger planets. . . . Thus anything accomplished in our time for mankind's benefit will in some way survive into future ages; and through this our existence acquires the only significance it can possess.

Having thus expressed in the Marxist idiom and in an atheistic spirit the ancient human longing for immortality, the immortality of mankind and of its genius, Yoffe went on to say that for twenty-seven years his life had had its full significance: he had lived for socialism; he had not wasted a single day, for

[1] Even while Yoffe was writing the letter to Trotsky his wife came to tell him that the Politbureau had declined his latest request for permission to go abroad for a month or two.

even while in prison he used every day to study and prepare
himself for future struggles. But now his life had become purposeless; and it was his duty to depart. Trotsky's expulsion and
the silence in which the party had witnessed it were the last
blows. Had he been in good health, he would have fought on
in the ranks of the Opposition. But perhaps his suicide, 'a small
event compared with your expulsion' (and 'a gesture of protest
against those who have reduced the party to such a condition
that it is unable to react in any way against this monstrosity')—
perhaps his suicide would contribute to arouse the party to the
Thermidorian danger. He feared that the hour of the party's
awakening had not yet come—all the same his death would be
more useful than his life.

With the utmost modesty, evoking their long friendship and
common work, Yoffe excused himself for 'using this tragic
opportunity' to tell Trotsky where, in his view, Trotsky's weakness lay. He had wanted to tell him this earlier, but could not
prevail upon himself to do so. He had never had any doubt that
Trotsky had been politically in the right ever since 1905. He had
heard Lenin himself saying this and admitting that not he but
Trotsky had been right in the old controversies over permanent
revolution. 'One does not tell lies before one's death, and once
again I am repeating this to you now.'[1] 'But I have always
thought that you have not enough in yourself of Lenin's unbending and unyielding character, not enough of that ability
which Lenin had to stand alone and remain alone on the road
which he considered to be the right road. . . . You have often
renounced your own correct attitude for the sake of an agreement or a compromise, the value of which you have overrated.'
In this, his last word, therefore, he wished that Trotsky should
find in himself that 'unyielding strength' which would help
their common cause to eventual even if delayed triumph.

The criticism, coming from the depth of a dying friend's devotion and love, could not but move and impress Trotsky: he
was to stand almost alone, 'unbending and unyielding', for the
rest of his life. Politically, however, Yoffe's suicide made no

---

[1] In his autobiography Trotsky relates that Yoffe had intended several times to
publish this conversation with Lenin and Lenin's admission but that Trotsky dissuaded him, because he feared that Yoffe would expose himself to attacks which
would ruin his health to the end. Yoffe's letter confirms this. The full text of the
letter is in *The Trotsky Archives*.

impact at all. His letter was not published—the G.P.U. had attempted to conceal it even from Trotsky who had as it were to wrest it from their hands. In the ranks of the Opposition the event spread depression; it was received as an act of despair. Trotsky feared that the example might be infectious. After the defeat of the 1923 Opposition several of its adherents—Eugene Bosch, a legendary heroine of the civil war in the Ukraine, Lutovinov, a prominent trade unionist and veteran of the Workers' Opposition, and Glazman, one of Trotsky's secretaries—took their lives. Now, when the Opposition was under an incomparably more brutal attack and saw no clear road ahead, there was even more ground for an outbreak of panic. Only after Yoffe's letter had been circulated in Opposition groups did the sense he had intended to give to his suicide become better known; and the deed came to be seen as an act of faith rather than of despair.[1]

On 19 November a long procession, headed by Trotsky, Rakovsky, and Ivan Smirnov, followed Yoffe's coffin through the streets and squares of Moscow to the cemetery of the Novodevichyi Monastery on the outskirts. It was the early afternoon of an ordinary working day—the authorities had arranged the funeral at this time in order to make it inconspicuous; but many thousands of people joined in the cortège and marched singing mournful tunes and revolutionary hymns. Representatives of the Central Committee and of the Commissariat for Foreign Affairs mingled with the Oppositionists—anxious to hush up the scandal, they had come to pay official homage to their dead adversary. When the cortège reached the Monastery —where Peter the Great once held his sister Sophia behind bars, and ordered several hundreds of her adherents to be slain under the window of her cell—police and G.P.U. tried to stop the procession outside the cemetery. The crowd forced its way into the alleys and gathered around the open grave. It received with an angry murmur an official spokesman who rose to make an oration. Then Trotsky and Rakovsky spoke. 'Yoffe left us', Trotsky said, 'not because he did not wish to fight, but because he lacked the physical strength for fighting. He feared to be-

---

[1] From the text which was circulated Trotsky omitted, as Yoffe had authorized him to do, those passages which expressed a certain pessimism about the immediate prospects of the Opposition.

come a burden on those engaged in the struggle. His life, not his suicide, should serve as a model to those who are left behind. The struggle goes on. Everyone remains at his post. Let nobody leave.'

This gathering at a cemetery haunted by Russia's fearful past was the Opposition's last public meeting and demonstration. This was also Trotsky's last public appearance—and this his cry for courage resounding amid graves his last public speech— in Russia.[1]

. . . .

'Everyone remains at his post! Let nobody leave!'—how often had not these words appeared in Trotsky's Orders of the Day at the worst moments of the civil war; and how many times had they not led back into battle routed and disheartened divisions, making them fight till victory! Now, however, the words had lost their power. Zinoviev, Kamenev, and their followers were already 'leaving their posts' and casting round in desperation for an avenue of retreat. On the eve of Yoffe's funeral Moscow was already astir with rumours about their surrender to Stalin. In a note, dated 18 November, Trotsky dismissed the rumours, declaring that Stalin had put them out in order to confound the Opposition. Once again Trotsky maintained that repression worked in the Opposition's favour; and he warned his adherents that they must continue to consider themselves as belonging to the party, and that even expulsion and imprisonment would not justify them in forming another party. But if the Opposition accepted expulsion, Zinoviev and Kamenev replied, it would inevitably, even against its will, constitute itself into another party. They were therefore obliged to do their utmost in order to obtain an annulment of the expulsion. 'Lev Davidovich,' they said, 'the time has come when we must have the courage to surrender.' 'If this kind of courage, the courage

---

[1] The speech as well as an obituary on Yoffe are in *The Archives*. L. Fischer, who witnessed the scene, writes that after the ceremonies 'everybody crowded towards Trotsky to give him an ovation. Appeals were made to the people to go home. They stayed, and Trotsky for a long time could not get out of the cemetery. Finally young men linked elbows and formed two human chains facing one another with a narrow corridor in between through which Trotsky could pass to the exit.' But the crowd surged into that corridor and meantime Trotsky waited alone in a shed on the cemetery; '. . . he never stood still. He walked like a pacing tiger. . . . I was nearby and had the definite impression that he feared assassination.' L. Fischer, op. cit., p. 94.

to surrender, were all that was needed,' Trotsky rejoined, 'the revolution should have been victorious by now the world over.'[1] They still agreed, however, to address a joint statement to the congress which was now convened for the beginning of December. In that statement, signed by 121 Oppositionists, they declared that they could not renounce their views, but that they recognized that the schism, leading to a struggle between two parties, was 'the gravest menace to Lenin's cause'; that the Opposition bore its share of responsibility, but not the major one, for what had happened; that the forms of inner-party contention must change; and that the Opposition, ready to disband its organization once again, appealed to the congress to reinstate the expelled and imprisoned Oppositionists.

It was clear that the congress would reject this appeal out of hand and that it would not agree to annul the expulsions. At this point the Joint Opposition was bound to dissolve and each of its two constituent groups to take its own road.

The congress was in session for three weeks; and it was wholly preoccupied with the schism. The Opposition had not a single delegate with voting rights. Trotsky did not attend; he had not even asked to be admitted in order to make a personal appeal against his expulsion. Unanimously the congress declared that expression of the Opposition's views was incompatible with membership in the party. Rakovsky tried to plead the Opposition's case; but he was driven from the rostrum. Then the assembly listened with amused astonishment to Kamenev as he gave a pathetic description of the Opposition's plight. He and his comrades, he said, were in this dilemma: either they must constitute themselves a second party—but this would be 'ruinous for the revolution' and would lead to 'political degeneration'; or else they must, 'after a fierce and stubborn struggle', declare their 'complete and thorough surrender to the party'. They had chosen surrender—they agreed, that is, to refrain from expressing any views critical of the official policy—because they were 'deeply convinced that the triumph of the correct Leninist policy could be secured only within and through our party, not outside it and despite of it'. They were therefore ready to submit to all decisions of the congress and to 'carry them out, no matter how hard they might be'.[2]

[1] Serge, *Le Tournant obscur*, p. 149.   [2] *15 Syezd VKP (b)*, pp. 245-6.

Having placed himself and his comrades at the mercy of the congress and going down on his knees, Kamenev then tried to stop half-way. The Oppositionists who capitulated, he said, acted as Bolsheviks; but they would not act as Bolsheviks if they were also to renounce their views. Never before had anyone in the party been asked to do this, he asserted, forgetting that he and Zinoviev had demanded it of Trotsky in 1924. 'If we should disclaim the views which we advocated a week or a fortnight ago, this would be hypocrisy on our part and you would not believe us.' He made another desperate attempt to save the capitulators' dignity: he pleaded for the release of the imprisoned Trotskyists: 'A situation in which people like Mrachkovsky are imprisoned while we are free is intolerable. We have been fighting together with those comrades. We are responsible for all their deeds.' He therefore implored the congress to give all Oppositionists the chance to undo what had happened. 'We beg you, if you wish this assembly to go down in history . . . as a congress of conciliation: give us a helping hand.'[1]

A week later the disintegration of the Joint Opposition was complete. On 10 December Zinovievists and Trotskyists separated and spoke in different voices. On behalf of the former, Kamenev, Bakaev, and Evdokimov announced their final acceptance of all decisions taken by the congress. On the same day Rakovsky, Radek, and Muralov declared that although they agreed with the Zinovievists about the 'absolute necessity' to maintain the single-party system, they nevertheless refused to submit to the decisions of the congress. 'For us to refrain from advocating our views within the party would amount to a renunciation of those views'; and in agreeing to this 'we would fail in our most elementary duty towards the party and the working class'.[2]

Zinoviev and his followers had in effect repeated what Trotsky had said in 1924—that the party was the only force capable of 'securing the conquests of October', the 'only instrument of historic progress', and that 'no one could be right against it'. It was this belief that led them to surrender. Trotsky and his adherents, on the other hand, were now convinced that they were 'right as against the party'; yet they resolved to fight on, thinking that they were fighting not against the party but for it—to save it from itself or rather from its bureaucracy. Both

[1] *15 Syezd VKP (b)*, p. 248.   [2] Ibid., pp. 1286–7.

Trotsky and Zinoviev tried in fact to square the same circle, only that each attempted to do it in a different way. The Zinovievists hoped that by remaining within the party they might be able, circumstances permitting, to 'regenerate' it; the Trotskyists were convinced that this could be done only from without. Both repeated in the same words that any attempt to set up another party would be disastrous to the revolution; and both thereby implicitly admitted that the working class was, in their view, politically immature, that it could not be relied upon to support two Communist parties, that as yet it was therefore futile to appeal to the workers against the party bureaucracy, which, despite all its faults and vices, still acted as guardian of the proletarian interest, as trustee of the revolution and agent of socialism. If they had not thought so, the horror with which both Trotsky and Zinoviev spoke about 'another party' would have been inexplicable and ridiculous. In that case they should have, on the contrary, considered it their duty to set up another party. Recognizing their adversaries, if only implicitly and with grave reservations, as the guardians and trustees of the prole- tarian dictatorship, and being in conflict with them, the Oppositionists were caught in a contradiction. Zinoviev in his conscience sought to resolve the contradiction by accepting the dictates of the ruling factions. Trotsky, convinced that the ruling factions could not remain the guardians of the revolution for long, obeyed the dictates of his conscience which told him that nothing could be gained by self-renunciation.

While around him the Joint Opposition crumbled, expulsions multiplied and thousands of Oppositionists capitulated, Trotsky remained undaunted and contemptuous of the 'dead souls'— Zinoviev and Kamenev—predicting that they would be driven from surrender to surrender and from disgrace to disgrace, each worse than the other. The ruling factions were now in a rage of triumph. They were all the more boisterous because they had not been sure up to the last moment whether Stalin would in- deed be able to manœuvre the Opposition into surrender. No sooner had Zinoviev and Kamenev announced their capitula- tion than the ruling factions declared that they did not accept it, and that the capitulators must fully repudiate their ideas and recant. At first Zinoviev and Kamenev had been given to understand that they would be reinstated if they agreed merely

to refrain from voicing their views. Now that they had agreed
to this, they were told that their silence would be an insult and
a challenge to the party. 'Comrades', Kalinin said at the congress, 'what will the working class think . . . of people who declare that they will not advocate views which they still hold to
be correct? . . . this is either deliberate deception . . . or these
Oppositionists have become Philistines, keeping their views to
themselves and not defending them.'[1] The ruling factions feared,
in truth, that if they accepted Zinoviev's and Kamenev's first
surrender, they would compromise themselves. What sort of a
party is it, people would wonder, that allows its members to
hold certain views but not to express them? The victors could
not stop half-way. To hold the ground they had just gained,
they had to gain more and drive their defeated opponents even
farther. Having forbidden them to express heresy, the congress
had to forbid them to profess it even by silence. Having deprived them of their voice, it had to rob them of their thought;
and it had to give them back a voice so that they should use it
to abjure their ideas.

Another week was filled with haggling over terms, a week
during which the Zinovievists strained and struggled in the
trap. They could not go back on their first capitulation; and in
order to save its sense and to achieve what they had hoped to
achieve through it, they stumbled into another capitulation.
On 18 December Zinoviev and Kamenev returned and knocked
at the doors of the congress to say that they condemned their
own views as 'wrong and anti-Leninist'. Bukharin, it is related,
received them with these words: 'You have done well to make
up your mind—this was the last minute—the iron curtain of
history is just coming down'—the iron curtain which, we may
add, was to crush Bukharin as well. Bukharin was undoubtedly
relieved to see Zinoviev and Kamenev return and submit, for
he, like some other members of the ruling factions, had wondered anxiously what would happen if Zinoviev and Kamenev
refused to recant and rejoined Trotsky. Even Ordjonikidze, who
on behalf of the Central Control Commission presented the
report and moved the motion for expulsion, showed his uneasiness when he said that the repressive measures hit men 'who
have brought a good deal of benefit to our party and have

[1] Ibid., p. 1211.

fought in our ranks for many years'. But Stalin and the majority, drunk with jubilation, went on to kick the prostrated. They refused to reinstate them even after the recantation. By a strange quirk it was Rykov, one day to share Zinoviev's and Kamenev's fate, who went out to see them as they waited at the door and to slam the door on them. He told them that they were not readmitted into the party; that they were to remain on probation for at least six months; and that only afterwards would the Central Committee decide whether to reinstate them.

The defection of the Zinovievists left Trotsky and his adherents isolated. It soothed the none too sensitive consciences of many Stalinists and Bukharinists who saw in it the final vindication of Stalin's action. Surely Trotsky must be absolutely in the wrong, they reflected, if even his erstwhile allies turned their backs on him. The party and the nation had their eyes glued to the congress and the astounding spectacle of capitulation enacted there; they were not greatly concerned with that section of the Opposition which was not involved in the spectacle. The Trotskyists themselves were stunned. They were overcome by a sense of the finality of their break with the party. They viewed with incredulity the gulf which had opened between themselves and the Zinovievists. They wondered whether they themselves had not acted foolhardily: should they have conducted their semi-clandestine propaganda? should they have 'appealed to the masses' on 7 November? should they have precipitated the schism? Such qualms induced them to receive the verdicts of expulsion with unending and exalted declarations of their undiminished fidelity to the party. A few went in the footsteps of the Zinovievists; others wavered. The majority remained determined to fight on and face persecution. Yet no one knew who was and who was not a 'capitulator'. Immediately after the congress 1,500 Oppositionists were expelled and 2,500 signed statements of recantation.[1] But among those who signed a few withdrew, when they saw that one act of surrender entailed another; and among those who had refused to sign some weakened in their resolve when they were subjected to further intimidation, temptation, and persuasion. Those of one set viewed those of another as blacklegs or traitors. As it was not known

[1] Popov, op. cit., vol. ii, p. 327.

where one set ended and the other began, confusion and suspicion spread all through the whole of the former Joint Opposition.

Trotsky, seeing the futility of Zinoviev's surrender, was confirmed in his conviction that he had chosen the right road. He worked feverishly to impart his belief to his disheartened followers. He told them that no prudence or procrastination would have helped them, because Stalin would in any case have found the excuses needed for driving them out. What mattered was to rally those who stood fast, to draw a sharp line of division between them and the renegades, to avoid ambiguous attitudes, and to make the causes of the breach clear for contemporaries and posterity alike. Moreover, the Opposition could no longer work as it had worked hitherto—it must 'go underground' for good, find new forms of contacts between its groups and new methods of work, and establish links with its co-thinkers abroad.

Very little time was left for all this. Even before the year was out Stalin arranged to deport the Oppositionists. Yet the remorseless master of the bloody purges to come was still curiously concerned with his alibi and with appearances. He wished to avoid the scandal of an undisguised and forcible deportation and he tried so to stage the banishment of his enemies that it should look like a voluntary departure. Through the Central Committee he offered the leading Trotskyists minor administrative posts in the far corners of the immense country: Trotsky himself was to leave of his 'own free will' for Astrakhan, on the Caspian Sea. Early in January 1928 Rakovsky and Radek, delegated by the Opposition, and Ordjonikidze were engaged in fantastic bargaining over these proposals. Radek and Rakovsky protested against Trotsky's assignment to Astrakhan, saying that his health, sapped by malaria, would not stand the vaporous and hot climate of the Caspian port. The game was cut short when Trotsky and his friends declared that they were ready to accept any provincial appointments provided that these were no mere excuses for deportation, that the Opposition's consent was obtained for every appointment, and that the assignments were fixed with an eye to the health and safety of those concerned and of their families.[1]

[1] An account of the 'negotiations' is given in a letter written by Trotsky himself or by one of his friends to the Central Control Commission and the Politbureau in the first days of 1928. *The Archives.*

On 3 January, while the bargaining was still on, the G.P.U. summoned Trotsky to appear before it. He ignored the summons. The farce then came to an end; and a few days later, on the 12th, the G.P.U. informed Trotsky that under article 58 of the criminal code, i.e. under the charge of counter-revolutionary activity, he would be deported to Alma Ata, in Turkestan, near the Chinese Frontier. The date of the deportation was set for 16 January.

Two writers, one a complete outsider, the other a Trotskyist, have given their impression of Trotsky during his last days in Moscow. Paul Scheffer, correspondent of the *Berliner Tageblatt*, interviewed him on 15 January. At a 'superficial glance' he could see nothing indicating that a police watch was kept over Trotsky. (It may be assumed that the eye of the German journalist was not very skilled in detecting such indications.) He noticed excitement at Trotsky's home, the comings, goings, and leave-takings of men who were all about to be exiled, and the packing off for a long journey. 'In all corridors and passages there were piles of books, and once again books—the nourishment of revolutionaries, as ox blood used to be the nourishment of the Spartans.' Against this background he describes the man himself, 'somewhat less than middle-size, with a very delicate skin, a yellowish complexion, and blue, not large eyes, which at times can be very friendly, and at times are full of flashes and very powerful.' A large animated face 'reflecting both strength and loftiness of mind', and a mouth strikingly small in proportion to the face. A delicate, soft, feminine hand. 'This man, who has improvised armies and filled primitive workers and peasants with his own enthusiasm, lifting them high above their understanding . . . is at first shy, slightly embarrassed . . . that is perhaps why he is so captivating.'

Throughout the conversation Trotsky, though courteous, was on his guard, content to express himself *pro foro externo*, but extremely reticent *vis-à-vis* the bourgeois journalist about domestic issues. Not a single mention of his adversaries, no complaint, no polemics. Only once did the talk skirt inner-party affairs, when the interviewer remarked that Lloyd George had prophesied 'a Napoleonic future for Trotsky'. This was the nearest that Scheffer came to alluding to the deportation, to Trotsky's plans for the future, and so on. Trotsky, however, seized a different facet of the comparison: 'It is a strange idea', he answered somewhat amused, 'that I should be the man to put an end to a revolution. This is not the first of Lloyd George's blunders.' Character-istically, the comparison with Napoleon brought to Trotsky's mind not the obvious and superficial parallel between their per-sonal fortunes as exiles, but the political idea, so abhorrent to him, of Bonapartism, the successor to Thermidor. With him the general problem took precedence over the personal. ('One is constantly reminded', Scheffer remarks, 'that this man is first and foremost a fighter.') He spoke mainly about the decay of capitalism and the prospects of revolution in Europe, prospects with which as always he linked the future of Bolshevik Russia. 'Trotsky's talk quickly loses its conversational tone, becomes oratorical, and soars high', and he illustrates the ups and downs of the curve of world revolution with 'beautifully melodious gestures'. The argument was interrupted by a comrade due to go into exile this very evening—he had come to ask whether there was anything he could still do for Trotsky. 'Trotsky's face, with the small upturned moustache, folds itself into many gay wrinkles: "You are going for a journey tonight, aren't you?" The man of controversy and irony will miss no opportunity. . . . The humour of the unshaken man is undimmed.' At the parting he invited Scheffer to come and visit him at Alma Ata.[1]

Unlike Scheffer, Serge described Trotsky's surroundings as 'watched day and night by comrades who were themselves watched by stool-pigeons'. In the street G.P.U. men on motor-cycles noted every car coming and going.

I went up by the back stairs. . . . He whom among ourselves we called with affectionate respect The Old Man, as we used to call Lenin, worked in a small room facing the courtyard and furnished only with a field bed and a table. . . . Dressed in a well-worn jacket, active and majestic, his high crop of hair almost white, his complexion sickly, he displayed in this cage a stubborn energy. In the next room messages which he had just dictated were being typed out. In the dining room comrades arriving from every corner of the country were received—he talked with them hurriedly between telephone calls. All might be arrested any moment—what next? Nobody

---

[1] Paul Scheffer, *Sieben Jahre Sowjet Union*, pp. 158-61.

knew . . . but all were in a hurry to benefit from these last hours, for surely they were the last. . . .[1]

The day of 16 January, taken up by conferences, instructions, further leave-takings, and last preparations for the journey, passed as if in a fever. The hour of departure was fixed for 10 p.m. In the evening the whole family, exhausted and tense, sat waiting for the G.P.U. agents to appear. The appointed time had passed, but they did not come. The family was lost in guesses until the G.P.U. informed Trotsky by telephone, without offering any explanation, that his departure was postponed by two days. Further guesses, interrupted by the arrival of Rakovsky and other friends, all greatly excited. They had come from the station where thousands had gathered to give Trotsky a farewell. There was a stormy demonstration at the train by which he was expected to travel. Many lay down on the tracks and swore not to allow the train to leave. The police tried to remove them and to disperse the crowd; but the powers that be, seeing what turn the demonstration had taken, ordered the deportation to be postponed. The Opposition congratulated itself on the effect and planned to repeat the manifestation in two days' time. The G.P.U., however, decided to catch the Opposition by surprise and to abduct its leader surreptitiously. The plan was to take him to another station; to bring him to a little stop outside Moscow, and only there to put him on the Central Asian train. They had told him to be ready to depart on 18 January; but already on the 17th they called to apprehend him. Curiously, his followers failed to keep watch at his home; and so when the G.P.U. men arrived, they found on the spot only Trotsky and his wife, their two sons, and two women, one of whom was Yoffe's widow.[2]

A scene of rare tragi-comedy followed. Trotsky locked himself up and refused to let the G.P.U. in. This was a token of passive resistance, with which in the old days he had invariably met any police trying to lay hands on him. Through the locked door the prisoner and the officer in charge conducted a parley. Finally, the officer ordered his men to smash the door; and they broke into the room. By a weird freak the officer who had come to arrest Trotsky had served on Trotsky's military train

[1] V. Serge, *Le Tournant obscur*, p. 155.   [2] *Moya Zhizn*, vol. ii, p. 287.

during the civil war, as one of the body-guards. Face to face
with his former chief, he lost countenance, broke down, and
muttered distraught: 'Shoot me, comrade Trotsky, shoot me.'
Trotsky did his best to comfort his jailer and even urged and
persuaded him to carry out orders. Then he resumed the posture
of disobedience and refused to dress. The armed men took off
his slippers, dressed him, and, as he declined to walk out, carried him down the staircase, amid the shouts and the booing
of Trotsky's family and of Yoffe's widow, who followed them.
There were no other witnesses, apart from a few neighbours,
high officials and their wives, who, startled by the commotion,
peeped out and quickly hid their frightened faces.

The deportee and his family were bundled into a police car
which then, in broad daylight, rushed through the streets of
Moscow carrying away unnoticed the leader of the October
Revolution and the founder of the Red Army. At the Kazan
station—it was there that the escort took him—he refused to
walk to the train; and armed men dragged him to a solitary
carriage waiting for him at a shunting yard. The station was
cordoned off and emptied of passengers, only a few busy railway
men moved around. Behind the escort there followed the deportee's family. His younger son, Sergei, exchanged blows with
a G.P.U. man, and the elder, Lyova, tried to arouse the railway
workers: 'Look, comrades', he shouted, 'look how they are
carrying off comrade Trotsky.' The workers stared with dry
eyes—not a cry or even a murmur of protest came from them.

.   .   .   .

Nearly thirty years had passed from the moment when the
young Trotsky saw the towers and the walls of Moscow for the
first time. He was then being transported from a jail in Odessa
to a place of exile in Siberia; and it was from behind the bars
of a prison van that he had his first glimpse of the 'village of the
Tsars', the future 'capital of the Communist International'. It
was from behind such bars also that he now had his last glimpse
of Moscow, for he was never to return to the city of his triumphs
and defeats. He entered it a persecuted revolutionary; and so
he left it.

CHAPTER VI

A Year at Alma Ata

AT a deserted little station, about 50 kilometres from Moscow, the single railway carriage in which Trotsky and his family had been taken away from the capital stopped; and it was hitched to a train bound for central Asia. Sergei, anxious to continue his academic curriculum, alighted and returned to Moscow. Sedova, ill with fever, and Lyova accompanied Trotsky into exile. A guard of about a dozen men escorted them. From the corridor through a half-open door the guardsmen kept watch on the prisoner and his wife slumped on the wooden benches inside a dark compartment dimly lit by a candle. The officer who had come to arrest Trotsky was still in command; his presence on this train was a grotesque reminder of that other and famous train, the *Predrevvoyen's*[1] field headquarters, on which he had served as Trotsky's body-guard. 'We were tired out', Sedova recalls, 'by the surprises, uncertainties, and tension of these last days; and we were resting.' As he lay in the dark or watched the endless white plain through which the train moved eastwards, Trotsky began to adjust his mind to his new circumstances. There he was, wrenched from the world with its tumult and fascination, cut off from his work and struggle, and isolated from adherents and friends. What was to follow now? And what was he to do? He bestirred himself to enter a few notes in his diary or to draft a protest; but he found—and this was something of a minor shock—that he had set out 'without writing utensils'—this had never happened to him before, not even during his perilous flight from the Far North in 1907. All was full of hazard now—he did not even know whether it was still to Alma Ata that he was being deported. Insecurity roused his defiant and contrary temper. He remarked to his wife that it was at least a consolation to know that he would not die a Philistine's death in a comfortable Kremlin bed.

On the next day the train stopped at Samara; and Trotsky

---

[1] *Predrevvoyen*—President of the Revolutionary Military Council.

telegraphed a protest to Kalinin and Menzhinsky saying that never during his long revolutionary career had any capitalist police treated him with such trickery and mendacity as the G.P.U. who had kidnapped him without telling him where they were taking him and made him travel without a change of linen and elementary amenities and without medicine for his sick wife.[1] The men of the escort were considerate and even friendly, however, as had been the Tsarist soldiers who had escorted him in 1907, as the convicted leader of the Petersburg Soviet. On the way they bought linen, towels, soap, &c., for the family; and they brought meals from railway stations. Their prisoner still inspired them with the awe with which a Grand Duke, deported under the old régime, might have inspired his guards: there was, after all, no knowing whether he might not be back in power soon. And so when the train arrived in Turkestan, the commander of the escort asked his prisoner to give him a certificate of good behaviour.[2] On the way Sermuks and Posnansky, Trotsky's two devoted secretaries, had joined the train, hoping to outwit the G.P.U. Such incidents broke up the monotony of the journey.

At Pishpek-Frunze[3] the railway journey came to an end. The stretch of road from there to Alma Ata, about 250 kilometres, had to be traversed by bus, lorry, sleigh, and on foot, across ice-covered and wind-swept mountain and through deep snow-drifts, with a night stop in an abandoned hut in the desert. At last, after a week's journey, on 25 January at 3 a.m., the party reached Alma Ata. The deportee and his family were put up at an inn called 'The Seven Rivers' in Gogol Street. The inn 'dated from Gogol's time'; and the spirit of the great satirist hovering over it seems to have suggested to Trotsky many of his observations on Alma Ata and the style of the frequent protests which he was to send from there to Moscow.

Towards the end of the 1920's Alma Ata was still a little town wholly Oriental in character. Although famous for gorgeous orchards and gardens, it was a slummy and sleepy Kirghiz backwater barely touched by civilization, and exposed to earthquakes, floods, icy blizzards and scorching heat waves. The

---

[1] *The Archives.*   [2] The text of the certificate ibid.
[3] The town Pishpek had just been renamed in honour of Frunze, Trotsky's successor as Commissar of War.

heat waves brought dense dust-clouds, malaria, and plagues of vermin. The town was to be developed as the administrative centre of Kazakhstan, but the republican administration was only begining to form itself; in the meantime officials requisitioned all available accommodation, and the local slums were more than usually overcrowded. 'In the bazaar at the centre of the town the Kirghizes sat in the mud at the doorsteps of their shops, warmed themselves in the sun, and searched their bodies for lice.'[1] Leprosy was not unknown; and during the summer of Trotsky's stay animals were struck by pestilence, and howling mad dogs swarmed in the streets.

In the same year life at Alma Ata was made even more miserable by continuous scarcity of bread. Within the first few months of Trotsky's arrival the price of bread trebled. Long queues waited outside the few bakers' shops. Foodstuffs other than bread were even scarcer. There was no regular transport. Mail was erratic; the local Soviet tried to regularize it with the help of private contractors. The gloom of the place and the helplessness and feeble-mindedness of the local caciques are well illustrated by this extract from Trotsky's correspondence: 'The other day the local newspaper wrote: "In town rumours are *functioning* to the effect that there is going to be no bread, whereas there are numerous carts coming with loads of bread." The carts are really coming, as they say; but in the meantime the rumours are functioning, malaria is functioning, but bread is not functioning.'

Here then Trotsky was to stay. Stalin was eager to keep him as far from Moscow as possible and to reduce him to his own resources. Trotsky's two secretaries were arrested, one *en route* from Moscow, the other at Alma Ata, and deported elsewhere. For the moment, however, Stalin appeared to have no further designs on his enemy; and the G.P.U. still treated Trotsky with consideration that would have been unthinkable later. It took care that his enormous library and archives, containing important state and party documents, should reach him—a lorryful of these presently arrived at Alma Ata. Trotsky protested to Kalinin, Ordjonikidze, and Menzhinsky against the conditions in which he was placed, demanding better accommodation, the right to go on hunting trips, and even to have his pet dog sent to

[1] *Moya Zhizn*, vol. ii, p. 296.

him from Moscow. He complained that he was kept at the inn at Gogol Street only to suit the G.P.U.'s convenience and that his banishment was virtual imprisonment. 'You could just as well have jailed me in Moscow—there was no need to deport me four thousand versts away.'[1] The protest was effective. Three weeks after his arrival he was given a four-roomed flat in the centre of the town, at 75 Krasin Street—the street was so named after his deceased friend. He was allowed to go on hunting trips. He showered further sarcastic telegrams on Moscow, making demands, some serious, others trivial, and mixing little quarrels with great controversy. 'Maya, my darling [Maya was his pet dog]', he wrote to a friend, 'does not even suspect that she is now at the centre of a great political struggle.' He refused, as it were, to consider himself a captive; and his persecutors made a show of leniency.

He appeared almost relaxed after so many years of ceaseless toil and tension. Thus, unexpectedly and oddly, there was a quasi-idyllic flavour about the first few months of his stay at Alma Ata. Steppe and mountain, river and lake lured him as never since his childhood. He relished hunting; and in his voluminous correspondence political argument and advice are often interspersed with poetic descriptions of landscape and humorous reports on hunting ventures. He was at first refused permission to go out of Alma Ata. Then he was allowed to go hunting but no farther than twenty-five versts away. He telegraphed to Menzhinsky that he would disregard the restriction because there were no suitable hunting grounds within that distance and he was not going to be bothered with small game—he *must* be allowed to go at least seventy versts away; and let Moscow inform the local G.P.U. about this so as to avoid trouble. He went; and there was no trouble. Then he protested to the chief of the local G.P.U. against being pursued rudely and conspicuously by sleuths and declared that because of this he would 'go on strike' and cease to hunt—unless this form of police supervision was prescribed directly by Moscow, in which case he understood the position of the local G.P.U. and waived his objections. The supervision became milder and less conspicuous.

He had begun to hunt soon after his arrival and went on as long as the spring migration of beasts along the river Ili lasted.

---

[1] From a protest sent out early in February. *The Archives.*

Some of the trips took as many as ten days and were strenuous and refreshing. In letters to friends he proudly described his hunting triumphs. At first he spent nights in Kirghiz mud huts or bug-ridden *yourtas*, sleeping alongside a dozen natives on the floor, boiling dirty water for tea, and barely containing nausea. 'Next time', he announced, 'I shall sleep in the open air and compel all my companions to do the same.'[1] Next time indeed —this was still before the end of March—the hunting party stayed in the open nine frosty days and nights. Crossing a river on horseback, Trotsky once slipped into the water. The booty was not large: 'about forty ducks in all'. True, he wrote to friends, bigger game could be found farther afield on the Balkhash Lake, even snow leopards and tigers; but 'I decided to make a pact of non-aggression with the tigers'. 'I enjoyed enormously . . . this temporary relapse into barbarity. One does not often have such experiences as spending nine days and nights in the open, without having to wash, dress, and undress, eating venison cooked in a pail, falling from a horse into the river (this was the only time I had to undress), and staying days and nights on a small log in the midst of water, stone and reed.'[2] The hunting season over, fishing began; and then even Natalya Ivanovna joined in, although the fishing was no townsman's lazy week-end playing with tackle, for every trip was a long and arduous job with large boats, heavy loads, and elaborate tacking about.

Early in June, when the heat waves hit Alma Ata, the family moved to a *dacha* in the foothills of the mountains just outside the town, where they had rented a reed-thatched farm-house surrounded by a large apple orchard. From the house they could see the town below and the steppe beyond on one side and snow-capped mountain ranges on the other. During heavy downpours the thatched roof leaked and everyone rushed to the loft with pails and pots and pans. In the orchard a wooden hut was put up—Trotsky's study and workroom. It was soon crammed with books, newspapers, and manuscripts; and it shook with the pounding of a well-worn typewriter, which resounded through the orchard. At his writing table Trotsky watched a shrub as it pushed through a chink in the floor and

[1] *The Archives.*
[2] From a letter dated 1 April 1928 (no addressee) in *The Archives.*

in no time shot up to his knees. All this underlined the 'ephemeral character' of the abode; but it was a relief to have escaped from the town where through the dust-clouds people now chased and shot mad dogs in the street. Throughout the earlier months both Trotsky and Sedova had suffered from malaria and lived on a 'quinine diet'; now the attacks of fever had almost ceased.[1]

The deportee had to earn a living. True, he received an official allowance but this was a mere pittance, and, although the household was small and its needs very modest, the allowance was not enough to meet the rising cost of food. *Gosizdat*, the State Publishers, had just ceased to publish Trotsky's *Works*, of which thirteen volumes had so far appeared. These were already banished from bookshops and public libraries. Trotsky's head was full of new literary projects. He thought of writing a study of revolution in Asia and assembled a sizeable collection of reference works on China and India. In another book he planned to sum up Russian and world developments since the October Revolution. Immediately after his arrival at Alma Ata he set to work on a full-scale statement of the Opposition's principles which was to be addressed to the sixth congress of the Communist International convened for the summer. His friends, especially Preobrazhensky, urged him to write his memoirs. In April he was already at work on these, recapturing, with the help of old southern newspapers and maps of Nikolayev and Odessa, the image of his childhood and youth with which he was to open *My Life*.

None of these writings, however, could bring him any earnings, for there was no chance of their being published. Yet even a man deported under article 58, for 'counter-revolutionary activities', could still try to earn a living as translator, sub-editor, and proof-reader. When it turned out that the authors whom Trotsky would be allowed to translate, or the translations of whose works he was to supervise, were Marx and Engels, he took to the job eagerly. Ryazanov, his old friend, at present Director of the Marx-Engels Institute in Moscow, was preparing the complete edition in Russian of the *Works* of Marx and Engels; and he asked Trotsky to translate *Herr Vogt*. In this long and little-known pamphlet Marx had replied to slanders thrown at him by Karl Vogt who, as it turned out later, was an agent of

[1] See Trotsky's letter to Rakovsky of 14 July. Ibid.

Napoleon III. Reading this broadside for the first time, Trotsky remarked that it took Marx several hundred pages to refute Vogt's charges, whereas it would take his translator 'a whole encyclopaedia' to refute Stalin's slanders. Ryazanov then asked Trotsky to edit the translations and read the proofs of the other volumes of Marx and Engels, which he did.[1]

Trotsky's correspondence with Ryazanov shows the modesty and conscientiousness with which Trotsky applied himself to the work: it contains detailed, almost pedantic, criticisms of the style of the translations and minute suggestions for improvements. The correspondence is wholly non-political and studiously business-like. There is no hint of any irony on Trotsky's part about the only gainful occupation now left open to him in the Soviet Union. The fees paid him by Ryazanov supplied the family's needs and covered the cost of Trotsky's huge correspondence.[2]

.   .   .   .

From the moment of his arrival at Alma Ata Trotsky worked hard to establish contact with friends and followers scattered all over the country and reduced to isolation and silence. At the beginning this could be done only by normal mail; and it had to be done in the most primitive conditions when it was sometimes a feat to obtain on the spot a pen, a pencil, a few sheets of rough paper, or a few candles. Lyova became his 'minister of foreign affairs and minister of post and telegraphs', body-guard, research assistant, secretary, and organizer of hunting trips. With his help a constant flow of letters and circulars began to pour out of Alma Ata in all directions. Twice or three times a week an invalid postman on horseback brought the mail bag bulging with letters, press clippings, and later even with books and newspapers from abroad. No doubt the censorship and the G.P.U. kept a watchful eye on the correspondence. Most of it was with Rakovsky, who had been deported to Astrakhan, Radek, who was at Tobolsk, Preobrazhensky, exiled to Uralsk, Smilga who was at Narym, Beloborodov, banished as far north as Ust-Kylom in the

---

[1] In one of his letters Trotsky mentioned that he was also translating the writings of Thomas Hodgkin 'the English Utopian Socialist'.

[2] Between April and October 1928 Trotsky mailed 800 political letters, many of essay length, and 550 telegrams; and he received 1,000 letters and 700 telegrams, apart from private mail.

Komi Republic, Serebriakov, who was at Semi-Palatinsk in Central Asia, Muralov at Tara, Ivan Smirnov at Novo-Bayazet in Armenia, and Mrachkovsky at Voronezh. Less systematically Trotsky corresponded with a host of other Oppositionists. Later in the year he related to Sosnovsky[1] that he was in more or less regular contact with all the major colonies of exiles in Siberia and Soviet Asia at large, with Barnaul, Kaminsk, Minussinsk, Tomsk, Kolpashevo, Yenisseisk, Novosibirsk, Kansk, Achinsk, Aktiubinsk, Tashkent, Samarkand, &c. With colonies in European Russia he communicated through Rakovsky, who from Astrakhan was in charge of Opposition centres along the southern Volga and in the Crimea, and through Mrachkovsky, who from Voronezh kept in touch with colonies in the north. In places where there were large centres of exiles, the correspondence and the circulars were duplicated and forwarded to minor colonies. Since April a secret postal service operated between Alma Ata and Moscow; it delivered and collected mail once every fortnight or three weeks.

In this way the groups of exiles, constantly growing in numbers and size, formed a community of their own with its own intense political life. Trotsky was the inspirer, organizer, and symbol of the Opposition in exile. The state of mind of the deportees was anything but settled. Some were stunned by what had happened. Others viewed the persecution to which they were subjected as little more than a bad joke. The majority at first appeared to be convinced that Stalin's triumph would not last and that soon events would vindicate the Opposition so that its adherents would return from exile to be hailed for their foresight, courage, and dedication to Marxism and Leninism.

As the conditions in which they found themselves, though painful and humiliating, were not yet crushingly oppressive, the Oppositionists reverted to a manner of existence which had been familiar to them before the revolution. The job of the political prisoners and exiles was to use enforced idleness in order to clear their thoughts, learn, and prepare for the day when they would once again have to shoulder the burdens of direct struggle or the responsibilities of government. For this kind of work the conditions seemed propitious. In many colonies there were educated men, brilliant theorists, and gifted writers whom their comrades

[1] Letter of 7 November in *The Archives*.

provided with a choice audience. Intensive exchange of ideas helped to keep up self-discipline and self-respect. From Alma Ata Trotsky eagerly followed this exchange and encouraged it, quoting, in letters to friends, Goethe's maxim that in intellectual and moral matters it is necessary in order to guard what one possesses to conquer it ever anew. Thus the colonies became centres of important intellectual and literary-political activity. Apart from memoranda and 'theses' on current affairs, which proliferated freely, major works were undertaken. Radek began to write a large-scale biography and study of Lenin; Rakovsky worked on a Life of Saint Simon and on the origins of Utopian socialism; Preobrazhensky wrote and completed books on the Soviet economy and on the economy of medieval Europe; Smilga was busy on a book about Bukharin and his school of thought; Dingelstedt produced essays on the social structure of India; and so on. However, these intellectual pursuits, valuable though they were, could not give any direct answer to the question which was uppermost in the thoughts of the deportees and which events were about to pose anew—the question: what next?

.   .   .   .

Even in the remoteness of Siberia and Central Asia the shock of a new social crisis could be felt before the end of the winter. The crisis had long been in the making; and it had reached danger point as early as the autumn, just before the deportation of the Oppositionists. The state granaries were half empty; hunger threatened the urban population; and it was not even certain whether the armed forces would be supplied with provisions. The interminable queues outside the bakers and the repeated rises in the price of bread, witnessed by Trotsky at Alma Ata, could be observed all over the Soviet Union.

Yet on the face of it the agricultural situation was not bad. Almost as much land had been sown as in the best of times; and there had been a succession of three excellent harvests. But once again the 'link' between town and country was broken. The peasants refused to deliver bread and to sell it at fixed prices. Grain collections were accompanied by riots: the official collectors were driven from the villages and returned empty-handed to town. The peasantry had little or no incentive to deliver or sell its produce when now as before it could not obtain in return clothing, footwear, agricultural tools, or other industrial goods.

It demanded a steep rise in the price of grain; and clamouring for this, it followed even more clearly than before the lead of the wealthy farmers.

At the Politbureau the Bukharinists and the Stalinists came to blows over this at the very moment when they were jointly expelling the Trotskyists and crushing the Zinovievists. The Bukharinists wished to calm the peasantry with concessions, while the Stalinists were inclined, although not yet determined, to resort to force. In the first week of January, ten days before Trotsky's banishment, the Politbureau had to come to a decision about the further course of the grain collection; and undoubtedly nervousness over the situation in the country caused it to speed up Trotsky's banishment. On 6 January the Politbureau secretly instructed party organizations to proceed with greater severity against peasants who obstructed the grain collection, to levy forced 'bread loans', to resist firmly pressure for higher food prices, and to keep a sharp watch on the kulaks. The instructions failed to yield results; and five weeks later the Politbureau had to repeat them with greater emphasis and less secrecy.

In the middle of February *Pravda* sounded the alarm: 'The kulak has raised his head!' Finally, in April, the Central Committee declared bluntly, as if it had borrowed its terms from the Trotskyists and Zinovievists, that the nation was threatened by a grave crisis, and that the threat had been created by the 'growth of the kulaks' economic power' which the government's fiscal policy had failed to keep in check. 'In connexion with the further differentiation of the peasantry, the kulaks, their economic weight growing . . . have acquired the power to exert considerable influence on the entire state of the market.'[1] Yet, the party, so the Central Committee said, had been and still was slack in curbing them. Emergency measures were decreed, under which compulsory loans were to be levied on kulaks to reduce their purchasing power; grain stocks were to be requisitioned; the fixed bread price was to be enforced; and finally, officials and party members inclined to treat the kulak indulgently were to be removed from their posts. These decisions were presented not as a departure from accepted policy but as *ad hoc* moves designed to deal with unexpected difficulties. The resolutions of the Central Committee contained no hint of 'wholesale collectivization'

[1] *KPSS v Rezolutsyakh*, vol. ii, p. 373.

—indeed, the idea was emphatically rejected. However, the manner in which the Central Committee explained the emergency and its insistence on the danger from the kulak and the party's failure to take counteraction already pointed to a fundamental change of policy. Within the Central Committee the Stalinists were gaining the upper hand. By obtaining powers to strengthen the party's hands against the kulak Stalin had strengthened his own hands against the Bukharinists; he was free to remove them from many posts at the lower and middle rungs of the administration and of the party machine.

The first reaction of the deported Trotskyists to these events was one of amusement, irony, even exultation. Had the predictions of the Opposition not come true? they asked. Was Stalin not being forced to adopt a 'left course', the course the Opposition had advocated? How could the party not realize now who had been right and who had been wrong in the great controversy of the last years? Most Oppositionists congratulated themselves, expecting even more confidently to be called back to play their part in overcoming the emergency and steering Bolshevik policy in the new direction. Trotsky, too, in his correspondence dwelt on the Opposition's foresight and appeared to be in a hopeful mood, although he did not share the most sanguine expectations of his followers.[1]

As the weeks passed and the 'left course' developed, while nothing changed in the official attitude towards the Opposition, the self-congratulatory mood in the colonies gave place to uneasiness and heart-searching. The turn that events had taken appeared to call into question some of the Opposition's major assumptions and predictions, especially its appraisal of the political trends within the party. Had we been right, some Trotskyists began to wonder, in denouncing Stalin as the protector of the kulak? Had we been justified in saying that once the left Opposition was defeated, the inner-party balance would be so upset that the Bukharinist right would assert itself and sweep away the Stalinist centre? Had we not overrated the strength of the

[1] See, for instance, his letter to Sosnovsky of 5 March 1928 in *The Archives*. *Inter alia* he recalls there the accusations of defeatism levelled against him after he had said that a good harvest, no less than a bad one, might, under Stalin's and Bukharin's policy, strengthen the kulak. Now *Pravda*, suddenly discovering the kulak's strength, wrote about the last three abundant harvests 'as if they had been three earthquakes'.

conservative elements in the party? The Stalinist faction, far
from being overwhelmed, was beginning to overwhelm the right
—had we then not exaggerated with our Cassandra cries about
the danger of Thermidor? And had we, generally speaking, not
gone too far in our struggle against Stalin?

The great majority of deportees would not even admit such
doubts to their thoughts. But a minority posed these questions
ever more persistently; and every question it asked entailed
other questions bringing under scrutiny ever more points of the
Opposition's programme and activity. The answers turned on
what view the Opposition took of the seriousness of Stalin's left
course. It was still possible to regard Stalin's action against the
kulak as an incidental tactical manœuvre which need not prevent him from resuming the pro-kulak policy. This was indeed
what most Oppositionists thought of it. But a few were already
convinced of the seriousness of the left course, saw it as the beginning of a momentous upheaval, and reflected uneasily on the
Opposition's prospects. How could the Opposition remain a passive onlooker, they asked, while the party was embarking upon a
dangerous struggle against the capitalist and quasi-capitalist elements in the nation, the struggle to which the Opposition had
summoned it?

The Opposition had to such an extent based its own action on
the idea that in all vital matters the right wing played the leading part and that the Stalinist faction, weak and vacillating,
merely followed it like a shadow that Stalin's first or preliminary
attack on the kulak shook the ground under its feet. Even in
December, during the fifteenth congress, Zinoviev and Kamenev
had excused their capitulation with the argument that Stalin
was about to embark upon a left course. Soon thereafter, two
eminent Trotskyists, Pyatakov and Antonov-Ovseenko, followed
this example and announced their break with Trotsky. They
had been the boldest and most energetic leaders of the 1923
Opposition; they had participated only half-heartedly in the
struggle of the later years; and they justified their capitulation
on the ground that Stalin was carrying out the Opposition's
programme. The deportees at first received Pyatakov's and
Antonov-Ovseenko's defection with the contempt and derision
reserved for renegades; but their arguments nevertheless made
an impression and stimulated self-interrogation.

Early in May Trotsky still knew little or nothing about the new ferment among the exiles; and he sent a letter to them in which he set out his views.[1] He declared that Stalin's left course marked the beginning of an important change. The Opposition, he said, had every right to regard itself with pride as the inspirer and prompter of the new policy. True, pride must be mingled with sadness when Oppositionists reflected on the price they had had to pay for their vicarious success. However, it has been the fate of revolutionaries more than once that, at the price of heavy or tragic sacrifice, they have compelled others, even enemies, to carry out parts of a revolutionary programme. Thus, the Commune of Paris had been drowned in blood but it triumphed over its hangmen, for its very hangmen had to carry out part of its programme: although the Commune had failed as a proletarian revolution, it made the restoration of the monarchy impossible in France and secured the establishment at least of a parliamentary republic. Such might be, *mutatis mutandis*, the Opposition's relation to Stalin's left course: the Opposition might be defeated; it might not see its full programme carried into effect; but at least its struggle had made it impossible for the ruling group to continue the retreat before the capitalist elements and to inaugurate a neo-N.E.P.

What was the Opposition to do? We were in duty bound, Trotsky replied, to lend critical support to Stalin's left course. Under no circumstances must we make common cause with Bukharin and Rykov against it. We should, on the contrary, encourage the vacillating Stalinist centre to break definitely with the right and make common cause with the left. An alliance between the Opposition and its Stalinist persecutors against the defenders of the kulak should not be ruled out, even though the possibility was remote. More than ever must the Opposition press for freedom within the party; and 'the left course facilitates the struggle for proletarian democracy'. In reasoning thus Trotsky was logically consistent with himself: he had, ever since 1923, maintained that the main 'function' of the Stalinist régime was to shield from the workers a party bureaucracy which protected the kulak and the N.E.P.-man. It was natural for him to conclude that once that bureaucracy had ceased to protect the kulak and the N.E.P.-man, it would draw closer to the working class, seek reconcilia-

[1] See his circular letter of 9 May in *The Archives*.

tion with its spokesmen, and restore to them freedom of expression. All the more resolutely should the Opposition, even while supporting the left course, resist Stalinist oppression and warn the party that as long as this persisted there was no guarantee that Stalin would pursue the new policy and would not once again yield to the kulak. Trotsky admitted that his was a 'dual attitude', difficult to adopt; but he claimed that it was the only attitude justified in the circumstances. Pyatakov had already described Trotsky's views as 'self-contradictory'. 'But all contradictions', Trotsky retorted, 'disappear in a man who [like Pyatakov] makes a suicide jump into a river.'

Trotsky's view had all the dialectical suppleness which the ambiguous situation demanded from him. He treated Stalin's drive against the kulak as a great and hopeful development; and he insisted all the more firmly on the need for freedom of criticism and discussion as the main guarantee of the soundness of the new policy. He offered the Opposition no axe to grind—only principles to defend. When his enemy took another leaf from his book, he acknowledged the leaf as his own and urged his followers to back his enemy in an undertaking which they had considered necessary. But there were many other leaves left in his book; and he was not going to throw them away. As to the Opposition's prospects, he shunned the extremes of optimism and pessimism: it was possible that events might compel the Stalinists to seek reconciliation with the Opposition, and in that case the Opposition would regain moral and political leadership; but the Opposition must also be ready to share the fate of the Commune of Paris and through its martyrdom to further the cause of socialism and progress.

The fact that Trotsky took a relatively favourable view of Stalin's left course and acknowledged its positive significance made a great and even bewildering impression on his followers. It added strength to the arguments of those among them who had begun to criticize the Opposition's record. If Trotsky was right now, they said, then had he not been wrong earlier in raising alarms about the Thermidorian peril? Had he not erroneously evaluated Stalin's policy? And would it be right for the Opposition to console itself with the thought that history would vindicate it, as it had vindicated the Commune of Paris? Should Trotskyists not lend a hand to the momentous struggle against private property that was going on in the country and thus help to make history rather than rely passively on history's anticipated verdict? Posterity may well extol the martyrdom of Communards; but Communards fight not for the glory of martyrdom, but for purposes which they believe to be practical and within their reach.

Such reasonings reflected a dilemma inherent in the Trotskyist attitude; and frustration injected bitterness. Exile, enforced idleness, and nagging doubts weighed down vigorous and strong-minded men who had made a revolution, fought civil wars, and built a new state. To be cast out of the party to which they had dedicated their lives, for which they had languished in Tsarist prisons, and in which they still saw humanity's highest hope—was a burden heavy enough in itself. The burden became unbearable when they realized that some of the crucial differences which had separated them from the Stalinists were vanishing and that the party was beginning to do what they had so ardently desired it to do. It is not so difficult for a political fighter to suffer defeat, privation, and humiliation as long as he knows clearly what he stands for and feels that his cause depends exclusively on what he and his comrades do for it. But even the most hardened fighter loses heart in a paradoxical situation when he sees his cause, or an important part of it, embraced by his persecutor. His cause no longer seems to depend on whether he fights for it or not. The fight itself suddenly appears to be purposeless and the persecution to which he has exposed himself—senseless. He begins to doubt whether he is justified in regarding his perse-cutor as an enemy.

Stalin had a cold and acute insight into the troubled mind of the Opposition; but he too had his dilemmas. Any Trotskyist commendation of his left course assisted him; but he was afraid of Trotskyist assistance. Hesitantly, falteringly, driven by circumstances, he was embarking upon an unknown and danger-ous road. He risked grave conflict with the peasantry. He did not and could not gauge beforehand the scope and the violence of the resistance with which he would meet. He had cautiously turned against his erstwhile allies, the Bukharinists, whose popu-larity and influence he did not underrate. He could not know how far this new struggle might carry him and what dangers it might create for him. No more than Trotsky could he rule out

the possibility that in an extremely critical situation he might
have to seek an alliance with the left Opposition. But he too
realized that this would be Trotsky's triumph; and he was determined to do all that lay in his power to defeat the Bukharinists
without having recourse to reconciliation with Trotsky. He
had reason to fear that the strength of his own faction would be
inadequate for this and that his followers alone would not be
able to manage the state machine and to cope with nationalized
industry and finance in the new and difficult phase of rapid
expansion. The Stalinists were primarily men of the party
machine. Theorists, policy-makers, economists, industrial administrators, financial and agricultural experts, and men of political talent were found among the Trotskyists, the Bukharinists,
and the Zinovievists. Stalin needed the assistance of men of
ability who would be eager to carry out an anti-kulak policy and
would carry it out with conviction and zeal. He could find
such men in the Left Opposition. He was therefore anxious to
win to his side as much Trotskyist and Zinovievist talent as he
could without yielding ground to Trotsky and Zinoviev. He
appealed to the Trotskyists behind Trotsky's back. Through his
agents he lured them with the left course and sought to persuade
them that their opposition to him had become pointless. At
first the deportees rejected these appeals almost unanimously; but
the appeals fell on fertile ground. In some of Trotsky's followers
they intensified the doubts and the inclination to review the
Opposition's record with disillusioned eyes.

Trotsky became aware of these developments only about the
middle of May. Beloborodov had sent him a report on the discussions in the colonies. Another Trotskyist, who was still in
Stalin's diplomatic service, informed him from Berlin about
Stalin's presumed plan of action. According to this correspondent, Stalin hoped to improve his difficult position by inducing
influential banished Oppositionists to recant—with their assistance he expected to put the left course into effect and to give
Trotsky the *coup de grâce*. He even delayed embarking full steam
upon the left course until he had secured the capitulation of many
important Trotskyists. Everything now depended on whether he
would succeed in this. If the Opposition could frustrate him, if it
were not weakened by defections, and if it held out at least until
the autumn, by which time Stalin would find his own faction

unable to cope with the difficulties, then the Opposition would have every chance to regain the initiative and return to power. But should Stalin succeed in sapping the Opposition's morale and should Trotskyist capitulators come to his succour, then he would maintain himself in power, crush the Bukharinists, and carry on with the left course without having to conciliate Trotsky and Trotsky's impenitent adherents. The correspondent feared that Stalin was about to succeed: the Opposition's morale was dangerously sagging, and all too many Oppositionists were ready to give up the fight.[1]

Trotsky, it appears, did not believe that the Opposition's morale was so low. There had been very few capitulations among the deportees. One notorious case was that of Safarov, the former leader of the Comsomol who had signed a formula of recantation and was recalled to Moscow. However, Safarov's case was exceptional in that he was not a Trotskyist. He had belonged to Zinoviev's faction but had at first refused to capitulate with his leader, had gone with the Trotskyists into exile, and only then, on second thoughts, capitulated. His behaviour, it seemed, was not related to the mood among the Trotskyists. Yet Safarov, as he tried to justify himself, expressed something that struck a chord in them as well: 'Everything is now going to be carried out without us!', he exclaimed. 'Everything' meant the drive against the kulak and the N.E.P.-man, the expansion of the socialist sector of the economy, accelerated industrialization, and possibly collectivization of farming, for all these aspects of the left course hung together. It was a galling thought for the Trotskyists also that the great change, this 'second revolution', might be carried out without them. The more disinterestedly Trotsky stressed the desirability and the progressive character of Stalin's latest moves and the more he insisted on the Opposition's duty to support them, the greater was the frustration among his followers, the more anxiously did they reflect over the rights and wrongs of the Opposition's policy, and the more poignantly did they feel that cast out of the party, in the wilderness where they

[1] This remarkable letter dated 8 May 1928 was written anonymously from Berlin. Trotsky had known the correspondent but towards the end of his life, when he sorted out the Archives, he could not remember who he was. In 1928 the correspondent was about to be recalled from his post and asked Trotsky whether he should not refuse to return to Moscow. Trotsky, it seems, had already advised him to return.

were, they could not possibly lend any practical support to the left course.

Before the end of May Trotsky again in several statements addressed his followers.[1] He defended the record of the Opposition and sought to outline new prospects. His argument may be summed up in these three points:

Firstly, it was not true that he had overrated the strength of the Bukharinist right. This was still formidable. Nor had the Opposition been wrong in seeking to arouse the party against the danger of Thermidor. In doing so it had helped to keep the Thermidorian forces at bay. The Opposition's action and pressure from the working class had compelled the Stalinists to break with the Bukharinists—otherwise the present bread crisis might have induced them to make far-reaching concessions to capitalist farming, and might thus have provoked, instead of the left course, a powerful shift to the right. He feared that those who maintained that the Opposition had magnified the danger from the right would in the end surrender to Stalin.

Secondly, the Opposition had no reason to reproach itself with having gone too far in its struggle. On the contrary, because of Zinoviev's and Kamenev's timidity, it had not gone far enough: 'All our activities had a propagandist and only a propagandist character.' The Opposition had hardly ever appealed to the rank and file strongly and boldly enough. When at last it sought to do so, on 7 November, Stalin tried to provoke it into civil war; and then it had to retreat.

Finally, the fact that Stalin was stealing the Opposition's thunder should not dishearten the Opposition. The Stalinist faction had initiated a left policy when it could do nothing else, but it would not be able to see it through to the end. Consequently, Trotsky assured his followers, 'the party is still going to need us'.

These arguments and assurances did not satisfy many of Trotsky's adherents. He offered them no clear perspective. They continued to ask whether Stalin had turned against the kulak for good or whether his left course was mere pretence; and they expected a plain answer. Trotsky did not possess it; and probably Stalin himself did not yet know definitely where he stood. Nor did Trotsky tell his followers how, in the position in which they

[1] See his letters to Beloborodov (23 May) and to Yudin (25 May) in *The Archives*.

were placed, they could act on his advice and how, in what manner, they could support and oppose Stalin at the same time.

Already in the spring of 1928 two distinct currents of opinion had formed themselves in the Trotskyist colonies. There were, on the one hand, those who took to heart, most of all, their obligation to support Stalin's left course, the obligation which Trotsky again and again impressed on them; and there were those, on the other hand, who were above all inclined to go on opposing Stalin, as Trotsky also urged them to do. Thus the differences that had existed within the Joint Opposition, between Trotskyists and Zinovievists, were now reproduced within the ranks of the Trotskyists themselves, splitting them into 'conciliators' and 'irreconcilables'. The conciliators were still far from the thought of surrendering to Stalin; but they wished the Opposition to mitigate its hostility towards his faction and to prepare for a dignified reconciliation with it on the basis of the left course. They held that integrity and the Opposition's own interest demanded from them that they should review critically, and modify in the light of events, the Opposition's accepted views. To this attitude rallied Oppositionists of the older generation, men of the reflective and sedate type, and those in whom the nostalgic feeling for their old party was extremely strong; and also the 'enlightened bureaucrats', economists and administrators, who had been interested more in the Opposition's programme of industrialization and economic planning than in its demands for inner-party freedom and proletarian democracy; and finally, people whose will to go on resisting the ruling group was already weakened by the ordeal they had undergone. As individuals were often moved by mixed impulses, it was in many cases wellnigh impossible to disentangle their motives.

The irreconcilable Trotskyists were mostly young men, to whom expulsion from the party had been less of a break in life than it had been to their elders; people whom the Opposition attracted by its call for proletarian democracy rather than by its economic and social *desiderata*; and the zealots of the Opposition, the doctrinaire enemies of bureaucracy, and the fanatics of anti-Stalinism. In this group too the motives of individuals could not be easily distinguished. Most often the young, those for whom the break with the party was no great moral upset, were also relatively indifferent to the complex economic and social issues, but responded ardently to the Opposition's call for freedom of expression, and viewed all bureaucracy with a fierce hostility, rendered even fiercer by persecution and exile.

Both wings of the Trotskyist Opposition tended to overlap with other groups outside it. The conciliators moved closer and closer towards the Zinovievists whom they had hitherto despised. They began to see them in a new light, and even if they were not ready to follow them, they began to appreciate the reasons for their surrender, to listen eagerly to their arguments, and to watch sympathetically their doings. The most extreme irreconcilables, on the other hand, found that they had much in common with the unrepentant Mohicans of the Workers' Opposition and of the Decemists, who were led by Sapronov and Vladimir Smirnov, and had been exiled together with the Trotskyists. In their enmity towards the bureaucracy they had been far less inhibited than the Trotskyists. More or less openly they had renounced all allegiance to the existing state and party. They proclaimed that the revolution and Bolshevism were dead, and that the working class had to begin from the beginning, that is to start a new revolutionary struggle in order to free itself from exploitation by the new 'state capitalism', the N.E.P. bourgeoisie, and the kulaks. To many a young Trotskyist this plain and single-minded message sounded more convincing than did Trotsky's carefully balanced analyses and 'dual policy'. It was easier to digest it, for in it yes was yes and no was no, without any dialectical complication. To denounce Stalin as the grave-digger of the revolution, the Decemists said, and to dwell, as Trotsky did, on the progressive implications of the left course was absurd; to fight Stalin meant to fight him and not to support him.

Both sets of Trotskyists looked to Trotsky for guidance, although each was inclined to accept only that part of his advice that suited it. Both sets evoked the Opposition's first principles and common interests. But as the differences widened, the sense of comradeship wore thin and mutual suspicions grew until the two sets had little more for each other than black looks and harsh words. To the irreconcilables their more moderate comrades were men of small faith, if not yet deserters. The moderates looked down on the irreconcilables as ultra-lefts or crude *anarchisants*, devoid of Marxist intellectual discipline and responsibility for the fortunes of the revolution. The irreconcilables suspected that knowingly or unknowingly the conciliators worked for Stalin, while the conciliators held that nothing compromised the Opposition and assisted Stalin more effectively than the exaggerations and the excesses of the doctrinaires and the zealots of Trotskyism.

The spokesmen for each of the two sets were Oppositionists of long standing and Trotsky's trusted and respected friends. Preobrazhensky was the first to speak of the need for a more conciliatory attitude towards Stalinism. He had never faltered as an Oppositionist, and not the slightest taint of self-regard or opportunism attached to his character. His weakness, if weakness it be, lay rather in his utter disregard of expediency and popularity and in the theoretical consistency of his views. He began to preach conciliation from deep conviction, which can be traced back to his writings of 1924–5. He had been, we know, the chief theoretical exponent of primitive socialist accumulation. 'The period of primitive socialist accumulation', he had written in *The New Economics*, 'constitutes the most critical era in the life of the socialist state after the conclusion of civil war. . . . To go through this period as rapidly as possible and to reach as soon as possible the stage at which the socialist system develops all its advantages *vis-à-vis* capitalism is for the socialist economy a matter of life and death.' During that period the socialist state was bound to get the worst of both worlds: it would benefit neither from the advantages of capitalism nor from those of socialism. It would have to 'exploit' the peasantry in order to finance accumulation in the socialist sector. On this point, it will be remembered, Preobrazhensky had clashed with Bukharin and the neo-Populist school, 'our Soviet Manchester school of thought', as he dubbed it. 'The pressure of [foreign, mainly American] capitalist monopolism', he argued then, 'can find a barrier only in socialist monopolism.' This must subordinate to itself, by means of fiscal policy and through a state-regulated price mechanism, the private sector of the economy, especially farming. To Bukharin's outcry of indignation Preobrazhensky replied: 'But can it be otherwise? To put it in the simplest terms: can the burden of the development of the state-owned industry . . . be thrown on to the shoulders of our three million industrial workers only—or should the twenty-two million of our peasant smallholders also contribute their share?'

Even he had not advocated the expropriation and forcible collectivization of the smallholders; but more than anyone else he had been aware of the inherent violence of the conflict between State and peasantry under 'the iron heel of the law of primitive socialist accumulation'.[1]

No wonder that Preobrazhensky responded eagerly to Stalin's left course. He received it as a confirmation of his own theory. He saw it as an inevitable and wholly desirable development. From the outset he was convinced of its momentous significance; and he was convinced of it more firmly than Trotsky was. The differences between him and Trotsky, hitherto only implicit in their writings but of no practical consequence, now began to affect their attitudes. Trotsky had never committed himself to the view that the workers' state must as a rule 'exploit' the peasantry—at any rate, he had never expounded this view as bluntly as Preobrazhensky had done it. Nor had he advocated a pace of industrialization as forcible as that which Preobrazhensky had anticipated. Preobrazhensky's theorem of *The New Economics* had not been incompatible with socialism in one country—it had implied that primitive accumulation, the most difficult part of the transition from capitalism to socialism, might be accomplished within a single and industrially underdeveloped nation-state. Finally, unlike Trotsky, Preobrazhensky had dwelt on the 'objective force of the laws' of the transition to socialism, a force which would assert itself and compel the party leaders to act *malgré eux-mêmes* as the agents of socialism. Nationalization of all large-scale industry, he held, led ineluctably to planned economy and rapid industrialization. In opposing these the Stalinists and Bukharinists opposed a historic necessity—a necessity which the Opposition alone saw in time and of which it sought to make the Bolsheviks aware. Stalin and Bukharin might defeat the Opposition; but 'they could not outwit the laws of history'. 'The structure of our state economy [which] often proves itself to be more progressive than is the whole system of our economic leadership' would eventually force them to carry out the Opposition's programme.

These ideas, which were little more than asides and hints in Preobrazhensky's earlier writings, now came to govern all his thoughts. Stalin declaring war on the kulak was in his eyes but

[1] See Chapter V, pp. 234–40.

the unconscious and reluctant agent of necessity. While Trotsky still viewed the left course somewhat incredulously and wondered whether it might not be only a temporary shift, Preobrazhensky had no doubt whatsoever that Stalin was not trifling, that he could not retreat from the left course, that he would be compelled to wage war on the kulak ever more ruthlessly, and that this created a completely new situation for the country at large and for the Opposition in particular. He insisted that the country was on the brink of a tremendous revolutionary upheaval. The kulaks, he said, would go on refusing to sell grain and would threaten the town with famine. The middle and poor peasants would not be able to supply enough food; and the official attack on the kulak would antagonize them too and would lead to a colossal clash between the government and the bulk of the peasantry. In a survey written in the spring of 1928 Preobrazhensky maintained that Stalin's threats and emergency measures had already aroused in the country a storm so violent that to calm it the government would have to make such vast and dangerous concessions to capitalism that not only Stalin but even Bukharin and Rykov would recoil and refuse to make them.[1] Only a drastically right or drastically left policy could avert a calamity; and everything indicated that Stalin would move farther to the left.

What was to be the Opposition's role in this upheaval? The Opposition, Preobrazhensky replied, had acted as the conscious interpreter of a historic necessity. It had displayed superior foresight: its ideas were 'reflected in Stalin's new policy as in a distorting mirror'. The present crisis would not have been as grave if the party had acted on the Opposition's advice earlier. The Opposition must still go on advocating accelerated industrialization; and it must call as insistently as ever for proletarian democracy. However, although the Opposition had correctly interpreted the needs of the time, it was not given to it to meet those needs in practice. Stalin and his adherents were taking charge of the practical task. They were the agents of the historic necessity, although they had not understood it and had long resisted it. Somewhere then the Opposition had gone wrong. It had exaggerated the danger from the right and the Stalinist connivance with the kulak. It had misjudged the trends within the

[1] See Preobrazhensky's *'Levyi Kurs v Derevnie i Perspektivy'* in *The Trotsky Archives*.

party and their relationship to the social classes without, a grave error for Marxists to commit. It was therefore incumbent on the Opposition to modify its attitude and to contribute to a *rapprochement* with the Stalinist faction.

With this aim in view Preobrazhensky proposed that the Opposition should ask for official permission to call a conference of its members, at which all exiled colonies should be represented, in order to discuss the new situation and the Opposition's conduct. Trotsky had spoken of the possibility and desirability of an alliance between left and centre against the right; but he had not proposed any move designed to bring it about. Preobrazhensky was not satisfied with this. If there was to be such an alliance, he argued, the time for it was now, when the Stalinists struck against the right; and the Opposition's duty was to act instead of waiting until events produced the alliance ready-made—they might never produce it.

Trotsky was dead against Preobrazhensky's proposal. He held that, desirable though a centre-left coalition was in theory, the Opposition could do nothing to bring it about. The jailer and the jailed were not allies. He feared that Preobrazhensky took too favourable a view of the left course; but, even if this were not so, the gulf between Stalinism and the Opposition remained fixed. Persecution continued. The party was still robbed of its freedom, and its régime was getting worse and worse. The dogma of the Leader's infallibility was established; and it was applied to past as well as present. The entire history of the party was falsified to suit the requirements of that dogma. Under such conditions the Opposition could take no step to meet the ruling faction half-way. It would be a disgrace for it to ask its persecutors for permission to hold a conference—the request alone would flavour of capitulation.[1]

In May the colonies discussed Preobrazhensky's proposal—this was the first test of the exiles' reaction to the left course. The proposal was rejected out of hand. The great majority was in an irreconcilable mood, sceptical about the left course, inclined as before to see in Stalin the defender of the kulak and the accomplice of the Thermidorians, confident in the Opposition's cause, and reluctant to contemplate any revision of its attitude.

Despite this rebuff to Preobrazhensky, his ideas began to

---

[1] See Trotsky's '*Pismo Drugu*' (24 June 1928) in *The Archives*.

germinate in many minds. Radek, it seems, was the first of the leaders of the Opposition to come under their influence. He had not so far belonged to those inclined to pull punches. Throughout 1927 he had urged the Opposition to attack the ruling group more boldly, to appeal to the factory workers who stood outside the party, and to voice aggressively their grievances, instead of contenting itself with 'honour-saving gestures' and highbrow theory. He had not recoiled from the idea of a new party and had favoured the admission to the Opposition of the Decemists who stood for it. He was still in this militant mood after his deportation, when he wrote scornfully of Zinoviev's and Pyatakov's recantations and the morbid odour of *Dostoevshchyna* they exuded. 'They have denied their own convictions and have lied to the working class—you cannot help the working class with lies.'[1] Even in May, when Preobrazhensky called for the conference, Radek still appeared to be opposed to the idea—at any rate, he criticized Preobrazhensky's conciliatory attitude.

Barely a month later, the man seemed to have completely changed; he preached conciliation himself, with all the ingenuity, verve, and wit peculiar to him. His accession enormously strengthened the 'moderate' wing, for he and Preobrazhensky were, next to Trotsky and Rakovsky, the most authoritative leaders in exile. Subsequently, as his prolific correspondence shows, his will to resist Stalinism crumbled almost from week to week, although nearly a year was to elapse before his actual surrender.

It would be too simple to attribute the change merely to Radek's volatility or lack of courage. His motives were tangled. No doubt he did not possess all the 'Bolshevik hardihood' that others had gained in underground politics, in Tsarist prisons, and through years of Siberian exile. His spells of underground work had been brief: up to 1917 he had spent his political life mainly in the open socialist movements of Austro-Hungary and Germany. He was essentially a Western European and a Bohemian, sociable, accustomed to breathe the air and the excitement of great cities and to be at the centre of public affairs. In the course of more than twenty-five years he had held famous Central Committees and great editorial offices spell-

[1] See Radek's letter to Zhenya written from Tobolsk, on 10 May 1928, and his letter to Preobrazhensky of 25 May in *The Trotsky Archives*.

bound by his views and witticisms. For ten years he had been one of the leading lights of the Bolshevik party and the Communist International. As long as he was surrounded by the bustle of political life, his confidence and mettle had not abandoned him—he had remained bold and active and had still been at the centre of affairs even in the Moabit prison of Berlin in 1919. But cast out suddenly into the empty, bleak, and severe wilderness of northern Siberia, his spirit began to sink. Solitude oppressed him. He felt as if he had been exiled from life itself. His sense of reality was shaken. Had all the years he had spent at Lenin's side, as valued comrade and adviser, helping to direct the affairs of a world-wide movement, been but a dream? Men of far greater resilience were beset by similar feelings. This, for instance, is what Ivan Smirnov, hero of the civil war, wrote to Radek, from southern Armenia to northern Siberia:

> You, dear Karlyusha,[1] are pained that we have found ourselves outside the party. To me, too, and to all the others this is agony indeed. At the beginning I was haunted by nightmares. I would suddenly awake at night and could not believe that I was a deportee —I, who had worked for the party ever since 1899, without a day's break, not like some of those scoundrels of the Society of Old Bolsheviks who after 1906 deserted the party for full ten years.[2]

But it was not only this predicament that troubled Radek and his friends. They brooded over the fate of the revolution. They were accustomed to regard themselves as the true guardians of the 'conquests of October' and as the sole depositaries of Marxism and Leninism which the Stalinists and Bukharinists had diluted and falsified. They were accustomed to think that whatever was beneficial to Marxism and the revolution was beneficial to the Opposition too, and that the Opposition's defeats were the revolution's defeats. They now saw the Opposition reduced to a small group, almost a sect, utterly impotent and estranged from the great state and party with which they had identified themselves. Was it possible, they wondered, that a movement claiming for itself so high a mission should be reduced to so low a state? They were confronted with this dilemma: if they really were the sole reliable and legitimate guardians of October, then their cruel defeat could not but bring irretrievable disaster to the

---

[1] Diminutive from Karl, Charlie.

[2] The letter, written in 1928 (no more precise date), is in *The Trotsky Archives*.

revolution, and the heritage of October was lost. But if this was not so, if the 'conquests of October' were more or less intact and the Soviet Union, despite all that had happened, was still a workers' state, then had the Opposition not been wrong and guilty of arrogance in regarding itself as the sole depositary of Marxism-Leninism and in denying its adversaries all revolutionary virtue? Were the few thousand Oppositionists all that was left of the great and world-shaking Bolshevik movement? Had the mountain of revolution brought forth a mouse? 'I cannot believe', Radek wrote to Sosnovsky, 'that Lenin's entire work and the entire work of the revolution should have left behind only 5,000 Communists in the whole of Russia.'[1] Yet, if one were to take literally some of the Opposition's claims and if one were to believe that the other Bolshevik factions merely paved the way for counter-revolution, then one could not escape this conclusion, from which both realism and the Marxist sense of history recoiled. Surely, the Bolshevik epic with all its heroism, sacrifice, hope, blood, and toil, could not have been mere sound and fury, signifying nothing. As long as Stalinists and Bukharinists had jointly protected the kulaks and the N.E.P.-men there was substance in the Opposition's claims and charges. But the left course, bringing the Stalinist faction into mortal conflict with private property, demonstrated that the work of Lenin and the October Revolution had left behind something more than a handful of righteous men, something more than 'five thousand communists in the whole of Russia'. The volcano of the revolution, far from having given birth to a mouse and becoming extinguished, was still active.

Preobrazhensky argued that it was the 'objective force' of social ownership that provided the impulse for Russia's further revolutionary and socialist transformation. The 'objective force' asserted itself through men, its subjective representatives. The Stalinist faction was the agent of historic necessity; and despite confusion, mistakes, and even crimes committed, it acted as guardian of the heritage of October and champion of socialism. The Stalinists, Radek discovered, had proved themselves worthier than the Opposition had thought them to be. The Opposition should and could admit this without any self-depreciation. In the new advance towards socialism the Opposition had acted as the

[1] The letter (dated Tomsk, 14 July 1928) is in *The Archives*.

vanguard while the Stalinist faction had formed the rearguard. The conflict between them had not been a clash of hostile class interests, but a breach between two sections of the same class, for both vanguard and rearguard belonged to the same camp. It was time to heal the breach. Many Oppositionists were startled by the idea of a reconciliation between Stalinists and Trotskyists; but, Radek remarked, such a regrouping would not be stranger than had been earlier reversals of inner-party alliances. 'There was a time when we thought that Stalin was a good revolutionary and that Zinoviev was hopeless. Then things changed—they may change once again.'

There was an unmistakable note of despair in these pleadings —but it was a despair which sought to escape from itself and to change into hope. The conciliators' mood was nurtured in the deepening isolationism of Bolshevik Russia. It was within the Soviet Union, not without, that Radek and Preobrazhensky— and many others—looked for a great and promising change in the fortunes of communism. And this fact accounts for much that was to follow.

This was the aftermath of the Chinese Revolution. In December 1927 the communist rising of Canton had been suppressed. The rising had been the last act or rather the epilogue of the drama of 1925–7. The shock of the defeat was making itself felt in all Bolshevik thinking: it sapped even further and submerged the internationalist tradition of Leninism; and it enhanced Russian self-centredness. More than ever socialism in one country appeared to offer the only way out and the only consolation. This time, however, the tide of isolationism affected the Opposition as well; it reached the remote colonies of deportees and worked on the thoughts of the conciliators. Like Stalin's turn to the left this latest defeat gave Preobrazhensky and Radek a fresh motive for disillusionment with the Opposition's record. The Opposition, they argued, had been partly mistaken in its estimate of internal Russian developments—had it not been mistaken in its view of the international prospects as well? Trotsky had erred over the Soviet Thermidor—was not his Permanent Revolution, too, a fallacy?

Barely a few weeks after their deportation Trotsky and Preobrazhensky were already in correspondence over the Canton rising. Knowing little about the actual circumstances of the event and trying to form an opinion from *Pravda*'s belated and scanty reports, Trotsky resumed an exchange of views which he had had with Preobrazhensky in Moscow. Like many an old Bolshevik in Opposition, Preobrazhensky had not accepted the idea of Permanent Revolution and its corollary that the Chinese Revolution could conquer only as a proletarian dictatorship. Like Zinoviev and Kamenev he held that China could not go beyond a bourgeois revolution. From their places of exile Trotsky and Preobrazhensky discussed the bearing of the Canton rising on this difference. *Pravda* had reported that the insurgents of Canton had formed a Council of Workers' Deputies and had set out to socialize industry. Although the rising had been crushed —so Trotsky wrote to Preobrazhensky on 2 March—it left a message and a significant pointer to the course of the next Chinese Revolution which would not be arrested in its bourgeois phase but would establish Soviets and aim at socialism. Preobrazhensky replied that the rising had been staged by Stalin merely in order to save his face after all his surrenders to the Kuomintang, that this had been a reckless venture, and that the 'Soviet' of Canton and its 'socialist' slogans, not having resulted organically from any mass movement, had not reflected the inherent logic of any genuine revolutionary process.[1] Preobrazhensky was, of course, closer to the facts than Trotsky, who in this case relied on dubious evidence for his conclusion about the character of the next Chinese Revolution. His conclusion was nevertheless correct: the revolution of 1948–9 was to transcend its bourgeois limits; and to this extent it was to be a 'permanent revolution', even if its course and the alignment of social classes in it were to prove very different from what the Trotskyist and indeed the Marxist and Leninist theories of revolution had envisaged.

'We, the old Bolsheviks in opposition, must dissociate ourselves from Trotsky on the point of permanent revolution', Preobrazhensky declared. The statement itself could not have been surprising to Trotsky, but its emphatic tone certainly was. Trotsky had been accustomed to hear such reminders of his non-Bolshevik past from his adversaries and lately again from Zinoviev and Kamenev, but hardly from Preobrazhensky, his close

[1] Preobrazhensky's (undated) answer is in *The Archives*.

co-thinker since 1922. He knew that such reminders never cropped up fortuitously. What surprised him even more was that Radek, too, produced a *critique* of Permanent Revolution —Radek, no old Bolshevik himself, had hitherto whole-heartedly defended that theory. Even now he acknowledged that Trotsky had in 1906 anticipated the course of the Russian Revolution more correctly than Lenin; but he added that it did not follow that the scheme of permanent revolution was valid in other countries. In China, Radek maintained, Lenin's 'democratic dictatorship of the proletariat and the peasantry' was preferable because it allowed for a possible hiatus between the bourgeois revolution and the socialist one.

Apparently this controversy had no direct bearing on the issues of the day; and Trotsky was drawn into it reluctantly. He replied that China had freshly demonstrated that any contemporary revolution which did not find its consummation in a socialist upheaval was bound to suffer defeat even as a bourgeois revolution. Whatever the pros and the cons, the fact that the two conciliators attacked Permanent Revolution was all the more symptomatic because Trotsky had not attempted to make of his theory the Opposition's canon. This was not the first time that frustration with defeats of communism abroad and isolationist propensities induced Bolsheviks to turn against the theory which in its very title challenged their isolationism. The result of all the dogmatic battles fought over Permanent Revolution since 1924 had been to make of it in the party's eyes the symbol of Trotskyism, Trotsky's master heresy, and the intellectual fount of all his political vices. To Stalin's and Bukharin's followers Permanent Revolution had become a horror-inspiring taboo. An Oppositionist beset by doubts and second thoughts and looking for a way back to the party—his lost paradise—sought instinctively to rid himself of any association with that taboo. It will be remembered that Trotsky, anxious to render it easier for Zinoviev and Kamenev to make common cause with him, had declared that his old writings on Permanent Revolution had their place in the historical archives and that he would not defend them on every point, even though for himself he was convinced that his idea had stood the test of time. Yet he did not succeed in relegating his theory to the archives. Not only his enemies dragged it out and forced him to defend it. Again and again his allies did likewise; and whenever they did so this was a sure sign that one of his political alliances or associations was about to break down.

Presently dissension came into the open over a more topical and less theoretical issue. The sixth congress of the Communist International was convened in Moscow for the summer of 1928. The Opposition had the statutory right to appeal to the congress against its expulsion from the Russian party; and it intended to do so. There was no chance that the appeal would obtain a proper hearing, or that the leaders of the Opposition would be allowed to appear before the congress to state their case. '. . . the Congress will probably make an attempt to cover us in a most authoritative manner with the heaviest of tombstones . . .', Trotsky wrote. 'Fortunately, Marxism will rise from this *papier-mâché* grave and like an irrepressible drummer sound the alarm!'[1] He intended to produce a brief and blunt criticism of the Comintern's policy and a concise declaration of the Opposition's purpose to be addressed to the congress. But the work grew in his hands into a massive treatise the writing of which kept him occupied throughout the spring and summer.[2] The congress was expected to adopt a new programme of which a draft, written largely by Bukharin and centred on socialism in one country, had been published. Trotsky gave his statement the form of a *Critique* of the new programme. He completed this in June; and in July he followed it up by a message to the congress under the title *What Next?* He summed up 'five years of the International's failures' and five years of the Opposition's work in a manner 'free from all traces of reticence, duplicity, and diplomacy' and calculated to mark clearly the gulf between the Opposition and its adversaries. He sent copies to the colonies just before the opening of the congress; and he asked all Oppositionists to endorse his statements in their collective and individual messages addressed to the congress.

Meantime Radek and Preobrazhensky had prepared statements of their own which were more conciliatory in content and tone. True, Preobrazhensky drew a devastating balance-sheet of the Comintern's policy of recent years; and he was outspoken about the differences which opposed Trotskyists of all shades to

[1] Trotsky's circular letter of 17 July 1928. *The Archives.*
[2] The work is known in English under the title *The Third International After Lenin.*

Stalinism and the Comintern. But in his conclusion he declared that 'many of these differences have disappeared as a result of the change that has occurred in the International's policy', because the International, following the Russian party, had also 'veered to the left'.[1] Radek expressed the same opinion and at once dispatched his statement to Moscow. 'If history shows', he wrote, 'that some of the party leaders with whom yesterday we crossed swords are better than the viewpoints they defended, nobody will find greater satisfaction in this than we shall.'[2]

The fact that Trotsky and Radek had addressed different and partly conflicting messages to the congress could only damage the Opposition's cause. Instead of demonstrating its unity, the Opposition spoke with two voices. When Trotsky learned what had happened, he telegraphed to the major centres of the Opposition asking all the exiles to dissociate themselves publicly from Radek. The colonies were agog with indignation, disavowed Radek, and sent appropriate statements to Moscow. In the end Radek himself informed the Congress that he was withdrawing his message and that he was in complete agreement with Trotsky. To his comrades he apologized for his *faux pas*, saying that it had been due to difficulties of communication with Trotsky, whose *Critique* of the Comintern had reached him too late. Trotsky accepted the apology; and there the matter rested for the moment. The Opposition, Trotsky said, had 'straightened out its front'. However, the incipient split was not mended—it was only thinly covered over.

.   .   .   .

An important event had helped Trotsky to rally the exiles. In July the Central Committee held a session at which Bukharin's faction appeared to have gained the upper hand over Stalin's. The critical issue was still the same: the bread crisis and the threat of famine suspended over urban Russia. The emergency measures earlier in the year had not averted the threat; and the situation was aggravated by a partial failure of winter crops in the Ukraine and in the northern Caucasus. The peasantry was in uproar. It delivered and sold only 50 per cent. of the grain it

---

[1] Preobrazhensky, 'Chto nado skazat Kongresu Kominterna' in *The Archives*.

[2] Radek's memorandum to the congress, written in Tomsk in June 1928, is in *The Trotsky Archives*. Trotsky must have read 'psychoanalytically' the passage quoted here: he underlined with red pencil the word 'yesterday' in Radek's phrase about the party leaders 'with whom yesterday we crossed swords'.

used to sell before the revolution. All exports of grain had to be stopped.[1] The strong-arm methods in grain collection had been just enough to enrage the farmers but not enough to intimidate them. The Central Committee noted 'the discontent among . . . the peasantry which showed itself in demonstrations of protest against arbitary administrative proceedings'; and it declared that such proceedings 'had helped capitalist elements to exploit the discontent and turn it against the Soviet Government . . . and had given rise to talk about the [forthcoming] abolition of N.E.P.'[2]

At the session of the Committee, after Mikoyan had made a report, the Bukharinist faction called for an end to the left course. Rykov demanded the cancellation of the antikulak policy; Frumkin, the Commissar of Finance, went even farther and asked for a revision of the entire peasant policy enunciated at the fifteenth congress (at which Stalin, to confound the Trotskyists and the Zinovievists, had adopted some of their ideas) and for a return to the predominantly Bukharinist policy of the previous congress. The Central Committee declared that it stood by the decisions of the fifteenth congress; but it cancelled its own emergency measures 'against the kulak'. It proclaimed that henceforth the 'rule of law' must prevail. It forbade searches and raids on barns and farmsteads. It stopped the requisitioning of food and the forcible levying of grain loans. Last but not least, it authorized a 20 per cent. rise in the price of bread, the rise it had so categorically prohibited three months earlier.[3] Seen in retrospect, this was the Central Committee's last attempt to appease the peasants, the last before it proceeded to suppress private farming. At the time, however, it looked as if the kulak had won a round, as if Stalin had abandoned the left course, and as if Bukharin and Rykov had dictated policy.

It may be imagined how the Trotskyist deportees received this. They were back on familiar ground. The old scheme of things, within which they had been accustomed to think and to argue, seemed re-established. They saw 'the defenders of the kulak' reasserting themselves. They saw Stalin's 'vacillating centre' yielding as always. Authorizing the higher bread price, the Central Committee had hit the industrial workers and had acted in the interests of the wealthy farmers. This was surely not

---

[1] *KPSS v Rezolutsyakh*, vol. ii, p. 392. [2] Ibid., p. 395. [3] Ibid., p. 396.

yet the end. The struggle was on: the right wing would resume
its offensive; and the Stalinists would continue to retreat. The
Thermidorian danger was closer than ever—the Thermidorians
were on the move. Trotsky thought likewise: 'In Rykov's
speech...', he declared, 'the right wing has thrown its challenge
at the October Revolution. . . . The challenge must be taken
up. . . .' The rise of the price of bread was only the beginning of
a neo-N.E.P. To appease the kulak, the right wing would soon
make a determined attempt to undermine the state monopoly of
foreign trade. He saw Rykov and Bukharin as the victors who
would soon 'hunt down Stalin as a Trotskyist, just as Stalin had
hunted down Zinoviev'. Rykov had said at the Central Committee that 'the Trotskyists regarded it as their main task to
prevent a victory of the right wing'. Trotsky replied that this
was indeed the Opposition's main task.[1]

Among the Trotskyists the conciliators were completely isolated for the moment. 'Where is Stalin's left course?' the deportees
exultantly demanded of Radek and Preobrazhensky. 'It was all
a flash in the pan. But this was enough for you to try and throw
overboard our old and well-tested ideas and views and to urge
us to conciliate the Stalinists!' Once again they saw Stalin's
ascendancy as a mere incident in the fundamental struggle
between themselves and the Bukharinists; and they believed
even more ardently than before that all Bolsheviks who had
remained faithful to the revolution would soon see the issues in
this light, as a conflict essentially between right and left, and
would opt for the left. Stalin's apparent discomfiture raised
their hopes sky-high. 'The day is not far off', wrote as eminent a
Trotskyist as Sosnovsky, 'when the call for Trotsky's return will
resound throughout the world.'[2]

＊　　＊　　＊　　＊　　＊　　＊　　＊　　＊　　＊　　＊

In the middle of all this political excitement tragedy visited
Trotsky's family. Both his daughters, Zina and Nina, had been
ill with consumption. The health of Nina, the younger of the
two—she was twenty-six—broke down after the imprisonment
and deportation of Nevelson, her husband. The news reached
Trotsky in the spring, during a fishing expedition. He was not
yet fully aware of the gravity of Nina's illness; but he spent the

[1] 'Yulskiye Plenum i Prava Opasnost' in The Archives.
[2] See Sosnovsky's letter to Rafail of 24 August in The Archives.

next weeks in anxiety and worry. He knew that both his daughters and their children lived in utter poverty, that they could not count on the help of friends, and that Zina, herself wasted by consumptive fever, spent her days and nights at Nina's bed. 'Am aggrieved', he telegraphed her, 'that cannot be with Ninushka to help her. Communicate her condition. Kisses for both of you. Papa.' Again and again he asked for news but received no answer. He wrote to Rakovsky begging him to make inquiries in Moscow. Finally, he learned that Nina had died on 9 June. Much later he received the last letter she had written him—it had been on the way and held up by the censors for over ten weeks. It was a painful thought for Trotsky that on her death-bed she had waited for his answer in vain. He mourned her as 'an ardent revolutionary and member of the Opposition' as well as a daughter; and to her memory he devoted the *Critique* of the Comintern's programme on which he had been working at the time of her death.

Messages of condolence from many deportees were still arriving at Alma Ata when another blow caused Trotsky much sorrow and grief. After Nina's death Zina had intended to go to Alma Ata. Her husband too had been deported and she had strained her health in nursing her sister. From week to week she delayed the journey until news reached Alma Ata that she was dangerously ill and unable to travel. Her malady was aggravated by a severe and protracted nervous disorder; and she was not to rejoin her father before his banishment from Russia.

A family reunion, nevertheless, occurred at the *dacha* outside Alma Ata, when Sergei arrived to spend his holiday there. With him came Lyova's wife and child. They stayed only a few weeks; and this was an anxious and mournful reunion.

. . . .

After the 'rightward turn' of official policy, the extreme and irreconcilable Trotskyists had the upper hand in nearly all the centres of the Opposition. The mass of deportees would not even hear of any attempt at narrowing the gulf between themselves and the Stalinists. However, the extreme irreconcilables had no spokesmen of Preobrazhensky's and Radek's authority and ability. Their views were formulated by men like Sosnovsky, Dingelstedt, Elzin, and a few others who expressed a mood rather than any definite political ideas.

Of this group Sosnovsky was the most gifted and articulate; and when he confidently asserted that 'the cry for Trotsky's return will soon resound throughout the world' he expressed the fervid hope of many of his comrades. He was Trotsky's trusted friend and one of the most effective Bolshevik journalists, very popular far outside the ranks of the Opposition. But he was no political leader or theorist. He was distinguished as a chronicler of Bolshevik Russia and a sharp-eyed critic of morals and manners. A rebel by temperament, animated by an intense hatred of inequality and injustice, he indignantly watched the rise, in the workers' state, of a privileged bureaucracy. He pungently exposed its greed and corruption (the 'harem-cum-motor-car-factor'), its snobbery and its upstart ambition to assimilate itself to the old bureaucracy and aristocracy and to intermarry with them. He felt only distaste for those who could even think of any conciliation with the ruling group. He was in this respect poles apart from Radek. It was to Sosnovsky that Radek had written that he could not believe that all that was left of Lenin's party was a mere handful of righteous Opposition-ists—to Sosnovsky the Opposition was indeed the sole guardian of the heritage of October. Nothing characterizes him more strikingly than a letter he wrote to Vardin, his old comrade, who had together with Safarov deserted the Opposition and 'capitula-ted'. Merciless in contempt, Sosnovsky recalled an old Jewish funeral custom which required that when a dead man was brought to the cemetery, his synagogue associates should shout into his ears: 'So-and-So, Son of So-and-So, know that thou art dead!' He, Sosnovsky, now shouted this into the ear of his old comrade, and he would shout it into the ear of every capitulator. Distrustfully he watched Radek's evolution, wondering whether he ought not to shout these words into Radek's ear as well.[1]

The other spokesmen of this wing of the Opposition were younger men of lesser stature. Dingelstedt was a promising scholar, a sociologist and economist; a Bolshevik since 1910, distinguished as an agitator in the Baltic Fleet in 1917, he was

---

[1] About the same time Radek also wrote to Vardin; and his and Sosnovsky's letters make a curious contrast. This was in May when Radek had only just begun to develop the conciliatory mood. He chided Vardin, but he did this gently and sympathetically and was far from treating the capitulator as 'morally dead'. Radek's and Sosnovsky's letters are in *The Archives*.

still in his early thirties. Elzin had been one of Trotsky's gifted secretaries. These men were not sure whether Trotsky himself was not showing signs of vacillation. Thus Dingelstedt wrote to him that 'some comrades were gravely disturbed' by his opinion that Stalin's left course was 'an indubitable step in our direction' and that the Opposition should 'support it unconditionally'.[1] They also reproached Trotsky for the 'indulgence' with which he treated Radek and Preobrazhensky. Nor did they share Trotsky's hope for a reform in the party and the revival in it of proletarian democracy.

Thus, while at one extreme the Opposition included those who were more and more anxious to come to terms with their persecutors, its other extreme became almost indistinguishable from the followers of V. Smirnov and Sapronov, the Decemists, and the remnants of the Workers' Opposition. These 'ultra-left' groups, we remember, had acceded to the Joint Opposition in 1926; but then they left it or were expelled. In the places of deportation their adherents mingled with the Trotskyists and endlessly argued with them. They carried the ideas of the Trotskyists to extreme conclusions, which were sometimes logical, sometimes absurd, and sometimes absurd in their very logicality. In an exaggerated manner they expressed all the emotions that stirred in Trotskyist hearts, even if many of Trotsky's reasonings were above their heads. They therefore occasionally said things which Trotsky at first indignantly rejected only to take them up and say them at a later stage. They criticized Trotsky for indecision and pointed out that it was hopeless to count on a democratic reform in the party. (It was to take Trotsky another five or six years to reach the same conclusion.) The party led by Stalin was 'a stinking corpse', V. Smirnov wrote in 1928. He and his adherents maintained that Stalin was the victorious chief of the Russian Thermidor, which had occurred as far back as 1923, and the authentic leader of the kulaks and of the men of property at large. They denounced the Stalinist régime as a 'bourgeois democracy', or 'a peasant democracy', which only a new proletarian revolution could overthrow. 'The liquidation in 1923 of inner-party democracy and proletarian democracy at large', Smirnov wrote, 'has proved to be a mere prologue to the

---

[1] See Dingelstedt's letters to Trotsky of 8 July and 24 August 1928 in *The Archives*. Also his letter to Radek of 22 August.

development of a peasant-kulak democracy.'[1] Sapronov held that 'bourgeois parties are already legally organizing themselves in this country'—and this in 1928![2] They thus accused Stalin of restoring capitalism just when he was about to destroy private farming, the main potential breeding ground of capitalism in Russia; and of favouring a bourgeois multi-party régime just when he was driving the single-party system to its ultimate conclusion and establishing himself as the single leader. This was Quixotry indeed. An element of it might be found in Trotsky too, but his realism and self-discipline kept it in check. V. Smirnov, Sapronov, and their followers were held back by no such inhibitions when they threw themselves on the windmills of Stalin's 'kulak-democracy'; and some of Trotsky's younger and unreasoning followers were tempted to join them, especially after the 'liquidation of the left course' in July had momentarily given the windmills the slightest semblance of a foe on the move.[3]

Amid all these cross-currents Trotsky did what he could to prevent the Opposition from falling to pieces. He saw its dissensions as a conflict between two generations of Oppositionists, a clash between 'fathers and sons', the former over-ripe and weary with knowledge and experience, the latter full of innocent ardour and audacity. He himself felt with both, understood both, and was apprehensive of both. He had forebodings about Radek and Preobrazhensky: in their mood and reasonings he discerned the impulses that were to lead them to capitulation. But he was wary of alienating them; he gave them the benefit of the doubt; and he defended them from abuse by over-zealous Trotskyists. Patiently but firmly he argued with the two men: he granted them that there was truth in what they said about the left course and the changing outlook of the country; but he begged them not to draw rash conclusions and not to exaggerate the chances of any genuine conciliation with Stalinism. At the same time he tried to curb the extremists on the other side, telling them

---

[1] The quotation is from a Decemist essay '*Pod Znamya Lenina*', the authorship of which Trotsky ascribes to V. Smirnov. *The Archives.*

[2] See Sapronov's statement of 18 June, addressed to an unknown friend, in *The Archives.*

[3] Trotsky described those who shared V. Smirnov's and Sapronov's views as the lunatic fringe of anti-Stalinism, but he favoured co-operation with the more moderate Decemists, such as Rafail, V. Kossior, Drobnis, and Boguslavsky. See his circular letter on the Decemists of 22 September 1928 in *The Archives.*

that they were taking an over-confident view of the Opposition's prospects and were courting disillusionment: they should not imagine that the latest attempt at appeasing the kulaks was 'Stalin's last word' which could be followed only by the 'inevitable collapse' of the Stalinist régime. The outlook, as he saw it, was far more complex: it was impossible to be sure what might emerge from the cauldron. At any rate, although he had said that 'the party will still need us', he was far less confident than Sosnovsky that 'the call for Trotsky's return will soon resound throughout the world'.[1]

He endeavoured to maintain the Opposition's unity on the ground of a 'sustained and uncompromising struggle for inner party reform'. His adamant rejection of 'illusions about a *rapprochement* with Stalinism' commended his attitude to the young irreconcilables, while his emphasis on inner party reform provided the link between himself and the conciliators. He repudiated the 'wholly negative and sterile' Decemist attitude towards the party; and he sought to counteract the nostalgic hankering after the party, the creeping feeling of isolation, and the sense of their own uselessness to which the older Oppositionists tended to succumb. He tried to rekindle the sense of mission—the conviction that even in exile they still spoke for the mute working class, that what they said still mattered, and that sooner or later it would reach the working class and the party. This conviction, he added, should not induce self-righteousness or arrogance in the Opposition: although it alone stood consistently for the Marxist and Leninist tradition, it must not dismiss all its adversaries as worthless—indeed, it must not assume that all that had been left of Lenin's party was a few thousand Oppositionists. The Opposition was right in exposing the party's 'bureaucratic degeneration'; but even in this a sense of proportion was necessary, because there were 'various degrees of degeneration'; and there were still many uncorrupted and sound elements in the party. 'Stalin has owed his position not only to the terror exercised by the machine, but also to the confidence or semi-confidence of a section of Bolshevik workers.' With those workers the Opposition must not lose touch—to them it must appeal.[2]

---

[1] See Trotsky's letter to 'V. D.' (Elzin?) of 30 August 1928.

[2] See his circular letter on the Opposition's differences with the Decemists of 11 November 1928 and also his letters of 15 July, 20 August, 2 October, and 10 November, dealing with the same subject.

Trotsky's finely balanced interventions were not always well received. The ultra-radicals went on carping at his leniency towards the conciliators, while Preobrazhensky and Radek reproached him with countenancing the 'Decemist attitude' of those Trotskyists who behaved as if the Opposition were a new party, not a faction of the old. The estrangement between the groups grew continually. But as long as Trotsky remained at Alma Ata and from there exercised his influence, and as long as Stalin's policy, being in a state of suspense, did not further accentuate the Opposition's dilemmas, Trotsky succeeded in preventing the various sets of his followers from straying too far apart and scuttling the Opposition.

In these trying circumstances he found the strongest moral support in Rakovsky. Their old and close friendship had now acquired a new depth of affection, intimacy, and intellectual concord. After his great career as head of the Bolshevik government in the Ukraine and diplomat, Rakovsky worked at Astrakhan, the place of his exile, as a minor official of the local Gosplan. His correspondence with Trotsky and eye-witness accounts give impressive evidence of the stoical calm with which he bore his fortune and of the intensity and range of his intellectual work in exile.[1] In the wanderer's bag he had brought to Astrakhan the works of Saint-Simon and Enfantin, of many French historians of the revolution, and of Marx and Engels, Dickens's novels, and classics of Russian literature. In the first weeks of deportation Cervantes was his favourite reading. 'In a situation like this', he wrote to Trotsky, 'I go back to *Don Quixote* and find enormous satisfaction.' Longing for his native Dobrudja, he reread Ovid. Concerned with economic planning in the Astrakhan area, he assiduously studied the 'geological profiles' of the Caspian steppes; and describing this work to Trotsky, he interspersed his remarks with references to Dante and Aristotle. Above all, he was eagerly restudying the French Revolution;[2]

---

[1] Louis Fischer, who visited Rakovsky at Astrakhan, relates that he once saw him employed by local authority to act as an interpreter to a group of American tourists. Rakovsky looked worn and haggard and, when he had finished interpreting, the American visitors tried to tip him. With a polite gesture, half-sad and half-amused, Rakovsky withdrew.

[2] As Ambassador in Paris Rakovsky had done much to promote the study by Soviet historians of the archives of the French Revolution, in which he himself took a close interest. Among the books he took with him into exile and cherished

and he wrote a *Life of Saint-Simon*. He reported to Trotsky on the progress of his work and quoted to him Saint-Simon's predictions about Russia and the United States as the two antagonistic giants of the future (predictions which are less known but more original than those made by Tocqueville later). Grumbling about the effect of age on his memory and imagination—he was fifty-five at the time of deportation—he nevertheless worked 'with enormous zest—*avec ardeur*!' With a hint of paternal tenderness, he urged Trotsky not to spend his energy and talents on current affairs only: 'It is extremely important that you should also choose a large subject, something like my Saint-Simon, which would compel you to take a fresh look at many issues and re-read many things from a definite angle.'[1] He procured for Trotsky books and periodicals which could not be obtained at Alma Ata. He kept in touch with Trotsky's children in Moscow, and shared in the family's sorrows. Politically, he supported Trotsky against both conciliators and ultra-radicals; and to no one of the leaders of the Opposition was Trotsky attached as strongly as he was to Christian Georgevich.[2]

Rakovsky's political temperament was in many respects different from Trotsky's. He did not, of course, possess Trotsky's powers of thought, passion, and expression, nor his tempestuous energy. But he had a very clear and penetrating mind; and perhaps also a greater capacity for philosophical detachment. For all his devotion to the Opposition, he was less of a partisan, at least in the sense that his views transcended in their largeness the Opposition's immediate aims and tactics. Convinced of the Opposition's rightness and its ultimate vindication, he was far less confident about its chances of political success. He stood back and took in the immense picture of the revolution and grasped clearly the tragic motif that ran through it and affected all the warring factions. That motif was 'the inevitable disintegration of the party of revolution after its victory'.

He developed this idea in his 'Letter to Valentinov,' an essay which caused a stir in the Trotskyist colonies in the summer of

greatly was a copy of Aulard's *Histoire politique de la Révolution Française* dedicated to him by the author.

[1] See Rakovsky's letter to Trotsky of 17 February 1928 in *Bulleten Oppozitsii*, nr. 35.

[2] 'To Christian Georgevich Rakovsky, Fighter, Man, and Friend' Trotsky had dedicated his *Literature and Revolution*.

1928.[1] How is one to account, Rakovsky asked, for the abysmal wickedness and moral depravity which had revealed itself in the Bolshevik party, a party that had consisted of honest, dedicated, and courageous revolutionaries? It was not enough to blame the ruling group or the bureaucracy. The deeper cause was 'the apathy of the masses and the indifference of the victorious working class after the revolution'. Trotsky had pointed to Russia's backwardness, the numerical weakness of the working class, isolation, and capitalist encirclement as the factors responsible for the 'bureaucratic degeneration' of state and party. To Rakovsky this explanation was valid but insufficient. He argued that even in a most advanced and thoroughly industrialized nation, even in a nation consisting almost entirely of workers and surrounded only by socialist states, the masses might, after the revolution, succumb to apathy, abdicate their right to shape their own life, and enable an arbitrary bureaucracy to usurp power. This, he said, was the danger inherent in any victorious revolution—it was the 'professional risk' of government.

Revolution and civil war are as a rule followed by the social decomposition of the revolutionary class. The French Third Estate disintegrated after it had triumphed over the *ancien régime*. Class antagonisms in its midst, the conflicts between bourgeois and plebeian, destroyed its unity. But even socially homogeneous groups were split because of the 'functional specialization' of their members, some of whom became the new rulers while others remained among the ruled. 'The function adjusted its organ to itself and changed it.' Because of the disintegration of the Third Estate, the social basis of the revolution narrowed and power was exercised by ever fewer people. Election was replaced by nomination. This process had been well advanced even before the Thermidorian *coup*; it was Robespierre who had furthered it and then became its victim. First it was the exasperation of the people with hunger and misery that did not allow the Jacobins to trust the fate of the revolution to the popular vote; then Jacobin arbitrary and terroristic rule drove the people into political indifference; and this enabled the Thermidorians to destroy Robespierre and the Jacobin party. In Russia similar changes had occurred in the 'anatomy and physiology' of the

---

[1] The text of the letter, written on 2 August 1928, is in *The Archives*. Valentinov had been editor in chief of *Trud* and was exiled as a Trotskyist.

working class and had led to similar results: the abolition of the elective system; the concentration of power in very few hands; and the replacement of representative bodies by hierarchies of nominees. The Bolshevik party was split between rulers and ruled; it disintegrated; and it changed its character so much that 'the Bolshevik of 1917 would hardly recognize himself in the Bolshevik of 1928'.

A deep and shocking apathy still paralysed the working class. Unlike Trotsky, Rakovsky did not think that it was the workers' pressure that had forced Stalin to embark upon the 'left course'. This was a bureaucratic operation carried out exclusively from above. The rank and file had no initiative and was all too little eager to defend its freedoms. Rakovsky recalled one of Babeuf's sayings in 1794: 'To re-educate the people in the love of liberty is more difficult than to conquer liberty.' Babeuf raised the battle-cry: 'Liberty and an Elected Commune!'; but his cry fell on deaf ears. The French had 'unlearned' freedom. It was to take them thirty-seven years, from 1793 to 1830, before they re-learned it, recovered from apathy, and rose in another revolution. Rakovsky did not explicitly pose the question which suggested itself: how long would it take the Russian masses to regain their political vitality and vigour? But his argument implied that a political revival could occur in Russia only in a relatively remote future, after great changes had taken place in society, and after the working class had grown, developed, become reintegrated, and had recovered from many shocks and disillusionments. He 'confessed' that he had never expected early political triumphs for the Opposition; and he concluded that the Opposition should direct its efforts mainly towards the long-term political education of the working class. In this respect, he said, the Opposition had not done or attempted to do much, although it had done more than the ruling group; and it should keep in mind that 'political education bears fruit only very slowly'.

The unspoken conclusion was that the Opposition had little chance, if any, to influence the course of events in its time, although it could confidently look forward to its ultimate, perhaps posthumous, vindication. Rakovsky threw into relief the Opposition's basic predicament: its position between a demoralized, treacherous, and tyrannical bureaucracy on the one side, and a hopelessly apathetic and passive working class on the other. 'I think', he emphasized, 'that it would be utterly unrealistic to expect any inner-party reform based on the bureaucracy.' Yet he anticipated no regenerative movement from the masses either, for many years to come. It followed (although Rakovsky did not say it) that the bureaucracy, such as it was, would remain, perhaps for decades, the only force capable of initiative and action in the reshaping of Soviet society. The Opposition was bound by its principles to persist in irreducible hostility towards the bureaucracy; but it could not effectively appeal against it to the people. Consequently, it could not play any practical part in the evolution of party and state; and it was eliminated in advance from the great historic process by which Soviet society was presently to be transformed. It could only hope to work for the future mainly in the field of ideas.

A conclusion of this kind, implicit in Rakovsky's 'Letter to Valentinov', may in certain situations satisfy a small circle of theorists and ideologues; but it spells the death sentence for any political movement. Rakovsky viewed the course of the revolution and the Opposition's prospects with cool, profound insight and stoical equanimity. No such detachment or equanimity could be expected from the several thousand Oppositionists who read the 'Letter to Valentinov'. Whether workers or intellectuals, they were practical revolutionaries and fighters, passionately interested in the immediate outcome of their struggle and in the upheavals which were shaking and shaping their nation. They had joined the Opposition as a political movement, not as a coterie of philosophers or ideologues; and they wished it to triumph as a political movement. Even the most heroic and selfless rebels or revolutionaries struggle as a rule for objectives which they believe to be in some measure within the reach of their generation—only few and very exceptional men, thinkers, can fight for a prize which history may award them posthumously.

The mass of the Oppositionists had striven to strengthen the socialist sector of the Soviet economy, to further industrialization, to revive the spirit of internationalism, and to restore some freedom within the party. They could not bring themselves to believe that these objectives were for them unattainable. They had already found out that they could not attain them by themselves, and that they had to look either to the masses or to the bureaucracy for help. They could not accept the view that it was hopeless to look to either. To exist politically, they had to believe either that the masses would sooner or later rise against the bureaucracy, or that the bureaucracy would, for its own reasons, carry out many of the reforms for which the Opposition stood. The radical Trotskyists looked to the masses; the conciliators to the ruling group or to a section of it. Each of these hopes was illusory, but not to the same extent. There was no sign in the country of any spontaneous mass movement in favour of the Opposition's objectives. But the bureaucracy was clearly in ferment; it was divided against itself over such issues as industrialization and peasant policy. The conciliators saw that on these issues the Stalinist faction had, after all, moved closer to the Opposition; and this encouraged them to expect that it might move closer in other respects as well. The fact that the bureaucracy was the only force showing effective social initiative induced the hope that the bureaucracy might even restore freedom to the party. The alternative was too gloomy to contemplate: it was that inner-party freedom and proletarian democracy at large were bound to remain empty dreams for a long time to come.

Trotsky was greatly impressed by Rakovsky's views and commended them to the Opposition; but he missed, so it seems, some of their deeper and relatively pessimistic implications. In Trotsky the detached thinker and the active political leader were now at loggerheads. The thinker accepted an analysis from which it followed that the Opposition was virtually doomed as a political movement. The leader could not even consider such a conclusion, let alone reconcile himself to it. The theorist could admit that Russia, like France before her, had 'unlearned freedom' and might not relearn it before the rise of a new generation. The man of action had to banish this prospect from his mind and try and give his followers a practical purpose. The thinker could run ahead of his time and work for the verdict of posterity. The chief of the Opposition had to go back to his time, live in it, and believe with his followers that they had a great and constructive part to play in it. Both as thinker and political leader, Trotsky refused to contemplate his country in isolation from the world. He remained convinced that the worst predicament of Bolshevism lay in its isolation and that the spread of revolution to other countries would help the peoples of the Soviet Union to relearn freedom much earlier than they could otherwise do.

.   .   .   .

Late in the summer of 1928 startling news, coming from clandestine Trotskyist circles in Moscow, reached Alma Ata. It brought detailed evidence that Stalin was about to resume the left course and that the breach between his faction and Bukharin's was complete and irreparable. Moreover, the reports from Moscow claimed that both the Bukharinists and the Stalinists mooted an alliance with the Left Opposition and that both were already vying for Trotskyist and Zinovievist support. It looked indeed as if the cry for Trotsky's return was about to go up, after all.

The Moscow Trotskyists were in fairly close contact with Kamenev, who gave them an account of talks he had had with Sokolnikov during the July session of the Central Committee. Sokolnikov, still a member of the Committee and himself something of a semi-Bukharinist and semi-Zinovievist, appeared to entertain the hope of forming a coalition of right and left against the Stalinist centre; and he himself tried to act as go-between. He related to Kamenev that Stalin had boasted at the Central Committee that in the struggle against the Bukharinists he would soon have the Trotskyists and Zinovievists on his side, and that indeed he had them 'in his pocket' already. Bukharin was dismayed. Through Sokolnikov he implored the Left Opposition to refrain from assisting Stalin and even suggested joint action against Stalin. However, the July session of the Central Committee ended with Bukharin's seeming success, or rather with a compromise between him and Stalin. But shortly thereafter they were at loggerheads again; and Bukharin secretly met Kamenev in Sokolnikov's presence. He told Kamenev that both he and Stalin were going to be compelled to turn to the Left Opposition and try and make common cause with it. Bukharinists and Stalinists still were afraid of appealing to their former enemies; but both knew that this course would become 'inevitable within a couple of months'. It was, in any case, certain, Bukharin said, that the expelled and deported Oppositionists would soon be recalled to Moscow and reinstated in the party.[1]

[1] The reports of the Moscow Trotskyists are in *The Archives*. The account of Sokolnikov's talks with Kamenev is dated 11 July 1928; and that of the meeting

Of his meeting with Bukharin, Kamenev wrote a detailed account for Zinoviev who was still in semi-exile at Voronezh; and this account allows us to reconstruct the scene with its peculiar colour and atmosphere. The Bukharin closeted with Kamenev and Sokolnikov was a very different man from the one who had only seven months earlier, at the fifteenth congress, helped to crush the Opposition. There was no trace in him now of that earlier self-confident and bragging Bukharin who had mocked Kamenev for 'leaning on Trotsky' and whom Stalin had congratulated for 'slaughtering' the leaders of the Opposition 'instead of arguing with them'. He arrived at Kamenev's home stealthily, terrified, pale, trembling, looking over his shoulders, and talking in whispers. He began by begging Kamenev to tell no one of their meeting and to make no mention of it in writing and over the telephone because they were both spied upon by the G.P.U. Broken in spirit, he had come to 'lean' on his old adversary who was himself morally crippled. Panic made his speech partly incoherent. Without pronouncing Stalin's name he repeated obsessively: '*He* will slay us', '*He* is the new Genghiz Khan', '*He* will strangle us'. On Kamenev Bukharin already made 'the impression of a doomed man'.

Bukharin confirmed that the crisis in the leadership had been caused by the conflict between government and peasantry. In the first half of the year, he said, the G.P.U. had had to quell 150 sporadic and widely scattered peasant rebellions—to such despair had Stalin's emergency measures driven the muzhiks. In July the Central Committee was so alarmed that Stalin had to feign a retreat: he revoked temporarily the emergency measures but he did so only in order to weaken the Bukharinists and to prepare himself better for a new attack. Since then he had succeeded in winning over to his side Voroshilov and Kalinin, who had been in sympathy with the Bukharinists; and this had given him a majority in the Politbureau. Stalin, so Bukharin related, was now ready for the final offensive against private farming. He had adopted Preobrazhensky's idea and argued that only by 'exploiting' the peasantry could socialism proceed with primitive

between Bukharin and Kamenev bears the date of 11 August. A further report on a meeting between the Trotskyists and Kamenev is of 22 September. The account of the talk between Kamenev and Bukharin was clandestinely circulated by the Trotskyists in Moscow a few months later, at the time of Trotsky's deportation from Russia.

accumulation in Russia, because, unlike early capitalism, it could not develop through the exploitation of colonies and with the help of foreign loans. From this Stalin drew the conclusion (which Bukharin characterized as 'illiterate and idiotic') that the further socialism advanced, the stronger would popular resistance to it become, a resistance which only 'firm leadership' could hold down. 'This meant a police state', Bukharin commented; but 'Stalin will stop at nothing'; 'his policy is leading us to civil war; he will be compelled to drown rebellions in blood'; and 'he will denounce us as the defenders of the kulak'. The party was on the brink of an abyss: if Stalin were to win, not a shred of freedom would be left. And again: '*He* will slay us','*He* will strangle us'. 'The root of the evil is that party and state are so completely merged.'

This was the situation in which Bukharin resolved to appeal to the left Opposition. The old divisions, as he saw it, had become largely irrelevant: 'Our disagreements with Stalin', he said to Kamenev, 'are far, far graver than those we have had with you.' What was now at stake was no longer normal differences of policy, but the preservation of party and state and the self-preservation of all of Stalin's adversaries. Though the Left Opposition stood for an anti-kulak policy, Bukharin knew that it would not wish to pursue it by the reckless and bloody methods to which Stalin would resort. In any case, it was not ideas that mattered to Stalin: 'He is an unprincipled intriguer who subordinates everything to his lust for power . . . he knows only vengeance and . . . the stab in the back. . . .' And so Stalin's opponents should not allow their old differences over ideas to prevent them from joining hands in self-defence.

Eager to encourage his would-be partners, Bukharin then enumerated the organizations and influential individuals whom he supposed to be ready to line up against Stalin. The workers' hatred of Stalin, he said, was notorious: Tomsky, when he was drunk, whispered into Stalin's ear: 'Soon our workers will start shooting at you, they will.' At party cells members were so disgusted with Stalin's lack of principles that, when the left course was initiated, they asked: 'Why is Rykov still at the head of the Council of People's Commissars, while Trotsky is exiled to Alma Ata?' The 'psychological conditions' for Stalin's dismissal were not yet ripe; but they were ripening, Bukharin claimed. True,

Stalin had won over Voroshilov and Kalinin; Ordjonikidze who had come to hate Stalin had no guts; but Andreev, the Leningrad leaders—was Kirov one of them?—and Yagoda and Trillisser, the two deputy chiefs of the G.P.U., and others, were ready to turn against Stalin. Alleging that the two effective chiefs of the G.P.U. were on his side, Bukharin nevertheless did not cease to speak in terror of the G.P.U.; his account of the forces that he could marshal against Stalin could not sound reassuring to his interlocutor.

A few weeks later the Muscovite Trotskyists reported to Alma Ata on another meeting they had had with Kamenev. 'Stalin is on the point of making overtures to the Left Opposition'—so confident was Kamenev about this that he had already warned Zinoviev not to compromise their position by responding too eagerly to Stalin's approaches. He held that a *dénouement* was imminent; and he was 'at one with Trotsky' in thinking that Stalin's policy had antagonized the entire peasantry, not merely the kulaks, and that the tension had reached explosion point. Consequently, a change in the party leadership was unavoidable: it 'was bound to occur even before the end of the year'. But Kamenev implored Trotsky to take a step which would ease his re-entry into the party. 'Lev Davidovich should make a statement now, saying: "Call us back and let us work together." But Lev Davidovich is stubborn. He will not do that; he will rather stay at Alma Ata until they send a special train to fetch him. But by the time they have made up their minds to send that train, the situation will be out of hand and Kerensky will be *ante portas.*'[1]

Stalin, however, did not make the direct approaches that Kamenev expected. Instead, he dropped many broad hints of a possible reconciliation; and he made sure that these hints reached Trotsky by roundabout ways. Thus he told a foreign, Asian, communist that he recognized that even in exile Trotsky and his followers had, unlike the Decemists, remained 'on the ground of Bolshevik ideology'; and that he, Stalin, was only wondering how to bring them back at the earliest opportunity. Stalin's entourage, Ordjonikidze in particular, talked about Trotsky's

---

[1] Kamenev resented Trotsky's attacks on the capitulators; nevertheless he and Zinoviev intervened with Bukharin and Molotov on Trotsky's behalf and protested against his being kept in exile in conditions detrimental to his health.

reinstatement openly and freely; and at the sixth Comintern congress foreign delegations had been told in confidence to reckon with the possibility or even probability of a coalition between Stalin and Trotsky.[1]

The sense of crisis had by now spread from the Russian party to the International. Despite a show of unanimity and official enthusiasm, the sixth congress was disappointed by Stalin's and Bukharin's joint conduct of the International's affairs. Trotsky's *Critique* of the new programme had, in a censured version, been circulated at the congress, where, according to Trotsky's correspondents, it made its impression.[2] Even those foreign communist leaders who passed as ardent Stalinists spoke in private with disgust about the dogmas and rites Stalin had imposed upon the Communist movement. Togliatti-Ercoli was reported to have complained about the unreality of the proceedings at the congress, the 'dull and sad parades of loyalty', and the arrogance of the Russian leaders. 'One felt like hanging oneself from sheer despair', he allegedly said. 'The tragedy is that one cannot speak the truth about the most important current issues. We dare not speak. . . .' Togliatti found Trotsky's *Critique* 'extraordinarily interesting . . . a very sensible analysis of socialism in one country'. Thorez, the French leader, characterized the mood at the congress as one of 'uneasiness, discontent, and scepticism'; and he too approved much in Trotsky's criticism of socialism in one country. 'How has it happened', he asked, 'that we have been made to swallow this theory?' Even if the Russian party had had to combat Trotskyism, it should not have accepted Stalin's dogma. He found the degradation of the International 'almost unbearable'. It was not possible to conceal from the congress the conflict between Stalin and Bukharin; and it was in this connexion that trusted foreign delegates were forewarned that, in the case of a definite breach with Bukharin, Stalin might consider it desirable or necessary to form a coalition with Trotsky.

Similar reports continued to reach Alma Ata from many sides throughout August and September. Stalin himself was

---

[1] See an undated letter entitled '*Podgotovka Kongresa*' and other undated correspondence from Moscow in *The Archives*.

[2] It was in this version that American Communists brought *The Critique* out of Russia and published it in the States in 1928.

undoubtedly still lending colour to the belief that he favoured Trotsky's imminent recall. In part this was deceit and *ruse de guerre*. By hinting that he was ready to make peace with Trotsky Stalin sought to intimidate Bukharin and Rykov, to confuse the Trotskyists and to make the conciliators among them even more impatient for conciliation than they were. But Stalin was not only bluffing. He could not yet be quite sure of the outcome of his show-down with Bukharin, Rykov, and Tomsky, and of his ability to cope simultaneously, and in the midst of a national crisis, with both oppositions, left and right. He worked tirelessly to bring both oppositions to their knees; but as long as he had not fully succeeded in this, he had to keep his door ajar to agreement with one of them. His position was already so much stronger than Bukharin's that he had no need to make direct overtures. But he threw out *ballons d'essai* and he watched how Trotsky and his associates received them.

Trotsky was well prepared to meet some of these developments; yet others caught him by surprise. The recrudescence in so dangerous a form of the conflict between town and country, the breach between Stalin and Bukharin, and the fact that the eyes of some of his adversaries and of the capitulators were once again turned on himself—all this corresponded to Trotsky's expectations. He was still inclined to think that the Stalinist faction would not be able to extricate itself and that it would be compelled to beg the Left Opposition to come to its rescue. He had repeatedly declared, in the most formal and solemn manner, that in such a situation the Opposition 'would do its duty' and would not refuse co-operation. He now reiterated this pledge. But he added that he spurned all 'bureaucratic combinations': he was not prepared to bargain behind the scenes for his seat in the Politbureau or to content himself with such share of control over the party machine as Stalin might offer him *in extremis*. He and his associates, he declared, would re-enter the party only on terms of proletarian democracy, reserving full freedom of expression and criticism—and on the condition that the party leadership would be elected by the rank and file in secret ballot instead of being picked by caucusdom through the familiar interfactional contrivances.[1]

Stalin's situation, difficult though it was, was not so desperate

[1] See, for instance, Trotsky's letter to S. A. (20 August 1928).

that he should accept Trotsky's conditions. Trotsky expected, however, that it would deteriorate further and then the bulk of the Stalinist faction, with or without its leader, might be compelled to seek agreement on his terms. As a matter of both principle and self-interest, he would not contemplate any other terms—after all his experiences he would not rely on the favours of the 'apparatus'.

Meantime, however, Trotsky was confronted by an unexpected turn of events. For years he had not ceased to speak of the 'danger from the right' and to warn the party against the defenders of the kulak and the Thermidorians. He had been prepared to form a 'united front' with Stalin against Bukharin. But it was Bukharin who implored the Left Opposition to make common cause against Stalin, their common enemy and oppressor. When Bukharin whispered in terror: '*He* will strangle us—*He* will slay us' Trotsky could not dismiss this as the imaginings of a befogged and panicky man—he himself had repeatedly spoken about the holocaust the 'grave-digger of the revolution' was preparing for the party. True, Bukharin's appeal had come very late in the day, after he had helped Stalin to crush the Opposition and to destroy the party's freedom. But he was not the first of Stalin's adversaries to behave in this manner. Zinoviev and Kamenev had done the same; yet this had not prevented Trotsky from joining hands with them. Should he then spurn Bukharin's outstretched hand? If Stalin was taking one leaf out of Trotsky's book, the left course, Bukharin took another: he appealed to the Left Opposition in the name of proletarian democracy. Trotsky was in a quandary: he could not turn a deaf ear on Bukharin's appeal without denying one of his own principles; and he could not respond to it without acting, or appearing to act, against another principle of his by which he was committed to support the left course.

Seeking a way out, he took a more reserved attitude towards Stalin's left course and became less emphatic in proclaiming the Opposition's support for it. Quite apart from Bukharin's approaches, he had his own reasons for this. From all over the Soviet Union followers wrote to him about the terror Stalin had let loose on the country in the spring and early summer and about the 'orgies of brutality' to which he had subjected the middle and even the poor peasants. Officialdom tried to disclaim

responsibility by telling the people that Trotskyist and Zinovievist pressure had provoked the drive against the peasants. Everything indicated that, if and when Stalin resumed the left course,
it would lead to a bloody cataclysm. Trotsky refused in advance
to bear any share of responsibility for this. In August 1928,
nearly a year before the 'liquidation of the kulaks' started, he
wrote to his followers that although the Opposition had pledged
itself to back the left course, it had never proposed to deal with
the peasantry in the Stalinist manner. It had stood for higher
taxes on the wealthy, for government support to the poor
farmers, for an equitable and equable treatment of the middle
ones, and for encouragement of voluntary collectivization—but
not for a 'left course' of which the chief ingredient was administrative force and brutality. In judging Stalin's policy 'it
was necessary to consider not only *what* he did but also *how* he
did it'.[1] Trotsky did not suggest that the Opposition should not
support the left course, but he stressed more than ever that it
must combine support with severe criticism. He set his face
against the conciliators who regained spirit from the latest
evidence that the breach between Stalin and Bukharin was
unhealed and that Stalin was about to resume the 'drive against
the kulak'. He rejected Kamenev's promptings with scorn and
contempt. He declared that he would do nothing to 'ease' his
own re-entry into the party and that he would not beg his
persecutors to recall him to Moscow. It was up to them to do so
if they wished, but even then he would not cease to attack them
and the capitulators as well.[2]

This was Trotsky's reply not only to Kamenev's suggestions,
but also to Stalin's vague and allusive blandishments. Conciliation between them was out of the question. He responded far
more favourably to Bukharin's appeal. He did this in 'A Frank
Talk with a Well-wishing Party-man', a circular letter of 12
September. The 'well-wishing party-man' was a Bukharinist
who had written to Trotsky inquiring about his attitude towards

[1] See Trotsky's letter of 30 August to Palatnikov, a 'red professor', an economist,
exiled to Aktiubinsk. In a letter to Rakovsky of 13 July Trotsky wrote that Radek
and Preobrazhensky imagined that the Stalinist faction, having moved leftwards,
had only a 'rightist tail' behind it and should be persuaded to rid itself of it. Even if
this were true, Trotsky remarked, it would help little: 'an ape freed of its tail is
not yet a human being.' *The Archives.*

[2] '*Pismo Druzyam*' of 21 October.

the right wing, now the Right Opposition. Trotsky replied that on major issues of industrial and social policy the gulf between them was as wide as ever. But he added that he was ready to co-operate with the right for one purpose, namely, the restoration of inner-party democracy. If Rykov and Bukharin were prepared to work with the left in order to prepare jointly an honestly elected and truly democratic party congress, he favoured an agreement with them.

This statement caused astonishment and even indignation in Trotskyist colonies. Many exiles, not only conciliators, protested against it and reminded Trotsky how often he himself had described coalitions of right and left directed against the centre as unprincipled, pernicious, and responsible for the wrecking of more than one revolution. Had Thermidor not been precisely such a combination of right and left Jacobins nefariously united against Robespierre's centre? Had not the whole conduct of the Opposition so far been determined by its readiness to coalesce, on conditions, with the Stalinists against the Bukharinists, not vice versa? Had Trotsky himself not solemnly restated this principle only quite recently, when he assured the Communist International that the Left Opposition would never enter into any combination with those who opposed Stalinism from the right?

Trotsky replied that he still viewed the Bukharinist right rather than the Stalinist centre as the chief antagonist. He had not proposed to Bukharin any coalition over issues of policy. But he saw no reason why they should not join hands for the one clearly defined purpose of re-establishing inner-party freedom. He was ready to 'negotiate with Bukharin in the same way that duellists parley through their seconds over the rules and regulations by which they will abide'.[1] The left could only wish to pursue its controversy with the right under rules of inner-party democracy; and if this was also what the right wanted, nothing would be more natural than that they should collaborate in order to make those rules prevail.

This plea carried little conviction with Trotsky's followers. They had been so much accustomed to see in Bukharin's faction their chief enemy that they could not contemplate any agreement with it. They had so long and so persistently assailed

[1] See 'Na Zloby Dnya' (no precise date), Trotsky's reply to his critics, in *The Archives*.

PLATE XI

Radio Times Hulton Picture Library

(*a*) Christian Rakovsky, as Soviet envoy at the Genoa Conference (1922)

(*b*) Karl Radek

(*c*) Adolfe Yoffe: committed suicide to protest against Trotsky's expulsion

(*d*) Antonov-Ovseenko, Trotskyist, as chief political commissar of the Red Army

PLATE XII

Trotsky and his family at Alma Ata in 1928

the Stalinists as the two-faced accomplices of the right that they were horrified to think that they themselves might appear as its accomplices. Nor could they accept Trotsky's explanation that he had proposed to the Bukharinists only a technical arrangement, something like the fixing of regulations for a duel. For one thing, this was not a duel but a three-cornered fight, in which any agreement between two sides was automatically directed against the third. For another, inner-party democracy was a political problem *par excellence* with a bearing on all major issues. An alliance of right and left, no matter how limited its purpose, would, if successful, result in the overthrow of the Stalinist faction, and this after the latter had initiated the left course. The left course would be brought to an immediate standstill. The sequel would hang on the uncertain outcome of the contest between right and left. If the right were to win, it would surely proclaim that neo-N.E.P., the danger of which had haunted the Trotskyists. Could they take such a risk? With the country on the brink of economic catastrophe and the peasantry in turmoil, should they expose the party to a convulsion in the course of which the Stalinists might be overthrown but the Bukharinists and the Trotskyists might be unable to resolve their differences democratically, let alone rule jointly? They might thus unwittingly ruin the party, and give anti-Bolshevik forces their opportunity. This would indeed be a classically Thermidorian situation, for it was precisely such a coalition of right and left, both exasperated by the terror, that had brought about Robespierre's downfall. Was not Trotsky now playing with Thermidorian fire—he who had all these years warned others against it?

Trotsky and the Opposition were in an *impasse*. If any chance of self-preservation was left to them, that chance lay in a broad alliance of all anti-Stalinist Bolsheviks. Yet they could hardly hope that even such an alliance would save them. They had reason to fear that its outcome might be the end of the Bolshevik party. In considering for a while the idea of a coalition, both Trotsky and Bukharin were moved by a fleeting reflex of self-defence. Neither, however, could act on this reflex any further. Both factions were more anxious to preserve the party as it was than to preserve themselves; or else they did not see clearly their inexorable dilemma. Undoubtedly, some of the leaders saw it.

Kamenev's account of his meeting with Bukharin contains these grim words: 'Sometimes I say to Yefim: "Is not our situation hopeless? If our nation is crushed we are crushed with it; and, if it extricates itself and Stalin changes course in time, we are still going to be crushed."' Radek, in a letter written to his comrades, described the choice before them as a choice 'between two forms of political suicide'—one which consisted in being cut off from the party, and the other in re-entering the party after having abjured one's convictions.[1]

Bukharin's panicky offer of an alliance and Trotsky's tentative answer had therefore no sequel. The Bukharinists could not but react to their leader's proposal with the same resistance with which the Trotskyists met their leader's reply. They had seen their chief enemies in the Trotskyists and Zinovievists; and their most recent charge against Stalin was that he had become a crypto-Trotskyist (or, as Bukharin put it, that he had adopted Preobrazhensky's ideas). How then could they themselves contemplate a partnership with the Trotskyists? They knew that the latter and the Zinovievists viewed the left course with a sneaking sympathy—Bukharin too must have inferred this from his talk with Kamenev. And if even the banished Trotskyists were frightened of the shock to which a right–left coalition might expose the party, how much more must the Bukharinists have dreaded this prospect—they who had been in and of the ruling group and were still in it. They were dismayed by Stalin's hints that if they misbehaved he would ally himself with Trotsky. They decided that they would not misbehave. They did not even try to carry the struggle against Stalin into the open as the Trotskyists and Zinovievists had done; or, if they did, they found that having robbed the Left Opposition of freedom of expression they had also robbed themselves of it. Bukharin therefore could not follow up his approaches or respond to Trotsky's idea of a 'limited agreement'.

These developments strengthened the Trotskyist conciliators. Three of the most authoritative leaders of the Opposition in exile, Smilga, Serebriakov, and Ivan Smirnov, were now with Radek and Preobrazhensky. It was clear, they argued, that Stalin had not said 'his last word' in July when he appeared to yield to the kulak—the left course was on. Trotsky had im-

[1] The letter dated 16 September is in *The Trotsky Archives*.

plicitly admitted that the Left Opposition could not persist in splendid isolation and that it ought to look for allies; but its natural allies were the Stalinists, not the Bukharinists. This is not to say that the conciliators were happy about the manner in which Stalin dealt with the right opposition. 'Today the régime strikes at Bukharin', Smilga wrote, 'in the same way in which it struck at the Leninist Opposition . . . [the Bukharinists] are being strangled behind the back of the party and the working class.' But 'the Leninist Opposition has no reason to express political sympathy for the right because of this': its watchword was still 'Down with the Right!'[1] This had been Trotsky's watchword in the summer, but hardly in the autumn. The relations between him and the conciliators grew tense and inimical. He was scarcely in touch with Preobrazhensky; and his correspondence with Radek became acrimonious and intermittent. Radek protested against Trotsky's scathing attacks on Zinoviev, Kamenev, and the other capitulators. 'It is ludicrous to think', Radek wrote, 'that they have surrendered only from cowardice. The fact that group after group one day speaks against capitulation and on the next day agrees to capitulate, and that this has happened repeatedly and many times shows that we are confronted here with a clash of principles and not merely with fear of repression.'[2] It was true that the capitulators committed political suicide; but so also did those who had refused to capitulate. There remained only this hope that further shifts within the party and its further evolution towards the left would clear the air and enable the Left Opposition to re-enter the party with dignity.

While he thus excused Zinoviev's and Kamenev's motives, Radek circulated among his comrades a long treatise which he had written in refutation of Trotsky's Permanent Revolution.[3] He did not, however, send it to Trotsky, who received it second-

---

[1] The quotation is from Smilga's *'Platforma Pravovo Kryla VKP (b)'* (23 October 1928) which was a comment on Bukharin's *'Zametki Ekonomista'* which had appeared in *Pravda* on 30 September. (This was Bukharin's only public statement of his objections to the left course.) Smilga was also writing a book on Bukharin and Bukharinism, but it is not known whether he completed it.

[2] See Radek's circular letter to comrades of 16 September.

[3] The text of the treatise *Razvitie i Znachenie Lozunga Proletarskoi Diktatury* (hitherto unpublished) is in *The Trotsky Archives*. In reply to this Trotsky wrote *Permanentnaya Revolutsia*, the most extensive historical-theoretical defence of his conception.

hand—from Moscow. With an ironic reply to Radek Trotsky enclosed Radek's own earlier writings in defence of Trotskyism, saying that there he would find the best rejoinder to his latest arguments.[1] He did not yet suspect Radek of the intention to capitulate. He trusted that Radek's sense of humour and European-Marxist habits of mind would not allow him to go through a 'Byzantine' ritual of recantation. Still fond of the man and admiring him, Trotsky ascribed Radek's behaviour to 'moodiness' and went on defending him and Preobrazhensky against the suspicions of the young irreconcilables.[2]

Even now all Oppositionists, conciliators and irreconcilables alike, still looked to Trotsky as to their undisputed leader. Their feelings for him are best expressed in a protest which no other than Radek sent to the Central Committee in October, when news of a deterioration in Trotsky's health greatly disturbed the exiles:

Trotsky's illness has brought our patience to an end [Radek wrote]. We cannot look on in silence while malaria wastes the strength of a fighter who has served the working class all his life and was the Sword of the October Revolution. If preoccupation with factional interests has extinguished in you all memories of a common revolutionary struggle, let intelligence and plain facts speak. The dangers against which the Soviet Republic is contending are piling up. . . . Only those who do not understand what is needed in order to meet those dangers can remain indifferent towards the slow death of that fighting heart that is Comrade L. D. Trotsky. But those among you —and I am convinced that they are not few—who think with dread of what the next day may bring . . . must say: Enough of this inhuman playing with Comrade Trotsky's health and life![3]

.   .   .   .

Since the summer Trotsky's health had indeed deteriorated. He suffered again from malaria, severe headaches, and the chronic stomach infection which was to trouble him till the end of his days. Reports of his illness brought forth a spate of letters

[1] See Trotsky's letter to Radek of 20 October in *The Archives*.
[2] Even many months later, towards the end of May 1929, in Prinkipo, Trotsky received the first news of Radek's capitulation with the utmost incredulity and wrote: 'Radek has behind him a quarter of a century of revolutionary Marxist work . . . it is doubtful whether he is capable of joining the Stalinists. In any case, he will not be capable of staying with them. For this he is, after all, too much a Marxist and too internationally minded.' *The Archives*.
[3] Quoted from the *Militant*, 1 January 1929.

and telegrams from exiles expressing sympathy with him and protesting to Moscow. Some of the deportees were anxious for more vigorous action in Trotsky's defence and planned a collective hunger strike. Trotsky had some difficulty in dissuading them from so desperate a decision. There was no need—he said in messages to the colonies—to worry greatly about his health which was not so bad as to prevent him working. It was advisable to circulate more widely the protests which the Opposition had already made; but it would be rash to resort to drastic action which might only worsen the lot of those involved.[1]

As the autumn advanced more clouds began to gather over Trotsky's head. In October he ceased to receive letters from friends and followers—only communications from men who were ready to desert the Opposition were still delivered to him. The censorship worked selectively. His own letters and messages failed to reach their destination. He could obtain no reply even to telegrams in which he inquired about Zina's health, which continued to cause him anxiety. He passed the days of the revolution's anniversary in loneliness and apprehension—none of the usual greetings had arrived. Thereafter the ill omens multiplied. A local official, who had secretly sympathized with the Opposition and had kept in touch with Trotsky, was suddenly imprisoned. An Oppositionist who had come all the way from Moscow, had taken a driver's job at Alma Ata, and used to meet Trotsky stealthily at the public baths, and who had, it seems, run the 'secret mail' between Moscow and Alma Ata, vanished without a trace. The household had by now moved back from the *dacha* with its orchards and flower-beds into the dreariness of the town. 'Since the end of October', Sedova wrote to a friend, 'we have received no letters from home. We get no answers to our telegrams. We are under a postal blockade. Things will not stop at this, of course. We are awaiting something worse. . . . There is a severe frost here. The cold in our rooms is agony. Houses here are not built for the cold weather. The price of wood is incredibly high.'

Finally, rumours reached Trotsky from many quarters that he

---

[1] This, for instance, is the text of a telegram to the deportees of Yenisseisk (14 October 1928): 'Categorically object to forms of protest contemplated by yourselves. . . . My illness not immediately dangerous. Please observe common line [of conduct]. Fraternal greetings. Trotsky.' *The Archives.*

would not be left at Alma Ata and that he was presently to be
deported farther away and isolated far more rigorously. At first
he dismissed the rumours. 'I do not expect this to happen—
where on earth could they send me?', he wrote to Elzin on
2 October. He looked forward to a winter of intensive study and
literary work at Alma Ata and, of course, to hunting trips in the
surrounding wilds. But the rumours persisted; and the postal
blockade and other signs indicated that 'something worse' was
indeed about to happen.

This was a strange autumn. On the anniversary of the revolution there resounded from the Red Square in Moscow these
official calls: 'The Danger is on the Right!', 'Strike Against the
Kulak!', 'Curb the N.E.P.-men!', 'Speed up Industrialization!';
and the slogans reverberated throughout the country, penetrating to the remotest backwaters, even to Alma Ata. How long
had not Trotsky sought to persuade the party to adopt this
policy! Only the year before on the same anniversary day, his
followers had descended on the streets of Moscow and Leningrad with the same slogans on their banners. They were dispersed, maltreated, and accused of counter-revolution. There
could be, one might have thought, no greater vindication of the
Opposition than the fact that the ruling group was compelled
to appropriate its ideas. No one who took the mildest interest in
public affairs could fail to notice it. The ferocious attacks on
Trotsky, the 'super-industrializer' and the 'enemy of the muzhik', were still fresh in everyone's mind. Now the dishonesty and
wretchedness of these attacks were exposed and cried to heaven.
Was not Stalin himself turning into a super-industrializer and
enemy of the peasants, many a Bolshevik wondered. Yet this
year as the year before, millions of citizens marched in the
official processions, followed the prescribed routes, and shouted
the prescribed slogans as if nothing unusual had occurred and
as if they had been unable to think, reflect, and act.

Popular apathy allowed Stalin to steal Trotsky's clothes with
impunity. Trotsky still consoled himself with the thought that
Stalin would not be able to wear them, because they would not
fit him. He still expected that as the national crisis deepened the
Stalinist faction alone would not be able to cope with it. The
crisis had indeed deepened. With the peasantry in rebellion and

the towns gripped by fear of hunger, the nation lived in unbearable tension. There was feverish nervousness in the air and a sense of danger and alarm. The party machine sternly marshalled its strength and called on all to be ready for a grim, though as yet undefined, emergency. But it showed no inclination to recall the exiled Oppositionists.

Towards the end of the year Stalin was in a position far stronger than that in which he had been in the summer. He was less afraid of having to contend with two Oppositions simultaneously. The right was cowed and demoralized and was already surrendering. The left was torn by dissensions and paralysed. Stalin watched the disputes between Trotsky, Radek, Preobrazhensky, the irreconcilables, and the Decemists, and concluded that time was on his side. He was still engaged in the preliminaries to his all-out drive for industrialization and collectivization; and already the Trotskyist conciliators felt that they must not stand aside. How much more would they feel this once he had passed from the preliminaries to real action? True, they were not yet in a mood to surrender; but they were steadily approaching that stage; and all that they needed to reach it was time and a little encouragement. Through his agents Stalin encouraged them by every means at his command: he invoked the revolution's supreme interest; he appealed to Bolshevik loyalty; he mixed cajolery with threat; and he intensified the terror against the irreconcilable Trotskyists and the Decemists.[1] In this way he expected to make good his boast, which was premature when he made it, that he had the left Opposition 'in his pocket'. He did, in fact, need the left's assistance for his new policy. But he was bent on getting that assistance, not by allying himself with the left, but by splitting it, taming a large section of it, and turning it against Trotsky. He hoped to inflict on Trotsky a defeat far more harrowing than all the blows he had aimed at him so far.

Yet, for all his strength, Stalin could not be sure that he would be able to achieve what he had set out to achieve. He was about to embark upon a gigantic enterprise such as no ruler had ever undertaken: he was to expropriate at a stroke twenty-odd

---

[1] In the autumn the police supervision over the deportees was suddenly tightened and many deportees were imprisoned. V. Smirnov was sent to jail because he was five minutes late in reporting to the local G.P.U. for a routine check. Butov, one of Trotsky's secretaries, died in prison after a hunger strike lasting fifty days.

million farmers and drive them and their families into collective farms; he was about to force urban Russia into an industrial drive in which the horrors of primitive capitalist accumulation were to be reproduced on an immense scale and condensed within a very short time. He could not know how the nation would take it, what despair, anger, violence, and revolt the upheaval might not breed; to what pass he himself might not be driven; and whether his adversaries might not then try and seize their opportunity. If they were to seize it, they were sure to look to Trotsky for leadership. Even from Alma Ata Trotsky's ideas and his personality, surrounded by the halo of heroic martyrdom, fascinated the Bolshevik *élite*. Despite all the confusion and dejection among the exiles, Trotskyism was gaining new followers in the party cells. The G.P.U. had to deal with so many of them that towards the end of 1928 between 6,000 and 8,000 Left Oppositionists were imprisoned and deported, whereas at the beginning of the year the strength of both Trotskyists and Zinovievists was estimated at between 4,000 and 5,000 only. Kamenev was not alone in thinking that in an emergency the party would have to 'send a special train' for Trotsky. There was much heart-searching among capitulators and even among Stalinists, some of whom wondered whether, if the left course was justified, Trotsky had not been right all along; they were therefore sick of the calumny and brutality with which he had been treated. Stalin knew that, for nearly every one of the six or eight thousand Oppositionists who rather than renounce their views had chosen prison and exile, there were one or two capitulators who at heart agreed with their less pliable comrades, and one or two doubters or 'conciliators' (*dvurushniki*, the double-faced, as he called them) in his own faction. They all lay low now; but would they not rise against him when the tide had turned?

Nor could Stalin take lightly the threat of an alliance between Trotsky and Bukharin. Although it had not materialized this time, the threat remained in being as long as Trotsky was the undisputed chief of the Left Opposition and could be brought back by a 'special train'. Stalin therefore redoubled his efforts to break the spirit of the Opposition. His agents held out every possible hope and temptation to Radek, Preobrazhensky, and their friends, promising rehabilitation, invoking common purposes, and speaking of the great, fruitful, and honourable work they could still perform for the party and for socialism. All these efforts, however, met with a formidable obstacle in the influence which Trotsky exercised from Alma Ata and which had so far prevented the Opposition in exile from disintegrating. Stalin was determined to remove this obstacle from his path.

But how was he to do it? He still shrank from sending the killer; he did not yet dare even to throw his enemy into jail. The odium would have been too heavy, because, despite all that had happened, Trotsky's part in the revolution was still too fresh and vivid in the nation's mind. He therefore planned to expel Trotsky from Russia. He knew that even this would shock; and he carefully prepared public opinion. First, he put out rumours about the new banishment; next he ordered the rumours to be denied; and, finally, he gave them fresh currency. In this way he blunted public sensitivity. Only after rumour, denial, and recurrent rumour had made the thought of Trotsky's expulsion from the U.S.S.R. familiar and therefore less shocking could Stalin carry out his intention.

· · · · · · · · · ·

Amid all the uncertainties about his future, Trotsky posed anew the great and baffling question: 'Whither is the revolution going?' The Soviet Union was now in the grey interval between two epochs—between N.E.P. and the Stalinist 'second revolution'.[1] The shape of things to come was blurred; at best, it could be seen only through a glass, darkly. Trotsky was becoming aware that some of the ideas he had expounded in recent years were on the point of being surpassed by events. He tried to go beyond these ideas, but their pull on him was strong. He attempted to outline new prospects; but habits of mind, formed during N.E.P. and suited to its realities, and historical memories of the French Revolution kept intruding upon his vision.

He realized, for instance, that his conception of the Soviet Thermidor had become untenable. It had become absurd to maintain that Bukharin and Rykov were still *the* defenders of

---

[1] I first used the term 'second revolution' in *Stalin, a Political Biography*, pp. 294 ff., and I have been criticized for using it. Collectivization and industrialization, the critics say, do not amount to a revolution. But if a change in property relations resulting from the dispossession at a stroke of twenty-odd million smallholders is not an economic and social revolution, what is?

private property, that Stalin was their will-less helpmeet, and that they were bound to be the ultimate beneficiaries of his policy. Trotsky therefore virtually abandoned his conception of the Soviet Thermidor.[1] In a 'Letter to Friends', written in October 1928,[2] one of his most remarkable essays of the Alma Ata period (although it is written in the Opposition's peculiar phraseology), he argued that Bukharin and the Bukharinists were Thermidorians *manqués* who had lacked the courage to act on their convictions. He gave this ironical and vivid description of their behaviour: 'Bukharin has gone farther than any of the leaders of the right [in promoting the interests of the kulak and of the N.E.P.-man], while Rykov and Tomsky have watched him from a safe distance. But every time Bukharin steps into the cold water [of Thermidor] he shivers, shudders, and jumps out; and Tomsky and Rykov run to the bushes for shelter.' Consequently, the kulak, the N.E.P.-man, and the conservative bureaucrat, disillusioned with the leaders of the Bolshevik right, were inclined to look for effective leadership elsewhere, notably to the army. With the French precedents in mind, Trotsky spoke about the closeness of the 'Bonapartist danger', implying that the Russian Revolution might skip Thermidor and pass directly from the Bolshevik to the Bonapartist phase.

The Bonapartist danger, he went on, could assume two different forms: it could either materialize as a classical military *coup d'état*, a Russian 18th Brumaire; or it could take the shape of Stalin's personal rule. He considered it probable that the army, appealing directly to the property-owning peasantry and backed by it, would attempt to overthrow Stalin and to put an end to the Bolshevik régime at large. It was to him a secondary question which of the army leaders might place himself at the head of the movement: in favourable conditions even mediocrities like Voroshilov or Budienny might take the initiative and succeed. (Trotsky quoted a proverb of which, he said, Stalin was fond: *Iz gryazi delayut Knyazia*—a Prince can be made out of filth.) The conditions favouring a *coup* were there: the peasantry felt nothing but hostility towards the party led by Stalin, and the working class was disgruntled and listless. A military

---

[1] He did, however, take it up again and defend it, after his exile to Turkey, but only to 'revise it' once again a few years later.

[2] *'Pismo Druzyam'* of 21 October in *The Archives*.

dictatorship, if it came into being, would therefore be broadly based. It would be counter-revolutionary in its character and consequences. It would seek to guarantee security, stability, and expansion to the private sector of the economy. It would dismantle or cripple the socialist sector. It would bring about the restoration of capitalism. Confronted with such a danger, Trotsky concluded, all Bolsheviks eager to defend socialism would have to unite; and the Left Opposition would have to co-operate with Stalin and his faction, because Stalin spoke not for the men of property, but for the 'proletarian upstart' and had so far avoided an open breach with the working class.

It was possible, on the other hand, that Stalin himself would become the Soviet Bonaparte. This would create a different situation for the country and the Opposition. Stalin could exercise his personal rule only through the party machine, not through the army. His dictatorship would not immediately have the counter-revolutionary consequences that would follow a military *coup*. But it would be based very narrowly; and it would be utterly insecure. Stalin would find himself in chronic conflict with all classes of society; he would try to overpower now this class and now that and play them against one another. He would have to struggle continuously in order to keep in subordination the party machine, the state bureaucracy, and the army; and he would rule in incessant and unrelievable fear of defiance from either of them. He would suppress all spontaneous social and political activity and all freedom of expression. In such conditions there could hardly be room for any 'united front' between the Left Opposition and the Stalinists—there would be only struggle beyond conciliation.

In this context Trotsky analysed succinctly and with powerful foresight the social background, the mechanics, the shape and the outlook of Stalin's rule as it was to evolve over the next twenty years. He portrayed in advance the General Secretary transformed into the fully fledged totalitarian dictator. However, having done this, he himself viewed the portrait rather incredulously; he thought that, on balance, the danger of a purely military dictatorship was more real. It seemed to him far more probable that Voroshilov, Budienny, or some other general would lead the army against Stalin, and that Trotskyists and Stalinists would then fight together 'on the same side of the barricade'.

He added that on the long historical view it might matter little which of them, Stalin or Voroshilov, 'rode the white horse' and which of them was trampled underfoot. In the short run, however, the difference was important—it was the difference between an open and immediate triumph of the anti-socialist forces (under a military dictator) and a far more complex, confused, and protracted development (under Stalin). In the long run, he held, Stalin's dictatorship too would be detrimental to socialism; and he saw the triumphant kulak and N.E.P.-man at the end even of Stalin's road. 'The film of revolution is running backwards, and Stalin's part in it is that of Kerensky in reverse.' Kerenskyism epitomized Russia's transition from capitalism to Bolshevism; and victorious Stalinism could mark only the return passage.

It is all too easy to see in retrospect the fallacies of this reasoning; and it is even easier to miss the core of truth they contained. That Trotsky could imagine Voroshilov or Budienny acting the part of Bonaparte must appear almost absurd. Out of this 'filth' no Prince was to be made. Yet as a political analyst Trotsky had to keep an eye on potentialities as well as actualities; and the potentiality of a military coup was there. Although it did not become an actuality, at least in the next thirty years, the threat repeatedly haunted first Stalin and then his successors; witness Stalin's conflicts with Tukhachevsky and other generals in 1937 and with Zhukov in 1946 and Khrushchev's clash with Zhukov in 1957. Here Trotsky touched a trend latent in Soviet politics; but he evidently overrated its strength. He also overrated the force of what was, in Marxist theory, the social impulse behind that trend: the determination and the power of the peasantry to defend its property, and its capacity to assert itself, through the army, against the town. Trotsky himself had written in 1906 that 'the history of capitalism is the history of the subordination of the country to the town'; and in this context he had analysed the amorphousness and the political helplessness of the Russian peasantry under the old régime.[1] That subordination of country to town characterizes *a fortiori* the history of the Soviet Union. Stalin's hammer blows were just about to descend upon private farming with a terrific impact and to crush the peasantry. They could not prevent the peasants from resisting collectivization.

[1] See *The Prophet Armed*, pp. 156 ff.

That resistance, shapeless, scattered, and protracted, was to result in the chronic inefficiency and backwardness of collectivized farming; but it could not focus itself into any effective political action on the national scale. And in the defeat of the property-loving muzhik lay the secret of the failures of the military candidates to the post of the Soviet Bonaparte.

The helplessness and dumbness of the peasantry were part and parcel of the political lethargy of the post-revolutionary society at large; and this formed the background to the extraordinary activity and seeming omnipotence of the ruling bureaucracy. Trotsky repeatedly grappled with this aspect of the situation; and repeatedly his mind ran away from it. Krupskaya once made the remark, which in all probability she had picked up from Lenin, that Trotsky was inclined to underrate the apathy of the masses.[1] In this Trotsky was true to himself and his character as a revolutionary. The revolutionary is in his element when society is in action, when it unfolds all its energies, and when all social classes pursue their aspirations with the maximum of vigour and *élan*. Then his perception is at its most sensitive, his understanding at its acutest, and his eye at its quickest and sharpest. But let society be overcome by torpor and let its various classes fall into a coma, and the great revolutionary theorist, be he Trotsky or even Marx, loses something of his vision and penetration. This condition of society is most uncongenial to him and he cannot intellectually accommodate himself to it. Hence Trotsky's errors of judgement. Even when he made the utmost allowance for the post-revolutionary weariness of the masses he still shrank from fathoming its full depth. Thinking ahead, he still envisaged all social classes and groups —kulaks as well as workers and army leaders as well as the various Bolshevik groupings—in action and motion, in a state of self-reliance and animation, ready to jump at one another and to fight their titanic battles. His thought was baffled at the sight of Titans drowsy and indolent whom a bureaucracy could tame and tie hand and foot.

Because ultimately he identified the process of revolution with the social awareness and activity of the toiling masses, the evident absence of that awareness and activity led him to conclude that, with Stalinism victorious, 'the film of the revolution was

[1] N. Krupskaya, '*K Voprosu ob Urokakh Oktyabrya*' in *Za Leninizm*, p. 155.

running backwards', and that Stalin's part in it was that of
Kerensky in reverse. Here again the fallacy is obvious; but the
core of truth in it should not be overlooked. The film was not
running as the precursors and the makers of the revolution had
expected: it was moving partly in a different direction—but not
backwards. Stalin's role in it was not that of Kerensky in reverse.
The film is still on; and it may still be too early to pass final
judgement on it. In theory it may yet be possible for it to end
in a setback for the revolution as grave as that which earlier
great revolutions, the French and the English, had suffered. But
this possibility appears to be extremely remote. When Trotsky
wrote that the film was running backwards he meant that it was
moving towards the restoration of capitalism. Actually it moved
towards planned economy, industrial expansion, and mass
education; and these, despite all bureaucratic distortion and
debasement, Trotsky himself recognized to be essential prerequisites for socialism, the *sine qua non* for the ultimate fulfilment
of the revolution's promise. The prerequisites were admittedly
not the fulfilment; and the Soviet Union of the 1950's had
enough reasons to look back upon the record of Stalinism, or
at least upon some of its facets, with sorely disillusioned eyes.
But it did not see the triumphant kulak and N.E.P.-man at the
end of Stalin's road.[1]

Was Stalin's record one of Bonapartism? Trotsky did not use
the term in the accepted meaning as signifying merely 'government by the sword' and personal rule. The wider Marxist
definition of Bonapartism is that of a dictatorship exercised by
the state machine or the bureaucracy at large, of which military
autocracy is only one particular form. What, in the Marxist
view, is essential to Bonapartism is that the State or the Executive should acquire *political* independence of all social classes and
establish its absolute supremacy over society. In this sense
Stalin's rule had, of course, much in common with Bonapartism.
Yet, the equation offers only a very general and vague clue to
the understanding of the phenomenon in all its complexity and
contradictoriness. Stalin exercised his rule not so much through
an 'independent' state machine as through the 'independent'

---

[1] Eastern Europe (Hungary, Poland, and Eastern Germany), however, found
itself almost on the brink of bourgeois restoration at the end of the Stalin era; and
only Soviet armed power (or its threat) stopped it there.

party machine through which he also controlled the state. The difference was of great consequence to the course of the revolution and the political climate of the Soviet Union. The party machine considered itself to be the only authorized guardian and interpreter of the Bolshevik idea and tradition. Its rule therefore meant that the Bolshevik idea and tradition remained, through all successive pragmatic and ecclesiastical re-formulations, the ruling idea and the dominant tradition of the Soviet Union. This was possible only because the idea and the tradition were firmly anchored in the social structure of the Soviet Union, primarily in the nationalized urban economy. If any partial parallel to this state of affairs were to be drawn from the French Revolution, it would have to be an imaginary one: we would have to imagine what revolutionary France would have looked like if the Thermidorians had never overthrown Robespierre, and if he had ruled France, in the name of a crippled and docile Jacobin party, throughout all those years that the historian now describes as the eras of the Directory, the Consulate, and the Empire—in a word, what France would have looked like if no Napoleon had ever come to the fore and if the revolution had run its full course under the banner of Jacobinism.[1]

We have seen that the rule of the party machine had in fact been initiated at the close of the Lenin era. It had been inherent in the dominance of the single party which Lenin himself saw as being essentially the dominance of the Bolshevik Old Guard. Lenin's government in his last years might therefore be described, in accordance with Trotsky's use of the term, as 'Bonapartist', although it lacked the feature which formed the true consummation of Bonapartism, namely, personal rule. Thus, when in 1928 Trotsky spoke about the danger of Bonapartism he saw a phase of development which had been largely accomplished many years earlier as still looming ahead. Since Lenin's day the despotism of the party machine had, of course, become

---

[1] Auguste Blanqui described Robespierre as *un Napoléon prématuré* or *un Napoléon avorté* while Madame de Staël said of the First Consul: *c'est un Robespierre à cheval.* (Daniel Guérin in *La Lutte de classes sous la Première République*, vol. ii, pp. 301–4, devotes some interesting passages to this subject.) However, the *Robespierre à cheval* had social forces behind him different from those behind the leader of the Jacobins: his mainstay was the army, not the *petite bourgeoisie*, and he was not constrained by Jacobin ideology. Of Robespierre Michelet said: 'Il eut le cœur moins roi que prêtre.' Napoleon was only King not Priest. Stalin was both Pope and Caesar.

increasingly aggressive and brutal. But the specific content of the stormy political history of these years, from 1921 till 1929, consisted not merely and not so much in this as in the transformation of the rule of a single party into the rule of a single faction. This was the only form in which the political monopoly of Bolshevism could survive and become consolidated. In the opening pages of this volume we found the single-party system to be a contradiction in terms. The various Bolshevik factions, groups, and schools of thought formed something like a shadowy multi-party system within the single party. The logic of the single-party system implicitly required that they be eliminated. Stalin spoke with the voice of that logic when he declared that the Bolshevik party must be monolithic or it would not be Bolshevik. (Up to a point, of course, the party ceased to be Bolshevik as it was becoming monolithic.)

The logic of the single-party system might not have asserted itself as strongly as it did, it might never have become as ruthless as it was and its implication might never have become explicit, or the system might even have been undone by the growth of a workers' democracy, if the whole history of the Soviet Union, encircled and isolated in its age-old poverty and backwardness, had not been an almost uninterrupted sequence of calamities, emergencies, and crises threatening the nation's very existence. Almost every emergency and crisis posed all major issues of national policy on the knife's edge, set the Bolshevik factions and groupings at loggerheads, and gave to their struggles that indescribable vehemence and intensity which led to the substitution of the rule of a single faction for that of the single party. At the point our narrative has reached, in the show-down between the Stalinists and the Bukharinists, this process was coming to a close. What still lay ahead was the quasi-Bonapartist consummation: the substitution, in the early 1930's, of the rule of the single leader for that of a single faction. It was this consummation —Stalin's autocracy—that Trotsky clearly foreshadowed, however he erred in other respects.

Even now, however, Trotsky did not perceive the ascendancy of Stalinism as an inevitable result of the Bolshevik monopoly of power. On the contrary, he saw it as the virtual end of Bolshevik government. Thus, while Stalin presented the undivided rule of his own faction as the consequence and final affirmation of the rule of the single party, Trotsky viewed it as a negation. In truth, the Bolshevik monopoly of power, as established by Lenin and Trotsky, found in Stalin's monopoly both its affirmation and its negation; and each of the two antagonists now dwelt on a different aspect of the problem. We have traced the transitions through which the rule of the single party had become the rule of the single faction and through which Leninism had given place to Stalinism. We have seen that the things that had been implicit in the opening phase of this evolution became explicit and found an extreme or exaggerated expression in the closing phase. To this extent Stalin dealt in realities when he claimed that in his conduct of party affairs he followed the line set by Lenin. But Trotsky's emphatic denial of this was no less strongly based on realities. The rule of the single faction was indeed an abuse as well as a consequence of the rule of the single party. Trotsky, and following him one Bolshevik leader after another, protested that when they had, under Lenin, established the Bolshevik political monopoly they had sought to combine it with a workers' democracy; and that, far from imposing any monolithic discipline on the party itself, they had taken the party's inner freedom for granted and had indeed guaranteed it. Only the blind and the deaf could be unaware of the contrast between Stalinism and Leninism. The contrast showed itself in the field of ideas and in the moral and intellectual climate of Bolshevism even more strongly than in matters of organization and discipline. Here indeed the film of revolution ran backwards, at least in the sense that Stalinism represented an amalgamation of Marxism with all that was primitive and archaically semi-Asiatic in Russia: with the illiteracy and barbarism of the muzhik on the one hand, and the absolutist traditions of the old ruling groups on the other. Against this Trotsky stood for undiluted classical Marxism, in all its intellectual and moral strength and also in all its political weakness—a weakness which resulted from its own incompatibility with Russian backwardness and from the failures of socialism in the West. In banishing Trotsky, Stalin banished classical Marxism from Russia.

Yet, such were the paradoxical fortunes of the two antagonists, that just when Trotsky was being ejected from his country Stalin set out to uproot, in his own barbaric manner, that Russian backwardness and barbarism which had as if regurgitated classical Marxism, and the Stalinist bureaucracy was about to put into effect Trotsky's programme of primitive socialist accumulation. Trotsky was the authentic inspirer and prompter of the second revolution of which Stalin was to be the practical manager in the coming decade. It would be futile to speculate how Trotsky might have directed that revolution, whether he would have succeeded in carrying out Russia's industrialization at a comparable pace and scale without condemning the mass of the Soviet people to the privation, misery, and oppression they suffered under Stalin, or whether he would have been able to bring the muzhik by persuasion to collective farming rather than to coerce him into it. These questions cannot be answered; and the historian has more than enough work in analysing events and situations as they were, without trying to ponder events and situations that might have been. As things were, the political evolution of the 1920's predetermined the manner in which Russia's social transformation was to be accomplished in the 1930's. That evolution led to autocracy and monolithic discipline and consequently to *forcible* industrialization and collectivization. The political instruments that would be needed for primitive socialist accumulation had been forged throughout the 1920's; and they were now ready for use. They had been forged not in any deliberate and conscious preparation for the task ahead but rather in the unpremeditated course of the inner-party struggles by which the Bolshevik monopoly of power had become the Stalinist monopoly. However, if autocracy and monolithic discipline formed, as the Marxist would say, the political superstructure of primitive socialist accumulation, they also derived from this a measure of self-justification. Stalin's adherents could argue that without autocracy and monolithic discipline that accumulation, on the scale on which he carried it out, could not be undertaken. To put it plainly, from the long contests of the Bolshevik factions there had emerged Stalin's 'firm leadership' for which he may have striven for its own sake. Once he wielded it, he employed it to industrialize the Soviet Union, to collectivize farming, and to transform the whole outlook of the nation; and then he pointed to the use he was making of his 'firm leadership' in order to vindicate it.

Trotsky repudiated Stalin's self-vindicatory claims. He continued to denounce his adversary as a Bonapartist usurper. He was to acknowledge the 'positive and progressive' aspects of Stalin's second revolution and to see them as the realization of parts of his own programme. He had, we remember, already compared his and the Opposition's fate with that of the Communards of Paris, who although they failed to conquer as proletarian revolutionaries in 1871 had nevertheless barred the way to a monarchist restoration. This had been their victory in defeat. The great transformation of the Soviet Union in the 1930's was Trotsky's victory in defeat. But the Communards had not been reconciled to the Third Republic, the *bourgeois* republic which might never have prevailed without them. They remained its enemies. Similarly, Trotsky was for ever to remain unreconciled to the *bureaucratic* second revolution; and against it he was to call for the self-assertion of the working classes in a workers' state and for freedom of thought in socialism. In doing this he was condemned to political solitude, because all too many of his closest associates allowed themselves, partly from frustration and weariness and partly from conviction, to be captivated or bribed by Stalin's second revolution. The Opposition in exile was on the point of virtual self-liquidation.

Was Trotsky then in conflict with his time? Was he fighting a hopeless battle 'against history'? Nietzsche tells us:

If you want a biography, do not look for one with the legend: 'Mr. So-and-So and his times', but for one in which the title page might be inscribed 'A fighter against his time'. . . . Were history nothing more than an 'all embracing system of passion and error' man would have to read it as Goethe wished *Werther* to be read—just as if its moral were 'Be a man and follow me *not!*' But, fortunately, history also keeps alive for us the memory of the great 'fighters against history', that is against the blind power of the actual . . . and it glorifies the true historical nature in men who troubled themselves very little about the 'Thus It Is', in order that they might follow a 'Thus It Must Be' with greater joy and greater pride. Not to drag their generation to the grave, but to found a new one—that is the motive that ever drives them onwards. . . .

These are excellent words despite their underlying subjectivist romanticism. Trotsky was indeed a 'fighter against his time', though not in the Nietzschean sense. As a Marxist he was greatly concerned with the 'Thus It Is' and was aware that the 'Thus

It Must Be' is the child of the 'Thus It Is'. But he refused to bow to 'the blind power of the actual' and to surrender the 'Thus It Must Be' to the 'Thus It Is'.

He fought against his time not as the Quixote or the Nietzschean Superman does but as the pioneers do— not in the name of the past but in that of the future. To be sure, as we scrutinize the face of any great pioneer we may detect in it a quixotic trait; but the pioneer is not a Quixote or a Utopian. Very few men in history have been in such triumphant harmony with their time as Trotsky was in 1917 and after; and so it was not because of any inherent estrangement from the realities of his generation that he then came into conflict with his time. The precursor's character and temperament led him into it. He had, in 1905, been the forerunner of 1917 and of the Soviets; he had been second to none as the leader of the Soviets in 1917; he had been the prompter of planned economy and industrialization since the early 1920's; and he was to remain the great, though not unerring harbinger of some future reawakening of the revolutionary peoples (—to that political reawakening the urge to transcend Stalinism which took hold of the Soviet Union in the years 1953–6 was an important pointer; still faint yet sure). He fought 'against history' in the name of history itself; and against its accomplished facts, which all too often were facts of oppression, he held out the better, the liberating accomplishments of which one day it would be capable.

.   .   .   .

At the beginning of December Trotsky protested to Kalinin and Menzhinsky against the 'postal blockade' under which he was held. He waited a fortnight for the answer. On 16 December a high official of the G.P.U. arrived from Moscow and presented him with an 'ultimatum': he must cease at once his 'counter-revolutionary activity' or else he would be 'completely isolated from political life' and 'forced to change his place of residence'. On the same day Trotsky replied with a defiant letter to the leaders of the party and of the International:

To demand from me that I renounce my political activity is to demand that I abjure the struggle which I have been conducting in the interests of the international working class, a struggle in which I have been ceaselessly engaged for thirty-two years, during the whole of my conscious life. . . . Only a bureaucracy corrupt to its roots can demand such a renunciation. Only contemptible renegades can give such a promise. I have nothing to add to these words!'[1]

A month of sleepless suspense followed at Alma Ata. The G.P.U. envoy did not return to Moscow, but waited on the spot for further orders. These still depended on the Politbureau's decision; and the Politbureau had not yet made up its mind. When Stalin urged it to sanction the expulsion order, Bukharin, Rykov, and Tomsky vehemently objected; and Bukharin, remorseful for what he had done to Trotsky and ever more dreading the 'new Genghiz Khan', screamed, wept, and sobbed at the session. But the majority voted as Stalin wished it to vote; and on 20 January 1929—it was a full year now since Trotsky had been deported from Moscow—armed guards surrounded and occupied the house at Alma Ata; and the G.P.U. official presented Trotsky with the new order of deportation, this time 'from the entire territory of the U.S.S.R.'. 'The decision of the G.P.U.', Trotsky wrote on the receipt, 'criminal in substance and illegal in form, was communicated to me on 20 January 1929.'[2]

Once again there followed tragi-comic scenes similar to those that had attended his arrest in Moscow. His jailers were embarrassed by their orders, and went in awe, as it were, of their charge; worrying because they did not know whither they were to take him, they made anxious inquiries of his family and showed him furtively their solicitude and friendliness. But their orders were harsh: they were to disarm him, to carry him off within twenty-four hours, and to tell him that only *en route* would he receive a message indicating whither he was being deported.

At dawn on 22 January the prisoner, his family, and a strong escort drove from Alma Ata towards Frunze through mountainous desert and the pass of Kurday. They had driven by the same road through a snow blizzard this time last year. The present journey was far worse. This was a winter memorable for its severity, perhaps the cruellest winter for a century. 'The powerful tractor which was to tow us over the pass got stuck and almost disappeared in the snow-drifts, together with the seven motor-cars behind it. Seven men and a good many horses were frozen to death. . . . We had to change to sleighs. It took us more than seven hours to advance about thirty kilometres.'[3]

---

[1] *The Archives.*   [2] Ibid.   [3] *Moya Zhizn*, vol. ii, p. 314.

At Frunze, Trotsky and his family were put on a special train bound for European Russia. Under way the message came through that he was being deported to Constantinople. He at once protested to Moscow. The government, he declared, had no right to banish him abroad without his consent. Constantinople had been an assembly place for the remnants of Wrangel's army who had come there from the Crimea. Did the Politbureau dare expose him to the vengeance of the White Guards? Could they not at least obtain for him an entry permit to Germany or another country? He demanded to be allowed to see those members of his family who lived in Moscow. This last demand was granted: Sergei and Lyova's wife were brought from Moscow and joined the deportees on the train. Once again Trotsky refused to proceed to Constantinople. The G.P.U. envoy, who accompanied him on the journey, forwarded his protests and waited for instructions. Meantime, the train was diverted from its route and stopped on a side-line 'near a dead little station'.

There it sinks into a coma between two thin stretches of woods. Day after day passes. More and more empty tins are lying by the side of the train. Crows and magpies gather for the feast in larger and larger flocks. Wasteland . . . solitude . . . the fox has laid his stealthy tracks to the very train. The engine, one carriage hitched to it, makes daily trips to a larger station to fetch our midday meal and newspapers. Influenza has invaded our compartments. We re-read Anatole France and Klyuchevsky's *History*. . . . The cold is 53 degrees below zero. Our engine keeps rolling back and forth . . . to avoid freezing . . . we do not even know where we are.[1]

Thus twelve days and twelve nights passed during which no one was allowed to leave the train. The newspapers brought the only echoes from the world—they were full of the most violent and threatening invective against Trotskyism and of reports about the discovery of a new 'Trotskyist centre' and arrests of hundreds of Oppositionists.[2]

After twelve days the journey was resumed. The train went full steam ahead southward, through familiar Ukrainian steppe. Since the German government had, as Moscow claimed, refused

---

[1] *Moya Zhizn*, vol. ii, p. 315.
[2] Among those imprisoned was Voronsky, editor of *Krasnaya Nov*, Budu Mdivani, and several of the Georgian Bolsheviks who had opposed Stalin since 1921, and 140 Moscow Oppositionists who had circulated Trotsky's 'Letter to Friends' quoted above.

to grant Trotsky an entry permit, it was, after all, at Constantinople that he was to be cast out. Sergei, anxious to continue his academic course, and Lyova's wife, returned to Moscow hoping for the family's early reunion abroad. The parents embraced them with forebodings; but uncertain of their own future they did not dare to ask them to share exile. They were never to see them again.

From this train, through the darkness of night, Trotsky saw Russia for the last time. The train ran through the streets and the harbour of Odessa, the city of his childhood and his first ambitions and dreams of the world. In his memories there always stood out the old Tsarist governor of Odessa who had exercised 'absolute power with an uncurbed temper' and who 'standing in his carriage, fully erect, shouted curses in his hoarse voice across the street, shaking his fist'. Another cursing and hoarse voice and another shaking fist—or was it the same?—now pursued the man in his fiftieth year through the streets of his childhood. Once the sight of the satrap made him shrink, 'adjust the school bag and hurry home'. Now the prison-train hurried through the harbour where he was to embark on a boat which would take him to the unknown; and he could only reflect on the incongruity of his fate. The pier in the harbour was densely surrounded by troops which had only four years earlier been under his orders. As if to mock him, the empty ship waiting for him bore Lenin's patronymic—*Ilyich*! She left harbour precipitately in the dead of night and in a gale. Even the Black Sea was frozen that year; and an ice-breaker had to force a passage to a distance of about sixty miles. As the *Ilyich* lifted anchor and Trotsky looked back at the receding shore, he must have felt as if the whole country he was leaving behind had frozen into a desert and as if the revolution itself had become congealed.

There was no power on earth, no human ice-breaker, to cut open a return passage.

VOLUME III

THE PROPHET OUTCAST

1929–1940

Trotsky in Mexico, 1940. On one of his last outings

PREFACE

THIS volume concludes my trilogy about Trotsky and relates the catastrophic *dénouement* of his drama. At the *dénouement*, the protagonist of a tragedy is usually more acted upon than acting. Yet Trotsky remained Stalin's active and fighting antipode to the end, his sole vocal antagonist. Throughout these twelve years, from 1929 to 1940, no voice could be raised against Stalin in the U.S.S.R.; and not even an echo could be heard of the earlier intense struggles, except in the grovelling confessions of guilt to which so many of Stalin's adversaries had been reduced. Consequently, Trotsky appeared to stand quite alone against Stalin's autocracy. It was as if a huge historic conflict had become compressed into a controversy and feud between two men. The biographer has had to show how this had come about and to delve into the complex circumstances and relationships which, while enabling Stalin to 'strut about in the hero's garb', made Trotsky into the symbol and sole mouthpiece of opposition to Stalinism.

Together, therefore, with the facts of Trotsky's life I have had to narrate the tremendous social and political events of the period: the turmoil of industrialization and collectivization in the U.S.S.R. and the Great Purges; the collapse of the German and European labour movements under the onslaught of Nazism; and the outbreak of the Second World War. Each of these events affected Trotsky's fortunes; and over each he took his stand against Stalin. I have had to go over the major controversies of the time; for in Trotsky's life the ideological debate is as important as the battle scene is in Shakespearian tragedy: through it the protagonist's character reveals itself, while he is moving towards catastrophe.

More than ever before I dwell in this volume on my chief character's private life, and especially on the fate of his family. Again and again readers will have to transfer their attention from the political narrative to what common parlance insists on describing as the 'human story' (as though public affairs were not the most human of all our preoccupations; and as if politics were not a human activity *par excellence*). At this stage Trotsky's family life is inseparable from his political fortunes: it gives a new dimension to his struggle; and it adds sombre depth to his drama. The strange and moving tale is told here for the first time on the basis of Trotsky's intimate correspondence with his wife and children, a correspondence to which I have been privileged to obtain unrestricted access. (For this I am indebted to the generosity of the late Natalya Sedova, who two years before her death asked the Librarians of Harvard University to open to me the so-called sealed section of her husband's Archives, the section that by his will was to remain closed till the year 1980.)

.   .   .   .

I would like to comment briefly on the political context in which I have produced this biography. When I started working on it, at the end of 1949, official Moscow was celebrating Stalin's seventieth birthday with a servility unparalleled in modern history, and Trotsky's name seemed covered for ever by heavy calumny and oblivion. I had published *The Prophet Armed* and was trying to complete the first draft of what is now *The Prophet Unarmed* and *The Prophet Outcast* when, in the latter part of 1956, the consequences of the Twentieth Congress of the Soviet Communist Party, the October upheaval in Poland, and the fighting in Hungary compelled me to interrupt this work and turn my whole attention to current affairs. In Budapest raging crowds had pulled down Stalin's statues while in Moscow the desecration of the idol was still being carried out stealthily and was treated by the ruling group as their family secret. 'We cannot let this matter go out of the Party, especially to the Press,' Khrushchev warned his audience at the Twentieth Congress. 'We should not wash our dirty linen before the eyes [of our enemies].' 'The washing of the dirty linen', I then commented, 'can hardly be carried on behind the back of the Soviet people much longer. It will presently have to be done in front of them and in broad daylight. It is, after all, in their sweat and blood that the "dirty linen" was soaked. And the washing, which will take a long time, will perhaps be brought to an end by hands other than those that have begun it—by younger and cleaner hands.'

The Prophet Outcast is appearing after some washing of the 'dirty linen' has already been done in public, and after Stalin's mummy has been evicted from the Red Square Mausoleum. A perceptive Western cartoonist reacted to this last event with a drawing of the Mausoleum in which Trotsky could be seen placed in the crypt just vacated, and next to Lenin. The cartoonist expressed an idea which probably occurred to many people in the U.S.S.R. (although it is to be hoped that the 'rehabilitation' of Trotsky, when it comes, will be carried out in a manner free from cult, ritual, and primitive magic). Meanwhile, Khrushchev and his friends are still exerting themselves to keep in force the Stalinist anathema on Trotsky; and in the controversy between Khrushchev and Mao Tse-tung each side accuses the other of Trotskyism, as if each were bent on providing at least negative evidence of the vitality of the issues raised by Trotsky and of his ideas.

All these events have sustained my conviction of the topicality as well as the historical importance of my theme. But—*pace* some of my critics—they have not significantly affected either my approach or even the design of my work. True, this biography has grown in scale beyond all my original plans: I have produced three volumes instead of one or two. However, in doing so I obeyed solely—and at first reluctantly—the literary logic of the work and the logic of my research, which was unexpectedly growing in scope and depth. The biographical material struggled under my hands, as it were, for the shape and the proportions proper to it, and it imposed its requirements on me. (I know that what I am saying will not exculpate me in the eyes of one critic, a former British Ambassador to Moscow, who says that he has 'always held that the Russian Revolution has never taken place' and who therefore wonders why I should devote so much space to so unreal an event.) As to my political approach to Trotsky, this has remained unchanged throughout. I concluded the first volume of this trilogy, in 1952, with a chapter entitled 'Defeat in Victory', where I portrayed Trotsky at the pinnacle of power. In the Preface to that volume I said that on completing his Life I would consider 'the question whether a strong element of victory was not concealed in his very defeat'. This precisely is the question I discuss in the closing pages of *The Prophet Outcast*, in a Postscript entitled 'Victory in Defeat'.

A Note about Sources and Acknowledgements

The narrative of this volume is based even more strongly than that of the previous volumes on Trotsky's archives, especially on his correspondence with the members of his family. Whenever I refer to *The Archives* in general, I have in mind their Open Section which is accessible to students at the Houghton Library, Harvard University. When I draw on the 'sealed' part of *The Archives* I refer to the 'Closed Section'. A general description of the Open Section was given in the Bibliography of *The Prophet Armed*. The Closed Section is described in the Bibliography attached to the present volume.

Most of the 20,000 documents of the Closed Section consists of Trotsky's political correspondence with adherents and friends; he stipulated that this should be sealed because at the time when he transferred his papers to Harvard University (in the summer of 1940), nearly the whole of Europe was either under Nazi or under Stalinist occupation and the future of many countries outside Europe looked uncertain; and so he felt obliged to protect his correspondents. But there was little or nothing strictly confidential or private in the political content of that correspondence. Indeed, with much of it I had become familiar in the nineteen-thirties—I shall presently explain in what way—so that re-reading it in 1959 I found hardly anything that could startle or surprise me. Trotsky's family correspondence, on the other hand, and even his household papers, also contained in the Closed Section, have revealed to me his most intimate experiences and feelings and have greatly enriched my image of his personality.

Some reviewers of the earlier volumes have complained that my references to *The Archives* are not detailed enough. I can only point out that whenever I cite any document from *The Archives*, I say, *either* in the text *or* in a footnote, by whom the document was written, when it was written, and to whom it was addressed. This is all that any student needs. More detailed annotation might have added impressively to my 'scholarly apparatus', but would be of no use either to the general reader, who has no access to *The Trotsky Archives*, or to the scholar, whom the indications I provide should enable to locate easily any paper I have referred to. Moreover, since I worked on my earlier volumes *The Archives* have been rearranged so that any more specific markings I might have given would have become valueless by now. (e.g. I might have indicated that document X or Y is in Section B, folder 17, but in the meantime Section A or B or C—has ceased to exist!) The material is now arranged in simple chronological order; and as I usually give the date of any document quoted the student should find the item at a glance in the excellent two-volume *Index* to *The Archives*, available at the Houghton Library.

One or two critics have wondered just how reliable are *The Archives* and whether Trotsky or his followers have not 'doctored documents'. To my mind the reliability of *The Archives* is overwhelmingly confirmed by the internal evidence, by cross-reference to other sources, and by the circumstance that *The Archives* provide Trotsky's critics as well as his apologists with all the material they may want. Trotsky indeed was above falsifying or distorting documents. As to his followers, these have, either from lack of interest or from preoccupation with other matters, hardly ever looked into the master's Archives. In 1950 my wife and I were the first students to work on Trotsky's papers since he had parted with them.

In relating the climate of ideas and describing the parties, groups, and individuals involved in the inner communist struggles. of the nineteen-thirties I drew *inter alia* on my own experience as spokesman of anti-Stalinist communism in Poland. The group with which I was associated then worked in close contact with Trotsky. His International Secretariat supplied us with very abundant documentation, some of it confidential, with circulars, copies of Trotsky's correspondence, &c. As writer and debater, I was deeply involved in nearly all the controversies described in this volume. In the course of the debates I had to acquaint myself with an enormous political literature, with Stalinist, Social-Democratic, Trotskyist, Brandlerist, and other pamphlets, books, periodicals, and leaflets published in many countries. Naturally enough, only a small part of that literature was available to me at the time of writing —just enough to check the accuracy of my impressions and memories and to verify data and quotations. My Bibliography and footnotes do not therefore pretend to exhaust the literature of the subject.

I have been fortunate in being able to supplement the material drawn from *The Archives* (and from printed sources) by information obtained from Trotsky's widow; from Alfred and Marguerite Rosmer, Trotsky's closest friends in the years of banishment; from Jeanne Martin des Paillères, who transmitted to me papers and correspondence of Leon Sedov, Trotsky's elder son; from Pierre Frank, Trotsky's secretary in the Prinkipo period; from Joseph Hansen, secretary and bodyguard at Coyoacan, and close eye-witness of Trotsky's last days and hours; and from many other people who were Trotsky's adherents at one time or another. (Of those listed here Natalya Sedova, Marguerite Rosmer, and Jeanne Martin died before I completed this volume.)

Outside the circle of Trotsky's family and followers, I am obliged to Konrad Knudsen and his wife, who were Trotsky's hosts in Norway, and to Mr. Helge Krog and Mr. and Mrs. N. K. Dahl for much information and vivid reminiscences about the circumstances of Trotsky's internment and deportation from Norway. I interviewed Mr. Trygve Lie, who was the Minister of Justice responsible for both the admission of Trotsky and his internment; but Mr. Lie, having spoken to me at great length and self-revealingly, then asked me to refrain from quoting him, saying that his memory had misled him and that, in addition, under a contract with an American publisher, he was not allowed to disclose this information otherwise than in his own memoirs. Mr. Lie was good enough, however, to send me the official Report on the Trotsky case which he had submitted to the Norwegian Parliament early in 1937. I have also had the benefit of interviewing Professor H. Koht, Norway's Minister of Foreign Affairs at the time of Trotsky's stay in that country, who was most anxious to establish in detail the truth of the case.

In investigating another important chapter in Trotsky's life, I approached the late John Dewey, who gave me an illuminating account of the Mexican counter-trial and spoke freely about the impression Trotsky made on him; and I am indebted to Dr. S. Ratner, Dewey's friend and secretary, for valuable information about the circumstances in which the old American philosopher decided to preside over the counter-trial. Of many other informants I would like to mention Mr. Joseph Berger, once a member of the Comintern Staff in Moscow who then spent nearly twenty-five years in Stalin's concentration camps —Mr. Berger has related to me his meeting in 1937 with Sergei Sedov, Trotsky's younger son, in the Butyrki prison of Moscow.

My thanks are due to the Russian Research Centre, Harvard University, especially to Professors M. Fainsod and M. D. Shulman for the facilities they offered me, and to Dr. R. A. Brower, Master of Adams House, and his wife, whose pleasant hospitality I enjoyed while working on the Closed Section of *The Trotsky Archives* in 1959. I am greatly obliged to Professor William Jackson and Miss C. E. Jakeman of Houghton Library for their infinitely patient helpfulness and to Mrs. Elena Zarudnaya-Levin for assisting me in reading some of the documents in *The Archives*.

To Mr. John Bell, Mr. Dan M. Davin, and Mr. Donald Tyerman who have read my MS and proofs I am grateful for criticisms and many suggestions for improvements.

My wife's contribution to this volume has been not only that of unfailing assistant and critic—in the course of many years, ever since 1950 when we first pored together over *The Trotsky Archives*, she absorbed the air of this tragic drama; and, through her sensitive sympathy with its *personae*, she has helped me decidedly in portraying their characters and narrating their fortunes.

I. D.

CHAPTER I

On the Princes' Isles

THE circumstances of Trotsky's banishment from Russia contained a foretaste of the years that lay ahead of him. The manner of the deportation was freakish and brutal. For weeks Stalin had delayed it, while Trotsky bombarded the Politbureau with protests denouncing the decision as lawless. It looked as if Stalin had not yet finally made up his mind, or was still consulting the Politbureau. Then, suddenly, the cat and mouse game was at an end: on the night of 10 February 1929, Trotsky, his wife, and elder son were rushed to the harbour of Odessa, and put on board the *Ilyich*, which sailed forthwith. His escort and the harbour authorities were under strict orders which had to be enforced at once, despite the late hour, the gales, and the frozen seas. Stalin would not now brook even the slightest delay. The *Ilyich* (and the ice-breaker that preceded her) had been especially detailed for the task; apart from Trotsky, his family, and two G.P.U. officers, she had not a single passenger on board and carried no cargo. Stalin was at last confronting the Politbureau with a *fait accompli*; he thus cut short all hesitation and prevented the repetition of scenes like those which had occurred when he first asked the Politbureau to authorize the banishment and when Bukharin protested, wrung his hands, and wept in full session, and together with Rykov and Tomsky voted against.[1]

The banishment was effected in the greatest secrecy. The decision was not made public until well after it had been carried out. Stalin was still afraid of commotion. The troops assembled in the harbour were there to prevent any demonstration of protest and any mass farewell such as the Opposition had organized a year earlier, before Trotsky's abduction from Moscow.[2] This time there were to be no witnesses and no

---

[1] See *The Prophet Unarmed* pp. 468–71. Rykov was still Chairman of the Council of People's Commissars, i.e. Soviet Prime Minister in succession to Lenin.

[2] Op. cit., p. 393.

eye-witness accounts. Trotsky was not to travel with a crowd of passengers before whose gaze he might resort to passive resistance. Even the crew were warned to keep to their quarters and avoid all contact with those on board. A nervous mystery surrounded the voyage. Stalin did not yet wish to burden himself with full responsibility. He was waiting to see whether communist opinion abroad would be shocked; and he did not know whether future developments might not compel him to recall his adversary. He took care to stage the deportation so ambiguously that it could be explained away, if need be, or even denied completely—for a few days afterwards communist newspapers abroad were suggesting that Trotsky had gone to Turkey on an official or semi-official mission or that he had gone there of his own accord, with a large suite.[1]

And so suddenly Trotsky found himself on board a bleak and almost deserted ship, heading through gales towards an empty horizon. Even after the year at Alma Ata, this void around him, made even more malignant by the hovering figures of the two G.P.U. officers, was disconcerting. What could it mean? What could it portend? Only Natalya and Lyova were by his side; and in their eyes he could read the same question. To escape the gale and the emptiness they went down to their cabins and stayed there throughout the voyage. The emptiness seemed to creep after them. What did it signify? What was to be the journey's end?

Trotsky was prepared for the worst. He did not think that Stalin would be content to deposit him on the other shore of the Black Sea and let him go. He suspected that Stalin and Kemal Pasha, Turkey's President and dictator, were in a plot against him, and that Kemal's police would seize him from the boat and either intern him or deliver him surreptitiously to the vengeance of White émigrés congregating in Constantinople. The tricks the G.P.U. had played on him confirmed this apprehension: he had repeatedly asked them to release from prison Sermuks and Posnansky, his two devoted secretaries and bodyguards, and to allow them to accompany him abroad; and the G.P.U. had repeatedly promised to do so but had broken the promise. They had evidently decided to put him on shore without a friend to guard him. En route the escorting officers tried to

[1] *Humanité*, February 1929.

reassure him: Sermuks and Posnansky, they said, would join him in Constantinople, and meanwhile the G.P.U. assumed responsibility for his safety. 'You have cheated me once,' he replied, 'and you will cheat me again.'[1]

Baffled and anguished, he recalled with his wife and son the last sea voyage they had made together—in March 1917 when, freed from British internment in Canada, they had set off for Russia on board a Norwegian steamer. 'Our family was the same then,' Trotsky reflects in his autobiography (although Sergei, his younger son, who had been with them in 1917 was not on the *Ilyich*), 'but we were twelve years younger.' More essential than this difference in age was the contrast in the circumstances, on which he makes no comment. In 1917 the revolution called him back to Russia for the great battles to come; now he was driven from Russia by a government ruling in the name of the revolution. In 1917, every day throughout the month spent in British internment, he had addressed crowds of German sailors behind barbed wire, prisoners of war, telling them of the stand taken by Karl Liebknecht in the Reichstag, in jail, and in the trenches against the Kaiser and the imperialist war, and arousing their enthusiasm for socialism. When he was released, the sailors had carried him shoulder high all the way to the camp gate, cheering him and singing the Internationale.[2] Now there was only the void around him and the howling gale. It was ten years now since the defeat of the *Spartakus* and the assassination of Liebknecht; and more than once already Trotsky had wondered whether he too was not fated to suffer 'Liebknecht's end'. A minor incident added a grotesque touch to this contrast. As the *Ilyich* was entering the Bosphorus one of the G.P.U. officers handed him the sum of 1,500 dollars, a grant which the Soviet Government had made their former Commissar of War 'to enable him to settle abroad'. Trotsky could see Stalin's mocking grin; but, being penniless, he swallowed the affront and accepted the money. This was the last wage he received from the state of which he had been a founding father.

[1] Trotsky's messages to the Central Committee, the Executive of the Comintern, and to 'Citizen Fokin, plenipotentiary of G.P.U.', dated 7–12 February 1929. *The Archives; Moya Zhizn*, vol. II, p. 318.

[2] *The Prophet Armed*, p. 247.

Trotsky would not have been himself if he had brooded over these melancholy incidents. Whatever the future held in store, he was resolved to meet it on his feet and fighting. He would not allow himself to be dispersed in the void. Beyond it there were unexplored horizons of struggle and hope—the past to live up to now and a future in which past and present would live on. He felt nothing in common with those historic personalities of whom Hegel says that once they have accomplished their 'mission in history' they are exhausted and 'fall like empty husks'.[1] He would struggle to break out of the vacuum in which Stalin and events were enclosing him. For the moment he could only record his final protest against expatriation. Before the end of the voyage he delivered to his escort a message addressed to the Central Committee of the Party and the Central Executive Committee of the Soviets. In it he denounced the 'conspiracy' which Stalin and the G.P.U. had entered with Kemal Pasha and Kemal's 'national fascist' police; and he warned his persecutors that a day would come when they would have to answer for this 'treacherous and shameful deed'. Then, after the *Ilyich* had dropped anchor and Turkish frontier guards appeared, he handed them a formal protest addressed to Kemal. Anger and irony broke through his restrained official tone: 'At the gates of Constantinople', he wrote, 'I have the honour to inform you that it is not by my own free will that I have arrived at the frontier of Turkey—I am crossing this frontier only because I must submit to force. Please, Mr. President, accept my appropriate sentiments.'[2]

He hardly expected Kemal to react to this protest, and he was aware that his persecutors in Moscow would not be deterred by the thought that one day they might be called to account for what they were doing. But even if at the moment it seemed vain to invoke history for justice, he could do nothing but invoke it. He was convinced that he spoke not for himself only but for his silent, imprisoned, or deported friends and followers, and that the violence of which he was the victim was inflicted on the Bolshevik Party at large and the revolution itself. He knew that, whatever his personal fortunes, his controversy with Stalin would go on and reverberate through

[1] Hegel, *Philosophie der Weltgeschichte*, p. 78.
[2] *The Archives; Moya Zhizn*, vol. II, p. 317.

the century. If Stalin was bent on suppressing all those who might protest and bear witness, then Trotsky, at the very moment when he was being driven into exile, would come forward to protest and bear witness.

.   .   .   .

The sequel to the disembarkation was almost farcical. From the pier Trotsky and his family were taken straight to the Soviet Consulate in Constantinople. Although he had been branded as a political offender and counter-revolutionary, he was received with the honours due to the leader of October and the creator of the Red Army. A wing of the Consulate was reserved for him. The officials, some of whom had served under him in the civil war, seemed eager to make him feel at home. The G.P.U. men behaved as if they meant to honour the pledge that they would protect his life. They met all his wishes. They went on errands for him. They accompanied Natalya and Lyova on trips to the city, while he stayed at the Consulate. They took care to unload and transport his bulky archives brought from Alma Ata, without even trying to check their contents—the documents and records which he was presently to use as political ammunition against Stalin. Moscow seemed to be still trying to disguise the banishment and soften its impact on communist opinion. Not for nothing did Bukharin once speak of Stalin's genius for gradation and timing: Stalin's peculiar gift for pursuing his aims by slow degrees, inch by inch, showed itself even in details like these.

It showed itself also in the way he had assured himself of Kemal Pasha's co-operation. The Turkish Government informed Trotsky shortly after his arrival that they had never been told that he was to be exiled, that the Soviet Government had simply requested them to grant him an entry permit 'for health reasons', and that, cherishing friendly relations with their northern neighbour, they could not go into the motives for the request and had to grant the visa. Yet Kemal Pasha, uneasy at seeing himself thus turned into Stalin's accomplice, hastened to assure Trotsky that 'it was out of the question that he should be interned or exposed to any violence on Turkish soil', that he was free to leave the country whenever he chose or to stay as long as he pleased; and that if he were to stay, the Turkish Government would extend to him every hospitality and ensure his safety.[1] Despite this respectful sympathy, Trotsky remained convinced that Kemal was hand-in-glove with Stalin. There was, in any case, no knowing how Kemal would behave if Stalin confronted him with further demands—would he risk embroiling himself with his powerful 'northern neighbour' for the sake of a political exile?

The ambiguous situation created by Trotsky's residence in the Soviet Consulate could not last. Stalin was only waiting for a pretext to end it; and it was unbearable to Trotsky as well. 'Protected' by the G.P.U., he remained their virtual prisoner, not knowing whom to fear more: the White émigrés outside the Consulate or his guards inside. He found himself deprived of the sole advantage that exile bestows upon the political fighter: freedom of movement and expression. He was anxious to state his case, to reveal the events that had led to his expulsion, to make contact with followers in various countries, and to plan further action. He could not safely do any of these things from the Consulate. In addition, both he and his wife were ill; and he had to earn his living, which he could do only by writing. He had to settle somewhere, to get in touch with publishers and newspapers; and to start work.

On the day he arrived he sent out messages to friends and well-wishers in western Europe, especially in France. Their response was immediate. 'We need hardly tell you that you can count on us body and soul. We embrace you from the depth of our faithful and affectionate hearts.' Thus Alfred and Marguerite Rosmer wrote to him three days after he had landed.[2] They had been his and Natalya's friends since the First World War, when they were in the Zimmerwald move-ment. In the early nineteen-twenties Alfred Rosmer had repre-sented the French Communist party on the Executive of the Communist International in Moscow; and for his solidarity with Trotsky he had been expelled from the party. The 'depth of our faithful and affectionate hearts' was no mere turn of phrase with the Rosmers—they were to remain Trotsky's only intimate friends in the years of his exile, despite later disagreements and

---

[1] Quoted from a letter to Trotsky, written on Kemal's order, by the Governor of Constantinople on 18 February 1929. Closed section of the Trotsky *Archives*.

[2] Correspondence between the Rosmers and Trotsky. Ibid.

discords. Boris Souvarine, a former Editor of the theoretical paper of the French Communist party, who alone among all foreign communist delegates in Moscow in May 1924 spoke up in Trotsky's defence, also wrote to offer help and co-operation.[1] Other well-wishers were Maurice and Magdeleine Paz, a lawyer and a journalist, both expelled from the Communist party, and in later years well known as socialist parliamentarians. Addressing him as '*Cher grand Ami*', they wrote of their anxiety about his precarious position in Turkey, tried to obtain for him entry permits to other countries, and promised to join him shortly in Constantinople.[2]

Through the Rosmers and Pazes Trotsky established contact with western newspapers; and while still at the Consulate, he wrote a series of articles which appeared in the *New York Times*, the *Daily Express*, and other papers in the second half of February. This series was his first public account of the inner party struggle of the last years and months. It was brief, forceful, and aggressive. He spared none of his enemies or adversaries, old or new, least of all Stalin whom he now denounced to the world as he had earlier denounced him to the Politbureau as 'the grave-digger of the revolution'.[3] Even before these articles appeared, he was in trouble with his hosts, who began to urge him to move from the Consulate to a compound inhabited by consular employees, where he would go on living under G.P.U. 'protection'. He refused to move, and the question was shelved until the publication of the articles brought matters to a head. Stalin now had the pretext he needed to bring the banishment into the open. Soviet newspapers spoke of Trotsky having 'sold himself to the world bourgeoisie and conspiring against the Soviet Union'; and their cartoonists depicted *Mister* Trotsky embracing a bag with 25,000 dollars. The G.P.U. declared that they no longer held themselves responsible for his safety and were going to evict him from the Consulate.[4]

For several days Natalya and Lyova, even now solicitously

---

[1] Souvarine to Trotsky, 15 February 1929, ibid.

[2] Maurice Paz to Trotsky, 18 February 1929, ibid.

[3] The original text bears the date of 25 February 1929. *The Archives; Écrits*, vol. I, pp. 19–52.

[4] Trotsky's correspondence with the G.P.U. representative in Constantinople of 5 and 8 March. *The Archives.*

accompanied by the G.P.U. men, searched breathlessly the suburbs and outskirts of Constantinople for some more or less safe and secluded accommodation. At last they found a house, not in or near the city, but on the Prinkipo Islands, out on the sea of Marmara—it took an hour and a half to reach the islands by steamer from Constantinople. There was a touch of irony in this hurried choice of residence, for Prinkipo, or the Princes' Isles, had once been a place of exile to which Byzantine Emperors confined their rivals and rebels of royal blood. Trotsky arrived there on 7 or 8 March. As he set foot on the shore at Büyük Ada, the main village of Prinkipo, he imagined that he was alighting there as a bird of passage; but this was to be his home for more than four long and eventful years.

.   .   .   .

Trotsky often described this period of his life as his 'third emigration'. The term, not quite precise, reveals something of the mood in which he came to Prinkipo. This was indeed the third time that he had been deported by Russian governments and that he had come to live abroad. But in 1902 and 1907 he had been deported to Siberia or the Polar Region, whence he fled and took refuge in the West; and wherever he came in those days he belonged to that large, active, and dynamic community that was revolutionary Russia in exile. This time he had not chosen to become an émigré; and abroad there was no community of Russian exiles to receive him as one of their own and to offer him the environment and the medium for further political activity. Many new colonies of political émigrés existed; but these formed the counter-revolutionary Russia in exile. Between him and them there was the blood of the civil war. Of those who in that war had fought on his side there was none to join hands with him.

His third exile was therefore different in kind from the previous two. It could not be related to any precedent, for in the long and abundant history of political emigration there hardly ever was a man banished into comparable solitude (except Napoleon who was, however, a prisoner of war). Unconsciously, as it were, Trotsky sought to soften for himself and his family the severity of his present ostracism by relating it to his pre-revolutionary experiences. The memory of those experiences was now comforting. His first period of emigration lasted less than three years—it was interrupted by the *annus mirabilis* of 1905; the second lasted much longer, ten years; but it was followed by the supreme triumph of 1917. Each time history had bounteously rewarded the revolutionary for his restless wait abroad. Was it too much to expect that she would do so again? He was aware that this time the outlook might prove less promising and that he might never return to Russia. But stronger than this awareness was his need for a clear-cut and encouraging prospect, and the optimism of the fighter who even when he courts defeat, or is engaged in a hopeless battle, still looks forward to victory.

This kind of optimism was never to forsake him. But whereas in later years he remained confident of the ultimate triumph of his cause rather than of his chance of living to see it, in the first years of this exile there was still a more personal note to his optimism. He did indeed look forward to his early vindication and return to Russia. He did not consider the political situation there as stable; and, amid the upheavals of collectivization and industrialization, he expected shifts in the nation to produce great shifts in the ruling party as well. He did not believe that Stalinism could achieve consolidation. Was it anything more than a patchwork of incompatible ideas, the shilly-shallying of a bureaucracy not daring to tackle the problems by which it was confronted? He was convinced that the 'interlude' of Stalin's ascendancy must be brought to an end either by a resurgence of the revolutionary spirit and a regeneration of Bolshevism or by counter-revolution and capitalist restoration. This stark alternative governed his thoughts, even if at times he reckoned with other possibilities as well. He saw himself and his co-thinkers as representing the only serious opposition to Stalin, the only opposition that stood on the ground of the October revolution, offered a programme of socialist action, and constituted an alternative Bolshevik government. He did not imagine that Stalin would be able to destroy the Opposition or even to reduce it to silence for long. Here too his hopes fed on pre-revolutionary memories. Tsardom had failed to stifle any opposition, even though it imprisoned, deported, and executed the revolutionaries. Why then should Stalin, who was not yet executing his opponents, succeed where the Tsars had failed?

True, the Opposition had had its ups and downs; but, having deep roots in social realities and being the mouthpiece of the proletarian class interest, it could not be annihilated. As its acknowledged leader he was in duty bound to direct its activity from abroad, as Lenin and indeed he himself had once led their followers from exile. He alone could now speak for the Opposition in relative freedom and make its voice heard far and wide.

In yet another respect, however, his position was unlike what it had been before the revolution. Then he was unknown to the world or known as a Russian revolutionary only to the initiated. This was not his present standing. He had not this time re-emerged from the dimness of an underground movement. The world had seen him as leader of the October insurrection, as founder of the Red Army, as architect of its victory, and as inspirer of the Communist International. He had risen to a height from which it is not given to descend. He had acted his part on a world stage, in the limelight of history, and he could not withdraw. His past dominated his present. He could not lapse back into the protective obscurity of pre-revolutionary émigré life. His deeds had shaken the world; and neither he nor the world could forget them.

Nor could he confine himself to his Russian preoccupations. He was conscious of his 'duty towards the International'. Much of the struggle of recent years had centred on the strategy and tactics of communism in Germany, China, and Britain, and on the manner in which Moscow, for the sake of expediency, emasculated the International. It was unthinkable that he should not carry on this struggle. On the face of it, banishment should have made it easier for him to do so. If, as the champion of internationalism and the critic of Stalinist and Bukharinist 'national narrow-mindedness', he incurred unpopularity in Russia, he had reason to hope for eager response from communists outside Russia, for it was their most vital interest that he sought to advance when to socialism in a single country he opposed the primacy of the international viewpoint. From Moscow and Alma Ata he could not address foreign communists, and Stalin had seen to it that they should either remain ignorant or get only a grossly distorted view of what he stood for. Now at last his enforced stay abroad enabled him to put his case before them.

He still viewed the 'advanced industrial countries of the West', especially those of western Europe, as the main battle-grounds of the international class struggle. In this he was true to himself and the tradition of classical Marxism which he represented in its purity. In fact, no school of thought in the labour movement, not even the Stalinist, yet dared openly to flout that tradition. For the Third as for the Second International western Europe was still the main sphere of activity. The German and the French Communist parties commanded large mass followings, while the Soviet Union was still industrially underdeveloped and extremely weak, and the victory of the Chinese revolution was twenty years off. Just as bourgeois Europe, even in this period of its decline, still ostensibly held the centre of world politics, so the western European working classes still appeared to be the most important forces of proletarian revolution, the most important next to the Soviet Union in the Stalinist conception, and potentially even more important in Trotsky's.

Trotsky, of course, did not believe in the stability of the bourgeois order in Europe. When he arrived at Prinkipo the 'prosperity' which the West enjoyed in the late nineteen-twenties was already nearing its end. But Conservatives, Liberals, and Social Democrats still basked in the sunshine of democracy, pacifism, and class co-operation which were to assure the indefinite continuation of that prosperity. Parliamentary government appeared to be firmly established; and fascism, entrenched only in Italy, seemed a marginal phenomenon of European politics. Yet in his first days in Constantinople Trotsky announced the approaching end of this fools' paradise and spoke of the decay of bourgeois democracy and the ground-swell of fascism: '. . . these post-war trends in Europe's political development are not episodic; they are the bloody prologue to a new epoch. . . . The [first world] war has ushered us into an era of high tension and great struggle; major new wars are casting their shadows ahead. . . . Our epoch cannot be measured by the standards of the nineteenth century, that classical age of expanding [bourgeois] democracy. The twentieth century will in many respects differ from the nineteenth even more than modern times differ from the middle ages.'[1] He had a sense of returning to Europe

[1] *Écrits*, vol. I, p. 47.

on the eve of a decisive turn of history, when socialist revolution
alone could offer the western nations the effective alternative to
fascism. Revolution in the West, he believed, would also free
the Soviet Union from isolation and create a powerful counterbalance to the immense weight of backwardness that had
depressed the Russian Revolution. This hope did not seem vain.
The western labour movement, with its mass organizations
intact and its fighting spirit subdued but not yet deadened, was
still battleworthy. The Communist parties, despite their faults
and vices, still had in their ranks the vanguard of the working
class. Trotsky concluded that what was necessary was to open
the eyes of that vanguard to the dangers and the opportunities,
to make it aware of its responsibilities, to shake its conscience,
and to arouse it to revolutionary action.

This view of the present as well as his own past cast Trotsky
for his peculiar role in exile. He came forward as the legatee of
classical Marxism and also of Leninism, which Stalinism had
degraded to a set of dogmas and to a bureaucratic mythology.
To restore Marxism and to reimbue the mass of communists
with its critical spirit was the essential preliminary to effective
revolutionary action, and the task that he set himself. No
Marxist, except Lenin, had ever spoken with a moral authority
comparable to his, the authority he wielded as both theorist and
victorious commander in a revolution; and none had to act in a
situation as difficult as his, being on all sides surrounded by
implacable hostility and being caught up in a conflict with the
state which had issued from revolution.

He possessed in abdundance and even superabundance the
courage and energy needed to cope with such a role and to
grapple with such a predicament. All the severe reverses he
had suffered, far from dulling his fighting instincts, had excited
them to the utmost. The passions of his intellect and heart,
always uncommonly large and intense, now swelled into a
tragic energy as mighty and high as that which animates the
prophets and the law-givers of Michelangelo's vision. It was
this moral energy that preserved him at this stage from any
sense of personal tragedy. There was as yet not even a hint of
self-pity in him. When in the first year of exile he concluded his
autobiography with the words: 'I know no personal tragedy',
he spoke the truth. He saw his own destiny as an incident in

the great flux and reflux of revolution and reaction; and it did
not greatly matter to him whether he fought in the full panoply
of power or whether he did so as an outcast. The difference
did not affect his faith in his cause and in himself. When a
critic remarked well-meaningly that despite his fall the ex-
Commissar of War had preserved the full clarity and power
of his thought, Trotsky could only mock the Philistine 'who saw
any connexion between a man's power of reasoning and his
holding of office'.[1] He felt the fullness of life only when he could
stretch all his faculties and use them in the service of his idea.
This he was going to do come what might. What sustained his
confidence was that his triumphs in the revolution and the
civil war still stood out more vividly in his mind than the defeats
that followed them. He knew that these were imperishable
triumphs. So mighty had been the climax of his life that it
over-shadowed the anti-climax and no power on earth could
drag him down from it. All the same, tragedy, relentless and
pitiless, was closing in on him.

.   .   .   .

Around 1930 Prinkipo was still as deserted as it probably was
when the disgraced brothers and cousins of the Byzantine
Emperors lingered away their lives on its shores. Nature itself
seemed to have designed the spot to be a regal penitentiary.
A 'red-cliffed island set in deep blue', Büyük Ada 'crouches
in the sea like a pre-historical animal drinking'.[2] In the blaze
of a sunset its purple unfurled gaily and challengingly like a
flame over the serene azure; then it burst into a red rage of
lonely defiance, gesturing angrily at the remote and invisible
world, until at last it sunk resentfully into the dark. The island-
ers, a few fishermen and shepherds, dwelling between the red
and the blue, lived as their forefathers did a thousand years
earlier; and 'the village cemetery seemed more alive than the
village itself'.[3] The horn of a motor-car never disturbed the
stillness; only the braying of an ass came down from the outlying
cliff and field into the main street. For a few weeks in the year
noisy vulgarity intruded: in the summer multitudes of holiday
makers, families of Constantinople merchants, crowded the

[1] *Moya Zhizn*, vol. II, p. 336.   [2] Max Eastman, *Great Companions*, p. 117.
[3] Quoted from Trotsky's unpublished diary (July 1933). *The Archives.*

beaches and the huts. Then calm returned, and only the braying of the ass greeted the still and splendid onset of the autumn.

On the fringe of Büyük Ada, closed in between high hedges and the sea, fenced off from the village and almost as aloof from it as the village was from the rest of the world, was Trotsky's new abode, a spacious, dilapidated villa rented from a bankrupt pasha. When the new tenants moved in, it was sunk in cobwebbed squalor. Years later Trotsky recollected the gaiety and zest for cleanliness, with which Natalya rolled up her sleeves and made her menfolk do the same to sweep away the filth, and paint the walls white. Much later they covered the floors with paint so cheap that many months after their shoes still stuck to it as they walked. At the centre of the house was a vast hall with doors opening on a veranda facing the sea. On the first floor was Trotsky's work room, the walls of which quickly became lined with books and periodicals arriving from Europe and America. On the ground floor was the secretariat with Lyova in charge. An English visitor described 'the dingy marbles, sad bronze peacock, and humiliated gilt betraying the social pretensions as well as the failure of the Turkish owner' —this faded *décor*, designed to give comfort and prestige to a retired pasha, contrasted comically with the Spartan aura the place assumed.[1] Max Eastman, who arrived there when the house was full of secretaries, bodyguards, and guests, compared it in its 'lack of comfort and beauty' to a bare barrack. 'In these vast rooms and on the balcony there is not an article of furniture, not even a chair! They are mere gangways and the doors to the rooms on each side are closed. In each of these rooms someone has an office table or a bed, or both, and a chair to go with it. One of them, downstairs, very small and square and white-walled with barely space for table and chairs, is the dining-room.' The hedonistically minded American visitor reflected that 'a man and woman must be almost dead aesthetically' to live in so severe an abode, when 'for a few dollars' they might have made of it a 'charming home'.[2] No doubt, the place had none of the cosiness of an American middle-class

---

[1] The *Manchester Guardian*, 17 March 1931. See also Rosmer in the 'Appendice' to Trotsky's *Ma Vie*, p. 592.

[2] Eastman, loc. cit.

home. Even in normal circumstances it would hardly have occurred to Trotsky or Natalya to set up a 'charming home' with pictures 'for a few dollars'; and their circumstances on Prinkipo were never normal. They sat there all the time as in a waiting-room on a pier, looking out for the ship that would take them away. The garden around the villa was abandoned to weeds, 'to save money' as Natalya explained to the visitor, who half expected Trotsky to cultivate his little plot of land. Effort and money had to be saved for a desperate struggle in which the Büyük Ada house was a temporary headquarters. Its clean and bare austerity suited its purpose.

· · · · · · · · · ·

From the moment of his arrival Trotsky was unreconciled to his isolation and apprehensive of remaining within such easy reach of both the G.P.U. and the White émigrés. Outside his gates two Turkish policemen were posted, but he could hardly entrust his safety to them. Almost at once he began the quest for a visa which he partly described in the last pages of his autobiography.[1]

Even before his deportation from Odessa he had asked the Politbureau to obtain for him a German entry permit. He was told that the German Government—a Social Democratic Government headed by Hermann Mueller—had refused. He was half convinced that Stalin cheated him; and so when soon afterwards Paul Loebe, the Socialist Speaker of the Reichstag, declared that Germany would grant Trotsky asylum, he at once applied for a visa. He was not deterred by the 'malicious satisfaction with which . . . newspapers dwelt on the fact that an advocate of revolutionary dictatorship was obliged to seek asylum in a democratic country'. This lesson, they said, should teach him 'to appreciate the worth of democratic institutions'. The lesson was hardly edifying, however. The German Government first asked him whether he would submit to restrictions on his freedom of movement. He answered that he was prepared to refrain from any public activity, to live in 'complete seclusion', preferably somewhere near Berlin, and devote himself to literary work. Then he was asked whether

---

[1] *Moya Zhizn*, vol. II, pp. 318–33. *The Archives.*

it would not be enough for him to come for a short visit, just to undergo medical treatment. When he replied that having no choice he would content himself even with this, he was told that in the government's view he was not so ill as to require any special treatment. 'I asked whether Loebe had offered me the right of asylum or the right of burial in Germany. . . . In the course of a few weeks the democratic right of asylum was thrice curtailed. At first it was reduced to the right of resistance under special restrictions, then to the right of medical treatment, and finally to the right of burial. I could thus appreciate the full advantages of democracy only as a corpse.'

The British House of Commons discussed Trotsky's admission as early as February 1929. The Government made it clear that it would not allow him to enter. The country was just about to have an election and the Labour Party was expected to return to office. Before the end of April two leading lights of Fabianism, Sidney and Beatrice Webb, arrived in Constantinople and respectfully asked Trotsky to receive them.[1] Despite old political animosities he entertained them courteously, eagerly enlightening himself on the economic and political facts of British life. The Webbs expressed their confidence that the Labour Party would win the election, whereupon he remarked that he would then apply for a British visa. Sidney Webb regretted that the Labour Government would depend on Liberal support in the Commons, and the Liberals would object to Trotsky's admission. After a few weeks Ramsay MacDonald did indeed form his second government with Sidney Webb, now Lord Passfield, as one of his Ministers.

Early in June, Trotsky applied to the British Consulate in Constantinople and cabled a formal request for a visa to MacDonald. He also wrote to Beatrice Webb, in terms as elegant as witty, about their talks at Prinkipo and the attraction that Britain, especially the British Museum, exercised on him. He appealed to Philip Snowden, the Chancellor of the Exchequer, saying that political differences should not prevent him from visiting England just as they had not prevented Snowden from going to Russia when Trotsky was in office. 'I hope to be able soon to return you the kind visit you paid me in

[1] The Webbs' correspondence with Trotsky is in *The Archives*, Closed Section. The letter in which they ask Trotsky to receive them is dated 29 April 1929.

Kislovodsk', he telegraphed George Lansbury.[1] It was all in vain. However, it was not the Liberals who objected to his admission. On the contrary, they protested against the attitude of the Labour Ministers; and Lloyd George and Herbert Samuel repeatedly intervened, in private, in Trotsky's favour.[2] 'This was a variant', he commented, 'which Mr. Webb did not foresee.' On and off, for nearly two years, the question was raised in Parliament and in the Press. H. G. Wells and Bernard Shaw wrote two statements of protest against the barring of Trotsky; and J. M. Keynes, C. P. Scott, Arnold Bennett, Harold Laski, Ellen Wilkinson, J. L. Garvin, the Bishop of Birmingham, and many others appealed to the Government to reconsider their decision. The protests and appeals fell on deaf ears. 'This "one act" comedy on the theme of democracy and its principles . . .', Trotsky observed, 'might have been written by Bernard Shaw, if the Fabian fluid which runs in his veins had been strengthened by as much as five per cent of Jonathan Swift's blood.'

Shaw, even if his satirical sting was not at its sharpest on this occasion, did what he could. He wrote to Clynes, the Home Secretary, about the 'ironic situation . . . of a Labour and Socialist government refusing the right of asylum to a very distinguished Socialist while granting it . . . to the most reactionary opponents. Now, if the government by excluding Mr. Trotsky could have also silenced him. . . . But Mr. Trotsky cannot be silenced. His trenchant literary power and the hold, which his extraordinary career has given him on the public imagination of the modern world, enable him to use every attempt to persecute him. . . . He becomes the inspirer and the hero of all the militants of the extreme left of every country.' Those who had 'an unreasoning dread of him as a caged lion'

---

[1] The copies of the application, cables, and letters are in *The Archives*, Closed Section. The letter to Beatrice Webb, written in French 'with Rosmer's help' says, *inter alia*: 'Je me souviens avec plaisir de votre visite. Ce fût pour moi une surprise agréable et, bien que nos points de vue se soient révélés irreductibles, ce que nous savions bien du reste, la conversation avec les Webbs m'a montré que celui qui a étudié la désormais classique histoire du trade-unionisme pouvait encore bien tirer profit d'un entretien avec ses auteurs.' Speaking of the attraction Britain had for him, Trotsky mentioned 'ma sympathie déjà ancienne pour le British Museum'.

[2] *The Archives*, Closed Section, British Files. Trotsky's British correspondent who kept him *au courant* with these developments was a cousin of Herbert Samuel. He quoted Samuel himself as the source of the information.

C

should allow him to enter Britain 'if only to hold the key of his cage'. Shaw contrasted Kemal Pasha's behaviour with Mac-Donald's and found 'hard to swallow an example of liberality set by a Turkish government to a British one'.[1]

Other European governments were no more willing to 'hold the key of his cage'. The French dug up the order of expulsion issued against Trotsky in 1916 and declared it to be still in force. The Czechs at first were ready to welcome him, and Masaryk's Socialist Minister, Dr. Ludwig Chekh, addressing him as 'Most Respected Comrade', informed him, in agree-ment with Beneš, that the visa had been issued; but the correspondence ended frigidly, with the 'Comrade' addressed as '*Herr*' and with an unexplained refusal.[2] The Dutch, who were giving refuge to Kaiser Wilhelm, would not give it to Trotsky. In a letter to Magdeleine Paz he wrote ironically that, as he did not even know the Dutch language, the govern-ment could rest assured that he would not interfere in domestic Dutch affairs; and that he was prepared to live in any rural backwater, incognito.[3] Nor were the Austrians willing to give 'an example of liberality' to others. The Norwegian Government declared that they could not allow him to enter their country, because they could not guarantee his safety. Trotsky's friends sounded out even the rulers of the Duchy of Luxemburg. He found that 'Europe was without a visa'. He did not even think of applying to the United States, for this 'the most powerful nation of the world was also the most frightened'. He concluded that 'Europe and America were without a visa' and, 'as these two continents owned the other three, the planet was without a visa'. 'On many sides it had been ex-plained to me that my disbelief in democracy was my cardinal sin. . . . But when I ask to be given a brief object lesson in democracy there are no volunteers.'[4]

The truth is that even in exile Trotsky inspired fear. Govern-ments and ruling parties made him feel that no one can lead a great revolution, defy all the established powers, and challenge

[1] Quoted from the copy of Shaw's letter to Clynes, the Home Secretary, pre-served in *The Archives*, ibid. Shaw intervened also with Henderson, the Foreign Secretary, who 'refused to interfere'.

[2] Trotsky's correspondence with Dr. Chekh (Czech), Czechoslovak Minister of Interior. *The Archives*, Closed Section.

[3] Ibid.   [4] *Moya Zhizn*, vol. II, p. 333.

the sacred rights of property with impunity. Bourgeois Europe gazed with amazement and glee at the spectacle, the like of which it had not seen indeed since Napoleon's downfall— never since then had so many governments proscribed one man or had one man aroused such widespread animosity and alarm.[1] Conservatives had not forgiven him the part he had played in defeating the anti-Bolshevik 'crusade of fourteen nations'. No one expressed their feelings better than Winston Churchill, the inspirer of that crusade, in a triumphantly mocking essay on 'The Ogre of Europe'. 'Trotsky, whose frown meted death to thousands, sits disconsolate, *a bundle of old rags*, stranded on the shores of the Black Sea.' Presently Churchill had second thoughts, and when he included the essay in *Great Contemporaries*, he replaced the '*bundle of old rags*' by the words 'Trotsky—*a skin of malice*'. Trotsky's first political statements made 'on the shores of the Black Sea' showed him to have remained unshaken as enemy of the established order, and to be still as defiant and self-confident as he was in the days when he led the Red Army and addressed the world from the rostrum of the Communist International. No, no, this was not 'a bundle of old rags'—this was 'a skin of malice'.[2]

Ignorance of the issues that had split Bolshevism magnified the hatred and the fear. Reputable newspapers could not tell whether Trotsky's deportation was not a hoax and whether he had not left his country in secret agreement with Stalin in order to foster revolution abroad. *The Times* had 'reliable information' that this was indeed the case and saw Trotsky's hand

---

[1] '. . . Sir Austen Chamberlain [the Foreign Secretary]', Trotsky wrote, 'has, according to newspaper reports . . . expressed the opinion that regular relations [between Britain and the Soviet Union] . . . will become perfectly possible on the day after Trotsky has been put against the wall. This lapidary formula does honour to the temperament of the Tory Minister . . . but . . . I take the liberty of advising him . . . not to insist on this condition. Stalin has sufficiently shown how far he is prepared to go to meet Mr. Chamberlain by banishing me from the Soviet Union. If he has not gone further, this is not for lack of good will. It would really be too unreasonable to penalize, because of this, the Soviet economy and British industry.' *Écrits*, vol. I, p. 27.

[2] Winston S. Churchill, *Great Contemporaries*, p. 197. My italics. Churchill wrote the original essay in reply to an article by Trotsky for *John o' London's Weekly*. Commenting on Churchill's profile of Lenin, Trotsky had pointed out that Churchill's dates were mostly wrong and that he showed a total lack of insight into Lenin's character because of the gulf that separated him from the founder of Bolshevism. 'Lenin thought in terms of epochs and continents, Churchill thinks in terms of parliamentary fireworks and *feuilletons*.'

behind Communist demonstrations in Germany.[1] The *Morning Post* reported, with circumstantial details, on secret negotiations between Stalin and Trotsky which were to bring the latter back to the command of the armed forces; the paper knew that in connection with this Trotsky's sister had travelled between Moscow, Berlin, and Constantinople.[2] The *Daily Express* spoke of 'this raven perched upon the bough of British socialism'— 'Even with the clipped wings and claws, he is not the sort of fowl that we in Britain can ever hope to domesticate.'[3] The *Manchester Guardian* and the *Observer* supported with some warmth Trotsky's claim to political asylum, but theirs were solitary voices. American newspapers saw Trotsky as the 'revolutionary incendiary' and Stalin as 'the moderate statesman' with whom America could do business.[4] The German right wing and nationalist Press was raucous and rabid: 'Germany has enough trouble . . . we consider it superfluous to add to it by extending hospitality to this most powerful propagandist of Bolshevism', said the *Berliner Boersenzeitung*.[5] 'Trotsky, the Soviet-Jewish bloodhound, would like to reside in Berlin', wrote Hitler's *Beobachter*. 'We shall have to keep a watchful eye on this Jewish assassin and criminal.'[6]

The Social Democratic parties, especially those which were in office, felt somewhat disturbed in their democratic conscience, but were no less afraid. When George Lansbury protested at a Cabinet meeting against the treatment of Trotsky, the Prime Minister, the Foreign Secretary, and the Home Secretary replied: 'There he is, in Constantinople, out of the way—it is to nobody's interest that he should be anywhere else. We are all afraid of him.'[7] Beatrice Webb, express-

[1] *The Times*, 10 May 1929.

[2] *Morning Post*, 6–8 July 1929. The report was reproduced in many European papers. See e.g. *Intransigeant* of 8–9 July.

[3] *Daily Express*, 19 June 1929.

[4] See e.g. *The New York American* and *The New York World* of 27 February 1929. 'Stalin, intelligent Russian,' wrote the latter, 'knows that power without money is a shadow, so he leans in the direction of money'; and this should 'interest America's conservative government'.

[5] *Berliner Börsenzeitung*, 1 February 1929.

[6] 9 February 1929. The more 'respectable' *Hamburger Nachrichten* of 25 January 1929 said: 'Stalin is reaping the consequence of his blunder in not having sent Trotsky and the Trotsky crowd into the Great Beyond. . . .'

[7] The source of this information is Lansbury himself. He related it to Trotsky's British correspondent, whom he assured that he remained opposed to the Cabinet decision and that 'anything I can do behind the scenes to advise you, I will'. *The Archives*, Closed Section.

ing admiration for his intellect and 'heroic character', wrote to Trotsky: 'My husband and I were very sorry that you were not admitted into Great Britain. But I am afraid that anyone who preaches the permanence of revolution, that is carries the revolutionary war into the politics of other countries, will always be excluded from entering those other countries.'[1] Historically, this was not quite true: Karl Marx and Friedrich Engels spent most of their lives as refugees in England 'preaching the permanence of the revolution'. But times had changed, and Marx and Engels had not been as fortunate and unfortunate as to turn first from obscure political exiles into leaders of actual revolution and then back into exiles. Trotsky was not greatly surprised by the feeling he evoked. He refused to go about the business of visas more diplomatically, as the Pazes urged him to do; he would not pull strings behind the scenes and refrain from making public appeals.[2] Even while he was seeking a refuge for himself, he was engaged in a battle of ideas. He knew that governments and ruling classes, in their fear of him, were paying him a tribute: they could not view him as a private supplicant; they had to treat him as an institution and as the embodiment of revolution militant.

.   .   .   .

Without waiting for the result of his many requests and the canvassing for visas, Trotsky settled down to work. There was an unusual bustle on Prinkipo in the very first weeks after his arrival. Reporters from all the continents rushed to interview him. Visitors and friends appeared—in a single month, in May, no fewer than seven came from France alone and stayed for weeks, even months. Young Trotskyists arrived to serve as bodyguards and secretaries. German and American publishers called to sign contracts for books and to offer advances on royalties. From everywhere dissident communists wrote to inquire about points of ideology and policy; and presently Trotsky, answering every question systematically and scrupulously filing away mountains of paper, found himself up to his eyes in a correspondence, amazing in volume, which

[1] Beatrice Webb wrote on 30 April 1930 to thank Trotsky for a complimentary copy of *My Life*. She concluded the letter by offering the 'subversive propagandist' help with books, periodicals, and documents.

[2] Magdeleine Paz to Trotsky on 14 June 1929. *The Archives*, Closed Section.

he was to carry on, regardless of circumstances, till the end of his life. He was getting ready the first issue of the *Bulletin Oppozitsii*, the little periodical—it began to appear in July— which was to be his main platform for the discussion of inner party affairs and his most important medium of contact with the Opposition in the Soviet Union. It was not easy to edit it in Büyük Ada and to find Russian printers for it first in Paris and then in Berlin. At the same time he set out to organize his international following.

In addition, during the very first months of his stay on the island, he prepared a number of books for publication. He was anxious to acquaint the world with the 1927 Platform of the Joint Opposition, which was to see the light under the title *The Real Situation in Russia*. He assembled a collection of documents, suppressed in the Soviet Union, which were to make the volume on *The Stalinist School of Falsification*. In *The Third International After Lenin* he presented his 'Critique of the Draft Programme of the Third International' and the message he had addressed to the Sixth Congress from Alma Ata. Shortened and partly garbled versions of these texts had already appeared abroad, which was one more reason why Trotsky was eager to produce the full and authentic statements. *Permanent Revolution* was the small book, also written at Alma Ata, in which he restated and defended his theory in controversy with Radek.

The main literary fruit of the season was, however, *My Life*. Urged by Preobrazhensky and other friends to write his autobiography, he had, at Alma Ata, jotted down the opening parts narrating his childhood and youth; and on Prinkipo he hurriedly went on with the work, sending out chapters, as he completed them, to his German, French, and English translators. His progress was so rapid that one may wonder whether he had not drafted much more at Alma Ata than just the opening parts. Less than three months after he had come to Büyük Ada he was already able to write to the Klyachkos in Vienna, an old Russian revolutionary family with whom he was friendly well before 1914: 'I am still completely immersed in this autobiography, and I do not know how to get out of it. I could have virtually completed it long ago, but an accursed pedantry does not allow me to complete it. I go on looking up references, checking dates, deleting one thing and inserting another. More than once I have felt tempted to throw it all into the fireplace and to take to more serious work. But, alas, this is summer, there is no fire in the fireplaces, and, by the way, there are no fireplaces here either.'[1] In May he had sent to Alexandra Ramm, his German translator, a large part of the work; a few weeks later she already had in hand the chapters on the civil war. But in July his 'accursed pedantry' pestered him again and he went back to rewrite the opening pages of the book. Early in the autumn the whole manuscript had already gone out and fragments were being serialized in newspapers. While he was still fastidiously correcting the German and the French translations, he was getting ready to start the *History of the Russian Revolution*, the first synopsis of which Alexandra Ramm received before the end of November.[2]

Amid this burst of activity he was never free from anxieties about children, grandchildren, and friends he had left 'beyond the frontier'. The sorrow of Nina's agony and death was still fresh with him when Zina's illness—Zina was his elder daughter from his first marriage—disturbed him. He inquired for news from her via Paris, where the Pazes kept in touch with his family in Moscow through a sympathizer on the staff of the Soviet Embassy. Zina suffered from consumption; and the death of her sister, the persecution of her father, the deportation to Siberia of Platon Volkov, her husband, and the difficulty of keeping herself and her two children alive, had strained her mental balance. She tried unsuccessfully to obtain official permission to leave the country and join her father. Trotsky supported her financially; and his well-wishers urged the Soviet Government to grant her an exit permit. Her mother, Alexandra Sokolovskaya, was still in Leningrad, though no one knew how long she would be allowed to stay there; and she took care of Nina's children—their father too, Man-Nevelson, was deported and imprisoned. This was not all: Lyova's wife and child were also left in Moscow, at fate's mercy.

---

[1] The letter was written on 1 June 1929. *The Archives*, Closed Section.

[2] Alexandra Ramm, of Russian origin, was the wife of Franz Pfemfert, editor of a radical weekly *Aktion*. Pfemfert had been expelled from the Communist party as an 'ultra-radical' after the third Congress of the Comintern, when Trotsky's influence was at its height; but he and his wife, disregarding political differences, retained to the end a warm friendship for Trotsky.

Thus, among Trotsky's next of kin no fewer than four families were broken up by the pitiless political conflict. And almost every week brought news about victimization of friends and untold miseries, illnesses in prison, starvation, clashes with jailers, hunger strikes, suicides, and deaths. Trotsky did what he could to arouse protests, especially against the persecution of Rakovsky, until lately the best known and the most respected of Soviet Ambassadors in the West, who was dragged from one place of deportation to another and suffered heart attacks, and from whom there was no news for several months.

Trotsky's vitality got the better of anxiety, worry, and fatigue. He drowned his sorrows in tenacious work and in intercourse with friends and followers; and he sought relief from the strain of work in rowing and fishing in the sky-coloured waters of the Marmara. Even while he rested he was unable to bring his energy to a standstill; he had to expend it in strenuous exertion all the time. As at Alma Ata his fishing was still a matter of elaborate expeditions with heavy boats, stones, and dragnets. He would go out for long trips, accompanied by two Turkish fishermen who gradually became part of the household; and with them he toiled, dragged the nets and stones, and carried back loads of fish. (Eastman, who found Trotsky's 'idea of relaxation' disagreeable, wondered 'if that is the mood in which he will go fishing—intense, speedy, systematic, organized for success, much as he went to Kazan to defeat the White Armies'.[1]) He was unable to use his strength, physical or mental, sparingly; and even chronic ill-health did not seem to impair his sinewy agility. Sometimes he sailed out by himself and, to the alarm of his family and secretaries, disappeared for long periods. A follower who arrived at such a moment wondered whether Trotsky was not afraid that the G.P.U. might lay a trap for him out at sea. Trotsky replied somewhat fatalistically that the G.P.U. were so powerful that once they decided to destroy him he would be helpless anyhow. In the meantime he saw no reason why he should become his own jailer and deny himself the little freedom left to him, and the colour and taste of life.[2]

---

[1] Eastman, loc. cit.

[2] M. Parijanine describes vividly a fishing escapade with Trotsky far in the waters of Asia Minor: '. . . he was bent on getting his trophy . . . one could sense his secret happiness . . . he is mastering the element.' At nightfall they were caught

The misgivings with which he had arrived in Turkey were somewhat allayed. The Turks behaved correctly, even helpfully. Kemal Pasha was as good as his word, though Trotsky was still incredulous. The police guards, placed at the gates of the villa, attached themselves so much to their ward that they also became part of the household, running errands, and helping in domestic chores. The White émigrés made no attempt to penetrate behind the high fences and hedges. Even the G.P.U. seemed remote and uninterested. This appearance, however, was deceptive: the G.P.U. were anything but aloof. All too often one of their agents, posing as an ardent follower, slipped into Trotsky's entourage as secretary or bodyguard. 'A Latvian Franck stayed at Prinkipo for five months', writes Natalya. 'Later we learned that he was an informer of the Russian Secret Service, just like one Sobolevicius, also a Latvian, who came to us for a short stay only (his brother Roman Well acted as *agent provocateur* in Opposition circles in Paris and central Europe . . .).'[1] The trouble was that not all those who were exposed as *agents provocateurs* necessarily acted that part, whereas the most dangerous spies were never detected. Sobolevicius, for instance, thirty years later imprisoned in the United States as a Soviet agent, confessed that he had indeed spied on Trotsky during the Prinkipo period.[2]

by a great storm. The boat was very nearly overwhelmed; the Turkish gendarme accompanying them was crying with fear; and Trotsky took the oars and struggled vigorously against the tide. Such was his calm, concern for companions, and humour that Parijanine thought of 'Don't fear . . . thou hast Caesar and his fortunes with thee'. They found refuge in an empty hut on a deserted little island. Next morning, left without food, they shot two rabbits. Parijanine, having only wounded his rabbit, killed it off. 'This is not the hunter's way,' Trotsky said, 'one doesn't kill a wounded animal.' In the meantime the Turkish authorities had begun a search; and some peasants came to the rescue. Trotsky received the help with self-irony, recalling Shchedrin's story about two Russian generals lost in an unknown land and unable to procure the barest necessities of life. 'Ah,' sighs one of them, 'if only we could find a *mouzhik* here!' 'And lo, the *mouzhik* appears at once; and in a moment he has done all that was needed'. 'A Léon Trotsky', *Les Humbles*, May-June 1934.

[1] V. Serge, *Vie et Mort de. Trotsky*, pp. 201-2.

[2] See *Hearing before the Subcommittee to Investigate the Administration of the Internal Security Act*, etc. *United States Senate*, 21 November 1957, pp. 4875-6, where Sobolevicius appears under the name of Jack Soble. In his correspondence with Trotsky he used the cover name Senin. His brother Dr. Soblen, also condemned, fled from the U.S.A. to Israel in 1962; but was denied refuge there. Being returned to the United States, via England, he committed two attempts on his life and died in London.

Yet his whole correspondence with Trotsky and the circumstances of their break throw doubt on the veracity of this part of his confession. Sobolevicius himself broke with Trotsky after he had openly and repeatedly expressed important political disagreements, which was not the manner in which an *agent provocateur* would behave. Trotsky denounced him in the end as a Stalinist, but did not believe that he was an *agent provocateur*. Whatever the truth, both Sobolevicius and his brother enjoyed Trotsky's almost unqualified confidence during the first three Prinkipo years. They were no novices to Trotskyist circles. Sobolevicius had been in Russia as correspondent of the left Marxist *Saechsische Arbeiterzeitung*, and there he joined the Trotskyist Opposition in 1927. Both he and his brother were later not only extremely active in France and Germany, they also supplied Trotsky with much useful information and with reference materials for his books; they helped him to publish the *Bulleten Oppozitsii*; and through their hands went much of his clandestine correspondence with the Soviet Union, codes, chemically written letters, cover addresses, etc.[1]

In an underground organization it is hardly ever possible to keep out the *agent provocateur* altogether. The organization is invariably the stool-pigeon's target; and it is just as easy to err on the side of too much suspicion, which may paralyse the entire organization, as on the side of too little vigilance. What made matters worse for Trotsky was that only very few of his western followers were familiar with the Russian language and background, and so he was unduly dependent on the few that were. His work would have been almost impossible without Lyova's assistance. But this was not enough; and Trotsky accepted his son's sacrifice with uneasiness, for it was a sacrifice on the part of a man in his early twenties to condemn himself to a hermit-like existence on Prinkipo. So Trotsky was all too often on the look-out for a Russian secretary, and this made it easier for the stool-pigeon to sneak in. Occasionally friends forestalled trouble with a timely warning. Thus, early in 1930, Valentine Olberg, of Russian-Menshevik parentage, posing as a Trotskyist, tried hard to obtain access to Prinkipo as a secre-

---

[1] The correspondence between Trotsky, Sobolevicius, and his brother R. Well (Dr. Soblen) fills two files in the Closed Section of *The Archives*.

tary. But from Berlin Franz Pfemfert and Alexandra Ramm, suspicious of the applicant, informed Trotsky of their fears and Olberg was turned away—in 1936 he was to appear as defendant and witness against Trotsky, Zinoviev, and Kamenev in the first of the great Moscow trials.[1] Such timely warnings were all too rare, however; and in years to come the shadowy figure of the *agent provocateur* was to follow Trotsky like a curse.

. . . .

Trotsky's financial circumstances during the Prinkipo period were much easier than he had expected. His literary earnings were large, life on the island was cheap, and his and the family's needs were extremely modest. As the household increased, with secretaries and long-staying guests always around, and as the correspondence became almost as voluminous as that of a minor government department, the expenses rose to 12,000 and even 15,000 American dollars per year.[2] A wide international readership assured Trotsky of correspondingly high fees and royalties. For his first articles written in Constantinople he received 10,000 dollars, of which he put aside 6,000 as a publication fund for the *Bulletin Oppozitsii* and French and even American Trotskyist papers. Later in the year he received considerable advances on the various editions of *My Life*, 7,000 dollars on the American edition alone. In 1932 the *Saturday Evening Post* paid 45,000 dollars for the serialization of the *History of the Russian Revolution*.[3] When he left the Soviet Consulate in Constantinople, Trotsky borrowed 20,000 French francs from Maurice Paz. A year later he repaid the debt and had no need to borrow any more. When in May 1929 Paz inquired whether he was not in any difficulties, Trotsky

[1] Pfemfert's correspondence with Trotsky, April 1930, ibid. Olberg was a member of the *Reichsleitung* of the German Opposition. He aroused suspicion by his insistent inquiries about Trotsky's contacts with followers in the Soviet Union. (See also the correspondence between Olberg and Lev Sedov.) Whether he was an *agent-provocateur* in 1930 or became one later is, as in the case of Sobolevicius, not definitely established. After the rise of Nazism, in 1933–4, Olberg is said to have lived in dire poverty as a political émigré in Czechoslovakia. He may, of course, have acted as a Stalinist stool-pigeon for 'ideological' reasons, without receiving any reward. He was a defendant and one of the Prosecution's chief witnesses in Zinoviev's trial in 1936; and was sentenced to death.

[2] Eastman, op. cit.

[3] These data are drawn from Trotsky's accounts and correspondence with his publishers and literary agents. *The Archives*, Closed Section.

answered that far from this being the case he could now afford
to assist financially his political friends in the West. This, as his
correspondence and preserved accounts show, he did with an
unstinting hand, on which some of the recipients presently
came rather unbecomingly to rely.

.   .   .   .

Long before their defeat Trotsky, Zinoviev, and even
Shlyapnikov had made attempts at organizing their followers
in foreign Communist parties. These efforts were not altogether unsuccessful at first, despite excommunications and
expulsions.[1] The tactical manœuvres and retreats, however, of
the Russian Opposition disorientated communists abroad as
strongly as Stalinist reprisals intimidated them. The final
capitulation of Zinoviev's faction demoralized its foreign
associates. Trotsky's reverses and deportation had not had quite
the same effect. In the eyes of communists not yet fully prepared
to submit to Stalinist dictates, his moral authority stood as high
as ever; and the legend which surrounded his name, the legend
of indomitable militancy and victory, was enriched with its
new note of martyrdom. Yet the Comintern had already
stigmatized Trotskyism with so much brutality and was so
ferociously stamping it out from foreign sections that no
communist could hope to gain any advantage by embracing the
heresy; and few were those prepared to follow the martyr on his
path.

From Prinkipo, Trotsky set out to rally anew his supporters,
past and present. That he had no power to share with them did
not in his eyes render the undertaking hopeless—this made
it in a way even more attractive. Knowing that self-seekers
and bureaucrats would not respond, he appealed only to the
thoughtful and disinterested. Had not the strength of a revolutionary organization always consisted in the depth of the
conviction held by its members and in their devotion rather
than in their numbers? At the turn of the decade Stalin's mastery
of the Comintern was still superficial. Almost anyone who spent

[1] In a letter written to Sobolevicius and Well on 4 November 1929, Trotsky
maintained that the German *Leninbund* carried on its activities for money which its
leaders had received from Pyatakov before the latter's capitulation. The scale of
these activities was so modest that quite a small amount of money would have
enabled them to carry on.

those years in the Communist party can relate from experience
the bewilderment and the reluctance with which cadres and
rankers alike began to conform to the new orthodoxy consecrated in Moscow. Underneath the conformity, still only skin
deep, there was malaise, incredulity, and restiveness; and there
were old Marxist habits of thought and uneasy consciences, to
which Trotsky's fate was a constant challenge. The good party
man considered it his supreme duty to practise solidarity with
the Russian revolution; and so he could not take it upon himself
to contradict the men who now ruled Moscow, who spoke with
the voice of the revolution, and who insisted that the foreign
communist should, at committees and cells, vote for resolutions
condemning Trotskyism. The party man voted as he was
required, but the whole 'campaign' remained to him a sad
puzzle. The venom with which it was pursued vaguely offended
him. He was unable to discern its motive. And sometimes he
wondered why he should be required to add his own modest
endorsement to the awe-inspiring anathemas pronounced from
so far above. Working-class members, except for the very young
and uninformed, recalled the days of Trotsky's glory, his
resounding assaults on world capitalism, and his fiery manifestoes that had stirred so many of them and even brought some
of them into the ranks. The change in the party's attitude
towards the man whom they remembered as Lenin's closest
companion seemed incomprehensible. Yet there was little or
nothing they could do about it. Here and there a few men
disgusted by this or that manipulation of the 'party line'
renounced membership; but most reflected that they should
not perhaps be unduly concerned over what looked like a
feud among the big chiefs, that Russia was anyhow far away
and difficult to understand, but that their own class enemies
were near at home, and against them the Communist party
fought reliably and bravely. They continued to give their
allegiance to the party, but they did so despite and not because
of Stalinism; and for some time yet they shrugged with embarrassment when they heard party officialdom rail against
Trotsky, the 'traitor and the counter-revolutionary'.

Trotsky's hold on the imagination of the left and radical
intelligentsia was still immense. When Bernard Shaw wrote of
him as becoming anew the 'inspirer and hero of all the militants

of the extreme left of every country' he was not as far from the
truth as may have seemed later.[1] We have seen the impressive
list of the celebrities of radical England who spoke up in
Trotsky's defence against their own government. (True,
the British Communist party was less 'infected with Trotskyism' than any other; yet in Trotsky's Prinkipo correspondence
one finds a thick file of extremely friendly and revealing letters
he exchanged with an English communist writer, later notorious for Stalinist orthodoxy.) Among European and American
poets, novelists, and artists, famous or about to gain fame,
André Breton and others of the Surrealist school, Henrietta
Roland Holst, the Dutch poetess, Panait Istrati, whose meteoric
and sad literary career was then at its zenith, Diego Rivera,
Edmund Wilson, the young André Malraux, and many
others, were under his spell. 'Trotsky continued to haunt the
communist intellectuals', says a historian of American communism; and by way of illustration he quotes Michael Gold the
well-known communist writer and editor who even after the
first anathemas on Trotsky 'could not resist extolling Trotsky
[in the *New Masses*] as "almost as universal as Leonardo da
Vinci" '! As late as 1930 Gold wrote, among some tritely
derogatory remarks, that ' "Trotsky is now an immortal part of
the great Russian Revolution . . . one of the permanent legends
of humanity, like Savonarola or Danton".'[2] 'The unbounded
admiration for Trotsky was not confined to Michael Gold',
testifies another American communist man of letters, 'it marked
all the extreme radicals of this country who followed Russian
events. . . .'

In most European countries groups of expelled Trotskyists

---

[1] Shaw had many times expressed his admiration for Trotsky with unusual
ardour. In one of his letters to Molly Tompkins, for instance, he wrote:
'Yesterday . . . I had with me a bundle of reports of the speeches of our great
party leaders, and a half-crown book by Trotsky. . . . For sheer coarse savage
bloodymindedness it would be hard to beat the orations of Birkenhead, Lloyd
George, and Churchill. For good sense, unaffected frankness, and educated mental
capacity give me Trotsky all the time. To turn from the presidential campaign in
your country and the general election here to his surveys of the position is to move
to another planet.' G. B. Shaw, *To a Young Actress*, p. 78. It was Shaw who first
compared Trotsky, the writer, with Lessing (in terms which he borrowed from
Heines *Zur Geschichte der Philosophie und Religion in Deutschland*). See my Preface to
The Prophet Armed. See also further, p. 369.

[2] Th. Draper, *American Communism and Soviet Russia*, p. 358; and *Roots of American
Communism*, p. 129. See also J. Freeman, *An American Testament*, pp. 383–4.

and Zinovievists, led by a few of the founders of the Communist International, were active. It was only five years or so since the Central Committee of the French party had unanimously protested to Moscow against the anti-Trotskyist campaign. Between 1924 and 1929 Alfred Rosmer, Boris Souvarine, and others went on contending against Stalinism.[1] Trotskyist sympathies were alive in the revolutionary-syndicalist circle of Pierre Monatte which had formed one of the constituent elements of the French Communist party but had since become estranged from it. The Zinovievists kept their own *côterie*. In Germany there were the Leninbund and also the Wedding Opposition (so called after Berlin's largest working-class district); but there Zinovievism, as represented by Arkadii Maslov and Ruth Fisher, rather than Trotskyism set the tone of the dissidence. Two important Italian communist leaders, Antonio Gramsci and Amadeo Bordiga, both Mussolini's prisoners, had declared themselves against Stalin: Gramsci, from his prison cell, had sent his declaration to Moscow, where Togliatti, the party's representative with the Comintern Executive, suppressed it.[2] Andrés Nin, the most able

---

[1] *The Prophet Unarmed*, pp. 140–1. In 1926 Pyatakov, then on the staff of the Soviet Embassy in Paris, sought to unite the various anti-Stalinist elements expelled from the French Communist party. In Moscow, Trotsky and Zinoviev were forming the Joint Opposition, and Pyatakov's task was to create a French counterpart to it. He held meetings with Rosmer, A. Dunois, Loriot, Souvarine, Monatte, Paz, and others, and initiated the publication of *Contre le Courant*. But Rosmer and Monatte, hostile towards any idea of a 'bloc' between Trotskyists and Zinovievists, refused to co-operate; and so *Contre le Courant* began to appear as the French organ of the Joint Opposition, under the editorship of the Pazes and Loriot. Rosmer and Monatte continued their anti-Stalinist activities independently.

[2] *Bulletin Oppozitsii*, nos. 17–18, 1930, see also Rosmer's letter to Trotsky of 10 April 1930 in *The Archives*, Closed Section. About this time three members of the Italian Politbureau, Ravazzoli, Leonetti, and Tresso, went over to the Trotskyist Opposition. They were friends and followers of Gramsci; and one of them informed Rosmer about Gramsci's letter to Togliatti and its suppression. In 1961 I asked Togliatti publicly, in the Italian Press, to explain the matter. He answered through a friend of his that Gramsci had indeed urged him in 1926 not to involve Italian communism in the Russian inner-party struggle. (Togliatti had backed Bukharin and Stalin against Trotsky.) Togliatti maintains that Gramsci's letter arrived in Moscow during an inner-party truce; and so, after consulting Bukharin, he decided that it had no relevance to the current situation. When the struggle between Stalin and Trotsky was resumed, the Comintern and the Italian party were nevertheless kept in ignorance about Gramsci's attitude. This attitude accounted for the oblivion to which Gramsci's memory was consigned during the Stalin era. Only after Stalin's death were Gramsci's merits 'rediscovered', and Togliatti initiated something like a posthumous Gramsci cult in the Italian party.

exponent of Marxism in Spain, had thrown in his lot with the Russian Opposition and had for years kept in touch with Trotsky.[1] In Holland Maring-Sneevliet, the first inspirer of Indonesian communism, led a fairly strong group of Dutch left trade unionists opposed to Stalinism. In Belgium Van Overstraeten and Lesoil, ex-chiefs of the Communist party, and their followers strongly entrenched in the large mining district of Charleroi, had also embraced Trotskyism.

The inner party controversy had some repercussions even in Asia. The germs of Trotskyism had been brought to Shanghai, Peking, Quantung, and Wuhan by former students of the Sun Yat-sen University in Moscow, witnesses of Trotsky's struggle over the Chinese issue in 1927. In 1928 they held the first national conference of the Chinese Opposition; and some of them looked forward to an alliance with Mao Tse-tung, on whom the Comintern frowned at this time, because his attitude in 1925–7 had often coincided with Trotsky's and because he was now, at the ebb of the revolution, embarking upon partisan warfare against the Kuomintang. In 1929 Chen Tu-hsiu, the party's leader up to 1927, came out with the Open Letter in which he revealed the sordid inner story of the relations between Moscow, the Kuomintang, and Chinese communism, and acknowledged that Trotsky's criticisms of Stalin's and Bukharin's policy had been only too well founded.[2] The Trotskyist

---

[1] Nin was in correspondence with Trotsky during the Alma Ata period. *The Archives.*

[2] Trotsky's interest in China was as sustained as his contacts with his Chinese followers were, in the circumstances, close. In the summer or autumn of 1929 Lin Tse (?), an Oppositionist *en route* from Moscow to China, visited him in Prinkipo, and thereafter, until 1940, Trotsky was in almost regular correspondence with several groups in China representing different shades of Opposition. As early as 1929–31 his Chinese followers reported to him the rivalries between Li Li-san, then official party leader, Chu Teh, and Mao Tse-tung, dismissing the former two as 'opportunists' and placing great hopes on Mao. Some of Trotsky's followers were not at all elated over Chen Tu-hsiu's 'conversion to Trotskyism'; they considered him a 'liquidator' and held that he had played out his role. Trotsky, to whom Mao's name could not yet mean much, attached great importance to Chen Tu-hsiu, the 'grand old man' of Chinese Marxism, and tried to reconcile the Chinese Trotskyists with him. Chen Tu-hsiu himself, in a letter to Trotsky of 1 December 1930, explained that he had first acquainted himself with the latter's views on the Chinese Revolution in the summer of 1929, and that no sooner had he done so than he became convinced of their correctness. (*The Archives*, Closed Section. Further reference to this correspondence is made later on pp. 423–24. Chen Tu-hsiu's part in the revolution of 1925–7 is described in *The Prophet Unarmed*, pp. 317–38.)

influence made itself felt in Indo-China, Indonesia, and Ceylon. About the same time Trotsky gained new adherents in America: James P. Cannon and Max Shachtman, members of the Central Committee in the United States, and Maurice Spector, chairman of the Communist party of Canada. Even in remote Mexico a group of communists, encouraged by Diego Rivera, rallied to the cause of the heretics defeated in Moscow.

Trotsky established liaison with all these groups, and tried to weld them into a single organization. Since his deportation from Moscow they had lived on crumbs of his thought and had published, in small papers and bulletins, fragments of his writings, surreptitiously brought out of the Soviet Union. His appearance in Constantinople gave them a fillip; his moral authority was their greatest asset; and they expected him to give life to a world-wide communist opposition to Stalinism. True, his authority was also a liability, for they were becoming accustomed to the constricting roles of disciples and devotees. Trotskyism was already, as Heinrich Brandler put it, a tiny boat overweighted by a huge sail. Even in the Russian Opposition Trotsky's personality had been pre-eminent; but there at least he had been surrounded by associates distinguished in the revolution, men of independent mind, strong character, and rich experience. There were, with one or two exceptions, no men of such weight among his associates outside Russia. He hoped that this weakness of the Opposition would soon be remedied and that new leaders would rise from the ranks. He did not imagine that he would remain the only expatriate leader of the Russian Opposition. He expected that Stalin would banish others beside him, especially Rakovsky and Radek, and that once these had emerged from Russia the international opposition would obtain a 'strong directing centre'.[1] These expectations were not to be fulfilled: Stalin had no intention of strengthening Trotsky's hand by further banishments.

   .   .   .   .

What, apart from the magic of a personality, did Trotskyism represent at this stage?

[1] *B.O.*, nos. 1–2, July 1929. From now on the initials *B.O.* are used for *Bulletin Oppozitsii*.

D

At its heart were the principles of revolutionary internationalism and proletarian democracy. Revolutionary internationalism belonged to the heritage of classical Marxism; the Third International had once rescued it from the failing hands of the Second; and now Trotsky defended it against both the Third and the Second Internationals. This principle was no mere abstraction to him: it permeated his thought and his political instincts. He never viewed any issue of policy otherwise than in the international perspective; and the supranational interest of communism was his supreme criterion. Hence he saw the doctrine of 'socialism in a single country' as a 'national socialist' distortion of Marxism and as the epitome of the national self-sufficiency and arrogance of the Soviet bureaucracy. That doctrine now ruled not only in the Soviet Union, where at least it met a psychological need; it was also the official canon of international communism, where it met no such need. In bowing to the sacred egoism of Stalinist Russia the Comintern had shattered its own *raison d'être*: an International hitched to socialism in a single country was a contradiction in terms. Trotsky pointed out that, theoretically, the conception of an isolated and self-contained socialist state was alien to Marxist thinking—it originated in the national-reformist theory of the German revisionists of the nineteenth century— and that practically it expressed renunciation of international revolution and the subordination of Comintern policy to Stalinist expediency.[1] Upholding the primacy of the inter-

[1] Trotsky traced the ancestry of Socialism in a Single Country to G. Vollmar, the well-known German reformist, who twenty years before Bernstein's 'revisionist' campaign expounded the idea of the 'isolated socialist state'. (This, we may add, was a socialist variation on the basic theme of List's economics.) Vollmar's conception, Trotsky pointed out, was more subtle than Stalin's or Bukharin's, because his isolated socialist state was to be a state like Germany, enjoying technological ascendancy, not an underdeveloped peasant nation. Vollmar saw in the technological superiority of the isolated socialist state over its capitalist neighbours the guarantee of its security and success, whereas Bukharin and Stalin (up to 1928) were satisfied that such a state could flourish even in industrial backwardness. (See Trotsky, *The Third International After Lenin*, pp. 43–4.) Vollmar also imagined that a socialist Germany, using the advantages of superior technology and planned economy, would vanquish its capitalist neighbours through peaceful economic competition and would thus render revolution in other countries more or less superfluous. With this idea, Vollmar anticipated not only and not so much the Stalinist-Bukharinist conception of the 1920s as the Khrushchevite theses of 'economic competition' and 'peaceful transition to socialism' adopted by the XX Congress of the Soviet Communist party in February 1956.

national interest *vis-à-vis* the national, Trotsky was, however, far from treating the national needs of the Soviet Union with any degree of nihilistic neglect, or from overlooking its specific diplomatic or military interests; and he insisted that the defence of the workers' first state was the duty of every communist. But he was convinced that Stalinist self-sufficiency weakened the Soviet Union, whose ultimate interest lay in overcoming its isolation and in the spread of revolution. He held therefore that at decisive stages of the international class struggle the workers' state should, on a long term view, be prepared to sacrifice immediate advantages rather than obstruct that struggle, as Stalin and Bukharin obstructed the Chinese Revolution in 1925–7. In the coming decade this controversy was to shift to issues of communist strategy and tactics *vis-à-vis* Nazism and the Popular Fronts; but underlying it still was the same conflict between (to use an analogy with contemporary American politics) Trotskyist internationalism and the isolationism which coloured Stalin's policies in the nineteen-twenties and thirties.

On the face of it Trotsky's attitude was, or should have been, much more congenial to communists outside the Soviet Union than was Stalin's, and he had reason to expect that it would meet with the stronger response, for he dwelt on their importance as independent actors in the international class struggle, whereas Stalinism assigned to them the parts of the mere clients of the 'workers' fatherland'.

Trotsky's advocacy of 'proletarian democracy' aimed at freeing the Communist parties from the rigidities of their ultra-bureaucratic organization and at the restitution in their midst of 'democractic centralism'. This principle, too, had been embedded in their Marxist tradition and was still inscribed in their statutes. Democratic centralism had sought to safeguard for the Socialist and later the Communist parties freedom in discipline and discipline in freedom. It obliged them to maintain the strictest concord and unity in action, and allowed them to entertain the widest diversity of views compatible with their programme. It committed minorities to carrying out majority decisions; and it bound the majority to respect the right of any minority to criticize and oppose. It invested the Central Committee of any party (and the leadership of the Internationa with the power to command effectively the rank and file during its tenure of office; but it made that Central Committee dependent on the will and the unhampered vote of the rank and file. The principle had therefore been of great educative and practical political value for the movement; and its abandonment and replacement by bureaucratic centralism crippled the International. If in the Soviet party the monolithic discipline and the over-centralization were part and parcel of the organic evolution of the Bolshevik monopoly of power, the extension of this régime to the foreign sections of the Comintern was wholly artificial and bore no relation to their national environments and conditions of existence.

Most western Communist parties had been accustomed to act within the multi-party system where, as a rule, they enjoyed the formal freedom of criticism and debate. Their leaders now found themselves in the paradoxical situation that within their own organization they denied their own followers the rights which the latter enjoyed outside the organization. By 1930 no German, French, or other communist could voice dissent from the party line; they had to accept as gospel all official pronouncements coming from Moscow. Thus every Communist party became in its own country something like a bizarre enclave, sharply separated from the rest of the nation not so much by its revolutionary purpose as by a code of behaviour which had little to do with that purpose. This was the code of a quasi-ecclesiastical order which subjected its members to a mental drill as severe as any that had been practised in any monastic body since the counter-reformation. It is true that by means of this drill the Stalinized Comintern achieved extraordinary feats of discipline. But discipline of this type was destructive of the efficacy of a revolutionary party. Such a party must be in and of the people among whom it works; it must not be set apart by the observances of an esoteric cult. Stalinism, with its devotions, burnt offerings, and incense, undoubtedly fascinated some intellectuals in search of a creed, those intellectuals who were later to curse it as the 'God that failed'. But the cult that captivated them rarely appealed to the mass of workers, to those 'sturdy proletarians' whom it was supposed to suit. Moreover, the strange discipline and ritual tied the party agitators hand and foot when what they needed was a free and easy approach to those whom they desired to win for their cause. When the European communist went out to argue his case before a working-class audience, he usually met there a Social Democratic opponent whose arguments he had to refute and whose slogans he had to counter. Most frequently he was unable to do this, because he lacked the habits of political debate, which were not cultivated within the party, and because his schooling deprived him of the ability to preach to the unconverted. He could not probe adequately into his opponent's case when he had to think all the time about his own orthodoxy and to check perpetually whether in what he himself was saying he was not unwittingly deviating from the party line. He could expound with mechanical fanaticism a prescribed set of arguments and slogans; but unforeseen opposition or heckling at once put him out of countenance. When he was called upon, as he often was, to answer criticisms of the Soviet Union he could rarely do so convincingly; his thanksgiving prayers to the workers' fatherland and his hosannahs for Stalin covered him with ridicule in the eyes of any sober-minded audience. This ineffectiveness of the Stalinist agitation was one of the main reasons why over many years, even in the most favourable circumstances, that agitation made little or no headway against Social Democratic reformism.

Trotsky set out to shake the Communist parties from their petrifaction and to reawaken in them the *élan*, the self-reliance, and the fighting ardour which were once theirs—and which they could not recover without freedom in their own ranks. Again and again he expounded the meaning of 'democratic centralism' for the benefit of communists who had never grasped it or who had forgotten it. He appealed to them in their own interest, in the name of their own dignity and future, hoping that they would not remain unresponsive. And indeed, if reason, Marxist principle, or communist self-interest had had any say in the matter, his arguments and pleas would not have fallen on deaf ears.

Apart from its fundamental principles, Trotskyism represented also a set of tactical conceptions varying with circumstances. An inordinately large proportion of Trotsky's writings in exile consists of comments on these topics, which are rarely exciting to outsiders, especially after the lapse of time. However, the range of Trotsky's tactical ideas was so wide and his views are in part still so relevant to working-class politics, that what he had to say is of more than historical interest.

It will be remembered that between 1923 and 1928, when the Comintern pursued a 'moderate' line, Trotsky and his adherents criticized it from the left.[1] After 1928 this changed to some extent. Since Stalin had initiated the 'left course' in the Soviet Union, the policy of the Comintern too had, by an automatic transmission to it of every movement and reflex from the Russian party, changed direction. Already at its Sixth Congress, in the summer of 1928, the International began to transpose its watchwords and tactical prescriptions from the rightist to an ultra-left pattern.[2] In the following months the new line was further evolved until it was in every respect diametrically opposed to the old.[3] While in previous years the Comintern spoke of the 'relative stabilization of capitalism', it now diagnosed the end of the stabilization and predicted the imminent and final collapse of capitalism. This was the crux of the so-called Third Period Theory, of which Molotov, who replaced Bukharin as head of the Comintern, became the chief exponent. According to that 'theory', the political history of the post-war era fell into three distinct chapters: the first, one of revolutionary strains and stresses, had lasted till 1923; the second, capitalist stabilization, had come to an end by 1928; while the third, now opening, was to bring the death agony of capitalism and imperialism. If hitherto international communism had been on the defensive, it was time now to pass to the offensive and to turn from the struggle for 'partial demands' and reforms to the direct contest for power.

The Comintern alleged that all the contradictions of capitalism were about to explode because the bourgeoisie would be unable to master the next economic crisis; and that the makings of a revolutionary situation were already evident all over the world, especially in a new radicalism of the working classes, who were shaking off reformist illusions and virtually waiting for the communists to place themselves at their head and lead them into battle. Almost any incident of class conflict now had

---

[1] See *The Prophet Unarmed*, Chapters II and V.
[2] *Kommunisticheskii Internatsional v Dokumentakh*, (ed. B. Kun), pp. 769–84.
[3] Op. cit., pp. 876–88, 915–25, 957–66.

incalculable revolutionary momentum and could lead to the 'struggle for the street', or, more explicitly, to armed insurrection. 'In the whole capitalist world', *Bolshevik* wrote in June 1929, 'the strike wave is mounting . . . elements of a stubborn revolutionary struggle and of civil war are intertwined with the strikes. The masses of unorganized workers are drawn into the fight. . . . The growth of dissatisfaction and the leftward swing embrace also millions of agricultural labourers and the oppressed peasantry.' 'One must be a dull opportunist or a sorry liberal . . .', Molotov told the Executive of the International, 'not to see that we have stepped with both feet into a zone of the most tremendous revolutionary events of international significance.' These words were not meant as long-term predictions but as topical forecasts and directions for action. Several European Communist parties tried indeed to turn the May Day parades of 1929 and anti-war demonstrations called for 4 August into direct 'struggles for the street', which resulted in fruitless and bloody clashes between demonstrators and police in Berlin, Paris, and other cities.

In accordance with this 'general line', the Comintern also changed its attitude towards the Social Democratic parties. In a truly revolutionary situation, it was said, those parties could only side with counter-revolution; and so no ground was left for communists to seek co-operation or partial agreements with them. As the bourgeoisie was striving to save its rule with the help of fascism, as the era of parliamentary government and democratic liberties was coming to a close, and as parliamentary democracy itself was being transformed 'from the inside' into fascism, the Social Democratic parties too were becoming 'social-fascist'—'socialist in words and fascist in deeds'. Because they concealed their 'true nature' under the paraphernalia of democracy and socialism, the Social Democrats were an even greater menace than plain fascism. It was therefore on 'social fascism' as 'the main enemy' that communists ought to concentrate their fire. Similarly, the left Social Democrats, often speaking a language almost indistinguishable from that of communism, were even more dangerous than the right wing 'social-fascists', and should be combated even more vigorously. If, hitherto, communists were required to form united fronts with the Social Democrats from 'above and below', with leaders and rank and file alike, the Comintern now declared a rigorous ban on any such tactics. 'Only from below' could the united front still be practised—communists were permitted to co-operate only with those of the Social Democratic rank and file who were 'ready to break with their own leaders'. To favour any contact 'from above' was to aid and abet 'social-fascism'.[1]

These notions and prescriptions were to govern the policies of all Communist parties for the next five or six years, almost up to the time of the Popular Front, throughout the fateful years of the Great Slump, the rise of Nazism, the collapse of the monarchy in Spain, and other events in which the conduct of the Communist parties was of crucial importance.

In the previous period, when Trotsky maintained that by its timid policies the Comintern was wasting revolutionary opportunities, he never proposed a reversal of its line as sweeping and extreme as the one now carried out. He therefore criticized the reversal as a 'turn by 180 degrees' and a 'swing from opportunism to ultra-radicalism': the new slogans and tactical prescriptions merely turned the old ones inside out and served to cover up their fiasco. In a devastating comment on Molotov's disquisitions on the Three Periods, Trotsky pointed out that if it was wrong to consider the 'second period', during which the Chinese Revolution and the British General Strike had occurred, as one of stabilization, it was even less realistic to envisage the imminent collapse of capitalism in the 'third period', and to deduce the need for an exclusively offensive policy. The Comintern, he said, had accomplished this 're-orientation' quite mechanically, without any attempt to elucidate what had gone wrong with its old tactics, and without any genuine debate and reappraisal of the issues. Prevented from discussing the rights and wrongs of their own policy, the Communist parties were condemned to veer from extreme to extreme and to exchange, on orders, one set of blunders for another. Their inner régime was no mere matter of organiza-tion—it affected the entire policy of the International, making it rigid and unstable at the same time. Nor did the feverish ultra-radicalism of the 'third period' testify to any reawakened revolutionary internationalism in official Moscow. That ultra-radicalism obstructed the growth of communism in the world

[1] Op. cit., pp. 946, 957–66, and *passim*.

not less effectively than did the earlier opportunism, and underlying it was the same cynical bureaucratic indifference to the international interests of the working class.[1]

Now as before Trotsky expounded the view that the whole epoch opened by the First World War and the Russian Revolution was one of the decline of capitalism, the very foundations of which were shattered. This, however, did not mean that the edifice was about to come down with a crash. The decay of a social system is never a single process of economic collapse or an uninterrupted succession of revolutionary situations. No slump was therefore *a priori* the 'last and final'. Even in its decay capitalism must have its ups and downs (although the ups tended to become ever shorter and shakier and the downs ever steeper and more ruinous). The trade cycle, however it had changed since Marx's time, still ran its usual course, not only from boom to slump but also from slump to boom. It was therefore preposterous to announce that the bourgeoisie had 'objectively' reached its ultimate impasse: there existed no such impasse from which a possessing class would not fight its way out; and whether it would succeed or not depended not so much on purely economic factors as on the balance of political forces, which could be tilted one way or the other by the quality of the communist leadership. To forecast an 'uninterruptedly mounting tide of revolution', to discover 'elements of civil war' in almost any turbulent strike, and to proclaim that the moment had come to pass from defensive to offensive action and armed insurrection was to offer no leadership at all and to court defeat. In class struggle as in war defensive and offensive forms of action could not be separated from and opposed to one another. The most effective offensive usually grows out of successful defence; and an element of defence persists even in armed insurrection, that climax of all revolutionary struggle. During slump and depression the workers had to defend themselves against attacks on their living standards and against the rise of fascism. To tell them that the time for such defence had passed and that they must be ready for the all-out attack on capitalism was to preach nothing but inaction or surrender, and to preach it at the very top of one's ultra-radical voice.

[1] Trotsky devoted to the criticism of the Third Period Policy a whole issue of the *B.O.*, no. 8 (January 1930), and returned to it in many subsequent issues.

Similarly, to ban all co-operation between Communist and Socialist parties was to invite disaster for the labour movement at large and communism in particular. The notion of the Third Period, Trotsky concluded, was a product of bureaucratic recklessness—'all that had been inaugurated', under the auspices of 'Maestro Molotov', was 'the third period of the Comintern's blunders'.

These early criticisms contained in a nutshell Trotsky's far larger controversy with the Comintern (over the latter's policy during Hitler's rise to power) which was to fill the early nineteen-thirties. Clearly, on these tactical issues Trotskyism now appeared to oppose the Comintern from the right and not, as hitherto, from the left. The change lay not in Trotsky's attitude, which remained consistent with the one which Lenin and he had adopted at the third and fourth Comintern congresses in 1921–2, but in the gyrations of Stalin's 'bureaucratic centralism' and in the 'alternation of its rightist and ultra-left zigzags'. Even so, the position of being Stalin's critic 'from the right' had its inconveniences for Trotsky. Communists accustomed to think of him as Stalin's critic from the left were apt to suspect inconsistency or lack of principle. In fact, the division between Trotskyism and the various rightist quasi-Bukharinist oppositions in the communist camp was blurred, at least in the tactical issues which loomed so large in these controversies. The right oppositions in Europe, of which the Brandlerites were by far the most important—Brandler and Thalheimer had just been expelled from their party—also severely criticized the new ultra-radicalism.[1] Yet what set Trotskyism apart from all other brands of opposition was the intellectual power, the aggressiveness, and the comprehensiveness of its criticism. Brandler and Thalheimer confined themselves to exposing only the latest, the ultra-left, 'zigzag' of the Comintern; Trotsky attacked its entire post-Leninist record. The Brandlerites, concerned mainly with the policies of their national parties, studiously refrained from offending the Soviet leadership: in internal Soviet conflicts they willy-nilly sided with Stalin, endorsing socialism in one country, excusing the bureaucratic régime as fitting Russia's

---

[1] Groups akin to the Brandlerites were those of Warski and Kostrzewa in Poland (who were demoted in 1929 but not yet expelled from the party), of Humbert Droz in Switzerland, and of Lovestone in the United States.

peculiar conditions, and even echoing Moscow's denunciations of Trotskyism.[1] They were convinced that no communist opposition which defied Moscow on principle could evoke response in communist ranks; and they hoped that the Comintern would sooner or later find the Third Period policy impracticable, discard it, and reconcile itself with those of its critics who had shunned an irreparable breach. Against this, Trotskyism insisted that the policies of the various national parties could not be corrected, or their faults remedied, within those parties alone, because the main source of their 'degeneration' lay in Moscow; and that it was therefore the duty of all communists to take the closest interest in domestic Soviet affairs and to oppose on that ground, too, the Stalinist bureaucracy. This call for the intervention of foreign communist opinion in Soviet affairs was peculiar to Trotskyism. It was a challenge, which struck horror in most communist hearts.

Despite the comprehensiveness of its criticism of the Comintern, Trotskyism did not aspire to set up a new communist movement. Now and for several years to come Trotsky was absolutely opposed to the idea of a Fourth International, already canvassed by the Workers' Opposition in the Soviet Union and by some survivors of the Zinovievist opposition in Europe. He declared that he and his adherents owed their loyalty to the Communist International even though they had been expelled from it. They formed a school of thought struggling to regain its place within the general communist movement—only persecution had forced them to constitute themselves into a faction; and a faction, not a rival party, they remained. Their sole purpose was to influence communist opinion, to make it realize that usurpers had seized the reins of the Soviet Government and of the Comintern, and to induce it to strive for the restoration of pristine Marxism and Leninism. They therefore stood for a reform of the International, not for a permanent break with it. Trotsky believed that with all their flaws and vices the Communist parties still represented the militant vanguard of the working classes. The Opposition's

[1] The Brandlerite *Arbeiterpolitik* maintained a consistently hostile attitude towards Trotskyism, and Trotsky repaid it in the same coin: 'Just as I do not discuss various trends in materialism with anyone who crosses himself when passing by a church, so I shall not argue with Brandler and Thalheimer', he wrote on one occasion.

place was with that vanguard. If he and his followers were to
turn their backs on it, they would voluntarily go out into the
wilderness into which Stalin was driving them. True enough,
Stalinism did not allow any current of opposition to assert
itself within the International; but this state of affairs could
not last: critical events inside or outside the Soviet Union
would presently stir the dormant *élan* of communism into
action again and give the Opposition its chance. Trotsky
warned those who stood for a Fourth International that it was
not enough for a group of dissidents to raise a new banner in
order to become a real factor in politics. Revolutionary
movements were not conjured up with banners and slogans,
but rose and grew organically with the social class for which
they spoke. Each of the Internationals represented a definite
stage in the historic experience of the working class and in the
struggle for socialism; and no one could ignore with impunity
the ties the Second and the Third Internationals had with the
masses or the weight of their political traditions. Moreover, the
Third International was the child of the Russian Revolution;
and the politically conscious workers extended to it the solidarity they felt with the Revolution. They were right in doing so,
Trotsky maintained, though they should not allow Stalinism to
abuse their loyalty. And so, as long as the Soviet Union
remained a workers' state, the workers should not be expected
or urged to renounce the Third International.

On this point, that the Soviet Union, however 'bureaucratically deformed', remained a workers' state, Trotsky was
adamant. What, in his view, determined the social character
of the Soviet state was the national ownership of the means of
production. As long as this, 'the most important conquest of
October', was unimpaired, the Soviet Union possessed the
foundations on which to base its socialist development. To be
sure, its working class had to assert itself against the bureaucracy
before it could even begin to make socialism a reality; but, once
again, it could not make that into a reality otherwise than on the
basis of public ownership. With this preserved, the workers'
state was still alive, as a potentiality if not an actuality.

This view was often to be challenged, among others by
Trotsky's own disciples; but he was never to compromise over it
or to yield an inch from it, even when he revised and modified

his other ideas. Thus, during the first half of this term of exile he preached reform, not revolution, in the Soviet Union; whereas in the second half he was to maintain that political revolution was the only answer to bureaucratic absolutism. He was also to revise his conception of the Opposition's role and to proclaim a new Communist Party and a new International. But even then he was never to waver in his insistence that the Soviet Union was a workers' state; he declared the 'unconditional defence of the Soviet Union' against its bourgeois enemies to be the elementary obligation of every member of the Opposition; and he was repeatedly to disown friends and adherents who were reluctant to accept this obligation.[1]

. . . .

The outcome of Trotsky's first attempts to organize his followers in the West was disappointing. He concentrated his attention on France where he had had a more influential following than elsewhere; and in the hope of setting up there a strong base for the Opposition he endeavoured to bring together various Trotskyist and quasi-Trotskyist groups and coteries and to unite these with the Zinovievists and with the syndicalist circle of *Revolution Prolétarienne*. At the outset Rosmer warned him about the political depression and demoralization which beset most of these groups. Five years had elapsed since the hey-day of Trotskyism in the French party; in this time the Comintern had managed to restore its influence there and to expel all dissenters and isolate them from the rank and file. The sense of their isolation and the defeats of the Opposition in Russia had disheartened many anti-Stalinists, among whom Rosmer noted a mood of *sauve qui peut* which led them to give up the fight and to wish 'they had never had anything to do with the Opposition'. Even those who withstood this mood were confused and at loggerheads with one another. 'The great misfortune of all these groups', Rosmer went on, 'is that they find themselves outside all action; and this fatally accentuates their sectarian character.'[2]

The truth of Rosmer's observations became evident when Trotsky, disregarding his advice, tried to 'regain' Souvarine

[1] *B.O.*, nos. 3–4, 5, and *passim*; *Écrits*, vol. I, pp. 213–74; *Militant*, December 1929.
[2] Rosmer to Trotsky, 16 April 1929.

and others for the Opposition. Souvarine had once distinguished himself by raising, in Moscow, a lonely voice in
Trotsky's defence; and Trotsky, valuing his journalistic talent,
expected him to be the Opposition's most articulate French
mouthpiece. To his surprise Souvarine displayed intolerable
airs and pretensions. He asked Trotsky to make no public
statements without 'previous agreements with the French
Opposition', that is with himself. Trotsky, anxious to avoid
dissension, answered that he would make no pronouncement
on French issues, but that so far he had spoken in public on
Soviet (and Chinese) affairs only, on which surely he was entitled
to have his say without asking for a French *placet*. Souvarine
replied with an immense epistle, running to over 130 pages,
packed with paradoxes, *bons mots*, odds and ends of shrewd
observation and analysis, but also with incredibly muddled
arguments, all advanced in a tone of venomous hostility
which made a breach inevitable. He asserted that Bolshevism
had 'once for all failed outside Russia', because 'it misunderstood the character of the epoch', underrated the power of
the bourgeoisie, and overrated the militancy of the workers;
it also committed the 'fatal error' of trying to fashion foreign
Communist parties in its own image. This was not a view,
whatever its merits, that Trotsky expected to be advanced by
someone reputed to be his adherent, or that he himself could
accept. He did not agree that Bolshevism was guilty of the 'fatal
errors' Souvarine attributed to it, and he blamed Stalinism,
not Leninism, for the failure of the Comintern. Far more
startling, however, was Souvarine's other reproach which,
despite his talk about Soviet 'state capitalism', had a pro-
Stalinist flavour—namely, the reproach that Trotsky and the
Opposition needlessly 'cultivated a revolutionary intransigence' which prevented them from attending properly to the
'tangible necessities of the Soviet state'. 'There is nothing more
important', these were Souvarine's words, 'for the entire
international workers' movement than the economic success of
the Soviet Union whose state capitalism marks . . . an undeniable advance upon imperialist capitalism. . . .' He went on
to deride the 'useless heroism' which prevented Trotsky and his
associates from serving the Soviet state even if there was no
room for them in the party: 'One can make oneself useful to the

revolution without being a member of the Politbureau or of the Central Committee or even of the party.' Had it not been for their sheer incongruity, these remarks would have sounded like a belated counsel to Trotsky to surrender to Stalin, for nothing short of surrender, if even that, might have enabled him to go on 'serving the revolution' without being a member of the party. Yet in the same breath Souvarine turned with savage sarcasm on Trotsky's loyalty to Bolshevism and Leninism, urging him to emancipate himself from these and 'return to Marx'.[1]

'I do not see anything left of the ties that united us a few years ago', Trotsky wrote back. In what Souvarine said he could not find 'a single reasoning based on Marxist doctrine and . . . the relevant facts'. 'What guides you and suggests your paradoxes to you is the pen of a disgruntled and frustrated journalist.' 'You are treating the party and the International as corpses. You see the great fault of the Russian Opposition in its insistent endeavour to influence the party and to re-enter its ranks. On the other hand you describe the Soviet economy as state capitalist . . . and you demand that the Opposition should lower itself to the role of a servant of that state capitalism. . . . You are crossing to the other side of the barricade.'[2] This brought the correspondence to an end, and Souvarine was forever to remain among Trotsky's adversaries. And although in 1929 he sought to instruct Trotsky 'how to be useful to the revolution' by serving a progressive state capitalism, in later years he was to castigate him from the opposite sin, for seeing any progress at all in the Soviet Union and for thinking that enough was left there of the heritage of the Revolution to be worth defending.

An attempt to come to terms with the syndicalists of the *Revolution Prolétarienne*, of whom Monatte and Louzon were the best known, also came to nothing. Trotsky had once, during the First World War, exercised a strong influence on them, overcoming their characteristic bias against all politics, including those of revolutionary Marxism; later they joined the Communist party only to be expelled from it at the time of the anti-Trotskyist campaign. Their personal attachment to Trotsky was still strong; but their experience with the Comintern confirmed them in their old distaste for politics, and in the

---

[1] Trotsky—Souvarine correspondence. *The Archives*, Closed Section.   [2] Ibid.

belief that militant trade union activity, culminating in the general strike, was *the* highway to socialist revolution. Hard as Trotsky tried, he did not manage to bring them back to the Leninist view of the paramount importance of the revolutionary party and induce them to join him in the struggle for a reform of the Comintern.

He fared no better in the mediation which he undertook between his own followers and the Zinovievists. The latter were a tiny sect, but they had a leader of renown in Albert Treint, who had been official chief of the French Communist party in 1924–5. It was Treint who, at the time when Zinoviev was directing the 'Bolshevization', had expelled the Trotskyists from the party, sparing them no denunciation or abuse. For this they bore him a grudge even after he too had been expelled; and they would not hear of making peace with him. Trotsky nevertheless invited him to Prinkipo, in May 1929, and throughout a whole month tried to bring about a reconciliation. But the old resentments were too strong, and Treint, trying to justify his behaviour in 1924, did nothing to assuage them. Trotsky, pressed by his own followers, had to part from Treint; but their parting was more friendly than that with Souvarine, and they remained in amicable though remote relations.

No sooner had Trotsky failed with Souvarine, the syndicalists, and Treint, than he had to deal with discords among the Trotskyists themselves. The story would hardly be worth relating had it not played its part in Trotsky's life and in the eventual failure of Trotskyism as a movement. There were several rival groups and coteries in Paris: the circle of Maurice and Magdeleine Paz who brought out a little periodical, *Contre le Courant*; Rosmer; and the young Trotskyists (with their own papers *Lutte des Classes* and *Vérité*), among whom Pierre Naville and Raymond Molinier formed two antagonistic sets. Of all these men Rosmer alone was a public figure of considerable standing: a member of the small élite of revolutionary internationalists, who had proved themselves in the First World War. Naville was a young writer who had participated in the literary rebellion of the Surrealists, had then joined the Communist party, gained some repute as a Marxist critic of Surrealism, witnessed sympathetically Trotsky's struggle in

Moscow in 1927, and had himself been expelled from the party. He possessed a theoretical education in Marxism, but had little political experience and hardly any ties with the working-class movement. Molinier, on the contrary, was an 'activist', full of energy and enterprise, very much at home in the movement, but not too fastidious in the choice of ways and means and rather crude intellectually. The antithetical types of intellectual and activist often formed a good working partnership when they were carried along by the impetus of practical day-to-day activity in a broad organization; but their antagonism usually wrecked small groups cut off from the mainstream of the movement and remaining 'outside all action'.

When early in the spring of 1929 Maurice and Magdeleine Paz came to Prinkipo, Trotsky urged them to unite their circle with the other groups, to transform *Contre le Courant* into a 'great and aggressive' weekly speaking with the voice of the Opposition, and to launch an ambitious recruiting campaign. He worked out with them the plan of the campaign and promised his own close co-operation. They accepted his suggestions, though not without reservations. On their return to Paris, however, they had second thoughts and refused to launch the great weekly. They saw, they said, no chance for the Opposition to succeed in any drive undertaken on the scale envisaged by Trotsky. Above all, they protested against his 'attempt to impose Rosmer's leadership'; and they spoke disparagingly of the young Trotskyists spoiling for a fight as a bunch of simpletons and ignoramuses. Nothing could be more calculated to convince Trotsky that the Pazes had in them little or nothing of the professional revolutionaries whom he was seeking to gather. They were in truth 'drawing-room Bolsheviks' successful in their bourgeois professions—Maurice, at any rate, was a prosperous lawyer—and indulging in Trotskyism as a hobby. While Trotsky was at Alma Ata they were glad to act as his representatives in Paris and to walk in his reflected glory; but when he emerged from Russia and confronted them in person with his exacting demands, they had no desire to commit themselves seriously. An embarrassing correspondence followed. Trotsky made them feel that he thought of them as philistines: 'Revolutionaries', he wrote to them, 'may be either educated or ignorant people, either intelligent or dull; but there can be no

E

revolutionaries without the will that breaks obstacles, without devotion, without the spirit of sacrifice.'[1]

The Pazes replied in a manner which was not less wounding to Trotsky than his strictures were to them. They dwelt on the strength and attraction of official communism and on the weakness of the Opposition, using the contrast, which was only too real, as an excuse for their lukewarmness. They explained that they would not launch *Contre le Courant* as a weekly because 'the Opposition's journal, if it is not to end in failure, must avail itself of other things besides the scintillating prose and the *nom de bataille* of Comrade Trotsky'—it must have a material and moral base and must be able to 'live with its readers and active sympathizers'. The paper would lack such a base, because the old communists, to whom Trotsky's name had meant so much, had lapsed into apathy; and the young were ignorant and inaccessible to argument. 'Don't give yourself too many illusions about the weight of your name. For five years the official communist Press had slandered you to such an extent that among the great masses there is left only a faint and vague memory of you as the leader of the Red Army. . . .' It was a far cry from the reverence with which the Pazes had a few months earlier addressed Trotsky as 'Cher grand Ami' to the insinuation that he was actuated by egotism and vanity. That his followers were isolated and that Stalinist propagandists made his name odious to the communist rank and file, or sought to bury it in oblivion, Trotsky was not unaware. But this was for him one more reason why his followers should undertake a large-scale counter-attack by which alone they might break through the apathy of the communist rank and file. He concluded that he could do nothing with the Pazes, although the breach with them, following closely upon the rupture with Souvarine, was all the more disagreeable because of the services and the attentions they had given him from the moment of banishment.

What now followed was more than a little pitiable, for Trotsky had at once to deal with the animosities that divided his remaining adherents, Rosmer, and the sets of Naville and Molinier. Molinier had come to Prinkipo with boisterous optimism and with a headful of plans for making Trotskyism

[1] Trotshy-Paz correspondence. *The Archives*, Closed Section.

into a great political force. He was convinced that the Opposition had golden opportunities in France, because the official party was riddled with discontent and could not remain insensitive to the Opposition's appeal—all the Opposition needed was to act with self-confidence and bold initiative. He had schemes for infiltrating the party with Trotskyists, for mass meetings, newspapers with a large circulation, &c. The implementation of the schemes required much more money than the Opposition could collect from its members; but he had his financial plans too, somewhat vague but not implausible. He was ready to plunge into all sorts of commercial ventures, and he budgeted ahead with the expected profits.[1]

Rosmer and Naville took a more cautious view of the chances, discounted the possibilities of 'mass action' which Molinier held out, and were inclined to content themselves for the beginning with a more modest but steady clarification of the Opposition's ideas and with propaganda among the mature elements of the left. They were afraid that Molinier's ventures might bring discredit on the Opposition; and they distrusted him. *'Ce n'est pas un militant communiste, c'est un homme d'affaires, et c'est un illettré'*, Rosmer said. Unpleasant tales about Molinier were being told in Paris: one was that he had deserted from the army and then before a court martial conducted his defence in a manner unworthy of a communist, describing himself as a conscientious objector of the religious type. Allegations and hints were thrown out about the shady character of his commercial activities, but it was difficult to pin down the allegations to anything specific.

Trotsky, admitting some of Molinier's limitations, nevertheless trusted him implicitly. He was captivated by the man's verve, inventiveness, and courage, qualities he usually valued in followers. There was a streak of the adventurer in Molinier; but there was also genuine revolutionary fervour and unconventionality. It was his unconventionality, Trotsky pleaded, that brought the philistines' displeasure and obloquy on Molinier's head; and he, Trotsky, knew very well that no revolutionary movement could do without such men, in whom some crudeness of thought is compensated for by energy and the will to venture and take risks—how often had he himself had recourse to such men in the years of revolution and civil war!

[1] The Molinier family ran a small bank in Paris, at the Avenue de la République.

Molinier endeared himself to Trotsky by the eagerness with which he did many small yet important chores for him, helping to organize the Prinkipo household and set up the secretariat, keeping an eye on publishing interests in Paris, &c.—he had indeed made himself an indispensable *factotum*. His family, too, his wife Jeanne, and his brother Henri, a modest engineer without political pretensions, all had rendered themselves helpful in the same manner, with the *'énergie Molinièresque'* which greatly pleased Trotsky. They travelled between Paris and Prinkipo and spent much time at Büyük Ada; their relations with Trotsky's family became close and warm. And so Trotsky was anxious to dispel gently Rosmer's doubts and suspicions; all the more so because, much though he valued Rosmer's integrity and judgement, he considered him to be ill-suited for the minutiae of organization and to be too easily disheartened by the petty irritations of factional work, which Molinier took in his stride. With Naville's objections to Molinier, Trotsky had less patience; he chided Naville with 'intellectual haughtiness', 'schematic thinking', political lukewarmness, and reluctance to face 'work among the masses'. Somehow, however, he managed to compose the rivalry for the time being. Rosmer, Molinier, and Naville accepted a 'settlement' and, agreeing to put aside personal dislikes and to work together, returned to Paris with the intention of building up not merely a national but an international organization of the Opposition.[1]

Trotsky was hopeful. True, the 'base' to be set up in France would be narrower than he had expected, but sufficient to become the nucleus of a wider organization. True, also, at this point a dilemma had already presented itself: should the Opposition aim at 'mass action' and come forward with its own agitation and slogans, or should it confine itself to the kind of work that had in the past been carried out, slowly but fruitfully, by small Marxist propagandist circles, expounding patiently their theories and dealing with ideas rather than slogans? But this dilemma did not pose itself clearly or acutely; and so it could be left in the air. The circumstance that the Opposition did not aspire to found a new political party but

---

[1] This account is based on the correspondence between Trotsky, R. Molinier, Naville, V. Serge, L. Sedov, and many others, a correspondence covering the whole of the nineteen-thirties. *The Archives*, Closed Section.

was a faction bent on reforming the old party suggested that it should concentrate on the theoretical propaganda of its ideas. To this form of activity Trotsky the thinker was certainly inclined. But the man of action in him, the great Commissar, and the leader of the Opposition, fretted at its limitations and yearned for the scope and impetus of a mass movement.

In the summer of 1929 Rosmer went on a tour of Germany and Belgium to inspect and rally groups of the Opposition there; and he established contact with Italian, Dutch, American, and other Trotskyists. In detailed reports he kept Trotsky informed about his findings. These were not encouraging, on the whole. Inaction, sectarian squabbles, and personal rivalries, which had so greatly weakened the Opposition in France, had done it great harm elsewhere too. From Trotsky's viewpoint no country was more important than Germany, the main arena of class struggle in Europe, where the Communist party, with a following of several million voters, was stronger than anywhere in the West. Rosmer reported that in Berlin he found several groups, all invoking Trotsky's authority, but frittering away their strength in internecine animosities. The so-called Wedding group comprised the Trotskyists proper, but far more influential was the Leninbund which published the *Fahne des Kommunismus* and was led by Hugo Urbahns. There were also other tiny, 'ultra-left' sects such as the Korschists, so-called after Karl Korsch, a theorist who had in 1923 been Minister of the Communist-Socialist Government of Thuringia. The Zinovievists, Maslov and Fischer, were by far the strongest group; but, paradoxically, after their inspirer had surrendered to Stalin, they themselves took up an extreme anti-Stalinist attitude, similar to that of the survivors of the Workers' Opposition in the Soviet Union; and in their attacks on official communism they went 'much further' than Trotsky was prepared to go. They argued that the Russian Revolution had run its full course, and that the Soviet Union had ushered in an epoch of counter-revolution; that nothing was left there of the proletarian dictatorship; that the ruling bureaucracy was a new exploiting and oppressing class basing itself on the state capitalism of a nationalized economy; that, in a word, the Russian Thermidor was triumphant. They added that even the foreign policy of Stalinism was becoming indistinguishable from that of the Tsarist imperialism. Consequently, no reform could resuscitate the rule of the working class—only another proletarian revolution could achieve that. They also considered it hopeless to aim at a reform of the Third International which was 'a tool of the Russian Thermidorians' and exploited the heroic October legend in order to prevent the workers from facing realities and to harness their revolutionary energy to the engine of a counter-revolution. It went without saying that those who held this view did not feel themselves bound by any solidarity with the Soviet Union, still less by the duty to defend it; and they pointed to the very fact of Trotsky's banishment as conclusive evidence in favour of their attitude. 'The expulsion of Trotsky', they wrote, 'marks the line at which the Russian Revolution has definitely come to a halt.'

Trotsky defended himself against *trop de zèle* on the part of his defenders. In controversies with the Leninbund and the *Révolution Prolétarienne* he elaborated his old argument against those who held that the Soviet Thermidor was an accomplished fact. Once again defining the Thermidor as a bourgeois counter-revolution, he pointed out that this could not occur without civil war. Yet the Soviet Union had not gone through another civil war; and the régime established in 1917 had, despite its degeneration, preserved continuity, which manifested itself in its social structure based on public ownership and in the uninterrupted exercise of power by the Bolshevik party. 'The Russian Revolution of the twentieth century', he wrote, 'is incontestably wider in scope and deeper than the French Revolution of the eighteenth century. The social class in which the October revolution has found its support is incomparably more numerous, homogeneous, compact, and resolute than were the urban plebeians of France. The leadership given to the October revolution has, *in all its currents*, been infinitely more experienced and penetrating than the leading groups of the French Revolution were or could be. Finally, the political, economic, social, and cultural changes the Bolshevik dictatorship has brought about are also incontestably far more profound than those initiated by the Jacobins. If it was impossible to wrest power from the hands of the French plebeians . . . without a civil war—and Thermidor was a civil war in which the *sans culottes* were vanquished—how can anyone think or believe that power could pass from the hands of the Russian proletariat into those of the bourgeoisie peacefully, by way of a quiet, imperceptible bureaucratic change? Such a conception of the Thermidor is nothing but reformism *à rebours*.' 'The means of production', he went on, 'which once belonged to the capitalists remain in the hands of the Soviet state till this day. The land is nationalized. Social elements that live on the exploitation of labour continue to be debarred from the Soviets and the Army.' The Thermidorian danger was real enough, but the struggle was not yet resolved. And just as Stalin's left course and attack on the N.E.P.-man and the kulak had not effaced the Thermidorian danger, so his, Trotsky's, banishment had not obliterated the October revolution. A sense of proportion was needed in the evaluation of facts and in theorizing. The concept of Soviet state capitalism was meaningless where no capitalists existed; and if those who spoke of it denounced state ownership of industry, they renounced an essential prerequisite of socialism. Nor was the bureaucracy a new exploiting class in any Marxist sense, but a 'morbid growth on the body of the working class'—a new exploiting class could not form itself in exercising merely managerial functions, without having any property in the means of production.[1]

The implications of this dispute became apparent when a conflict flared up, in the summer of 1929, between the Soviet Union and China over the possession of the Manchurian Railway. China claimed the railway which the Soviet Government held as a concessionaire. The question arose whose side the Opposition ought to take. The French syndicalists, the Leninbund, and some Belgian Trotskyists held that the Soviet Government should give up the railway (which had been built by Russia in the course of the Tsarist expansion to Manchuria); and in Stalin's refusal to do so they saw evidence of the imperialist character of his policy. To their surprise Trotsky declared that Stalin was right in holding on to the railway and that it was the Opposition's duty to side with the Soviet Union against China.[2] This was, in the first year of his exile, Trotsky's first great controversy with his own followers—we shall see him

---

[1] *Écrits*, loc. cit.; *B.O.*, loc. cit.
[2] Trotsky's role in 1926 as Chairman of the Politbureau's Chinese Commission, concerned *inter alia* with securing Soviet influence in Manchuria, is related in *The Prophet Unarmed*, pp. 322–3.

again, in his last year, during the Soviet-Finnish war of 1939–40, engaged in another, his last, dispute with his own followers, a dispute again centring on the Opposition's attitude towards the Soviet Union; and in that dispute he would again adopt essentially the same view as in 1929.

He saw no reason, he argued, why the workers' state should yield a vital economic and strategic position to Chiang Kai-shek's Government (which had recognized the Soviet concession in Manchuria). He criticized severely Stalin's manner of dealing with the Chinese, his disregard of their suscepti-bilities, and his failure to appeal to the people in Manchuria —a more considerate and thoughtful policy might have averted the conflict. But once the conflict had broken out, he asserted, communists had no choice but to back the Soviet Union. If Stalin gave up the railway to the Kuomintang he would have yielded it not to the Chinese people but to their oppressors. Chiang Kai-shek was not even an independent agent. If he obtained control of the railway, he would not be able to main-tain it but would sooner or later lose it to Japan (or else allow American capital to bring the Manchurian economy under its influence). Only the Soviet Union was strong enough to keep this Manchurian position out of Japan's hands. China's national rights, invoked by the critics, were, in Trotsky's view, not relevant to this case, which was an incident in a complex and many-sided contest between the various forces of world imperialism and the workers' state. He concluded that the time for the Soviet Union to do historic justice and return the Manchurian outpost to China would come when a revolution-ary government was established in Peking; and this forecast was to come true after the Chinese revolution. In the meantime, the Soviet Government was obliged to act as the trustee of revolutionary China and keep for it the Manchurian assets.[1]

[1] In 1935, Stalin, anxious in view of the approaching war to ward off a Japanese attack on the U.S.S.R., sold the Railway to the Japanese puppet government of Manchukuo. In 1945 the Soviet Union regained control of the Railway; and it was not before September 1952 that Stalin, after some hesitation, ceded it to Mao Tse-tung's government. This was one of Stalin's last important acts of policy. Until that time he had pursued a course of economic penetration of China, and the cession foreshadowed the final abandonment of that course by his successors. In this, as in so many other acts, Stalin and his successors were the reluctant and half-hearted executors of a policy which Trotsky outlined nearly a quarter of a century earlier.

One may imagine the consternation which Trotsky caused among the zealots of the Opposition. They were puzzled by his 'inconsistency', thinking that he was missing a great opportunity to strike at Stalin. He was, indeed, not out to score points; but his behaviour was consistent with what he was saying about the Soviet Union as the workers' state. For that state he felt, as an outcast, the same responsibility that he had felt as a member of the Politbureau and of Lenin's government. He found the displays of self-righteous indignation over Soviet policy, in which some of his pupils indulged, wrong-headed and cheap; and he told them bluntly that he had nothing in common with 'Trotskyists' who refused to give the workers' state unshakable, if critical, allegiance.

The rigour with which he stuck to his principles, refusing to dilute them with demagogy, offended many of his past and would-be admirers. Indeed, the movement he was sponsoring was hemmed in, on the one hand, by his severe scrupulousness about ideas and, on the other, by the unscrupulous ruthlessness of the Stalinist persecution. The persecution kept his followers at an impassable distance from the only people in whom his ideas could strike a chord, the large communist audience in Europe. His fastidiousness in the choice of his argumentative weapons was estranging him from the scattered yet growing anti-Stalinist public consisting of former party members, who felt tempted to meet the Stalinists on their own ground, to return blow for blow, to counter villainy with faithlessness and to match venom with virulence. That public was in no mood to accept Trotsky's self denying ordnances.

And so, after a year or two of argument and recruiting, those who followed him on his arduous path were still very few. New groups came over here or there; another member, say, of the Italian Politbureau or of the Belgian Central Committee, or a small band of Czech or even British activists saw the light and hopefully joined the Opposition. But their accession failed to change anything in the state of the Opposition. Even though some of the newcomers were until quite recently influential in the party and had many ties with the working class, cultivated over the years, they lost influence and ties once the party expelled them, pursued them with every imaginable calumny, and chased them away like lepers. They had against them the authority of Moscow, the prestige of their own party, the hallowed discipline of the proletarian vanguard, an array of massive caucuses, and legions of propagandists and agitators, some of whom were no better than gangsters, but most of whom turned out of a passionate but blind devotion to their cause into the moral assassins of their erstwhile comrades. The new converts to Trotskyism started out with a determination to shake the party they loved and to make it see the light which they themselves, studying Trotsky's writings, had excitedly seen; but soon they found themselves shut in within small, hermetic circles, where they were to accustom themselves to live as noble lepers in a political wilderness. Tiny groups which cannot hitch themselves to any mass movement are quickly soured with frustration. No matter how much intelligence and vigour they may possess, if they find no practical application for these, they are bound to use up their strength in scholastic squabbling and intense personal animosities which lead to endless splits and mutual anathemas. A certain amount of such sectarian wrangling has, of course, always marked the progress of any revolutionary movement. But what distinguishes the vital movement from the arid sect is that the former finds in time, and the latter does not, the salutary transition from the squabbling and the splits to genuine political mass action.

The Trotskyist groups did not lack men of brains, integrity, and enthusiasm. But they were unable to break through the ostracism which Stalinism imposed on them; and, in their beyond-the-pale existence they could never rid themselves of their internal dissensions. Thus, soon after the reconciliation Trotsky brought about among his French followers, the latter fell out again. Rosmer and Naville renewed their complaints against Molinier, charging him with irresponsibility and recklessness, while he reproached them with too little faith and obstructing all plans for action. The puny organization, giving itself the airs and the constitution of a much larger body, had its National Executive and its Paris Committee. On the former, Rosmer and Naville were in a majority, and they proposed to exclude Molinier on the ground that his financial deals threatened to bring the Opposition into disrepute. But Molinier had behind him the Paris Committee and—Trotsky's support. Rosmer implored Trotsky to save the National Executive this embarrassment and to cease sheltering Molinier under his wing.[1] By now Trotsky's attachment to Molinier was little short of infatuation; and his relations with Rosmer became strained and their correspondence somewhat acid. The rivalry also affected the two shadowy international bodies the Opposition had given itself, the International Bureau and the International Secretariat which were equally at loggerheads.[2] In the summer of 1930 Trotsky once again asked his French adherents to come to Prinkipo and settle the differences. They came, patched up another 'peace', and Trotsky sent them back to Paris confident that now at last they would launch in unison the long-delayed drive from which he expected so much. But after a few weeks the quarrel broke out again; and in November Rosmer, hurt by Trotsky's partiality for Molinier, resigned. This was a blow to the organization and to Trotsky personally, who knew that of all his followers in Europe none had Rosmer's qualities or prestige. But he was convinced that Molinier's energy would soon jerk the organization out of the impasse and that then Rosmer would return. Even in resigning Rosmer gave Trotsky proof of a rare disinterested devotion, for he refrained from entering into any controversy, and rather than openly clash with Trotsky withdrew from all factional activity. Yet he resented Trotsky's behaviour so strongly that for several years he refused to meet him or even to exchange views.

Similar dissensions, in which it is well-nigh impossible to disentangle the personal from the political, became a chronic

[1] See the Trotsky-Rosmer correspondence for June and July 1930, and also Trotsky's letters to M. Shachtman, of 18 August 1930, to R. Molinier of January-February 1931, and to the Federation of Charleroi of 28 June 1931. *The Archives*, Closed Section.

[2] The International Bureau, formed at a conference of Trotskyists from several countries, in April 1930, consisted of Rosmer (with Naville as deputy), the American Shachtman, the German Landau, the Spaniard Nin, and the Russian Markin. Under the cover name Markin, L. Sedov (Lyova) represented the Russian Opposition. (He did not, however, participate in the conference.) The Bureau could not function, because Shachtman returned to the States, Nin was imprisoned in Spain shortly after, and Markin could not get out of Prinkipo. An International Secretariat was then formed in Paris, of which Naville was the mainstay, with the Italian Suzo and the American Mill as members. Mill was presently exposed as a Stalinist; and the Secretariat was no more effective than the Bureau. Trotsky then sought to overhaul it with the help of Senin-Sobolevicius and Well. (See Trotsky's letter to Well of 15 December 1931.)

distemper of most, if not all, Trotskyist groups; the French example was infectious if only because Paris was now the centre of international Trotskyism. The personalities were, as a rule, of so little weight, the issues so slight, and the quarrels so tedious that even Trotsky's involvement does not give them enough significance to earn them a place in his biography. With the years his involvement assumed piteous and at times quite grotesque forms. As almost every quarrel shook the entire organization, these triflings devoured much of his time and nerves. He took sides; he acted as arbiter. Being in contact with groups in every corner of the world, he had to deal with an incredibly large number of such altercations; and as he encouraged the various sections of the Opposition to interest themselves in each other's activities, he wrote interminable circulars and epistles explaining, say, to the Belgians why the French fell out, to the Greeks why the German comrades were in disagreement, to the Poles what were the points at issue between different sets of the Belgian or of the American Opposition, and so on, and so forth.[1]

He did all this in the belief that he was educating and training a new levy of communists, new cadres of revolution. The extreme paucity of the Opposition's resources and the feebleness of its organization did not deter him. He held that the worth of a movement lay in the power of its ideas which was bound to prevail eventually; that the chief task was 'to maintain the continuity' of the Marxist school of thought; that only an organization could assure that continuity; and that any organization had to be built in the circumstances that were given and with such human material as was available. Sometimes, the bickering of his followers was enough to drive him to despair and to make him wonder whether his efforts were not wasted. Then he consoled himself with the recollection that Lenin, in the years of his 'factional émigré squabbles', often invoked an image of Tolstoy's which described a man squatting in the middle of a road and making incoherent, maniacal gestures which suggested to passers-by that he was a madman;

---

[1] Of over 300 files, containing about 20,000 documents of the Closed Section of *The Archives* approximately nine-tenths consist of Trotsky's correspondence with his followers. A very large proportion of the Open Section of *The Archives* also consists of his writings on the policy, tactics, and organization of various Trotskyist groups.

but on coming nearer one saw that the queer gesticulation was a purposeful activity—the man was sharpening a knife on a grindstone. And so Trotsky, however purposeless his own dealings with his followers might at times appear, told himself that he was in fact sharpening the mind and the will of a new Marxist generation. He suppressed his distaste at mingling great principles with the pettiest of wrangles, and mustered all his patience and persuasiveness to give freely to his followers. Yet he could not help sensing that the human material with which he was working was quite unlike that with which either he or Lenin had worked before the revolution. Then, whatever the miseries of émigré politics, those involved were genuine and serious fighters, wholly dedicated to their cause and sacrificing to it every interest in life and life itself—human flames of revolutionary enthusiasm. His present followers in the West were made of different stuff: they had in them only little of the passion and heroism that could storm the heavens. They were certainly not or 'not yet' 'genuine Bolsheviks', he reflected; and this accounted for an irreducible psychological distance between him and them. In his thoughts he preferred to dwell with his other friends and disciples, those who were scattered over the prisons and punitive colonies of the Urals and Siberia, and there were fighting, starving, freezing, and wrestling with their problems unto death. Even the most mediocre of the people over there now seemed to him worthier as fighters and closer than almost any of his followers in the West. Sometimes he unwittingly vented this feeling as, for instance, in an obituary on Kote Tsintsadze which he wrote early in 1931. Tsintsadze, a Bolshevik since 1903, head of the Caucasian Cheka during the civil war, and then a leading Oppositionist, had been deported, jailed, and tortured. Ill with tuberculosis, suffering from haemorrhages of the lungs, he fought on, went on hunger strikes, and died in prison. In the obituary, published in the *Bulletin*, Trotsky quoted these prescient words from a letter Tsintsadze had written him at Alma Ata: 'Many, very many of our friends and of the people close to us will have to . . . end their lives in prison or somewhere in deportation. Yet in the last resort this will be an enrichment of revolutionary history: a new generation will learn the lesson.'

'The Communist parties in the West', Trotsky remarked,

'have not yet brought up fighters of Tsintsadze's type'; this was their besetting weakness; and it affected the Opposition as well. He confessed that he was amazed to find how much cheap ambition and self-seeking there was even among Oppositionists in the West. It was not that he deprecated all personal ambition—desire for distinction was often a stimulus to effort and achievement. But 'the revolutionary begins where personal ambition is fully and wholly subordinated to the service of a great idea. . . .' Unfortunately, only too few people in the West had learned to take principles seriously: 'Flirtation with ideas' or dilettante dabbling with Marxism-Leninism was all too common.[1]

It was rarely that Trotsky allowed himself such a complaint. He saw no use in wringing hands over the limitations of the human material produced by history—it was only from this material that the 'new Tsintsadzes' could be formed.

.   .   .   .

Meantime, in the Soviet Union the Opposition was breaking up and the fighters 'of Tsintsadze's type' were either perishing physically or shrinking morally. They were caught in the double vice of the Stalinist terror and of their own dilemmas. Even as early as 1928, while Trotsky was still sustaining their spirit of resistance from Alma Ata, they showed signs of being unequal to the strain. A division of opinion, it will be remembered, arose among them as they watched the end of the coalition between the Stalinists and the Bukharinists and the beginnings of Stalin's left course.[2] These events rendered obsolete some of the Opposition's major demands and battle-cries. The Opposition had called for rapid industrialization and for the gradual collectivization of farming and had charged Stalin with obstruction and with favouring the wealthy farmer. When in 1928 Stalin accelerated the tempo of industrialization and turned against private farming, the Oppositionists first congratulated themselves on the change, in which they saw their vindication; but then they felt themselves robbed of their ideas and slogans and deprived of much of their political *raison d'être*.

---

[1] *B.O.*, no. 19, March 1931.
[2] See the chapter 'A Year at Alma Ata' in *The Prophet Unarmed*.

Under any régime allowing a modicum of political controversy, a party or faction which has the misfortune of seeing its rivals steal its clothes may still be permitted to assist with dignity at the realization of its own programme by others. The deported Trotskyists were not free even to hint that their clothes had been stolen or to point out, in the hearing of the nation, how worthless and hypocritical had been the accusations the Stalinists had heaped on them when they branded them as 'super industrializers' and 'enemies of the peasantry'. Stalin's left course, which implicitly vindicated the Opposition, sealed its defeat; and the Opposition no longer knew clearly whether or on what ground it was to go on opposing him, especially as up to the middle of 1929, before Stalin decided on 'wholesale collectivization' and the 'liquidation of the kulaks', his policy followed the Opposition's demands quite closely. If it is a galling experience for any party or group to see its programme plagiarized by its adversaries, to the Trotskyists, who in advocating their ideas exposed themselves to persecution and slander, this was a shattering shock. Some began to wonder for the sake of what they should go on suffering and let their next of kin endure the most cruel privations. Was it not time, they asked themselves, to give up the fight and even to reconcile themselves with their strange persecutors?

Those who succumbed to this mood eagerly assented to Radek's and Preobrazhensky's argument that there would be nothing reprehensible in such a reconciliation, and that the Opposition, if it was not merely to grind its axe, should indeed rejoice in the triumph of its ideas, even though its persecutors gave effect to them. It was true, they said, that Stalin showed no willingness to restore within the party the proletarian democracy for which the Opposition had also clamoured; but as he was carrying out so much of the Opposition's programme there was reason to hope that he would eventually carry out the rest of it as well. In any case, Oppositionists would be better able to further the cause of inner-party freedom if they returned to the ranks than if they remained in the punitive colonies, from where they could exercise no practical influence. Whatever it was that they were striving for, they must strive for it within the party, which was, as Trotsky once put it, 'the only historically given instrument that the working class possessed' for furthering the progress of socialism; only through it and inside it could the Oppositionists achieve their purposes. Neither Radek nor Preobrazhensky as yet suggested surrender—they merely advised a more conciliatory attitude, which would make it possible for them to negotiate the terms of their reinstatement.

Another section of the Opposition, for which Sosnovsky, Dingelstedt, and sometimes Rakovsky spoke, rejected these promptings and did not believe that Stalin was in earnest about industrialization and the struggle against the kulaks. They treated the left course as a 'temporary manœuvre' to be followed by sweeping concessions to rural capitalism, the neo-N.E.P., and the triumph of the right wing. They denied that the Opposition's programme was surpassed by events and saw no reason to modify any of their attitudes. The more sanguine were as hopeful as ever that time was working for them. If Stalin were to pursue the left course, they said, its logic would compel him to call off his fight against the left Opposition; and if he were to launch the neo-N.E.P., the subsequent 'shift to the right' would so endanger his own position that again, in order to redress the balance, he would have to come to terms with the Trotskyists. The Opposition would therefore be foolish to try to barter principles against reinstatement, especially to waive its demand for freedom of expression and criticism. This, broadly, was the 'orthodox Trotskyist' view.

The conviction that the Opposition's programme was obsolescent was gaining ground not only among the conciliators, however. It was held with even greater fervour, but for reasons diametrically opposed to Radek's and Preobrazhensky's, by those who formed the most extreme and irreconcilable wing of the Opposition. There the view was already becoming axiomatic that the Soviet Union was no longer a workers' state; that the party had betrayed the revolution; and that the hope to reform it being futile, the Opposition should constitute itself into a new party and preach and prepare a new revolution. Some still saw Stalin as the promoter of agrarian capitalism or even the leader of a 'kulak democracy', while to others his rule epitomized the ascendancy of a state capitalism implacably hostile to socialism.

Up to the end of 1928 these cross currents were not yet so

strong as to destroy the Opposition's outward unity. A ceaseless discussion went on in the colonies; and Trotsky presided over it, holding the balance between the opposed viewpoints. After his banishment to Constantinople, however, the force of the disagreements grew and the opposed groups drifted farther and farther apart. The conciliators eager for reinstatement gradually 'curtailed' the conditions on which they were prepared to come to terms with Stalin, until the conciliation for which they were getting ready became indistinguishable from surrender. On the other hand, the irreconcilables worked themselves up into such a frenzy of hostility towards all that Stalin stood for that they were no longer concerned with changes in his policy or even with what was going on in the country at large; they repeated obsessively their old denunciations of Stalinism regardless of whether these still bore any relation to the facts, old and new. The members of these extreme groups viewed one another as renegades and traitors. The irreconcilables branded their conciliatory comrades in advance as 'Stalin's lackeys', while the latter looked upon the zealots as upon people who had lost their bearings, had ceased to be Bolsheviks, and were turning into *anarchisants* and counter-revolutionaries. The two extreme wings were growing and only the shrinking rump of the Opposition remained 'orthodox Trotskyist'.

Scarcely three months after Trotsky's banishment not a trace was left even of the outward unity of the Opposition. While he was cut off from his followers—it took him a few months to re-establish contacts—Stalin found it all the easier to divide them and demoralize them by means of terror and cajolery. The terror was selective: the G.P.U. spared the conciliators but combed the punitive colonies, picking out the most stubborn Oppositionists and transferring them to jails, where they were subjected to the harshest treatment: placed under military guards; crowded in damp and dark cells unheated in the Siberian winter; kept on a meagre diet of rotten food; and denied reading matter, light, and facilities for communication with their families. They were thus deprived of the privileges which political prisoners had obtained in Tsarist Russia and which the Bolsheviks had, since the end of civil war, granted to anti-Bolshevik offenders. (About this time, as if to mock his former comrades even further, Stalin ordered the release of quite a few Mensheviks and Social Revolutionaries.) As early as March 1929 Trotskyists describing their life at the hard labour prison of Tobolsk compared it with Dostoevsky's haunting image of *katorga* in *The House of the Dead*.[1] If this terror aimed at intimidating and softening the conciliators, it also seemed designed to drive the irreconcilables to demonstrations of such unthinking hostility towards all aspects of the existing régime that it should be easy to brand them as counter-revolutionaries and to drive an even deeper wedge between them and the conciliators.

However, Stalin could not break the Opposition by terror alone—his far more potent weapon was the left course. 'Without severe persecution', Rakovsky remarked, 'the left course would have only brought fresh adherents into the ranks of the Opposition, because it marked the bankruptcy [of the earlier Stalinist policy]. But persecution alone, without the left course, would not have had the effect it has had.'[2] In the months that followed Trotsky's arrival in Constantinople Stalin's hesitation over policy was coming to an end. His break with Bukharin was consummated at the February session of the Politbureau, while Trotsky was *en route* to Turkey. In April the conflict was carried from the Politbureau to the Central Committee, and then to the sixteenth party conference. The conference addressed the nation with a rousing call for a radical speeding up of industrialization and collectivization, a call which reproduced, in part literally, Trotsky's earlier appeals.[3] It became increasingly difficult to maintain, as Trotsky and some of the Trotskyists were still doing, that Stalin's change of policy was a 'temporary manœuvre'. It turned out that Preobrazhensky and Radek who had held all along that Stalin was not trifling with the left course (and that circumstances would not allow him to do so even if he wanted to) had in this point a much better grasp of reality.

At a stroke the Opposition's dilemmas were immensely aggravated. It became almost ludicrous for its members to

[1] See the report of 20 March 1929 in *B.O.*, no. 1.

[2] Ibid., no. 7, November–December 1929.

[3] *V.K.P.* (*b*). *Profsoyuzakh*, p. 515. In the resolutions of the conference Trotsky's appeal for socialist competition, now ten years old, was literally, but of course anonymously, reproduced. *K.P.S.S. v. Rezolutsyakh*, vol. II, pp. 496–7; see also my *Soviet Trade Unions*, pp. 95–97.

chew over old slogans, to clamour for more industrialization, to protest against the appeasement of rural capitalism, and to speak of the threatening Neo-N.E.P. The Opposition either had to admit that Stalin was doing its job for it or it had to re-equip itself and 'rearm' politically for any further struggle. Trotsky, Rakovsky, and others were indeed working to bring the Opposition's ideas up to date. But events moved faster than even the most quick-minded of theorists.

The state of the nation not less than changes in official policy contributed to the disarray of the Opposition. This was a time of the gravest emergency. Stalin described it in these terms;[1] but so also did all the leaders of the Opposition, however they differed among themselves. Preobrazhensky, not given to dramatic overstatement, compared the tension of the spring of 1929 with that which had led to the Kronstadt rising, the rising the Bolsheviks had regarded as more dangerous to themselves than any critical phase of the civil war.[2] Radek, speaking of the conflict between Stalinists and Bukharinists in the Central Committee, said that 'the Central Committee looked like the Jacobin Convention on the very eve of the 9 Thermidor', the day that brought the ruin of Jacobinism. Rakovsky described the moment as 'the most fateful since the civil war'.[3] Indeed, there was a complete agreement about this among all observers.

For several years now the gulf between town and country had widened and deepened. The 25–6 millions of small and mostly tiny and archaic farmsteads could not feed the rapidly growing urban population. The towns lived under an almost constant threat of famine. Ultimately, the crisis could be resolved only through the replacement of the unproductive smallholding by the modern large-scale farm. In a vast country accustomed to extensive agriculture, this could be achieved either by the energetic fostering of agrarian capitalism or by collectivization—there was no other choice. No Bolshevik government could act as the foster parent of agrarian capitalism —if it had so acted it would have let loose formidable forces

[1] Stalin, *Sochinenya*, vol. XII, pp. 118ff.

[2] Preobrazhensky, 'Ko Vsem Tovarishcham po Oppozitsii' (*The Archives*), to which reference is made in further pages also; and Rakovsky's report in *B.O.*, loc. cit.

[3] Loc. cit.

hostile to itself and it would have compromised the prospects of planned industrialization.[1] There was thus only one road left, that of collectivization, even though the all-important questions of scale, method, and tempo had still to be resolved. Years of official hesitation had led only to this, that the decisions had now to be taken under conditions far worse than those under which they might have been taken earlier. Stalin's attempts to combine the most contradictory policies, to appease the well-to-do farmers and then to requisition their produce, had infuriated the peasantry. His long-lasting reluctance to press on with industrial development had been no less disastrous. While the country was unable and unwilling to feed the town, the town was unable to supply the country with industrial goods. The peasant, not being able to obtain shoes, clothes, and farm tools, had no incentive to raise his output, still less to sell it. And so both the starving town and the country famished of industrial goods were in turmoil.

The decisions about tempo and scale of industrialization and collectivization were taken in conditions of an acute scarcity of all the human and material elements needed for the two-fold drive. While workers went short of bread, industry was short of skilled labour. It was also short of machinery. Yet machines stood idle for lack of fuel and the raw materials whose supply depended on the rural economy. Transport was disrupted and could not cope with increased industrial traffic. The supply of nearly all goods and services was grievously inadequate to the demand. Inflation was rampant. Controlled prices bore no relation to the uncontrolled ones, and neither reflected genuine economic values.

All the ties and links between the various parts of the body politic were cut, except for the bonds of misery and desperation. Not only had economic intercourse between town and country once again broken down, so had all normal relations between citizenry and state and even between party and state. There

---

[1] Large scale capitalist farming formed the rural background to the industrialization of Britain and the United States; the Junkers' estates and the *Grossbauerwirtschaft* were dominant in Germany's agriculture during her industrial rise. In all these countries large-scale farming had been in existence at the outset of industrialization, whereas in the Russia of the nineteen-twenties it was not. The concentration of farming by any normal processes of capitalist competition would have required much time and much *laissez faire*.

was no extreme of deception and violence to which both the
rulers and the ruled were not prepared to go in the scramble.
The kulaks, and many 'middle' and even poor peasants, were
implacable in their hatred of the 'commissars'. Arson and
killings of party agents and agitators were daily occurrences in
the villages. The mood of the peasantry communicated itself to
the working class among whom newcomers from the country
were very numerous. In the twelfth year of the revolution the
poverty of the nation and the neglects and the abuses of government provoked a revulsion so bitter and widespread that
something great and terrible had to happen or had to be done
soon in order either to suppress or to release the pent-up
emotions. Under the surface forces were boiling up for what
might have become a gigantic explosion of the kind of which,
on a small scale, Hungary was to give an example in 1956.
Almost cornered, Stalin and his followers fought back with
mounting fury.

'The revolution is in danger!' was the cry which the Trotskyists raised in their places of deportation and prison cells. Both
the 'orthodox' Trotskyists and the conciliators were seized
with equal alarm; but whereas the former did not see what
course of action was open to them in the conditions in which
they were placed and thought that they should keep themselves
in readiness for the approaching crisis, the conciliators, on the
contrary, felt impelled to 'act at once'; and it was with the cry:
'The revolution is in danger!' that they marched to surrender.
The best of them did so from the deep conviction that when the
fate of Bolshevism and of the revolution was at stake, it was a
crime to cling to factions and to cherish sectional interests and
ambitions. The worst among them, the weary opportunists,
found in the 'revolution's danger' a convenient pretext for
wriggling out of commitment to a lost cause. Those who were
neither the best nor the worst, the average conciliators, may not
have been aware of their own motives, which were probably
mixed or ambivalent.

In April 1929 Preobrazhensky drew the conciliators together
with an appeal 'To All Comrades-in-Opposition!'[1] This was
an extraordinary document: in it the conciliator for the last
time, before surrender had sealed his lips, expressed himself

[1] *The Archives.*

frankly as he looked back on the Opposition's road and turned his gaze on the tortuous and stony path ahead of him. Preobrazhensky described how the Opposition had been driven to an impasse by the very triumph of its ideas. He found that many of his comrades would rather deny the triumph than admit the impasse. They still behaved as if their forecasts about the Neo-N.E.P. and the 'shift to the right' had come true; as if there had been no left course. To be sure, Stalin had initiated the left course in a manner very different from the one they had championed. The Opposition wanted industrialization and collectivization to be carried out in the broad daylight of proletarian democracy, with the consent of the masses and free initiative 'from below'; whereas Stalin relied on the force of the decree and coercion from above. All the same, the Opposition had stood for what he was doing even if the way he was doing it was repugnant to them. If they refused to acknowledge this, they would turn into an Opposition for opposition's sake; and then to justify themselves they would drift away from their own principles. He, Preobrazhensky, did not repudiate the Opposition's past: 'In fighting against the Central Committee we have done our duty.' But the Opposition's present duty was to come closer to the party and then return to it—and here spoke the theoretical pioneer of 'primitive socialist accumulation'—in order 'to hold out together against the pressure of that discontent which must be aroused in a peasant country by a policy of socialist accumulation and a struggle against agrarian capitalism'.

Preobrazhensky spoke of the resentment Stalin had aroused, even among conciliators, by banishing Trotsky 'with the help of the class enemy' (i.e. of the Turkish Government). The Oppositionists 'cannot forgive this', he said; but he suggested that this outrage should not be allowed to obscure considerations of a more general character; and he added that Trotsky too had confounded the Opposition by carrying the struggle against Stalin into the bourgeois Press of the West. Preobrazhensky had few illusions about the fate that awaited the conciliators: he was aware of the blows and humiliations that would fall on them in the 'difficult, critical years ahead', although even he could hardly have glimpsed all the mud and blood through which they were to wade and in which they were to perish. But he was clear-eyed enough to indicate plainly to his comrades that the course to which he was summoning them would be full of anxiety and torment. His hopes for a genuine and dignified reconciliation, the hopes he had entertained in the previous year, had sagged. He now saw reinstatement as a virtual surrender. 'Those of us', he concluded, 'who have fought in the ranks of the party ten, twenty or more years [Preobrazhensky himself had been a Bolshevik since 1904] will return to it with feelings very different from those with which they once joined it for the first time.' They would go back without their early enthusiasm, as broken-hearted men. They could not even be sure that the Central Committee would agree to reinstate them on any terms. 'Such are all the circumstances of this return and such is the inner party situation that, if readmitted, we shall have to bear responsibility for things against which we have warned and to submit to [methods] to which we cannot give our assent. . . . If we are reinstated we shall, each of us, receive back the *partbilet* [membership card] as one accepts a heavy cross.' Yet for those who wish to serve the cause of socialism effectively nothing was left but to take the cross.

In May, Preobrazhensky was allowed to travel to Moscow in order to try and 'make peace with the party'. At first he sought to obtain favourable terms for the Opposition at large, pleading for a cessation of the terror, for a halt to deportations, for a rehabilitation of party members victimized under Article 58 on the charge of counter-revolutionary activity, and—last but not least—for the rescinding of Trotsky's banishment. He negotiated with Ordjonikidze and Yaroslavsky and other members of the Central Committee and Central Control Commission who acted under Stalin's personal supervision.

To Stalin the capitulation of a large section of the Opposition was important enough because of the effect this was bound to have on the party's morale and on Trotsky's fortunes. Anxious to entice the conciliators and wary of blasting all their hopes at once, he at first feigned readiness to consider some of their desiderata. But he could not in truth accept any. Above all, he could not allow the Oppositionists to say on their reinstatement that they had come back because the party leadership had adopted *their* programme—this would have

amounted not merely to a vindication of Trotsky and Trotskyism and to a refutation of all the charges against them, but also
to an exposure of the lawlessness of the reprisals by which
Stalin had overwhelmed them. He could not permit anyone
even to allude to the fact that he had taken a leaf—and what a
leaf!—out of Trotsky's book. If he did he would have destroyed
his own claim to infallibility and power. The capitulators must
declare that he, and not they and Trotsky, had been right.
They must denounce and recant their own past. They could not
be tolerated to come back as misunderstood trail-blazers; they
could return only as the remorseful saboteurs of the left
course and of all the policies that had consistently led up to it.
Even then they must not be allowed to arouse in the party
the feelings due to rueful prodigal sons—they could count only
on the forgiveness granted to broken sinners and criminals;
they must make their way back on their knees. To get them to
do this Stalin had to wear down, by slow and stubborn bargaining, their mental defences, and induce them to give up one
demand after another until they were brought to the point of
unconditional surrender. Stalin's behaviour was not surprising:
the terms on which Zinoviev, Kamenev, Antonov-Ovseenko,
Pyatakov, and so many others had capitulated, and the process
by which they had been brought to do it were still fresh in
everyone's memory. But such was the power of self-deception
that many conciliators who from afar anxiously watched Preobrazhensky's parleys in Moscow—he was allowed to communicate with the colonies of deportees—still hoped that they
would be spared the indignities inflicted on earlier capitulators.

After a month the result of Preobrazhensky's 'negotiations'
was already discernible in the behaviour of his closest comrades.
In the middle of June, Radek and Smilga also travelled, under
G.P.U. convoy, to Moscow to join Preobrazhensky. Their train
stopped at a small Siberian station, where by chance they were
met by a group of Oppositionists, who described the encounter
in a letter preserved among Trotsky's papers. They spoke only
to Radek—Smilga was ill and had to stay in his compartment.
Radek told them of the purpose of the journey and made the
by now familiar argument for surrender: the nation-wide
famine, the shortage of bread felt even in Moscow, the workers'
discontent, the threat of peasant risings, the discords in the

Central Committee (where 'Bukharinists and Stalinists were plotting to arrest each other'), &c. The situation, he said, was as grave as in 1919 when Denikin stood at the gates of Moscow and Yudenich stormed Petrograd. They must all rally to the party. On what terms? they asked. Would he demand in Moscow that paragraph 58 of the Criminal Code, the stigma of counter-revolution, be lifted from the deportees? No, he replied; those who persisted in opposition deserved the stigma. 'We ourselves', he shouted, 'have driven ourselves into exile and prison.' Would he demand that Trotsky be brought back? It was only a few weeks since Preobrazhensky had declared that the Opposition 'could not forgive' Trotsky's banishment, and only a few months since Radek himself, the author of the celebrated essay 'Trotsky the Organizer of Victory', had protested to the Central Committee against its causing the 'slow death' of that 'fighting heart of the revolution' and concluded his protest with the words: 'Enough of this inhuman playing with Comrade Trotsky's health and life.' But in the last few weeks the logic of the surrender to Stalin had done its work. And so to their amazement Radek's interlocutors heard this reply: 'I have definitely broken with Lev Davidovich— we are political enemies now. With the contributor to Lord Beaverbrook's papers I have nothing in common.' (Radek himself had often contributed to the bourgeois Press and was to do so again, but in Stalin's interest.)[1] In the very violence of his answer Radek betrayed his guilty conscience. He went on to speak bitterly against the new recruits to the Opposition, the angry young men, who, he alleged, had nothing Bolshevik about them, but joined the Trotskyists from sheer anti-Soviet spite. Once more he appealed to his interlocutors: 'The last party conference has adopted our Platform which has brilliantly proved itself. What can you still have against the party?' Radek's escort provided the answer: while he was arguing, his G.P.U. guards interrupted him, shouting that they would

---

[1] Trotsky often had to defend himself against this reproach, which was at first made even by his French followers, as Rosmer informed him in a letter of 24 February 1929. Rosmer's and Trotsky's answer was that Marx too had to earn his living by writing for the bourgeois Press. In a special note in the first issue of the *Bulletin Oppozitsii* Trotsky explained his position to Soviet readers and emphasized that even in the bourgeois Press he spoke as a Bolshevik and a Leninist, defending the revolution.

not allow him to agitate against Trotsky's banishment; and they pushed him and kicked him back into the train. Radek burst out with hysterical laughter: 'I? Agitating against Trotsky's banishment!' Then he apologized plaintively: 'I am only trying to persuade these comrades to return to the party'; but the guard would not even listen and kept on pushing him back to the compartment. The year before Radek had scorned Zinoviev and Pyatakov for the 'morbid odour of *Dostoevshchyna*' they and their recantations exuded—now he himself, the prince of pamphleteers, appeared to his erstwhile co-thinkers and co-sufferers as a Smerdyakov descended from Dostoevsky's pages on to the little god-forsaken Siberian station.[1]

After another month of haggling, on 13 July, Radek, Preobrazhensky, Smilga, and 400 other deportees finally announced their surrender.[2] The advantages that Stalin derived from this were many. No event since Zinoviev's and Kamenev's capitulation at the Fifteenth Congress, in December 1927, had done so much to bolster Stalin's prestige. As he was just engaged in a heavy attack on Bukharin's faction, the disintegration of the Trotskyist Opposition relieved him of the need to fight on two fronts simultaneously. Trotsky had often said that in the face of an acute 'danger from the right' Trotskyists and Stalinists would join hands. Well, they were now doing so, but on Stalin's own terms—he was winning them over to his side without and even against Trotsky. Many of the capitulators were men of high talent and experience with whom he would fill industrial and administrative posts from which the Bukharinists were being squeezed out. He knew that the capitulators would throw themselves heart and soul into the industrial drive—many of them were to serve under Pyatakov, the arch-capitulator who was the moving spirit of the Commissariat of Heavy Industry. Radek alone was, as a propagandist, worth more to Stalin than hosts of his own scribes.

Trotsky at once attacked the 'capitulators of the third draft'. (Those of the 'first draft' were Zinoviev, Kamenev, and their followers, and those of the second were Antonov-Ovseenko, Pyatakov, and their friends.) 'They state', Trotsky wrote, 'that the differences between Stalin and the Opposition have almost vanished. How then do they explain the furious character of the

[1] *The Archives; B.O.*, no. 6, 1929.   [2] *Pravda*, 13 July 1929.

reprisals? If in the absence of the most irreconcilable and profound differences the Stalinists banish and inflict *katorga* on Bolsheviks, then they do it from sheer bureaucratic banditry, without any political idea. This is how the Stalinist policy presents itself if one looks at it from Radek's viewpoint. How then dare he and his friends raise their voices to advocate unity with political bandits . . . ?' This was not the view that he, Trotsky, took of Stalinist policy; he held that for all its lack of scruple Stalinism had deep political motives for its implacable hostility towards the Opposition; the fundamental differences had lost none of their force. Radek and Preobrazhensky overlooked them or pretended to do so because they broke down morally. Revolution was a great devourer of characters; and every period of reaction took its toll of a tired generation of fighters who knuckled under. But sooner or later the old and weary were replaced by the young who entered the struggle with fresh courage and learned their lessons even from the prostration of their elders. 'We have before us the prospect of a long, tenacious struggle and of a long labour of education.'[1]

In truth, Trotsky received the first news of Radek's surrender with some incredulity; and he attributed Radek's behaviour to 'impulsive character, isolation, and lack of moral support' from comrades. He recalled with warmth of feeling that 'Radek had behind him a quarter of a century of revolutionary Marxist work', and doubted whether he would really be able to make his peace with Stalinism: 'He is too much of a Marxist for that and, above all, he is too internationally minded.' But when *Pravda* came out with Radek's letter of recantation, he found that 'Radek has fallen much lower than I had supposed'. Even now the fall was so incredible that Trotsky imagined that his bargain with Stalin was only temporary and that, having frequently wavered between right and left in the party, he would soon join hands with the Bukharinists. Yet what a tangle this was: 'Radek and a few others with him consider this the most propitious moment for capitulation. Why indeed? Because the Stalinists, you see, are chastising Rykov, Tomsky, and Bukharin. Has it then been our task to make one part of the ruling group chastise the other? Has the approach to fundamental political questions changed? . . . Has the anti-Marxist régime

[1] *Écrits*, vol. I, pp. 157–63.

of the Communist International not been maintained? Is there any guarantee for the future?' Radek and Preobrazhensky saw in the first Five Year Plan a radically new departure. 'The central issue', Trotsky replied, 'is not the statistics of this bureaucratic Five Year Plan *per se*, but the problem of the party', the spirit in which the party was led, because this determined also its policy. Was the Five Year Plan, in its formulation and execution, subject to any control from below, to criticism and discussion? Yet on this depended also the results of the Plan. 'The inner party régime is for the Marxist an irreplaceable element of control over the political line . . .'—this had always been the Opposition's essential idea. 'But the renegades usually have, or think that others have, a short memory. One can say with reason that a revolutionary party embodies the memory of the working class: its first and foremost task is to learn not to forget the past in order to be able to foresee the future.' Trotsky still viewed Stalin's left course as a by-product of the Opposition's struggle and pressure; he still thought that Stalin might reverse his policy and that his conflict with Bukharin was, despite all its harshness, only 'superficial'.

Trotsky's arguments did not reach the Oppositionists in the Soviet Union until the autumn; and they could hardly suffice to stop the capitulation stampede. The upheaval in the Soviet Union had already gone deeper, and its impact on the Opposition was far more violent, than he realized. As yet there was in his remarks no hint of the gravity and alarm that one finds in the writings of all, even the most irreconcilable, Oppositionists in Russia. He still viewed the scene of 1929 through the prism of 1928 and was half-unaware of the 'eve of civil war' atmosphere that hung over the country. The full force of the cry 'The Revolution is in Danger' somehow escaped him, as did also the momentum the left course was gathering and the depth of the breach between Stalin and Bukharin. These, however, were the matters that weighed on the minds of all Opposition groups.

The sense that the revolution was threatened by a mortal danger, which the Opposition must ward off jointly with the Stalinists, soon prompted many who had hitherto belonged to its irreconcilable wing to follow in Preobrazhensky's and Radek's footsteps. Ivan Smirnov, the victor over Kolchak and one of Trotsky's closest associates, Mrachkovsky, a fighter of legendary heroism, Byeloborodov, the Commissar in whose home Trotsky found refuge when he left the Kremlin in November 1927, Ter-Vaganyan, Boguslavsky, and many others asked to be reinstated. They began to parley with Stalinist headquarters in a less sombre mood than Preobrazhensky had done, hoping that the general situation would induce Stalin to reinstate them on terms less humiliating.[1] This time the bargaining went on for nearly five months, from June to the end of October, in the course of which Smirnov's group prepared four different political declarations. In an early draft, produced in August and preserved among Trotsky's papers, they gave, as the reasons for their step, agreement with the Five Year Plan, and the 'danger from the right'. But they also advanced clear criticisms of Stalin's policy, saying that insufficient thought was given in the Five Year Plan to the need to raise the depressed standards of living of the workers; that the 'selection of party cadres' was such as to make the expression of critical opinions impossible; and that the doctrine of socialism in one country served as a 'screen for opportunism', as did also the continued official bias in favour of the 'middle' peasant. Having in all these points upheld the Opposition's attitudes, the applicants admitted also its errors. They had been mistaken, they stated, in thinking that the Central Committee would, in the search for a way out of the crisis, turn rightwards and pave the way for the Thermidor—only the behaviour of the Bukharinist minority justified that fear. They agreed that in the present grave circumstances the party leadership should allow no freedom to factions, because only the right elements would benefit. The Trotskyist Opposition should therefore disperse its organization, disband its own leading centre 'which under various names had existed for years', and stop any form of clandestine activity. But they also demanded an end to the reprisals against the Opposition and they pleaded fervently for the recall of Trotsky, 'whose fate is tied to the fate of the working class', and with whose services neither the Soviet Union nor international communism could dispense.[2]

Only slowly, defending every one of their points, did Smirnov and his associates allow their demands to be whittled down.

---

[1] *Vide* Rakovsky's account in *B.O.*, no. 7, 1929.   [2] *The Archives*.

As the year advanced and his difficulties mounted, Stalin was indeed more anxious than before to secure fresh capitulations; and he did not extract from this group a recantation quite as abject as the one he got from Radek and Preobrazhensky. Smirnov and his friends, in softening or dropping their criticisms of Stalin and waiving various demands, still insisted that they be allowed, in the very act of surrender, to call for Trotsky's return—it was mainly over this that the bargaining dragged on for five months. When at last they gave way, they still refused to denounce or renounce Trotsky; and their statement of submission, which appeared with hundreds of signatures in *Pravda* on 3 November 1929, was more restrained and dignified than any previous act of this kind.

The mood of surrender now touched the inner core of the Opposition, the most faithful of Trotskyists. However, Rakovsky, who, gravely ill and suffering from heart attacks, was transferred from Astrakhan to Barnaul, still managed to rally them. Under his inspiration a section of the Opposition as large as that which followed Smirnov stopped just on the brink of capitulation. 'We are fighting for the *whole* programme of the Opposition', Rakovsky declared. Those who made their peace with Stalin, because he was carrying out the economic part of that programme and who hoped that he would carry out the political part as well, were behaving like old-type reformists contenting themselves with the piecemeal realization of their demands. The political ideas of the Opposition were inseparable from its economic desiderata: 'As long as the political part of our programme remains unfulfilled, the whole work of socialist construction is in danger of being blown sky high.' Even more important to Rakovsky was integrity of conviction and honesty in one's attitude towards adversaries. A party leadership which extracted from Oppositionists confessions of imaginary errors merely imitated the Catholic Church, which made the atheist recant on his deathbed—such a leadership 'loses every title to respect; and the Oppositionist who changes his conviction overnight deserves only utter scorn'.[1]

It took Rakovsky's group several months to define its attitude; its 'Open Letter to the Central Committee' was not ready before the end of August. To collect about 500 signatures

[1] *B.O.*, no. 6, 1929.

from about ninety places of deportation was not easy; but it was even more difficult to accommodate in the document all the shadings of opinion that could be found among the signatories. The tenor of the Letter, which was in form also an application for reinstatement, bore witness to the prevalence of the conciliatory mood. Like Preobrazhensky and Smirnov, Rakovsky and those who followed him—Sosnovsky, Muralov, Mdivani, Kasparova and others—declared that it was the national emergency and the party's decision to sponsor the first Five Year Plan that prompted them to approach the Central Committee. The success of the Plan, they held, would strengthen the working class and socialism; failure would reopen the door to Thermidor and Restoration. Confronted by the 'gravest conflict between the forces of capitalism and those of socialism', they preferred to dwell on the issues on which they were at one with the party rather than on those on which they were not. To them too the 'danger from the right' was close and acute; and what they still criticized in the party's policy was the lingering desire to appease the 'middle' peasants. They were so whole-heartedly in favour of rapid industrialization that from their punitive colonies they pleaded for higher labour discipline in the factories and for determined action against those who tried to exploit the workers' discontent for counter-revolutionary purposes. But they also held it to be vital for the success of the industrial drive that it should be backed by the mass of the people who still resented the neglect of their living conditions, the run-away inflation, the many unkept official promises, and bureaucratic high-handedness. Having for years championed the course of action the party had taken, the applicants felt that they were entitled to reinstatement, all the more so as they also welcomed the 'left turn' in Comintern policy and admitted the harm of all faction. They regretted the exacerbation of feeling between the Opposition and the Central Committee, to which Trotsky's banishment had contributed so much. 'We appeal to the Central Committee, the Central Control Commission, and the entire party', the statement concluded, 'to ease our way back to the party by freeing the Bolshevik-Leninists, lifting the 58 paragraph, and bringing back Lev Davidovich Trotsky.'

When the statement reached Prinkipo, on 22 September,

Trotsky's satisfaction was mingled with apprehension. He was pleased to see at last a declaration from his followers—the first for many months—which did not ooze utter resignation. Yet he was apprehensive of its tenor. Having by now arranged his contacts with the Soviet Union via Berlin, Paris, and Oslo, he undertook to forward the Letter to those colonies of deportees which had not yet received it. But he added a gloss of his own design to give the statement a sharper edge. He said that he endorsed the Letter because, although it was 'moderate', it was 'not equivocal'. Only those could refuse to sign it who were of the opinion that the Soviet Thermidor was already accomplished, that the party was dead, and that nothing less than a new revolution was necessary in the U.S.S.R. 'Although this opinion has been attributed to us dozens of times, we have nothing in common with it. . . . Despite repression and persecution, we declare that our loyalty to Lenin's party and the October revolution remains unshakeable.' He too acknowledged that with the 'left turn' and the break between Stalin and Bukharin a new situation had arisen: 'If previously Stalin fought the Left Opposition with arguments borrowed from the Bukharinist right, he now attacks the right exclusively with arguments borrowed from the left.' In theory this should have led to a *rapprochement* between the centre and the left; in practice it did not. Stalin's adoption of the Opposition's policy was superficial, fortuitous, or merely tactical; basically they remained poles apart. Stalin conceived the Five Year Plan within the framework of socialism in one country, while the Opposition viewed the whole process of constructing socialism in the context of international revolution. This fundamental difference was as sharp as ever; and while Rakovsky and his friends had declared their solidarity with the new Comintern policy, Trotsky briefly but firmly stated his objections to it. Nevertheless, he agreed that Rakovsky was right in expressing readiness 'to subordinate the struggle we are waging for our ideas to the statutory norms and the discipline of a party that would base itself on proletarian democracy'. They had been willing to defend their views *within* the party at the time when the party was ruled by the right-centre coalition; and they must *a fortiori* be prepared to do so when the right was no longer in control. But to renounce their views because of this would be dishonest and 'unworthy of Marxism and of the Leninist school of thought'. Trotsky trusted implicitly Rakovsky's integrity and courage; but he sensed the press and the pull of the stampede under which Rakovsky acted. In another gloss he excused Rakovsky's conciliatory tone as designed to 'test openly the inner party régime' in changed political circumstances: 'Was that régime or was it not, after all the recent lessons, capable of making good, at least partly, the immense harm it had done to the party and the revolution?' Was a self-reform of the Stalinist 'apparatus' still possible? Rakovsky's 'reticence, his silence on Stalin's mistakes in the international field, and his emphasis on the recent shifts to the left' were all calculated to facilitate the beginning of such a self-reform. Rakovsky had once again demonstrated that what mattered to the Opposition was the essence, not the form, of things, and the interest of the revolution, not the ambitions of persons or groups. 'The Opposition is ready to take the most modest place inside the party, but only if it can remain true to itself. . . .'[1]

Even while he wrote this, Trotsky wondered how many of those who had signed Rakovsky's statement might yet defect, and in a confidential message he warned Rakovsky that in his quest for conciliation he had gone to the limit and must not go 'even one step further!'. In the same *Bulletin* in which Rakovsky's statement appeared Trotsky published also an anonymous letter from a correspondent in Russia, criticizing Rakovsky for pandering to the capitulators. The writer, one of the few 'optimists' still left, was confident that soon 'Stalin will be on his knees before us as Zinoviev was in 1926'.

At the close of the year only a small minority of the Oppositionists still held out. According to one report not more than about a thousand Trotskyists remained in places of exile and prisons, whereas before the capitulations there were several thousands. Not for the first or the last time Trotsky had to say to himself: 'Friends who set forth at our side, Falter, are lost in the storm!' In the last days of November he wrote to a group of his Soviet disciples:[2] 'Let there remain in exile not 350

---

[1] 'Pismo druzyam' ('Not for Publication') of 25 September 1929. *The Archives; B.O.*, loc. cit.

[2] The letter, dated 26 November 1929, was provoked by a communication from an Oppositionist who was obviously inclined to join the capitulators. *The Archives.*

G

people faithful to their banner, but only 35. Let there remain even three—the banner will remain, the strategic line will remain, the future will remain.' He was ready to struggle on even alone. Did he at this moment think of Adolf Yoffe's farewell message? 'I have always thought', so Yoffe in the hour of his suicide wrote to Trotsky, 'that you have not enough in yourself of Lenin's unbending and unyielding character, not enough of that ability which Lenin had to stand alone and remain alone on the road he considered to be the right road. . . .'[1]

.   .   .   .

Paradoxically, Stalin viewed with some uneasiness the rush of the capitulators to Moscow, much though he benefited from it. Many thousands of Trotskyists and Zinovievists were now back in and around the party, forming a distinctive *milieu*. Stalin did not allow a single one of them to occupy any office of political importance. But the administrators, the economists, and the educationists were assigned to posts on all rungs of the government, where they were bound to exercise an influence. Although Stalin could not doubt their zeal for the left course, especially for industrialization, he knew what value to attach to the recantations he had extracted from them. They remained Oppositionists at heart. They considered themselves the wronged pioneers of the left course. They hated him not merely as their persecutor, but as the man who had robbed them of their ideas. True, he had turned them, politically, into his slaves. But the hidden hatred of slaves can be more dangerous than open hostility; it can lie silently in ambush, follow the master with a thousand eyes, and set upon him when he slips or makes a false step.

The capitulators now had a chance to influence, directly or indirectly, even the Stalinists and Bukharinists, some of whom also were bewildered when they saw Stalin appropriate the ideas and slogans which they had sincerely believed pernicious when Trotsky and Zinoviev had proclaimed them. After all his triumphs over all his opponents, Stalin was therefore at logger-heads with some of his own followers, among whom he began to discover crypto-Trotskyists and crypto-Bukharinists. 'If we

[1] See *The Prophet Unarmed*, p. 382.

were right in 1925-7', such people said, 'when we rejected the
Opposition's demand for rapid industrialization and for an
offensive against the kulak, and when we branded Trotsky
and Zinoviev as the wreckers of the alliance between workers
and peasants, then surely we are wrong now. And if we are right
now, and if nothing but the left course can save the revolution,
should we not have adopted it earlier, when the Opposition
urged us to do so?' 'And was it not vile on our part', the most
conscientious added, 'to abuse and crush the Opposition?'
The answers varied, of course: some drew one conclusion, others
another.[1] Enough that as early as the summer and autumn of
1929, while the capitulators were re-entering the party, a few
good old Stalinists were being expelled from it, and some even
sent to the places of deportation which the capitulators had
just vacated. The most notorious cases were those of Uglanov,
secretary of the Moscow organization, and other members of
the Central Committee, branded as Bukharinists, and of
Shatskin, Sten, and Lominadze, eminent propagandists and
leaders of the 'young Stalinists', who were all three unmasked as
semi-Trotskyists.

These cases revealed something of the ferment in the ruling
group itself, a ferment which made it no unmixed advantage
for Stalin to have so many capitulators around. Stalin knew that
they still looked up to Trotsky as their guide and inspirer and
indeed as the true leader of the revolution. Every batch of them,
as they negotiated terms of surrender, had asked for Trotsky's
return and stuck to this demand even while yielding on all other
points of policy and discipline. When at last they were brought
to renounce Trotsky, most of them did so with despair in their
hearts and tears in their eyes. Few, very few, were those who
like Radek perversely quelled their qualms and railed against
Trotsky; and Radek's outbursts aroused disgust even among old
Stalinists. To most capitulators Trotsky represented all that
they had stood for in their better and prouder days. Their
débacle and self-abasement had isolated him politically, but
threw into fresh relief his moral grandeur. The capitulators, the
Bukharinists, and the doubting Stalinists took in avidly every
word of his that penetrated into the Soviet Union. At critical

[1] Such discussions went on even as late as 1931, during the writer's stay in
Moscow.

moments, when important decisions were pending, the whisper: 'What does Lev Davidovich say about this?' was often heard even in Stalin's antechambers.[1] The *Bulletin* circulated in Moscow—party men returning from assignments abroad, especially members of embassies, smuggled it home and passed it on to friends. Although only very few papers got about in this way—the *Bulletin* seems never to have been printed in more than 1,000 copies—Trotsky's comments and forecasts and the choice morsels of his invective spread quickly by word of mouth. Stalin could not rest on his laurels and contemplate the ferment with equanimity.

.   .   .   .

The Blumkin affair gave him an opportunity to strike. Jacob Blumkin, a high official of the G.P.U.'s foreign department, had a strange career behind him, and stranger still was his present role. Just before the revolution he had, as an adolescent, joined the terrorist organization of the Social Revolutionary Party. Something of a poet, he was a romantic idealist, with a precocious, simple-minded, and boundless devotion to his cause. In October 1917 he was among the Left Social Revolutionaries who made common cause with the Bolsheviks; and he represented his party on the Cheka under Dzerzhinsky—thus as a youngster of twenty—Revolution picks her lovers young!—he was one of the original founders of the Cheka. When his party broke with the Bolsheviks over the peace of Brest Litovsk, Blumkin shared his comrades' fierce conviction that in concluding that peace the Bolsheviks had betrayed the revolution. When his comrades decided to stage a rising against Lenin's government and to force the Soviet Republic into war against Germany, they assigned two men to make an attempt on the life of Count Mirbach, the German Ambassador in Moscow. Blumkin was one of the two. He succeeded; and this event was the signal for the insurrection which Trotsky suppressed. The Bolsheviks seized Blumkin and brought him before Trotsky.

It will be remembered that the Bolshevik party had itself been deeply divided over the Brest Litovsk peace; and so

[1] It was in the lobbies of the Central Committee that the writer, to his surprise, repeatedly heard that whisper.

although the Party outlawed the Left Social Revolutionaries, many Bolsheviks felt a warm sympathy for Mirbach's assassin, even though they condemned the deed. Trotsky appealed to the insurgents' revolutionary sentiment and sought to impress on them how misguided their action had been and to convert them to Bolshevik views. When Blumkin was brought before him, he engaged the young and impressionable terrorist in a long and serious argument. Succumbing to superior powers of persuasion, Blumkin repented and asked to be allowed to redeem himself. *Pro forma* he was condemned to death, and the German Government was even informed of his execution; but he was pardoned and given the chance to 'prove his devotion to the revolution'. He undertook to carry out the most dangerous missions for the Bolsheviks; and during the civil war he worked for them behind the lines of the White Guards. The Left Social Revolutionaries considered him a traitor and made several attempts on his life. After one attempt, while he was recovering in a hospital, they threw a hand grenade into his ward; he seized it and flung it out of the window at the very moment of the explosion. Rehabilitated by the Bolsheviks, he then served on Trotsky's military staff, studied at the Military Academy, gained some repute as a writer on military affairs, and was active in the Comintern. After the civil war he rejoined the Cheka or G.P.U. and was a senior officer of its Counter Intelligence Department. His faith in Trotsky knew no bounds; he was attached to the Commissar of War with the whole force of his emotional temperament. He was also in close friendship with Radek, whom he 'adored' and who was more accessible and responsive than Trotsky. When Trotsky and Radek went into opposition, Blumkin made no secret of his solidarity with them. Although the nature of his work prevented him from engaging in the Opposition's activities, he considered it his duty to make his attitude clear to Menzhinsky, the chief of the G.P.U. But, as his skill at counter intelligence was greatly valued, and as he did not participate in the Opposition's work and never committed any breach of discipline, he was allowed to hold his views and remain in his post. He stayed in the party and the G.P.U. even after the Opposition had been expelled.

In the summer of 1929, while travelling on duty from India to Russia, Blumkin stopped at Constantinople where, as

Trotsky maintains, he met Lyova by chance in the street. One may doubt whether this was in fact a chance encounter. It is implausible that Blumkin should have arrived in Turkey without intending to make contact with Trotsky. Having met the son, accidentally or not, he asked for an appointment with the father. Trotsky at first refused, considering the risk too great. But when Blumkin imploringly repeated the request, he agreed to receive him.

Blumkin arrived to pour out his heart to the man before whom eleven years earlier he had stood as Mirbach's assassin. He was, as were most Oppositionists, confused; and he was a prey to a conflict of loyalties. He found it hard to reconcile his position in the G.P.U. with his sentiment for the Opposition. He was torn between the Oppositionists who had capitulated and those who resisted, and between his faith in Trotsky and his friendship for Radek. He did not believe that the breach between the two was irreparable; and in his simple-mindedness he hoped to reconcile them. For hours he remained closeted with Trotsky, relating news from Moscow and listening avidly to Trotsky's arguments about the Opposition's responsibilities and duties and the futility of surrender.

He put before Trotsky his own *cas de conscience* and spoke of his wish to resign from the G.P.U. Trotsky firmly dissuaded him. Difficult as his situation was, Trotsky said, he must go on working loyally for the G.P.U. The Opposition was committed to defend the workers' state; and no Oppositionist should withdraw from any official post in which he acted in the broad interest of the state and not in that of the Stalinist faction. Was the Opposition not on the side of the Soviet Union in the conflict over the Manchurian Railway? Blumkin's activity was directed entirely against the external enemy; and it was perfectly consistent with the Opposition's attitude that he should carry on.

Blumkin accepted the advice and asked Trotsky to give him a message or instructions to Oppositionists at home. He also volunteered to help in arranging contacts and in organizing, with the help of Turkish fishermen, the *Bulletin's* clandestine despatch across the frontier.

Trotsky gave him the message, a copy of which is preserved in *The Archives*. The document contains nothing that could by any stretch of the imagination be described as conspiratorial. Its terms were so general and in part so trivial that it was feckless of Trotsky and Blumkin to take any risk at all in transmitting it. Trotsky forecast that in the autumn Stalin would find himself in great difficulties and that the capitulators would then realize how useless their surrender had been. He appealed, of course, to his followers to hold out, and poured scorn on the faint-hearted. He gave them notice of the attack on Radek he was preparing to publish and reproduced the gist of it. For the nth time he denied the charge, which Radek now echoed, that he was trying to form a new party; and he repeated that the Opposition remained part and parcel of the old party. He gave an account of what he was doing to set up the international organization of the Opposition and explained in humdrum detail the quarrels among the German, French, and Austrian Trotskyists and Zinovievists; he begged the Russians not to be disappointed by all this, but to be confident that the international Opposition would eventually emerge as a vital political force. It is a pathetic thought that the deportees placed such great hopes on this, and that Trotsky had to reassure them. In the whole message there was nothing that he had not said or was not about to say in public, especially in the *Bulletin*.[1] It is, of course, possible to suspect that he gave Blumkin more definitely conspiratorial instructions orally. But, strangely, even the G.P.U. never maintained that he did so; and the inner evidence of his attitude, activity, and correspondence indicates that he had in fact nothing to say to his followers in private that he did not or could not tell them in public. With this message in hand Blumkin departed in high spirits, confident that now he would be able to prove to Radek and others that their charges were

---

[1] The text of the message (undated) is in *The Archives*, Closed Section, Russian files. I have not been able to ascertain the exact date of Blumkin's visit. On internal evidence it appears to have occurred either in July or in August 1929. Trotsky's message contained in addition these organizational 'instructions': he asked his followers not to send him communications through Urbahns, the leader of the German *Leninbund*, with whom he was in political controversy; and he warned them to beware of one Kharin, an official of the Soviet Embassy in Paris, whom he denounced as a Stalinist *agent-provocateur*. (It was partly through Kharin, it seems, that Trotsky, immediately after the banishment, maintained contact with Russia.) These 'instructions' too had nothing conspiratorial or even confidential about them. In any movement of this kind warnings against an *agent provocateur* are normally given the widest publicity so as to put on guard as many people as possible.

groundless, that Trotsky was as loyal and as great a Bolshevik as ever, and that the Opposition should, under his leadership, restore its unity.

Shortly after his return to Moscow, Blumkin was arrested, charged with treason, and executed. It is not easy to determine how the G.P.U. came to learn about his moves. Some said that he had confided his secret to a woman whom he loved and who, being herself a secret service agent, denounced him. Others maintained that on his return Blumkin went straight to Radek who, fearing to draw suspicion on himself or being anxious to convince Stalin of the sincerity of his own recantation, betrayed his friend. This account gained wide credence and made Radek despised and hated. According to yet another version, upheld by Victor Serge, Radek's role was pitiable rather than sinister. Serge relates that back in Moscow Blumkin felt at once that the G.P.U. knew where he had been and that their agents were shadowing him in order to find out with whom of the Oppositionists he was in touch. Radek was worried about Blumkin's plight and advised him to approach Ordjonikidze, chairman of the Central Control Commission, and make a clean breast of everything. This was the only way, he allegedly said, in which Blumkin could save himself: Ordjonikidze, although a strict disciplinarian, was a conscientious and in his way even a generous man, the only one in the hierarchy who could be expected to treat the case sternly indeed but not without humanity. It was not known, however, whether Blumkin was arrested after or before he approached Ordjonikidze.[1] The whole puzzle may perhaps be explained more simply: the vigilant eye of a member of the Soviet Consulate in Constantinople may have caught sight of Blumkin taking the boat to Prinkipo; or an *agent provocateur* in Trotsky's house may have discovered the identity of the mysterious visitor with whom Trotsky had shut himself up for so many hours.

Blumkin 'carried himself with remarkable dignity' during the interrogation, relates a former G.P.U. officer. 'He went courageously to his execution and when the fatal shot was about to be fired he shouted, "Long live Trotsky!" '[2] More and more

[1] Trotsky's letter to Rosmer, 5 January 1930; *B.O.*, nos. 9 and 10, 1930; and Serge, *Mémoires d'un Revolutionnaire*, pp. 277–9.

[2] A. Orlov, *The Secret History of Stalin's Crimes*, p. 202.

frequently in years to come was this cry to resound amid volleys fired by execution squads.

This was the first execution of its kind. True, other Trotskyists had already paid for their convictions with their lives, perishing from hunger and exhaustion—the year before, for instance, Butov, one of Trotsky's secretaries, died in prison after a long hunger strike. Nevertheless, the rule that the Bolsheviks must never repeat the mortal error of the Jacobins and have recourse in their internecine struggles to execution had hitherto been respected, at least in form. Now that rule was broken. Blumkin was the first party member on whom capital punishment was inflicted for an inner party offence, an offence no graver than being in contact with Trotsky.

Stalin had been apprehensive lest the capitulations should blur the line of division between the Opposition and the party; and Blumkin's venture heightened his apprehension. He could not tolerate a senior G.P.U. officer on active service visiting Trotsky in a comradely manner and mediating between Trotsky and the capitulators—to tolerate this would be to make a mockery of all the official accusations of Trotsky and encourage further contacts. Stalin himself may not have believed in the relatively innocuous character of Blumkin's mission and of Trotsky's message to the Opposition. The thought may have occurred to his suspicious mind that it would be unsafe to assume that Mirbach's assassin would never again vent his simple but strong political passions in a terrorist act. In any case Blumkin's execution was to serve as a warning to others: it was to show them that official charges of counter-revolution must not be trifled with, that paragraph 58 was paragraph 58, and that henceforth comradely connexions with the Prinkipo outcast would be punished with the whole severity of a garbled and perverted law. Curiously enough, no capital punishment was as yet inflicted on the avowed Trotskyists, who from their prisons and punitive colonies were in communication with their leader, who sent him collective greetings on October anniversaries and May Days, and whose names appeared under articles and 'theses' in the *Bulletin Oppozitsii*. For the time being, the warning was meant only for party members, holders of official posts, especially in the G.P.U., and reinstated capitulators. The line of division between party and Opposition was redrawn in blood.

Trotsky learned of the execution from an anonymous Oppositionist who, being still in government service, was on an official mission in Paris.[1] But Moscow was silent; and when a rumour percolated through to the German Press, communist papers denied it. For several weeks Trotsky waited for further information, and in his letters to Russian followers made no allusion to Blumkin—until early in January 1930 a message from Oppositionists in Moscow dispelled all doubts. Trotsky at once disclosed the circumstances of his meeting with Blumkin. He declared that it was Stalin personally who had ordered the execution and that Yagoda gave effect to the order without even referring it to Menzhinsky, the nominal head of the G.P.U. The *Bulletin* published the correspondence from Moscow, the writers of which maintained that it was Radek who had betrayed Blumkin. Trotsky himself, on second thoughts, doubted whether this was so and intimated that Radek had probably acted irresponsibly and stupidly but in good faith. 'Blumkin's misfortune', Trotsky wrote, 'was that he trusted Radek and that Radek trusted Stalin.'

Trotsky enjoined his followers in the West to raise a 'storm of protests'. 'The Blumkin affair', he wrote to Rosmer on 5 January 1930, 'should become the Sacco-Vanzetti affair of the Left Opposition.' Some time earlier the execution in Boston of Sacco and Vanzetti, two Italian-American anarchists, had been the object of a memorable world-wide protest raised by communists, socialists, radicals, and liberals. Trotsky's call found no response. Blumkin's fate did not arouse even a fraction of the indignation that the execution of Sacco and Vanzetti had provoked. It was far easier to arouse the conscience of the left against a miscarriage of justice by the judiciary of a bourgeois state than to move it against a *Justizmord* committed in a workers' state. Barely a few weeks later Trotsky was already having to protest, and to ask others to protest, against two further executions of Oppositionists and against harsh reprisals to which Rakovsky and his friends were subjected.

---

[1] The news was transmitted to Trotsky by R. Molinier in a letter of 10 December 1929, together with a rather gloomy account of the Opposition's disintegration. *The Archives*, Closed Section.

And once again he failed even to dent the stony indifference of those whom he had hoped to move.[1]

. . . .

The year 1929 ended in the Soviet Union with an upheaval the violence of which surpassed all expectations. Early in the year Stalin's policy had still been hesitant and uncertain. The industrial drive was gaining momentum, but the government had not yet thrown all caution to the wind; in April, the Sixteenth Party Conference called for speedier collectivization, but proclaimed that the private farms would for many years yet predominate in the rural economy—the Five Year Plan provided for the collectivization of only 20 per cent. of all smallholdings by 1933; the kulak was to pay higher taxes and to deliver more grain, but there was no thought yet of his 'liquidation'. By the end of the year it was as if a whirlwind had swept away these plans and the prudence that had inspired them. The industrial drive burst all bounds: again and again the targets were raised; and the call went out that the Plan must be carried out in four, three, or even two and a half years. On the twelfth anniversary of the revolution Stalin, confronted by the 'difficulties' Trotsky foresaw, the peasantry's refusal to deliver grain, pronounced death sentence on private farming: 'Immediate and wholesale collectivization' was the order of the day; and only four months later he announced that 50 per cent., about 13 million, of the farmsteads had already been collectivized. The whole power of state and party drove the kulaks from the land and forced millions of other peasants to pool all their possessions and accept a new mode of production.[2]

Almost every village became a battlefield in a class war, the like of which had never been seen before, a war which the collectivist state waged, under Stalin's supreme command, in order to conquer rural Russia and her stubborn individualism. The forces of collectivism were small but well armed, mobile,

---

[1] In no. 10 of the *B.O.*. Trotsky named the two executed men as Silov and Rabinovich, saying that they had been charged with 'sabotage of railway transport'. According to Orlov (op. cit., loc. cit.) the real 'crime' of Rabinovich, himself a G.P.U. officer, was that he had informed clandestine Trotskyist circles in Moscow of Blumkin's execution.

[2] See *K.P.S.S. v Rezolutsyakh*, vol. II, pp. 449–69, 593ff.; Stalin, *Sochinenya* vol. XII, pp. 118–35; *Pravda*, 6 January 1930; Deutscher, *Stalin*, 317–22.

and directed by a single will; rural individualism, its great strength scattered, was caught by surprise, and was armed only with the wooden club of despair. As in every war so in this, there was no lack of manœuvres, inconclusive skirmishes, and confused retreats and advances; but eventually the victors seized their spoils and took uncounted multitudes of prisoners, whom they drove into the endless and empty plains of Siberia and the icy wastes of the Far North. As in no other war, however, the victors could neither admit nor reveal the full scope of hostilities; they had to pretend that they carried out a salutary transformation of rural Russia with the consent of the overwhelming majority; and so even after several decades the precise numbers of the casualties, which must have gone into millions, remained unknown.

Such were the suddenness, the magnitude, and the force of the upheaval that few who witnessed it were able to absorb and focus mentally its immensity. Until recently the Trotskyist Opposition could maintain that Stalin, by initiating the left course, was only giving effect to its demands; but the Great Change exceeded those demands to an extent that took away the breath of Trotskyists and Stalinists alike, not to speak of the Bukharinists. Among the Trotskyists, the conciliators showed a clearer awareness of the scope and the finality of events; the resisters still clung to premises and reasonings formed in earlier years. Rakovsky, for instance, treated Stalin's orders for the annihilation of the kulaks as 'ultra-left rhetoric' and asserted that 'the specific weight of the wealthy farms in the national economy will grow even further, despite all the talk about fighting agrarian capitalism'.[1] Just before the twelfth anniversary of the revolution, Trotsky himself claimed that 'the slow development of the rural economy . . . and the difficulties which the countryside experiences favour the growth of the power of the kulaks and the progress of their influence . . .'.[2] He did not imagine that at a stroke, or within a very few years, 25 million private smallholdings could be wiped out by force.

At the beginning of 1930, however, Trotsky began to realize what was happening and in a series of essays devoted to a critique of the Five Year Plan he evolved a new line of attack on Stalin's policy. The new criticism was marked by dialectical

[1] B.O., no. 7, 1929.   [2] Écrits, vol. I, p. 76.

duality: he made a sharp distinction between the 'socialist-progressive' and the 'bureaucratic-retrograde' trends in the Soviet Union and illumined their perpetual conflict. He began, for instance, an essay on 'Economic Recklessness and its Perils' with these words:[1]

The success of the Soviet Union in industrial development is acquiring global historical significance. Social Democrats who do not even try to evaluate the tempo which the Soviet economy proves itself capable of attaining deserve but contempt. That tempo is neither stable nor secure . . . but it provides practical proof of the immense possibilities inherent in socialist economic methods. . . . On the basis of the Soviet experience it is not difficult to see what economic power a socialist bloc comprising central and eastern Europe and large parts of Asia would have wielded if the Social Democratic Parties had used the power that the 1918 revolution had given them and carried out a socialist upheaval. The whole of mankind would have had a different outlook by now. As it is, mankind will have to pay for the betrayal committed by the Social Democratic Party with additional wars and revolutions.

Having so emphatically restated his appreciation of the socialist trend in Soviet developments, he attacked Stalin's domestic policy in the same terms in which he had characterized the new Comintern line—as an 'ultra-left zigzag that had come to replace the previous rightist zigzag'. This was consistent with Trotsky's view that Stalin, as a 'centrist', acted under alternate pressures from right and left, a view which properly described Stalin's place in the inner party alignments of the nineteen-twenties, but fitted the realities of later years less well. By and large Trotsky still held that intensive industrialization and collectivization were merely a transient phase of Stalin's policy. He was not aware, and he was never to become fully aware, that in 1929–30 Stalin had gone beyond a point of no return, where he could neither halt the industrial drive in its tracks nor, having destroyed the kulaks, try and make peace with them. This basic error in Trotsky's judgement, to which we shall return later, does not, however, invalidate his specific criticisms, in which he anticipated most of the revisions of policy that Stalin's successors were to carry out after 1953. Just as in the nineteen-twenties Trotsky was the pioneer of primitive socialist

[1] The essay was written in February 1930 and published in the *B.O.*, no. 9.

accumulation, so in the early nineteen-thirties he was the precursor of economic and social reforms that were to be undertaken only several decades later.

He attacked at the outset the rate set by the first Five Year Plan, in its final version, for industrial expansion.[1] From the 'snail's pace', he observed, Stalin had switched over to the 'race-track gallop'. In its early versions the Plan had aimed at an 8–9 per cent rate of annual expansion; and the Opposition's proposal to double the tempo had been decried as fanciful, irresponsible, and dangerous. Now the tempo was trebled. Instead of striving for *optimum* results, Trotsky pointed out, the planners and managers were ordered to strain always for the *maximum*, regardless of the fact that this threw the national economy out of balance, and so reduced the effectiveness of the drive. Production targets grossly exceeded available resources; and so an incongruity arose between manufacturing and primary production, between heavy and light industry, and between investment and private consumption. Worse still was the contrast between the advance of industry and the lag in farming. There is no need to dwell here on these and other disproportions which Trotsky often analysed in detail—it has since become a truism that these disproportions did indeed mark and mar the whole process of industrialization in the Stalin era. But, as happens so often, the truisms of one generation were the dreaded heresy of its predecessor; and communists, but not only they, received Trotsky's criticisms with indignation or derision.

Yet when one re-examines after this lapse of time what Trotsky said on these matters, one is struck by his political restraint rather than by his polemical heat. He usually prefaced almost every piece of criticism by emphatic acknowledgement of the progress achieved under the direction of his adversary, although he insisted that the mainspring of progress lay in the national ownership and planning of industry and that Stalin not only used but also abused these advantages of the Soviet economy. He did not believe that the administrative whip did or

[1] See also Trotsky's 'Open Letter' to party members in *B.O.*, no. 10 (April 1930); his comments on the XVI Congress, ibid., nos. 12–13 (June–July 1930); and 'The Successes of Socialism and the Perils of Recklessness', ibid., nos. 17–18 (November–December 1930).

could accelerate the industrial advance—the whip was all too often the very cause of a halt and a breakdown. National ownership led to central planning and required it; but bureaucratic over-centralization led to the concentration and magnification of the errors committed by those in power, to paralysis of social initiative, and to tremendous wastage of human and material resources. An irresponsible and 'infallible' Leader had to boast all mistakes and reverses out of existence and to flaunt all the time spectacular achievements, unheard-of records, and dazzling statistics. Stalinist planning dwelt on the quantitative side of industrialization to the exclusion of everything else; and the higher the quantity of goods that had to be produced at any price, the lower the quality. For rational planning a comprehensive system of economic coefficients and tests was needed, which would measure continuously not merely the growth of production but changes in quality, costs, the purchasing power of money, comparative rates of productivity, &c. Yet all these facets of the economy were wrapt in obscurity: Stalin conducted the industrial drive 'with all lamps extinguished', amid a complete blackout of vital information.

Trotsky's criticism of the collectivization was even more thoroughgoing. He condemned the 'liquidation of the kulaks' as a monstrosity; and he did so long before the horrors that attended it had become known. In the years when he himself was stigmatized as the 'enemy of the peasantry', he had urged the Politbureau to raise the taxation of well-to-do farmers, to organize farm labourers and poor peasants, to encourage them to form collective farms on a voluntary basis, and to throw the state's resources (agricultural machinery, fertilizers, credit and agronomic assistance) behind the collective farms so as to promote them in their competition with private farming. These proposals had expressed the full extent of his anti-kulak policy; and he had never gone beyond them. It had never occurred to him that a social class as numerous as the rural bourgeoisie could or should be destroyed by decree and violence—that millions of people should be dispossessed and condemned to social, and many also to physical, death. That socialism and private farming were ultimately incompatible and that the capitalist farmer would vanish in a society evolving towards socialism, had, of course, been an axiom of Marxism and Leninism. But Trotsky, like all Bolsheviks until quite recently, envisaged this as a gradual process, in the course of which the smallholder would succumb to the more productive collective method of farming in a way similar to, but far less painful than, the way the independent artisan and small farmer had succumbed to modern industry and large-scale agriculture under capitalism.

There was therefore no element of demagogy in the angry denunciation with which Trotsky met the liquidation of the kulaks. Not only was this to him a malignant and sanguinary travesty of all that Marxism and Leninism had stood for—he did not believe that the *kolkhozy* which Stalin was forcing into existence would be viable. He argued that collectivized agriculture required a technological base far superior to that on which individual husbandry had rested; and such a base did not exist in the Soviet Union: the tractor had not yet replaced the horse.[1] In an expressive simile (of which it could, however, be said that *comparaison n'est pas raison*) he asserted that without modern machinery it was just as impossible to turn private smallholdings into a viable collective farm as it was to merge small boats into an ocean-going liner. Stalin intended, of course, to supply the machinery over the years, as he eventually did. What Trotsky maintained was that collectivization should not outrun the technical means needed for it. Otherwise, the collectives would not be economically integrated; their productivity would not be higher than that of private farming; and they would not bring the peasants the material advantages which could compensate them for the loss of private property.[2] Meantime, before the collectives were technologically in-

---

[1] *Pravda* of 15 January 1930 estimated that 1,500,000 tractors were needed for the full collectivization of Soviet farming. This degree of mechanization was not reached until 1956, when the 'Tractor Park' (calculated in 15 h.p. units) passed the 1,500,000 mark—in actual, nearly 30 h.p., units, it consisted of 870,000 tractors.

The annual output of (15 h.p.) tractors was only a little over 3,000 in 1929 and 50,000 in 1932. The amounts of other available agricultural machinery were altogether negligible. At the beginning of the first Five Year Plan, in 1928, there were fewer than 1,000 lorries on the farms; and there were only 14,000 in 1932. *Narodnoe Khozyaistvo S.S.S.R. v 1958 g.*, Soviet Statistical Yearbook, 1959, pp. 243, 487.

[2] 'The collectivization of *sokhas* [wooden ploughs] . . . is a fraud', Trotsky wrote. His argument was controverted by some Trotskyist economists (see, e.g. Ya. Gref's study on collectivization and overpopulation in *B.O.*, no. 11) and, of course, by the Stalinists, who maintained that the collective farm, even when technologically

tegrated, the peasantry's resentment would show in a decline or stagnation of agricultural output; and it would threaten to blow up the collectives from the inside. So acute was Trotsky's insight into the state of mind of the peasantry that from Prinkipo he warned Moscow about the coming calamitous mass slaughter of cattle; and he did this in plenty of time, five years before Stalin admitted the fact.[1] Even much later Trotsky remained convinced that the collectivist structure of farming was chronically in a state of near collapse.

In retrospect it may appear that Trotsky took too black a view: the collective farms did not collapse, after all. Yet Stalin's rural policy throughout the nineteen-thirties, with its whimsical combination of massive terror and petty concessions, was dictated precisely by the fear of a collapse: only with iron bands could he hold together the collective farm. The decline and subsequent stagnation in farm output were all too real, and became the great theme of official policy twenty-five and thirty years later.

The state of affairs in the country reacted upon all aspects of national policy. Industrialization proceeded on a dangerously narrow and shattered agricultural base, amid famines or a perpetual dearth of foodstuffs. It was therefore accompanied by a universal and almost zoologically fierce scramble for the necessities of life, by widespread discontent, and by low productivity of labour. The government had continuously to quell the discontent and to force up productivity by intimidation and subornation. The violent shock of 1929–30 drove the Soviet Union into a vicious circle of scarcities and terrors from which it was not to break out for a long time to come.

primitive, would be more productive than the old smallholding. Trotsky's critics argued from an analogy with British manufacture which, even before the Industrial Revolution (when it was still manufacture in the strict, etymological sense), was more productive than individual handicraft, because, as Marx pointed out in *Das Kapital*, it enjoyed the advantages first of 'simple co-operation,' and then of the division of manual labour. In strict theory, Trotsky's critics were right: collectivization, even without the prior existence of a technological basis proper to it, should result in higher productivity, as it did in China for a time, during the middle nineteen-fifties. Practically, however, and as far as the collectivization of 1929–32 was concerned, Trotsky was right: any advantages which the collective farm might have obtained from the co-operation and division of manual labour were nullified by the peasants' resentful attitude towards work and by the initial destruction of agricultural stock.

[1] *B.O.*, no. 9, 1930.

II

Stalin had now proclaimed the end of N.E.P. and the abolition of the market economy. Surveying Trotsky's views at an
earlier stage we saw that in these there was 'no room for any
sudden abolition of N.E.P., for the prohibition of private trade
by decree . . .' and that socialist planning 'could not one day
supersede N.E.P. at a stroke, but should develop within the
mixed economy until the socialist sector had by its growing
preponderance gradually absorbed, transformed, or eliminated
the private sector and outgrown the framework of N.E.P.'[1]
Trotsky still stuck to this view. He considered the 'abolition of
N.E.P.' a coinage of the bureaucratic brain—only a bureaucracy which, through long neglect of industrialization and a
faulty approach to the peasantry, had failed to cope with the
forces of the market economy and allowed these to grow out of
control could try to decree the market out of existence. But
'thrown out by the door the market would come back by the
window', Trotsky said. As long as farming was not socialized
organically and securely, and amid an all-round scarcity of
goods, it was impossible to eliminate the play of supply and
demand and to substitute for it the planned distribution of
goods. The spontaneous pressures of the market were bound to
break through in farming first, then in those areas where
farming and industry overlapped, and finally even within the
nationalized sector of the economy, where they would often
upset and distort planning. There was ample evidence of this,
especially during the early nineteen-thirties, in the chaos of
official and unofficial prices of consumer goods, in a fantastic
spread of black markets, in the depreciation of the rouble, and
in a steep fall of the purchasing power of wages. The planners
worked 'without yardstick and scale', unable to assess genuine
values and costs and to appraise productivity. 'Regain yardstick and scale', was Trotsky's insistent advice. Instead of
pretending that they had overcome the pressures of the market,
the planners would do better to acknowledge their existence, to
make allowance for them, and to try and bring them under
control. Even in later years, after the runaway inflation of the
early nineteen-thirties was overcome, these criticisms retained
validity; and here, too, much of what Soviet economists said,
in the first decade after Stalin, about the importance of value

[1] *The Prophet Unarmed*, pp. 100–1.

measurement and cost accountancy sounded like an echo of Trotsky's arguments.

The Stalinist blackout of economic information obscured other crucial questions as well. Who was paying for the industrialization, which social classes—and how much? Which classes and groups benefited from it—and to what extent? In the early nineteen-twenties the leaders of the Opposition, especially Preobrazhensky, had maintained that the peasantry would have to contribute heavily to the investment funds of the nationalized industry. Stalin hoped to ensure through collectivization that the peasantry should indeed make this contribution, by increasing the output and the supply of foodstuffs and raw materials. But the peasantry foiled him. 'Let my soul perish with the commissars!' was the cry of the smallholder as he left his holding; and, although he did not manage to bring down the pillars upon the collectivist state, he refused to yield up to it a large part of the sinews of industrialization that he was expected to provide. This was what the destruction of farmstock and the decline in output amounted to in practice.

All the heavier was the burden the urban working class was called upon to carry. The major part of industry's huge investment fund was in effect a deduction from the national wages bill. In real terms, a greatly increased working class had to subsist on a shrunken mass of consumer goods while it built new power stations, steel mills, and engineering plants.[1] Ten years earlier Trotsky had said that the working class 'can

[1] The urban population of the U.S.S.R. rose in the course of the nineteen-thirties from about 30,000,000 to nearly 60,000,000; and the most intensive rise occurred in the first half of the decade. The gross output of agriculture fell from 124 in 1928 (1913—100) to 101 in 1933, and was only 109 in 1936, while that of cattle farming declined from 137 in 1928 to 65 in 1933 and then rose slowly to 96 in 1936. Throughout the nineteen-thirties the grain crops did not exceed the pre-1913 level or were somewhat below it. (*Narodnoe Khozyaistvo S.S.S.R.*, pp. 350–2.) In 1928, however, the marketable surplus of farm produce amounted to only half the pre-revolutionary volume; and only the requisitions of 1929–32 doubled (approximately) the grain stocks available for urban needs. Supplies of sugar, meat, and fat fell very sharply in the years of the first plan (ibid. p. 302). The output of cotton clothing declined or was stationary between 1928 and 1935 (ibid. p. 274). The same is true of footwear, the scarcity of which was aggravated by the disappearance of home industry. (Ibid. p. 293.) Throughout the decade, marked by shortage of labour and materials on which heavy industry had first claim, urban overcrowding, which had been bad enough even earlier, was calamitous. New building provided not more than an average of four square yards of space per new town-dweller.

approach socialism only through the greatest sacrifices, by straining all its strength, and giving its blood and nerves. . . .' Stalin now exacted those sacrifices in blood and nerves. 'There may be moments', Trotsky said in 1923, 'when the government pays you no wages, or when it pays you half your wages and when you, the worker, have to lend the other half to the state in order to enable it to rebuild the nationalized industry.'[1] Stalin now seized that 'other half' of the worker's wages. But whereas Trotsky had excused his proposal by the ruin of the economy after war and civil war and sought to obtain the worker's consent to this method of accumulation, Stalin did what he did after many years of reconstruction and told the worker that his real earnings were doubled and that he was entering the promised land of socialism. For a time inflation concealed the realities from the workers, on whose enthusiasm, endurance, or at least willingness to work the success of the Plan depended.[2]

At the outset the Plan was launched in a spirit which if not egalitarian was nevertheless one of common service and common sacrifice, untarnished by any shocking inequality of rewards. This spirit stirred the fervour of the *Komsomoltsy* and *Udarniki* who rushed to build the *Magnitostroys* and the *Tractorstroys*.[3] But as the first elation sagged and as the great weariness of the workers began to show, the government prodded them on with incentive wages, piece rates, Stakhanovism, rewards for production records, &c. On a par with the bureaucracy and the managers, the labour aristocracy attained

---

[1] *The Prophet Unarmed*, p. 102.

[2] In the resolution of the Central Committee of 10 January 1933 (*K.P.S.S. v Rezolutsyakh*, vol. II, p. 723) the 'average' rise of the incomes of workers and peasants under the first Five Year Plan is given as 85 per cent. In the same period the total sum of retail sales by state-owned and co-operative stores rose from nearly 12 billion to over 40 billion roubles. (*Narodnoe Khozyaistvo v S.S.S.R.*, p. 698.) As apart from bread which was rationed at a fixed price, and perhaps of potatoes, the mass of goods sold was either stationary or rose only to a small extent over these years, it follows that the purchasing power of the rouble, even if measured only in controlled prices, fell to between one-fourth and one-third of that of 1928. In uncontrolled prices the fall was far steeper. Thus, even if the 'average' nominal wage was doubled, the average real wage was in 1932 only half the 1928 wage. It was therefore in a literal sense that, by means of inflation, Stalin took half the worker's wage to finance industrialization.

[3] This enthusiasm was fed by the illusion that the Soviet Union would 'catch up with and surpass' western industrial countries *in two or three years* and so build 'an armoured wall around socialism in one country'. *B.O.*, no. 17–18, 1930.

a markedly privileged status. Henceforth, while Stalin hurled imprecation after imprecation upon 'petty bourgeois levellers', the anti-egalitarian trend gained immense force. Against it Trotsky invoked 'the tradition of Bolshevism which has been one of opposition to labour aristocracy and bureaucratic privilege'. He did not preach levelling. 'It is altogether beyond dispute', he pointed out, 'that at a low level of productive forces and consequently of civilization at large, it is impossible to attain equality of rewards.' He even stated that the egalitarian wages policy of the early revolutionary years had gone too far and impeded economic progress. Yet he held that a socialist government was in duty bound to keep inequality within the limits of what was necessary, to reduce it gradually, and to defend the interests of the great unprivileged mass. 'In the conflict between the working woman and the bureaucrat, we, the Left Opposition, side with the working woman against the bureaucrat . . . who seizes her by the throat. . . .' In the fact that Stalin acted as the protector of privilege, he saw a 'threat to all the conquests of the revolution'.[1]

Trotsky now also redefined his view of proletarian democracy. Only when the toilers were free to express their demands and criticize those in power, he argued, could they arrest the growth of privilege; and from the standpoint of socialism the supreme test 'by which the country's economic condition should be judged is the standard of living of the workers and the role they play in the state'. If in the years of N.E.P. he held that only the strength of proletarian democracy could counterbalance the combined forces of the N.E.P.-men, the kulaks, and the conservative bureaucrats, he now regarded that democracy as the only political setting within which a planned economy could attain its full efficiency. It was therefore a vital economic, and not merely a political, interest of the U.S.S.R. that proletarian democracy be revived. Contrary to a myth of vulgar Trotskyism, he did not advocate any 'direct workers' control over industry', that is management by factory committees or works' councils. This form of management had failed in Russia shortly after the revolution, and Trotsky had ever since been a most determined advocate of one-man management and central control, arguing that management by factory

[1] *B.O.*, no. 23 (August 1931) and no. 27 (March 1932).

committees would become possible only if and when the mass of producers became well educated and imbued with a strong sense of social responsibility. He had also been absolutely opposed to the 'anarcho-syndicalist' schemes of the Workers' Opposition for the transfer of industrial management to trade unions or 'producers' associations'. He did not significantly alter these views when he found himself in Opposition and exile. He conceived proletarian democracy as the workers' right and freedom to criticize and oppose the government and thereby to shape its policies, but not necessarily as their 'right' to exercise direct control over production. He saw in central planning and central direction the essential condition of any socialist economy and of any economy evolving towards socialism. But he pointed out that the process of planning, to be efficacious, must proceed not only from above downwards but also from below upwards. Production targets must not be decreed from the top of the administrative pyramid, without preparatory nation-wide debates, without careful on-the-spot assessment of resources and capacities, without the preliminary testing of the state of mind of the workers, and without the latter's genuine understanding of the plan and willingness to carry it out. When working-class opinion was not allowed to check, correct, and modify schemes presented by a planning authority, the severe disproportions which characterized the Soviet economy under Stalin were inevitable.[1]

Trotsky turned his criticism against the assumption of national self-sufficiency which underlay Stalin's conduct of economic affairs. Socialism in one country remained to him a 'reactionary, national-socialist utopia', unattainable no matter whether it was to be striven for at racing speed or at the snail's pace. With an emphasis which was sometimes exaggerated or misplaced, he pointed out that the Soviet Union could not with its own resources and by its own exertions surpass or even reach the productivity of the advanced western capitalism, the productivity which was the *sine qua non* of socialism. The spread of revolution remained in any case the essential condition for the achievement of socialism in the U.S.S.R. The Stalinist isolationism affected not only the grand strategy of revolution and of socialist construction but even immediate

[1] Loc. cit.

trade policies: Stalin took no account of the advantages of 'international division of labour', and he virtually ignored the importance of foreign trade for Soviet industrialization, especially after the Great Slump when the terms of trade turned sharply against the Soviet Union. Trotsky then urged Moscow to enhance its trading position by political means and appeal to the many millions of the unemployed workers of the West to raise a clamour for trade with Russia (and for export credits) which would assist Russia but would also help to create employment in the capitalist countries. In his own name and on behalf of his tiny organization, Trotsky published several persuasive manifestoes to this effect; but the idea evoked no response from Moscow.[1]

These detailed criticisms culminated in Trotsky's sustained and passionate protest against the moral discredit that Stalin's policy was bringing upon communism. In 1931 Stalin proclaimed that the Soviet Union had already laid the 'foundations of socialism'—even that it had 'entered the era of socialism'; and his propagandists had to back up this claim by contrasting a fantastically bright image of Soviet society with a crudely overdrawn picture of the miseries of life under decaying capitalism.[2] Exposing the double distortion, Trotsky pointed out that to tell the Soviet masses that the hunger and the privations, not to speak of the oppression, which they endured amounted to socialism was to kill their faith in socialism and to turn them into its enemies. In this he saw Stalin's 'greatest crime', for it was committed against the deepest hopes of the working classes and threatened to compromise the future of the revolution and of the communist movement.[3]

. . . .

We have said that Trotsky's criticism was in all its aspects consistent with the tradition of classical Marxism and also that it anticipated the reforms of the post-Stalin era. The question

[1] 'Trotsky urges us to make ourselves more dependent on the capitalist world', Kaganovich said, to which Trotsky retorted that 'autarchy is Hitler's ideal, not Marx's and not Lenin's'. 'Sovetskoe Khozyaistvo v Opasnosti' in *B.O.*, no. 31, November 1932. The value of Soviet exports shrank to one-third and that of imports to one-fourth between 1930 and 1935. Part of this fall was due to adverse trade terms.

[2] See, for instance, *K.P.S.S. v Rezolutsyakh*, vol. II, pp. 717–24. *Pravda, Bolshevik*, and the entire Soviet Press of the nineteen-thirties are full of this contrast.

[3] *B.O.*, loc. cit. and *passim*.

may now be asked whether or to what extent it was relevant to the situation of the nineteen-thirties? Were Trotsky's proposals practicable at the time when he made them? Was a deep divorce between Marxist theory and the practice of the Russian Revolution not an inherent characteristic of that era? And had circumstances not made that divorce inevitable? Only very few questions with which the historian has to deal can tax his confidence in his own judgement as severely as these questions do. Trotsky himself, in his less polemical moods, stressed that the immense difficulties which beset the Soviet Union were rooted in its poverty, backwardness, and isolation. His main charge against Stalin's rule was that it aggravated these difficulties rather than created them; and it was not easy for Trotsky, nor is it for the historian, to draw a line between the 'objective' and the 'subjective' factors of the situation, between the miseries to which the Russian Revolution was heir and those which Stalinist arbitrariness and cruelty produced. Moreover, there was a real 'unity of opposites' here, a dialectical interplay of the objective and the subjective: bureaucratic arbitrariness and cruelty were themselves part and parcel of the Russian backwardness and isolation—they were the backward responses of the inheritors of the revolution to native backwardness.

It was now the commonly (though in part only tacitly) held view of both Trotsky and Stalin that the Soviet Union could achieve rapid industrial ascendancy only through primitive socialist accumulation, a view historically justified by the fact that no underdeveloped nation has, in this century, achieved an advance comparable to Russia's on any other basis. Primitive accumulation, however, presupposed that the workers and peasants should bear more than the 'normal' burden of economic development. Some of the basic disproportions of Stalinist planning were inherent in these conditions. Investment had in any case to expand much faster than consumption. Priority had to be given to heavy over light industry. The theorists of the Opposition had argued that with industrialization the national income would grow so rapidly that popular consumption would rise together with investment, even if not at the same rate. Instead, consumption shrank disastrously in the crucial years of the early nineteen-thirties. Trotsky maintained that this would have been avoided and that the industrial drive would have been carried on under less severe strains and stresses if it had been started several years earlier and in a more rational manner. The argument was plausible; but its truth could not be proved. The Stalinist counter argument, held esoterically rather than stated openly, was also plausible: it was that the Great Change would have been just as cataclysmic even if it had been initiated earlier and more mildly. The threat of famine had hung over urban Russia most of the time since the revolution (and it had recurred periodically before the revolution). Industrialization and the rapid growth of the urban population were, in any case, bound to aggravate it, as long as agriculture remained as fragmented and archaic as it was. Having refused to allow capitalist farming to take charge of the provisioning of the feverishly expanding towns, the Bolsheviks had to opt for collectivization. If they had attempted the gradual collectivization for which Trotsky stood, so the Stalinist argument went on, they would have had the worst of both worlds: the great mass of the smallholders would have been antagonized anyhow; and progress would have been, as under capitalist farming, too slow to secure the provisioning of the towns during rapid industrialization. Trotsky believed, on the contrary, that it was possible to induce the peasantry to a voluntary and economically sound collectivization; and it is a moot point whether he did not underrate the extent to which any form of collectivism offended the stubborn 'irrationality' of the muzhik's attachment to private property. Stalin acted on the Machiavellian principle that nothing was as dangerous for a ruler as to offend and at the same time to seek to propitiate his enemies; and to Stalin his subjects became his enemies. He hurled all the resources of his power against the smallholders; and a whole generation was to labour under the consequences of the economic cataclysm. Yet at this price Stalin, from his viewpoint, scored an immense political gain: he broke the backbone of the archaic rural individualism which threatened to thwart industrialization. Having made this gain, he could not give it up; he had to defend it tooth and nail.

Trotsky did not believe in the solidity of this Machiavellian achievement; he denied to the end that Stalin had vanquished the peasantry's individualism. Convinced that the latter was still able to destroy the collective farms or to bend them to its own interests and needs, he forecast that a new class of kulaks would rise within the kolkhozy and take command.[1] Here again Trotsky grasped a real tendency; but he overemphasized its strength. The peasantry's acquisitiveness did indeed reassert itself in many ways, and Stalin had to struggle against the resurgence of kulaks in the kolkhozy. By a combination of economic measures and terror, however, he succeeded in keeping the recrudescence of private property within narrow and severely restricted bounds; and the peasantry's individualism was never to recover from the mortal blow he inflicted on it, although its death rattle was to sound in Russia's ears for a quarter of a century.

From exile Trotsky repeatedly implored the Stalinist Politbureau to withdraw from their savage enterprise, to call a halt to the barbarous warfare against rural barbarism, and to revert to the more civilized and humane courses of action to which their Marxist-Leninist heritage committed them. He urged the Politbureau to initiate a great act of reconciliation with the peasantry, to declare before the whole nation that in imposing collectivization they had acted wrongly, and that the peasants who wished to leave the collective farms and resume private farming were free to do so. He had no doubt that this would result in the dissolution of many or perhaps most collective farms; but as, in his view, these were not viable anyhow, little would be lost; and the kolkhozy that survived (if they were supplied with machines, credits, and agronomic assistance and so enabled to offer their members material benefits which were beyond the smallholder's reach) could still become the pioneers of a genuine, voluntary collectivist movement, which would in time transform the whole of agriculture and raise its productivity to the level required by a modern and expanding economy. This, Trotsky proclaimed, was what the Opposition would do if it returned to power.[2]

For the Stalinist Politbureau it was too late to seek such a reconciliation with the peasantry. Ever since the autumn of 1929 all the forces of party and state had been fully engaged in

---

[1] See, e.g., the chapter on 'Social Contradictions in the Collective Village' in *The Revolution Betrayed*, pp. 128–35.

[2] *B.O.*, no. 29–30, 1932.

the struggle, and an attempt to disengage them for a deep retreat could well end in their rout. So many had from the outset been the victims of the campaign, so bitter were the passions aroused, so much violence had been inflicted on the villagers and so fierce was their urge for revenge, so immense and bloody was the upheaval, that it was more than doubtful whether any rational way out could be found as long as the generation that had experienced the shock held the stage. If the government had proclaimed that the peasants were free to leave the collective farms, the whole agricultural structure would have come down with a crash, and hardly any collectives would have survived. It would then have taken time before private farming got back into its grooves and began to work in its accustomed ways. Meanwhile, production and supply of food would have further declined and industrial development would have suffered a severe setback. Nor was it likely that a mass exodus from the collective farms could proceed peacefully. The peasants would have felt entitled to get their own back on government and party. The reconciliation would have required that the expropriated and the deported be amnestied and indemnified; and one may well imagine the mood in which trainloads of deportees returning from concentration camps would have been received in their native villages. De-collectivization might have let loose violence as furious as that which had accompanied collectivization. Perhaps a new government with a clean record, a government formed by the Opposition, could have sought to appease the country without bringing it to the brink of counter-revolution—this was what Trotsky believed. For Stalin's government any such attempt would have been suicide. Any sign of weakness on its part would have set ablaze the hatreds smouldering in millions of huts. There was nothing left for Stalin but to remain locked in the struggle, even though, as he confessed to Churchill years later, this was more frightful than even the ordeals of the Second World War.[1]

[1] 'It was now past midnight . . .' writes Churchill. "Tell me," I asked, "have the stresses of this war been as bad to you personally as carrying through the policy of the Collective Farms?" This subject immediately roused the Marshal. "Oh, no," he said, "the Collective Farm policy was a terrible struggle." . . . "Ten millions [of peasants]", he said, holding up his hands. "It was fearful. Four years it lasted. It was absolutely necessary for Russia. . . ." Winston S. Churchill, *The Second World War*, vol. IV, p. 447.

We have seen that the condition of rural Russia prevented any rational change in industrial policy as well; that a new and huge industrial structure, many times larger than that of pre-revolutionary Russia, had to be mounted on an agricultural base narrower than that of the *ancien régime*; and that for many years the subsistence of an ever-growing mass of town dwellers —their numbers, we know, were to rise from 30 to 60 million people in the nineteen-thirties alone—was to depend on a diminished or highly inadequate stock of foodstuffs. It was beyond the power of any government to correct this dis-proportion: of any government, that is, not prepared to call a halt to the industrial drive or to slow it down radically and accept the prospect of economic stagnation. If Trotsky and his followers had, at any time after 1929–30, returned to office, they too would have had to reckon with the consequences of the catastrophic destruction and deterioration of agricultural stock; and committed as they were to industrialization they too would have had to suit their policies to these severely restrictive circumstances.

Years earlier Preobrazhensky had asserted that primitive socialist accumulation, which he expected to take place under far less astringent conditions, would be 'the most critical era in the life of the socialist state . . . it will be a matter of life and death that we should rush through this transition as quickly as possible . . .'.[1] How much more was this a matter of life and death for Stalin, who had cut all his avenues of retreat. He rushed through this transition at a murderous pace, paying no heed to warnings and counsels of moderation. Preobrazhensky had urged the Bolsheviks to 'take the productionist and not the consumptionist point of view . . .' because 'we do not live yet in a socialist society with its production for the consumer —we live under the iron heel of the law of primitive socialist accumulation'. How much heavier, how crushingly heavy, that iron heel had now become! How much sterner also was the 'productionist' viewpoint that, after all that had happened and with all his commitments, Stalin had to adopt! Preobrazhensky had foreseen that a relative shortage of consumer goods would in any case accompany accumulation and result in economic

[1] The conclusions of Preobrazhensky's *New Economics* are summarised in *The Prophet Unarmed*, pp. 234–8.

inequality between administrators and workers, and between skilled, unskilled, and semi-skilled labourers; and that this inequality would be necessary in order to promote skill and efficiency; but that it would not produce new and fundamental class antagonisms. Actually, inequality grew in proportion to scarcity; and both surpassed all expectation.

Stalin employed every ideological device to increase, conceal, and justify the gulf between the privileges of the few and the destitution of the many. But ideological prevarication was not enough; and terror held its dreadful vigil over the gulf. Its fierceness corresponded to the tenseness of all social relations. Outwardly the violence of the nineteen-thirties looked like the recrudescent terror of the civil war. In fact it far surpassed it and immensely differed from it in scale and blind force. In the civil war it was the hot breath of a genuine revolutionary anger that struck at the forces of the *ancien régime* which plotted, organized, armed, and fought against the new republic. The agents of the Cheka were freshly recruited from insurgent workers, were steeped in the experience of their class, shared its privations and sacrifices, and relied on its support. Their terror was as discriminating as it could be amid the chaos of civil war: it aimed at the real and active enemies of the revolution, who, even if they were not 'a mere handful', were in any case a minority. And in the stern atmosphere of war communism, it also guarded the utopian Spartan equality of those years.

The terror of the nineteen-thirties was the guardian of inequality. By its very nature it was anti-popular; and being potentially or actually directed against the majority, it was indiscriminate. Yet even this does not fully account for its all-pervasiveness and fury. Mass executions, mass purges, and mass deportations were not needed merely to safeguard differential wage scales or even the privileges of the bureaucracy— far greater inequalities and privileges are normally safeguarded by far milder means. The great burst of violence came with collectivization; it was primarily the need to perpetuate the Great Change in the countryside that perpetuated the terror. Only the presence in the villages of punitive brigades and Political Departments could prevent the peasants from reverting to private farming. Brute force kept in being the kolkhoz which lacked intrinsic economic coherence. The need to bring that force to bear on the great majority of the nation—the peasantry still formed 60 to 70 per cent. of the population—and to bring it to bear at every season of the year, during the ploughing, the sowing, the harvesting, and finally when the farmers were due to deliver their produce to the state—all this resulted in a constant injection of such huge doses of fear into so vast a part of the social organism that the whole body was inevitably poisoned. Once the machine of terror, far more massive than anything hitherto seen, was mounted and set in motion, it developed its own incalculable momentum. Urban Russia could not insulate herself from the convulsions in which rural Russia was caught: the despair and the hatred of the peasantry overflowed into the cities and towns, catching large sections of the working class; and so also overflowed the violence let loose to meet the despair and the hatred.

. . . .

For all their irrational course, the changes of 1929–30 added up to social revolution, quite as irreversible as that of October 1917, although utterly unlike it. What manifested itself in this upheaval was the 'permanence' of the revolutionary process that Trotsky had prophesied—only that the manifestation was so different from what he had expected that he could not and did not recognize it as such. He still thought, as all Bolsheviks had done until quite recently, that revolution was necessary only for the overthrow of feudal and bourgeois rule and the expropriation of landed estates and big capital; but that after this had been accomplished, the 'transition from capitalism to socialism' should proceed in an essentially peaceful and evolutionary manner. In his approach to domestic Soviet issues the author of 'Permanent Revolution' was in a sense a reformist. True, earlier than anyone he had realized that the Soviet Republic would be unable to resolve its inner conflicts and problems within the framework of national reform; and so he looked forward to international revolution to solve them ultimately. His revolutionary approach to the international class struggle and his reformist approach to domestic Soviet issues were the two sides of a single coin. By contrast, Stalin had, up to 1929, been confident that national reform alone could cope with the conflicts of Soviet society. Having found that this was not so, he too had to go beyond the framework of national reform; and he staged another national revolution. What he discarded was the reformist not the nationalist element of his policy. His pragmatic indifference to international revolutionary perspectives and the quasi-revolutionary character of his domestic policy were also two sides of a single coin.

In its own ironic way the historic development now confirmed the essential truth of the idea which underlay Trotsky's scheme, but controverted, at least in part, that scheme. 'Left to itself alone, the working class of Russia', Trotsky had written early in the century, 'will inevitably be crushed by the counter-revolution at the moment when the peasantry turns its back upon the proletariat.' That moment seemed very close, first in 1921 and then again in the late nineteen-twenties, when the peasantry did turn its back upon the Bolsheviks. 'The workers will have no choice', Trotsky had further written, 'but to link the fate . . . of the Russian Revolution with that of the socialist revolution in Europe.' Since 1917 he kept on repeating that Russia could not by herself achieve socialism, but that nevertheless the momentum of her revolution was not yet spent: 1917 had been but the prelude to international revolution. It now turned out that the dynamic force of the Russian Revolution had indeed not yet come to a rest, although its impulse had failed to ignite revolution in Europe. But having failed to work outwards and to expand and being compressed within the Soviet Union, that dynamic force turned inwards and began once again to reshape violently the structure of Soviet society. Forcible industrialization and collectivization were now substitutes for the spread of revolution, and the liquidation of the Russian kulaks was the *Ersatz* for the overthrow of bourgeois rule abroad. To Trotsky, his idea was inseparable from his scheme: only a German, French, or at least a Chinese October would provide the real sequel to the Russian October; the consummation of the revolutionary process in Russia could come only with its internationalization. Historically this was still true; but immediately Stalin acted as the unwitting agent of permanent revolution within the Soviet Union. Trotsky refused to acknowledge this and to accept the *Ersatz* for the real thing.

His view had in it the rationality of classical Marxism. Stalin's Great Change was shot through with irrationality. The classical revolution conceived by Marxism was carried on the high tide of social awareness and of the political activity of the masses; it was the supreme manifestation of their will to live and remake their lives. The upheaval of 1929–30 came at the lowest ebb of the nation's social awareness and political energy—it was a revolution from above, based on the suppression of all spontaneous popular activity. Its driving force was not any social class, but the party machine. To Trotsky whose thought had imbibed and embodied all the rich and varied European tradition of classical revolutions, this upheaval was therefore no revolution at all—it was merely the rape of history committed by the Stalinist bureaucracy. Yet, however 'illegitimate' from the classical Marxist viewpoint, Stalin's revolution from above effected a lasting and as to scale unprecedented change in property relations, and ultimately in the nation's way of life.[1]

.   .   .   .

In the course of our narrative we have repeatedly considered the peculiarity of Russian history which consisted in the state's extraordinary power over the nation. The old Tsarist absolutism had drawn its strength from the primitive, undifferentiated, and formless fabric of Russian society. 'Whereas in the West', Miliukov observed, 'the Estates had created the State, in Russia the State had brought into being the Estates.' Even Russian capitalism, Trotsky added, came into being 'as the child of the state'. The immaturity of Russia's social classes had induced the leaders of the intelligentsia and tiny groups of revolutionaries to substitute themselves for the people and to act as its proxies.[2] After a relatively brief but immense upsurge of Russia's popular energies during the first two decades of this century, the exhaustion of these energies in the civil war and the post-revolutionary disintegration of society produced a similar effect. In 1921–2, with the working class unable to uphold its own class interest, Lenin and his Old Guard assumed the roles of its trustees. The logic of this 'substitutism' led them to

[1] See Chapter VIII in Deutscher, *Stalin*.
[2] *The Prophet Armed*, pp. 151ff., 189–90, and *passim*.

establish the political monopoly of the Bolshevik Party, which then gave place to the much narrower monopoly of the Stalinist faction. In order to grasp the further course of events and the struggle between Stalin and Trotsky, we should now briefly re-examine the condition of the various classes of Soviet society a decade after the civil war.

The shrinkage and dispersal of the working class characteristic of the early nineteen-twenties were now a matter of the past. Under N.E.P., as industry recovered, a new working class grew up almost as numerous as the old. After only a few years, by 1932, industrial employment had risen further from 10 to 22 million; and in the course of the decade so many new recruits were drafted to the factories and mines that by about 1940 the working class was nearly three times larger than ever before.[1] Yet, despite this immense growth, the weight of the working class did not make itself felt politically. The workers' direct influence on political life was immeasurably less than it had been in the last years of Tsardom, not to speak of 1917; they were quite unable to assert themselves against the bureaucracy. It was not that in a workers' state they had no need to do so—none other than Lenin insisted, in 1920–1, that the workers needed to defend themselves against their own state; and if they needed to do so in 1921 they needed to do so *a fortiori* in 1931. Yet they remained passive and mute.

What accounted for this phenomenon of a prolonged eclipse of social awareness and paralysis of political will? It could not be terror alone, not even totalitarian terror, for this is effective or ineffective in proportion to the resistance which it meets or fails to meet. There must have been something in the working class itself that was responsible for its passivity. What was it?

The millions of new workers came to industry mostly from the primordially primitive countryside, at first 'spontaneously', driven by rural over-population, and then in the course of that planned transfer of manpower from farm to factory, which the government effected using the collective farms as convenient recruiting centres. The recruits brought with them (into the towns and factory settlements) the illiteracy, the listlessness, and the fatalistic spirit of rural Russia. Uprooted and bewildered by

---

[1] *Narodnoe Khozyaistvo S.S.S.R.*, pp. 656–7. The figures include both workers and employees.

I

unfamiliar surroundings, they were at once caught up in the tremendous mechanism which was to process them into beings very different from what they had been, to break them into the rhythm and discipline of industrial life, to train them in mechanical skills, and to drum into them the party's latest commandments, prohibitions, and slogans. Crowded into huge compounds and barracks, clothed in rags, undernourished, bullied in the workshops, and often kept under quasi-military discipline, they were unable to resist the pressures that bore down on them. Basically, their experience was not very different from that of generations of uprooted peasants thrown into the industrial melting-pots of early capitalism. But whereas under *laissez faire* it was the spontaneous action of the labour market, the fear of unemployment and hunger, that slowly transformed and disciplined the peasant into an industrial worker, in Stalinist Russia it was the state that took care of this and compressed the whole process of transformation into a much shorter time.

So violent was the wrench the industrial recruit suffered, so intensive was the drilling to which he was subjected, so forsaken by God and men did he feel, and so overwhelmed by the hugeness of the forces that shaped his life, that he had neither the mind nor the strength to form any opinion or utter any protest. Sporadically, his resentment found outlet in a drunken brawl, in the stealthy wrecking of a machine, or in the attempt to escape from one factory to another. He tried to fend for himself and improve his own lot without reference to the situation of his class. His atavistic individualism as much as the prohibition of strikes prevented him from associating in self-defence with his fellow-workers and acting in solidarity with them. Stalin, who was stamping out that individualism on its native ground, in the village, encouraged it and played upon it in the industrial workshops, where Stakhanovism and 'socialist competition' excited to the utmost the workers' acquisitiveness and prodded them to compete against one another at the bench.

Thus, while the peasantry was being collectivized, the working class was reduced to such a state that little was left of its traditionally collectivist outlook. 'While our peasantry is being "proletarianized", our working class is becoming completely infected with the peasantry's spirit', observed sadly a deported sociologist of the Opposition.[1] This is not to say that class solidarity and Marxist militancy were completely wiped out. These were still alive in the survivors of the 'October genera-tion' and in quite a few younger people brought up in the nineteen-twenties—as anyone was aware who around 1930 watched the self-sacrificing enthusiasm with which the early *udarniki* set out to build, often on their own bones almost, new steel mills and power plants amid the bare rocks of the Urals or farther to the East. Stalinist propaganda, self-contradictory as it was, continued to inculcate much of the Marxist tradition even while distorting or mutilating it. The workers imbued with that tradition resented the intrusion of peasant individualism into the factories and the scramble for wages and bonuses. But such workers were in a minority and were swamped by the millions of proletarianized muzhiks. Moreover, state and party continually drained the intellectual and political resources of the working class by picking out from its midst the most class-conscious, educated, and energetic individuals in order to fill with them newly created managerial and administrative posts or to draft them into the special brigades whose task it was to collectivize the peasants. Deprived of its élite, the working class was all the more strongly torn by centrifugal forces and split. It was, of course, also deeply divided over collectivization. The drive in the country at first aroused high hope among the proletarians with a strong urban background, who had all along distrusted the rural bourgeoisie. But the labourers who had come from the villages were outraged, filled the towns with tales about the horrors perpetrated in the country, and aroused much sympathy. The sociologist whom we have just quoted observes that in the years of the first Five Year Plan towns were full of people whom he describes as *sans culottes à rebours*. Ever since the French Revolution, he explains, the *sans culotte*, the man without property, had been the enemy of property; but in the Soviet Union, at this time, he was the fiercest defender of property. His presence and mood were felt even in the oldest strongholds of Bolshevism, which was not surprising when, for instance, in the Donetz Coal Basin no fewer than

[1] Ya. Gref in the essay on Collectivization and Overpopulation (*B.O.*, no. 11, 1930). This is a most original, though somewhat dogmatic, analysis of Soviet society during the upheaval.

40 per cent. of the miners were, in 1930, expropriated kulaks and other peasants. In the older layers of proletarian communities the moods ranged from a sullen enmity towards authority to the feeling that party and state did, after all, express the aspirations of the working class and that opposition to them was inadmissible. But there could be no doubt that the mass of the *sans culottes à rebours* and the numerous Lumpenproletarians, displaced peasants who could not fit in with any industrial environment and who filled the suburbs and outskirts with drunkenness and crime, formed potentially a large reserve of cannon-fodder for any 'Thermidorian', counter-revolutionary, or even fascist movement.

In its fragmentation, confusion, and lack of political identity, the new working class partly resembled the proletariat of the early capitalist era, whom Marx had described as a 'class *in* itself' but not *'for* itself'. A class in itself performs its economic function in society, but is unconscious of its place in society, unable to conceive its own corporate and 'historic' interest and to subordinate to it the sectional or private strivings of its members. Marxists had tacitly assumed that once the working class achieved the social self-integration and political awareness that made of it a 'class *for* itself' it would maintain itself indefinitely in that position and would not sink back into immaturity. Instead, the working class of Russia, having overthrown the Tsar, the landlords, and the capitalists, relapsed into the inferior condition of a class unconscious of its interest and inarticulate.

The state of the peasantry was, of course, even worse. The blows that fell on it utterly disorganized and deranged it. Yet before 1929 the peasantry appeared to have achieved a degree of inner cohesion which it had hardly ever attained in the past. In its mass, it seemed, and to some extent was, united in the hostility with which it confronted Bolshevik collectivism. Its antagonism to party and state overshadowed its inner divisions, that is the conflicts between well-to-do and poor farmers. The kulak was at the head of the village community; and farm labourers and *byedniaks*, who had for years watched Bolshevik efforts to come to terms with him, refrained from challenging his position and willy-nilly accepted his leadership. And so the collectivizers, when they first appeared on the scene, found it hard to breach the villagers' solidarity. So inflated had been the kulak's self-confidence and so strongly had the poorer peasants been impressed by it that they did not believe the commissars who threatened the kulak with annihilation to be in earnest. Many thought that it was still safer to side with the kulak and defend the old mode of farming than to follow the call of the commissars. But, as it became clear that the government was in no mood to retreat and that the kulak was indeed doomed, the unity of the village crumbled; the long-subdued but now stoked-up hostility of the poor towards the well-to-do came back into its own. The great mass was torn between conflicting interests, calculations, and sentiments. As the government attacked not only rural capitalism but private farming at large, and as even the poorest farmers were asked to give up their small-holdings, the peasants still tended to remain united in clinging to their possessions. The instinct for property was often as strong in the poorest as it was in the wealthiest peasant; and this instinct and the common sense of humanity were shocked and revolted by the arbitrariness and the inhumanity of the collectivization. Yet these sentiments were disturbed and weakened by the cold reflection of the poor peasants that they might, after all, benefit from the dispossession of the well-to-do and the pooling of the farmsteads; and then, when it was no longer in doubt who was winning the day, many rushed to the victors' band waggon.

The idea of collective farming had, of course, not been alien to rural Russia. The belief that the land was the common good of those who tilled it, not intended by the Creator to enrich some and impoverish others, had once been deeply held; and the *Mir* or *Obshchina*, the primordial rural commune within which the land had been periodically redistributed among members, had survived until shortly before the revolution—it was not till 1907 that Stolypin's government enabled the 'strong farmer' to leave the *Mir* and so to withdraw his possessions from the redistribution and escape its levelling effect. True, since 1917 the peasant's attachment to his own, enlarged, plot of land had grown immensely. Nevertheless, the party agitators were still able to present the kolkhoz as the legitimate successor to the *Mir* and to commend it to the villagers, not as a subversive innovation but rather as the revival, in modified form, of a

native institution, which though corroded by capitalist greed
and rapacity was still hallowed in memory. Thus the impulses
and influences that determined the peasantry's behaviour
were intricate and contradictory, with the result that fear
and faith, horror and hope, despair and reassurance wrestled
in the muzhik's thoughts, leaving him unnerved, resentful
yet unresisting, and nourishing his grievances in sluggish
submission.

While the peasants were being rapidly reduced to this state,
they still took a fiercely insane plunge into dissipation. In the
first months of collectivization they slaughtered over 15,000,000
cows and oxen, nearly 40,000,000 goats and sheep, 7,000,000
pigs, and 4,000,000 horses; the slaughter went on until the
nation's cattle stock was brought down to less than half what it
had been. This great shambles of meat was the main dish at
the feast with which the smallholder celebrated his own funeral.
The kulak began the carnage and incited others to follow suit.
Seeing that he had lost all, that he, the nation's provider, was
to be robbed of his property, he set out to rob the nation of its
food supply; and rather than allow the collectivizers to drive
away his cattle to communal assembly stations, he filled his own
larders with the carcasses so as to let his enemies starve. The
collectivizers were at first taken aback by this form of 'class
warfare' and watched with helpless amazement as the 'middle'
peasants and even the poor joined in the butchery, until the
whole of rural Russia was turned into an abbatoir.

So began the strange carnival over which despair presided
and for which fury filled the fleshpots. An epidemic of orgiastic
gluttony spread from village to village, from *volost* to *volost*,
and from *gubernia* to *gubernia*. Men, women, and children gorged
themselves, vomited, and went back to the fleshpots. Never
before had so much vodka been brewed in the country—
almost every hut became a distillery—and the drinking was, in
the old Slav fashion, hard and deep. As they guzzled and
gulped, the kulaks illuminated the villages with bonfires they
made of their own barns and stables. People suffocated with
the stench of rotting meat, with the vapours of vodka, with the
smoke of their blazing possessions, and with their own despair.
Such was often the scene upon which a brigade of collectivizers
descended to interrupt the grim carouse with the rattle of

machine-guns; they executed on the spot or dragged away the crapulous enemies of collectivization and announced that henceforth all remaining villagers would, as exemplary members of the kolkhoz, strive only for the triumph of socialism in agriculture. But after the kulaks and the *podkulachniki*, their helpmeets, had been disposed of, the slaughter of cattle and the feasting went on—there was no way of stopping it. Animals were killed because no fodder was left or because they had become diseased from neglect; and even the *bednyaks* who, having joined the kolkhozes, had every interest in preserving their wealth, went on dissipating it and stuffing their own long-starved stomachs. Then followed the long and dreadful fast: the farms were left without horses and without seed for the sowing; the kolkhozniki of the Ukraine and of European Russia rushed to central Asia to buy horses, and, having returned empty-handed, harnessed the few remaining cows and oxen to the ploughs; and in 1931 and 1932 vast tracts of land remained untilled and the furrows were strewn with the bodies of starved muzhiks. The smallholder perished as he had lived, in pathetic helplessness and barbarism; and his final defeat was moral as well as economic and political.

But the collectivizers too were morally defeated; and, as we have said, the new system of agriculture was to labour under this defeat in years to come. Normally, a revolution does not depend for the success of its constructive task on the social class it has overthrown, be it the landlords or the bourgeoisie; it can rely on the classes that have rallied to its side. The paradox of the rural revolution of 1929–30 was that the realization of its positive programme depended precisely on the vanquished: collective farming could not flourish when the smallholder-turned-kolkhoznik was in no mood to make it work.[1]

The lack of moral and political cohesion among the workers and the peasants made for the apparent omnipotence of the state. If after the civil war bureaucratic rule was established against the background of economic disintegration and the dispersal of the working class,[2] that rule now gained virtually unlimited power from the opposite processes, from economic growth and expansion, which were to give new structure and shape to society, but immediately made society even more

[1] Ya. Gref, op. cit. [2] See *The Prophet Unarmed*, Chapter I.

shapeless and increased its mental atrophy. In years to come all the energies of the Soviet Union were to be so intensely occupied with material progress and the prodigious efforts which this required that little or no resources were left for the assertion of any moral and political purposes. And, as the power of the state was all the greater when it was exercised over a nation politically reduced to pulp, those in power did all they could to keep the nation in just that condition.

Yet even the bureaucracy was not truly united by any common interest or outlook. All the divisions which split the other classes were reflected in its midst. The old estrangement between the communist and the non-communist civil servants was still there; it was sharply revealed in the frequent monster trials of 'specialists' denounced as saboteurs and 'wreckers'. Throughout the years of N.E.P. most of these 'specialists' and their friends had hopefully waited for the moment when the dynamic force of the revolution would come to rest and Russia would once again become a 'normal' state. They had indeed prayed for that Neo-N.E.P. and that Thermidor the spectres of which haunted the Trotskyists and the Zinovievists; they had first banked on Stalin and Bukharin against Trotsky; and then they longed to see Bukharin, or any other 'authentic Thermidorian', prevail against Stalin. These hopes were now frustrated; and those who had held them, often unable or unwilling to adjust themselves to the new situation, were in disarray. In the Bolshevik section of the bureaucracy Bukharinists and Stalinists were at loggerheads. The former, strongly entrenched during the years of N.E.P., were tracked down and ejected from the administration. New men from the working class and from the young intelligentsia filled their places and the many other vacancies which were opening all the time. The bureaucracy's composition was therefore highly unstable, and its outlook heterogeneous. Even the one bond that might have been expected to unite it, the bond of privilege, was extremely tenuous when not only individuals but entire groups of the bureaucracy could be, and frequently were, stripped of all privileges almost overnight, turned into pariahs, and driven into concentration camps. And even the strictly Stalinist elements, the men of the party machine and the leaders of the nationalized industry, who formed the ruling groups proper, were by no means exempt from the insecurity in which all the hierarchies trembled under Stalin's autocracy.

Thus the feverish economic expansion, the general unsettlement which accompanied it, the eclipse of social awareness in the masses, and the emaciation of their political will formed the background to the development by which the rule of the single faction now became the rule of a single leader. The sheer multiplicity of the conflicts between the classes and within each class, conflicts which society itself was unable to resolve, called for constant arbitrament, which could come only from the very pinnacle of power. The greater the unsettlement, the flux, and the chaos down below the more stable and fixed that pinnacle had to be. The more enfeebled and devoid of will all social forces were, the stronger and more wilful grew the arbitrator; and the more powerful he became the more impotent were they bound to remain. He had to concentrate in himself all the vigour of decision and action which they lacked. He had to focus in himself the whole dispersed *élan* of the nation. To the extent to which the bulk of the people sunk below the level of higher human aspiration he must appear superhuman. His infallible mind had to dominate their absent-mindedness. His sleepless vigilance had to protect them against all the dangers of which they were unaware and against which they were unable to protect themselves. Everyone had to be blind in order that he, the only seer, might lead. He must be proclaimed the sole trustee of the revolution and of socialism; and his colleagues who had hitherto exercised that trusteeship jointly with him had to renounce all claim to it, and yet had to be crushed as well. To put his pre-eminence beyond any challenge the multitudes had to acclaim him ceaselessly; and he himself had to guard his pre-eminence with the utmost care and see to it that the popular adulation should rise in endless crescendo. Like History's Elect in Hegel, he embodied a great phase in the nation's, and indeed in mankind's, life. But for the obsessive megalomania, which his position bred in him, even this was not enough: the Superman's elbows burst the frame of his time: in him must live and merge past, present, and future: the past with the ghosts of the early Empire-building Tsars incongruously jostling the shades of Marx and Lenin; the present with its tremendous eruptive and creative force; and the future glowing with the fulfilment of mankind's most sublime dreams. The secret of this grotesque apotheosis, however, lay less in Stalin than in the society he ruled: as that society forfeited its own political identity and the sense of its own tremendous movement, that identity and the whole movement of history became personalized in the Leader.

The process by which Stalinist government became Stalin's government was far less distinct and consecutive than the evolution that had led to it, the transformation of the rule of the Bolshevik party into the rule of the Stalinist faction. From the outset the faction's political monopoly had to some extent been Stalin's own, because his supporters had always been far more rigidly disciplined than those of his rivals. He had always been in sole command of his followers in a way neither Trotsky nor Bukharin nor Zinoviev had ever been of theirs. Nevertheless, having crushed all his opponents, Stalin still had to complete a full ascendancy over his own followers. It now turned out that the rule of a single faction no less than that of a single party was a contradiction in terms. Just as in the single party, as long as members could express themselves freely, the various groups and schools of thought formed a shadowy multi-party system incompatible with it, so the single faction tended to reproduce within itself patchy reflections of the factions and schools of thought which it had just suppressed. Stalin had to ferret out the crypto-Trotskyists and crypto-Bukharinists among his own followers. He had to deny all these followers the restricted liberties still left to them. It was now their turn to discover that, having deprived all their opponents of freedom, they had robbed themselves of it as well, and that they had placed themselves at the mercy of their own Leader. Having once proclaimed that the party must be monolithic or it would not be Bolshevik, he now insisted that his own faction must be monolithic or it would not be Stalinist. Stalinism ceased to be a current of opinion or the expression of any political group— it became Stalin's personal interest, will, and whim.

The personalization of all political relations affected Trotsky's position as well. As Stalin was becoming the sole official and orthodox embodiment of the revolution, Trotsky was becoming its sole unofficial and unorthodox representative. This had not been quite the case up to 1929. The Trotskyist Opposition was in no sense his personal domain, even though he was its out-standing leader. Its directing centre consisted of strong-minded and independent men: Rakovsky, Radek, Preobraz-hensky, Smirnov, Pyatakov, and others, none of whom could be described as Trotsky's creature; and the rank and file struggling for freedom within the party preserved it within the narrower confines of their own faction. In the Joint Opposition, Zinoviev and Kamenev, though conscious of Trotsky's superiority, were extremely jealous of their own authority and treated with him on a footing of equality. Not only did he not impose his dictates but often, as we have seen, he was hamstrung in his action against Stalin by the concessions he made to his adherents or temporary allies. Until 1929 also Bukharin's school of thought represented an alternative to both Stalinism and Trotskyism, an alternative which appealed to many in and out of the party. Thus, despite the growing concentration of power in Stalin's hands and the increasing conformism, Bolshevik hopes and expectations did not as yet focus on any single leader and policy, but attached themselves to various personalities, teams of leaders, and various attitudes and shades of attitudes.

The events of 1929–30 changed all this. The Bukharinist school of thought was wrecked even before it managed to come out openly against Stalin. It could not go on arguing against the accomplished facts of the Great Change: it could not resist the industrial drive or bank on the strong farmer any longer. The alpha and omega of Bukharinism had been its approach to the peasantry; and this had become pointless. From the moment the smallholder vanished the Right Opposition had no ground to stand on. Therein lay the essential difference between the defeat of Trotsky and Zinoviev and that of Bukharin and Rykov: to vanquish the former, Stalin had to steal their political weapons, while the latter had themselves to throw away their own weapons as antiquated. This was why Bukharin, Rykov, and Tomsky, when, in November 1929, they were expelled from the Politbureau, left with a barely audible whimper, whereas even Zinoviev and Kamenev had in their time left with a battle cry.

The capitulation of the Zinovievists and the quietus of Bukharinism left Stalinism and Trotskyism as the sole con-tenders for Bolshevik allegiance. But now, by a strangely parallel though antithetical development, these two factions too were disintegrating, each in its own way, the Trotskyists through endless defections and the Stalinists through doubt and confusion in their own midst. And just as Stalinism, in victory, was being reduced to Stalin's autocracy, so Trotskyism, in defeat, was becoming identified with Trotsky alone. To be sure, even after all the surrenders there were still unrepentant Oppositionists in the prisons and places of deportation; and in the early nineteen-thirties, while Rakovsky guided them, their ranks were at times reinforced by new adherents and by the return of capitulators disillusioned with surrender. Yet, despite such accessions, Trotskyism could not regain the coherence and confidence which it still had even in 1928. At best it was only a loose congeries of splinter groups conscious of their isolation, despairing of the prospects, yet persisting in their allegiance to Trotsky, to what he stood for or was supposed to stand for. They still argued among themselves and produced controversial theses and papers; but these circulated only within prison walls. Even before the terror mounted to the climax of the great purges, the Trotskyists were unable to use the prisons and places of exile as bases for political action in the way revolutionaries had used them in Tsarist times: their ideas did not reach the working class and the intelligentsia. With the years their contact with Trotsky became more and more tenuous until in 1932 even their correspondence ceased altogether. They no longer knew exactly what he stood for; and he could no longer ascertain whether or not his views accorded with theirs. He had no choice but to substitute himself for the Opposition at large; and they had no choice but to acknowledge him, expressly or tacitly, as their sole trustee and by definition the sole trustee of the revolution. His voice alone was now the voice of the Opposition; and the immense silence of the whole of anti-Stalinist Russia was his sounding board.

Thus, against Stalin, the sole trustee of Bolshevism in office, Trotsky stood alone as the proxy of Bolshevism in opposition. His name, like Stalin's, became something of a myth; but whereas Stalin's was the myth of power sponsored by power, his was the legend of resistance and martyrdom cherished by the martyred. The young people who in the nineteen-thirties faced executioners with the cry 'Long Live Trotsky!' often had no more than a mere inkling of his ideas. They identified themselves with a symbol rather than a programme, the symbol of their own anger with all the misery and oppression that surrounded them, of their own harking back to the great promise of October and of their own, rather vague, hope for a 'renascence' of the revolution.

Not only Trotsky's avowed supporters and most of the capitulators viewed him thus. The sense that he represented the sole alternative to Stalinism persisted even among party members who silently carried out Stalin's orders, and outside the party, among politically minded workers and the intelligentsia. Whenever people feared or felt that Stalin was driving them to the brink of catastrophe and whenever even their meekness was shocked by some excess of his brutality, their thoughts went out, if only fleetingly, to Trotsky, of whom they knew that he had not laid down arms and that in foreign lands he continued his lonely struggle against the corruption of the revolution.

Stalin was apprehensively aware of this; and he treated Trotsky as in older times an established monarch treated a dangerous Pretender, or as under the Double and Triple Schisms the Pope treated the Anti-Pope. It was for the role of an Anti-Pope that the ironies of history now cast Trotsky, the legatee of classical Marxism, who was utterly ill-suited for such a role and was neither able nor willing to act it. Throughout a decade crowded with the most momentous and explosive events, the transformation of Soviet society, the great slump in the West, the rise of Nazism, and the rumblings of approaching war—throughout the nineteen-thirties the duel between Stalin and Trotsky remained at the centre of Soviet politics, often overshadowing all the other issues. Not for a moment did Stalin himself slacken, or allow his propagandists and policemen to relax, in the anti-Trotskyist campaign which he carried into every sphere of thought and activity, and which he stepped up from year to year and from month to month. The fear of the Pretender robbed him of his sleep. He was constantly on the look-out for the Pretender's agents, who might be crossing the frontiers stealthily, smuggling the Pretender's messages, inciting, intriguing, and rallying for action. The suspicion that haunted Stalin's mind sought to read the hidden thoughts that the most subservient of his own subjects might have about

Trotsky; and he discovered in the most innocuous of their utterances, even in the flatteries of his courtiers, deliberate and sly allusions to the legitimacy of Trotsky's claims. The bigger Stalin himself looked and talked and the more abjectly Trotsky's old adherents rolled before him in the dust, the more delirious was his obsession with Trotsky, and the more restlessly did he work to make the whole of the Soviet Union share his obsession. The frenzy with which he pursued the feud, making it the paramount preoccupation of international communism as well as of the Soviet Union and subordinating to it all political, tactical, intellectual, and other interests, beggars description: there is in the whole of history hardly another case in which such immense resources of power and propaganda were employed against a single individual.

Morbid though the obsession was, it had a basis in reality. Stalin had not conquered power once and for all; he had to reconquer it over and over again. His success should not obscure the fact that at least up to the end of the Great Purges his supremacy remained unconsolidated. The higher he rose the greater was the void around him and the larger was the mass of those who had reason to fear and hate him and whom he feared and hated. He saw that the old divisions among his opponents, the differences between Right and Left Bolsheviks, were becoming blurred and obliterated; and so he was frightened of those 'Right-Left conspiracies' and 'Trotskyist-Bukharinist blocs' which his police had to unearth or to invent again and again, and the makings of which were indeed inherent in the situation. Finally, his ascendancy over his own faction turned even authentic old Stalinists into potential allies of the Trotsky-ists, the Zinovievists, and the Bukharinists. Elevated above the whole Bolshevik party, he saw, not without reason, the whole party as one potential coalition against himself; and he had to use every ounce of his strength and cunning to prevent the potential from becoming actual. He knew that if that coalition ever came into being, Trotsky would be its unrivalled leader. Having brought the chiefs of all the oppositions to prostrate themselves before him, he himself worked unwittingly to exalt Trotsky's unique moral authority. He then had to do all he could, and far more than he could, to destroy it. He resorted to ever more drastic means and to ever more absurd slanders; but his efforts were self-defeating. The more loudly he denounced his adversary as the chief or sole prompter of every heresy and opposition, the more strongly did he turn all the mute anti-Stalinist feelings, with which Bolshevik Russia was overflowing, towards the outcast's remote yet towering figure.

CHAPTER II

Reason and Unreason

THROUGHOUT the nineteen-thirties Trotsky's mind battled with the tide of irrationality surging up in world politics. Yet some of his Russian followers feared that, although his criticisms of Stalin's policy were justified and even irrefutable, he somehow failed to make allowance for the irrational element in the situation of the Soviet Union.[1] It was he himself who had maintained a few years earlier, in a controversy with Bertrand Russell, that it was impossible 'to map out the revolutionary road beforehand in a rationalistic manner' and that 'revolution is an expression of the impossibility of reconstructing class society by rationalist methods'.[2] It now turned out that it was impossible to reconstruct society by such methods even after the revolution, under a system which had given up the advantages of capitalism but could not yet avail itself of the advantages of socialism. Most, if not all, of the factors that made for the irrationality of class society—basic conflicts of interests, the fetishism of commodity and money, the inadequacy or absence of social control over productive forces—all these were still intensely at work in the Soviet Union. The Bolshevik aspiration to industrialize and educate Russia, to build up a planned economy, and to achieve control over social chaos became itself infected with the irrationality of the environment to which it was confined. This situation, though it could be explained theoretically and even predicted, gave rise to such monstrous absurdities that the analytical and dialectical mind was at times baffled in its attempts to disentangle reason from unreason.

In the West these were the years of the Great Slump; and history's record of folly and crime was suddenly enlarged by the rise and triumph of Nazism. In one way or another the Nazi triumph from now on overshadows the life of our chief character. Without running too far ahead of the narrative, it may be

[1] *B.O.*, no. 11, 1930.   [2] *The Prophet Unarmed*, p. 222.

said here that Trotsky's attempt to arouse the working class of Germany to the danger that threatened it was his greatest political deed in exile. Like no one else, and much earlier than anyone, he grasped the destructive delirium with which National Socialism was to burst upon the world. His commentaries on the German situation, written between 1930 and 1933, the years before Hitler's assumption of power, stand out as a cool, clinical analysis and forecast of this stupendous phenomenon of social psychopathology and of its consequences to the international labour movement, to the Soviet Union, and to the world. What underlines even further the political insanity of the times is with what utter unconcern about the future and venomous hostility the men responsible for the fate of German communism and socialism reacted to the alarm which Trotsky sounded, from his Prinkipo retreat, in these decisive three years. An historical narrative can hardly convey the full blast of slander and derision with which he was met. He represented in effect the self-preservation of the labour movement against the movement itself, which was as if bent on self-destruction. He had to watch the capitulation of the Third International before Hitler as a father watches the suicide of a prodigal and absent-minded child, with fear, shame, and anger—he could not forget that he had been a founding father of the International.

And there was a fierce flash of fate's extravagant cruelty in the inroad which the insanity of the time made even in Trotsky's own family circle.

.   .   .   .

Only a few months had passed since the beginning of the world-wide economic crisis, the Wall Street panic of October 1929, and the whole edifice of the Weimar Republic was shattered. The Great Slump had struck Germany with devastating force and thrown six million workers out of employment. In March 1930 Hermann Müller, the Social Democratic Chancellor, was forced to resign: the Socialist-Catholic coalition on which his government rested had collapsed. The coalition partners could not agree whether or by how much the government should cut the dole it paid out to the unemployed. Field-Marshal Hindenburg, the relic and symbol of the Hohenzollern Empire, now the Republic's President, dissolved

Parliament and appointed Heinrich Brüning *Reichskanzler*. Brüning ruled by decree, enforced a rigidly 'deflationary' policy, cut expenditure on social insurance, dismissed government employees *en masse*, reduced wages and salaries, and crushed small businessmen with taxes, thus aggravating the distress and the despair of all. In elections held on 14 September 1930, Hitler's party, which had polled only 800,000 votes in 1928, won six and a half million votes; from the smallest party in the Reichstag it became the second largest. The Communist party, too, increased its vote from about three million to over four and a half. The Social Democrats, who had for years ruled the Weimar Republic, lost; and so did the Deutschnazionale and the other parties of the traditional right wing. The election revealed the instability and the acute crisis of parliamentary democracy.

The leaders of the Weimar Republic refused to read the omens. Conservatives viewed the emergence of the Nazi movement with mixed feelings: disconcerted by their own losses and by the violence of Nazism, they were nevertheless reassured by the rise of a great party which declared implacable war on all working-class organizations; and they hoped to find in Nazism an ally against the left and possibly a junior partner in government. The Social Democrats, frightened by Hitler's threats—he strutted the country proclaiming that 'the heads of Marxists and Jews would soon roll in the sand'—decided to 'tolerate' Brüning's government as 'the lesser of the two evils'. The Communist party exulted in its gains and made light of the huge increase in the vote for Hitler. On the day after the election, the *Rote Fahne*, then the most important communist paper in Europe, wrote: 'Yesterday was Herr Hitler's "great day", but the so-called electoral victory of the Nazis is only the beginning of their end.' 'The 14th of September [*Rote Fahne* repeated a few weeks later] was the high watermark of the National Socialist movement in Germany—what follows now can be only ebb and decline.'

Several months later, after the towns and cities of Germany had had their first taste of the terror of Hitler's Stormtroops, Ernest Thaelmann, the leader of the Communist party, told the Executive of the Comintern in Moscow: 'After 14 September, following the sensational success of the National

Socialists, their adherents all over Germany expected great things from them. We, however, did not allow ourselves to be misled by the mood of panic which showed itself . . . in the working class, at any rate, among the followers of the Social Democratic party. We stated soberly and seriously that 14 September was in a sense Hitler's best day after which there would be no better but only worse days.' The Executive of the Comintern endorsed this view, congratulated Thaelmann, and confirmed its Third Period policy which committed the Communist party to reject the idea of any Socialist-Communist coalition against Nazism and obliged it to 'concentrate fire on the Social-Fascists'.[1]

We know that Trotsky had subjected this policy to severe criticism as early as 1929. In March 1930, six months before the crucial elections, he repeated this criticism in an 'Open Letter' to the Soviet Communist party, where he spoke again of the growing force of fascism all over Europe, but especially in Germany, and insisted on the need for joint Socialist-Communist action.[2] No sooner had the results of the September elections become known than he commented on them in a special pamphlet which he took care to publish in several European languages. 'The first quality of a truly revolutionary party is the ability to face realities', he wrote, dismissing the Comintern's self-congratulations and pointing out that the communist gain of over a million votes was almost insignificant compared with the Nazi gain of nearly six million. The 'radicalization of the masses', of which the Comintern boasted, had benefited counter-revolution rather than revolution. What accounted for the 'gigantic' upsurge of Nazism was 'a profound social crisis', which had upset the mental balance of the lower middle classes, and the inability of the Communist party to cope with the problems posed by that crisis. If communism expressed the revolutionary hopes of the worker, Nazism voiced the counter-revolutionary despair of the *petit bourgeois*. When the

---

[1] The session of the Comintern's Executive took place in April 1931. Manuilsky was the *rapporteur* on the international situation. He expounded the Third Period policy with an uninhibited zeal which only served to underline its absurdity. See *Kommunistische Internationale*, nos. 17–18, 1931.

[2] *B.O.*, no. 10, April 1930. See also his devastating attack on "The Third Period of the Comintern's Blunders", published in *Vérité, Permanente Revolution, Militant*, and other Trotskyist papers in January and February 1930.

party of socialist revolution is in the ascendant it carries with it not only the working class but also large sections of the lower middle class. In Germany, however, the opposite was happening: the party of counter-revolutionary despair had captured the lower middle class and important layers of the working class as well. Comintern analysts consoled themselves with the idea that Nazism was merely a remote aftermath of the crisis of 1923 and of subsequent social tensions. Trotsky argued that far from representing a belated reaction to any crisis of the past, Nazism mobilized forces for a crisis that lay ahead; and that 'the fact that fascism has been able to occupy so strong a starting position on the eve of a revolutionary period, and not at its end, is a source of weakness to communism, not to fascism'. He concluded that 'despite the parliamentary success of the Communist party, proletarian revolution . . . has suffered a serious defeat . . . a defeat which may become decisive'.[1]

In this brochure Trotsky had already outlined an analysis of National Socialism, which he was to develop presently in a series of books and articles. Thirty years later some of his ideas may seem truisms; they were all heresies when he put them forward. In the main, his view of Nazism has retained freshness and originality; it still remains the only coherent and realistic analysis of National Socialism (or of fascism at large) that can be found in Marxist literature. It will therefore not be out of place to summarize his view, which he himself developed mostly in controversial form, in the context of a debate over communist tactics.[2]

The crux of Trotsky's conception lies in his description of National Socialism as 'the party of counter-revolutionary despair'. He saw National Socialism as the movement and ideology of the *wildgewordene Kleinbürger*, the small bourgeois run amok. This set it apart from all other reactionary and counter-revolutionary parties. The forces of conventional reaction worked usually from above, from the top of the social pyramid, to defend established authority. Fascism and National Socialism were counter-revolutions from below, plebeian

---

[1] L. Trotsky, *Écrits*, vol. III, pp. 25–46. *The Archives*.

[2] His most important works on this subject are: *Nemetskaya Revolutsia i Stalinskaya Burokratiya* (published under the title *Was Nun?* in German, and *What Next?* in English) and *Edinstvennyi Put'* (*Der einzige Weg*), essays and articles in *B.O.* and other Trotskyist papers. *Écrits*, vol. III.

movements rising from the depths of society. They expressed the urge of the lower middle class to assert itself against the rest of society. Usually subdued, that urge becomes aggressive in a national catastrophe with which established authority and the traditional parties are unable to cope. During the 'prosperity' of the nineteen-twenties Hitler's party had been on the lunatic fringe of German politics. The slump of 1929 brought it to the fore. The great mass of shopkeepers and white collar employees had hitherto followed the traditional bourgeois parties and had seen themselves as upholders of parliamentary democracy. They now deserted those parties and followed Hitler, because sudden economic ruin filled them with insecurity and fear, and aroused their craving for self-assertion.

The *Kleinbürger* normally resented his social position: he looked up with envy and hatred to big business, to which he so often helplessly succumbed in competition; and he looked down upon the workers, jealous of their capacity for political and trade union organization and for collective self-defence. Marx once described what, in June 1848, had driven the French *petite bourgeoisie* to turn furiously against the insurgent workers of Paris: the shopkeepers, he said, saw access to their shops blocked by the workers' barricades in the streets; and they went out and smashed the barricades. The German shopkeepers of the early nineteen-thirties had no such reason for running amok—no barricades blocked access to their shops. But they were ruined economically; they had cause to blame the Weimar Republic at the head of which they had for years seen the Social Democrats; and they were frightened of the threat of communism, which even if, or because, it did not materialize, kept society in permanent ferment and agitation. In the *Kleinbürger's* eyes big business, Jewish finance, parliamentary democracy, social-democratic governments, communism and Marxism at large, all merged into the image of a many-headed monster which strangled him—all were partners in a sinister conspiracy responsible for his ruin. At big business the small man shook his fists as if he were a socialist; against the worker he shrilled his bourgeois respectability, his horror of class struggle, his rabid nationalist pride, and his detestation of Marxist inter-nationalism. This political neurosis of impoverished millions gave National Socialism its force and impetus. Hitler was the small man writ large, the small man with all these neurotic obsessions, prejudices, and fury. 'Not every *Kleinbürger* run amok can become a Hitler', said Trotsky, 'but there is something of Hitler in every *Kleinbürger* run amok.'

Yet the lower middle class was normally 'human dust'. It had none of the workers' capacity for self-organization, for it was inherently amorphous and atomized; and, despite bluster and threats, it was cowardly wherever it met with genuine resistance. The whole record of European class struggles and the Russian Revolution proved this. The small bourgeoisie could no longer play any independent part—ultimately it had to follow either the upper bourgeoisie or the working class. Its rebellion against big business was impotent—the small artisan and shopkeeper could not prevail against monopolistic capitalist oligarchies. National Socialism in office could not therefore keep any of its 'socialistic' promises. It would reveal itself as an essentially conservative force; it would seek to perpetuate capitalism; it would crush the working class, and hasten the ruin of the same lower middle class which had brought it to power. But in the meantime the lower middle class and its *Lumpenproletarian* fringe were in feverish motion and their imagination was inflamed with the dream of the social and political supremacy which Hitler was to bring them.

This 'human dust', Trotsky argued, is attracted by the magnet of power. It follows in any struggle that side which shows the greater determination to win, the greater audacity, and the ability to cope with a catastrophe like the Great Slump. That was why in Russia, Bolshevism, having assumed the leadership of the working class in 1917, carried also, at decisive moments, the great hesitant and dispersed mass of the peasantry and even part of the small urban bourgeoisie. Similarly, the German working class would still attract to itself the multitudes of the lower middle classes if these felt its strength and determination to win; that is, if socialist and communist policies did not lack direction and purpose. The inflated ambitions of the *Kleinbürger* and the strength of Nazism sprang from the weakness of the working class. The Social-Democratic leaders sought to ingratiate themselves with the middle classes, lower and upper, first by acting, under the Weimar Republic as business managers of the bourgeois state, then by submitting meekly to the Brüning régime, and throughout by defending the social and political *status quo*. Yet it was precisely against the Weimar Republic and its Brüning sequel and against the *status quo* that the lower middle classes were in revolt. Social-Democratic policy therefore contributed decisively to the dangerous estrangement between the organized working class and the small bourgeoisie, the estrangement on which Nazism thrived. The Social-Democrats went on preaching moderation and prudence when moderation and prudence were bankrupt; and they continued to defend the *status quo* when this had become so unbearable that the masses preferred almost anything else, even the abyss into which Hitler was plunging them.

In their ostrich-like behaviour the Social Democrats were true to character. All the greater, Trotsky pointed out, was the responsibility of the Communist party. Yet its leaders were unaware of the magnitude and the nature of the peril. With sham ultra-radicalism they refused to make any distinction between fascism and bourgeois democracy. They maintained that as monopolistic capitalism was bent on rendering bourgeois democracy fascist, all parties standing on the ground of capitalism were bound to undergo this process. All cats then were equally brown: Hitler was a fascist; but so were the leaders of the traditional bourgeois parties, right and centre; so in particular was Brüning, who already ruled by decree; and so even were the Social Democrats, who formed the 'left wing of fascism'. This was no mere abuse of polemical invective, for underlying it was a wrong political orientation and a false strategy. Again and again communist propagandists proclaimed that 'Germany was already living under fascist rule', and that 'Hitler could not make matters worse than they were under Brüning, the Starvation Chancellor'.[1] But, Trotsky countered, in proclaiming that fascism had already won the day they were in fact declaring the battle lost before it had even

[1] Throughout the year 1931 (and in the first half of 1932) these profound diagnoses and prognostications figured almost daily in the *Rote Fahne*; and they were authoritatively supported by the *Internationale Presse Korrespondenz* and the *Kommunistische Internationale* (see also *XI Plenum IKKI*, and *Kommunisticheskii Internatsional*, 1932, nos. 27–30). Not only Molotov, Manuilsky, Pyatnitsky, and other Russian leaders, but such spokesmen of European communism as Togliatti (Ercoli), Thorez, Cachin, Lenski, Kuusinen, and others dutifully reassured themselves and their followers that the only road to salvation was the one along which Thaelmann was guiding the German party.

begun; at any rate, in telling the masses that Hitler would not be worse than Brüning they were morally disarming them before Hitler. Yet it was folly for a working-class party to deny or blur the distinction between fascism and bourgeois democracy. True enough, both were 'only' different forms and methods of capitalist rule; but, circumstances being what they were, the difference of form and method was of the utmost importance. In a parliamentary democracy the bourgeoisie maintained its domination by means of a broad social compromise with the working class, a compromise which necessitated constant bargaining and presupposed the existence of autonomous proletarian organizations, political parties, and trade unions. From the standpoint of the revolutionary Marxist, these organizations formed 'islands of proletarian democracy within bourgeois democracy', strongholds and ramparts from which the workers could fight against bourgeois rule at large. Fascism meant an end to the social compromise and the bargaining between the classes; it had no use for the channels through which that bargaining had been done; and it could not tolerate the existence of any autonomous working-class organization. Drawing a lesson from the evolution of Italian fascism and, no doubt, reasoning also from the experience of the Bolshevik single party system, Trotsky in advance forcefully described Hitler's totalitarian monopoly of power, under which there would be no room for labour parties and independent trade unions. For this reason alone Marxists and Leninists were bound in duty to defend bourgeois democracy, or rather the 'islands of proletarian democracy within it', against fascist attack. In saying that the Social Democrats formed 'the left wing of fascism' and that they would sooner or later 'make a deal with the Nazis', Stalinist propaganda overlooked the objective impossibility of such a deal.[1] (It should be added that the Social Democratic leaders also entertained this illusion; in 1933 they did indeed make a suicidal effort to reach an accommodation with Hitler.[2]) Trotsky had no doubt that

[1] Trotsky *What Next?* Preface and Chapters I–II, *Écrits*, vol. III, pp. 109–13.

[2] Otto Wels, the leader of the Social Democrats in the Reichstag, used one of his last opportunities to speak from the parliamentary rostrum in order to proclaim his party's readiness to support Hitler's government in the field of foreign policy. At this price he hoped to save his party from destruction by the Nazis; but Hitler did not accept the offer.

Hitler would destroy every vestige of the labour movement, reformist as well as communist. His prognostication followed from the view that National Socialism could not but aim at the complete atomization of German society.

It was thus wrong to treat the Brüning régime as fascist, even though it marked the virtual end of the broad compromise between capital and labour on which the Weimar Republic had been based. Brüning was unable to crush the labour movement (and unable also to hold his ground against National Socialism). Apart from the shaky support of the Catholic Centre Party and apart from Social Democratic 'toleration', he could rely only on the normal resources of the bureaucratic establishment. With these alone he could not suppress the organized working class; and so the political structure still remained what it had been under the Weimar Republic. Only the dynamic force of National Socialism could pulverize it. The breakdown of the compromise between the classes had set the stage for a civil war in which Nazism and the labour movement as a whole would be the real antagonists. The Brüning régime was 'like a ball on the top of a pyramid'; it rested on a fleeting equilibrium between the two hostile camps. Meanwhile, the Nazis recruited millions, whipped up hysteria, and mounted an immense striking force; while socialists and communists alike only marked time and virtually sabotaged the mobilization of their own strength.

. A few quotations will convey something of the urgency, and even exasperation with which Trotsky argued:

> The Brüning régime is a transitional short-lived prelude to catastrophe. . . . The wiseacres who claim that they see no difference between Brüning and Hitler are in fact saying: it makes no difference whether our organizations exist or whether they are already destroyed. Beneath this pseudo-radical verbiage hides the most sordid passivity. . . . Every thinking worker . . . must be aware of this and see through the empty and rotten talk about . . . Brüning and Hitler being one and the same thing. You are blundering! we reply. You are blundering disgracefully because you are afraid of the difficulties that lie ahead, because you are terrified by the great problems that confront you. You give in before the fighting has begun, you proclaim that we have already suffered defeat. You are lying! The working class is split . . . weakened . . . but it is not yet annihilated.

Its forces are not yet exhausted. Brüning's is a transitional régime. It marks the transition to what? Either to the victory of fascism or to the victory of the working class . . . the two camps are only preparing for the decisive battle. If you identify Brüning with Hitler, you identify the situation before the battle with conditions after defeat; you acknowledge defeat beforehand; you appeal in effect for surrender without a battle. The overwhelming majority of workers, of communists in particular, do not want this. The Stalinist bureaucracy does not want it either. But one must take into account not their good intentions with which Hitler will pave the road to his hell. . . . We must expose to the end the passive, timidly hesitant, defeatist, and declamatory character of the policy of Stalin, Manuilsky, Thaelmann, and Remmele. We must show the revolutionary workers that the Communist party still holds the key to the situation but that the Stalinist bureaucracy is attempting to lock with this key the gates to revolutionary action.[1]

The Social Democratic leaders promised to launch a 'major offensive' if and when Hitler tried to seize power; in the meantime they demanded calm and restraint from the workers. The Stalinists bragged that if Hitler seized power the workers would sweep him away. A leading communist parliamentarian, Remmele, said in the Reichstag: 'Let Hitler take office—he will soon go bankrupt, and then it will be our day.' To this Trotsky replied:

The major offensive must be launched before Brüning is replaced by Hitler, before the workers' organizations are crushed. . . . It is an infamy to promise that the workers will sweep away Hitler once he has seized power. This prepares the way for Hitler's domination. . . . Should the German working class . . . permit fascism to seize power, should it evince so fatal a blindness and passivity, then there are no reasons whatsoever to suppose that after the fascists have seized power the same working class will at once shake off its lethargy and make a clean sweep. Nothing like this has happened in Italy [after Mussolini's rise]. Remmele reasons altogether in the manner of those French petty bourgeois phrase-mongers who [in 1850-1] were convinced that if Louis Bonaparte were to place himself above the Republic the people would rise. . . . The people, however, who permitted the adventurer to seize power proved, sure enough, incapable of sweeping him away thereafter . . . historic earthquakes and a war had to occur before he was overthrown. [In exactly the same way was to end this kind of 'struggle' against Hitler, compared

[1] Trotsky, *What Next?* pp. 38–39; *Écrits*, vol. III, pp. 129–30.

with whom Mussolini and Napoleon III would look like some 'mild, almost humanitarian small town apothecaries'.] 'We are the victors of to-morrow', Remmele brags in the Reichstag. 'We are not afraid of Hitler assuming power.' This means that the victory of to-morrow will be Hitler's not Remmele's. And then you may as well carve it on your nose: the victory of the communists will not come so soon. 'We are not afraid' of Hitler's assuming power—what is this if not the formula of cowardice turned inside out? 'We' do not consider ourselves capable of preventing Hitler from assuming power; worse yet: We, bureaucrats, have so degenerated that we dare not think seriously of fighting Hitler. Therefore 'we are not afraid'. What is it that you are not afraid of: fighting against Hitler? Oh, no . . . they are not afraid of Hitler's victory. They are not afraid of refusing to fight. They are not afraid of confessing their own cowardice. Shame![1]

Warning while there was still time, Trotsky expected the socialists and communists to rally. Their situation was far from hopeless; but it was deteriorating rapidly; and he called for nothing less than preparation and readiness for civil war. To the Social Democratic preachers of moderation and to the Stalinists who defied Hitler to seize power, his call sounded like irresponsible and malignant provocation or, at best, the raving of a Quixote. Events were to prove all too grimly on which side were the irresponsibility, the malice, or the quixotry. They were to demonstrate that, of all courses of action open to the German left, civil war that might have prevented Hitler's assumption of power was in fact the least risky, indeed the only one that might have spared Germany and the world the terrors of the Third Reich and the cataclysms of world war. Early in his campaign Trotsky was convinced that a united left could still rout the Nazis almost without a fight, as the Bolsheviks and Mensheviks had routed Kornilov in August 1917, an example he frequently evoked. He argued that a demonstration of socialist-communist strength might still dissolve Hitler's following, that 'human dust' which had assumed the power of an avalanche only because it moved in a political vacuum and met with no coherent resistance. What favoured the left to some extent was also the fact that the traditional right wing had not yet made common cause with Hitler, even though some

[1] Trotsky, *What Next?* pp. 60–62; *Écrits*, vol. III, pp. 143–5.

potentates of German industry and banking were already backing him. In careful surveys of all the strategic and tactical circumstances, Trotsky analysed the ambiguous attitudes of the capitalist oligarchies, the Junkers, the army, the Stahlhelm, and the police, who were all torn between their desire to use Nazism and their fear of it, between their hope to crush labour with Hitler's hands and their apprehension that he might plunge Germany into a bloody civil war the outcome of which could not be foreseen. Hindenburg, the industrial magnates, and the officers' corps were still in a quandary—hence the quarrels and rows between them and the Nazis. Vigorous Social-ist-Communist action was needed to make the quandary even more difficult, to heighten in the eyes of all the conservative leaders the risks of their support to Hitler, to deepen their vacillations and divisions, and to neutralize at least some of them. Disorientation and inaction on the left, by reducing the risks, would only drive the big bourgeoisie, the army, and Hindenburg into Nazi arms.

A 'united front' between socialists and communists could thus still transform the whole political scene. The same mortal menace now hung over both parties, even if neither was aware of it. This alone should have been enough for them to join forces. The very thought was, of course, repugnant to the Social Democratic chiefs. Anti-communism had been the mainspring of their policy ever since 1918, and had caused them to cling to the 'lesser evil' of Hindenburg-cum-Brüning rather than ally themselves with communism against Hitler. Again and again Trotsky showed how by clinging to the 'lesser evil' they were merely opening the gates to the greater evil of Nazism. But this was for him one more reason why the communists should have made of the united front the central issue of all working-class policies. They failed to do so because they were entangled in the Comintern's 'Third Period' line. The Communist party could not even try to open the eyes of the millions of Social Democratic workers to the danger that threatened all of them when its own leaders were blind to the danger; and Moscow's ban on agreement with the Social Democratic party did not permit effective communist approach to that party. The daily Stalinist vituperation against 'social fascists' incessantly deep-ened the division in the working class, provided the Social

Democratic chiefs with a plausible excuse for their anti-communism, and made it all the easier for them to pursue their disastrous course. Only a genuine and convincing communist appeal to the social democratic conscience and self-interest alike, an appeal untiringly repeated in the hearing of the entire working class, could have broken the barriers between the two parties..

Their united front would have had to be not a diplomatic or parliamentary game with empty and insincere cordialities, in the style of the Anglo-Soviet Committee of 1924–6 (or, one may add, of the Popular Front of 1936–8), but joint preparation and organization for common combat. The two parties and their trade unions would have to 'march separately but strike unitedly' and agree among themselves 'how to strike, whom to strike, and when to strike'. For this they had no need to give up any of their principles or seek any ideological accommodation. Communists must never forget that the Social Democrats could at best be only their 'temporary and uncertain allies', who would always be afraid of extra-parliamentary action and might contract out of the struggle at its most critical turn. Yet it was the communists' duty to bring the strongest pressure to bear on them in order to arouse them to action. If they yielded to the pressure, all would be well; if not, millions of their followers would at least see where each party stood and would be more inclined to respond to a purely communist call to action. Already now, in 1930–1, hardly a day passed without scattered but bloody encounters between workers and Stormtroops; but in these the workers' militancy was being dissipated to no purpose. Only sporadically did socialists and communists agree to repel a Nazi attack jointly. Commenting on one such case Trotsky remarked: 'Oh, supreme leaders! Oh, sevenfold sages of strategy! Learn from these workers . . . do as they do! Do it on a wider, on a national scale.' In the course of the year 1931 Hitler's Stormtroops had grown from 100,000 to 400,000. Trotsky urged the German left to raise their own anti-Nazi militias and to concert the mutual defence of their party offices, factory councils, trade unions, &c. With the Russian Red Guards in mind, he wrote: 'Every factory must become an anti-fascist bulwark, with its own commanders and its own battalions. It is necessary to work with a map of fascist barracks and strongholds in every city and every district. The fascists are attempting to encircle the proletarian strongholds. The en-circlers must be encircled.'[1]

The chiefs of the German labour movement could not bring themselves to think and act in terms of civil war, partly because Hitler, as he advanced on his road to office, disavowed from time to time any thought of a *coup d'état* and any intention of using violence. He declared that he would assume and exercise office in the constitutional manner; and these assurances had their effect. 'He lulls his antagonists', Trotsky warned, 'in order to catch them napping and deal them a mortal blow at the right moment. His curtsey to parliamentary democracy may help him to set up in the immediate future a coalition in which his party will obtain the most important posts in order to use these later for a *coup d'état*.' 'This military cunning, no matter how plain and simple, secretes a tremendous force because it is calculated to meet the psychological needs of the intermediate parties who would like to settle everything peacefully and law-fully, and—this is far more dangerous—because it satisfies the gullibility of the popular masses.'[2]

Pravda and *Rote Fahne* now spoke of Trotsky as the 'panic-monger', 'adventurer', and 'Brüning's stooge', who urged communists to abandon proletarian revolution, to defend bourgeois democracy, and to forget that 'without a prior victory over social fascism we cannot vanquish fascism'.[3] Not without anger yet with infinite patience Trotsky dealt with even the most preposterous arguments in order to make his views clear to those befuddled by polemical tricks. Untiringly he went on exploding the fallacy that there could be 'no victory over fascism without a prior victory over social fascism', point-ing out that, on the contrary, only when fascism had been

---

[1] Trotsky, *Germany, the Key to the International Situation*, p. 41; *B.O.*, no. 27.

[2] *What Next?*, pp. 147–8

[3] An anthology of German Stalinist polemics against Trotsky would make instructive though unendurably monotonous reading. Even a man like W. Münzen-berg wrote: 'Trotsky proposes . . . a bloc between the Communist and Social Democratic Parties. Nothing could be as detrimental to the German working class and communism and nothing would promote fascism so much as the realization of so criminal a proposal. . . . He who proposes such a bloc . . . only assists the social-fascist leaders. His role is indeed . . . plainly fascist.' (*Rote Aufbau*, 15 February 1932.) Münzenberg ended this polemical campaign by committing suicide in exile.

defeated could the communists contend effectively against the social democrats, and that proletarian revolution in Germany could develop only out of a successful resistance to Nazism.

It was all to no avail. As late as September 1932, a few months before Hitler became Chancellor, Thaelmann, at a session of the Comintern Executive, still repeated, what Münzenberg had said: 'In his pamphlet on how National Socialism is to be defeated, Trotsky gives one answer only, and it is this: the German Communist Party must join hands with the Social Democratic Party. . . . This, according to Trotsky, is the only way in which the German working class can save itself from fascism. Either, says he, the Communist party makes common cause with the Social Democrats, or the German working class is lost for ten or twenty years. This is the theory of an utterly bankrupt Fascist and counter-revolutionary. This is indeed the worst, the most dangerous, and the most criminal theory that Trotsky has construed in these last years of his counter-revolutionary propaganda.'[1]

'One of the decisive moments in history is approaching', Trotsky rejoined, '. . . when the Comintern as a revolutionary factor may be wiped off the political map for an entire historic epoch. Let blind men and cowards refuse to notice this. Let slanderers and hired scribblers accuse us of being in league with the counter-revolution. Has not counter-revolution become anything . . . that interferes with the digestion of communist bureaucrats . . . nothing must be concealed, nothing belittled. We must tell the advanced workers as loudly as we can: After the "third period" of recklessness and boasting the fourth period of panic and capitulation has set in.' In an almost desperate effort to arouse the communists, Trotsky put into words the whole power of his conviction and gave them once again the ring of an alarm bell: 'Workers-communists! There are hundreds of thousands, there are millions of you. . . . If fascism comes to power it will ride like a terrific tank over your skulls and spines. Your salvation lies in merciless struggle.

---

[1] Compare *Rote Aufbau*, loc. cit. with *XII Plenum IKKI*, part 3; *Kommunistichesky Internatsional*, 1932, nos. 28–29, pp. 102–3, 111 and *passim*. Thaelmann was serenely confident that 'Germany will of course not go fascist—our electoral victories are a guarantee of this . . . the irresistible advance of communism is a guarantee of this'.

Only a fighting unity with social democratic workers can bring victory. Make haste, communist workers, you have very little time to lose.'[1]

.   .   .   .

To have to let, at such a time, the grass grow under his feet at Prinkipo was for Trotsky more and more painful. Letters and newspapers from the continent reached him with much, sometimes with a fortnight's, delay; it took even longer for his brochures and manifestoes to reach Germany. In 1923, when Germany seemed on the verge of revolution, he had asked the Politbureau to relieve him from his official posts and allow him to go to Germany and direct, as the German party had asked, revolutionary operations there. How much more anxious was he to find himself nearer the scene of action now, when the future of communism and the political fortunes of the world were being decided for decades ahead. In 1931 there was talk about his going on a short lecture tour to Germany; but, of course, nothing came of it. There was no chance of his getting out of Turkey. Worse still, his few followers in the Reich were making no headway. They published a tiny paper *Permanente Revolution*, which appeared once a month, filling its columns with Trotsky's writings, and had almost no impact (although his brochures were quite widely read and discussed). He planned to set up an International Secretariat in Berlin where the brothers Sobolevicius were very active, and whither the *Bulletin Oppozitsii* had already been transferred from Paris. To improve his contact with the Secretariat it was decided that Lyova should leave for Berlin and act there as his father's representative, or, as organizational punctilio demanded, as the 'representative of the Russian Section of the Left Opposition'.

Lyova, we know, had shared with his parents all the vicissitudes of their exile and was Trotsky's right-hand man. Yet relations between father and son had not been unruffled. They were in full political concord, and Lyova's adoration for his father amounted to identification with him. Yet it was this identification that was also a cause of strain. Trotsky had an uneasy feeling that· his own personality and interests had

---

[1] Trotsky, *Germany, the Key*, etc., p. 44.

imposed themselves too overwhelmingly on Lyova, and that he had reduced Lyova to the frustrating part of the great man's little son. Yet he craved the filial devotion. The more lonely he was the more he depended on it. Lyova was the only man with whom he could freely thrash out his ideas and plans and share innermost thoughts, his most trusted critic, and, as he liked to think, his 'link' (in later years, his only link) with the young Russian revolutionary generation. Yet at times Lyova's absolute devotion disturbed him: he wanted greater independence in his son and almost wished for some signs of filial dissent. But dissent, when there was a hint of it, upset him and made him fear estrangement. Seclusion and incessant intercourse deepened the mutual dependence and also heightened the stresses which, though not unnatural between father and son, had in them something of the irritable tension between two prisoners who have shared a dungeon for too long. Trotsky was exacting towards his assistants and secretaries, but his demands were never as severe as those he made on himself and his son. With strangers he was self-controlled and polite; but under great nervous strain his self-control was liable to break down when he was alone with his next of kin. Harsh reproaches would then come down upon Lyova's head on account of 'disorder' in the secretariat, 'sloth and sloppiness', and 'letting down' his father, reproaches which could not but hurt the dedicated, industrious and conscientious young man.[1]

Some relief was therefore mixed with sadness when parents and son agreed on separation. There was probably yet another reason for this decision: Raymond Molinier's wife, Jeanne, had left her husband and chosen to stay with Lyova. Molinier, however, was still a frequent and helpful visitor at Prinkipo; and Lyova's and Jeanne's departure may well have spared them all embarrassing encounters. It was doubtful at first whether Lyova would obtain a German entry permit. (The year before he had in vain applied for a French visa: the French police replied that they knew of his revolutionary activities and did not wish to see him in Paris.) But, having inscribed himself as a student at the *Technische Hochschule* in Berlin, he finally

---

[1] Relations between father and son are characterized here (and in the following pages) on the basis of the family correspondence, which fills forty folders in the Closed Section of the Trotsky *Archives* and consists of 1,244 items.

obtained the German visa in February 1931. The academic purpose of his sojourn was no mere pretext, for at the *Hochshule* he did indeed take with much application courses in physics and mathematics; but his chief preoccupations remained, of course, political.[1]

A few weeks before Lyova's departure, in the middle of January, something occurred that was to affect the life of the entire family: Zina and her five-year-old son Seva arrived from Moscow. For several months she had been expected at Büyük Ada; but hope of her coming had been nearly given up, because the Soviet Government had repeatedly refused her permission to make the journey. Her husband, Platon Volkov, was deported; and she herself had been detained twice because of her involvement with the Opposition. Only after the intervention of western European friends who appealed to Soviet Ambassadors on compassionate grounds—her health had broken down after the death of her sister Nina whom she had nursed to the end—did she obtain the exit permit. But there was a catch. She was allowed to take with her only one child and had to leave behind another, a little daughter, a six- or seven-year-old hostage to Stalin. Alexandra Lvovna, Trotsky's first wife, who, herself under a cloud, was bringing up Nina's two children, took care of this infant too, and urged Zina to leave, join her father, and repair her health abroad.

Zina came to Prinkipo a nervous wreck, though this did not show at once in the flush of reunion. Her father received her with the utmost tenderness. 'In the first period of my stay', she wrote later to her mother in Leningrad, 'he was so soft and attentive to me that I cannot even describe it. . . .' Of all his children she, his first-born, resembled him most. She had the same sharp, dark features, the same fiery eyes, the same smile, the same sardonic irony, the same deep-running emotions, and something also of his untameable mind and of his eloquence. She seemed to have inherited his political passions, his militancy, and craving for activity. 'She was', as

[1] Lyova's mathematical exercise books, densely and neatly filled, with entries dated and marked by his academic teachers, served later as evidence of his alibi in the Mexican counter-trial of 1937. The exercise books are preserved in *The Archives*. In an undated letter to Dr. Soblen (Well), Lyova explained the reasons of organization which impelled him to move to Berlin. (It took seven or eight months before he obtained the German visa.)

her mother put it, 'more public-spirited than family-minded.'[1]

In Trotsky's feeling for her there was a touch of remorse. Ever since those days in 1917 when, addressing multitudes at the *Cirque Moderne* in Petrograd, he had felt the loving eyes of his two adolescent daughters staring up at him from the audience, and fixed on him, he had been aware of Zina's intense emotion for him. Yet she was to him almost a stranger. It was nearly thirty years now since he had left his first wife and their two babies in the eastern Siberian settlement of Verkholensk (the place of his first exile)—nearly thirty years since he had arranged in his bed there the dummy of a man in order to deceive the police and delay their pursuit.[2] It was as if that dummy had deceived the offspring of his first marriage also. In fifteen years, up to 1917, he had seen his daughters only twice or thrice, fleetingly; and he could give them only very little time and attention thereafter, in the years of the revolution, the civil war, and the cruel struggles that followed. His heart went out to them when he was exiled to Alma Ata; but then it was too late: Nina presently died; and Zina was too ill to undertake the journey from Moscow, too ill even to come later to the family's sad farewell meeting on the train when he was being deported from Russia. She arrived at Prinkipo heart-broken yet overwhelmed with joy, love, and pride in her father; she had come not merely as a sick and suffering daughter but as a dedicated follower, hoping to be of use to him, offering her services, and yearning to be admitted to his confidence. They wept together over Nina's death; they talked about friends and comrades and deported relatives; and they argued about politics. She listened all ecstasy and read, with a thrill, the manuscripts of the *History of the Russian Revolution* and his other writings, acquainted herself with the controversies in which he was engaged, absorbed their dramatic gravity, and relished his sarcasm and wit. She was convulsed with laughter when she came across Churchill's essay on the 'Ogre of Europe': and it was as the 'ogre' that she liked to address her father.[3]

---

[1] The quotation is from Sokolovskaya's letter to Trotsky, written after Zina's death. See its summary on pp. 197–8, *The Archives*, Closed Section.

[2] *The Prophet Armed*, p. 55.

[3] These details are drawn from Zina's correspondence. *The Archives*, Closed Section. In *The Archives* I found a picture of her which she presented to her father with the inscription: 'To the ogre'.

The other members of the family also gave her affection and compassion and did their best to make her feel at home. Natalya Ivanovna's position was admittedly delicate; but she had been closer to the children of Trotsky's first marriage than he himself, and had not only tried to overcome estrangement with friendship but had behaved towards them like a second mother. Not deceived by the apparent improvement in Zina's condition, she took her to the doctors and gave meticulous attention to her health. Too sensitive to imagine that the hidden strains could ever vanish altogether, she tried to efface herself whenever she felt that father and daughter would best be left by themselves. Curiously, Lyova's relation with his sister was far more tense. Their characters were discordant. Resembling his mother rather than his father, Lyova was reserved, modest, and even-tempered; he was easily disconcerted by his sister's intensity and impassioned expansiveness, while her feelings were tinged by a jealousy of Lyova's closeness to their father. In the warmth of reunion, and while Lyova was preparing for his move to Berlin, these strains were subdued. The whole family went into raptures over Zina's child, whose chatter and pranks brought an unfamiliar note into the austere and industrious existence of the household. This was, it seems, the first time that Trotsky, who already had five grandchildren, could freely indulge in the sentiments of grandfatherhood.

Shortly after Zina's arrival, in the dead of night, a great fire broke out in the house, consuming most of the family's belongings and Trotsky's library. With difficulty he wrested from the flames his archives and the manuscript of the just completed first volume of his *History*. A suspicion of arson crossed everyone's mind: was this perhaps an attempt by the G.P.U. to destroy the archives? An investigation was opened; witnesses were cross-examined, but nothing was found out. 'All of us felt dejected and were very much disturbed . . .', writes one of Trotsky's secretaries, 'all, except Trotsky himself.' The household moved to a near-by hotel; and 'no sooner were we settled than he laid out his manuscripts on the table, called the stenographer, and began to dictate a chapter of his book, as if nothing had happened during the night'.[1] After a few days they

---

[1] Jan Fraenkel in *Militant*, 2 January 1932. See also *Journal d'Orient*, 8 April 1931.

moved to Kodikoy, an Anglo-American residential suburb on the eastern fringe of Constantinople, into a wooden house surrounded by high barbed wire fences, where the household, complete with secretaries, policemen, and fishermen, stayed for about a year, until the Büyük Ada house was habitable again.

A few months after the move to Kodikoy another fire broke out. Once again the archives were hastily removed; and the family had to bivouac in barns and shacks near by; and once again the thought of an incendiary hand occurred to everyone. But it turned out that the fire was caused by Zina's child playing with matches and a pile of wood, rags, and sawdust in the loft. It was a relief after all the scares; and everyone laughed and teased the 'little G.P.U. agent'.

As the weeks passed Zina's illness came back. Her lungs were diseased; she had to undergo several operations; she could not bear the heat of the eastern Mediterranean; and she was tormented by anxiety over her husband and the child she had left behind. Under the stress of illness and worry, her shaky nervous balance gave way. Hidden tensions and conflicts, probably rooted in the misery of her childhood and nurtured by later experiences, came to the surface. Her behaviour became explosive and incoherent. She gave vent to memories, desires, and grievances that had hitherto lurked beyond the threshold of her consciousness. She was obsessed by the sense of being an unwanted daughter, unwanted by the father whom she adored with all her passion as the life-giving genius of revolution. It was her faith in him, she herself wrote, that kept her alive and gave her the strength to grapple with her predicament—without him life would have been empty. Yet she felt an unsurmountable barrier between herself and him. 'I know, I know', these are words she threw at him, 'that children are not wanted, that they come only as punishment for sins committed.'[1] It was as if the shock she may have suffered as an infant, on that day when she found instead of him the mere dummy of a man in his bed, reverberated in the reproach.

In this emotional turmoil she struggled to suppress her inner resentment at her father's second marriage. Outwardly her attitude towards Natalya Ivanovna was one of affection and care; but there was an unnatural exaltation in it. She walked

[1] Zina's letter of 26 February 1932.

around her stepmother on tiptoe, insistently inquiring and worrying about her, and lavishing caresses and apologies. Yet the resentment was close enough to the surface for father and stepmother to feel it; every now and then it broke through and hit them in their faces. Much though they tried to ignore or soothe it, relations became tense. To avoid making them worse, Trotsky withdrew within himself. The more he did so, the more frustrated was Zina's yearning for his confidence and closeness. She had hoped to work at least as one of his assistants. He, worried about her health and mindful of her possible return to her child in Russia, did not encourage this ambition. He wished her to use her stay abroad for a cure and in the meantime to avoid compromising her politically, as if being his daughter had not already compromised her finally and irretrievably. The worsening of her illness, he felt, necessitated even greater reserve on his part and made work in common almost impossible. He could not take her into his confidence over the affairs of the Opposition in Russia; and it was in these precisely that she was breathlessly interested. At this time his correspondence with his Russian followers was still fairly abundant, part of it being despatched openly but part clandestinely, with coded signatures and addresses. The greatest discretion about the codes had to be exercised; and secrecy had to be redoubled *vis-à-vis* an ill and unbalanced person who on return to Russia might be subjected to inquisitorial interrogation. Elementary rules of underground communications required such safeguards; but the unfortunate woman took these as a slur on her, a sign of her father's distrust. 'To Papa', she often repeated, 'I am a good-for-nothing.' More resentment, more reproach and self-reproach, more gloom, and more and graver mental disturbance made everyone feel worse. In the summer she left home, and in a near-by sanatorium underwent the operations on her lungs. She returned, her physical health somewhat restored, but her misery unrelieved.

Distressed and shaken with pity, Trotsky was a prey to guilt and helplessness. How much easier it was to see in what way the great ills of society should be fought against than to relieve the sufferings of an incurable daughter! How much easier to diagnose the turmoil in the collective mind of the German petty bourgeoisie than to penetrate into the pain-laden recesses of

Zina's personality! How much superior was one's Marxian understanding of social psychology to one's grasp of the troubles of the individual psyche! He watched Zina's features and eyes overcast with insanity—they were his features, his eyes. For him, the prodigy of intellectual lucidity and self-discipline, it was unbearable to see her so incoherent, so distraught. It was as if reason itself had discovered in unreason its closest progeny and its double. Tenderness and horror, compassion and revulsion, pride and humiliation were at odds in him. He was wounded; he was helpless; he grew irritable. Sometimes, when Zina's jealousy burst out to hurt Natalya Ivanovna, he raised his voice demanding tact and courtesy. His raised voice reduced her to utter prostration. Remembering some such scene, she wrote to him a year later: 'Don't shout at me, Papa, don't— your shouting is the one thing I cannot endure; in this I am like my mother.' And she added: 'There is nothing I desire so much, if only I have enough strength to do it, as to soften for Natalya Ivanovna that of which I have turned out without guilt to be guilty towards her.'[1]

With tempers frayed and Zina's illness becoming quite alarming—she began to suffer fits of delirium—she could not stay on. For some time he had thought that she should undergo psychoanalytical treatment, and he had written about this to the Pfemferts in Berlin. She resisted. She had no wish, she said, to submerge herself in the 'filth' of her subconsciousness; and she could not bear the thought that, having overcome so many obstacles and borne so many sacrifices to rejoin her father, she should again be separated from him. She would also have to be separated from her son, for it was very difficult for her to take care of his upbringing. But she yielded to persuasion; and in the autumn of 1931, leaving Seva behind, she went to Berlin. The parting was a torment to both father and daughter. This is how she related it to Lyova: ' "You are an astonishing person, [her father told her in their last talk] I have never met anyone like you." ' 'He said that', she added, 'in an expressive and severe voice'.

This was the voice of reason baffled and thwarted by unreason.

· · · · · · · · ·

[1] The Russian expression is: '*Bez viny vinovata.*' The letter is undated.

Life in the German capital, when Zina arrived there, was a crescendo of chaos and topsy-turviness. She arrived a few weeks after a plebiscite, arranged on the initiative of Hitler and Goebbels, the purpose of which was to overthrow the Social Democratic *Landesregierung* of Prussia. The Nazis had let loose a savage chauvinistic campaign calling for a 'People's Revolution' against the party that 'had accepted the slavery and humiliation of the Versailles Peace'. The Communist party reacted by addressing to the Social Democratic Ministers of Prussia, Braun and Severing, an ultimatum in which it offered to defend their government if they agreed to certain demands, but threatened to vote against it if the demands were rejected. On the face of it, this was a depature from the 'third period tactics', at least in so far as the communists had made a direct approach to Social Democratic leaders. Actually they 'concentrated fire on the social-fascists'; and when the Prussian Government refused their demands, they called upon the workers to cast their votes against it. Thus, instead of making a united front with the Social Democrats, conditionally or unconditionally, they formed an unavowed but all too real, and unconditional, united front with the Nazis; and to save face they called the enterprise *der Rote Volksentscheid*, the Red Plebiscite.

A fatal and deeply demoralizing ambiguity now appeared in communist policy, which was to persist until Hitler's seizure of power and even thereafter. Not infrequently the same slogans appeared on communist and Nazi banners. The Nazis, seeking to win socially discontented and radical elements, promised that their 'People's Revolution' would settle accounts with finance capital. The Communist party, wary of calling for a proletarian socialist revolution, spoke, instead, of the 'People's Revolution' which would achieve Germany's 'social and national liberation' and break the shackles of Versailles. The spirit of nationalism insinuated itself more and more strongly into its propaganda just at a time when nothing was more urgent in Germany than the need to stem the mounting tide of racial and chauvinist fanaticism. Although the plebiscite went in favour of the Social Democrats, its effect was to deepen the breach in the working class and to make confusion worse confounded.

Trotsky attacked Thaelmann's and the Comintern's 'national communism' with the utmost vigour, exposing the absurdities of the 'Red Plebiscite'. The whole venture, he argued, was all the more repugnant because communists and Nazis remained, and could not help remaining, mortal enemies. In self-justification, the Stalinists pointed out that the Social Democrats were paving the way for Nazism. This was all too true, Trotsky remarked, but if the Social Democrats paved the way for a Nazi victory, should the communists shorten it? It happens sometimes that the parties of revolution and counter-revolution attack the same 'moderate' enemy from their opposite poles. But a Marxist party can afford to do this only when the tide runs in its favour, not when it runs, as it did in Germany, in favour of counter-revolution. 'To go out into the street with the slogan "Down with the government of Brüning and Braun" is a reckless adventure when the whole balance of strength is such that the government of Brüning and Braun can be replaced only by a government of Hitler and Hugenberg. The same slogan would acquire quite a different meaning if and when it presaged the direct struggle for power by the working class.' Even now he did not doubt the good intentions of the Communist party; but 'unfortunately, the Stalinist bureaucracy is trying . . . to act against fascism by using the weapons of the latter. It borrows colours from the political palette of Nazism and tries to outdo Nazism at an auction of patriotism. These are not methods of a principled class struggle, but tricks of a petty market competition . . . a betrayal of Marxism . . . a display of concentrated bureaucratic stupidity.' Those who talked about the 'People's Revolution' and about freeing Germany from the chains of Versailles had forgotten Karl Liebknecht's maxim that for the working class 'the main enemy stands in their own country'. The insinuation of nationalism into communist thinking had begun with Stalin's 'socialism in one country' and it now produced Thaelmann's 'national communism'. 'Ideas have not only their own logic but their own explosive force'; and the lack of scruple with which the Comintern tried to outbid Hitler in nationalist demagogy showed up the 'spiritual emptiness of Stalinism'.[1]

What, according to Trotsky, was at stake was not only all the hard-won achievements of the German labour movement but

[1] 'Protiv Natsjonal-Kommunizma (Uroki Krasnovo Referenduma)', *B.O.*, no. 24. The article was published as a pamphlet in Germany.

the future of civilization: with Nazism the shadow of the dark ages was returning to Europe. Hitler, if victorious, would not merely preserve capitalism but reduce it to barbarism. The enraged *Kleinbürger* 'repudiated not only Marxism but even Darwinism', and to the rationalism and materialism of the eighteenth, nineteenth, and twentieth centuries he opposed the myths of the tenth or eleventh century, the mystique of race and blood. This, their supposed racial superiority, was to boost the pride of Germany's lower middle classes, and give them an imaginary escape from the miseries of their life. In its rabid anti-Marxism and rejection of the 'economic view of history', 'National Socialism descends lower down: from economic materialism to zoological materialism'. Nazism collected 'all the refuse of international political thought . . . to make up the intellectual treasure of the new Germanic Messianism'. It stirred and rallied all the forces of barbarism lurking under the thin surface of 'civilized' class society. It tapped inexhaustible reserves of darkness, ignorance, and savagery. In a memorable phrase, alive with a premonition of the *autos da fé* and gas chambers of the Third Reich, Trotsky thus described the essence of Nazism: 'Everything which society, it if had developed normally [i.e. towards socialism], would have rejected . . . as the excrement of culture is now bursting out through its throat: capitalist civilization is disgorging undigested barbarity —such is the physiology of National Socialism.'[1]

That communist (as well as non-communist) opinion of the early nineteen-thirties was insensitive to such a philosophical-historical view of Nazism need not perhaps surprise the historian. What he must find more difficult to comprehend is how the leaders of the Soviet Union and the great mass of communists all over the world could remain deaf to what Trotsky was saying about the threat to the Soviet Union. In November 1931, ten years before the battle of Moscow, he wrote: 'A victory of fascism in Germany would signify the inevitability of war against the U.S.S.R.'[2] At that time Moscow still saw France as the chief western antagonist of the Soviet Union; and it feared an imminent attack from Japan, which had just embarked upon the invasion of Manchuria. The progress of

---

[1] *Écrits*, vol. III, pp. 391–9. 'Qu'est-ce que c'est le national-socialisme?'
[2] Op. cit., pp. 100–1.

Nazism had as yet aroused little or no apprehension in Stalin and his advisers, even though Hitler was loudly proclaiming that he was out to destroy Bolshevism and conquer the East. Stalin assumed that these were the ravings of Hitler the 'rebel', but that Hitler the Chancellor would not easily forgo the advantages which Germany derived from her relations with Russia, under the Rapallo Treaty. Stalin expected that Hitler's striving to rearm Germany would bring him into conflict with France and compel him to abate his hostility towards the Soviet Union. It was not for nothing that the Comintern encouraged the German communists to lend ambiguous support to Hitler's campaign against Versailles: that campaign was to divert Hitler from his ambition to lead a western crusade against Bolshevism.

Trotsky struggled against this unawareness of the international implications of Nazism. He did not believe that France was still Russia's chief enemy, as in the years of intervention. 'Not a single one of the normal bourgeois parliamentary governments', he maintained, 'can at present risk a war against the U.S.S.R.: such an undertaking would entail incalculable domestic complications. But once Hitler has seized power . . . and pulverized and demoralized the German working class for many years to come, his will be the only government capable of waging war against the U.S.S.R.'[1] Nor did he believe that the Soviet Union was seriously threatened by Japan. He forecast that by invading Manchuria, Japan would involve herself in a long and exhausting war with China, which would divert Japanese strength from the Soviet Union and hasten revolution in China. 'The basic conditions of the East—immense distances, huge populations, and economic backwardness imply that the whole process [of Japanese conquest] will be slow, creeping, and wasteful. In any case, in the Far East no immediate and grave danger threatens the Soviet Union. The crucial events of the coming period will unfold in Europe, in Germany', where 'the political and economic antagonisms have reached an unprecedented sharpness . . . and the dénouement is close at hand.' And again: 'For many years to come, not only the fate of Germany . . . but the destinies of Europe and the destinies of the entire world will be decided in Germany.' 'Socialist

[1] Loc. cit.

construction in the Soviet Union, the march of the Spanish revolution, the growth of a pre-revolutionary situation in England, the future of French imperialism, the fate of the revolutionary movement in China and India, all these issues reduce themselves . . . to this single question: who is going to win in Germany in the course of the coming months? Communism or fascism?'[1]

Trotsky assumed that for an anti-Soviet crusade Hitler could gain the support of world capitalism, and that this would entail 'a frightful isolation of the Soviet Union and the necessity to fight a life-and-death struggle under the hardest and most dangerous conditions'. 'If fascism were to crush the German working class, this would amount to at least half the collapse of the Republic of the Soviets.' Only if the workers succeeded in barring Hitler's road to power would Germany, the U.S.S.R., and the world be saved from catastrophe. Stalin's policy in Germany was therefore directed against the vital interests of the Soviet Union as well as of German communism. Soviet security and the international proletarian interest were inextricably bound up. For years Stalin and the Comintern had screamed about the imminence of an anti-Soviet crusade; but now, when the peril was real, they were silent. Yet it should be 'an axiom' that a Nazi attempt to seize power 'must be followed by a mobilization of the Red Army. For the workers' state this will be a matter of revolutionary self-defence. . . . Germany is not only Germany. It is the heart of Europe. Hitler is not only Hitler. He is the candidate for the role of a super-Wrangel. But the Red Army is not only the Red Army. It is the instrument of proletarian world revolution.'[2]

A few months later, in April 1932, he restated this idea even more strikingly. Routine-ridden politicians and diplomats, he said, were blind to what was coming, just as they had been on the eve of the First World War. 'My relations with the present government of Moscow are not of such a nature as to permit me to speak in its name or refer to its intentions. . . . With all the greater frankness can I state how, in my view, the Soviet government should act in case of a fascist upheaval in Germany. In their place, I would, at the very moment of receiving telegraphic news of this event, sign a mobilization order calling up

---

[1] Loc. cit., p. 95.   [2] Ibid., p. 101.

several age groups. In the face of a mortal enemy, when the logic of the situation points to inevitable war, it would be irresponsible and unpardonable to give that enemy time to establish himself, to consolidate his positions, to conclude alliances . . . and to work out the plan of attack. . . .' And again: 'War between Hitlerite Germany and the Soviet Union would be inevitable and this in the short term', in view of which even the question who would attack first was of secondary importance. With an eye to those in France and Britain who hoped to save the *status quo* in the West and the Versailles system by diverting German imperialism eastwards, Trotsky wrote that 'whatever illusions are entertained in Paris one can safely predict that the Versailles system would be one of the first to be consumed in the flames of a war between Bolshevism and fascism'.[1]

The Comintern Press at once branded Trotsky as a 'treacherous warmonger' seeking to embroil Russia and Germany; and to many outside the Comintern too the boldness of his statements seemed reckless. His attitude, however, will not appear quite so reckless if it is remembered that, even in the early nineteen-thirties, with Germany, Britain, and the United States disarmed, the Soviet Union was the greatest military power of the world. But Trotsky did not in fact urge the Soviet Government to wage war against Germany, even a Nazi Germany. In 1933, after Hitler had become Chancellor, Trotsky declared that in the existing circumstances mobilization of the Red Army would serve no purpose. He had advocated it, he explained, on the assumption that Hitler would have to shoot his way to office—he had refused to believe that the German labour movement would allow Hitler to become the master of their country without having to fire a shot. It was in this context of an assumed civil war in Germany that he had insisted on the Red Army's duty to intervene.[2] Admittedly this would have been a hazardous course, but less so than was waiting passively for Hitler's ascendancy and Germany's rearmament. Trotsky's attitude, revolutionary in its political aspect, was in its military aspect similar to that which Winston

[1] Ibid., pp. 104–5.
[2] The article appeared originally in the American *Forum*, 15 April 1932. *Écrits*, vol. III, pp. 233–40. See also 'Hitler i Krasnaya Armija', *B.O.*, no. 34, May 1933.

Churchill was to adopt four or five years later, when he called the British and French Governments to counter Hitler's march into the Rhineland by measures of mobilization and preparation for war. This attitude earned Churchill the unrivalled moral authority he needed to become Britain's leader in the Second World War. Vilification was all it earned Trotsky.

Meanwhile, the Nazi avalanche moved on. In the spring of 1932 Germany was to elect a President, and Hitler posed his candidature. A Socialist-Communist candidate was still sure to poll more votes than Hitler or any other contestant—at the repeated parliamentary elections of that year Communists and Social-Democrats invariably obtained more than 13 million votes. But the Social Democrats decided to uphold the candidature of Hindenburg, the nearly nonagenarian retiring President, whom they had opposed at the previous election as the very symbol of the old Imperial reaction, but behind whose senile back they now sought to shelter. The Communist party called the workers to vote for Thaelmann. Hindenburg was re-elected; and at once he delivered the *coup de grâce* to the parliamentary régime and struck at the Social Democrats. He dismissed Brüning, who had just made a half-hearted attempt to ban Hitler's Stormtroops and had also incurred the enmity of the East Prussian Junkers. Hindenburg's new Chancellor, von Papen, lifted the ban on the Stormtroops; and, on 20 July 1932, he deposed by decree the Social-Democratic government of Prussia which the Nazis had in vain tried to overthrow by plebiscite. The event was remarkable for its tragi-comedy: a lieutenant commanding a section of soldiers turned out of their offices the Prussian Prime Minister and Minister of Interior, who nominally had the whole Prussian police under their orders. Too late and perfunctorily the communists advised the Social Democrats to call a general strike and offered support. Once again the Social Democrats refused to make common cause with their 'enemies on the left'; and they deluded themselves that von Papen and Hindenburg's camarilla (of which General Schleicher was the moving spirit), would somehow outmanœuvre Hitler and keep him at bay. This was a widespread illusion in these last months of the Weimar Republic: von Papen, having so easily seized the Social Democratic 'fortress' in Prussia, seemed very powerful; he appeared to have

stolen Hitler's thunder; and the Nazi movement was momentarily losing impetus.[1]

All the more must one marvel at the accuracy and precision
of Trotsky's analyses and predictions. 'The less the workers were
prepared to fight', he commented, 'the greater was the impression of strength which Papen's government gave. . . .'
However, this is not yet the fascist upheaval—that is still to
come. Papen will not be able to outmanœuvre Hitler and
prevent a Nazi dictatorship, for he does not even have the
limited strength Brüning possessed: he is backed only by
the most archaic elements of the Prussian bureaucracy. He
will not be able to control the fury and the rage of the
millions that follow Hitler—only the determination and the
militancy of millions of workers might do that. But how could
the workers have that determination when they see the
Prussian Socialist government allowing itself to be overthrown
by a 'flick on the nose', and when the communists, after telling
them for years that Germany is already fascist, now call
them to rise in general strike against Papen's 'fascist' *coup
d'état* and in defence of the 'social-fascist' government of
Prussia. Yet, confused though the workers are, the alternative
is still a victory of Nazism or a victory of the working class—
tertium non datur. Papen, Trotsky insisted, will have no more
than 'a hundred days'; and so will Schleicher who will
follow him as Chancellor. Then the Reichswehr and the
Junkers will form a coalition with the Nazis in the hope of
taming the latter. It will all be in vain: 'All conceivable
[governmental] combinations with Hitler must lead to the
absorption of the bureaucracy, the courts, the police, and the
army by fascism.' Even now, he held, it was not yet too late for
a 'united front' of the workers; but—'how much time has been
wasted without purpose, senselessly, and shamefully!'[2]

.   .   .   .

About this time Trotsky was also in controversy with the
Comintern over the Spanish revolution. Primo de Rivera's
dictatorship came to an end in 1930 and the collapse of the
monarchy followed in April 1931. While Germany was

[1] W. L. Shirer, *The Rise and Fall of the Third Reich*, pp. 158–60, 170–2, and
passim.
[2] *Der Einrige Weg*; see also *B.O.*, nos. 29–30, September 1932.

developing from a bourgeois democracy to an authoritarian régime, in Spain the opposite was happening. Yet in both countries the Comintern clung to the third period policy. While the German party declared that the antagonism between fascism and bourgeois democracy was irrelevant, the Spanish party made light of the conflict between monarchy and republic. In Moscow, Manuilsky told the Comintern Executive in February 1930, after the fall of Primo de Rivera: 'Movements of this kind pass across the historic screen as mere incidents and leave no deep traces in the mind of the working masses. . . . A single strike . . . may be of greater importance than a "revolution" like the Spanish. . . .'[1] The revolution that was to occupy the world for nearly a decade was still referred to in quotation marks. The abdication of King Alfonso caught the party by surprise. When subsequently Spain resounded with the demand for a democratically elected Cortes, the official communists, like the Anarcho-Syndicalists, maintained that the workers and peasants would gain nothing from any parliament; and they favoured the boycott of elections. Yet, at the same time, the Comintern declared that the Spanish revolution, in view of the country's backwardness, must keep within 'bourgeois democratic' limits, and that 'proletarian dictatorship was not on the order of the day'. It is easy to recognize there the Stalinist canon developed as antithesis to Trotsky's Permanent Revolution and applied in China in 1925–7. This canon was to underlie Stalinist policy in Spain through all its phases. At a later stage, in 1936–8, it was invoked to justify the communist coalition with bourgeois republican parties in the Popular Front, the 'moderate' policy of the Communist party and its repressive action against the P.O.U.M., the Trotskyists, and the radical Anarcho-Syndicalists. In the early nineteen-thirties, however, the same canon was incongruously combined with ultra-left tactics and with the rejection of the demands for a Constituent Assembly and democratic liberties, the classical desiderata of bourgeois revolution.

Trotsky asserted that the Spanish revolution would have to pass, as the Russian revolution had done, from the bourgeois

---

[1] Yet later in the year the organ of the Comintern Executive blamed the Spanish Communists for having missed the revolutionary significance of the events. See *Kommunisticheskii Internatsional*, 1930, nos. 34–35,

into the socialist phase, if it was not to be defeated. Of all European countries Spain was closest to pre-1917 Russia in social structure, in the alignment of political forces—and in Spain as in Russia Workers' Councils or Juntas were destined to be the organs of revolution. While insisting on the 'permanence' of the revolution, Trotsky urged the communists to adopt more realistic tactics, to raise or support demands for general franchise, for a Constituent Assembly, for the self-determination of the Catalans and Basques, and, above all, to support the peasantry's struggle for land. The peasants were bound to look to the Cortes for a solution of the land problem; and communists were in duty bound to state their agrarian programme from the parliamentary platform, if only to promote the peasantry's extra-parliamentary action. They could not do this under their 'third period' policy and while they were inclined to ignore and boycott parliament. 'Parliamentary cretinism is a detestable disease, but anti-parliamentary cretinism is not much better', he remarked. Had not the Bolsheviks called for a Constituent Assembly in 1917? In Spain parliamentary politics were bound to be even more important than in Russia, because the rhythm of the revolution would be slower; and the Spanish communists should in their action 'take less into account the Russian experience than that of the great French Revolution. The Jacobin dictatorship was preceded by three parliamentary assemblies'; and something similar might happen in Spain.[1]

The Spanish party was not only disoriented, small, and weak; it was also disorganized by the divisions and splits which were inseparable from Stalinist orthodoxy. It had already expelled several Trotskyist and semi-Trotskyist groups and Andres Nin its founder and one-time leader. The splits were to be the cause of much demoralization in republican Spain in later years, and the baiting of Nin was to end in his assassination. Already in April 1931, only a few days after the overthrow of the monarchy, Trotsky protested in a confidential message to the Politbureau in Moscow against the heresy hunt in Spain. He recalled that in 1917 the Bolsheviks had, under Lenin's guidance, joined hands with all groupings close to them, regardless of past differences—he himself had then entered the Bolshevik

---

[1] *Écrits*, vol. III, pp. 451–71 and *passim*; B.O., nos. 21–22, 1931.

M

party—and they found that this, and their ability to base their unity and discipline on freedom of internal debate, decisively strengthened their hands in the struggle for power. 'Are there any other ways or methods', he asked, 'which would permit the proletarian vanguard of Spain to work out its ideas and to become permeated with the unshakeable conviction of the truth and justice of these ideas—a conviction which alone would enable them to lead the popular masses to the decisive assault on the old order?' The heresy hunts confused and demoralized the ranks and facilitated a fascist victory which would have 'grave repercussions for the whole of Europe and the U.S.S.R.' He asked the Politbureau to advise—'precisely to advise, not to order'—the Spanish communists to call a unity congress; and he offered to advise his followers to co-operate in this. 'The march of events in Spain will daily confirm the need for unity in communist ranks. A grave historic responsibility will burden those who promote the splits.'[1] There was no answer from Moscow to this message; but in it were laid bare the seeds of the defeat which the Spanish revolution was to suffer seven to eight years later.

.   .   .   .

At the height of these controversies Stalin deprived Trotsky of Soviet nationality and of the right ever to return to Russia. *Pravda* published a decree to this effect on 20 February 1932, giving as reason Trotsky's 'counter-revolutionary activity', without specifying his offences. This was an unprecedented reprisal. The Menshevik and Social Revolutionary émigrés, who sat on the leading bodies of the Second International and had, with the material and moral support of that International, conducted their agitation against the Bolsheviks, had not so far been deprived of Soviet nationality. To make good this omission and to conceal somewhat the real target, the decree of 20 February also stripped about thirty Menshevik émigrés of citizenship.

There was a studied malice in this 'amalgam'. Unlike Trotsky, the Menshevik leaders had not been deported: most of them were, in 1921–2, 'advised' to leave if they wished to avoid persecution; and they left. It was Lenin who decided to give them that 'advice'; and Trotsky undoubtedly endorsed the

[1] The letter to the Politbureau was published later in *B.O.* See *Écrits*, vol. III, pp. 447–8.

decision. His hostility towards the Mensheviks remained unabated even in exile and led him into a grievous error of judgement only a few months before the decree of 20 February.
In 1931, during the ill-famed trial of the Mensheviks, which
took place in Moscow, Trotsky accepted the prosecution's
charges against them at face value. The defendants Sukhanov,
Groman, and others were accused of economic sabotage and
conspiracy with their émigré comrades. The charges were
based on faked evidence and 'confessions'.[1] What accounted in
part for Trotsky's attitude was the element of truth in the
prosecution's assertion that the chief defendant, Groman,
formerly economic adviser to the State Planning Commission,
had sought to obstruct the first Five Year Plan. Groman had in
fact for a long time backed Stalin's and Bukharin's policy and
had strenuously opposed Trotsky's programme of industrialization. During his trial Trotsky commented that it was with
Stalin's connivance that Groman and his group had 'sabotaged'
the Soviet economy; and that only the 'left course' had brought
Stalin's connivance to an end and the Mensheviks to the dock.[2]
While these circumstances account for Trotsky's acceptance of
the prosecution's case, they do not justify it. Later Trotsky
himself publicly regretted his mistake.[3] But the incident
illustrates how intense his enmity towards the Mensheviks
remained; and one may well imagine with what perverse
pleasure Stalin pilloried both Trotsky and the Menshevik
'saboteurs' in the same decree simultaneously depriving them of
citizenship.

This event followed shortly after the somewhat enigmatic

[1] The Prosecutor alleged that the defendants had taken orders from R. Abramovich, the Menshevik émigré leader, and that the latter had come clandestinely
to Russia to inspect the conspiratorial organization. Abramovich was able to prove
that at the time when, according to the Prosecutor, he was supposed to have travelled in Russia, he was present at sessions of the Executive of the Second International in Brussels and spoke together with Leon Blum, Vanderwelde, and other
Social Democratic leaders from public platforms.

[2] Trotsky's first opinion on the trial of the Mensheviks is in *B.O.*, nos. 21–22,
1931. Thirty years later in July–September 1961, the Menshevik *Sotsialisticheskii
Vestnik* published N. Jasny's reminiscences on Groman which confirmed that
Groman's role in the struggle between the Bolshevik factions had indeed been such
as Trotsky described it, though he was, of course, innocent of the crimes imputed
to him.

[3] See *B.O.*, no. 51, July–August 1936. Trotsky was prompted by Lyova to
admit his mistake; and he did so shortly before the great Zinoviev–Kamenev trial.

'Turkul affair'. On 31 October 1931, *Rote Fahne* published an article alleging that General Turkul, an émigré who had commanded White Guards in the civil war, was about to organize an attempt on Trotsky's life, taking advantage of the fact that Trotsky was not guarded well enough on Prinkipo; and that if the attempt succeeded, the perpetrators would shift the blame on the Soviet Government. These allegations sounded plausible enough; but it was puzzling that the *Rote Fahne*, of all papers, should have come out with them. On Trotsky's prompting, his friends made representations at the Soviet Embassies in Berlin and Paris, reminding the Soviet Government that it had promised to protect his life in exile and asking what it was going to do to honour the pledge. Moscow left the query unanswered; and Trotsky concluded that *Rote Fahne* had had only one purpose: to provide an alibi for Stalin in case of an attempt. His followers then addressed to the Soviet Government a statement, showing clearly the marks of Trotsky's style, which affirmed that 'Stalin was concerned not to prevent the men of the White Guards carrying out their design, but only to prevent them shifting the responsibility for the terroristic act on Stalin and his agents'.[1] Stalin replied indirectly, through the Comintern, chiding Trotsky for the black ingratitude with which he repaid the solicitude he, Stalin, had shown him— the reply suggested that Trotsky's life was indeed threatened by the White Guards.[2] Stalin now punished the 'ingratitude' by rendering Trotsky stateless and depriving him even of the modicum of formal protection that any government owes its subjects in foreign parts.

The reprisal was intended to accomplish what the execution of Blumkin had failed to do, to cut off all contacts between Trotsky and his followers in the Soviet Union. Despite censorship and interception, Trotsky still received much mail from the colonies of deportees and from prisons. In Berlin, Lyova was trying to establish connexions with old comrades who arrived there on official business; and he reported to Prinkipo

---

[1] The message was despatched to Moscow confidentially. Trotsky published it only after he had been deprived of Soviet citizenship. *B.O.*, no. 27, March 1932.

[2] The reply took the form of a secret circular sent out by the Executive of the Comintern to the Central Committees of all Communist parties. A copy of the circular came into Trotsky's possession and is in *The Archives*, Closed Section.

on his successes and failures. Thus, in the spring of 1931, he ran by chance into Pyatakov; but that close friend of earlier years, now 'the Judas, the red-haired'—so Lyova wrote— 'turned away his head and pretended not to see me'. Later, in July, while wandering in one of the city's big stores, Lyova met unexpectedly Ivan Smirnov, who since his capitulation had held a high managerial post in Soviet industry. They embraced; Smirnov warmly inquired about Trotsky and all members of his family; and pouring out the capitulator's bitter heart, he spoke about the grim situation and the discontent rife in the Soviet Union. Although disillusioned in the hopes with which he had surrendered to Stalin, he was in no mood to resume the fight; he preferred to wait and see. He said, however, that he and his friends would welcome a 'bloc' with Trotsky and his followers, the immediate purpose of which was to be merely exchange of information. At the very least he wished to keep up a contact with Trotsky; and, as he was about to return to Moscow, he promised to send through a trusted friend a document surveying the state of the Soviet economy and the political moods in the country. They agreed on a password which the messenger was to use. Early in the autumn E. S. Golzman, an old Bolshevik, a capitulator, brought a memorandum from Smirnov, which was to appear in the *Bulletin Oppozitsii* a year later and to reveal, for the first time, the full extent of the destruction of agricultural stock during collectivization, the grave disproportions in industry, the effects of inflation on the whole economy, &c. The memorandum ended with this pregnant conclusion: 'In view of the incapacity of the present leadership to get out of the economic and political impasse, the conviction is growing about the need to change the party leadership.' Lyova and Golzman often met and discussed developments in the Soviet Union.[1]

Smirnov and Golzman spoke not only for themselves but for many capitulators who, timidly yet unmistakably, once again turned their eyes to Trotsky. Their anxiety was aroused by the storm gathering over Germany as well as by the domestic

[1] This account is based on Lyova's correspondence with his father, and on his deposition to the French Commission of Inquiry which, in 1937, conducted investigations preparatory to the Mexican counter-trial. *The Archives*, Closed Section.

situation. They were alarmed by the paralysis of German communism and sympathetically followed Trotsky's campaign. Most of them already thought what Radek was to express later, in 1933, when, speaking to a trusted German communist, he pointed to Stalin's office in the Kremlin and said: 'There sit those who bear the guilt for Hitler's victory.'[1] Seeing no way to change the Comintern's policy, exasperated and frustrated, the capitulators moved some way back towards the Trotskyist Opposition. This did not escape the notice of Stalin, who was more than ever bent on insulating the party from Trotsky's influence. He now regretted banishing Trotsky from Russia, for the banishment enabled Trotsky to broadcast his ideas all over the world. Stalin decided to make good this 'error': Trotsky, deprived of Soviet nationality, was branded as an outcast once and for all. Henceforth, any Soviet citizen trying to communicate with Trotsky would be guilty of association not just with a disgraced leader of a domestic opposition, but with a *foreign* conspirator.

Trotsky replied with an 'Open Letter' to the Presidium of the Central Executive Committee, in whose name the decree of 20 February was published.[2] He exposed the lawlessness of the decree (which he described as a 'consummate amalgam in the Thermidorian style', and 'an impotent and even pitiable' act of Stalin's personal vengeance); and he also drew the balance of a decade of the inner-party struggle. 'Do you think that with this false scrap of paper . . . you will stop the growth of Bolshevik criticism? Prevent us from doing our duty? Intimidate our co-thinkers? . . . The Opposition will step over the decree of 20 February as a worker steps over a dirty puddle on the way to his workshop.' He was aware that this reprisal was not Stalin's 'last word'. 'We know the arsenal of his methods . . . and you know Stalin as well as I know him. Many of you have more than once, in conversations with me or people close to me, given your own estimate of Stalin, and given it without illusions.' He was addressing Stalin's entourage, the 'men of the apparatus'. He appealed to their conscience, but also to their

[1] E. Wollenberg, a former editor of the *Rote Fahne* and leader of the *Rotfrontbund* writes in *The Red Army*, p. 278: 'Early in 1933 Zinoviev said to me: "Apart from the German Social-Democrats, Stalin bears the main responsibility to history for Hitler's victory" '.

[2] *B.O.*, no. 27, March 1932.

interest. He sought to persuade them that they too had nothing to gain but much to lose under Stalin's autocracy. He described tellingly the humiliation which together with the whole party they were suffering at Stalin's hands.

You started the fight against 'Trotskyism' under the banner of the Old Bolshevik Guard. To Trotsky's imaginary ambitions of personal leadership, ambitions which you yourselves had invented, you opposed the 'collective leadership of the Leninist Central Committee'. What remains of that collective leadership? What is left of the Leninist Central Committee? The apparatus, independent of the working class and of the party, has set the stage for Stalin's dictatorship which is independent of the apparatus. And now for anyone to take the oath of loyalty to the 'Leninist Central Committee' is almost the same as to call openly for insurrection. Only an oath of loyalty to Stalin may be taken—this is the only permitted formula. The public speaker, the propagandist, the journalist, the theorist, the educationist, the sportsman—all are obliged to include in their speeches, articles, or lectures the phrase . . . 'under Stalin's leadership'; all must proclaim the infallibility of Stalin who rides on the back of the Central Committee. Every party man and Soviet official, from the head of the government to the humble clerk in any backwater, has to swear. . . that in case of any differences arising between the Central Committee and Stalin, he, the undersigned, will support Stalin against the Central Committee.

Stalin was suppressing his own faction which had helped and was still helping him to suppress all his opponents. Within his own faction he had set up a narrower faction of his own, working through secret agents, passwords, codes, &c. He was desperately anxious to destroy the opposition to the end—hence the decree of 20 February—in order to be free to settle accounts with his own followers and his own entourage. The men of the 'apparatus' should therefore in their own interest refuse to do Stalin's bidding—only in this way could they save themselves.

Stalin's strength has always lain in the machine, not in himself. . . . Severed from the machine. . . . Stalin . . . represents nothing. . . . It is time to part with the Stalin myth. It is time that you should place your trust in the working class and its genuine, not its counterfeit, party. . . . You wish to proceed along the [Stalinist] road any further? But there is no road further. Stalin has brought you to an impasse. . . . It is time to bring under review the whole Soviet system and cleanse it ruthlessly from all the filth with which it has overgrown. It is time to carry out at last Lenin's final and insistent advice: 'Remove Stalin!'

It was emphatically to the chiefs of the Stalinist bureaucracy rather than to the Bolshevik rank and file that Trotsky was appealing here. Committed as he was to work for the reform of the ruling party, not for its overthrow, he had to appeal to them, because only the Central Committee, composed almost entirely of Stalinists, could start a reform in a constitutional manner. Trotsky was in effect prompting the chiefs of the old Stalinist faction to initiate—in 1932!—the de-Stalinization that some of them were to carry out twenty-odd years later, after Stalin's death. This appeal, though it was not to be heeded, was by no means pointless, for the conflict between Stalin and his old associates and followers was to end fatally for most of the latter. Trotsky, watching their conflict, was by no means inclined to belittle its significance, even though he played it down in some of his more exoteric writings. This, we know, was the most dangerous and gloomy moment in Soviet history, when the nation came to feel the full force of the calamity in agriculture and of famine, and when inflationary chaos threatened to disrupt its toilsome industrial advance. 'Adversities and frustrations piled up upon one another; Stalin's popularity was at its nadir. He watched tensely the waves of discontent rising and beating against the walls of the Kremlin', so we have described this moment elsewhere.[1] The discontent, it should be added, not only beat against the walls of the Kremlin; it breached them.

The discord between Stalin and his entourage had shown itself as early as 1930, when, in the statement 'On Dizziness from Success', he demonstratively disavowed the use of violence in collectivization and, over the head of the Central Committee, presented himself to the country as the peasantry's sole protector. The Central Committee protested; and Stalin had to tell the nation that the whole Committee and not he alone had called for a halt to the violence. The next dissension was occasioned by Yaroslavsky's temporary eclipse in the same year. Yaroslavsky was a pillar of the Stalinist faction, the most ferocious guardian of its orthodoxy, and the author of a textbook on party history, a feat of falsification which had been

---

[1] Deutscher, *Stalin*, p. 332.

hailed as a reliable guide through the doctrinal maze of the inner party struggle and had been crammed into the party's mind. It was precisely this textbook that now brought about Yaroslavsky's disgrace. Stalin suddenly found it teeming with heresies and ordered it to be banned. Yaroslavsky, having composed the book in the nineteen-twenties, could not carry falsification to the point that suited Stalin in 1931. The forger of history does not work in a vacuum: the scope he can give himself and the insolence he can afford depend on how large and heavy is the oblivion which time, indifference, and previous falsification have already cast on men and events; and in the nineteen-twenties, Yaroslavsky had to reckon with the fact that many of his readers still had relatively fresh memories of the years of revolution and civil war. In 1931 Stalin required forgeries far more massive. As he grew in sheer power, he required the cloth of history to be cut to his measure ever anew. A few years earlier it was enough for any Stalinist text to denounce Trotsky as a 'deviator' from Bolshevism and to hail Stalin as the reliable interpreter of Leninism. Now the writer of any textbook had to brand Trotsky as one who had always been a rabid counter-revolutionary; depict him as a traitor even at the time when he was President of the Petrograd Soviet and Commissar of War; make people forget that the villain had ever held such exalted posts; clothe Stalin with all splendour of which Trotsky had been stripped; and establish unquestionably the apostolic succession of Marx-Engels-Lenin-Stalin. It was not in the interest of the Stalinist faction at large, but only in that of Stalin's autocracy, that falsification should be carried to such extremes. Yaroslavsky's *History* had represented the Stalinists' viewpoint at the time when they still treated Stalin as their *primus inter pares*: it had therefore extolled Stalinism but had not glorified Stalin himself and the superhuman genius that entitled him to set himself above his own faction. Yaroslavsky had therefore to be struck down. But such was the dismay this caused even among Stalin's henchmen that soon his disgrace had to be lifted.[1]

More dramatic was the deposition, also in 1931, of Ryazanov from the post of Director of the Marx-Engels Institute. The

[1] The author was in Moscow at that time and heard many agitated expressions of that dismay from most 'orthodox' party members.

celebrated Marxian scholar had long since withdrawn from political activity and had, despite his old friendship with Trotsky, behaved towards Stalin with complete loyalty, devoting all his energy to the Institute's rich archives and library. Yet by his mere presence at the Institute he kept alive a scholarly tradition of classical Marxism just when Stalin was anxious to turn the Institute into a shrine of his personal cult. Ryazanov was therefore expelled and deported from Moscow under the pretext that he had plotted with the Mensheviks to suppress some of Marx's unpublished writings.[1]

Connected with these affairs was Stalin's notorious attack on the editors of *Proletarskaya Revolutsia*, whom he accused of trafficking in 'Trotskyist contraband'. The journal had published an historical essay on the pre-1914 Bolshevik attitude towards Rosa Luxemburg, duly acknowledging her revolutionary and Marxist merits. There was nothing unusual in this, for ever since Luxemburg's assassination in 1919, communists paid regular and solemn tribute to her memory; after 1924 the anniversaries of Lenin's, Luxemburg's, and Liebknecht's deaths were annually observed in a single solemn celebration of the 'Three L's'. Stalin now denounced Luxemburg's ideas as inherently hostile to Bolshevism and akin to Trotskyism. The kinship was undeniable; but hitherto the Stalinists had fought against the living leader of the Opposition, not against a ghost. Stalin came to suspect that in paying homage to the ghost they slyly aimed at rehabilitating Trotsky.

I think [he wrote] that the editors have been actuated by that rotten liberalism which is now fairly widespread among some Bolsheviks. Some think that Trotskyism is a school of thought within communism, a faction which has, to be sure, committed mistakes, done not a few silly things, and even behaved at times in an anti-Soviet manner; but that it is all the same a communist faction. It is hardly necessary to point out that such a view of

---

[1] Trotsky's defence of Ryazanov is in *B.O.*, nos. 21–22, May–June 1931. As director of the Marx-Engels Institute Ryaznov had done more than anyone to assemble at the Institute the papers of Marx and Engels. He obtained among other things a number of Marx's letters to Kautsky, which Kautsky yielded on condition that some of them, containing strictures of him, would not be published in his lifetime. Ryazanov, bound by his word, refrained from publishing these; and no one held this against him until Stalin needed a pretext for squeezing him out of the Institute and discrediting him.

Trotskyism is profoundly mistaken and harmful. Actually, Trotskyism is the spearhead of the counter-revolutionary bourgeoisie, waging
the struggle against communism. . . . Trotskyism is the vanguard of
the counter-revolutionary bourgeoisie. That is why liberalism towards it . . . borders on crime and on betrayal of the working
class.[1]

It was not only with the 'rotten liberalism' of his own
entourage that Stalin was at loggerheads. He had to contend
with more direct challenges. Within the Central Committee
and around it ever new groups of malcontents formed. The
affairs of Riutin, Slepkov, Syrtsov, and Lominadze had dragged
on for over two years now. All four had in turn been demoted,
denounced, half-rehabilitated, and once again branded as
conspirators. Stalin and the Central Committee could not agree
on just how guilty these men were and what was to be the
measure of their punishment. In 1932 several new 'conspiratorial factions' were unmasked, a group led by A. Smirnov, former
Commissar of Agriculture, Eysmont, a Commissar of Supplies,
and Tolmachev, a Transport Commissar; another group, that
of Konor, Kovarsky, and Vulf, was uncovered in the Commissariat of Agriculture; and 'networks of opposition' were
found to exist in the trade unions and various Commissariats.[2]
The leaders of these groups had not engaged in any real
conspiracy. Those of them who were members of the Central
Committee had merely exercised their statutory right in trying
to persuade their colleagues that Stalin's policies were pernicious, that he was guilty of abusing his power, and that the
Central Committee should depose him as its General Secretary.
They circulated memoranda to this effect and sought to obtain
the moral support of previous oppositions. Thus Riutin sought
Zinoviev's and Kamenev's advice; while Eysmont and Tolmachev appealed to Tomsky and Rykov. In the course of the
years 1931 and 1932 Stalin pressed the Politbureau and the
Central Committee to give him a free hand in dealing with these

[1] Stalin, *Sochinenya*, vol. XIII, pp. 98–99.
[2] Popov, N., *Outline History of the C.P.S.U.* (b), vol. II, pp. 391, 399, 418–19,
434; *K.P.S.S. v Rezolutsyakh*, vol. II, p. 742. The cases of all these 'deviationists'
were the subjects of various 'confessions' in the Moscow trials of 1937–8—see the
Verbatim Reports of the trials. See also Serge, *Mémoires d'un Révolutionnaire*, pp. 280–1,
and *B.O.*, no. 31 and *passim*.

critics. He met with resistance in the Committee; and even the
G.P.U. was reluctant to act.[1]

Only after many delays could he, in November 1932 and
January 1933, expel some of the malcontents and pronounce a
new excommunication on Zinoviev and Kamenev, who were
once again banished from Moscow, this time to Siberia.
During this, his second deportation, Zinoviev allegedly stated
that the greatest mistake of his life, greater even than his
opposition to Lenin during the days of the October revolution,
had been his decision to desert Trotsky and to capitulate to
Stalin in 1927. Soon thereafter Preobrazhensky, Ivan Smirnov,
Mrachkovsky, Muralov, Ter-Vaganyan, and many other
capitulators were once again expelled and imprisoned; they
were persecuted even more cruelly than the Oppositionists who
had never surrendered. Towards the end of the year it seemed
that the Opposition had regained the ground it had lost since
1927. A contemporary report thus describes the effect of the
persecution of the capitulators: 'These old revolutionaries,
experienced political leaders, have made an attempt to find a
common language with the men of the apparatus. The attempt
lasted nearly four years and has ended in failure. When they
capitulated the party cells were told that "all the old Bolsheviks
had broken with the Opposition". This argument undoubtedly
made a great impression. . . . Now the arrest of the [capitul-
ators] is making an even stronger impression, but in the
opposite direction: "Well", say many, "the Left Opposition
has been right after all, if so many of those who deserted it are
now returning to it." '[2] They were not in truth returning of their
own accord—Stalin drove them out of the party because he
feared their presence there during this early phase of his conflict
with his own followers and the disarray in his own entourage.
Just at the time of Zinoviev's and Kamenev's second deportation, Nadia Aliluyeva, Stalin's wife, committed suicide: she had
broken down under the burden of remorse at the way her
husband managed the affairs of party and state.

Such then were the circumstances in which Trotsky urged

[1] In his 'secret' speech at the Twentieth Congress N. Khrushchev made public a
telegram which Stalin and Zhdanov sent to the Politbureau on 25 September
1936, chiding the G.P.U. for being *four years behind* in 'unmasking' Trotskyist-
Zinovievist conspiracies. N. Khrushchev, *The Dethronement of Stalin*, p. 12.

[2] See Correspondence from Moscow in *B.O.*, no. 33.

Stalin's entourage to carry out at last Lenin's will and 'remove Stalin'. This was not on his part merely an impulsive reaction to the decree which deprived him of citizenship. He reckoned with the possibility that Stalin's autocratic ambition might at last shock the men of the ruling group and arouse them to act in their self-defence. When one considers that five or six years hence Stalin was to order the execution of 98 out of the 139 members and deputy members of the Central Committee (and of 1,108 out of the 1,966 delegates to the Seventeenth Party Congress) and thus to exterminate the majority of the *Stalinist* 'cadres', nearly three quarters of their élite, one may well admit that Trotsky, in addressing these cadres, had enough reason to invoke not only his, the Opposition's, and the party's interests, but also the dictates of their own self-preservation. 'Save yourselves—this is your last chance!' he said in effect to those Stalinists who were presently to become victims of Stalin's terror. He urged men like Khrushchev and Mikoyan to 'cleanse the Soviet state of the filth with which it was overgrown' twenty-four years before they were ready to start with this, and when there was still far less filth to be cleansed than there would be later. He knew, of course, that even if they decided to act against Stalin they would do so half-heartedly and would be held back by a thousand inhibitions. He nevertheless envisaged a 'united front' with them and offered them his critical support, confident that once the movement against Stalin was started, he and his followers would come to the fore.[1]

He did what he could to give heart to the Stalinist malcontents. Lyova, who from Berlin was in closer touch with the turmoil in Moscow, was especially eager that he should do so. Reports from Moscow continued to dwell on the exasperation among the Stalinists and on the talk about the need to 'remove Stalin'. But the same reports indicated that the Stalinist malcontents were terrified at the mere thought of Trotsky's return. 'If Trotsky came back', they said, 'he would shoot us all.' Or: 'He will revenge himself for all that we have done to him and his followers and he will put thousands of us before the firing squads.' Stalin played on this fear and whipped it up. 'This indicates along what line we ought to move', Trotsky

[1] Ibid., no. 27. During the year 1932 Trotsky often returned to this subject in his correspondence with Lyova.

wrote to his son. 'In no case should we frighten people with slogans or formulas which could be interpreted as expressing any intention . . . to take revenge. The closer the showdown . . . the softer and the more conciliatory should be the manner in which we speak, although we should not, of course, make any concessions of principle.'[1] In the *Bulletin* and in a special leaflet designed for circulation in Russia, Trotsky thus sought to reassure those who feared his revenge:

> An end must, of course, be put to the Bonapartist régime of a single leader whom every one is forced to worship—an end must be put to this shameful distortion of the idea of a revolutionary party. But what matters is that the system be changed not that individuals be ostracized. The Stalinist clique assiduously spreads the rumour that the Left Opposition will return . . . sword in hand, and that its first job will be to wreak ruthless revenge on its adversaries. . . . This poisoned lie must be repudiated. . . . Revenge is not a political sentiment. Bolsheviks-Leninists have never been guided by it; least of all shall we be guided by it. We know all too well the . . . causes that have driven tens of thousands of party men into the blind alley. . . . We are prepared to work hand in hand with everyone who is willing to reconstitute the party and forestall a catastrophe.[2]

However, this was the year 1932, not 1953 or 1956. Despite the signs that seemed to augur it, the movement against Stalin did not materialize. The 'men of the apparatus' were unable to act against their chief. The fear of Trotsky's return and revenge was not the most important of the inhibitions that held them back. It was the very decomposition of the Stalinist faction that rendered them incapable. Stalin dominated them by dividing them, setting up rival caucuses and forming his pretorian guard, the members of which knew no loyalty to erstwhile comrades and were willing to promote his personal rule. This was the 'secret staff' working through its own agents with 'secret passwords and codes' which Trotsky had mentioned; and these were the 'quintets', 'sextets', and 'septets' which, according to Khrushchev, Stalin set up within the Politbureau and the Central Committee and through which he reduced the latter to impotence. The arts which had gained him power did not fail to maintain it. He was able to spot any hostile stirring within the Central Committee before it had the

---

[1] Trotsky's letters to Lyova of 17, 24 and 30 October 1932.   [2] *B.O.*, no. 33.

time to spread. No group of malcontents, not even one composed of the most influential Stalinists, could voice any criticism and try to influence others in the hierarchy, for no sooner
had they tried than they were 'unmasked' and stigmatized as
traitors.

Yet the secret caucuses, the 'quintets', the 'sextets', and
Stalin's other conspiratorial devices would have counted for
little if the malcontents had not been paralysed by a fear that
had hamstrung all previous oppositions. They were afraid that
any move against Stalin might become the signal for an explosion of popular discontent and set the stage for a counter-
revolution which would engulf together with Stalin all his
Bolshevik adversaries. This fear haunted Trotsky as well. He
still saw no solution to the dilemma that had beset him in the
ninteen-twenties. Shortly after he had made his dramatic
appeal and concluded it with the words 'Remove Stalin', he
had second thoughts. In October 1932 he wrote to his son:

> The slogan 'remove Stalin' is correct in a definite, specific sense
> [the sense in which Lenin used it when he advised the Central
> Committee to elect another General Secretary]. . . . If we were
> strong now . . . there would be no danger at all in advancing this
> slogan. But at present Miliukov, the Mensheviks, and Thermidor-
> ians of all sorts . . . will willingly echo the cry 'remove Stalin'. Yet,
> it may still happen within a few months that Stalin may have to
> defend himself against Thermidorian pressure, and that we may
> have temporarily to support him. We have not yet left this stage
> behind us. . . . This being so, the slogan 'down with Stalin' is
> ambiguous and should not be raised as a war cry at this mo-
> ment. . . .[1]

At the same time Trotsky stated in the *Bulletin*: 'If the bureaucratic equilibrium in the U.S.S.R. [i.e. Stalin's rule] were to
be upset at present, this would almost certainly benefit the
forces of counter-revolution.'[2]

To the Stalinist malcontents in Moscow, not to speak of the
capitulators, this euphemism amounted to advising them to
hold their fire. If even Trotsky thought 'Down with Stalin'
was too hazardous, how much more risky must that cry have

---

[1] *The Archives*, Closed Section.

[2] *B.O.*, ibid. It is interesting to note that it was partly on Lyova's prompting that
Trotsky came out with this disavowal of the slogan 'Down with Stalin'.

sounded to them. What then were they to do? 'You wish to proceed along the Stalinist road any further? But there is no road further', Trotsky had told them in March. 'Stalin has brought you to an impasse.' They now learned that there was no way back either, and that all they could do was to try to survive in the impasse and hope that time and the nation's progress would lead them out of it. They concluded that in the meantime they had to bow to the inevitable; and they were to bow to it for over two decades, till Stalin's death.

.   .   .   .

Zinoviev or Kamenev had once told Trotsky that Stalin would revenge himself on him and his children and grand-children 'until the third and fourth generation'. Now indeed the biblical vengance struck Trotsky's family. The decree which deprived him of Soviet nationality robbed of it also those of his relatives who shared his exile; and it forbade them to return to the Soviet Union. This immediately affected Zina. She found herself cut off from her husband and younger child, and without the hope of ever being able to rejoin them.

She had now spent over four months in the German capital. The unfamiliar city and its political drama at first so engrossed her that to her doctors' satisfaction she appeared to recover her balance. The improvement was superficial, and the doctors may have been misled by a patient too proud to reveal to them her disturbed mind. She stubbornly resisted psychoanalytical investigation. 'The doctors have only confused me,' she con-fessed later, 'but I have confused them, poor creatures, much more. . . .' Her emotional strains were undiminished. Her adoration for her father was still at odds with her grievance. In her thoughts and correspondence she returned to their last parting: she resented its strange coolness and his remoteness and Olympian superiority. She brooded over his words: 'You are an astonishing person, I have never met anyone like you'; and she pined over their uncomprehending severity. She yearned for warmer contact by correspondence; but he wrote rarely, more rarely, at any rate, than she wished; and in his letters, though full of concern for her, she still felt him frigid and distant.

There was also her discord with Lyova. She could not get

along with him even though there was no one in Berlin closer
to her, and even though their father begged them to sustain
each other in their plight. She reproached Lyova too with
lack of compassion; and the mere sight of him aroused all
her agonizing jealousy. 'Every time I see him', she wrote very
shortly after she had come to Berlin, 'I suffer a nervous breakdown.'[1] She avoided meeting him; and he was, anyhow, too
busy with his political work and the *Hochschule*. His very busyness,
which came from his close bonds with their father, excited her
envy: she contrasted it with her own 'passivity and uselessness'
and despised herself as 'Zina the idler'.

The *ukase* which deprived her of the prospect of a return to
Russia sharpened her loneliness and insecurity. Her father
advised her to protest at the Soviet Embassy, calmly and
moderately: perhaps if they realized in Moscow that she was
not engaged in political activity but only trying to repair her
health, they might exempt her from the decree.[2] We do not
know whether she acted on this advice; she did not, in any case,
regain her nationality. Meanwhile, her doctors reached the
conclusion that to recover she should rejoin her family in Russia
and resume as soon as possible a normal existence in her proper
environment. This was precisely what she could not do. An
outcast, lonely in the huge and alien city, feeling estranged from
one half of her family, and reproaching herself with having
abandoned the other, her nervous breakdowns and fits of
absent-mindedness became more frequent. She had no choice
but to return reluctantly to the psychoanalyst's couch, from
which she emerged to stare at the vast political lunacy that was
overtaking the nation in whose midst fate had thrown her.

In her letters she described the misery and the torment of
Germany, interspersing her descriptions with acute political
observations and mordant *Galgenhumor*. When she first wrote to
her father to tell him how worried she was at being cut off
from Russia and her next of kin there, she told him also that she
was quite as much depressed by the 'Red plebiscite' and the
confusion and demoralization in the German working class.[3]

---

[1] See e.g., Zina's letters and postcards to her father of 26 February, 30 May,
7 June 1932.
[2] See Trotsky's correspondence with his children of March 1932.
[3] See her letter of 26 February 1932.

She followed eagerly Trotsky's 'German campaign'; but the gratification this gave her was spoiled by the sense that she was excluded from his work and political interests: 'There is no purpose in corresponding with Papa . . . the doubting Thomas', she said in a letter. 'He is further and further above the clouds in the regions of high policy . . . and I am mostly stuck in psychoanalytical swinishness'.[1] Her own vision of the political turmoil was heightened by the convulsive insight of the insane eye. There are phrases in her correspondence as rich and sarcastic as if they had come from the pen of her own father. Like a refrain there occurs an image of Berlin, hungry and drunken, full of the tramping of heavy boots, and swelling up with despair and bloodthirstiness. 'Berlin is singing . . . all the time, often in a voice hoarse with drunkenness or hunger. . . . This is a gay city, very gay indeed. . . . And think only that old Krylov was so rash as to say that no one would ever sing on an empty stomach.'[2]

The doom-laden city bewitched her; she became attached to it as if she belonged to it; she lived through all its tremblings and fevers. Early in June 1932, when Hitler's Stormtroops, unscathed by Brüning's ban, re-emerged in riotous triumph, Lyova urged her to leave Berlin, to go to Vienna, and there, in a calmer atmosphere, to continue the psychoanalytical cure. Himself inconvenienced by the police, he feared that she too would be troubled. She resented the advice, dismissed the fears, and complained to Prinkipo that Lyova bossed and bullied her. When her father repeated Lyova's advice, she answered in a strangely reverential tone, saying that she did not even dare to protest; but then she dwelt on her fondness for Berlin and refused to budge. Even her father's and brother's concern humiliated her. Had not her father said so many times that the fate of Europe, nay, of mankind, was being decided in Berlin for decades ahead? Was this not why he had wished Lyova to be on the spot? Had he not refused to accept a German Trotskyist as a secretary, saying that it would be a shame if at such a time a single one of his followers absented himself from the political battlefield? Why then should she be asked to leave? She felt rejected and degraded.[3]

As loneliness was grinding her down, the doctors asked that

[1] Letter of 30 May.   [2] Letters of 7 June and 17 August 1932.   [3] Ibid.

at least the child she had left on Prinkipo should be brought
to her to occupy her mind and give her some responsibility.
But the child, too, was affected by the decree of 20 February:
at the age of six Seva was a 'stateless political émigré', officially
registered as such—a problem for consular dispensers of travelling permits and visas. Applications were turned down on the
ground that he could travel only with one of his parents or
grandparents. The child had been badly upset by his mother's
absence and by her messages imploring him not to forget
her and promising that she would return very soon—it was
with difficulty that she was persuaded not to send such messages.
Now the expectation of a reunion and the suspense put on edge
the child's nerves—and the nerves of the whole family.

In her distress Zina was less and less able to look after herself,
even to manage reasonably her monthly allowance and
expenses.[1] She reproached herself with being a burden to her
father; and she moved to a low-grade boarding-house, where
she lived among tramps and rowdies, and often had to stand
between them, and separate them when they came to
blows. Any attempt by her brother or even father to get her
out of such circumstances and to manage her money affairs for
her aroused her resentment and provoked nervous attacks.
After one breakdown she wrote an angry postcard to her father
blaming him for the attack and asking to be left in peace.[2]

Zina's sufferings and the strain they put on Trotsky did something to trouble his relations with Lyova, whom he expected to
show more patience and affection towards her. Yet his reliance
and dependence on Lyova grew ever stronger and more
vulnerable. He lavished praise for the way he managed the
Bulletin and the political work; and he went on confiding his
thoughts, consulting him, and inviting criticism. He was
touched by Lyova's self-denial and dedication, of which he
had a thousand proofs. (Again and again he remonstrated with
Lyova for being over-scrupulous with money accounts and
spending his living allowance on the *Bulletin*.[3]) Yet again and
again he suspected that the concord in their views and ideas

---

[1] This is how Lyova described her condition in a letter to his father of 26 November 1932.

[2] Zina to Trotsky, 5 and 24 October 1932.

[3] See, for instance, Trotsky's letter of 11 May 1932.

sprang from filial piety only, that filial piety which he found so gratifying and so irritating. The more tense and weary he became, the more exacting, even whimsical, grew the demands he made on his son. His loneliness and isolation, as Natalya put it, showed itself in the impatience with which he awaited letters from Lyova. When for a few days there was no mail from Berlin he exploded with anger, accused Lyova of indifference, and even insulted him; then he grew angry with himself, full of pity for his son, and even more fretful.[1]

Lyova's pack of personal troubles was also heavy enough. From Moscow his wife wrote harrowing letters about their broken lives and their child's unhappiness. He had gone abroad despite her protests and tears, she reminded him, in order to be with his parents and protect his father; now he was neither with his parents nor with his wife and child. It was no use trying to explain to her what his lot would have been in Russia—she was a simple working woman, ill, poverty-stricken, and in despair; and she threatened to commit suicide.[2] He could do nothing to relieve her plight, except to send her money. Nor did his liaison with Jeanne Molinier turn out to be much happier. Only devotion to his father's cause helped him to get away from his private worries and frustrations. Unflinchingly he carried out the thousand-and-one instructions from Prinkipo; kept in touch with all the scattered Trotskyist groups; harassed the Russian printers to bring out the *Bulletin* on time; saw to it that his father's topical brochures were promptly translated into German and published; bargained with literary agents; and for hours roamed, often hungry, the streets of Berlin in the hope of meeting a countryman on assignment abroad or a western tourist *en route* to Russia, through whom a piece of information could be obtained or a message transmitted. On top of this, he followed pedantically his course in mathematics and physics; and in the small hours of the night he conversed with his parents by correspondence. Nothing made him feel more wretched than his father's ill-humour or any intimation that his efforts did not come up to expectations. He

---

[1] The description is based on Natalya's correspondence, especially her letter to Lyova of 27 July 1932 in the Closed Section of *The Archives*.

[2] Her letter to this effect is among the family correspondence in the Closed Section of *The Archives*.

found it hard to dispel paternal displeasure, to explain himself, to ask for an explanation, or to apologize; it was only to his mother that he grieved and complained.

Natalya, frail and suffering, caught in the dangerous tangle of Zina's emotions, and torn sometimes between husband and son, did what she could. She had enough insight to grasp clearly the predicament of each of them, enough love to feel with each, and enough fortitude to try and sustain each. In her letters she explained to Lyova Zina's problem, and again and again she conveyed to both Lyova and Zina the unbearable tension in which their father lived, presenting all the time a heroic front to a hostile world—what was the wonder that now and then within the family circle his endurance snapped? 'The trouble with father, as you know, is never over the great issues, but over the tiny ones'. In the great problems his patience was infinite; over trivialities he was easily annoyed and even petulant. This, she begged the children, must never make them forget or doubt his deep and passionate love for them. 'Your pain is the pain of all three of us', she wrote to Lyova, imploring him to write more often to father, and to write 'inspiring' letters, and also to give Zina more warmth and attention. Yet at times the blows were too heavy even for Natalya's vigilant fortitude. 'What is to be done—nothing can be done', these resigned words occur not rarely in her letters to Lyova; and once she confessed to him: 'I am writing as you are, with my feelings closed and my eyes closed.'[1]

.   .   .   .

This was the late summer of 1932. It was now three and a half years since Trotsky had arrived in Prinkipo. All this time he had worked hard, pursuing his various interests, neglecting none of his correspondents, filling the pages of the *Bulletin*, and writing, apart from a dozen minor books and brochures, *My Life* and the three large volumes of the *History*. (He sent out the last Appendix closing the third volume to Alexandra Ramm on 29 June.) These had been years of prodigious labour, all the more so because, spurning easy writing, he had repeatedly redrafted almost every chapter of every one of his books, slaving patiently over every page and almost every phrase.

[1] Many of Natalya's letters are undated.

The great toil had tired him. His head was full of new literary plans: he intended to write a History of the civil war, a Life of Lenin, a joint Life of Marx and Engels, and other books. But circumstances did not favour his settling down to a major work; and he needed a rest. More than ever he chafed at his confinement to Prinkipo[1]; and political events made him restless. The trickle of news that was coming out of Russia was just enough to exasperate him. In Germany socialists and communists were moving along their beaten tracks at the very brink of disaster. His campaign was making no impact. The strength of the Trotskyist group there was less than negligible. And in the Opposition's international organization trouble was brewing: in its Berlin Secretariat the brothers Sobolevicius, who had only recently supported him in his controversy against the ultra-left Leninbund, now adopted a disquietingly conciliatory attitude towards Stalinism. Oh, if only he could get away from his enchanted and accursed island and find himself closer to the main currents of political life and to—civilization!

Early in the autumn Danish Social Democratic students invited him to come to Copenhagen and lecture on the fifteenth anniversary of the October Revolution. He had received quite a few such invitations before; but there had never been any chance of his being allowed to appear anywhere in Europe.[2] He doubted whether the Danish Social-Democratic Government would give him a visa, but this time he accepted the invitation. When he received the visa, he was at once ready for the journey. At the back of his mind was a vague hope that he might not need to return, although he was prudent enough to secure the Turkish re-entry permit. He and Natalya also hoped to be able to take Seva to Copenhagen, and from there to send him to Zina. But they could not obtain travelling permits for the child; and they had to leave him at Prinkipo under the care of one of the secretaries.

On 14 November, accompanied by Natalya and three secretaries, Trotsky sailed from Constantinople. He registered as Mr. Sedov, a stateless passenger; but his incognito could not

[1] During all his Prinkipo years Trotsky went out to Constantinople only once or twice to visit the Basilica of St. Sophia and to see a dentist.

[2] *Inter alia* a group of Edinburgh students asked him for permission to put forward his candidature in the elections of a Rector of their University—he politely declined the honour. (*The Archives.*)

shield him from public curiosity—it only thickened the aura
of mystery and scandal that surrounded him. *Pravda*, paraphrasing Bernard Shaw, jeered at the 'escaped lion'; and the jeer
unintentionally conveyed something of the nervousness with
which governments, police headquarters, and the Press of
many countries watched his progress. Had he traversed Europe
as the head of a real and powerful conspiracy, and had multitudes of followers hailed him, his journey could not have
aroused more commotion than it did, when he travelled as an
outcast, denied the protection of any government, and accompanied only by an elderly ailing woman and a few young
devotees; and when his sole set purpose was to deliver a lecture.
Wild rumour ran ahead. Newspapers speculated on the real
purpose of his trip; they had no doubt that the lecture was a
mere pretext: some said that he was to meet secretly an envoy of
Stalin somewhere in Europe; others that he was about to
mount his final conspiracy against Stalin. At Greek and Italian
ports of call reporters besieged him, but he refused to talk to
them. He was not allowed to visit Athens. At Naples he left
ship and under police escort visited the ruins of Pompeii. The
French forbade him to disembark at Marseilles; out at sea
their police ordered him to transfer to a small motor-boat
which took him to a forsaken little jetty outside Marseilles,
where he landed. He was rushed through France by car and
train, with only one hour's stop in Paris, so that reporters who
pursued him all the way from Marseilles were able to pick up
his trail only at Dunkirk, where he boarded a ship for Denmark.
Across France he was followed by the curses of right-wing
newspapers, whose leader writers were beside themselves at the
thought that the 'traitor of Brest Litovsk', the man who had
'robbed of their savings the widows and orphans' of French
rentiers, should have been allowed to set foot on French soil.
He tried to calm the excitement and assured reporters that he
was on 'a strictly private journey, devoid of all political
significance'.[1]

On 23 November he arrived in Denmark and was ordered to
disembark at Esbjaerg so as to be 'brought to Copenhagen by a
backstairs entrance', as *Politiken* put it. A crowd of communists

[1] His statements to the French Press of the 21 and 22 November 1932. *The
Archives.*

had come to boo and hiss him; but, according to the same paper, 'the moment Trotsky showed himself there was a deep silence—the sense of a historic personality and perhaps of a historic occasion'[1]. Reporters noted Trotsky's 'perfect calm' and the nervousness of his secretaries and of the organizers of the trip. He had hardly entered Copenhagen when a member of the Royal family, Prince Aage, echoed by a section of the Press, denounced 'the murderer of the Tsar's family': the Danish Court had not forgotten that the mother of the last Tsar had been a Danish princess. At the same time the Soviet Ambassador expressed his government's concern over the visit. The Social Democrats gave Trotsky a warm welcome; but the warmth did not last. As both the Royal family and the Soviet Embassy continued to vent displeasure, the embarrassed Socialist Ministers became impatient for his early departure.

Trotsky did his best to keep out of public sight. He stayed in somewhat eccentric surroundings, in a villa Raymond Molinier had hired from a famous danseuse who was away on a tour—the rooms were crammed with trinkets and the walls covered with alluring pictures of the absent hostess. Then a newspaper disclosed Trotsky's whereabouts by publishing a photograph of the villa; and so he and his companions hurriedly moved away to a pension in a suburb. There were various minor incidents. Molinier's car, which Trotsky used, vanished mysteriously. After a few hours the police returned it without an explanation and took the owner's . . . fingerprints. There were rumours that Trotsky's enemies were preparing to disrupt the meeting at which he was to lecture. And all the time he was guarded by the police as well as by his followers; only once or twice did he go out for short drives through the city.

The lecture passed without obstruction or disturbance. For two hours, speaking in German, he addressed an audience of about 2,000 people. His theme was the Russian Revolution. As the authorities had allowed the lecture on the condition that he would avoid controversy, he spoke in a somewhat professorial manner, giving his listeners the quintessence of the three volumes of his just concluded *History*. His restraint did not conceal the depth and force of his conviction; the address was a

[1] *Politiken*, 24 November 1932; see also *Berlingske Tidende* and *Informacion*, of the same date.

vindication of the October Revolution, all the more effective because free of apologetics and frankly acknowledging partial failures and mistakes. Nearly twenty-five years later members of the audience still recalled the lecture with vivid appreciation as an oratorical feat.[1] This, incidentally, was the last time that Trotsky addressed any large public meeting in person.

Of his other activities in Copenhagen his interviews and a broadcast in English to the United States may be mentioned. 'My English, my poor English', he said in the broadcast, 'is in no proportion to my admiration for Anglo-Saxon culture.' Against those who, dwelling on retrograde developments in the Soviet Union (and on his own fate), denied the *raison d'être* of the October Revolution, he pointed out that 'in criticism as in creative activity perspective is needed'. The fifteen years since October were only 'a minute on the clock of history'. The American Civil War too had outraged contemporaries. Yet 'out of the Civil War came the present United States, with its unbounded practical initiative, its rationalized technology, its economic *élan*. These achievements . . . will [form] part of the basis for the new society.'[2] He told American interviewers that although the 1929 slump had hit their country so severely, the position of the United States *vis-à-vis* the rest of the capitalist world was strengthened. He declared to French reporters that he would never refuse Stalin his collaboration, if the defence of the Soviet Union required it: '*La politique ne connaît ni ressentiment personnel ni l'ésprit de vengeance. La politique ne connaît que l'éfficacité.*'[3]

Four years later, during the Great Purges and at the trial of Zinoviev, Kamenev, and others, the prosecution was to base a crucial part of its case against Trotsky and the defendants on the allegation that it was from Copenhagen, in this last week of November 1932, that he pulled the strings of a gigantic conspiracy and ordered his adherents to assassinate Stalin, Voroshilov, and other members of the Politbureau, to sabotage industry, to poison masses of Russian workers, and to wreck

[1] In 1956, I lectured in Copenhagen, and was approached by quite a few members of the audience who spoke to me about the memorable meeting of 1932 at which they had been present.

[2] He made the statement for the Columbia Broadcasting System. The Danish Radio had refused to broadcast his lecture. *The Archives.*

[3] Ibid.

the country's economic and military power in order to restore capitalism. According to Vyshinsky, the Prosecutor-General, it was in Copenhagen that, in the presence of his son, Trotsky received Golzman, Fritz David, and Berman Yurin, three men who sat behind Zinoviev and Kamenev in the dock, and through them transmitted his orders. There is no need to refute here in detail these accusations and the defendants' 'confessions' by which they were supported. Stalin's successors, who upheld these accusations for twenty years, no longer do so; at the 20th and 22nd Congresses of the Soviet Communist party, Khrushchev, still haunted by Trotsky's ghost, described how such charges were concocted and how such 'confessions' were produced. Even much earlier, during the trials, Trotsky knocked the bottom out of the prosecution's case by exposing its absurdities and contradictions. Thus the Hotel Bristol, which Vyshinsky was imprudent enough to name as Trotsky's headquarters in Copenhagen, did not exist in 1932, having been demolished many years earlier. Lyova, whom Vyshinsky depicted as acting in Copenhagen as chief of staff to the leader of the terrorists, was not with his father in the Danish capital. Trotsky was able to reconstruct every incident of his trip to Denmark from his pedantically systematic records, and also to call numerous eye-witnesses to testify in his favour.[1]

His entourage in Copenhagen was larger than usual. Apart from the three secretaries who had come with him, twenty-five of his followers, Germans, Frenchmen, Italians, and others had arrived, among them Molinier, Naville, Sneevliet, and Gerard Rosenthal, Trotsky's French attorney. A group of students from Hamburg had come to meet him and guard him. Another visitor was Oscar Cohn, an eminent German lawyer, Karl Liebknecht's associate, who acted as Trotsky's attorney in Germany. The presence of so many followers gave Trotsky an opportunity to hold an informal 'international conference', at which they discussed the situation in Germany and the affairs of the various Trotskyist groups. Nothing could be less like a meeting of conspirators than this little gathering of thrilled and rather garrulous devotees of an ineffectual sect. 'Everyone talked endlessly', says the only British participant, 'except Trotsky, who worked hard nearly all the time in his room, either

---

[1] *The Case of Leon Trotsky*, pp. 135–73 and Closed Section of *The Archives*.

writing or dictating something.'[1] Five years later every one of those present, if he was not in a Nazi prison or concentration camp, was to testify that none of the men who, according to Vyshinsky, took orders from Trotsky in Copenhagen, was there or could have slipped unnoticed through the numerous guards. The only man with a Russian connexion whom Trotsky received was Senin-Sobolevicius. He had come to clear himself of the suspicion of being a Stalinist agent, and he spent an hour or two with Trotsky, who treated him not as an *agent provocateur* but as a political opponent: in their correspondence Sobolevicius had frankly and in part correctly criticized Trotsky for underrating Stalin's industrial achievement and the lasting effects of collectivization. As far as one can judge from their subsequent letters, their meeting in Copenhagen ended in a patching up of differences. In any case, Sobolevicius was not to appear as witness at any of the Moscow trials. Nor did he, apparently, make any other contribution to the trials, for if he had done so, he would have given the prosecution a description of Trotsky's surroundings in Copenhagen far more realistic than that which Vyshinsky presented.

Trotsky's stay in Denmark was thus rather uneventful. After his public lecture he spoke only once to a small group of the Danish students who had invited him. His host has recorded this curious incident:

Trotsky and five or six others were in my home when suddenly I had a telephone call from a friend, who told me that a newspaper had just come out with a telegram from Moscow that Zinoviev had died. Trotsky rose, deeply moved . . . 'I have fought against Zinoviev . . .', he said. 'In some matters I was united with him. I know his mistakes, but at this moment I will not think about them, I will think only about the fact that throughout he tried to work for the labour movement. . . .' Trotsky continued to honour in eloquent phrases the memory of his dead adversary and co-fighter . . . it was very moving to hear his solemn speech in this little group.[2]

No outsider, not even Trotsky's friends and secretaries, was

---

[1] The British participant, to whom I am obliged for his impressions, was Mr. Harry Wicks. He was to try to transmit Trotsky's writings to the U.S.S.R. through Russian sailors calling at British ports; and Trotsky gave him a letter authorizing him to do so.

[2] *The Case of Leon Trotsky*, p. 147. The rumour about Zinoviev's death was denied next day.

aware of the frustration and pain he lived through in Copenhagen. It was galling enough for him to have to cross the whole
of Europe, with all the precautions this required and amid all
the hostile uproar, only in order to deliver a lecture in Denmark
and then to have to go back to Prinkipo. He made piteous
efforts to postpone return, if not to escape it. To American
journalists he remarked wistfully how much he would have liked
to be able for a time to 'watch the world panorama from New
York', which would be like surveying a horizon 'from the top
of a skyscraper'. 'Is it a Utopian dream, I ask you, to think that
I should be able to work in one of the great American libraries
for two or three months? The good example set by the Danish
Government will not, I hope, be wasted on other countries.'[1]
That 'example' was far from edifying, however: the Danish
Government refused him any short-term asylum. In vain did
Oscar Cohn appeal to Stauning, the Socialist Prime Minister
and Cohn's personal friend; in vain did Trotsky himself request
Stauning for a prolongation of the visa for a fortnight only so
that he and his wife could undergo medical treatment in
Copenhagen. In vain did he also appeal for a Swedish visa.
This was refused him, allegedly because of objections from the
Soviet Ambassador, none other than Alexandra Kollontai,
former leader of the Workers' Opposition.

More oppressive than the hermetic hostility into which he
had run afresh was the worry about Zina, whose health was
going from bad to worse. It was probably during his Danish
trip that Trotsky received this lurid letter which sounds like
an accusatory farewell: 'You act . . .' she wrote to him, 'too
impatiently and therefore sometimes impetuously. Do you
know the meaning of something as complex and yet as elementary as instinct—something one must not trifle with . . .?
Who says that instinct is blind . . .? That is not true. Instinct
has terribly keen eyes which see in the dark . . . and overcome
time and space—it is not for nothing that instinct is the memory
of generations and begins where life itself starts. It may direct
itself to all sorts of purposes. What is most frightful is that it hits
infallibly and mercilessly those who are in its way.' She dwelt
on the 'premonitions', the 'suspicious imaginings', and the
'terribly sharpened sensitivity' that make out instinct; and she

[1] From a statement for American journalists in *The Archives*.

went on: 'It will not frighten you if I tell you that there was a moment when I felt that something like this touched me; but with a terrible frenzy, I threw myself into the struggle. And no one supported me. The doctors have only confused me . . . do you know what sustained me? *Faith in you*. Despite all that was so plain and obvious, despite everything. . . . And is this not instinct?'[1]

Lyova was to have come to Copenhagen in order, among other things, to consult his parents about Zina; but insuperable passport and visa difficulties detained him in Berlin. Meanwhile, he was sending alarming letters about Zina's behaviour: her mind was getting more and more deranged; she would not be able to look after Seva, if they sent him to her; and she was less and less able to look after herself. He was uneasy about her erratic politics: she had apparently entered into contact with the German Communist party; and he was afraid that she would expose herself to police persecution. 'Don't you see, don't you see', she was telling him, in the days after Papen's resignation, 'that Germany is now heading straight towards a [communist] revolution?'[2] He advised his parents to do their utmost to send her away to Austria. Day after day, and some-times twice daily, either Trotsky or Natalya anxiously talked with Lyova over the telephone, asking for further news, inquiring whether the doctors too considered it unsafe to entrust Zina with the care of her child, and urging Lyova to come to Copenhagen.

Eight days passed in this way; those days, the world was presently to be told, that Trotsky had used to stage his mon-strous conspiracy against the Soviet Government. He spent these days 'conspiring' against the tyranny with which ordinary passport and visa regulations confront the stateless and the homeless. He employed every influence and accidental circum-stance, every innocent stratagem and trick of publicity to gain a few more weeks or even days in Denmark, or elsewhere in Europe. Meanwhile, Natalya appealed to Edouard Herriot the French Prime Minister, begging him to allow Lyova to meet her in France while she and Trotsky were on their way

---

[1] The letter is undated, but internal evidence indicates that it was written in November 1932.

[2] Quoted from Lyova's letter to his parents of 26 November 1932.

back to Turkey. As the eight days, for which Trotsky's Danish visa was granted, were up, he declared that he had missed his boat and was not yet ready to leave. Perhaps, he thought Lyova would arrive while he was waiting for the next boat? Perhaps they would make up their minds whether and how to send the child to Zina? Perhaps, perhaps the heart of some government would melt and a visa would be obtained somewhere on this inhospitable continent? But the Danish Ministry insisted that his time was up and that he must go; and they rushed him out of the country by car so that he should embark before his visa expired. And so, on 2 December, Trotsky, Natalya, and the secretaries left Denmark. This time no one booed or hissed from the quay, and no one had come to say farewell, either.

.　　.　　.　　.　　.　　.　　.　　.　　.

As the ship sailed into Antwerp, the harbour was black with police and cordoned off. Frontier guards came on board to interrogate Trotsky; he refused to answer questions, saying that, as he was not disembarking in Belgium, the interrogation was illegal. There was a wrangle; there were threats of arrest; and none of his companions was allowed to go ashore.

At this moment a memory ten years old came back to him. In 1922, when Dora Kaplan was tried in Moscow for her attempt on Lenin's life, Emil Vanderwelde, the famous Belgian Socialist and President of the Second International, asked to be admitted as Counsel for the defence. His request was granted; and Vanderwelde used the opportunity to attack, in a Soviet court, the Soviet system of government. He did the same in an Open Letter to Trotsky. Having left the Letter unanswered in 1922, Trotsky decided to answer it now, while his ship was in Belgian waters. Vanderwelde had in the meantime been his King's Prime Minister, and even in opposition occupied a most exalted place in Belgian politics.

The government of which I was a member [Trotsky wrote to him] allowed you not only to come to the Soviet Union but even to act in court as attorney for those who had attempted to assassinate the leaders of the workers' first state. In your plea of defence, which we published in our press, you repeatedly invoked the principles of democracy. That was your right. On 4 December 1932 I and my companions stopped in transit at Antwerp harbour. I have no intention of preaching proletarian dictatorship here, or of acting as defence council for any imprisoned Belgian communists and strikers, who, as far as I know, have not made any attempt on the lives of Ministers. [Yet] the part of the harbour where our ship stopped has been thoroughly cordoned off. On both sides, right and left, police boats are on the alert. From our deck we have had the opportunity to review a parade of democracy's police agents. . . . This has been an impressive spectacle! There are more cops and *flics* here—excuse my using such vulgar terms for brevity's sake—than sailors and stevedores. Our ship looks like a temporary prison, and the adjacent part of the harbour like a prison yard.[1]

He knew, of course, that this reception and the vexations which went with it 'were triflings compared with the persecution which militant workers and communists commonly suffered'; he mentioned the facts only to give Vanderwelde the long-overdue answer to his 1922 philippic about Bolshevism and democracy:

I am not mistaken, I trust, in counting Belgium among the democracies. The war [of 1914–18] which you have fought was a war for democracy, was it not? Since the war you have been at the head of Belgium as Minister and Prime Minister. What more has been needed to bring democracy to fruition? . . . Why then does this your democracy reek so much of the old Prussian police state? How can anyone suppose that a democracy, which suffers a nervous shock when a Bolshevik by chance approaches its frontiers, that such a democracy may ever be able to neutralize class struggle and guarantee the peaceful transformation of capitalism into socialism?

Oh yes, he, Trotsky, knew all about the G.P.U. and political persecution in the Soviet Union. But the Soviet Government had at least not boasted of democratic virtues; it openly identified itself with a proletarian dictatorship; and the sole test by which it should be judged was whether it secured the transition from capitalism to socialism.

The dictatorship has its own methods and its own logic, which are rather severe. Not rarely . . . revolutionaries who had established the dictatorship are themselves the victims of its logic. . . . Before class enemies, however, I assume full responsibility not only for the October revolution . . . but even for the Soviet Republic such as it is

[1] *B.O.*, no. 32, December 1932.

to-day, including that government which has banished me and deprived me of Soviet citizenship. [But] you—you are defending capitalism allegedly in the name of democracy. Where then is that democracy? It was in any case not to be found at Antwerp harbour.

For all that, he was leaving the waters of Antwerp 'without the slightest pessimism'. He had before his eyes the picture of 'sturdy, severe Flemish dockers, thickly covered with coal-dust', who, separated from his boat by a police cordon, 'eyed the scene in silence, took the measure of everyone', recognized 'their own', winked ironically at the cops, exchanged friendly smiles with the dangerous passenger on deck, and 'with their gnarled fingers touched their caps' in greeting. 'When the steamer sailed down the Scheldt in the mist, past cranes brought to a standstill by the economic crisis, farewell shouts of unknown yet faithful friends resounded from the quay. Finishing these lines between Antwerp and Flüssingen, I send fraternal greetings to the workers of Belgium.'

.   .   .   .

On 6 December, Trotsky and Natalya alighted in Paris, at the Gare du Nord, where they were again surrounded by a strong police cordon and separated from the crowd of passengers. Waiting for them there was Lyova: Herriot had granted Natalya's request. At the frontier Trotsky had been told that in Marseilles he would have to wait nine days for a boat to Constantinople. He rejoiced at the delay. Molinier rented accommodation near Marseilles; and Trotsky asked friends to come there and spend the few days with him. But no sooner had he arrived at Marseilles than the police told him that he could not stay even a single day and must board at once an Italian cargo vessel which happened to be leaving that night. He embarked under protest; but having found out that the vessel had no passenger accommodation and would be under way for fifteen days, and fearing that he was being led into a trap, he came back on shore. It was midnight. The police tried to force him back but failed. Sparring with gendarmes, the whole party camped in the harbour through the small hours of a wintry and windy night. From the harbour Trotsky addressed telegrams of protest to Herriot, to the Ministry of the Interior, to Blum and Thorez; he also sent a request to Rome

PLATE XIII

Trotsky and his wife, returning from Copenhagen to Prinkipo, 1932

PLATE XIV

Zina, Trotsky's daughter, shortly before her suicide

for an Italian transit visa. Before dawn the police took him and
Natalya to a hotel, warning them to await imminent deportation.

Day came, hours passed, and there was no reply from Herriot
or anyone else in Paris. Ironically, Mussolini's Foreign Ministry
immediately answered and granted the transit visa. The police
then rushed Trotsky and Natalya to the first train departing for
Italy. Across the police cordon both embraced Lyova. They had
spent only a day with him, a day so full of agitation that they
had no chance, as Natalya put it, to have a look at each other, let
alone to unburden themselves of the troubles that weighed on
their minds—only petty vexations and misunderstandings,
arising out of the circumstances, had come between them.

In the train Trotsky and Natalya reflected on the absurdity of
it all. They were hurt and weary. It was as if the burdens of their
life, the heavy dull-witted spite of governments and gendarmes,
Zina's misfortune and uncertainty about her child, had all
come down on them at once. Well inside Italy, Natalya wrote
to Lyova, 'we long, long sat with Papa in the dark compartment and wept. . . .'[1]

Next morning they awakened in Venice, which they had
never seen before; and through tears their eyes opened wide to
the lustre and the glory of San Marco.

.   .   .   .

On 12 December they landed at Prinkipo. The 'escaped lion'
was back in his 'cage'; but he appeared reconciled to the
return. Perhaps his nerves were soothed by the beauty of
the island, the courtesy Turkish officials had shown him on the
frontier, and the honest faces of the fishermen of Büyük Ada
beaming a friendly welcome. The bookshelves and desks, with
piles of correspondence and papers, urged him back to his
labour. 'It is good to work pen in hand in Prinkipo', he noted
later in his diary, 'especially in the autumn and the winter,
when the island is empty and woodcocks appear in the park'.
Beyond the windows, the sea, with shoals of fish coming right
up to the shore, was like an unruffled lake. After all the agitation

---

[1] Natalya to Lyova, 16 December 1932. Closed Section of *The Archives*. See
also Trotsky's statement to the Press made at Brindisi on 8 December. *The
Archives.*

o

and uproar of recent weeks, the stillness of the island, never disturbed by a motor horn or a telephone bell, offered a respite and induced reflection.

And so the last weeks of the year passed off quietly and restfully. The only discordant yet minor incident was the final break with Senin-Sobolevicius, who in Berlin had moved a motion dissociating the International Secretariat of the Opposition from one of Trotsky's sharp attacks on Stalin.[1] The incident surprised Trotsky, even though he had months earlier written to Sobolevicius that 'the party is exercising a strong pull on you'. But he had thought that they had come to an agreement in Copenhagen. 'You told me', he wrote to Senin on 18 December, 'that your journey to the Soviet Union had finally convinced you that the Opposition was right.' Even now Trotsky suspected no foul play, but thought that Senin was yielding to 'the party's pull' and that this might lead him to capitulation. 'Capitulation', he warned Senin, 'is political death'; and he advised him to take time off and think matters over. He evidently regretted losing an intelligent and helpful follower; but the break was accomplished, and soon Senin disappeared from Trotsky's horizon.[2]

In these weeks of repose Trotsky found in fishing the old 'diverter of sadness and calmer of unquiet thoughts'. In diary pages, written just before he left Prinkipo, he describes it in a rather Waltonian manner, and draws affectionate character sketches of fellow fishermen, especially of a young, almost illiterate Greek, Kharalambos, with whom he often ventured out.[3] The young Greek 'had angling in his bones'; his forebears, as far as memory reached back, were all fishermen. 'His own world extends approximately to four kilometres around

---

[1] See Trotsky's correspondence with the brothers Senin—Soblen-Sobolevicius of 15, 16, 18 and 22 December 1932. Trotsky's attack on Stalin ('Obeimi rukami'), to which they objected appeared in *B.O.*, no. 32 in the same month. In it Trotsky had charged Stalin with unprincipled wooing of American capitalism—he based the accusation on an interview Stalin had given to a certain Thomas Campbell, an American engineering expert and author of a book on Russia. Campbell quoted Stalin as saying that the first reason for the break between himself and Trotsky was Trotsky's eagerness to spread revolution to other countries and his, Stalin's, desire 'to limit all his efforts to his own country'. Stalin later denied that he had made this statement, but the denial was rather unconvincing. The brothers Sobolevicius held that Trotsky's attack was unjust and ultra-left.

[2] *The Archives*, Closed Section.

[3] These diary pages, dated 15 July, are in *The Archives*.

Prinkipo. But he knows this world'; and finds in it enough magic to fill his life (as in Walton, 'somewhat like poetry' and somewhat 'like the mathematics that it can never be fully learned'). 'He could read like an artist the beautiful book of Marmara'; and he diverted to it from distant wanderings the mind of the old revolutionary. They talked to each other only in gestures, grimaces, and a few Turkish, Greek, or Russian monosyllables. These were enough for Kharalambos to convey what was going on in the depth of the sea, to tell, by the horizon, the skies, the season and the winds, how the nets should be cast—straight, in spirals, or in semicircles—how weights should be thrown from the boat to bring lobsters into traps, and how the catch should be guarded against dolphins lurking round. The author of *Permanent Revolution* learned eagerly and humbly this 'intricate and primordial art which has not changed for thousands of years'. He noticed 'the annihilating glance' Kharalambos gave him whenever he threw a weight the wrong way. 'From kindness and a sense of social discipline he admits that, on the whole, I do not throw the weights badly. But it is enough that I should compare my work with his and my pride abandons me at once.' It was not so bad, after all, to come back to Kharalambos, to read with him the book of the Marmara, and to write a book of one's own as well.

This idyllic interval ended abruptly and grimly. On 5 January 1933 Lyova informed his parents by cable that Zina had committed suicide. She killed herself a week after her child had at last been brought to her. The child's presence, it seems, far from steadying her nerves, finally shattered them. Among the papers she left was this note written in German: 'I feel the approach of my terrible disease. In this condition I do not trust myself, not even with the handling of my child. *In no circumstances* should he come here. He is very sensitive and nervous. He is also frightened of Frau B. [the landlady]. He is with Frau K. [address follows]. He does not speak a word of German. Telephone my brother.'[1] Her brainstorms had been recurring with ever greater force and frequency; she felt useless even to her child; she had no strength to struggle on; and, on top of all this, the police had just told her that she must leave Germany. These were the last days of General Schleicher's government—

[1] The note written in German bears no date.

before the end of the month Hitler was to be acclaimed as
Chancellor. Louder than ever Berlin was resounding with the
trampling of heavy boots and hoarse and drunken singing; and
one song, coarse and cruel, *Die Strassen frei für die braunen
Batallionen* drowned all the others. The 'terrific tank' of Nazism
was rolling in to crush the German worker. The *Horst Wessel
Lied* in her ears, her own country closed to her, and herself
torn from her family, driven from Germany, and too sick to
look for another refuge, Zina locked and barricaded herself
in her room and opened the gas taps. So massive was the
barricade she put up that any attempt at saving her was
hopeless—her doctor was amazed at the 'rare energy' she
had displayed in the very act of dying. And in her last
minutes the consciousness of release brought a faint smile
to her face, an expression of relief and calm. She was thirty
years old.[1]

Lyova's message about the suicide was laconic, but, to quote
Trotsky, 'one sensed unbearable moral tension in every line of
it' for he 'found himself alone with the corpse of his elder
sister. . . .' How was the child to be told what had happened?
And how was the news to be broken to Alexandra Sokolovskaya,
Zina's mother, in Leningrad? Lyova tried to obtain a telephone connexion with his brother in Moscow. 'Was it because
the G.P.U. were disconcerted . . . or because they hoped to overhear some secret—enough that, against all expectations, Lyova
obtained the telephone connexion and . . . communicated the
tragic news. . . . Such was the last talk of our two sons, the
doomed brothers, over their sister's still warm body.'[2]

Six days after Zina's suicide Trotsky wrote an 'Open Letter'
to the party leaders in Moscow. He described how the decree
of 20 February had broken Zina's spirit: she 'did not choose
death of her own will—she was driven to it by Stalin'. 'There
was not even a shadow of any political sense in the persecution
of my daughter—there was nothing in it but purposeless,
naked vengeance.' He ended the letter on a note in which grief
stifled anger: 'I am confining myself to this communication

[1] A moving description of Zina's death and funeral is in Franz Pfemfert's letter
to Trotsky of 20 January 1933 (*The Archives*, Closed Section). Lyova's telegram,
ibid.
[2] Quoted from Trotsky's obituary of Lyova, written six years later. *B.O.*, no.
64, March 1938.

without drawing further conclusions. The time for draw-ing such conclusions will come—a revived party will draw them.'[1]

From Leningrad, from Zina's mother, came a cry of pain, reproach, and despair. She had now lost both her children, both born during their father's first exile and both struck down during his last exile. 'I shall go mad myself if I do not learn everything', she wrote to Trotsky on 31 January, asking for an explanation of all the circumstances. She quoted what Zina had written her only a few weeks earlier: 'It is sad that I can no longer return to Papa. You know how I have adored and worshipped him from my earliest days. And now we are in utter discord. This has been at the bottom of my illness.' Zina had complained about his coolness towards her. 'I explained to her', these are her mother's words, 'that all this comes from your character, from the fact that you find it so difficult to show your feelings even when you would like to show them.' (To those familiar only with the public face of Trotsky, the passionate rhetorician, his first wife's testimony about his undemonstrative intimate character may come as a surprise.) Then followed this poignant reproach: 'Yet have reckoned only with her [Zina's] physical condition, but she was an adult and a fully developed being in need of intellectual intercourse.' She had yearned for political activity and she needed scope, for she had taken after her father; and—'you, her father, you could have saved her'. And what, Alexandra asked, had been behind the conflict between Zina and Lyova, of which Zina had also written? And why had Trotsky insisted on a psychoanalytic treatment when 'she was closed in herself—as we both are—and one should not have pressed her to talk about things she did not want to talk about!' Yet, as the mother confronted Trotsky with these reproaches, she softened them with the reflection that if Zina had remained in Russia, she would have perished anyhow —she would have died of consumption. 'Our children were doomed', Alexandra added and described the fear with which she looked on the grandchildren left with her: 'I do not believe in life any longer. I do not believe that they will grow up. All the time I am expecting some new disaster.' And she con-cluded: 'It has been difficult for me to write and mail this letter.

[1] *B.O.*, no. 33, March 1933.

Excuse my cruelty towards you, but you too should know everything about our kith and kin.'[1]

We do not know whether or how Trotsky answered this
letter—perhaps the wound was too deep for words. Some time
later, apologizing to friends for not having acknowledged condolences, he wrote that he had been struck down by malaria
and 'half deaf'.[2]

.   .   .   .

To the last, Trotsky refused to believe that the German
labour movement was so devoid of any power of self-preservation as to put up almost no resistance to Nazism and to collapse
ignominiously under its first onslaught. For nearly three years
he had argued that it was inconceivable that Hitler should win
without a civil war. The inconceivable had now happened:
on 30 January 1933 Hitler had become Chancellor, before
socialists and communists had even begun to marshal their
immense resources for a fight. A week later Trotsky stated:
'Hitler's accession to power is a terrible blow to the working
class. But this is not yet the final, the irretrievable defeat.
The enemy, whom it was possible to rout while he was still
climbing up, has now occupied a whole series of commanding
posts. He has thus gained a great advantage, but the battle
has not yet been fought.' Even now there was still time, for
Hitler had not yet seized total power; he had to share it with
Hugenberg and the Deutschnazionale. The coalition he headed
was unstable and riddled with contradictions. He still had to
strip his partners of all influence, and to obtain exclusive
control of all the resources of the state. Until then his position
remained vulnerable. Socialists and communists could still
strike back—but it was desperately late: 'what is at stake is the
head of the German working class, the head of the Communist
International and . . . the head of the Soviet Republic!'[3]

We know now from numerous German archives and diaries

---

[1] Alexandra Sokolovskaya's letter, dated 31 January 1933, is in the Closed
Section of *The Archives*.

[2] Trotsky to Franz Pfemfert, 5 February 1933, ibid. According to Pierre Frank,
who was at Büyük Ada then, Trotsky shut himself in his room for several days;
Natalya was with him; and she alone came out now and then. When he emerged
at last, his secretaries noticed how grey his hair had grown during those days.

[3] *B.O.*, no. 33, 1933.

how great indeed was the vulnerability of Hitler's first government, as it came into being.[1] Even a month later, on 5 March, after the Nazi raid on the Karl Liebknecht House in Berlin and after the Reichstag fire, in elections held under an unbridled Nazi terror, the socialists and the communists still polled 12 million votes, not to speak of the nearly 6 million votes cast for the Catholic opposition to Hitler. We also know of the quarrels, the rows, and the mutual distrust between Hitler and his partners, which might well have disrupted their coalition if those millions of socialists and communists had moved into action. As early as 6 February Trotsky observed that the working class 'was not conducting any defensive battle but was retreating, and tomorrow the retreat may well turn into a panic-stricken rout'. He concluded rather abruptly with this grave passage:

> In order to expose more clearly the historic significance of the party's decisions . . . in these days and weeks, it is, in my view, necessary to pose the issue before Communists . . . with the utmost sharpness and irreconcilability: the party's [continued] refusal to form a united front and to set up local defence committees, committees which might become Soviets tomorrow, will be nothing less than a surrender to fascism, an historic crime tantamount to the liquidation of the party and of the Communist International. Should such a disaster happen, the working class will have to make its way towards a Fourth International; and it will have to make it through mountains of corpses and years of unbearable sufferings and calamities.[2]

Even before these words appeared in print, the great mass organizations of German labour, its parties and trade unions, its many newspapers, cultural institutions, and sports organizations all lay in ruins.

The great defeat at once affected the fate of Trotsky's family. The *Bulletin* was banned in Berlin, and Lyova had to go into hiding and steal across the frontier. On 24 March, Trotsky wrote to the Pfemferts (whose home the Nazis had already wrecked): 'We have all the time been very anxious about L.L. [i.e. Lyova]. German friends think that if he fell into fascist hands he would not come out alive. I thought the same. But yesterday we received a telegram from him: "I am moving

---

[1] A. Bullock, *Hitler*, pp. 229–33ff.   [2] *B.O.* Loc. cit.

to Paris." Let us hope that he will have good luck in completing
the move. We have not yet had any further news from him.'[1]

.   .   .   .

In these weeks Trotsky renounced his allegiance to the Third
International. In an article under the title 'The Tragedy of the
German Proletariat' (and the sub-title: 'The German workers
will rise again—Stalinism never!'), he thus summed up the
situation: what the labour movement had suffered in Germany
was not a temporary reverse or a tactical setback, but a decisive
strategic defeat, which would leave the working class prostrated
and paralysed for a whole epoch. The Second and Third
Internationals alike refused to admit this, spoke of Hitler's
'ephemeral' success, and now, when it was too late, declaimed
about a united front. But 'before any decisive struggles become
possible in Germany once again, the vanguard of the working
class must orientate itself anew, grasp clearly what has happened, fix the responsibility for . . . defeat, clear new roads,
and thus regain self-confidence and self-respect'. For years the
'key to the situation' had been in communist hands; it was no
longer there. All positions in Germany were lost for years to
come; all the more important was it for the labour movement to
fortify its strongholds and to fight in the countries surrounding
Germany, in Austria, Czechoslovakia, Poland, the Netherlands,
and France. 'Austria, most immediately threatened by a
fascist upheaval, is now the forward bastion.' It was the height
of irresponsibility on the Comintern's part to announce that the
German workers were 'on the eve of great battles' because they
had cast 5 million votes for the communists. 'Yes, five million
communists still managed, each individually, to make their way
to the polling booths. But in the factories and the streets their
presence is not felt. They are lost, dispersed, demoralized. . . .
The bureaucratic terror of Stalinism has paralysed their will
even before the gangster terror of fascism has started its
work.'[2]

He concluded that Stalinism had had its '4 August', a
collapse as ignominious as that which the Second International

[1] *The Archives*, Closed Section.
[2] 'The Tragedy of the German Proletariat', dated 14 March, appeared in the
May issue of *B.O.* (no. 34).

had suffered at the outbreak of the First World War. Then Lenin, Trotsky, Rosa Luxemburg, Karl Liebknecht, and their associates had declared that the Second International was dead and had proclaimed the idea of the Third International. The analogy with 4 August suggested that Trotsky would now proclaim the idea of the Fourth International. He did not yet do this, however. He called only for the formation of a new Communist party in Germany. 'The advanced workers of Germany will henceforth speak about the time when the Stalinist bureaucracy dominated [German communism] not otherwise than with burning shame. . . . The official Communist party of Germany is doomed. From now on it will only disintegrate, crumble, and dissolve into nothing.' He still reckoned with the possibility that the defeat might come as a salutary shock to the other Communist parties, induce them to delve into the causes, to find out where the responsibilities lay, and perhaps to break with Stalinism. Should this happen, then the Comintern (or a segment of it) might still save its revolutionary honour and *raison d'être*. But 'in Germany at any rate the sinister song of Stalinist bureaucracy is at an end. . . . Under the enemy's terrible blows advanced German workers will have to build a new party'. It might be argued that it was illogical to call for a new Communist party, but not for a new International; but the historic development did not proceed altogether according to the rules of logic; and one should wait and see whether any Communist parties would draw the lessons from the German experience.[1]

If Trotsky had any such hopes these were soon dispelled. The Executive of the Comintern, at its first session after Hitler's victory, declared that victory devoid of significance. It asserted that the strategy and tactics of the German party had been flawless from beginning to end; and it forbade any Communist party to open any debate over the issue.[2] Not a single party dared to defy the ban. The spectacle was so shocking that it led Trotsky to state that 'an organization which has not been wakened up by the thunderbolt of fascism . . . is dead and cannot be revived'. In July, he declared that it was not enough to build a new Communist party in Germany; the

[1] Ibid.
[2] *Kommunisticheskij Internatsional*, 1933, no. 36, p. 17; *B.O.*, nos. 36–37, 1933.

time had come to lay the foundations of a new International.[1]

Even now he could not make up his mind whether the new International should extend its activities to the Soviet Union; that is, whether his followers there should cease to consider themselves a faction of the old party and form a new party of their own. For several months he advised them against such a course and insisted that the activities of the Fourth International must stop at the frontiers of the Soviet Union. He still saw in the Bolshevik monopoly of power, abused though it was by Stalin, the *sine qua non* of the revolution's survival. The Opposition, he argued, would be justified in constituting itself an independent party only if it abandoned any hope of reforming the régime and reoriented itself for a revolutionary struggle against Stalinism; this it must not do. A new International could well refrain from working inside the Soviet Union because 'the key to the situation' in the labour movement was no longer in the Soviet Union: the Opposition had hardly any chance of developing its activity there, at any rate in the near future; and so the issue of a new Communist party was academic. Only if and when the new International grew into a vital political force in other countries, could the alignment of forces change in the U.S.S.R. as well. Above all, it would be the advance of revolution in the West, an advance which could not be achieved under Stalin's leadership, that would weaken the stranglehold of Stalinism on the Soviet Union and give fresh strength to the communist opposition.[2]

This was clearly an untenable position; and the logic of his new venture soon got the better of Trotsky once again. It had been inconsistent to advocate a new party in Germany but not a new International; and it was just as inconsistent for the new International to refrain from action within the Soviet Union. And so in October 1933 Trotsky concluded that the Opposition should constitute itself into a new party in the U.S.S.R. as well.[3]

[1] *B.O.* Loc. cit.

[2] Ibid. Pierre Frank relates that during the weeks and months when Trotsky tried to make up his mind on these points his secretaries saw him every day walking in his room for hours, silent, tense and absorbed in his dilemmas. 'His face was profusely covered with sweat; and one sensed the physical exertion of his thought and hesitancy.'

[3] Loc. cit. Trotsky carried out this revision in his essay 'The Class Character of the Soviet State', the writing of which he concluded, according to *The Archives*, on 1 October 1933. In the *B.O.*, nos. 36–37 the date has been misprinted as 1 October 1932.

It had taken him about six months to draw this conclusion. Having done so he had to revise some of the views by which he had stood unflinchingly for ten years. He had ceased to uphold the political monopoly of the ruling party. The new party, if and when it came into existence, was to work not for the reform and the constitutional replacement of the Stalinist government but for its revolutionary overthrow. Did he then still consider the Soviet Union to be a workers' state? Or did he now view its régime as a Thermidorian or Bonapartist variety of counter-revolution? And was the Opposition, or was it not, to remain committed to the unconditional defence of the Soviet Union?

Trotsky argued that after all the experiences of recent years it would be childish to think that it was possible to depose Stalin at a Congress of the Party or of the Soviets. 'No normal constitutional ways are left for the removal of the ruling clique. Only *force* can compel the bureaucracy to hand over power into the hands of the proletarian vanguard.' That vanguard, however, was dispersed and crushed—it would not be able to fight for power in the near future. The question of Reform or Revolution was therefore basically a matter of long term orientation. The Opposition could not claim office unless it had the support of the majority of the working class; and it could not obtain that without previous social shifts at home and radical changes on the international scene, in the first instance, without an advance of revolution outside the Soviet Union. After such shifts and changes 'the Stalinist apparatus would find itself suspended in a vacuum'; and the Opposition, assisted by popular pressure, might be able to win even without revolution or civil war. If Stalin and his adherents, despite their isolation, still continued to cling to power, the Opposition would oust them by means of a 'police operation'. Confronted by an upsurge of political energy in the working class, Stalinism would be utterly weak precisely because it had 'its roots in the working class and nowhere else': only with the acquiescence and submissiveness, if not the active support, of the workers was Stalin strong—without these he could be overthrown by a push.[1]

The Soviet Union, Trotsky reasserted, remained a workers'

[1] *B.O.* Loc. cit.

state. Social ownership of the means of production prevailing, Soviet society was engaged in the transition from capitalism into socialism, even though it paid an exorbitant price for every step forward. The bureaucracy, no matter how privileged, was still only 'a malignant growth on the body of the working class, not a new possessing class'. Privileges and growing social inequality reflected not a new type of exploitation, as the ultra-radicals alleged, but were the consequences of poverty and material scarcities. To some extent, as incentives to efficiency and production, privileges and inequality were 'the bourgeois tools of socialist progress'. Bureaucratic rule, parasitic and tyrannical, might endanger all the conquests of the revolution and provoke counter-revolution; but it might also turn out to be 'the instrument'—a poor and expensive one—'of socialist development'. 'Wasting . . . an enormous portion of the national income, the Soviet bureaucracy is at the same time . . . interested in promoting the economic and cultural growth of the nation: the higher the national income the more abundant is the fund of the bureaucracy's privileges. Yet, the economic and cultural advance of the working masses, achieved on the social foundations of the Soviet state, should undermine the basis of bureaucratic rule.' Thus, twenty years before the end of the Stalin era, Trotsky foresaw that by industrializing the Soviet Union and spreading education among its people, Stalinism might destroy the soil on which it had grown and which nourished it, the soil of primordial poverty, illiteracy, and barbarism.[1]

Having ceased to defend the single party system in the U.S.S.R., Trotsky nevertheless repeated his earlier warning that 'if the bureaucratic equilibrium in the Soviet Union were to be shaken at present, this would almost certainly be to the advantage of counter-revolutionary forces'. He restated his commitment to the unconditional defence of the Soviet Union: '. . . the new International . . . before it can reform the Soviet state, must take upon itself the duty to defend it. Any political grouping which disavows this commitment, under the pretext

[1] B.O. Loc. cit. 'It is clear', Trotsky concluded, 'that in this happy historical variant, the bureaucracy would turn out to be only the tool—a poor and expensive tool—of the socialist state.' But he did not take it for granted that this 'happy variant' would materialize.

that the Soviet Union is no longer a workers' state, risks becoming a passive tool of imperialism. . . .' The adherents of the new International, he added, 'must in an hour of mortal danger fight on the last barricade' in defence of the U.S.S.R.[1]

Yet, while he insisted so forcefully that the Soviet Union, judged by its economic structure, remained a workers' state, he now took the view that as a factor of international revolution it was little more than an extinct volcano. 'From the beginning of the First World War, and more explicitly since the October revolution, the Bolshevik party has played a leading role in the global revolutionary struggle. Now this leading position has been lost.' Not only official Bolshevism, that 'parody of the party', but the Bolshevik Opposition as well, was, because of the difficult conditions in which it worked, unable to 'exercise any international leadership'. 'The revolutionary centre of gravity has definitely shifted to the West, where the immediate possibilities for building a new party are much wider.' He proclaimed the idea of the Fourth International in the belief that new impulses for revolution would come from the West, not from the Soviet Union.[2]

We have seen with how much hesitation Trotsky had made up his mind to renounce his allegiance to the Third International. The causes of his hesitancy were not far to seek, for he himself had many times stated his objections to the step he was now taking. It was to the Third International, he had argued, that the revolutionary workers of all countries looked for guidance; it was in it that they saw the legitimate successor to the Second and First Internationals and the very embodiment of the idea of the Russian Revolution; and as long as the Soviet Union remained a workers' state and the Comintern retained its association with it, the class-conscious *élite* of the workers were justified in their loyalty to the Comintern. He was not quite sure that this reasoning had now lost its validity. Nor was it easy for him, in view of the part he had played in the Third International, to announce his final break with it. It is extremely rare for one of the principal architects of a great and vital movement to find in himself the strength to declare that movement worthless. It was far more difficult for Trotsky to turn his back on the Third International than it had been to renounce

[1] *B.O.* Loc. cit.   [2] Ibid.

the Second in 1914. Only the Comintern's stunning failure in Germany brought him to do it. He admitted that there was a difference between 1914 and 1933. In 1914 the leaders of the Second International had, by supporting an imperialist war, betrayed their trust deliberately and with their eyes open; whereas in 1933 the Comintern had facilitated Hitler's victory from sheer irresponsibility and blindness. Yet the catastrophe of 1933 was in other respects even worse than that of 1914. In the First World War revolutionary Marxism soon recovered from the blow: Zimmerwald, Kienthal, and the Russian Revolution registered a powerful protest against the 'social imperialist' perversion of Marxism. No comparable protest against the enormity of 1933 had come or was to come from within the communist movement. Not only had the Comintern's policy contributed to the loss by German labour of all it had gained in over eighty years of struggle; and not only had that policy allowed the danger, nay, the certainty of another world war to come about—in addition, all this had occurred amid an uncanny indifference and apathy on the part of the entire movement. What had happened, Trotsky asked, to the political conscience and understanding of the great mass of communists?

He concluded that reformism and Stalinism had between them stultified the minds and destroyed the will of the workers. That all his own warnings, so clear, so loud, so strikingly confirmed by events, could have gone so unheeded confirmed him in this conclusion. No one knew better than he himself how unheeded his warnings had gone, for in a letter to Sobolevicius he remarked, early in 1932, that the Trotskyist Opposition had failed to recruit in Germany even 'ten native factory workers' (and had won over only a few intellectuals and immigrants).[1] In the First World War at least a few thousand German workers joined the clandestine *Spartakus* and echoed the denunciation of the '4 August', which Rosa Luxemburg and Karl Liebknecht voiced from their prison cells. Now, after Hitler's triumph, all the Communist parties of the world received the Comintern's self-justifications and self-congratulations in numbed silence. Was there no spark of intelligence, of international solidarity, and of responsibility left in all those

[1] Letter to Senin-Sobolevicius, 6 March 1932, *The Archives*, Closed Section.

parties? Trotsky asked again and again. If not, then Stalinism had so irretrievably debased the entire communist movement that to try and reform it was a Sisyphean labour. He had been performing that labour for ten years now; and he refused to go on rolling the heavy rock up the dismal mountain.

It was even more painful for him to renounce finally the Soviet party, the party which Lenin had founded, which had accomplished the revolution, and within which he had achieved greatness. The year before, after the second deportation of Zinoviev, Kamenev, Smirnov, Preobrazhensky, and others, it looked as if the Joint Opposition of 1925–7 was coming back into being. Every message from Moscow indicated that amid the nation-wide turmoil even Stalin's entourage longed to rid itself of him. Since 1932, however, Stalin had once more gained the upper hand. He succeeded in this in part because he once more adopted some of the measures Trotsky had advocated: he gave the economy a 'breathing space' at the end of the first Five Year Plan; he set lower and more realistic targets for the second Plan; he made concessions to the collectivized peasantry. Consequently, the chaos, the turmoil, and the inner party ferment subsided. The German catastrophe instead of weakening Stalin strengthened his hand. Those who realized its implications felt that this was not the time to sap the stability of government in Moscow. The establishment of totalitarian rule in Germany gave a new impetus to the totalitarian trend in the Soviet Union. When the cry *Ein Führer, eine Partei, ein Volk!* thundered over Germany, the Soviet hierarchy and many of the rank and file felt that only under a single leader could the revolution and the Soviet Union survive. In May 1933 Zinoviev and Kamenev once again capitulated and returned from exile. At their first capitulation, in 1927, they had surrendered to Stalinism, but had not gone, and no one expected them to go, on their knees before Stalin's person. When this was required of them in 1932 they could not yet bring themselves to do it. This, however, was what they did in 1933: in their new recantations they glorified Stalin's infallibility and unique genius.

All this occurred while Trotsky was committing himself to the Fourth International, but was not yet ready to call for a new party in the Soviet Union. Stalin's triumphant emergence from the crisis, the new autocratic aura around him, and the spectacle of the latest capitulations impelled Trotsky to sever the last tie which in theory still bound him to the old party. Commenting on Zinoviev's and Kamenev's 'tragic fate', he wrote: 'The future historian, who will wish to show how ruthlessly an epoch of great upheavals devastates characters, will take Zinoviev and Kamenev as his examples . . . the Stalinist apparatus has become a machine for crushing the backbones [of former revolutionaries].' And: 'Like Gogol's hero, Stalin collects dead souls for the lack of living ones.'[1] Trotsky's hope for any regeneration of the Soviet party was now destroyed. It was futile to go on appealing to men with broken backs and to dead souls; and, anyhow, the Marxist-Leninist traditions had gone from a party that could bow to an autocrat. Only in complete independence from it and beyond its confines could Bolshevism have a rebirth.

This, briefly, was Trotsky's case for a new International. Having made it and, after a discussion, obtained for it the endorsement of all his groups, he did not, however, proclaim these groups to be the Fourth International. Aware of their weakness, he contented himself with launching the idea in the hope that it would gain many more adherents presently. He repeated in a way his own experience of the Zimmerwald era, the memory of which is discernible in his writings and behaviour. From the moment when Lenin and he had begun to advocate the Third International in 1915, it took four years of propaganda and preparatory work before they called a foundation congress of the International. Similarly, now there was 'no question of any immediate proclamation of . . . the International, but only of preparatory work. The new orientation means . . . that the talk about "reforming" [the Stalinist organization] and all demands for the reinstatement of expelled Oppositionists should be definitely abandoned. . . . The Left Opposition ceases to think of itself and to act as an [inner-party] Opposition.'[2] It was to take four years exactly before he would be ready to convene a foundation congress.

His hopes for the new International were not as wild in 1933 as they appeared later. Over the German issue the Comintern was in fact utterly discredited, while Trotskyism had scored a

[1] *B.O.*, no. 35, 1933.   [2] *B.O.*, no. 36, 1933.

striking moral victory. If hitherto, so Trotsky thought, all his appeals to European communist opinion had met with all too little response, this had been partly because the main issues of his controversy with Stalin, domestic Soviet affairs and the Chinese revolution, had been too remote from European communists or too obscure. In its latest phase the controversy had centred on Germany, 'the heart of Europe'. Hitler's advent affected immediately every Communist party. It posed problems of life and death. It pointed to war. It threatened communism with extinction. Both he and the Comintern had conducted the argument publicly and with the utmost vigour until the very moment when the differences were tested by events. The outcome of the test was in no doubt. The pros and cons were, or should have been, fresh in everyone's mind: every communist could review and ponder them anew. The conclusion to be drawn was in no doubt either: those who had led the most powerful Communist party of the West to so shameful a débâcle were guilty of incompetence bordering on treason, and had forfeited every title to leadership. By the same token the Opposition had, or should have had, established its claim to leadership.

Some awareness of all this was undoubtedly penetrating into Stalinist ranks. The more spitefully the Comintern had attacked and mocked Trotsky for 'playing the bogey-man', 'exaggerating the Nazi menace', and 'urging a united front with social-fascists', the more did these mockeries rebound on their authors. Embarrassment and shame took hold of many a party cell. Even hardened Stalinists felt a sneaking admiration for Trotsky's clear-sighted and intrepid stand.[1] New Trotskyist and quasi-Trotskyist groups formed themselves among German refugees from Hitler's terror and among Polish, Czech, Dutch, American, and other communists. The groups were small, but their influence could not be ignored. They drew to themselves alert-minded and devoted party members. They assailed the conscience of communism. They forced Stalinism on to the defensive. Only by frantic appeals to party patriotism, threats of expulsion, and actual expulsion could the leaders subdue the

[1] They themselves admitted this 'sneaking admiration' many years later when they were freer to do so; some went out of their way to be able to speak about it to Trotsky's present biographer.

P

malaise in the ranks; and eventually the Comintern could dispel it only by reversing all its attitudes, by throwing overboard the slogans about social-fascism, and by adopting the tactics of the united front (and going beyond them, to the Popular Front). Moreover, the collapse of the Weimar Republic had shaken the Social-Democratic parties too. Their belief in parliamentary democracy had received a rude blow. There was hardly a Socialist party in Europe which did not, under the impact of the German experience, solemnly inscribe some form of 'proletarian dictatorship' in its programme. Inside those parties radical and leftish groups looked up to Trotsky and found his ideas much more rational and alluring than all that official communism could offer. This was indeed the high water mark of his political influence in exile. If he had any chance at all to found an independent Communist party it was now.

Yet the arguments which he himself had so frequently and cogently advanced against the course of action he was now taking had lost none of their strength. It was still true that as long as national ownership in the means of production remained intact in the Soviet Union and as long as the banner of Bolshevism was hoisted over Moscow, the association of international communism with the Soviet Union was indissoluble. To the mass of those who were in sympathy with communism the workers' first state was still the bulwark of international revolution; and the official Communist parties exercised an overwhelming attraction on them. They saw no alternative to the Stalinist leadership which, in their eyes, had come to represent the Russian Revolution and the Bolshevik tradition. The Stalinist bureaucracy had actually succeeded in identifying itself with Leninism and with Marxism at large. Militant French dockers, Polish coalminers, and Chinese guerilla fighters alike saw in those who ruled Moscow the best judges of the Soviet interest and reliable counsellors to world communism. Hence the unreasoning obedience with which they so often accepted the twists and turns and the most preposterous dictates of Stalinist policy. Its opponents appeared to them as the enemies of the Soviet Union and of communism just as to the devout Roman Catholic the enemies of the Holy See were the enemies of Christianity.

All this boded ill for Trotsky's venture. His ideas and

slogans were such that only those who were in sympathy with communism could be sensitive to them—yet these were the people who would be least inclined to rally to a new International. Having for so long remained unimpressed by Trotsky's call for a reform in their parties, they were even less likely to be moved when he urged them to break with these parties.

Nor did or could the aftermath of the German débâcle favour the new International, no matter how discredited the old Internationals were. Each of the old Internationals had arisen on a high tide of the labour movement; and at the moment of formation none of them had had to contend against any established rival.[1] The Fourth International set out to challenge two established and powerful rivals during a deep depression of the movement. In Germany the working class was indeed, as Trotsky had predicted, unable to recover politically for many years to come; but precisely because of this Trotskyism could derive no practical benefit from the moral advantage it had gained over the German issue. Elsewhere in Europe, the working class was to remain in retreat for the rest of the decade, despite the upsurge of its energies in France and Spain in 1936. The long leaden sequence of retreats and defeats produced a moral sickness, amid which even the most persuasive pleas for a new International fell flat. Trotsky argued that the working class needed a new leadership precisely in order to bring the retreat to a halt and to regroup for defence and counter-offensive. But the mass of communists (and of socialists), those of them who had not yet lost heart, felt that they must not swap horses mid-stream. And so the two established Internationals flourished even on their blunders and defeats: their followers, whatever misgivings they felt, refused to look for new leaders and new methods of struggle under the hail of blows Nazism and fascism were inflicting on them. They were prepared to flounder under old and familiar banners, from defeat to defeat, rather than rally to a new standard behind which they could see only the giant but enigmatic or suspect figure of the standard-bearer.

Trotsky was convinced that the Comintern had, as a

---

[1] For a continuation of this argument, especially for the case of the Polish Trotskyists against the foundation of the Fourth International, see Chapter V, pp. 421–22.

revolutionary organization, played out its role. He was not altogether mistaken. Ten years later Stalin was to disband the organization and declare that it no longer served any purpose; and in those ten years the Comintern was only to add to its German bankruptcy new failures in France and Spain and the ambiguities of its policy under the Stalin-Hitler pact of 1939–41. Yet the movement behind the Comintern was anything but a 'corpse'. All that Stalin did to wreck it morally could not kill it. At the very time he disbanded the Comintern its western European parties were gaining fresh strength from their resistance to the Nazi occupation; and it was still under Stalinist banners, though in implicit conflict with Stalin, that the Yugoslav and the Chinese revolutions were to achieve their victories. No matter how much Stalin had done to degrade all Communist parties to mere pawns, the Yugoslav, the Chinese and some other parties had enough vitality to live their own lives, to wage their own struggles, and to change the fortunes of their countries and of the world. Moreover, they were to take fresh impetus and new revolutionary *élan* from the triumphs of Soviet arms in the Second World War.

The idea that new impulses for revolution would come from the West but not from the Soviet Union was the *leitmotif* of Trotsky's advocacy of the Fourth International. Again and again he asserted that, while in the Soviet Union Stalinism continued to play a dual role, at once progressive and retrograde, it exercised internationally only a counter-revolutionary influence. Here his grasp of reality failed him. Stalinism was to go on acting its dual role internationally as well as nationally: it was to stimulate as well as to obstruct the class struggle outside the Soviet Union. In any case, it was not from the West that the revolutionary impulses were to come in the next three or four decades. Thus the major premiss on which Trotsky set out to create the Fourth International was unreal. Yet, since all his attempts to reform the Comintern had been in vain, he could not, as we have seen, go on with that Sisyphean task. He had to look for another solution. His new task, however, was to prove at least as barren as the old one. Sisyphus had only moved hopefully from one side of his dismal mountain to the other; and there he started to roll his rock again.

.   .   .   .

We have seen how Trotsky, when he turned his back on the Comintern, re-committed his adherents to remain the last-ditch defenders of the Soviet Union. He himself, when he addressed western bourgeois opinion in his articles, sought to arouse it to the fact that the Third Reich spelt world war. As early as the spring of 1933 he urged the Western Powers to enter into an alliance with the Soviet Union. These were the first weeks and months of the Third Reich, when hardly a single western statesman contemplated the idea. Hitler now assumed pacifist postures, and at an International Disarmament Conference accepted, to the relief and delight of official London, Austen Chamberlain's and John Simon's disarmament schemes. On 2 June 1933 Trotsky wrote in an essay on 'Hitler and Disarmament': 'The greatest danger is to underrate an enemy . . . the leaders of the German labour movement did not wish to take Hitler seriously. . . . The same danger may arise on the plane of world politics.' He noted how ready the British Government was to respond to Hitler's 'moderation' and 'peaceful intentions': 'Diplomatic routine has its advantages as long as things move within familiar grooves. It is at once disconcerted when it has to face new and important facts.' Austen Chamberlain and John Simon 'had expected to meet [in Hitler] a madman brandishing an axe; instead they met a man hiding his revolver in a pocket—what a relief!' This was Hitler's first great diplomatic success. His purpose was to rearm Germany, which had since Versailles recovered its place as Europe's mightiest industrial nation, but was still unarmed. 'This combination of potential power and actual weakness determines both the explosive character of Nazi objectives and the extreme caution of Hitler's first steps leading towards those objectives.' Hitler had endorsed the British disarmament schemes knowing full well that France could not accept them—this gave him the chance to play off Britain against France and to place on the latter the odium for the arms race to follow. 'Hitler's love for peace is not an accidental diplomatic improvisation, but a necessary element in a large manœuvre, designed to turn the balance of power radically in Germany's favour and to prepare the onslaught of German imperialism on Europe and the world.' He forecast that, if Hitler's moves were not countered, they would inevitably lead to world war within five to ten years. 'It is against the Soviet Union that Hitler is eager to march. But should this not prove to be the line of the least resistance, the eruption may well turn in the other direction. . . . Weapons that can be used against the East can just as well be used against the West.'[1] He remarked that he did not consider himself 'called upon to act as guardian of the Treaty of Versailles. Europe needs a new organization. But woe if this job falls into the hands of fascism!'

In statements for the American Press Trotsky urged the United States Government (which in this, the sixteenth, year of the revolution had not yet recognized the Soviet Government) to move closer to the Soviet Union in order to meet threats from Japan and Germany.[2] We do not know whether these promptings had any influence on President Roosevelt's decision, taken shortly thereafter, to establish diplomatic relations with Moscow. But Trotsky's views certainly impressed Stalin's diplomacy, which presently took up the theme of the anti-Nazi alliance. Where the security of his own government was concerned, Stalin was quite willing to benefit from the advice of his adversary, even if he did it often belatedly and always in his own crudely perverse manner.

Meanwhile, the Soviet Government prolonged its Rapallo agreements with Germany; and this tempted ultra-radical anti-Stalinists to denounce yet another of Stalin's 'betrayals'. Trotsky found the issue too serious to make a debating point of it. He did not tire of exposing Stalin's and the Comintern's share of responsibility for Hitler's ascendancy. But he did not deny Stalin the right to act in the diplomatic field from expediency. Two years earlier, we know, he had urged the Soviet Government to mobilize the Red Army if Hitler threatened to seize power; but he had done this imagining that the German left would be up in arms against Nazism, in which case the Red Army would be in duty bound to assist. Hitler's bloodless victory and the total destruction of the German left, Trotsky now pointed out, turned the balance against the Soviet Union,

---

[1] *B.O.*, no. 35, 1933. The article appeared in the *Manchester Guardian* of 21–22 June 1933 (three weeks after it had been written). It was from this article that Litvinov, Stalin's Foreign Minister, borrowed the much-quoted phrase that 'a gun that can fire to the East can fire westwards as well'.

[2] See, e.g., Trotsky's interview with *The New York World Telegram* given on 4 July 1933.

especially as the Soviet Union was also weakened internally by the Stalinist collectivization. Soviet diplomacy was therefore entitled to bide its time, to parley, and even to seek a temporary accommodation with Hitler. With a somewhat startling disinterestedness Trotsky declared that if the Opposition were to assume office in present circumstances, it would not be able to act differently: 'In its *immediate practical actions* the Opposition would have to start from the existing balance of power. It would be compelled in particular to maintain diplomatic and economic connexions with Hitler's Germany. At the same time it would prepare the *revanche*. This would be a great task, requiring time—a task that could not be accomplished by spectacular gestures, but would demand a radical reshaping of policy in every field.'[1] His judgement remained unclouded by any personal emotion against Stalin, and severely objective.

⋅ ⋅ ⋅ ⋅ ⋅ ⋅ ⋅ ⋅ ⋅ ⋅

These were Trotsky's last months on Prinkipo. For some time his French friends, especially Maurice Parijanine, his translator, had urged the French Government to cancel the order under which Trotsky had, in 1916, been expelled from France 'for ever', and to grant him asylum. Trotsky was sceptical: he assumed that the Radical government, just formed under Edouard Daladier, would be anxious to improve relations with the Soviet Union and would not tolerate his presence in France. But he did what he could to help. He had just arranged to publish in New York an unflattering character study of Edouard Herriot, written shortly after the nocturnal tussle with the police at Marseilles; and he refrained from publishing lest it provided grist to the opponents of his admission to France. He also wrote to Henri Guernut, the Minister of Education, who as a member of the government pleaded for Trotsky's right to asylum; and he solemnly promised to behave with the utmost discretion in France and to cause the government no trouble.[2]

Weeks passed without a decision, the weeks during which he drafted his ideas on the Fourth International and also wrote a few minor essays on French political and literary topics. Uncertainty about his immediate future caused him to put

[1] *B.O.*, no. 35, 1933.   [2] *The Archives*, Closed Section.

aside larger literary plans and entailed financial troubles such as he had not known since 1929. The trip to Copenhagen, Zina's illness, Lyova's move to France, and the transfer of the *Bulletin* to Paris had involved him in large expenses just when his income was greatly reduced. In Germany, where his major works had had a wide reading public, the Nazis banned and burned his writings, along with all Marxist and Freudian literature, just after the third volume of the *History of the Russian Revolution* had come off the press. In the United States the *History* did not fare too well either. Already in March he had written to a British admirer: 'The world's financial crisis has become my crisis also, especially as the sales of the *History* are quite pitiable.' He contributed occasionally to the *Manchester Guardian* and other papers, but the fees amounted to little. To speed up the decision about the French visa, he wrote, on 7 July, to Henri Molinier that he would be content with a residence permit that would allow him to stay not in metropolitan France but in Corsica, for even there he would be in closer contact with European politics and somewhat farther from the G.P.U. than on Prinkipo.[1] His French friends, however, demanded asylum for him in France, and their insistence was soon rewarded. Before the middle of July he received the visa. This was by no means an unqualified residence permit: he would be allowed to stay only in one of the southern *départements*; he would not be permitted to come, even for the shortest trip, to Paris; and he would have to keep a strict incognito and submit to stringent police surveillance.

He accepted these terms as an incredible piece of good luck. At last he would be out of his Turkish backwater! And he was going to France, whose way of life and culture were so congenial to him, and which was now the main centre of working-class politics in the West. Preparing, full of hopeful anticipation, for the journey, he yet cast a backward glance on his Prinkipo years. 'Four and a half years ago when we came here', he wrote in his diary, 'the sun of prosperity still shone over the United States. Now those days seem as remote as prehistory, or as a fairy tale. . . . Here on this island of quiet and oblivion echoes from the great world reached us delayed and muffled.' It was not without a tug of emotion that he took leave of the splendour

[1] *The Archives*, Closed Section.

of the Sea of Marmara and the fishing expeditions and that he thought of his faithful fishermen, some of whom, 'their bones saturated through and through with the salt of the sea', had recently found their rest in the village cemetery, while others had, in these years of slump, to struggle harder and harder to sell their catch. 'The house is already empty. The wooden cases are already downstairs; young hands are driving in the nails. The floor of our old and dilapidated villa was painted with such queer paint in the spring that even now, four months later, tables, chairs, and our feet keep sticking to it. . . . Oddly, I feel as if my feet had got somewhat rooted in the soil of Prinkipo.'[1]

Fate had not spared him disappointment and suffering on this island. The shadow of death had darkened for him many a day there, even the hours of the departure. The last thing he wrote on Prinkipo (apart from a farewell message of thanks to the Turkish Government) was an obituary on Skrypnik, the old Bolshevik, a leader of the October insurrection, later a fervent Stalinist, who, having come into conflict with Stalin, had just committed suicide.[2]

Yet, despite all the adversities, the years Trotsky had spent on Prinkipo were the calmest, the most creative, and the least unhappy time of his exile.

[1] 'Pered Otyezdom', 15 July 1933 in *The Archives*.
[2] The obituary bears the date of 15 July; it appeared in *B.O.* in October, nos. 36–37.

CHAPTER III

The Revolutionary as Historian

Like Thucydides, Dante, Machiavelli, Heine, Marx, Herzen, and other thinkers and poets, Trotsky attained his full eminence as a writer only in exile, during the few Prinkipo years. Posterity will remember him as the historian of the October Revolution as well as its leader. No other Bolshevik has or could have produced so great and splendid an account of the events of 1917; and none of the many writers of the anti-Bolshevik parties has presented any worthy counterpart to it. The promise of this achievement could be discerned in Trotsky very early. His descriptions of the revolution of 1905 provide till this day the most vivid panorama of that 'general rehearsal' for 1917. He produced his first narrative and analysis of the upheavals of 1917 only a few weeks after the October insurrection, during the recesses of the Brest Litovsk peace conference; and in subsequent years he went on working at his historical interpretation of the events in which he had been a protagonist. There was in him a twofold *vis historica*: the revolutionary's urge to make history and the writer's impulse to describe it and grasp its meaning.

All banished men brood over the past; but only a few, very few, conquer the future. Hardly any one among them however, has had to fight for his life, morally and physically, as Trotsky fought. Stalin at first inflicted exile on him in the way the Romans used to inflict it—as a substitute for the death penalty; and he was not to remain content with the substitute. Even before Trotsky was assassinated physically, his moral assassins were at work for years, first effacing his name from the annals of the revolution and then reinscribing it as the eponym of counter-revolution. Trotsky the historian was therefore doubly embattled: he defended the revolution against its enemies; and he defended his own place in it. No writer has ever created his major work in similar conditions, designed to inflame all his passions, to rob him of every calm thought, and to distort his vision. In Trotsky all passions were aroused, but his thought remained calm and his vision clear. He often recalled Spinoza's maxim: 'Neither weep nor laugh but understand'; but he himself could not help weeping and laughing; yet he understood.

It would not be quite right to say that as historian he combined extreme partisanship with rigorous objectivity. He had no need to combine them: they were the heat and the light of his work, and as heat and light belonged to each other. He scorned the 'impartiality' and 'conciliatory justice' of the scholar who pretends 'to stand on the wall of a threatened city and behold at the same time the besiegers and the besieged'.[1] His own place was, as it had been in the years 1917–22, within the revolution's threatened city. Yet his involvement in the struggle, far from blurring his sight, sharpens it. His antagonism to Russia's old ruling classes and their willing and unwilling supporters makes him see clearly not only their vices or weaknesses but also such feeble and ineffective virtues as they possessed. Here, as in the best military thinking, extreme partisanship and scrupulously sober observation indeed go hand in hand. To the good soldier nothing is of greater importance than to get a realistic picture of the 'other side of the hill', unclouded by wishful thinking or emotion. Trotsky, the commander of the October insurrection, had acted on this principle; and Trotsky the historian does the same. He achieves in his image of the revolution the unity of the subjective and the objective elements.

His historical writing is dialectical as is hardly any other such work produced by the Marxist school of thought since Marx, from whom he derives his method and style. To Marx's minor historical works, *The Class Struggle in France*, *The 18th Brumaire of Louis Bonaparte*, and *The Civil War in France*, Trotsky's *History* stands as the large mural painting stands to the miniature. Whereas Marx towers above the disciple in the power of his abstract thought and gothic imagination, the disciple is superior as epic artist, especially as master of the graphic

[1] Trotsky referred in particular to L. Madelin, 'the reactionary and therefore fashionable' French historian. Preface to *History of the Russian Revolution*, Vol. I.

portrayal of masses and individuals in action. His socio-
political analysis and artistic vision are in such concord that
there is no trace of any divergence. His thought and his
imagination take flight together. He expounds his theory of
revolution with the tension and the *élan* of narrative; and his
narrative takes depth from his ideas. His scenes, portraits, and
dialogues, sensuous in their reality, are inwardly illumined
by his conception of the historical process. Many non-Marxist
critics have been impressed by this distinctive quality of his
writing. Here, for instance, is what a British historian, A. L.
Rowse, says:

> The real importance of Trotsky's *History* does not lie in his power
> of word painting, either of character or of scene, though indeed
> his gift is so brilliant and incisive that one is continually reminded
> of Carlyle. There is something of the same technique, the same
> mannerism even, in the way the rapid lights shift across the scene
> and particular odd episodes are brought out in singular sharpness
> of relief and made to bear general significance; something of the
> same difficulty in following the sequel of events—the lights are so
> blinding—one may add. But where Carlyle had but his magnificent
> powers of intuition to rely on, Trotsky has a theory of history at
> his command, which enables him to grasp what is significant and
> to relate things together. The same point can be illustrated more
> appositely by comparison with Winston Churchill's *The World
> Crisis*, for the two men are not dissimilar in character and gifts of
> mind. But here again one notices the difference; for Mr. Churchill's
> history, for all its personality, its vividness, and vitality, points
> which it has in common with Trotsky—has not a philosophy of
> history behind it.[1]

The remark about the similarity between Trotsky and
Churchill is correct: at their opposite poles the two men
represent the same blend of realism and romanticism, the
same pugnacity, the same inclination to look, and to run,
ahead of their class and milieu, and the same urge to make
and to write history. One need not deny Churchill a 'philosophy of history' even if he holds it only instinctively; but
it is true that Trotsky's is a fully formed and elaborate theory.
What is important is that his theoretical *Weltanschauung*
permeates his sensitivity, amplifies his intuition, and heightens

---

[1] A. L. Rowse, *End of an Epoch*, pp. 282–3.

his vision. And, although he has in common with Carlyle the intensity and dazzling brilliance of imagery, he also has the compactness and clarity of expression and the balance of the greatest classical historians. He is indeed the only historian of genius that the Marxist school of thought has so far produced and so far—rejected.[1]

.   .   .   .

Of Trotsky's two major historical works, *My Life* and *The History*, the former is, of course, the less ambitious. He wrote it too early in a sense, though if he had not written it in 1929, or shortly thereafter, he might not have written it at all. It tells in the main one half of his story, that of his revolutionary triumph; it only sketches the beginning of the other half, which was still unfolding. He concluded the book after a few months in exile, only five years or so after the struggle between him and Stalin had begun in earnest. The conflict was still too fresh, and in relating it he was handicapped by tactical considerations and lack of perspective. What he was to live through in the coming eleven years was not only to be of great weight in itself, but was to reflect back upon all his earlier experience: the whole of his life was to take on the glow of tragedy from its grave and gloomy epilogue. He concluded *My Life* with a statement defying those who spoke of his tragedy: 'I enjoy the spectacle every scene of which I understand . . .' he repeated after Proudhon. 'What makes others wither, elevates . . . inspires, and fortifies me; how then . . . can I lament destiny . . .?'[2] Would he have repeated these words a few years later? In a sense, if it were to be held that tragedy necessarily includes the protagonist's penance, there was indeed no tragedy in Trotsky—there was no penance in him to the end. Like Shelley, who could not bear that his Prometheus should end by humbling himself before Jupiter, Trotsky was 'averse from a catastrophe so feeble'. His was the modern tragedy of the precursor in conflict with his contemporaries, the tragedy an example of which he himself saw in Babeuf—only that his was a far larger drama, of far

---

[1] This is true, however, only to the extent to which it may be permissible to characterize the communist movement under Stalin and Khrushchev as Marxist.

[2] *Moya Zhizn*, vol. II, p. 338.

greater catastrophic force. Yet even of this kind of tragedy
there is no premonition in his autobiography, which consequently leaves the impression of a certain superficiality in
the writer's view of his own fortunes, the superficiality characteristic of the protagonist of a tragedy just before disasters
assault him from all sides.

The least convincing part of *My Life* is in the last chapters
where he relates his struggle with Stalin. Even there he gives
us a wealth of insight, incident, and characterization; but he
does not go to the root of the matter and he leaves Stalin's
ascendancy only half explained. He portrays Stalin too much
as villain *ex machina*; and he views him still as he had viewed
him years earlier, as too insignificant to be his antagonist, let
alone to dominate the stage of the Soviet state and of international communism for full three decades. 'To the leading
group of the party (to wider circles he was not known at all)
Stalin always seemed a man destined to play second and third
fiddle', he says; and he suggests that although Stalin had come
to play first fiddle he would soon, very soon, play out his tune.[1]
It may be recalled that Lenin in his will described Stalin as
one of the 'two most able men of the Central Committee', the
other being Trotsky, and warned the party that the animosity
of these two men was the gravest danger to the revolution.
Trotsky could not gloss over the wider political reasons for
Stalin's ascendancy, and he shows Stalin as the incarnation
of the party machine and of the new bureaucracy greedy for
power and privileges. Yet he could not explain convincingly
why the leading cadre of Bolsheviks first assisted in the usurpation and then connived in it, and why all this led to such
extraordinary forms of the inner party struggle. As auto-
biographer no less than as leader of the Opposition, Trotsky
virtually ignores the intrinsic connexion between the suppression by Bolshevism of all parties and its self-suppression,
of which Stalin was the supreme agent. He does not see why
the party should have turned against itself the weapons it had
wielded, far less savagely, against its enemies; and that it did
so appears to him to be the result of a mere 'conspiracy'.[2]

Yet *My Life* remains an autobiographical masterpiece.
François Mauriac rightly compares its opening chapters with

[1] Op. cit., vol. II, p. 247.   [2] Ibid., pp. 227-34.

Tolstoy's and Gorky's descriptions of childhood.[1] Trotsky has the same 'childlike' freshness of the eye and the same almost inexhaustible visual memory, the same power in the evocation of atmosphere and mood, and the same seeming ease in bringing characters and scenes to life. With one or two small strokes describing a grimace, a gesture, or the glimmer of an eye he conveys the inwardness and moral flavour of a human being. In this manner he portrays entire galleries of relatives, domestic servants, neighbours, schoolmasters, and so on. Here are a few examples, although his prose is too close-textured for any excerpt to be even remotely as vibrant with life as it is in its context. He describes his headmaster at his school in Odessa: 'He never looked at the person with whom he talked; he moved about the corridors and the classrooms noiselessly on rubber heels. He spoke in a small, hoarse, falsetto voice which, without being raised, could be terrifying. . . . A humanity-hater by nature . . . he seemed even-tempered, but inwardly was in a state of chronic irritation.' One of the masters was 'thin, with a prickly moustache on a greenish-yellow face; his eyeballs were muddy, his movements as sluggish as if he had just awakened. He coughed noisily and spat in the classroom . . . he would stare beyond his pupils. . . . Several years later he cut his throat with a razor.' Another master: 'A large and imposing man with gold-rimmed glasses on a small nose, with a manly young beard around his full face. Only when he smiled did it suddenly appear . . . that he was weak-willed, timid, torn within himself. . . .' And yet another: 'A huge German with a large head and a beard which reached to his waist line, he carried his heavy body, which seemed a vessel of kindliness, on almost childlike limbs. He was a most honest person and suffered over the failures of his pupils. . . .'[2]

We are made to see the 'seal of doom' on the families of landowning neighbours, who 'were all progressing with extraordinary rapidity, and all in the same direction, towards downfall'. To one of these families 'the whole countryside had once belonged; but now their scion lives by writing petitions, complaints, and letters for the peasants. When he came to see us he used to hide tobacco and lumps of sugar up his sleeve,

[1] F. Mauriac, *Memoires Interieures*, pp. 128–32.   [2] *Moya Zhizn*, vol. I, pp. 67–71.

and his wife did the same. With dribbling lips she would tell us stories of her youth, with its serfs, its grand pianos, its silks, and its perfumery. Their two sons grew up almost illiterate. The younger, Victor, was an apprentice in our machine shop.' And here is a glimpse of a Jewish landlord: he 'had received an education of the aristocratic kind. He spoke French fluently, played the piano. . . . His left hand was weak, but his right hand was fit, he said, to play in a concert. . . . He would often stop in the midst of playing, get up, and go to the mirror. Then, if no one was present, he would singe his beard on all sides with his burning cigarette—this was his idea of keeping his beard tidy.' And behind these galleries of bankrupt land-lords and upstart farmers, emaciated labourers and diverse relatives, there is always the breath of the Ukrainian steppe: 'The name of Falz-Fein [a landlord, the 'king of sheep'] rang like the sound of the feet of ten thousand sheep in motion, like the bleating of countless sheep, like the sound of the whistle of a shepherd in the steppes . . . like the barking of many sheepdogs. The steppe itself breathed this name both in summer heat and winter cold.'[1]

From the environment of his childhood Trotsky takes us to the first revolutionary circles of Nikolayev, the prisons of Odessa and Moscow, the colonies of exiles in Siberia; and then he shows us the galaxy of *Iskra*'s editors, the schism at the second Congress of the party, and the birth of Bolshevism. In the whole literature about that period there is not a single memoir or eye-witness account that fixes so graphic a picture of the schism as that which we get from *My Life*. The fact that Trotsky had been a Menshevik in 1903 but wrote as a Bol-shevik has much to do with his rendering of the atmosphere and his portrayal of the personalities. In retrospect he sides with Lenin; but he also has to do justice to himself, to Martov, Axelrod, and Zasulich, and to explain why they all went against Lenin. Unlike nearly all Bolshevik and Menshevik memoirists, he shows each of the opposed groups from the inside; and although he now condemns politically the Mensheviks and himself, he does it with understanding and sympathy. Even before he introduces us to the political controversy, he makes us feel the underlying clash of characters:

[1] Op. cit., vol. I, chapter II.

Working side by side with Lenin, Martov, his closest companion in arms, was already beginning to feel not quite at his ease. They still addressed each other in second singular, but a certain coolness was beginning to creep into their relations. Martov lived much more in the present. . . . Lenin, although firmly entrenched in the present, was always trying to pierce the veil of the future. Martov evolved innumerable, often ingenious, guesses, hypotheses, and propositions which he himself promptly forgot; whereas Lenin waited until the moment when he needed them. The elaborate subtlety of Martov's ideas made Lenin shake his head. . . . One can say that even before the split . . . Lenin was 'hard' and Martov 'soft'. And they both knew it. Lenin would glance at Martov, whom he highly esteemed, with a critical and somewhat suspicious look; and Martov, feeling this glance, would look down and his thin shoulders would twitch nervously. When they met and talked afterwards, at least in my presence, one missed the friendly inflection and the jests. Lenin would look beyond Martov as he talked, while Martov's eyes would grow glassy under his drooping and never quite clean pince-nez. And when Lenin spoke to me of Martov, there was a peculiar intonation in his voice: 'Who said that? Julius?'—and the name Julius was pronounced in a special way, with a slight emphasis, as if to give warning: 'A good man, no question about it, even a remarkable one, but much too soft.'[1]

One has at once the sense of destiny coming at this moment between the two 'closest comrades in arms', and of defeat suspended over Martov's frail and untidy figure. Trotsky does not forget how much as a young man he owed to Martov; and so, even as he passes his final judgement on him, he does it with sorrowful warmth: 'Martov [was] . . . one of the most tragic figures of the revolutionary movement. A gifted writer, an ingenious politician, a penetrating thinker, he stood far above the . . . movement of which he became the leader. But his thought lacked courage; his insight was devoid of will. Sheer doggedness was no substitute. His first reaction to events always tended to be revolutionary. In his second thoughts, however, lacking the support of an active will, he usually slid back.' The lack of active will is depicted here as the basic infirmity crippling a daring mind and noble character. How different is this sketch of Plekhanov drawn with discreet antipathy:

[1] Op. cit., vol. I, pp. 175–6.

... he apparently sensed something. .... At least he told Axelrod referring to Lenin: 'Of such stuff the Robespierres are made.' Plekhanov himself did not play an enviable part at the Congress. Only once did I see and hear him in all his power. That was at a session of the Programme Commission. With a clear, scientifically exact scheme of the Programme in mind, sure of himself, his knowledge and superiority, with a gay ironic sparkle in his eyes, his greying moustache alert and bristling, with slightly theatrical, lively and expressive gestures, Plekhanov as Chairman illumined the entire large gathering with his personality, like a live firework of erudition and wit.[1]

How devastating is this seemingly flattering picture of the man, with his self-satisfaction and vanity breaking through his brilliance, and with the suggestion of the firework about to fizzle out in darkness.

No less suggestive and memorable are the character sketches of the leaders of European socialism in the pre-1914 era: August Bebel, Karl Kautsky, Jean Jaures, Victor Adler, Rudolf Hilferding, Karl Renner, and many others. In a brief, often humorous passage, dealing with an outwardly trivial incident, Trotsky tells us about the time and the men more than do many learned volumes. He relates, for instance, how in 1902, after his first escape from Siberia, he stopped, penniless, hungry, but full of the importance of his mission, in Vienna and called at Social Democratic headquarters to ask the celebrated Victor Adler for help in arranging his further journey to London. It is Sunday: the offices are closed. On the staircase he meets an old gentleman 'looking none too amiable', whom he tells that he must see Adler. 'Do you know what day it is?' the gentleman replies sternly. 'It is Sunday', and tries to by-pass the intruder. 'No matter, I want to see Adler.' At this the accosted man 'replies in the voice of one who is leading a battalion to the attack: "I am telling you Doctor Adler cannot be seen on a Sunday." ' Trotsky tries to impress the old man with the urgency of his business; but he thunders back: 'Even if your business were ten times as important— do you understand?—even if you brought the news—you hear me?—that your Tsar was assassinated, that a revolution had broken out in your country—do you hear me?—even that

[1] Op. cit., vol. I, p. 189.

would not give you the right to disturb the Doctor's Sunday rest.' This was Fritz Austerlitz, famous editor of the *Arbeiterzeitung*, the 'terror of his office', who in 1914 was to become a most chauvinistic war propagandist.[1]

On that staircase the young revolutionary, freshly emerged from the Russian underground, ran straight into the embodiment of the orderly, hierarchical, routine-ridden bureaucracy of European socialism. In a few sentences he relates his meeting with Adler, whom he managed to reach after all: 'A short man, with a pronounced stoop, almost a hunch, and with swollen eyes in a tired face.' Trotsky apologized for disturbing the Sunday rest. ' "Go on, go on," Adler replied with seeming sternness, but in a tone which encouraged instead of intimidating me. One could see intelligence emanating from every wrinkle of his face.' Told about the strange staircase encounter, Adler wondered: 'Who could it have been? A tall man? And did he speak to you like that? He shouted? Oh, that was Austerlitz. You say he shouted? Oh, yes, it was Austerlitz. Do not take it to heart. If you ever bring news of revolution in Russia you may ring my bell even at night.' These few lines at once confront us with another element of European pre-1914 socialism: the sensitive intelligence of the old pioneer leader, who, however, becomes gradually the glorified prisoner of the party's sergeant-major. The book is strewn with hundreds of such laconic and expressive incidents and dialogues.

When he comes to the climax of his life, the October Revolution and the Civil War, Trotsky describes it with the utmost restraint, with sparse, often pointillistic, touches. This, to take a random illustration, is how he shows the current of popular feeling underlying the brief triumph of reaction in the hungry and stormy July days of 1917, when Bolshevism seemed to be down and out, and Lenin, branded as German spy, had gone into hiding. Trotsky takes us into the canteen of the Petrograd Soviet:

I noticed that Grafov (a soldier in charge of the canteen) would slip me a hotter glass of tea, or a sandwich better than the rest, avoiding looking at me. He obviously was in sympathy with the Bolsheviks but had to hide this from his superiors. I began to look

[1] Op. cit., vol. I, p. 165.

about me more attentively. Grafov was not the only one: the whole lower staff of the Smolny—porters, messengers, watchmen—were unmistakably with the Bolsheviks. Then I felt that our cause was half won. But so far only half.[1]

A child's remark, a glimpse of Lenin's 'soiled collar' on the day after the October rising, the view of a long, dark, crowded corridor in the Smolny, alive like an anthill, a grotesque episode occurring in the middle of a decisive battle, and a terse dialogue—it is mostly through such details that he conveys the colour and the air of an historic scene. His artistry is in his indirect approach to events too immense to be depicted frontally (in an autobiography) and too big for big words.

It has been said of *My Life* that it shows up Trotsky's egotism and 'self-dramatization'. Autobiography being 'egotistical' by definition, this criticism amounts to saying that he should not have indulged in it. He himself had his 'Marxist' scruples, which lingered on even while he was putting the title to the book. 'If I had been writing these memoirs in different cir-cumstances,' he apologizes, 'although in other circumstances I should hardly have written them at all—I should have hesitated to include much of what I say in these pages.' But he was compelled to counter the avalanche of Stalinist falsi-fication which covered every part of his life story. 'My friends are in prison or in exile. I am obliged to speak of myself. . . . It is a question not merely of historical truth but also of a political struggle that is still going on.' He was in the position of a man in the dock, charged with every imaginable and unimaginable crime, who tries to vindicate himself by giving the court a full account of his doings and is then shouted down for his preoccupation with himself.

This is not to deny that there was an unmistakable streak of self-centredness in Trotsky. It belonged to his artistic nature; it developed during the pre-revolutionary years, when he walked by himself, neither a Bolshevik nor a Menshevik; and Stalinist vilification, forcing him into an intensely personal self-defensive attitude, brought it to the fore. Yet, of his self-dramatization' one would be entitled to speak only if his autobiography, or any biography of him, could at all make his life appear more dramatic than it actually was. To the

[1] Op. cit., vol. II, pp. 36–7.

extent to which in *My Life* he was not yet conscious of the tragic quality of his fate, it would be more correct to say that he under-dramatized himself. Nor, as we shall see later, can there be any question of his having over-stated his role in the revolution. In both *My Life* and the *History*, his real hero is not himself but Lenin, in whose shadow he deliberately placed himself.

Others have criticized *My Life* for its lack of introspection and the author's failure to reveal his subconscious mind. True enough, Trotsky produces no 'interior monologue'; he does not dwell on his dreams or complexes; and he observes an almost puritanical reticence about sex. This is, after all, a political autobiography, political in a very wide sense. Still, the author's respect for the rational core of psychoanalysis shows itself in the care he takes with the description of his childhood, where he does not omit such possible clues for the psychoanalyst as experiences and 'accidents' of the infantile years, toys, &c. (The narrative begins with the words: 'At times it has seemed to me that I can remember suckling at my mother's breast. . . .') He gives this incidental explanation of his caution about Freudian introspection: 'Memory is . . . not disinterested', he says in the Preface. 'Not rarely it suppresses or relegates to an obscure corner episodes which go against the grain of the individual's controlling vital instinct. . . . This, however, is a question for "psychoanalytical" criticism, which is sometimes ingenious and instructive, but more often whimsical and arbitrary.' He had gone into the subject of psychoanalysis deeply and sympathetically enough to know its pitfalls; and he had neither the time nor the patience for 'whimsical and arbitrary' guesses about his subconscious. Instead, he offered a self-portrait remarkable for its conscious integrity and human warmth.

As a political work *My Life* failed to achieve its immediate purpose: it made no impression on the communist public at whom it was primarily aimed. To average party members the mere reading of it was an impiety; and they did not read it. The few who did felt offended or antagonized. They were either committed to the Stalin cult, and the book only confirmed for them Stalinist imputations about Trotsky's personal ambition; or they were shocked to see that a leader of the revolution should at all engage in self-portraiture. 'Here is

Trotsky, the Narcissus, in the act of self-adulation' was a typical comment. And so communists overlooked the rich historical material Trotsky put before them, his insights into revolution, and his interpretation of Bolshevism from which they might have drawn many lessons for themselves. On the other hand, the book found a wide bourgeois reading public, which admired its literary qualities, but had little or no use for its message. '*Mein Leid ertönt der unbekannten Menge, Ihr Beifall selbst macht meinem Herzen bang . . .*', Trotsky might have said of himself.

.   .   .   .

The *History* is his crowning work, both in scale and power and as the fullest expression of his ideas on revolution. As an account of a revolution, given by one of its chief actors, it stands unique in world literature.

He introduces us to the scene of 1917 with a chapter 'Peculiarities of Russia's Development' which sets the events in deep historical perspective; and one recognizes in this chapter at once an enriched and mature version of his earliest exposition of Permanent Revolution, dating back to 1906.[1] We are shown Russia entering the twentieth century without having shaken off the Middle Ages or passed through a Reformation and bourgeois revolution, yet with elements of a modern bourgeois civilization thrust into her archaic existence. Forced to advance under superior economic and military pressure from the West, she could not go through all the phases of the 'classical' cycle of western European progress. 'Savages throw away their bows and arrows for rifles all at once, without travelling the road which lay between those two weapons in the past.' Modern Russia could not enact a Reformation of her own or a bourgeois revolution under bourgeois leadership. Her very backwardness impelled her to advance politically all at once to the point western Europe had reached and to go beyond it—to socialist revolution. Her feeble bourgeoisie being unable to cast off the burden of a semi-feudal absolutism, her small but compact working class, eventually supported by a rebellious peasantry, came forward as the leading revolutionary force. The working class could not content itself with a revolution resulting in the

[1] See *The Prophet Armed*, chapter VI.

establishment of a bourgeois democracy—it had to fight for the realization of the socialist programme. Thus by a 'law of combined development' the extreme of backwardness tended towards the extreme of progress, and this led to the explosion of 1917.

The 'law of combined development' accounts for the force of the tensions within Russia's social structure. Trotsky, however, treats the social structure as a 'relatively constant' element of the situation which does not account by itself for the events of the revolution. In a controversy with Pokrovsky, he points out that neither in 1917 nor in the preceding decade did any fundamental change occur in Russia's social structure—the war had weakened and exposed that structure but not altered it.[1] The national economy and the basic relations between social classes were in 1917 broadly the same as in 1912–14, and even in 1905–7. What then accounted directly for the eruptions of February and October, and for the violent ebb and flow of revolution in between? The changes in mass psychology, Trotsky replies. If the structure of society was the constant factor, the temper and the moods of the masses were the variable element which determined the flux and reflux of events, their rhythm and direction. 'The most indubitable feature of a revolution is the direct intervention of the masses in historic events. The revolution is there in their nerves before it comes out into the street.' The *History* is therefore to a large extent a study in revolutionary mass psychology. Delving into the interconnexion between the 'constant' and 'variable' factors, he demonstrates that what makes for revolution is not merely the fact that the social and political institutions have long been in decay and crying out to be overthrown, but the circumstances that many millions of people have for the first time heard that 'cry' and become aware of it. In the social structure the revolution had been ripe well before 1917; in the mind of the masses it ripened only in 1917. Thus, paradoxically, the deeper cause of revolution lies not in the mobility of men's minds, but in their inert conservatism; men rise *en masse* only when they suddenly realize their mental lag behind the times and want to make it good all at once. This is

[1] Preface to vol. I and introduction to vols. II and III of the *History*.

the lesson the *History* drives home: no great upheaval in society follows automatically from the decay of an old order; generations may live under a decaying order without being aware of it. But when, under the impact of some catastrophe like war or economic collapse, they become conscious of it, there comes the gigantic outburst of despair, hope, and activity. The historian has therefore to 'enter into the nerves' and the minds of millions of people in order to feel and convey the mighty heave that overturns the established order.

The academic pedant burrowing in mountains of documents in order to reconstruct from them a single historical incident may say that no historian can 'enter into the nerves' of millions. Trotsky is aware of the difficulties: the manifestations of mass consciousness are scrappy and scattered; and this may lead the historian to arbitrary constructions and false intuitions. But he points out that the historian can nevertheless verify the truth or untruth of his image of mass consciousness by certain severely objective tests. He must follow faithfully the internal evidence of the events. He can and must check whether the motion of mass consciousness, as he sees it, is consistent with itself; whether every phase of it follows necessarily from what went before it, and whether it leads clearly to what comes after it. He must further consider whether the flow of mass consciousness is consistent with the movement of events: are the moods of the people reflected in the events and do they in turn reflect these? If it be argued that the answers to such questions must be vague and subjective, Trotsky replies by referring, in the Marxist manner, to practical action as the final criterion. He points out that what he is doing as an historian, he and other Bolshevik leaders did while they were making the revolution: relying upon analysis and observation they made guesses about the state of mind and the moods of the masses. All their crucial political decisions rested on those 'guesses'; and the course of the revolution is there to show that, despite trial and error, these had been broadly correct. If in the heat of battle the revolutionary was able to form an approximately correct image of the political emotions and thoughts of millions, there is no reason why the historian should not be able to form it after the event.

The manner in which Trotsky depicts the mass in action

has much in common with Eisenstein's method in the classical
Potemkin. He picks out of the crowd a few individuals, exposes
them in a moment of excitement or apathy, and lets them
express their mood in a phrase or gesture; then he shows us
the crowd again, a dense and warm crowd, swayed by a tidal
emotion or moving into action; and we recognize at once that
this is the emotion or action which the individual phrase or
gesture had foreshadowed. He has a peculiar gift for over-
hearing the multitudes as they think aloud and for letting us
hear them for ourselves. In conception and image he leads
perpetually from the general to the particular and back to the
general; and the passage is never unnatural or strained. Here
one is again reminded of the comparison between Trotsky
and Carlyle; but the comparison lights up a contrast rather
than a similarity. In the Histories of both much of the ethos
depends on the mass scenes. Both make us feel the elemental
force of an insurgent people, so that we view it as if we were
watching landslides or avalanches on the move. But whereas
Carlyle's crowds are driven only by emotion, Trotsky's think
and reflect. They are elemental; yet they are human. Carlyle's
mass is enveloped in a purple haze of mysticism, which suggests
that the revolutionary people of France are God's blind
scourge bringing retribution upon a sinful ruling class. His
mass fascinates us and repels us. He 'enters into its nerves',
but only after he has worked himself up into a frenzy—he
himself is all nerves and hallucinatory fever. Trotsky draws
his mass scenes with not less imaginative *élan*, but with crystalline clarity. He lets us feel that here and now men make
their own history; and that they do it in accordance with the
'laws of history', but also by acts of their consciousness and
will. Of such men, even though they may be illiterate and
crude, he is proud; and he wants us to be proud of them. The
revolution is for him that brief but pregnant moment when
the humble and downtrodden at last have their say. In his
eyes this moment redeems ages of oppression. He harks back
to it with a nostalgia which gives the re-enactment a vivid
and high relief.

He does not, however, overstate the role of the masses. He
does not oppose them to the parties and leaders as, for instance,
does Kropotkin, the great anarchist historian of the French

Revolution, who seeks to prove that every advance of the revolution is due to spontaneous popular action and every setback to the scheming and the 'statesmanship' of politicians. Trotsky sees the masses as the driving force of the upheaval, yet a force which needs to be concentrated and directed. Only the party can provide direction. 'Without a guiding organization the energy of the mass would dissipate like steam not enclosed in a piston box. But nevertheless what moves things is not the piston or the box but the steam.' The great contrast which he draws between the two revolutions of 1917 is based on this idea. The February revolution was essentially the work of the masses themselves, whose energy was powerful enough to force the Tsar to abdicate and to bring the Soviets into existence, but then dissipated before having solved any of the great issues, allowing Prince Lvov to become the head of the government. The October Revolution was primarily the work of the Bolsheviks who focused and directed the energy of the masses.

The relationship between classes and parties is much more complex in Trotsky's presentation, however, than any mechanistic simile might suggest. He shows the subtle interplay of many objective and subjective factors. What guides a party in its action is basically a definite class interest. But the connexion between class and party is often involved and sometimes ambiguous; in a revolutionary era it is also highly unstable. Even if a party's behaviour is ultimately governed by its nexus with one particular class, it may recruit its following from another, a potentially hostile, class. Or it may represent only one phase in the development of a social milieu, a phase to which some leaders remain mentally fixed, while the milieu has left it far behind. Or else a party may be ahead of its class and expound a programme which the latter is not yet ready to accept, but which events will force it to accept; and so on and so forth. In a revolution the traditional political balance collapses, and new alignments take shape abruptly. Trotsky's *History* is a grand inquiry into the dynamic of these processes.

.   .   .   .

We have said that Trotsky does not disguise his hostility

towards the enemies of the October Revolution. To put it more accurately, he confronts them before the tribunal of history as Counsel for the Prosecution; and there he inflicts upon them for a second time the defeat he had inflicted on them in the streets of Petrograd. As a rule this is not a role that fits the historian. Yet in history as in law it happens that the Counsel for the Prosecution may present the fullest possible truth of a case—namely, when he charges the men in the dock with offences they have actually committed; when he does not exaggerate their guilt; when he enters into their conditions and motives and gives due weight to mitigating circumstances; when he supports every count of the indictment with ample and valid evidence; and, finally, when the defendants, having full freedom to refute the evidence, not only fail to do so, but loudly quarrelling among themselves in the dock only confirm it. Such is the manner in which Trotsky discharges his duty. When his *History* was published, and for many years thereafter, most of the chiefs of the anti-Bolshevik parties, Miliukov, Kerensky, Tseretelli, Chernov, Dan, Abramovich, and others were alive and active as émigrés. Yet none of them has exposed a single significant flaw in the fabric of fact which he presented; and none, with the partial exception of Miliukov, has seriously attempted an alternative account.[1] And so (since no History worthy of the name has so far been produced in the Soviet Union either), Trotsky's work is still, in the fifth decade after October, the only full-scale history of the revolution. This is no accident. All the other major actors, again with the partial exception of Miliukov, were so entangled in their contradictions and failures as to be incapable of presenting in full their own more or less coherent versions. They refused to go back as historians to the fatal battlefield where every landmark and indeed every inch of land reminded them of their disgrace. Trotsky revisits the battlefield, his conscience clear and his head up.

Yet his story has no real villains. He does not, as a rule,

[1] Miliukov, however, himself partly renounced his own work as being from an historical viewpoint inadequate. Miliukov, *Istorya Vtoroi Russkoi Revolutsii*, Preface. The main, or rather the only, point of fact on which Kerensky seeks to refute Trotsky is in reiterating the old accusation that Lenin and the Bolshevik party were spies in German pay. Kerensky, *Crucifixion of Liberty*, pp. 285ff.

depict the enemies of Bolshevism as corrupt and depraved men. He does not strip them of their private virtues and personal honour. If they nevertheless stand condemned, it is because he has shown them as defending indefensible causes, as lagging behind the times, as elevated by events to heights of responsibility to which they had not risen mentally and morally, and as perpetually torn between word and deed. The villainy he exposes lies in the archaic social system rather than in individuals. His determinist view of history allows him to treat adversaries, not indulgently indeed, but fairly, and at times generously. When he depicts an enemy in power he shows him complacent, talking big, throwing his weight about; and he crushes him with irony or indignation. Not rarely, however, he stops to pay a tribute to an adversary's past achievement, integrity, even heroism; and he sighs over the deterioration of a character worthy of a better destiny. When he describes a broken enemy, he dwells on the necessity of what had happened and exults in its historic justice; but sometimes the exultation subsides and he casts a commiserating glance—usually his last glance—at the prostrate victim.

He never paints the enemies of the revolution blacker than they have painted one another. Often he paints them less black, because he dissects their mutual animosities and jealousies and makes allowance for exaggeration in the cruel insults they exchanged. He treats the Tsar and the Tsarina no more mercilessly than Witte, Miliukov, Denikin, and even more orthodox monarchists have treated them. He even 'defends' the Tsar against Liberal critics, who have held that by means of timely concessions the Tsar might have averted the catastrophe. Nicholas II, Trotsky argues, made quite a few concessions, but could not yield more ground than self-preservation permitted. As in Tolstoy's *War and Peace*, so in Trotsky the Tsar is a 'slave of history'. 'Nicholas II inherited from his ancestors not only a giant empire, but also a revolution. And they did not bequeath him one quality which would have made him capable of governing an empire, or even a province, or a county. To that historical flood which was rolling its billows each one closer to the gates of his palace, the last Romanov opposed only a dumb indifference.'[1] He draws

[1] Trotsky, op. cit., vol. I, p. 71.

a memorable analogy between three doomed monarchs: Nicholas II, Louis XVI, and Charles I, and also between their Queens. Nicholas's chief characteristic is not just cruelty, of which he was capable, or stupidity, but 'meagreness of inner powers, a weakness of the nervous discharge, poverty of spiritual resources'. 'Both Nicholas and Louis XVI give the impression of people overburdened by their job, but at the same time unwilling to give up even a part of those rights which they are unable to use.' Each went to the abyss 'with the crown pushed down over his head'. But, Trotsky remarks, 'would it be any easier . . . to go to an abyss which you cannot escape anyway with your eyes wide open?' He shows that at the decisive moments, when the three sovereigns are overtaken by their fate, they look so much like each other that their distinctive features seem to vanish, because 'to a tickle people react differently, but to red hot iron alike'. As for the Tsarina and Marie Antoinette, both were 'enterprising but chickenheaded' and both 'see rainbow dreams as they drown'.[1]

And here is how he portrays the Cadets, the Mensheviks, and the Social Revolutionaries. Miliukov: 'Professor of history, author of significant scholarly works, founder of the Cadet Party . . . completely free from that insufferable, half-aristocratic and half-intellectual, political dilettantism which is proper to the majority of Russian Liberal men of politics. Miliukov took his profession very seriously and that alone distinguishes him.' The Russian bourgeoisie did not like him because 'prosaically and soberly, without adornment [he] expressed the political essence of the Russian bourgeoisie. Beholding himself in the Miliukov mirror, the man of the bourgeoisie saw himself grey, self-interested, and cowardly; and, as so often happens, he took offence at the mirror'. Rodzianko, the Tsar's Lord Chamberlain who became one of the leaders of the February régime, cuts a grotesque figure: 'Having received power from the hands of conspirators, rebels, and tyrannicides, [he] wore a haunted expression in those days . . . sneaked on tiptoe round the blaze of the revolution, choking from the smoke and saying: "Let it burn down to the coals, then we will try to cook up something." '[2]

Trotsky's Mensheviks and Social Revolutionaries have, of

[1] Ibid., pp. 108–18.   [2] Ibid., pp. 197–8.

course, little in common with the faceless counter-revolutionary
phantoms usually shown in Stalinist and even post-Stalinist
literature. Each of them belongs to his species, but has his
individual traits of character. Here is a thumbnail sketch of
Chkheidze, the Menshevik President of the Petrograd Soviet:
'He tried to consecrate to the duties of his office all the resources of his conscientiousness, concealing his perpetual lack
of confidence in himself under an ingenious jocularity. He
carried the ineradicable imprint of his province . . . mountainous Georgia . . . the Gironde of the Russian revolution.'
The 'most distinguished figure' of that Gironde, Tseretelli, had
for many years been a hard labour convict in Siberia, yet

remained a radical of the southern French type. In conditions of
ordinary parliamentary routine he would have been a fish in water.
But he was born into a revolutionary epoch and had poisoned himself in youth with a dose of Marxism. At any rate, of all the Mensheviks, Tseretelli . . . revealed the widest horizon and the [strongest]
desire to pursue a consistent policy. For this reason he, more than
any other, helped on with the destruction of the February régime.
Chkheidze wholly submitted to Tseretelli, although at moments he
was frightened by that doctrinaire straightforwardness which
caused the revolutionary hard labour convict of yesterday to unite
with the conservative representatives of the bourgeoisie.[1]

Skobelev, once Trotsky's disciple, looks like an undergraduate
'playing the role of a statesman on a home-made stage'.
And as for Lieber:

If the first violin in the orchestra . . . was Tseretelli, the piercing
clarinet was played by Lieber, with all his lung power and blood
in his eyes. This was a Menshevik of the Jewish Workers' Union
(the Bund) with a long revolutionary past, very sincere, very
temperamental, very eloquent, very limited, and passionately
desirous of showing himself an inflexible patriot and iron statesman . . . beside himself with hatred of Bolsheviks.

Chernov, the ex-participant in the Zimmerwald movement,
now Kerensky's Minister:

A well-read rather than educated man, with a considerable but
unintegrated learning, Chernov always had at his disposition a
boundless assortment of appropriate quotations, which for a long

[1] Trotsky, op. cit., vol. I, p. 243.

time caught the imagination of the Russian youth without teaching them much. There was only one single question which this many-worded leader could not answer: Whom was he leading and whither? The eclectic formulas of Chernov, ornamented with moralisms and verses, united for a time a most variegated public who at all critical moments pulled in different directions. No wonder Chernov complacently contrasted his methods of forming a party with Lenin's 'sectarianism'. . . . He decided to evade all issues, abstaining from the vote became for him a form of political life. . . . With all the differences between Chernov and Kerensky, who hated each other, they were both completely rooted in the pre-revolutionary past—in the old, flabby Russian society, in that thin-blooded and pretentious intelligentsia, burning with a desire to teach the masses of the people, to be their guardian and benefactor, but completely incapable of listening to them, understanding them, and learning from them.[1]

What distinguishes Trotsky's Bolsheviks from all other parties is precisely the ability to 'learn from the masses' as well as to teach them. But it is not without reluctance and inner resistance that they learn and rise to their task; and when Trotsky concludes with an apotheosis of the revolution and its party, he leaves us wondering for just how long the Bolsheviks will go on 'learning from the masses'. The party he shows us is very different from the 'iron phalanx' which, in the official legend, marches steadfastly and irresistibly, free from all human frailty, towards its predetermined goal. It is not that Trotsky's Bolsheviks lack 'iron', determination and audacity; but they possess these qualities in doses appropriate to the human character and distributed rather unevenly among leaders and rankers. We see them in their finest moments, when isolated, insulted, and battered, they hope and struggle on. In selfless devotion to a cause none of their adversaries is their equal. Greatness of purpose and character is ever present in their picture. But we see them also in disarray and confusion, the leaders shortsighted and timid, the rankers groping tensely and awkwardly in the dark. Because of this Trotsky has been accused of presenting a caricature of Bolshevism. Nothing is further from the truth. His picture is superbly true to nature precisely because he exposes all the weaknesses, doubtings, and waverings of Bolshevism. At the decisive

[1] Ibid., pp. 244–6.

moment the hesitancy and the divisions are subdued or overcome, and doubt gives place to confidence. That the party had
to struggle with itself as well as with its enemies in order to
rise to its role does not derogate from its accomplishment—
it makes the accomplishment all the greater. Trotsky does not
detract from the political honour even of Zinoviev, Kamenev,
Rykov, Kalinin, and the others who shrank from the great
leap of October; if his narrative brings discredit upon them,
it is only because after the event they posed as the unflagging
leaders of the iron phalanx.

The *History* highlights two great 'inner crises' of Bolshevism
in the year of the revolution. In the first Lenin, just returned
from Switzerland, presents his April Theses and politically
'rearms' his party for warfare against the February régime;
in the second, at the penultimate stage of the revolution, the
advocates and opponents of insurrection confront each other
in the Bolshevik Central Committee. In both crises the limelight rests for a long time on a narrow circle of leaders. Yet
the scenes engrave themselves on our mind as deeply as do the
broader, majestic images of the February rising and of the
October Revolution or as does the sombre interval of the July
days, when the movement is shown at its nadir. In both crises
we are made to feel that it is on the few members of the Central
Committee that the fate of the revolution hangs: their vote
decides whether the energies of the masses are to be dissipated
and defeated or directed towards victory. The problem of
masses and leaders is posed in all its acuteness; and almost at
once the limelight is focused even more narrowly and intensely
on a single leader—Lenin.

Both in April and October, Lenin stands almost alone, misunderstood and disavowed by his disciples. Members of the
Central Committee are on the point of burning the letter in
which he urges them to prepare for insurrection; and he
resolves to 'wage war' against them and if need be to appeal,
disregarding party discipline, to the rank and file. 'Lenin did
not trust the Central Committee—without Lenin . . .', Trotsky
comments; and 'Lenin was not so wrong in his mistrust'.[1] Yet
in each crisis he eventually won the party for his strategy and
threw it into battle. His shrewdness, realism, and concentrated

[1] Op. cit., vol. III, p. 131.

will emerge from the narrative as the decisive elements of the historic process, at least equal in importance to the spontaneous struggle of millions of workers and soldiers. If their energy was the 'steam' and the Bolshevik party the 'piston box' of the revolution, Lenin was the driver.

Here Trotsky is grappling with the classical problem of personality in history; and here he is perhaps least successful. His factual account of Lenin's activity is irreproachable. At no stage is it possible to say that here, at this or that point Lenin did not act and the other Bolsheviks did not behave as Trotsky tells us they did. Nor is he out to present Lenin as a self-sufficient maker of events. 'Lenin did not oppose the party from outside, but was himself its most complete expression', he assures us; and he repeatedly demonstrates that Lenin merely translated into clear formulas and action the thoughts and moods which agitated the rank and file, and that because of this he eventually prevailed. Leader and mass act in unison. There is a deep concord between Lenin and his party, even when he is at cross purposes with the Central Committee. Just as Bolshevism had not made its historic entry by chance, so Lenin's part was not fortuitous: he was 'a product of the whole past . . . embedded in it with the deepest roots. . . .' He was not 'a demiurge of the revolutionary process'; but merely a link, 'a great link', in a chain of objective historic causes.[1]

· However, having placed Lenin as a link in this chain, Trotsky then intimates that without the 'link' the 'chain' would have fallen to pieces. He asks what would have happened if Lenin had not managed to return to Russia in April 1917—'Is it possible . . . to say confidently that the party without him would have found its road? We would by no means make bold to say that. . . .' It is quite conceivable, he adds, that 'a disoriented and split party might have let slip the revolutionary opportunity for many years'. If in the *History* Trotsky expresses this view with caution, he dots the i's elsewhere. In a letter he wrote to Preobrazhensky from Alma Ata he says: 'You know better than I do that had Lenin not managed to come to Petrograd in April 1917, the October Revolution would not have taken place.' In his French Diary he makes the

[1] Op. cit., vol. I, pp. 341–2.

R

point categorically: 'Had I not been present in 1917 in Petro-grad the October Revolution would still have taken place—*on the condition that Lenin was present and in command.* If neither Lenin nor I had been present in Petrograd, there would have been no October Revolution: the leadership of the Bolshevik Party would have prevented it from occurring—of this I have not the slightest doubt!'[1] If Lenin is not yet a 'demiurge of history' here, this is so only in the sense that he did not make the revolution *ex nihilo*: the decay of the social structure, the 'steam' of mass energy, the 'piston box' of the Bolshevik party (which Lenin had designed and engineered)—all these had to be there in order that he should be able to play his part. But even if all these elements had been there, Trotsky tells us, without Lenin the Bolsheviks would have 'let slip the revolu-tionary opportunity for many years'. For how many years? Five—six? Or perhaps thirty—forty? We do not know. In any case, without Lenin, Russia might have continued to live under the capitalist order, or even under a restored Tsardom, per-haps for an indefinite period; and in this century at least world history would have been very different from what it has been.

For a Marxist this is a startling conclusion. The argument admittedly has a flavour of scholasticism, and the historian cannot resolve it by reference to empirical evidence: he cannot re-enact the revolution, keep Lenin out of the spec-tacle, and see what happens. If the issue is nevertheless pur-sued a little further here, this is done not for the sake of the argument but for the light it throws on our chief character. On this point the views of Trotsky, the historian, are closely affected by the experience and the mood of Trotsky, the leader of the defeated Opposition—it is doubtful whether earlier in his career he would have expressed a view which goes so strongly against the grain of the Marxist intellectual tradition.

Of that tradition Plekhanov's celebrated essay *The Role of the Individual in History* is highly representative—like Plek-hanov's other theoretical writings it exercised a formative influence on several generations of Russian Marxists. Plek-hanov discusses the issue in terms of the classical antinomy of

[1] *Trotsky's Diary in Exile*, pp. 53–54. The letter to Preobrazhensky, written in 1928, is in the Trotsky *Archives*.

necessity and freedom. He does not deny the role of the personality; he accepts Carlyle's dictum that 'the great man is a beginner': 'This is a very apt description. A great man is precisely a beginner because he sees *farther* than others and desires things *more strongly* than others.' Hence the 'colossal significance' in history and the 'terrible power' of the great leader. But Plekhanov insists that the leader is merely the organ of an historic need or necessity, and that necessity creates its organ when it needs it. No great man is therefore 'irreplaceable'. Any historic trend, if it is deep and wide enough, expresses itself through a certain number of men, not only through a single individual. In discussing the French Revolution, Plekhanov asks a question analogous to that which Trotsky poses: what would have been the course of the revolution without Robespierre or Napoleon?

> Let us assume that Robespierre was an absolutely indispensable force in his party; but even so he was not the only one. If the accidental fall of a brick had killed him in, say, January 1793, his place would, of course, have been taken by someone else; and although that other person might have been inferior to him in every respect, events would have nevertheless taken the same course as they did with Robespierre. . . . The Gironde would probably not have escaped defeat, but it is possible that Robespierre's party would have lost power somewhat earlier . . . or later, but it would have certainly fallen. . . .[1]

What Trotsky suggests is that if a brick had killed Lenin, say in March 1917, there would have been no Bolshevik revolution in that year and 'for many years after'. The fall of the brick would consequently have diverted a tremendous current of history in some other direction. The discussion about the individual's role turns out to be a debate over accident in history, a debate with a close bearing on the philosophy of Marxism. Plekhanov concludes his argument by saying that such accidental 'changes in the course of events might, to some extent, have influenced the subsequent political . . . life of Europe', but that 'in no circumstances would the final outcome of the revolutionary movement have been the "opposite" of what it was. Owing to the specific qualities of their minds and their characters, influential individuals can change the *individual features of events and some of their particular consequences*, but they cannot change their general *trend*, which is determined by other forces'. Trotsky implies that Lenin's personality changed not merely the 'individual features of events', but the general trend—without Lenin the social forces that made that trend or contributed to it would have been ineffective. This conclusion accords ill with Trotsky's *Weltanschauung* and with much else besides. If it were true that the greatest revolution of all time could not have occurred without one particular leader, then the leader cult at large would by no means be preposterous; and its denunciation by historical materialists, from Marx to Trotsky, and the revulsion of all progressive thought against it would be pointless.

Trotsky evidently succumbs here to the 'optical illusion' of which Plekhanov speaks in his argument against historians who insist that Napoleon's role was decisive because no one else could have taken his place with the same or a similar effect. The 'illusion' consists in the fact that a leader appears irreplaceable because, having assumed his place, he prevents others assuming it.

Coming forward [as the 'saviour of order'] . . . Napoleon made it impossible for all other generals to play this role; and some of them might have performed it in the same or almost the same way as he did. Once the public need for an energetic military ruler was satisfied, the social organization barred the road to this position . . . for all other gifted soldiers. . . . The power of Napoleon's personality presents itself to us in an extremely magnified form, for we credit him with the power of the social organization which had brought him to the fore and held him there. His power appears to us quite exceptional because other powers similar to his did not pass from the potential to the actual. And when we are asked: 'What would have happened if there had been no Napoleon?' our imagination becomes confused, and it seems to us that without him the social movement upon which his strength and influence were based could not have taken place.[1]

Similarly, it may be argued, Lenin's influence on events appears to us greatly magnified because once Lenin had assumed the post of the leader, he prevented others from

[1] Plekhanov, op. cit., pp. 325–6. (English ed., loc. cit.)

assuming it. It is, of course, impossible to say who might have taken his place had he not been there. It might have been Trotsky himself. Not for nothing did revolutionaries as important as Lunacharsky, Uritsky, and Manuilsky, discussing, in the summer of 1917, Lenin's and Trotsky's relative merits, agree that Trotsky had at that time eclipsed Lenin—and this while Lenin was there, on the spot; and although Lenin's influence on the Bolshevik party was decisive, the October insurrection was in fact carried out according to Trotsky's, not to Lenin's, plan. If neither Lenin nor Trotsky had been there someone else might have come to the fore. The fact that among the Bolsheviks there was apparently no other man of their stature and reputation does not prove that in their absence such a man would not have emerged. History has indeed a limited number of vacancies for the posts of great chiefs and commanders; and once the vacancies are filled, potential candidates have no opportunity to develop and achieve 'self-fulfilment'. Need it be held that they would not have achieved it in any circumstances? And could Lenin's or Trotsky's part not have been played by leaders smaller in stature, with this difference perhaps that the smaller men instead of 'allowing destiny to direct' them would have been 'dragged' by it?

It is a fact that almost every great leader or dictator appears irreplaceable in his lifetime; and that on his demise someone does fill his place, usually someone who to his colleagues appears to be the least likely candidate, a 'mediocrity' 'destined to play second or third fiddle'. Hence the surprise of so many at seeing first Stalin as Lenin's successor and then Khrushchev as Stalin's heir, the surprise which is a by-product of the optical illusion about the irreplaceable colossus. Trotsky maintains that only Lenin's genius could cope with the tasks of the Russian Revolution; and he often intimates that in other countries too the revolution must have a party like the Bolshevik and a leader like Lenin in order to win. There is no gainsaying Lenin's extraordinary capacity and character, or Bolshevism's good fortune in having him at its head. But have not in our time the Chinese and the Yugoslav revolutions triumphed under parties very different from that of the Bolsheviks of 1917, and under leaders of smaller, even much smaller, stature? In each case the revolutionary trend found or created its organ in such human material as was available. And if it seems implausible to assume that the October revolution would have occurred without Lenin, this is surely not as implausible as is the opposite assumption that a brick falling from a roof in Zurich early in 1917 could have altered the fortunes of mankind in this century.

Let us add that this last view accords so ill with Trotsky's basic philosophy and conception of the revolution that he could not uphold it consistently. Thus, in the *Revolution Betrayed*, written a few years later, he asserts:

> The quality of the leadership is, of course, far from being a matter of indifference . . . but it is not the only factor, and in the last analysis is not decisive. . . . The Bolsheviks . . . conquered . . . not through the personal superiority of their leaders, but through a new correlation of social forces. . . . [In the French Revolution too] in the successive supremacy of Mirabeau, Brissot, Robespierre, Barras, and Bonaparte, there is an obedience to objective law incomparably more effective than the special traits of the historic protagonists themselves.[1]

As indicated, Trotsky's 'optical illusion' about Lenin sheds a light on himself and his state of mind in these years rather than on Lenin. He produced the *History* after the orgy of the Stalinist 'personality cult' had begun; and his view of Lenin was a negative reflex of that cult. He appealed against the 'irreplaceable' Stalin to the 'irreplaceable' Lenin. Moreover, in view of the apathy and amorphousness of Soviet society, the leader did indeed loom incomparably larger in those years than in 1917, when the whole mass of the nation was seething with political energy and activity. On the one hand Stalin was emerging as autocrat; on the other, Trotsky was of necessity exercising a sort of ideal, moral autocracy as sole mouthpiece of the Opposition. He too, in his defeat, loomed as an individual exceptionally, even uniquely, large. As historian, he projected the leader's huge apparition back on to the screen

---

[1] Trotsky, *The Revolution Betrayed*, pp. 87–88. Characteristically, Sidney Hook in his reaction against Marxism (and Trotskyism) leaned heavily on the subjectivist note in Trotsky's treatment of Lenin, and concluded that the October Revolution 'was not so much a product of the whole past of Russian history as a product of one of the most event-making figures of all time'. Hook, *The Hero in History*, pp. 150–1.

of 1917, and drew this self-defensive moral: 'From the extra-ordinary significance which Lenin's arrival acquired, it should only be inferred that leaders are not accidentally created, that they are gradually chosen out and trained up in the course of decades, that they cannot be capriciously replaced, that their mechanical exclusion from the struggle gives the party a living wound, and in many cases may paralyse it for a long period.'[1] In his Diary he draws the moral even more explicitly:

. . . I think that the work on which I am engaged now [the opposition to Stalin and the foundation of the Fourth International], despite its extremely insufficient and fragmentary nature, is the most important work of my life—more important than 1917, more important than the period of the civil war, or any other. . . . I cannot speak of the 'indispensability' of my work, even in the period of 1917 to 1921. But now my work is 'indispensable' in the full sense of the word. There is no arrogance in this claim at all. The collapse of the two Internationals has posed a problem which none of the leaders of these Internationals is at all equipped to solve. The vicissitudes of my personal fate have confronted me with this problem and armed me with important experience in dealing with it. There is now no one except me to carry out the mission of arming a new generation with the revolutionary method. . . . I need at least about five more years of uninterrupted work to ensure the succession.[2]

He needed to feel that the leader, whether Lenin in 1917 or he himself in the nineteen-thirties, was irreplaceable—from this belief he drew the strength for his solitary and heroic exertions. And now, when alone of a whole Bolshevik genera-tion he spoke against Stalin, no one indeed was in a position to take his place. But, precisely because he was alone and irreplaceable did so much of his labour run to waste.

Quite apart from the pros and cons of this argument, Trotsky's feelings towards Lenin need further elucidation. The opinions of two contemporaries may be cited. 'Trotsky is prickly and imperative. Only in his relations with Lenin, after

---

[1] *History of the Russian Revolution*, vol. I, p. 342. There is, however, a *non sequitur* in this moral, for if leaders are 'not accidentally created' they are not accidentally (or 'capriciously') eliminated either.

[2] *Diary in Exile*, p. 54.

their union, did he show always a touching and tender deference. With the modesty characteristic of truly great men, he
recognized Lenin's priority',[1] thus wrote Lunacharsky in 1923,
at the beginning of the anti-Trotsky campaign. Krupskaya,
speaking, in the early nineteen-thirties, to a famous foreigner,
a non-communist, and knowing that she was eavesdropped
upon and that her words would be reported to Stalin, also
remarked on Trotsky's 'domineering and difficult character',
but added: 'He loved Vladimir Ilyich very deeply; on learning
of his death, he fainted and did not recover for two hours.'[2]
This love and recognition of Lenin's priority are evident in
all of Trotsky's post-revolutionary utterances on Lenin. As
early as September 1918, after Dora Kaplan's attempt on
Lenin's life, he paid this tribute to the wounded leader:

All that was best in Russia's revolutionary intellectuals of earlier
times, their spirit of self-denial, their audacity, their hatred of
oppression—all this is concentrated in the figure of this man. . . .
Supported by Russia's young revolutionary proletariat, utilizing
the rich experience of a world-wide workers' movement, he has
risen to his full stature . . . as the greatest man of our revolutionary
epoch. . . . Never yet has the life of any one of us seemed to us so
secondary in importance as it does now, at a moment when
the life of the greatest man of our epoch is in peril.[3]

There was not a hint of sycophancy in these words. Lenin
was not yet surrounded by any cult; and Trotsky was more
than once yet to voice strong disagreement with him. In 1920,
on the occasion of Lenin's fiftieth birthday, he published an
essay, more restrained in tone, on Lenin as a 'national type'
embodying the best sides of the Russian character.[4] In exile,
after he had left Prinkipo, he began to work on Lenin's full-
scale biography, of which he finished only the few opening
chapters. His failure to complete this work is partly made
good by a wealth of biographical sketches he had written and
published in the early nineteen-twenties. These deal with two
decisive periods of Lenin's life, the years 1902–3 and 1917–18,
and give a portrait throbbing with life and suffused with the
tenderness of which Lunacharsky spoke.[5]

[1] Lunarharsky, *Revolutsionnye Siluety*.   [2] *Memoirs of Michael Karolyi*, p. 265.
[3] Trotsky, *Lénine*, pp. 211–18.   [4] Op. cit., pp. 205–10.   [5] Op. cit.

What Trotsky admired in Lenin was his '*tseleustremlennost*', his being completely geared up to his great purpose, his *tension vers le but*—but also the personality, in which high-mindedness is matched by zest for life, gravity of purpose by rich humour, fanatical devotion to principle by suppleness of thought, ruthlessness and cunning in action by delicate sensitivity, high intellect by simplicity. He shows the 'greatest man of our epoch' as a fallible being; and so he demolishes the Stalinist icon of Lenin. Yet he himself approaches Lenin bare-headed, as it were, and, unabashed, reveres him. But he does not genuflect. He pays a manly tribute not to an idol but to the man as he knew him. Even while he depicts Lenin's heroic character, he does not make a demigod of him. He presents a lifesize and workaday figure, not a solemn statue. He employs the most ephemeral genre, the journalistic sketch, to create an enduring picture; and his sketches of Lenin have far greater artistic effect than those drawn by two eminent contemporary novelists, Gorky and Wells. He watches Lenin avidly from every angle: he catches his mind at work; the way he constructs an argument; his appearance and manner on the platform; his gesticulation and the movements of his body; the tone of his laughter; even his practical jokes. We see Lenin's brow clouded with indignation and anger; we observe him playing gently with a dog in a dramatic moment, while he is making up his mind on a grave issue; we catch a glimpse of him as he races like a schoolboy across the Kremlin Square to the government's conference room eager to play an amusing trick on his fellow Commissars. And all the time there is in the painter's searching eye a glimmer of love for the 'prosaic genius of the revolution'.

There is also a flicker of remorse in the painter's eye. Trotsky had spent by Lenin's side, in close partnership, only about six years, his best, his epoch-making years. He had passed the earlier thirteen or fourteen years in factional struggle against Lenin, assailing him with ferocious personal insults, as 'slovenly attorney', as 'hideous caricature of Robespierre, malicious and morally repulsive', as 'exploiter of Russian backwardness', 'demoralizer of the Russian working class', &c., insults compared with which Lenin's rejoinders were restrained, almost mild. Though Lenin had never, since 1917, even hinted at all this, the invective had been too wounding not to have left any scar. Even between 1917 and 1923, when they were in the closest political union, their relations lacked a note of personal intimacy—there was a certain reserve in Lenin.[1] Trotsky, in his 'touching deference', made tacit and tactful amends. In his writings he is still, perhaps only half consciously, anxious to compensate Lenin posthumously for all the abuse. He admits that in 1903, when he broke with Lenin, the revolution was still largely a 'theoretical abstraction' to himself, while Lenin had already fully grasped its realities. Again and again he speaks of the inner resistance he had to overcome, while 'moving towards Lenin'. But having overcome it and rejoined Lenin, he placed himself in his shadow; and there he still keeps himself as historian. He relates conscientiously all their differences; but his memory shrinks from the recollection. It shortens instinctively the time of their separation, softens the harshness of the antagonism, and dwells with delight on the years of friendship, seeking to extend them as it were backwards and forwards. Sometimes in reverie he seems to relive his life in continuous undisturbed harmony with Lenin. He thinks of writing a book about the intimate, fruitful, and lifelong friendship of Marx and Engels, his ideal of friendship which it was not given him to achieve in his own life. Eleven years after Lenin's death he notes in the Diary:

Last night . . . I dreamt I had a conversation with Lenin. Judging by the surroundings, it was on a ship on the third class deck. Lenin was lying in a bunk, I was standing or sitting near him. . . . He was questioning me anxiously about my illness. 'You seem to have accumulated nervous fatigue, you must rest. . . .' I answered that I had always recovered from fatigue quickly, but . . . that this time the trouble seems to lie in some deeper processes. . . . 'Then you should *seriously* (he emphasized the word) consult the doctors

[1] *The Prophet Armed*, pp. 92–93. When I remarked to Natalya Sedova on the lack of the note of personal intimacy between Lenin and Trotsky and suggested that the wounding character of Trotsky's pre-revolutionary polemics had rendered this impossible, she replied that she had never thought about it in this way. On reflection, however, she added: 'Perhaps such was indeed the reason for a certain reserve on Lenin's part. Those old factional struggles were conducted in a savage and beastly manner (*Eto byla zverinnaya borba*)'.

(several names . . .).' I answered that I had already had many consultations . . . but looking at Lenin I recalled that he was dead. I immediately tried to drive away this thought. . . . When I had finished telling him about my therapeutic trip to Berlin in 1926, I wanted to add, 'This was after your death'; but I checked myself and said, 'After you fell ill . . .'.[1]

Dream and reverie shield Trotsky in his vulnerability; and in wish-fulfilment he sees himself protected by Lenin's care and affection.

. . . .

The 'optical illusion' about Lenin is the sole instance of subjectivist thinking in the *History*. Otherwise it is as an objective thinker that Trotsky presents the events. To be sure, only an actor and an eye-witness could feel as intimately as he does the inwardness, the colour, and the flavour of every fact and scene. But as historian he stands above himself as actor and eye-witness. What is said of Caesar—that as author he was only the shadow of the commander and politician—cannot be said of Trotsky. He submits his work to the most exacting tests and supports the narrative by the most rigorous testimony, which as a rule he draws from enemies rather than friends. He never refers to his own authority; and only very rarely does he introduce himself as a *dramatis persona*. He devotes, for instance, only one brief dry sentence to his assumption of the Presidency of the Petrograd Soviet, which was one of the great scenes and momentous events of the time.[2] It is perhaps a defect of the *History* that if one tried to deduce from it alone just how important was Trotsky's role in the revolution, one would form a wrong idea. Trotsky looms incomparably larger, in 1917, on every page of *Pravda*, in every anti-Bolshevik newspaper, and in the records of the Soviets and the party than he does in his own pages. His silhouette is the only almost empty spot on his vast and animated canvas.

. . . .

Hazlitt held that oratorical genius and literary greatness are incompatible. Yet Trotsky who had in such full measure the orator's quickness of perception, spontaneous eloquence, and

[1] *Diary in Exile*, pp. 130–1. [2] *History*, vol. II, p. 347.

responsiveness to audience, possessed in the same degree the habits of deep and sustained reflection, the indifference to ephemeral satisfaction, and the 'patience of soul' indispensable to the true writer. Lunacharsky, himself a most prominent speaker, describes Trotsky as 'the first orator of his time' and his writing as 'congealed speech'. 'He is literary even in his oratory and oratorical even in literature.'[1] This opinion applies well to Trotsky's early writings; and Lunacharsky expressed it in 1923 before Trotsky the writer rose to his full height. In *My Life* and in the *History* the rhetorical element is sternly disciplined by the needs of narrative and interpretation, and the prose has an epic rhythm. It is still 'congealed speech' in the sense in which all narrative is.

For decades Trotsky's major works have been read only in translations. As the man was exiled, so his literary genius was banished into foreign languages. He found skilful and devoted translators in Max Eastman, Alexandra Ramm, and Maurice Parijanine who acquainted the European and American public with his major works. Yet something of his spirit and style is missing from any translation, although Trotsky, having absorbed so much of the European literary tradition, is the most cosmopolitan of Russian writers. But it was from his native sources that he drank most deeply, imbibing the vigour, subtlety, colour, and humour of the Russian tongue. He is, in his generation, the greatest master of Russian prose. To the English ear his style may sometimes seem to suffer from that 'too muchness' in which Coleridge saw the flaw of even the best German, or continental, style. This is a matter of taste and accepted stylistical standards, which vary not only from nation to nation, but within the same nation from epoch to epoch. Emotional vigour and strong, repetitive emphasis belong to the style of a revolutionary era, when speaker and writer expound to great masses of people ideas over which a life and death struggle is being waged; and, of course, the raised voices in which people communicate on a battlefield or in a revolution are unbearable at the quiet fireplace of the Englishman's castle. However, *My Life* and the *History* are free from 'too muchness'. Here Trotsky exercises a classical economy of expression. Here he is an 'objective word maker',

[1] Lunacharsky, op. cit.

striving for the utmost precision in nuance of meaning or mood—a heavy worker in the field of letters. He moulds his work with a watchful eye on the structure of the whole and the proportions of the parts, with an unflagging sense of artistic unity. So closely does he weave his theoretical argument into the narrative that try to disentangle them and the fabric loses texture and pattern. He knows when to contract and when to expand his story as very few narrators know. Yet it is not by arbitrary design that he expands or contracts it: the pace and cadences are attuned to the pulse of events. The whole has the torrential flow proper to a presentation of revolution. But for long stretches he keeps his rhythms even and regular, until, when they approach a climax, they rise and grow, passionate and tempestuous, so that the Red Guards' assault on the Winter Palace, the sirens of the battleships on the Neva, the final cut and thrust between the parties in the Soviet, the collapse of a social order, and the triumph of revolution are reproduced with symphonic effect.[1] And in all this grand sweep his *Sachlichkeit* is never lost—his originality lies in the combination of classical grandeur and sober modernity.

Over his pages he strews dazzling similes and metaphors; these spring spontaneously from his imagination, but he never loses control over them. His imagery is as precise, conceptually, as it is vivid. He uses metaphor with a definite purpose: to accelerate thought; to illumine a situation; or to clip tightly together two or more threads of ideas. The image may flash out in a single sentence; it may shape itself more slowly over the length of a passage; or it may grow in a chapter like a plant, push up a shoot first, blossom forth a few pages later, and come to fruition before the end of the chapter. Note, for instance, the use of metaphor in a passage describing the beginning of the February· revolution: the scene is a demonstration of 2,500 Petrograd workers which, in a narrow place, runs into a detachment of Cossacks, 'those age-old subduers and punishers' of popular revolt:

Cutting their way with the breasts of their horses, the officers first charged through the crowd. Behind them, filling the whole width of the Prospect, galloped the Cossacks. Decisive moment! But the horsemen, cautiously, in a long ribbon, rode through the

[1] Compare, e.g., pp. 301, 305, 313, 315–16, 377–8 in the *History*, vol. III.

corridor just made by the officers. 'Some of them smiled,' Kayurov recalls, 'and one of them gave the workers a good wink.' This wink was not without meaning. The workers were emboldened with a friendly, not hostile, kind of assurance, and slightly infected the Cossacks with it. The one who winked found imitators. In spite of renewed efforts from the officers, the Cossacks, without openly breaking discipline, failed to force the crowd to disperse, but flowed through it in streams. This was repeated three or four times and brought the two sides ever closer together. Individual Cossacks began to reply to the workers' questions and even to enter into momentary conversations with them. Of discipline there remained but a thin transparent shell that threatened to break through any second. The officers hastened to separate their patrol from the workers, and, abandoning the idea of dispersing them, lined the Cossacks out across the street as a barrier to prevent the demonstrators from getting to the centre. But even this did not help: standing stock-still in perfect discipline, the Cossacks did not hinder the workers from 'diving' under their horses. The revolution does not choose its paths: it made its first steps towards victory under the belly of a Cossack's horse.[1]

The generalizing image of the revolution diving under the belly of a Cossack's horse emerges naturally from the descriptive passage: it illumines all the novelty, hopefulness, and uncertainty of the situation. We feel that this time the workers will not be trampled upon though their positon is not yet quite secure. But turn another twenty pages, which narrate the progress of the rising, and the metaphor reappears in modified form, as a reminder of the distance the revolution has travelled:

One after another came the joyful reports of victories. Our own armoured cars have appeared! With red flags flying, they are spreading terror through the districts to all who have not yet submitted. Now it will no longer be necessary to crawl under the belly of a Cossack's horse. The revolution is standing up to its full height.[2]

Not less characteristic is a different kind of image in which the writer depicts a peculiar scene with such intensity that the scene itself grows into a haunting symbol. He describes the antagonism between officers and men in the disintegrating Tsarist army:

[1] *History*, vol. I, pp. 122–3.   [2] Ibid., p. 143.

The blind struggle had its ebbs and flows. The officers would try to adapt themselves; the soldiers would again begin to bide their time. But during this temporary relief, during these days and weeks of truce, the social hatred which was decomposing the army of the old régime would become more and more intense. Oftener and oftener it would flash out in a kind of heat lightning. In Moscow, in one of the amphitheatres, a meeting of invalids was called, soldiers and officers together. An orator-cripple began to cast aspersions on the officers. A noise of protest arose, a stamping of shoes, canes, crutches. 'And how long ago were you, Mr. Officer, insulting the soldiers with lashes and fists?' These wounded, shell-shocked, mutilated people stood like two walls, one facing the other. Crippled soldiers against crippled officers, the majority against the minority, crutches against crutches. That nightmare scene in the amphitheatre foreshadowed the ferocity of the coming civil war.[1]

This sternly realistic reportage is all terse passion. The scene is rendered in six clipped and harsh sentences. A few words transfer us into the amphitheatre and hit our ears with the 'stamping of shoes, canes, crutches'. A commonplace simile stresses the uncommonness of the spectacle: the cripples stand 'like two walls, one facing the other'. How much tragic pathos is condensed in these few and apparently artless sentences.

Sarcasm, irony, and humour pervade all his writings. He has turned against the established order not only from indignation and theoretical conviction but also from a sense of its absurdity. In the midst of the most tense and merciless struggle his eye catches the grotesque or comic incident. He is struck, and struck for ever afresh, by men's weakmindedness, meanness, and hypocrisy. In *My Life* he recollects how in New York, early in 1917, Russo-American socialists reacted to his forecast that the Russian Revolution would end in the overthrow of bourgeois rule as well as of Tsardom:

Almost everyone I talked with took my words as a joke. At a special meeting of 'worthy and most worthy' Russian Social Democrats I gave a lecture in which I argued that the proletariañ party would inevitably assume power in the next phase of the Russian revolution. The effect was like that of a stone thrown into a puddle alive with puffed up and phlegmatic frogs. Dr. Ingerman did not hesitate to point out that I was ignorant of the

[1] *History*, vol. I, p. 273.

rudiments of political arithmetic and that it was not worth while wasting five minutes to refute my nonsensical dreams.[1]

It is with this kind of amused disdain that Trotsky most often laughs at his adversaries. His laughter is not kindly, except on rare occasions, or in recollections of childhood and youth when he could still laugh disinterestedly. Later, he is too much absorbed in too bitter a struggle; and he derides men and institutions in order to turn the people against them. 'What!' he says in effect, 'Are we going to allow those puffed up and phlegmatic frogs to have it all their way and to manage our human affairs for us?' His satire was to make the oppressed and the downtrodden look down upon the mighty in their seats; and the mighty squirmed under the lash. Like Lessing (in Heine's famous portrait), he not only cuts off the head of his enemy, but 'is malicious enough to lift it from the ground and show the public that it is quite empty'. Never does he cut off so many heads, and show them to have been empty, as when he revisits, with Clio, the great battlefield of October.

[1] *Moya Zhizn*, vol. I, p. 315.

CHAPTER IV

'Enemy of the People'

'FOR the very reason that it fell to my lot to take part in great events, my past now cuts me off from chances of action', Trotsky remarks in his Diary. 'I am reduced to interpreting events and trying to foresee their future course.'[1] This appears to be the only such observation he made about himself; and it expresses more than he probably intended to say. To judge from the context, what he had in mind was that his ostracism made it impossible for him to engage in any large-scale political activity. In truth, his past 'cut him off from chances of action' in another and deeper sense as well. His ideas and methods and his political character belonged to an epoch towards which the present, the period of his banishment, was hostile; and because of this they did not have their impact. His ideas and methods were those of classical Marxism and were bound up with the prospect of revolution in the 'advanced' capitalist West. His political character had been formed in the atmosphere of revolution from below and proletarian democracy, in which Russian and international Marxism had been nurtured. Yet in the period between the two world wars, despite the intense class struggles, international revolution stagnated. The staying power of western capitalism proved far greater than classical Marxism had expected; and it was further enhanced as Social Democratic reformism and Stalinism disarmed the labour movement, politically and morally. Only in the aftermath of the Second World War was international revolution to resume its course; but then its main arena was to be in the underdeveloped East, and its forms, and partly also its content, were to be very different from those predicted by classical Marxism. To eastern Europe revolution was to be brought, in the main, 'from above and from outside' —by conquest and occupation; while in China it was to rise not as a proletarian democracy, spreading from the cities to

[1] *Trotsky's Diary in Exile*, p. 21.

S

the country, but as a gigantic *jacquerie* conquering the cities from the country and only subsequently passing from the 'bourgeois democratic' to the socialist phase. In any case, the years of Trotsky's exile were, from the Marxist viewpoint, a time out of joint, an historic hiatus; and the ground crumbled under the champion of classical socialist revolution. In the stormy events of the nineteen-thirties, especially in those outside the U.S.S.R., Trotsky was essentially the great outsider.

Yet his past, which had 'cut him off from chances of action', did not allow him to be inactive either: the man of October, the founder of the Red Army, and the erstwhile inspirer of the Communist International could not possibly reconcile himself to the outsider's role. It was not that such a part would have been incompatible with his Marxist outlook. Marx and Engels themselves were, for long periods, detached from 'practical' politics, engaged in fundamental theoretical work, and content to 'interpret' events—they were in a sense outsiders. Not they but Lassalle led the first socialist mass movement in Germany; not they but Proudhon and Blanqui inspired French socialism; and their influence on the British labour movement was remote and less than skin deep. They did not take their own philosophical postulate about 'unity of theory and practice' so narrowly as to feel obliged to engage in *formal* political activity at all times.[1] When they had no chance to build their

---

[1] In February 1851, after the defeat of revolution in Europe had become clear, Engels wrote to Marx: 'Now at last we have again . . . the opportunity to show that we need no popularity, no "support" from any party in any country, and that our position is altogether independent of such trifles. . . . Really we should not even complain when these *petits grands hommes* [the leaders of the various socialist parties and sects] are afraid of us; since so many years we have behaved as if rag, tag, and bobtail were our party, whereas we had in fact no party at all, and the people whom we counted as belonging to our party, at least officially, *sous reserve de les appeller des bêtes incorrigibles entre nous*, did not grasp even the rudiments of our problems.' 'From now on we are responsible only for ourselves; and when the moment comes when these gentlemen need us we shall be in a position to dictate our terms. Till then we have at least peace. To be sure, with this goes some loneliness. . . . [Yet] how can people like ourselves, who shun any official post like the plague, fit into a "party" . . . i.e. into a band of asses who swear by us because they think we are of their sort. . . . At the next occasion we can and must take this attitude: we hold no official position in the state, and as long as possible no official party post either, no seats in committees, &c., no responsibility for asses [but instead we exercise] merciless criticism of all and enjoy a cheerfulness of which the plotting of all the blockheads cannot deprive us. . . . The main thing for the

party and fight for power, they withdrew into the realm of ideas. The work they did there was historically, but not immediately, of the utmost practical importance, for, steeped in rich experience of social struggle, it pointed to future action. As to Trotsky, neither his character nor his circumstances permitted him to resign from formal political activity. He would not and could not contract out of the day-to-day struggle. The time of his banishment was not an uneventful political interval like the decades after 1848, when Marx wrote *Das Kapital*; it was an era of world-wide social battles and catastrophes, from which a man of Trotsky's record could not stand apart. Nor was he for a moment free to withdraw from his ceaseless and ferocious duel with Stalin. His past drove him to action as pitilessly as it cut him off from the prospect of action.

All his behaviour in exile is marked by this conflict between the necessity and the impossibility of action. He senses the conflict, but is never clearly conscious of it. Even when he glimpses the impossibility, he sees it as extraneous, temporary, and resulting merely from persecution and physical isolation. This unawareness of his deeper predicament gives him the strength to struggle on against odds perhaps more fearful than any historic figure has ever faced. Necessity impels him to formal political activity. Yet he recoils again and again, not in his conscious mind, which is ever hopeful, but in his involuntary moods and instinctive reflexes. His will wrestles with these moods and never succumbs. But this is a fierce, desperate, and exhausting collision.

During the Prinkipo years sheer physical isolation made his dilemma less pressing. He fretted and longed to come closer to a scene of political action, convinced that this would enable him to intervene effectively. In the meantime he had no choice but to plunge into literary historical work. He withdrew, though not completely, into the realm of theoretical ideas, where his enduring strength now lay. This is why the four Prinkipo years were his most creative period in exile. His emergence from Prinkipo was bound to heighten and sharpen

moment is that we should have the possibility to publish what we write. . . . either in quarterlies or in bulky volumes. . . . What will be left of all the prattle-tattle, in which this entire émigré mob may indulge at your expense, once you have come out in reply with your economic treatise?' Marx-Engels *Briefwechsel*, vol. I, pp. 179–82.

his dilemma. Not only was he presently to experience the full blast of that implacable hostility from which seclusion had partly shielded him. Closeness to a scene of political action was to excite in him all that passion for action, in which his weakness now lay. He was to discover or rediscover that the current of events was passing him by; yet he would exert himself to turn it. In the eight years left to him he was to produce no single work as weighty and enduring as his *History* or even his autobiography, although his hand never dropped the pen. He left Prinkipo planning to write a History of the Civil War which, because of his unique authority, would have been as important as the *History of the Revolution*, and perhaps even more illuminating. He started a large-scale biography of Lenin, which, as he confided to Max Eastman and Victor Gollancz, he expected to be 'the major work of my life' and the occasion for a comprehensive, 'positive and critical', exposition of the philosophy of dialectical materialism.[1] He did not carry out these and other plans, partly because wanderings and persecution did not allow him to concentrate, but mainly because he sacrificed them to his formal political activity, to his untiring labour for the Fourth International.

Thus his whole existence was torn between the necessity and the impossibility of action. Just now, at the moment of departure from Prinkipo, he had a foreboding of the gravity of the conflict. He was leaving in high spirits, full of hope and great expectations, yet with a chilling dread in the innermost recesses of his being.

· · · · · · · · ·

With Natalya, Max Shachtman, and three secretaries, van Heijenoort, Klement, and Sara Weber, he sailed from Prinkipo on board a slow Italian boat *Bulgaria*, on 17 July 1933. The voyage to Marseilles took a full week. Once again all precautions taken to keep the move secret failed. As on the trip to Denmark, he travelled under his wife's name and did his best to remain inconspicuous; but when the boat called at the port of Piraeus, many eager reporters were already

---

[1] Trotsky to Eastman, 6 November 1933, and to Gollancz, 28 September 1933. *The Archives*, Closed Section. In his letter to Gollancz Trotsky wrote that he would like Arthur Ransome to edit the English edition of this work.

waiting for him. He told them that his journey was 'strictly private'; that he and his wife would devote the next few months to medical treatment; and he refused to be drawn into any political statement: 'Our journey has no right to engage public attention, especially now when the world is occupied by infinitely more important questions.' But the Press once again watched suspiciously and speculated on his purpose. There was a rumour that he was going to France on Stalin's initiative to meet Litvinov, the Soviet Commisssar of Foreign Affairs, and to discuss the terms of his return to Russia. So widespread and persistent was the rumour that the *Vossische Zeitung*, a serious German paper, asked him whether it was true, and the Soviet Telegraph Agency issued an official denial.[1]

He spent most of his time *en route* in his cabin, working out his ideas about the Fourth International. He wrote an article, 'One Cannot Remain in One "International" with Stalin . . . and Co.' (He also reviewed, briefly and warmly, a novel just published by one of his young Italian followers, Ignazio Silone's *Fontamara*.[2]) After a few industriously spent days, he fell ill as the boat was nearing France: a severe attack of lumbago laid him low.[3] 'It was very hot', Natalya recollects, 'the pain tormented him . . . he was unable to get up. We called the ship's doctor. The steamer was approaching its destination. We were afraid of disembarking.' His pain, which made even breathing difficult, was somewhat relieved when a good way outside Marseilles, the ship was suddenly stopped and the French police ordered him and Natalya into a small tug, while his secretaries were to go on to Marseilles. He was uneasy at being separated from the secretaries and was about to protest when he noticed Lyova and Raymond Molinier

---

[1] Trotsky suspected that the *Vossische Zeitung* (already Nazified) had made the inquiry on Hitler's orders; and that Stalin hastened to reassure Hitler that he was not thinking of any reconciliation with the man who had suggested that the Soviet Government should reply to Hitler's seizure of power with the mobilization of the Red Army. See the note 'Stalin reassures Hitler' of 19 July 1933 in *The Archives*.

[2] *The Archives*, B.O., nos. 36–37, 1933.

[3] According to *Black's Medical Dictionary* (p. 731), 'an attack of lumbago may be due not to any disease of the muscles of the back, but to emotional disturbances which literally prevent the individual from standing up to the stresses and strains of life.'

waiting for him in the tugboat. He descended slowly, gasping with pain. It was Lyova who had arranged that he should be taken off in order to remove him from the public gaze and to escape the swarm of reporters, who were waiting at the harbour, and among whom G.P.U. agents were sure to be planted. Unobtrusively Trotsky landed at Cassis, near Marseilles, where an officer of the *Sûreté Générale* handed him an official paper revoking the order under which he had, in 1916, been expelled from France 'for ever'. 'It is a long time', Trotsky noted, 'since I acknowledged the receipt of any official document with so much pleasure.'[1]

The pleasure was at once somewhat spoiled by the outcry of right-wing newspapers against his admission.[2] Ironically, on the day of his arrival, 24 July, *Humanité* also protested against the annulment of the 1916 expulsion order—an order issued at the instigation of Count Isvolsky, the Tsar's last Ambassador, as reprisal for Trotsky's anti-war activity. *L'Humanité* also published a resolution of the French Politbureau, calling upon the whole Communist party to keep a watch on Trotsky's movements. Lyova's fears and precautions proved well justified. From Cassis, accompanied by a few young French Trotskyists, they drove towards Bordeaux, then northwards to St. Palais, near Royan, on the Atlantic coast, where Molinier had rented a villa. Meanwhile, the secretaries disembarked at Marseilles, unloaded Trotsky's library, archives, and luggage, despatched these to Paris, and went there themselves. G.P.U. sleuths concluded from this that Trotsky too had gone to Paris—on this guess Vyshinsky was to base, during the Moscow trials four years later, an essential part of his allegations about Trotsky's terroristic activities in France.

Trotsky's party travelled slowly towards Royan, and because of Trotsky's persistent pain, stopped at a village inn in the Gironde department—at night Lyova and a young Frenchman stood guard at Trotsky's doors. Only next afternoon did they reach St. Palais. On arrival Trotsky went to bed with high fever. But within an hour he had to dress and leave the house in a hurry—a fire had broken out, the rooms were full of smoke; the verandah, the garden, and the fences stood in

---

[1] *The Archives.*
[2] See, e.g., *Le Matin* and *Le Journal*, of 24, 25, and 26 July 1933.

flames. There was something symbolic in this opening incident: more than once during Trotsky's stay in France the ground would catch fire beneath his feet and he would have to rush out and take to the road. But the mishap at St. Palais was quite accidental; the summer was exceedingly hot; and not a few woods and houses were ablaze. The accident might have become embarrassing if Trotsky's identity had been found out; he was under an obligation to keep his incognito. Outside the villa, a crowd had gathered; and to avoid being recognized, he rushed across the road, hid in Molinier's car at the roadside, and there waited until his wife, son, and friends, helped by a change of wind, extinguished the fire. People approached him; but he pretended to be an American tourist, speaking hardly any French; and he noticed with relief that his accent had not given him away. Next day the local paper reporting the event mentioned an 'elderly American couple' who had moved into the villa just before the fire broke out.

He stayed at St. Palais from 25 July to 1 October, remaining all this time indoors, mostly in bed. His health, according to Natalya, deteriorated every time there was something the matter; he suffered from insomnia, headaches, and fevers. 'He could not raise himself up to have a look at the garden or to get out to the beach, and he postponed this "undertaking" from day to day.' When he was a little better, he received visitors; but he tired quickly and spent long hours on a couch indoors or a deckchair in the garden. Visitors were to recall that he could not sustain a conversation for longer than fifteen or twenty minutes and that he perspired profusely and almost fainted, so that some of them stayed at St. Palais for a few days in order to have several short talks with him.[1]

Yet, during the two months at St. Palais, he received no fewer than fifty callers. Among them were, apart from French and other Trotskyists: Jenny Lee (Aneurin Bevan's wife) and A. C. Smith of the British Independent Labour party; Jacob Walcher and Paul Frölich, formerly leaders of the German Communist party, then of the Sozialistische Arbeiterpartei;

[1] See Natalya Sedova's statement before the Dewey Commission (of 1 March 1937) and depositions by Klement and 'Erde' (of 31 March 1937) in *The Archives*, Closed Section.

Maring-Sneevliet, once Comintern representative in Indonesia and China, now member of the Dutch Parliament and leader of an Independent Socialist party; Paul-Henri Spaak, future General Secretary of the North Atlantic Treaty Organization, at this time leader of Belgium's Socialist Youth and something of a disciple of Trotsky's, over-awed by the master and diligently yet apprehensively submissive; Ruth Fischer; Carlo Rosselli, the eminent Italian anti-fascist; André Malraux; and others.

Most visitors called in connexion with a conference, convened in Paris at the end of August, of parties and groups interested in the idea of a new International. Trotsky, unable to attend the conference, was active in its preparation, wrote 'Theses' and resolutions for it, and took a close interest in the details of organization. He hoped to win over many of those who stood outside the established Internationals. But of the fourteen small parties and groups represented at the conference only three, the German Sozialistische Arbeiterpartei and two Dutch groups, joined the Trotskyists in working for the Fourth International. All the others were frightened by the fierceness of Trotsky's opposition to both reformism and Stalinism; even the three who joined did so with reservations; and they did not form an International but merely a preliminary organization. Outwardly, Trotsky was pleased with this start, and saw in it an event as significant as the Zimmerwald Conference had been in its time.[1]

Yet he could not fail to sense how feeble a start it really was; and this certainly contributed to his despondency. Of his mood in these weeks we find an intimate expression in his correspondence with Natalya, who early in September left for Paris to consult doctors. Their letters, sad and tender, show him forlorn and morally dependent on her in a way he could hardly ever have been in any of the earlier, more active periods of his life. Her stay in Paris reminded him of the far-off years when they had lived there together; and he had a poignant feeling of declining strength and of advancing age. A day or two after her departure he wrote to her: 'How painfully I long to see your old picture, our common picture, showing us

[1] B.O. nos. 36–37, 1933. Trotsky signed some of the resolutions and 'theses', he wrote for the conference with the pen-name 'G. Gurov'.

when we were so young. . . . You are in Paris . . . the day you left . . . I was unwell. . . . I went into your room and touched your things. . . .' Again and again, he strained to recapture the image of their youth, and complained of sleeplessness, lassitude, and loss of memory, 'caused by the sufferings of recent years'. But he reassured her that he felt his intellectual powers to be unimpaired and that he was well looked after by a good doctor, a comrade who had come from Paris and was staying with him. 'Dearest, dearest mine', he wrote on 11 September, 'it was quieter on Prinkipo. Already the recent past seems better than it was. Yet we looked forward with so much hope to our stay in France. Is this definitely old age already? Or is it only a temporary, though all too sharp a decline, from which I shall still rally? We shall see. Yesterday two elderly workers and a schoolmaster came to see me. Naville was also here. . . . I felt weary; there was little relevance in the talk. But I watched with curiosity the elderly provincial workers.'[1]

A week later he recovered somewhat and described to Natalya how, still bedridden, he had received a group of followers and had argued with them vigorously; and how Lyova, having seen them off, had come back, embraced him over the blanket, kissed him, and whispered: 'I love you, Father'—this filial affection and admiration moved him after years of separation. But a few days later he wrote again that he felt very old among the young men who visited him, and that at night he awoke and 'like an abandoned child' called for Natalya—'did not Goethe say that old age catches us by surprise and finds us children?' 'How sad you are', Natalya answered. 'You have never been like that. . . . I see you pale, weary, doleful—this is terribly depressing. This is quite unlike you. . . . You are making superhuman demands on yourself and speak of old age when one should be amazed at how much you are still able to shoulder.' He quailed inwardly before the impossibility of his task; and the visits, the talks, mostly turning round in circles, and the intrigues of tiny cliques, could hardly raise his spirits.[2]

By the beginning of October his health had improved; and to get a complete rest he went with Natalya to Bagnères de

---

[1] *The Archives,* Closed Section.   [2] Ibid.

Bigorre in the Pyrenees, where they spent three weeks, made trips and visited Lourdes, which amused and irritated him as a monument to human credulity. He came to himself and longed to be back at work. From Bagnères he wrote to Gollancz, who had been urging him to get on with the *Lenin*, that he would now concentrate on this book and put aside his plan for the *History of the Red Army*.[1]

Thus three months passed from his landing in France. The protests against his admission had subsided; he had managed to keep his incognito; his whereabouts were unknown to the Press; and few even of the friends and well-wishers who called at St. Palais knew his exact address—so cautiously had Lyova arranged their visits. The Stalinists were unable to trace him and to stage their planned demonstrations against his presence. A Trotskyist sympathizer, who was still a party member, came to Royan to watch what was going on in the cells there and, if need be, to give a warning to St. Palais; but the local Stalinists had no inkling that Trotsky was in the neighbourhood. The government, reassured by his discretion, lifted some of the restrictions on his freedom of movement and permitted him to stay anywhere, except in Paris and the Seine department. And so on 1 November he moved to Barbizon, the little town near Paris which has given its name to a famous school of painting. He lived there in a house outside the town, in a small park on the edge of the Fontainebleau forest, well hidden from prying eyes, guarded by sentries and watchdogs. He kept in close touch with his followers in Paris—messengers regularly carried the correspondence to and fro; and in the winter, escorted by a bodyguard, he made two or three trips to the capital. At Barbizon he hoped to work undisturbed on the *Lenin* at least for a year.

There seemed to be no trace of his recent lassitude. He resumed his customary routine: at six in the morning, while everyone in the house was still asleep, he was at work; and, pausing only for breakfast, he went on until noon. After lunch and an hour's rest he was at work again; at 4 p.m. he, Natalya, and the secretaries took tea standing; then everyone was back at his job till supper. In the evenings the members of the

---

[1] Letter to Gollancz of 25 October 1933. In reply to these assurances Gollancz offered Trotsky an advance of £1,500 on the *Life of Lenin*. Ibid.

household and visitors formed a debating circle, over which he presided, of course. He resumed solid research and literary work: he assembled materials for the *Lenin*; delved into the Ulyanovs' family background and Lenin's childhood and adolescence, studied the Russia of the eighteen-seventies and eighteen-eighties, and the formative phases of Lenin's intellectual growth, the topics that fill the first and the only completed part of the biography. Preparing to deal with Lenin's philosophical writings, and conscious of gaps in his own knowledge, he went back to the classics of logic and dialectics, Aristotle and Descartes, but especially to Hegel. He did not allow other projects to tempt him away. About this time Harold Laski urged him to write a book 'Where is America Going?', somewhat on the pattern of *Where is Britain Going?* 'I know no one', wrote the mentor of the British Labour party, himself renowned as an authority on American constitutional history and politics, 'I know no one whose book on this subject would be more interesting to the Anglo-American public.'[1] But Trotsky was not to be diverted.

More than ever he now followed *con amore* French politics and letters. For relaxation he wrote or rewrote character sketches of Briand, Millerand, Poincaré, Herriot; and he reviewed quite a few French novels. Of these minor writings, his essay on Céline's *Voyage au bout de la nuit* and Poincaré's · *Memoirs* deserve to be briefly summarized.[2] The occasion for it was Céline's debut with *Voyage*. 'Céline has entered great literature as others enter their homes', Trotsky said, praising the writer's indifference to respectability, his wide experience, fine ear and daring idiom. 'He has shaken up the vocabulary of French literature' and brought back into it words long banished by academic purism. Rooted in a rich tradition, deriving from Rabelais, he had written the *Voyage* 'as if he had been the first to use French words'. He also defied the conventionalities of the French bourgeoisie, of which Poincaré was a perfect embodiment. The juxtaposition of Céline and Poincaré was suggested to Trotsky by the opening scene in *Voyage* which depicts Poincaré inaugurating a dog show. The 'incorruptible

[1] Laski to Trotsky, 15 November 1933, ibid.
[2] The essay is dated 10 May 1933, but Trotsky was still working on it after he had moved to France.

notary of the French bourgeoisie' and patron saint of the
Third Republic had 'not a single individual note of his own'—
everything in him was conventional and imitative; his personality, as it appeared in his speeches and memoirs, was like
a 'barbed-wire skeleton wrapped up in paper flowers and
golden tinsel'. 'I am a bourgeois, and nothing bourgeois is
alien to me', Poincaré might have said. His rapacity, displayed
in exacting reparations from defeated Germany, and his
hypocrisy, 'so absolute that it became a kind of sincerity', were
dressed up as traditional French rationalism. Yet the logic and
clarté of bourgeois France stood to that high philosophical tradition 'as medieval scholasticism stood to Aristotle': 'it viewed
the world not in the three dimensions of reality but in the
two dimensions of documents'. The famous French sense of
proportion was in Poincaré a 'sense of the small proportions'.
The French bourgeoisie had 'inherited from its ancestors a
wardrobe rich in historic costumes', which it used to cover its
stubborn conservatism; and next to rationalism, the 'religion
of patriotism' was to it what religion was to the Anglo-Saxon
middle classes. 'The free-thinking French bourgeois', for whom
Poincaré spoke, 'projected into his own nation all the attributes
that other people vest in Father, Son and Holy Ghost'; France
is to him the Holy Virgin. 'The liturgy of patriotism is an
inevitable part of the political ritual.'

Céline's merit was that he exposed and rejected these sanctities. He depicted a way of life in which murder for small profit
was not the rare exception or the excess which conventional
morality pretended it to be, but almost a natural occurrence.
Yet, an innovator in style rather than in ideas, Céline was
himself a bourgeois, weary, despairing, and 'so disgusted by his
own image in the mirror that he smashes the glass until his
hands bleed'. With only his intense hatred of the lie and his disbelief in any truth, Céline would not be able to write another book
like the *Voyage*, Trotsky concluded—if no radical change were to
occur in him he would sink into darkness. (Presently Céline was
indeed captivated and carried away by the tide of Nazism.)

Trotsky's remarks on Malraux are also noteworthy, for he
was one of the first, if not the first, reviewer of *La Condition
Humaine* which he hailed as the revelation of a great and
original talent. He urged a New York publisher to bring out

an American edition of the book and recommended it in these terms: 'Only a great superhuman purpose for which man is ready to pay with his life gives meaning to personal existence. This is the final import of the novel which is free from philosophical didacticism and remains from beginning to end a true work of art.'[1] In an earlier review, however, he spoke of the streak of 'cheap Machiavellianism' in Malraux, who was fascinated not so much by revolution and its genuine fighters as by pseudo-revolutionary adventurers and 'bureaucratic super-men' seeking to dominate and boss the working class. Fascination with this kind of 'superman' as we now know, was to make it so easy for Malraux to become associated first with Stalinism and then with Gaullism. At this time, however, he was still trying to reconcile his Stalinist inclinations with sympathy and admiration for Trotsky.[2]

. . . .

At Barbizon Trotsky was able to take a close look at his western European followers, especially the French ones; and he tried to go beyond the narrow confines of his faction in recruiting adherents for the Fourth International. He set great store by the accession of Ruth Fischer and Maslov who were émigrés in France; he often received Fischer at Barbizon and, to the annoyance of the German Trotskyists, introduced her as a member to the International Secretariat. He wrote an enthusiastic preface to a brochure by Maria Reese, formerly a communist member of the Reichstag, who exposed the confusion and panic in which the German party had collapsed in 1933 and announced her adherence to Trotskyism. Shortly thereafter, however, Reese deserted the Trotskyists, returned to Germany, and declared for National Socialism.[3] The

[1] Trotsky to Simon and Schuster, New York, 9 November 1933. *The Archives*, Closed Section.

[2] Trotsky first wrote about Malraux in 1931. *B.O.*, nos. 21–22. Some time after Trotsky's arrival in France Malraux was a member of a *Comité pour contribuer à la securité de Leon Trotzky*. The Committee made a money collection which was to cover the expenses of providing Trotsky with a bodyguard; and in an appeal signed *inter alia* by Malraux it addressed itself '*à tous ceux qui refusent de livrer un proscrit dont toute la vie a été au service de l'avenement d'une société meuilleure aux balles de la reaction*'. (Among those who lent support to the appeal was Romain Rolland, who later, however, also justified Stalin's purges.) Quoted from *Les Humbles*, May–June 1934.

[3] *B.O.*, nos. 38–39, 1934.

recruitment of new adherents was hard going. The few groups that had agreed to work together for the new International were at loggerheads. Some old Trotskyists like Nin and his friends broke away to form an independent party, the P.O.U.M. of Catalonia. In France all the Trotskyist groups aggregated about a hundred members at the most, and *Verité* had a circulation of less than 3,000. Rosmer kept aloof: 'During the two years of Trotsky's stay in France', he says, 'we never saw each other. Probably he was waiting for me to make the first step towards him, and I waited for a first step from him.'[1] By now Trotsky was discovering that it was not without reason that Rosmer had refused to associate with Raymond Molinier; he himself was taken aback by Molinier's 'political irresponsibility', even though the Molinier family was very helpful to him during his French peregrinations. He was also irked by Naville's 'arrogance' and 'lack of revolutionary spirit and initiative'.[2] He spent many an hour in discussions with Simone Weil, a 'Trotskyist' at this time, but found her a 'muddlehead', 'without any understanding for working-class politics and Marxism'—in later years she gained fame as a philosophical convert to Catholicism and mystic. The impression which most of his French intellectual adherents made on him is well conveyed in his letter to Victor Serge, written two years later, where he describes them as 'Philistines': 'I have been even in their homes and have felt the smell of their petty bourgeois life—my nose has not deceived me.' All he could count on were a few fervent and young workers and students; yet even these lacked political knowledge and experience and vegetated outside the labour movement. 'We must look for roads to the workers,' he concluded, 'and in the process must avoid ex-revolutionaries and even push them discourteously aside. . . .'[3]

This was the time of the Stavisky affair, the scandal which

---

[1] This tallies well with what Trotsky wrote later (on 29 April 1936) to V. Serge: 'Rosmer, disagreeing with me over a secondary issue, got over-excited. . . . Because of this we did not meet during [my] stay in France; but our respect and sympathy for both of them, Alfred and Marguerite, are as great as ever. Rosmer is a man on whom one can always count in a difficulty.' *The Archives*, Closed Section.

[2] Trotsky to Lyova, 27 December 1935, *The Archives*, Closed Section. He characterized another one of his French followers, David Rousset, as 'a mixture of opportunism and anarchism'. Ibid.

[3] Trotsky to Serge, 30 July 1936, ibid.

revealed shocking corruption in the Third Republic, its Ministers, Deputies, police chiefs, and Press. The Parliamentary mainstay of the Republic, the Radical party, was deeply involved; and the government was nearly choking in the fumes of the affair. Fascist and quasi-fascist leagues, especially the *Croix de Feu*, or the Cagoûlards, led by Colonel de la Rocque, battened on the popular indignation and threatened to overthrow the parliamentary régime. On 6 February 1934 they staged a semi-insurrection and with the cry '*Daladier au poteau*' assailed the Chamber of Deputies. The *coup* failed, however; and within a week it provoked a General Strike of the workers of Paris, in which socialists and communists spontaneously formed a united front, the first time for years. This happened just when the Comintern was abandoning its 'ultra-left' tactics; and the united front of 12 February set a precedent. In July socialists and communists reached a formal agreement to 'defend jointly the Republic against every fascist attack'. The Radical party did not join them yet —the Popular Front, which was to include it, was to come into existence only the following year. But a new chapter was opened: the Daladier government had been saved by the united front and was increasingly dependent on its support; the political balance of France had shifted; there was an upsurge of energy among the workers and a revival of class struggle.

In these circumstances, Trotsky held, it was all the more urgent that his followers should find themselves within the mass movement. As they could not go back to the Communist party, which slandered them and persecuted them mercilessly, he advised them to join the S.F.I.O., the Socialist party, which, directed by Leon Blum, still held sway over the majority of workers. (The S.F.I.O. was not yet the party of the white-collar man and the *petite bourgeoisie* which it was to become after the Second World War.) Trotsky advised his followers to join that party, not in order to accept its ideas, but on the contrary in order to defy reformism within its own stronghold and to 'carry their revolutionary programme to the masses'. The S.F.I.O. was not a centralized body but a federation of various groups and factions openly competing for influence: in such an organization it should have been possible for the

Trotskyists to convert people to the idea of the Fourth International. This was the 'French turn', which all Trotskyist groups were debating in 1934–5—eventually Trotsky advised nearly all of them to follow a similar course in their own countries, i.e. to join, as distinct groups, the Social Democratic parties.[1]

In this way he implicitly acknowledged that his scheme for the new International was unreal; the 'French turn' was a desperate attempt to salvage it. It could not succeed. Trotskyism could not appeal, except episodically, to the rank and file of a Social Democratic party; it went too strongly against their habits of thought and deep-rooted reformist tradition. Trotsky could not defeat Blum's influence on Blum's native ground, which was what he indirectly undertook to do. His followers entered the S.F.I.O. as a tiny group without authority or prestige, proclaiming in advance their enmity to the party's established leaders and accepted tenets. They made a few converts among the young, but soon ran up against a wall of hostility. Yet the 'French turn' removed the Trotskyists even further from the mass of communists and provided grist to Stalinist propaganda. To the communist rank and file the claim that they had joined the S.F.I.O. only in order to 'give battle to reformism' sounded like a flimsy pretext. Communists saw the Social Democrats making for a time political capital out of the Trotskyists' adherence; and they heard the latter inveighing against Stalinism from Social Democratic platforms. Their old distrust of Trotskyism turned into a blind hatred of the 'renegades and traitors'. True enough, presently they did indeed see the Trotskyists assailing the Social Democratic leaders and their policies and being expelled from the S.F.I.O. But this happened during the Popular Front; and the Communist party applauded and even instigated the expulsion. All the same, the 'French turn' helped to change the antipathy the ordinary French communist felt for Trotskyism into an intense animosity; and even if the difference was only one of a nuance, it was not unimportant: it was by such imperceptible

---

[1] 'Entrism' is the term by which the Trotskyists described and discussed this move even thirty years later, when they still kept entering, leaving, and re-entering other parties, splitting and dispersing their own ranks in the process, and still 'building the Fourth International'.

gradations that the mood of western communists was being worked up to that furious abhorrence of Trotskyism in which they were to receive the Great Purges.

. . . .

Six months had not yet passed since Trotsky's arrival at Barbizon when the comparative peace in which he lived there was suddenly destroyed. He had again preserved his incognito and concealed his whereabouts so well that even his friends did not know where he was and corresponded with him at a cover address. Not a single letter of his was ever posted from Barbizon; a secretary acted as messenger and carried letters between Barbizon and Paris. A trivial incident undid all those prudent arrangements. One evening in April the police stopped Trotsky's messenger for a minor traffic offence. Puzzled by his vague answers and foreign accent—the messenger was Klement, a German political émigré—the police stumbled on the discovery that Trotsky was at Barbizon. As the headquarters of the *Sûreté* had cautiously withheld this information from them, the local gendarmes, flushed with their feat of detection, broke the news with all drums beating. The local *Procureur*, followed by a platoon of gendarmerie and by reporters from Paris, came to interrogate Trotsky. The rightwing Press at once renewed its clamour, and *Humanité* once again vied with it. The government was frightened. The fascist leagues had already attacked it for granting Trotsky asylum: this, they screamed, was one of the crimes of the 'rotten and degenerate' régime, the true face of which had been shown up in the Stavisky affair. From Berlin, Goebbels' Ministry of Propaganda spread the tale that Trotsky was preparing a communist insurrection. The *petite bourgeoisie*, terrified by the slump, incensed against the Third Republic, and fed by sensational headlines about Trotsky's mysterious doings, readily believed that the 'ogre of Europe' was after them. *Humanité* maintained that he was conspiring against the French national interest. To appease the hostile clamour the Ministry announced that it was about to expel Trotsky, and it served him an order of expulsion. It did not, however, enforce the order, because no country was prepared to accept him.

T

On 16 or 17 April the police instructed him to move out of Barbizon. His house was besieged by crowds; an attack either from the Cagoûlards or from the Stalinists was to be feared. He shaved off his beard, did what else he could to make himself unrecognizable, and slipped out of the house. He went to Paris and stayed for a few days with his son in a poor student's garret. But Paris was out of bounds for him and too dangerous; and so, leaving Natalya, he took to the road again. With Henri Molinier and van Heijenoort he drove southwards without any definite destination. He was still to stay in France for another fourteen months; but he had either to lead a vagrant life or to take shelter in a remote village in the Alps; and all the time he had to hide his high and all too conspicuous head.

Followed by a police detective, he moved from place to place and from hotel to hotel until he arrived at Chamonix. Almost at once a local newspaper came out with the hot news. 'Apparently the police suspected', he noted, 'that I had some intentions concerning Switzerland or Italy, and gave me away. . . .' He had to move on. The police forbade him to remain in the frontier area and ordered him to find a refuge in a small town or village situated at least 300 km. from Paris. At Chamonix, Natalya rejoined him; and, while Molinier or van Heijenoort looked for a new dwelling-place, they had to be put up in a pension. To enter a pension was 'a very complicated operation', because he could not present himself under his name, and the police would not allow him to use any cover name. He introduced himself finally as Monsieur Sedov, a French citizen of foreign extraction; and to obtain complete privacy he and Natalya pretended to be in deep mourning and took meals in their room. Van Heijenoort posing as a nephew kept an eye on the surroundings. Tragi-comically, the pension turned out to be the centre for local royalists and fascists with whom the 'loyal republican' agent of the *Sûreté*, who continued to escort Trotsky, engaged in acrimonious discussions at table. 'After each meal our "nephew" would tell us about these Molièresque scenes; and half an hour of merry though suppressed laughter (we were, of course, in mourning) repaid us at least partially for the discomfort of our existence. On Sunday Natalya and I went out "to Mass", really for a walk. This heightened our prestige in the house.' From this pension they moved .to a cottage in the country. But when the local Prefect learned the address, he wrung his hands: 'You have chosen the most inappropriate place! That is a hotbed of clericalism. The *maire* is a personal enemy of mine.' Having rented the cottage for a few months and being 'bankrupt' by now, Trotsky refused to depart, until another indiscretion in a local newspaper compelled him to leave in a hurry.[1]

After nearly three months of such wanderings he came at last, early in July, to Domesne, near Grenoble, where he and Natalya stayed with a Monsieur Beau, the village teacher. There they remained for nearly eleven months, in complete isolation, without a secretary or a bodyguard. Only two or three visitors, who had come especially from abroad called at Domesne. Once in several weeks a secretary would arrive from Paris; and every now and then a few schoolmasters from the neighbourhood visited Monsieur Beau, and then his two tenants joined them in discussing local school affairs. 'Our life here differs very little from imprisonment', Trotsky noted. 'We are shut up in our house and yard and meet people no more often than we would at visiting hours in a prison . . . we have acquired a radio, but such things probably exist even in some penitentiaries. . . .' Even their daily walks reminded them of taking exercise in a prison yard: they skirted the village to avoid people and could not go far without straying into a neighbouring hamlet. Mail from Paris arrived only twice a month. In democratic France they had far less freedom than they had had on Prinkipo and even at Alma Ata.[2]

He worked less than usual and less fruitfully, and made almost no progress with the *Lenin*. In October he wrote under the title *Où va la France?* a pamphlet about French politics on the eve of the Popular Front. The pamphlet contained many brilliant passages, but it failed to answer, or rather gave the wrong answer, to the question posed in its title. He viewed the French scene through the same prism through which he had viewed the German scene; yet the prism through which he had seen Hitler's advent so clearly blurred his view of the French

---

[1] *Diary in Exile*, p. 104.
[2] Ibid., pp. 37, 92, and *passim*; also Pierre Naville, *Trotsky Vivant*.

prospects. Once again he diagnosed, rightly, a crisis of bourgeois democracy; but once again he saw, mistakenly, the lower middle classes 'running amok', producing a dynamic fascist mass movement, and confronting the working class with their violence. The February *coup* of the *Croix de Feu* seemed to lend some colour to this view. But Colonel de la Rocque was not to be the French Hitler; nor was the French *petite bourgeoisie* to engender a movement like National Socialism, either because the Popular Front forestalled it, or because its outlook and traditions were different from those of the German *Klein-bürgertum*. It was one of the peculiarities of French political history in the nineteen-thirties, the nineteen-forties and the nineteen-fifties that attempts to launch fascist mass movements were repeatedly made and repeatedly failed. When the Third Republic collapsed in 1940, it did so under the blast of German invasion; even then not a native fascism but Pétain's sclerotic dictatorship doddered over its ruins. Eighteen years later the Fourth Republic too succumbed to a military *coup*. The French reaction against bourgeois democracy took, as it had done in the nineteenth century, a quasi- or pseudo-Bonapartist form, resulting in the 'rule of the sabre', the methods and impact of which were very different from those of totalitarian fascism.[1]

From his premisses Trotsky expounded his ideas about the strategy and tactics of the French labour movement. He criticized the united front, as Thorez and Blum practised it, on the grounds that its action was confined to parliamentary manœuvres and electoral alliances; and that it did not seek to arouse the workers to an extra-parliamentary struggle against fascism, a struggle which might have opened up the prospect of socialist revolution as well. He poured out his sarcasm on

---

[1] Trotsky was, in his time, the only political theorist to produce a precise definition of fascism. Yet on some occasions he applied it rather imprecisely. He saw the imminence of fascism in France; and he insisted on labelling Pilsudski's pseudo-Bonapartist dictatorship over Poland as fascist, although Pilsudski did not rule in a totalitarian fashion and had to put up with the existence of a multi-party system. On the other hand, Trotsky described, rather unconvincingly, the ephemeral governments of Schleicher and Papen, and also Doumergue's feeble government of 1934, as Bonapartist. (Only in 1940 did he at last describe the Petain régime as pseudo-Bonapartist rather than fascist.) I argued on these points with Trotsky in the nineteen-thirties; but the issue is perhaps of too little historical significance and too involved to be taken up here.

the Comintern which had denounced him for urging German socialists and communists to bar jointly Hitler's road to power and which had now, without turning a hair, adopted the united front only to pervert it into a tactic of evasion, 'parliamentary cretinism', and opportunism. Ironically, it was Thorez who now urged Blum to extend their alliance to the Radicals in order to 'associate the *petite bourgeoisie* with the anti-fascist struggle of the working class'. This—the Popular Front—Trotsky argued, would not associate the lower middle classes with the workers but would open up a chasm between them, because the lower middle classes were turning their backs on the Radicals, their traditional party. He appealed to communists and socialists to form workers' militias and prepare to fight fascism arms in hand, if need be; and he repeated these views in another pamphlet, *Encore une fois: Où va la France?*, written in March 1935.

The eventual failure of the Popular Front was to justify most of Trotsky's criticisms. For the moment, however, the joint socialist-communist action succeeded in throwing back the fascist leagues, which never recovered from their defeat; and the Popular Front undeniably aroused the working class for a time and gave a tremendous impulse to its movement. Only subsequently was the policy of the Popular Front to break the energy of the workers, to estrange the *petite bourgeoisie*, and thus to throw the country into the mood of reaction and prostration, in which the outbreak of the Second World War found it. But in 1934–5, as the danger of fascism had receded, Trotsky's call for extra-Parliamentary action and for workers' militias sounded out of season, and evoked no response. Watching from his retreat in the Alps the first manœuvres of the Popular Front, he noted in his Diary that 'this order has hopelessly undermined itself. It will collapse with a stench.'[1] Only a few years lay between the triumphs of the Popular Front and the great stench of the 1940 collapse.

. . . .

Up to the end of 1932 Trotsky was still in contact with his followers in the Soviet Union, and received letters and bulletins from many penal settlements and prisons. Written in Russian,

[1] *Diary in Exile*, p. 48.

French, and German, mostly on rough wrapping sheets, some-times even on cigarette paper, and dealing with political and theoretical matters or bringing personal greetings, this cor-respondence was despatched with incredible ingenuity: once, for instance, there landed on Trotsky's desk a matchbox inside which he found a whole political treatise penned in the tiniest of handwritings. This correspondence, preserved in his Arch-ives, brought to Prinkipo the breath of Siberian and sub-Polar winds, the smell of dungeons, the echoes of savage struggles, the cries of doomed and despairing men, but also some lucid thoughts and unbroken hopes. As long as it went on reaching him, he felt the throbbing of Soviet reality. Gradually, however, the correspondence dwindled to a trickle; and even before he left Prinkipo it ceased altogether.

In France he had no contact at all with the Opposition in the Soviet Union. Its silence, made even deeper by the capitu-lators' unending recantations, was on his mind when he stated that the Russian movement had lost the power of revolutionary initiative and that only a new International could regain it. In February 1934, while he was still at Barbizon, the news of Rakovsky's capitulation reached him. It may well be imagined how this affected him. Rakovsky had been closer to him as 'friend, fighter, and thinker' than any other associate; despite his age, he had, unbroken by persecution, held out against Stalin after nearly all the other leaders of the Opposition had surrendered; and in the prisons and places of deportation his moral authority had been second only to Trotsky's. In almost every issue of the *Bulletin* Trotsky had published some-thing by Rakovsky or about him: an article, a letter, an extract from an old speech, or a protest against his persecution. After every defeat of the Opposition and after every series of capitu-lations, he had pointed to Rakovsky as the shining example and as proof that the Opposition was alive. Rakovsky's defection filled him therefore with immense sadness; it marked for him the passing of an epoch. 'Rakovsky', he wrote, 'was virtually my last contact with the old revolutionary generation. After his capitulation there is nobody left. . . .'[1] Was it weariness, he wondered, that had at last overcome the old fighter? Or was he, as he stated, guided by the conviction that when the

[1] Op. cit., pp. 41, 53; also *B.O.*, no. 40, 1934.

Soviet Union was threatened by the Third Reich, he too had to 'rally behind Stalin'? In any case, Stalin's triumph could not be more complete. And in the next few months the reconciliation between Stalin and his many repentant opponents seemed more genuine than ever, although the party still ceaselessly expelled 'disloyal elements' from its ranks.

Then suddenly, before the end of the year, this appearance of reconciliation was exploded. On 1 December, Sergei Kirov, who had nine years earlier replaced Zinoviev as the head of the Leningrad organization and in the Politbureau, was assassinated. The first official version claimed that a body of White Guard conspirators stood behind Nikolaev, the assassin; and that a Latvian consul had pulled the wires—there was no question of any inner party opposition being involved. A second version, however, described the assassin as a follower of Zinoviev and Kamenev and made no mention of White Guards. Nikolaev and fourteen other young men, all Komsomoltsy, were executed. Zinoviev and Kamenev were expelled from the party for the third time; they were imprisoned, and awaited trial by a court martial. Press and radio linked Trotsky with Zinoviev and Kamenev and assailed him as the real instigator. A mass terror was let loose against 'Kirov's assassins', Trotskyists, Zinovievists, and disgruntled Stalinists; many thousands were deported to concentration camps. Finally, several high officers of the Leningrad G.P.U. were charged with 'neglect of duty' and sentenced, with surprising mildness, to two or three years.

At the cottage in the Alps Trotsky, glued to his wireless set and listening to transmissions from Moscow, followed the unfolding of the plot and recorded his comments.[1] In the clamour rising from Moscow he discerned at once a prelude to events far vaster and more sinister than the Kirov affair. He was convinced that Zinoviev and Kamenev had not been implicated in the attempt on Kirov—old Marxists that they were, nothing could have been more unlike them than a cloak-and-dagger action, which hit an individual holder of office without changing the system. He had no doubt that Stalin was using the assassination as a pretext for a new assault

---

[1] B.O., no. 41 (the issue for January 1935) was entirely taken up by Trotsky's current commentary on the Kirov affair.

on the Opposition. On 30 December, a fortnight before the news about the trial of the chiefs of the Leningrad G.P.U. was broadcast, Trotsky asserted, on the internal evidence of the official announcements, that the G.P.U. had known about the preparations of the attempt and had, for their own reasons, condoned them. What were those reasons? Nikolaev had been one of the Komsomoltsy who had grown up after the suppression of the oppositions and, who, disillusioned, robbed of any way of expressing themselves legally, and uninhibited by Marxist tradition, sought to protest with bomb and revolver. Not the Opposition, Trotsky asserted, but the ruling group was responsible for this. The G.P.U. had known about Nikolaev's intentions and had used him as their pawn. What aims did they pursue? Nikolaev had allegedly confessed that the Latvian consul had urged him to enter into contact with Trotsky and to write a letter to him. The 'consul', Trotsky pointed out, had been acting for the G.P.U., who had planned to 'discover' Nikolaev's plot only after they could produce 'evidence' that he was in correspondence with Trotsky. As long as they had not obtained that 'evidence', they left Nikolaev at large, and were confident that they were able to watch him closely and direct all his moves. They miscalculated: Nikolaev aimed his revolver at Kirov before the G.P.U. had achieved their purpose. Hence the contradictions between the various official versions; hence the secrecy in which Nikolaev's trial had been held; and hence the trial of the G.P.U. officers for 'neglect of duty' and the mildness of their sentences.

Trotsky concluded that the G.P.U., having failed to obtain false evidence against him from Nikolaev, would try to get it from—Zinoviev and Kamenev. Meanwhile, Zinoviev and Kamenev had been sentenced to ten and five years prison respectively, but had been allowed to state in public that they had had no dealings with Nikolaev and that they could be held co-responsible only indirectly, in so far as their criticisms of Stalin in bygone years might have influenced the terrorist. The court accepted their plea; and Trotsky concluded that behind the scenes a bargain was being struck between Stalin and Zinoviev and Kamenev: Stalin must have promised to rehabilitate them if they agreed to denounce Trotsky as the leader of a terroristic conspiracy. 'As far as I can judge . . .', Trotsky wrote, 'the strategy which Stalin displayed around Kirov's corpse has brought him no laurels': the incongruities of the affair had given rise to comment and to rumour which placed the odium on Stalin and his entourage. 'Precisely because of this Stalin can neither halt nor retreat. He must cover up the failure of this amalgam by new amalgams which must be conceived on a much wider scale, on a world scale, and more . . . successfully.'[1] Dissecting the Kirov affair, Trotsky predicted the great trials, which were indeed to be conceived 'on a world scale' with Hitler, instead of a mere Latvian consul, being cast by Stalin as Trotsky's ally.

. . . .

The Kirov affair at once affected the fortunes of Trotsky's family. His two sons-in-law, Nevelson and Volkov, deported since 1928, were arrested, and without trial the terms of their deportation or internment were prolonged. His first wife— now over sixty—was expelled from Leningrad, first to Tobolsk and then to a remote settlement in the Omsk province. His three grandchildren who had been under her care were now put up with an old aunt and were at fate's mercy. 'I receive letters from the little ones', Alexandra wrote to Lyova, 'but I do not have a clear idea of their life. My sister is probably having a hard time . . . although she keeps reassuring me. My health is so-so, there is no doctor here so that I must keep well.'[2] This time the terror also hit Sergei, Trotsky's youngest son who, we remember, was a scientist, shunned politics, and avoided contact with his father. In all the years since 1929 he had been writing only to his mother, confining himself to such matters as his health and his progress in academic work, and inquiring about the family's well-being—there had never been even the slightest political allusion in his letters and postcards. Just a few days after Kirov's assassination he wrote again to his mother about his professional work, describing the variety of the subjects on which he lectured at the Higher Technological Institute in Moscow, the effort this demanded

[1] See 'Letter to American Friends' of 26 January 1935 in *The Archives*; and *B.O.*, no. 42, February 1935.
[2] *Diary in Exile*, p. 79.

of him, and so on. Only in the closing lines he hinted that 'something unpleasant is brewing, so far it has taken the form of rumours, but how all this is going to end I do not know'. A week later, on 12 December, he wrote again about his academic work, and concluded alarmingly: 'My general situation is very grave, graver than one could imagine.'[1] Was it possible, the parents wondered in anguish, that the G.P.U. would seize Sergei as a hostage? For many a week they lived in expectation of another letter from him. None came. An old friend of the family, the widow of L. S. Klyachko, domiciled in Vienna, visited Moscow and inquired about Sergei, with the result that she was ordered to leave the country at once, without any explanation.

For weeks and months, through many a sleepless night, his parents' thoughts went out to Sergei. They were tormented by uncertainty. Perhaps his trouble was of a personal and private nature, not political? Perhaps the G.P.U. had only expelled him from Moscow but not imprisoned him? Surely they must realize that he was not politically minded at all? Could they have imprisoned him without Stalin's knowledge? Natalya asked, as if she entertained a faint, unspoken hope that perhaps an appeal to Stalin would help. No, Trotsky replied, only on Stalin's order could they have imprisoned him—only Stalin could have contrived such an act of vengeance. Would they try to extract from Sergei a confession with accusations against his own father? But of what use could these be to Stalin? Would their falsity not be obvious? Yet for what other reason could they have seized him? Would they torture him? Would he break down?[2]

For days and nights on end his parents were haunted by the image of their son facing his inquisitors. They feared that in his political innocence he would not be able to take the blows. They saw him bewildered and crushed; and they reproached themselves for not having insisted that he should go with them into exile. But could they try and tear him away from his academic preoccupations and routine when they themselves did not know what awaited them? It was different with Lyova, whose mind and passions were completely engaged in the political struggle. They remembered Zina whom they

[1] *The Archives*, Closed Section.   [2] *Diary in Exile*, pp. 61–72.

had been unable to save after she had joined them abroad. They recollected Sergei's jolly childhood, his reaction against his father and elder brother, his distaste for politics, his restless yet gay adolescence, and finally his serious and dedicated concentration on science. No, they could not have asked him to become involved in his father's affairs. But was he thinking now that they had abandoned and forgotten him? They searched Russian newspapers to see whether there was any mention of him. In the mounting avalanche of abuse against the 'dregs of Zinovievists, Trotskyists, former Princes, Counts and gendarmes' they came across names of relatives and friends; but there was dead silence about Sergei. Stalin, Trotsky noted, 'is clever enough to realize that even today I would not change places with him. . . . But if revenge on a higher [moral-political] plane has not succeeded—and clearly it will not succeed—it is still possible [for Stalin] to reward himself by striking at people close to me'.[1]

The feeling that Stalin had laid hands on the son because he could not reach the father gave Trotsky a sense of guilt. In his Diary, between entries about Sergei, he tells, seemingly out of context, the story of the execution of the Tsar and the Tsar's family. In his anxiety over Sergei falling a victim to his conflict with Stalin, he evidently thought also about those other innocent children, the Tsar's, on whom the sins of the father had been visited. He records in the Diary that he had no part in the decision about the Tsar's execution—the decision having been Lenin's primarily—and that he was taken aback when he first learnt about the fate of the Tsar's family. He does not recall this, however, to dissociate himself from Lenin or to exculpate himself. Seventeen years after the event he defends Lenin's decision as necessary and taken in the interest of the revolution. In the midst of civil war, he says, the Bolsheviks could not leave the White Armies with a 'live banner to rally around'; and after the Tsar's death any one of his children might have served them as the rallying symbol. The Tsar's children 'fell victim to that principle which constitutes the axis of Monarchy: dynastic succession'. The unspoken conclusion of this digression is clear enough: even if one granted Stalin the right to exterminate his adversaries—

[1] Op. cit., pp. 66–67.

and Trotsky was, of course, far from granting him that—
Stalin still had not a shred of justification for persecuting the
children of his adversaries. Sergei was not bound to his father
by any principle of dynastic succession. Immediately after
this digression Trotsky notes: 'No news about Seriozha, and
perhaps there won't be any for a long time. Long waiting has
blunted the anxiety of the first days.'[1]

Yet the anxiety began to tell on Trotsky. He was depressed.
He brooded again over his advancing age and death. He was
not yet fifty-five, but repeatedly he recalled Lenin's, or rather
Turgeniev's, dictum: 'Do you know what is the greatest vice?
To be more than fifty-five years old.' With a hint of envy he
remarked: 'But Lenin did not live long enough to develop
this vice.' 'My condition is not encouraging. The attacks of
illness have become more frequent, the symptoms are more
acute, my resistance is obviously getting weaker.' 'Of course,
the curve may yet take a temporary turn upwards. But in
general I have a feeling that liquidation is approaching.'
With a clear prescience of what was to come he observed that
Stalin 'would now give a great deal to be able to retract the
decision to deport me. He will unquestionably resort to a
terroristic act . . . in two cases . . .: if there is a threat of war,
or if his own position deteriorates greatly. Of course, there
could also be a third case, and a fourth . . . we shall see. And
if we don't, then others will.' He began to think of suicide,
and reflected that he should commit it if and when his physical
strength gave out and he could no longer continue his struggle.
Perhaps, it occurred to him, in this way he might save Sergei?
But these were fleeting thoughts. Although his energy was
sapped, he was still to show astonishing vitality and vigour
in years to come, when events were to confront him with their
challenge even more directly. Meanwhile, he was experiencing
something as ordinary and human as the crisis of middle age;
he succumbed to bouts of hypochondria and to the weariness
of prolonged isolation and passivity.[2]

He was now at his nadir. The ambitious plans and sanguine
hopes with which he had left Turkey were in the doldrums.
His great campaign against the Stalinist surrender to Hitler
had brought him no political rewards. Stalinism was even

[1] Op. cit., p. 82.   [2] Ibid., pp. 51, 109 and *passim*.

exploiting this surrender to make fresh political capital: playing on the fear of Nazism, it ingratiated itself with the European left. Trotsky sensed, although he could not admit it even to himself, that the Fourth International was stillborn. He could neither escape his circumstances nor make peace with them. And so he found some solace in exalted reflections on his 'historic mission' in founding the Fourth International. It was in this context that he contemplated what would have been the course of the Russian Revolution without Lenin and himself and that he asserted that his work for the new International was 'indispensable' in a sense in which even his work in the October insurrection and the Civil War was not. 'There is no arrogance in this claim at all', he noted. 'The collapse of the two Internationals has posed a problem which none of the leaders of these Internationals is at all equipped to solve. . . . There is now no one except me to carry out the mission of arming a new generation with a revolutionary method over the heads of the leaders of the Second and the Third Internationals. And . . . the worst vice is to be more than fifty-five years old! I need at least about five more years of uninterrupted work to ensure the succession', that is to form an International capable of leading the working class to revolution.[1]

At his nadir he challenged fate, which was to grant him exactly 'five more years' yet was not to allow him to 'ensure the succession'.

.   .   .   .

In all the years of their life together—now thirty-three—Trotsky and Natalya had never been as alone as they were during these eleven months at Domesne. Solitude and suffering drew them even closer to each other. In tragic hours, he said, he was 'always amazed at the reserves of her character'. Their love had survived triumph and defeat; and the afterglow of their past happiness broke through even the gloom of these days. Her face was becoming wrinkled and tense with worry and anxiety, and he thought with pain of her bright and gaily defiant youth. 'Today on our walk we went up a hill. Natalya got tired and unexpectedly sat down, quite pale, on the dry leaves. . . . Even now she still walks beautifully, with-

[1] Ibid., p. 54.

out fatigue and her gait is quite youthful, like her whole figure. But for the last two months her heart has been playing up now and then. She works too much. . . [she] sat down all of a sudden —she obviously just *could not* go any further—and smiled apologetically. What a pang of pity I felt for her youth. . . .' She bore her lot with quiet fortitude, and her life was wholly absorbed in his. Every storm that passed over him shook her; every current of his emotion permeated her being as well; and every reflex of his thought was mirrored in her. She had not been to him the kind of political comrade Krupskaya had been to Lenin; for Krupskaya, being childless, had been a political worker in her own right and sat on the party's Central Committee. Natalya was not only less active but less politically minded. 'Even though she is interested in the small daily facts of politics [these are Trotsky's words] she does not usually combine them into one coherent picture.' The loving husband could not express more clearly a doubt about his wife's political judgement. But this was not important: '. . . when politics go deep down and demand a complete response Natalya always finds in her inner music the right note'.[1]

To this, her 'inner music', he often referred; and, incidentally, when he described her in his Diary it was mostly while she was listening to music. Her independent interests were, as always, in the arts; and she had uncommon gifts of insight, observation, and expression, which appear strikingly in her own Diary pages. Her husband's disciples sometimes raised eyebrows at her political remarks, which caused Trotsky to say that 'sensitive people . . . instinctively feel the depth of her nature. Of those who pass her by with indifference or condescension without noticing the forces concealed in her, one can almost always say with certainty that they are superficial and trivial. . . . Philistinism, vulgarity, and cowardice can never be concealed from her, even though she is exceptionally lenient towards all minor human vices'. Of her 'inner forces' there can indeed be no doubt. At the worst moments, when he was almost at the end of his endurance, it was she who raised him back to his feet and revived in him the strength to carry his burden. At Domesne he noted with gratitude that she never reproached him for Sergei's misfortune and that she concealed

[1] Op. cit., pp. 51, 56.

her suffering from him. Only exceptionally did her anguish break out in a remark like this: 'They will not deport Sergei . . . they will torture him in order to get something out of him, and after that they will destroy him.' She hid her feelings in work, housekeeping, helping her husband in his writing, and discussing the French and Russian novels they read together. 'Her voice made me feel a sudden pang . . . slightly hoarse, [it] comes from deep in her chest', he remarked. 'When she suffers it withdraws even deeper, as if her soul were speaking directly. How well I know this voice of tenderness and suffering.' And on one occasion he noticed that for days she had been thinking more about his first wife than about Sergei, saying that Sergei might after all not be in any trouble and fearing that Alexandra, in her old age, would not survive deportation.[1]

In the slender hope that perhaps an appeal to the conscience of the world might save Sergei, Natalya wrote an 'Open Letter' in his defence and published it in the *Bulletin*.[2] She explained Sergei's complete innocence and, doing some violence to her pride, related how his distaste for politics had been caused by his reaction against his father. Had recent developments changed Sergei's attitude and drawn him to the opposition? 'I would be happy for him if I could think so, since under those conditions it would be immeasurably easier for Seriozha to bear the blow. . . .' Unfortunately, this supposition was unreal: she knew from various people that 'during the last few years [he] had been keeping as much out of politics as before. But personally I would not need even this evidence. . . .' The G.P.U. and the university authorities must know this, for they had undoubtedly watched him; and Stalin, 'whose son was a frequent guest in our boys' room', knew it too. She appealed to famous humanitarians and 'friends of the U.S.S.R.', such as Romain Rolland, André Gide, Bernard Shaw, and others, to speak up; she proposed that an international commission should investigate the mass reprisals that followed the Kirov affair. 'The Soviet bureaucracy cannot stand above the public opinion of the working class of the world. As far as the interests of the workers' state are concerned, these would only benefit by a serious examination of

[1] Ibid., pp. 51, 71, 121–2.   [2] *B.O.*, no. 44, July 1935.

its actions. I . . . offer all the necessary information and documents concerning my son. If, after long hesitation I openly raise the question of Sergei, it is not only because he is my son: that reason would be only too sufficient for a mother, but not adequate for . . . political action. But Sergei's case is a completely clear, simple, and indisputable instance of conscious and criminal abuse of power, and a case which can be examined very easily.' The appeal brought no answer.

By a curious coincidence, about the time when Natalya made this appeal, Trotsky was re-reading the autobiography of Protopop Avakuum, a famous and colourful Russian arch-priest and preacher of the Old Belief, who lived in the seventeenth century, after the Time of Trouble. Avakuum defended 'true' Greek Orthodoxy against Patriarch Nikon, his harsh rival, who had for temporal reasons changed the Church rites and the prayer book; and he exposed the corruption of the ecclesiastical hierarchy, and took up the cause of the oppressed peasants. He was unfrocked, jailed, banished first to Siberia and then to the Mongolian frontier, starved and tortured; but he refused to recant. His family suffered with him, and he, a loving husband and father, wondered for a while whether he should not give up the struggle and save his next of kin. His children died of disease and starvation in exile. It was in Siberia that he wrote his autobiography, a work which made an epoch in Russian literature; and he continued to preach with such effect that his fame as 'hero and martyr for truth' grew in the country. Banished, he was even more dangerous to his enemies than he had been when he stood near the Throne. They brought him back to Moscow and burned him at the stake.[1] Across the chasm of centuries and ideologies Trotsky could not help feeling with a shudder his affinity with this legendary rebel—how much and how little had changed in Russia! And even the spirit of Avakuum's wife stood before him as if embodied in Natalya:

Reflecting on the blows that had fallen to our lot I reminded Natasha the other day of the life of the Archpriest Avakuum. They were stumbling on together in Siberia, the rebellious priest and his faithful spouse. Their feet sunk in the snow, and the poor exhausted

[1] A new edition of *Zhizn Protopopa Avakuma*, with an interesting Preface not lacking topical allusions, was brought out in Moscow in 1960.

woman kept falling in the snowdrifts. Avakuum relates: 'And I came up and she, poor soul, began to reproach me, saying "How long, Archpriest, is this suffering to be?" And I said: "Markovna, unto our very death." And she, with a sigh, answered: "So be it, Petrovich, let us be getting on our way."'[1]

And so it was to be with Trotsky and Natalya: the suffering was to be 'unto our very death'.

.   .   .   .

They could not now remain at Domesne much longer. Any political swing to the right, bringing forward the fascist leagues, and any swing to the left, adding strength to the Communist party, threatened to rob Trotsky of his precarious refuge. It was the swing to the left that came. Since the Kirov affair the Stalinist incitement against 'the leader of world counter-revolution' had grown so brutal and venomous that it was all too likely to provoke an act of violence.[2] He could not feel secure even in the remote village in the Alps. He describes how once in these days he and Natalya, alone in their cottage, listened in tense silence to two men who as they approached were singing the Internationale. In past times only a friend could come with that song; now it might be an enemy and an assailant. They felt like those old Narodniks who, two generations earlier, went out into the country to enlighten and emancipate the muzhiks, and were beaten up and lynched by the muzhiks themselves.

The Government could no longer afford to ignore the Stalinist clamour. In May 1935 Laval had gone to Moscow to negotiate the Soviet-French alliance with Stalin, and he returned with that startling declaration by which Stalin pledged his support to Daladier's and Laval's defence policy. The French communist leaders, who had hitherto opposed that policy on principle, at once took up a 'patriotic' line; and the Popular Front took shape. Trotsky had every reason to believe that the Government would presently enforce the

---

[1] *Diary in Exile*, p. 121.

[2] An article by Jacques Duclos in *Humanité*, in December 1934, spoke of 'Trotsky's hands covered with Kirov's blood'; and the *Secours Rouge International*, the French section of M.O.P.R. (the international organization for the defence of political prisoners and exiles) clamoured for Trotsky's deportation from France.

expulsion order it had served on him the year before; and as no other country was willing to accept him, he feared deportation to a remote French colony, possibly to Madagascar.

In the spring of 1935 he asked for asylum in Norway. An election had just been held there and the Labour party had taken office. This was a Social Democratic party with a difference: it had belonged to the Comintern; and although it had broken with it in 1923, it did not adhere to the Second International. It was only natural to expect that such a party should give Trotsky refuge. Walter Held, a German Trotskyist, living as an émigré in Oslo, approached Olav Schöffle, one of the party's outstanding leaders, who headed its radical wing and was greatly devoted to Trotsky. It took many weeks before an official reply came. Trotsky supposed that the Norwegians had been stung by an article of his which taunted them for abandoning, on the assumption of office, their republican tradition and making peace with their King. Early in June, however, he was informed that they had granted him asylum. On 10 June he left Domesne and went to Paris, where he was to obtain the visa. But there was a hitch: high Norwegian officials, displeased with the government's decision, sought to obstruct it; he did not receive the visa and he had to cancel the arrangements for the voyage. The French police, suspecting that he had used all this as a pretext for descending on Paris, ordered him to leave France at once, within twenty-four or at the most forty-eight hours. He was resigned to returning to Domesne but was not allowed to do so. He proposed to wait for the final answer from Oslo in a private clinic; but the police, imagining that he was playing another trick on them, objected to this too. For a day or two he found refuge in the home of Doctor Rosenthal, a well-known Parisian surgeon. On 12 June he cabled a reproachful message to the Norwegian Prime Minister, saying that he had left his place of residence, relying on the Norwegian promise and now: 'The French government believes that I have deceived it, and demands that I leave France within twenty-four hours. I am sick and my wife is sick. Situation is desperate. I solicit immediate favourable decision.'[1] To make matters worse, he was

[1] From Trotsky's telegram to Nygaardsvold, Prime Minister of Norway (12 June 1935), *The Archives*, Closed Section.

penniless and had to borrow money for the journey. The Norwegians still asked him to secure a French re-entry permit, which he had no chance of obtaining, before they would allow him to come to Norway. At last, thanks to Schöffle's efforts, they granted him the visa, with a residence permit for six months only. He parted hurriedly from his French followers: 'I was seeing numerous Parisian comrades. The worthy doctor's apartment had unexpectedly been transformed into the headquarters of the Bolshevik-Leninist group. There were meetings going on in all the rooms, the telephone was ringing, more and more new friends kept arriving.'[1] He described the scene in a manner calling back to one's mind the moment of his deportation from Moscow in 1928. But this description is something of a pastiche: the farewells in Moscow had concluded one great epoch of his struggle and opened another; the farewells in Paris concluded and opened nothing.

He once again wrote, as he had done before his expulsion from France in 1916, an 'Open Letter' to the French workers. He told them that during his stay he had been condemned to silence. 'The most "democratic" Ministers like the most reactionary ones see their task in defending capitalist slavery. I belong to a revolutionary party which sees its task in the overthrow of capitalism.' He lashed out at the Stalinists: 'Two years ago *Humanité* reported every day that "the fascist Daladier has called the social-fascist Trotsky to France in order to organize with his assistance military intervention against the Soviets. . . ." Today the same gentlemen have formed . . . an anti-fascist "Popular Front" with the "fascist" Daladier. They have ceased to talk . . . about any French imperialist intervention against the U.S.S.R. Now they see the guarantee of peace in the alliance of French capital with the Soviet bureacracy and . . . say that Trotsky's policy serves not Herriot and Daladier but Hitler. . . .' He concluded vehemently that Stalinism was a 'festering sore' on the labour movement, which should be burned out with 'red hot iron', and that the workers should reassemble under the banner of Marx and Lenin. 'I am leaving with a deep love for the French people and ineradicable faith in the future of the working class. Sooner or later they will render me the hospitality that the bourgeoisie

[1] *Diary in Exile*, pp. 125–6.

refuses me.'[1] After two dismal and wasted years he was leaving
France never to return.

    .   .   .   .

The tale of Trotsky's sojourn in Norway reads like a large
variation on Ibsen's *Enemy of the People*. Ibsen presents the
drama of Doctor Stockman, revered for his nobility by all his
fellow-citizens, until he threatens to destroy their prosperity
by disclosing the truth about the poisoned source of their
wealth. Then his own brother, the town Mayor, and his own
'radical' friends, turn against him with cold and murderous
fury. We are now in Ibsen country once again. It does not
greatly matter that this time the Enemy of the People is a
fugitive from abroad; that he speaks not about the contaminated conduit pipes of a Norwegian resort but about a revolution
that has been perverted. The drama and the stage are essentially the same; and so are the family traits of the actors, especially of the sons and grandsons of Ibsen's pseudo-radicals—even
their *People's Messenger* is still there, as of old, changing sides
overnight and manipulating public opinion. In the crowd we
may also discern one or two descendants of the modest and
courageous captain Horster, who stood up for the Enemy of
the People. Only the times are changed; the forces in action
are far more potent; and the conflict more cruel.

From the outset the auguries were not promising. Not only
had the Norwegians been niggardly in granting Trotsky
asylum; they placed him under restrictions not very different
from those under which he had lived in France, and they
reserved the right to fix the place of his residence at some
distance from the capital. No sooner had he disembarked on
18 June than the National Farmers' Union protested against
his admission; and on 22 June the Storting was already debating the protest. This had no immediate sequel, but it was
clear that the Opposition would use his presence to embarrass
the government. The conservative bourgeoisie was scared of the
'ogre'; it was impossible to find lodgings for him; no house-
holder dared to accept him as tenant. The government asked
him to pledge himself to refrain from political activity. He did
this, on the understanding that what was demanded from him

[1] *B.O.*, no. 44, July 1935.

was that he should not interfere in Norway's domestic affairs. The government was to claim later that it had asked him to refrain from any political activity, a demand to which no political exile can normally submit or is asked to submit. The circumstance that he was thus treated by men still thinking of themselves as schismatics from official communism underlined the meanness of their behaviour.

However, on his arrival, the chiefs of the government and the Labour party made a great show of generosity. 'The working class of this country and all right thinking and un-prejudiced people'—this is how their newspaper *Arbeider-bladet* welcomed him—'will be delighted with the government's decision. The right of asylum must not be a dead letter but a reality. The Norwegian people feel . . . honoured by Trotsky's presence in their country.' Without going into the pros and cons of his dispute with Stalin, on which they held no definite views, they denied Stalin the right to 'persecute and banish a man like Leon Trotsky whose name will stand together with Lenin's in the history of the Russian revolution. Now that, despite his great and imperishable services, he has been exiled from his own country, any democratic nation must consider it a welcome duty to offer him refuge. . . .'[1] Martin Tranmael, the party's founder and leader, came out with personal greetings. Various ministers intimated that the terms of Trot-sky's admission, the six months' limit and the restrictions on his freedom of movement, were so many formalities. The govern-ment asked Konrad Knudsen, a Socialist editor, to assist in settling Trotsky; and Knudsen, seeing that it was impossible to lease a house, invited him and Natalya to move into his own home.[2]

Presently three party chiefs, Tranmael, Trygve Lie, the Minister of Justice, and the Editor of *Arbeiderbladet* paid Trotsky a formal visit. The meeting was rather awkward. The Nor-wegians reminded Trotsky that in 1921 they had been in Moscow and negotiated with him, Lenin, and Zinoviev the terms of their adherence to the Comintern; but before they

---

[1] H. Krog, *Meninger*, p. 220; (I am obliged to Mr. Krog and to Mr. N. K. Dahl for the English translations of passages from this book and of other Norwegian documents quoted later); *Diary in Exile*, pp. 128–9.

[2] This is how Konrad Knudsen has related the facts to me.

proceeded further Trygve Lie wished to make sure that Trotsky was aware of his obligation to refrain from political activity. He answered that he had not the slightest intention of meddling in Norwegian affairs—Trygve Lie later maintained that he, Lie, had demanded there and then that Trotsky should abstain from all action 'hostile towards any friendly government'. An eye-witness recollects that 'Trotsky refused to be drawn into any political discussion with us and talked only about the weather'. But the visitors, having gone through with the official part of the business, were eager to change over to a tone of comradeship, to talk politics, and to bask in the greatness of the man to whom they had given refuge. They begged him to give *Arbeiderbladet* a long and exhaustive interview on the major issues of world politics. According to the same eye-witness, he replied frigidly that the Minister of Justice had just forbidden him to indulge in any form of political activity. His interlocutors shrugged and laughed off the prohibition as a piece of make-believe which they had to go through *pro forma* in order to appease their parliamentary opponents; and the Minister of Justice reassured Trotsky that by expressing his opinions he would in no way offend against the terms of his residence. The Minister himself then turned into an eager journalistic interviewer; and Trotsky answered his questions at length, availing himself of the opportunity to denounce Stalin's policy and the terror unleashed since Kirov's assassination. On 26 July *Arbeiderbladet* published the interview, with much editorial flourish, leaving readers in no doubt that the Minister of Justice himself had been instrumental in making the benefit of Trotsky's views available to them. Thus the 'misunderstandings' of the first days seemed dispelled. The party in office treated Trotsky as an illustrious guest rather than as a refugee on sufferance. Parliamentarians and journalists vied with one another in paying him respects; and for a time nothing bestowed greater distinction on a person in Oslo's leftish circles than the ability to boast of having been received by the great exile.

Before the end of June, Trotsky and Natalya were installed in Knudsen's home at Vexhall, a village near Honnefoss, about thirty miles north of Oslo. Amid the quiet and peace of the country, sharing in the domesticities of a modest, warm-hearted and fairly large family they could recover from recent harassments. Knudsen was a moderate, suave Social Democrat, very remote from Trotskyism—it was from sheer sensitiveness and from defiance of philistinism that he had invited the man of October under his roof. By tacit agreement they never touched on their political differences. And so 'during his entire stay with us', these are Knudsen's words, 'we were not troubled even once by the slightest misunderstanding. Trotsky was too much concentrated on his work to waste time in fruitless discussion. He worked very hard. I have never met anyone as precise, punctual, and pedantic in his habits. When he was not ill, he used to get up at 5.20 or 5.30 in the morning, go down to the pantry, take a little food, and set to work. He did it all very quietly, on tiptoe, so as not to disturb anyone. I have no words to describe his tact and consideration for all who lived in our house. Natalya's behaviour was the same; we nicknamed her affectionately "the little lady of the big house". Their needs were quite incredibly modest.'[1]

For the first time since 1917 Trotsky did not have to live under the protection of a 'comradely bodyguard' or under police surveillance and incognito. The yard gate was wide open day and night, with village folk straying in for amiable chats. Occasionally, visitors came from abroad, German refugees living in Scandinavia, Frenchmen, Belgians, and Americans. Among the Americans was Harold Isaacs who had just returned from China, after a stay of several years, and was a source of valuable information on that country and its communist movement. (He was just writing a book, *The Tragedy of the Chinese Revolution*, to which Trotsky was to contribute a preface.) Shachtman and Muste, the well-known American socialist who had joined the Trotskyists, also came to Vexhall. The French arrived several times with their disputes and quarrels, asking Trotsky to act as umpire. They could not agree whether they should leave the S.F.I.O. and reconstitute themselves as an independent party. Raymond Molinier had set up his own paper, *La Commune*, advocating disaffiliation. This brought the quarrel into the open and at last led Trotsky to break with Molinier. The incident would

[1] I am quoting again Knudsen's account and also his Preface to the Norwegian edition of Trotsky's *My Life*.

not be worth mentioning had it not been for the fact that the feud was to go on for years and to become grotesquely intertwined with the fortunes of Trotsky's family. Amid all this and while his correspondence with his followers, which he could not well carry on from France, grew to enormous bulk, Trotsky began writing a new book, *The Revolution Betrayed*.[1]

Towards the end of the summer, however, on 19 September, he entered the Municipal Hospital of Oslo because of the persistence of his fevers and a general debility. In the stillness of his ward he gave himself to melancholy musings. 'It is nearly twenty years', he wrote, 'since I lay on a bunk in a Madrid prison and wondered in amazement what on earth had brought me there. I remember I burst into a fit of laughter . . . and laughed and laughed until I fell asleep. Now once again I am wondering in amazement what on earth has brought me here, into an Oslo hospital?'[2] A Bible on his bedside table sent his mind wondering farther back, to a prison cell in Odessa where thirty-seven years before he had been learning foreign languages from a multilingual copy of the Bible. 'Unfortunately, I cannot promise that this new encounter with the old and so familiar book will help in saving my soul. But reading the Gospel in Norwegian may help me to learn the language of the country which has shown me hospitality, and its literature which I have . . . loved since my early years.' After many tests and examinations he left hospital, his soul not saved and his body not restored to health. He spent the greater part of December in bed—this, he said later, was 'the worst month of my life'.

His recovery was impeded by old and new anxieties and worries. He was depressed by the futility of his 'organizational' work. He was irritated by the French Trotskyists, who did not cease to pester him with their quarrels; and he wrote to Lyova: 'It is absolutely necessary that I should get at least four weeks' "leave" and should not be approached with any letters from the Sections. . . . Otherwise it will be impossible for me to recover my capacity for work. These disgusting

---

[1] The enormous growth of Trotsky's correspondence with his French, German, Belgian, Dutch, Austrian, American, Greek, and other followers is reflected in the files of *The Archives*, Closed Section. Harold Isaacs' report on China, ibid.

[2] Quoted from Trotsky's Preface to the Norwegian edition of *My Life*; and from *The Archives*.

trivia (*eckelhafter Kleinkramm*) not only rob me of the ability to occupy myself with more serious affairs, but give me insomnia, fever, etc. . . . I request you to be quite ruthless about this. Then I may perhaps be at your disposal again, say, by 1 February.'[1] In the following weeks and months, however, he repeatedly reproached Lyova for harassing him with the '*eckelhafte Kleinkrämmerei*' and vented his 'despair' at the 'silly intrigues' of the 'French cliques'.[2] His correspondence shows all too clearly that things were no better in most of the other Sections of the would-be Fourth International. And there was the anguish over events in Russia and the uncertainty about Sergei. Indirect inquiries in Moscow brought forth an official explanation that Sergei was not imprisoned but 'placed under police surveillance' to keep him from communicating with his father. But when Natalya tried to transmit a small money order to Sergei's wife in Moscow, this was returned to a bank in Oslo with the note that the addressee was unknown. On top of all this, he was troubled by lack of money. Publishers' advances had just enabled him to cover the expenses of settling in Norway and to pay off a debt to Henri Molinier, which he was anxious to do before he broke with the Molinier set. In what bad straits he was can be seen from a letter to Harold Isaacs which he wrote from the Oslo hospital on 29 September, begging for help in a 'financial catastrophe': He had to pay 10 Krones per day in hospital, and had only 100 Krones left.[3]

Just before Christmas he went with Knudsen and a few young Norwegians to the wild rocky country north of Honnefoss, hoping that a few days of physical activity in the open air might improve his health. The time of this trip should be noted—a year later, at Radek's and Pyatakov's trial, Vyshinsky was to claim that at this time Pyatakov paid Trotsky a secret visit; and Pyatakov himself was to confess that he had come to Oslo by plane from Berlin and had gone by car straight from the airfield to meet Trotsky. These allegations were refuted by Norwegian authorities, who ascertained that no German plane had landed at Oslo airfield at the end of December

[1] The letter, dated 27 December 1935, was addressed to Lyova and also, it seems, to another member of the International Secretariat. *The Archives*, Closed Section.

[2] Letters of 14 January and 22 March 1936, ibid.

[3] Correspondence with Harold Isaacs, ibid.

1935 and for several months before and after that; and Trotsky's companions proved that no one could have come by car to the place where they stayed with Trotsky. 'The winter was extremely severe; the roadless country was completely submerged by snowdrifts, and gripped by Arctic ice. We remember this well, because once during the trip Trotsky was trapped by snow and ice. We were on skis, and he was not good at skiing; and so we had to organize a regular rescue operation, and we were very worried.'[1]

Soon after, by one of those abrupt changes in his health which puzzled his doctors, he recovered, and resumed the writing of *The Revolution Betrayed*. This kept him busy for the next six months until he completed the book.

. . . .

The Revolution Betrayed occupies a special place in Trotsky's literary work. It is the last book he managed to complete and, in a sense, his political testament. In it he gave his final analysis of Soviet society and a survey of its history up to the middle of the Stalin era. His most complex book, it combines all the weakness and the strength of his thought. It contains many new and original reflections on socialism, on the difficulties with which proletarian revolution has to grapple, and on the role of a bureaucracy in a workers' state. He also surveyed the international position of the Soviet Union before the Second World War and tried to pierce the future with daring and partly erroneous forecasts. The book is a profound theoretical treatise and a tract for the time; a creative restatement of classical Marxist views; and the manifesto of the 'new Trotskyism' calling for revolution in the Soviet Union. Trotsky appears here in all his capacities: as detached and rigorously objective thinker; as leader of a defeated Opposition; and as passionate pamphleteer and polemicist. The polemicist's contribution forms the more esoteric part of the work and tends to overshadow the objective and analytical argument. Because of the wealth of its ideas and its imaginative force, this has been one of the seminal books of this century, as instructive as confusing, and destined to be put to adventitious use more often

[1] This is what Mr. and Mrs. N. K. Dahl relate, who accompanied Trotsky on this trip. See also *The Case of Leon Trotsky*, pp. 204–23.

than any other piece of political writing. Even its title was to become one of the shibboleths of our time.

The Revolution Betrayed was Trotsky's critical reaction to a crucial moment of the Stalin era. Official Moscow had just proclaimed that the Soviet Union had already achieved socialism—until recently it had contented itself with the more modest claim that only 'the foundations of socialism' had been laid. What emboldened Stalin to proclaim nothing less than the advent of socialism was the progress of industrialization, the first superficial signs of the consolidation of collective farming, and the nation's fresh relief at having left behind the famines and massacres of the early nineteen-thirties. A new Constitution, 'the most democratic in the world', was to be the epitome of the new epoch: it nominally abolished discrimination against members of the former possessing classes, and introduced general and equal franchise for all. This presupposed that the proletarian dictatorship no longer needed any special constitutional guarantees, because a virtually classless society had come into being. Yet while it gave all citizens the equal right to vote, the Constitution deprived all of the right to choose for whom to vote, and unlike previous Soviet Constitutions, it formally consecrated the single party system. That system and the monolithic party, the propagandists maintained, conformed to the very nature of a socialist community, which was not torn by any conflict of class interests, whereas any multi-party system reflected the inherent antagonisms of bourgeois society.

Yet this was also a time of growing inequality, when discrepancies between high and low earnings widened rapidly, when 'socialist competition' degenerated into a wild scramble for privileges and necessities of life, when Stakhanovism carried that scramble to every factory bench and coal seam in the country, and when the contrast between the affluence of the few and the pauperism of the many took on most offensive forms. Stalin, conducting a ferocious drive against the 'levellers', placed himself at the head of the *nouveaux riches*, whetted their appetites, ridiculed the faint scruples that inhibited them, and glorified the new inequality as an accomplishment of socialism. A new hierarchical organization was taking shape. It was elaborately graded, with ranks, titles, and prerogatives sharply differentiated, and with every little rung on all the multiple steep ladders of authority marked out with bizarre precision. Nowhere was this reversal from earlier 'proletarian democratic' ways to the new authoritarianism as pronounced as in the armed forces, where the ranks and distinctions of Tsarist times were reintroduced. Amid the celebrations of the advent of socialism there was thus the flavour of something like Restoration in the air. The educational system and the nation's spiritual life were deeply affected. The progressive school reforms of the nineteen-twenties, which had aroused the admiration of many foreign educationists, were decried as ultra-left aberrations; and a heavy, increasingly nationalist traditionalism and an old-fashioned paternalistic discipline invaded classrooms and lecture halls, stifling the spirit of the young generation. The bureaucratic tutelage over science, literature, and the arts grew unbearably tyrannical. In every field the state exercised absolute power provocatively and brazenly, glorifying itself as the supreme guardian of society. And the autocratic bearer of power was exalted as Father of the Peoples, fount of all wisdom, benefactor of mankind, and demiurge of socialism.

Trotsky set out to refute Stalin's claims; and he did this by confronting the realities of Stalinism with the classical Marxist conception of socialism. He pointed out that the predominance of social forms of ownership did not yet constitute socialism, even though it was its essential condition. Socialism presupposed an economy of abundance; it could not be founded on the want and poverty that prevailed in the Soviet Union and that led to the recrudescence of glaring inequality. Stalin had invoked Marx's dictum about the two stages of communism, a lower one where society would reward its members 'each according to his work', and the higher where it would reward them 'each according to his needs'—it was at the lower stage, Stalin declared, that the Soviet Union found itself. Trotsky pointed out that Stalin was abusing the authority of Marx in order to justify the inequality he was promoting. While it was true that Marx had foreseen that inequality would persist in the early phase of socialism, it would not have occurred to him that it would grow, and even grow by leaps and bounds, as it did under Stalin's rule. Soviet society was still only half-way between capitalism and socialism. It could advance or slide back; and only to the extent to which it overcame inequality would it advance. The growth of inequality indicated backsliding.

The orgies of Stalinist absolutism were part and parcel of the same retrograde trend. Lenin had, in his *State and Revolution*, wrested from oblivion the Marxian notion of the 'withering away of the state' and made of it the household idea of Bolshevism; and Trotsky now defended the idea against Stalinist manipulation. He insisted that socialism was inconceivable without the withering away of the state. It was from class conflict that the state had arisen; and it existed as an instrument of class domination. Even in its lower phase socialism meant the disappearance of class antagonisms and of political coercion—only the purely administrative functions of the state 'the management of things, not of men' were to survive under socialism. Lenin had imagined the proletarian dictatorship as a 'semi-state' only, modelled on the Commune of Paris, whose officials would be elected and deposed by vote and paid workers' wages, so that they should not form a bureaucracy estranged from the people. In backward and isolated Russia this scheme had proved unworkable. All the same, the advance towards socialism must be measured by the degree to which the coercive power of the state was on the decline. Massive political persecution and the glorification of the state in themselves refuted the Stalinist claim about the achievement of socialism. Stalin argued that the state could not wither away in a single country; to Trotsky this was only an indirect admission that socialism could not be achieved in a single country either. But it was not the 'capitalist encirclement' that was the chief reason for the increased power of the state, for the Stalinist terror aimed primarily at 'domestic enemies', i.e. at communist opposition.

To the non-Marxist much of this critique must seem 'doctrinaire'. To the Marxist it was vital because it stripped Stalinism of 'ideological' pretensions and dissociated Marxism from Stalin's practices. Trotsky sought to establish for the Marxist school of thought a position, from which it could disclaim the moral liabilities which Stalinism was creating for it, and from which it could declare that its ideas were no

more responsible for Stalin's reign of terror than the Ten
Commandments and the Sermon on the Mount had been for
the Holy Inquisition. Nor is the significance of this argument
only moral and historical, for it still has a profound bearing on
communist thinking. The notion, which Khrushchev has
expounded in the late nineteen-fifties and early nineteen-sixties,
that the Soviet Union is passing from socialism to communism
is predicated on the Stalinist claim about the achievement of
socialism in the nineteen-thirties, and is just as unreal as that
claim. Seen from Trotsky's standpoint Soviet society is, as yet,
despite its immense strides forward, very far from having
achieved socialism. As all the thinking of Soviet ideologues,
economists, sociologists, philosophers, and historians is still
entangled in the canon about the completion of socialism, and
is moving within a circle of fictions construed around that
canon, the application of Trotsky's criteria to present Soviet
reality would entail a revision of the legacy of Stalinism far
more thoroughgoing than that undertaken in the Soviet Union
in the first decade after Stalin.

The Revolution Betrayed is Trotsky's classical indictment of
bureaucracy. Once again, in the 'conflict between the ordinary
working woman and the bureaucrat who has seized her by
the throat' he 'sided with the working woman'. He saw the
mainspring of Stalinism in the defence of privilege, which alone
gave a certain unity to all the disparate aspects of Stalin's
policy, connecting its 'Thermidorian' spirit with its diplomacy
and the debasement of the Comintern. The ruling group
shielded the interests of an acquisitive minority against popular
discontent at home and the shocks of revolutionary class struggle
abroad. Trotsky analysed the social composition of the managerial groups, of the party machine, of the civil servants and of
the officer corps, who between them formed 12 to 15 per cent.
of the population, a massive stratum, conscious of its weight,
rendered conservative by privilege, and straining with all its
might to preserve the national and the international *status quo*.

Not content with indicting the bureaucracy, Trotsky considered again how and why it had achieved its power in the
Soviet Union and whether its predominance was not inherent
in socialist revolution at large. He went beyond his earlier
answers and threw into bolder relief the objective causes for

the recrudescence of inequality amid all the 'want and poverty' in the Soviet Union. But he also stated with emphasis that some of these factors would recur in every socialist revolution, for none would be able to abolish inequality immediately. Even the United States, the wealthiest industrial nation, did not yet produce enough to be able to reward labour 'according to needs'; it still suffered from a relative scarcity which would compel it, under communist government, to maintain differential wages and salaries. Consequently, tensions and social conflicts would persist, although they would be much milder than in an underdeveloped country. And so 'the tendencies of bureaucratism . . . would everywhere show themselves even after a proletarian revolution'.[1] Marx and Lenin had been aware of this. Marx had spoken of 'bourgeois law', safeguarding unequal distribution of goods, as being 'inevitable in the first phase of communist society'. Lenin had described the Soviet republic as being in some respects a 'bourgeois state without the bourgeoisie', even if it were governed in the spirit of proletarian democracy. But only the experience of the Stalin era had revealed the full dimensions of the problem and allowed real insight into the contradictions of post-capitalist society. A revolutionary government had to maintain inequality and had to struggle against it; and it had to do both for the sake of socialism. It had to provide incentives to technicians, skilled workers, and administrators in order to ensure the proper functioning and the rapid expansion of the economy; yet it had also to aim at the reduction and the eventual abolition of privileges.

Ultimately, this contradiction could be resolved only by an increase in social wealth, surpassing all that mankind had hitherto dreamt of, and by the attainment of so high and universal a level of education that the gulf between manual labour and intellectual work would vanish. In the meantime before these conditions are fulfilled, the revolutionary state assumes 'directly and from the very beginning a dual character': it is socialist in so far as it defends social property in the means of production; and it is bourgeois in so far as it directs an unequal, differential distribution of goods among the members of society. The clear formulation of this contradiction and

[1] *The Revolution Betrayed*, pp. 57–59.

duality as inherent in the transition to socialism is one of Trotsky's important contributions to the Marxist thought of his time.[1]

Returning to the analysis of Soviet society he admitted that Lenin and he had not foreseen that a 'bourgeois state without a bourgeoisie' would prove inconsistent with genuine Soviet democracy; and that the state could not 'wither away' as long as there was 'the iron necessity' for it to foster and support a privileged minority. The destruction of Soviet democracy was thus due not merely to Stalin's conspiracy, which was the subjective aspect of a wider objective process. He went on to say that the Stalinist government had preserved the 'dual character' inherent in any revolutionary government; but that the bourgeois element in it had gained immense weight and power at the expense of the socialist element. The bureaucracy was by its very nature 'the planter and protector of inequality'; it acted like a policeman who during an acute shortage of goods 'keeps order' while crowds queue up at food-shops—when food is abundant there are no queues and the policeman becomes superfluous. Yet 'nobody who has wealth to distribute ever omits himself. Thus out of a social necessity there has developed an organ which has far outgrown its socially necessary function, and has become an independent factor and therewith the source of great danger for the whole social organism. . . . The poverty and cultural backwardness of the masses have again become incarnate in the malignant figure of the ruler with the great club in his hand.'[2]

Had the bourgeois element in the Soviet state acquired enough force to destroy the socialist element? Trotsky asked. Once again he firmly rejected the view that the bureaucracy was a 'new class' or that the Soviet masses were exploited by 'state capitalism'. State capitalism without a capitalist class was to the Marxist a contradiction in terms. As for the bureaucracy, it lacked the social homogeneity of any class which owed its place in society to the ownership and the command of the means of production. The exercise of mere managerial functions had not turned the directors of the Soviet industry and state into such a class, even though they treated both state

[1] See in particular op. cit., chapter II: 'Socialism and the State.'
[2] Op. cit., p. 111.

and industry as if these were their private domains. The in-equality which Stalinism promoted was still confined to the sphere of private consumption. The privileged groups were not permitted to appropriate means of production. Unlike any exploiting class, they could not accumulate wealth in the form that would give them command over the labour of others and enable them to appropriate more and more wealth. Even their privileges and power were bound up with the national ownership of productive resources; and so they had to defend that ownership and thereby to perform a function which, from the socialist viewpoint, was necessary and progressive, though they performed it at an exorbitant cost to society.

But the social balance of the Stalinist state, Trotsky went on, was unstable. In the long run either the socialist element or the bourgeois one must prevail. The continuous growth of in-equality was a danger signal. The managerial groups would not indefinitely content themselves with consumer privileges. Sooner or later they would seek to form themselves into a new possessing class by expropriating the state and becoming the shareholding owners of trusts and concerns. 'One may argue that the big bureaucrat cares little what are the prevailing forms of property, provided only that they guarantee him the necessary income. This argument ignores not only the stability of the bureaucrat's own rights, but also the question of his descendants. . . . Privileges have only half their worth if they cannot be transmitted to one's children. But the right of testa-ment is inseparable from the right of property. It is not enough to be director of the trust; it is necessary to be a stockholder. The victory of the bureaucracy in this decisive sphere would mean its conversion into a new possessing class.' Stalin, Trotsky pointed out, could not preside over this 'conversion'; his régime was based on national ownership and a planned economy. Turning into a new bourgeoisie, the bureaucracy would there-fore necessarily come into conflict with Stalinism; and Stalin, by encouraging its acquisitiveness, was unwittingly under-mining not only his own rule, but all the conquests of the revolution. So close did this danger appear to Trotsky that he had no hesitation in stating that the 1936 Constitution 'creates the political premises for the birth of a new possessing class'. As in the nineteen-twenties so in the nineteen-thirties, he

w

considered the bureaucracy, or a section of it, as the potential agent of a capitalist restoration; but while earlier he saw it as an auxiliary of the kulaks and the N.E.P. men, now, after the 'liquidation' of those classes, he regarded it as an independent agent.[1]

This view appears altogether erroneous in retrospect. Far from laying its hands on and appropriating the means of production, the Soviet bureaucracy was, in the coming decades, to remain the guardian of public ownership. It should be remarked, however, that Trotsky spoke of the bureaucracy's metamorphosis into a new bourgeoisie as of one of several possibilities; he was careful to point out that the potentiality should not be mistaken for actuality. He dealt, as he emphasized, with an unprecedented, complex, and enigmatic phenomenon, at a time when the Stalinist anti-egalitarianism and reaction against early Bolshevism were at the highest pitch. The theorist could take nothing for granted; he could not rule out the possibility that these trends might release powerful and independent forces utterly inimical to socialism. Stalin, representing an ambiguous combination of 'Leninist orthodoxy' with a revulsion against revolutionary principle, did indeed appear at times to lead Russia to the very brink of Restoration. That he could not cross that brink Trotsky had no doubt. He feared that others might cross it, even if over Stalin's body.[2]

The same fear, however, haunted Stalin as well; and this was why he raged against his own bureaucracy and, on the pretext of fighting Trotskyism and Bukharinism, decimated it in each of the successive purges. It was one of the effects of the purges that they prevented the managerial groups from consolidation as a social stratum. Stalin whetted their acquisitive instincts and wrung their necks. This was one of the most obscure, least discussed and yet important consequences of the permanent terror. While on the one hand the terror annihilated the old Bolshevik cadres and cowed the working class and the peasantry, it kept, on the other, the whole of the bureaucracy in a state of flux, renewing permanently its composition, and not allowing it to grow out of a protoplasmic or amoeboid condition, to form a compact and articulate body

[1] Op. cit., pp. 240, 257, and *passim*.   [2] Ibid., pp. 236–7.

with a socio-political identity of its own. In such circumstances the managerial groups could not become a new possessing class, even if they wanted to—they could not start accumulating capital on their own account while they were hovering between their offices and the concentration camps. Just as he had 'liquidated' the kulaks, so Stalin was constantly 'liquidating' the embryo of the new bourgeoisie; and in this he once again acted, in his own barbaric autocratic manner, from Trotsky's tacitly accepted premiss. In any case, the bureaucratic would-be bourgeoisie was no mere figment of Trotsky's imagination. But he patently exaggerated its vitality and capacity for self-realization, just as he had exaggerated the power of the kulaks; and he underrated once again Stalin's cunning, tenacity, and ruthlessness. The manner in which Stalin both promoted and repressed the bourgeois element in the state was utterly alien and even incomprehensible to Trotsky, who, as always, thought that only a conscious and active working class could check the anti-socialist tendencies of the state.

Yet Trotsky also realized that the Soviet workers were unwilling to rise against the bureaucracy, for even if they were hostile to it 'in their vast majority', they feared 'lest in throwing out the bureaucracy they would open the way for a capitalist restoration. . . .' The workers felt that for the time being 'the bureaucracy continues to fulfil a necessary function' as the 'watchman' guarding some of *their* conquests. 'They will inevitably drive out the dishonest, impudent, and unreliable watchman as soon as they see another possibility.' What a paradox this was! The same social group which might turn into a new possessing class and destroy the revolution was to some extent the revolution's protector. Trotsky knew that 'doctrinaires would not be satisfied' with his appraisal of the situation: 'They would like categorical formulas: yes—yes, and no—no'; and, of course, sociological analysis would be simple 'if social phenomena had always a finished character'. But he refused to force realities into any neat scheme and to give 'for the sake of logical completeness' 'a finished definition to an unfinished process'. Confronted by a completely new and 'dynamic social formation', the theorist could produce only working hypotheses and let events test them.[1]

[1] Ibid., pp. 241–2, 269–70.

Events disproved the hypothesis about the transformation of the bureaucracy into a new possessing class already in the nineteen-thirties; but even more so during and after the Second World War. Then the needs of national defence and the destruction of the bourgeois order in eastern Europe and China powerfully reinforced the nationalized structure of the Soviet economy. The Stalinist state, by promoting or assisting for its own reasons revolution in eastern Europe and Asia, created formidable counter-checks to its own bourgeois tendencies. The post-war industrialization, the immense expansion of the Soviet working class, the growth of mass education, and the reviving self-assurance of the workers tended to subdue the bourgeois element in the state; and after Stalin's death the bureaucracy was compelled to make concession after concession to the egalitarianism of the masses. To be sure, the tension between the bourgeois and the socialist elements of the state continued; and, being inherent in the structure of any post-capitalist society, it was bound to persist for a very long time to come. The managers, the administrators, the technicians, and the skilled workers remained privileged groups. But the gulf between them and the great mass of the toilers was narrowing in the middle and late nineteen-fifties and the early nineteen-sixties; and so the balance between the contradictory elements in the state was very different from what it had been when Trotsky wrote *The Revolution Betrayed*. Trotsky himself anticipated such a development:

Two opposite tendencies are growing up out of the depth of the Soviet régime. To the extent that, in contrast to a decaying capitalism, [that régime] develops the productive forces, it is preparing the economic basis of socialism. To the extent that, for the benefit of an upper stratum, it carries to more and more extreme expression bourgeois norms of distribution, it is preparing a capitalist restoration. This contrast between forms of property and norms of distribution cannot grow indefinitely. Either the bourgeois norms must in one form or another spread to the means of production, or the norms of distribution must be brought into correspondence with the socialist property system.[1]

It is this latter course that events were to take twenty and twenty-five years later, when Stalin's successors began grudg-

[1] Op. cit., pp. 231–2.

ingly yet unmistakably to bring the norms of distribution into
closer correspondence with the socialist property system. Trotsky's hypothesis about the rise of a new possessing class appears
therefore unduly pessimistic, even though it reflected a situation
in which the balance was strongly and dangerously weighted
against the socialist elements. Yet, despite the 'pessimism',
Trotsky's analysis of the dynamic contradictions of the post-
revolutionary state still offers the best clue to the subsequent
social evolution.

It was against a 'greedy, mendacious, and cynical caste of
rulers', against the germ of a new possessing class, that Trotsky
formulated his programme of a 'political revolution' in the
U.S.S.R. 'There is no peaceful outcome . . .' he wrote. 'The
Soviet bureaucracy will not give up its positions without a
fight . . . no devil has ever yet voluntarily cut off his own
claws.' 'The proletariat of a backward country was fated to
accomplish the first socialist revolution. For this historic
privilege it must, according to all the evidence, pay with a
second supplementary revolution—against bureaucratic absolutism.' He preached 'a political, not a social revolution',
a revolution, that is, which would overthrow the Stalinist
system of government, but would not change the existing
property relations.[1]

This was a completely new prospect: Marxists had never
imagined that after a socialist revolution they would have to
call upon the workers to rise again, for they had taken it for
granted that a workers' state could be only a proletarian
democracy. History had now demonstrated that this was not
so; and that, just as the bourgeois order had developed various
forms of government, monarchical and republican, constitutional and autocratic, so the workers' state could exist in
various political forms, ranging from a bureaucratic absolutism
to government by democratic Soviets. And just as the French
bourgeoisie had to 'supplement' the social revolution of
1789–93 by the political revolutions of 1830 and 1848, in
which ruling groups and methods of government were changed
but not the economic structure of society—so, Trotsky argued,
the working class too had to 'supplement' the October Revolution. The bourgeoisie had acted consistently within its class

[1] Op. cit., pp. 271–2.

interest when it asserted itself against its own absolutist rulers; and the working class would also act legitimately in freeing its own state from a despotic stranglehold. A political revolution of this kind had, of course, nothing to do with terroristic acts: 'Individual terror is a weapon of impatient and despairing individuals, belonging most frequently to the young genera- tion of the bureaucracy itself.' For Marxists it was axiomatic that they could carry out the revolution only with the open support of the majority of the workers. It was therefore not with a call for any immediate action that Trotsky came out, for as long as the workers saw in the bureaucracy the 'watch- man of their conquests', they would not rise against it. Trotsky advanced the idea, not the slogan, of a revolution; he offered a long-term orientation for the struggle against Stalinism, not guidance for direct action.

This is how he formulated the programme of the revolution:

It is not a question of substituting one ruling clique for another, but of changing the very methods of administering the economy and guiding the culture of the country. Bureaucratic autocracy must give place to Soviet democracy. A restoration of the right of criticism and genuine freedom of elections is the necessary con- dition for the further development of the country. This assumes a revival of freedom of Soviet parties, beginning with the party of Bolsheviks, and a renascence of the trade unions. The bringing of democracy into industry means a radical revision of plans in the interests of the toilers. Free discussion of economic problems will decrease the overhead expense of bureaucratic mistakes and zig- zags. Expensive playthings—Palaces of the Soviets, new theatres, showy Metro subways—will be abandoned in favour of workers' dwellings. 'Bourgeois norms of distribution' will be confined within the limits of strict necessity, and, in step with the growth of social wealth, will give way to socialist equality. Ranks will be immedi- ately abolished. The tinsel of decorations will go into the melting pot. Youth will receive the opportunity to breathe freely, criticise, make mistakes, and grow up. Science and art will be freed of their chains. And, finally, foreign policy will return to the traditions of revolutionary internationalism.[1]

He reiterated here all the familiar desiderata of the period when he still stood for reform. Only in one point did he make a new departure—namely, in his demand for 'genuine freedom

[1] Op. cit., p. 273.

of elections'. On this point, however, he was confronted with a dilemma: he had discarded the principle of the single party; but he did not advocate unqualified freedom of parties. Going back to a pre-1921 formula, he spoke of a 'revival of freedom of *Soviet* parties', that is of the parties that 'stood on the ground of the October Revolution'. But who was to determine which were and which were not 'Soviet parties'? Should the Mensheviks, for instance, be allowed to benefit from the 'revived' freedom? He left these questions in suspense, no doubt because he held that they could not be resolved in advance, regardless of circumstances. He was similarly cautious in discussing equality: he did not speak of any 'abolition' of 'bourgeois norms of distribution'—these were to be maintained, but only 'within the limits of strict necessity'; and dispensed with gradually, 'with the growth of social wealth'. The political revolution was thus to leave some privileges to managers, administrators, technicians, and skilled workers. As he himself sometimes, in polemical utterances, spoke loosely of the 'overthrow' or 'abolition' of bureaucracy, this gloss put the problem in a more realistic perspective. What he envisaged on calm reflection was a drastic curtailment, not the obliteration, of bureaucratic and managerial privilege.

Over a quarter of a century after its formulation, this programme has remained relevant; and most of its ideas have reappeared in the post-Stalinist movement of reform. Yet the question must be asked whether in insisting on the necessity of a political revolution in the U.S.S.R. Trotsky had not taken too dogmatic a view of the prospect and, against his own advice, given 'too finished a definition to an unfinished process'. From the tenor of *The Revolution Betrayed* it is clear that he saw no chance of any reform from above; and there was indeed no chance of it in his lifetime and for the rest of the Stalin era. But during that time there was no chance in the Soviet Union of any political revolution either. This was a period of deadlock: it was impossible either to cut or to untie the Gordian knots of Stalinism. Any programme of change, whether revolutionary or reformist, was illusory. This could not prevent a fighter like Trotsky from searching for a way out. But he was searching within a vicious circle, which only world-shaking events began to breach many years later. And

when that happened the Soviet Union moved away from Stalinism through reform from above in the first instance. What
forced the reform was precisely the factors on which Trotsky
had banked: economic progress, the cultural rise of the
masses, and the end of Soviet isolation. The break with
Stalinism could only be piecemeal, because at the end of the
Stalin era there existed and could exist no political force
capable and willing to act in a revolutionary manner. Moreover, throughout the first decade after Stalin there did not
emerge 'from below' any autonomous and articulate mass
movement even for reform. Since Stalinism had become an
anachronism, nationally and internationally, and a break with
it had become an historic necessity for the Soviet Union, the
ruling group itself had to take the initiative of the break. Thus,
by an irony of history Stalin's epigones began the liquidation
of Stalinism and thereby carried out, *malgré eux mêmes*, parts of
Trotsky's political testament.[1]

But can they continue this work and complete it? Or is a
political revolution still necessary? On the face of it, the
chances of revolution are still as slender as they were in
Trotsky's days, whereas the possibilities of reform are far more
real. The conditions for any revolution, as Lenin once put it,
are (*a*) that the rulers should not be able to go on ruling as
they used to; (*b*) that the ruled, in their misery, despair, and
fury, should refuse to go on living as before; and (*c*) that there
should exist a revolutionary party determined and able to
seize its chance. These conditions are not likely to materialize
in a country with a vital and expanding economy and with
rising standards of living, when the masses, having unprece-

---

[1] I underlined this circumstance in my book *Russia After Stalin* (1953) and in
many articles published just at the end of the Stalin era. The American Trotskyists
then devoted a whole issue of their theoretical organ *The Fourth International* (Winter
1954) to the theme: '*Trotsky or Deutscher*'; and James P. Cannon, their leader,
vehemently denounced me as a 'revisionist' and as 'the Bernstein of Trotskyism'.
My sin was that I forecast that in the next few years there would be no chance
for a 'political revolution' in the U.S.S.R. and that a period of 'reform from above'
was opening. (This was indeed to be the chief political characteristic of the
first decade after Stalin.) I based my argument, *inter alia*, on the fact that the
extermination of all oppositions, especially of the Trotskyist Opposition, had left
Soviet society politically amorphous, inarticulate, and incapable of 'initiative from
below'. It was paradoxical that Trotskyists in the West should have been so utterly
unaware of this consequence of the extermination of the Trotskyists (and other anti-
Stalinist Bolsheviks) in the U.S.S.R.

dented access to education, see before them prospects of continuous social advance. In such a nation any conflict between popular aspirations and the selfishness of a ruling group, a conflict under which Soviet society is still labouring, is more likely to give rise to pressure for continuous reform than to lead to a revolutionary explosion. History may therefore yet vindicate the Trotsky who had for twelve or thirteen years struggled for reform rather than the Trotsky who, in his last five years, preached revolution.

This, however, can be only a tentative conclusion. The problem of a bureaucracy in a workers' state is indeed so new and complex that it allows little or no certitude. We cannot determine in advance how far a bureaucracy can go in yielding up privileges; what strength and effectiveness popular pressure for reform can acquire under a single party system; and whether a 'monolithic' régime can gradually dissolve and transform itself into one allowing freedom of expression and association on a socialist basis. How far do the social tensions inherent in 'primitive socialist accumulation' soften or abate as the accumulation loses its primitive, forcible, and antagonistic character? To what extent does the rise in popular well-being and education resolve antagonisms between the bureaucracy and the people? Only experience, in which there may be more surprises than are dreamt of in any philosophy, can provide the answer. At any rate, the present writer prefers to leave the final judgement on Trotsky's idea of a political revolution to a historian of the next generation.

.   .   .   .

Mention should be made here of the revision, which Trotsky carried out in *The Revolution Betrayed*, of his conception of the Soviet Thermidor. We have described earlier the passions and the turbulence which this abstruse historical analogy had aroused in the Bolshevik party in the nineteen-twenties; and we have said that this was a case of *le mort saisit le vif*.[1] About ten years later we find Trotsky, under a Norwegian village roof, still wrestling with the French phantom of 1794. We remember that as long as he stood for reform in the Soviet Union, he rejected the view, originally held by the Workers'

[1] *The Prophet Unarmed*, pp. 312–14.

Opposition, that the Russian Revolution had already declined into the Thermidorian or post-Thermidorian phase. Thermidor, he argued, was the danger with which Stalin's policy was fraught, but not yet an accomplished fact. He still defended this attitude against friend and foe alike in the first years of his banishment. But having decided that the Opposition must become an independent party and that political revolution was inevitable in the Soviet Union, he thought again and stated that the Soviet Union had long since been living in the post-Thermidorian epoch.[1]

He admitted that the historical analogy had done more to obfuscate minds than to enlighten them; yet he went on elaborating it. He and his friends, he argued, had committed a mistake in thinking that Thermidor amounted to a counter-revolution and restoration; and having so defined it, they had been right in insisting that no Thermidor had occurred in Russia. But the definition was wrong and unhistoric: the original Thermidor had not been a counter-revolution, but only 'a phase of reaction *within* the revolution'. The Thermidorians had not destroyed the social basis of the French Revolution, the new bourgeois property relations, that had taken shape in 1789–93; but they had on that basis set up their anti-popular rule and set the stage for the Consulate and the Empire. The comparable development in the Soviet Union occurred as early as 1923, when Stalin suppressed the Left Opposition and established his anti-proletarian régime on the social foundations of the October Revolution. With the calendar of the French Revolution before his eyes all the time, Trotsky went on to say that Stalin's rule having assumed a Bonapartist character, the Soviet Union was living under its Consulate. Within this perspective the danger of restoration appeared all too real—in France twenty years had passed between Thermidor and the return of the Bourbons; and Trotsky's call for a new revolution and a return to Soviet democracy echoed the cry raised by the Conspiracy of Equals for a return to the First Republic.

---

[1] Trotsky first 'revised' his Thermidor analogy in an essay 'The Workers State, Thermidor, and Bonapartism', written during the latter part of his stay in France and published in *B.O.*, no. 43 in April 1935. That essay contained in a nutshell the argument of *The Revolution Betrayed*.

Thus, Trotsky involved himself deeper and deeper in that 'summoning up of the ghosts of the past' which Marx had seen as a peculiar feature of bourgeois revolutions. The English Puritans had conjured up the prophets of the Old Testament; and the Jacobins the heroes and the virtues of Republican Rome. In doing so, Marx said, they did not just 'parody the past', but 'genuinely strove to rediscover the spirit of revolution'.[1] Marx was confident that a socialist revolution would not need to borrow its costumes from the past because it would have a clear awareness of its own character and purpose. And indeed, in 1917 the Bolsheviks did not dress up in such costumes and had no use for the pageantry and the symbols of earlier revolutions. In later years, however, they derived from Jacobinism all their nightmares and fears, the nightmares of the *épurations* and the fears of Thermidor; and they magnified these by their own actions and in their own imagination. They did so not from sheer imitativeness, but because they were struggling with similar predicaments and sought to master them differently. They consulted the gloomy experiences of the past in order to avoid their repetition. And although it is true that the Bolsheviks did not escape the horrors of a fratricidal struggle in their midst, yet they did manage to avoid the whole fatal cycle through which Jacobinism had moved to its doom and through which the French Revolution was driven to its end. The fear of Thermidor that haunted the Bolsheviks was a reflex of self-defence and self-preservation. But the reflex often worked irrationally. Trotsky now admitted that for more than ten years the Opposition had raised the alarm about Thermidor without perceiving clearly the meaning of the precedent Thermidor represented. Was he himself more clear about it now?

The original Thermidor was one of the most involved, many-faceted, and enigmatic events in modern history; and this accounts partly for the confusion about it. The Thermidorians overthrew Robespierre after a series of internecine Jacobin struggles, in the course of which Robespierre, leading the centre of his party, had destroyed its right and left wings, the Dantonists and Hebertists. The end of his rule marked the downfall of his faction and of the Jacobin party at large.

---

[1] *The Eighteenth Brumaire of Louis Bonaparte.*

Soon after Thermidor the Jacobin Club was disbanded and ceased to exist. The Thermidorians replaced Robespierre's 'reign of terror' by the rule of 'law and order' and inflicted final defeat on the plebs of Paris, which had suffered many reverses even earlier. They abolished the quasi-egalitarian distribution of food, which Robespierre had maintained by fixing 'maximum' prices. Henceforth, the bourgeoisie was free to trade profitably, to amass fortunes, and to gain the social dominance which it was to preserve even under the Empire. Thus, against the background of ebbing revolutionary energies and of disillusionment and apathy in the masses, the revolutionary régime passed from the popular to the anti-popular phase.

It is enough to outline briefly these various aspects of Thermidor to see where Trotsky was wrong in his assertion that Russia had gone through her Thermidor in 1923. The defeat of the Opposition in that year was not in any sense an event comparable to the collapse and dissolution of the Jacobin party; it corresponded rather to the defeat of the left Jacobins which had taken place well before Thermidor. While Trotsky was writing *The Revolution Betrayed* the Soviet Union was on the eve of the great purge trials—in France the *épurations* were part and parcel of the Jacobin period; only after Robespierre's downfall was the guillotine brought to a halt. Thermidor was in fact an explosion of despair with the permanent purge; and most of the Thermidorians were ex-Dantonists and ex-Hebertists who had survived the slaughter of their factions. The Russian analogy to this would have been a successful coup against Stalin carried out, after the trials of 1936–8, by remnants of the Bukharinist and Trotskyist oppositions.

Another difference is even more important: Thermidor brought to a close the revolutionary transformation of French society and the upheaval in property. In the Soviet Union these did not come to a halt with Stalin's ascendancy. On the contrary, the most violent upheaval, collectivization of farming, was carried out under his rule. And it was surely not 'law and order', even in a most anti-popular form, that prevailed either in 1923, or at any time during the Stalin era. What the early nineteen-twenties had in common with the Thermidorian period was the ebbing away of the popular revolutionary energies and the disillusionment and apathy of the masses. It was against such a background that Robespierre had sought to keep the rump of the Jacobin Party in power and failed; and that Stalin struggled to preserve the dictatorship of the Bolshevik rump (i.e. of his own faction) and succeeded.

Admittedly, there was a strong Thermidorian flavour about Stalin's anti-egalitarianism. But that was not absent from Lenin's N.E.P. either. Curiously, when in 1921 the Mensheviks described N.E.P. as the 'Soviet Thermidor', neither Lenin nor Trotsky protested. On the contrary, they congratulated themselves on having carried out something like Thermidor peacefully, without breaking up their own party and losing power. 'It was not they [the Mensheviks]', Trotsky wrote in 1921, 'but we ourselves who formulated this diagnosis. And, what is more important, the concessions to the Thermidorian mood and tendencies of the petty bourgeoisie, necessary for the purpose of maintaining the power of the proletariat, were made by the Communist party without effecting a break in the system and without quitting the helm.'[1] Stalin also made the most far-reaching 'concessions to the Thermidorian moods and tendencies' of his bureaucracy and managerial groups, 'without effecting a break in the system and without quitting the helm'. In any case, an historical analogy which led Trotsky, in 1921, almost to boast that he and Lenin had carried out a semi-Thermidor, then to deny that any Soviet Thermidor had occurred, and finally, in 1935, to maintain that the Soviet Union had for twelve years lived under a Thermidor, without Trotsky himself noticing it—such an analogy did indeed serve more to obfuscate minds than to enlighten them.

The historically far more justified charge that Trotsky could have levelled against Stalin was that he instituted a reign of terror like Robespierre's, and that he had monstrously outdone Robespierre. However, Trotsky's own past and the Bolshevik tradition did not allow him to say this. It will be remembered that in 1903–4, when he first dissociated himself from Bolshevism, he levelled the accusation of Jacobinism against Lenin; and in reply Lenin proudly identified himself as the 'proletarian Jacobin' of the twentieth century.[2] The

---

[1] Trotsky, *Between Red and White*, p. 77. (Trotsky concluded the writing of this book in February 1922.)

[2] See *The Prophet Armed*, pp. 91–97.

two men were thinking of two different Robespierres: Lenin of the one who had secured the triumph of the revolution against the Gironde, Trotsky of the one who had sent his own comrades to the guillotine. Not only in Lenin's eyes, but in those of most western Marxists, the Conductor of the Purges had, after a century, receded behind the great Incorruptible hallowed in the Pantheon of the Revolution. Trotsky the Bolshevik regretted that he had ever raised the charge of Robespierrism against Lenin; and he was wary of throwing it at Stalin. Having in the meantime accepted the Bolshevik glorification of Jacobinism, he virtually identified himself with Robespierre; and this led him to see his enemies as Thermidorians, which they were not. True, his alarms did much to rouse all Bolsheviks, including the Stalinists, to vigilance. Moreover, something of the Thermidorian mood still survives in the Soviet Union; and it can be found (together with the 'bourgeois element' and 'bourgeois norms of distribution') in any workers' state. All the same, we who have seen, in the nineteen-forties and nineteen-fifties, the Russian Revolution in its full Protean power, by far surpasssing the French Revolution in scale and momentum—we can only wonder over the strange *quid pro quo* through which the Thermidorian phantom strayed on to the Russian scene and kept itself there for a whole historic epoch.

.   .   .   .

The pessimism, real and apparent, underlying *The Revolution Betrayed* shows itself also in those pages where Trotsky tried to anticipate the impact of the Second World War on the Soviet Union. He noted that the new social system had provided 'national defence with advantages of which the old Russia could not dream'; that in a planned economy it was relatively easy to switch from civilian to military production and 'to focus on the interests of defence even in building and equipping new factories'. He underlined the progress of the Soviet armed forces in all modern weapons and stated that 'the correlation between the living and mechanical forces of the Red Army may be considered by and large as on a level with the best armies of the West'.[1] This was not, in 1936, a view

[1] *The Revolution Betrayed*, pp. 196–7.

generally accepted by western military experts; and the emphasis with which Trotsky expressed it was undoubtedly calculated to impress the Governments and the General Staffs of the western powers. But he saw the weakness of the Soviet defences in the Thermidorian spirit of its officer corps, in the army's rigidly hierarchical structure which was replacing its revolutionary-democratic organization, and above all in Stalin's foreign policy. He argued that Stalin, having first neglected the danger from the Third Reich, was now, to counter it, relying mainly on alliances with western bourgeois Governments, on the League of Nations, and on 'collective security', for the sake of which he would in case of war refrain from making any genuinely revolutionary, appeal to the armed workers and peasants of the belligerent nations.

'Can we . . .' Trotsky asked, 'expect that the Soviet Union will come out of the approaching great war without defeat? To this frankly posed question we will answer as frankly: if the war should remain only a war, the defeat of the Soviet Union would be inevitable. In a technical, economic, and military sense, imperialism is incomparably stronger. If it is not paralysed by revolution in the West, imperialism will sweep away the régime which issued from the October Revolution.'[1] Divided though the West was against itself, it would eventually unite 'in order to block the military victory of the Soviet Union'. Well before the Munich crisis, Trotsky observed that France was already treating her alliance with the Soviet Union as a 'scrap of paper' and she would continue to do so, no matter how much Stalin tried to secure the alliance through the Popular Front. Only if Stalin were to yield further to French, British and American economic and political pressures, would the alliance assume reality; but even then the allies would take advantage of the Soviet Union's wartime difficulties and seek to sap the socialist foundations of its economy and exact far-reaching concessions to capitalism. At the same time the peasantry's individualism, stirred up by war, would threaten to disrupt collective farming. These external and domestic pressures, Trotsky concluded, would bring the danger of counter-revolution and restoration closer to Russia. The situation was not hopeless, however, because the war

[1] Op. cit., p. 216.

would also bring revolution closer to Europe; and so, on balance, 'the Soviet régime would have more stability than the régimes of its probable enemies'. 'The Polish bourgeoisie' could only 'hasten the war and find'in it . . . certain death'; and 'Hitler has far less chance than had Wilhelm II of carrying a war to victory'. Trotsky's confidence in European revolution was as strong as was his despondency about the prospects of the Soviet Union in the absence of such a revolution:

> The danger of war and defeat of the Soviet Union is a reality, but the revolution is also a reality. If the revolution does not prevent war, then war will help the revolution. Second births are commonly easier than first. In the new war it will not be necessary to wait a whole two years and a half for the first insurrection [as it was after 1914]. Once it is begun, moreover, the revolution will not this time stop half way. The fate of the Soviet Union will be decided in the long run not on the maps of the General Staffs, but on the map of the class struggle. Only the European proletariat, implacably opposing its bourgeoisie . . . can protect the Soviet Union from destruction, or from an 'allied' stab in the back. Even a military defeat of the Soviet Union would be only a short episode, if there were to be a victory of the proletariat in other countries. And, on the other hand, no military victory can save the inheritance of the October revolution if imperialism holds out in the rest of the world. . . . Without the Red Army the Soviet Union would be crushed and dismembered like China. Only its stubborn and heroic resistance to the future capitalist enemy can create favourable conditions for the development of the class struggle in the imperialist camp. The Red Army is thus a factor of immense significance. But this does not mean that it is the sole historic factor.
>
> It is not under the banner of the *status quo* [which Stalin's diplomacy defended in the nineteen-thirties] that the European workers and the colonial peoples can rise. . . . The task of the European proletariat is not the perpetuation of boundaries, but, on the contrary, their revolutionary abolition, not [the preservation of] the *status quo* but a socialist United States of Europe.[1]

The outcome of the Second World War was to be far less clear cut than this alternative; and nothing would be easier than to compile from *The Revolution Betrayed* a list of Trotsky's errors in prognostication. Yet each of his errors contains important elements of truth and follows from premisses which

[1] Op. cit., pp. 219–20.

retain validity; and so more can still be learned from his mistakes than from the correct platitudes of most political writers. Trotsky is in this respect not unlike Marx: his thought is 'algebraically' correct, even when his 'arithmetical' conclusions are wrong. Where his forecasts were erroneous, they were so because too often he viewed the Second World War in terms of the first; but his general insights into the relationship between war and revolution were deep and are still essential to an understanding of the revolutionary aftermath of the Second World War.[1]

The Revolution Betrayed has exercised its influence in a strange, often self-defeating, manner—*pro captu lectoris*. It was published in May 1937, right in the middle of the slaughter of the Old Bolsheviks, just after the trial of Radek, Pyatakov, and Sokolnikov and on the eve of the execution of Tukhachevsky and the other Generals. The volleys of Stalin's execution squads gave a peculiar resonance to the title of the book: it came as a desperate and piercing cry of protest. Focusing all of Trotsky's tragic invective, it suggested that the October Revolution had suffered its last and irretrievable débâcle and that Trotsky and his followers had abandoned all allegiance to the Soviet Union. Thus, the 'revolution betrayed' became a startling, memorable, yet vacuous slogan; and for a long time the title page of the book made a stronger impression than the book itself; often it closed minds to Trotsky's complex and subtle argument. His speculations about the possible emergence of a new possessing class caught readers' attention to the exclusion of his qualifying clauses and counter-balancing ideas. Quite a few of his disciples saw actuality where he saw mere potentiality. The very brilliance of his controversial style helped to produce this distorting response, for it tempted hosts of lesser writers to imitate the master's invective, which was so much easier to do than to enter critically into his thought. Not only did *The Revolution Betrayed* become the Bible of latter-day Trotskyist sects and chapels, whose members piously mumbled its verses long after Trotsky's death. The effect of the book was felt more widely, in the literature of disillusionment produced by western ex-communists in the nineteen-forties and nineteen-fifties. Some of them lived on

[1] The argument is further developed in the Postscript to this volume.

mere crumbs, and not the best ones, from Trotsky's rich table; and they gained a reputation for originality by serving these up in their own brands of sauce. James Burnham, a Trotskyist in the nineteen-thirties, based his *Managerial Revolution* on a few fragments of Trotsky's theory torn out of context.[1] *The Revolution Betrayed* re-echoes through the early writings of Ignazio Silone and Arthur Koestler. George Orwell was strongly impressed by it. The fragments of 'The Book', which take up so many pages in his *1984* were intended to paraphrase *The Revolution Betrayed* just as Emmanuel Goldstein, Big Brother's enigmatic antagonist, is modelled on Trotsky. And last but not least, in the nineteen-forties, and nineteen-fifties, many of the intellectually ambitious 'Sovietologists' and propagandists of the cold war drew, directly or indirectly, their arguments and catch phrases from this source.[2]

Despite the adventitious use made of it, *The Revolution Betrayed* remains a classic of Marxist literature. But this is Trotsky's most difficult book; and only the reader who approaches it with discrimination, without accepting or rejecting it *in toto*, can benefit from it. Goethe once said of Lessing that, being the greatest thinker of his generation, his influence on contemporaries was only slight and partly even harmful, because only an intelligence equal to Lessing's could absorb the full complexity of his thought; he therefore swayed the mind of Germany only indirectly and posthumously. This is also true of the author of *The Revolution Betrayed*, and accounts for the distorted and distorting influence of this book in the West. In our time, however, its ideas are already in the air in the U.S.S.R., where Trotsky's writings are still banned. The Soviet Jourdains who nowadays unknowingly speak his prose are legion: they are to be found in universities, factories, literary clubs, Komsomol cells, and even in the ruling circles. To give only a few random illustrations: Trotsky's verdict that the Stalin era 'will go down in the history of artistic creation pre-

---

[1] See further, pp. 471–5.

[2] In 1961 an American Government agency brought out a pamphlet under the title *The Revolution Betrayed*, the purpose of which was to justify the American campaign against Cuba. The man whom the State Department, the Pentagon, ex-owners of Cuban sugar plantations, and some 'radicals' denounced as traitor to the revolution was Fidel Castro. An American sponsored invasion of Cuba aimed presumably at restoring to the Cuban revolution its pristine purity.

eminently as an epoch of mediocrities, laureates, and toadies' has come to be generally accepted. Who does not now agree with him that under Stalinism 'the literary schools were strangled one after the other' and that

The process of extermination took place in all ideological spheres, and it took place more decisively since it was more than half unconscious. The present ruling stratum considers itself called not only to control spiritual creation politically, but also to prescribe its roads of development. The method of command-without-appeal extends in like measure to the concentration camps, to scientific agriculture, and to music. The central organ of the party prints anonymous directive editorials having the character of military orders, in architecture, literature, dramatic arts, the ballet, to say nothing of philosophy, natural science, and history. The bureaucracy superstitiously fears whatever does not serve it directly, as well as whatever it does not understand.[1]

If fortunately not all of this is any longer true, much of it still is; and as critic of the legacy of Stalinism the dead Trotsky still speaks more powerfully than all the living 'de-Stalinizers':

The school and the social life of the student are saturated with formalism and hypocrisy. The children have learned to sit through innumerable deadly dull meetings, with their inevitable honorary presidium, their chants in honour of the dear leaders, their pre-digested debates in which, quite in the manner of their elders, they say one thing and think another. . . . The more thoughtful teachers and children's writers, in spite of the enforced optimism, cannot always conceal their horror in the presence of this spirit of repression, falsity, and boredom. . . . Independent character, like independent thought, cannot develop without criticism. The Soviet youth, however, are simply denied the elementary opportunity to exchange thoughts, make mistakes, and try out and correct mistakes, their own as well as others'. All questions. . . . are decided for them. Theirs only to carry out the decision and sing the glory of those who made it. . . . This explains the fact that out of the millions upon millions of communist youth there has not emerged a single major figure.

In throwing themselves into engineering, science, literature, sport, or chess playing, the young people are, so to speak, winning their spurs for future great action. In all these spheres they compete with the badly prepared older generation, and often equal and beat

[1] Trotsky, *The Revolution Betrayed*, p. 173.

them. But at every contact with politics they burn their fingers.

And how alive still is the prophetic anger, faith, and vision which inspired words like these:[1]

> . . . the actual establishment of a socialist society can and will be achieved, not by these humiliating measures of a backward capitalism, to which the Soviet government is resorting, but by methods more worthy of a liberated humanity—and above all not under the whip of a bureaucracy. For this very whip is the most disgusting inheritance of the old world. It will have to be broken into pieces and burned at a public bonfire before one can speak of socialism without a blush of shame.

.   .   .   .

The months during which Trotsky wrote *The Revolution Betrayed* were, despite intense work, a respite. Life at Vexhall was uneventful and tranquil. The daily routine was rarely interrupted for visitors or for an outing in the bare and rocky countryside to the north. Once a week the Trotskys and Knudsens went to the cinema at Honnefoss to view an old and faded American film. So well did Trotsky progress with his work that, having concluded *The Revolution Betrayed*, he looked forward to taking up the *Lenin* at once. He had found, so it seemed, the security of a real asylum at last. Yet now and then a small cloud showed itself. Elections were due in the autumn; and already in the summer a small pro-Nazi party, the National Sammling, had begun to attack the government for jeopardizing peace and prosperity by harbouring Trotsky. The party's leader was Major Quisling, who a few years later, under German occupation, was to become head of a puppet government, and whose name then became the by-word for 'collaboration' with the occupant. At this time, however, his following was small and it belonged to the lunatic fringe; little notice was therefore taken. More disturbing were the attacks of *Arbeideren*, the communist paper. Although it too had few readers, it voiced the views of the Soviet Embassy, when it charged Trotsky with using Norway as 'a base for terroristic activities directed against the Soviet Union and its leaders, above all against the greatest leader of the world proletariat in our time—Stalin. . . .' 'How long', the paper asked,

[1] Op. cit., p. 125.

'will the Norwegian workers tolerate this? What has the Central Bureau of the Norwegian Labour Party to say? What has the Norwegian Government to say?' This was the first time it was alleged that Trotsky 'was using Norway as a base for terroristic activities'—the charge was to be taken up by Vyshinsky a few months later.

The Labour party firmly rejected the allegation. 'What is the purpose of this?' Schöffle replied. 'To make the Norwegian workers believe a lie . . . and to compel the Labour government to place Trotsky under arrest? Well, gentlemen, neither will happen. You will not so easily make fools either of Norwegian workers or of the Norwegian Labour government. . . .' Other spokesmen for the party in office replied in the same vein.[1]

The Norwegian police nevertheless kept Trotsky under surveillance and regularly reported not only their own findings but communications received from the Belgian and the French police to the Minister of Justice. A Sherlock Holmes in Brussels had discovered that Trotsky was the actual inspirer and leader of the Fourth International; and at Oslo police headquarters cautious minds inquired whether that disquieting piece of information was correct. The French police confirmed it and expressed concern over the comings and goings of Trotsky's secretaries, all agents of the Fourth International. The Norwegian Ministers could only be amused by this feat of detection—a little earlier they themselves, or some among them, might even have been inclined to join the subversive organization. All the same, to appease his police, the Minister of Justice ordered the deportation of Jan Fraenkel, one of Trotsky's secretaries. His place, however, was soon taken by Erwin Wolf, who stayed at Vexhall for about a year unmolested and married Knudsen's daughter. To avoid needless irritation, Trotsky asked his followers to delete his name from the list of the 'International Executive' of their organization; and he published articles on internal Trotskyist affairs anonymously or under a pen-name.[2] He refused to give interviews to

---

[1] *Arbeideren*, 12 December and *Soerlandet*, 16 December 1935.

[2] 'Crux' was the pen-name Trotsky used most often at this time; he also conducted part of his correspondence with his adherents in Paris and Amsterdam in code. The key to the code is preserved in *The Archives*, Closed Section. See also Krog, op. cit., pp. 245–6

foreign newspapers. And so scrupulously did he avoid even the slightest involvement in Norwegian politics that when Knudsen, who stood for Parliament, invited him to attend his election meetings as spectator, Trotsky refused; he used to accompany Knudsen and wait for him outside, in his car, until the meeting was over.[1] The police dutifully reported to the Minister that Trotsky's behaviour was in this respect irreproachable. 'We knew, of course, that Trotsky continued to write his commentaries on international affairs', says Koht, the Foreign Minister, 'but we considered it our duty to respect his right to do so under the democratic principle of asylum.'[2] The government was so satisfied that it twice prolonged Trotsky's residence permit automatically, without raising any question.

Nevertheless, when in the summer of 1936 Koht went on a mission to Moscow and was ostentatiously fêted there, Trotsky awaited his return with misgivings. 'They are bargaining over my head in the Kremlin', he said to Knudsen. 'Do you believe', Knudsen asked with shocked incredulity, 'that we, the Norwegian Labour party, are ready to sell your head?' 'No', Trotsky replied, sparing the feelings of his host, 'but I believe that Stalin is ready to buy it.'[3] According to Koht himself, he had gone to Moscow only on a courtesy visit: having previously been in Warsaw as guest of the Polish Government, he had been anxious to avoid giving Moscow the impression that he had 'ganged up' with the Poles. During his visit, he says, the question of Trotsky's asylum was never raised—only once in Geneva, at a session of the League of Nations, had Litvinov blandly alluded to it in a private talk.[4] Koht's testimony may well be accepted: Stalin would hardly have bargained over Trotsky's head with Koht, a gentle and somewhat unworldly scholar-diplomat—for that he had to find a much tougher character.

Trotsky's suspicion arose out of the stupendous growth of

---

[1] This is Knudsen's account given to me.

[2] Professor Koht made this statement early in 1937; and he emphatically repeated it to me during my visit in Oslo in 1956.

[3] Trotsky, *Stalin's Verbrechen; The Case of Leon Trotsky*, p. 33; Knudsen's statement to the writer.

[4] This is how Koht explained his motives to me (adding that he had long been in contact with Moscow's academic circles in connexion with his research on the early history of Russo-Norwegian relations).

the anti-Trotskyist terror in the Soviet Union. He had recently received first-hand accounts about this from three followers who had come straight from Soviet prisons and concentration camps. They were: A. Tarov, a Russian worker and old Bolshevik; Anton Ciliga, former member of the Politbureau of the Yugoslav Communist party; and Victor Serge, to whose role in the Russian Opposition we have frequently referred.[1] Serge owed his freedom to Romain Rolland's personal intervention with Stalin; Ciliga was released at the instance of western European friends; and Tarov had secretly crossed the frontier. Tarov related that, impressed by the rise of Nazism, he had been ready to make his peace with Stalinism and had negotiated with the G.P.U. over the terms of his capitulation. 'Do you agree or do you not', they asked him, 'that Trotsky is the chief of the vanguard of bourgeois counter-revolution?' This was the formula the capitulators were now required to accept. Tarov replied that to his mind 'Trotsky is the man most devoted to the cause of the world proletariat, an unflinching revolutionary, whom I consider my friend and comrade in a common cause'. Throughout many a night he was interrogated and pressed to renounce Trotsky; but he could not bring himself to do that.[2]

All three described the new, cataclysmic violence of the terror: the huge concentration camps set up all over the U.S.S.R.; the pitiless brutality with which the inmates were being treated since Kirov's assassination; and the torture and deceit by which the G.P.U. extracted 'confessions'. For all the severity of his criticisms of Stalin, Trotsky had not been fully aware how far things had gone. Like any political émigré, he had to some extent preserved the image of his country as he had known it, when the terror had been much narrower in scope and milder. The new accounts (and André Gide's just published *Retour de l'U.R.S.S.*) filled him with shame and

---

[1] *The Archives*, Closed Section. Tarov's 'Letter of an Escaped Bolshevik-Leninist' appeared in *B.O.*, no. 45, 1935. Ciliga's account of the Stalinist terror is in *B.O.*, nos. 47, 48, 49. Victor Serge's 'Open Letter to André Gide', exposing the Stalinist régime to Gide, who was then still favourably disposed towards Stalin, appeared in *B.O.*, no. 51, 1936. These issues of the *B.O.* contained an abundance of fresh information from the U.S.S.R. See also the correspondence between Lyova and Serge of April 1936 in *The Archives*, Closed Section.

[2] Tarov, loc. cit.

anger, and confirmed him in his determination to renounce all 'reformist illusions', and to give the sharpest possible expression to his break with the Comintern.

These reports, it should be added, left hardly any ray of hope for the Opposition, for while they dwelt on the depravity of the ruling group and the hatred and contempt which surrounded it, they described also, in the grimmest terms, the total dispersal and impotence of the Opposition.[1] It must have been only a bitter consolation for Trotsky to learn how people like Tarov still defended his honour in the dungeons and prison camps. These people appeared to be the last Mohicans of the Opposition. Yet, before the end of 1935, fresh mass expulsions from the party were announced. On 30 December, Khrushchev, then Secretary of the Moscow Committee, stated that in the capital alone 10,000 members had been expelled; from Leningrad Zhdanov reported the expulsion of 7,000. All over the country at least 40,000 people had been deprived of membership; many more had been expelled from the Komsomol; and most were branded as Trotskyists and Zinovievists. Even if only one-half or one-third of this mass had been genuine oppositionists, their numbers would have been far greater than the 4–6,000 who had put their signatures to the Platform of the Joint Opposition in 1927.[2] Was this a new tide? Trotsky wondered; and, despite Serge's and Ciliga's depressing accounts, he struck an optimistic note:

. . . under the influence of the Stalinist press and its agents (of the type of Louis Fischer and his like) not merely our enemies but many of our friends in the West without noticing it have become accustomed to thinking that if Bolshevik-Leninists still exist in the U.S.S.R., they do so only as hard labour convicts. No, this is not so! It is impossible to eradicate the Marxist programme and a great revolutionary tradition by police methods. . . . If not as a doctrine then as a mood, a tradition, and a banner, our movement has now a mass character in the U.S.S.R. and is evidently absorbing new and fresh forces. Among the 10 to 20,000 'Trotskyists' expelled in

[1] Ciliga presently came out with a full-scàle description of the situation in his book, *Au pays du grand mensonge*. Serge in his correspondence with Lyova also described the disintegration of the Opposition. Such, according to the old Elzin, an eminent Trotskyist (whom Serge quoted), was the disarray that 'no two comrades can be found to hold the same view—what unites us is the G.P.U.'
[2] *The Prophet Unarmed*, p. 370.

the last months there are no more than a few tens, perhaps a few hundreds . . . of men of the older generation, oppositionists of the 1923–8 vintages. The mass is made up of new recruits. . . . It can be said with confidence that in spite of thirteen years of baiting, slander, and persecution, unsurpassed in wickedness and savagery, in spite of capitulations and defections, more dangerous than persecution, the Fourth International possesses already today its strongest, most numerous, and most hardened branch in the U.S.S.R.[1]

This seemed to contradict Trotsky's earlier resigned statements that no revolutionary initiative could be expected from the Soviet Union, even from his followers. As a 'mood, tradition, and banner' even if not as an organized party, Trotskyism was still as alive as ever. And both Stalin and Trotsky knew that in favourable circumstances 'a mood and a tradition' could easily cohere into a party. Stalin was therefore preparing his final onslaught on Trotskyism. Meanwhile, in the spring and early summer of 1936, there was still an uneasy lull.

In western Europe this was the hey-day of the Popular Front. The parties of the Popular Front had gained an overwhelming electoral victory in France; and this encouraged the workers to raise demands, join trade unions by the million, occupy factories, and stage nationwide strikes and demonstrations. 'The French revolution has begun', Trotsky proclaimed in the title of an article he wrote for the American *Nation*. (The conservative *Le Temps* spoke of '*les grandes manœuvres de la révolution*'.) He pointed to the collapse of the French economy, the sharpening of all class antagonisms, the panic in the possessing classes and their parties, and the impetus of the mass movement. 'The whole working class has begun to move. This gigantic mass will not be halted by words. The struggle is bound to end either with supreme victory or with the most terrible of defeats.' The leaders of the Popular Front courted defeat; they did what they could to subdue the energy and the self-confidence of the workers and to reassure the bourgeoisie. 'The Socialists and Communists had been working with all their strength for a Ministry headed by Herriot, at the worst by Daladier. What have the masses done? They have

[1] *B.O.*, no. 48, 1936.

imposed on them Blum's Ministry. Does this not amount to a direct vote against the policy of the Popular Front?' For the time being counter-revolution lay low, waiting for the storm to blow over and preparing a comeback. 'It would be frivolous to maintain that its calculations are groundless. With the help of Blum, Jouhaux, and Cachin, the counter-revolution may yet achieve its purpose.' For years the Communist party had clamoured *Les Soviets partout*; but now, when it was time to pass from words to deeds, to rally and arm the workers, and to form Workers' Councils, it declared the slogan to be 'untimely'. He also addressed this warning to his own followers: 'The party or group which cannot find a foothold in the present strike movement and establish solid ties with the embattled workers is not worthy of the name of a revolutionary organization.' Not for the first and not for the last time his followers were unable to find the 'foothold'.

On 4 August, having just mailed to his publishers his Preface to *The Revolution Betrayed*, Trotsky left with Knudsen for a holiday, which they intended to spend on a wild and deserted little island in a southern fjord. They travelled by car and on the way Knudsen noticed that a few men, whom he recognized as Quisling's adherents, were pursuing them. At a ferry, however, he managed to put them off the track; and pleased with this, he and Trotsky crossed the fjord, reached the island and settled down for the night in a fisherman's hut.

Next morning they were aroused by an urgent message from Vexhall. During the night Quisling's followers, disguised as policemen, had broken into Knudsen's house and, claiming that they had orders to carry out a search, had tried to force their way into Trotsky's rooms. Knudsen's daughter, suspecting a fraud, resisted them, while her brother alarmed neighbours. The intruders fled, having seized only a few sheets of typescript from a table. Apprehended by the police, they declared that they had planned to break into the house during Trotsky's absence, and that, having tapped Knudsen's telephone, they had known when he and Trotsky would be away. There was no question then of any attempt on Trotsky's life. Their purpose was to obtain evidence of Trotsky's political activity and of his transgression against the terms of his residence in Norway, evidence which Quisling's party intended to use in the elections. The intruders claimed that they had achieved their purpose.

The incident seemed ludicrous. Trotsky was sure that Quisling's men could not possibly have obtained proof of a transgression he had not committed. Nor could they have seized anything of importance from his archives, which Knudsen had, as a precaution, placed in a bank safe before the departure. And so, after a moment of excitement, he and Knudsen went back to climbing the rocks and to fishing. A week later, on 13 or 14 August, a small aircraft landed on the island; and from it emerged the chief of the Norwegian criminal police. He had come on Trygve Lie's orders to interrogate Trotsky in connexion with the forthcoming trial of Quisling's men. The questions concerned the papers the latter had seized at Knudsen's house, a copy of Trotsky's private letter to a French follower and his article 'The French revolution has begun', to which we have just referred. Trotsky answered all questions put to him; and the police officer left to tell the Press that he had found the Nazi charges against Trotsky absolutely groundless.[1]

Early next morning Knudsen listened as usual to the news. The reception was indistinct: there was no electricity on the island, and he had only a small portable wireless set. But what he heard was enough to send him breathless to Trotsky: Moscow had just announced that Zinoviev, Kamenev, and fourteen other defendants would presently stand trial, charged with treason, conspiracy, and attempts at the assassination of Stalin. A long indictment was then broadcast which branded Trotsky as their chief abettor. Knudsen was not sure of the details, but he had no doubt that Zinoviev and Kamenev were accused of terrorism and also of collusion with the Gestapo. Trotsky was dumbfounded. 'Terrorism? Terrorism?', he kept on repeating. 'Well, I can still understand this charge. But Gestapo? Did they say Gestapo? Are you sure of this?' he asked in amazement. 'Yes, this is what they said', Knudsen confirmed. Later in the day they learned that the indictment

---

[1] Trotsky, *Stalin's Verbrechen*; Krog, op. cit.: *The Archives*; statements by Knudsen and various official Norwegian personalities.

also claimed that it was from Norway that Trotsky was des-
patching terrorists and assassins to the Soviet Union. They
felt as if the rocks of the tranquil island had suddenly errupted
with flames and lava. They rushed back to Vexhall.

On the same day, 15 August, Trotsky refuted the charges,
describing them to the Press as 'the greatest forgery in the
world's political history'. 'Stalin is staging this trial in order
to suppress discontent and opposition. The ruling bureaucracy treats every criticism and every form of opposition as
conspiracy.' The charge that he was using Norway as a base for
terroristic activity, he said, was designed to rob him of asylum
and of the possibility of defending himself. 'I emphatically
assert that since I have been in Norway I have had no connexion with the Soviet Union. I have not received here even
a single letter from there, nor have I written to anyone either
directly or through other persons. My wife and I have not
been able to exchange even a single line with our son, who was
employed as a scientist and has had no political connexion
with us whatsoever.' He proposed that the Norwegian Government should investigate the charges—he was ready to place
before it all relevant papers and materials. And he also
appealed to the labour organizations of all countries for an
impartial and international Commission of Inquiry.[1]

Thus the culmination of the terror, which he had so many
times predicted, had come. It was more hideous and more
menacing than anything he had foreseen. His ears once again
glued to the wireless set, he listened, from 19 to 24 August, to
the accounts of the trial. Hour by hour he absorbed its horror,
as prosecutor, judges, and defendants acted out a spectacle, so
hallucinatory in its masochism and sadism that it seemed to
surpass human imagination. It was clear from the outset that
the heads of the sixteen defendants were at stake, and with them
the heads of Trotsky and Lyova. (In the indictment Lyova
figured as his father's chief assistant.) As the proceedings went
on, it became obvious that the trial could only be the prelude
to the destruction of an entire generation of revolutionaries.
But worst of all was the manner in which the defendants were
dragged through the mud, and made to crawl to their death
amid indescribably nauseating denunciations and self-de-

[1] Quoted from the originals in *The Archives*.

nunciations. Compared with this all the nightmares of the French Revolution, the tumbrils, the guillotine, and the Jacobins' fratricidal struggles, looked now like a drama of almost sober and solemn dignity. Robespierre had put his adversaries in the dock amid thieves and felons and had loaded them with fantastic accusations; but he had not prevented them from defending their honour and dying as fighters. Danton was at least free to exclaim: 'After me it will be your turn, Robespierre!' Stalin hurled his broken adversaries to unfathomable depths of self-humiliation. He made the leaders and thinkers of Bolshevism behave like the wretched medieval women who had to relate to the Inquisition every act of their witchcraft and every detail of their debauchery with the Devil. Here, for instance, is Vyshinsky's dialogue with Kamenev, conducted in the hearing of the whole world:

Vyshinsky: What appraisal should be given to the articles and statements you wrote in which you expressed loyalty to the Party? Was this deception?
Kamenev: No, it was worse than deception.
Vyshinsky: Perfidy?
Kamenev: Worse than that.
Vyshinsky: Worse than deception, worse than perfidy? Then find the word for it. Was it treason?
Kamenev: You have found the word.
Vyshinsky: Defendant Zinoviev, do you confirm this?
Zinoviev: Yes.
Vyshinsky: Treason? Perfidy? Double-dealing?
Zinoviev: Yes.

And this was how Kamenev wound up his *mea culpa*:

Twice my life was spared, but there is a limit to everything, there is a limit to the magnanimity of the proletariat, and that limit we have reached. . . . We are sitting here side by side with the agents of foreign secret police departments. Our weapons were the same, our arms became intertwined, before our fate became intertwined here, in this dock. We have served fascism, we have organized counter-revolution against socialism. Such has been the path we took, and such is the pit of contemptible treachery into which we have fallen.[1]

---

[1] *Sudebnyi Otchet po Delu Trotskistkovo-Zinovievskovo Terroristskovo Tsentra*; the quotations are from the official English version of the proceedings, pp. 68, 169-70.

Zinoviev followed:

> I am guilty of having been organizer, second only to Trotsky, of the Trotskyist-Zinovievist bloc, which set itself the aim of assassinating Stalin, Voroshilov, and other leaders. . . . I plead guilty to having been the principal organizer of the assassination of Kirov. We entered into an alliance with Trotsky. My defective Bolshevism became transformed into anti-Bolshevism and through Trotskyism I arrived at fascism. Trotskyism is a variety of fascism, and Zinovievism is a variety of Trotskyism.[1]

Ivan Smirnov, who had defeated Kolchak in the civil war and had sat by Trotsky's side on the Revolutionary Military Council, stated:

> There is no other path for our country but the one that it is now treading; and there is not, nor can there be, any other leadership than that which history has given us. Trotsky, who sends directions and instructions on terrorism and regards our state as a fascist state, is an enemy. He is on the other side of the barricade.[2]

Mrachkovsky, another one of Trotsky's old companions and also a hero of the civil war, said:

> Why did I take the counter-revolutionary path? My connexion with Trotsky brought me to this. From the time I made that connexion I began to deceive the party, to deceive its leaders.[3]

Bakayev, the intrepid chief of the Leningrad Cheka during the civil war and leader of the Opposition's demonstrations in 1927, confessed:

> The facts revealed before this court show to the whole world that the organizer of this . . . counter-revolutionary terrorist bloc, its moving spirit, is Trotsky. . . . I have staked my head over and over again in the interests of Zinoviev and Kamenev. I am deeply oppressed by the thought that I became an obedient tool in their hands, an agent of counter-revolution, and that I raised my arm against Stalin.[4]

For hours, Vyshinsky, the ex-Menshevik who had climbed on the Bolshevik band-wagon well after the civil war, and was now Prosecutor-General, fumed and raged in a deliberate affectation of hysteria:

[1] Op. cit., p. 170. [2] Op. cit., pp. 171–2. [3] Op. cit., p. 165. [4] Op. cit., p. 168.

These mad dogs of capitalism tried to tear limb from limb the best of the best of our Soviet land. They killed one of the men of the revolution who was most dear to us, that admirable and wonderful man, bright and joyous as the smile on his lips was always bright and joyous, as our new life is bright and joyous. They killed our Kirov, they wounded us close to our very heart. . . . The enemy is cunning, a cunning enemy must not be spared. . . . Our whole people is quivering with indignation; and on behalf of the State Prosecution I am joining my angry and indignant voice to the rumbling voices of millions. . . . I demand that dogs gone mad should be shot, every one of them![1]

After five days filled with coarse vituperation and obscene insults, days during which the prosecution had not submitted a single piece of evidence, the court pronounced a verdict condemning all defendants to death and concluding that:

Lev Davidovich Trotsky and his son Lev Lvovich Sedov . . . convicted . . . as having directly prepared and personally directed the organization in the U.S.S.R. of terroristic acts . . . are subject, in the event of their being discovered on the territory of the U.S.S.R., to immediate arrest and trial by the Military Collegium of the Supreme Court of the U.S.S.R.[2]

Stalin had timed the trial to be staged just after Hitler's march into the Rhineland and shortly after the Popular Front had formed its government in France. In doing so he blackmailed the labour movement and the left intelligentsia of the West, who looked to him as their ally against Hitler. He threatened in effect that if there were any protests against his purges, he would retaliate by breaking up the Popular Front and leaving western Europe alone to face the Third Reich. He was assisted in his purpose by the sombre irrationality of the trial, which confounded people who might have raised their voices against an infamy they understood, but were utterly reluctant to protest against a dark and bloody mystery and thereby to become involved in it.

Oppressive though the trial and the executions were, they aroused in Trotsky all his fighting spirit. He was determined to meet the challenge with all the concentrated power and confidence with which he had once directed the first battles of

[1] Op. cit., pp. 120, 164.   [2] Op. cit., p. 180.

the civil war. He had been the chief defendant in the Zinoviev-Kamenev trial; and he knew that there would be further trials, in which he would be made to bear an ever heavier load of ever more stupendous accusations. He fought for his head and honour, for his surviving children, and for the dignity of all the doomed old Bolsheviks who could not defend themselves. He showed up contradictions and absurdities with which the trial was riddled. He strained every nerve to expose its falsehood and to shatter its mystery. He knew that he stood alone against Stalin's huge power and the legions of propagandists who served it. But at least he was free to speak and organize his counteraction; and he was determined to make the fullest use of this. On the second day of the trial he gave an exhaustive interview to *Arbeiderbladet*, which published it next day, 21 August, on the front page (under the title 'Trotsky claims that Moscow's accusations are false'), and left its readers in no doubt about its sympathy with Trotsky's case. He prepared statements for American, British, and French telegraph agencies and for many reporters, who rushed to Oslo. He was in the thick of battle; and time was of its essence: He had to refute Stalin's accusations before the world's amazed and shocked sensitivity was blunted. All that he needed was the freedom to defend himself.

Of that freedom he was suddenly and insidiously robbed; and those who robbed him of it were the men who had just professed friendship for him, had honoured him, and had prided themselves in having given him refuge. On 26 August, a day after the end of the Moscow trial, two senior police officers called on him to tell him, on the orders of the Minister of Justice, that he had offended against the terms of his residence permit. They asked him to sign an undertaking that henceforth he would refrain from interfering 'directly or indirectly, orally and in writing, in political questions current in other countries'; and that as author he would 'strictly limit his activity to historical works and general theoretical observations not directed towards any specific country'.[1] The demand sounded like a mockery. How could he refrain from expressing

[1] Norwegian Ministry of Justice and Police, *Storting Report no. 19*, submitted by Mr. Trygve Lie on 18 February 1937; Krog, op. cit.; Trotsky, '*Ich fordere ein Gerichtsverfahren über mich!*' in *The Archives*; and *Stalin's Verbrechen*.

himself on 'questions current in other countries' now, when Stalin had denounced him as Hitler's accomplice and ringleader of a gang of wreckers and assassins? How could he confine himself to 'theoretical observations not directed towards any specific country'? His silence would only lend colour to all the calumny against him which Stalin was drumming into the world's ears. He flatly refused to sign. Thereupon the police put him under house arrest, placed guards at his doors, and forbade him to make any statement for publication.

What accounted for this sudden change in the Norwegian Government's attitude? On 29 August, Yakubovich, the Soviet Ambassador, delivered in Oslo a formal Note demanding Trotsky's expulsion. The Note insisted that Trotsky was using Norway as 'the base for his conspiracy'; it invoked the verdict of Moscow's Supreme Court; and it ended with this slightly veiled threat: 'The Soviet Government wishes to state that the continued granting of asylum to Trotsky . . . will . . . impair friendly relations between the U.S.S.R. and Norway and will violate . . . rules governing international intercourse.'[1] This was three days after Trotsky had been placed under house arrest, a circumstance which enabled Trygve Lie to maintain that it was not because of Soviet intervention that he had taken action against Trotsky. However, the Soviet Ambassador had already asked for Trotsky's expulsion a few days earlier in an oral *démarche*. 'The difficulty', says Koht, 'in establishing the exact date when the Soviet Ambassador first asked that we should deny Trotsky asylum arises from the fact that he did this in an oral communication, of which no record seems to exist. I was away from Oslo at that time, touring my constituency in the far north; and at the Ministry of Foreign Affairs Trygve Lie acted as my deputy.'[2] In fact, the Ambassador saw Trygve Lie shortly after *Arbeiderbladet* had published its interview with Trotsky about the Moscow trial; it is inconceivable that he should not have protested against the publication of the interview in the paper of the ruling party and demanded that Trotsky be denied asylum. Oslo was astir with rumours that he also threatened to cut off trade with

[1] The Note is attached as an appendix to the *Storting Report no. 19*. *Izvestya* of 30 August 1936 spoke merely of a statement by the Soviet Ambassador.
[2] Koht's statement to the writer.

Norway; and that the shipping companies and the fishing industry were pressing the government not to endanger their interests at a time of slump and unemployment. 'My colleagues in the government', says Koht, 'were afraid of economic reprisals, although the Russians did not say that they would apply them. I did not believe that they would resort to a commercial boycott; and I held that, in any case, our trade with Russia—herring was our main export—was not large enough for us to be afraid. I was therefore opposed to the proposal that we should intern Trotsky; but I was overridden by my colleagues in the Cabinet.'[1]

The Ministers were afraid of a break with Russia and of losing the elections over this issue. And so, although they knew that the allegation that Trotsky was using Norway as a base for terroristic activities was sheer humbug, and although they denied it in their reply to the Soviet Note, they yielded to the pressure. They could not, however, expel Trotsky, because no other country would accept him. Nor could they hand him over to the Soviet Government, which did not ask for extradition, despite the fact that Trotsky had defied Stalin to ask for it. (Such a demand would have necessitated a hearing of the case before a Norwegian court; and this would have given Trotsky the opportunity to refute the charges.) Afraid of incensing Moscow by allowing Trotsky to conduct his defence in public, the Ministers therefore decided to intern him. Democratic conscience and ministerial self-importance, however, did not allow them to admit that they were yielding to threats and that in their own country they could not give shelter to a man of whose innocence they were convinced and whose greatness they had extolled. They had therefore to cast a slur upon his innocence. They did not dare to take up Vyshinsky's accusations, for although they lacked the courage to stand up for the truth, they did not have the audacity to embrace so big a falsehood either. They were small men capable of telling a small lie only. They decided to accuse Trotsky of having abused their confidence by engaging in criticisms of foreign governments and by being involved with the Fourth International, although they admitted that none of these activities was illegal. They now looked for proof of

[1] Idem.

his misconduct. But where was it to be found? At Oslo's Court, Quisling's men were flaunting from the dock the few sheets of paper they had managed to snatch at Knudsen's house, the copy of Trotsky's article 'The French Revolution has begun'. Had he not attacked in it the French Popular Front and Blum's Ministry? Was this not an activity 'directed against a friendly government'? There was, however, nothing clandestine or illegal about it: the article had appeared in the American *Nation* and in two small Trotskyist periodicals, *Verité* and *Unser Wort*: and it would be unseemly for Labour Ministers to make use of papers stolen from Trotsky's desk by Quisling's men. The Minister of Justice had in his files the police reports about Trotsky's contacts with the Fourth International. But the government had taken these contacts for granted and had shrugged off the police reports as recently as June, when they gladly prolonged his residence permit. Wherever they turned they could find no respectable motive for denying him asylum.

Yet deny it they had to, even if the legal motivation was to be bungled. As the days passed and Moscow's wrath grew louder and louder, they became more and more terrified to see their Lilliputian interests and reputations involved in a contest of giants; and they cursed the hour when they had allowed the man-mountain to come into their country. He was in their hands, however, and they were free to make him their prisoner. They did this fumblingly, ashamed of turning into Stalin's accomplices. But, to quote a Norwegian writer: 'A guilty conscience and the sense of shame seldom lead a wrongdoer to penitence . . . he must obtain an imaginary justification of his misdeeds. And it is not unusual for the wrongdoer to come to hate his victim.'[1] And the *amour propre* of the Ministers had been so enormously flattered when they acted as hosts to 'Lenin's closest companion' that they grew fretful and irascible when they became his jailers.

On 28 August, Trotsky appeared, under police escort, at the Court of Oslo to give, for a second time, testimony in the case of Quisling's men. He found himself almost at once put into the position of a defendant rather than of a witness. Quisling's men pleaded that they had exposed his 'disloyal'

[1] Krog, op. cit., p. 220.

behaviour in Norway; and the presiding judge subjected him to close questioning. Had he during his stay in Norway engaged in correspondence with his comrades abroad? Had he offered them political guidance? Had he criticized any foreign government in his articles? Trotsky answered all these questions in the affirmative, although they had no legal bearing on the case before the court, which was whether the men in the dock, in disguising themselves as policemen and breaking into Knudsen's house, had been guilty of fraud and burglary. The judge then declared that Trotsky had, on his own showing, violated the terms on which he had been admitted into the country. Trotsky replied that he had never assumed the obligation to refrain from expressing his views and communicating with his comrades; and that he was prepared to prove there and then that he had not engaged in any illegal or conspiratorial activity. At this point the judge interrupted him and ordered him to leave the witness stand.

Straight from the courtroom the police took him to the Ministry of Justice, where the Minister, surrounded by officials, asked him peremptorily to sign on the spot the following statement:

I, Leon Trotsky, declare that I, my wife, and my secretaries shall not engage, while in Norway, in any political activity directed against any state friendly to Norway. I declare that I will reside at such place as the government may select or approve . . . that I, my wife, and my secretaries, will in no way . . . involve ourselves in political questions current either in Norway or abroad . . . that my activities as author shall be limited to historical works, biographies, and memoirs . . . that [my] . . . writings of a theoretical nature . . . shall not be directed against any government of any foreign state. I further agree that all mail, telegrams, telephone calls, sent or received by myself, my wife, and my secretaries be censored. . . .[1]

Twenty years later eye-witnesses of the scene still remembered the flashes of scorn in Trotsky's eyes and the thunder of his voice as he refused to comply. How, he asked, did the Minister dare to submit to him so shameful a document? Did he really expect a man of his, Trotsky's, record, to sign it? What the Minister asked of him was complete submission and renunciation of any right to express a political opinion. Had he,

[1] *Storting Report no. 19.*

Trotsky, ever been prepared to accept such terms he would not have been in exile now and would not be dependent on Norway's dubious hospitality. Did Trygve Lie believe himself to be so powerful as to obtain from him what Stalin could never obtain? In admitting him to the country the Norwegian Government knew who he was—how then dare they ask that even his theoretical writings should not be directed against any foreign government? Had he ever allowed himself even the most trivial interference in Norwegian affairs—had they the slightest reproach against him on this count? The Minister admitted that they had none. Did they then believe that he was using Norway as a base for terroristic activities? No, the government definitely refused to believe that, Trygve Lie answered. Did they accuse him of conspiratorial or illegal action against any foreign government? No, the Minister replied again, there was no question of any conspiratorial or illegal activity. The government's case against Trotsky was that he had broken his pledge to refrain from any political activity; and his article 'The French Revolution has begun' and his contacts with the Fourth International were proof of this. Trotsky denied having ever given such a pledge. No communist, no socialist can ever commit himself to refrain from all political activity. What sort of idea did the Minister have of socialism and socialist morality? In what respect was the article on France more reprehensible than the interview for *Arbeiderbladet* he, Trotsky, had given to Trygve Lie himself, when Lie assured him that by expressing his political opinion he would not be offending against the terms of the residence permit? And how dare the government base the charge against him on a document supplied by Nazi burglars? Were they allowing a gang of Hitler's stooges to determine their conduct?

At this point Trotsky raised his voice so that it resounded through the halls and corridors of the Ministry: 'This is your first act of surrender to Nazism in your own country. You will pay for this. You think yourselves secure and free to deal with a political exile as you please. But the day is near—remember this!—the day is near when the Nazis will drive you from your country, all of you together with your *Pantoffel-Minister-President*.' Trygve Lie shrugged at this odd piece of soothsaying. Yet after less than four years the same government had

indeed to flee from Norway before the Nazi invasion; and as
the Ministers and their aged King Haakon stood on the coast,
huddled together and waiting anxiously for a boat that was
to take them to England, they recalled with awe Trotsky's
words as a prophet's curse come true.[1]

After this encounter Trygve Lie put Trotsky in more
stringent internment, deported his two secretaries, and placed
guards inside Knudsen's house, so as to prevent Trotsky from
communicating even with Knudsen. In ordering all this he
exceeded his powers, for the Norwegian Constitution did not
allow him to deprive of freedom any person not convicted by a
court of justice. Many people, including Conservatives, were
scandalized and protested; and so, three days after he had
ordered Trotsky's arrest, Lie obtained the King's signature for
a decree which invested him with extra-constitutional power
for this exceptional occasion; and on 2 September he ordered
that Trotsky and Natalya be transferred from Knudsen's
house to Sundby, in Hurum, to a fjord twenty miles to the
south of Oslo, where they were interned in a small house which
the Ministry had rented for this purpose. Guarded day and
night, they had to share the house with twenty jack-booted,
stamping, pipe-smoking, and card-playing policemen. No one
was allowed to visit Trotsky, except his Norwegian lawyer—
even his French lawyer was not admitted. He was denied the
prisoner's normal right to take physical exercise or a short
walk outdoors. To obtain a newspaper he had to apply for
special permission; and he had to submit all his correspondence
to censorship. The censor was a member of Quisling's party;
and so was one of the two officers in charge of the guard, Jonas
Lie, who was to become chief of police under Quisling's govern-

---

[1] In his War Memoirs Professor Koht thus describes the scene: 'After the meeting [with the King and the German Ambassador] I called together the members of
Parliament . . . and explained to them the new German demands. . . . I had no
doubt that the government would turn these down . . . that we would be on the run
again . . . and would have to get out of the country. I remembered the words
Trotsky had said to Trygve Lie . . .: "In a few years you and your government
will be political refugees, without home and country, as I am now." We had
brushed his words aside, such things had seemed to us utterly impossible. . . .
Several times I had to interrupt my speech to keep back my tears.' *Barricade to
Barricade* (Norwegian edition), p. 47. Norwegian parliamentarians who witnessed
this scene have described it to me in the same terms. One of them maintains
that it was King Haakon who reminded Trygve Lie of 'Trotsky's curse'.

ment. 'Trotsky's isolation was so strict', Knudsen recalls, 'that Trygve Lie repeatedly refused me permission to go to Hurum, even after I had become a Member of Parliament. Only after much trouble and delay was I allowed to send Trotsky a wireless set—at first he had been forbidden even to listen to the radio.'[1]

All this was to prevent Trotsky from replying to Stalin's charges. Yet he did not give in. He wrote articles exposing in detail the trial of Zinoviev and Kamenev; and in letters to his followers and to Lyova he instructed them how to conduct a campaign against the purges and how to assemble factual evidence disproving every count of Vyshinsky's indictment. Under protest he submitted the articles and letters to the censor, and then for weeks waited impatiently for answers. None came. The censor confiscated all his writings without informing him. Meantime, Trotsky and Natalya listened day after day to Moscow radio as it thundered out the accusations and made these re-echo through the world like an apocalyptic cacophony. How many people, Trotsky wondered, were by now beginning to recover from their first shocked astonishment and to give credence to the incredible? Had not the huge clouds of poisonous dust that had risen from Moscow begun to settle on peoples' minds and harden into a crust? The fact that the Norwegian Government had seen fit to intern him inevitably prejudiced many against him: people reasoned that if he had been quite innocent then surely his friends, the Norwegian socialists, would not have deprived him of freedom. His very silence seemed to cry out against him; and his enemies made the most of it. Barely a fortnight after the internment, Vyshinsky pointed out in *Bolshevik* that Trotsky evidently had nothing to say in self-defence, for otherwise he would have spoken up.[2]

Straining in the trap, Trotsky then tried to sue for defamation two Norwegian editors, a Nazi and a Stalinist who had in their newspapers, *Vrit Volk* and *Arbeideren*, endorsed Vyshinsky's accusations. On 6 October, Puntervold, his Norwegian lawyer, initiated the suit. The court had already issued the summonses—the case was to be heard before the end of the month—

---

[1] I am quoting the words that Knudsen spoke to me.

[2] *Bolshevik*, 15 September 1936. Lyova reported this indignantly to his father in a letter of 26 October.

when the government stopped the proceedings. Having interned Trotsky so as to make it impossible for him to answer Stalin, the government could not allow him now to use the court as his forum. Yet in law it could not prevent him from doing that, for even a jailbird had the right to defend himself in court against libel and slander. But Trygve Lie was not to be put off by legal niceties; and just as he had secured the decree which, after the event, sanctioned Trotsky's internment, so, on 29 October, he obtained another 'Provisional Royal Decree' stating that 'an alien interned under the terms of the decree of 31 August 1936 [Trotsky was the only alien interned under that decree] cannot appear as plaintiff before a Norwegian court without the concurrence of the Ministry of Justice'. The Ministry, of course, refused its 'concurrence,' and it forbade the court to hear Trotsky's suit against the two editors.

Trotsky then asked his French lawyer to sue for defamation Stalinist editors in France, Czechoslovakia, Switzerland, Belgium, and Spain, hoping that, even if he were not to be summoned as witness, he would at least be able to state his case through legal representatives. To this, it would seem, the Norwegians could have no objection—they had no legal ground whatsoever for preventing him from defending his reputation before foreign courts. By now, however, the government's zeal for appeasing Stalin knew no limits. 'The Ministry of Justice', Trygve Lie declared, 'after having conferred with the government, has decided that it will oppose Leon Trotsky's attempts to take legal action before a foreign tribunal, while he remains in Norway.'[1] In addition the Minister forbade Trotsky to communicate with any lawyers abroad. Now at last he had trapped and gagged him completely.

'Yesterday I received the official statement forbidding me to sue anyone even abroad', Trotsky informed Gérard Rosenthal, his French lawyer, on 19 November. 'I am refraining from any comment in order to make sure that this letter reaches you.' To Lyova he wrote: 'You must take into account that the Minister of Justice has confiscated all my important letters relating to my personal defence. I am now confronted by

[1] *Storting Report no. 19*; Krog, op. cit.; Trotsky's letters to Gerard Rosenthal of 19 and 22 November; and *Stalin's Verbrechen*.

slanderers, burglars, scoundrels . . . and am completely defenceless. You must act on your own initiative and tell all our friends about this.' In the next letter he gave even stronger vent to exasperation. He remarked that *Arbeiderbladet* was just conducting a campaign for the release of Ossietzky, the famous radical writer, from a Nazi concentration camp, but had nothing to say about his own internment in Norway—'Ossietzky at least was not slandered by his jailers'. 'This letter too naturally goes through [the censor's hands], but I have ceased to pay any attention to this. I am writing these words, privately and confidentially, to my son who is pursued by bandits in Paris and whose life may be in danger, while [I am] imprisoned and tied hand and foot. At stake are matters on which . . . [our] physical and moral existence may depend; and I must speak out.'[1]

There was probably something of a *ruse de guerre* in these letters. Trygve Lie claims that Trotsky communicated with his son by illegal means; that he wrote some of his letters in chemical ink; that he communicated stealthily with his followers while he was allowed to visit a dentist in town; and that his followers smuggled letters to him in cakes sent to Hurum; and so on. For once the charges appear to be based on facts, although Natalya, when asked, twenty years later, whether Lie's allegations were true, did not know what to say about them. But political prisoners use such devices to maintain clandestine contact with their comrades; and it would be strange if Trotsky had not used them, when he was subjected to so much violence, trickery, and chicanery.

. . . .

In view of Trotsky's enforced silence, the burden of the first public campaign against the Moscow trials fell on Lyova. Shy, somewhat inarticulate, and accustomed to keep himself in his father's shadow, he was suddenly brought to the fore in this great and grim affair. Vyshinsky had depicted him as a pillar of the 'terroristic conspiracy', and as his father's deputy and chief of staff, who instructed eminent old Bolsheviks about how to conduct their action inside the U.S.S.R.; and the Court's verdict had referred to him in the same

[1] *The Archives*, Closed Section.

terms as to his father. Now he was indeed compelled to act
in his father's place. Within a few weeks of the Zinoviev-
Kamenev trial he published his *Livre Rouge sur le proces de Moscou*,
the first factual refutation of the Stalinist charges, and the
first detailed exposure of their incongruities. He produced
proof that he had never been with his father in Copenhagen,
and that the Hotel Bristol where he was supposed to have
met the conspirators was non-existent. He delved into the
mystery of the confessions, saying that 'with their self-accusatory
statements based on no facts and no evidence, with their literal
repetition of the Prosecutor's pronouncements, and with their
zeal for self-defamation, the defendants were in effect saying
to the world: "Don't believe us, don't you see that all this is a
lie, a lie from beginning to end!" '[1]

He was, however, shaken to his depths by the misfortune
and the self-humiliation of the old Bolsheviks. He had known
them all from his childhood, had played with their sons in
the squares and corridors of the Kremlin, and had, as adolescent, looked up to them as the great men of the revolution
and his father's friends. With these feelings still alive, he thus
defended their honour: '. . . the inner moral strength of
Zinoviev and Kamenev was very considerably above the
average, though it proved to be insufficient in these quite
exceptional circumstances. Hundreds of thousands . . . would
not have been able to stand even one-hundredth part of the
continuous and monstrous pressure to which Zinoviev, Kamenev, and the other defendants were subjected.' But—'Stalin
wants Trotsky's head—this is his main purpose; and he will
resort to the most extreme and villainous concoctions to get
it. . . . He hates Trotsky as the living embodiment of the ideas
and traditions of the October Revolution. . . .' Not content
with 'triumphs' at home, the G.P.U. were in fact seeking to
exterminate Trotskyism abroad as well. They accused the
Spanish Trotskyists of wrecking the Popular Front and trying
to assassinate its leaders; and they branded the Polish Trotskyists as agents of the Polish political police, and the German
ones as agents of the Gestapo. 'Stalin aims at reducing all
political differences in the labour movement to this formula:
G.P.U. or Gestapo? Who is not with the G.P.U. is with the

[1] *B.O.*, no. 52–53, October 1936; *Livre Rouge sur le procès de Moscou.*

Gestapo.' 'Today he uses this method mainly in the struggle against Trotskyism, tomorrow he will turn it against other groupings in the working class. . . . Woe, if the world's labour movement proves unable to defend itself against this mortal poison.'[1]

Trotsky describes the relief with which he received at Hurum the first copy of the *Livre Rouge*: 'There are forms of paralysis under which one can see, hear, and understand everything, but is unable to lift a finger in order to turn away a mortal danger. To such political paralysis the Norwegian 'Socialist' Government had subjected us. What an inestimable gift Lyova's book was for us in these conditions. . . . The opening pages, I remember, seemed pallid to me: they reiterated a [familiar] political evaluation. . . . But from the moment the writer began his independent analysis of the trial I became completely absorbed. Every chapter seemed better than the previous one. "Our brave dear Lyova", I and my wife said to each other, "We have a defender!".'[2] In their correspondence, full of pain, anxiety, and tenderness, Lyova described all he was doing to set afoot a campaign against the purges; and he conveyed to his parents every word of sympathy and encouragement he could pick up from their all too few well-wishers.

Yet the horrible spectacle in which he was involved was probably more than Lyova's sensitivity could bear. He was, next to his father, the G.P.U.'s most important target. The feeling that he was being spied upon and that his mail was intercepted by a mysterious hand never left him. He feared that he would be kidnapped. He was lonely, defenceless, and completely dependent on the comradeship of the little band of Trotskyists around him. He found some solace in the friendship of Alfred and Marguerite Rosmer, who had now rallied to his father's defence, forgetting and forgiving all past misunderstandings. But within the narrow circle of his comrades he confided most of all in Mark Zborowski, a young and well-educated man, who had studied medicine and philosophy and who worked in the organization under the pseudonym Étienne, helping to publish the *Bulletin* and sitting on a little Russian Committee supposed to deal with the Opposition in

[1] Ibid.   [2] *B.O.*, no. 64, March 1938.

the U.S.S.R. Being of Polish-Ukrainian origin, Étienne knew Russian and had an intimate feeling for Soviet affairs—this enabled him to render Trotsky many small services and to gain Lyova's confidence.

This well-educated and fervent 'friend', however, was a Stalinist *agent provocateur*. Such was his knack for dissimulation that he never incurred the slightest suspicion on the part of Lyova and Trotsky. And so complete was Lyova's trust in him that he held the key to Lyova's letter-box and collected the mail for him. The mysterious hand that 'intercepted' Lyova's correspondence was Étienne's. He was also in charge of the most confidential files of Trotsky's archives; he kept these in his own home.[1]

A few months before the internment Trotsky asked Lyova to place a section of his archives with the Dutch Institute for Social History. He did this in part because he was pressed for money, and the Institute was willing to pay for the papers he offered them the modest sum of 15,000 (depreciated) French francs; but he was actuated mainly by a fear that the G.P.U. might try to seize his archives and he was anxious to deposit these in safe hands. In the first days of November, Lyova and Étienne delivered a number of files at the Paris branch of the Institute, at 7, rue Michelet—the branch was then under the management of Boris Nikolayevsky, the well-known Menshevik and one time associate of the Marx-Engels Institute in Moscow. The transaction was made tentatively, as an experiment; and the bulk of the archives, including the most confidential papers, remained with Étienne.[2]

No sooner had the files been delivered at the rue Michelet than a burglary was perpetrated there, on the night of 6–7 November; and some of the files were stolen. At once the suspicion arose that this was the G.P.U.'s work. The burglars

---

[1] Étienne (Mark Zborowski) has since made his confession; and in December 1955 he was sentenced by an American court to five years' imprisonment on a charge of perjury. My account of the relations between Étienne and Lyova is based on their correspondence with Trotsky and depositions which each of them made to the French police and magistrate. Étienne's story has been told in the *New Leader* by H. Kasson (on 21 November 1955) and by David J. Dallin (on 19 and 26 March 1956). See also *Hearing before the U.S. Senate Subcommittee on Internal Security*, Part 51, 14–15 February, 1957, pp. 3423–9. See also Isaac Don Levine, *The Mind of an Assassin*.

[2] Lyova's, 'Memoire pour l'Instruction', 19 November 1936. *The Archives, Closed Section.*

had left untouched valuables and money they had found and carried away only Trotsky's papers—who but G.P.U. agents would have done that? The French police were puzzled by the technical skill of the house-breaking; and they decided that this could not have been the work of French criminals but only of a powerful international gang. They interrogated Lyova, who accused the G.P.U. But how and from whom, they asked, did the G.P.U. learn so quickly that the files had been delivered at the rue Michelet? Who had been acquainted with the transaction? Lyova declared that apart from himself only three people had known about it: Nikolayevsky, a certain Madame Estrine, an employee of the Dutch Institute, and Étienne. He vouched for the integrity of all three, although he suspected that Nikolayevsky might have unwittingly, through careless talk, given the G.P.U. a clue. What about Étienne, the police inquired. Étienne, Lyova replied, was absolutely above suspicion: the proof of it was that at the very moment of the burglary he was guarding the most valuable parts of the archives in his own home.[1] Thus the question from whom the G.P.U. had learned about the deposition of the files appeared insoluble.

It turned out that the burglars had seized only Press cuttings and relatively unimportant papers; but no one doubted that, disappointed by the meagre spoils, the G.P.U. would make another and far more serious attempt. To the end of his days Trotsky was to remain almost as much concerned about the safety of his archives as about the safety of his own person. Yet the G.P.U. never made that other, much feared, attempt to seize his papers; and this was another puzzle. In the light of the facts stated here it is clear that they had no need to get hold of the archives, for they could have them, or copies of them, directly from Zborowski. They evidently staged the burglary in Paris as a feint to shield Étienne and enhance Trotsky's and Lyova's trust in him. Nothing, indeed, could more definitely divert all suspicion from him and turn it in other directions than the fact that, while the G.P.U. appeared to do their utmost to seize the archives, Étienne had 'reliably' guarded them in his apartment.

. . . .

[1] Ibid.

At Hurum the months dragged on with leaden monotony; and nothing promised to open or even to loosen the trap in which Trotsky found himself. American followers were trying to obtain for him asylum in Mexico; but it was far from certain that they would succeed; and Trotsky, though anxious to get out of Norway, was reluctant, at so critical a moment, to seek shelter in a country at once so remote and so ill-famed for its cloak-and-dagger politics (where, as Lyova reminded him, 'an assassin is hired for a few dollars'[1]). He still had a glimmer of hope that he would be able to make himself heard even in Norway. On 11 December he was to reappear as witness in the protracted trial of the Quisling men who had broken into his home at Honnefoss; and he reckoned that this time the government would not dare to stop the proceedings. However, the Minister of Justice intervened once again, not indeed to stop the trial, but to order that the case be heard *in camera*. And so, when Trotsky appeared in the witness-box, surrounded by a platoon of police, the public and the reporters were removed from the courtroom. In contrast to what happened during the previous open hearing, now that everything had been done to suppress Trotsky's testimony, the presiding judge treated him with exquisite consideration and courtesy; and for several hours Trotsky pleaded his case, refuting the Stalinist charges, with as much power and gravity as if he were speaking to a world-wide audience. Not once did the President of the Court interrupt him, not even when he attacked the Norwegian Minister of Justice as Stalin's accomplice. It was almost grotesque for Trotsky to make this plea, which was a forensic masterpiece, in the course of an almost trivial trial and in a closed and empty courtroom. But so uncertain was he now of his future and so doubtful whether he would ever have a chance to state his case, that he availed himself of this opportunity to state it, even if only for the record.[2]

.   .   .   .

A few eye-witnesses offer vivid glimpses of Trotsky in internment. Askvik, one of the officers in charge of the guard, decribes, in unpublished memoirs, his calm dignity, pride, and

---

[1] Lyova to his parents, 7 December 1936. *The Archives*, Closed Section.
[2] Trotsky, *Stalin's Verbrechen*, pp. 37ff. (He spoke in German.)

self-discipline. Trotsky, Askvik says, met every restriction on his freedom with a protest and firmly claimed his rights, without ever offending his guards, whom he addressed in correct and fluent Norwegian.[1] Puntervold, the Norwegian lawyer, recalls how intently Trotsky followed the elections—he was worried that Knudsen, who stood for Parliament in a predominantly conservative constituency and was attacked as Trotsky's host, might be defeated. Puntervold was at Hurum when the news came that Knudsen had been elected with an unexpectedly large majority; and he relates that Trotsky, overjoyed, jumped up, seized Natalya in his arms, and danced with her in celebration of his friend's success (which was also something of a slap in the government's face). Knudsen's steadfast loyalty was one of the few consolations left to him in these dreary months, as was also the campaign in Trotsky's defence which Helge Krog, a radical writer, conducted with fire and brilliance in *Dagbladet*, Oslo's Liberal paper.[2]

Twice or perhaps thrice Trygve Lie visited Trotsky at Hurum. He came first on 11 or 13 December to warn Trotsky that he was going to be transferred from Hurum to a more remote and inaccessible place of internment in the north, because the Ministry 'could not afford to go on paying for the large police guard' it had had to keep at Hurum. Trotsky then told Lie that his friends—he mentioned Diego Rivera—intended to take him over to Mexico, and that he would rather go there than allow himself to be moved to the desert of Norway's far north. While they were talking, Lie noticed Ibsen's *Works* on Trotsky's table. 'Are you reading Ibsen here?' Lie asked. 'Yes, I am re-reading his *Works*; Ibsen used to be the love of my youth, and I have gone back to him.' The dialogue which now followed would be worthy of Ibsen himself. Trotsky remarked how relevant the idea of the *Enemy of the People* was to the situation in which he himself and the Minister were

---

[1] I am obliged for some of these details to Mrs. Askvik, the widow of the police officer. In April 1956, hearing that I was in Oslo, she brought the manuscript of her husband's memoirs to Knudsen, requesting him to submit it to me. It was with surprise that Knudsen, translating to me the relevant passages, learned about Trotsky's command of the Norwegian language. At Honnefoss they had usually conversed in German.

[2] Trotsky, *Stalin's Verbrechen*, pp. 77–78. Every detail of this account is confirmed by other sources.

involved. Lie replied evasively that 'Ibsen could be variously interpreted'. 'No matter how you interpret him', Trotsky said, 'he will always testify against you. Remember Burgomaster Stockman?' The Minister asked whether Trotsky really intended to compare him with the villain of Ibsen's play, who for the sake of authority and vested interests destroys his own brother? 'With Burgomaster Stockman? . . . at best, Mr. Minister, at best', Trotsky replied. 'Your government has all the vices of a bourgeois government without any of its virtues.' Stung by this remark, the Minister inveighed against Trotsky's 'ingratitude', saying that he made 'a silly mistake' when he allowed Trotsky to come to Norway. 'And this silly mistake you now wish to make good by crime?' Trotsky retorted; and opening Ibsen's drama he read out the challenge with which Dr. Stockman meets his villainous brother: 'We shall yet see whether meanness and cowardice are strong enough to close the mouth of a free and honest man.' This brought the conversation to an end. The Minister rose, yet before leaving he turned to his prisoner with an outstretched hand; but Trotsky refused the handshake.[1]

A week later Lie returned to tell Trotsky that Mexico had granted him asylum and that he, Lie, had already chartered a petrol tanker on board which Trotsky and his wife would sail the following day, under the escort of Jonas Lie, the commander of the Hurum police guard. The haste and the details of the deportation aroused Trotsky's forebodings. Why, he asked, was the Minister leaving him only twenty-four hours to prepare for the voyage? Why did he not release him from internment? He demanded that he should be allowed to leave as a free man, to consult friends, to wind up his affairs and collect his papers, to communicate with the Mexican Government, to chose his own route, and to make his own safety arrangements. 'And what', he asked, 'if Stalin knows about your tanker? We may be torpedoed on the high seas and never reach the English Channel.' (He even inquired whether the vessel had any defences.) The Minister refused all his demands, but tried to reassure him about the safety of the voyage, saying that no one knew about the plan except he himself and

[1] Trotsky, *Stalin's Verbrechen*, pp. 77–78; and Trotsky's diary pages in *The Archives*, Closed Section; Krog, op. cit.

the shipowner. Trotsky then asked to be allowed to travel via France: surely the French would give him a transit visa now that he had asylum in Mexico? Lie declined this demand too. He was in great haste to get Trotsky out of the country before Parliament assembled to debate the affair. His haste seemed to Trotsky more sinister than it was. 'Of course', he said, 'you are in a position to destroy us physically, but morally you will break your necks just as the German Social Democrats broke theirs on Karl Liebknecht and Rosa Luxemburg.' He repeated his prophecy: 'In three to five years . . . you will all be émigrés . . .'; and once again he turned his back on the Minister, refusing to shake hands.[1]

He had the feeling that he was being driven from one trap into another, and he was not sure what might happen to him and Natalya on the way. While Natalya was packing luggage, he wrote, in chemical ink, an article under the title 'Shame!'. This was to be 'a reply to slanderers', especially to well-known British and French lawyers who had 'vouched' for the legal correctness of the Zinoviev-Kamenev trial. One of these lawyers was a King's Counsel; another was an eminent member of the *Ligue des Droits d'Homme*; and both had praised the Moscow Court for not having sentenced Trotsky to death *in absentia*. 'Whoever knows anything at all about revolutionary history, human psychology and . . . the biographies of the men involved', Trotsky commented, 'will agree . . . that there is a thousand times more ground to assume that [these lawyers] are in Stalin's service than to admit for a minute that Trotsky can be an ally of the Gestapo. . . . All the Leagues of the Rights of Man of the whole solar system will not be able to prove this. . . . I shall give the final answer to the accusers and their lackeys . . . in Mexico, *if ever I arrive there*.' Before starting on the voyage, he wanted to leave this article behind 'as the ship-wrecked sailor leaves a bottle in the sea'.[2] To Lyova he wrote: 'It seems that tomorrow we are going to be sent to Mexico. This then is our last letter from Europe. If something happens to us *en route* or elsewhere you and Sergei are my heirs. *This letter should have testamentary value. . . .* As you know, I have in

[1] Ibid.
[2] The article appeared in the first issue of *B.O.* (nos. 54–55 March 1937) published after Trotsky's deportation from Norway.

mind future royalties on my books—apart from these I possess nothing. If you ever meet Sergei . . . tell him that we have never forgotten him and do not forget him for a single moment.'[1] As he was writing these words, his doctor, his lawyer, and his tax collector presented their bills; and to secure their claims they sequestrated his bank account.[2]

On 19 December the petrol tanker, the *Ruth*, sailed from Norway, with Trotsky, Natalya, and their police escort as the only passengers. The deportation was carried out in such secrecy that for several days afterwards police sentries stood outside the internment place at Hurum to give the impression that Trotsky was still there. The seas were rough at first; and in their cabin Trotsky and Natalya read books about Mexico and wondered what the future held in store for them. Then, as the sea calmed down, Trotsky began to write, partly in diary form, his analysis of the trial of Zinoviev and Kamenev, which he included in his book *Stalin's Crimes*. He worked hard for three weeks while the vessel tacked about, changed course, and avoided normal routes. But the world had already learned about the deportation, and Press agencies were anxious to interview Trotsky by radio. The captain of the *Ruth*, however, was ordered from Oslo not to allow him to use the transmitter. On board the empty ship Trotsky and Natalya were still treated as internees; even at their meals they remained flanked by their police escort.

'This was Cain's year', runs the entry in Trotsky's diary dated 31 December 1936. On the next morning the *Ruth* greeted the New Year with her sirens. No one returned the greetings; and there were no Wishes of the Season. Only the fascist police officer came to the dining table, flourishing New Year greetings which he personally had received from his socialist Minister. The world seemed engulfed in absurdity.

By one of those strange coincidences which run through Trotsky's life, it was exactly twenty years since Trotsky had last sailed from Europe, also as an exile expelled from a country which had given him temporary refuge.[3] But in 1917 the world was at war and the seas were infested with submarines. Now the world seemed at .peace, and no submarines

---

[1] The letter, dated 18 December 1936, was written in French.
[2] *The Archives*, Closed Section.   [3] *The Prophet Armed*, pp. 238–41.

lurked in the ocean. Yet there was an almost warlike tension on board the tanker; and Trotsky noted in his diary that the captain and the crew kept alluding to the G.P.U., but avoided uttering the name, 'as if they were hinting at underwater rocks'.[1] And twenty years before Trotsky had written from his voyage: 'This is the last time I am casting a glance on that old *canaille* Europe'—only to hurry back across the ocean three months later. Now he had indeed cast his last glance on the 'old *canaille*'. But as he departed from Europe, his head and heart were full of its infernal turmoil; and his thoughts hovered over the graves he was leaving behind, the graves of his two daughters, the graves of so many friends and followers, and the graves of so many hopes.

[1] Some parts of this diary are included in *Stalin's Verbrechen*; others have not yet been published and are in *The Archives*.

CHAPTER V

The 'Hell-black Night'

As the *Ruth* sailed into the great oil harbour of Tampico, on 9 January 1937, Trotsky and Natalya were still so apprehensive of what might await them on the Mexican shore that they refused to land unless they were met by friends. The Norwegian police were threatening to disembark them by force when a small boat approached from which a Mexican general, accompanied by officials, emerged, bringing a message of welcome from Lazaro Cardenas, the President of Mexico. (The President had sent his official train to take Trotsky and Natalya from Tampico.) On the pier two American Trotskyists, George Novack and Max Shachtman, waved greetings; and Frida Kahlo, Diego Rivera's wife, was waiting to offer hospitality. The contrast between the warm reception in Mexico and the icy send-off from Norway was so sharp as to seem unreal. Entering the Presidential train Trotsky and Natalya ran into a police guard and again shrank back. 'A fear crossed our minds . . .', she notes, 'that perhaps we were being taken to just another place of captivity.' At a small station near Mexico City Diego Rivera received them with expansive enthusiasm and took them to Coyoacan, a suburb of the capital, and to his Blue House—this was to be their home for the next two years. The place might have been designed to soothe weary nerves: it was spacious, sunlit, covered with a profusion of pictures, full of flowers and objects of Mexican and Indian art. At every step the newcomers found comforting signs of the care with which their Mexican and American friends had prepared the new abode for them, and had thought of their personal protection and provided facilities for work. Thus, the first few days in Mexico brought quite unexpected relief—there was even a touch of the fleeting idyll about them.[1]

[1] This is evident from Trotsky's first Mexican letters to Lyova, in which he expresses delight with the country of his new refuge, its climate, and even with its fruit and vegetables.

The country's political climate also offered attractions. The Mexican Revolution was still at its height. Quite recently Cardenas had signed a decree, under which some of the *latifundias* were shared out among the poor peasants; and he was about to nationalize the American and British owned oil and railway companies. Foreign investors, native land-lords, and the Catholic Church fought back; and relations between Mexico and the United States were strained. But Cardenas had behind him the peasants and the Confederation of Mexican Workers which had suddenly grown into a great political force.

In admitting Trotsky, at Rivera's request and on promptings from his own entourage, Cardenas had acted from a sense of revolutionary solidarity. He declared that he had not merely granted Trotsky asylum, but invited him to stay in Mexico as the government's guest. From the outset he did his utmost to protect his guest's head against the storms of hatred gathering over it; and he was to go on doing this till the end. However, his own situation was rather delicate. On the one hand, his political enemies soon began to insinuate that Trotsky was the inspirer of his revolutionary policy, and the insinuation found its way into American newspapers.[1] On the other, the Con-federation of Mexican Workers, on whose support he depended, was a Stalinist stronghold; its leader Lombardo Toledano and the Communist party protested fiercely against Trotsky's admission and warned the President that they would not rest until that 'chief of the vanguard of the counter-revolution' was expelled. Cardenas was careful to lend no colour to the charge that he was expropriating British and American investors at Trotsky's instigation; and he was even more anxious to calm the Confederation of Mexican Workers. He was himself po-litically very far from any form of Trotskyism and indeed of communism. The son of poor peasants, he was guided by agrarian radicalism and the empirical experience of his patriotic struggle against foreign predominance. He was

---

[1] Cardenas later found it necessary to refute the insinuation publicly (*La Prensa*, 12 November 1938); and Trotsky thought of suing an American paper (*The New York Daily News*) which had violently attacked him as Cardenas's evil spirit. He desisted only when he was told by Albert Goldman that he had no legal grounds for action. See Trotsky's correspondence with Goldman in December 1938. *The Archives*, Closed Section.

therefore wary of getting involved in any of the internal conflicts of communism. In these difficult circumstances he repudiated with dignity the Stalinist clamour against Trotsky's admission; but he kept studiously aloof from his 'guest'—they never met in person. He asked Trotsky to pledge himself that he would not interfere in Mexico's domestic affairs. Trotsky gave this pledge at once, but, taught by his bitter Norwegian experience, he was on his guard and explicitly reserved his 'moral right' to reply in public to any accusations or slanders.[1] Cardenas was satisfied with this. It never occurred to him to ask Trotsky to refrain from political activity; and he himself stood up for Trotsky's right to defend himself against Stalinist attacks. In this attitude of aloof but vigilant benevolence he was to persist. Trotsky often expressed his gratitude and, strictly observing his pledge, never ventured to state any opinion on Mexican politics even in private, although his view of Cardenas' policy, which did not go beyond the 'bourgeois stage' of the revolution, must have been critical to some extent.

During his first years in Mexico, Diego Rivera was Trotsky's most devoted friend and guardian. A rebel in politics as well as in art, the great painter had been one of the founders of the Mexican Communist party and a member of its Central Committee since 1922. In November 1927 he witnessed the Trotskyist street demonstrations in Moscow and the expulsion of the Opposition, which gravely disturbed him. Subsequently he broke with the party, and also with David Alfaro Siqueiros, another of Mexico's great painters, his closest friend and political comrade, who sided with Stalin. The dramatic pathos of Trotsky's fate stirred Rivera's imagination: here was a figure of heroic dimensions who might have been destined to take a central place in his epic frescoes—he had indeed put Trotsky and Lenin in the forefront of that famous mural glorifying class struggle and communism with which he had, to the horror of all respectable America, decorated the walls of the Rockefeller Centre in New York. For Rivera it was a moment of rare sublimity when strange fortunes brought his leader and prophet under his roof at Coyoacan.

Trotsky had long admired Rivera's work. He probably first saw his paintings in Paris during the First World War;

---

[1] *'Aux Representants de la Presse Mexicaine'*, 12 January 1937. *The Archives.*

and references to them occur in Trotsky's Alma Ata correspondence of 1928.[1] Rivera's restless search for new artistic expression aptly illustrated Trotsky's own view that the malaise in contemporary painting was rooted in its divorce from architecture and public life, a divorce which was inherent in bourgeois society and could be overcome only by socialism. The striving for the reunion of painting, architecture, and public life animated Rivera's art, in which Renaissance traditions and Goya's and El Greco's influences merged with Indian and Mexican folk art and cubism. This interplay of tradition and innovation suited Trotsky's taste; he was captivated by Rivera's defiant courage and the soaring and passionate imagination with which he brought motifs of the Russian and Mexican revolutions into his monumental murals. Nor could Trotsky help being fascinated and puzzled by Rivera's elemental temperament, somnambulism, and 'Gargantuan size and appetites', which made of him a riotous and roaring prodigy like any of the chimerical figures appearing in his paintings. And in counterpoint, as it were, to Diego there was his wife Frida, herself a painter of delicate melancholy, introspective and symbolist, and a woman of exquisite beauty—she emanated exotic grace and dreaminess as she moved about in long-flowing, richly shaded, and embroidered Mexican robes which concealed a deformed leg. After the dreary months of internment, it was gratifying, even thrilling, for Trotsky and Natalya to find refuge with such friends.

An onlooker with some insight into the characters might have wondered how Trotsky and Rivera would get along and whether a clash between them was not bound to occur. Not satisfied with his artistic eminence, Rivera saw himself also as a political leader. He was not exceptional in this: painters and sculptors played an extraordinarily large part in Mexican politics—most members of the Politbureau of the Communist party were painters. (Political agitation carried out by means of brush and chisel may have appealed to masses of illiterate but artistically sensitive *campesinos* more directly than any other form of agitation.) Yet as a politician Rivera was even less

---

[1] Andres Nin had sent to Trotsky at Alma Ata a volume of reproductions of Rivera's paintings and sculptures, and Trotsky wrote back to thank him for the book and express appreciation of the artist. *The Archives.*

than an amateur; he frequently fell a prey to his restless temperament. However, in Trotsky's presence, at least at the beginning, he kept his political ambition under control and modestly assumed the disciple's role. As to Trotsky, he had always treated the political vagaries of artists with tender understanding, even those of lesser artists, to whom he was not indebted for anything. All the more willing was he in Rivera's case to say that 'genius does what it must'.

Thus Trotsky might have been in a mood to count the blessings of his new refuge had he not been driven back into his grim struggle almost at once. He was daily the object of threats from the local Stalinists and from Moscow. President Cardenas had to order police guards to be placed outside the Blue House. Inside, American Trotskyists, who had come to serve as secretaries and bodyguards, kept watch. Trotsky's American followers were aiding him unstintingly in organizing his defence and his campaign against the Moscow trials. They were few and poor; but they assisted him as well as they could in re-establishing his contacts with friends and followers all over the world and in resuming his work. 'What good luck it is', he wrote to Lyova on 1 February 1937, 'that we have managed to come to Mexico just before the start of the new trial in Moscow.'[1]

.   .   .   .

The new trial opened less than a fortnight after his landing at Tampico. Radek, Pyatakov, Muralov, Sokolnikov, Serebriakov, and twelve others took their place in the dock; and Trotsky was once again the chief defendant *in absentia*. The accusations piled up ever more incongruously and incredibly. Vyshinsky now spoke of Trotsky's formal agreement with Hitler and the Emperor of Japan: in exchange for their aid in the struggle against Stalin, Trotsky, he maintained, was working for the military defeat and dismemberment of the Soviet Union, for he had pledged himself *inter alia* to cede the Soviet Ukraine to the Third Reich. Meanwhile he was organizing and directing industrial sabotage in the Soviet Union; catastrophes in coal mines, factories, and on the railways, mass poisonings of Soviet workers, and repeated attempts on the lives

[1] *The Archives*, Closed Section.

of Stalin and other members of the Politbureau. The defendants echoed the prosecutor and elaborated his charges. One of them, Romm, who had been *Izvestya's* correspondent in France, confessed that he had seen Trotsky in Paris in July 1933 and taken terroristic instructions from him. Pyatakov told the court that he had visited Trotsky in Oslo in December 1935 and there taken orders from him.[1]

'We listened to the radio, we opened the mail and the Moscow newspapers', Natalya writes, 'and we felt that insanity, absurdity, outrage, fraud, and blood were flooding us from all sides here in Mexico as in Norway. . . . With pencil in hand Lev Davidovich, over-tense and overworked, often in fever, yet tireless, lists the forgeries which have grown so numerous that it becomes impossible to refute them.'[2] The trial lasted a week and was followed by executions—Radek and Sokolnikov, however, were sentenced to ten years' imprisonment each.

For Trotsky to refute the accusations was indeed like wrestling and arguing with monsters in a nightmare. The trials were more and more unreal in their horror, and horrible in their unreality. They seemed designed to paralyse every critical thought and to render every argument grotesquely inadequate. Yet even before Trotsky had had the time to marshal his facts and arguments some of the charges were pricked. The Norwegian Ministry of Foreign Affairs investigated the statement that Pyatakov had arrived in Oslo by plane from Berlin in December 1935 and seen Trotsky; and it ascertained that no plane coming from Berlin had landed at Oslo Airport in that month and for many weeks before and after; the Airport Authority issued a statement to that effect. Trotsky then telegraphed these questions to the Moscow tribunal: when exactly, on what day and at what hour, had Pyatakov landed? And where, when, in what circumstances had he, Trotsky, received him? He asked similar questions about his alleged meetings with Romm.[3] The Prosecutor and the judges ignored the questions, knowing full well that if the defendants tried to answer they would involve themselves in glaring contradictions and discredit the show. On 29 January, just before the end of the proceedings, Trotsky once again challenged

---

[1] *Sudebnyi Otchet po Delu Anti-Sovietskovo Trotskistskovo Tsentra.*
[2] In V. Serge, *Vie et Mort de Leon Trotsky*, p. 258.   [3] *B.O.*, nos. 54–5, 1937.

Stalin to demand his extradition. In an appeal to the League of Nations he declared himself ready to submit his case to a Commission on Political Terrorism which the League was supposed to set up on Soviet initiative—he had already made one such appeal from Norway. The League kept silent; and Stalin once again disregarded the demand for extradition.[1] In another effort to come to grips with his accusers Trotsky stated in a message to a public meeting in New York:

> . . . I am ready to appear before a public and impartial Commission of Inquiry with documents, facts, and testimonies . . . and to disclose the truth to the very end. I declare: *If this Commission decides that I am guilty in the slightest degree of the crimes which Stalin imputes to me, I pledge in advance to place myself voluntarily in the hands of the executioners of the G.P.U.* . . . I make this declaration before the entire world. I ask the Press to publish my words in the farthest corners of our planet. But, if the Commission establishes—do you hear me? do you hear me?—that the Moscow trials are a conscious and premeditated frame-up, I will not ask my accusers to place themselves voluntarily before a firing squad. No, the eternal disgrace in the memory of human generations will be sufficient for them! Do the accusers in the Kremlin hear me? I throw my defiance in their faces, and I await their reply![2]

About this time Trotsky's two sons were finally linked with him in his ordeal—and here the story turns into the modern version of the Laocoön legend. Lyova, feeling that he was pursued by the G.P.U., published in a French newspaper a statement saying that if he were to die suddenly the world should know that he had found his death at Stalinist hands— no other version should deserve credence, for he was in good health and was not harbouring any thought of suicide. Sergei had been arrested at Krasnoyarsk in Siberia, according to the Russian Press, and charged with attempting, on his father's orders, a mass poisoning of workers in factories. 'Stalin intends to extract a confession from my own son against me,' Trotsky noted. 'The G.P.U. will not hesitate to drive Sergei to insanity and then they will shoot him.' Natalya came out with another appeal addressed in vain 'To the Conscience of the World'.[3] 'There were moments', she recollected later, 'when

---

[1] '*Trebovanie Moei Vidachy*', 24 January 1937. *The Archives.*
[2] 'I Stake my Life', Appendix II in *The Revolution Betrayed.*
[3] *B.O.*, nos. 54–55.

L.D. felt crushed' and 'remorseful at still being alive. "Perhaps my death could save Sergei?" he once told me. . . .'[1] She alone knew of those moments. In the eyes of the world Trotsky remained indomitable, unflinching, and possessed of unconquerable energy. He never tired of summoning his followers to action and rousing flagging friends. This, for instance, is what he wrote to Angelica Balabanoff, his old Zimmerwald associate, when he heard that the Moscow trials had plunged her into deep pessimism: 'Indignation, anger, revulsion? Yes, even temporary weariness. All this is human, only too human. But I will not believe that you have succumbed to pessimism. . . . This would be like passively and plaintively taking umbrage at history. How can one do that? History has to be taken as she is; and when she allows herself such extraordinary and filthy outrages, one must fight her back with one's fists.'[2] So he himself fought back.

He undertook to establish his full alibi, to prove that not a single one of the Stalinist charges was or could have been true and to bring to light the political meaning of the gigantic frame-up. This was, in the view of many, an impossible task. He had to retrace all his whereabouts and activities through all the years of his banishment; to assemble evidence from his enormous and partly scattered archives and from newspapers in many languages; to collect testimonials and affidavits from former secretaries and bodyguards and from adherents, some of whom had turned into opponents; and from Ministries, Consulates, police headquarters, travel agencies, landlords, householders, inn-keepers and casual acquaintances in various countries. Yet in a sense this vast and costly undertaking was bound to be useless. Those who wished to know the truth could very well grasp it without such a mass of detailed evidence, while people with indifferent or closed minds were not to be persuaded anyhow. Nor was it likely that posterity would ever require such an accumulation of testimonies in order to be able to form its opinion. Trotsky, the great controversialist might well have been satisfied with exposing the trials on their internal evidence alone, as Lyova and a few

[1] Serge, op. cit., p. 266.
[2] Trotsky to A. Balabanoff, who was then living as exile in New York. Letter of 3 February 1937 in *The Archives*, Closed Section.

friends—and Bernard Shaw—urged him to do[1]. But it was characteristic of the man's relentless meticulousness that once he had resolved to put the whole record straight, he left nothing to chance, allowed not a single relevant incident to remain undocumented and omitted not a single affidavit from the dossier. He behaved as if he were reckoning with the possibility that Stalin's forgery might endure for ages; and for the ages he was preparing a foolproof and indestructible alibi.

This nerve-racking labour took him many months. He put all his strength into it and drove his secretaries and adherents remorselessly, and above all Lyova, who in Paris performed the major part of the work. He brooked no delay, no contradiction, no excuse. At the slightest sign of a let-down he threatened to 'break off all relations' first with Shachtman and then with Naville and to 'denounce their sabotage or even worse', although both men did their best to assist him. In the first letter to Lyova from Mexico he was already venting disappointment at not having received a pile of testimonies he had expected to find on arrival. After a fortnight or so he was bursting with impatience; and every letter to Lyova was bitter with reproach. Why had the papers relating to his Copenhagen trip not yet come? Was this not 'a plain crime'? Why were some testimonies not validated legally by Commissioners of Oaths? Why were the signatures under others illegible? Why were the dates not precise? Why were certain place-names not indicated beyond all possibility of misunderstanding? From week to week his tone grew more scolding and brutal. 'Today I have received your letter . . . with the usual excuses . . . and the usual promises . . .' he wrote to Lyova on 15 February, 'but I have had enough of excuses and have long since ceased to believe in promises!' Lyova's 'slovenliness bordered on treachery'. 'After all the experiences of recent months I must say that I have not yet had a day as black as this one, when I opened your envelope, confident I would find the affidavits in it and instead found only apologies and assurances.' 'It is difficult to say which are the worst blows, those that come from Moscow or those from Paris.'[2] He planned the opening of

---

[1] For Bernard Shaw's opinion see further pp. 369–70. Lyova expressed his misgivings in a letter to his mother (8 March 1937), *The Archives*, Closed Section.

[2] *The Archives*, Closed Section. Letters of 1 and 15 February 1937.

a counter-trial for the spring; and he was afraid that the dossier would not be ready in time. The Blue House looked almost like a sweat shop in these days, with the secretaries, Trotsky himself, and Natalya translating, copying, and typing endless papers. At the same time he filled pages in American newspapers with his comments, tried to make his views intelligible to the Mexican Press, and arranged for 'Commissions of Inquiry' to be set up in various countries. Obsessed with the importance of what he was doing, suspicious of every hitch, apprehensive of interference by the G.P.U., and despairing perhaps of ever finishing the job, he felt no inhibition about prodding and chiding Lyova, whose life and honour were as much at stake as his own. So indeed might Laocoön have upbraided his sons and goaded them on to strain every nerve in fighting off the giant snakes in whose strangulating coils they had all been caught, father and sons.

Lyova was hurt and wounded in his filial devotion. While Trotsky was interned in Norway he had stepped bravely into the breach. But the incubus with which he was struggling was stronger than himself; and he had looked forward to the day when his father would be released and take the burden on his own broad shoulders. He was distressed now to see that his father was so wrought up and irate. He still doubted the value of the whole undertaking and wrote to Natalya that *Stalin's Crimes*, the short book Trotsky had written *en route* to Mexico, was a far more effective riposte than any 'counter-trial', or the work of any Commissions of Inquiry, could be. Yet, once his father had decided to establish his alibi, Lyova put all his heart into the job. It was not his fault that progress was slow and misunderstandings arose. From Hurum, for instance, Trotsky had directed him to arrange a counter-trial in Switzerland; but in the meantime it had been decided to hold it in America. Lyova, not knowing about this, was still busy with preparations in Switzerland. This brought him a severe rebuke from his father, who threatened to cut off all the money needed and to take all further work out of Lyova's hands, and entrust it to Naville (in whom he had always had so little confidence).[1] The gathering of testimonies was impeded by the animosities of the Trotskyist sects: Lyova had to obtain many statements

[1] Trotsky to Lyova, 24 February, 5 and 16 March 1937, ibid.

from members of the Molinier group whom Trotsky had disowned; and he had to use tact and diplomacy. He was overworked and depressed. He too was engaged in the Press campaign against the trials: his articles appeared now and then in the *Manchester Guardian*. He went on looking after his father's publishing affairs, collected royalties, forwarded them regularly to Mexico, paid parental debts in Norway and France, and brought out the *Bulletin*. Offended by his father's censoriousness, sensing that he was being ensnared by the G.P.U., deeply unhappy in his family life, he began at the age of thirty to suffer from persistent insomnia. He grew weary and exhausted.

As usual, he opened his heart only to his mother: ('Darling Mamochka, I have no doubt that you alone are not cross with me for my silence or for anything else.') But he also met his father's reprimands with this poignant reproach: '. . . I have had to carry out, in very difficult conditions, part of the work which would otherwise have burdened yourself; and I have had to do it without the necessary authority and without the assistance you have; sometimes I do not even have the money to buy postage stamps. I thought that I could count on your support. Instead you are making me your butt and are telling all and sundry about my "criminal carelessness". . . . Even if I bear a share of responsibility for the delay with the Copenhagen documents this does not . . . justify your attitude towards me.'[1] Harassed, and dejected, Lyova confided all the more trustingly in Étienne, whom no one seemed to equal in ingenuity, industry, and devotion to the cause.

Trotsky at first hoped that the counter-trial would be set on a scale appropriate to the provocation, that it would be conducted in such a way as to shake the conscience of the international labour movement. He sought to associate the Second International with it and the so-called Amsterdam International of the Trade Unions. On his advice, Lyova had approached Friedrich Adler, the Secretary of the Second International, who had of his own accord denounced the Moscow purges as 'medieval witch hunts'. Adler did what he could; yet all he achieved was that after much delay the Executive of the International issued a statement condemning

[1] Lyova to Trotsky, 8 March 1937, ibid.

the purges; it refused to take part in any inquiry or counter-trial. So did the Trade Unions' International. Both these organizations, their German and Austrian sections suppressed by Hitler and Dolfuss, were under the thumb of Leon Blum; and as head of the Popular Front government he depended on Stalinist support. Blum was embarrassed even by the International's platonic declaration against the purges; and he used his influence to prevent any further action by his own party and by 'fraternal sections'. And so the western European Social Democrats, usually so eager to defend the 'freedoms and rights of the individual' against communism, preferred this time to observe a diplomatic silence, or even to exculpate Stalin. 'The International', as Trotsky put it, 'boycotted its own Secretary.' This reduced in advance the effectiveness of any counter-trial: without the Socialist parties and the Trade Unions no campaign could engage the attention of the working classes.[1]

Trotsky's adherents then tried to enlist the support of eminent intellectuals of the left. This did not quite suit Trotsky, who often derided the 'peace committees', 'peace congresses', and 'Anti-fascist parades' for which the Stalinists assembled galaxies of literary and academic 'stars'; he despised the showy snobbery of such stage effects, especially when the Comintern substituted them for solid and united action by the labour movement. He reproached his American followers for failing to draw workers into the 'Committees for Trotsky's Defence'; but he had no choice in the matter.[2]

Yet the response of the intelligentsia was also disappointing, for the Stalinists, who in France, Spain, Britain, and the United States exercised a strong influence on them, brought to bear upon the intelligentsia every means of moral pressure to prevent them from lending the slightest support to any protest against the purges. From Moscow, where the flower of Russian literature and art was being exterminated, the voices of Gorky, Sholokhov, and Ehrenburg could be heard, joining in the chorus that filled the air with the cry, 'Shoot the mad dogs!' In the West literary celebrities like Theodore Dreiser, Leon

[1] *B.O.*, nos. 56–57, 1937; Lyova's correspondence with F. Adler in 1936. *The Archives*, Closed Section.
[2] See the *Internal Bulletin* of the S.W.P. (the American Trotskyist party), March-April 1940. (The question was raised then, in the course of Trotsky's controversy with Shachtman and Burnham.)

Feuchtwanger, Barbusse, and Aragon echoed the cry; and a man like Romain Rolland, the admirer of Ghandi, the enemy of violence, the 'humanitarian conscience' of his generation, used his sweetly evangelical voice to justify the massacre in Russia and extol the master hangman—with such zeal that Trotsky thought of suing him for defamation. Where Gorky and Rolland gave the cue, hosts of minor humanitarians and moralists followed suit with little or no scruple. Their manifestoes and appeals in support of Stalin make strange reading. In the United States, for instance, they declared a boycott on the Commission of Inquiry set up under John Dewey's auspices. They warned 'all men of good will' against assisting the Commission, saying that critics of the Moscow trials were interfering in domestic Soviet affairs, giving aid and comfort to fascism, and 'dealing a blow to the forces of progress'. The manifesto was signed by Theodore Dreiser, Granville Hicks, Corliss Lamont, Max Lerner, Raymond Robins, Anna Louise Strong, Paul Sweezy, Nathaniel West, and many professors and artists, quite a few of whom were to be in the forefront of the anti-communist crusades of the nineteen-forties and nineteen-fifties.[1] Louis Fischer and Walter Duranty, popular experts on Soviet affairs, vouched for Stalin's integrity, Vyshinsky's veracity, and the G.P.U.'s humane methods in obtaining confessions from Zinoviev, Kamenev, Pyatakov, and Radek. Even Bertram D. Wolfe, a member of the Lovestonite Opposition long expelled from the Communist party, still gave Stalin credit for saving the revolution from the Trotskyite-Zinovievite conspiracy.[2] In the Jewish-American Press

---

[1] See, e.g., the manifesto published in *Soviet Russia To-day*, issue of March 1937.

[2] 'Today, whatever his [Trotsky's] subjective intentions may be, and I shall not try to judge them, his objective role is to mobilize labour sentiment against the Soviet Union. He has ordered his followers in France to enter the Socialist International. He has departed ever further from communist fundamentals. . . . He has even come out for civil war in the Soviet Union and thus become an open enemy of the class and land he once served so faithfully.' Thus Bertram D. Wolfe wrote about Trotsky in 1936! (*'Things we want to know'* Workers' Age Publications.) Only when the Great Purges were coming to a close, shortly before Bukharin appeared in the dock, did Wolfe, the 'Communist fundamentalist', express (in *The New Republic* of 24 November 1937) his regret at having given moral support to the purges. This led Trotsky to remark that Wolfe had still a lot of things to learn and un-learn in order to avoid committing grievous mistakes in the future. In later years Wolfe attacked other writers (who had always denounced the Stalinist purges) as 'apologists for Stalin'.

PLATE XV

Arriving in Mexico. Trotsky and Natalya at Tampico, 1937

Associated Press

PLATE XVI

Diego Rivera

Paul Popper

writers who had hitherto described themselves as 'Trotsky's admirers' turned against him when he spoke of the anti-semitic undertones of the Moscow trials. The editor of one such paper wrote: 'This is the first time that we of the Jewish Press have heard such an accusation. We have been accustomed to look to the Soviet Union as to our only consolation, as far as anti-semitism is concerned. . . . It is unforgivable that Trotsky should raise such groundless charges against Stalin.'[1]

Hypocrisy, bigotry, and the simple-minded fear of aiding Hitler by criticizing Stalin were not the only motives. Some of the intelligentsia saw no point in Trotsky's refutations. Charles A. Beard, America's distinguished historian, held that it was not 'incumbent upon Trotsky to do the impossible, that is to prove a negative by positive evidence. It is incumbent upon his accusers to produce more than confessions, to produce corroborating evidence. . . .'[2] Bernard Shaw also rejected the idea of a counter-trial and wrote: 'I hope Trotsky will not allow himself to be brought before any narrower tribunal than his reading public where his accusers are at his mercy. . . . His pen is a terrific weapon.' A month later he wrote less sympathetically: 'The strength of Trotsky's case was the incredibility of the accusations against him. . . . But Trotsky spoils it all by making exactly the same sort of attacks on Stalin. Now I have spent nearly three hours in Stalin's presence and observed him with keen curiosity, and I find it just as hard to believe that he is a vulgar gangster as that Trotsky is an assassin.'[3] Shaw was, of course, evading the issue, for Trotsky did not make 'exactly

[1] B. Z. Goldberg in the New York *Tag* of 26 and 27 January 1937. At this time Trotsky re-formulated his views on the Jewish problem. In an interview with the *Forwärts*, another American-Jewish daily, he admitted that recent experience with anti-semitism in the Third Reich and even in the U.S.S.R. had caused him to give up his old hope for the 'assimilation' of the Jews with the nations among whom they lived. He had arrived at the view that even under socialism the Jewish question would require a 'territorial solution', i.e. that the Jews would need to be settled in their own homeland. He did not believe, however, that this would be in Palestine, that Zionism would be able to solve the problem, or that it could be solved under capitalism. The longer the decaying bourgeois society survives, he argued, the more vicious and barbarous will anti-semitism grow all over the world. *The Archives*, 28 January 1937.

[2] Quoted from *The Case of Leon Trotsky*, p. 464.

[3] G. B. Shaw in letters to the Secretary of the British Committee for the Defence of Leon Trotsky, 20 June and 21 July 1937. Quoted from the Archives of the Committee and the Trotsky *Archives*, Closed Section.

the same sort of attacks on Stalin'. Yet, unlike Rolland, Shaw did not carry his friendship for Stalin to the point of justifying the purges. He saw there a conflict not between right and wrong but between right and right, an historic drama of the kind he had depicted in *St. Joan* (which he had written about the time of the first anathema on Trotsky), a clash between the revolutionary fighting for the future and the established power defending the legitimate interests of the present. André Malraux declared likewise that 'Trotsky is a great moral force in the world, but Stalin has lent dignity to mankind; and just as the Inquisition did not detract from the fundamental dignity of Christianity, so the Moscow trials do not detract from the fundamental dignity [of communism].'[1]

Berthold Brecht's response was similar. He had been in some sympathy with Trotskyism and was shaken by the purges; but he could not bring himself to break with Stalinism. He surrendered to it with a load of doubt on his mind, as the capitulators in Russia had done; and he expressed artistically his and their predicament in *Galileo Galilei*. It was through the prism of the Bolshevik experience that he saw Galileo going down on his knees before the Inquisition and doing this from an 'historic necessity', because of the people's spiritual and political immaturity. The Galileo of his drama is Zinoviev, or Bukharin or Rakovsky dressed up in historical costume. He is haunted by the 'fruitless' martyrdom of Giordano Bruno; that terrible example causes him to surrender to the Inquisition, just as Trotsky's fate caused so many communists to surrender to Stalin. And Brecht's famous duologue: 'Happy is the country that produces such a hero' and 'Unhappy is the people that needs such a hero' epitomizes clearly enough the problem of Trotsky and Stalinist Russia rather than Galileo's quandary in Renaissance Italy.[2]

To Stalin's apologists and to those who washed their hands,

---

[1] Quoted from a summary of Malraux's speech at a banquet given in his honour by the editorial staff of *The Nation*. (The summary was sent to Trotsky by one of his followers and is in *The Archives*, Closed Section.) Malraux had come to the United States with Stalinist backing and was trying to rally support for the International Brigades fighting in Spain. Somewhat earlier Trotsky had attacked him for his attitude towards the purges.

[2] Brecht wrote the original version of *Galileo Galilei* in 1937–8, at the height of the Great Purges.

Trotsky replied with an anger which, however justified, made him look like the proverbial *animal méchant* and gave lukewarm 'defenders of the truth' an excuse for silence. That Sidney and Beatrice Webb refused to join in the protest was not surprising; they had by now become Stalin's admirers. But even men like André Gide and H. G. Wells, whose first impulse was to support the counter-trial, decided in the end to keep aloof. The scope of the campaign thus remained rather narrow; and the various Committees in Defence of Trotsky were composed mostly of declared anti-Stalinists and some anti-communists of long standing; and this restricted still further the effect of their action.

In March 1937 the American, the British, the French, and the Czechoslovak Committees formed a Joint Commission of Inquiry which was to conduct the counter-trial. Its members were: Alfred Rosmer; Otto Rühle, distinguished as the member of the Reichstag, who alone with Karl Liebknecht had voted against war in 1914–15; Wendelin Thomas, also a former communist member of the Reichstag; Carlo Tresca, a well-known anarcho-syndicalist; Suzanne La Follette, a radical, strongly anti-Marxist American writer; Benjamin Stolberg, and John R. Chamberlain, journalists; Edward A. Ross, Professor of Wisconsin University; Carlton Beals, a University lecturer; and Francisco Zamorra, a leftish Latin American writer. Apart from Rosmer, none of the members had ever been associated with Trotsky—most of them were his political opponents. The Commission owed its authority mainly to John Dewey, its chairman, America's leading philosopher and educationist who was also reputed to be a friend of the Soviet Union. John F. Finerty, famous as Counsel of Defence in great American political trials, especially those of Tom Mooney and Sacco and Vanzetti, acted as the Commission's legal counsel.

Trotsky was not at first confident that the Commission would be up to its task. The names of most of its members told him little or nothing; and he had doubts even about its chairman. He wondered whether Dewey, who was nearly eighty, was not too old and too remote from the issues before the Commission. Would he not fall asleep during the hearings? Would he be able to cope with the enormous documentary evidence? And would he as 'friend of the Soviet Union' not be inclined to whitewash Stalin? James Burnham, who was active in organizing the Commission, laid these doubts at rest: 'Dewey is old . . .', he wrote to Trotsky, 'but his mind is still keen and his personal integrity beyond question. It was he, you will recall, who wrote the most searching analysis of the Sacco-Vanzetti case. He will judge the evidence not perhaps as a politician . . . but as a scientist and a logician. He will not sleep during the hearings. . . . It would be a great error to underestimate him. . . . Dewey is, of course, not a Marxist; and all his personal integrity and intelligence does not prevent him from being politically on the fence. In that sense we cannot, obviously, be "quite sure" of him. . . .'[1]

Dewey's accession to the Committee was an act almost heroic. Philosophically he was Trotsky's adversary—they were presently to clash in public controversy over dialectical materialism. For all his radicalism, he stood for the 'American way of life' and parliamentary democracy. As a pragmatist, he was inclined to favour the 'undoctrinaire' and 'practical' Stalin against Trotsky, the 'dogmatic Marxist'. In taking upon himself, at his age, the burden of presiding over the inquiry, he had to break many old associations and give up old friendships. The Stalinists went out of their way to dissuade him. When they failed, they shrank from no obloquy and slander— their mildest aspersion on him was that he had 'fallen for Trotsky' from sheer senility. The *New Republic*, of which he had been a founder and on whose editorial board he had sat for nearly a quarter of a century, turned against him; and he resigned from it. His next of kin implored him not to tarnish the lustre of his name by participating in a shady and shabby business. Intrigue and harassment only hardened his resolve. The fact that so many influences were set in motion to obstruct his action, openly and surreptitiously, was to him an argument in its favour. He put aside work on a treatise *Logic: the Theory of Inquiry*, which he regarded as his *magnum opus*, in order to plunge into the practical experience of this particular inquiry. In the course of weeks and months he pored over the blood-reeking pages of the official reports of the Moscow trials, over Trotsky's voluminous writings and correspondence, and

[1] Burnham to Trotsky, 1 April 1937, *The Archives*, Closed Section.

mountains of other documents. He took notes, compared facts, dates, and allegations, until he was thoroughly versed in all aspects of the case. Again and again he had to resist intimidation and threats. Nothing shook his equanimity or weakened his energy. The Commission was to cross-examine Trotsky as chief witness; and as there was no chance that the American Government would allow him to come to New York, Dewey decided to carry out the investigation in Mexico. He was warned that the Mexican Federation of Workers would not allow the counter-trial to take place; that he and his companions would be met with hostile demonstrations on the frontier; and that they would be mobbed. Unmoved, the old philosopher pursued his course. His mind was open. Though he was convinced that Trotsky's guilt had not been proven in Moscow, he was not yet sure of Trotsky's innocence. Determined not only to maintain strict impartiality, but to make the impartiality evident to all, he never met Trotsky outside the Commission's public sessions, although he 'would have liked to talk to him informally as man to man'.[1]

The Commission opened its hearings on 10 April. It had intended to hold them in a large hall in the centre of Mexico City; but it gave up the idea in order to avoid public disturbance and to save money. The sessions were held at the Blue House, in Trotsky's study. 'The atmosphere was tense. There was a police guard outside . . . visitors were searched for guns and identified by a secretary of Trotsky who was, himself, armed.' The French windows of the room facing the street 'were covered, and behind each of them there were six-foot barricades of cemented brick and sand bags. . . . These brick barricades had been completed the night before.' About fifty people were present, including reporters and photographers. The hearings were conducted in accordance with American judicial procedure. Dewey had invited the Soviet Embassy and the Communist parties of Mexico and the United States to send representatives and take part in the cross examination; but the invitations were ignored.[2]

---

[1] This account is based on what Dewey himself and Dr. Ratner, his secretary, told me in 1950.

[2] *The Case of Leon Trotsky*, appendix III; See also James Farrell in *John Dewey*, (A *Symposium*, edited by Sidney Hook) p. 361.

In a brief inaugural statement Dewey declared that the Commission was neither a court nor a jury but merely an investigating body. 'Our function, is to hear whatever testimony Mr. Trotsky may present to us, to cross-examine him, and to give the results of our investigation to the full Commission of which we are part. . . .' The title of the American Committee for the Defence of Leon Trotsky did not mean that the Committee stood for Trotsky; it acted 'in the American tradition', on the belief that 'no man should be condemned without a chance to defend himself'. Its aim was to secure a fair trial where there was a suspicion that the accused man was denied such a trial. The case was comparable with the cases of Mooney and of Sacco and Vanzetti; but the latter could at least make their pleas before a legally constituted court, whereas Trotsky and his son had twice been declared guilty in their absence by the highest Soviet tribunal; and his repeated demands that the Soviet Government ask for his extradition, which would have brought him automatically before a Norwegian or a Mexican court, had been ignored. 'That he has been condemned without the opportunity to be heard is a matter of utmost concern to the Commission and the conscience of the whole world.' Explaining his own motives for participation, Dewey said that having given his life to social education, he treated his present work as a great social and educational task—'to act otherwise would be to be false to my life's work'.

The proceedings lasted a full week and took up thirteen long sessions. Dewey, Finerty, A. Goldman, Trotsky's lawyer, and others cross-examined Trotsky on every detail of the charges and the evidence. At times the cross-examination almost turned into a political dispute, when some of the examiners insisted on Trotsky's and Lenin's moral co-responsibility for Stalinism, and Trotsky refuted the imputation. There was not a single question into which he refused to go or which he dodged. Despite the controversial interludes, the hearings proceeded calmly and smoothly; they were disturbed only once by the so-called Beals incident.

Carlton Beals, a member of the Commission, repeatedly addressed to Trotsky questions which were more or less irrelevant but showed a marked pro-Stalinist bias and were extremely offensive in form. Trotsky answered composedly and to the point. Towards the end of a long session on 16 April, Beals went into a political argument and maintained that while Stalin, the expounder of socialism in one country, represented the mature statesmanship of Bolshevism, Trotsky was something of an incendiary bent on fomenting world revolution. Trotsky replied that in the Moscow trials he had been described as the fomentor not of revolution but of counter-revolution and as Hitler's ally. Beals then asked him whether he knew Borodin, Stalin's former emissary to China and adviser to Chiang Kai-shek. Trotsky replied that he had not met him personally although he had, of course, known of him. But, Beals asked, had Trotsky not sent Borodin to Mexico in 1919 or 1920 in order to found the Communist party there? The question suggested that Trotsky had lied to the Commission and moreover that he had tried to foment revolution even in the country that was giving him shelter at present. The exchange grew hot. With his Norwegian experience still fresh, Trotsky suspected that the question might have been designed to incite Mexican opinion against him, to rob him of asylum, and to disrupt the counter-trial. He pointed out that he had always set his hopes on world revolution, but had sought to promote it by politically legitimate means, not by staging coups in foreign countries. The allegation that he had sent Borodin to Mexico in 1919–20 was fantastic. At that time, at the height of civil war, he hardly ever left his military train; he had his eyes fixed on the maps of his fronts and had nearly forgotten 'all his world geography'.

Beals emphatically reiterated his allegation and added that Borodin himself had declared that Trotsky had sent him to Mexico, and also that already in 1919 the Soviet Communist party was torn between the statesmen and the fomentors of revolution. 'May I ask the source of this sensational communication?', Trotsky inquired. 'Is it published?' 'It is not published', said Beals. 'I can only give the advice to the Commissioner to say to his informant that he is a liar', Trotsky retorted. 'Thank you, Mr. Trotsky. Mr. Borodin is the liar.' 'Very possible', was Trotsky's laconic reply. Before the end of the hearing he protested against Beals's 'tendentious Stalinist tone'. The incident looked to him more and more sinister.

The Borodin affair had nothing to do with the Moscow trials
and seemed to have been dragged in only to embarrass him
and the Mexican Government. And so at the opening of the
next session he once again denied Beals's assertion and asked
the Commission to throw light on its source. If Beals had his
information directly from Borodin, let him say where and
when he obtained it. If, indirectly, then in what way, through
whom and when did he get it? A probing into these questions
should reveal a design aiming at disrupting the counter-trial.
'If Mr. Beals himself is not consciously and directly involved
in this new intrigue, and I will hope that he is not, he must
hasten to present all the necessary explanations in order to
permit the Commission to unmask the true source of the
intrigue.' As Beals refused to reveal that source, the Commission censured him in private session; and he resigned from
the Commission. The incident had no further sequel.[1]

The results of the cross-examination were summed up by
Trotsky himself in his final plea on 17 April.[2] Showing signs
of strain and fatigue, he asked to be allowed to read his statement sitting. He began by pointing out that either he and nearly
all members of Lenin's Politbureau were traitors to the Soviet
Union and communism, as the accusers in Moscow claimed,
or else Stalin and his Politbureau were forgers. *Tertium non
datur*. It was said that to delve into this question was to interfere with the domestic affairs of the Soviet Union, the Fatherland of the workers of the world. It would be 'a strange
Fatherland' whose affairs the workers were not allowed to
discuss. He himself and his family had been deprived of Soviet
citizenship; they had no choice but to place themselves 'under
the protection of international public opinion'. To those who,
like Charles A. Beard, held that the onus of the proof lay on
Stalin, not on him, and that it was anyhow impossible to
'disprove a negative with positive evidence', he replied that the
legal conception of an alibi presupposed the possibility of
such a disproof and that he was in a position to establish his alibi
and to demonstrate the 'positive fact' that Stalin had organized
'the greatest frame-up in history'.

The juridical examination of the case, however, was 'concerned with the *form* of the frame-up and not with its *essence*',

[1] *The Case of Leon Trotsky*, pp. 411–17.   [2] Ibid., pp. 459–585.

which was inseparable from the political background of the purges, the 'totalitarian oppression, to which . . . all are subjected, accused, witnesses, judges, counsel, and even the prosecution itself'. Under such oppression a trial ceases to be a juridical process and becomes a 'play, with the roles prepared in advance. The defendants appear on the scene only after a series of rehearsals which give the director in advance complete assurance that they will not overstep the limits of their roles'. There was no room for any contest between prosecution and defence. The chief actors performed their parts at pistol point. 'The play can be performed well or badly; but that is a question of inquisitorial technique and not of justice.'

In evaluating the accusation one must consider the political record of the defendants. A crime usually arises from the criminal's character or is at least compatible with it. The cross-examination was therefore necessarily concerned with his and the other defendants' work in the Bolshevik party and with their roles in the revolution; and in the light of these the crimes imputed to them were utterly incompatible with their characters. That was why Stalin had to falsify their records. The classical criterion *Cui prodest?* had to be applied here. Was or could the assassination of Kirov be of any advantage to the Opposition? Or was it of advantage to Stalin, whom it provided with a pretext for the extermination of the Opposition? Could the Opposition hope to benefit in any way from acts of sabotage in coal mines, factories, and on the railways? Or did the government, whose insistence on over-hasty industrialization and whose bureaucratic neglect had caused many industrial disasters, seek to exculpate itself by blaming the Opposition for these disasters? Could the Opposition gain anything from an alliance with Hitler and the Mikado? Or was Stalin making political capital out of the defendants' confessions that they were Hitler's allies?

It would have been suicidal folly for the Opposition to commit any of these crimes. The unreality of the accusation accounted for the prosecution's inability to produce any valid evidence. The conspiracy of which Vyshinsky spoke was supposed to have gone on for many years and to have had the widest ramifications in the Soviet Union and abroad. Most of its supposed leaders and participants had all these years been in the G.P.U.'s hands. Yet the G.P.U. could not adduce any realistic data or even a single factual piece of evidence for the gigantic conspiracy—only confessions, confessions, endless confessions. The 'plot had no flesh and blood'. The men in the dock related not any specific events or actions of the conspiracy but only their conversations about it—the court proceedings were a conversation about conversations. The lack of all psychological verisimilitude and factual content showed that the spectacle had been enacted on the basis of an especially prepared 'libretto'. Yet 'a frame-up on such a colossal scale is too much even for the most powerful police . . . too many people and circumstances, characteristics and dates, interests and documents . . . do not fit . . . the ready-made libretto!' 'If one approaches the question in its artistic aspect, such a task —the dramatic concordance of hundreds of people and of innumerable circumstances—would have been too much even for a Shakespeare. But the G.P.U. does not have Shakespeares at its beck and call.' As long as they were concocting events supposed to have taken place inside the U.S.S.R. they could still maintain a semblance of coherence. Inquisitorial violence could force defendants and witnesses to be consistent in some of their fantastic tales. The situation changed when the threads of the plot had to be extended to foreign countries; and the G.P.U. had to extend them there in order to implicate him, the 'public enemy number one'. Abroad, however, the facts, dates, and circumstances could be verified; and whenever this was done the story of the conspiracy fell to pieces. Not a single one of the 'threads' that were supposed to lead to Trotsky had led to him. It was established that the few defendants, David, Berman-Yurin, Romm, and Pyatakov, to whom he had allegedly given terrorist orders (in the presence of his son or otherwise) had not and could not have seen him (and his son) at the places and on the dates indicated, because either he (and his son), or they, were not and could not have been there. Yet, these contacts disproved, the whole accusation collapsed because his alleged contacts with Radek (through Romm) and Pyatakov were crucial to the 'conspiracy'. All other accusations and testimonies had been based on, or derived from, Pyatakov's and Radek's confessions that they had acted as Trotsky's chief agents and as the twin pillars of the conspiracy. 'All the testimony of the other accused rests upon our own testimony', Radek himself had declared in court; and their own testimony, which centred on the meetings with Trotsky in Paris and Oslo, rested on nothing. 'It is hardly necessary to demolish a building brick by brick once the two basic columns on which it rests are thrown down', Trotsky pointed out; yet he went on demolishing the building 'brick by brick'.

He asked the Commission to consider that his own versions were full of that psychological and historical authenticity which was so conspicuously lacking in Moscow's versions; that the documentation he had placed before the Commission reflected with extraordinary fullness his life and work over many years: and that had he committed any of the crimes, surely his papers would betray him at one point or another. People who easily swallowed camels but strained at gnats were saying that he could have arranged all his archives and all the files of his correspondence so as to camouflage his real designs. Yet for the purpose of camouflage one can compose five, ten, even a hundred documents—not thousands of letters addressed to hundreds of persons, not hundreds of articles and dozens of books. No, he had not 'built a skyscraper to camouflage a dead rat'. If someone had declared, for instance, that Diego Rivera was a secret agent of the Catholic Church, would not any jury investigating the accusation inspect Rivera's frescoes? And would anyone dare to say that the impassioned anti-clericalism evident in those frescoes was mere camouflage? No one can 'pour out his heart's blood and nerves' sap' in works of art, history, and revolutionary politics just in order to deceive the world. How hollow by comparison with his documentation was Vyshinsky's: all it consisted of were Trotsky's letters: two to Mrachkovsky, three to Radek, one to Pyatakov, and one to Muralov—all faked!

But why had the defendants made their confessions? He could hardly be expected to offer precise information about the G.P.U.'s inquisitorial techniques. 'We could not here question Yagoda (he is now himself being questioned by Yezhov) or Yezhov, or Vyshinsky, or Stalin, or . . . their victims, the majority of whom have already been shot.' However, the Commission had before it the affidavits of Russian and

European communists who had themselves been subjected to
the G.P.U.'s techniques. It was all too often forgotten that
those who made the confessions had not been active opposition
leaders but capitulators, who had for years prostrated themselves before Stalin. Their last confessions were the consummation of a long series of surrenders, the conclusion of a truly
'geometric progression of false accusations'. In the course of
thirteen years Stalin had with their help erected a 'Babel
tower' of slander. A dictator who used terror without inhibition
and 'could buy consciences like sacks of potatoes' was well able
to perform such a feat. But Stalin himself was terrified by his
tower of Babel, for he knew that it must collapse after the first
breach in it had been made—and made it would be!

Trotsky ended with an apotheosis of the October Revolution
and of communism. Even under Stalin, he said, despite all
the horror of the purges, Soviet society still represented the
greatest progress in social organization mankind had so far
achieved. The blame for the tragic degeneration of Bolshevism
lay not on the revolution but on its failure to extend beyond
Russia. For the time being Soviet workers were confronted with
a choice between Hitler and Stalin. They preferred Stalin;
and in this they were right: 'Stalin is better than Hitler.' As
long as they saw no other alternative, the workers remained
apathetic even in the face of the monstrosities of Stalinist rule.
They would shed the apathy the very moment when any
prospect appeared abroad of new victories for socialism.
'That is why I do not despair . . . I have patience. Three
revolutions made me patient.'

The experience of my life, in which there has been no lack either
of success or of failures, has not only not destroyed my faith in the
clear, bright future of mankind, but, on the contrary, has given it
an indestructible temper. This faith in reason, in truth, in human
solidarity, which at the age of eighteen I took with me into the
workers' quarters of the provincial Russian town of Nikolayev—
this faith I have preserved fully and completely. It has become
more mature, but not less ardent.

With these words, and with thanks to the Commission and
its chairman, he concluded this *apologia pro vita sua*.

For a long while the Commission sat in silence deeply
shaken. Dewey had intended to sum up and close the

proceedings in a formal manner; instead he brought the hearings to an end with this single sentence: 'Anything I can say will be an anti-climax.'[1]

The record of the cross-examination is all the more remarkable because of the handicaps Trotsky had imposed upon himself. He often pulled his punches so as not to embarrass the Mexican Government unduly. He sought to explain the many involved issues between himself and Stalin not in his accustomed Marxist idiom, which might have been unintelligible to his audience, but in the language of the pragmatically minded liberal—the difficulty of such a translation can be appreciated only by those who have ever attempted it. Eager for personal contact with his listeners, he conducted his defence not in his native tongue or even in German or French but in English. His vocabulary was limited. His grammar and idiom were shaky. Stripped of the splendours of his mighty eloquence, denying himself the advantages which even the humdrum speaker finds in the use of his native language, he answered impromptu the most varied, complex, and unexpected questions. Day after day, and hearing after hearing, he searched for expression and struggled with the resistance of the language, frequently halting or stumbling into unintentionally comic sentences, and sometimes saying almost the opposite of what he meant to say, or failing to understand questions put to him. It was as if Demosthenes, his stammer uncured and his mouth full of pebbles, had come to court to fight for his life. Thus he recounted the events of his long career, expounded his beliefs, described the many changes in the Soviet régime, analysed the issues that had separated him from Stalin and Bukharin, but also from Zinoviev and Kamenev, portrayed the personalities, and delved into every phase of the terrible contest.

By the end no question had been left unanswered, no important issue blurred, no serious historic event unilluminated. Thirteen years later Dewey, who had spent so much of his life in academic debate and was still as opposed as ever to Trotsky's *Weltanschauung*, recalled with enthusiastic admiration 'the intellectual power with which Trotsky had assembled and

---

[1] Dewey added only a few formal announcements concerning the Commission's further work.

organized the mass of his evidence and argumentation and conveyed to us the meaning of every relevant fact'. The incisiveness of Trotsky's logic got the better of his unwieldy sentences, and the clarity of his ideas shone through all his verbal blunderings. Even his wit did not succumb; it often relieved the gloom of his subject-matter. Above all, the integrity of his case allowed him to overcome all external restraint and constraint. He stood where he stood like truth itself, unkempt and unadorned, unarmoured and unshielded yet magnificent and invincible.

.   .   .   .

It was to be several months before the Dewey Commission got ready with its verdict. Meanwhile, Trotsky had still to supplement the evidence he had laid before it; and he kept the whole household busy. The cross-examination and the work connected with it had worn him out; and he did not recuperate during a brief stay in the country. For the rest of the spring and the summer he suffered again from severe headaches, dizziness, and high blood pressure and complained again about old age that had 'caught him by surprise'. The first echoes of the counter-trial were less than faint.[1] The strains in the family were scarcely diminished. 'Dear Papa', Lyova wrote towards the end of April, 'you continue to subject me to your ostracism . . . it is more than a month since I received any letter from you.' Trotsky, still dissatisfied with the way Lyova was managing the *Bulletin*, had again proposed to transfer it to New York; in reply Lyova calmly pointed out that the paper should remain in Europe where most of its readers were; and he again bitterly complained to his mother about the rough treatment he was getting. In a long and somewhat apologetic letter, Trotsky then tried to smooth matters out.[2] He

---

[1] Both the British and the French Committees for the Defence of Leon Trotsky reported to Coyoacan that the newspapers of their respective countries were ignoring the counter-trial almost completely.

[2] Lyova to Trotsky, 27 April; Trotsky to Lyova, 29 May, 1937. *The Archives,* Closed Section. Over twenty years later Natalya told me that Trotsky had written 'a very long and very cordial letter' to Lyova which 'cleared away all these misunderstandings'. She promised to find that letter, though she feared that it might have been laid astray. She probably had in mind the letter summarized here. This, however, did not quite succeed in 'clearing the misunderstandings'.

explained to Lyova that having lost so many months in Norway before he could prepare for the counter-trial, he was then irritated by further delays and anxious to be able to place his full dossiers before the Dewey Commission; and he was convinced that the delays had been caused by Lyova's reluctance to co-operate with comrades. He advised him to take a rest and steady his nerves: 'great trials are still ahead for both of us'.

The advice was timely enough. Lyova too was suffering from headaches and fevers; and he did not have his father's resilience. 'What is left of my old strength?' he wrote to his mother, hinting that he would presently need 'a small operation'. He lived in poverty, but thought of helping his parents financially by earning a living as a factory worker or gaining an academic scholarship. When Natalya urged him to write for newspapers instead, he replied with a note of frustration: 'Writing . . . comes with difficulty to me—I have to read, study, reflect, which requires time. . . . Yet since I have been in emigration I have been burdened almost continually with technical and other chores. I am a beast of burden, nothing else. I do not learn, I do not read. I cannot aspire to do any literary work: I do not have the light touch and the talent that can partly replace knowledge.'[1] This mood of frustration was suffused with tenderness and devotion. When his parents sent him back cheques he had collected from French publishers and forwarded to them, Lyova took only a little for himself and divided the rest among needy comrades or paid it into the organization's funds. He worried lest his father was expending his strength too recklessly and shattering his nerves. Why, he asked Natalya, had they not bought a car in Mexico and organized hunting or fishing trips? Why did L.D. not play croquet of which he used to be so fond? 'My dear darling Mamochka', he wrote in reply to a rather sad letter from her, '. . . think only what might have happened if Stalin had not committed the "mistake" of banishing Papa? Papa would have been dead long ago. . . . Or if I had been allowed to return to the U.S.S.R. in 1929, if Sergei had been active in politics, òr if Papa had been in Norway now, or, worse still, in Turkey? Kemal would have handed him over . . . things might have been far, far worse.'[2] These

---

[1] Lyova to his mother, 29–30 June 1937.
[2] Letter of 7 July 1937. *The Archives*, Closed Section.

were poor consolations, of course; yet no better ones were at hand.

About this time there occurred a somewhat tragi-comic incident in the family's intimate life. Amid all these grim events and amid all her anguish, Natalya was troubled by marital jealousy. What caused it exactly is not quite clear: she is most discreet about this even in her letters to her husband, which leave no doubt on one point only—namely that this was the first time she felt she had reason to be jealous. Perhaps a less self-assured woman would have been jealous earlier, for Trotsky's behaviour towards women, in those rare moments when he could notice them, was characterized by a sort of articulate gallantry, not free from male vanity and sensitiveness to female admiration. At any rate, a woman's presence sometimes stimulated him to dashing displays of seductive verve and wit. There was old-fashioned chivalry and artistic finesse in these 'flirtations'; yet they were somewhat at variance with his high seriousness and his almost ascetic life. Natalya, however, was confident enough of his love not to take them amiss. But at Coyoacan she became acutely jealous of someone to whom she referred in her letters only by the initial F. To judge from circumstantial evidence, this may have been Frida Kahlo. Members of the household soon noticed a discord between the two women and a slight cooling off between their husbands. We do not know whether Frida's uncommon delicate beauty and artistry excited in Trotsky more than the normal gallantry or whether Natalya, now fifty-five, fell a prey to the jealousy that often comes with middle age. Enough that a 'crisis' ensued and both Trotsky and Natalya were unhappy and miserable.[1]

In the middle of July he left Coyoacan and with his bodyguard went to the mountains to get physical exercise, to do farmwork on a large estate, and to ride and hunt. Daily, sometimes even twice daily, he wrote to Natalya. He had promised her to say nothing in his letters about her upset but 'could not help breaking the promise': he implored her to 'stop competing with a woman who meant so little' to him while she, Natalya, was all to him. He was full of 'shame and self-hatred' and

[1] See their correspondence of July 1937. *The Archives*, Closed Section.

PLATE XVII

Leon Sedov (Lyova)

PLATE XVIII

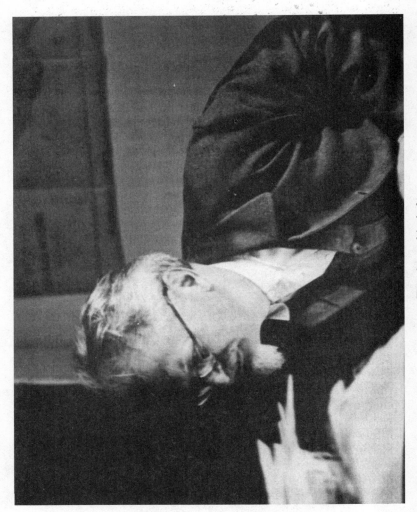

Trotsky at his desk

signed himself 'your old faithful dog'. 'How I love you, Nata, my only one, my eternal one, my faithful one, my love, my *victim.* . . .' 'Ah, if only I could still bring a little joy into your life. As I am writing this, after every two or three lines, I get up, walk about my room, and weep with tears of self-reproach and of gratitude to you; and I weep over old age that has caught us by surprise.' Again and again the note of self-pity, which no stranger and no member of his household could ever detect in him, breaks through in these letters. '. . . I am still living with our yesterdays, with our pangs and memories, and with the torments of my suffering.' Then his resilience and even joy of life come back: 'All will be well, Nata, all will be well—only you must recover and get stronger.' Once he relates to her somewhat teasingly how he 'charmed' a group of men, women, and children—'especially the women'—who had visited him in the mountains. His vitality surges up and he feels a sexual craving for Natalya. He relates to her that he had just re-read the passage in Tolstoy's memoirs where Tolstoy describes how at the age of seventy he would come back from his riding full of desire and lust for his wife—he, Trotsky, at fifty-eight, was returning in the same mood from his strenuous escapades on horseback. In his craving for her he breaks into the slang of sex, and then feels 'abashed at putting such words on paper for the first time in my life' and 'behaving just like a young cadet officer'. And as if to prove the *nihil humanum* . . ., he indulges in an odd marital recrimination. He rakes up a love affair Natalya was supposed to have had as far back as 1918; and he pleads that as he had never made her the slightest reproach and had never even mentioned that affair, she should not be too severe on him, who had not given her any ground for jealousy. In reply she explains the 'affair' of 1918. This was just after she had been appointed Director of the Museums Department in the Commissariat of Education; she did not quite know how to organize her work; and one of her assistants, a comrade who was admittedly 'infatuated' with her, helped her. She was grateful and treated him with sympathy; without, however, reciprocating his feelings or allowing him any intimacy. This gently comic recrimination, in which, after thirty-five years of common life, husband and wife found no other 'infidelity' with which to reproach each other, reveals in quite unexpected a manner the steadfastness of their love.[1]

In her letters Natalya appears reserved, somewhat embarrassed by his outbursts, and anxious to bring him back to himself from his introspective and effusive moods. To his harping on old age she invariably has this answer: 'One is old only when one has no prospect ahead' and when one no longer strives for anything—and this surely could not be true of him! 'Pull yourself together. Get back to work. If only you do this, your cure will have begun.' Before long she was again mistress of her emotions; and, though herself ill and tense, she was pre-occupied with the diseases, fevers, misfortunes, and strivings of every member of the family, and was calmer and stronger than any of them. He knew her fortitude and relied on it. In one of his letters to her there occur these telling words: '*You will still carry me on your shoulders, Nata, as you have carried me throughout our life.*'[2]

.   .   .   .

Meanwhile, in the Soviet Union hardly a day passed without its human hecatomb. Towards the end of May the G.P.U. announced that they had discovered a conspiracy at the head of which had stood Marshal Tukhachevsky, the deputy Commissar of Defence, the modernizer and actual Commander-in-Chief of the Red Army. Outstanding generals Yakir, Uborovich, Kork, Putna, Primakov and others, including Gamarnik, the chief Political Commissar of the armed forces, were charged with treason. With the exception of Gamarnik, who committed suicide, all were executed. Of the four marshals whose signatures appeared under the death sentence, Voroshilov, Budienny, Blucher, and Yegorov, the last two presently also faced the firing squad. All these men had risen to their positions of command while Trotsky was Commissar of War; but most of them had never belonged to the Opposition and none of them had been in contact with Trotsky since his banishment. Yet all were accused of being his and Hitler's accessories and

[1] Natalya's 'explanatory' letter is undated; judging from internal evidence, it was written around 15 July. On 19 July Trotsky answered with two letters. He also wrote in these days a special diary meant (as he repeatedly underlined) only for Natalya's eyes.

[2] Trotsky to Natalya on 18 July 1937. *The Archives*, Closed Section.

of working for the military defeat of the Soviet Union and its dismemberment. Their executions were the prelude to a purge which affected 25,000 officers and decapitated the Red Army on the eve of the Second World War. Twenty-five years later, after the formal rehabilitation of Tukhachevsky and most of the other generals, no light has yet been thrown on the background to this purge. According to various anti-Stalinist sources, Tukhachevsky, alarmed by the terror which was sapping the nation's morale and defences, had planned a *coup d'état* in order to overthrow Stalin and break the power of the G.P.U.; but he had done this without any connexion with Trotsky, let alone with Hitler or any foreign power. Trotsky did not believe that there had been any plot, but described Tukhachevsky's fall as a symptom of a conflict between Stalin and the officer corps, a conflict which might place a military *coup* 'on the order of the day'.[1]

By this time the G.P.U. were already rehearsing the 'trial of the twenty-one', casting Rykov, Bukharin, Tomsky, Rakovsky, Krestinsky, and Yagoda, for the main roles. (Of all these, Tomsky alone, by committing suicide, escaped the humiliation of a public trial and confession.) Even before the curtain rose on this spectacle, the terror struck at the Stalinist faction too. Rudzutak, Mezhlauk, Kossior, Chubar, Postyshev, Yenukidze, Okuzhava, Elyava, Chervyakov, and others, members of the Politbureau, party secretaries of Moscow, of the Ukraine, Byelorussia, and Georgia, trade union leaders, heads of the State Planning Commission and of the Supreme Council of the National Economy, nearly all of them Stalinists of long standing, were branded as traitors and foreign spies, and executed. Ordjonikidze, who had been devoted to Stalin for more than thirty years but became troubled in his conscience and began to oppose him, died in mysterious circumstances, or, as some believed, was driven to commit suicide. If the Trotskyists, Zinovievists, and Bukharinists were disgraced publicly, these Stalinists were destroyed secretly without open trials. The havoc which Stalin's rage wrought among them was hidden in obscurity. The terror spread beyond the Bolshevik party and caught many German, Polish, Hungarian, Italian, and Balkan communists who had lived in the Soviet Union as

[1] *B.O.*, nos. 56–57, 1937.

refugees from prisons and concentration camps in their own countries. Then the 'drive against Trotskyism' was carried into foreign lands. In Spain, the G.P.U. established themselves early in the civil war and launched an attack on the P.O.U.M. Andres Nin, the leader of the P.O.U.M., had his differences with Trotsky, who criticized him for his participation in the loyalist government of Catalonia and for adopting a 'timid and semi-Menshevik' attitude in the revolution. Even so, Nin's policy was far too radical and independent for the Stalinism of the Popular Front period; and so he and his party were denigrated as Franco's 'fifth column'; in the end he was kidnapped and assassinated. Whoever dared to protest, exposed himself to G.P.U. vengeance. The witch hunts, the assassinations, and the cynicism with which Stalin used the Spanish revolution demoralized the Republican camp and prepared its defeat. And as if in mockery, Stalin sent none other than Antonov-Ovseenko, the ex-Trotskyist and hero of 1917, to preside over the purge in Catalonia, the stronghold of the P.O.U.M.; then, after Antonov had done his job, he denounced him too as a wrecker and spy and ordered his execution.

In Moscow no one was safe now, not even the inquisitors and the hangmen. After Yagoda's arrest, the G.P.U. and all secret services were purged. Their agents in Europe were lured back to face the usual accusations. As a rule, these agents knew or guessed what awaited them, but as if hypnotized they obeyed the summons—many preferred self-immolation to asylum in any capitalist country. It was therefore a startling event, when Ignaz Reiss, chief of a network of the Soviet secret service in Europe, resigned from his post in protest against the purges. When he made up his mind to do this, he had not even been summoned back to Moscow. Shaken by the purges, he approached Sneevliet, the Dutch Trotskyist parliamentarian (and through him Lyova), in order to warn Trotsky that Stalin had decided to 'liquidate Trotskyism' outside the Soviet Union by the same means he was using to destroy it inside. Reiss described the infernal sadism and blackmail, the long and horrible interrogations, through which the G.P.U. had obtained the confessions in the Moscow trials and the moral torture and confusion in which the old generation of Bolsheviks was meeting its doom; but he also depicted the young communists who refused to submit and still filled prison yards and execution places with the cry: 'Long live Trotsky!'[1]

On 18 July, Reiss addressed a message from Paris to the Central Committee in Moscow announcing his break with Stalinism and 'adherence to the Fourth International'. 'The day is not far', he stated, 'when international socialism will sit in judgement over all the crimes committed in the last ten years. Nothing will be forgotten, nothing forgiven. . . . The "leader of genius, Father of the peoples, Sun of Socialism" will have to give account for all his deeds.' 'I am returning to you the Order of the Red Banner awarded to me in 1928. To wear it . . . would be beneath my dignity.'[2]

Six weeks later, on 4 September, Reiss was found dead, his body bullet-ridden, on a Swiss road near Lausanne. The G.P.U. had known about his decision even before he handed his letter of resignation to an official of the Soviet Embassy in Paris. Knowing the disgust which the purges had aroused even among his former colleagues in the secret service, he had hoped to persuade some of them to follow his example. With this purpose in mind he had arranged to meet in Lausanne Gertrud Schildbach, a Soviet agent resident in Italy, who had been a friend of his for close on twenty years. They met; she pretended sympathy; and after their first talk, she lured him to another meeting on the outskirts of Lausanne. There the G.P.U. had laid a trap for him.

The Swiss and French police soon brought to light some of the circumstances. Using clues found in an abandoned blood-stained car and in luggage left in hotels, they established the identity of the assassins. These, it turned out, had been members of the Society for the Repatriation of Russian Émigrés in Paris, a society sponsored by the Soviet Embassy.

The police ascertained that the gang which had killed Reiss had long kept a watch on Lyova also. A woman in whose name the blood-stained car was hired, had been detailed to shadow him. (He recalled that a year earlier she had followed him to the south of France, where he had gone for a short rest, had installed herself in his *pension* and had occasionally

---

[1] '*Zapiski Ignatya Reissa*', *B.O.*, nos. 60–61, December 1937.
[2] I. Reiss, '*Pismo v Ts.K. V.K.P.*' in *B.O.*, nos. 58–59, September-October 1937.

urged him with strange insistence to go out with her on sailing trips.) Further investigation disclosed that the same gang had laid a trap for Lyova in Mulhouse, near the Swiss border, in January 1937, when he was planning to go there in order to discuss with a Swiss lawyer a lawsuit against Swiss Stalinists. He avoided the trap because ill-health prevented him from making the journey; but the gang had gone on shadowing him throughout the first half of the year and he sensed it. In July and August he was puzzled to notice that the watch on him had almost ceased—evidently his pursuers were then busy keeping track of Reiss. Now they could be expected to return to their old hunt.[1]

Lyova was startled to learn from the interrogation how quickly and accurately the G.P.U. agents were as a rule informed about all his plans and moves. By whom? And who had informed them about Reiss's intentions? Some Trotsky-ists already wondered whether an *agent provocateur* was not to be found among Lyova's closest friends; and suspicion turned on Étienne (who had quite recently worked for the Society for the Repatriation of Russian Émigrés). Sneevliet's distrust of Étienne was so strong that after Reiss had approached him, he at first refused to put him in touch with the Trotskyist centre in Paris, fearing that this would be dangerous.[2] Lyova, however, refused to countenance any suspicion of his 'best and most reliable comrade'.

With the feeling that a mysterious noose was tightening around his neck, Lyova wrote Reiss's obituary for the *Bulletin*.[3] 'The "Father of the Peoples" and his Yezhovs know all too well how many potential Reisses there are around. . . . Stalin's designs will be defeated. . . . No one can bring history to a halt with a gun. Stalinism is doomed; it is rotting and dis-integrating before our eyes. The day is near when its stinking corpse will be thrown into the sewers of history.' Yet Reiss's fate deterred potential imitators. In the next few weeks only two of these came forward: Walter Krivitsky, another senior agent of the secret service, and Alexander Barmin, Soviet

---

[1] See Lyova's cable to Coyoacan of 16 September and his letters to Trotsky of 4 and 12 October 1937. *The Archives*, Closed Section. See also N. Markin's (Lyova's pen-name) account of the assassination in *B.O.*, nos. 58–59.

[2] In addition to Lyova's letters quoted above see his letter of 7 August 1937.

[3] *B.O.*, nos. 58–59.

chargé d'affaires in Athens. They too, having broken with their government, sought contact with Trotsky, whose adherents they had never been, because, as Krivitsky put it, Trotsky was 'surrounded by an aureole' even in the eyes of the G.P.U. men assigned to the struggle against Trotskyism.[1] These were strange converts. Krivitsky feared that Trotsky and his adherents would distrust and despise him as one who had spent so many years in Stalin's service. He was therefore anxious to justify his past at the very moment he was breaking with it. Reiss's widow accused him of complicity in the assassination of her husband. He bowed his head and confessed that he was not blameless.[2] He was eager to wipe out his guilt by revealing the truth about the purges; yet he was also anxious to guard the many secrets in his possession which had a bearing on Soviet military security. Lyova listened to his tortured confidences with some distaste. But he considered it his duty to transmit the information to his father and also to help, comfort, and as far as possible protect any Soviet citizen who broke with Stalinism. Trotsky, on his part, urged Krivitsky and Barmin, for their own safety and for the sake of political clarity, to come out against Stalin unequivocally and in broad daylight; he was uneasy about their contortions and impatient with Lyova's indulgence. This led to renewed altercations between father and son.[3]

Meanwhile, the presence of an *agent provocateur* in Lyova's circle caused more and more suspicion and confusion. Krivitsky had confirmed Reiss's warnings about the forthcoming assassinations of Trotskyists and said that the G.P.U. had their 'eyes and ears' inside the Trotskyist centre in Paris. He was, however, unable to identify the *agent provocateur*, and he cast a suspicion on Victor Serge, of all people. The G.P.U., he said, would not have released Serge and allowed him to leave the Soviet Union unless they were sure that he would spy for them on the Trotskyists. No one was, of course, less suited to act such a part than Serge. He was one of Trotsky's early adherents, a gifted and generous, though politically

[1] *B.O.*, nos. 60–61, December 1937.

[2] Lyova to Trotsky on 19 November 1937 and Trotsky to Lyova on 22 January 1938. *The Archives*, Closed Section.

[3] See Trotsky, '*Tragicheskii Urok*', *B.O.* ibid.; and Lyova's letters of 16 and 19 November and 17 December 1937.

ingenuous, man of letters. The worst that might be said of him was that he had a foible for vainglorious chatter and that this was a grave fault in a member of an organization which had to guard its secrets from the G.P.U. In any case suspicion began to cling indiscriminately to anyone, even to Lyova himself, while the actual *agent provocateur* went on collecting and reading Trotsky's mail, shared all of Lyova's secrets, and used his wiles to keep his own reputation clear by casting distrust upon others.[1]

The French police, continuing to investigate the Reiss case, discovered that one of the gang of assassins had applied for a Mexican visa and had supplied himself with detailed plans of Mexico City. Lyova at once conveyed the warning to Coyoacan. The police also took a grave view of the danger to Lyova's life and assigned a special guard to him.[2] One of his comrades —almost certainly Klement ('Adolf')—took Lyova's plight so much to heart that he wrote to Trotsky and Natalya begging them to ask Lyova to leave France at once and join them in Mexico. Lyova, he warned them, was ill, nearly exhausted, exposed to constant danger, yet convinced that he was 'irreplaceable' in Paris and that he must 'remain at his post'. This was not so, however, for his comrades could replace him; and if he were to stay on in Paris, he would be 'quite helpless against the G.P.U.' At the very least his parents should ask him to come over to Mexico for a time, to rest and convalesce there. 'He is able, brave, and energetic; and we must save him.'[3]

This touching solicitude did not have the effect it should have had. Trotsky was well aware, of course, that Lyova's life was in jeopardy. He had urged him unceasingly to be prudent and avoid any contact with people 'on whom the G.P.U. might have a hold', especially with nostalgic Russian émigrés. Just before the Reiss affair he had written: 'If an attempt is made on your life or mine, Stalin will be blamed, but he has nothing to lose, in honour anyhow.' Yet he discouraged the idea of Lyova's move from France. When Lyova insisted that he was 'irreplaceable in Paris' and assured him that to protect himself

---

[1] In addition to Lyova's letters just referred to, Étienne's own correspondence with Trotsky (*The Archives*, Closed Section) reveals all these details.

[2] Lyova's letters to Trotsky of 1 and 5 November 1937.

[3] The letter, written in German and dated 5 November 1937, is signed only with the initial A. (which probably stands for Adolf). *The Archives*, Closed Section.

he was assuming an incognito (as Trotsky had done at Bar-bizon), Trotsky wrote back that Lyova would gain nothing by leaving France: the United States was not likely to admit him and Mexico would offer him even less security than France. He did not wish his son to shut himself up in the Coyoacan 'semi-prison'; and the discords between father and son perhaps made both of them reluctant to contemplate reunion. Trotsky's final letter about this ended with these spare and tense sentences: '*Voilà, mon petit,* this is what I can tell you. It isn't much. But . . . it's all. . . . You ought to keep now whatever you can cash from the publishers. You will need it all. *Je t'embrasse. Ton Vieux.*'[1] There was in this letter (of which Trotsky was to think with bitter self-reproach a few months later) something of the message sent out to a fighter holding out in a doomed forward position beyond all succour. Yet Trotsky had some ground for thinking that Mexico would offer Lyova even less security than France. Many G.P.U. agents, often disguised as refugees from Spain, had just installed themselves in Mexico; and the clamour for Trotsky's expulsion was growing more and more strident. Before the turn of the year the walls of Mexico City were covered with posters accusing him of conspiring with reactionary generals to overthrow President Cardenas and to establish a fascist dictatorship in Mexico. There was no saying whither the vilification might lead.

The gloom of these months was only momentarily relieved in September, when the Dewey Commission concluded the counter-trial and pronounced the verdict. This stated pointedly: 'On the basis of all evidence . . . we find that the [Moscow] trials of August 1936 and January 1937 were frame-ups . . . we find Leon Trotsky and Leon Sedov not guilty.'[2] Trotsky received this verdict with joy. Yet its effect was small, if not negligible. Dewey's voice commanded some attention in the United States; but it was ignored in Europe, where opinion was preoccupied with the critical events of the year, the last year before Munich, and with the vicissitudes of the French Popular Front and the Spanish Civil War. Trotsky was again

[1] Letter of 18 November 1937, ibid.
[2] *Not Guilty!* (Report of the Commission of Inquiry into the Charges made against Leon Trotsky in the Moscow Trials). See also Trotsky's letter to Lyova of 21 January 1938.

disappointed; and when the *Bulletin* which was to carry the verdict was slow in appearing, he was so irritated that he chided Lyova for 'this crime' and 'political blindness'. 'I am utterly dissatisfied', he wrote to him on 21 January 1938, 'with the way the *Bulletin* is conducted and I must pose anew the question of its transfer to New York.'

By this time Lyova's strength had ebbed away. He had lived, as Serge puts it, 'an infernal life'. He endured poverty and personal frustrations more easily than blows to his faith and pride. To quote Serge again: 'More than once, lingering until dawn in the streets of Montparnasse, we tried together to unravel the tangle of the Moscow trials. Every now and then, stopping under a street lamp, one of us would exclaim: "We are in a labyrinth of sheer madness!" '[1] Overworked, penniless, and anxious about his father, Lyova lived permanently in this labyrinth. He went on echoing his father's arguments, denunciations, and hopes. But with each of the trials something snapped in him. His brightest memories of childhood and adolescence had been bound up with the men in the dock: Kamenev was his uncle; Bukharin almost an affectionate play-mate; Rakovsky, Smirnóv, Muralov, and so many others— elder friends and comrades, all ardently admired for their revolutionary virtues and courage. He brooded over their degradation and could not reconcile himself to it. How had it been possible to break every one of them and make them crawl through so much mud and blood? Would at least one of them not stand up in the dock, abjure his confession, and tear in shreds all the false and terrible accusations? In vain Lyova waited for this to happen. He was shocked and pained when Lenin's widow was reported to have come out in support of the trials. For the *n*th time he repeated that the Stalinist bureau-cracy, aspiring to become a new possessing class, had finally betrayed the revolution. But even this interpretation failed to account for all the blood and fury. Yes, this was the laby-rinth of sheer madness—would even his father's clear-sighted genius be able to find the way out?

Sickness of heart, despair, fever, insomnia. Reluctant to leave his 'post', he delayed an operation for appendicitis, despite recurrent sharp attacks. He ate little, was unnerved,

---

[1] Serge, *Mémoires d'un Révolutionnaire*, p. 375.

and moved about droopingly. Yet in the first days of February he at last brought out the *Bulletin* with the verdict of the Dewey Commission; he joyfully reported this to Coyoacan, enclosing the proofs; and outlined his plans for further work, without giving any hint about his health. This was the last letter he wrote to his parents.

On 8 February he was still working, but ate nothing the whole day and spent much time with Étienne. In the evening he had another attack, the worst of all. He could not delay the operation any longer; and he wrote a letter, which he sealed and handed to his wife, telling her to open it only if some 'accident' happened to him. He talked to Étienne again, and wished to see no one else. They agreed that he must not enter a French hospital and register under his own name; for, if he did, the G.P.U. would easily discover his whereabouts. He was to go to a small private clinic run by some Russian émigré doctors; he was to present himself as Monsieur Martin, a French engineer; and he was to speak only French. No French comrade, however, was to know where he was or to visit him. Having agreed on all this, Étienne ordered the ambulance.[1]

Even on the face of it this was an incredibly absurd arrangement. Russian émigrés were the last people among whom Lyova could hope to pass for a Frenchman. He was all too likely to lapse into his native tongue in fever or under an anaesthetic. It was preposterous that in the whole of Paris the only hospital or clinic found for him should be one staffed by the very people whom, since Reiss's assassination, he had avoided like the plague. Yet he agreed at once to go, although, when his wife and Étienne took him there, he was neither delirious nor unconscious. Evidently, his critical sense and instinct of self-preservation were blunted.

He was operated on that same evening. In the next few days he seemed to recover well and rapidly. Apart from his wife, only Étienne came to see him. The visits cheered him up: they talked about politics and matters of organization; and he invariably begged Étienne to come back as soon as possible. When some French Trotskyists wished to see him, Étienne

---

[1] See depositions of Madame Estrine, Elsa Reiss, Rous, Jeanne Martin, and of Étienne himself made during the police investigation; also the Report of the Police Prefecture in *The Archives*, Closed Section.

told them, with the appropriate air of mystery, that they could not do so and that the address must be kept secret even from them if it was to remain a secret to the G.P.U. When one of the French comrades was startled by this excess of caution, Étienne promised to talk the matter over with Lyova; but no one was admitted to the patient's bedside. Four days passed. Then, all of a sudden, the patient suffered a grave relapse. He was seized by attacks of pain and lost consciousness. On the night of 13 February he was seen wandering half-naked and delirious through corridors and wards, which for some reason were unattended and unguarded. He was raving in Russian. Next morning his surgeon was so surprised by his state that he asked Jeanne whether her husband might not have attempted to take his own life—had he not been recently in a suicidal mood? Jeanne denied this, burst into tears, and said that the G.P.U. must have poisoned him. Another operation was carried out urgently, but it brought no improvement. The patient suffered terrible agony, and the doctors tried to save him by repeated blood transfusions. It was in vain. On 16 February 1938 he died at the age of thirty-two.

Did he, as his widow claimed, die at the hands of the G.P.U.? Much of the circumstantial evidence suggests that this was the case. In the Moscow trials he had been branded as his father's most active assistant, indeed, as the chief of staff of the Trotskyist-Zinovievist conspiracy. 'The youngster is working well; without him the Old Man would have found the going much harder', it had often been said at G.P.U. headquarters in Moscow, according to Reiss's and Krivitsky's testimony. It was in the G.P.U.'s interest to deprive Trotsky of his help, especially as this was sure to gratify Stalin's vengefulness. The G.P.U. had a most reliable informer and agent at his side who had brought him to the spot where he was to meet his death. The G.P.U. had every reason to hope that once Lyova was out of the way, their agent would take his place at the Russian 'section' of the Trotskyist organization and establish direct contact with Trotsky. At the clinic not only doctors and nurses but even cooks and porters were Russian émigrés, some of them members of the Repatriation Society. Nothing would have been easier for the G.P.U. than to find an agent among them, who would somehow administer poison to the patient. With so many murders on their conscience, would the G.P.U. have scrupled over this one?

But there is no certainty. An inquest held at Jeanne's demand yielded no proof of foul play. Police and doctors emphatically denied poisoning or any other attempt on Lyova's life; they attributed his death to a post-operational complication ('intestinal occlusion'), heart failure, and low powers of resistance. An eminent doctor who was also a friend of the Trotsky family accepted their opinion. On the other hand, Trotsky and his daughter-in-law asked a number of pertinent questions which remained unclarified. Was it by sheer accident that Lyova found himself in the Russian clinic? (Trotsky did not know that no sooner had Étienne called the ambulance than he informed the G.P.U. as Étienne himself has since confessed.) The staff of the clinic maintained that they had been unaware of Lyova's identity and nationality. But eye-witnesses maintain that they had heard him raving and even arguing about politics in Russian. Why had Lyova's surgeon been inclined to attribute the deterioration of his state to a suicidal attempt rather than to any natural cause? According to Lyova's widow, that surgeon lapsed into terrified silence as soon as the scandal blew up; and he took cover behind his duty to guard his professional secrets. It was in vain that Jeanne tried to bring these obscure circumstances to the notice of the examining magistrate; and that Trotsky pointed out that the routine inquest took no acount of the G.P.U.'s 'perfected and recondite' techniques of assassination. Did the French police, as Trotsky surmised, hush up the matter in order to cover their own inefficiency? Or were there, within the Popular Front, powerful political influences at work to prevent a thorough investigation? Nothing was left for the family but to demand a new inquest.[1]

. . . .

When the news reached Mexico, Trotsky was away from Coyoacan. A few days earlier Rivera had noticed unknown

[1] The depositions, eye-witness accounts, doctors' testimonials, and Trotsky's correspondence are quoted partly from *The Archives*, Closed Section, and partly from Lev Sedov's Papers which Jeanne Martin has transmitted to me through the courtesy of Pierre Frank.

people prowling around the Blue House and spying on its inhabitants from an observation post in the neighbourhood. He was alarmed; and he arranged that Trotsky should move out and stay for some time with Antonio Hidalgo, an old revolutionary and Rivera's friend, at Chapultepec Park. There, on 16 February, Trotsky was working on his essay, *Their Morals and Ours*, when evening papers announced Lyova's death. Rivera, when he read the news, telephoned to Paris hoping for a denial, and then went to Trotsky at Chapultepec Park. Trotsky refused to believe it, exploded with anger, and showed the door to Rivera; but then went back with him to Coyoacan to break the news to Natalya. 'I was just . . . sorting out old pictures, photographs of our children', she writes. 'The bell rang, and I was surprised to see Leon Davidovich coming in. I went out to meet him. He entered, his head bowed as I had never seen it, his face ash-grey and his whole look suddenly age-worn. "What has happened?" I asked in alarm. "Are you ill?" He answered in a low voice: "Lyova is ill. Our little Lyova . . .".'[1]

For many days he and Natalya remained closed in his room, petrified with pain, and unable to see secretaries, receive friends, or answer condolences. 'None spake a word unto him; for they saw that his grief was very great.' When after eight days he emerged, his eyes were swollen, his beard overgrown, and he could not bring out his voice. Several weeks later he wrote to Jeanne: 'Natalya . . . is not yet capable of answering you. She is reading and re-reading your letters and weeping, weeping. When I manage to free myself from work . . . I weep with her.'[2] Mingled with his grief was compunction for the harsh rebukes he had not spared his son this last year and the advice he had given him to stay on in Paris. This was the third time he was mourning a child; and each time there was greater remorse in the mourning. After Nina's death, in 1928, he reproached himself for not having done enough to comfort her and not even having written to her in her last weeks. Zina was estranged from him when she killed herself; and now Lyova had met his doom at the post where he had urged

---

[1] Natalya Sedova, 'Father and Son' in *Fourth International* (August 1941) and in *Vie et Mort de Leon Trotsky*.

[2] Trotsky to Jeanne Martin on 10 March 1938, *The Archives*, Closed Section.

him to hold out. With none of his children had he shared so much of his life and struggle as with Lyova; and no other loss had left him so desolate.

In these days of mourning he wrote Lyova's obituary, a threnody unique in world literature.[1] 'Now as together with Lev Sedov's mother I write these lines . . . we cannot yet believe it. Not only because he was our son, faithful, devoted, and loving . . . but because like no one else he had entered our life and grown into it with all his roots. . . .'

The old generation with whom . . . we once embarked upon the road of revolution . . . has been swept off the stage. What Tsarist deportations, prisons, and katorga, what the privations of life in exile, what civil war, and what illness had not done, Stalin, the worst scourge of the revolution, has accomplished in these last few years. . . . The better part of the middle generation, those . . . whom the year 1917 awakened and who received their training in twenty-four armies on the revolutionary front, have also been exterminated. The best part of the young generation, Lyova's contemporaries, . . . has also been trampled down and crushed. . . . In these years of exile we have made many new friends, some of whom have become . . . like members of our family. But we first met all of them . . . when we were already approaching old age. Lyova alone knew us when we were young; he participated in our life from the moment he acquired self-awareness. Remaining young, he became almost like our contemporary. . . .

Simply and tenderly he recollected Lyova's short life, depicting the child, scuffling with his father's jailers, bringing food parcels and books to the prison, making friends with revolutionary sailors, and hiding under a bench in the Soviet Government's conference hall so as to see 'how Lenin directed the revolution'. He portrayed the adolescent, who during the 'great and hungry years' of civil war would bring home, in the sleeves of a tattered jacket, a fresh roll given him by baker's apprentices, among whom he worked as a political agitator; and who, detesting bureaucratic privilege, refused to travel with his father by motor car and left the parental home in the Kremlin for a proletarian students' hostel and, joining voluntary workers' teams, swept the snow off Moscow's

[1] '*Lev Sedov, Syn, Drug, Borets*' In *B.O.*, no. 64, March 1938. (English pamphlet edition: *Leon Sedoff, Son, Friend, Fighter.*)

streets, unloaded bread and timber from trains, repaired locomotives, and 'liquidated' illiteracy. He recalled the young man, the oppositionist, who 'without a moment's hesitation' left his wife and child to go with his parents into banishment; who, at Alma Ata, where they lived surrounded by the G.P.U., assured his father's contact with the outside world, and went out, sometimes in the dead of night, in rain or snow storm, to meet a comrade clandestinely in woods outside the town, in a crowded bazaar, in a library, or even in a public bath. 'Each time he would return animated and happy, with a bellicose little fire in his eyes and with a treasured trophy under his coat.' 'How well he understood people—he knew many more Oppositionists than I did . . . his revolutionary instinct allowed him, without hesitation, to tell the genuine from the false. . . . His mother's eyes—and she knew the son better than I did— shone with pride.'

Here the father's feelings of remorse found their outlet. He mentioned his exacting demands on Lyova and explained these apologetically by his, Trotsky's, 'pedantic habits of work' and his inclination to demand the utmost from those who were closest to him—and who had been closer than Lyova? It might appear that 'our relationship was marked by a certain severity and estrangement. But underneath there . . . lived a deep, a burning mutual attachment, springing from something im- measurably greater than blood kinship—from commonly held views, from shared sympathies and hates, from joys and sufferings experienced together, and from great hopes cherished in common.' Some saw Lyova as merely 'a great father's little son'. But they were mistaken as were those who for a long time thought in this way of Karl Liebknecht; only circumstances had not allowed Lyova to rise to his full stature. Here comes a perhaps over-generous acknowledgement of Lyova's share in his father's literary work: 'On almost all my books written since the year 1929 his name should in justice have figured next to mine.' With what relief and joy his parents, in their Norwegian internment, had received a copy of Lyova's *Livre Rouge*, 'the first crushing retort to the slanderers in the Kremlin'. How right the G.P.U. men were who had said that 'without the youngster the old man would have found the going much harder'—and how much harder it would be now!

He again contemplated the ordeals which this 'very sensitive and delicate being' had had to endure: the endless hail of lies and calumnies; the long series of desertions and surrenders of former friends and comrades; Zina's suicide; and finally the trials which 'deeply shook his moral organism'. Whatever the truth about the direct cause of Lyova's death, whether he died exhausted by these ordeals or whether the G.P.U. had poisoned him, in either case 'it was *they* [and their master] that were guilty of his death'.

The great lament ended on the note on which it had begun:

> His mother, who was closer to him than anyone in the world, and I, as we are living through these terrible hours, recall his image feature by feature; we refuse to believe that he is no more and we weep because it is impossible not to believe. . . . He was part of us, our young part. . . . Together with our boy has died everything that still remained young in us. . . . Your mother and I never thought, never expected, that fate would lay this task on us . . . that we should have to write your obituary. . . . But we have not been able to save you.

It was almost certain by now that Sergei had also perished, although there was no official information about this—and none was to be available even twenty-five years later. From a political prisoner, however, who early in 1937 shared a cell with him in Moscow's Butyrki we have this account:[1] for several months in 1936 the G.P.U. pressed Sergei to renounce publicly his father and all his father stood for. Sergei refused, was sentenced to five years' labour in a concentration camp, and was deported to Vorkuta. There towards the end of the year the Trotskyists were being assembled from many other camps. It was there, behind the barbed wire, that Sergei first came into close contact with them; and although he refused to consider himself a Trotskyist even now, he spoke with deep gratitude and respect of his father's adherents, especially those who had held out without any surrender for nearly ten years. He took part in a hunger strike which they proclaimed and which lasted more than three months; and he was near death.[2]

[1] This account of Sergei's behaviour in prison comes from Mr. Joseph Berger, who, having helped to found the Communist Party of Palestine and having served on the Middle Eastern division of the Comintern, spent twenty-three years in Stalin's prisons and concentration camps. He was freed and rehabilitated in 1956.

[2] See later, p. 416.

CI

At the beginning of 1937 he was brought back to Moscow for yet another interrogation (it was then that the prisoner from whom we draw our account met him). He did not hope to be freed or to get any relief, for he was convinced that all his father's followers—and he with them—would be exterminated. Yet he behaved with stoic equanimity, drawing strength from his intellectual and moral resources. 'Discussing the G.P.U.'s methods of interrogation, he expressed the opinion that any educated man . . . should be equal to them; he pointed out that a century earlier Balzac had described all these tricks and techniques very accurately and that they were still almost exactly the same. . . . He faced the future with complete calm and would under no circumstances make any statement that would implicate in the slightest degree either himself or anyone else.' He evidently stuck it out to the end, for if he had not—if the G.P.U. had succeeded in wresting any confession from him —they would have broadcast the fact all over the world. He guessed that his parents must fear that he, their 'non-political' son, might lack the conviction and courage necessary to endure his lot; and 'he regretted most of all that no one would ever be able to tell them, especially his mother, about the change that had occurred in him, for he did not believe that anyone of all those whom he had met since his imprisonment would live to tell the story'. The author of this account soon lost sight of Sergei, but heard of his execution from other prisoners. Much later, in 1939, a message of dubious trustworthiness, which reached Trotsky through an American journalist, claimed that Sergei had still been alive late in 1938; but after that nothing more was heard about him.[1]

. . . .

Of Trotsky's offspring, only Seva, Zina's son who was now twelve years old, was left alive outside the U.S.S.R. Nothing was or is known of what happened to Trotsky's other grandchildren. Seva had been brought up by Lyova and Jeanne, who, herself childless, had been a mother to him and had become passionately and obsessively attached to him. In his first letter after Lyova's death, Trotsky invited her to come with the child to Mexico. 'I love you greatly, Jeanne', he wrote,

[1] *The Archives*, Closed Section.

'and for Natalya you are not only . . . a daughter loved tenderly and discreetly as only Natalya can love, but also part of Lyova, of what is left of his most intimate life. . . .' They both wished nothing more than that she and Seva should live with them in Mexico. But if this was not Jeanne's wish, let her at least visit them; 'and if you think that it would be too difficult for you now to separate yourself from Seva, we shall understand your feelings.'[1]

Here, however, the sorrowful tale shades off into the grotesque, and becomes entangled in the squabbles of the Trotskyist sects in Paris. Lyova and Jeanne had belonged to two different groups, he to the 'orthodox Trotskyists', she to the Molinier set. It says much for his tact and dignity that in the letter he left in lieu of a will, he declared that despite this difference (and despite, one may add, their unhappy marital life) he held her in the highest esteem and had unreserved confidence in her. Yet the furious competition of the rival sects did not spare even Lyova's dead body; it fastened on the little orphan; and it involved Trotsky himself in a preposterous situation.[2] Jeanne, pressing desperately for a new inquest on Lyova, authorized a lawyer who was a member of the Molinier set to represent the family interest vis-à-vis the French magistrates and police. The 'orthodox Trotskyists' (and Gérard Rosenthal, who was Trotsky's lawyer) denied Jeanne the right to do this and maintained that Lyova's parents alone were entitled to speak for the family. The conflicting claims only made it easier for the police and the magistrates to ignore the demand for the inquest.[3]

Another rumpus broke out over Trotsky's archives. Since Lyova's death these had been in Jeanne's possession and so, indirectly, in the hands of the Molinier group. Trotsky asked that the archives be returned to him through one of his 'orthodox' French followers. Jeanne refused to hand them over. The relations between her and Lyova's parents cooled off abruptly and even grew hostile. Trotsky eventually recovered the archives, but not before he sent an American follower of his to Paris to collect them. Despite repeated urgings, Jeanne

[1] Trotsky to Jeanne, 10 March 1938. *The Archives*, Closed Section.
[2] Trotsky to Rosmer, Jeanne, Rous, and Camille (Klement) on 12 March.
[3] See Trotsky's correspondence with G. Rosenthal in *The Archives*, Closed Section.

refused to come to Mexico or to send the child there. She was neurotic; her mind was quite unsettled now; and she would not agree to part with her ward even temporarily. The rival factions kicked up a row over this too; and, much though Trotsky tried to conciliate his daughter-in-law, they rendered any agreement impossible. Whether because after the loss of all his children Trotsky was more than eager to recover his grandchild, the only one he could recover, or because he was afraid of leaving the orphan, as he put it, under the care of '*un ésprit très ombrageux et malheureusement déséquilibré*', or for both these reasons, he decided to go to law. An unseemly litigation followed, which dragged on for a year, providing grist for sensational newspapers and sectarian sheets.[1] In her despair at losing the child, Jeanne sought to invalidate Trotsky's claim by asserting that he had never legalized either his first or his second marriage; and Trotsky had to prove that this was not true. Even under this provocation he expressed (in a letter to the court) his understanding of Jeanne's emotional predicament; recognized her moral, though not her legal, right to the child; and renewed the invitation to her, offering to pay the cost of her journey to Mexico. He even declared himself willing to consider returning Seva to her, but not before he had had the chance to see him.[2] Twice the court adjudicated in Trotsky's favour and appointed trustees to ensure that the orphan was given back to the grandfather; but Jeanne refused to comply, took the boy away from Paris, and hid him. Only after a long search and a 'winter expedition' to the Vosges, did Marguerite Rosmer trace the child and wrest him from his aunt's hands. This was not the end yet, for Jeanne's friends made an attempt to abduct the child; and it was not until October 1939 that the Rosmers at last brought him to Coyoacan.

[1] Trotsky to the Rosmers on 19 September and to G. Rosenthal on 27 October 1938; Rosenthal to Trotsky, 7 October 1938. *Paris-Soir*, among other papers, reported the affair on the 26 March 1939; and Molinier's *Vérité* (no. 4, April 1939) devoted a special supplement to it under the title: '*Tous les moyens sont bons*', presenting Jeanne's case and attacking Trotsky for laying claims to the child.

[2] Trotsky's statement to M. Hamel, the official trustee, of 7 February 1939; reports of court proceedings, legal communications, and correspondence between Trotsky, his secretaries, and his attorney, especially letters of 22, 27, 29 March and 17 and 29 April 1939. *The Archives*, Closed Section. Also Trotsky's letter to the Rosmers of 26 May 1939.

In a pathetic letter Trotsky tried to explain to Seva why he insisted on his coming to Mexico. As he avoided making any derogatory remark about Jeanne, he could not give the child his main reason, and so the explanation was awkward and unconvincing:

Mon petit Seva . . . uncle Leon is no more, and we should keep in direct touch with each other, my dear boy. I do not know where your father is or whether he is still alive. In his last letter to me, written over four years ago, he asked insistently whether you had not forgotten the Russian language. Although your father is a very intelligent and educated man, he does not speak foreign languages. It would be a terrible blow to him if finding you one day he were unable to communicate with you. The same goes for your sister. You may imagine what a sad reunion this would be if you could not talk with your little sister in your native tongue. . . . You are a big boy now, and so I want to talk to you also about something else that is of great importance, the ideas that were and are common to your mother and father, to your Uncle Leon, and to me and Natalya. I greatly desire to explain to you personally the high value of these ideas and purposes, for the sake of which our family . . . has suffered and is suffering so much. I bear full responsibility for you, my grandson, before myself, before your father if he is alive, and before yourself.

And in words which were strangely stiff and out of place in a letter to a child, he concluded: 'That is why my decision about your journey is irrevocable.'[1]

. . . .

Meanwhile the G.P.U. continued to weave their intrigue. Étienne had no difficulty in taking Lyova's place in the Trotskyist organization in Paris: he now published the *Bulletin*, was Trotsky's most important correspondent in Europe, and kept in touch with new refugees from the Stalinist terror who sought contact with Trotsky. The 'Russian section' of the organization had only three or four members in Paris, of whom none was as well versed in Soviet affairs and as educated and industrious as Étienne. From Lyova's letters Trotsky knew that Lyova had regarded him as his most intimate and reliable friend; and the *agent provocateur* now did what he could to

[1] The letter dated 19 September 1938 is in *The Archives*, Closed Section.

confirm this opinion of himself. Playing on Trotsky's paternal grief and sensibilities, he sought to arouse Trotsky's distrust of people who were in his, Étienne's, way. Within a week of Lyova's death, he wrote to Trotsky with all due indignation that Sneevliet was spreading the 'slanderous rumour' that Lyova had been responsible for Reiss's death; and with seeming casualness he reminded Trotsky of Lyova's complete trust in him, Étienne, who had all the time held the key to Lyova's letter box and collected all his mail.[1] Trotsky, who had his political differences with Sneevliet, replied with an angry outburst against the 'slanderer'.[2] The *agent provocateur* was, of course, the model of an orthodox Trotskyist, never dissenting from the 'Old Man', yet never appearing as a contemptible yes-man either. Careful to give abundant yet not over-ostentatious proof of devotion, he inquired with touching concern about the Old Man's health and well-being, addressing, however, such questions not to Trotsky himself but to one of the secretaries. With Trotsky directly he discussed political questions and the contents of the *Bulletin*, which now appeared more regularly than it had done for a long time. He asked Trotsky for a commemorative article on Reiss, which, he said, he was anxious to publish on the anniversary of Reiss's death. He saw to it that the paper should come out with a proper tribute to Lyova, too, on his first anniversary. He gave Trotsky notice that the *Bulletin* was going to come out with an article, 'Trotsky's Life in Danger', exposing the activities of G.P.U. agents in Mexico. He supplied Trotsky with data and quotations drawn from files of old Russian newspapers and from other, not easily accessible, publications, data and quotations which Trotsky needed for his *Stalin*. In a word, he made himself indispensable, almost as indispensable as Lyova had been. And all the time he unobtrusively added fuel to the feud between the sects and the quarrel between Trotsky and Jeanne, until Trotsky refused to support Jeanne's application for a new official inquiry into the circumstances of Lyova's death. Étienne himself did what

---

[1] Étienne corresponded with Trotsky sometimes in his own name, sometimes on behalf of the 'International Secretariat', and sometimes as editor of the *Bulletin Oppozitsii*. See, e.g., letter of International Secretariat to Trotsky of 22 February 1938 (signed by Étienne and Paulsen).

[2] Trotsky to the International Secretariat, 12 March 1938. *The Archives*, Closed Section.

he could to obstruct the inquiry: presenting himself to the French police as 'Leon Sedov's closest friend', he dismissed any suspicion of foul play, saying that Lyova's death had been due to the feeble resistance of his constitution.[1]

The *agent provocateur* was also at the centre of the preparations which the Trotskyists were making for the 'foundation congress' of the Fourth International. In the very middle of the preparations, on 13 July 1938, Rudolf Klement, the German émigré who had been Trotsky's secretary at Barbizon and was the secretary of the would-be International, vanished mysteriously from his home in Paris. About a fortnight later Trotsky received a letter, ostensibly written and signed by Klement, but posted from New York, which denounced Trotsky's alliance with Hitler, collaboration with the Gestapo, &c. Having repeated the usual Stalinist accusations, the writer announced his break with Trotsky. (Several French Trotskyists received copies of this letter which had been posted at Perpignan.) The letter contained so many incongruities and blunders, which Klement could not possibly have committed, that Trotsky at once concluded that it was plain forgery or that Klement had written it under duress, while a G.P.U. man pointed a revolver at him. 'Let Klement, if he is still alive, come forward and state before the judiciary, the police, or any impartial commission everything he knows. One can foretell that the G.P.U. will in no case let him out of their hands.'[2] Shortly thereafter Klement's body, horribly mutilated, was found washed ashore by the waters of the Seine. The gang that had assassinated Reiss had evidently killed him too; and one of the killers had assumed in Klement's name the attitude of a 'disillusioned follower' breaking with Trotsky—two years later Trotsky's assassin was to adopt the same pose.

Why had the G.P.U. picked Klement? He had not been outstanding among the Trotskyists for any special ability;

---

[1] Étienne's deposition during the police interrogation quoted above; his letter to Trotsky of 6 June 1938; and Trotsky's·letter to 'Comrades Lola and Étienne', 17 February 1939. Van Heijenoort, Trotsky's secretary, wrote to Naville on 29 April 1938: 'J'ai reçu des lettres de divers amis de France (*Étienne en particulier*) s'inquiétant de la situation du Vieux et demandant des informations'. My italics. *The Archives*, Closed Section. See also *B.O.*, nos. 66–67, 68–69, and 70, 1938, and no. 74, 1939.

[2] *B.O.*, nos. 68–69, 1938.

but he had been a modest and selfless worker who kept his eyes wide open to what was going on in the organization. It was, we think, he who had urged Trotsky and Natalya to ask Lyova to leave France. Had he recently come into possession of some important G.P.U. secret? Had he been on the track of their *agent provocateur*, perhaps about to unmask him? This, Trotsky guessed, would plausibly explain why the G.P.U. pounced and why they killed him in so vindictive and cruel a manner.[1]

By this time Sneevliet's suspicion of Étienne had hardened into a certainty; and both he and Serge voiced it openly. The *agent provocateur* was so brazen as to ask Trotsky what to do about it. Trotsky replied that he should at once challenge his accusers to lay their charges before a competent commission: 'Comrade Étienne should take this step; and the sooner, the more categorically and firmly he does it the better.' Trotsky could give no other advice: in such cases it was customary and obligatory for a man who had come under suspicion to ask for an investigation and for a chance to clear his honour. But Trotsky himself did not believe the accusation.[2]

To make the strange tale stranger, another warning reached Trotsky within a month. It came from a senior officer of the G.P.U., now a refugee in the United States. The author of the warning was, however, so afraid of the G.P.U. that he refused to disclose his identity and pretended to be an old American Jew of Russian origin conveying the message to Trotsky from a relative of his, a G.P.U. officer who had fled to Japan. The correspondent begged Trotsky to beware of a dangerous stool-pigeon in Paris, who was called 'Mark'. He did not know 'Mark's' family name, but gave so detailed and accurate a description of Étienne's person, background, and relations with Lyova, that Trotsky could have no doubt to whom he was referring. The writer was amazed at the credulity and carelessness of the Trotskyists in Paris, whose suspicions had not been aroused even by the fact (which he claimed was well known) that 'Mark' had worked in the notorious Society for the Repatriation of Russian Émigrés;

---

[1] *B.O.*, nos. 68–69, 1938.

[2] Trotsky to Étienne on 2 December 1938—the letter was formally addressed to the editors of the *Bulletin*. *The Archives*, Closed Section. Referring to Sneevliet's accusations, Trotsky put 'accusations' in quotation marks.

and he assured Trotsky that if only they watched the stool-pigeon they would find that secretly he was still meeting officials of the Soviet Embassy. Whether 'Mark' was guilty of Lyova's death, the correspondent did not know; but he feared that 'what was on the agenda now' was Trotsky's assassination, which was to be carried out either by 'Mark' himself or by some Spaniard posing as a Trotskyist. This was a weighty warning. 'The main thing, Lev Davidovich', the correspondent urged, 'is that you should be on your guard. Distrust any man or woman whom this *agent provocateur* may send or recommend to you.'[1]

Trotsky did not leave the warning altogether unheeded. Through a note in a Trotskyist paper, he asked the correspondent to get in touch with his followers in New York. The correspondent, afraid of revealing himself to them, tried to speak to Trotsky over the telephone from New York, but failed to contact him. The apparent lack of response on the correspondent's part and the strange form of his warning made Trotsky doubt his trustworthiness. Nevertheless, a small commission was formed at Coyoacan to investigate the matter; but it found no substance in the charges against Étienne. Trotsky wondered whether the denunciation was not a G.P.U. hoax, designed to discredit the man who appeared to be the most efficient and devoted of his assistants, who spoke and wrote Russian, was thoroughly versed in Soviet affairs, and edited the *Bulletin*. All too many accusations had already been bandied about in the small Trotskyist circle in Paris anyhow; and if all of these were to be taken seriously, there would be no end to the chasing of *agents provocateurs*. He knew all too well what a curse stool-pigeons were in any organization; but he also knew that constant suspicion and witch-hunting could be even worse. He decided not to lend ear to any accusation unless it was unequivocally presented and substantiated. He preferred to take the gravest risks and to expose himself to

---

[1] Both my wife and I found the letter among Trotsky's papers (in the 'open' section of *The Archives*) early in 1950, and copied it *in extenso*. Since then Alexander Orlov, a former G.P.U. officer, has claimed authorship of this letter. (See his deposition in *Hearings* of the U.S. Senate Committee on the Judiciary, sub-committee dealing with the scope of Soviet activity in the U.S. Part 51, pp. 3423-9.) For Orlov's role in the G.P.U., especially during the purges in Spain, see Jesus Hernandez, *La Grande Trahison*, and Orlov's own *Stalin's Crimes*.

extreme danger rather than to infect and demoralize his followers with distrust and scares. And so the *agent provocateur* went on acting as his factotum in Paris until the outbreak of the war.[1]

. . . .

Within a fortnight of Lyova's death, Bukharin, Rykov, Rakovsky, Krestinsky, and Yagoda appeared in the dock in Moscow. It might have seemed that in the previous trials the macabre imagination of the stage producer had reached the limit. But those trials looked almost like essays in moderate realism compared with the new fantasmagoria. Once again Prosecutor and defendants denounced Trotsky as the chief of the conspiracy, which this time included the Bukharinists, who had been his deadly enemies. Lyova loomed as his father's accomplice even larger than in the earlier indictments. After a feeble attempt to deny the accusations, Krestinsky confessed that he had repeatedly conspired with Trotsky personally and Lyova in Berlin and various European resorts; that he had contacted Lyova with General von Seeckt, chief of the *Reichswehr*; and had paid out two million goldmarks, nearly a million dollars, and various other sums to finance the conspiracy. Trotsky and the defendants were now depicted as the agents not only of Hitler and the Mikado, but of British Military Intelligence as well, and even of the Polish *Deuxième Bureau*. To the familiar tales about attempts on the lives of Stalin, Voroshilov, and Kaganovich, and about railway catastrophes, colliery explosions, and mass poisonings of workers, were added stories about the assassination of Gorky, Menzhinsky, Kuibyshev, and even of Sverdlov, who had died in 1919— all these Trotsky had on his conscience. With each confession, the conspiracy not only grew in scope and swelled beyond the

[1] Mrs. Lilia Dallin (the 'comrade Lola' of the Russian Section of the International Secretariat in Paris in the late nineteen-thirties) testified in the U.S. that when she came to Coyoacan in the summer of 1939, Trotsky showed her the letter warning him against Étienne. 'I felt a bit uncomfortable because the details were very unpleasant. . . . I said: "That is certainly a dirty job of the N.K.V.D., who want to deprive you of your few collaborators . . ." and . . . he [Trotsky] had another letter from another unnamed correspondent telling him that a woman, meaning me, is coming to visit him and will poison him. So we both decided . . . that . . . it was a hoax of the N.K.V.D. . . . And the first thing I did [on returning to Paris] was to tell Étienne about it. . . . I trusted him'. Étienne had a 'hearty laugh' about the matter. Isaac Don Levine, *The Mind of an Assassin*, p. 60.

bounds of reason; it also extended back in time, to the very first weeks of the Soviet régime, and even to earlier periods. Like ghosts, Kamkov and Karelin, once leaders of the left Social Revolutionaries, came to the courtroom to testify that in 1918, when they staged their anti-Bolshevik insurrection, they had acted in secret accord with Bukharin, who was out to assassinate Lenin. Yagoda, who had for ten years been in charge of the persecution of the Trotskyists, had deported them *en masse*, had introduced torture in prisons and concentration camps, and had prepared the trial of Zinoviev and Kamenev, now claimed to have been all this time a mere tool in Trotsky's hands. Alongside former members of the Politbureau or the Central Committee and Ministers and Ambassadors, a group of distinguished doctors sat in the dock. One of them, Doctor Levin, a septuagenarian, had been Lenin's and Stalin's personal physician since the revolution; and he was charged with having, on Yagoda's orders, poisoned Gorky and Kuibyshev. For many hours in the course of several sessions the doctors related how they plied their poisonous trade within the walls of the Kremlin, describing all manner of sadistic procedures in which they had allegedly indulged.[1]

Trotsky compared this trial with the Rasputin affair, for the trial, he said, reeked with 'the same rot and decay of an autocracy'. Perhaps nothing shows more tellingly than this comparison how his mind boggled at the spectacle. The Rasputin affair had, of course, been a puny and almost innocuous incident, compared with any of these trials; and the trials can hardly be said to have hastened Stalin's downfall even though they were to cover his memory with shame and disgrace. Yet Trotsky found no more adequate precedent or parallel, because none existed. Stalin had in a sense surpassed all historical experience and imagination: he set a new scale to the terror and imparted to it a new dimension. As the trials proceeded, any rational reaction to them became more and more helpless. Trotsky went on exposing the absurdities of the case, elaborating methodically his alibi, and proving that neither he nor Lyova could have conspired with any of the defendants, let alone with General von Seeckt, at the places and the dates indicated.

[1] *Sudebnyi Otchet po Delu anti-Sovietskovo i Pravo-Trotskistskovo Bloka.*

In this criminal activity [he commented] Prime Ministers, Ministers, Generals, Marshals, and Ambassadors, appear invariably to have taken their orders from a single quarter—not from their official leader but from a banished man. A wink from Trotsky was enough for veterans of the revolution to become Hitler's and the Mikado's agents. On Trotsky's 'instructions', transmitted through the first and best Tass correspondent, the leaders of industry, agriculture, and transport were destroying the nation's productive resources and shattering its civilization. On an order from the 'enemy of the people', sent out from Norway or Mexico, railway-men wrecked military transports in the Far East and highly respectable doctors poisoned their patients in the Kremlin. This is the astounding picture . . . drawn by Vyshinsky. . . . But here a difficulty arises. In a totalitarian régime it is the apparatus [i.e. the party and state machine] that exercises the dictatorship. If my underlings have occupied all the crucial positions in the apparatus, how is it that Stalin is in the Kremlin and that I am in exile?[1]

He referred to the international setting and the consequences of the trials: Hitler's troops had just marched triumphantly into Austria and were getting ready for further conquests:

Is Stalin still chuckling behind the scenes? Has this unforeseen turn of events not yet taken his breath away? True, he is separated from the world by a wall of ignorance and of servility. True, he is accustomed to think that world opinion is nothing and the G.P.U. is everything. But the threatening and multiplying symptoms must be visible even to him. The working masses of the world are seized by acute anxiety. . . . Fascism is gaining victory after victory and finding its chief aid . . . in Stalinism. Terrible military perils knock at all the doors of the Soviet Union. And Stalin has chosen this moment to shatter the army and trample over the nation. . . . Even this Tiflis impostor . . . must find it harder to chuckle. An immense hatred is growing around him; a terrible resentment is suspended over his head. . . .
It is quite possible that a régime which exterminates . . . the nation's best brains may eventually provoke a genuinely terroristic opposition. What is more: it would be contrary to all laws of history if [it did not do so]. . . . But this terrorism of despair and revenge is alien to the adherents of the Fourth International. . . . Individual revenge . . . would be all too little for us. What political and moral satisfaction indeed could the working class derive from the assassination of Cain-Djugashvili, whom any new bureaucratic 'genius'

[1] B.O., no. 65, 1938.

would replace without difficulty? In so far as Stalin's personal
fortunes can be of any interest to us at all, we should only wish that
he should survive the crumbling of his own system; and that is
not very far off.

He forecast 'another trial, a genuine one', at which the
workers will sit in judgement over Stalin and his accomplices.
'No words will then be found in the human language to defend
this most malignant of all the Cains that can be found in
history. . . . The monuments he has erected to himself will be
pulled down or taken into museums and placed there in
chambers of totalitarian horrors. And the victorious working
class will revise all the trials, public and secret, and will erect
monuments to the unfortunate victims of Stalinist villainy and
infamy on the squares of a liberated Soviet Union.'[1]

Again, this prophecy was to come true, but not for many
years. In the meantime, the purges, by their scale and force,
acted like an immense natural cataclysm, against which all
human reaction was vain. The terror crushed brains, broke
wills, and flattened all resistance. The immense hatreds and
resentments of which Trotsky spoke were there; but they were
pressed deep down, where they were to remain stored for the
future; at present and for the rest of the Stalin era they could
find no outlet. All those—the Trotskyists in the first instance
—in whom such emotions were allied with a political consciousness and who had ideas and programmes of action to offer—
all such people were being exterminated systematically and
pitilessly.

For over ten years Stalin had kept the Trotskyists behind
bars and barbed wire, and subjecting them to inhuman persecution, demoralized many of them, divided them, and almost
succeeded in cutting them off from society. By 1934 Trotskyism
seemed to have been stamped out completely. Yet two or
three years later Stalin was more afraid of it than ever. Paradoxically, the great purges and mass deportations that had
followed the assassination of Kirov gave fresh life to Trotskyism. With tens and even hundreds of thousands of newly-
banished people around them, the Trotskyists were no longer
isolated. They were rejoined by the mass of capitulators, who

[1] Ibid. The leading article.

ruefully reflected that things might have never come to the present pass if they had held out with the Trotskyists. Oppositionists of younger age groups, Komsomoltsy who first turned against Stalin long after Trotskyism had been defeated, 'deviationists' of every possible variety, ordinary workers deported for trivial offences against labour discipline, and malcontents and grumblers who began to think politically only behind barbed wire—all these formed an immense new audience for the Trotskyist veterans.[1] The régime in the concentration camps was more and more cruel: the inmates had to slave ten or twelve hours a day; they starved; and they wasted away amid disease and indescribable squalor. Yet the camps were once again becoming schools and training grounds of the opposition, with the Trotskyists as the unrivalled tutors. It was they who were at the head of the deportees in nearly all the strikes and hunger strikes, who confronted the administration with demands for improvements in camp conditions, and who by their defiant, often heroic behaviour, inspired others to hold out. Tightly organized, self-disciplined, and politically well informed, they were the real élite of that huge segment of the nation that had been cast behind the barbed wire.

Stalin realized that he would achieve nothing by further persecution. It was hardly possible to add to the torment and the oppression, which had only surrounded the Trotskyists with the halo of martyrdom. They were a menace to him as long as they were alive; and with war and its hazards approaching, the potential threat might become actual. We have seen that since he had first seized power he had to reconquer it over and over again. He now decided to rid himself of the necessity to go on reconquering it; he was out to ensure it once for all and against all hazards. There was only one way in which he could achieve this: by the wholesale extermination of his opponents; above all, of the Trotskyists. The Moscow trials had been

[1] M. Fainsod in *Smolensk Under Soviet Rule* quotes, from captured G.P.U. documents, cases when even in 1936-7, at the height of the purges, workers who were asked who should be considered an exemplary Bolshevik replied: Trotsky (and/or Zinoviev); and when school children, at a meeting called to commemorate Kirov, proposed that Trotsky be included in the honorary praesidium (p. 302 and *passim*). Trotskyism had not been especially popular in the Smolensk province; and such cases were more frequent in other parts of the country. All culprits, often even the children, were deported as 'Trotskyists.' For a description of the orgy of the denunciation of 'Trotskyists' in the Smolensk area, see ibid., pp. 232-7.

staged to justify this design, the main part of which was now carried out, not in the limelight of the courtrooms, but in the dungeons and camps of the East and far North.

.　　.　　.　　.　　.　　.　　.　　.　　.　　.

An eye-witness, an ex-inmate of the great Vorkuta camp but not a Trotskyist himself, thus describes the last activities of the Trotskyists and their annihilation.[1] There were, he says, in his camp alone about a thousand old Trotskyists, calling themselves 'Bolsheviks-Leninists'. Roughly five hundred of these worked at the Vorkuta colliery. In all the camps of the Pechora province there were several thousands of 'orthodox Trotskyists', who 'had been in deportation since 1927' and 'remained true to their political ideas and leaders till the end'. The writer probably includes former capitulators among the 'orthodox Trotskyists', for otherwise his estimate of their number would appear greatly exaggerated.[2] 'Apart from these genuine Trotskyists', he goes on to say, 'there were about this time more than one hundred thousand inmates of the camps in Vorkuta and elsewhere, who as party members or Komsomoltsy had joined the Trotskyist Opposition and had then, at various times and for various reasons, . . . been forced to "recant and admit their mistakes" and to leave the ranks of the Opposition.' Many deportees, who had never been party members, also regarded themselves as Trotskyists. These numbers again must include oppositionists of every possible shade, even some of Rykov's and Bukharin's adherents, and newcomers of the young and youngest age groups, as our eye-witness himself indicates.

'All the same', he remarks, 'the Trotskyists proper, the followers of L. D. Trotsky, were the most numerous group.' Among their leaders he lists V. V. Kossior, Posnansky, Vladimir Ivanov, and other authentic Trotskyists of long standing. 'They arrived at the colliery in the summer of 1936 and were put up . . . in two large shanties. They refused categorically to work in the pits. They worked only at the pitheads and for not more than eight hours a day, not ten or twelve hours, as the

---

[1] This report ('*Trotskisty na Vorkute*'), signed M.B., appeared in the émigré-Menshevik *Sotsialisticheskii Vestnik*, nos. 10–11, 1961.

[2] Compare Chapter I, p. 81.

regulations required and as all other inmates laboured. They ignored the camp regulations ostentatiously and in an organized manner. Most of them had spent about ten years in isolation, first in jails, then in camps on the Solovky Islands, and finally at Vorkuta. The Trotskyists were the only groups of political prisoners who openly criticized the Stalinist 'general line' and openly and in an organized manner resisted the jailers.' They still proclaimed, as Trotsky did abroad, that in case of war they would defend the Soviet Union unconditionally, but seek to overthrow Stalin's government; and even 'ultra-lefts', like Sapronov's adherents, shared this attitude, though with reservations.

In the autumn of 1936, after the trial of Zinoviev and Kamenev, the Trotskyists arranged camp meetings and demonstrations in honour of their executed comrades and leaders. Shortly after, on 27 October, they began a hunger strike—this was the strike in which, according to the account quoted earlier, Sergei, Trotsky's younger son, took part. The Trotskyists of all the Pechora camps joined in and the strike lasted 132 days. The strikers protested against their transfer from previous places of deportation and their penalization without open trial. They demanded an eight-hour working day, the same food for all inmates (regardless of whether they fulfilled production norms or not), separation of political and criminal prisoners, and the removal of invalids, women, and old people from sub-Polar regions to areas with a milder climate. The decision to strike was taken at an open meeting. Sick and old-age prisoners were exempted; 'but the latter categorically rejected the exemption'. In almost every barrack non-Trotskyists responded to the call, but only 'in the shanties of the Trotskyists was the strike complete'.

The administration, afraid that the action might spread, transferred the Trotskyists to some half-ruined and deserted huts twenty-five miles away from the camp. Of a total of 1,000 strikers several died and only two broke down; but those two were not Trotskyists. In March 1937, on orders from Moscow, the camp administration yielded on all points; and the strike came to an end. In the next few months, before the Yezhov terror reached its height, the Trotskyists benefited from the rights they had won; and this raised the spirits of all other deportees so much that many of them looked forward to the twentieth anniversary of the October Revolution, hoping that a partial amnesty would be promulgated. But presently the terror came back with fresh fury. The food ration was reduced to 400 gr. of bread a day. The G.P.U. armed criminal prisoners with clubs and incited them against the Opposition-ists. There were indiscriminate shootings; and all political prisoners were isolated in a camp within the camp, surrounded by barbed wire, and guarded by a hundred heavily armed soldiers, day and night.

One morning, towards the end of March 1938, twenty-five men, mostly leading Trotskyists, were called out, given a kilogram of bread each, and ordered to collect their belong-ings and prepare for a march. 'After a warm leave-taking with friends, they left the shanties; there was a roll call and they were marched out. In about fifteen or twenty minutes a volley was suddenly fired about half a kilometre from the shanties, near the steep bank of a little river, the Upper Vorkuta. Then a few disorderly shots were heard, and silence fell. Soon the men of the escort were back, and they passed by the shanties. Everyone understood what march it was the twenty-five had been sent on.'

On the next day no fewer than forty people were called out in this way, given their bread ration, and ordered to get ready. 'Some were so exhausted that they could not walk; they were promised they would be put on carts. With bated breath the people in the shanties listened to the creaking of the snow under the feet of those who were marched away. All sounds had already died down; yet everyone was still listening tensely. After about an hour shots resounded across the tundra.' The crowd in the shanties knew now what awaited them; but after the long hunger strike of the previous year and many more months of freezing and starvation, they had not the strength to resist. 'Throughout April and part of May the executions in the tundra went on. Every day or every other day thirty to forty people would be called out. . . .' Com-muniqués were broadcast over loudspeakers: 'For counter-revolutionary agitation, sabotage, banditry, refusal to work, and attempts to escape, the following have been executed. . . .' 'Once a large group, about a hundred people, mostly

DI

Trotskyists, were taken out. . . . As they marched away, they sang the Internationale; and hundreds of voices in the shanties joined in the singing.' The eye-witness describes the executions of the families of the Oppositionists—the wife of one Trotskyist walked on her crutches to the execution place. Children were left alive only if they were less than twelve years of age. The massacre went on in all the camps of the Pechora province and lasted until May. At Vorkuta 'only a little over a hundred people were left alive in the huts. About two weeks passed away quietly. Then the survivors were sent back to the colliery, where they were told that Yezhov had been dismissed and that Beria was in charge of the G.P.U.'

By this time hardly any of the authentic Trotskyists or Zinovievists were left alive. When about two years later hundreds of thousands of new deportees, Poles, Latvians, Lithuanians, and Estonians, arrived in the camps, they found among the old inmates many disgraced Stalinists and even a few Bukharinists, but no Trotskyists or Zinovievists. An old deportee would tell the story of their extermination in whispers or hints, because nothing was more dangerous even for a wretched deportee than to draw on himself the suspicion of harbouring any sympathy or pity for the Trotskyists.[1]

The terror of the Yezhov period amounted to political genocide: it destroyed the whole species of the anti-Stalinist Bolsheviks. During the remaining fifteen years of Stalin's rule no group was left in Soviet society, not even in the prisons and camps, capable of challenging him. No centre of independent political thinking had been allowed to survive. A tremendous gap had been torn in the nation's consciousness; its collective memory was shattered; the continuity of its revolutionary traditions was broken; and its capacity to form and crystallize any non-conformist notions was destroyed. The Soviet Union was finally left, not merely in its practical politics, but even in its hidden mental processes, without any alternative to Stalinism. (Such was the amorphousness of the popular mind that even after Stalin's death no anti-Stalinist movement could spring from below, from the depth of the

---

[1] I am indebted for detailed and perceptive descriptions of life in the Vorkuta camps during the later period to Bernard Singer, the well-known Polish journalist, who was deported there in the early years of the Second World War.

Soviet society; and the reform of the most anachronistic features of the Stalinist régime could be undertaken only from above, by Stalin's former underlings and accomplices.)

While the trials in Moscow were engaging the world's awe-struck attention, the great massacre in the concentration camps passed almost unnoticed. It was carried out in such deep secrecy that it took years for the truth to leak out. Trotsky knew better than anyone that only a small part of the terror revealed itself through the trials; he surmised what was happening in the background. Yet even he could not guess or visualise the whole truth; and had he done so, his mind would hardly have been able to absorb its full enormity and all its implications during the short time left to him. He still assumed that the anti-Stalinist forces would presently come to the fore, articulate and politically effective; and in particular that they would be able to overthrow Stalin in the course of the war and to conduct the war towards a victorious and revolutionary conclusion. He still reckoned on the regeneration of the old Bolshevism to whose wide and deep influence Stalin's ceaseless crusades seemed to be unwitting tributes. He was unaware of the fact that all anti-Stalinist forces had been wiped out; that Trotskyism, Zinovievism, and Bukharinism, all drowned in blood, had, like some Atlantis, vanished from all political horizons; and that he himself was now the sole survivor of Atlantis.

.   .   .   .

Throughout the summer of 1938 Trotsky was busy preparing the 'Draft Programme' and resolutions for the 'foundation congress' of the International. In fact this was a small conference of Trotskyists, held at the home of Alfred Rosmer at Périgny, a village near Paris, on 3 September 1938. Twenty-one delegates were present, claiming to represent the organizations of eleven countries.[1] The conference was overshadowed by the recent assassinations and kidnappings. It elected the three young martyrs: Lyova, Klement, and Erwin Wolf, as

[1] This account is based on the 'Minutes of the World Congress of the Fourth International' held on 3 September 1938. *The Archives*, Closed Section. (An identical copy of the Minutes obtained from former British Trotskyists has been in my possession.) In 1938, I remember, I read a more detailed, critical report of the 'Congress' by its Polish participants.

its honorary Presidents.[1] Along with Klement, the organizing secretary of the conference, reports on Trotskyist work in various countries, the draft of the statutes of the Fourth International, and other documents had vanished. In order to prevent another *coup* by the G.P.U. the conference held only one plenary session, which lasted a whole day without a break; and it refused to admit observers from the Catalonian P.O.U.M. and the French *Parti Socialiste Ouvrier et Paysan*.[2] To assure the 'deepest secrecy' a communiqué issued after the conference spoke of the 'congress held at Lausanne'. At the conference, however, Étienne 'represented' the 'Russian section' of the International. Two 'guests' were also present; one of them was a certain Sylvia Agelof, a Trotskyist from New York, who served as an interpreter. She had come over from the States some time earlier and in Paris met a man calling himself Jacques Mornard, whose mistress she became. He hovered somewhere outside the conference room, pretending to take no interest in the highly secret gathering and waiting only for Sylvia to come out.

Max Shachtman presided over the conference, which during its one-day session voted on the reports of the commissions and on the resolutions most of which had come from Trotsky's pen. The formal agenda was so crowded that it would have kept any normal congress busy for a week. Naville delivered the 'progress report', which was to justify the organizers' decision to proclaim the foundation of the Fourth International. Unwittingly, however, he revealed that the International was little more than a fiction: none of its so-called Executives and International Bureaus had been able to work in the past few years. The 'sections' of the International consisted of a few dozen, or at most, a few hundred members each —this was true even of the American section, the most numerous of all, which claimed a formal membership of 2,500.[3] The

[1] Erwin Wolf, Trotsky's secretary in Norway and Konrad Knudsen's son-in-law, had gone to Spain in 1936 and perished there at the hands of the G.P.U.

[2] Both P.O.U.M. and the *Parti Socialiste Ouvrier et Paysan* (a small, lively French party led by Marceau Pivert) 'sympathized' with Trotskyism, but had their differences with it.

[3] In the *Internal Bulletins* of the American Trotskyists the membership was given as 1,000. Dwight Macdonald says in *Memoirs of a Revolutionist*, p. 17: 'We had about eight hundred members'.

conference, however, remained unshaken in its determination to constitute itself a 'foundation congress', as Trotsky had advised. Only two Polish delegates protested that 'the Polish section as a whole was opposed to the proclamation of the Fourth International'. They pointed out that it was hopeless to try to create a new International while the workers' movement, as a whole, was on the ebb, during 'a period of intense reaction and political depression', and that all previous Internationals had to some extent owed their success to the fact that they had been formed in times of revolutionary upsurge. 'The creation of every one of the earlier Internationals constituted a definite threat to bourgeois rule. . . . This will not be the case with the Fourth International. No significant section of the working class will respond to our manifesto. It is necessary to wait. . . .' The Poles agreed with Trotsky that the Second and the Third Internationals were 'morally dead'; but they warned the conference that it was frivolous to underrate the hold those Internationals had on the allegiance of the working class in many countries; and although the Poles endorsed Trotsky's 'Draft Programme' they appealed again and again to their comrades to refrain from 'making an empty gesture' and 'committing a folly'.[1]

These were weighty objections; and they came from the only Trotskyist group outside the U.S.S.R. which had behind it many years of clandestine revolutionary work and a solid tradition of Marxist thought going back to Rosa Luxemburg. Much of the conference was taken up by rejoinders to the Poles; but no serious attempt was made to refute their argument. Naville declared that the moment was 'uniquely suitable' for the creation of the new International. 'It was essential to put an end to the present indeterminate situation and to have a definite programme, a definitely constituted international leadership, and definitely formed national sections.'

[1] Of the two Polish delegates one, 'Stephen', a young scientist studying in France, had spent several years of his adolescence in a Polish prison for juveniles because of his political activity; and the other 'Karl', an elderly Jewish worker, had spent twelve years in prisons under the Tsar and Pilsudski, had taken part in the October revolution in Moscow, and had fought in the first battles of the civil war in Russia, after which he returned to Poland; was sentenced to death there for his revolutionary activity and escaped while he was being led to his execution. I was the author of the argument against the foundation of the Fourth International which these two delegates advanced at the conference.

Shachtman dismissed the historical arguments of the Poles as 'irrelevant and false' and described them as 'the Mensheviks in our midst', for only Mensheviks could show so poor a grasp of the importance of organization and so little faith in the future of the International. In the vote the conference decided by a majority of nineteen against three to proclaim the Fourth International there and then.

After a hurried and almost unanimous acceptance of all other resolutions, the delegates proceeded to elect an Executive Committee. At this point Étienne, who had been the chief speaker on the 'Russian question', protested that the 'Russian section' had not been allocated a seat. The conference made good this oversight and nominated Trotsky as a 'secret' and Honorary Member of the Executive. As Trotsky could not participate in the Executive's work, the *agent provocateur* was to go on representing the 'Russian section'.

. . . .

Trotsky decided to 'found' the new International at a time when, as the Poles warned him, the act could make no impact. His adherents in the Soviet Union ('the strongest section of the Fourth International') had been exterminated. His following in Europe and Asia was dwindling. In nearly all countries east of the Rhine and south of the Alps the labour movement was crushed. No Marxist organization could engage in systematic clandestine activity under Hitler's rule in Germany, Austria, and presently in Czechoslovakia. In France the Popular Front was crumbling in disappointment and apathy. In Spain the civil war was drawing to an end, with the left self-defeated morally even before it was vanquished militarily. The whole of the European continent was politically prostrate, waiting only for Hitler's armed might to roll over it. Years of Nazi occupation and unbearable oppression and humiliation were needed to force the working classes of some countries back into political activity or into the *Résistance*. But then the workers, at least in France and Italy, turned to the Stalinist parties, which were associated with the Soviet Union, the greatest and since 1941 the most effective force of the *Résistance*. Whatever the changing circumstances, the influence of Trotskyism was bound to remain negligible.

The prospects were no better for it in Asia, even though Asia was full of revolutionary ferment. Trotsky devoted much time and attention to the social and political developments in China, Japan, India, Indo-China, and Indonesia. In all these countries he exercised an influence on small groups of communist intellectuals and workers. But nowhere, with the peculiar exception of Ceylon, were his followers able to form an effective political party. Even in China, where his opposition to Stalin's policy in 1925–7 might have been expected to make the greatest impression, the Fourth International did not possess a section worthy of the name. Trotskyist groups, working clandestinely, under the pressure of terrible poverty, and persecuted by Kuomintang and Stalinists alike, consisted of two dozen men in Shangai, a few dozen in Hongkong, and smaller circles scattered over the central and eastern provinces. Even after Chen Tu-hsiu had embraced Trotskyism they never managed to break out of their isolation. Chen Tu-hsiu spent six years in prison; on his release he was banished to a remote village in the Chungking province and forbidden to engage in politics or publish his writings. He lived in starvation and fear, weighed down by the odium of his responsibility for the defeat of 1927, distrusted even by the Trotskyists, calumniated by the Maoists, surrounded by spies, and threatened with murder by Chiang Kai-shek's police who eventually, in 1943, were to imprison him again and assassinate him. In 1938 and 1939 Trotsky tried desperately to bring him out of China, hoping that 'he could play in the Fourth International a role comparable to that Katayama played in the Third, but . . . with greater advantage to the cause of revolution'. But Chen Tu-hsiu was already breaking down under the strain and sinking into the blackest pessimism. He nevertheless occasionally still surveyed the Chinese scene with great perspicacity and pointed out where and why Trotskyism was failing. In a statement written two months after the proclamation of the Fourth International he explained, for instance, why the revolutionary movement in China must base itself on the peasantry, and not (as Trotsky and he himself had expected) on the urban workers. The Japanese had dismantled industry in China's most advanced provinces; consequently 'the Chinese working class was reduced numerically, materially, and spiritually, to the condition in which it had been thirty or forty years earlier'. It was therefore vain to assume that the revolution could find its main centres in the towns. 'If we do not grasp now what are likely to be the political circumstances of the future and if we do not recognize clearly the weakness of the Chinese proletariat and the condition of its party, we shall be shutting ourselves up in our small holes, shall slumber away our chances, and, taking great pride in ourselves, feed on consolations.' The Trotskyists, he went on, by their sectarian arrogance, their purely negative attitude towards Maoism, and their insensitivity to the needs of the war against Japan were cutting themselves off from political realities. He feared that the proclamation of the Fourth International would merely encourage them in their 'conceits and illusions'; and that the venture would end in bankruptcy. He himself leaned towards reconciliation now with the Kuomintang and now with Maoism; but was unable or unwilling to come to terms with either; and it was as a broken man that he lived out his last tragic years. His warnings and his fate summed up the predicament of Trotskyism in his part of the world.[1]

The only country where Trotskyism stirred a little was the United States. In January 1938, after various splits and mergers, the Socialist Workers' party formed itself, and soon gained the title of 'the strongest section' of the Fourth International. It had to its credit some militant activity in trade unions and industry; and it published regularly two periodicals: *The New International*, a 'theoretical monthly', and *The Militant*. At its head there was a fairly large team of, by American standards, experienced and able leaders, of whom James P. Cannon, Max Shachtman, and James Burnham were the best known.[2] Trotsky was always at the party's call, willing to advise, criticize, praise, prod, and settle disputes and squabbles. Emissaries travelled between New York and Mexico City; and

[1] See Trotsky's letters to 'Comrade Glass' of 5 February and 25 June 1938; and H. Fleetman's account of impressions from a journey to China and meetings with Chinese Trotskyists. (19 February 1940.) Trotsky's abundant correspondence with his Chinese followers testifies to his never-flagging intense interest in prospects of the Chinese revolution. I am quoting Chen Tu-hsiu's views from a long essay of his, written in Szechwan and dated 3 November 1938. *The Archives*, Closed Section.

[2] James P. Cannon, *The History of American Trotskyism*; M. Pablo, 'Vingt ans de la Quatrième Internationale' in *Quatrième Internationale*, 1958–9; and M. Shachtman, 'Twenty-five Years of American Trotskyism' in *The New International*, 1954.

contact was facilitated by the circumstance that the secretaries and bodyguards at the Blue House were nearly all Americans. New York rather than Paris was now the centre of Trotsky-ism. Even so, the American party too was a feeble shoot planted in a soil from which it could draw all too little nourishment.

Why then, despite such unpropitious auguries, did Trotsky go ahead with the proclamation of the Fourth International?

It was more than five years now since he had decided that it was impossible 'to sit in one International with Stalin, Manuilsky, & Co.'. In these years the Third International had deteriorated so much further and had become so depraved that he was impelled to sever himself and his following from it as sharply and dramatically as possible. Lenin, in his re-vulsion against the Second International, had once urged the Bolsheviks to throw off the old 'dirty shirt' of Social Democracy and call themselves Communists. Trotsky spoke of the 'syphilis of Stalinism' or of the 'cancer that must be burned out of the labour movement with a hot iron'; and he believed that he was bringing to life an organization that would play a decisive part in the revolutionary class struggles to come.[1]

What is less clear is whether he hoped for success in the near future or whether he was working 'for history', without any such hope. His own statements are contradictory. 'All great movements', he wrote once, referring to the smallness of his following, 'have begun as "splinter groups" of old movements. Christianity was at the beginning a "splinter" of Judaism. Protestantism—a "splinter" of Catholicism, that is of de-generate Christianity. The grouping of Marx and Engels came into being as a "splinter" of the Hegelian left. The Communist International was prepared during the last war by "splinters" of the Social Democratic International. The initiators of all these movements were able to gain mass followings only be-cause they were not afraid of remaining isolated.' A passage like this, for all its historical optimism, suggests that Trotsky did not expect any early and decisive success. On the other hand, the Draft Programme, which he wrote for the Inter-national, was not so much a statement of principles as an

[1] *B.O.*, no. 71, November 1938, speech in English on the 'Foundation Congress'.

instruction on tactics, designed for a party up to its ears in trade union struggles and day-to-day politics and striving to gain practical leadership immediately. In a message on the 'foundation congress' he wrote: 'Henceforth the Fourth International is confronted with the task of a mass movement. . . . It is now the only organization which has not merely a clear idea of what are the driving forces of this . . . epoch, but also a full set of day-to-day demands capable of uniting the masses for the revolutionary struggle for power. . . .' And he went on: 'The disproportion between our strength today and our tasks tomorrow is clearer to us than to our critics. But the severe and tragic dialectic of our epoch is working for us. The masses whom [war will] drive to utter despair and indignation will find no other leadership than that which the Fourth International offers them.' In an address to his American followers he exalted the mission of the new International in an almost mystical vein and even more confidently: '. . . in the course of the coming ten years the programme of the Fourth International will gain the adherence of millions, and these revolutionary millions will be able to storm heaven and earth.' In the days of the Munich crisis he stated again that though the Fourth International might be weak at the beginning of the next war, 'each new day will work in our favour. . . . In the very first months of the war a stormy reaction against the fumes of chauvinism will set in among the working masses. Its first victims will be, along with fascism, the parties of the Second and Third Internationals. Their collapse will be the indispensable condition for an open revolutionary movement . . . led . . . by the Fourth International.' To Kingsley Martin, who visited him in 1937, he exclaimed: 'I tell you that in three to five years from now the Fourth International will be a great force in the world.'[1]

[1] B.O., loc. cit. and nos. 66–67 and 71, 1938. The meeting with Kingsley Martin, described by the latter in *The New Statesman* of 10 April 1937, was rather unfriendly because of Martin's concern with 'defending the honour' of his friend D. N. Pritt, King's Counsel and M.P. who was busy justifying the Moscow trials before the British public from the legal viewpoint. The British Editor's sensitivity about Pritt's honour, and insensitivity about the honour of all the defendants in the Moscow trials and of Trotsky himself, may have irritated Trotsky and provoked him into making a rash statement. A rather piquant description of Martin's visit at Coyoacan is given by Trotsky himself in his correspondence with the International Secretariat in Paris.

His expectations were based on the twin premiss that the coming world war would be followed by a revolutionary aftermath similar to that which had followed the first world war, but larger in scope and force; and that the Stalinist parties, like the Social Democratic ones, would use all their strength to stem the tide of revolution. More than ever he saw the advanced industrial countries of the West as the main battlefields of socialism; from their working classes was to come the salutary revolutionary initiative that alone could break the vicious circle—socialism in a single country and bureaucratic absolutism—in which the Russian Revolution was imprisoned. It was almost unthinkable to him that western capitalism, already shattered by the slumps and depressions of the nineteen-thirties, should be able to survive the coming cataclysm. He had no doubt that Hitler would endeavour to unify Europe under German imperialism, and would fail. But Europe needed to be united and only proletarian revolution could unite it and bring into existence the United States of Socialist Europe. Not only Germany, with its Marxist heritage, and France and Italy, with their revolutionary traditions, but even North America would be drawn into the social upheaval. In his Introduction to *Living Thoughts of Karl Marx*, written in 1939, he refuted the Rooseveltian New Deal and all attempts to rejuvenate and reform capitalism as 'reactionary and helpless quackery'; he pointed out how relevant *Das Kapital* was to the problems of the American economy; and he greeted the dawn of a new epoch of Marxism in the United States. In Marxism too 'America will in a few jumps catch up with Europe and outdistance it. Progressive technology and a progressive social structure will pave their own way in the sphere of doctrine. The best theoreticians of Marxism will appear on American soil. Marx will become the mentor of the advanced American worker.'[1]

Trotsky did not overlook the vast potentialities of revolution in the underdeveloped countries, especially in China—he dwelt on these more than any other writer of the nineteen-thirties. But he visualized those prospects as subordinate to the prospect of revolution in the West: 'Once it begins, the socialist revolution will spread from country to country with immeasurably greater force than fascism is spreading now. By the example

[1] *Living Thoughts of Karl Marx*, p. 38.

and with the aid of the advanced nations, the backward nations will also be brought into the mainstream of socialism.' By carrying to an extreme the logic of classical Marxism, which had postulated 'progressive technology and a progressive social structure' as the basis for socialist revolution, he was unwittingly exposing the discrepancy between theory and facts. Had the advanced industrial countries played the part for which classical Marxism had cast them in theory, no country should have been more congenial to Marxism and socialism than the United States. Trotsky did not and could not foresee that in the next few decades the backward nations would form the 'mainstream of socialism'; that the 'advanced West' would seek to contain it or to throw it back; and that the United States in particular, instead of evolving its own ultra-modern version of Marxism, would become the world's greatest and most powerful bulwark against it.[1]

He expected the working classes of the West to rise, as they had risen in 1848, 1871, 1905, and 1917–18. Applying the traditional Marxist conception even to China, he viewed with distrust Mao Tse-tung's 'peasant armies', fearing that, like many such armies in China's history, they might turn into instruments of reaction and come into conflict with the workers, if the latter failed to resume the revolutionary initiative. Despite Chen Tu-hsiu's warnings, he believed that the Chinese working class would recover its political *élan* and reassert itself as the leading force of the revolution. It remained an axiom with him that in all modern class struggle supremacy belongs of necessity to the towns; and the idea of an insurgent movement conquering the cities from the outside—from the countryside—was to him both unreal and retrograde. In West and East alike, he insisted, the revolution would either be proletarian in the true sense or it would not be at all. Least of all could he envisage the situation which was to arise during and after the Second World War, when the course of the class struggle in East and West alike was to be governed, and in a sense distorted, first by the alliance between Stalin's Russia and the West, and then by their world-embracing antagonism.

---

[1] Whether Trotsky's prognostications about the 'advanced West', especially the United States, will look as unreal towards the end of this century as they did at its middle, must, of course, remain an open question.

From his premisses Trotsky could not but pose the question: who—which party—was going to direct the forthcoming revolutionary struggles? The Second International, he answered, was a rotting prop of the old order. The Third was a tool in Stalin's hands, a tool Stalin would throw away when this suited him or use as a mere bargaining counter in his dealings with the capitalist powers. Stalin and his bureaucracy lived in fear of revolution abroad, a revolution which might arouse the working class of the Soviet Union as well and endanger bureaucratic absolutism and privilege. Thus the workers, as they entered a new epoch of social convulsions, had no revolutionary Marxist party at their head. Lack of leadership had been responsible for the long sequence of débâcles they had suffered in the nineteen-twenties and nineteen-thirties; and without revolutionary leadership they would suffer further and even more catastrophic defeats. If Marxism was not a fallacy, if the working class was the historic agent of socialism, and if Leninism was right in insisting that the workers could not win unless they were led by a 'vanguard', then the protracted 'crisis of leadership' could be resolved only by the formation of a new Communist party and International. In his pre-Bolshevik years, Trotsky, like Rosa Luxemburg and so many other Marxists, had been inclined to rely on the untutored activity of the working class and to neglect the directing and organizing functions of the party—the functions that had been at the centre of Lenin's preoccupations. He had since come to see in this the greatest single mistake he had committed in his long political career; and he was not going now to place his trust once again in the 'spontaneous' flow of the tide of revolution. And when all his reasonings led him to set himself a task, he would not shrink from any difficulties, not even from its apparent hopelessness. 'The Second and the Third Internationals are dead—Long Live the Fourth!' His duty, as he conceived it, was to proclaim this; as for the rest, let the future take care of it.

.   .   .   .

In one milieu, among the radical American intelligentsia, especially in literary circles, Trotskyism was making headway at this time. Under the impact of the great slump, the rise of

Nazism, and the Spanish Civil War, many American intellectuals had been drawn towards the Communist party; but the
most critically minded baulked at the Popular Front opportunism which caused the party to court Roosevelt and hail the
New Deal; and they were shocked and disgusted by the Moscow
trials and the equivocal manœuvres and bizarre rituals of
Stalinism. Trotskyism appeared to them as a fresh breeze
breaking into the stuffy air of the left and opening new horizons.
Men of letters responded to the dramatic pathos of Trotsky's
struggle and to his eloquence and literary genius. Trotskyism
became something of a vogue which was to leave many marks
in American literature. Among the writers, especially critics,
affected by it, were Edmund Wilson, Sidney Hook, James T.
Farrell, Dwight Macdonald, Charles Malamud, Philip Rahv,
James Rorty, Harold Rosenberg, Clement Greenberg, Mary
McCarthy, and many, many others.[1]

Partisan Review became the centre of that 'literary Trotskyism'. Edited by Philip Rahv and William Phillips, the paper
had been published under the auspices of the John Reed Clubs
and, indirectly, of the Communist party. The editors, however,
irritated by the party's meddling in literature, uneasy at its
political gyrations, and shaken by the Moscow trials, suspended
publication. Before the end of 1937 they brought the paper out
again, but changed its orientation: *Partisan Review* was to stand
for revolutionary socialism and against Stalinism. The editors
invited Trotsky to contribute. He refused at first, and treated
the venture with reserve. 'It is my general impression', he
wrote to Dwight Macdonald, 'that the editors of *Partisan
Review* are capable, educated, and intelligent, but have nothing
to say.'[2] The leaders of the Socialist Workers party did not like
to see his prestige thrown behind the periodical; and he himself
wondered just how serious was the *Partisan Review*'s commitment

---

[1] Dwight Macdonald, op. cit., pp. 12–15.

[2] Trotsky to Macdonald on 20 January 1938. The Editors of *Partisan Review* had
invited Trotsky to contribute to a Symposium on Marxism in which Harold
Laski, Sidney Hook, Ignazio Silone, Edmund Wilson, August Thalheimer, John
Strachey, Fenner Brockway and others were to participate. The theme was defined
as 'What is alive and what is dead in Marxism?' The fact that *Partisan Review*
intended to start its 'new chapter' by questioning the validity of Marxism did not
recommend it to Trotsky. See his correspondence with the Editors of *Partisan
Review* in *The Archives*, Closed Section. The Editors gave up the idea of the symposium.

to revolutionary socialism. Most of its contributors had known Marxism and Bolshevism only through the Stalinist distortion—would they not now in their disillusionment with Stalinism react also against Marxism and Bolshevism? On the other hand, he reproached the editors with reacting too feebly against the Moscow trials and attempting to remain on friendly terms with *New Masses*, *The Nation*, and *The New Republic*, which either defended the trials or were vague about them. 'Certain measures', Trotsky wrote to Rahv, 'are necessary for a struggle against incorrect theory, and others for fighting a cholera epidemic. Stalin is incomparably nearer to cholera than to a false theory. The struggle must be intense, truculent, merciless. An element of "fanaticism" . . . is salutary.'[1] Later in the year, as *Partisan Review* grew more outspoken in its anti-Stalinism, the ice was broken. The moment of the paper's closest association with Trotsky came when Breton and Rivera, inspired by Trotsky, published in its pages their *Manifesto* for the freedom of art and called for an International Federation of Revolutionary Writers and Artists to resist totalitarian encroachments on literature and the arts.[2]

André Breton, the French Surrealist poet, arrived at Coyoacan in February 1938. He had long been one of Trotsky's ardent admirers; and nothing characterizes better his—but not only his—feeling towards Trotsky than a letter he wrote him after the visit to Mexico, on board the ship that was taking him back to France: '*Très cher Lev Davidovich*. In addressing you now in this way I am suffering less from lack of confidence than I did in your presence. I felt so often the desire to address you thus—I am telling you this so that you should realize of what inhibition I am the victim whenever I am trying to make a move towards you and trying it *under your eyes*.' That inhibition came from 'boundless admiration', it was a 'Cordelia complex' which got hold of him whenever he came face to face with Trotsky. He succumbed to this inhibition only when he had to approach the greatest of men: 'You are one of these . . . the only one alive. . . . I need a long process of

[1] Trotsky to Rahv on 21 March 1938, ibid.
[2] *Partisan Review*, Fall 1938; Trotsky's letters to Rahv of 12 May and 30 July 1938. *The Archives*, Closed Section, contain James Burnham's biting characterization of the personnel of *Partisan Review*, coupled with a gossipy *chronique de scandale* (Burnham to Trotsky, 12 April 1938).

adjustment to persuade myself that you are not beyond my reach.' (Trotsky's answer to this letter was not less character-istic: 'Your eulogies seem to me so exaggerated that I am becoming a little uneasy about the future of our relations.')[1]

During his stay at Coyoacan, Breton, Trotsky, and Rivera went for long walks and trips into the country, arguing, some-times heatedly, about politics and art. In France the Sur-realists and the Trotskyists (especially Naville, the ex-Surreal-ist) were at loggerheads. Trotsky's attitude towards Surrealism, however, as towards any artistic innovation, was rather friendly, though not uncritical: he accepted the Surrealists' quasi-Freudian concentration on dream and subconscious experi-ence, but shook his head over a 'strand of mysticism' in the work of Breton and his friends. Remote though these issues were from Trotsky's present preoccupations (Breton's visit coincided with Lyova's death and the Bukharin trial), he nevertheless argued at length with Breton and Rivera about communism and art and the philosophy of Marxism and aesthetics. Out of these discussions emerged the idea of the *Manifesto* to writers and artists and of the International Federa-tion. The *Manifesto*, of which Trotsky was co-author, appeared under Breton's and Rivera's signatures in the *Partisan Review*.[2] Trotsky himself thus commented on the venture in letters to Breton and to the *Review*:

I welcome whole-heartedly [he wrote to Breton] your and Rivera's initiative in founding an International Federation of genuinely revolutionary and genuinely independent artists—and why not add of genuine artists? . . . Our planet is being turned into a filthy and evil-smelling imperialist barrack. The heroes of democracy . . . do all they can to resemble the heroes of fascism . . . and the more ignorant and obtuse a dictator is, the more does he feel destined to direct the development of science, philosophy, and art. The intelligentsia's herd instinct and servility are yet another and not inconsiderable symptom of the decadence of contemporary society.

[1] Breton to Trotsky, 9 August 1938; and Trotsky's answer, 31 August, in *The Archives*, Closed Section. See also Breton *La clé des champs*, pp. 142–54; and *Entretiens*, pp. 118–19 and 187–90; M. Nadeau, *Histoire du Surrealisme*, pp. 242–4.

[2] *Partisan Review*, Fall, 1938. Breton maintains that Rivera contributed only his signature; and that Trotsky was the chief author of the Manifesto, but thought it improper to sign.

The ideas of the *Manifesto* were essentially those which he had expressed in *Literature and Revolution* fifteen years earlier, when he sought to forestall the Stalinist tutelage over literature and the arts. He now attacked the sycophants of Stalinism, 'the Aragons, Ehrenburgs, and other petty tricksters', the 'gentlemen who [like Barbusse] compose with the same enthusiasm biographies of Jesus Christ and of Joseph Stalin', and Malraux, whose 'falsehood' in his latest descriptions of the German and Spanish scenes was 'all the more repulsive because he sought to give it an artistic form'. He saw Malraux's behaviour as 'typical of a whole category, almost of a generation of writers: so many of them tell lies from alleged "friendship" for the October Revolution, as if the revolution needed lies'. The struggle for artistic truth and for the artist's unyielding faithfulness to himself had therefore become a necessary part of the struggle for the ideas of the revolution.

In art man expresses . . . his need for harmony and a full existence . . . which class society denies him. [The quotation is from Trotsky's letter to *Partisan Review*.] That is why there is always implied, a conscious or unconscious, active or passive, optimistic or pessimistic, protest against reality in any genuine artistic creation. . . . Decaying capitalism is incapable of assuring even the minimum conditions necessary for their development to those currents of art which to some extent meet the needs of our epoch. It is superstitiously terrified of any new word. The oppressed masses live their own life. The Bohemian artistic milieu is shut in in its own narrowness. . . . The artistic schools of the last decades, Cubism, Futurism, Dadaism, Surrealism, have superseded each other without any of them coming to fruition. . . . It is impossible to find a way out of this impasse by artistic means alone. This is a crisis of the entire civilization. . . . If contemporary society does not succeed in reconstructing itself, art will inevitably perish as Greek art perished under the ruins of the slave civilization. . . . Hence the function of art in our epoch is determined by its attitude towards the revolution.

But here precisely history has laid a tremendous trap for the arts. A whole generation of the 'left' intelligentsia has . . . turned its eyes eastwards and has tied . . . its fate not so much to the revolutionary working class as to a victorious revolution, which is not the same. In that victorious revolution there is not only the revolution, but also a new privileged stratum . . . [which] has strangled artistic

E I

creation with a totalitarian hand. . . . Even under absolute monarchy Court art was based on idealization, but not on falsification,
whereas in the Soviet Union official art—and none other exists
there—is sharing in the fate of official justice; its purpose is to
glorify the 'Leader' and to manufacture officially a heroic
myth. . . .

The style of official Soviet painting is being described as 'socialist
realism',—the label could have been invented only by a bureaucrat
at the head of an Arts Department. The realism consists in imitating
provincial daguerrotype pictures of the third quarter of the previous
century; the 'socialist' style—in using tricks of affected photo-
graphy to represent events that have never taken place. One
cannot without revulsion and horror read the poems and novels or
view the pictures and sculptures, in which officials armed with pen,
brush, or chisel, and surveyed by officials, armed with revolvers,
glorify the 'great leaders of genius' in whom there is not a spark
either of genius or of greatness. The art of the Stalin epoch will
remain the most striking expression of the deepest decline of proletarian revolution.

The problem, he pointed out, was not limited to the
U.S.S.R.:

Under the pretence of a belated recognition of the October
Revolution, the 'left' intelligentsia of the West has gone down on
its knees before the Soviet bureaucracy. . . . A new era has opened
with all sorts of centres and circles, . . . with the inevitable epistles
by Romain Rolland, and with subsidized editions, banquets, and
congresses (where it is difficult to draw any line between art and the
G.P.U.). Yet, despite its wide sweep, this militarized movement has
not brought forth a single artistic work capable of surviving its
author and his Kremlin inspirers.

Art, culture, and politics need a new perspective. Without it
mankind will not move forward. . . . But a genuinely revolutionary
party cannot and will not wish to 'guide' art, let alone take it under
command. . . . Only an ignorant and insolent bureaucracy run
amok with arbitrary power could conceive such an ambition. . . .
Art can be the revolution's great ally only in so far as it remains
true to itself.[1]

Despite these rousing appeals, the International Federation
of writers and artists never assumed reality. In Europe its

[1] *B.O.*, no. 74, 1939.

call for the defence of artistic freedom was soon drowned in the rumblings of approaching war; and in America the hey-day of 'literary Trotskyism' was of short duration. As Trotsky had feared, the intelligentsia's revulsion against Stalinism was turning into a reaction against Marxism at large and Bolshevism.

For the nth time we can follow here the strange cycle through which ran the emotions roused by Trotsky in his intel-lectual followers. Most of them had turned towards him with an exalted reverence and in most he had evoked the 'Cordelia complex', of which Breton spoke. But gradually they found his way of living and thinking an unbearable moral strain; they found him indeed 'beyond their reach'. Their King Lear, they discovered, was still the hardest of revolutionaries. He was not out to gather around him a retinue of lyrical admirers— he strove to rally fighters to the most impossible of causes. He sought to set his followers, as he himself was set, against every power in the world: against fascism, bourgeois democracy, and Stalinism; against every variety of imperialism, social-patriotism, reformism, and pacifism; and against religion, mysticism, and even secularist rationalism and pragmatism. He required his adherents to 'defend the Soviet Union un-conditionally' despite Stalin, and to assail Stalinism with a vehemence matching his own. Himself never yielding an inch from his principles, he would not tolerate yielding in others. He demanded of his adherents unshakeable conviction, utter indifference to public opinion, unflagging readiness for sacri-fice, and a burning faith in the proletarian revolution, whose breath he constantly felt (but they did not). In a word, he expected them to be made of the stuff of which he himself was made.

They balked; and their exalted reverence for him gave place first to uneasiness and doubt, or to a weariness which was still mingled with awe, then to opposition, and finally to a covert or frank hostility. One by one the intellectual *Trotskisants* came to abjure first timidly then angrily their erstwhile enthusiasms and to dwell on Trotsky's faults. As nothing fails like failure, they brought up whatever mistakes or fiascos of his, real or imaginary, they could seize on until they came to denounce him as a fanatical and dogma-ridden day-dreamer, or until they decided that there was not much to choose between him and Stalin.

Behind the persistent pattern of these disillusionments and broken friendships there was the growing exasperation of the radical intelligentsia of the West with the experience of the Russian revolution in all its aspects, and with Marxism. This was one of those recurrent processes of political conversion by which the radicals and revolutionaries of one era turn into the middle-of-the-roaders or conservatives and reactionaries of the next—among the literary *Trotskisants* of the nineteen-thirties there were only a very few who would not be found at the head of the propagandist crusaders against communism of the late nineteen-forties and nineteeen-fifties. To those crusades they were to bring a familiarity with communism, an acute though one-sided grasp of its vulnerable points, and a passionate hatred which Trotsky had inculcated in them, in the hope that Stalinism, not communism, would be its object. (Of course, many former Stalinists, who had never succumbed to any Trotskyist influence, were also to be prominent in the anti-communist crusades, but more often as vulgar informers than as ideological inspirers.)

The beginnings of this conversion are half hidden in the confusion of a few minor controversies. During the winter of 1937–8 Eastman, Serge, Souvarine, Ciliga, and others raised the question of Trotsky's responsibility for the suppression of the Kronstadt revolt in 1921. The context in which they raised it was an attempt to find out where and when exactly that fatal flaw in Bolshevism had shown itself from which Stalinism took its origin. It had shown itself, they answered, at Kronstadt, in the suppression of the 1921 revolt. That was the decisive turn, the original sin, as it were, that led to the fall of Bolshevism! But was not Trotsky responsible for the suppression of the Kronstadt revolt? Did he not appear in that act as the true precursor of the Stalinist terror? The critics found it all the easier to condemn him, as they had a highly idealized image of the Kronstadt rising and glorified it as the first truly proletarian protest against the 'betrayal of the revolution'. Trotsky replied that their image of Kronstadt was unreal and that if the Bolsheviks had not suppressed the rising they would have opened the floodgates to counter-revolution. He assumed full political responsibility for the Politbureau's decision about this, a decision he had supported, and denied only the allegation that he had personally directed the attack on Kronstadt.[1]

The polemic was full of a strange and unreasonable passion. There was no need to accept Trotsky's version to see that his critics greatly inflated the importance of the Kronstadt rising, detaching it, as it were, from the historic flux and the many cross-currents of events. Kronstadt as the prelude to Stalinism overshadowed in their eyes the fundamental factors that favoured Stalinism such as the defeats of communism in the West, the poverty and isolation of the Soviet Union, the weariness of its working masses, the conflicts between town and country, the 'logic' of the single party system, and so on. And such at times was the venom of the discussion over the relatively distant and ambiguous episode that Trotsky remarked: 'One would think that the Kronstadt revolt occurred not seventeen years ago but only yesterday.' What angered him was that his supposed well-wishers should have chosen to heckle him about Kronstadt right in the middle of his campaign against the Moscow trials. Moreover, while he was denouncing the present executions of the wives and children of the anti-Stalinists, Serge and Souvarine blamed him for the shooting of hostages during the Civil War. Did not this 'hue and cry' aid Stalin? And did they not see the moral and political difference between his use of violence in civil war and Stalin's present terror? Or were they denying the Bolshevik government of 1918–21 the right to defend itself and impose discipline?

[1] *B.O.*, no. 70, 1938. In a letter to Lyova (19 November 1937) Trotsky relates that, when the issue came before the Politbureau, he was for attacking Kronstadt while Stalin was against it, saying that the rebels, if left to themselves, would surrender within two or three weeks. Curiously, in his public polemics against Stalin (and in his biography of Stalin) Trotsky never mentioned this fact, although he usually made the most of any instance of Stalin's political 'softness' or deviation from Lenin's line. Is it that Trotsky somehow felt that in this case 'softness' might redound to Stalin's credit? The debate about Kronstadt went on in *The New International* (Trotsky, 'Hue and cry over Kronstadt', April 1938; Serge, 'Letter to the Editors', February 1939, etc.) and in books (Ciliga's *Au pays du Grand Mensonge* and Serge's *Mémoires d'un Révolutionnaire*). One of Trotsky's American secretaries, Bernard Wolfe, who spent a few months at Coyoacan in 1937, has since written a novel, *The Great Prince Died*, the main idea of which is that Trotsky's conscience and life were corroded by his guilt over Kronstadt. Unfortunately, the novel is as crude and cheap artistically as it is unreal historically.

I do not know . . . whether there were any innocent victims [at Kronstadt]. . . . I cannot undertake to decide now, so long after the event, who should have been punished and in what way. . . especially as I have no data at hand. I am ready to admit that civil war is not a school of humane behaviour. Idealists and pacifists have always blamed revolution for 'excesses'. The crux of the matter is that the 'excesses' spring from the very nature of revolution, which is itself an 'excess' of history. Let those who wish to do so reject (in their petty journalistic articles) revolution on this ground. I do not reject it.

The critics accused him of 'Jesuitic' or 'Leninist immorality', that is of holding that the end justifies the means. He replied with his essay *Their Morals and Ours*, an aggressive and eloquent statement on the ethics of communism.[1] The essay begins with a burst of invective against those democrats and anarchists of the 'left' who at a time when reaction triumphs 'exude double their usual amount of moral effluvia, just as other people perspire doubly in fear'; but who preach morality not to the mighty persecutors but to persecuted revolutionaries. He did not indeed accept any absolute principles of morality. Such absolutes had no meaning outside religion. The Popes at least derived them from divine revelation; but whence did his critics, those 'petty secularist priests', draw their eternal moral truths? From 'man's conscience', 'moral nature' and similar concepts which are but metaphysical circumlocutions for divine revelation.

Morality is embedded in history and class struggles and has no immutable substance. It reflects social experience and needs; and so it always must relate means to ends. In a striking passage he 'defended' the Jesuits against their moralistic critics. 'The Jesuitic Order . . . never taught . . . that *any* means, though it be criminal . . . is permissible, if only it leads to the "end". . . . Such a . . . doctrine was malevolently attributed to the Jesuits by Protestant and partly by Catholic adversaries, who had no scruples in choosing the means for the attainment of *their* ends.' Jesuit theologians expounded the truism that the use of

---

[1] Trotsky was concluding the first draft of this essay when Rivera brought him the news of Lyova's death; and he devoted the essay to Lyova's memory. *B.O.*, nos. 68–69, 1938, and *The New International*, June 1938. The essay also appeared as a pamphlet in many languages.

any means, which by itself may be morally indifferent, must be justified or condemned according to the nature of the end it serves. To fire a shot is morally indifferent; to shoot a mad dog threatening a child is a good deed; to shoot to murder is a crime. 'In their practical morals the Jesuits were not at all worse than other priests and monks . . . on the contrary, they were superior to them, at any rate more consistent, courageous, and perspicacious. They represented a militant, closed, strictly centralized and aggressive organization, dangerous not only to enemies but also to allies.' Just like the Bolsheviks, they had had their heroic era and periods of decadence, when from warriors of the Church they turned into bureaucrats, and 'like all good bureaucrats were quite good swindlers'. In the heroic period, however, the Jesuit differs from the average priest as a soldier of the church differs from one who is a merchant in it. 'We have no reason to idealize either of them. But it is altogether unworthy to look upon the fanatic warrior with the eyes of the obtuse and slothful shopkeeper.'

The idea that the end justifies the means, Trotsky argued, is implicit in every conception of morality, not least in that Anglo-Saxon utilitarianism, from the standpoint of which most of the attacks against Jesuitic and Bolshevik 'immorality' are made. In so far as the ideal of 'the greatest possible happiness of the greatest possible number' implies that what is done to achieve that end is moral, that ideal coincides with the 'Jesuitic' notion of ends and means. And all governments, even the most 'humanitarian', who in time of war proclaim it the duty of their armies to exterminate the greatest possible number of the enemy, do they not accept the principle that the end justifies the means? Yet, the end too needs to be justified; and ends and means may change places, for what is seen as an end now may later be the means to a new end. To the Marxist the great end of increasing man's power over nature and abolishing man's power over man is justified; and so is the means to it—socialism; and so is the means to socialism— revolutionary class struggle. Marxist-Leninist morality is indeed governed by the needs of revolution. Does this signify that all means—even lies, betrayal, and murder—may be used if they further the interests of revolution? All means are per- missible', Trotsky replied, 'which genuinely lead to mankind's emancipation'; but such is the dialectic of ends and means that certain means *cannot* lead to that end. 'Permissible and obligatory are those and only those means which impart solidarity and unity to revolutionary workers, which fill them with irreconcilable hostility to oppression, . . . which imbue them with the consciousness of their historic tasks, and raise their courage and spirit of self-sacrifice. . . . Consequently, *not* all means are permissible.' He who says that the end justifies the means says also that the end 'rejects' certain means as incompatible with itself. 'A wheat grain must be sown in order that wheat should grow.' Socialism cannot be furthered by fraud, deceit, or the worship of leaders which humiliates the mass; nor can it be imposed upon the workers against their will. As Lassalle put it:

> Show not only the goal; show also the road.
> So inseparably grow goal and road into each other,
> That the one always changes with the other;
> Another road brings another goal into being.

Truthfulness and integrity in dealing with the working masses are essential to revolutionary morality, because any other road is bound to lead to a goal other than socialism. The Bolsheviks, in their heroic period, were 'the most honest political party in the whole of history'. Of course, they deceived their enemies, especially in civil war; but they were truthful with the working people whose confidence they gained to an extent to which no other party had ever gained it. Lenin, who repudiated all ethical absolutes, gave the whole of his life to the cause of the oppressed, was supremely conscientious in ideas and fearless in action, and never showed the slightest attitude of superiority towards the plain worker, the defenceless woman, the child. As to his own, Trotsky's, immorality in decreeing that families of White Guard officers be taken as hostages, he assumed full responsibility for that measure, which was dictated by the necessities of civil war, although to his knowledge not a single one of those hostages had ever been executed. 'Hundreds of thousands of lives would have been saved, if the revolution had from the outset shown less super-fluous magnanimity.' He trusted that posterity would judge his behaviour as it judged Lincoln's ruthlessness in the American

Civil War: 'History has different yardsticks for the cruelty of the northerners and that of the southerners. A slave owner who uses cunning and violence to shackle the slave, and a slave who uses cunning and violence to break the chains—only contemptible eunuchs will tell us that they are equal before the court of morality!'

It was a perversion of the truth to blame the October Revolution and 'Bolshevik immorality' for the atrocities of Stalinism. Stalinism was the product not of revolution or Bolshevism but of what had survived of the old society—this accounted for Stalin's pitiless struggle against the old Bolsheviks, a struggle through which the primordial barbarity of Russia was taking revenge on the progressive forces and aspirations that had come to the top in 1917. Moreover, Stalinism was the epitome of all the 'untruths, brutality, and baseness' that made up the mechanics of any class rule and of the state at large. The apologists of class society and of the state, including the defenders of bourgeois democracy, were therefore hardly entitled to feel morally superior: Stalinism was holding up to them their own mirror, even if it was partly a distorting mirror.

Of the many rejoinders to *Their Morals and Ours* John Dewey's deserves to be mentioned here.[1] Dewey accepted Trotsky's view of the relationship between means and ends and of the relative historical character of moral judgements. He agreed also that 'a means can be justified only by its end . . . and the end is justified if it leads to the increase of man's power over nature and the abolition of man's power over man.' But he differed from Trotsky in that he did not see why this end should be pursued mainly or exclusively by means of class struggle—to his mind Trotsky, like all Marxists, treated the class struggle as an end in itself. He detected a 'philosophical contradiction' in Trotsky, who on the one hand asserted that the nature of the end (i.e. of socialism) determines the character of the means and, on the other, deduced the means from 'historical laws of the class struggle' or justified them by reference to such 'laws'. To Dewey the assumption of *fixed laws*, allegedly governing the development of society, was irrelevant. 'The belief that a law of history determines the particular way in

[1] John Dewey, 'Means and Ends' in *New International*, August 1938.

which the struggle is to be carried on certainly seems to tend to
a fanatical and even mystical devotion to the use of certain ways
of conducting the class struggle, to the exclusion of all other
ways. . . . Orthodox Marxism shares with orthodox religionism
and . . . traditional idealism the belief that human ends are
interwoven into the very texture and structure of existence
—a conception inherited presumably from its Hegelian
origins.'

Dewey's conclusion became the keynote of nearly all the
attacks on Trotsky that presently came from his former disciples
and friends—all aimed at the 'Hegelian heritage of Marxism',
dialectical materialism, and the 'religious fanaticism' of
Bolshevism. Max Eastman, for instance, spoke of the final
collapse of the 'dream about socialism'. 'I advocate that we
abandon those utopian and absolute ideals.' Not only was
Marxism in his eyes now an 'antique religion' or a 'German
romantic faith', but it was the progenitor of fascism as well as
of Stalinism. 'Do not forget that Stalin was a socialist. Mussolini
was a socialist. Hundreds of thousands of the followers of
Hitler were socialists or communists. . . .' Sidney Hook likewise renounced the idea of proletarian dictatorship and
finally abandoned Marxism in favour of pragmatic liberalism.
So did Edmund Wilson, Benjamin Stolberg, James Rorty,
and others.[1]

With forty years of 'ideological' controversy behind him,
Trotsky found little new or original in these arguments. They
must have reminded him of Tikhomirov's *Why I ceased to be a
Revolutionary*, the almost classic statement of recantation by an
old Narodnik who left the revolutionary movement to make
peace with the established order. Since then in every generation,
in every decade, the weary and disillusioned, as they withdrew
from the fray or changed sides tried to answer this question.
What was new this time was the vehemence of the disillusionment: it matched the savage blows that Stalinism was inflicting on faith and illusion. Never yet had men withdrawn
from a revolutionary struggle with so much deep-felt emotion
and genuine indignation; and never yet had any cause looked as
hopeless as Trotsky's began to look to the professors, authors,

[1] Max Eastman, *Marxism, is it Science?* pp. 275–97; Sidney Hook, *Political
Power and Personal Freedom.*

and literary critics who were deserting him. They came to feel that by opting for Trotskyism they had needlessly involved themselves in the huge, remote, obscure and dangerous business of the Russian revolution; and that this involvement was bringing them into conflict with the way of life and the climate of ideas which prevailed in their universities, editorial offices, and literary coteries. It was one thing to lend one's name to a Committee for the Defence of Trotsky and to protest against the purges, but quite another to subscribe to the Manifestoes of the Fourth International and to echo Trotsky's call for the conversion of the forthcoming world war into a global civil war. What was galling to Trotsky was to see even such old friends and associates as Eastman and Serge turn their back on him. He emptied the vials of his scorn on them and 'their ilk'; and like another great controversialist, not too fastidious in the choice of his victims, he preserved in his prose—as one preserves insects in amber—the names of quite a few scribblers who would otherwise have been long forgotten. Here is a sample of his polemic—with Souvarine as his target:

> Ex-pacifist, ex-communist, ex-Trotskyist, ex-democrato-communist, ex-Marxist . . . almost ex-Souvarine is all the more insolent in his attacks on proletarian revolution . . . the less he knows what he wants. This man loves . . . to collect and file . . . documents, excerpts, quotation marks, and commas; and he has a sharp pen. He once imagined that this equipment would do him for his lifetime. Then he had to learn that it was also necessary to know how to think. . . . In his book on Stalin, despite an abundance of interesting quotations and facts, he himself produced the certificate of his own intellectual poverty. He understands neither revolution nor counter-revolution. He applies the criteria of a petty *raisonneur* to the historic process. . . . The disproportion between the critical bent and the creative impotence of his mind corrodes him like an acid. Hence he is constantly in a state of savage irritation and lacks elementary scruple in appraising ideas, men, and events; and he covers all this by dry moralizing. He is, like all misanthropes and cynics, drawn towards reaction. But has he ever openly broken with Marxism? We have never heard about this. He prefers equivocacation; that is his native element. In his review of my pamphlet [*Their Morals and Ours*] he writes: 'Trotsky once again mounts his hobby horse of class struggle.' To the Marxist of yesterday class

struggle is already 'Trotsky's hobby horse'. He, Souvarine, prefers to sit astride the dead dog of eternal morality.[1]

In such polemical excursions Trotsky was eagerly accompanied by two of his disciples: James Burnham and Max Shachtman, who sprang fiercely on 'The Intellectuals in Retreat', tearing them to pieces for their 'Stalinophobia' and 'treason to the working class and Marxism'. Before long these disciples too were to desert the master and join 'The Intellectuals in Retreat'.[2]

.   .   .   .

After a friendship which lasted two years, Trotsky and Rivera fell out. The quarrel broke out rather suddenly, just after the manifesto on the freedom of art had appeared in *Partisan Review*. In the summer Trotsky, hoping that Rivera would attend the 'foundation congress' of the Fourth International, had written to the organizers in Paris: 'You should invite him . . . personally . . . and underline that the Fourth International is proud to have in its ranks, him, the greatest artist of our epoch and an indomitable revolutionary. We should be at least as attentive towards Diego Rivera as Marx was towards Freiligrath and Lenin towards Gorky. As an artist he is far superior to Freiligrath and Gorky and he is . . . a genuine revolutionary, whereas Freiligrath was only a petty bourgeois sympathizer and Gorky a somewhat equivocal fellow-traveller.'[3] It was therefore a rude shock to Trotsky when, before the end of the year, Rivera bitterly attacked President Cardenas as 'an accomplice of the Stalinists', and in the Presidential elections backed Cardenas' rival, Almazar, a right-wing general who promised to bring the trade unions to heel and tame the left. Rivera too had caught the 'virus of Stalinophobia' (but such was the whimsicality of his political behaviour that a few years hence he was to return contritely to the Stalinist fold). Trotsky was wary of becoming involved in Mexican politics; and he would in any case have nothing to do with the kind of anti-Stalinism for which Rivera now stood and with his campaign against Cardenas. He tried to dissuade Rivera, but failed. As in the public eye he was extremely closely associated

[1] *B.O.*, nos. 77–78, 1939 and *New International*, August 1939.
[2] *New International*, January 1939.
[3] Trotsky to the International Secretariat in Paris, 12 June 1938.

with the painter, nothing short of an open break with him
could free Trotsky of responsibility for his political vagaries.
In a special statement Trotsky deplored Rivera's stand in the
Presidential elections and declared that henceforth he could
not feel any 'moral solidarity' with him or even benefit from
his hospitality.[1] However, when the Stalinists attacked Rivera
as one who 'sold himself to reaction' Trotsky defended him
against the charge of venality and expressed undiminished
admiration for the 'genius whose political blunderings could
cast no shadow either on his art or on his personal integrity'.[2]

The break with Rivera and the decision to leave the Blue
House put Trotsky in a difficult financial situation. His earnings had been greatly reduced, which had not mattered much
as long as he did not have to pay for the roof over his head.
Now he was compelled to do what he could to raise his earnings; and in the meantime he had to borrow from his friends
to be able to run his household.[3] He had undertaken to write
a biography of Stalin; but work being frequently interrupted
he progressed with it slowly. His publishers, disappointed that
his *Lenin* had not been forthcoming, were cautious with advances.[4] He thought of writing a short and popular book that

---

[1] Trotsky's statement to the Mexican Press of 11 January 1939. *The Archives*.
See also Van Heijenoort's letter to Breton (11 January 1939) informing him, on
Trotsky's instruction, about the breach. Breton, replying to Trotsky on 2 June,
refused to take sides in the quarrel between Trotsky and Rivera.

[2] Trotsky's article ('Ignorance is not a Weapon of Revolution') for *Trinchera
Aprista*, written on 30 January 1939. *The Archives*.

[3] I am told that a Mexican publisher and bookseller of Russian origin, a descendant of Russian revolutionaries, was Trotsky's creditor on this and other occasions.
I have also heard fantastic tales about the 'financial side' of Trotsky's existence in
exile. Thus, the Editor of a great American magazine has assured me that Trotsky
drew money from a large American bank account which Lenin had opened in his
and Trotsky's name during the civil war, when he reckoned with the possibility
of a Bolshevik defeat and with the need to resume the revolutionary struggle from
abroad. The story would be interesting if it were true. It is not.

[4] *The Archives* (Closed Section) contain Trotsky's correspondence with his
publishers, detailed royalty statements, accounts, etc. which give a clear idea of
his financial difficulties in the year 1939. Thus, Doubleday had paid him as far
back as 1936 an advance of 5,000 dollars on the *Lenin* and now pressed for the
manuscript. They had paid him, also in 1936, 1,800 dollars and a smaller amount
later on, for *The Revolution Betrayed*; but until 1939 the sales had not covered the
advances. Trotsky had signed contracts for *Stalin* with Harpers in New York and
Nicholson and Watson in London in the first half of 1938; but before the end of
the year Harpers already refused him advances on the ground that he was slow
with delivering portions of the MS.

might become a best-seller and free him from journalistic chores; but he could not bring himself to do this. He negotiated with the New York Public Library and the Universities of Harvard and Stanford about the sale of his Archives. Eager to place his papers in safety, he had asked an almost ludicrously low price for them; but the prospective buyers were in no hurry, and the negotiations dragged on for over a year.[1] Even in journalism his stock had slumped badly; and literary agents often found it difficult to place his articles, although he wrote on subjects of burning topicality such as the Munich settlement, the state of the Soviet armed forces, American diplomacy, Japan's role in the coming war, and so on.[2]

Financial difficulties led him to a strange quarrel with *Life* magazine.[3] At the end of September 1939, on Burnham's initiative, one of *Life*'s editors came to Coyoacan, and commissioned him to write a character sketch of Stalin and also an article on Lenin's death. (Trotsky had just concluded the chapter in *Stalin* in which he suggested that Stalin had poisoned Lenin, and he was to present this version in *Life*.) His first article appeared in the magazine on 2 October. Although it contained relatively inoffensive reminiscences, the article raised the ire of pro-Stalinist 'liberals', who flooded *Life* with vituperative protests. *Life* printed some of these to the annoyance of Trotsky, who maintained that the protests had come from 'a G.P.U. factory' in New York, and were defamatory of him. He nevertheless sent in his second article, the one on Lenin's death; but *Life* refused to publish it. Ironically, the objections of the editors were reasonable enough: they found Trotsky's surmise that Stalin had poisoned Lenin unconvincing; and they demanded from him 'less conjecture and more unquestionable facts'. He threatened to sue *Life* for breach of contract; and in a huff submitted the article to the *Saturday Evening Post* and *Collier's*, where he again met with refusals,

[1] Trotsky to Albert Goldman, 11 January 1940. As late as March 1940 Harvard University offered to pay for the archives not more than 6,000 dollars. Eventually, the University bought the archives for 15,000 dollars, a small sum for the 'value' it received.

[2] Among Trotsky's several articles in which American and British Editors found no 'news-value' was one written early in the summer of 1939 and saying that Stalin was about to sign a pact with Hitler.

[3] See Trotsky's letter to J. Burnham of 30 September 1939 and his correspondence with *Life* magazine. *The Archives*, Closed Section.

until *Liberty* finally published it. It is sad to see how much time in his last year the irate and futile correspondence about this matter took. In the end *Life* paid him the fee for the rejected article. This and a few other earnings, he could report to his friends, 'insured' him financially for 'a few months' and allowed him to go on bargaining a little longer about the sale of his Archives.

.   .   .   .

In February or March 1939 he rented a house at the Avenida Viena on the far outskirts of Coyoacan, where the long street grew empty, stony, and dusty, with only a few *campesino* hovels scattered on either side. The house was old and roughly built, but fairly solid and spacious; and it stood in its own grounds, separated by thick walls from the road and the surroundings. No sooner had the Trotskys moved in than a rumour spread that 'the G.P.U. was about to buy up the property'. To forestall this, Trotsky himself purchased it, although he had to borrow money for this his 'first deal in real estate'. In view of the unceasing Stalinist threats of physical violence it was necessary, or so it seemed, to fortify the house. Later on a watch tower was to be erected at the entrance gate; immediately doors were heavily barred, sand bags were put up against walls, and alarm signals were installed. Day and night five policemen were on duty in the street outside; and eight to ten Trotskyists guarded the house inside. The Trotskyists lived in; after a turn of duty at the gate, they worked as secretaries and participated in domestic activities, especially in the regular debates which took place in the evenings—unless the arrival of visitors turned day into debating time.

The visitors were sometimes political refugees from Europe, but more often Americans, radical educationists, liberal professors, journalists, historians, occasionally a few Congressmen or Senators, and, of course, Trotskyists. The debates ranged from dialectics and Surrealism to the condition of the American Negroes, and from military strategy to Indian agriculture or the social problems of Brazil and Peru. Every visitor was a source of fresh knowledge to Trotsky, who listened, interrogated, took notes, argued and questioned again—there seemed to be no limit to his curiosity and capacity to absorb

facts. The men of his bodyguard were uneasy at the unconcern
with which he received strangers, but they could do nothing
about it. Only when his curiosity turned to his immediate
neighbourhood and he peeped into the hovels across the road
to find out how people lived there and 'what they thought of
the land reform', his guards stopped him. They considered it
safer for him to go under their protection on long trips into
the country than to slip past the gate and wander around
outside the house.

The trips into the country had to be undertaken suddenly
and in great secrecy. He usually went by car, accompanied by
Natalya, a friend, and the bodyguard. When they passed
through Mexico City, he had to crouch down in his seat and
cover his face—otherwise a crowd on the pavements would
recognize him and cheer or boo. Just as at Alma Ata and on
Prinkipo these trips were 'military expeditions', with much
marching, climbing, and toiling. Since there was less chance
of fishing and hunting, he developed a new hobby and collected
rare, huge cacti on the rocky pyramid-shaped mountains.
When he was not ill, he still had enormous physical strength,
although with his white head and deeply lined face he sometimes looked prematurely aged. He had also preserved his
military bearing; and the strongest of his bodyguards could not
easily keep pace with him as he climbed up a steep slope with
a load of heavy 'bayonet-bladed' cacti on his back. 'On one
occasion', a secretary relates, 'we accompanied some friends
to Tamazunchale, a distance of about 380 kilometres from
Coyoacan, in hopes of finding a special variety of cactus.
We were unsuccessful, but on the way down, nearer to Mexico
City, L.D. had noticed some *viznaga*s. He decided, despite
the fact that we reached the spot long after dark, to stop and
collect a carful. It was a .balmy night; L.D. was in a cheerful
mood; he moved briskly about the little group, digging cactus
by the light from the headlamps of the cars.'[1] More often his
companions had to follow him in the heat of the blazing sun,
as he climbed among the boulders, his figure, in a blue French
peasant jacket, sharply outlined against the rocks and his

---

[1] Karl Mayer, 'Lev Davidovich' in *Fourth International*, August 1941; Charles
Cornell, 'With Trotsky in Mexico', ibid., August 1944; A. Rosmer in Appendix II
to the French edition of Trotsky's *My Life*.

white thatch of hair torn by the wind. Natalya teasingly called
these outings 'days of penal labour'. 'He was in a frenzy', she
recollects, 'always the first on the job and the last to leave . . .
hypnotically driven by an urge to *complete* the job in hand.'[1]

With time, and with the growing violence of Stalinist threats,
even these outings seemed more and more risky; and all of
Trotsky's existence was becoming compressed within the walls
of his half court half prison. This showed itself even in his
manner of taking physical exercise and in his hobbies. He took
to planting the most exotic cacti in his garden and to raising
chickens and rabbits in his yard. Even in these melancholy
chores he remained rigorously methodical: every morning
he spent a long while in the yard, feeding the rabbits and
chickens (according to 'strictly scientific' formulas), tending
them, and scrubbing the coops and hutches. 'When his health
was poor', says Natalya, 'the feeding of rabbits was a strain on
him; but he could not give it up, for he pitied the little animals.'

.   .   .   .

How remote, how infinitely remote, was now his tumultuous, world-shaking past; and how poignant his and Natalya's
loneliness. Very rarely a face or a voice from that past would
come back, but only to bring it home to him that nothing
bygone could be recaptured or revived. In October 1939
Alfred and Marguerite Rosmer at last came to Coyoacan.
They were the Trotskys' only surviving friends of the years of
the First World War. They stayed with them at the Avenida
Viena, nearly eight months, till the end of May 1940, during
which they spent many an hour in intimate talk and reminiscences. Trotsky and Rosmer went over the archives together
sorting them out, and pondering old documents. Sometimes
they were joined by Otto Rühle, another veteran, who as
an exile also lived in Mexico. Rühle, we know, had at the
beginning of the First World War distinguished himself as one
of the two socialists in the Reichstag—the other was Karl
Liebknecht—who voted against the war. He had been one of
the founding members of the German Communist party and
one of the first dissenters to break with it. In emigration he

[1] Natalya Sedova in 'Father and Son', *Fourth International*, August 1941 and in
Vie et Mort de Leon Trotsky.

devoted himself to a study of Marx and kept aloof from political activity, though he agreed to sit on Dewey's Commission of Inquiry. Since the counter-trial he had become a frequent guest at the Blue House and then at the Avenida Viena; and Trotsky, who respected his scholarship, showed him a warm friendship and helped him as much as he could—together they brought out *The Living Thoughts of Karl Marx.*[1]

In the first days of the war the thoughts of the three men, naturally enough went back to the days when they had all been engaged in the same revolutionary opposition to war, the days of the Zimmerwald movement. Trotsky (the author of the Zimmerwald Manifesto) proposed that they should come out with a new manifesto to assert and to symbolize the continuity of the revolutionary attitude in both world wars. Rosmer was all for it; but as Rühle had his differences with them and anyhow would not allow himself to be tempted into political action, the idea of the 'new Zimmerwald Manifesto' was abandoned. The past was too remote to answer even with an echo.

.   .   .   .

With the Rosmers, Seva had come to Coyoacan; and Trotsky and Natalya hugged the recovered grandchild. It was nearly seven years since they had sent him away from Prinkipo. The child had lived those years in Germany, Austria, and France, had changed guardians, schools, and languages, and had almost forgotten how to speak Russian. His grandfather's huge drama was as if mirrored in the tiny compass of his childhood. He had scarcely left the cradle when his father was torn away from him; and no sooner had he rejoined his mother in Berlin than she killed herself. Then Lyova, who had become father to him, died suddenly and mysteriously; and the child became the object of the family quarrel, was abducted, hidden, and seized again until he was brought to his grandfather, whom he could scarcely remember but whom he had been brought up to adore. And now the bewildered orphan stared

---

[1] Trotsky had advised the American Publishers Longmans, Green and Co. to ask Rühle, who had written a biography of Marx, to be the sole author of this book, assuring them that after Ryazanov Rühle was 'the greatest living Marx scholar'. The Publishers agreed that Rühle should select and edit the Marxian texts, but insisted that Trotsky write the Introduction.

restlessly at the strange and crowded fortress-like house to which he had been brought, a house already marked by death.

Behind the most welcome guests, the Rosmers, an ominous shadow was to creep in, the shadow of Ramon Mercader-'Jacson'. This was the 'friend' of Sylvia Agelof, the American Trotskyist who had attended the foundation conference of the Fourth International at the Rosmers' home. Some claim that it was then or shortly thereafter that 'Jacson' had been introduced to the Rosmers; and that ever since he had unobtrusively sought their company and rendered them, with seeming disinterestedness, many small services and favours. Rosmer emphatically denies this and asserts that he met him only in Mexico; and Rosmer's version is confirmed by 'Jacson' himself.[1] 'Jacson' posed, plausibly enough, as a non-politically minded businessman, sportsman, and *bon viveur*; it was supposedly as an agent of an oil company that he went to Mexico City at the time when the Rosmers arrived there. He kept himself in the background, however, and for many months sought no access to the fortified house at the Avenida Viena. But he was getting ready for his dreadful assignment.

.   .   .   .

Stalin was the only full-scale book, his last, on which Trotsky worked in these years. As posthumously published, the volume is pieced together from seven completed chapters and a mass of diverse fragments, arranged, supplemented, and linked up by an editor, not always in accordance with Trotsky's trend of thought. No wonder that the book lacks the ripeness and balance of Trotsky's other works. But perhaps even if he had lived to give it final shape and to eliminate the many tentative statements and overstatements of its early drafts, the *Stalin* would probably have remained his weakest work.

Trotsky had no awareness at all that he was somehow lowering himself by assuming the role of his rival's and enemy's portraitist. He never found any literary or journalistic work beneath him provided he could carry it out conscientiously. It is said that his publishers pressed him to tackle the biography

[1] See A. Rosmer, 'Une Mise au Point sur L'Assassinat de Léon Trotsky' in *La Révolution Prolétarienne*, Nr. 20, November 1948. See also 'Jacson's' statement in A. Goldman, *The Assassination of Leon Trotsky*, pp. 11, 15 and 25.

of Stalin, and that financial necessity compelled him to yield. This is not quite borne out by the evidence. The publishers were at least as keen, if not more so, on the *Life of Lenin* he had promised to complete.[1] If the need of money played its part in causing him to give priority to *Stalin*, he was nevertheless mainly actuated by a literary-artistic motive. He was eager to reassess Stalin's character in the fresh and fierce light of the purges; and his fascination with this task was stronger than any pride or vanity that might have prevented him becoming Stalin's biographer. His chief character, the Super-Cain now revealed, was to some extent unfamiliar even to him. He scrutinized Stalin's features anew, dug deep into archives, and searched his own memories for those scenes, incidents, and impressions that now seemed to acquire new meanings and new aspects. He delved with unrelenting suspicion into the hidden nooks and crannies of Stalin's career; and everywhere he discovered, or rediscovered, the same villain. Yes, he concluded, the Cain of the Great Purges had been there all the time, concealed in the Politbureau member, in the pre-1917 Bolshevik, in the agitator of 1905, even in the pupil of the Tiflis Seminary and the boy Soso. He drew the sinister, malignant, almost ape-like figure, stealthily making its way to the highest seat of power. The image, rough, lop-sided, sometimes unreal, derives an artistic quality from the force of the passion that animates it. It does present the torso of a terrifying monster.

There is no question that even here Trotsky treats the facts, dates, and quotations with his usual historical conscientiousness. He draws a clear line of distinction between the established facts, the deductions, the guesses, and the hearsay, so that the reader is able to sift the enormous biographical material and form his own opinion. Such indeed is Trotsky's pedantry here that his method of inquiry and exposition is exceptionally repetitive and wearisome. Armed with a formidable array of quotations and documents, he polemicizes at great length against hosts of Stalin's flatterers and courtiers, without realizing what a grotesque honour he pays them by doing so. Nevertheless, in composing the portrait, he uses abundantly and far too often the

---

[1] See Trotsky's correspondence with Curtis Brown, the Literary Agents. *The Archives*, Closed Section.

material of inference, guess, and hearsay. He picks up any piece of gossip or rumour if only it shows a trait of cruelty or suggests treachery in the young Djugashvili. He gives credence to Stalin's schoolmates and later enemies who in reminiscences about their childhood, written in exile thirty or more years after the events, say that the boy Soso 'had only a sarcastic sneer for the joys and sorrows of his fellows': that 'compassion for people or for animals was foreign to him'; or that from 'his youth the carrying out of vengeful plots became for him the goal that dominated all his efforts'. He cites Stalin's adversaries who depict the youngster and the mature man as almost an *agent provocateur*; and although Trotsky does not accept the accusation, he attaches 'significance' to it as showing what Stalin was held to be capable of by his former comrades![1]

There is no need to go into many examples of this approach. The most striking is, of course, Trotsky's suggestion, mentioned earlier, that Stalin had poisoned Lenin. He relates that in February 1923 Lenin, paralysed and losing speech, wanted to commit suicide and asked Stalin for poison—Stalin himself confided this to Trotsky, and to Zinoviev and Kamenev. He recalls the queer expression Stalin's face bore at that moment; and he makes his accusation on the ground that Lenin's death—a year later—came 'unexpectedly', and that Stalin was just then in so severe a conflict with Lenin that 'he 'must have made up his mind' to hasten Lenin's death. 'Whether Stalin sent the poison to Lenin with the hint that the physicians had left no hope for his recovery or whether he resorted to more direct means, I do not know. But I am firmly convinced that Stalin could not have waited passively when his fate hung by a thread, and the decision depended on a small, very small, motion of his hand.'[2] And here Trotsky presents in a startlingly new context the story he had told so many times before, of how Stalin manœuvred to keep him, Trotsky, away from Moscow during Lenin's funeral: 'He might have feared that I would connect Lenin's death with last year's conversation about poison, would ask the doctors whether poisoning was involved, and demand a special autopsy.' He

---

[1] Trotsky, *Stalin*, pp. 11–12, 53, 100, 116, 120 and *passim*.
[2] Op. cit., pp. 372–82.

recalls that on his return to Moscow after the funeral, he found that the physicians 'were at a loss to account' for Lenin's death; and that even two and three years later Zinoviev and Kamenev eschewed all talk about this and answered Trotsky's questions 'in monosyllables and avoiding my eyes'. Yet ·he never states whether he himself had conceived the suspicion or conviction of Stalin's guilt already in 1924 or whether he formed it only during the purges, after Yagoda and the Kremlin doctors had been charged with using poison in their murderous intrigues. If he had felt this conviction or suspicion in 1924, why did he never voice it before 1939? Why did he, even after Lenin's death, describe Stalin as a 'brave and sincere revolutionary' to none other than Max Eastman? Even in this denunciatory biography, Trotsky still expresses the opinion that if Stalin had ever foreseen in what bloody convulsions the inner party struggle would end, he would never have started it.[1] Thus he still treats the Stalin of 1924 as a basically honest though short-sighted man, who would have hardly been capable of poisoning Lenin. Such inconsistencies suggest that in charging Stalin with this particular crime, Trotsky is projecting the experience of the Great Purges back to 1923–4. He concludes that Stalin, the hangman of all of Lenin's disciples was surely capable of killing Lenin as well, and that he did kill him. Yet it is difficult not to wonder whether the 'enigma' of Lenin's death, the suspicion of foul play, the tricks Stalin used to avoid a post-mortem, whether all these parts of the story are not so many transposed circumstances, say, of the story of Lyova's death.

Stalin's personality admittedly confronts any biographer with this difficult problem. His character was undoubtedly a vital element in the purges; and it is the biographer's task to trace the formation of that character and to show how early, at what stages, and to what extent its propensities had revealed themselves. The task, however, is not different from that which the student analysing the life course of a criminal has to solve. The potentiality of the criminal act may be present in the given character early enough; but it must not be presented as an actuality before it has turned into one. To be sure, deep suspiciousness, secretiveness, and a resentful craving for

[1] Op. cit., p. 393, and M. Eastman, *Since Lenin Died*, p. 55.

power reveal themselves in Stalin long before his rise; yet for many years they are only his secondary characteristics. The biographer ought to treat them with a sense of proportion and with an eye to the dynamics of the personality and the all-important interplay of circumstance and character. Trotsky's Stalin is implausible to the extent to which he presents the character as being essentially the same in 1936–8 as in 1924, and even in 1904. The monster does not form, grow, and emerge —he is there almost fully-fledged from the outset. Any better qualities and emotions, such as intellectual ambition and a degree of sympathy with the oppressed, without which no young man would ever join a persecuted revolutionary party, are almost totally absent. Stalin's rise within the party is not due to merit or achievement; and so his career becomes very nearly inexplicable. His election to Lenin's Politbureau, his presence in the Bolshevik inner cabinet, and his appointment to the post of the General Secretary appear quite fortuitous. Trotsky himself sums up his approach in a single sentence: 'The process of [Stalin's] rise took place somewhere behind an impenetrable political curtain. At a certain moment his figure, in the full panoply of power, suddenly stepped away from the Kremlin wall. . . .'[1] Yet even from Trotsky's disclosures it is evident that Stalin did not at all come to the fore in this way: that he had been, next to Lenin and Trotsky, the most influential man in the party's inner councils at least since 1918; and that it was not for nothing that Lenin in his will described Stalin as one of the 'two most able men of the Central Committee'.

As biographer not less than as leader of the Opposition Trotsky underrates Stalin and the forces and circumstances favouring him. 'The current official comparisons of Stalin to Lenin are simply indecent', he rightly remarks. 'If the basis o comparison is sweep of personality', he then adds, 'it is impossible to place Stalin even alongside Mussolini or Hitler. However meagre the "ideas" of fascism, both the victorious leaders of reaction, the Italian and the German, from the beginning of their respective movements, displayed initiative, roused the masses to action, pioneered new paths through the political jungle. Nothing of the kind can be said about Stalin.'

[1] Trotsky, op. cit., p. 336.

These words were written while the U.S.S.R. was entering into the second decade of planned economy; and there was an unreal ring about them even then. They sounded altogether fantastic a few years later when Stalin's role could be viewed against the background of the Second World War and its aftermath. 'In attempting to find an historical parallel to Stalin', Trotsky went on, 'we have to reject not only Cromwell, Robespierre, Napoleon, and Lenin, but even Mussolini and Hitler. [We come] closer to an understanding of Stalin [when we think in terms of] Mustapha Kemal Pasha or perhaps Porfirio Diaz.'[1] Here the lack of historical scale and perspective is striking and disturbing.

What guides Trotsky's pen in passages like these is, of course, his holy anger and disgust with the monstrosities of the Stalin cult. He reduces to less than life-size the autocrat who has puffed himself up to superhuman stature, the self-deified despot. In doing so, Trotsky paves the way, as it were, for those who will many years later pull down Stalin's monuments, evict his body from the Red Square Mausoleum, efface his name from the squares and streets, and even rename Stalingrad Volgograd. With a lucid premonition of all this, Trotsky recalls that Nero too had been deified, but that 'after he perished his statues were smashed and his name was scraped off everything. The vengeance of history is more powerful than the vengeance of the most powerful General Secretary. I venture to think that this is consoling.'[2] About to be struck down by the ultimate act of Stalin's treachery, Trotsky already savours history's coming retribution and his own victory beyond the grave. He prepares that retribution in words weighty enough to serve as texts for posterity's judgement. He treats Stalin as the symbol of an immense vacuum, the product of an epoch in which the morality of the old order has dissolved and that of the new one has not yet formed.

L'état c'est moi is almost a liberal formula by comparison with the actualities of Stalin's totalitarian régime. Louis XIV identified himself with both the state and the Church—but only during the epoch of temporal power. The totalitarian state goes far beyond Caesaro-Papism. . . . Stalin can justly say, unlike le *Roi Soleil*, *la société c'est moi.*

[1] Op. cit., p. 413.   [2] Op. cit., p. 383.

And this is how Trotsky conveys in a single epigram the whole tragic tension between Stalin and the old Bolsheviks:

Of Christ's twelve Apostles Judas alone proved to be traitor. But if he had acquired power, he would have represented the other eleven Apostles as traitors, and also all the lesser Apostles whom Luke numbers as seventy.[1]

.   .   .   .

Trotsky's comments on the events leading up to the war and on the prospects of war and revolution could be the subject of a special monograph. In these writings one is struck more strongly than ever by the contrast between his lucid and almost flawless analyses of the strategic-diplomatic elements of the world situation and his blurred vision of the prospects of revolution. He saw the Second World War as being basically a continuation of the First, a prolongation of the struggle of the great imperialist powers for a redivision of the world. At the time of the Munich Crisis he saw 'Hitler's strength (and weakness) in . . . his readiness to use . . . blackmail and bluff and to risk war', whereas the old colonial powers, having nothing to win but much to lose, were frightened of armed conflict. 'Chamberlain would give away all the democracies of the world —and not many are left—for one-tenth of India.' The Munich settlement, in his view, hastened the outbreak of war; and so did Franco's successes in Spain, in so far as they freed the bourgeois governments from the fear of revolution in Europe. Stalin's policy had the same effect: selling out the labour movement, 'as if it were petrol or manganese ore', he too was helping capitalism to regain self-confidence.[2] But it was the attitude of the United States that was decisive, for both Chamberlain and Stalin were afraid of committing themselves against Hitler as long as the United States remained un-committed. Yet as the world's leading imperialist power, in-heriting Britain's place, the United States could not remain

[1] Op. cit., pp. 416, 421.

[2] In an article dated 22 September 1938 (B.O., no. 70) Trotsky wrote: 'One may now be sure that Soviet diplomacy will attempt a rapprochement with Germany. . . .' 'The compromise made over Czechoslovakia's dead body . . . gives Hitler a more convenient base for starting the war. Chamberlain's flights [to Munich] will enter history as [the] symbol of the diplomatic convulsions which a divided, greedy, and helpless imperialist Europe lived through on the eve of the new bloodbath awaiting our planet.' See also B.O., nos. 71, 74, and 75–76.

isolationist; it was vitally interested in stopping the expansion of German and Japanese imperialism; and it would be compelled to join in the Second World War 'much earlier than it had entered the First'. The United States was also destined to play a far more decisive part in the peace-making, for 'if peace is not concluded on the basis of socialism, then the victorious United States will dictate the conditions of peace'.

One may well imagine the thunderous denunciation with which Trotsky met the German-Soviet pact of August 1939: the master of the Great Purges now stood self-exposed as Hitler's accomplice. Ever since 1933 Trotsky had repeated that nothing would suit Stalin better than an accommodation with Hitler. Now, after the decapitation of the Red Army, the fear of his own weakness had driven Stalin into Hitler's arms. 'While Hitler is conducting his military operations, Stalin is acting as his *intendant*', Trotsky remarked in the first days of the war.[1] But Stalin's purpose, he added, was not to help the Third Reich to victory, but to keep the Soviet Union out of the war for as long as possible, and in the meantime to obtain a free hand in the Baltic states and in the Balkans. When Stalin and Hitler, applauded by the Comintern, proceeded to partition Poland, Trotsky commented: 'Poland will resurrect, the Comintern never.' But even in his most vehement assaults on Stalin's lack of principle and cynicism, he did not put all the blame on Stalin. He reiterated that 'the key to the Kremlin's policy is in Washington', and that in order that Stalin should change his course the United States must throw its weight against Hitler. He repeated the same thought during the 'phoney war' in the winter of 1939–40, saying that France and Britain, in avoiding real military collision with Germany, were conducting a sort of 'a military strike' against the United States. From East and West alike Hitler was abetted in the conquest of Europe. The Polish and Czech Governments had already fled to France. 'Who knows', Trotsky wrote on 4 December 1939, many months before the collapse of France, 'whether the French Government, together with the Belgian, Dutch, Polish and Czechoslovak Governments, will not have to seek refuge in Great Britain?' He did not accept 'even for a

[1] The article 'Stalin, Hitler's *Intendant*' bears the date '2 September 1939, 3 a.m.' *The Archives.*

moment' the possibility of a Nazi victory; 'but before the hour of Hitler's defeat strikes, many, very many in Europe will be wiped out. Stalin does not want to be among them and so he is wary of detaching himself from Hitler too early'.[1]

When France capitulated and nearly the whole of Europe succumbed to Hitler's armed might, Trotsky stigmatized Stalin and the Comintern for their share in bringing about the catastrophe. 'The Second and Third Internationals . . . have deceived and demoralized the working class. After five years of propaganda for an alliance of the democracies and collective security, and after Stalin's sudden passage into Hitler's camp, the French working class was caught unawares. The war provoked a terrible disorientation, a mood of passive defeatism. . . .' Now the U.S.S.R. was 'on the brink of the abyss'. All Stalin's territorial gains in eastern Europe counted little in comparison with the resources and the power which Hitler had seized and which he would use against the Soviet Union.[2]

Having said all this, Trotsky insisted with the utmost firmness that the Soviet Union remained a workers' state, entitled to be unconditionally defended against all its capitalist enemies, fascist and democratic. He did not even deny Stalin the right to bargain with Hitler, although he himself thought that the Soviet-German Pact had not brought the Soviet Union any significant advantage; he would have preferred a Soviet coalition with the West. But he held that the question with whom the Soviet Union should align itself should be decided solely on grounds of expediency; and that no political or moral principle was involved in the choice, because the western powers no less than the Third Reich fought only for their imperialist interests. What Trotsky repudiated in Stalin's policy was not so much his choice of ally or partner, but his making a virtue of the choice and his proclaiming ideological solidarity with whoever happened to be his partner at the moment. Stalin and Molotov now extolled the German-Soviet friendship 'cemented with blood'; their underlings, conniving in Hitler's atrocities, declared that Poland would never rise again; and their propagandists, like Ulbricht,

---

[1] 'The twin stars: Hitler–Stalin'; quoted from *The Archives*.
[2] A statement for the Press ('The Kremlin's role in the European catastrophe'), 17 June 1940. Ibid.

turned all their 'anti-imperialist' zeal exclusively against the western powers. This was, Trotsky concluded, how 'Stalinism exercised its counter-revolutionary influence on the international arena'; and this was one more reason why the Soviet workers must overthrow it by force. But he reasserted that even under Stalin's rule, the workers' state remained a reality, which must be protected against any foreign enemy and fought for to the last.[1]

He was well aware that his ideas would again seem paradoxical to many—but was reality not just as paradoxical? Having in collusion with Hitler annexed Poland's eastern marches, Stalin proceeded to expropriate the big landlords there, to divide their estates among the peasants, and to nationalize industry and banking. Anxious to secure military control over the annexed territories, his new 'defensive glacis', he adjusted in every respect their social and political régime to that of the Soviet Union. Thus an act of revolution resulted from Stalin's co-operation and rivalry with the most counter-revolutionary power in the world. At a stroke, Stalin fulfilled the main desiderata which had always figured in every programme of Polish and Ukrainian socialists and communists, the desiderata they themselves had not been able to realize. The social upheaval in the annexed lands was, of course, the work of the Soviet occupation forces, not of the Polish and Ukrainian toilers— it was the first of the long series of revolutions from above which Stalin was to impose upon eastern Europe. And while he was expropriating the possessing classes economically, he expropriated the workers and the peasants politically, depriving them of freedom of expression and association.[2]

Trotsky, contemptuous of Stalin's 'bureaucratic methods' and 'horse-trading with Hitler', acknowledged the 'basically progressive' character of the social changes in Poland's eastern marches. He argued that Stalin overthrew the old order there only because the workers' state was a reality in the Soviet Union—only *that* had stopped him from coming to terms with the Polish landlords and capitalists. In other words, the revolutionary dynamic of the Stalinist state had now overlapped the

[1] 'The U.S.S.R. in War', *New International*, November 1939; articles in subsequent issues of this periodical; and *In Defence of Marxism*.
[2] *New International*, loc. cit.

boundaries of the U.S.S.R. However, in making this assertion Trotsky involved himself in a contradiction. Had he not maintained that Stalinism continued to play a 'dual', progressive and reactionary part, *only* within the Soviet Union, but that its role 'on the international arena' was 'exclusively counter-revolutionary', i.e. directed towards the preservation of the capitalist order? Had this not been Trotsky's chief argument in favour of the creation of the Fourth International? He still held that the wider international influence of Stalinism remained counter-revolutionary; and that the social upheaval on Poland's eastern marches was only a local phenomenon. He pointed out how little the expropriation of landlords and capitalists in the western Ukraine (or later in the Baltic states) weighed against the demoralization by Stalinism of the French workers, the betrayal by it of the Spanish revolution, and the services it had rendered Hitler. Again and again he returned to the disparity of the two facets of Stalinism, the domestic and the foreign; and he sought to explain it by the fact that inside the U.S.S.R. the elements of the workers' state (national ownership, planning, and revolutionary traditions) refracted themselves even through Stalin's bureaucratic despotism and limited Stalin's freedom of movement; whereas in the 'international arena' Stalinism acted without any such inhibition, pursuing only its narrow interests and following freely its opportunistic bent.[1]

The argument, although it contained some truth, could not resolve or even conceal the theoretical and political difficulty which now beset Trotskyism, a difficulty that was to grow immensely with the events of the coming decade. How real indeed was the distinction Trotsky had drawn between the domestic (partly still progressive) and the international (wholly counter-revolutionary) functions of Stalinism? Could any government or ruling group have for any length of time one character at home and quite a different one abroad? If the Soviet body politic preserved the quality of a workers' state, how could this leave unaffected its relationship with the outside world? How could the government of a workers' state be consistently a factor of counter-revolution?

Trotsky and his disciples could deal with this problem in only one of two ways: Either they had to declare that the

[1] Ibid.

Soviet Union had ceased to be a workers' state; that this accounted for the anti-revolutionary direction of Stalin's policies both at home and abroad; and that consequently Marxists had no reason whatsoever to go on 'defending the Soviet Union'. Or else, they had to admit that Stalinism was continuing to act a dual or ambivalent (progressive and reactionary) role both abroad and at home; that this was consistent with the contradictory character of the régime of the U.S.S.R., with the survival of the workers' state within the bureaucratic despotism; and that Marxists could cope with this intricate situation only by opposing Stalinism yet defending the Soviet Union.

Quite a few of Trotsky's disciples tried to find a way out of the predicament by declaring that the Soviet Union was no longer a workers' state, because its bureaucracy formed a new class, exploiting and oppressing the workers and peasants. This idea, we know, had been in the air since 1921, when the Workers' Opposition first voiced it in Moscow; and although Trotsky had always rejected it, the idea never ceased to appeal to some of his followers. In 1929 Rakovsky startled them when he wrote that the Soviet Union had already changed from a proletarian state which was bureaucratically deformed into a bureaucratic state with only a residual proletarian element.[1] Trotsky approvingly quoted the epigram (which underlay some of his reasonings in *The Revolution Betrayed*); but he drew no conclusions from it. Some of his disciples now wondered what could possibly be left of that 'residual proletarian element' after ten years—and what years! Was it not, they asked, preposterous to go on talking about a workers' state? They found encouragement for such a conclusion in some of Trotsky's speculations, hints, and *obiter dicta*. In *The Revolution Betrayed* he had argued that the Soviet managerial groups were preparing to denationalize industry and to become its stock-holding owners—in other words, that the Stalinist bureaucracy was incubating a new capitalist class. Years had passed and of such a development there was no sign. Was Trotsky then not mistaken in his conception of Soviet society? He saw the Stalinist bureaucracy hatching out a new bourgeois class and a new capitalism; but was not that bureaucracy itself

[1] See *B.O.*, nos. 15–16, 1930; Correspondence from the U.S.S.R.

the new class hatched out by the October revolution and fully fledged already?

Just before the outbreak of the war an Italian ex-Trotskyist, Bruno Rizzi, answered this question affirmatively in a little noticed but influential book, *La Bureaucratisation du Monde*, published in Paris. Rizzi was the original author of the idea of the 'managerial revolution', which Burnham, Shachtman, Djilas and many others were to expound later in far cruder versions. He based himself on part of Trotsky's argument, as stated in *The Revolution Betrayed*, in order to reject the argument as a whole. The Russian revolution, he maintained, having set out, like the French, to abolish inequality had merely replaced one mode of economic exploitation and political oppression by another. Trotsky, haunted by the phantom of a capitalist restoration in the U.S.S.R., failed to see that 'bureaucratic collectivism' had established itself there as the new form of class domination. He refused to treat the bureaucracy as the 'new class' because it did not own the means of production and did not accumulate profits. But the bureaucracy, Rizzi replied, did own the means of production and did accumulate profits, only it was doing that collectively and not individually, as the old possessing classes had done. 'In Soviet society the exploiters do not appropriate surplus value directly, as the capitalist does when he pockets the dividends of his enterprise; they do it indirectly, through the state, which cashes in the sum total of the national surplus value and then distributes it among its own officials.'[1] *De facto* possession of the means of production, possession *through* the state and possession *of* the state, had taken the place of bourgeois possession *de jure*. The new state of affairs was not, as Trotsky supposed, a bureaucratic interval or a transient phase of reaction, but a new stage in the development of society, even an historically necessary stage. Just as feudalism was followed not by Equality, Liberty, Fraternity, but by capitalism, so capitalism was being followed not by socialism but by bureaucratic collectivism. The Bolsheviks were 'objectively' just as incapable of achieving their ideal as the Jacobins had been of realizing theirs. Socialism was still utopia! The workers inspired by it were once again cheated of the fruits of their revolution.

[1] Bruno, R., *La Bureaucratisation du Monde*.

In so far, Rizzi went on, as bureaucratic collectivism organized society and its economy more efficiently and pro-
ductively than capitalism had done, or could do it, its triumph
marked historic progress. It was therefore bound to supersede
capitalism. State control and planning were predominant not
only in the Stalinist régime, but also under Hitler, Mussolini,
and even under Roosevelt. In different degrees Stalinists,
Nazis, and New Dealers were the conscious or unconscious
agents of the same new system of exploitation, destined to
prevail the world over. As long as bureaucratic collectivism
stimulated social productivity, Rizzi concluded, it would be
invulnerable. The workers could only do what they had done
under early capitalism—struggle to improve their lot and wrest
concessions and reforms from their new exploiters. Only after
the new system had begun to decay and to retard and shackle
social growth, would they be able to resume the fight for socialism successfully. This was a remote prospect, yet it was not
unreal: bureaucratic collectivism was the last form of man's
domination by man, so close to classless society that bureaucracy, the last exploiting class, refused to acknowledge itself
as a possessing class.[1]

Trotsky, knowing that Rizzi had expressed a trend of ideas
that was gaining ground among Trotskyists, dealt with his
argument in an essay 'The U.S.S.R. in War', written in the
middle of September 1939.[2] 'It would be a piece of monstrous
nonsense', he began, 'to break with comrades who differ
from us in their views about the social nature of the U.S.S.R.
as long as we are in agreement about our political tasks.'
The argument whether the U.S.S.R. was a workers' state or
not was often only a quibble—Rizzi had at least the merit of
having 'raised it to the height of historical generalization'.
He identified bureaucratic collectivism as the new order of
society, essentially the same behind the different façades of
Stalinism, Nazism, Fascism, and the New Deal. His equation
of Stalinism and Nazism (Trotsky replied) might sound
plausible enough in the days of the pact between Hitler and
Stalin. That pact, many argued, had merely brought out
the kinship of the two régimes, a kinship so evident in their

[1] Bruno, R., op. cit.
[2] *New International*, November 1939 and *In Defence of Marxism*, pp. 8-11.

techniques of government; and, in Rizzi's opinion, it was only a matter of time before the Nazi and Fascist (but also the Rooseveltan) state would carry its control of the economy to a logical conclusion and nationalize all industry. Against this, Trotsky asserted that whatever the resemblances between Hitler's and Stalin's methods of government, the economic and social differences were qualitative and not merely quantitative—this was the gulf between their régimes. Neither Hitler nor Roosevelt would or could go beyond 'partial nationalization'—each was only superimposing state intervention upon an essentially capitalist order. Stalin alone exercised control over a truly post-capitalist economy. To be sure, the growth of bureaucracy was evident in various countries and under different régimes. But bureaucratic collectivism as a distinctive social order, if it existed at all, was still confined to a single country; and there it rested upon foundations created by a socialist revolution.

It was therefore rash, Trotsky pointed out, to speak of any 'universal trend', by dint of which bureaucratic collectivism was the real successor to capitalism. If this had been so, then any socialist revolution, even in the most advanced industrial country (or in several such countries), would inevitably usher in something like the Stalinist régime. This was indeed Rizzi's view. Against this Trotsky referred to the empirical evidence which showed how decisively Russia's backwardness, poverty, and isolation had contributed to the ascendancy of Stalinism. The Russian Revolution had deteriorated under the burden of circumstance; and there was no reason to assume that any socialist revolution must, regardless of circumstance, deteriorate likewise. Stalinism was not the norm of the new society, as Rizzi thought, but an historic abnormality; not the final outcome of the revolution, but an aberration from the revolutionary course. Soviet bureaucracy was still a parasitic outgrowth of the working class, as dangerous as such an outgrowth can be; but it was not an independent body. Contrary to Rizzi's view, bureaucratic collectivism did not represent any historic progress—the progress the Soviet Union was making was due to collectivism not to bureaucracy. Stalinism could survive only as long as the Soviet Union was merely borrowing, imitating, and assimilating superior western technology. Once this stage was left behind, the requirements of social life would become more complex; and social initiative would have to reassert itself. A major conflict between bureaucracy and social initiative was therefore looming ahead; and the conflict would be all the deeper, because unlike the French bourgeoisie after the revolution the bureaucracy 'is not the bearer of a new economic system', which could not function without it. On the contrary, in order to function properly the new system would have to free itself from the stranglehold of bureaucracy.

The idea that underlay all the theories about bureaucratic collectivism was that the working class had shown itself incapable of accomplishing the socialist revolution which Marxism had expected it to accomplish. Yet capitalism too had shown itself unable to function and survive. Some form of a collectivist economy was therefore bound to replace it. But as the working class had failed to cope with this task, the bureaucracy was performing it; and not socialist but bureaucratic collectivism was superseding the old order. Trotsky agreed that here was the crux of the controversy.[1] The question whether the Soviet Union was a workers' state or whether its régime was one of bureaucratic collectivism was secondary. All that he himself intended to say when he spoke of the 'workers' state' was that its potentiality and its elements were preserved in the social structure of the Soviet Union—it had not occurred to him to suggest that the Stalinist régime was a workers' state in the ordinary and political sense of the term. One might, on the other hand, speak of 'Soviet' bureaucratic collectivism and still hold that this included the potentiality of the workers' state. What was far more important was whether one held that bureaucratic collectivism had come to stay because the working class was inherently incapable of achieving socialism.

That the record of the labour movement was compounded of failures and disappointments was undeniable. The workers had not been able to bar Mussolini's, Hitler's, and Franco's roads to power; they had allowed themselves to be manœuvred into defeat by Popular Fronts, and they had not prevented two world wars. But how were these failures to be diagnosed? As

[1] Loc. cit.

faults of leadership, faults which could be remedied? Or as the historic bankruptcy of the working class and evidence of its inability to rule and transform society? If the leadership was at fault, the way out was to create a new leadership in new Marxist parties and a new International. But if the working class was at fault, then the Marxist view of capitalist society and socialism must be admitted to have been wrong, for Marxism had proclaimed that socialism would either be the work of the proletariat or it would not be at all. Was Marxism then just another 'ideology' or another form of the false consciousness that causes oppressed classes and their parties to believe that they struggle for their own purposes when in truth they are only promoting the interests of a new, or even of an old, ruling class? Viewed from this angle, the defeat of the pristine Bolshevism would indeed appear to have been of the same order as the defeat of the Jacobins—the result of a collision between Utopia and a new social order—and Stalin's victory would present itself as the triumph of reality over illusion and as a necessary act of historic progress.

Thus at the close of his days Trotsky interrogated himself about the meaning and the purpose of all his life and struggle and indeed of all the struggles of several generations of fighters, communists, and socialists. Was a whole century of revolutionary endeavour crumbling into dust? Again and again he returned to the fact that the workers had not overthrown capitalism anywhere outside Russia. Again and again he surveyed the long and dismal sequence of defeats which the revolution had suffered between the two world wars. And he saw himself driven to the conclusion that if major new failures were to be added to this record, then the whole historic perspective drawn by Marxism would indeed come under question. At this point he indulged in one of those overemphatic and hyperbolic statements which from time to time occur to any great controversialist and man of action, but which taken literally lead to endless confusion. He declared that the final test for the working class, for socialism, and for Marxism was imminent: it was coming with the Second World War. If the war were not to lead to proletarian revolution in the West, then the place of decaying capitalism would indeed be taken not by socialism, but by a new bureaucratic and totalitarian system of exploitation.

And if the working classes of the West were to seize power, but then prove incapable of holding it and surrender it to a privileged bureaucracy, as the Russian workers had done, then it would indeed be necessary to acknowledge that the hopes which Marxism placed in the proletariat had been false. In that case the rise of Stalinism in Russia would also appear in a new light: 'We would be compelled to acknowledge that . . . [Stalinism] was rooted not in the backwardness of the country and not in the imperialist environment, but in the congenital incapacity of the proletariat to become a ruling class. Then it would be necessary to establish in retrospect that . . . the present U.S.S.R. was the precursor of a new and universal system of exploitation. . . . However onerous this . . . perspective may be, if the world proletariat should actually prove incapable of accomplishing its mission . . . nothing else would remain but to recognize openly that the socialist programme, based on the internal contradictions of capitalist society, had petered out as a Utopia.'[1]

Perhaps only Marxists could sense fully the tragic solemnity which these words had in Trotsky's mouth. True, he uttered them for the sake of the argument; but even for the sake of argument he had never yet contemplated the possibility of an utter failure of socialism so closely; he insisted that the final 'test' was a matter of the next few years; and he defined the terms of the test with painful precision. He went on to state: 'It is self-evident that [if the Marxist programme turned out to be impracticable] a new minimum programme would be required—to defend the interests of the slaves of the totalitarian bureaucratic system.' The passage was characteristic of the man: if bureaucratic slavery was all that the future had in store for mankind, then he and his disciples would be on the side of the slaves and not of the new exploiters, however 'historically necessary' the new exploitation might be. Having lived all his life with the conviction that the advent of socialism was a scientifically established certainty and that history was on the side of those who struggled for the emancipation of the exploited and the oppressed, he now entreated his disciples to remain on the side of the exploited and the oppressed, even if history and all scientific certainties were against them. He, at

---

[1] Loc. cit., and *passim.*

any rate, would be with Spartacus, not with Pompey and the Caesars.

Having explored this dark prospect, he did not, however, resign himself to it. Was there, he asked, sufficient evidence for the view that the working class was incapable of overthrowing capitalism and transforming society? Those who held this view, including some of his disciples, had never seen the working class in revolutionary action. They had watched only the triumphs of fascism, Nazism, and Stalinism; or they had known only bourgeois democracy in decay. All their political experience was indeed compounded of defeat and frustration; no wonder that they had come to doubt the political capacity of the proletariat. But how could he doubt it, he who had seen and led the Russian workers in 1917? 'In these years of world-wide reaction we must proceed from the possibilities which the Russian proletariat revealed in 1917.' The revolutionary intelligence and energy the Russian workers had shown then was surely latent in German, French, British, and American workers as well. The October Revolution was therefore still 'a colossal asset' and 'a priceless pledge for the future'. The subsequent record of defeats must be blamed not on the workers but on their 'conservative and utterly bourgeois leaders'. Such was the 'dialectics of the historic process that the proletariat of Russia, a most backward country . . . has brought forth the most far-sighted and courageous leadership, whereas in Great Britain, the country of the oldest capitalist civilization, the proletariat has even today the most dull-witted and obsequious leaders'. But leaders come and go, the social class remains. Marxists must still work for the renewal of the leadership and must stake everything on the 'organic, deep, irrepressible urge of the toiling masses to tear themselves free from the sanguinary chaos of capitalism. . . .'

He reasserted his Marxist conviction not with the flamboyant optimism of his earlier years, but with a hard-tested and enduring loyalty:

. . . the basic task of our epoch .has not changed for the simple reason that it has not been solved. . . . Marxists do not have the slightest right (if disillusionment and fatigue are not considered 'rights') to draw the conclusion that the proletariat has forfeited its revolutionary possibilities and must renounce all aspirations. . . .

Twenty-five years in the scales of history, when it is a question of most profound changes in economic and cultural systems, weigh less than an hour in a man's life. What good is the individual who, because of setbacks suffered in an hour or a day, renounces a goal he has set for himself on the basis of all the experience . . . of his life?

If this war provokes, as we firmly believe it will, a proletarian revolution, this must inevitably lead to the overthrow of the bureaucracy in the U.S.S.R. and to the regeneration of Soviet democracy on an economic and cultural basis far higher than that of 1918. In that case the question whether the Stalinist bureaucracy was a 'new class' or a malignant growth on the workers' state will be solved . . . it will become clear to everyone that in the world wide process of revolution the Soviet bureaucracy was only an *episodic* relapse.

To 'put a cross' over the Soviet Union because of this 'episodic relapse' and so to lose all historic perspective, would be unpardonable. The Soviet Union—and for the time being the Soviet Union alone—contained within itself the socio-economic framework for a reborn socialist democracy; and this must be defended. 'What do we defend in the Soviet Union? Not the features in which it resembles the capitalist countries, but precisely those in which it differs from them', not privilege and oppression, but the elements of socialism. This attitude 'does not at all mean any *rapprochement* with the Kremlin bureaucracy, any acceptance of its policies or any conciliation with the policies of Stalin's allies. . . . We are not a government party; we are the party of irreconcilable opposition. . . . We realize our tasks . . . exclusively through the education of the workers . . . by explaining to them what they should defend and what they ought to overthrow.'

Turning again to Stalin's moves in eastern Poland, Trotsky pointed out that if Stalin had left private property untouched there then it would have been necessary to reassess thoroughly the nature of the Soviet state. But Stalin acted as Napoleon had done when, having tamed revolution at home, he carried it abroad on bayonets. (Here Trotsky tacitly revised the notion about the 'wholly counter-revolutionary' character of Stalin's foreign policy.) To be sure, this was not the Marxist method of revolution: 'We were and remain against seizures of new territories by the Kremlin. We are for the independence of the Soviet

Ukraine and . . . of Soviet Byelorussia. At the same time, in the provinces of Poland which are occupied by the Red Army, the adherents of the Fourth International must be most active in expropriating the landlords and capitalists, in sharing out the land among the peasants, in creating soviets, workers' councils, &c. In doing so they must preserve their political independence; they must fight in elections for the complete independence of the soviets and the factory committees *vis-à-vis* the bureaucracy; and they must conduct their revolutionary propaganda in a spirit of distrust of the Kremlin and its local agencies.'

Trotsky could not offer his Polish and Ukrainian followers any other advice and remain true to himself; yet they had no chance whatsoever to act on his advice. They were weak; they held lost positions; and the G.P.U. crushed them in no time. They too were caught, as he had been, between the necessity and the impossibility of action.

.   .   .   .

This dispute was to last till the end of May 1940, that is until the armed raid on Trotsky's home. James Burnham, Max Shachtman, and other American Trotskyists, members of the S.W.P., held views similar to Rizzi's, though they were less definite. With the outbreak of war and the Stalin-Hitler Pact these views crystallized rapidly. Early in September 1939 Burnham submitted to the National Committee of the S.W.P. a statement saying that 'it is impossible to regard the Soviet Union as a workers' state in any sense whatever.'[1] Before the end of the month Shachtman tabled a motion branding the Soviet occupation of the western Ukraine and Byelorussia as 'imperialist'; denying that the occupation had any of the progressive consequences of which Trotsky spoke; and urging the party to disavow its pledge to defend the Soviet Union. Burnham, as Professor of Philosophy at New York University, and Shachtman, the party's popular spokesman, exercised a strong influence on the Trotskyist intelligentsia. They had hitherto been committed to oppose war with revolutionary defeatism, if the war was waged by a bourgeois government, even a democratic one; and to defend the Soviet Union no matter to which

---

[1] See the *Internal Bulletin* of S.W.P. and the *New International* of the last months of 1939; Dwight Macdonald, *Memoirs of A Revolutionist*, pp. 17–19.

imperialist camp it was allied. For men like Burnham and Shachtman it was easy enough to expound such a view theoretically before the outbreak of the war, when it was generally assumed that the Soviet Union would be the ally of the western democracies. But with the Stalin-Hitler pact and the beginning of hostilities much had changed. The national mood, even in the years of American neutrality, was one of cautious sympathy with Britain and France and furious indignation against the German-Soviet Pact. Even Trotskyists found it hard to resist that mood. Burnham and Shachtman could not help feeling that if they went on 'defending' the Soviet Union, they would take upon themselves an unbearable odium. Yet in order to refuse 'defending' it they had, in Marxist terms, to declare that the U.S.S.R. was no longer a workers' state, but just another counter-revolutionary power fighting for imperialist aggrandizement. If Rizzi still argued that bureaucratic collectivism was 'historically necessary' and to some extent progressive, Burnham and Shachtman denied it any such merits. The logic of the argument led them further to deny that there was anything progressive in the Soviet economy. Implicitly or explicitly, they attacked national ownership of industry and national planning, saying that these served as the foundations for bureaucratic collectivism and totalitarian slavery. Gradually every principle of the Marxist-Leninist programme, including dialectics and morality, came again under debate. Burnham, Shachtman, and those who followed them, found themselves rejecting the programme point after point. This was, in fact, a continuation of that 'Retreat of the Intellectuals' which they themselves had just described, when they attacked Eastman, Hook, and others in the pages of *The New International*—only that now the attackers joined in the retreat.

In his criticism of Rizzi, Trotsky had said all that he had to say in this debate. The controversy with Burnham and Shachtman was conducted on far lower levels of political thought and style. The argument was remarkable mainly as an outburst of the disillusionment and pessimism pent-up among Trotsky's followers, and as Trotsky's last stand against them—the finale of all his controversies.[1]

[1] Trotsky's most characteristic statements in this debate are collected in *In Defence of Marxism*.

All the issues under debate were brought to a head before the end of the year 1939, when Stalin ordered his armies to attack Finland. Trotsky in his commentaries castigated Stalin's 'stupid and incompetent' conduct of the Finnish War, which had outraged the world and exposed the Red Army to humiliating defeats.[1] He nevertheless insisted that what Stalin was trying to do in Finland was to secure an exposed flank of the Soviet Union against a probable attack from Hitler. This was a legitimate endeavour; and any Soviet government, acting in the circumstances in which Stalin acted (circumstances which were, however, partly of Stalin's making), might well be compelled to protect its frontiers at Finland's expense. The strategic interest of the workers' state must take precedence over Finland's right to self-determination.[2] As Stalin's invasion of Finland was met in the Allied countries by a campaign for 'switching the war', and for armed intervention in favour of Finland, Trotsky called all the more emphatically for the 'defence of the Soviet Union'. This brought an outcry from his erstwhile disciples: 'Has Trotsky become Stalin's apologist?! Does he want us to become Stalin's stooges?!' 'No, Comrade Trotsky, . . .', Burnham replied, 'we will not fight alongside the G.P.U. for the salvation of the counter-revolution in the Kremlin.'[3]

Words like these echoed the language Trotsky himself had used in connexion with the Great Purges, when he called on 'every honest man' to expose the murderous G.P.U. plots, and to 'burn out with iron the cancer of Stalinism,' and when he inveighed against those 'friends of the Soviet Union' who, in the name of the sacrosanct interests of the workers' state, condoned Stalin's crimes. True, even in the heat of the most furious polemics, he had always reiterated that, despite everything, he and his followers would defend unconditionally the U.S.S.R. against all foreign enemies. But quite a few of his followers had treated these declarations as merely his *façon de parler*; and they were

---

[1] Trotsky's commentaries on the Finnish war appeared in American and British newspapers; and he summed up his view in an article 'Stalin After the Finnish Experience' written in March 1940. *The Archives.*

[2] *In Defence of Marxism*, pp. 56–59 and *passim.*

[3] The controversy was conducted within the S.W.P., in its *Internal Bulletin* (which published the resolutions of the Majority and of the Minority in December 1939) and finally in the *New International.*

dismayed to find that he meant what he had said. They charged him with inconsistency, duplicity, even betrayal. They searched his reasonings and arguments for the loose threads that could be found in them; and out of these threads they spun their own theories. Had Trotsky not said that 'internationally' Stalinism was only a factor of reaction and counter-revolution? How could he now dwell on the 'progressive and revolutionary consequences' of Stalinist expansion in eastern Europe? When they spoke about the Soviet Union's 'new class' and bureaucratic collectivism, he reproached them with abandoning Marxism and said that it was preposterous to speak of any new mode of exploitation in a country where the means of production were nationalized. Yet had he himself not declared that if within the next few years socialism were to fail in the West, bureaucratic collectivism would supersede capitalism as the new and universal system of exploitation? If bureaucratic collectivism was conceivable as the new, universal system of exploitation, why was it inconceivable as the national system of the U.S.S.R.? In saying that if the working classes of the West did not overthrow capitalism by the end of the Second World War, Marxism and socialism would be bankrupt—he knocked all his followers on the head.[1] They had watched so many of his prophecies come true that they were not inclined to take this prophecy lightly. The faithful and naïve among his disciples spent the next few years looking for the signs of revolution in the West and having visions of revolution. The sceptics and cynics concluded (at once or somewhat later) that on Trotsky's own showing Marxism and socialism were already bankrupt; and that the epoch of bureaucratic collectivism—had set in. Burnham was the first to dot the i's. He had been a 'good Bolshevik-Leninist', even a 'fierce enemy of American imperialism', as long as he felt that he was riding the tide of history. But having, with Trotsky's unwitting assistance, convinced himself that the managerial class was riding it, he hastened to cast off the ideological ballast of Marxism and to proclaim the advent of the managerial

---

[1] 'Some comrades evidently were surprised', Trotsky remarked, 'that I spoke in my article of the system of "bureaucratic collectivism" as a theoretical possibility. They even discovered in this a complete revision of Marxism.' *In Defence of Marxism*, p. 30.

revolution.[1] Shachtman accepted Burnham's prognosis; but being more strongly attached to Marxism, he viewed the prospect with grief rather than exhilaration; and he tried to fit it in with the wreckage of his earlier beliefs.[2]

In terms of the new Trotskyism which they had culled from *The Revolution Betrayed*, Burnham and Shachtman used fairly strong arguments; and both now claimed to defend Trotskyism against Trotsky himself. 'Then I am not a Trotskyist', the master replied paraphrasing Marx.[3] But to counter their arguments he had to disavow, at least implicitly, his own polemical exaggerations and excesses. 'The comrades are very indignant about the Stalin-Hitler Pact', he said in a letter. 'This is comprehensible. They wish to get revenge on Stalin. Very good. But today we are weak, and we cannot immediately overthrow the Kremlin. Some comrades try then to find a purely verbalistic satisfaction: they take away from the U.S.S.R. the title Workers' State, as Stalin deprives a disgraced functionary of the Order of Lenin. I find it, my dear friend, a bit childish. Marxist sociology and hysteria are absolutely irreconcilable.'[4] After all he had suffered at Stalin's hands, nothing distressed him more than to see the judgement of his own disciples clouded by Stalinophobia; and to his last breath he pleaded with them 'against hysteria' and for 'objective Marxist thinking.'

The American Trotskyists had split into a 'majority' which, led by James P. Cannon, accepted Trotsky's view, and a 'minority' which followed Burnham and Shachtman. Trotsky urged all of them to exercise tact and tolerance; and while he encouraged the 'Cannonites' to conduct the argument against Burnham and Shachtman vigorously, he also warned them that Stalinist agents in their ranks would seek to exacerbate the quarrel; and he advised them to allow the minority to express itself freely and even to act as an organised faction within the S.W.P. 'If someone should propose . . . to expel comrade Burn-

[1] See Burnham's 'Science and Style (A Reply to Comrade Trotsky)' (reprinted as Appendix in Trotsky's *In Defence of Marxism*). 'The Politics of Desperation' in *New International*, March-April 1940, and *The Managerial Revolution*.
[2] Shachtman's 'The Crisis of the American Party—An Open Letter to Trotsky' and 'The U.S.S.R. and the War' also appeared first in the *Internal Bulletin* and then in *New International* of March-April 1940.
[3] Trotsky, op. cit., p. 168.　　　[4] Ibid., p. 23.

ham', he gave notice, 'I would oppose it energetically.'[1] Even after the minority had held its own National Convention, Trotsky still counselled the majority not to treat this as an excuse for expulsions.

The minority, however, of its own accord constituted itself as a new party and appropriated *The New International*, the 'theoretical monthly' of the S.W.P. Almost at once the new party also split, for Burnham broke with it, declaring that 'of the most important beliefs, which have been associated with the Marxist movement, whether in its reformist, Leninist, Stalinist, or Trotskyist variants, there is virtually none which I accept in its traditional form. I regard these beliefs as either false, or obsolete, or meaningless. . . .' This was a startling confession coming as it did from someone who had been a leading Trotsky-ist these last years. Only a few weeks earlier Burnham and his friends had felt offended by Trotsky's remarks about his 'un-Marxist' way of thinking, 'On the ground of beliefs and interests. . .', Burnham now stated, 'I have for several years had no real place in a Marxist party.'[2] Whether this was true or not, whether the future author of *The Managerial Revolution* was merely trying to make his ideological somersault appear less indecently sudden, or whether he had in fact only posed as a zealous Marxist and Leninist all these years, nothing that Trotsky said against him was even remotely as devastating as was Burnham's present picture of himself. After the event Trotsky was not sorry to lose so dubious a 'disciple' whom he had characterized in private letters with epithets of which 'intellectual snob' is the mildest.[3] He expected others to follow in Burnham's footsteps: 'Dwight Macdonald is not a snob, but a bit stupid. . . . [He] will abandon the party just as Burnham did, but possibly because he is a little lazier, it will come later.' He was, however, truly saddened by the break with Shacht-man, for whom he had a soft spot, even though he was often annoyed by his 'clownishness', 'superficiality', &c. Their con-nexion dated back to Shachtman's visit to Prinkipo early in 1929; and it had become close through many subsequent

---

[1] Ibid., pp. 97, 101, 148 and *passim*.
[2] Burnham's letter of resignation is appended to *In Defence of Marxism*, pp. 207–11.
[3] This epithet appears also in *In Defence of Marxism*, p. 181.

meetings, letters and proofs of Shachtman's devotion. In the present fight between the factions Trotsky, of course, supported Cannon, but on personal grounds he felt much closer to Shachtman. 'If I could do so', he wrote to him at the height of the controversy, 'I would immediately take an aeroplane to New York City in order to discuss with you for forty-eight or seventy-two hours uninterruptedly. I regret very much that you do not feel . . . the need to come here to discuss the questions with me. Or do you? I should be happy.'[1]

The split might be said to have ruined the Fourth International, if so shadowy an organization could be ruined at all. Trotsky trusted that after the exit of the 'petty bourgeois and careerist elements', the S.W.P. would strike deeper roots in the American working class. This was not to happen: the S.W.P. remained a tiny chapel, the members of which were zealously devoted to the letter of Trotsky's teaching, and later to his memory, but which was never able to acquire any political weight; while its rival, Shachtman's group, devoid even of such virtues as may keep the feeblest of sects alive for decades, renounced more and more of its 'Trotskyism' until it crumbled away and vanished.[2] Trotskyist groups in other countries were also affected, for everywhere, but especially in France, quite a few members accepted Burnham's or Shachtman's views.

Thus at his sunset Trotsky watched for the last time the rock he rolled up his dreary mountain rolling down the slope again.

.   .   .   .

On 27 February 1940 Trotsky wrote his testament. He had drafted several brief wills earlier, but he had done so for legal purposes only, to ensure that Natalya and/or Lyova inherited the copyright on his books. The present document was his real last will and testament; every line of it was permeated by his sense of the approaching end. In writing it he supposed, however, that he might die a natural death or commit suicide—he did not think of dying at the hand of an assassin. 'My high (and still rising) blood pressure is deceiving those near me about my

---

[1] Ibid., p. 64.
[2] Shachtman and his group have since formally and categorically renounced every connexion with Trotskyism and Leninism and joined the Social Democratic group led by Norman Thomas, whose influence on American politics has also been negligible.

actual condition. I am active and able to work. But the end is evidently near.' Yet in the course of the six months which he still had before him, his health, despite the usual ups and downs, was not so bad as to justify this gloomy foreboding. In a postscript, dated 3 March, he repeated: '. . . at present I feel . . . a surge of spiritual energy because of the high blood pressure; but this will not last long.' He suspected that he was in an advanced stage of arteriosclerosis and that his doctors were hiding the truth from him. Evidently, Lenin's last illness and protracted paralysis often came to his mind; and he declared that rather than suffer such agony, he would commit suicide or, to put it more accurately, 'cut short . . . the too slow process of dying'. Yet he hoped that death would come to him suddenly, through a brain hemorrhage, for 'this would be the best possible end I could wish for'.[1]

Unwittingly he modelled his testament to some extent on Lenin's. Both documents consist of the main texts and postscripts added a few days later. In content, however, they reflect all the striking contrast of characters and circumstances. Lenin's will is absolutely impersonal. He gave it the form of a letter to the forthcoming party congress; and he did not say or even hint that he was writing it with his approaching death in mind. Although he too was tormented by the gravest dilemmas, he felt no need to make of his will a *credo*, knowing full well that his principles and beliefs would be taken for granted. His mind was occupied exclusively with the crisis in Bolshevism (which he knew his death would precipitate), and with the means and ways to prevent it. He told the party what he thought about the virtues and the failings of every one of its top leaders; he submitted to it his scheme for the reorganization of the Central Committee; and he advised the Committee to remove Stalin from the post of the General Secretary. To his last breath he remained, in his whole being, the chief of a great movement. Trotsky's testament on the other hand is intensely personal. He states briefly that there is no need for him to refute Stalin's 'stupid and vile slander' for there is 'not a single spot' on his revolutionary honour; and that a new 'revolutionary generation will rehabilitate the political honour' of himself and of thousands of other victims. In a single sentence he thanks friends

[1] *The Archives*; and *Trotsky's Diary in Exile*, pp. 139–41.

and followers who kept faith with him in his most difficult hours; but he offers them no advice—the testament contains not a single mention of the Fourth International. About half the text is devoted to Natalya:

In addition to the happiness of being a fighter for the cause of socialism, fate gave me the happiness of being her husband. During almost forty years of our common life she has remained an inexhaustible source of love, magnanimity, and tenderness. She has undergone great sufferings . . . but I find some comfort in the fact that she has also known days of happiness.

He interrupts this tribute to her with a profession of faith:

For forty-three years of my conscious life I have been a revolutionary; and for forty-two I have fought under the banner of Marxism. If I were to begin all over again, I would . . . try to avoid making this or that mistake, but the main course of my life would remain unchanged. I shall die a proletarian revolutionary, a Marxist, a dialectical materialist, and consequently an irreconcilable atheist. My faith in the communist future of mankind is not less ardent, indeed it is firmer today, than it was in the days of my youth.

As he penned these lines he looked out of the window, saw Natalya approaching the house, and the sight of her stirred him to conclude with this poetic passage:

Natasha has just come up to the window from the courtyard and opened it wider so that the air may enter more freely into my room. I can see the bright green strip of grass beneath the wall, and the clear blue sky above the wall, and sunlight everywhere. Life is beautiful. Let the future generations cleanse it of all evil, oppression, and violence, and enjoy it to the full.

In an addendum he bequeathed to Natalya his literary rights and started another paragraph with the words: 'In case we both die. . . '; but he did not finish the sentence and left a blank. In the postscript of 3 March he went again into the nature of his illness and recorded that he and Natalya had more than once agreed that it was preferable to commit suicide rather than allow old age to turn one into a physical wreck. 'I reserve the right to determine for myself the time of my death. . . . But whatever may be the circumstances . . . I shall die with unshaken faith in the communist future. This faith in man and in his future gives me even now such power of resistance as cannot be given by any religion.'[1]

.   .   .   .

By now Stalin had decided that he could no longer allow Trotsky to live. This may seem strange. What, it might be asked, had he still to fear? Had he not exterminated all of Trotsky's adherents and even their families so that no avenger should rise? And what could Trotsky, from the other end of the world, alone undertake against him? A few years earlier Stalin might have feared that Trotsky could place himself at the head of a new communist movement abroad; but did he not realize now that the Fourth International had come to nothing?

The fact remains that Stalin was not reassured. He could not bring himself to believe that his violence and terror had indeed accomplished all that he wanted, that the old Bolshevik Atlantis had really vanished. He scrutinized the faces of the multitudes that acclaimed him, and he guessed what terrible hatred might be hidden in their adulation. With so many existences destroyed or broken up and with so much discontent and despair all around him, who could say what the unforeseeable shocks of war might not bring? Might not Atlantis somehow re-emerge, with new denizens, but with the old defiance? And even if the Fourth International was quite impotent now, who could say how the cataclysms of war might change the political landscape, what mountains they might not flatten and what hillocks they might not raise into mighty peaks? All the prospects that were so real to Trotsky in his hopes were equally real to Stalin in his fears; and Trotsky alive was their supreme and never-resting agent. He remained the mouthpiece of Atlantis, still uttering all its undying passions and all its battle cries. At every critical turn, when the inglorious Finnish campaign came to an end, when Hitler occupied Norway and Denmark, and when France collapsed, his voice rose from beyond the ocean to thunder on the consequences of these disasters, on Stalin's blunders that had helped to bring them about, and on the mortal perils threatening the Soviet Union. True, his indictments, condemnations, and warnings, did not reach the Soviet people; but they appeared in American, British, and other newspapers; and as the war spread to the East, they

[1] *The Archives* and *Trotsky's Diary in Exile*, pp. 139–41.

PLATE XIX

Two views of the 'little fortress' at Coyoacan

Associated Press

PLATE XX

Trotsky, Natalya, and Seva. At the end of 1939

might, in the turmoil and confusion of military defeats and retreats, penetrate there too.

At the end of April 1940 Trotsky addressed to 'Soviet workers, peasants, soldiers, and sailors' a message entitled 'You are being Deceived'. It is said that a leaflet with the message was smuggled into the U.S.S.R. by sympathetic sailors; but it must be doubted whether the message ever reached its destination.[1] Still, every sentence in it was dynamite. 'Your newspapers', he told the Soviet workers and soldiers, 'are telling you lies in the interest of Cain-Stalin and his depraved commissars, secretaries, and G.P.U.-men.' 'Your bureaucracy is bloodthirsty and ruthless at home, but cowardly *vis-à-vis* the imperialist powers.' Stalin's infamies were robbing the Soviet Union of sympathy abroad, isolating it, and strengthening its enemies; these infamies were 'the main source of danger to the Soviet Union'. He called the workers and soldiers 'never to surrender to the world bourgeoisie the nationalized industry and the collectivized economy, because upon this foundation they could still build a new and happier society'. 'It is the duty of revolutionaries to defend tooth and nail every position gained by the working class . . . democratic rights, wage scales, and an achievement as colossal as the nationalization of the means of production and a planned economy.' But these 'conquests' of the October revolution would benefit the people only if they proved themselves capable of dealing with the Stalinist bureaucracy as they had once dealt with the Tsarist bureaucracy. No, Stalin could not allow Trotsky's voice to go on summoning insurrection.

Several former G.P.U. officers and foreign communists have since described how the final assault on Trotsky was prepared.[2] At the end of the Spanish Civil War, G.P.U. agencies specialized in the 'liquidation of Trotskyism' were transferred to Mexico. Mexican Stalinists did what they could to whip up

---

[1] I am quoting the text, dated 23 April 1940, from *The Archives*. About this time shortly before the German invasion of Norway, Walter Held, the German Trotskyist, left that country, hoping to reach America via the U.S.S.R. and Japan. En route, however, he vanished without trace. He was almost certainly arrested and executed in the U.S.S.R. It is possible, but not very probable, that he tried to convey Trotsky's message to people in the U.S.S.R.

[2] See, e.g., Budenz, *This is my Story*, pp. 257–63; and Orlov's deposition quoted above.

mass hysteria against 'the traitor sheltering at Coyoacan'. Day in, day out, they accused him not only of plotting against Stalin, but of conspiring, in the interest of the American oil magnates, against Cardenas, and preparing a general strike and a fascist *coup d'état* in Mexico. Even so, at the beginning of the year 1940 Moscow charged the leaders of the Mexican Communist party with adopting 'a conciliatory attitude towards Trotskyism'; and these leaders were demoted. The anti-Trotskyist campaign rose to a new pitch; and a minor blunder committed by Trotsky himself provided grist to his enemies. Just before the end of the year 1939 he agreed to go to the United States and appear as witness before the so-called Dies Committee of the House of Representatives, a body which carried out 'investigations into un-American activities' (and which did this in a manner anticipating the witch-hunts conducted by Senator McCarthy in the nineteen-fifties). Senator Dies, chairman of the Committee, demanded the suppression of the American Communist party on the ground that it was the agency of a foreign power. Trotsky intended to use the Committee as a forum from which he would expose the G.P.U.'s murderous activities directed against himself and his followers. But he made it clear beforehand that he would speak up against the suppression of the Communist party and would call the workers of the world to turn world war into world revolution. Nothing came of the plan, partly because Trotsky's own followers, especially Burnham, strongly objected to it; and partly because the Dies Committee, forewarned about the kind of deposition Trotsky was ready to make, did not wish to hear him; and the American Government refused him the entry visa. Yet whatever the terms on which he had intended to appear before the Committee, the mere fact that he had been willing to do so made it easy for the Stalinists to accuse him of 'intriguing with Dies and the oil magnates against the Mexican people'. On 1 May 1940, 20,000 uniformed communists marched through Mexico City with the slogan 'Out with Trotsky' on their banners. He replied with denials, published his correspondence concerning the Dies Committee, and asked for an official Mexican inquiry into the matter.[1] President Cardenas

---

[1] 'Why did I agree to appear before the Dies Committee?' Trotsky's statements to the Press of 11 and 12 December 1939. *The Archives*.

shrugged off the Stalinist accusations; yet these had made an impression; and Trotsky's well-wishers wondered whether he would not be deprived of asylum, especially if Cardenas were to lose at the forthcoming elections.

.   .   .   .

At this time the assassin already stood at the gate of the house at Avenida Viena. This was the man who had, in the summer of 1938, introduced himself as Jacques Mornard, the son of a Belgian diplomat, to Sylvia Agelof, the American Trotskyist who was present at the founding conference of the Fourth International. What his real name was has not yet been officially established, although it seems quite certain that he was Ramon Mercader, the son of Caridad Mercader, a Spanish communist well known in her country during the civil war *inter alia* for her close connexions with the G.P.U. Mornard's meeting with Sylvia Agelof in Paris was not accidental; it had been carefully prearranged. G.P.U. agents had for some time past watched Sylvia and her sister: both were Trotskyists; and Sylvia's sister travelled occasionally as courier to Coyoacan and did secretarial work for Trotsky. As to Sylvia, she had studied philosophy under Sidney Hook and psychology at Columbia University; she knew Russian, French, and Spanish, and could be especially helpful to the 'Old Man,' who so often complained that he was 'paralysed at work' because of the lack of a Russian secretary. A lonely spinster of rather unattractive appearance, she found herself all of a sudden assiduously courted by the handsome and well-groomed Mornard. She succumbed, and spent with him several absent-minded, dream-like months in France. Now and then she was puzzled by his behaviour. He exhibited so complete a lack of any interest in politics that this seemed to amount to an indolence of mind, quite surprising in the educated 'son of a diplomat'. He had impenetrably obscure connexions in commerce and journalism; even his family background was enigmatic. The stories he told her about himself were odd, even incoherent; and he spent lavishly, as if from a horn of plenty, on feasts and amusements.[1]

In February 1939, Sylvia Agelof returned to the States. In

---

[1] M. Craipeau, 'J'ai connu l'assassin de Trotsky', *France-Observateur*, 19 May 1960.

September he joined her in New York. Again she was somewhat perplexed by his behaviour. He had given her notice that he would come to the States as the American correspondent of a Belgian newspaper; instead he arrived with a false Canadian passport, assumed the name of Frank Jacson, and said that he had done this in order to avoid military service in Belgium. He claimed that he had never been in New York before; yet he knew his way about the City like someone familiar with the place. But to any puzzled query he had a plausible answer; and as he never dropped his role of playboy and *bon viveur*, he aroused not a shred of political suspicion. The worst she could reproach him with was frivolity and a penchant for fanfaronade. She tried to improve him and to get him interested in Trotskyism; but he invariably met these attempts with a closed mind and a bored face. And so, when soon after his arrival in New York, he told her that he was going to Mexico as sales agent or manager of an import-export firm, she found nothing strange in this; and when he urged her to join him in Mexico, she eagerly consented.

He was in Mexico before the middle of October; she came in January. She went at once to worship at the shrine in the Avenida Viena—she certainly delivered there messages from American Trotskyists. She soon returned to help with secretarial work. 'Jacson' usually drove her to the Avenida Viena in his expensive car; and, when her work was done, he awaited her at the gate. The guards came to know him and often chatted with him. Yet for several months he never ventured into the compound. (He still pretended to have only a condescending smile for Sylvia's political activities; but just to please her he began to show a little more curiosity about them.) At the gate he ran into Alfred and Marguerite Rosmer who presently became familiar with him as the 'obliging young man', 'Sylvia's husband'. He invited them to dinners in Mexico City and took them out into the country on sightseeing trips.

During the hours which he was supposed to work as a business agent, he kept in touch with G.P.U. men from whom he took orders and, it seems, with his mother who, according to several sources, was in Mexico then. Of these contacts of his Sylvia never had the slightest glimpse; he never brought his 'wife' and his mother together. Only sometimes he committed an indiscretion that for a moment put even Sylvia on guard. He gave her the address of his business office; and this turned out to be fictitious. He apologized for the 'mistake' and gave her another address. Sylvia, remembering that he had made a similar 'mistake' in Paris once, was so worried that she asked Marguerite Rosmer, a shrewd and observant person, to investigate the matter. However, the new address was found to be genuine; and even the Rosmers were so convinced that if there was anything slightly *louche* in Mornard-'Jacson's' affairs it had nothing to do with politics, that no one tried to pry into the nature of his 'business office'. (Only much later was it discovered that the same 'office' was used by various local Stalinist big-wigs.) Sylvia was scrupulous enough never to bring 'Jacson' into Trotsky's home—she even told Trotsky that as her husband had come to Mexico on a false passport, his visit might needlessly embarrass Trotsky. And when, in March, she left for New York, she took from 'Jacson' a formal promise that he would never in her absence enter the house in Avenida Viena.

Soon thereafter, however, he did enter. Rosmer had fallen ill, and 'Jacson' was asked to take him to the French hospital in Mexico City; then to bring him back, to buy medicines, &c. While chance thus smoothed his way, he was cautious enough to write to Sylvia and explain apologetically why he had 'broken his promise'. And although he was now becoming more and more familiar with Trotsky's household, three more months were to pass before he would meet Trotsky himself.

It seems that so far 'Jacson' had not yet been assigned the job of assassin. His task was rather to reconnoitre the house, its layout and defences, to ferret out details of Trotsky's daily routine, and to get any other information that might be useful for a massive armed assault which others were to carry out.

The man in charge of this attack was to be David Alfaro Siqueiros, Rivera's former friend, the celebrated painter, communist, and leader of Mexican miners. The year before he had returned from Spain, where he had commanded several brigades during the Civil War—he withdrew from the fighting at the head of only two or three score survivors. That so eminent and even heroic an artist should have agreed or volunteered to become Trotsky's murderer speaks volumes about the morals of Stalinism in these years; but it was, of course, a national habit in Mexico to settle political accounts gun in hand. In Siqueiros art, revolution, and gangsterism were inseparable— he had in himself much of the Latin American buccaneer. In Spain he had entered into a close connexion with the G.P.U. and, some say, with the Mercader family. Yet, despite the zealous services he had rendered, the Communist party had censured him recently for a misdemeanour in his handling of party funds. He was hurt and eager to regain favour by a conspicuous and hazardous act of devotion. He worked out the plan of an armed raid on Trotsky's home, and for its execution he called on men who had fought under him in Spain, and on Mexican miners.[1]

At Avenida Viena everyone had lived in the expectation of such an attack. Reading the local Stalinist papers railing against him, Trotsky remarked: 'People write like this only when they are ready to change the pen for the machine-gun.' True, at the insistence of his American followers, the house had been fortified: heavily barred doors, electrified wires, automatic alarm signals, and machine guns were in the way of would-be assailants. The guards had been increased. Ten Mexican policemen were on duty outside and around the house. Inside, sentries kept watch at the gate, day and night; and four or five men were at the ready in the guards' quarters. No doubt some of the guards, American boys from middle-class homes and just out of college, were little suited for their duty; but this could not be helped: the few workers who were members of the Trotskyist organization could rarely afford to give up jobs, leave families, and come to Coyoacan. Men came and went—after a few months of the monotonous routine a member of the bodyguard easily became jaded, undisciplined, and had to be replaced. It was therefore unavoidable that now and then the sentry at the entrance door should be an inexperienced recruit. Robert Sheldon Harte, who was to be on duty on the night of the Siqueiros raid, had come from New York on 7 April. During his six weeks at Coyoacan his comrades and Trotsky himself found him a warm-hearted and devoted

---

[1] General L. A. S. Salazar, *Murder in Mexico*. (I am obliged for some of the details about Siqueiros's character and background to an American writer who knew him well in the nineteen-thirties.)

but rather gullible and feckless creature.[1] Much later his comrades were to recall that he had struck up a quick friendship
with Mornard-'Jacson' and that they had often been seen
going out together. Clearly, Trotsky's security depended now on
quite a few accidental circumstances. However, even these
circumstances were not quite accidental, for they reflected his
general situation, the heavy odds against him, and the extreme
scantiness and the limitations of his following.

On 23 May, Trotsky worked hard the whole day, went late
to bed; and could not fall asleep until he took a sleeping pill.
About 4 a.m. a noise like the rattling of machine-guns awakened
him. He was tired and drowsy and for a moment he thought
that Mexicans outside were celebrating with fireworks one of
their uproarious religious or national holidays. But 'the explosions were too close, right here within the room, next to me and
overhead. The odour of gunpowder became more acrid, more
penetrating . . . we were under attack'.[2] Natalya had already
jumped out of bed and shielded him with her body. A moment
later, under a hail of bullets, she pushed him down to the floor,
into a corner between the bed and the wall; and, pulled by
him, she went down herself, again covering him with her body.
Silent and motionless, they lay in the darkness, while unseen
assailants kept the room under a steady cross-fire coming
through windows and doors. Perhaps 200 shots were fired; a
hundred fell on and near the beds—over seventy holes were
later counted in walls and doors. Natalya raised herself a little;
he dragged her down again; and again they lay without stirring, breathed the gunpowder, and wondered what had happened to the guards and the police outside.

Suddenly a high-pitched cry 'Grandpa!' came from behind a
wall or door. The attackers had broken into Seva's bedroom.
'The voice of the child', Trotsky said later, 'remains the most
tragic recollection of that night.' 'This cry', Natalya recalls,
'chilled us to the marrow.' Then silence fell. 'They have

---

[1] Trotsky relates that shortly after Sheldon's arrival he saw him giving away the
key to the front gate of the house to one of the builders working there. Trotsky
warned him not to do this and said: 'If you behave like this, you will in case of an
attack be its first victim.' Trotsky's statement on Sheldon of 15 July 1940. *The
Archives*.

[2] Trotsky's account of the event, written on 8 June 1940, appeared posthumously under the title 'Stalin Seeks my Death' in *Fourth International*, August 1941.

kidnapped him', Trotsky whispered. As in a dream Natalya saw a man's silhouette which was illumined by the flare of an incendiary bomb exploding in the child's room, 'the curve of a helmet, shining buttons, an elongated face'. The man stopped at the doorstep between the Trotskys' bedroom and the child's, as if to check whether there was any sign of life and, though there seemed to be none, he fired another volley at the beds and vanished. The shooting now resounded through the courtyard, and the child's bedroom was on fire. Seva was not there—amid the flames a thin trail of blood could be seen leading out into the patio. 'Then all was silence . . . unbearable silence', Natalya recalled. ' "Where can I hide you safely?" [she was thinking] I was losing my strength from the tension and the hopelessness. Any moment now, they will return to finish him.' Where were all the members of the household, the Rosmers, the secretaries, the guards, the police? Were they all killed? '. . . we felt the stillness of the night, like the stillness of the grave, of death itself. . . . And suddenly there came again the same voice, the voice of our grandson; but this time it came from the patio and sounded quite differently, ringing out like a staccato passage of music, bravely, joyously: "Al-fred! Mar-gue-rite!" It returned us to the living!' Seva had saved himself also by hiding under his bed; and even before the shooting had ceased, thinking that his grandparents were dead, he went out with a wound in his toe, to look for the Rosmers.[1]

Within a few minutes the household assembled in the patio. No one had been killed or seriously wounded. The guards were still so dazed that they had not even checked what had happened to the police outside. Trotsky rushed out into the street and found the sentries disarmed and tied up. Brief, rapid, excited accounts: just before 4 a.m. over twenty men, in police and army uniforms, surprised the sentries and overpowered them without firing a shot. Then the assailants, led by a 'major', approached the gate; and one of them spoke to Robert Sheldon Harte who was on duty. The latter at once opened the gate. The attackers rushed into the courtyard, surprised and terrorized the other guards, placed machine guns behind trees at various points opposite Trotsky's bedroom, took up other positions, and opened fire. They were obviously out to kill

[1] Natalya Sedova in *Vie et Mort de Leon Trotsky*, pp. 309–10.

Trotsky and his family—they aimed not a single shot at anyone else. The raid lasted twenty minutes. Convinced that neither Trotsky nor his wife and grandchild could have survived, the raiders withdrew, throwing incendiary grenades into the house and a powerful bomb (which failed to explode) into the patio. Some left in two cars which belonged to Trotsky and usually stood in the yard ready to depart at a moment's notice, with the ignition keys in the locks. Sheldon disappeared with the raiders. The policemen, who had seen him, maintained that he had put up no resistance, but that two of the raiders had led him out, holding him fast by the arms.

Relief and joy at the 'miraculous escape' were the first emotions; and Trotsky's sense of irony was aroused. It amused him to see that so heavy an attack, so laboriously mounted, should have failed so miserably—only because he, Natalya, and the child had, in their utter helplessness, done the only thing they could do and thrown themselves under their beds! Now Stalin and his agents stood exposed and covered with ridicule! There could be no doubt for whose benefit, at whose instigation, and by whose orders the raid had been carried out. But with the exhilaration and the triumphant irony there mingled some perplexity. How familiar the raiders had been with the layout and the defences of the little fortress—they even knew that they could drive away in their victim's cars! How had Sheldon come to let them in, apparently without hesitation? He was feckless and gullible; but surely before he opened the gate, he must have been approached by someone whom he trusted and whose voice he knew? Who was it? Or had the raiders climbed into the courtyard over the high walls and electrified wires? Why then did they abduct Sheldon (whom they must certainly be going to kill)?

Within half an hour Colonel Salazar, chief of the Mexican Secret Police, was on the spot; and this is how he describes the scene:[1] 'I asked to see Trotsky, who soon arrived accompanied by his wife . . . [he] was in pyjamas, over which he had slipped a dressing-gown. They greeted me with friendliness . . . but they preserved a surprising calm. One might have thought that nothing had happened. . . . Trotsky smiled, with his eyes bright

[1] Salazar, op. cit., pp. 6–10.

and clear behind his tortoiseshell glasses—eyes always keen and piercing—his glance sharp and penetrating, with a jesting, sarcastic, slightly Mephistophelian air. His hair . . . almost white . . . seemed a little untidy, thrown back from his forehead, with stray locks falling at the sides. . . .' There was a 'striking contrast' between Trotsky and Natalya: 'He, energetic and authoritative . . . his features still young, firm; she sweet, calm, and almost resigned.' But both behaved with a coolness and 'perfect self-control' which seemed quite unnatural to the police chief. At once a suspicion crossed his mind: 'Had there really been an attempt on their lives or was it a put-up job?' As he listened to Trotsky, giving him, in his study, 'without the slightest emotion', a full and precise account of what he had just experienced, Salazar reflected again: 'So many attackers, so many fire-arms, even bombs, and nothing has happened to them! It is all very strange!' They went back into the garden which looked, with its lovingly tended cacti, as peaceful as ever; and the officer asked Trotsky whether he suspected anyone as 'the author of the attempt'.

'I most certainly do!' he replied in a very decided tone of voice. 'Come. . . .'

He put his right arm on my shoulder and slowly led me towards the rabbit hutches. . . . He stopped, glanced all round him, [as if] to make sure that we were alone, and, placing his right hand near his mouth, as though wishing to make the confidence more secret, he said in a low voice and with deep conviction:

'The author of the attack is Joseph Stalin, through the medium of the G.P.U.'

Now the officer was sure that Trotsky was pulling his leg. 'I looked at him stupefied. . . . My first suspicion became a certainty. Again I said to myself, "It is a put-up job! There is not the least doubt of it." ' And when Trotsky advised him to interrogate some of the 'most conspicuous' local Stalinists, from whom he might learn a lot about the raid, Salazar concluded that 'the old revolutionary was trying to distract my attention from the real path'. He ordered the arrest first of three domestic servants, a cook, a parlour maid, and a handyman, and then of two of Trotsky's secretaries, Otto Schüssler and Charles Cornell. The turn the investigation now took bred the most sensational rumours. Some said that Diego Rivera had organized the attack and that the raiders had broken into the house with the cry 'Long live Almazar'. (Almazar was the name of the reactionary general whose candidature for the Presidency Rivera backed against Cardenas.) Others maintained that Trotsky or his followers had staged the attack in order to turn suspicion on the Stalinists and discredit them.[1]

Curiously, the chief of the Secret Police felt no hostility towards Trotsky and had no axe to grind. But to the mind of a professional soldier and policeman, unfamiliar with the issues, the personalities, and the atmosphere of the terrible struggle which the raid was to have brought to an end—the whole affair did indeed appear extremely enigmatic. He had just counted seventy-three bullet holes in the wall over Trotsky's bed and the 'miraculous escape' seemed to him all the more mysterious. He observed Trotsky's and Natalya's self-possession and reflected that he, a veteran of Mexico's many civil wars, had never seen anyone behaving with such calm so soon after facing such dangers.[2] The precision and the humour of Trotsky's talk seemed quite out of place and all the more suspect. (Only in the next few months, when his duties brought him to Trotsky very frequently, was he to realize that the man's 'unnatural' calm, courage, and humour were his nature.) On the other hand, the raid was so gross a scandal even by Mexican standards that Salazar found it hard to believe that the Stalinists, Cardenas' supporters (of whom he was no friend), could have been behind it. The behaviour of Trotsky's guards also aroused his distrust: why had they been so strangely passive? Why had none of them been shot at? Salazar was convinced that Sheldon had been in collusion with the raiders and had left with them of his own free will. Trotsky vehemently asserted that Sheldon was their victim, not their accomplice; but he could offer no proof. And there was this grain of truth in Salazar's reasoning: the raid could not have been carried out without the co-operation of someone in Trotsky's entourage or at least of someone in close contact with his household. Who was it? This question

---

[1] Salazar, op. cit., pp. 18–25. Not only the pro-Stalinist newspapers of Mexico but even *The Nation* of New York published a correspondence suggesting that Trotsky himself or members of his household had staged the raid. 'What an infamous reptile breed', Trotsky commented, 'these "radicals" of *The Nation* are.' 18 June 1940. *The Archives.*

[2] Salazar, op. cit., pp. 10–11 and 100.

should now have engaged all their attention and aroused all their vigilance.

A week after the attack, Trotsky, outraged by the suspicions directed towards himself and Rivera, protested to President Cardenas against the arrest of his two secretaries.[1] Referring to what he knew (*inter alia* from Reiss and Krivitsky) about the workings of the G.P.U. in many countries, he demanded that the magistrate or the police interrogate the present and former General Secretaries of the Mexican Communist party and also Siqueiros and Lombardo Toledano. The President ordered the immediate release of Trotsky's secretaries. But for some time yet the investigation followed wrong tracks; and Trotsky was busy refuting imputations made against him, defending his collaborators, and affirming the innocence of Robert Sheldon Harte. 'If Harte', he said, 'had been a G.P.U. agent he could have stabbed me on the quiet', without all the hubbub of a massive and sensational raid. In the meantime the police apprehended several of the raiders, who confirmed that Siqueiros had been their leader; and Siqueiros himself went into hiding.[2] Finally, on 25 June, Salazar's men dug out Sheldon Harte's corpse from the grounds of a little farm outside Mexico City— the farmhouse had been rented by two well-known painters, both Stalinists.

At 4 a.m., the hour when a month and a day earlier the raid took place, Salazar came with this news to Trotsky's house. The guards refused to awaken Trotsky; and so he returned to the farmhouse with one of the guards to identify the body.

We arrived at the foot of the slope at dawn. The soaked earth made the ascent extraordinarily difficult. The body was lying on the stretcher where I had left it, outside the house. . . . Otto . . . immediately recognized his comrade.

'It was daylight when we arrived at San Angel. The corpse was placed in a courtyard. General Nunez arrived shortly afterwards, and gave the order for it to be washed. Then he had the guard

---

[1] Trotsky's letter to President Cardenas of 31 May 1940. *The Archives*.

[2] Salazar, op. cit., p. 184. Arrested on 4 October 1940, (after Trotsky's assassination), Siqueiros did not deny his participation in the May raid, but maintained that the Communist Party had nothing to do with it; and that his purpose was not to kill Trotsky but to produce a 'psychological shock' and to protest against Trotsky's presence. Released on bail, Siqueiros disappeared from Mexico for several years.

strengthened, for the news had spread throughout the town and inquisitive crowds began to arrive. The formalities finished, the magistrate left.

All at once a movement occurred among the crowd.

'Trotsky! Trotsky!'

It was indeed he. Ten o'clock struck. The old Russian exile approached the body. He looked sad and depressed. He stood for a long moment looking at his ex-secretary: his eyes were filled with tears. This man had directed a great revolution, had survived bloody battles, had seen his friends and his family disappearing one by one, had remained unmoved by an attack which had almost cost him not only his, but his wife's and grandson's lives— and now he wept in silence.[1]

The enigma of Harte's role was not definitely solved, however. Salazar still maintained that Harte had been a G.P.U. agent; but that the G.P.U. killed him because they feared that he would fall into the hands of the Mexican police and talk too much. This supposition was partly confirmed by eye-witnesses who said that they had seen Harte moving around the farmhouse freely and going out for walks without any guard or escort. Against this Trotsky insisted that this was the eighth of his secretaries to perish and that all that he and his American comrades knew of Harte contradicted Salazar's version.[2] He sent a moving message of condolence to the victim's parents and put up a plaque commemorating 'Bob'—opposite that plaque Trotsky's own tombstone was soon to be raised.

After 24 May the mist of doom hung still and stifling over the 'little fortress' at Avenida Viena. From week to week and from day to day another attack was expected. To Trotsky himself it was a freak of fortune that he was still alive. He would get up in the morning and say to Natalya: 'You see, they did not kill us last night, after all; and you are still dissatisfied.' Once or twice he added pensively: 'Yes, Natasha, we have had a reprieve.'[3] He remained as active and energetic as ever, intervened in every phase of the police investigation, appeared in

[1] Salazar, op. cit., pp. 76–77.

[2] Trotsky listed the following secretaries and assistants of his who had perished as victims of Stalinist vengeance: Glazman, Butov, Blumkin, Sermuks, Posnansky, Klement, and Wolf. Statement of 25 June 1940 in *The Archives*.

[3] Natalya Sedova, 'Tak eto bylo', *B.O.*, no. 85, March 1941; 'How it happened', *Fourth International*, May 1941.

the court, replied to never-ending calumny, commented on such events as the capitulation of France and Molotov's declaration of support to the Third Reich, and went on debating the position of the Negroes in the U.S.A., the tactics of revolutionary defeatism, and so on. A group of American friends, who visited him before the middle of June, implored him to 'go underground', assume an incognito, and allow himself to be smuggled into the United States, where they were confident they could provide him with a safe clandestine retreat. He refused to listen to their entreaties. He could not, he said, skulk for his life and do his work furtively; he had to meet foe and friend in the open—his bare head had to endure the 'hell-black night' to the end.[1] Reluctantly, he yielded to friends and to Mexican authorities who urged that the defences of his house be strengthened by higher concrete walls, new watch towers, armoured doors, and steel shutters on windows. He dutifully inspected the 'fortification works', suggested changes and improvements, but then shrugged with distaste: 'This reminds me of the first jail I was in', he remarked to Joseph Hansen, his secretary. 'The doors make the same sound. . . . This is not a home; it is a medieval prison.' 'One day [Hansen says] he caught me gazing at the new towers. His eyes twinkled in one of those warm, intimate smiles of his. . . . "Highly advanced civilization—that we must still make such constructions." '[2] He was indeed like a man awaiting the fatal day in the condemned cell—only that he was determined to make judicious use of every hour, and his irony and humour did not abandon him.

He went on his last drives into the country over muddy, boulder-strewn roads; and his mind wandered back to Russia's roads in the years of civil war. On this last trip 'he slept much more than usual, as if he were exhausted and this were his first opportunity in a long time to rest. He relaxed in the seat beside me and slept from Cuernavaca almost to Ameccamecca, where the volcanoes, Popocatapetl and Ixtaccihuatl, the Sleeping Woman, gather great fleecy clouds about their white summits . . . we stopped beside an ancient hacienda with towering, strongly buttressed walls. The Old Man regarded the walls with interest: "A fine wall, but medieval. Like our own

---

[1] This has been related to me by one of those who put the proposal to Trotsky.
[2] Joseph Hansen, 'With Trotsky to the End', *Fourth International*, October 1940.

prison." [1] In this description 'medieval', which so often came to his lips, he expressed not merely his repugnance for his own incarceration, but his sense that the world was relapsing from what might have been the age of progress and triumphant humanity into the savage cruelties of the Dark Ages; and that even he, by surrounding himself with turrets, buttresses, and ramparts, was somehow involved in the general backsliding. After the raid friends presented him with a bullet-proof vest; and even as he thanked them he could not hide his displeasure; he put the vest away and suggested that it would best be worn by the sentry on duty in the watch tower. His secretaries repeatedly proposed to search visitors for concealed weapons and objected when he received strangers alone in his study. 'He could not bear having his friends submit to search', says Hansen. 'No doubt he felt that in any case this would be useless and could even give us a false sense of security . . . a G.P.U. agent . . . would find some way of setting at nought what search we could make.' He frowned when any of his bodyguards tried to be present while he talked with visitors, some of whom 'had personal problems [and] would not talk freely in the presence of a guard'.[2]

.   .   .   .

It was on 28 May, a few days after the raid, that the assassin came for the first time face to face with Trotsky. The encounter could not have been more casual. The Rosmers were about to leave Mexico and board a ship at Vera Cruz; and 'Jacson' had offered to take them there in his car, pretending that he had to go to Vera Cruz anyhow, on one of his regular business journeys. He came to fetch them early in the morning and was asked to wait in the courtyard until they were ready. As he entered, he ran into Trotsky, who was still at the hutches feeding the rabbits. Without interrupting his chores, Trotsky shook hands with the visitor. 'Jacson' behaved with exemplary discretion and amiability: he did not stare at the great man, try to engage him in conversation or hang around; he went instead to Seva's room, gave the child a toy glider, and explained its working. At a hint from Trotsky Natalya then asked him to join the family and the Rosmers at the breakfast table.[3]

[1] Hansen, loc. cit.   [2] Hansen, loc. cit.   [3] Ibid.

After his return from Vera Cruz, 'Jacson' did not show himself at Avenida Viena for a fortnight. When he reappeared there on 12 June, he came for a few minutes to say that he was going to New York and leaving his car with the guards so that they might have its use in his absence. He returned to Mexico a month later, but did not call at Avenida Viena for three weeks, until the Trotskys invited him and Sylvia to have tea with them on 29 July. This was his longest visit—it lasted a little over an hour. According to the detailed records kept by the guards, he crossed the gate only ten times between 28 May and 20 August; and he saw Trotsky only twice or thrice. This was enough for him to survey the scene, to take the measure of his victim, and to put the finishing touches to his plan. He could not have behaved more unobtrusively, obligingly, innocuously; he came with a modest bouquet or a box of sweets for Natalya—'gifts from Sylvia'. He offered, as an experienced Alpinist, to accompany Trotsky in climbing mountains; but he did not dwell on the offer or take it up. When he chatted with the guards, he threw out with familiarity the names of well-known Trotskyists of various nationalities so as to give the impression that he was in and of the movement; *en passant* he mentioned his own donations to party funds. In Trotsky's and Natalya's presence, however, he behaved almost bashfully as befitted an outsider who was just being converted into a 'sympathizer'. This was the time of the split among the American Trotskyists. Sylvia had sided with Burnham and Shachtman; but she was as welcome as ever at Avenida Viena—only when she and 'Jacson' were invited to tea there was a lively argument at table. 'Jacson' did not take part, but let it be understood that he was on Trotsky's side, that he agreed that the Soviet Union was a workers' state and had to be defended 'unconditionally'. With the secretaries he was less reserved and he told them of the heated arguments he had about this with Sylvia. Yet he was careful not to appear over-zealous —had Trotsky not warned his followers that *agents provocateurs* in their midst would show *trop de zèle* and seek to exacerbate the quarrel? Well, 'Jacson' did nothing of the sort; he only tried judiciously to bring Sylvia round to the right viewpoint.

Yet even this master dissembler (who during the twenty years of his imprisonment was to foil all investigators, judges,

PLATE XXI

Trotsky searching for rare cacti. 1940

PLATE XXII

Still arguing—a few days before his assassination

Associated Press

doctors, and psychoanalysts attempting to discover his real identity and his connexions) began to lose nerve as his deadline approached. He returned from New York, where he probably got the final briefing on his assignment, in a brooding mood. Usually robust and gay, he became nervous and gloomy; his complexion was green and pale; his face twitched; his hands trembled. He spent most of his days in bed, silent, shut up in himself, refusing to talk to Sylvia. Then he had fits of gaiety and garrulousness which startled Trotsky's secretaries. He boasted of his Alpinist exploits and of the physical strength which enabled him 'to split a huge ice-block with a single blow of an ice-axe'. At a meal he demonstrated the 'surgical skill' of his hands by carving a chicken with unusual dexterity. (Months later those who witnessed this 'demonstration' recalled that he had also said that he had known Klement well, Klement whose dead body had been found dismembered with such 'surgical skill'.) He talked of the 'financial genius' of his commercial 'boss' and offered to carry out with him some operations on the Stock Exchange in order to help the Fourth International financially. One day, watching with Trotsky and Hansen the 'fortification works' at Avenida Viena, he remarked that these were worthless because 'in the next attack the G.P.U. would use quite a different method'; and asked what method that might be, he answered with a shrug.

Members of the household were to recall these and similar incidents only three and four months later when they realized how ominous they had been. For the time being they saw in them nothing worse than signs of 'Jacson's' erratic temper. Trotsky alone, who knew him so little, became apprehensive. True, even he had defended 'Jacson' rather half-heartedly when someone said with indignation that 'Jacson', during his trip to New York, had not even called at the Trotskyist headquarters there. Well, well, Trotsky replied, Sylvia's husband was, of course, a flippant fellow who might never be of much use as a comrade, but perhaps he would improve—it took all sorts of people to make a party. But 'Jacson's' talk about his 'boss', the 'financial genius', and the Stock Exchange speculations he would undertake for the 'movement', made Trotsky bristle. 'These brief conversations', says Natalya, 'displeased me; Leon Davidovich was also struck by them. "Who is this very rich 'boss'?", he said to me. "One should find out. It may, after all, be some profiteer of the fascist type perhaps—it might be better for us not to receive Sylvia's husband any more. . . ." ' He had broken with Molinier who had also had his 'financial plans'; but he had never had the slightest doubt about Molinier's political sincerity; and he was quite willing to forgive him his offences even now. But in 'Jacson' he sensed something sinister— was he perhaps connected with the fascists? Yet despite this vague intuition, he would not affront him without verifying the grounds for the distrust.[1]

On 17 August, 'Jacson' returned, saying that he had written an article against Burnham and Shachtman (with some references also to the situation in German-occupied France)— would Trotsky go over the draft and suggest corrections? He touched cunningly a sensitive chord in his victim, the urge to instruct and improve comrades and followers. Reluctantly but dutifully, Trotsky invited 'Jacson' to come with him to the study. There they remained alone and discussed the article. After only ten minutes Trotsky came out disturbed and worried. His suspicion was suddenly heightened; he told Natalya that he had no wish to see 'Jacson' any more. What upset him was not what the man had written—a few clumsy and muddled clichés— but his behaviour. While they were at the writing table and Trotsky was looking through the article, 'Jacson' seated himself on the table and there, placed above his host's head, he remained to the end of the interview! And all the time he had his hat on and clutched his coat to himself! Trotsky was not only irritated by the visitor's discourtesy; he sensed a fraud again. He had the feeling that the man was an impostor. He remarked to Natalya that in his behaviour 'Jacson' was 'quite unlike a Frenchman',—yet he presented himself as a Belgian brought up in France. Who was he really? They should find this out. Natalya was taken aback; it seemed to her that Trotsky 'had perceived something new about "Jacson", but had not yet reached, or rather was in no hurry, to reach, any conclusions'. Yet the implication of what he had said was alarming: if 'Jacson' was deceiving them about his nationality, why was he doing it? And was he not deceiving them about other things as well? About what? These questions must have been on Trotsky's

<hr />

[1] Natalya Sedova in *Vie et Mort de Leon Trotsky*, p. 319.

mind, for two days later he repeated his observations to Hansen, as if to ascertain whether similar misgivings had occurred to anyone beside himself. However, the assassin moved faster than the victim's intuition and instinct of self-preservation: it was on the day before the attempt on his life that Trotsky confided his vague suspicions to Hansen.[1]

The interview on 17 August was for Jacson his dress-rehearsal. He had enticed Trotsky into the study for a *tête-à-tête*, made him read a manuscript, and placed himself above his head. He had come to the dress-rehearsal with ice-axe, dagger, and pistol concealed in the coat he clutched in his arms. In his pocket he may already have had the letter purporting to explain his motives—the text had been typed out well ahead of time; on the day of the attempt he had only to insert the date and to sign it. In that letter he presented himself as Trotsky's 'devoted follower' who had been ready to give the 'last drop of blood' for him, who had gone to Mexico on instructions from the Fourth International, and for whom meeting Trotsky was 'the realization of a dream.' But in Mexico 'a great disillusionment' awaited him: the man whom he had imagined to be *the* leader of the working class unmasked himself as a criminal counter-revolutionary and urged him 'to go to Russia to organize there a series of attempts against various persons and, in the first place, against Stalin'. He found Trotsky conspiring 'with certain leaders of capitalist countries'—'the consul of a great foreign nation paid him frequent visits'—and conspiring against both the Soviet Union and Mexico.[2] The purpose of the letter was to make even Trotsky's death corroborate all the Stalinist accusations, except that, in view of the pact between Stalin and Hitler, the charge that Trotsky was Hitler's accomplice was replaced by a hint that he was in the service of American imperialism. Even the trick by which Trotsky's 'disillusioned follower' was to confirm the Stalinist charges was not new: the hand that had murdered Klement had written the same 'disclosures' of a 'disillusioned Trotskyist' in Klement's name. To make the concoction even shabbier, 'Jacson' added that Trotsky had urged him to 'desert his wife' because she had joined the Shachtman

[1] Natalya Sedova, ibid., and *B.O.*, no. 85, 1941; *Fourth International*, May 1941.
[2] The full text of 'Jacson's' 'Confession' is in Albert Goldman's *The Assassination of Leon Trotsky*, pp. 5–8.

group; but he, 'Jacson', could not live or go to Russia without Sylvia. The forgery was crude, but not too crude for the gullible; and, anyhow, who would find the time and patience to scrutinize it carefully now, during the interval between the capitulation of France and the Battle of Britain, when the existence of so many peoples and the foundations of so many states were shattered?

.   .   .   .

And so the last day, Tuesday, 20 August, had come. Whoever recalled it later remembered the exceptional peace and serenity that prevailed in the house up to the fatal hour. The sun shone brightly. The Old Man emanated calm, confidence, and energy. When he got up at 7 a.m. he turned to his wife not with the grim and by now habitual joke, 'You see, they did not kill us last night', but with an expression of physical well-being. 'It is a long time since I felt so well', he said to her; and added that the sleeping drugs he had taken had a good effect on him. 'It is not the drug that does you good', she replied, 'but sound sleep and complete rest.' 'Yes, of course', he chimed in contentedly. He looked forward to a 'really good day's work', dressed quickly, and 'vigorously walked out into the patio to feed his rabbits'. He had neglected them somewhat, for, on doctor's orders, he had spent the Sunday in bed; so he now tended them diligently for a full two hours. At breakfast he again assured Natalya of his excellent health and mood. He was eager to get back to work on 'my poor book', *Stalin*, which he had to put aside after the May raid in order to give his time to the police investigation and to current polemics. But now he had said all that he had to say about the raid; the investigation was moving in the right direction and he hoped that he would not be bothered with it any more. But before going back to the *Stalin*, he still wanted to write an 'important article', not for the great bourgeois Press but for the little Trotskyist periodicals, and speaking with some excitement about the article he went into the study.

He found the morning mail satisfactory. He had at last placed his archives in safety. A cable from the librarian of Harvard University had just acknowledged their receipt. There had been some uneasiness about these, because of hitches *en route* caused either by the G.P.U. or the F.B.I.; and a couple of days earlier Trotsky had instructed Albert Goldman, his American lawyer and comrade, to take action if the F.B.I. tried to pry into his papers. 'I personally have nothing to hide', he wrote, 'but in my letters many third persons are mentioned.' He had deposited the archives at Harvard on condition that one section of them would remain closed until the year 1980.[1] But the hitch *en route* was evidently not serious; and this matter was now happily settled. In his characteristic English, he wrote a few brief, kindly, and jovial, letters to American Trotskyists.[2] He inquired about the health of one who, after a spell as secretary at Coyoacan, had returned home; he thanked the comrade and his wife for a dictionary of American slang they had sent him and he promised to study it diligently so as to be able to follow his bodyguard's conversation at mealtimes. He sent greetings to two comrades who had been imprisoned for strike activities and were about to be released. And then he settled down to record his last article on a dictaphone.[3]

The tentative shapeless text of the article suggests that his mind was in a ferment and that he was trying to modify an old idea of his or to produce a new one. He had until quite recently expounded 'revolutionary defeatism', as Lenin had done during the First World War, telling the workers that their task was not to defend any imperialist fatherland, be it democratic or fascist, but to turn the war into revolution. But now, after the Nazis had conquered virtually the whole of Europe and while the British and American working classes were reacting to this with militant anti-fascism, he felt that the mere repetition of old formulae was of no use. 'The present war, as we have stated on more than one occasion, is a continuation of the last war. But a continuation is not a repetition [but] a development, a deepening, a sharpening.' Similarly, the continuation of the Leninist policy of 1914–17 should not be mere repetition, but 'development, deepening'. Lenin's revolutionary defeatism had rendered the Bolshevik party immune to the fetishes of bourgeois

[1] Trotsky to Goldman, 17 August 1940. *The Archives*, Closed Section. This section of the archives contained his correspondence with his followers. At a time when nearly the whole of Europe was controlled either by the Gestapo or by the G.P.U. he felt it to be his duty to protect his correspondents in this way.

[2] See 'Trotsky's Last Letters' in *Fourth International*, October 1940.

[3] Trotsky's 'Last Article', ibid.

patriotism; but—contrary to a widespread belief—'it could not win the masses who did not want a foreign conqueror'. The Bolsheviks had gained popular support not so much by their 'refusal to defend the bourgeois fatherland' as by the positive aspects of their revolutionary agitation and action. Marxists and Leninists in this war must realize this, he concluded; and he came out against Shachtman's group and the pacifists among the Trotskyists who opposed conscription in the United States. In a letter written a few days earlier he had commented on a Public Opinion Poll which had shown that 70 per cent. of American workers favoured conscription. 'We place ourselves on the same ground as the 70 per cent. of the workers. [We say] you, workers, wish to defend . . . democracy. We . . . wish to go further. However, we are ready to defend democracy with you, only on condition that it should be a real defence, and not a betrayal in the Pétain manner.' In the article his mind wandered between France, humiliated and saddled with a 'treacherous senile Bonapartism', and the vastly different American scene. But he had no time to develop these inchoate thoughts; his voice in the dictaphone was to remain the only trace of his last inconclusive groping in a new direction.

.   .   .   .

At one o'clock Rigault, his Mexican attorney, came to see him to advise him to reply at once to an attack in *El Popular*, Toledano's paper, which had accused him of defaming the Mexican trade unions. Trotsky feared that this would drag him back into arid polemics with the local Stalinists, but he agreed that he had to answer *El Popular* at once; and he put aside the article on revolutionary defeatism 'for a few days'. 'I will take the offensive and will charge them with brazen slander', he said to Natalya. He was defiant, but cheerful; and he assured her once more that he was in excellent form. After a brief siesta he was at his desk again, taking notes from *El Popular*. 'He looked well', says Natalya, 'and was in an even mood all the time.' Somewhat earlier she saw him standing in the patio, bareheaded under the scorching sun; and she hastened to fetch his white cap so as to protect his head. Now from time to time she slightly opened the door to his study 'so as not to disturb him'; and she saw him 'in his usual position, bent over his desk, pen in hand'. On tiptoe, from behind the door, the modern Niobe cast her last fond glances at the only beloved being left to her.

Shortly after 5 p.m. he was back at the hutches, feeding the rabbits. Natalya, stepping out on a balcony, noticed an 'unfamiliar figure' standing next to him. The figure came closer, took off the hat, and she recognized 'Jacson'. ' "Here he is again," it flashed through my mind. "Why has he begun to come so often?" I asked myself.' His appearance deepened her foreboding. His face was grey-green, his gestures nervous and jerky, and he pressed his overcoat to his body convulsively. She remembered suddenly that he had boasted to her that he never wore a hat and a coat even in winter; and she asked him why he had the hat and the coat on on so sunny a day. 'It might rain', he replied; and saying that he was 'frightfully thirsty' asked for a glass of water. She offered him tea. 'No, no, I dined too late and I feel the food up here', he pointed at his throat: 'it's choking me.' His mind wandered; he did not seem to catch the meaning of what was said to him. She asked whether he had corrected his article and he, clutching his coat with one hand, showed her several typewritten pages with the other. Pleased that her husband would not have to strain his eyes over an illegible manuscript, she went with 'Jacson' towards the hutches. As they came near, Trotsky turned to her and said in Russian that 'Jacson' was expecting Sylvia to come and, as they would both be leaving for New York the next day, Natalya ought perhaps to invite them to a farewell meal. She answered that 'Jacson' had just refused tea and was not feeling well. 'Lev Davidovich glanced at him attentively, and said in a tone of slight reproach: "Your health is poor again, you look ill. That's no good." '[1] There was a moment of awkward silence. The strange man stood waiting with the typewritten pages in hand and Trotsky, having advised him to rewrite the article, felt obliged to have a look at the result of his fresh effort.

'Lev Davidovich was reluctant to leave the rabbits and was not at all interested in the article', Natalya relates. 'But controlling himself, he said: "Well, what do you say, shall we go over your article?" Unhurriedly, he fastened the hutches and took off his working gloves. . . . He brushed his blue jacket and slowly, silently, walked with myself and "Jacson" towards the

[1] Natalya Sedova, as above.

house. I accompanied them to the door of L.D.'s study; the door closed and I went into the adjoining room.' As they entered the study, the thought 'this man could kill me' flashed across Trotsky's mind—so at least he told Natalya a few minutes later when he lay bleeding on the floor. However, thoughts like this must have occurred to him sometimes—only to be dismissed—when strangers visited him singly or in groups. He had resolved not to let his existence become cramped by fear and misanthropy; and so now he suppressed this last faint reflex of his self-protective instinct. He went to his desk, sat down, and bent his head over the typescript.

He had just managed to run through the first page, when a terrific blow came down upon his head. 'I had put my raincoat . . . on a piece of furniture', 'Jacson' testifies, 'took out the ice-axe, and, closing my eyes, brought it down on his head with all my strength.' He expected that after this mighty blow his victim would be dead without uttering a sound; and that he himself would walk out and vanish before the deed was discovered. Instead, the victim uttered 'a terrible, piercing cry'—'I shall hear that cry all my life', the assassin says.[1] His skull smashed, his face gored, Trotsky jumped up, hurled at the murderer whatever object was at hand, books, inkpots, even the dictaphone, and then threw himself at him. It had all taken only three or four minutes. The piercing, harrowing cry raised Natalya and the guards to their feet, but it took a few moments for them to realize whence it had come and to rush in its direction. During those moments a furious struggle went on in the study, Trotsky's last struggle. He fought it like a tiger. He grappled with the murderer, bit his hand, and wrenched the ice-axe from him. The murderer was so confounded that he did not strike another blow and did not use pistol or dagger. Then Trotsky, no longer able to stand up, straining all his will not to collapse at his enemy's feet, slowly staggered back. When Natalya rushed in, she found him standing in the doorway, between the dining-room and the balcony, and leaning against the door frame. His face was covered with blood, and through the blood his blue eyes, without the glasses on, shone on her sharper than ever; his arms were hanging limply. ' "What has happened?" I asked. ' "What's happened?" I put my arms

[1] Sálazar, op. cit., p. 160.

around him . . . he did not answer at once. For a second I wondered whether something had not fallen on him from the ceiling—repair work was being done in the study—and *why was he standing here?* Calmly, without anger, bitterness, or sorrow he said: "Jacson." He said it as if he wished to say: "Now it has happened." We took a few steps, and slowly, aided by me, he slumped down on to a mat on the floor.'[1]

' "Natasha, I love you." He uttered these words so unexpectedly, so gravely, almost severely that, weak from inner shock, I swayed towards him.' 'No one, no one,' she whispered to him, 'no one, must be allowed to see you without being searched.' Then she carefully placed a cushion under his broken head and a piece of ice on his wound; and she wiped the blood off his forehead and cheeks. 'Seva must be kept out of all this,' he said. He spoke with difficulty, his words were becoming blurred but he seemed unaware of it. 'You know, *in there*'— he turned his eyes towards the door of the study—'I sensed . . . I understood *what he wanted to do* . . . he wanted . . . me . . . once more . . . but I did not let him.' He said this 'calmly, softly, with a breaking voice'; and as if with a note of satisfaction he repeated: 'But I did not let him'. Natalya and Hansen knelt by his sides, opposite each other; and he turned towards Hansen and spoke to him in English, while she 'strained all her attention to catch the meaning of his words, but failed'.

'This is the end,' he said to his secretary in English; and he wanted to find out what exactly had happened. He was convinced that 'Jacson' had fired at him and was incredulous when Hansen told him that he had been hit with an ice-axe and that the wound was superficial. 'No, no, no,' he replied pointing to his heart, 'I feel here that this time they have succeeded.' When he was assured again that the wound was not very dangerous, he smiled faintly with his eyes as if it amused him to see that someone sought to comfort *him* and to conceal the truth from *him*. Most of the time he was pressing Natalya's hands to his lips. 'Take care of Natalya,' he went on in English; 'she has been with me many, many years.' 'We will', Hansen promised. 'The Old Man pressed our hands convulsively, tears suddenly in his eyes. Natalya cried brokenly, bending over him, kissing his wound.'[2]

[1] Natalya Sedova, loc. cit.   [2] Hansen, loc. cit.

Meanwhile, in the study the guards fell upon the assassin, beat him with revolver butts; and his whining and moaning were heard outside. 'Tell the boys not to kill him', Trotsky said, struggling to articulate his words clearly. 'No, no, he must not be killed—he must be made to talk.' The guards related that under the blows 'Jacson' said: 'They have got something on me, they have imprisoned my mother . . . Sylvia has nothing to do with this . . .'; and when they tried to get out of him who had imprisoned his mother, he denied that it was the G.P.U. and said that he had 'nothing to do with the G.P.U.'

When the doctor arrived, Trotsky's left arm and leg were already paralysed. As the stretcher-bearers came—simultaneously with them the police entered—Natalya shrank away: she thought of Lyova's death in the hospital, and she did not want her husband to be moved. He too had no wish to be taken away. Only when Hansen promised that the guards would accompany him, he replied: 'I leave it then to your decision', as if aware that for him 'all the days of making decisions were gone'. While he was being placed on the stretcher, he whispered again: 'I want everything I own to go to Natalya . . . .You will take care of her.'[1]

At the gate the guards, with belated vigilance, stopped the stretcher-bearers; afraid of another attack, they would not allow Trotsky to be taken away unless General Nunez, Chief of Police, came to take charge of the escort. 'I noticed [an ambulance worker relates] that the wounded man's wife had covered her husband with a white shawl. The Señora sobbed and held his bleeding head between her two hands. Señor Trotsky neither spoke nor groaned. We thought that he was dead, but . . . he was still breathing.'[2] They carried him to the ambulance between two lines of police; and as they were about to start, another ambulance arrived to fetch the assassin.

'Through the roaring city, through its vain tumult and din, amidst its garish evening lights, the emergency ambulance sped, winding its way through the traffic and overtaking cars; the sirens were incessantly wailing and the police cordon on motor-cycles whistled shrilly. With unendurable anguish in our hearts and alarm increasing with every minute, we were bearing the wounded man. He was conscious.' His right hand

---

[1] Hansen, loc. cit. [2] Salazar, op. cit., pp. 102–3.

described circles in the air as if it could not find a place to rest; then it wandered above the blanket, touched a water basin overhead, and at last found Natalya. She, bending over him, asked how he felt. 'Better now.' Then he motioned Hansen to himself and in a whisper instructed him how to conduct the investigation. 'He is a political assassin . . . a member of the G.P.U. . . . or a fascist. More likely the G.P.U. . . . but possibly aided by Gestapo.' (Almost simultaneously in the other ambulance the assassin was handing to his escort the letter giving his 'motives' and making it clear that the Gestapo had nothing to do at least with this crime.)

A large crowd was already gathered outside the hospital when Trotsky was lifted out of the ambulance. 'There may be enemies among them. . .' Natalya worried. 'Where are our friends? They should surround the stretcher.' A few minutes later he lay on a narrow hospital bed and doctors examined his wound. A nurse started to cut his hair; and he, grinning at Natalya, who stood at the head of the cot, recalled that only the day before they had wanted to send for a barber to cut his hair: 'You see,' he winked, 'the barber has also come.' Then, his eyes almost closed, he turned towards Hansen with the question with which he had turned to him so many times: 'Joe, you . . . have . . . notebook?' He remembered that Hansen did not know Russian and he made a great effort to dictate a message in English. His voice was barely audible, his words blurred. This is what Hansen claims to have taken down: 'I am close to death from the blow of a political assassin . . . struck me down in my room. I struggled with him . . . we . . . entered . . . talk about French statistics . . . he struck me . . . please say to our friends . . . I am sure . . . of victory . . . of Fourth International . . . go forward.' When he started dictating, he evidently still hoped to be able to give his account of the attempt on his life as well as a political message. But suddenly he felt that his life was ebbing; and he cut short the account and hastened to give his followers his last encouragement.

The nurses began to undress him for the operation, cutting with scissors his jacket, shirt, and vest, and unstrapping the watch from his wrist. When they began to remove his last garments, he said to Natalya 'distinctly but very sadly and gravely': 'I do not want them to undress me . . . I want you to undress me.' These were the last words she heard from him. When she finished undressing him, she bent over him and pressed her lips against his. 'He returned the kiss. Again. And again he responded. And once again. This was our final farewell.'[1]

About 7.30 the same evening he fell into a coma. Five surgeons carried out the trepanning of the skull. The wound was two and three-quarter inches deep. The right parietal bone was broken, its splinters embedded in the brain; the meninges were damaged and part of the brain substance was ruptured and destroyed. He 'bore the operation with extraordinary strength' but did not regain consciousness; and he struggled with death for more than twenty-two hours. Natalya 'dry-eyed, hands clenched', watched him day and night, waiting for his awakening. This is the last image she retained of him:

They lifted him up. His head drooped on to his shoulder. The arms fell just as the arms in Titian's 'Descent from the Cross'. Instead of a crown of thorns the dying man wore a bandage. The features of his face retained their purity and pride. It seemed that any moment now he might still straighten up and become his own master again.[2]

Death followed on 21 August 1940 at 7.25 p.m. The autopsy showed a brain of 'extraordinary dimensions', weighing two pounds and thirteen ounces; and 'the heart too was very large'.[3]

. . . .

On 22 August, in accordance with a Mexican custom, a large funeral cortège marched slowly behind the coffin carrying Trotsky's body, through the main thoroughfares of the city, and also through the working-class suburbs, where ragged, barefoot, silent crowds filled the pavements. American Trotskyists intended to take the body to the United States; but the State Department refused a visa even to the dead. For five days the body lay in state; and about 300,000 men and women filed past, while the streets resounded with the *Grand Corrido de*

---

[1] Natalya Sedova, loc. cit.   [2] Ibid.
[3] Salazar, op. cit., p. 110.

Leon Trotsky, a folk ballad composed by an anonymous bard.[1]

On 27 August the body was cremated; and the ashes were buried in the grounds of the 'little fortress' at Coyoacan. A white rectangular stone was raised over the grave, and a red flag was unfurled above it.

Natalya was to live on in the house for another twenty years; and every morning, as she rose, her eyes turned to the white stone in the courtyard.

---

[1] Salazar, loc. cit. Here are a few lines of the *corrido*, which breathes truly plebeian contempt for the 'sly and cowardly' assassin:

> Murio Trotsky asesinado
> de la noche a la mañana
> porque habian premeditado
> venganza tarde o temporano.

>   .   .   .

> Fué un dia martes por la tarde
> este tragedia fatal,
> Que ha conmovido al pais
> y a todo la Capital.

Pravda announced the event in a few lines, saying that Trotsky had been killed by a 'disillusioned follower'.

Postscript: Victory in Defeat

In the whole history of the Russian Revolution, and in the history of the labour movement and Marxism no period has been as difficult and sombre as the years of Trotsky's last exile. This was a time when, to paraphrase Marx, 'the idea pressed towards reality' but as reality did not tend towards the idea—a gulf was set between them, a gulf narrower yet deeper than ever. The world was riddled with extraordinary contradictions. Never had capitalism been so close to catastrophe as during the slumps and depressions of the nineteen-thirties; and never had it shown so much savage resilience. Never had the class struggle driven so stormily towards a revolutionary climax and never yet had it been so incapable of rising to it. Never had such vast masses of people been inspired by socialism; and never had they been so helpless and inert. In the whole experience of modern man there had been nothing as sublime and as repulsive as the first Workers' State and the first essay in 'building socialism'. And perhaps never yet had any man lived in so close a communion with the sufferings and the strivings of oppressed humanity and in such utter loneliness as Trotsky lived.

What was the meaning of his work and the moral of his defeat?

Any answer must be tentative, for we still lack the long historical perspective; and our appraisal of Trotsky follows primarily from our judgement on the Russian Revolution. If the view were to be taken that all that the Bolsheviks aimed at—socialism—was no more than a *fata morgana*, that the revolution merely substituted one kind of exploitation and oppression for another, and could not do otherwise, then Trotsky would appear as the high priest of a god that was bound to fail, as Utopia's servant mortally entangled in his dreams and illusions. Even then he would attract the respect and sympathy due to the great utopians and visionaries— he would stand out among them as one of the greatest. Even if it were true that it is man's fate to stagger in pain and blood from defeat to defeat and to throw off one yoke only to bend his neck beneath another—even then man's longings for a different destiny would still, like pillars of fire, relieve the darkness and gloom of the endless desert through which he has been wandering with no promised land beyond. And no one in our age has expressed those longings as vividly and sacrificially as Trotsky.

But has the Russian Revolution been able only to give the people one yoke instead of another? Is this to be its final outcome? Such a view seemed plausible to people who contemplated Stalinism in the last years of Trotsky's life and later. Against them Trotsky asserted his conviction that in the future, after Soviet Society had progressed towards socialism, Stalinism would be seen as merely 'an episodic relapse'. His optimism seemed gratuitous even to his followers. After nearly twenty-five years, however, his forecast may still sound bold, but hardly gratuitous. It is clear that even under Stalinism Soviet society was achieving immense progress in many fields, and that the progress, inseparable from its nationalized and planned economy, was disrupting and eroding Stalinism from the inside. In Trotsky's time it was too early to try to draw a balance of this development—his attempts to do so were not faultless; and the balance is not yet quite clear, even a quarter of a century later. But it is evident that Soviet society has been striving, not without success, to rid itself of the heavy liabilities, and to develop the great assets, it had inherited from the Stalin era. There has been far less poverty in the Soviet Union, far less inequality and far less oppression in the early nineteen-sixties than in the nineteen-thirties or the early nineteen-fifties. The contrast is so striking that it is an anachronism to speak of the 'new totalitarian slavery established by bureaucratic collectivism'. The issues over which Trotsky argued with his disciples in his last controversy are still being debated, not within tiny sects but before a world-wide audience. It is still a matter of argument whether the Soviet bureaucracy is 'a new class' and whether reform or revolution is needed to bring its arbitrary rule to an end. What is beyond question is that the reforms of the first post-Stalin decade, however inadequate and self-contradictory, have greatly mitigated and limited bureaucratic despotism and that fresh currents of popular aspirations are working to transform Soviet society further and more radically.

Even so, Trotsky's belief that one day all the horrors of Stalinism would appear to have been merely 'an episodic relapse' may still outrage contemporary sensitivity. But he applied the grand historical scale to events and to his own fate: 'When it is a question of the profoundest changes in economic and cultural systems, twenty-five years weigh less in history than an hour does in a man's life.' (His inclination to take the long historical view did not blunt his sensitivity to the injustices and cruelties of his time—on the contrary, it sharpened it. He denounced the Stalinist perversion of socialism so passionately because he himself never lost sight of the vista of a truly humane socialist future.) Measured by his historical scale, the progress which Soviet society has achieved since his day is merely a modest, an all too modest, beginning. Yet even this beginning vindicates the revolution and his basic optimism about it, and lifts the dense fog of disillusionment and despair.

Trotsky's huge life and work are an essential element in the experience of the Russian Revolution and, indeed, in the fabric of contemporary civilization. The uniqueness of his fortunes and the extraordinary moral and aesthetic qualities of his endeavour speak for themselves and bear witness to his significance. It cannot be, it would be contrary to all historical sense, that so high an intellectual energy, so prodigious an activity, and so noble a martyrdom should not have their full impact eventually. This is the stuff of which the most sublime and inspiring legends are made—only the Trotsky legend is woven throughout of recorded fact and ascertainable truth. Here no myth is hovering above reality; reality itself rises to the height of myth.

So copious and splendid was Trotsky's career that any part or fraction of it might have sufficed to fill the life of an outstanding historic personality. Had he died at the age of thirty or thirty-five, some time before 1917, he would have taken his place in one line with such Russian thinkers and revolutionaries as Belinsky, Herzen, and Bakunin, as their Marxist descendant and equal. If his life had come to a close in 1921 or later, about the time Lenin died, he would have been remembered as the leader of October, as founder of the Red Army and its

PLATE XXIII

(*a*) Trotsky's assassin

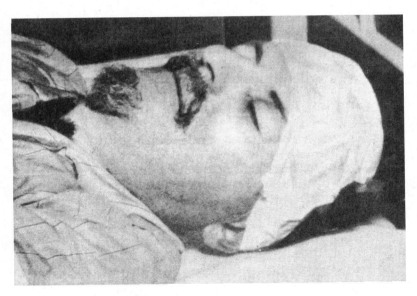

(*b*) 'Trotsky is dead'

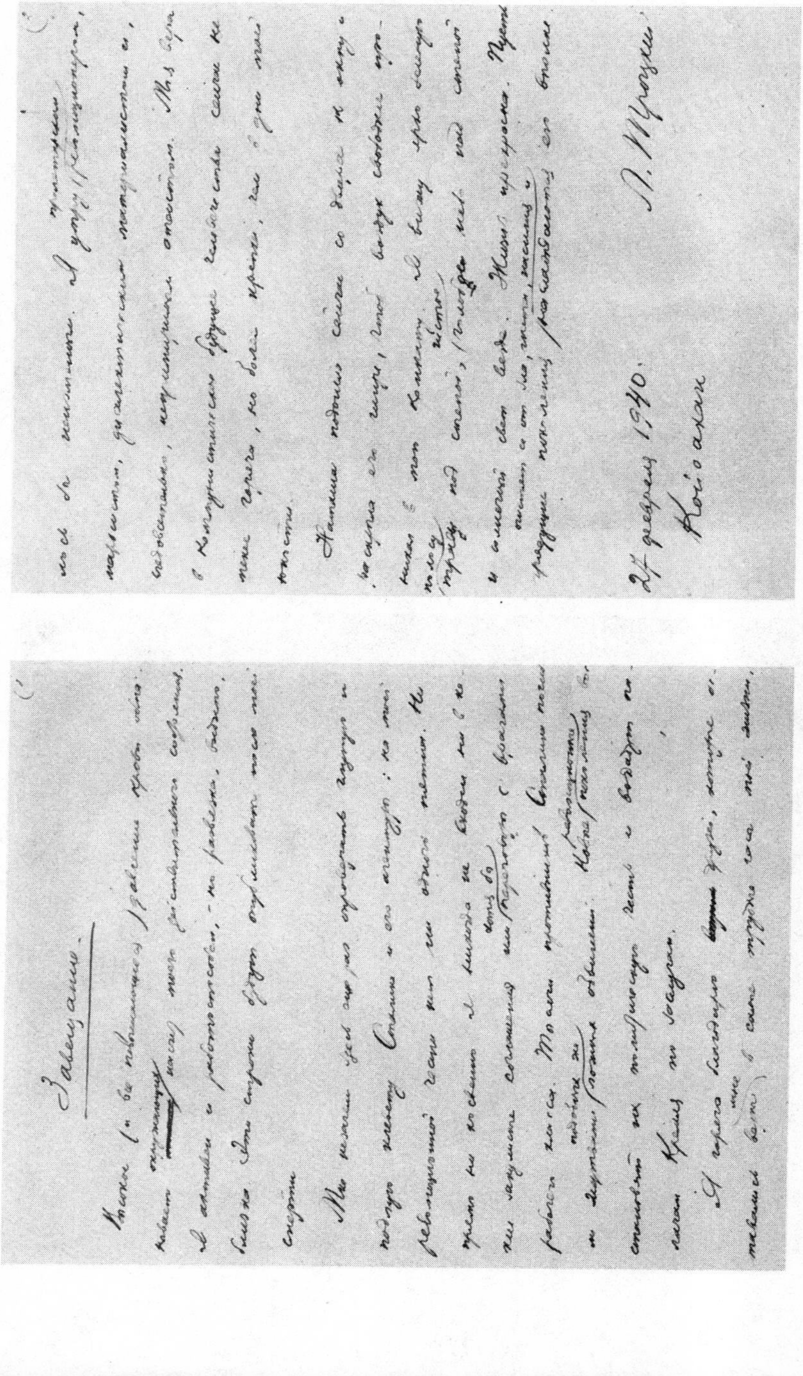

Trotsky's testament. A facsimile.

captain in the Civil War, and as the mentor of the Communist International who spoke to the workers of the world with Marx's power and brilliance and in accents that had not been heard since the *Communist Manifesto*. (It took decades of Stalinist falsification and slander to blur and erase this image of him from the memory of two generations.) The ideas which he expounded and the work which he performed as leader of the Opposition between 1923 and 1929 form the sum and substance of the most momentous and dramatic chapter in the annals of Bolshevism and communism. He came forward as protagonist in the greatest ideological controversy of the century, as intellectual initiator of industrialization and planned economy, and finally as the mouthpiece of all those within the Bolshevik party who resisted the advent of Stalinism. Even if he had not survived beyond the year 1927, he would have left behind a legacy of ideas which could not be destroyed or condemned to lasting oblivion, the legacy for the sake of which many of his followers faced the firing squad with his name on their lips, a legacy to which time is adding relevance and weight and towards which a new Soviet generation is gropingly finding its way.

On top of all this come his ideas, writings, struggles, and wanderings of the period narrated in this volume. We have reviewed critically his fiascos, fallacies, and miscalculations: his fiasco with the Fourth International, his mistakes about the prospects of revolution in the West, his fumblings about reform and revolution in the U.S.S.R., and the contradictions of the 'new Trotskyism' of his last years. We have also surveyed those of his campaigns which are now fully and incontrovertibly vindicated: his magnificently far-sighted, although vain, efforts to arouse the German workers, the international Left, and the Soviet Union to the mortal danger of Hitler's ascendancy; his sustained criticisms of Stalin's hideous abuses of power, not least in the conduct of economic affairs, especially in collectivization; and his final titanic struggle against the Great Purges. Even the epigones of Stalinism, who are still doing all they can to keep Trotsky's ghost at bay, admit by implication that on these great issues he was right—all that after so many years they themselves have been able to do, with all the courage that the dead Stalin has inspired in them, is to echo disparately Trotsky's protests, accusations, and criticisms of Stalin.

It must be emphasized again that to the end Trotsky's strength and weakness alike were rooted in classical Marxism. His defeats epitomized the basic predicament by which classical Marxism was beset as doctrine and movement—the discrepancy and the divorce between the Marxist vision of revolutionary development and the actual course of class struggle and revolution.

Socialist revolution made its first, immense conquests not in the advanced West but in the backward East, in countries, where not the industrial workers but the peasants predominated. Its immediate task was not to establish socialism but to initiate 'primitive socialist accumulation'. In the classical Marxist scheme of things revolution was to occur when the productive forces of the old society had so outgrown its property relations as to burst the old social framework; the revolution was to create new property relations and the new framework for fully grown, advanced, and dynamic productive forces. What happened in fact was that the revolution created the most advanced forms of social organization for the most backward of economies; it set up frameworks of social ownership and planning around underdeveloped and archaic productive forces, and partly around a vacuum. The theoretical Marxist conception of the revolution was thereby turned upside down. The new 'productive relations' being above the existing productive forces were also above the understanding of the great majority of the people; and so the revolutionary government defended and developed them against the will of the majority. Bureaucratic despotism took the place of Soviet democracy. The State, far from withering away, assumed unprecedented, ferocious power. The conflict between the Marxist norm and the reality of revolution came to permeate all the thinking and activity of the ruling party. Stalinism sought to overcome the conflict by perverting or discarding the norm. Trotskyism attempted to preserve the norm or to strike a temporary balance between norm and reality until revolution in the West resolved the conflict and restored harmony between theory and practice. The failures of revolution in the West were epitomized in Trotsky's defeat.

How definite and irrevocable was the defeat? We have seen that as long as Trotsky was alive Stalin never considered him to have been finally vanquished. Stalin's fear was no mere paranoiac obsession. Other leading actors on the political stage shared it. Robert Coulondre, French ambassador to the Third Reich, gives a striking testimony in a description of his last interview with Hitler just before the outbreak of the Second World War. Hitler had boasted of the advantages he had obtained from his pact with Stalin, just concluded; and he drew a grandiose vista of his future military triumph. In reply the French ambassador appealed to his 'reason' and spoke of the social turmoil and the revolutions that might follow a long and terrible war and engulf all belligerent governments. 'You are thinking of yourself as victor . . .', the ambassador said, 'but have you given thought to another possibility—that the victor may be Trotsky?' At this Hitler jumped up (as if he 'had been hit in the pit of the stomach') and screamed that this possibility, the threat of Trotsky's victory, was one more reason why France and Britain should not go to war against the Third Reich. Thus, the master of the Third Reich and the envoy of the Third Republic, in their last manœuvres, during the last hours of peace, sought to intimidate each other, and each other's governments, by invoking the name of the lonely outcast trapped and immured at the far end of the world. 'They are haunted by the spectre of revolution, and they give it a man's name', Trotsky remarked when he read the dialogue.

Were Hitler and the ambassador quite wrong in giving the spectre Trotsky's name? It may be argued that although their fear was well grounded, they should have given the spectre Stalin's name, not Trotsky's—it was, at any rate, Stalin who was to triumph over Hitler. Yet as so often in history so here the underlying realities were far more confused and ambiguous than the surface of events. Stalin's victory over Trotsky concealed a heavy element of defeat while Trotsky's defeat was pregnant with victory.

The central 'ideological' issue between them had been socialism in one country—the question whether the Soviet Union would or could achieve socialism in isolation, on the basis of national self-sufficiency, or whether socialism was conceivable only as an international order of society. The answer events have given is far less clear-cut than were the theoretical arguments, but it comes much closer to Trotsky's view than to Stalin's. Long before the Soviet Union came anywhere near socialism, revolution had spread to other countries. History, it might be said, did not leave the Soviet Union alone long enough to allow a laboratory experiment with socialism in a single country to be carried into any advanced stage, let alone to be completed. In so far as in the struggle between Trotskyism and Stalinism revolutionary international-ism had clashed with Bolshevik isolationism it is certainly not Stalinism that has emerged with flying colours: Bolshevik isolationism has been dead long since. On the other hand, the staying power of the Soviet Union, even in isolation, was far greater than Trotsky sometimes assumed; and, contrary to his expectations, it was not the proletariat of the West that freed the Russian Revolution from isolation. By a feat of history's irony, Stalinism itself *malgré lui-même* broke out of its national shell.

In his last debate Trotsky staked the whole future of Marxism and socialism upon the sequel to the Second World War. Convinced that war must lead to revolution—the classical Marxist revolution—he asserted that if it failed to do so Marx-ism would be refuted, socialism would lose once and for all by default, and the epoch of bureaucratic collectivism would set in. This was, in any case, a rash, dogmatic, and desperate view; historic reality was once again to prove immeasurably more intricate than the theorist's scheme. The war did indeed set in motion a new series of revolutions; yet once again the process did not conform to the classical pattern. The western prole-tariat again failed to storm and conquer the ramparts of the old order; and in eastern Europe it was mainly under the im-pact of Russia's armed power, advancing victoriously to the Elbe, that the old order broke down. The divorce between theory and practice—or between norm and fact—deepened even further.

This was not a fortuitous development. It represented a continuation of the trend which had first announced itself in 1920-1, when the Red Army marched on Warsaw and when it occupied Georgia.[1] With those military acts the revolutionary

---

[1] See *The Prophet Armed*, pp. 463-77.

cycle which the First World War set in motion had come to a close. At the beginning of that cycle Bolshevism had risen on the crest of a genuine revolution; towards its end the Bolsheviks began to spread revolution by conquest. Then followed the long interval of two decades, during which Bolshevism did not expand. When the next cycle of revolution was set in motion by the Second World War, it started where the first cycle had ended—with revolution by conquest. In military history there exists, as a rule, a continuity between the closing phase of one war and the opening phase of another: the weapons and the ideas about warfare invented and formed towards the end of one armed conflict dominate the first stage of the next conflict. A similar continuity exists also between cycles of revolution. In 1920–1 Bolshevism, straining to break out of its isolation, tried, rather fitfully, to carry revolution abroad on the point of bayonets. Two and three decades later Stalinism, dragged out of its national shell by war, imposed revolution upon the whole of eastern Europe.

Trotsky had expected the second revolutionary cycle to begin in the forms in which the first had begun, with class struggles and proletarian risings, the outcome of which would, in the main depend on the balance of social forces within each major nation and on the quality of national revolutionary leadership. Yet the new cycle started not where the previous one had begun, but where it had ended, not with revolution from below, but with revolution from above, with revolution by conquest. As this could be the work only of a great power applying its pressure in the first instance to its own periphery, the cycle ran its course on the fringes of the Soviet Union. The chief agents of revolution were not the workers of the countries concerned, and their parties, but the Red Army. Success or failure depended not on the balance of social forces within any nation, but mainly on the international balance of power, on diplomatic pacts, alliances, and military campaigns. The struggle and the co-operation of the great powers superimposed themselves upon class struggle, changing and distorting it. All criteria by which Marxists were wont to judge a nation's 'maturity' or 'immaturity' for revolution went by the board. Stalin's pact with Hitler and the division between them of spheres of influence provided the starting-point for the social upheaval in eastern Poland and in the Baltic States. The revolutions in Poland proper, in the Balkan countries, and in eastern Germany were accomplished on the basis of the division of spheres which Stalin, Roosevelt, and Churchill carried out at Teheran and Yalta. By dint of that division the western powers used their influence and force to suppress, with Stalin's connivance, revolution in western Europe (and Greece) regardless of any local balance of social forces. It is probable that had there been no Teheran and Yalta compacts, western rather than eastern Europe would have become the theatre of revolution—especially France and Italy, where the authority of the old ruling classes was in ruins, the working classes were in revolt, and the Communist parties led the bulk of the armed Resistance. Stalin, acting on his diplomatic commitments, prevailed upon the French and Italian Communists to resign themselves to the restoration of capitalism in their countries from the virtual collapse and even to co-operate in the restoration. At the same time Churchill and Roosevelt induced the bourgeois ruling groups of eastern Europe to submit to Russia's preponderance and consequently to surrender to revolution. On both sides of the great divide the international balance of power swamped the class struggle. As in the Napoleonic era, revolution and counter-revolution alike were the by-products of arms and diplomacy.

Trotsky saw only the opening of this great chain of events. He did not realize what it portended. All his habits of thought made it difficult, if not impossible, for him to imagine that for a whole epoch the armies and diplomacies of three powers would be able to impose their will upon all the social classes of old Europe; and that consequently the class struggle, suppressed at the level on which it had been traditionally waged, would be fought at a different level and in different forms, as rivalry between power blocs and as cold war.

From theoretical conviction and political instinct alike Trotsky felt nothing but distaste for revolution by conquest. He had opposed the invasions of Poland and Georgia in 1920–1, when Lenin favoured these ventures. As Commissar of War he had categorically disavowed Tukhachevsky, the early exponent of the neo-Napoleonic method of carrying revolution into foreign countries. Twenty years before the Second World War he had castigated the armed missionary of Bolshevism, saying that 'it were better that a millstone be hanged about his neck and he cast into the sea'. His attitude in 1940 was still the same as in 1920. He still saw in revolution by conquest the most dangerous aberration from the revolutionary road. He was still confident that the workers of the West were impelled by their own circumstances to struggle for power and for socialism and that it would be as criminal on the part of the Soviet Government to try to make the revolution for them as it would be to act directly against their revolutionary interests. He still saw the world pregnant with socialism; he still believed that the pregnancy could not last long; and he feared that any tampering with it would result in abortion. He was not quite wrong: Stalin's armed tampering with revolution has produced many a stillbirth—and many a live monstrosity.

Yet, confronted with revolution by conquest, Trotsky once again found himself in a grave quandary. He was for revolution and against conquests; but when revolution led to conquest or when conquest promoted revolution, he could not press his opposition to it beyond the point of an open and irrevocable breach. He did not press it to that point over Georgia and Poland in 1920–1; and he did not do so over Poland and Finland in 1939–40 either. Had he lived to witness the aftermath of the Second World War, he would have found his dilemma aggravated, huge, insoluble. We need not doubt that he would have denounced Stalin for bargaining away the interests of communism in the West; and also that the logic of his attitude would have compelled him to accept the reality of the revolution in eastern Europe, and, despite all distaste for the Stalinist methods, to recognize the 'Peoples' Democracies' as workers' states. Such an attitude, whatever its merits and integrity, could provide no clue to practical political action; and so Trotsky, the man of practical action, would hardly have found any effective role for himself in the whole post-war drama. There was no room for classical Marxism in this cycle of revolution.

This cycle, however, like the previous one was to end differently from the way it had begun. It culminated in the Chinese revolution which was neither imposed from above nor brought in on the point of foreign bayonets. Mao Tse-tung and his party struggled for power despite Stalin (who in 1945–8, as in 1925–6, aimed at a deal with the Kuomintang and Chiang Kai-shek); and having seized power they did not stop at the 'bourgeois democratic' stages of the upheaval but, obeying the logic of 'permanent revolution', carried it to the anti-bourgeois conclusion. This, the 'Chinese October' was, in a sense, yet another of Trotsky's posthumous triumphs.

Yet here again 'grey is all theory and evergreen is the tree of life'. The industrial proletariat was not the driving force of the upheaval. Mao's peasant armies 'substituted' themselves for the urban workers and carried the revolution from country to town. Trotsky had been convinced that, if these armies were to remain confined to the rural areas for long, they would become so assimilated with the peasantry as to champion its individualistic interests against the urban workers, and against socialism, and become the mainstay of a new reaction. (Had not rebellious Chinese peasant armies in the past fought jacqueries and overthrown established dynasties only to replace them by new dynasties?) This analysis was correct in terms of classical Marxism, which assumed that a party of socialist revolution needs not only to 'represent' the urban workers, but must necessarily live with them and act through them—otherwise it must become socially displaced and express alien class interests. And it may indeed be that if this revolution had depended solely on the social alignments within China, Mao's partisans would have become, during their Yenan period, so closely assimilated to the peasantry that, despite their communist origin, they would have been unable to bridge the gulf between jacquerie and proletarian revolution. But the outcome of the struggle was even in China determined as much by international as by national factors. Amid the cold war and in face of hostile American intervention, Mao's party secured its rule by attaching itself to the Soviet Union and transforming the social structure of China accordingly. Thus the revolutionary hegemony of the Soviet Union achieved (despite Stalin's initial obstruction) what otherwise only the Chinese workers could have achieved—it impelled the Chinese revolution into an anti-bourgeois and socialist direction. With the Chinese proletariat almost dispersed and absent from the political stage, the gravitational pull of the Soviet Union turned Mao's peasant armies into agents of collectivism.

With this the tide of revolution had moved farther to the east, farther away from the 'advanced' west; and it became once again embedded in a primitive and destitute pre-industrial society. More than ever classical Marxism appeared to be practically irrelevant to the problems of East and West alike. Yet such were the dialectics of the situation that at the same time processes were at work which were in an unexpected manner investing it with fresh validity. Thanks to intensive industrialization the backward East was becoming less and less backward. The Soviet Union emerged as the world's second industrial power, its social structure radically transformed, its large industrial working class striving for a modern way of life, and its standards of living and mass education rising rapidly, if unevenly. The very pre-conditions of socialism which classical Marxism had seen as existing only in the highly industrialized countries of the West were being created and assembled within Soviet society. In relation to the new needs of that society Stalinism, with its amalgamation of Marxism and barbarity, was anachronistic. Its methods of primitive accumulation were too primitive; its anti-egalitarianism was too shocking; its despotism absurd. The traditions of Marxism and of the October Revolution, having survived in a state of hibernation, as it were, began to awaken in the minds of millions and to struggle against bureaucratic privilege, the inertia of Stalinism, and the dead-weight of monolithic dogma. Through the forcible modernization of the structure of society Stalinism had worked towards its own undoing and had prepared the ground for the return of classical Marxism.

The return has been slow and accompanied by confusion and endless ambiguities. The conflict between Stalinism or what was left of it and a renascent socialist consciousness filled the first decade after Stalin.. Had the Trotskyist, Zinovievist, Bukharinist Oppositions survived into the nineteen-fifties, the task of de-Stalinization would have fallen to them; and they would have accomplished it with honour, whole-heartedly and consistently. But as they had all gone down with the old Bolshevik Atlantis, and as de-Stalinization was an inescapable necessity, Stalin's acolytes and accomplices had to tackle the job; and they could not tackle it otherwise than half-heartedly, with trembling hands and minds, never forgetting their own share in Stalin's crimes, and for ever anxious to bring to a halt the shocking disclosures and the reforms they themselves had had to initiate. Of all the ghosts of the past none dogged them as mockingly and menacingly as the ghost of Trotsky, their arch-enemy, to whom each of their disclosures and reforms was an unwitting tribute. Nothing indeed troubled Khrushchev more than the fear that young men, not burdened by responsibility for the horrors of the Stalin era, might become impatient with his evasions and quibblings and proceed to an open vindi-cation of Trotsky.

The open vindication is bound to come in any case, though not perhaps before Stalin's ageing epigones have left the stage. When it does come, it will be more than a long-overdue act of justice towards the memory of a great man. By this act the workers' state will announce that it has at last reached maturity, broken its bureaucratic shackles, and re-embraced the classical Marxism that had been banished with Trotsky.

How all this may affect the rest of the world is a question too large to be discussed in a postscript to a biographical study. Suffice it to say here that if the historic development has al-ready been cancelling out Trotsky's defeat by obliterating the old antithesis between *backward* Russia and the *advanced* West, the antithesis in which his defeat had been rooted, then the regeneration of the Russian revolution must help to obliterate that antithesis to the end. The West, in which a Marxism debased by Mother Russia into Stalinism inspired disgust and fear, will surely respond in quite a different manner to a Marxism cleansed of barbarous accretions; in that Marxism it will have to acknowledge at last its own creation and its own vision of man's destiny. And so history may come full circle

till Hope creates
From its own wreck the thing it contemplates.

Trotsky sometimes compared mankind's progress to the barefooted march of pilgrims who advance towards their shrine by moving only a few steps forward at a time, and then retreat or jump sideways in order to advance and deviate or retreat again; zigzagging thus all the time they approach laboriously their destination. He saw his role in prompting the 'pilgrims' to advance. Mankind, however, when after some progress it succumbs to a stampede, allows those who urge it forward to be abused, vilified, and trampled to death. Only when it has resumed the forward movement, does it pay rueful tribute to the victims, cherish their memory and piously collect their relics; then it is grateful to them for every drop of blood they gave— for it knows that with their blood they nourished the seed of the future.

BIBLIOGRAPHY

The Prophet Armed

(This list includes only such sources as have been quoted or directly referred to by the author).

AKIMOV, V. L., *Materialy dlya Kharakteristiki Razvitya RSDRP.* Geneva, 1905.

ANTONOV–OVSEENKO, V. A., *Zapiski o Grazhdanskoi Voine,* vol. i. Moscow, 1924.

ARSCHINOFF, P., *Geschichte der Machno-Bewegung (1918–1921).* Berlin, no date.

AVDEEV, N., and others, *Revolutsia 1917 (Khronika Sobytii),* vols. i–v. Moscow, 1923–6.

AXELROD, P. B., *Pisma P. B. Axelroda i Yu. O. Martova.* Berlin, 1924.

———*Perepiska G. V. Plekhanova i P. B. Axelroda.* Moscow, 1925.

BADAEV, A. E., *Bolsheviki v Gosudarstvennoi Dume.* Moscow, 1930.

BALABANOFF, A., *My Life as a Rebel.* London, 1938.

BEATTY, BESSIE, *The Red Heart of Russia.* New York, 1918.

BEER, M., *Fifty Years of International Socialism.* London, 1937.

BERKMAN, A., *Der Aufstand von Kronstadt,* Reprint, *Der Monat.* Berlin, no date.

———*The Bolshevik Myth.* London, 1925.

Bolsheviki, Dokumenty Okhrannovo Otdelenia (Dokumenty po Istorii Bolshevisma s 1903 po 1916 g. byvshevo Moskovskovo Okhrannovo Otdelenia), Ed. M. A. Tsyavlovskii. Moscow, 1918.

Borba za Petrograd, 15 Oktyabrya–6 Noyabrya, 1919, with Foreword by G. Zinoviev. Petrograd, 1920.

BRUPBACHER, F., *60 Jahre Ketzer.* Zürich, 1935.

BRYANT, LOUISE, *Six Red Months in Russia.* London, 1919.

BUBNOV, A., and others, *Grazhdanskaya Voina, 1918–1921,* vols. i–iii. Moscow, 1928.

BUCHANAN, SIR GEORGE, *My Mission to Russia.* London, 1923.

CHEREVANIN, N., *Organisatsionnyi Vopros*, with preface by Martov. Geneva, 1904.

CHERNOV, V., *The Great Russian Revolution*. New Haven, 1936.

——(Tchernov) *Mes Tribulations en Russie Soviétique*. Paris, 1921.

CZERNIN, COUNT OTTOKAR, *In the World War*. London, 1919.

DAN, F., *Proiskhozhdenie Bolshevisma*. New York, 1946.

DABSKI, JAN, *Pokój Ryski*. Warsaw 1931. (The second edition of J. Dąbski's memoirs, published in Polish at a later date, contains much more information about the background to the Russo-Polish peace treaty of 1921. It was not available during the writing of this book.)

DENIKIN, A. I., GENERAL, *Ocherki Russkoi Smuty*, vols. i–v. Paris–Berlin, 1921–6.

Doklad Russkikh Sotsial-Demokratov Vtoromu Internatsionalu. Geneva, 1896.

DUBNOV, S. M., *History of the Jews in Russia and Poland*. Philadelphia, 1918.

EASTMAN, M., *Leon Trotsky: The Portrait of a Youth*. New York, 1925.

EGOROV, A., *Lvov-Varshava*. Moscow, 1929.

ENGELS, F., *The Peasant War in Germany*. London, 1927.

FRUNZE, M. V., *Sobranie Sochinenii*, vols. i–iii, with preface by Bubnov. Moscow, 1929.

GARVI, P. A., *Vospominanya Sotsial-Demokrata*. New York, 1946.

GORKY, M., *Lénine et le Paysan Russe*. Paris, 1924.

——*Days with Lenin*. London, 1931.

HARD, WILLIAM, *Raymond Robins' Own Story*. New York, 1920.

History of the Communist Party of the Soviet Union (Bolsheviks); Short Course. Moscow, 1943.

HOFFMANN, MAX, *Die Aufzeichnungen des Generalmajors Max Hoffmann*. Berlin, 1929.

ILIN-ZHENEVSKII, A. F., *Bolsheviki u Vlasti*. Leningrad, 1929.

JAURÈS, J., *L'Armée Nouvelle*. Paris, 1911.

KAKURIN, N., *Kak Srazhalas Revolutsia*, vols. i–ii. Moscow, 1925.

KERENSKY, ALEXANDER, *Izdaleka, Sbornik Statei*. Paris, 1922.

——*The Crucifixion of Liberty*. London, 1934.

KNOX, SIR ALFRED, Major General, *With the Russian Army 1914–1917*. London, 1921.

KOLLONTAI, A. M., *The Workers' Opposition in Russia*. London, 1923. KRUPSKAYA, N. K., *Memories of Lenin*. London, 1942.

KÜHLMANN, RICHARD VON, *Erinnerungen*. Heidelberg, 1948.

LATSIS (Sudbars), *Chrezvychainye Komissii po Borbe s Kontrrevolutsiei*. Moscow, 1921.

LENIN, V. I., *Sochinenya*, vols. i–xxxv. Moscow 1941–50. All quotations from Lenin's Works are from this, the fourth edition, unless otherwise stated.

——*Sobranie Sochinenii*. This is the first edition of Lenin's Works published between 1920–6, of which occasional use has been made for quotation of passages omitted from later editions.

——*Letters of Lenin*. London, 1937.

Leninskii Sbornik, vols. iv–xx. Moscow, 1925–32.

Lenin's correspondence with Trotsky and other party leaders and military commanders, some of it hitherto unpublished, has been quoted from *The Trotsky Archives*. Harvard.

LLOYD GEORGE, D., *War Memoirs*. London, 1938.

LOCKHART BRUCE, R. H., *Memoirs of a British Agent*. London, 1932.

LUDENDORFF, E., *Meine Kriegserinnerungen 1914–1918*. Berlin, 1919.

LUNACHARSKY, A., *Revolutsionnye Siluety*. Moscow, 1923.

LYADOV, M. N., *Kak Nachala Skladyvatsya R. K. P.* Moscow, 1925.

——*Iz Zhizni Partii*. Moscow, 1926.

LYADOV, M. N., (M. LYDIN), *Material zur Erläuterung der Parteikrise in der S. D. Arbeiterpartei Rußlands*. Geneva, 1904.

MARTOV, L., MASLOV, P., POTRESOV, A., *Obshchestvennoe Dvizhenie v Rossii v Nachale XX-Veka*, vols. i–ii. Petersburg, 1909–10.

MARTOV, L., (Yu.) *Pisma Axelroda i Martova*. Berlin, 1924.

——*Istoria Rossiiskoi Sotsial-Demokratii*. Moscow, 1923.

——*Spasiteli ili Uprazdniteli*. Paris, 1911.

MARX, K. and ENGELS, F., *Selected Correspondence*. London, 1941.

————*Perepiska Marxa i Engelsa s Russkimi Politicheskimi Deyatelyami*. Moscow, 1947.

MEDEM, VLADIMIR, *Von Mein Leben*, vols. i–ii (Yiddish). New York, 1923. MILIUKOV, P. N., *Istorya Vtoroi Russkoi Revolutsii*. Sofia, 1921.

————*Kak Proshli Vybory vo Vtoruyu Gos. Dumu*. Petersburg, 1907.

MILL, JOHN, *Pioneers and Builders*, vols. i–ii (Yiddish). New York, 1946.

Mirnye Peregovory v Brest-Litovske, Records of the peace conference of Brest Litovsk. Ed. A. A. Yoffe (V. Krymsky), preface by Trotsky. Moscow, 1920.

MORIZET, A., *Chez Lénine et Trotski*. Paris, 1922.

NOULENS, JOSEPH, *Mon Ambassade en Russie Soviétique*, vols. i–ii. Paris, 1932.

OLGIN, M. J., 'Biographical Notes' in the American edition of Trotsky's *Our Revolution*. New York, 1918.

PALÉOLOGUE, MAURICE, *La Russie des Tsars pendant la Grande Guerre*, vols. i–iii. Paris, 1922.

PARVUS (HELPHAND, A. L.), *Rossia i Revolutsia*. Petersburg, 1906.

PAVLOVICH, *Pismo k Tovarishcham o Vtorom Syezde RSDRP*. Geneva, 1904.

PLEKHANOV, G. V., *God na Rodine*, vols. i–ii. Paris, 1921.

————*Perepiska Plekhanova i Axelroda*. Moscow, 1925.

POKROVSKY, M. N., *Oktyabrskaya Revolutsia*. Moscow, 1929.

————*Ocherki po Istorii Oktyabrskoi Revolutsii*, vols. i–ii. Moscow, 1927.

POPOV, N., *Outline History of the C.P.S.U.* (b), vols. i–ii (English translation from 16th Russian edition). London, no date.

POTRESOV, A. N., *Posmertny Sbornik Proizvedenii*. Paris, 1937.

PRICE PHILIPS, M., *My Reminiscences of the Russian Revolution*. London, 1921. *Pyat Let Vlasti Sovietov*. Moscow, 1922.

RADEK, K., *Portrety i Pamphlety*. Moscow, 1927.

————*Pyat Let Kominterna*. Moscow, 1924.

RANSOME, ARTHUR, *Six Weeks in Russia in 1919*. London, 1919.

Raskol na Vtorom Syezde RSDRP i Vtoroi Internatsional (Sbornik Dokumentov). Moscow, 1933.

RASKOLNIKOV, F. F., *Kronshtadt i Piter v 1917 g*. Moscow, 1925.

REED, JOHN, *Ten Days that Shook the World*. London, 1934.

ROWER, A., *Le Mouvement Ouvrier pendant la Guerre*. Paris, 1936.

SADOUL, JACQUES, *Notes sur la Révolution Bolchevique*. Paris, 1919.

SERGE, V., *Mémoires d'un Révolutionnaire*. Paris, 1951.

SIBIRYAK, *Studencheskoye Dvizhenie v Rossii*. Geneva, 1899.

SLEPKOV, A., *Kronshtadtskii Myatezh*. Moscow, 1928.

SMILGA, I., *Ocherednye Voprosy Stroitelstva Krasnoi Armii*. Moscow, 1921.

STALIN, J. V., *Sochinenya*, vols. i–xiii. Moscow, 1946–51.

Stalin's correspondence with Lenin, Trotsky, and other members of the Politbureau, some of it unpublished, is quoted from *The Trotsky Archives*.

STEINBERG, I., *Als ich Volkskommissar war*. Munich, 1929.

SUKHANOV, N., *Zapiski o Revolutsii*, vols. i–vii. Moscow, 1922.

SVERCHKOV, D., *Na Zarie Reuolutsii*. Leningrad, 1925.

TROTSKY, L. D.

———*The Trotsky Archives* (Houghton Library, Harvard University). The earliest document in this collection is dated Brest Litovsk 31 January 1918; the last bears the date 17 August 1940, three days before the assassination of Trotsky. The Archives consist of four parts:

Section A: contains about 800 letters and messages exchanged between Trotsky, Lenin, and other Soviet leaders (1918–22), and various other unpublished documents;

Section B: contains, in twenty-five dossiers, Trotsky's manuscripts and correspondence up to 1929;

Section C: contains, also in twenty-five dossiers, letters and memoranda from Zinoviev, Yoffe, Lunacharsky, Radek, Rakovsky, Preobrazhensky, Sosnovsky, and many others. Most of this correspondence belongs to the period of Trotsky's exile at Alma Ata. This section also includes many documents relating to the work of the Trotskyist opposition within the Soviet Union;

Section D: contains Trotsky's correspondence with groups and members of the Fourth International in various countries. This section is sealed and is not to be made available for research before 1980.

The references to *The Archives*, which occur in this volume are mainly to Section A. Only in a few instances are documents belonging to Sections B and C referred to. Extensive use of Sections B and C is made by the author in *The Prophet Unarmed*, the next volume in this series.

————*Sochinenya*. (This was planned to be the complete edition of Trotsky's *Works*, but its publication was discontinued in 1927, at the time of Trotsky's expulsion from the party. The following volumes, published in 1925–7, were available to the author:

Vol. II (parts 1 and 2) *Nasha Pervaya Revolutsia*;

Vol. III: (part 1) *Ot Fevralya do Oktyabrya*; (part 2) *Ot Oktyabrya do Bresta*;

Vol. IV: *Politicheskaya Khronika*;

Vol. VI: *Balkany i Balkanskaya Voina*;

Vol. VIII: *Politicheskie Siluety*;

Vol. IX: *Evropa v Voine*;

Vol. XII: *Osnovnye Voprosy Proletarskoi Revolutsii*;

Vol. XIII: *Kommunisticheskii Internatsional*;

Vol. XV: *Khozaistvennoe Stroitelstvo v Sovetskoi Rossii*;

Vol. XVII: (part 2) *Sovietskaya Respublika i Kapitalisticheskii Mir*;

Vol. XX: *Kultura Starovo Mira*;

Vol. XXI: *Kultura Perekhodnovo Vremeni*.

TROTSKY, L. D., *Kak Vooruzhalas Revolutsia*, vols. i–iii. Moscow, 1923–5. (The collection of Trotsky's military writings, orders of the day and speeches.)

————*Vtoroi Syezd RSDRP (Otchet Sibirskoi Delegatsii)*. Geneva, 1903. (In the signature over this and the next work Trotsky used the initial N., not L.)

————*Nashi Politicheskie Zadachi*. Geneva, 1904.

————*Istoria Revolutsii 1905–06*. Petrograd, 1917.

————*Our Revolution*. New York, 1918.

————*Itogi i Perspektivy*. Moscow, 1919.

————*Terrorism i Kommunism*. Petersburg, 1920.

————*Between Red and White*. London, 1922.

————*Die Russische Revolution 1905*. Berlin, 1923.

————*Pyat Let Kominterna*. Moscow, 1924.

————*Lénine*. Paris, 1924.

————*Pokolenie Oktyabrya*. Moscow, 1924.

————*Moya Zhizn.* vols. i–ii, Berlin, 1930.

————*Permanentnaya Revolutsia.* Berlin, 1930.

————*History of the Russian Revolution,* vols. i–iii. London, 1932–3.

————*Vie de Lénine, Jeunesse.* Paris, 1936.

————*The Stalin School of Falsification.* New York, 1937.

————*Stalin.* New York, 1946.

(Apart from the sources listed above, the author has quoted extensively from Trotsky's speeches printed in many published records of party and Soviet congresses and in the proceedings of the Central Committee. For Trotsky's early writings the author has drawn *inter alia* on the files of *Iskra, Nachalo,* the 'Viennese' *Pravda, Golos, Nashe Slovo,* &c., sources rarely, if ever, used by previous writers on the history of Russian revolutionary movements. These papers are in the Hoover Library, Stanford University, California.)

TUKHACHEVSKY, M., *Voina Klassov.* Moscow, 1921.

VANDERVELDE, E., *Souvenirs d'un Militant Socialiste.* Paris, 1939.

VOITINSKY, V., *Gody Pobied i Porazhenii.* Berlin, 1923.

VOROSHILOV, K., *Stalin i Krasnaya Armia.* Moscow, 1929.

WHEELER–BENNETT, JOHN W., *Brest Litovsk. The Forgotten Peace.* London, 1938.

WITTE, S. Yu., *Vospominania,* vols. i–iii. Petrograd, 1923–4.

ZELIKSON–BOBROVSKAYA, Ts., *Pervaya Russkaya Revolutsia v Peterburge 1905,* vols. i–ii. Moscow, 1925.

ZETKIN, KLARA, *Reminiscences of Lenin.* London, 1929.

ZINOVIEV, G. *Sochinenya,* vols. i–xvi. Moscow, 1924–9.

Ziv, G. A., *Trotsky. Kharakteristika po Lichnym Vospominaniam.* New York, 1925.

The following editions of protocols and verbatim reports have been quoted:

Protokoly Tsentralnovo Komiteta RSDRP (August 1917–February 1918). Moscow, 1929.

2 Syezd RSDRP. Moscow, 1932.

5 Syezd RSDRP. Moscow.

6 Syezd RSDRP. Moscow, 1934.
7 Syezd RKP (b). Moscow, 1923.
8 Syezd RKP (b). Moscow, 1933.
9 Syezd RKP (b). Moscow, 1934.
10 Syezd RKP (b). Moscow, 1921.
1 Vserossiiskii Syezd Sovetov. Moscow, 1930.
3 Vserossiiskii Syezd Sovetov. Petersburg, 1918.
5 Vserossiiskii Syezd Sovetov. Moscow, 5918.
3 Vserossiiskii Syezd Profsoyuzov. Moscow, 1920.
2 Kongress Kommunisticheskovo Internatsionala. Petrograd, 1921.

Newspapers and periodicals:

Ekononticheskaya Zhizn', Forward—Vorwärts (New York),
Golas (Paris), *Iskra* ('old' and 'new'), *Izvestya, Izvestya
Tsentralnovo Komiteta RKP (b), Krasnaya Letopis, Luch
Nachalo, The New International, Nashe Slovo* (Paris), *Nasha
Zarya, Novaya Zhizn, Neue Zeit, Pechat i Revolutsia, Pravda*
('Viennese'), *Pravda, Proletarskaya Revolutsia, Przeglad
Socjal-Demokratyczny, Rabocheye Delo* (Geneva, 1899),
*Russkaya Gazeta, Rabochyi Put, Ryech, Sotsial-Demokrat,
Sotsialisticheskii Vestnik, The Times, Vestnik Russkoi
Revolutsii, Voprosy Istorii.*

The Prophet Unarmed

BAJANOV, B., *Avec Staline dans le Kremlin.* Paris, 1930.
BALABANOFF, A., *My Life as a Rebel.* London, 1938.
BELOBORODOV, Unpublished Correspondence with Trotsky,
quoted from *The Archives.*
BRANDT, S CHWARTZ Fairbank, *A Documentary History of
Chinese Communism.* London, 1952.
BRUPBACHER, F., *60 Jahre Ketzer,* 1935.
BUBNOV, A., 'Uroki Oktyabrya i Trotskizm', in *Za Leninizm,*
1925.
———*Partiya i Oppozitsia, 1925 g.* Moscow, 1926.
———*VKP (b).* Moscow–Leningrad, 1931.
BURHARIN, N., *Proletarskaya Revolutsia i Kultura.* Petrograd,
1923.

————*Kritika Ekonomicheskoi Platformy Oppozitsii.* Leningrad, no date.

————*K Voprosu o Trotskizme.* Moscow, 1925.

————'Teoriya Permanentnoi Revolutsii,' in *Za Leninizm.*

————*V Zashchitu Proletarskoi Diktatury.* Moscow, 1928.

————(co-author with Preobrazhensky, E.) *The ABC of Communism.* London, 1922.

CHEN TU-HSIU, 'Open Letter to members of the Chinese Communist Party'. The American translation under the title 'How Stalin–Bukharin destroyed the Chinese Revolution' was published in *The Militant*, November 1930 (and not 1929, as stated on p. 867, n. 1 of this volume).

DEGRAS, J. (ed.), *Soviet Documents on Foreign Policy.* London, 1952.

DINGELSTEDT, I., Unpublished essays, articles, and letters to Trotsky, Radek, and others, quoted from *The Trotsky Archives.*

DZERZHINSKY, F., Izbrannye Stati i Rechi. Moscow, 1947.

EASTMAN, M., *Since Lenin Died.* London, 1925.

ENGELS, F., *Dialektik der Natur.* Berlin, 1955.

FISCHER, L., *Men and Politics.* New York, 1946.

————*The Soviets in World Affairs*, vols. i–ii. London, 1930.

FISCHER, R., *Stalin and German Communism.* London, 1948.

FOTIEVA, L. A., 'Iz Vospominanii o Lenine', in *Voprosy Istorii KPSS*, nr. 4, 1957.

FROSSARD, L-O., *De Jaurès d Lénine.* Paris, 1930.

————*Sous le Signe de Jaurès.* Paris, 1943.

GUÉRIN, D., *La Lutte de Classes sous la Première République*, vols. i–ii. Paris, 1946.

HERRIOT, E., *La Russie Nouvelle.* Paris, 1922.

HOLITSCHER, A., *Drei Monate in Sowjet Rußand.* Berlin, 1921.

ISAACS, H., *The Tragedy of the Chinese Revolution.* London, 1938.

KAMEGULOV, A. A., *Trotskizm v Literaturovedeni.* Moscow, 1932.

KAMENEV, L., 'Partiya i Trotskizm' and 'Byl-li Deistvitelno Lenin Vozhdem Proletariata i Revolutsii', in *Za Leninizm.*

————His letter about his meeting with Bukharin in the summer of 1928 is quoted from *The Trotsky Archives*, as are also other documents of which he was co-author.

———His speeches are quoted from the records of party congresses and conferences.

KAROLYI, M., *Memoirs*. London, 1956.

KHRUSHCHEV, N., *The Dethronement of Stalin* (this is the *Manchester Guardian* edition of the 'secret' speech at the XX Congress), 1956.

KOLLONTAI, A., *The Workers' Opposition in Russia*. London, 1923.

KPSS v Rezolutsyakh, vols. i–ii. Moscow, 1953.

KRITSMAN, L., *Geroicheskii Period Velikoi Russkoi Revolutsii*. Moscow, 1924 (?).

KRUPSKAYA, N., 'K. Voprosu o Urokakh Oktyabrya', in *Za Leninizm*.

———Speeches, quoted from party records.

KUUSINEN, O., 'Neudaysheesya Izobrazhenie "Nemetskovo Oktyabrya"', in *Za Leninizm*.

LATSIS (SUDBARS), *Chrezvychainye Komissii po Borbe s Kontrrevolutsiei*. Moscow, 1921.

LENIN, V., *Sochinenya*, vols. i–xxxv. Moscow, 1941–50. All quotations are from this, the fourth, edition of Lenin's Works, except in one case, indicated in a footnote, where the 1928 edition (vol. xxv) is quoted.

———*Sochinenya*, vol. xxxvi. Moscow, 1957. (The first of the additional volumes of the fourth edition, published after the XX Congress and containing Lenin's previously suppressed or unknown writings.)

———Still unpublished parts of Lenin's correspondence with Trotsky and others are quoted from *The Trotsky Archives*.

Leninskii Sbornik, vol. xx. Moscow, 1932.

Manifest der Arbeitergruppe der Russischen Kommunistischen Partei. Berlin, 1924.

MAO TSE-TUNG, *Izbrannye Proizvedeniya*, vols. i–ii. Moscow, 1952–3.

MARX, K., *Das Kapital*.

———*Das Kommunistische Manifest*.

———*Der 18 Brumaire des Louis Bonaparte*.

———*Herr Vogt*.

MOLOTOV, V., 'Ob Urokakh Trotskizma', in *Za Leninizm*.

———Speeches quoted from records of party congresses and conferences.

MORIZET, A., *Chez Lénine et Trotski*. Paris, 1922.

MURALOV, N., Unpublished correspondence with Trotsky and others in *The Trotsky Archives*.

MURPHY, J. T., *New Horizon*. London, 1941.

POKROVSKY, M. N., *Oktyabrskaya Revolutsia*. Moscow, 1929.

————*Ocherki po Istorii Oktyabrskoi Revolutsii*, vols. i–ii. Moscow, 1927.

POPOV, N., *Outline History of the C.P.S. U. (b)*, vols. i–ii (English translation from 16th Russian edition). London, no date.

PREOBRAZHENSKY, E., *Novaya Ekonomika*, vol. i, part 1. Moscow, 1926.

————Essays, memoranda ('Levyi Kurs v Derevnie i Perspektivi' 'Chto Nado Skazat Kongresu Kominterna', &c.,) and his correspondence with Trotsky, Radek, and others, quoted from *The Trotsky Archives*.

————(co-author with Bukharin), *The ABC of Communism. Pyat Let Sovietskoi Vlasti*. Moscow, 1922.

RADEK, K., *In den Reihen der Deutschen Revolution*. Munich, 1921.

————'Noyabr, iz Vospominanii', *Krasnaya Nov*, nr. to, 1926.

————*Pyat Let Kominterna*, vols. i–ii. Moscow, 1924.

————*Portrety i Pamflety*. Moscow, 1927. (This edition includes the essay, omitted from later editions, 'Lev Trotski, Organizator Pobedy' [Trotsky, the Organizer of Victory], which originally appeared in *Pravda*, 14 March 1923.)

————*Kitai v Ognie Voiny*. Moscow, 1924.

————*Razvitie i Znachenie Lozunga Proletarskoi Diktatury*. (This is Radek's long, unpublished, treatise about Trotsky's theory of permanent revolution, written in exile in 1928 and available in *The Trotsky Archives*. It was in reply to this treatise that Trotsky wrote his book *The Permanent Revolution*.)

————Unpublished correspondence with Trotsky, K. Zetkin, Dingelstedt, Sosnovsky, Preobrazhensky, Ter-Vaganyan, and others, *The Trotsky Archives*.

————Speeches quoted from party and Comintern records.

RAKOVSKY, CH., 'Letter to Valentinov', unpublished memoranda and correspondence with Trotsky and others, *The Trotsky Archives*. A French translation of the 'Letter to Valentinov' is in *Les Bolcheviks contre Staline*. Paris 1957.

RANSOME, A., *Six Weeks in Russia in 1919*. London, 1919.

ROSMER, A., *Moscou sous Lénine*. Paris, 1953.

ROY, M. N., *Revolution und Kontrrevolution in China*. Berlin, 1930.

RYKOV, A., 'Novaya Diskussiya' in *Za Leninizm*.

————Speeches quoted from records of party congresses and conferences.

SAPRONOV, T., Memoranda and Correspondence in *The Trotsky Archives*.

SCHEFFER, P., *Sieben Jahre Sowjet Union*. Leipzig, 1930.

SEDOVA, N. (part author with V. Serge), *Vie et Mort de Trotsky*. Paris, 1951.

SERGE, V., *Le Tournant Obscur*. Paris, 1951.

————*Mémoires d'un Revolutionnaire*. Paris, 1951.

————*Vie et Mort de Trotsky*. Paris, 1951.

SHERIDAN, C., *Russian Portraits*. London, 1921.

SMILGA, I., Correspondence and essays ('Platforma Pravovo Kryla VKP [b]') are quoted from *The Trotsky Archives*.

SMIRNOV, I., Unpublished correspondence with Trotsky, Radek, and others. Ibid.

SMIRNOV, V., *Pod Znamya Lenina* (an unpublished essay expounding the Decemist viewpoint in 1928. Trotsky attributes its authorship to V. Smirnov, but is not certain of it.)

SOKOLNIKOV, G., 'Teoriya tov. Trotskovo i Praktika Nashei Revolutsii' and 'Kak Podkhodit k Istorii Oktyabrya', in *Za Leninizm*.

SORIN, V., *Rabochaya Gruppa*. Moscow, 1924.

SOSNOVSKY, L., *Dela i Lyudi*, vols. i–iv. Moscow, 1924–7.

————Unpublished correspondence with Trotsky and others quoted from *The Archives*.

STALIN, J., *Sochinenya*, vols. v–x. Moscow, 1947–9.

TANG LEANG-LI, *The Inner History of the Chinese Revolution*. London, 1930.

THALHEIMER, A., *1923, Eine Verpasste Revolution?*. Berlin, 1931.

TROTSKY, L., *Sochinenya*. Moscow, 1925–7. The following volumes of this edition of Trotsky's collected writings are quoted or referred to in this work:

Vol. III: (part 1) *Ot Fevralya do Oktyabrya*; (part 2) *Ot Oktyabrya do Bresta*. It is as a preface to this volume that the much debated 'Uroki Oktyabrya' (*The Lessons of October*) first appeared.

Vol. XII: *Osnovnye Voprosy Proletarskoi Revolutsii.*
Vol. XIII: *Kommunisticheskii Internatsional.*
Vol. XV: *Khozaistvennoe Stroitelstvo v Sovietskoi Rossii.*
Vol. XVII: *Sovietskaya Respublika i Kapitalisticheskii Mir.*
Vol. XX: *Kultura Starovo Mira.*
Vol. XXI: *Kultura Perekhodnovo Vremeni.*
————*Kak Vooruzhalas Revolutsia*, vols. i–iii. Moscow, 1923–5.
————*Pyat Let Kominterna*, vols. i–ii. Moscow, 1924–5. An American edition under the title *The First Five Tears of the Communist International*, vols. i–ii, appeared in New York, 1945 and 1953.
————*Moya Zhizn*, vols. i–ii. Berlin, 1930. The English edition *My Life*. London, 1930.
————*Terrorism i Kommunism*. Petersburg, 1920.
————*Voina i Revolutsia*. Moscow, 1922.
————*Literatura i Revolutsia*. Moscow, 1923. An American edition *Literature and Revolution* appeared in New York, 1957.
————*Voprosy Byta*. Moscow, 1923. The English edition *Problems of Life*. London, 1924.
————*Mehzdu Imperializmom i Revolutsiey*. Moscow, 1922.
————*Novyi Kurs*. Moscow, 1924. The American edition *The New Course*. New York, 1943.
————*O Lenine*. Moscow, 1924.
————*Zapad i Vostok*. Moscow 1924.
————*Pokolenie Oktyabrya*. Moscow, 1924.
————*Kuda idet Angliya?*. Moscow, 1925. The English edition *Where is Britain Going?*, with a preface by H. N. Brailsford, appeared in London, 1926.
————*Kuda idet Angliya? (Vtoroi Vypusk)*. Moscow 1926. This is not, as the title may suggest, a second edition of the previous work, but a collection of criticisms by British authors, Bertrand Russell, Ramsay MacDonald, H. N. Brailsford, George Lansbury, and others, and of Trotsky's replies to his critics.
TROTSKY, L., *Europa and Amerika*. Berlin, 1926.
————*Towards Socialism or Capitalism*. London, 1926.
————*The Real Situation in Russia*. London, no date. The English version of the 'Platform' of the Joint Opposition of which Trotsky and Zinoviev were the co-authors.
————*Problems of the Chinese Revolution*. New York, 1932.

————*The Third International After Lenin*. New York, 1936. The American edition of the Critique of the Programme of the Third International, written in 1928.

————*Chto i Kak Proizoshlo?*. Paris, 1929.

————*Permanentnaya Revolutsia*. Berlin, 1930.

————*Stalinska Shkola Falskatsii*. Berlin, 1932. The American edition *The Stalin School of Falsification*. New York, 1937.

————*The Suppressed Testament of Lenin*. New York, 1935.

————*Écrits*, vol. i. Paris, 1955.

————*The Revolution Betrayed*. London, 1937.

————*Stalin*. New York, 1946.

————*The Case of Leon Trotsky*. London, 1937. Trotsky's depositions and cross-examination before the Dewey Commission in Mexico in 1937.

This list of Trotsky's published works includes only books and pamphlets quoted or referred to in this volume.

The Trotsky Archives, Houghton Library, Harvard University. A description of *The Archives* was given in the bibliography of *The Prophet Armed*. Speeches and statements by 'Trotsky are quoted either from *The Archives* or from published records of party congresses and conferences, as indicated in footnotes.

YAROSLAVSKY, E., *Rabochaya Oppozitsia*. Moscow, no date.

————*Protiv Oppozitsii*. Moscow, 1928.

————*Vcherashny i Zavtrashny Den Trotskistov*. Moscow, 1929.

————*Aus der Geschichte der Kommunistischen Partei d. Sowjetunion*, vols. i–ii. Hamburg–Berlin, 1931.

————*Ocherki po Istorii VKP (b)*. Moscow, 1936.

YOFFE, A., 'Farewell letter to Trotsky'. The full text is in *The Trotsky Archives*.

Za Leninizm, Leningrad, 1925. A collection of the most important contributions by Stalin, Zinoviev, Kamenev, Rykov, Bukharin, Sokolnikov, Krupskaya, and others to the discussion on Trotsky's *Lessons of October*. It includes also *The Lessons of October*.

Zayavlenie o Vnutripartiinom Polozheni. The statement of the 'Forty Six', of 15 October 1923, is in *The Trotsky Archives*.

ZINOVIEV, G., *Sochinenya*, vols. i, ii, v, xvi. Moscow, 1924–9.

————*Dvenadtsat Dney v Germanii*. Petersburg, 1920.

————'Bolshevizm ili Trotskyizm', in *Za Leninizm*.
————*Istoriya RKP (b)*. Moscow, 1924.
————*Lenin*. Leningrad, 1925.
————*Leninizm*. Leningrad, 1926.

Memoranda, essays, and other unpublished documents are quoted from *The Trotsky Archives*, and speeches from the published party records.

The following editions of protocols and verbatim reports have been quoted: Congresses and conferences of The Communist Party of the Soviet Union:

10 Syezd RKP (b). Moscow, 1921.
11 Konferentsya RKP (b). Moscow, 1921.
11 Syezd RKP (b). Moscow, 1936.
12 Syezd RKP (b). Moscow, 1923.
13 Konferentsya RKP (b). Moscow, 1924.
13 Syezd RKP (b). Moscow, 1924.
14 Syezd VKP (b). Moscow, 1926.
15 Konferentsya VKP (b). Moscow, 1927.
15 Syezd VKP (b), vols. i–ii. Moscow, 1935.
Protokoly Tsentralnovo Komiteta RSDRP. Moscow, 1929.
Congresses of Soviet trade unions:
3 Syezd Profsoyuzov. Moscow, 1920.
4 Syezd Profsoyuzov. Moscow, 1921.
5 Syezd Profsoyuzov. Moscow, 1922.
6 Syezd Profsoyuzov. Moscow, 1925.
7 Syezd Profsoyuzov. Moscow, 1927.
Congresses of Soviets:
8 Vserosiiskii Syezd Sovetov. Moscow, 1921.
9 Vserosiiskii Syezd Sovetov. Moscow, 1922.
The Communist International:
International Congresses:
3 Vsemirnyi Kongress Kominterna. Petrograd, 1922.
4 Vsemirnyi Kongress Kominterna. Moscow, 1923.
5 Vsemirnyi Kongress Kominterna, vols. i–ii. Moscow, 1925.
Sessions of the Executive:
Rasshirenny Plenum IKKI. Moscow, 1923.
Rasshirenny Plenum IKKI. Moscow, 1925.

Shestoi Rasshirenny Plenum IKKI. Moscow, 1927.

Puti Mirovoi Revolutsii (session of November–December 1926), vols. i–ii. Moscow, 1927.

Rasshirenny Plenum IKKI, vols. i–xii. Moscow, 1930–.

The Lessons of the German Events. London (?), 1924. (Report on the discussion at the Praesidium of the Executive on the 'German Crisis' of 1923.)

Varia:

The Second and Third International and the Vienna Union (report of the 1922 conference of the Three Internationals in Berlin), no date.

Newspapers and periodicals:

Bolshevik, Bulleten Oppozitsii, Ekonomicheskaya Zhizn, Die Freiheit, L'Humanité, Izvestya Ts. K. RKP (b), Iskusstvo Kommuny, Internationale Presse Korrespondenz, Kommunist, Kommunisticheskii Internatsional, Krasnaya Letopis, Krasnaya Nov, Kuznitsa, Labour Weekly, Labour Monthly, The Militant, The New International, Na Postu, The Nation, The New Leader, The New York Times, Oktyabr, Pechat i Revolutsia, Pod Znamyenem Marksizma, Pravda, Proletarskaya Revolutsia, Przegląd Socjal-Demokratyczny, Revolutsionnyi Vostok, Trud, Voprosy Istorii KPSS, Znamya, Z Pola Walki.

The Prophet Outcast

AVAKUM, PETROV, *Zhizn Protopopa Avakuma.* Moscow, 1960.

BRECHT, B., *Galileo Galilei.*

BRETON, A., *La clé des champs.* Paris, 1953.

————*Entretiens.* Paris, 1960.

————Correspondence with Trotsky in *The Trotsky Archives,* Closed Section.

BUDENZ, L. F., *This is My Story.* New York, 1947.

BULLOCK, A., *Hitler—A Study in Tyranny.* London, 1953.

BURNHAM, J., articles and essays in *New International* and *Internal Bulletin* of the S.W.P. (the American Trotskyist organization).

————Correspondence with Trotsky in *The Trotsky Archives,* Closed Section.

————*Managerial Revolution*. New York, 1941.

————*The Coming Defeat of Communism*. New York, 1950.

CANNON, J. P., *History of American Trotskyism*. New York, 1944.

————Articles in *Fourth International*, and *Internal Bulletin* of the S.W.P.

————Correspondence in *The Trotsky Archives*, Closed Section.

CÉLINE, L.-F., *Voyage au bout de la nuit*.

CHEN TU-HSIU, unpublished memoranda, essays, and correspondence in *The Trotsky Archives*, Closed Section.

CHURCHILL, W. S., *Great Contemporaries*. London, 1939.

————*The Second World War*, vol. iv. London, 1951.

CILIGA, A., *Au pays du grand mensonge*. Paris, 1937.

————Articles in *Bulletin Oppozitsii* and *Sotsialisticheskii Vestnik*.

COULONDRE, R., *De Staline à Hitler, Souvenir de deux Ambassades*. Paris, 1950. (Trotsky commented on Coulondre's report of his last meeting with Hitler on the basis of Coulondre's article in *Paris-Soir*.)

CRAIPEAU, M., 'J'ai connu l'assassin de Trotsky', *France-Observateur*, 19 May 1960.

DEWEY, JOHN, 'Means and Ends', in *New International*, 1938. (*See* also *The Case of Leon Trotsky*, and *John Dewey, Philosopher of Science and Freedom, A Symposium*, ed. S. Hook.)

DRAPER, TH., *American Communism and Soviet Russia*. New York, 1960.

————Roots of American Communism. New York, 1957.

EASTMAN, MAX, *Since Lenin Died*. London, 1925.

————*The End of Socialism in Russia*. London, 1937.

————*Marxism, is it Science?* London, 1941.

————*Stalin's Russia and the Crisis in Socialism*. London, 1940.

————*Great Companions*. London, 1959.

————Correspondence with Trotsky in *The Trotsky Archives*, Closed Section.

ENGELS, F., and MARX, K., *Briefwechsel*. Berlin, 1949–50.

FAINSOD, M., *Smolensk under Soviet Rule*. London, 1959.

FARRELL, J. T., 'Dewey in Mexico' in *John Dewey, A Symposium*, ed. Hook, S.

FREEMAN, J. *An American Testament*. London, 1938.

GIDE, ANDRÉ, *Retour de l'U.R.S.S.* Paris, 1936.

GOLDMAN, A., *The Assassination of Leon Trotsky*. New York, n.d.

GREF, YA., Contributions in *Bulletin Oppozitsii*.

GUÉRIN, D., *Jeunesse du Socialisme Libertaire*. Paris, 1959.

———*Fascisme et Grand Capital*. Paris, 1936.

HANSEN, J., Reminiscences about Trotsky in *Fourth International*.

HEGEL, G. W. F., *Philosophie der Weltgeschichte*.

HERNANDEZ, J., *La Grande Trahison*. Paris, 1953.

HOOK, S., *The Hero in History*. London, 1945.

———*Political Power and Personal Freedom*. New York, 1955.

———Ed. *John Dewey, Philosopher of Science and Freedom, A Symposium*. New York, 1950.

LES HUMBLES, Cahiers 5–6, *A Leon Trotsky*. Paris, 1934.

ISAACS, H., *The Tragedy of the Chinese Revolution* (Preface by Trotsky). London, 1938.

———Reports on China and correspondence with Trotsky in *The Archives*, Closed Section.

KAGANOVICH, L., speeches in Reports of party congresses.

KAROLYI, M., *Memoirs*. London, 1956.

KERENSKY, A., *The Crucifixion of Liberty*. London, 1934.

KHRUSHCHEV, N., *The Dethronement of Stalin*. (*Manchester Guardian* publication June 1956.)

———Speeches in *22 Syézd K.P.S.S.* Moscow, 1962.

KNUDSEN, K., Preface to Norwegian edition of Trotsky's *My Life*, Oslo.

KOHT, H., *Barricade to Barricade*. (Norwegian edition.) Oslo.

KROG, H., *Meninger*. Oslo, 1947.

KUN, BELA, (ed.) *Kommunisticheskii International v Dokumentakh, 1919–32*. Moscow, 1933.

LENIN, V. I., *Sochinenya*. Moscow, 1941–50.

LEVINE, I. DON, *The Mind of an Assassin*. New York, 1959.

LIE, TRYGVE (On behalf of the Norwegian Ministry of Justice and Police), *Storting Report*, nr. 19 (concerning Trotsky's internment and deportation from Norway), submitted on 18 February 1937.

LUNACHARSKY, A., *Revolutsionnye Siluety*. Moscow, 1923.

MACDONALD, DWIGHT, *Memoirs of a Revolutionist*. New York, 1958.

MALRAUX, A., *La Condition Humaine*.

MANUILSKY, D., *The Communist Parties and the Crisis of*

Capitalism. Report at II Plenum of Comintern Executive, March–April 1931. London, n.d.

————Other articles and speeches quoted from Reports of Party Congresses and *Kommunisticheskii International.*

MARX, K., *Das Kapital.*

————and ENGELS, F., *Das Kommunistische Manifest.*

————*Der 18 Brumaire des Louis Bonaparte.*

————and ENGELS, F., *Briefwechsel.* Berlin, 1949–50.

————*Living Thoughts of Karl Marx* (ed. by L. Trotsky and O. Rühle) London, 1946.

MAURIAC, F., *Mémoires Intérieures.* Paris, 1959.

M.B. 'Trotskisty na Vorkute', *Sotsialisticheskii Vestnik*, 1961. (An eyewitness's report on the extermination of the Trotskyists at the Vorkuta concentration camp in 1938.)

MERLEAU-PONTY, M., *Les Aventures de la Dialectique.* Paris, 1955.

————*Humanisme et terreur.* Paris, 1947.

MILIUKOV, P. N., *Istorya Vtoroi Russkoi Revolutsii.* Sofia, 1921.

MOUNTER, RAYMOND and HENRI, Correspondence with Trotsky and Leon Sedov quoted from *The Trotsky Archives*, Closed Section, and Leon Sedov's Papers.

MOLOTOV, V., speeches and reports in Reports of Party Congresses.

NADEAU, M., *Histoire du Surréalisme.* Paris, 1945.

NAVILLE, P., *Trotsky Vivant.* Paris, 1962.

————Correspondence in *The Trotsky Archives*, Closed Section.

NIN, A., Correspondence in *The Trotsky Archives*, Closed Section.

ORLOV, A., *The Secret History of Stalin's Crimes.* London, 1953.

ORWELL, G., *Homage to Catalonia.*

————*1984.*

PABLO, M., 'Vingt Ans de la Quartrième Internationale' in *Quatrième Internationale*, 1958–9.

PARIJANINE, M., 'Léon Trotsky ou la Revolution Bannie' in *Les Humbles.* Paris, 1934.

————Correspondence in *The Trotsky Archives*, Closed Section.

PAZ, MAURICE and MAGDELEINE, Correspondence with Trotsky in *The Archives*, Closed Section.

PFEMFERT, FRANZ, Correspondence with Trotsky, *The Trotsky Archives*, Closed Section.

PLEKHANOV, G., *Izbrannye Filosofskie Proizvedenya* (vol. ii). Moscow, 1956.

———*The Role of the Individual in History*. London, 1940.

POPOV, N., *Outline History of the C.P.S.U. (b)*, vols. i–ii. English translation from the 16th Russian edition. London, n.d.

PREOBRAZHENSKY, E., *Novaya Ekonomika*, vol. i, part i. Moscow, 1926.

———Essays and memoranda (including Manifesto 'Ko Vsem Tovarishcham po Oppozitsii') are quoted from *The Trotsky Archives*.

PRITT, D. N., *The Zinoviev Trial*. London, 1936.

RADEK, K., 'Ot Oppozitsii v Kloaku Kontrrevolutsii' in *Partiya v Borbe z OpPozitsijami*. Moscow, 1936.

———Articles in *Izvestya* and other Soviet newspapers. His 'Confession' at his trial is in *Sudebnyi Otchet po Delu Antisovietskovo Trotskistskovo Tsentra*. Moscow, 1937.

RAHV, PH., Correspondence with Trotsky. *The Trotsky Archives*, Closed Section.

RAKOVSKY, CH., Essays, articles, and correspondence in *Bulletin Oppozitsii* and *The Trotsky Archives*.

RAMM, A., Correspondence in *The Trotsky Archives*, Closed Section.

REISS, I., 'Letter to Central Committee' and 'Zapiski' in *Bulletin Oppozitsii*, 1937.

R(IZZI), BRUNO, *La Bureaucratisation du Monde*. Paris, 1939.

ROSMER, A., *Moscou sous Lévine*. Paris, 1953.

———Introduction and Appendixes in Trotsky's *Ma Vie*, Paris, 1953.

———Articles in Trotskyist periodicals and *La Révolution Proletarienne*.

———Correspondence with Trotsky in *The Trotsky Archives*, Closed Section.

———Correspondence with the author.

ROWSE, A. L., *End of an Epoch*. London.

RÜHLE, O. (and L. TROTSKY), *Living Thoughts of Karl Marx*. London, 1946.

SALAZAR, L. A. S. *Murder in Mexico*. London, 1950.

SAYERS, M., and KAHN, A. E., *The Great Conspiracy*. New York, 1947.

SEDOV, LEON, *Livre Rouge sur le procès de Moscou*. Paris, 1936.

The Russian text of this appeared simultaneously as a special issue of the *Bulletin Oppozitsii*. Articles and essays in *Bulletin Oppozitsii* (sometimes signed N. Markin), *Manchester Guardian* and other papers.

――――Correspondence with Trotsky, Natalya, and other members of the family, *The Trotsky Archives*, Closed Section.

――――L. Sedov papers transmitted to the author by Jeanne Martin des Paillères.

SEDOVA, NATALYA, (with V. SERGE), *Vie et Mort de Trotsky*.

――――Reminiscences about Trotsky and Lev Sedov in *Bulletin Oppozitsii* and *Fourth International*, 1941.

――――Family correspondence in *The Trotsky Archives*, Closed Section.

――――Correspondence with the author.

――――*Hommage à Natalia Sedova-Trotsky*. (Funeral orations and reminiscences) Paris, 1962.

SERGE, V., (and NATALYA SEDOVA) *Vie et Mort de Trotsky*. Paris, 1951.

――――*Mémoires d'un Révolutionnaire*. Paris, 1951.

――――Articles and letters in *The New International*, and other Trotskyist or near Trotskyist papers. Correspondence in *The Trotsky Archives*, Closed Section.

SHACHTMAN, M., Articles and essays in *New International, Militant, Internal Bulletin* of S.W.P. etc.

――――Correspondence in *The Trotsky Archives*, Closed Section.

SHAW, G. B., *Saint Joan*.

――――*To a Young Actress*. London, 1960.

――――Correspondence quoted from the Archives of the British Committee for the Defence of Leon Trotsky and from *The Trotsky Archives*, Closed Section.

SHIRER, W. L., *The Rise and Fall of the Third Reich*. London, 1960.

SMIRNOV, IVAN, Memoranda and correspondence quoted from *Bulletin Oppozitsii* and *The Trotsky Archives*.

SOBOLEVICIUS-SENIN, *alias* JACK SOBLE, and his brother, DR. SOBLEN (*alias* ROBERT WELL), correspondence with Trotsky and Leon Sedov in *The Trotsky Archives*, Closed Section.

SOKOLOVSKAYA, (BRONSTEIN) ALEXANDRA, correspondence with Trotsky and Leon Sedov, *The Trotsky Archives*, Closed Section.

SOUVARINE, B., *Stalin*, London, n.d.

———Correspondence in *The Trotsky Archives*, Closed Section.

STALIN, J., *Sochinenya*, vols. xii–xiii. Moscow, 1949–51.

TAROV, A., Contributions in *Bulletin Oppozitsii*.

TOGLIATTI (ERCOLI), P., Speeches and articles in *Kommunist-icheskii Internatsional* and Reports of Comintern Congresses and Conferences.

THAELMANN, E., speeches, reports, and articles quoted from *II Plenum IKKI, 12 Plenum IKKI, Rote Fahne, Internationale*, and *Kommunistische Internationale* (or the Russian edition of the latter).

TROTSKY, L., *Chto i Kak Proizoshlo?* Paris, 1929.

———*Moya Zhizn*, vols. i–ii. Berlin, 1930. (The English edition, *My Life*, London, 1930; the French, *Ma Vie*, with Introduction and Appendix by Alfred Rosmer, Paris 1953; the German *Mein Leben*, Berlin, 1929.)

———*The History of the Russian Revolution*, vols. i–iii. Translated by Max Eastman. London, 1932–3.

———*Écrits*, 1928–40, vols. i–iii, with Introductions by Pierre Frank. Paris, 1955–9.

———*O Lenine*. Moscow, 1924. (French edition *Lénine*. Paris, 1925), a collection of character sketches about Lenin, not be to confused with the biography of Lenin, of which Trotsky concluded only the first part and which has so far been published only in French as

———*Vie de Lénine, Jeunesse*. Paris, 1936.

———*The Third International after Lenin*. New York, 1936.

———*Nemetskaya Revolutsia i Stalinskaya Burokratiya*. Berlin 1932. (In German: *Was Nun?* Berlin, 1932; in English *What Next?* New York, 1932; French version *Écrits*, vol. iii.)

———*Edinstvennyi Put'* (in German: *Der einzige Weg*). Berlin, 1932.

———*Germany, the Key to the International Situation*. London, 1931.

———*Où va la France?* and *Encore une Fois, Où va la France?* Paris, 1936. (Reproduced in *Écrits*, vol. ii.)

———*The Revolution Betrayed*. London, 1937.

———*Permanent Revolution*. Calcutta, 1947.

TROTSKY, L. *Problems of the Chinese Revolution*. New York, 1932.

———*Trotsky's Diary in Exile*. London, 1958.

————*Stalins Verbrechen.* Zürich, 1937.

————*The Real Situation in Russia.* London, n.d.

————*Stalinskaya Shkola Falsifikatsii.* Berlin, 1932. (The American edition: *The Stalin School of Falsification.* New York, 1937.)

————*Between Red and White.* London, 1922.

————*Stalin.* New York, 1946.

————*Their Morals and Ours.* New York, 1939.

————*Leon Sedov, Son, Friend, Fighter.* New York, 1938.

————Articles, essays, treatises, and theses in *Bulletin Oppozitsii*, 1929–40, *New International*, and other Trotskyist periodicals.

The Trotsky Archives, Houghton Library, Harvard University. A description of these was given in the Bibliography in *The Prophet Armed.* Since then *The Archives* have been reorganized. The documents are no longer divided into Sections A, B, and C, but have been rearranged in chronological order. An Index, in two volumes, is available to students of this (the 'Open') part of *The Archives.* All references in *The Prophet Armed* and *The Prophet Unarmed* were to this part of *The Archives.*

What was described in the Bibliography in *The Prophet Armed* as 'Section D' is now described as 'The Closed Section of *The Archives.* It covers only the years 1929–40 and contains Trotsky's correspondence with groups and members of the Fourth International and with other well-wishers and friends, his family correspondence, household papers, correspondence with publishers, documentation prepared for The Dewey Commission, papers of the Fourth International, &c. According to Trotsky's wish, this Section of *The Archives* was not to be opened before the year 1980; but Harvard University gave the author access to it on the basis of a special authorization from Natalya Sedova, Trotsky's widow. (In references to *The Trotsky Archives* at large, the open section of *The Archives* is meant.)

The Closed Section of *The Archives* consists of forty-five boxes, containing 309 folders with documents and correspondence. Thus folders 1–16 contain Trotsky's family correspondence; folders 17–25, his household papers; folders 26–33, correspondence with publishers and literary agents; 34–35, documentation for the Mexican Counter-trial; while

Fourth International papers are in folders 36–40. The rest of the material is arranged according to countries, for instance, folders 65–70 contain Trotsky's correspondence concerning China; folders 90–121 refer to France; the German correspondence is in folders 122–6; the British 165–75; folders 254–86 contain correspondence with U.S.A.; folders 287–92 correspondence with the U.S.S.R., and 293–309 letters to and from Soviet citizens exiled from the U.S.S.R. To this Section of *The Archives* some papers were added by Trotsky's widow in 1953.

    See also: *The Case of Leon Trotsky*, London, 1937 (Trotsky's depositions and cross-examination before the Dewey Commission in Mexico).

————*Not Guilty*. Report of the Dewey Commission. London, 1938.

VOLKOV, ZINAIDA (ZINA, Trotsky's daughter), correspondence in *The Trotsky Archives*, Closed Section.

WEBB, SIDNEY and BEATRICE, *Soviet Communism, a New Civilization*. London, 1944.

————Correspondence with Trotsky. *The Trotsky Archives*, Closed Section.

WEIL, SIMONE, *Oppression et Liberté*. Paris, 1955.

WILSON, E. *To the Finland Station*. London, 1941.

WOLFE, B., *The Great Prince Died*. New York, 1959.

WOLFE, BERTRAM, D., Articles in *Things we Want to Know*. Workers' Age Publications, New York, 1936, and *The New Republic*, 1937.

WOLLENBERG, E., *The Red Army*. London, 1940.

YAROSLAVSKY, E., *Partiya v Borbe z Oppozitsiami*, with contributions by K. Radek, A. Pankratova, and others. Moscow, 1936.

————*O Noveishei Evolutsii Trotskizma*. Moscow, 1930.

————*Vcherashny i Zavtrashny Den Trotskizma*. Moscow, 1929.

ZBOROWSKI, MARK (ÉTIENNE) Correspondence with Trotsky and other documents, concerning his relationship with Leon Sedov are in *The Trotsky Archives*, Closed Section.

The following are the official reports of the Moscow Trials:
Sudebnyi Otchet po Delu Trotskistskovo-Zinovievskovo Terroristskovo Tsentra. Moscow, 1936.

Sudebyni Otchet po Delu Anti-Sovietskovo Trotskistskovo Tsentra.
Moscow, 1937. *Sudebnyi Otchet po Delu Anti-Sovietskovo i
Pravo-Trotskistskovo Bloko.* Moscow, 1938.

(Official English versions or *Reports of Court Proceedings* were
published simultaneously by the People's Commissariat of Justice
in Moscow:)

The following official Protocols, Verbatim Reports, and
Collections of documents have been referred to:
    16 Syezd V.K.P.(b). Moscow, 1931.
    17 Syezd V.K.P.(b). Moscow, 1934.
    20 Syezd K.P.S.S. Moscow, 1956.
    22 Syezd K.P.S.S. Moscow, 1962.
    11 Plenum IKKI. Moscow, 1932.
    12 Plenum IKKI. Moscow, 1933.
Kommunisticheskii Internatsional v Dokumentakh. Moscow, 1933.
K.P.S.S. v Rezolutsyakh, vols. i–ii. Moscow, 1953.
V.K.P. (b) o Profsoyuzakh. Moscow, 1940.
Narodnoe Khozyaistvo S.S.S.R. Moscow, 1959.
*Hearing before the Subcommittee to Investigate the Administration
    of the Internal Security Act, U.S. Senate* (14–15 February
    1957), part 51. Washington, 1957.
*Hearing before the Subcommittee to Investigate the Administration
    of the Internal Security Act, U.S. Senate* (21 November 1957),
    part 87. Washington, 1958.

Newspapers and periodicals:

*Bolshevik, Bulletin Oppozitsii, Izvestya, Pravda, Proletarskaya
    Revolutsia, Sotsialisticheskii Vestnik, Kommunisticheskii
    Internatsional.* (Stencilled or hand-copied periodicals circu-
    lated by Trotskyist deportees and prisoners in the U.S.S.R.
    are in *The Trotsky Archives.*)
*Internationale, Internationale Presse Korrespondenz, Kommunisti-
    sche Internationale, Rote Fahne, Roter Aufbau, Rundschau
    Unser Wort, Permanente Revolution, Arbeiterpolitik, Aktion,
    Berliner Borsenzeitung, Hamburger Nachrichten, Vossische
    Zeitung.*

Militant, New International, Fourth International, Partisan Review, Internal Bulletin Fourth International (International Secretariat), The Times, Manchester Guardian, Daily Express, The Observer, Morning Post, The New Statesman and Nation, The New York Times, The New York American, The New York Daily News, The New York World Telegram, Life, The Nation, The New Republic, The New Leader, Soviet Russia To-day.

New York Tag, and *Vorwärts* (Yiddish–U.S.A.).

Vérité Quatrième Internationale France-Observateur, Intransigeant, Paris-Soir, Le Matin, Le Journal, Le Temps, Humanité, Journal d'Orient.

Politiken, Berlingske Tidende, Information, Arbeiderbladet, Dagbladet, Arbeideren, Soerlandet.

La Prensa, Trinchera Aprista.

INDEX